READER'S DIGEST FAMILY GUIDE TO

Alternative Medicine

FAMILY GUIDE TO ALTERNATIVE MEDICINE
was edited and designed by
The Reader's Digest Association Limited,
London

First Edition
Copyright © 1991
The Reader's Digest Association Limited,
Berkeley Square House,
Berkeley Square, London W1X 6AB
Copyright © 1991 Reader's Digest
Association Far East Limited
Philippines Copyright © 1991 Reader's Digest
Association Far East Limited

Printed in Great Britain

ISBN 0 276 42010 1

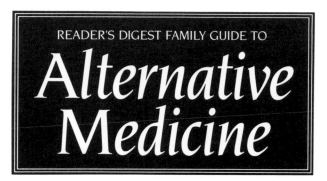

READER'S DIGEST FAMILY GUIDE TO

Alternative Medicine

Published by The Reader's Digest Association Limited
LONDON · NEW YORK · SYDNEY · MONTREAL · CAPE TOWN

Contributors

The publishers wish to express their thanks to the following who, as contributors and consultants, assisted in the preparation of this book.

Consultant editor

Dr Patrick C. Pietroni, FRCGP, MRCP, DCH
Senior Lecturer in General Practice,
St Mary's Hospital Medical School, London
Founder-member and past Chairman of the
British Holistic Medical Association
Principal partner in Marylebone Health
Centre, London

Contributors and consultants

Anthony Attenborough
Kinesiotherapist

Dr Daniel J. Benor, MD
Medical adviser to the Confederation of
Healing Organisations

John Blackwood, MA

Paul T. Brown, PhD, DipPsych, FBPsS
Chartered clinical and occupational
psychologist

Simon Brown
Director of the Community Health
Foundation
Co-director of the Kushi Institute
Registered Shiatsu practitioner

Brian H. Butler, BA
Principal of The Academy of Systematic
Kinesiology

Dr Derek Chase, MRCGP
General practitioner

**Jean Coleman, BSc, MScPsychol,
MScPsycoth**
Principal Clinical Psychologist,
Fairmile Hospital
Secretary of the International Committee on
Autogenic Training

**Dr James Cox, MB, BS, MRCGP,
DObst.RCOG**
General practitioner

Keir Davidson

**Arnold Desser, BA, CAc (Nanjing),
MRTCM**
Senior Lecturer,
London School of Acupuncture and
Traditional Chinese Medicine

Dr David Dowson, MB, ChB
Partner, Centre for the Study of
Complementary Medicine

Dr James A. Dyson, MRCS, LRCP
Medical Director, Park Attwood Clinic

Dr Sarah Eagger, MB, BS, MRCPsych
Secretary of the British Holistic Medical
Association

Mark Evans, MNIMH
Vice-President of the National Institute of
Medical Herbalists

Simon Fielding, DO, MRO
Registered osteopath

**Theophilus Gimbel, DCE, MIACT, NFSH,
MLHRC**
Principal, Hygeia College for Colour Therapy

**Dr Waguih R. Guirguis, DPM,
MRCPsych**

Nicola M. Hall, FBRA
Director, Bayly School of Reflexology
Chairman of the British Reflexology
Association

Fiona Harrold
Founder and Director, London College of
Massage and Shiatsu

Gabriella Hatfield

Leslie Hawkins, BSc, PhD, MIBiol, CBiol
Senior Lecturer in Applied Physiology and
Head of the Occupational Health Unit,
Robens Institute, University of Surrey

Eileen Herzberg

Sara Holden, BA, MInstGA
Senior Dance Movement Therapist,
Springfield Hospital

Ian M. Hutchinson, DC
Former President of the British Chiropractic
Association

Dr Julian N. Kenyon, MD, MB, ChB
Partner, Centre for the Study of
Complementary Medicine

**Dr Kai Kermani, BSc, DRCOG, MRCGP,
MBFATT**
General practitioner

**Dr George T. Lewith, MA, MRCP,
MRCGP**
Partner, Centre for the Study of
Complementary Medicine

Glynn Macdonald, BA, MSTAT

Dr Isaac M. Marks, MD, FRCPsych
Professor of Experimental Psychopathology, Institute of Psychiatry, Maudsley Hospital

Dr Sheena Meredith, MB, BS

Beverley Milne
Founder, School of T'ai-chi Ch'uan Centre for Healing

Robin Monro, MA, PhD
Founder/Director of the Yoga Biomedical Trust

Dr Susan Morrison, MB, BS, MRCGP
General practitioner at Marylebone Health Centre, London
Occupational and Student Health Physician, Polytechnic of Central London

Dr Roger Neighbour, MA, FRCGP

Paul Newham, BA
Voice consultant

John Newman

Miriam Polunin

Shirley Price, DipEd, MBABTAC, MISPA, MIFAT, MIFA
Founder, Shirley Price Aromatherapy School

Melanie Reinhart, BA, DFAstrolS

Stanley Richardson, FSSCh, FMAA, MSF, MSAAc
Principal, Richardson Clinic

Ray Ridolfi, MRSS
Registered Shiatsu practitioner

Dr Alan J. Riley, MSc, MB, BS, MRCS, DObst.RCOG, MFPM
Medical Director (Advanced and Clinical Research), Institute of Sexual and Reproductive Medicine, Newlands Medical Centre

Dr Brian Roet, MB, BS, DA, FFARACS
Psychotherapist and hypnotherapist

Gaston Saint-Pierre, BA
Founder/Director of the Metamorphic Association

Dr Farida Sharan, MD, MH, ND, FBRI
Founder and Director, School of Natural Medicine and British School of Iridology

Franklyn Sills, MA, RPT
Dean, Polarity Therapy Education Trust

Michael Turner, PhD, FIFST, FRSH, FIBiol
Nutritionist

Roger Newman Turner, BAc, ND, DO, MRO, MRN
Registered naturopath, osteopath and acupuncturist

Dr Paul Wallace, MSc, MRCGP
General practitioner

Diane Waller, MA, DipPsych, ATC, DPhil
Head of Art Psychotherapy Unit, Goldsmiths' College, University of London

Auriel Warwick, RMTh

Clive Wood, MSc, DPhil

Dr David Zigmond, MB, ChB, MRCGP, DPM
Psychotherapist and medical practitioner

Artists
Andrew Aloof

Richard Bonson

Baird Harris Limited

Biz Hull

Rosalyn Kennedy

Tim Pearce

Malcolm Porter

Photographers
Chapman/Collins & Partners

Diana Miller

Vernon Morgan

Andra Nelki

Introduction

Your guide to alternative medicine

oday's unorthodoxy, the Prince of Wales told a meeting of the British Medical Association (BMA) in 1982, 'is probably tomorrow's convention'. Few of those present at the time doubted that by 'today's unorthodoxy' he meant alternative or complementary medicine.

It is difficult now to imagine the effect of his words on a medical profession that viewed alternative medicine with a scepticism amounting in some quarters to outright scorn. For in less than ten years a remarkable change of attitude has emerged not only among ordinary people but also among doctors and scientists. The medical establishment, for so long critical or downright dismissive of claims made by alternative practitioners, has become more neutral and open-minded.

A year after Prince Charles's address – and almost certainly as a direct result of it – the BMA set up a scientific committee to 'consider the feasibility and possible methods of assessing the value of alternative therapies, whether used alone or to complement other treatments'. The committee produced a report listing the things that could account for the growing popularity of alternative therapies:

• Alternative practitioners were generally able to offer patients more time, and were more prepared to listen than busy doctors, who could not stop to discuss problems in detail.

• Patients felt that the therapists were more compassionate and concerned, providing care for the whole person rather than simply treating an illness.

• Patients also like the use of touch as a way of

communicating healing in therapies such as massage, acupressure, and laying on of hands – something often lacking in orthodox medicine, when technology could come between doctor and patient.

● As ordinary medicine became more familiar, patients seemed to be seeking therapists who had 'magical' qualities, their strange words and unfamiliar practices conveying the feeling of benefiting from a powerful healing force.

The committee concluded that modern conventional medicine was failing to give patients something they wanted. However, they also felt that the effectiveness of the therapies themselves was impossible to prove scientifically.

The committee did acknowledge, however, that so many people reported good effects from using acupuncture for pain relief and chiropractic or osteopathy for back problems that these therapies should have a place in orthodox treatment. They also endorsed the use of hypnotherapy, biofeedback and some special diets for a number of other conditions.

Sorting out the therapies

A major problem facing anybody trying to evaluate alternative medicine is that the term covers a wide range of different practices. Some therapies call for a training as long as that undertaken by conventional doctors, while others demand no more than a few weekend courses.

To differentiate between the various therapies, they can be grouped into four categories: complete healing systems, diagnostic techniques, complementary therapies and self-help measures.

Complete healing systems are the most highly developed. They incorporate theories about the cause of illness, methods of diagnosing and investigating problems, and treatments which often have something in common with conventional medicine. Some have existed for many thousands of years; others are relatively new.

In Britain, the best known systems include acupuncture, herbal medicine, osteopathy, chiropractic, homoeopathy and naturopathy. Ayurvedic medicine, the traditional healing system of India, is also becoming increasingly popular.

Most of these systems have well-established training programmes and strict ethical guidelines that regulate the way in which practitioners operate, in much the same way as the General Medical Council regulates the activities of doctors. Practitioners generally consider themselves competent to deal with most of the problems they encounter, but are prepared to refer patients with life-threatening complaints to conventional doctors.

Diagnostic techniques include kinesiology, which tests muscle strength to detect allergies; iridology, which examines the eyes for clues to hidden disorders; and hair analysis, which looks for nutritional deficiencies. Aura diagnosis, using the mystical 'aura' surrounding a person, is perhaps the most unconventional of these approaches, and the hardest for orthodox investigators to accept.

There are many more of these techniques, some

of which, such as 'intuitive diagnosis', do not even need the patient to be present. Some claim to be 'scientific' and use impressive-looking machines; others say that they call on powers 'unknown to science'. Anecdotal evidence supporting the claims is easy to find, but proof is still lacking.

Complementary therapies are treatments such as massage, reflexology, aromatherapy, spiritual healing and hydrotherapy. They do not offer to diagnose a patient's condition or advance theories about the cause of illness; they simply claim – with the support of many orthodox practitioners – that their methods can and do work. These methods are generally offered to complement, rather than replace, orthodox forms of treatment.

Self-help measures include breathing and relaxation exercises, meditation, visualisation, yoga and special diets. They, too, make no attempt to replace conventional treatment, but offer ways in which people may be able to relieve their symptoms, improve their health or simply stay well.

A *wider choice of treatment*

This book outlines the major approaches in each category, as explained by leading practitioners in their fields. It offers alternative treatments for common ailments and health problems – along with an orthodox view of those treatments and a brief outline of what your GP might prescribe.

It also outlines natural approaches to good health – diet, exercise, minimising environmental hazards and so on – and to the general 'management' of life itself, from family planning through pregnancy, childbirth and adolescence, to growing old and accepting that life must have an end. The overall aim is to increase understanding of all aspects of alternative medicine, and to provide readers with a wider choice in the matter of their own health care.

But greater choice is a two-edged sword, bringing with it the need for each individual to take responsibility for his or her own well-being. In challenging the traditional 'doctor knows best' attitude, the problem arises: which expert to believe?

For minor conditions, which will in any case get better on their own, this is unlikely to be a serious problem. But for someone with arthritis or cancer the confusion can add a further burden to the condition itself. In such cases it is often a good idea to ask your family doctor for advice. Many younger general practitioners in particular are interested in alternative medicine, and a recent survey found that 38 per cent had received additional training in at least one form of unconventional therapy.

However, many people turn to alternative medicine for the very reason that their GP is unsympathetic, so his advice may not be helpful. In such a case, you can contact one of the organisations whose addresses are given in this book. Self-help groups also offer information and support. Details of many such groups are given in the book, or you may be able to get information from your local library or Citizens Advice Bureau.

In any event, there is much you can do for

yourself. Indeed, therapists will expect you to take an active part in your own treatment by, for example, changing your diet or joining a relaxation class. It may well prove useful to try one or more of the self-help measures described in this book before even visiting a therapist.

If you do choose to consult an alternative practitioner, do not expect miracles any more than you would from an ordinary doctor. But, even if the practitioner is unable to cure you, your visit is unlikely to be wasted, since he or she will almost certainly be able to help you adjust to the discomfort or distress you are experiencing.

Is it available on the NHS?

While this book was in preparation, Britain's National Health Service (NHS) was undergoing the most far-reaching changes since it began in 1948. As a result some alternative practitioners may soon find it easier to operate within the NHS. Information on what is currently available can be found in the entry on the National Health Service on page 254.

Dr Patrick Pietroni

ABSENT HEALING
Projecting healing powers over a distance

As its name suggests, absent or distant healing is performed in a patient's absence. The healers, including those who practise SPIRITUAL HEALING, use prayer, MEDITATION or VISUALISATION THERAPY to link themselves to divine or mystical healing forces which are then channelled to patients, activating their power to heal themselves. The patients may not even know that they are being healed, although most healers will send healing only when requested by a patient.

Healers usually discover this ability by accident, and see it as a gift which they must use in the service of others. Most regard themselves as channels for powers which come from beyond them, and not as being personally able to heal. Often, training or religious belief helps them to develop their gifts, and many belong to church or spiritual groups. They work alone or in groups, and regular meetings are held at which people are prayed for or meditated upon.

Who it can help Any mental, physical or spiritual distress can be treated. The patient need take no active part, and may still benefit, although it is thought that a relaxed and positive patient may be more receptive to healing energies liberated within him. Because the patient does not have to participate actively, absent healing is said to be particularly suitable for babies, young children and animals, for very ill or unconscious patients, or for the mentally disordered.

Chronically ill people whose vitality and self-healing powers have been exhausted by lengthy illness may gain special benefit.

Absent healing is also particularly suitable for those who are too ill to travel.

Finding a healer Many therapists work only as healers, while others offer healing among a variety of treatments. Appointments with healers can be made by contacting one of the 16 associations affiliated to the Confederation of Healing Organisations. For advice, write to the National Federation of Spiritual Healers, Old Manor Farm Studio, Church Street, Sunbury on Thames, Middlesex TW16 6RG.

Healing also forms part of the ministry of most religions, and an approach can often be made through a minister or other religious worker. Healing meetings are also sometimes advertised in local newspapers and church notices.

The General Medical Council allows a doctor to prescribe healing, provided that the doctor remains in charge of the patient's treatment, and an increasing number of orthodox practitioners will now refer patients to healers and counsellors.

Most healers offer their services free, or accept only voluntary donations; others ask a fee which they may reduce or waive in cases of need. The code of conduct drawn up between the Confederation of Healing Organisations, The Royal Colleges of Medicine and General Medical Council prohibits healers who belong to affiliated groups from promising results or claiming cures.

Other healers who do make claims for themselves may not necessarily be charlatans – their claims may simply reflect an absolute faith in the powers they work with.

Consulting a healer Healers within the Confederation do not attempt to examine or diagnose patients, and will advise you to see a doctor if you have not already done so. Healing is usually a gradual process of helping patients to heal themselves. Instant cures cannot be expected, especially where illness is the result of long-term factors such as unhealthy diet or ongoing STRESS.

In such cases, healing MAY help, but it is not offered as a replacement for more direct, orthodox therapies.

Often, healing is sought as a last resort, when the body's defences are already depleted and, although it has proved successful in some cases regarded by orthodox medicine as incurable, patients should not expect healing to succeed immediately where all else has failed. Progress is often slow – sometimes even preceded by worsening symptoms as the body seeks to regain its ability to fight the illness.

Spiritual healers never accept that a case may be incurable, and this alone encourages many seriously ill patients. Healing of any type is likely to have positive psychological effects, and even where a condition cannot be reversed or improved, a patient may be relieved of distress and brought to accept his or her condition.

Many people even experience a sense of inner harmony through this kind of therapy.

The only danger arises when conventional treatment, which may help, is neglected in favour of absent healing, which may not.

An orthodox view

Most medical authorities remain sceptical of the benefits of absent healing.

Many good results are ascribed by doctors to temporary psychological effects; the patient is helped by what he or she believes will help them – at least in the short term. In recent years, some orthodox doctors have cooperated with healers. Whatever their attitude, however, practitioners of all kinds agree that absent healing can do no harm, provided it does not take the place of other treatment and provided the patient's hopes are not raised unrealistically.

ACID STOMACH

A variety of symptoms is covered by this emotive term. Usually, it refers to regurgitation of acid or partly digested food from the stomach into the oesophagus (food pipe) or mouth. Other symptoms may include heartburn (a burning sensation behind the breastbone), belching and a feeling that food is becoming stuck after swallowing.

Causes include overeating or drinking, wearing constrictive clothes, or bending, lying down or physical exertion too soon after eating. Regular attacks accompanied by a feeling of burning or constriction in the throat may be caused by a loose muscle at the base of the oesophagus, allowing acid to flow back from the stomach. Occasionally the symptoms indicate a more serious disorder, such as a stomach ULCER or hiatus hernia – if they persist, consult a doctor.

What the therapists recommend
NATUROPATHY
Self help Eat small, regular meals based on wholefoods such as fruit, vegetables, wholegrain cereals and moderate amounts of proteins such as lean meat, fish, eggs, cheese and nuts. Cut out fatty foods and those that contain possible irritants such as chemical FOOD ADDITIVES or hot spices. Avoid drinking immediately before meals, and drink sparingly during meals.

Hot compresses (see p. 193) over the stomach are said to improve the blood supply in the area and relax the muscles.

Consultation You will be given individual advice about improving your diet, and reducing STRESS – factors considered most important for regulating the digestive system.

HERBAL MEDICINE
Consultation In addition to advice about diet and way of living, practitioners may recommend comfrey root, marsh-mallow root and slippery elm to reduce irritation and inflammation of digestive organs. Despite rumours, comfrey has not been shown to cause liver damage, but it is advisable to use the remedy only on a short-term basis – for up to three weeks. For persistent problems see a qualified medical herbalist.

Comfrey and marsh-mallow would be taken as infusions or decoctions (p. 184);

Meadowsweet blooms prolifically at Wicken Fen, Cambridgeshire, in July. It can relieve an acid stomach when taken as an infusion.

slippery elm can be taken either in tablet form or a teaspoon of powder dissolved in a cup of hot water.

To tone and heal the whole digestive system, the bitter herbs wormwood, rue, gentian and golden seal may be suggested, but should not be taken for long periods or in large doses because of potentially poisonous effects. This is particularly true during pregnancy, because these herbs tend to stimulate the uterine muscles or, especially in the case of rue, can cause vomiting.

Centaury, yarrow and sweet flag are said to have the same action, but with a milder effect. Yarrow can be taken as an infusion, but take centaury, which is very bitter, as a weak infusion only.

Do's and don'ts for acid stomach

_Do_ take time to relax, allowing about 20 minutes of leisure before and after eating. Eat slowly, chew each mouthful well, and make meals enjoyable, unstressful occasions.
Don't smoke – it will irritate the stomach lining.
_Do_ make sure you get enough sleep.
Don't take aspirin in large quantities – it can cause gastrointestinal bleeding.
_Do_ make sure that your clothing is always loose and comfortable – especially over the stomach – and avoid tight belts and girdles.
_Do_ reduce the amount of coffee and tea you drink, and avoid them entirely during an attack.
Don't drink alcohol.

Other alternative treatments

Acupuncture This is said to relieve many digestive disorders, including excess acidity and inflammation of the stomach lining.
Homoeopathy _Nux vomica_ is used to relieve discomfort due to overeating or to relieve a HANGOVER. Take one tablet every hour for three hours, then one every two hours, if required.

Use the 6 or 30 centesimal potency.

An orthodox view

Doctors agree that diet is important in treating acid stomach. They recommend a bland diet of small, regular meals which include foods such as rice, milk, fish, chicken and cereals to reduce acidity. Fried and fatty foods are excluded, as are heavy meals, large amounts of alcohol, coffee, tea, and hot, spicy or very acid foods.

If the symptoms persist, the doctor may also prescribe an antacid preparation – an alkaline substance such as aluminium hydroxide or magnesium trisilicate that neutralises acidity in the stomach. Alternatively, if one of the more serious disorders mentioned earlier is diagnosed, some other form of treatment may be advised.

ACNE

The facial spots and scars of acne usually appear at puberty, the time when young people are most concerned about their looks (SEE PUBERTY AND ADOLESCENCE). The chest, shoulders and back can also be affected. The cause of acne is not fully understood, but heredity, hormonal fluctuations, hygiene and diet may all play a part.

An oily substance called sebum, produced by the skin's sebaceous glands, acts as a natural lubricant for the skin, but when too much is produced the glands can became blocked and inflamed, causing blackheads and pimples. Sometimes the blocked glands become infected – pus and sebum build up under the skin, forming larger pimples or cysts which can leave scars and pitting.

The fluctuating hormone levels of puberty are known to have an important role in the onset of acne. In particular, the hormone androgen, produced in large quantities during puberty, appears to affect the amount of sebum released. The severity of an attack can vary from week to week as hormone levels change, and women often find that the condition gets worse just before a period. The problem usually clears up as the sufferer reaches the early twenties.

What the therapists recommend
NATUROPATHY
Self help Keep the skin scrupulously clean, washing frequently – up to five times daily – but taking care that it does not become too dry. Use gentle cleansers made from natural ingredients or herbs, rather than harsher chemical preparations. If you prefer soap, use a mild, unscented brand. To remove as much oil as possible, first wash the skin then apply a hot facecloth for two minutes, splash with cold water and wipe gently with a ball of cotton wool soaked in witch hazel. Repeat as necessary and always use a clean facecloth, towel and cotton wool to prevent the spread of infection.

Women should avoid heavy make-up, but light, non-greasy products will do no harm and may boost self-confidence. Remove make-up thoroughly every evening with a natural cleanser followed by toner and moisturiser if the skin feels taut or dry. Most health food shops stock natural cosmetics and skin-care products, and some can easily be made at home. For example, you can make a cheap, effective toner by mixing equal parts of rose water and witch hazel (SEE NATURAL AIDS TO BEAUTY).

Other natural skin remedies include GARLIC, which acts as a natural antibiotic when rubbed onto spots. An ointment made with propolis (a resin substance extracted from flowers by bees) can be dabbed on several times a day. For the chest, shoulders and back, vigorous body rubbing with a loofah or dry towel stimulates circulation to the skin, and regular outdoor exercise is also an important factor.
Consultation Practitioners regard acne as a sign of some underlying disorder or imbalance in the body. Skin eruptions are seen as the body's attempt to rid itself of poisons from a system too overburdened with impurities for normal methods of elimination. Treatment is long term and the body

Other herbal remedies

To make an antiseptic lotion for spots that have been picked or squeezed Squeezing pimples is never advisable, but if you are tempted to do so, prevent infection spreading by bathing the whole face with a lotion made from a teaspoon of calendula tincture or Tincture of Hypercal (available from many chemists and health shops) in a glass of cold water.

To bring pustules to a head Make a paste from a teaspoon of powdered marsh-mallow root or slippery elm mixed with hot water. Spread it onto the acne and leave for about 20 minutes. Wash the mixture off with comfrey infusion.

To heal damaged skin An infusion of comfrey leaves also makes an excellent facial wash, and comfrey in any form will promote healing and the growth of new tissue.

To improve circulation and disinfect the area Paint lemon juice onto spots.

To cleanse the skin from within Take the following herbs as infusions, tablets or medicinal extracts: blue flag, echinacea, nettle, dandelion root.

---

must first be helped to cleanse itself and eliminate waste products.

Correct skin care is important. The therapist will advise on natural methods and may also recommend purifying treatments.

The therapist may recommend a diet to fortify the body against infection and as an aid in regulating hormone levels. The diet will be rich in natural wholefoods – wholegrain cereals, fresh fruit salads and vegetables, and free from oily, refined products such as cheese, fatty meat, cakes, white bread and sweets (see EATING FOR HEALTH).

Vegetables are eaten raw or lightly cooked, as high temperatures destroy many vitamins and enzymes (see RAW FOOD DIET). Food is grilled, steamed or baked, rather than roasted or fried. Carob replaces chocolate and skimmed milk replaces full-cream milk. Supplements of vitamin A and zinc may also be advised.

HERBAL MEDICINE

Self help For an anti-inflammatory and antibacterial skin wash there is a choice of three homemade preparations:

Calendula Mix a teaspoon of tincture of calendula (available from health food shops or made following instructions on p. 184) in a glass of water.

Camomile Simmer a teaspoon of dried flowers or a camomile tea bag for ten minutes in a cup of water, covered.

Yarrow, elder or lavender Pour a cup of boiling water over a handful of fresh or dried flowers, cover, and steep for ten minutes.

To use the preparations, strain as necessary and then bathe the affected areas with the solution, dabbing on gently with cotton wool. Alternatively, use the solution to make a compress (see p. 184).

Some therapists recommend a facial steam bath to reduce inflammation and infection by pouring a jug of boiling water into a bowl containing a handful of camomile flowers. Use lime flowers or sage leaves instead to detoxify; or lavender, to promote healing. Place the bowl on a table, sit with your face a comfortable distance above it, and cover your head and the bowl with a towel. Steam your face for as long as is comfortable, but never longer than 15 minutes. Take great care not to knock over the bowl or to scald the skin, and always stop if in doubt. Afterwards apply a toner to close the skin pores.

Consultation To remove toxins from the system a herbalist may make up an individual prescription for each patient, using herbs such as burdock leaves, artichoke leaves, greater celandine leaves, sage flowers and marsh-mallow roots and flowers.

For women, certain herbs such as chasteberry, dried beth root and false unicorn root may be recommended with the aim of regulating the hormonal system. However, these must be used only under the therapist's direct supervision.

Other alternative treatments

Biochemic Tissue Salts For outbreaks of acne during adolescence, *Calcarea sulph.* is prescribed. Take four tablets an hour for the first two days, then four times a day until the skin improves – usually within about two to four weeks.

Aromatherapy Bathe the affected skin with distilled water containing six drops of essential oil (two each of lavender, juniper and cajuput). Stir well, as essential oils do not dissolve easily in water. Afterwards apply a vegetable oil or non-greasy lotion containing any or all of these oils – use a total of 20 drops in 2fl oz (60ml) of water. Tea-tree oil applied directly onto spots with a cotton bud is claimed to stop infection.

Bach Remedies These may help to cope with the emotional problems that often accompany acne. Try Wild oat and Walnut for adolescent emotional problems, Crab apple for shame and embarrassment, Gorse for feelings of hopelessness.

Homoeopathy Practitioners recommend *Kali bichromicum* for chronic acne, and *Sulphur* for inflamed or infected pustules that are worse when washed. *Psorinum* is advised for severe and itchy infections.

An orthodox view

Some doctors will, like alternative practitioners, advise a change of diet – again avoiding fatty or oily foods. Others believe that diet has little or nothing to do with acne, and scientific research has so far found no evidence to support the view that diet can make acne worse.

Chemists sell many anti-acne preparations such as Acnegel, Acetoxyl and Quinoderm. However, a doctor can recommend the best product for your skin, and may prescribe antibiotic creams such as Actinax or NeoMedrone. Serious cases of acne will be treated with a six-month course of antibiotic pills or capsules such as Minocin, Erythrocin, Bactrim or Septrim.

Do not use a sun lamp and do not sunbathe a lot without a doctor's advice, as too much ultraviolet light can damage the skin (see SUNBURN).

ACUPRESSURE
An ancient massage skill

We all use this instinctive form of healing when we press our hands against our foreheads to soothe a headache. Massage is an inborn skill, but traditional oriental medicine, practised over 3000 years ago in China and Japan, developed this skill into a healing art with a system of special massage points. Acupressure is a mixture of MASSAGE and ACUPUNCTURE, and is thought to be the forerunner of acupuncture. It is still widely used at home by Japanese families.

Instead of inserting needles, practitioners use firm thumb or fingertip massage on pain-relieving 'pressure points', which are the same as those used in acupuncture.

Acupressure is said to improve the body's own healing powers, increase vitality and prevent illness. Like acupuncture, it is used to balance a flow of energy called *Qi*, which is believed to run through invisible channels known as meridians.

Who it can help Acupressure can only relieve symptoms and must be used in conjunction with other treatments, such as NATUROPATHY. Practitioners claim success in relieving many ailments, including ALLERGY, ARTHRITIS, ASTHMA, BACK PAIN, CIRCULATION PROBLEMS, DEPRESSION, DIGESTIVE PROBLEMS, INSOMNIA, MIGRAINE and TENSION.

But remember that some painful symptoms are warnings of serious illness, so always consult your doctor before using acupressure for any but everyday ailments you would normally treat at home.

Finding a therapist A register of reputable therapists who have completed training courses is available from the Shen Tao Foundation, Middle Piccadilly Natural Healing Centre, Holwell, Sherborne, Dorset DT9 5LW, or the Shiatsu Society, 19 Langside Park, Kilbarchan, Strathclyde PA10 2EP.

Consulting a therapist There are several forms of acupressure including Shin Tao, Jin Shin Do and SHIATSU. The difference lies mainly in the combination of pressure points and the amount of pressure used. However, all practitioners start by compiling your case history. You are then questioned about your diet and way of life, and your pulses are taken, as in acupuncture.

For treatment, you are asked to sit or lie on a firm table or a mattress on the floor. No equipment or oils are used and you do not undress, but you are advised to wear loose-fitting clothes that will not obstruct the therapist's touch.

Each therapist has his own way of working and applies pressure in a variety of ways to tone or sedate the energy channels. He may use his thumbs, fingers, palms, knees, elbows – even feet.

The points may be tender and you may feel some discomfort such as a deep chill or pain. However, this massage is believed to produce swift results, so that the tenderness soon decreases.

Sessions last between 30 and 60 minutes, and the number of sessions varies according to your condition and response to therapy. Weekly treatments are advised for specific disorders, or you can go whenever you feel in need of a 'tune-up'.

Pain relief for sudden conditions may be rapid, but long-standing problems may take longer. Dietary changes, EXERCISE and a self-healing technique such as VISUALISATION THERAPY may also be prescribed.

Some acupressure treatments are not recommended for women during PREGNANCY. Your therapist will advise you.

Self help Acupressure is safe to use at home for common ailments such as HEAD-ACHES and nausea (see right) but may occasionally induce minor aggravations – such as a short-term worsening of symptoms – if pressure points are overstimulated. Although you can use acupressure on yourself, it is better to get a friend or relative to massage you. A course with a qualified practitioner is the best way to learn. If common ailments persist, you should see your doctor.

How to do acupressure massage Make sure that anyone you are treating is calm and relaxed; that the room is comfortably warm and that his clothing is not too tight. Ask him to sit or lie down on a firm mattress or soft rug, preferably on the floor. If seated, the spine should be straight.

Find the pressure points you need to work on by pressing deeply over the body and noting those areas which are tender – if an organ is not functioning properly, its corresponding point on the body may be tender to the touch.

Start deep, firm massage on the tender points, using your thumbs or fingertips. Exert a downward pressure of about 10lb (4.5kg) and appreciably less for small children and babies. (You can practise this by pushing down on your bathroom scales.) Massage must be in the direction of the meridian's energy flow. Your pressure should cause some discomfort, but not pain. The tenderness will soon pass. Be sure to avoid any painful pressure on the face, abdomen or directly over joints.

Use rapid movements, about 50-100 times a minute and do not use oils or creams – they are not necessary. Take your time, adults need about 5-15 minutes of massage at each pressure point; small children about

Treating some common ailments

These recommendations are only general guidelines, as there are several points that can be used for each condition.

For headache, toothache, menstrual cramps and constipation Squeeze the point 'Large Intestine 4' firmly for about five minutes between thumb and forefinger of either hand. This point is located in the web of flesh between the thumb and index finger. The pressure should be towards the index finger. Most facial aches and pains may be relieved at this pressure point.

For nausea from any cause, such as travel sickness, pregnancy or anxiety Press with your thumb on the point 'Pericardium 6' as shown, about 2in (50mm) from the wrist, for five to ten minutes.

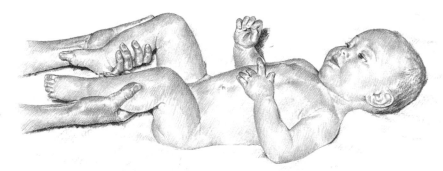

To stimulate energy and to soothe babies' colic and babies' and adults' digestive problems The point 'Stomach 36' is used for these disorders and to tone-up the system generally. This point is about 3in (75mm) below the knee joint on the outer side of the leg. It is often

slightly tender to touch, so it is usually easy to find. The point is considered to be one of the great Qi or energy 'balancers' in traditional Chinese medicine and is used often in both acupuncture and acupressure. Press deeply with your thumb for five to ten minutes.

five minutes; and babies half a minute using gentle pressure.

With self-help acupressure you can repeat the massage as often as necessary. Two or three treatments every hour are usually enough for sudden, painful conditions. Up to 20 treatments may be necessary for long-standing painful conditions, given two or three times a week, with a longer interval between as the condition improves.

Do not try to learn complicated routines or treat specific illnesses such as arthritis – know your limitations. For best results, visit a trained therapist first.

An orthodox view

There has been little direct research into how acupressure works, but the use of acupressure bands ('sea bands') on the wrists to combat MOTION SICKNESS and other forms of nausea (see NAUSEA AND VOMITING) has been scientifically studied. Research at the Department of Anaesthetics at Belfast University has shown clearly that acupressure or an acupressure band worn on a point called the 'Pericardium 6' (see p. 13) does relieve nausea caused by general anaesthesia, pregnancy, travel sickness and some drugs.

ACUPUNCTURE
Using needles to treat diseases and ailments

In this ancient Chinese therapy, patients are treated by sticking needles into their skin at particular points. These acupuncture points lie along invisible energy channels called 'meridians', which are believed to be linked to internal organs. The needles are said to unblock, increase or decrease a flow of energy (called *Qi*) through the meridians.

Traditional Chinese medicine views the body as a balance between two opposing yet complementary natural forces called 'yin' – the female force – and 'yang' – the male.

Yin force is passive and tranquil, and represents darkness, coldness, moisture and swelling. Yang force is aggressive and stimulating, and represents light, heat, dryness and contraction.

An imbalance of yin and yang is believed to cause diseases and ailments. For example, too much yang may cause sudden PAIN, inflammation, spasms, HEADACHES and high BLOOD PRESSURE; too much yin may cause dull aches and pains, chilliness, fluid retention, discharges and TIREDNESS.

In acupuncture, diagnosis and therapy are aimed at identifying any imbalance and

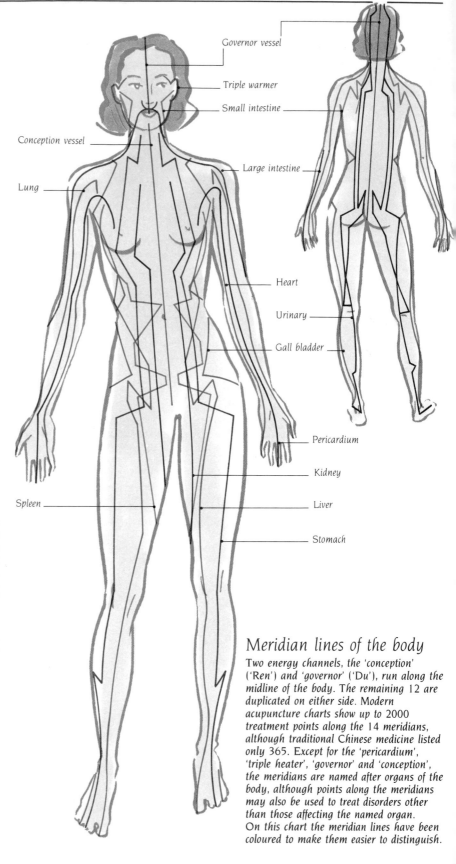

Meridian lines of the body

Two energy channels, the 'conception' ('Ren') and 'governor' ('Du'), run along the midline of the body. The remaining 12 are duplicated on either side. Modern acupuncture charts show up to 2000 treatment points along the 14 meridians, although traditional Chinese medicine listed only 365. Except for the 'pericardium', 'triple heater', 'governor' and 'conception', the meridians are named after organs of the body, although points along the meridians may also be used to treat disorders other than those affecting the named organ.
On this chart the meridian lines have been coloured to make them easier to distinguish.

correcting it by inserting needles at appropriate points. There are by tradition 365 points, but many more have been discovered over the centuries and there are up to 2000 on modern charts (see illustration).

Most of the important points are on the 14 meridians, each named after an organ which it represents – the heart, small intestine, bladder, kidney, gall bladder, liver, lungs, colon, stomach and spleen, plus two organs not recognised in Western medicine – the pericardium, which controls circulation and is important in sexual activity, and the 'triple heater' (or 'warmer') which controls endocrine (glands) activity and acts as the body's thermostat. Two extra meridians called the 'Ren' (or 'conception') and the 'Du' (or 'governor') run vertically up the midline of the body.

Physical, emotional and environmental disorders are said to alter the flow of *Qi* (also called *Ch'i* or *Shi*), making it either too fast or too slow; or it may even be blocked or diverted to the wrong organ. An acupuncturist aims to return the flow to its normal rate.

Who it can help In the West acupuncture is used mostly to treat painful conditions such as ARTHRITIS, BACK PAIN and RHEUMATISM, but it has also been found to help people suffering from ALLERGY, ANGINA, ANXIETY, ASTHMA, BRONCHITIS, COLITIS, DIGESTIVE PROBLEMS, gall-bladder problems, INSOMNIA, STRESS, tiredness and ULCERS. Success has been claimed in relieving withdrawal symptoms after giving up SMOKING and other types of ADDICTION.

Finding an acupuncturist As the law stands, anyone may use the title 'acupuncturist' whether or not he is properly trained. So it is important that you only consult a practitioner who belongs to one of the four professional bodies affiliated to the Council for Acupuncture: the British Acupuncture Association and Register (whose members use the initials MBAcA); the International Register of Oriental Medicine UK (MIROM); the Register of Traditional Chinese Medicine (MRTCM); and the Traditional Acupuncture Society (MTAS). These organisations have strict codes of ethics and practice. Training lasts for three years and qualifications in the subjects of anatomy, physiology, pathology and diagnosis are required for membership. Some conventional doctors are also trained traditional acupuncturists, and lists of these doctors can be obtained from the British Medical Acupuncture Society, Newton House, Newton Lane, Lower Whitley, Warrington, Cheshire WA4 4JA.

For a register of acupuncturists which lists the names of all the members of these bodies, contact The Council for Acupuncture, 38 Mount Pleasant, London WC1X 0AP. You may also find practitioners listed in your local *Yellow Pages* directory under Acupuncture Practitioners. Look for the designation MBAcA or FBAcA (Membership or Fellowship of the BAAR) and the qualifications LicAc (Licentiate in Acupuncture); BAc (Bachelor of Acupuncture); and DrAc (Doctorate in Acupuncture).

Consulting an acupuncturist A traditional acupuncturist uses Chinese diagnosis and follows an ancient set of rules to select the points. He will inspect your tongue, skin texture and colouring, hair texture, posture and movement, and listen to your breathing and the sound of your voice.

He will ask about your way of life, diet, exercise, quality of sleep, phobias and reactions to stress. He will also feel the 12 pulses of traditional acupuncture, six in each wrist, each pulse representing one of the 12 main organs and functions in acupuncture. This process is called 'palpating' and is the means used by acupuncturists to diagnose disturbance in the flow of *Qi* and any disease of the internal organs.

Fine, stainless-steel needles are then inserted – usually a quick, painless and bloodless procedure – and rotated between his finger and thumb, to 'draw or disperse energy' from a point. You will feel a slight numbness or tingling sensation over each point. Most lay acupuncturists insert the needles so that they just penetrate the skin, or go in a quarter to half an inch. The Chinese use even deeper insertion into the muscle tissue – up to three or four inches.

The number of needles used varies from one to as many as 15, but in general the more experienced the acupuncturist, the fewer needles he uses. They may be left in for just a few minutes or up to half an hour (depending on the patient, reaction to previous treatment, and the condition being treated), during which time there may be a heaviness of the limbs and a pleasant feeling of relaxation. A good acupuncturist now uses disposable acupuncture needles from sealed, sterilised packs, or he will sterilise them in a machine called an autoclave.

Boiling water is not adequate, as acupuncture needles can transmit blood-borne diseases such as hepatitis and the HIV virus responsible for AIDS.

Consultations may last up to an hour, particularly if a detailed history and 'palpation' is necessary.

Patients usually start feeling better within the first four to six visits – especially if the condition is long-standing, with clear and persistent symptoms. However, a complex problem such as asthma may need more sessions before there is a clear improvement.

Sometimes the patient may even feel worse after initial treatment – but this usually means that the acupuncturist has over-stimulated the body's energies, and will use fewer needles for a shorter time in the next session. In general, acupuncture works in

The acupuncturist places needles in the neck and shoulder of a patient sent to her by an osteopath, to relieve pain and muscle tension caused by thinning discs in the neck vertebrae.

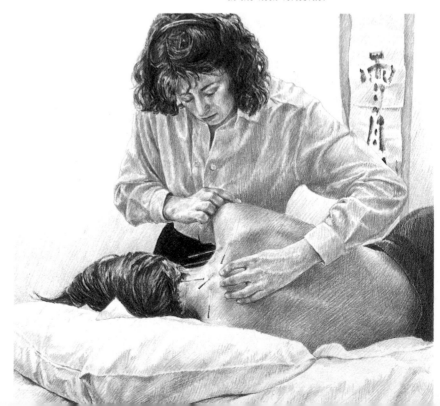

How acupuncture developed

The word 'acupuncture' is a European term meaning 'to prick with a needle'. It was coined by a Dutch physician called Willem Ten Rhyne who introduced the practice to Europe following a two-year stay in Nagasaki, Japan, in 1683.

Acupuncture has been practised in China for some 3500 years, but the exact date of its origin is unknown. A legend says that this complex healing system developed when it was noticed that soldiers who survived arrow wounds in battle sometimes also recovered from other long-standing ailments.

The first medical textbook on acupuncture was the *Nei Ching Su Wen* (the 'Yellow Emperor's Classic of Internal Medicine'), which dates from about 400 BC. The first therapeutic success with acupuncture appears in records of around the same time, when a physician named Pein Chueh used it to revive a dying patient in a coma.

The practice was gradually developed and refined until the Ching dynasty (AD 1644-1911), when Western medicine became more popular. Since the Communist revolution, however, acupuncture has been revitalised and is now widely used throughout China.

Acupuncture was used extensively by

This Chinese amulet shows the yin (black) and yang (red) symbol.

British doctors in the early 19th century for the relief of pain and also for the treatment of FEVER. In 1823 the first edition of *The Lancet*, the famous medical journal, carried a detailed report of the successful use of acupuncture in treating RHEUMATISM.

Acupuncture points can also be stimulated by a low-frequency electrical current applied with a probe (electro-acupuncture), or with finely tuned laser beams. Electro-acupuncture may also be used to detect acupuncture points (which pass an electric current more easily than other areas of skin), and to give a greater stimulation effect to acupuncture needles.

See also ACUPRESSURE; AURICULAR THERAPY; MOXIBUSTION; REFLEXOLOGY.

Moxibustion, related to acupuncture, as shown in a 700-year-old Chinese picture.

stages and improvement should build up in successive sessions. However, if there is no improvement after six to eight sessions, acupuncture is unlikely to work.

Many traditional acupuncturists recommend three or four visits a year at changes of season for a general body 'tune up' to balance the pulses and maintain health.

An orthodox view

The Chinese have published volumes of research into the use of acupuncture to treat many conditions, claiming a high success rate, but their methods of conducting clinical trials do not meet Western standards, and their conclusions are interpreted with caution. However, orthodox research based on a number of experiments involving animals, and the use of drugs on humans, has now discovered that it is possible to stop a 'pain signal' reaching the brain by 'closing a gate' on the nerve along which the signal travels from the source of pain.

This stops you feeling pain, and it is thought that acupuncture may work in a similar way. But doctors point to a danger that acupuncture may mask certain symp-

toms – including some associated with CANCER – which are warnings that call for orthodox treatment.

A further discovery has revealed that the body produces opiates called endorphins and enkephalins, which dull the senses and are part of its pain-relieving system. Worldwide studies have shown that acupuncture releases these opiates into the body's central nervous system, and that the amount of pain relief felt after acupuncture relates directly to the amount of opiates that are released.

This may explain the successful use of acupuncture to relieve pain during dentistry, childbirth and surgery. It is used widely in China as a replacement for chemical anaesthetics, where it is held to be 90 per cent effective for suitable patients. A small number of Western teaching hospitals and pain clinics also use acupuncture to relieve pain after operations, if they have doctors trained in the skill.

There is considerable evidence to suggest that acupuncture points are important medically. Western doctors recognise that treating areas of skin made tender by disease with injections, massage and heat can give

pain relief. These areas, called 'trigger points', are often some distance from the diseased organ and recent research has shown that over 70 per cent of them are also Chinese acupuncture points.

Research also shows that acupuncture points can be detected with electronic instruments because they have a lower electrical resistance than the surrounding skin. There is, however, no evidence as yet to prove the physical existence of 'meridians'.

ADDICTION
Vicious cycle of dependence

To most people the word 'addiction' conjures up pictures of heroin addicts injecting themselves with dirty needles, or Mafia gangs, pushers and street fights. But hard drug addiction is only one aspect of a growing problem – and is not even the most common or the most important. For addiction has become a part of everyday life.

In Britain alone, SMOKING is responsible for 100,000 premature deaths every year, and alcoholic drinks for about 40,000. Hundreds of thousands of men and women are addicted to tranquillisers such as Valium and Librium, and a large proportion of the population needs its 'fix' of coffee several times a day.

Addicts can be people of all ages from all kinds of backgrounds. The underlying cause is often a problem or situation in life which they cannot face or escape from, social pressure to conform, or simply a wish to experiment, out of curiosity.

As the body gets accustomed to the stimulation induced by the mood-changing substance, more and more of it is needed to get the same effect.

Addiction is a dependence on a substance which alters the body chemistry and so changes the user's moods. Illegal drugs such as cannabis, cocaine, crack (a form of cocaine that is smoked), acid (LSD) and heroin all do this. However, medically prescribed tranquillisers and sleeping pills, the nicotine in cigarettes and the caffeine in coffee also have a similar effect.

This is known as acquiring a 'tolerance' for it. For example, the heavy drinker starts to need an extra scotch or two, the caffeine addict makes his coffee ever stronger and the smoker gets through more cigarettes each day. This process eventually levels out, but by then the next stage has set in – withdrawal symptoms if the addicts cannot get the substance to which they are addicted.

These symptoms may include stomach pain, ANXIETY, loss of appetite, HEADACHES, INSOMNIA, muscle cramps, NAUSEA AND VOMITING, PALPITATIONS, panic attacks, shaking, sweating and tearfulness. In severe cases there will be CONVULSIONS and hallucinations – usually seeing frightening things that are not really there.

At this stage addicts have to continue taking whatever fix they are hooked on just to feel normal, and a cycle of dependence is established. Curing dependence means giving up all illegal drugs, and doctors avoiding the over-prescription of potentially addictive medical drugs (see DRUGS AND THEIR DANGERS); it means stopping smoking and reducing alcohol intake to moderate levels (see ALCOHOLISM); it means cutting down on stimulants such as tea and coffee – using decaffeinated coffee to reduce caffeine intake, for example.

What the therapists recommend

ACUPUNCTURE
Practitioners believe this to be an effective treatment for breaking addiction habits,

Signs and symptoms of drug abuse

The earlier an addiction is discovered, the better chance the addict has of recovery. General symptoms are:
Behaving out of character when there is no obvious explanation.
Mood swings, anxiety, depression, fear, bad temper, lethargy and tiredness.
Unusual laziness and unreliability; poor performance at school or work.
Neglecting food and appearance.
Constant sniffing, dry cough and skin peeling around the lips.
Specific symptoms include Pinpoint-size eye pupils – a sign of heroin and morphine addicts.
Unsteadiness, trembling of the limbs and confusion, sometimes resembling drunkenness, are indicators of tranquilliser dependence.
Red eyes, over-relaxed and drowsy are the signs of a cannabis user.
Disorientated or giggly: telltale behaviour of an LSD user (and terror during a 'bad trip').
Signs to look for include Unusual smells or substances around the house – tubes of glue, tablets, capsules and powder, greenish-brown 'tobacco', homemade cigarette stubs and hypodermic needles.
Uncharacteristic dishonesty – stealing, perhaps to buy drugs.
Changes in the person's circle of friends, attitudes and interests.
Needle injection marks and/or bruises on the inside of the elbow.

because it deals with the problem at every level – investigating the underlying cause of addiction, alleviating withdrawal symptoms, breaking the habit and rekindling enthusiasm for life. Diet (see EATING FOR HEALTH) and EXERCISE will be recommended, and the therapist may advise professional counselling or PSYCHOTHERAPY such as group therapy. The therapist will probably treat points in the arms and legs, corresponding to the small and large intestines, heart and lungs and also points in the ear, corresponding to the brain. Recent research by conventional doctors in the USA has confirmed that acupuncture works well against alcoholism.

BACH REMEDIES
Agrimony is prescribed for those who maintain a cheerful façade and drink to conceal tension and inner pain: Larch for addiction masking a lack of confidence; Star of Beth-

lehem where addiction follows a shock or sudden loss; Clematis for desire to escape reality; Wild oat for difficulty finding one's way in the world; Gorse for hopelessness; Willow for resentment, feeling victimised by life; Rescue Remedy for withdrawal symptoms. See also DEPRESSION.

HOMOEOPATHY
Consultation A homoeopath will deal with each patient's individual needs. Treatment is said to help reduce withdrawal symptoms; increase the addict's ability to succeed in breaking his habit; and help him come to terms with the underlying cause.

On a self-help basis, advice may be offered that *Nux vomica* is recommended for tranquilliser addicts and alcoholics when the underlying cause is TENSION, pressure or irritability. For a sudden, acute attack take a dose of 200th potency half-hourly – three or four doses should suffice. For an ongoing, chronic problem, take 3rd or 6th potency three times daily for a month.

NATUROPATHY
Consultation Whatever the addiction, a balanced diet is advised to build stamina and help the body to heal itself. FASTING may be recommended to clear poisons from the system, as well as exercise and relaxation routines such as MEDITATION. Naturopathy treatment can be combined with ACUPUNCTURE, psychotherapy and HYPNOTHERAPY.

Cravings for stimulants like tobacco have sometimes been found to be associated with low blood sugar, which could induce tiredness. The therapist will advise cutting out sugar, honey and sweet foods.

To overcome mild tranquilliser addictions a high-potency vitamin B-complex (100mg twice a day with food) and vitamin C (500iu twice a day) may be recommended; smokers are said to need extra vitamin B_1, B_6, B_{12} and C to make up for the loss of B vitamins in the body, which are destroyed by the presence of nicotine.

An orthodox view

There are several approaches to treatment, but one thing is essential to them all – addicts have to realise that they have a problem, and be convinced that they *want* to change. Although many people are reluctant to talk to their doctor about these problems, most doctors are only too happy to offer help and advice.

For most forms of addiction it is best to start with self help. Read about how to tackle the problem – a doctor can advise on pamphlets and publications. Addicts should seek counselling and support from self-help organisations such as Alcoholics Anonymous, Tranx (for tranquilliser addicts) and

Weightwatchers. Narcotics Anonymous offer help to anyone addicted to hard drugs. They can be contacted through a local community health council or health education service (usually at the nearest main hospital); or try the local library for a book of contacts.

If the doctor feels that the addict is really motivated, he may arrange to see him regularly during a withdrawal period. And if specialist help is required (which may include going into hospital) he can usually arrange it. Alcoholics may need detoxification and psychotherapy. Group psychotherapy may also be used to help the families of alcoholics and drug addicts.

Prescribed-drug addicts will have to work with their doctor, coming off the drug gradually, perhaps aided by psychotherapy or hypnotism. Illegal drug users may be given less-harmful substitute drugs in limited amounts, and sent to special detoxification clinics and rehabilitation centres.

ADENOIDS

The body, like an exclusive club, has a team of 'bouncers', whose job it is to keep out undesirables. One of the most effective of these is the pharyngeal tonsil, a small pad of tissue at the back of the nose. Just as a bouncer can get the worst of a tussle, so the tonsil can suffer in its battle against infections or ALLERGY. It can become enlarged or inflamed – rather like the palatine tonsils in an attack of TONSILLITIS. When an infection persists, or the pharyngeal tonsil has to deal with repeated infections, it can become chronically enlarged, causing breathing problems. This is commonly called 'adenoids'.

Babies are born with a small pharyngeal tonsil, which grows from the age of three until about five years later, after which it shrinks. Most cases of adenoids are in children aged between five and seven. They seldom occur after puberty.

The child breathes through the mouth and snores as the flow of air from the nose to the throat is blocked by swollen tissue. Sometimes he will also have a blocked nose or nasal speech, or the Eustachian tube connecting the middle ear to the throat may become blocked, causing deafness. Usually the pharyngeal tonsil returns to normal size, but see a doctor if the symptoms last more than a month, or there is earache or deafness.

What the therapists recommend
NATUROPATHY
Self help If a child has frequent infections and adenoid problems, his general health

should be improved. Strengthen general resistance to infection by introducing a wholefood diet (see EATING FOR HEALTH) rich in vitamin C and including foods such as citrus fruit, berries, leafy green vegetables, potatoes, sweet potatoes, tomatoes, onions, garlic and leeks.

Consultation The naturopath will examine the child thoroughly before beginning treatment. He will then give advice about improving the child's health in a variety of ways, including diet, relaxation and EXERCISE.

Food supplements such as VITAMINS and MINERALS may be suggested, depending on the child's individual needs. Dairy products (milk, butter and cheese) may also be cut from the diet for a short time, and replaced with soya milk and other calcium-rich foods.

HERBAL MEDICINE
Self help Herbal infusions (see p. 184) made from red sage, horehound, marshmallow and fenugreek may all help to relieve discomfort. A useful mixture can also be made from horehound, mullein, eucalyptus, coltsfoot leaves and wild-cherry bark. Use a teaspoon of each to a cup of boiling water.

Extracts of the following herbs are used to counteract infections: echinacea as tablets or drops, myrrh and wild indigo. Garlic – the fresh herb or in capsule form – can also be effective against infections.

A herb said to be useful for any inflammation connected with the lymphatic system is cleavers (also known as goosegrass or clivers). Make an infusion by pouring a cup of boiling water onto 2-3 teaspoons of the dried herb and leave it to infuse for 10-15 minutes. Make and drink the infusion three times a day, or take 2-4ml of the tincture (see p. 184) three times a day.

Other alternative treatments
Ionisation An ioniser placed in a bedroom at night can help if there is nasal congestion.
Hydrotherapy Adding mustard to a hot bath may be useful in all cases of infection.

An orthodox view
Doctors feel that vitamin and mineral food supplements may act simply as a PLACEBO, there being no good evidence to suggest that such preparations offer any specific help against adenoids.

Most cases of adenoids will be left untreated. When the child's body overcomes the infection, the swollen tissue shrinks and the symptoms disappear.

Severe infections are treated with antibiotics. Very occasionally surgery may be decided on to remove the pharyngeal tonsil, sometimes together with the palatine tonsils. However, this is now done far less frequently than it was 30 years ago.

AEROBICS

Any exercise that increases the body's need for oxygen is a form of aerobics. This includes activities such as walking, as well as sports such as rowing, JOGGING, swimming, and the popular 'aerobics' fitness exercises.

Aerobic exercise is a vital part of body fitness, since it strengthens the heart and lungs and builds up stamina, or the ability to keep going without running out of breath. Everybody needs regular aerobic exercise, but it is vitally important to start slowly and follow a sensible plan (see EXERCISE).

AGORAPHOBIA
When going out is a nightmare

People with an irrational fear of open spaces are suffering from agoraphobia. The term also applies to the state of acute ANXIETY suffered by those who dread finding themselves in public places of any kind. Faced with such situations, they become agitated, break into a sweat and their pulse rate soars. Their fear is very real to them, even though they admit it is unreasonable. Often, agoraphobics will go to any length to avoid public places; many become housebound, making it impossible for them and their families to lead normal lives.

What causes agoraphobia is not really understood, but the condition is thought to be strongly connected with other psychological states of anxiety.

Sometimes it develops in people who suffer from panic attacks, as a response to a general fear of panicking in public. Or it can be an unconscious mental device used to evade responsibilities in the outside world.

What the therapists recommend
NATUROPATHY
Self help A wholefood diet (see EATING FOR HEALTH), with an emphasis on raw foods and juices, is said to be beneficial. For example, a mixture of lettuce juice and carrot juice – ¼ pint (150ml) of each – might be taken, twice during the day and once at bedtime. This should have a gentle, calming effect on the nervous system. Dietary supplements may also include a high-potency vitamin B stress complex (vitamins B1, B6 and pantothenic acid are held to be particularly important). In addition, you can take vitamins C, E, and zinc, calcium and magnesium in chelated

form – in which the minerals are easier for the body to absorb.

These supplements are all thought to help regulate the nervous system's functioning and, in particular, its ability to cope with STRESS. The amino acid tryptophan is also said to have calming and relaxing effects.

Consultation The practitioner will pay attention to the patient's way of life as well as his symptoms. The practitioner will ask about diet, how any stressful experiences are dealt with, and how much time is devoted to EXERCISE and relaxation.

On the basis of this information, the patient is then told which aspects of his life may be causing or building anxiety, and ways of changing them will be suggested.

The patient will also be shown RELAXATION AND BREATHING exercises to help at times of stress, and will be told how to relax generally. The practitioner will probably work in conjunction with other therapists (see HYPNOTHERAPY, REFLEXOLOGY).

HERBAL MEDICINE

Self help To allay fear or anxiety, try a tea made from three or four sprigs of lemon balm – fresh leaves taste best – infused in a cup of boiling water. This is said to be relaxing and can be drunk as often as the sufferer feels it necessary.

AROMATHERAPY

Self help Several oils are recommended, including marjoram, basil and Roman camomile. Put a few drops of any of these, or mix a drop of two of them, or all three, on a ball of cotton wool or paper tissue and put it into your blouse or shirt, or sprinkle a few drops on your clothing. Use only pure essential oils obtainable at health shops, and not those which are in a vegetable carrier oil.

Other alternative treatments

Homoeopathy Usually, remedies are chosen to suit individual patients, but some general ones which are believed to help agoraphobics are: *Aconitum* for sudden panic attacks, fears and confusion; *Arsenicum album* for chronic anxiety with occasional panic attacks, especially in overtidy or obsessive people.

Bach Remedies Try Mimulus if the fear is well-defined; Aspen if there is apprehension or a secret dread, and Rock rose if it escalates into panic. If there is a fear of losing control or of doing something dreadful, try Cherry plum. Larch should ease the loss of confidence caused by fear, and Pine a tendency towards self-reproach.

Biochemic Tissue Salts *Kali phos.* is recommended for anxiety: take four tablets every two or three hours.

Acupuncture and Reflexology Both these therapies are claimed to relieve anxiety and to restore tranquillity.

Psychological Therapies Practitioners offer many different kinds of psychological therapy. There is no register of these therapists in Britain – so choose one with whom you are in sympathy and feel you can trust.

Some use techniques that are also part of orthodox therapies, such as psychoanalysis and BEHAVIOURAL THERAPY. More often, treatments use methods based on HUMANISTIC PSYCHOLOGY or transpersonal psychology that are not generally accepted by conventional psychology.

For more about these approaches, see ROGERIAN THERAPY, ENCOUNTER GROUPS, GESTALT THERAPY, PSYCHODRAMA, TRANSACTIONAL ANALYSIS, CO-COUNSELLING, BIOENERGETICS, POLARITY THERAPY, METAMORPHIC TECHNIQUE, REBIRTHING, PSYCHOSYNTHESIS.

An orthodox view

Some doctors use methods similar to those of alternative therapists – such as listening to a patient's problems and discussing them sympathetically. But when necessary, a general practitioner will also prescribe tranquillisers such as Valium (diazepam), Librium (chlordiazepoxide), Ativan (lorazepam) or Inderal (propranolol) to help to cope with anxiety. If these do not work, the patient may be referred to a psychiatrist or psychotherapist (see PSYCHOTHERAPY).

Psychiatrists are medically qualified physicians who specialise in psychological disorders, which they treat with drugs. Psychotherapists treat disorders through behaviour therapy or psychoanalysis.

For agoraphobia, behavioural therapy is often successful. Psychiatry, however, has a poor track record for treatment of agoraphobia and, as the drugs and other therapies are often drastic or involve side effects such as sleepiness or memory loss, many general practitioners avoid it. Psychotherapy is difficult to obtain through the NATIONAL HEALTH SERVICE and, when it is available, patients have no choice of a particular therapy, so often turn to alternatives.

AIDS

The body has no defence against Acquired Immune Deficiency Syndrome (AIDS) because the complex, everchanging virus that causes the disease attacks the very cells that should be helping the body to fight off infection. This Human Immunodeficiency Virus (HIV) is usually – though not always – passed on through casual sexual intercourse, or by injecting drugs with a needle already used by someone who carries the virus. Before tests for infected blood were developed, a number of people caught the HIV from blood transfusions.

The catastrophic damage that the HIV can cause to the IMMUNE SYSTEM can leave the body prey to infections of the lungs, skin, nervous and digestive systems, and a variety of cancers. This is AIDS, which develops in two or three out of every ten people who catch the HIV. Although the others usually remain symptomless, they also remain carriers of the virus and can pass it on.

There is no known cure, and the fear of AIDS that has spread worldwide since 1981, when cases were first diagnosed in the USA, has led to serious misconceptions about the disease, with distressing social consequences for sufferers.

It cannot, as many think, be passed on simply by touching a sufferer, or by drinking from the same glass or using the same cutlery – or even by kissing, as long as there are no cuts or sores on the mouth. The virus dies in the air and is also destroyed outside the body by soap and detergent. The disease is not, as many think, confined to homosexual men – it can be spread by unprotected sexual contact with any infected person.

As a protection against sexually transmitted AIDS, the Department of Health recommends using the condom, designed originally as a contraceptive. This works because the virus can be passed on through prolonged contact of body fluids – and the condom prevents contact with fluids such as the partner's semen or vaginal secretions during intercourse. For drug addicts, who can get the virus from a used syringe contaminated by the infected blood of an HIV carrier, official advice is to use a new disposable syringe for each injection.

People with haemophilia have also caught the HIV after being given transfusions of HIV-infected blood or blood products. However, in Britain blood donors have been screened for infection since 1985. Also at risk are babies whose mothers carry the HIV.

Symptoms of AIDS infection include weight loss, EXHAUSTION, DIARRHOEA, FEVER, coughing, breathlessness and swollen glands in the groin, armpits and neck. Some sufferers develop Kaposi's sarcoma, a rare skin cancer. Others suffer less serious complaints such as THRUSH, COLD SORES, milder SKIN DISORDERS or BOWEL DISORDERS.

Nobody knows why those HIV carriers who do not develop AIDS remain well. However, there is a general feeling among both conventional and alternative practitioners that healthy living, a positive mental attitude and learning to cope with STRESS can help.

AIDS is prevalent worldwide. It is endemic

in some places, such as parts of central and southern Africa, where those people affected are mostly heterosexuals.

Alternative treatments Because AIDS is a relatively new disease, and because those infected can get a wide range of complaints, alternative therapists have been unable to lay down hard-and-fast overall methods of treatment. Generally, however, practitioners tend to concentrate on a holistic approach, trying to treat simultaneously the sufferer's body, mind, emotions and spirit.

To achieve this, collaboration between the various different specialist therapies would be advisable. These might include the following therapies: ACUPUNCTURE, AUTOGENIC TRAINING, HERBAL MEDICINE, HOMOEOPATHY, MASSAGE, NATUROPATHY, REFLEXOLOGY and SPIRITUAL HEALING.

What the therapists recommend
NATUROPATHY
Self help A preparation of natural fats known as AL721 has been patented in the United States and reportedly used with beneficial effects there and in Israel. (AL stands for 'active lipids', which are fatty substances; 7:2:1 is the ratio of the ingredients used.) The mixture is designed to protect mucous membranes and blood cells which fight viruses. The preparation is available in powder and capsule form in the United Kingdom.

HERBAL MEDICINE
Self help For secondary infections, particularly thrush, two tablets of dried golden seal root are recommended twice a day; one to three GARLIC capsules a day are also very effective. For bowel disorders, about 20 drops of golden seal in liquid form should be taken three times a day between meals. Acidophilus is also believed to be effective against thrush and bowel infections: take ¼ teaspoon of Superdophilus twice a day between meals.
Consultation For protection against viruses, a herbalist might recommend the powerful herb echinacea. Dosage would be 500mg of dried root powder. Up to three garlic capsules a day might also be prescribed.

BACH REMEDIES
Self help If you or your partner is found to be HIV positive, you might benefit from learning about the Bach Remedies in some depth, to support you through the crisis. They include: Mimulus for fear of getting ill; Mimulus and Aspen for apprehensiveness and fear of death; Holly and Willow for anger, resentment and desire for revenge; Gorse for feelings of hopelessness; Sweet chestnut for extreme despair; Walnut to assist the transition in lifestyle and values; Pine for guilt and self-blame; Wild rose for

apathy, resignation or collapse; Honeysuckle for regrets over the past. See also GRIEF and TERMINAL ILLNESS.

An orthodox view
The only conventional drug which has been shown to be effective on a limited scale in some cases is Retrovir (AZT). But one of its side effects can be to inhibit bone-marrow production, which in turn necessitates continual blood transfusions for a few patients.

Since relatively few of those with HIV infection get AIDS, it is thought that a number of other important factors make particular individuals more susceptible.

A doctor will recommend EXERCISE, which will be dependent on the victim's ability to take it. A simple, nutritious diet, with plenty of FIBRE, fresh fruit and vegetables may also be advised. If thrush is present, mushrooms, sugar and yeast should be avoided.

In addition, to improve the state of the immune system, supplements such as amino acids, vitamins and trace elements may be prescribed. The most important vitamins include A (preferably in the form of beta-carotene, 12,500iu up to three times a day), B group, C (up to 6g a day, depending on tolerance and side effects), and E (100iu daily). The recommended trace elements include selenium (100-300 micrograms daily) and zinc (15-300mg, depending on the basic salt that is taken).

ALCOHOLISM

One of the most common forms of ADDICTION is alcoholism. It develops when the drinkers' bodies become so used to absorbing large amounts of alcohol that they can no longer function normally when they do not drink. The symptoms are a continual craving for alcohol, an inability to drink moderately and, as the illness develops, a need to drink more to get the same effect.

Mostly, alcoholism develops slowly over years of steadily increasing consumption. The victim may start by drinking to be 'one of the crowd', or to give himself a lift, or to help him to forget his worries. Later his system becomes dependent on alcohol and, if he cannot get it, he suffers withdrawal symptoms such as feverishness, sleeplessness and tremors accompanied by hallucinations – *delirium tremens* (DTs).

Alcoholism should always be treated by a doctor, since continual heavy drinking can cause serious LIVER DISORDERS, brain damage, mouth, throat and pancreatic CANCER, OBESITY, ANAEMIA, SEXUAL PROB-

LEMS, and disorders of the stomach, nervous system and heart. There may be high BLOOD PRESSURE, and vitamin deficiencies if meals are neglected. Social and psychological problems are also common.

Self help Prevention is the best method of dealing with alcoholism. Control social drinking by counting and measuring all drinks – even at home. Set a daily limit and stick to it; and eat something while drinking, to slow down the absorption of alcohol into the blood. If you meet friends in a pub, buy your own drinks rather than taking part in rounds. Drink slowly – no more than one unit (see caption) in half an hour – and make every second drink non-alcoholic. Do not drink at all if you are going to drive, and ask your doctor first if you are taking medicine.

What the therapists recommend
Naturopathy The practitioner will advise about diet, EXERCISE, avoiding drink, and coping with STRESS and other emotional problems. Naturopathic remedies are believed to be particularly effective when they are used in conjunction with PSYCHOTHERAPY, ACUPUNCTURE and HYPNOTHERAPY.

Herbal Medicine Evening-primrose oil is said to be helpful, since it is rich in GLA (gamma-linolenic acid) which the body of an alcoholic is often unable to manufacture for itself. It is believed to help in preventing mood swings and liver damage.

Milk thistle, which is gentle in its action, is believed to help liver cells to regenerate. Herbal remedies are also said to help in overcoming any withdrawal symptoms, by relieving TENSION and relaxing both the sufferer's body and his mind.

Infusions of skullcap, pasque flower (use carefully in low doses), motherwort, oats and

Facts about alcohol abuse

Heavy drinking is associated with 66 per cent of attempted suicides, 52 per cent of deaths from fire and with 45 per cent of fatal road accidents to young people in Britain.

The total cost of alcohol abuse is over £2 billion a year, of which £723 million is the cost of absence from work through sickness.

Up to 14 million working days a year are lost through heavy drinking.

Half of all people seen in hospital accident and emergency departments have alcohol or drug-related problems, and one in every five beds in medical wards is taken by a patient with an alcohol-related problem.

About 21 units of alcohol a week for men but only 14 for women is the recommended 'safe' intake. One unit is any one of the drinks illustrated above: a third of a pint of strong beer or ale, half a pint of ordinary beer or lager, a glass of wine, a small glass of sherry, or a single measure of spirits or aperitif. Pregnant women should preferably avoid all forms of alcohol. If they do drink, they should never drink more than four units in a week – and on no account drink more than two units in any single day.

lavender are recommended. Oats (the easiest way is to eat them in porridge) are said to be the safest of these relaxants. They are also believed to help in controlling blood sugar.

Bach Remedies These remedies are said to help people to deal with the reasons for their drinking problems: Agrimony is used where cheerfulness hides deep anxiety; Larch where there are feelings of failure; and Crab apple where the drinkers feel ashamed of themselves. White chestnut is recommended to overcome obsessive thoughts, and Aspen for fear or paranoia.

Hypnotherapy Treatment under hypnosis involves strengthening the willpower and determination needed to stop drinking, and planting subconscious 'drinking is bad' thoughts deeply in the patient's mind.

An orthodox view

A doctor may recommend AVERSION THERAPY, using a drug such as Antabuse (disulfiram), which makes you violently ill if you drink anything alcoholic. Forms of psychotherapy, including BEHAVIOURAL THERAPY and group therapy, are also used.

In addition, a general practitioner, perhaps working in liaison with a community nurse and social worker, can give advice and help both to sufferers and their families. Or he may refer the patient to a local organisation or clinic like those given on the right.

Where to seek help

For advice and information, write to Alcohol Concern, 305 Gray's Inn Road, London WC1X 8QF. For help with drinking problems contact Alcoholics Anonymous, P.O. Box 1, Stonebow House, Stonebow, York YO1 2NJ.

Advice, information and counselling are available from The Accept Clinic, 200 Seagrave Road, London SW6 1RQ. Families are helped by Al-Anon Family Groups, 61 Great Dover Street, London SE1 4YF.

ALEXANDER TECHNIQUE
Improving your health through better posture

By using the Alexander Technique you can learn to improve your posture so that your body is able to work in a more natural, relaxed and efficient manner. It is said to be entirely safe, to promote a harmonious state of both mind and body, and to help a number of medical conditions, ranging from BACK PAIN to HEADACHES.

The method was developed by an Australian actor, Frederick Matthias Alexander (see box), who found himself losing his voice on stage and discovered that he could cure the condition by improving his posture. His discovery became the basis for a whole technique for retraining the body's movements and positions. Today there are Alexander training schools and teachers in many parts of the world. People are taught individually and teachers refer to them as 'pupils' rather than patients.

Anyone feeling that they could benefit from the technique can test themselves by observing their posture in front of a mirror and performing some of the simple procedures illustrated.

Who it can help Teachers claim that the Alexander Technique has helped people of all ages and from all walks of life, by improving their health, emotional well-being, mental alertness and resistance to STRESS. The British writer Aldous Huxley said that the technique not only improved his physical and mental health, but caused a 'general heightening of consciousness on all levels'.

The Dutch zoologist and ethologist Professor Nikolaas Tinbergen, awarded the Nobel Prize for Physiology and Medicine in 1973, said in his acceptance speech that the Alexander Technique had brought 'striking improvements in such diverse things as high blood pressure, breathing, depth of sleep, overall cheerfulness and mental alertness . . . and also in such a refined skill as playing a stringed musical instrument'. He had become a pupil of the technique while working at Cambridge.

As a result of improved posture, those who have benefited from the training actually become taller because they stand more upright. The training has also been used to improve the performances of athletes, dancers, and public speakers. Success has been claimed in treating EXHAUSTION, DEPRESSION, ANXIETY, tension HEADACHES, high BLOOD

PRESSURE, RESPIRATORY DISORDERS, peptic ULCERS, IRRITABLE BOWEL SYNDROME, COLITIS, RHEUMATOID ARTHRITIS, OSTEOARTHRITIS, lower back pain, SCIATICA and ASTHMA.

Finding a teacher In Britain all reputable teachers of the technique have completed a three-year course at one of four London training schools recognised by the Society of Teachers of the Alexander Technique (STAT). Many, though not all, put STAT after their names. To find the one nearest to you, write to the society at 10 London House, 266 Fulham Road, London SW10 9EL.

Seeing a teacher The teacher begins by watching how you use your body. Even simple activities such as walking or reading a book involve the use of many muscles, and a certain amount of muscular tension and 'spring' is needed just to react against the pull of gravity. Children move naturally, but usually acquire bad habits as they grow. In addition, stress can result in misplaced muscular effort, seen in such simple actions as holding a pen too tightly, opening a jam jar or driving a car.

Some people suffer from chronic muscular tension, which throws the head, neck and back out of alignment, causing rounded

Even the way you stand can cause problems . . .

For much of the time people do not adopt the right posture, even when simply standing up. This may lead to aches and pains. They may stand in a slouched, round-shouldered way that looks and can feel uncomfortable (right). And in trying to correct themselves, they may stand too stiff and upright (centre) which can be equally harmful. A teacher can show you how to 'stand tall' in an aligned and balanced way (far right).

This is one of the many means by which the technique aims to rehabilitate – or redeploy – the body's entire muscular system. The goal is to return to the natural stance and movements of childhood which need the minimum of muscular effort.

Slouched   Over-correct   Aim for

Teachers use gentle manipulation to set pupils on the right path. A teacher may help a pupil to relax, then carefully pull her neck, stretching her body (below). Others employ gentle pushing techniques, of the hips, stomach and back, for example.

F.M. Alexander 1869-1955

An answer in the mirror

The originator of the Alexander Technique, Australian actor Frederick Matthias Alexander, found his career faltering when he began to lose his voice on stage. Medical treatment did not help, but he noted that his condition improved with rest and wondered whether something he was doing while on stage might be causing the problem. Acting out his stage role before a mirror, he saw that when the moment came for him to speak a startling physical change occurred: he shrank in height and had difficulty breathing.

He decided that the combined effort of having to remember his lines and project them for an audience was causing him to lower or duck his head, a natural reflex action to stress. He could feel that this put pressure on his vocal cords and tightened his throat, interfering with his breathing and creating tension throughout his body. Further, he found that even the thought of projecting his voice triggered off these reactions, leading him to believe that mind and body must be closely related.

By constantly observing and correcting himself, Alexander began slowly to change the way he thought about his task and to overcome what he called his 'startle reflex pattern'. Gradually he recovered his stage voice and came to use his body in a more natural way.

Alexander began to teach his technique. In 1904 he came to London where he was soon much in demand by the acting profession, which quickly saw the benefits of his method. And so did many public figures, including Aldous Huxley (1894-1963), the British author of *Brave New World*.

Alexander moved to America, and the technique rapidly gained international recognition. He suffered a stroke when he was 78, but astonished his doctors by using his method to regain the entire use of his body and faculties.

shoulders, a bowed head and arched back. If this is not corrected the spine develops a curve, and a hump may appear at the base of the neck. This causes back pain and strains the heart, lungs and digestive system.

The teacher shows you how to change these harmful postures and regain the habit of using muscles with minimum effort and maximum efficiency. While you stand, sit or lie down, the teacher gently manipulates your body into a more natural position. Meanwhile, you should concentrate on the teacher's instructions about posture. You are encouraged to think of the technique as a way of working not just on your body, but on your total awareness.

Gradually, by constantly practising and thinking about good posture, you should learn to release tension and use your body correctly. The teacher uses no force and

How to help yourself

Bad habits, such as a bad posture, are often so ingrained that they feel natural, and it may be difficult to rehabilitate your muscles to get rid of them. The technique is learnt from a qualified teacher, but you can help yourself: like Alexander watch yourself in a mirror, while standing, walking or sitting, for example, and aim for a relaxed stance and movements, with minimum muscular effort.

Walking
Avoid Slouched posture, with head down, shoulders stooped and tense (above).
Aim for Keeping the balance of the head on top of the spine, freely poised and shoulders relaxed. Feel yourself transferring your weight onto alternate feet as you walk (right).

Alexander Technique

Sitting

<u>Aim for</u> Holding your head freely poised, shoulders relaxed, knees a little apart (crossed legs twist the pelvis and spine) and feet firmly on the floor (right).

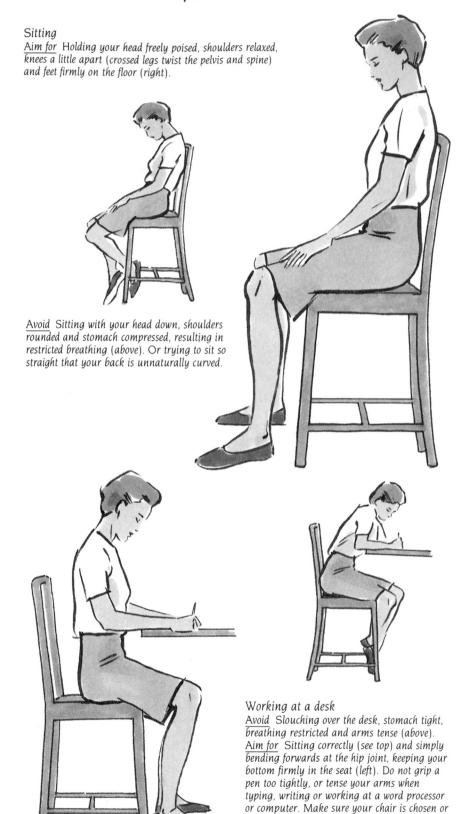

<u>Avoid</u> Sitting with your head down, shoulders rounded and stomach compressed, resulting in restricted breathing (above). Or trying to sit so straight that your back is unnaturally curved.

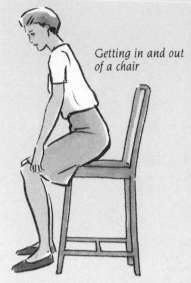

Getting in and out of a chair

<u>Aim for</u> Keeping your spine and neck in alignment and simply bending at the hip, knees and ankles. When getting into a chair imagine you are squatting down. Adopt the same posture when rising.

Getting into a chair
<u>Avoid</u> Collapsing into a chair by throwing your head back, sticking your bottom out and arching your lower back.

Rising from a chair
<u>Avoid</u> Jutting your head forwards, folding your body and then straightening up.

Working at a desk
<u>Avoid</u> Slouching over the desk, stomach tight, breathing restricted and arms tense (above).
<u>Aim for</u> Sitting correctly (see top) and simply bending forwards at the hip joint, keeping your bottom firmly in the seat (left). Do not grip a pen too tightly, or tense your arms when typing, writing or working at a word processor or computer. Make sure your chair is chosen or adjusted to be a comfortable height in relation to the desk top.

there is no wrenching or clicking of joints – just a subtle adjustment as you learn to walk, sit, stand and move all over again, in a free, released way.

Lessons last about 30 or 45 minutes, and a course of 30 is usual, after which you should have learnt enough about the technique to be able to continue on your own.

An orthodox view

Recent scientific research has confirmed Alexander's views about natural posture and the connection between anxiety and physical tension. The technique does not conflict with orthodox opinion and although doctors may not always suggest this therapy, they do not oppose it.

ALLERGY

Streaming eyes, sneezing and skin rashes are just three of the many symptoms resulting from the body's allergic reactions to substances to which it is abnormally sensitive, such as pollen, house dust and certain types of food. See A BATTLE GOING ON IN YOUR BODY, p. 26.

ALLOPATHIC MEDICINE
The cure of opposites

When the 18th-century German physician Samuel Hahnemann developed a new system of medicine, he needed to distinguish it from the conventional medicine of the day. He described the conventional system as 'allopathic' – from the Greek words *allos* meaning 'different' and *pathos* meaning 'suffering' – because it treated illness by prescribing drugs that had effects opposite from the symptoms. He called his new system HOMOEOPATHY – from the Greek words for 'the same' and 'suffering' – and it was based on the principle that 'like cures like'.

In allopathic medicine, a patient who develops a high temperature as a result of infection is treated with a drug such as aspirin to lower the temperature. A homoeopath prescribes (in minute amounts) a remedy that *causes* a high temperature in a healthy person, so using 'like to cure like'.

Allopathic medicine views symptoms of illness as something wrong with the body that treatment will put right. Homoeopathy

treats symptoms as signs of the body's *resistance* to disease, and works with them rather than against them. Allopathy is sometimes wrongly used to refer to all conventional medicine. In fact, orthodox medicine today makes use of many different techniques, some of which (such as inoculation) rely on principles closer to those of homoeopathy.

ALZHEIMER'S DISEASE
Growing old at an early age

This early onset of 'old age' is also known as pre-senile dementia. Symptoms are similar to those of senile dementia, or senility, but strike in middle age or even earlier. The patients' intellect, personality and physical condition all deteriorate in a way similar to the normal process of ageing. They become confused and forgetful, unable to think clearly and incapable of carrying on a conversation. They lose track of time – often wandering about at night – and movements become stiff and uncoordinated. Eventually they become bedridden and incontinent.

The cause is a loss of nerve cells in the brain, which shrinks, but how this comes about is not fully understood. However, recent research has found that both types of dementia – and particularly Alzheimer's disease – may be linked to levels of aluminium in the body. A shortage of the B-complex vitamin choline may also be involved.

A doctor should be consulted if any of the symptoms start interfering with normal activities or cause social problems.

What the therapists recommend
ACUPUNCTURE
A practitioner may advise treatment to alleviate symptoms and to improve general health, depending on the patient's condition.

HERBAL MEDICINE
Rosemary, which is believed to stimulate circulation and have a tonic effect on the nervous system, would be advised, but results are likely to be limited to reducing symptoms and slowing the rate of decline.

An orthodox view
There is as yet no cure, conventional or alternative, but a doctor may use drugs to alleviate symptoms and treat any attendant disease, and arrange for care in a nursing home or hospital if necessary.

AMNESIA

Loss of memory is seldom caused by the fiction-writer's favourite device of a knock on the head, though such an injury can be a cause. More usually it is brought on by severe emotional SHOCK, HYSTERIA, drink, or drug ADDICTION. A number of diseases can also cause amnesia, including meningitis, syphilis, brain tumour and EPILEPSY.

There are several forms of memory loss, and sufferers are said to have 'retrograde' amnesia if they cannot recall events before losing memory, or 'anterograde' amnesia if they cannot recall events afterwards. If an emotional disturbance is the cause, sufferers may also lose their identity.

In many cases, memory returns when the underlying condition clears up. However, if the cause is concussion, memories prior to a head injury may be lost for ever.

What the therapists recommend
HYPNOTHERAPY
Consultation The technique known as hypnoanalysis can be used as a drug-free alternative to narco-analysis (see below), but because it is impossible for an unwilling patient to be hypnotised, not everyone is susceptible to this treatment. In a state of hypnosis, the conscious mind is bypassed so that the hypnotist can communicate directly with the subconscious mind (which monitors mental and physical functions, and is believed to remember most – if not all – of our life experiences). In this state it may be possible for someone with amnesia to recall repressed painful memories.

BACH REMEDIES
Self help Clematis for lapses in consciousness, disorientation, mental numbness and vagueness; Star of Bethlehem if the cause was shock or grief; and Rescue Remedy if the cause is an accident or trauma.

An orthodox view

When the cause is an underlying mental illness, a doctor may give anaesthetic drugs to make the patient feel drowsy, yet talkative, and able to speak about emotional problems in a way that would not have been possible normally. This therapy, narco-analysis, may be given in hospital or to outpatients.

It may also be used with exploratory PSYCHOTHERAPY, in which a counsellor (usually a psychiatrist or psychiatric social worker) explores and assesses the patient's personality and situation by asking a series of intimate questions, the aim of which is to enable him to cope with problems.

A battle going on in your body

A number of seemingly unrelated ailments such as ASTHMA, HAY FEVER and ECZEMA all have something in common – they are caused by allergies. They erupt when your body reacts to something it is abnormally sensitive to – pollen, house dust, animal fur, foods such as shellfish, eggs and chocolate, to name but a few of these 'allergens', as they are called. If you are allergic, eating, breathing in or simply touching even tiny amounts of an allergen will cause your body to defend itself by releasing substances known as 'antibodies' – proteins designed to neutralise allergens and other antigens (see IMMUNE SYSTEM).

The ensuing battle between antibodies and allergens triggers the release of histamine and other chemicals from surrounding cells, which causes the allergic symptoms. Doctors use drugs called 'antihistamines' to control symptoms produced by allergies.

Some medical authorities believe that one person in every six has some kind of allergy; others argue that this figure is far too high. One reason for their disagreement is the difficulty in telling the difference between a true allergy, sensitivity and intolerance.

Unlike a true allergy, a sensitivity depends on how much of the substance you come into contact with. For example, almost everyone is sensitive to chlorine, but while some people have painful eyes after just a few minutes in a chlorine-treated swimming pool, others can tolerate it for much longer without ill effects. If you are among those quickly affected, you are more sensitive to chlorine than most, but probably not allergic to it.

An intolerance is different again – an adverse reaction, which may have psychological overtones, and which is particular to you. For example, a certain cheese may make you ill, but other cheeses may not affect you. In this case, you are almost certainly not allergic to the offending cheese, more likely simply intolerant of it.

The controversy deepens when such conditions as DEPRESSION, INSOMNIA, HYPERACTIVITY and inability to concentrate are attributed to allergy. There is no doubt that this is sometimes the case, but to suggest that it is always so (as some 'fringe' allergy clinics may do) would be misleading. Because orthodox medicine has, until now, not been very successful in detecting and treating allergies, a host of these clinics has opened to fill the gap. Many employ unqualified staff, and their techniques are dubious. However, other alternative treatments offer genuine help.

Causes of allergies

Environment Grass pollen, dust mites, animal hair, feathers, certain plants, and chemical and industrial pollutants can all provoke allergic responses such as runny, itchy eyes; HEADACHE; rashes and skin irritation; COUGHS and SNEEZING; WHEEZING, asthma, hay fever and eczema.

Diet Almost any food can bring on an allergic response, such as NAUSEA AND VOMITING and DIARRHOEA. The commonest allergens in order of frequency are: milk and other dairy products such as cheese; eggs; nuts; fish and shellfish; wheat and flour; chocolate; and artificial colourants. Some young babies suffer WIND, CONSTIPATION and diarrhoea because they are allergic to milk protein, and they may go on to develop asthma and eczema.

COELIAC DISEASE is due to a sensitivity to wheat protein (gluten). MIGRAINES seem sometimes to be brought on by certain foods, particularly chocolate, cheese and red wine. And it is now widely accepted that some children are affected by FOOD ADDITIVES, especially tartrazine and benzoate, leading to hyperactivity and behaviour problems.

Other factors It is possible to be allergic to almost anything. Soaps, perfumes, detergents, printers' ink, insect bites, stings, nickel in jewellery, antibiotics, cosmetics – all can be culprits.

Coping with an allergy

Like any problem, such as a cold or flu, that affects the immune system, the severity of an allergic attack depends as much upon your general health as on the allergen. Eating sensibly, relaxing and taking care of yourself will help you to cope with, and minimise, an allergic response. In addition to

---

Do's and don'ts for allergy

Do try to trace a pattern in your symptoms. Sneezing when doing housework might mean that you have an allergy to house dust, while an allergic reaction to perfume could show as a rash on the neck or wrist.

Do breastfeed a new baby for the first six months if possible. It will strengthen the baby's immune system and avoid the allergens in cow's milk. This is especially important if the mother suffers from asthma or eczema or other allergic symptoms, as the baby may also be allergic.

Do take steps to deal with STRESS, ANXIETY and TENSION, as these can increase the frequency and severity of allergic reactions.

Do try to improve your general health as much as possible. Good nutrition from a balanced diet (see EATING FOR HEALTH), and adequate rest and relaxation will all be beneficial.

Don't assume without first consulting your doctor that your symptoms are caused by an allergy – they could also indicate another kind of illness. For example, a rash that may develop if you are treated with penicillin could be due to your illness rather than an allergy to the antibiotic itself.

maintaining your health, there are three steps to be taken when dealing with an allergy. Firstly do all you can to identify the cause, or allergen; secondly, avoid it; and thirdly, if avoidance is impossible, treat the symptoms.

Food and chemical-induced allergies can be extremely difficult to track down. Your doctor may use skin testing to identify the cause, or suggest elimination dieting (cutting suspected foods out of your diet one at a time and observing the effect).

Warning Many fringe clinics' techniques are not always reliable, and their suggested treatments, especially full-scale elimination dieting undertaken without medical supervision, can be dangerous. Always check with your doctor first.

Self help Tracking down an allergen calls for good record-keeping.

Keep a diary Note everything you do and eat. It may establish a link between your allergic reaction and a particular food, or something like scent that you wear or cat's fur.

Elimination dieting On a small scale, elimination dieting may be helpful. If you suspect that a certain food – eggs or chocolate, for example – is at the root of your problem, cut it completely out of your diet for a week or two and see what happens. (In cases of eczema, you may have to eliminate a food for up to three weeks to be sure of its effect.) Otherwise, follow your normal diet. Under no circumstances should you drop more than one food at a time; it not only makes identification of the allergen more difficult, it can also lead to an unbalanced diet.

Warning While it is possible to suffer from multiple allergies, or that the particular allergen affecting you is present in a wide variety of foods, do not attempt an ambitious elimination programme without medical help. Without proper controls, the results will be virtually impossible to interpret correctly.

Alternative identification methods Despite the reputation of some dubious allergy clinics, alternative practitioners can be very successful in identifying allergens. Avoid using anyone who claims to be able to make a diagnosis by post, get your doctor's advice before going on an elimination diet, and you should come to no harm.

Clinical ecology The study of how the physical environment affects health focuses mainly on food allergies and chemical sensitivities. Many practitioners are trained doctors, and combine orthodox techniques with others such as cytotoxic testing (which uses white blood cells), muscle testing and electrical testing. If you suspect that you are suffering from

an allergy, consulting a clinical ecologist could prove helpful. See CLINICAL ECOLOGY.

Kinesiology This is a more controversial technique. Practitioners believe that muscle power is affected by allergy, and measure your muscular response to suspected substances to identify an allergen. Evidence in support is limited, but kinesiology can do you no harm.

Avoiding an allergen

Avoidance is the most effective way to deal with an allergy, but it is not always easy. However, there are precautions:

Check food labels Choose fresh, unprocessed foods; if you suspect food additives, read labels carefully and avoid those additives as far as you can.

Choose household products with care When using detergents, particularly biological detergents, take extra care. Rinse your washing thoroughly. Wear rubber gloves when using any household cleaners or chemicals. Keep notes of what you use, and a process of elimination may help.

Vacuum frequently To get rid of dust mites and prevent a build-up of animal hairs, vacuum daily.

Change your garden Few people are driven to such desperate lengths, but if your hay fever is really troublesome you could try paving over the lawn and growing non-flowering foliage plants. This will not, of course, prevent pollen drifting from your neighbours' gardens, but some hay fever sufferers say that their weekends have been made bearable by such drastic action.

If your efforts to avoid or eliminate the allergen have failed or are impracticable, the solution is to treat the symptoms. Remember that most allergens are, in themselves, harmless. It is your body's abnormal response, not the allergen, that does the damage, so coming into contact with the offending substance will not hurt you as long as you can control your reaction to it.

Other alternative treatments

Homoeopathy You may have to take far more personal responsibility for your cure than if you had consulted a conventional doctor. You may also have to change your diet and lifestyle as well as taking prescribed remedies.

Ionisation An ionising machine artificially produces negatively charged particles of air (ions) which are found naturally by running water, at the seaside and in pure mountain air. IONISATION may help symptoms such as asthma and hay fever.

Bach remedies Clematis is prescribed for general oversensitivity; Mimulus for fear of getting an allergic reaction; Impatiens if there is irritation of the skin or mucous membranes. Beech is claimed to be able to help various food intolerances and other allergies. Rescue Remedy cream may soothe allergic rashes.

Biofeedback Practitioners train you to recognise your body's response to an allergen by electrically measuring such functions as skin resistance and brain waves. When you have learned to identify the onset of an allergic reaction you can take steps to control it.

Hypnotherapy Just how HYPNOTHERAPY works to counter allergies is hard to define, but sufferers have successfully used stress reduction and desensitisation techniques to alleviate, or even entirely remove, allergic conditions such as asthma and eczema.

See also ACUPUNCTURE and RELAXATION AND BREATHING.

An orthodox view

A doctor may prescribe antihistamines, cortisone sprays and creams, nose drops or bronchodilators to treat various allergic reactions. All of these may provide effective relief, but some of the drugs used cause side effects, such as drowsiness, and others, particularly nose drops containing isoprenaline, can be habit forming (see ADDICTION). Desensitising injections, once used to combat allergies, are no longer given because of the risk of a dangerous reaction.

ANAEMIA

The name anaemia is given to a range of illnesses that involve a lack of the oxygen-carrying substance haemoglobin in the blood. Anaemia can be caused by loss of blood, an inability to produce enough red blood cells, or an inherited abnormality.

Symptoms include DIZZINESS, TIREDNESS, HEADACHES, INSOMNIA, shortness of breath, paleness, disturbances of vision, swollen ankles, loss of appetite, PALPITATIONS and, in older people, chest pains. The four main types of anaemia are iron deficiency, pernicious, megaloblastic and sickle cell.

Iron deficiency anaemia, the commonest form, results from a shortage of iron, through poor diet, blood loss, illness or infection. Pregnant women are particularly at risk.

Pernicious anaemia develops when a lack of a stomach enzyme called 'the intrinsic factor' prevents the body from absorbing enough vitamin B12 to make an adequate supply of blood. This may be due to a disorder of the IMMUNE SYSTEM or certain drugs. It affects vegans and people with blood group A particularly.

Megaloblastic anaemia arises from a shortage of folic acid (one of the many B vitamins), which is found in liver and fresh vegetables. Pregnant women and elderly people are most affected.

Sickle cell anaemia is an inherited blood disorder found among some people of African and Middle Eastern descent. Symptoms appear in childhood and include yellowing of the skin and whites of the eyes (JAUNDICE), FEVER, and weakness after physical exertion.

Always consult a doctor if you suspect anaemia, as medical diagnosis is necessary before beginning any type of treatment.

What the therapists recommend

NATUROPATHY
Self help   Plenty of iron-rich foods such as dark green leafy vegetables, walnuts, raisins, brewer's yeast, wheat germ, strawberries, parsley, nettles, apricots and pumpkin seeds are prescribed, and meats such as liver and kidneys. In moderation, full-bodied red wines may also help.

For pernicious anaemia caused by inadequate diet, you may be advised to eat foods rich in vitamin B12, such as dairy products, eggs, liver and kidneys. About 400iu of vitamin E a day may help in sickle cell anaemia.

All forms of anaemia may benefit from raw juices such as spinach, carrot, nettle and horseradish. Molasses is held to be good for building strong red blood cells, and high potencies of pollen may also help.

Consultation   The cause will be investigated before treatment. You will be referred to a doctor or, if the naturopath is a doctor, given orthodox treatment if the symptoms are severe, if another illness is causing the anaemia, or if you are losing blood regularly or in large quantities.

The naturopath will then give detailed individual advice about STRESS, diet and lifestyle. Dietary supplements may be prescribed – for example, iron gluconate (a naturally occurring form of iron) taken together with 500mg to 1g of vitamin C at each meal, plus zinc, since extra iron can interfere with zinc absorption.

HOMOEOPATHY
Self help   Therapists may prescribe *China* to strengthen red blood cells and give energy, particularly after a severe illness with loss of fluids. *Ferrum metallicum* can help replace iron in the blood. Pernicious anaemia is said to respond to *Arsenicum*; and pale, sensitive people who overexert themselves and become weak and breathless may be helped by *Phosphorus*, which is said also to be good for children who outgrow their strength.

MOXIBUSTION
Consultation   Anaemia can be treated with regular applications of MOXIBUSTION, usually given over six to eight sessions spread over four to six months. The points stimulated are on the back, lower trunk, abdomen, arm and leg. ACUPUNCTURE may also be given in the same areas. The therapist may suggest blood-fortifying foods and herbs such as liver, watercress, eggs, honey and spinach.

AROMATHERAPY
Self help   The essential oils of Roman camomile and lemon are recommended. Add ten drops of each to about 3 tablespoons (50ml) of vegetable oil or bland white lotion (see p. 36), and apply daily to the whole body after a bath or shower. A tea (see p. 36) made with two drops of lemon and one of Roman camomile oil may also help.

HERBAL MEDICINE
Self help   Remedies include infusions (see p. 184) of angelica, centaury or wild chicory leaves, horsetail, nettle, rosemary flowers or leaves, strawberry and thyme, and decoctions (see p. 184) of wild chicory root, dock root, plantain and walnut. Take about three cups a day. Carrot as a juice or vegetable is also said to significantly increase red blood cell production.

Alternatively, you may find herbal remedies in the form of tonic wines more palatable. They can be made easily at home, but always use a good quality wine and sterilise all containers, which must be non-metallic,

with boiling water before you start. Two tonics recommended for anaemia are:
Centaury wine   Soak 2oz (60g) of centaury leaves, flowers and stems and a few juniper berries in 1¾ pints (1 litre) of white wine for about a week. Then strain off the herbs, sweeten to taste with honey, and take a wineglass before each meal. This mixture stimulates the digestive tract, and juniper stimulates the kidneys. But it is recommended only for one or two weeks, and for occasional use if digestion is sluggish.
Dock wine   Soak together for 24-48 hours in 3½ pints (2 litres) of red wine in a covered container: 6oz (180g) yellow dock root, ¼oz (8g) liquorice root, ⅛oz (4g) juniper berries, 4oz (120g) brown sugar. Then boil the mixture gently in a double boiler until reduced by a third, strain and bottle. Drink half a wineglassful every morning before eating.

Consultation   The underlying cause of the anaemia must always be properly diagnosed by a doctor beforehand. Pernicious anaemia may be treated with vitamin B12 and dock root – especially yellow dock – is used for iron deficiency. Herbs containing iron, vitamins B and C – such as parsley, nettle and turnip tops – may be given, while the bitter herb gentian is said to tone the digestive system and increase the absorption of nutrients such as iron.

An orthodox view

Doctors agree that taking supplements such as iron, vitamin B12 or folic acid and eating foods rich in these nutrients will help many people with anaemia, provided that treatment is based on an accurate diagnosis.

Deficiencies are made up with iron or vitamin tablets or injections, and, if another disorder is causing the anaemia, this will also be treated.

Sickle cell anaemia cannot be cured, but regular blood transfusions can keep it under control. Crises can often be prevented by inoculating sufferers against infections, prescribing folic acid and antibiotics, and taking care that patients do not become dehydrated, breathless, or cold and wet.

ANAL PROBLEMS

An itching bottom is a common irritation, often aggravated by scratching, which inflames the skin. Sweat, poor hygiene, rough or tight clothing, WORMS, THRUSH, rashes, PILES, irritating soaps or lotions and sitting down for lengthy periods of time – all of these may be causes.

Anal bleeding or pain can also have a

number of causes, including piles, BOWEL DISORDERS, ULCERS or anal fissures – splits in the skin lining the anal passage made by passing hard motions.

Occasional anal pains that disappear after a few hours and do not recur are probably due to muscular spasms. Always consult a doctor if itching, irritation or pain persists, or when there is bleeding.

What the therapists recommend

NATUROPATHY

Self help Wear loose cotton underwear to allow air to circulate. Avoid using harsh soaps or detergents on skin and clothes. Chronic itching may be helped by scrupulous hygiene: wash the anal area several times a day with warm water, dry with a soft, clean towel and apply wheat-germ oil. Vitamin E cream may also be applied.

Occasional itches may be soothed by applying a paste made from baking soda or oatmeal and water; calamine lotion; lemon juice; witch-hazel lotion; or wintergreen alcohol. You can also try wetting the area and rubbing in a little salt, if it does not irritate your skin.

Consultation If signs indicate that the problem is a symptom of a bowel disorder or other illness, you will be given tests to investigate the cause. Treatment will depend on diagnosis, but is likely to include advice on diet and exercise.

For a simple fissure you will probably be advised to increase the amount of FIBRE in your diet, which should soften motions and so prevent constipation.

HERBAL MEDICINE

Self help Fissures may be eased by making a decoction (see p. 184) of a handful of calendula flowers in a litre of milk, and adding this to a hip bath. If the fissures are caused by constipation, try infusions (see p. 184) of laxative herbs such as linseed and psyllium seed to soften the motions and reduce straining.

A decoction of dandelion root can also be used for a gentle laxative effect.

A strong infusion of the plant chickweed, added to your bath water, is also believed to relieve anal itching.

AROMATHERAPY

Self help For itching, therapists recommend a warm bath containing three drops of Roman camomile and three drops of tea-tree essence. Stay in it for at least ten minutes.

Alternatively, mix three drops of sandalwood oil, three drops of lavender oil, two drops of camomile oil and one drop of peppermint oil in about 3 tablespoons (50ml) of vegetable oil, and apply to the affected area as required.

An orthodox view

Doctors approach anal problems in similar ways to those of alternative therapists. Small fissures usually heal themselves and pain can be eased by a hot bath; holding a hot, wet sponge to the anus; using a painkilling ointment such as Anusol or Anacal; or eating plenty of laxative foods – fruit and bran, with ample fluid – to soften the motions.

In all cases of anal itching, avoid scratching and keep the area clean and dry. If you use talcum powder, choose a mild type and stop using it if irritation returns.

ANGINA

The symptoms of angina are sudden, vice-like spasms in the upper chest. They can be extremely frightening, but are seldom life-threatening. However, the first attack can come as a shock, and it is advisable to seek immediate medical help.

The pains usually occur when the victim is involved in some activity or exertion. They last a few minutes and may spread to one or both arms – particularly the left – and the neck, throat, jaw or back. They are often accompanied by feelings of exhaustion, choking, suffocation, nausea or impending death. The pains vary from mild to severe and may crush, burn, ache or numb the chest – but they are not sharp or throbbing.

The cause of angina – properly called _angina pectoris_ – is an inadequate supply of blood to the heart. In moments of extra exertion, such as climbing stairs, running for a bus – even losing your temper – the body needs extra oxygen. To meet this need, the heart beats faster, and BLOOD PRESSURE rises to speed the circulation of the blood and so take more oxygen to the body tissues.

Sometimes, however, the heart cannot function properly because the arteries carrying the blood are too narrow for an adequate flow (see ARTERIES [HARDENING]). This is when angina pains are felt – a warning sign that the heart cannot work any harder, and that you should stop and rest immediately. Or, if you are emotionally upset, you should calm down and relax.

Angina itself does not cause permanent damage. Except during an attack, the narrowed coronary arteries of an angina patient are able to supply the heart muscle with sufficient blood for normal activities – the supply is never completely cut off and there is no death of heart tissue. But if the arteries continue to narrow, the risk of a heart attack increases (see HEART DISORDERS).

Warning No alternative practitioner should treat chest pains without first finding out the cause. The advice given below is for _diagnosed_ cases of angina.

What the therapists recommend

NATUROPATHY

Consultation Practitioners advise that diet is important as a way of stopping cholesterol from clogging the arteries and reducing any strain on the heart. In general, the diet should be based on raw or lightly cooked vegetables, fresh fruit and salads, whole grain cereals, pulses such as beans and lentils, fish, and lean meat and chicken.

Oatmeal porridge and oat bran are believed to reduce the level of blood cholesterol and should be eaten regularly, along with grilled, oily fish such as mackerel and herring. You will be asked to replace animal and dairy fats with unsaturated margarine, vegetable oil and low-fat products and avoid large amounts of sugar, salt and alcohol to reduce blood pressure, although a glass or two – no more – of wine daily may help.

Avoid coffee – even decaffeinated – and other caffeine-containing drinks such as tea, cola drinks and cocoa, as they increase blood pressure and pulse rate. Drink herbal teas and coffee substitutes made from figs, chicory and cereals instead.

Treatment will then focus on relieving STRESS. You may be advised to change your attitude to work or even change your job, and organise your day to allow plenty of time for rest and relaxation. You will be encouraged to develop a positive outlook and a non-competitive way of relating to others.

RELAXATION AND BREATHING techniques will be recommended as may regular, gentle EXERCISE such as walking, swimming and cycling – depending on your general state of health. The therapist will give you individual advice about how much exercise is safe, but good general advice is never to do more than allows you to stop and hold a conversation at any time. Patients taking conventional drugs prescribed by a doctor, such as glyceryl trinitrate and beta blockers, will, however, be told to avoid vigorous exercise.

Dietary supplements may be suggested, including calcium and magnesium, which are believed to promote a healthy heart and nervous system. Vitamin B-complex is recommended for anyone suffering from stress or TIREDNESS, and vitamin C to counteract cholesterol in the blood.

If you eat a lot of margarine and vegetable oils, you may be told to take extra vitamin E, which is said also to help the coronary arteries to function normally. You will start with low doses of 100-200iu a day – especially if your blood pressure is high – and gradually increase to 400-600iu if there is no increase in blood pressure.

Some naturopaths may recommend raw juice, FASTING or a raw fruit and vegetable diet – to be taken under supervision – as means of lowering blood pressure and improving circulation to the heart and lungs.

HERBAL MEDICINE

Self help A herbal remedy that may be prescribed for angina is an infusion (see p. 184) of hawthorn berries, mixed with yarrow, for high blood pressure, or an infusion of lime blossom for arteriosclerosis.

Garlic, added to food, or in capsule form, is said to bring down the level of cholesterol in the blood and to reduce the risk of blood clots blocking already narrowed arteries. Oats, usually taken as porridge, are another effective way of reducing cholesterol.

When to get help

If it is your first attack (see symptoms, main text).
If the attacks become more frequent or occur for reasons other than those which usually cause them.
If the pain is worse than it usually is, follows a different pattern or simply feels 'different'.
If the attack includes a cold sweat.
If you have pain at night, keeping you from sleep, or if it wakes you.
If angina recurs after treatment for a heart attack.
If your usual methods of dealing with an attack have no effect.
If the pain lasts longer than usual – if it lasts more than ten minutes call a doctor immediately.

Other alternative treatments

Acupuncture Angina patients are likely to be considered too *yang* – or active and assertive – by an acupuncturist, who will give treatment to restore the correct balance of *yin* and *yang* to body and mind. Acupuncture can also relieve the pain of angina and help the patient to relax.
Osteopathy and Chiropractic Many angina sufferers also experience tension in the neck, shoulders and back, which aggravates their chest pains. Osteopathy and chiropractic can relieve muscular tension.
Bach Remedies Try Elm if overwhelmed by responsibility; Hornbeam for mental exhaustion; Impatiens for impatience or tension; Olive for overwork; White chestnut for insomnia; Rescue Remedy for shock and fear.

Other useful relaxing and healing therapies recommended for angina sufferers include: ALEXANDER TECHNIQUE, AUTOGENIC TRAINING, MASSAGE – especially SHIATSU and DO-IN – and REFLEXOLOGY.

An orthodox view

Doctors, like alternative practitioners, believe that there is more than one cause of angina. Most significant is a hardening of the coronary arteries – arteriosclerosis. Stress, TENSION and emotional upsets can also cause or contribute to angina. If you are in a competitive job, or are constantly experiencing tensions or domestic conflicts, reactions within your nervous system mount up and increase your chances of developing angina.

The doctor will carry out tests, and if you do have angina, further tests will determine the causes. Once they are found, drugs such as glyceryl trinitrate or beta blockers may be prescribed, to prevent attacks or to treat them. The doctor will also advise you to avoid stress and prescribe a low-fat diet.

Coronary bypass operations are often performed when the arteries are badly blocked. A piece of healthy vein is taken from another part of the body, and grafted so that blood can flow around the blockage.

ANOREXIA
Fighting the 'slimmer's disease'

Teenage dieting, or sudden weight loss due to illness or STRESS, often trigger off this so-called 'slimmer's disease'. The victims become addicted to being thin, seeing it as some sort of solution to their problems: pressures at home and at school, feelings of insecurity and low self-esteem, and the traumas of growing up.

Adolescent girls in particular may feel that they are losing control of their bodies as they start to menstruate and develop a womanly shape. They see starvation as a way of turning back the clock and regaining control; the body reverts to its pre-adolescent shape, periods stop and the worry and attention that their emaciated state arouses in others makes them feel special.

Some doctors and practitioners also see a connection between anorexia and media tendencies to promote a trim figure as a recipe for health, success and happiness. Even women in their twenties are vulnerable, and statistics reveal that men – especially young, ambitious professionals – are also increasingly susceptible to the illness.

Whatever influences are at work on the victim, anorexia is a food phobia which is thought to be caused by an underlying mental disturbance of some kind. Anorexics do have an appetite, but choose to ignore their hunger, occasionally overeating then getting rid of the food by self-induced vomiting, or taking laxatives and diuretics (see BULIMIA), or by fasting and taking too much exercise. Paradoxically, anorexics are often obsessed with food, and feel a need to cook, or to study recipes and menus.

As a sufferer's condition deteriorates, a number of serious side effects occur – and are endured – in order to stay slim. These include DEPRESSION, ANXIETY, INSOMNIA, ANAEMIA, INFERTILITY, loss of sexual drive, impaired thinking, CONSTIPATION, perspiration, slow pulse rate, low BLOOD PRESSURE, reduced body temperature, changes in colour and texture of hair, nails and skin, and excessive hair growth on the body.

Eventually chronic illness sets in and if the condition is not treated, the sufferer may die from malnutrition, HYPOTHERMIA or dehydration. Since the weight loss is apparent to everyone but the sufferer (who imagines that his or her body is larger than it really is), family pressure to eat properly can make matters worse. A doctor must be consulted and he will stress that a proper understanding of the problem by the family is crucial.

What the therapists recommend

Home treatment is not advisable. Most alternative practitioners agree that help in hospital is essential in the early stages of recovery. All alternative therapies should be used in conjunction with orthodox treatment or COUNSELLING. Some which may help are:

ACUPUNCTURE

Practitioners believe that this can help to relieve stress, balance the body's energy and promote well-being.

ART THERAPY

The therapy gives patients a creative outlet for pent-up feelings, and a discussion of the work they produce can, in return, give the therapist and patient pointers to emotional states and the progress being made. For example, patients may at first paint 'pretty' pictures which they assume will please the therapist. Later, however, they may paint pictures that reflect their inner turmoil.

DANCE THERAPY

This is a good outlet for pent-up feelings and has proved especially useful in treating adolescents who are withdrawn and suffer with neurotic illnesses. It may encourage them to feel a sense of purpose and identity.

HYPNOTHERAPY

The therapist will discuss a patient's problems and try to establish a rapport, so that the sufferer is receptive to hypnosis. Ideally

Despite their weight loss, anorexia victims imagine they are heavier than they really are. The priority in treatment is persuading them to accept medical advice and help.

the patient is then susceptible to any suggestions the hypnotist may make about changes in behaviour, and will be given post-hypnotic suggestions, among which will be a positive feeling towards eating, instead of a revulsion to food. In addition, the patient should try to maintain an 'ideal' weight.

NATUROPATHY

Supplements containing multivitamins, minerals and high doses of zinc are given to build up strength until the appetite returns. A wholefood diet (see EATING FOR HEALTH) is gradually introduced, with plenty of freshly squeezed fruit and vegetable juices.

BACH REMEDIES

Heather is recommended if the patient's refusal of food is seen as a plea for attention; Beech is suitable for an emotional inability to accept food (or love). If the patient collapses, Wild rose is suggested. In the case of adolescents, Wild oat and Walnut could be offered.

An orthodox view

Because, as most therapists would admit, alternative treatments are on the whole supplementary, the first vital step in treating anorexia is to persuade the patient to accept orthodox medical help.

As sufferers tend to make themselves vomit after eating, in many cases the best course is close supervision in hospital by experienced nurses, who will encourage the patient to reach a target weight.

Once discharged, the patient needs supportive counselling and the help of a psychiatrist or psychotherapist to prevent the condition recurring. Underlying problems, general health and lifestyle are explored, and patients are encouraged to adopt a more positive outlook.

Doctors have found that some anorexics recover spontaneously if their personal problems resolve themselves.

See also PUBERTY AND ADOLESCENCE.

ANTHROPOSOPHICAL MEDICINE
Illness and the path to spiritual growth

In the early 1920s a group of doctors working on the Continent began practising a new system of holistic medicine. They were followers of the ideas of Rudolf Steiner (1861-1925), an Austrian scientist and philosopher and founder of anthroposophy – from the

Greek words meaning 'man' and 'wisdom' – which was the basis of the new system.

Steiner believed that the structure and functioning of a living organism could not be explained in purely physical or chemical terms. Instead, he maintained that as well as a physical body, all living things possessed an 'etheric' body which opposed the force of gravity and allowed them to grow upwards away from the earth. In addition, he thought that animals and man had 'astral' bodies which represented their emotions; and that man alone had an individual spiritual core, which he called the ego.

Steiner was not a qualified doctor and only assumed an advisory role in medical matters. He collaborated with the Dutch physician Dr Ita Wegman (1867-1943), leading to the foundation of the first anthroposophical clinic in Arlesheim, Switzerland, and their joint authorship of *Fundamentals of Therapy*. In anthroposophical medicine, Steiner's four aspects of man – the physical, etheric and astral bodies, and the ego – are held to correspond to the four ancient Greek elements: earth, water, air and fire. They are connected to each other by means of three interpenetrating bodily systems called the digestive/movement system, the nerve/sense system and the rhythmic system.

The digestive/movement system is governed mainly by the physical and etheric bodies, and includes processes such as excretion and the functioning of the glandular system, as well as all the restoring and rebuilding processes that take place in the body without our knowledge.

The nerve/sense system, by contrast, is dominated by the ego and the astral body, which control conscious processes such as thought, perception and self-awareness. It controls the body during the day, but gives way at night, when the digestive/movement system takes over. This allows the physical and etheric bodies to replenish themselves every night, and repair the wear and damage caused during the day by the activities of the astral body and the ego.

The rhythmic system is formed by the alternation of the other two systems, and controls processes such as circulation and breathing. Steiner believed that tension between the two types of activity was an inevitable part of life, and went on until the moment of death. Good health was a sign that a temporary balance between the two states had been achieved, but this could not continue for any length of time, or the individual would stop developing. Instead, anthroposophical doctors believe that by becoming more aware of these two opposing processes, each individual can start to take responsibility for his own development and the course of his life. Illness can in some cases be the key which starts off this process.

As anthroposophy is also founded on a belief in reincarnation, practitioners consider that all illness has a deeper meaning either in terms of a previous life or as preparation for a future life, and never view it as a simply physical problem. A wide variety of different treatments is used to help patients, including special anthroposophical medicines (see box); herbal remedies (see HERBAL MEDICINE); homoeopathic remedies (see HOMOEOPATHY); and a type of movement called EURHYTHMY, developed by Rudolf Steiner; and also conventional drugs and surgery when they are necessary.

Who it can help   All anthroposophical doctors are fully medically qualified, so they can be consulted for any sort of physical or mental illness. People who want to use drugs or surgery as little as possible, while still being safely treated, may find anthroposophical medicine a good alternative, since the broad range of therapies used by practitioners often allows them to prescribe conventional treatment more sparingly than orthodox doctors.

Finding a therapist   All anthroposophical practitioners are qualified medical doctors who have completed a post-graduate course recognised by the Anthroposophical Medical Association in Britain. In addition to their medical studies, most anthroposophical doctors have also undertaken a general study of anthroposophy, and many also follow an anthroposophical path of inner development, such as MEDITATION and attention to diet.

Some anthroposophical doctors work as general practitioners within the National Health Service, some practise privately, and many also work in Rudolf Steiner schools and homes for children in need of special care – there are about 35 such communities in Britain alone. Residential treatment in private clinics is also available. Further information and the names and addresses of doctors in your area can be obtained from the Anthroposophical Medical Association, c/o Rudolf Steiner House, 35 Park Road, London NW1 6XT.

Consulting a therapist   Consultations are much like visits to a family doctor, but in addition to describing your symptoms you will probably be asked about other aspects of your life and daily routine, such as how well you sleep, what foods you eat, and whether you often feel anxious or tense. A diagnosis is made in the normal way, and appropriate treatment given which could be either

Anthroposophical remedies

A whole range of special medicines is used by anthroposophical doctors. Some of them date from the early days of anthroposophy and Steiner's own instructions, others were developed by his followers, and new ones are continually being investigated.

The remedies are composed of mineral, plant and animal substances which are thought to counterbalance specific ailments.

Steiner believed that many natural substances were related to aspects of physical health – for example, seven metals (lead, tin, iron, gold, copper, mercury and silver) corresponded to bodily organs. So an anthroposophical doctor may prescribe a homoeopathic remedy or ointment made from tin for a patient with liver trouble, or one with copper to regulate the kidneys.

The essential oils of plants (see AROMATHERAPY) are also used to improve circulation, or cause a temperature rise in patients with degenerative diseases such as cancer, MULTIPLE SCLEROSIS and DIABETES.

The scientist and philosopher Rudolf Steiner (1861-1925; left) founded the Anthroposophical Society to explore new approaches in education, science, religion – and medicine. It has its headquarters in the Steiner-designed Goetheanum (above) in Switzerland. An earlier version of the building was destroyed by fire in 1923.

The anthroposophical view of illness

According to anthroposophical medicine, illnesses are divided into two main groups – inflammatory, or feverish, conditions, which are more common during childhood; and degenerative, or hardening, conditions, which tend to affect older people.

Inflammatory diseases are thought to arise when the individual's digestive/movement system becomes too strong, producing a heating, dissolving effect on the body. Such diseases include all fevers, and childhood diseases such as CHICKENPOX and MEASLES, which are believed to strengthen the child's IMMUNE SYSTEM and prevent the ageing process from setting in too soon. For this reason, anthroposophical doctors do not necessarily always try to reduce a fever.

Degenerative diseases, by contrast, are said to arise from the hardening, contracting influence of the astral body and ego on the nerve/sense system. They include conditions such as CANCER, hardening of the arteries and diseases in which the immune system is deficient, and are often accompanied by symptoms such as INSOMNIA, ANXIETY and a low temperature. Anthroposophical doctors believe that these conditions often develop as a result of events much earlier in the patient's life.

Anthroposophical practitioners say that the pattern of illness has changed during the 20th century, with inflammatory diseases becoming less common, but degenerative conditions alarmingly on the increase. They attribute this to the growing intellectual and materialistic emphasis in education and society, which is held to be reinforcing the astral and ego forces, while at the same time depleting healing physical and etheric ones in man and the earth as a whole. Consequently, they consider humanity to be fast approaching a critical point when a new approach to illness and health could be crucial for our survival.

anthroposophical, homoeopathic, herbal or conventional, depending on the condition.

While they aim first of all to relieve suffering, anthroposophical doctors often also try to treat the underlying imbalance that they think is causing an illness. They may suggest eurhythmy, ART THERAPY or MUSIC THERAPY, and send the patient to a specialist in one of these. Some Steiner doctors also work with therapists qualified in a special type of rhythmic massage designed to harmonise the breathing and circulatory systems, and stimulate general vitality. The relationship between doctor and patient is considered an important part of the therapy, and many practitioners will also refer patients in need to qualified counsellors.

Although anthroposophical doctors believe that illness is connected with the patient's personal destiny, they do not claim to have any special insight into his past or future lives. Nevertheless, some do feel that their philosophy helps them to work with difficult or incurable conditions, and that active therapy will benefit patients in a future life, even when a physical cure is not possible during the present one.

An orthodox view

Most doctors are not aware of the underlying principles of anthroposophical medicine, but those who are tend to agree that its treatment may be beneficial and can in any case do little harm.

ANXIETY

Everyone needs to feel anxious at times – it causes a reaction which pumps the hormone stimulant adrenaline into the system. It spurs people to do challenging and uncongenial tasks and prepares them to cope with difficult situations. What is not desirable is for anxiety to become a problem – for normal, temporary feelings of uncertainty, worry or fear to become persistent states of mind.

Normal anxiety almost always has a cause of which you are aware – for example, an important interview or a test of some kind may be looming up. But anxiety can become a problem when worry or apprehension is experienced for no apparent reason, or is much worse than the situation warrants.

Although anxiety is an emotional state, it can induce physical symptoms that are not 'all in the mind' – PAIN (particularly in the head, chest, abdomen and back), INSOMNIA, muscular TENSION and DIZZINESS. Often there is NAUSEA AND VOMITING, DIARRHOEA or frequent urinating. The sufferer may show signs

of panic such as SWEATING, PALPITATIONS and abnormally deep breathing, or feel tired, weak and listless. Generally, the symptoms disappear when there is no longer a reason to be anxious. Yet some people suffer from recurrent attacks over a period of years – an illness known as 'chronic anxiety'.

What the therapists recommend

NATUROPATHY

Self help A wholefood diet (see EATING FOR HEALTH) is advisable, with plenty of raw fruit, vegetables and salads, and extra protein if required. Raw carrot juice and lettuce juice are believed to strengthen the nervous system and have a calming effect. Try two cups of either during the day and a third before going to bed. Cups of camomile tea may be used instead if desired.

Consultation You will be given advice about coping with STRESS, taking EXERCISE, and RELAXATION AND BREATHING techniques. KINESIOLOGY can test for ALLERGY.

Dietary supplements may be recommended, including vitamin B-complex and vitamin C to help in coping with stress; vitamin E, said to improve the functioning of the central nervous system; and minerals such as calcium, magnesium and zinc.

HERBAL MEDICINE

Self help As sedatives and to treat insomnia, try infusions (see p. 184) of camomile, valerian root and lime flowers. Other useful remedies recommended for anxiety include infusions of hawthorn flowers, rosemary, betony (not more than two small cups a day, or it may cause vomiting), hops (but avoid if you are depressed), passion flower, and hyssop (avoid if pregnant).

HOMOEOPATHY

Self help If the anxiety is in anticipation of some sort of test or unpleasant event, and you feel fearful, go weak at the knees, or tremble all over, try *Gelsemium*.

If you suffer from fear and apprehension – such as stage fright – or panic in a crowd or closed space, or are compelled to do things in a hurry, *Argentum nitricum* may help. In such cases, a dose of 30th or 200th potency taken the night before, and hourly for two or three hours beforehand on the day itself, should be adequate. Remember that such symptoms are worse in hot weather.

For panic, shock, fear or feelings of being restlessly troubled, try *Aconite*. *Arsenicum album* is recommended for persistent anxiety with occasional panic attacks.

Other alternative treatments

Biofeedback Stress-related complaints, especially anxiety, were among the first areas to be tackled using biofeedback. A method

called respiration biofeedback, in which the patient listens to his own amplified breathing and tries to regulate it accordingly, is claimed to have been successful in treating anxiety.

Biochemic Tissue Salts To combat general anxiety three doses of *Kali phos.* should be taken daily for a month. An adult dose is four tablets and a child's is two tablets. A dose every half-hour on the day of a test or event – such as going for a daunting job interview – can be helpful.

Aromatherapy If struck by panic, deeply inhale a few drops each of essential oils of basil, clary sage, lavender and sandalwood on a tissue. If your anxiety is accompanied by a headache, or is causing muscular tension, add drops of marjoram and camomile oils to the others already recommended. In order to relax, try some drops of frankincense and patchouli. Ylang-ylang is believed to combat insomnia, and melissa is said to help to raise your spirits.

Hydrotheraphy Try a tepid bath, cold friction or hot-and-cold compresses.

Bach Remedies An acute attack of anxiety may be helped by Rescue Remedy. White chestnut is recommended for anxious thoughts that go round and round in your mind, possibly preventing sleep. For anxiety accompanied by indecision, take Scleranthus. Agrimony helps to present a bright and cheerful front, although you may be troubled and anxious underneath.

Acupuncture Treatment depends on the cause of the anxiety – such as disturbed sleep or exhaustion – but can be very successful. A practitioner will advise you.

Other therapies that can help anxiety victims – mainly by teaching relaxation – include AUTOGENIC TRAINING, DANCE THERAPY, HYPNOTHERAPY, MEDITATION, OSTEOPATHY, REFLEXOLOGY and YOGA.

An orthodox view

Like alternative therapists, a doctor will be concerned to uncover the root cause of a patient's anxiety, but will also check whether any physical symptoms are being caused by some other illness.

You will be asked to discuss aspects of your life that may be causing anxiety – such as marriage problems, money worries and difficulties at work. Most doctors are skilled, sympathetic listeners who can offer support and advice, but if this is not sufficient, tranquillisers or sedatives may be prescribed. They are not a long-term cure, however; they are simply a way of helping you to cope with some of the symptoms of anxiety and they can be addictive if used for long periods.

If your anxiety is so severe that it interferes with your work or relationships, you may be referred to a psychiatrist, who will probably prescribe stronger tranquillisers and may also offer PSYCHOTHERAPY.

APHRODISIACS
Do they really stimulate sexual desire?

Over the centuries, many foods, drugs and herbs have been held to stimulate or enhance sexual desire, from such folklore favourites as oysters and nasturtium leaves to exotic concoctions made from crushed, dried beetles (in a toxic drug called 'Spanish Fly') and powdered rhinoceros horn. Most have been discredited, but other natural stimulants are used in alternative medicine.

What the therapists recommend

AROMATHERAPY
Aromatherapists list several essential plant oils which they believe to be aphrodisiacs: jasmine, patchouli and ylang-ylang.

Jasmine is considered a sensual stimulant and antidepressant and it is said also to ease pain in the female reproductive system. Patchouli is thought to be an antidepressant and stimulant for the nerves and mind, and

ylang-ylang's exotic scent is held to stimulate the senses and induce feelings of well-being. Use the oils for MASSAGE, inhale them (see p. 36), or add five to ten drops to a full bath, relax and breathe deeply.

HERBAL MEDICINE

The herbal therapists' most favoured stimulant is GINSENG. Buy it in the form of tablets, tonics or teas from your health food shop, or make an infusion by adding half a teaspoon of the powdered root to a cup of boiling water and simmering it gently for ten minutes. Drink the infusion three times a day. Therapists say that ginseng must be taken for several months before results can be expected. However, take care if using it over a prolonged period as it can slightly raise the blood pressure.

Damiana – a shrub from Central America – is believed by herbalists to have an antidepressant, tonic effect on the nerves and hormonal system. Make an infusion from a teaspoon of berries in a cup of water, brought to the boil and simmered gently for five minutes. Drink three times a day.

A stimulating infusion said to strengthen the reproductive system can be made from a mixture by weight of the following herbs: damiana leaves, 8 parts; ginseng root, 3 parts; saw palmetto berries, 2 parts; false unicorn root, crushed, 6 parts; Irish moss, whole or flakes, 2 parts; and motherwort leaves, 3 parts.

To make the infusion put a teaspoon of the mixture in a cup of water and simmer for five minutes. To test its effectiveness, drink two or three cupfuls a day for a month.

NATUROPATHY

Practitioners might suggest 1-5g of pollen or one or two generous teaspoons of royal jelly (the food of queen bees) every day to aid male or female potency by increasing stamina and combating fatigue.

An orthodox view

Conventional doctors recognise the complexity of the factors that influence sexual desire, but do not accept that it can be aroused by simply taking any particular substance. However, many doctors do accept some of the claims made for ginseng as an overall tonic and stimulant. Research indicates that the herb may help the body to cope with STRESS, overcome fatigue, boost energy and enhance its powers of recovery. Aromatherapy, too, has gained some acceptance, since research has shown that scents can affect the mind.

A doctor will treat IMPOTENCE and FRIGIDITY by dealing with any underlying physical problems and referring the patient to a counsellor or psychotherapist.

APPENDICITIS

This fairly common complaint occurs when the appendix – a small, blind tube attached to the beginning of the large intestine – becomes inflamed or infected. There are, however, two kinds of appendicitis, one more serious than the other, and the symptoms must be watched carefully.

A mild inflammation of the appendix causes occasional discomfort in the lower right quarter of the abdomen – this is called chronic appendicitis. Although dull pains may persist on and off for months, they seldom develop into a more severe illness.

Symptoms of a serious inflammation – known as acute appendicitis – take from four to 48 hours to develop, and begin with a dull pain near the navel, nausea and sometimes vomiting. The sufferer usually refuses food and drink, and is often constipated. After a few hours the pain increases and moves to the lower right section of the abdomen. The temperature may rise slightly and the breath smell unpleasant. Sometimes the pain disappears after a few hours, but this does not necessarily mean that the illness has passed.

Call a doctor as soon as possible for symptoms of acute appendicitis. If you delay, the appendix may burst, causing an inflammation of the lining of the abdominal cavity – known as peritonitis – which can cause death. Even if the inflammation is confined to a small area, the result will be an abscess on the appendix, which will have to be drained. If the appendix is not removed, acute attacks will probably recur.

Warning Always consult a doctor before seeking any alternative treatment for chronic appendicitis. There is no safe alternative treatment for acute appendicitis. In China the condition is sometimes treated by acupuncture, but in the Western world it would be considered too dangerous to delay surgery while trying this method.

Do's and don'ts if you suspect appendicitis

Do lie down, keep warm and use a hot-water bottle to ease the pain.
Don't eat or drink. Rinse your mouth with a little water if necessary.
Don't take laxatives, painkillers or any other types of medicine.
Do call a doctor if the pain gets worse, or it becomes constant or it has not gone after four hours.

What the therapists recommend

HERBAL MEDICINE

Self help For chronic symptoms, an infusion (see p. 184) of agrimony, which is used as an anti-inflammatory herb, is suggested. Take one cupful three times a day.

ACUPUNCTURE

Consultation Treatment would probably begin with acupuncture in the neck, followed by acupuncture and/or MOXIBUSTION at points in the abdomen or leg.

AROMATHERAPY
The healing power of plant essences

Treating illness with highly concentrated oils extracted from plants is known as aromatherapy. These highly scented extracts – called essences or essential oils – contain the substances that give plants their smell. Aromatherapists believe that many also have medicinal properties.

Essential oils are produced by tiny glands in the petals, leaves, stems, bark and wood of many plants and trees. In nature they are released slowly, but when heated or crushed the oil glands burst, releasing the plant's aroma more strongly. To extract pure essential oil a distillation process is used, which involves vaporising the plant essence in steam which is then cooled down and separated into water and essential oil. If the oil is dissolved in alcohol, or some other solvent, the product is called a resin or absolute. Though less pure than essential oil, since traces of the solvent remain, even after purification, many resins and absolutes also have valuable therapeutic properties.

Essential oils are used in a variety of ways, but in Britain mostly for MASSAGE treatments. They can also be inhaled, added to baths or used for compresses (see p. 36). Oils of guaranteed purity are sometimes swallowed. Inhaling is believed to work quickest, because smell has been shown to have an immediate effect on the brain. Scientists have shown that the oils can also penetrate the skin – possibly through sweat pores and hair follicles – and are absorbed into the body fluids and bloodstream, to work internally.

Warning Concentrated oils, resins and absolutes must be used with care as they sometimes cause an ALLERGY or skin damage. Oils must be ingested only when prescribed by a medically qualified practitioner.

Who it can help Practitioners believe that aromatherapy is free from side effects and suitable for people of all ages, even babies. It is thought to be most helpful in treating long-term conditions, or a recurring illness. Therapists claim particular success in treating patients that orthodox medicine has been unable to help, or who are continually in and out of hospital, sometimes with extra problems caused by the side effects of drugs.

Aromatherapists claim that they can treat almost all illness, and often see immediate improvement in nervous problems such as DEPRESSION, anger, STRESS and related symptoms such as HEADACHES and INSOMNIA.

Revival of an ancient art

Nobody knows exactly where and when the ancient healing art of aromatherapy began. The medicinal use of plant oils is recorded in some of the earliest Chinese writings. The ancient Persians, too, valued flower waters distilled from roses and orange blossom, and used them both as cosmetics and as remedies for sickness. In the 11th century the Persian philosopher and physician Avicenna refined the distillation process and produced much purer essential oils.

Chinese knowledge of medicinal oils is thought to have reached the West by way of the Greeks and Romans, but the first recorded use of plant oils in Britain was in the 13th century. From then on, manufacture increased and the oils became widely used as perfumes, antiseptics and medicines, until the 19th century. Cheaper, chemical copies of the oils were then made; they did not have the same medicinal properties, but they almost ended the therapeutic use of natural oils.

The early 20th century saw a revival of interest in natural treatments, and with it an increasing demand for genuine plant oils. The pioneer of their use in modern medicine was a French chemist, Professor René Gattefosse, who accidentally discovered the healing power of lavender essence when he plunged his hand into it after receiving a bad burn. In a short time the burn had healed without forming a blister or leaving a scar.

Gattefosse went on to treat soldiers wounded in the First World War, and discovered many other healing oils. Later, his work was built on by a French physician, Dr Jean Valnet, and Marguerite Maury, a French biochemist and beautician. Valnet used essential oils to treat CANCER, tuberculosis, DIABETES and other serious illnesses, and claimed many successful cures. Marguerite Maury developed techniques such as massage and various beauty and skin-care treatments using essential oils.

The pressing of flowers to make medicines is shown in this Egyptian relief of about 600 BC.

When the oils have to penetrate the skin as well as being inhaled, the results may be slower – this is the case with complaints such as PAIN, ARTHRITIS and CRAMP, or the skin problems ECZEMA and ACNE.

In addition, almost all the oils have proven antiseptic qualities and many, such as lavender, tea tree and geranium, are said to be highly effective against infections caused by bacteria, fungi or viruses. Apart from treating illnesses, the oils are valued for their gently stimulating or calming effects and their ability to bring about a sense of harmony and well-being. They are also said by practitioners to be able to prevent illness.

Finding a therapist Professional aromatherapists have usually completed a three to 12 month diploma course in the subject. Many different organisations offer training in Britain, and most courses include medical subjects such as anatomy and physiology as well as massage, SHIATSU, ACUPRESSURE and REFLEXOLOGY techniques, and aromatherapy itself. To find a qualified therapist in your area, contact the International Federation of Aromatherapists, 4 Eastmearn Road, West Dulwich, London SE21 8HA.

Consulting a therapist The visit begins with a discussion of your general health and way of life, including diet, exercise, posture, appearance and sleeping habits. The therapist does not diagnose at this stage. He may test your foot reflexes to help him build up a picture of your overall health.

The therapist then selects the oils that are considered right for you as a whole person and, depending on the nature of the problem, mixes them for you to use at home, or offers an aromatherapy massage treatment: about 30 minutes for a part treatment and 90 minutes for the whole body. Therapists believe that massage treatments often lead to a permanent improvement, which can be maintained by using the oils at home. In other cases, repeated treatments may be considered necessary.

Self help Many workshops and short courses are available which teach the basic principles of aromatherapy for home use. See box, *Aromatherapy at home*, for an introduction to self help with aromatherapy.

Aromatherapy at home

Here are methods by which you can treat yourself at home, using the oils recommended for your condition:

Bath Add six to eight drops of essence to a hot bath, lie back and breathe deeply. Stay in the bath for 10-15 minutes. Bath treatments with appropriate oils are recommended for INSOMNIA, TENSION, sore muscles, poor circulation, PERIOD PROBLEMS, COUGHS, COLDS, HEADACHES and fluid retention.

Inhalation Put ten drops of the appropriate essential oil onto a paper towel or handkerchief and inhale. Placing the paper towel or hankie on your pillow at night should ease breathing if you have a blocked nose. Steam inhalations can be made by placing ten drops of the appropriate essence and half a cup of hot water into a bowl on a table. Sit with your head a comfortable distance above the bowl and cover head and bowl with a towel to keep the vapour in. Breathe deeply through your nose until the smell has almost gone, and repeat three times a day. Avoid steam treatments if you have ASTHMA.

Foot and hand baths Add eight to ten drops of suitable essential oil to a large bowl of hand-hot water. Soak the hands or feet in

A leg is massaged to relieve a circulation problem (above). Oils such as sage and lemon are used, and strokes must be applied upwards, from foot to knee.
Tense shoulder and neck muscles caused by stress are massaged with firm, circular finger movements for about three minutes (left). Juniper, lavender, sweet marjoram, camomile, neroli or rose otto oil can be used.

it for 10-15 minutes, swirling them around occasionally, and adding additional warm water if the bath gets cold. Complete the treatment by wrapping your hands or feet in a dry towel for another 15 minutes and then rubbing in aromatherapy massage oil (see below).

Compresses Add eight to ten drops of oil to half a cup of water. In it soak a piece of plain, unmedicated cotton wool or old sheeting folded into four thicknesses and large enough to cover the area being treated. Wring it out, place it over the affected area and cover with cling film.

A warmed towel or blanket placed over the compress should make it more efficient and keep the area warm. Leave the compress in place for at least two hours. Compresses using two or three drops of undiluted essence can be applied to small areas to treat conditions such as SPRAINS, BRUISING, burns, scalds and BOILS.

Massage Normal massage techniques are used to apply essential oils in a plant oil base to the skin. To mix an aromatherapy massage oil, combine in a 2fl oz (6oml) glass bottle: 1 teaspoon wheatgerm oil; 1 teaspoon avocado oil or hazelnut oil; 15-30 drops total of appropriate essential oils; grapeseed oil to fill bottle. A teaspoon is enough to treat the whole back, and less is needed for smaller areas. Massage the oil well into the skin to relieve stress, muscular aches and pains, breathing problems, arthritis and skin disorders.

Essential oil teas Do not take essential oils as a medicine except on the advice of a qualified practitioner, but it is safe to drink two or three drops of a suitable oil in a cup of black tea, hot or cold, twice a day for DIGESTIVE PROBLEMS, URINARY PROBLEMS and STRESS.

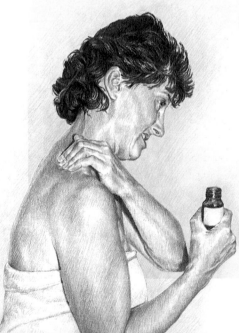

An orthodox view

Doctors and nurses are becoming increasingly aware of the benefits of aromatherapy, and many hospitals now offer it as an additional treatment.

Scientists have proved the medicinal properties of many plants, and accept that these properties are present in many aromatherapy oils. Research has shown that the scent of the oils affects the cells in the nose which send messages to the brain, and that the oils can, indeed, penetrate the skin.

Little more is known about how aromatherapy works, but research is in progress at a number of universities and hospitals in many parts of the world.

Do's and don'ts for aromatherapy

Practitioners say that aromatherapy is safe and suitable for home use, provided that you follow these guidelines:
Do buy only high quality oils, from a specialist aromatherapy supplier. The label should say that the contents are pure, undiluted essential oil, or an essential oil diluted with vegetable oil or alcohol. If the label says that the oil can be applied directly to the skin, it has probably been diluted, since pure oils are too strong for this. Diluted oils can be used for massage, but only pure oils are suitable for other types of treatment.
Don't apply pure, undiluted oils directly to the skin except in emergencies such as insect bites and stings, or if using tea tree on its own.
Don't swallow any oils unless they are supplied by a trained aromatherapist and used under his supervision.
Don't be afraid to use more than one oil at a time. Aromatherapy actually seems to work better when essences are combined. The quantities given are for the total number of drops to use, whether of one or more types of oil.

Oils for mind and body

Hundreds of plants have been used to produce essential oils, but aromatherapists generally rely on a repertoire of about 30 to treat most conditions. The oils fall into three general groups: those which invigorate the body and raise the spirits; those which tone and regulate the main bodily functions; and those which have a sedative, calming effect on body and mind. The list (right) is a guide to some of the better-known oils.

Aromatherapy oils

OIL	EFFECTS	USES
Basil	Uplifting, refreshing	Depression, stress, breathing problems, digestive problems
Benzoin (resin, not essential oil)	Warming, relaxing	Tension, cystitis, chest complaints, arthritis
Bergamot	Uplifting, refreshing, relaxing	Herpes, ulcers, sore throat
Black pepper	Stimulating	Digestive problems, food poisoning, catarrh
Camphor	Cooling, stimulating	Constipation, insomnia, acne, rheumatism
Cedarwood	Sedative	Anxiety, bronchitis, coughs
Clary sage	Warming, relaxing	High blood pressure, period problems
Cypress	Relaxing, refreshing	Varicose veins, diarrhoea, menopause
Eucalyptus	Clears head	Headaches, fluid retention, muscular pain
Fennel	Eases wind, stomach pains	Digestive problems, kidney stones
Frankincense	Relaxing, rejuvenating	Cystitis, stress, skin problems
Geranium	Refreshing, relaxing	Urinary disorders, viral infections
Hyssop	Decongestant	General poor health, breathing problems
Jasmine (absolute, not pure oil)	Relaxing, soothing	Apathy, catarrh, dry skin
Juniper	Refreshing, relaxing, stimulating	General poor health, rheumatoid arthritis, insomnia
Lavender	Refreshing, relaxing therapeutic	Good for children, depression, digestive problems
Lemon	Refreshing, stimulating	Poor circulation, high blood pressure, acne
Lemon grass	Toning, refreshing	Indigestion, oily skin, colitis
Marjoram	Warming, strengthening	Migraine, bruises, cramp
Myrrh	Cooling, toning	Mouth ulcers, thrush, catarrh
Orange blossom (neroli)	Deeply relaxing	Panic, stress, insomnia
Patchouli	Relaxing	Depression, dry skin, wounds
Peppermint	Cooling, refreshing	Motion sickness, headaches, indigestion
Pine needle	Refreshing, antiseptic	Asthma, cystitis, influenza
Roman camomile	Refreshing, relaxing	Good for children, depression, headaches
Rose (rose otto)	Relaxing, soothing	Good for children, depression, headaches
Rosemary	Invigorating, refreshing	Poor memory, mental fatigue, bronchitis
Sage	Improves circulation	Poor circulation, viral infections, rheumatism
Tea tree	Antiseptic, cleansing	Thrush, colds, sore throats

ARTERIES (HARDENING)

Hardening of the arteries is a natural process that occurs as you grow older and your arteries lose some of their original elasticity and flexibility. In itself, normal hardening of the arteries – also known as arteriosclerosis – does not cause illness, but combined with STRESS, SMOKING, an unhealthy, fatty diet or high BLOOD PRESSURE, it can become a serious condition.

Depending on which arteries are affected, symptoms of severe arteriosclerosis can include chest pains (see ANGINA), leg pains, and temporary disturbances of sight, speech, balance and use of the limbs. A common cause of artery damage is when arteriosclerosis is associated with high levels of cholesterol and other fatty substances in the blood. They form deposits on the artery walls, where they harden, prevent blood from flowing freely, increase the risk of blood clots, and sometimes cause a complete blockage. Drinking too much (see ALCOHOLISM) and being overweight (see OBESITY) can also cause problems.

Arteriosclerosis tends to run in families and affects men more than women. It is also more common in the West, where a fatty diet often accompanies a sedentary lifestyle.

Warning See your GP if you have symptoms indicating hardening of the arteries.

What the therapists recommend

NATUROPATHY
Self help Adopt a wholefood diet based on fresh fruit, vegetables and salads, wholegrain cereals, fish and lean meat. Reduce your intake of saturated animal and dairy product fat, salt, sugar and alcohol (see EATING FOR HEALTH) as much as possible. Eat plenty of oatmeal porridge, oat bran, lentils and beans for FIBRE to help lower your cholesterol level.
Consultation You will be advised about diet, the adverse effects of stress and smoking, and the advantages of EXERCISE and relaxation. Supplements may be prescribed, for example vitamin B-complex, said to relieve stress, or vitamin C, believed to reduce cholesterol and prevent blocked arteries. Eating more unsaturated fats is also thought to increase the body's need for vitamin E – you will be advised to start with small daily doses of 100-200iu if you have high blood pressure, and increase slowly to 400-600iu if your blood pressure does not rise. A teaspoon of lecithin taken with meals, and vitamin A, may also be prescribed in order to counteract cholesterol.

Eating to help your arteries

Here are some healthy alternatives to foods that can damage your arteries:

FOOD	HEALTHY ALTERNATIVES
Butter, animal fats such as suet and lard	Margarine (read the label and look for a polyunsaturated kind), vegetable oils
Milk, cream	Skimmed or low-fat milk, soya milk, yoghurt
Meat	Fish, chicken, lean cuts of meat, venison, vegetable protein such as beans, TOFU and soya dishes
Hard and high-fat cheeses	Cottage cheese, low-fat cheese, tofu for cooking
Fried foods such as chips	Boiled, grilled, steamed or baked foods such as baked or boiled potatoes
White bread and white flour, potatoes, products such as pasta	Wholegrain bread, oats, brown rice
White sugar	Brown sugar, fructose, honey, in moderation. Eat fresh or dried fruit if you want something sweet
Salt	Low-sodium Biosalt, vegetable salt
Alcohol	One or two glasses of wine a day will do no harm, and may even help if you have high blood pressure. Drink beer and spirits only occasionally; try low/non-alcoholic beers and wines, or fruit and vegetable juices and spring water

HERBAL MEDICINE
Self help Garlic, onions and ginger, raw or cooked, are believed to reduce cholesterol in the system. Yarrow infusions are said to help to prevent blood clots, lime flowers to improve circulation generally, and lemon to lower blood pressure.

An orthodox view

Doctors agree that not smoking, switching to LOW-FAT DIETS, taking moderate exercise and adopting a less stressful lifestyle will help many people with arteriosclerosis. In addition, conventional medicine can offer drugs to reduce high blood pressure, and surgery to replace blocked sections of artery with pieces taken from healthy veins.

ARTHRITIS

There are more than 100 different types of arthritis, all involving some disorder or inflammation of the joints. Two of the most common forms are osteoarthritis and rheumatoid arthritis, which affect millions of people in Britain; a third common form is GOUT, caused by crystals of a body waste, uric acid, collecting in the sufferer's joints.

Osteoarthritis causes swelling, pain and stiffness and sometimes deforms the joints. The parts most affected are the hips, knees, spine and hands. Shock-absorbing cartilage between the bones of the joints becomes rough and worn, allowing the bones to rub together and wear when the joints are flexed. Muscles and ligaments are also weakened. Women are more at risk than men.

Rheumatoid arthritis also affects more women than men. During an attack the tissue, tendons and ligaments of the joint become inflamed. Feet and fingers are usually the first parts to be affected; then the wrists, knees, shoulders, ankles and elbows. Symptoms include swelling, stiffness and pain in the joints; red, shiny skin over the joints; and a general feeling of stiffness and restricted movement. Sometimes there is numbness in the hands (see CARPAL TUNNEL SYNDROME), loss of weight or appetite, FEVER, or a general sense of being unwell.

The causes of arthritis are largely unknown, but various factors such as heredity, injury and stress on the joints may play a part. Many therapists believe that certain forms may be associated with a breakdown of the IMMUNE SYSTEM – possibly triggered off by an ALLERGY or by VIRUS INFECTIONS.

Always see your doctor if you suspect that you may have arthritis.

Arthritic joints

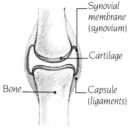

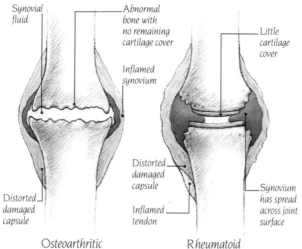

Normal joint

Osteoarthritic joint

Rheumatoid arthritic joint

A normal joint is cushioned by cartilage and synovial fluid. In osteoarthritis the bone is pitted and the cartilage disappears. In rheumatoid arthritis the synovium spreads between the joint surfaces.

What the therapists recommend

NATUROPATHY

Self help A wholefood, largely vegetarian diet (see EATING FOR HEALTH) with plenty of salads and lightly cooked vegetables is recommended. Cut out foods, such as dairy products, that can cause allergies. However, modest amounts such as one or two eggs a week and a little fish or chicken every second day may do no harm.

Avoid red meat and white flour products. Use goat's milk and the cheese and yoghurt made from it, instead of cow's milk and its products. Avoid also acid fruits such as lemons, oranges, grapefruit and strawberries, rhubarb, spinach, tomatoes, salt and sugar (use honey), tea, coffee, alcohol and products containing FOOD ADDITIVES. Drinking raw fruit and vegetable juices may also help. For cases of acute inflammation, two to four cups of celery juice and one cup each of carrot, cucumber and beetroot juice daily are recommended.

Consultation Before prescribing a course of treatment, the naturopath will examine you, ask general questions about your health, and possibly do some tests – for example, to find out if you have any allergies. Correct diet is thought to be effective in controlling the symptoms of arthritis, so the therapist will then advise about the best diet for your individual needs. He may suggest a RAW FOOD DIET one day a week, or recommend sulphur-rich foods (see MINERALS) such as garlic and live yoghurt. If necessary you will be urged to lose weight (see SLIMMING THE NATURAL WAY).

Arthritis sufferers with vitamin or mineral deficiencies may be recommended to take vitamins A, B-complex, especially B12, C and E, and minerals such as zinc and calcium. Other supplements used include evening primrose oil, pollen tablets, kelp or seaweed, and green-lipped mussel extract, which is reputed to have good short-term effects.

You will probably be advised to keep active and use your joints with specific exercises, except in severe stages of rheumatoid arthritis, when it is better to rest.

TRADITIONAL MEDICINE

Self help Remedies include a warming lotion made from glycerine and cayenne pepper (not if the skin is broken), and hot poultices and compresses (see p. 184) of pounded fresh ginger, powdered sulphur or green clay (available at health food shops or from chemists, to special order). Another lotion may be made by mixing one part cayenne to four parts olive oil and eight parts spirit of camphor.

Cider vinegar, honey and cod-liver oil are traditional cures – try 2 teaspoons of cider vinegar in a glass of water with a little honey, first thing in the morning and again at every meal; or take 2 teaspoons of cod-liver oil for five days before going to bed. Some sufferers also claim to have been helped by copper bracelets (see COPPER THERAPY).

HYDROTHERAPY

Self help Swimming and bathing take the weight off joints and warm water relaxes muscles and relieves pain. Sea water is believed to be particularly beneficial (see THALASSOTHERAPY), as are seaweed baths. You can buy dried seaweed for this purpose sold as bladderwrack at major chemists, health food shops or herbalists. An Epsom salts bath may also help – simply add 3-4 tablespoonsful to a hot bath.

HOMOEOPATHY

Self help Two general homoeopathic remedies are _Ruta_ and _Rhus tox._ The second is also claimed to be a specific remedy for pains that become worse after resting and in damp weather, and are relieved somewhat by continuous activity. For very painful joints that hurt if moved, try _Bryonia_, and after an injury, _Arnica._ If pain is eased by pressure and cold, and increased by heat and movement, _Bryonia_ may help. _Pulsatilla_ is used when pains seem to move from joint to joint, neck and shoulders 'crack' on movement, legs feel heavy in daytime and ache at night. Symptoms tend to worsen in a hot and stuffy atmosphere. Gentle movement and pressure can give relief.

MOXIBUSTION

Consultation Arthritis is seen as due to a blockage of _Qi_, or energy. The therapist will diagnose the organs affected and base his treatment on the diagnosis. The general treatment for all forms of arthritis is moxibustion at points in the back, abdomen, arms and legs. ACUPUNCTURE may be given also at points in the neck, back, abdomen and legs. Additional local treatment will also be given at the affected joints.

HERBAL MEDICINE

Self help Devil's claw is claimed to have given good results – research by drug companies has confirmed that the herb contains several glycosides that are powerful anti-inflammatory agents. For this reason, however, it is best not used during pregnancy. Alfalfa (lucerne) – as tablets or infusion (see p. 184, do not boil) – is used as a nutritional supplement, as is celery. Infusions of parsley and ginger root are said to clear poisons from the system, and extracts or infusions of willow, primula, aloe vera, feverfew and bogbean are all believed to reduce inflammation. Wild yam and lignum vitae may be helpful for attacks of rheumatoid arthritis.

ACUPRESSURE

Self help For the best results you should carry out self treatment daily, morning and evening until the symptoms are relieved. In each case press the points indicated firmly for one to two minutes – and massage in a clockwise direction if required.

Hands: Press the point at the end of the crease between forefinger and thumb towards the finger bone. _Hips:_ Press strongly inwards at the hollow at the sides of the hips at the joint between pelvis and leg. _Knees:_ Press in and under the kneecap in the outer depression. Or – and this is said to be particularly effective – press inwards at the point three thumbs' width down from the kneecap in the hollow on the outer edge of the shin.

Other alternative treatments

Acupuncture Practitioners treat more patients with arthritis than any other complaint. Both osteoarthritis and rheumatoid arthritis are said to respond well to acupuncture techniques. In addition, good results have been achieved in other similar diseases such as BURSITIS and fibrositis, or 'muscular rheumatism'. All are best treated before they become chronic and cause degenerative changes that lead to restricted movement and severe pain.

Bach Remedies Oak for those who are dutiful, stoic and long-suffering; Beech for rigidity and intolerance; Pine for those with autocratic, domineering personalities. When there is resentment and bitterness, Willow. Rock water for the self-critical, with punishingly high standards, and Vervain if the arthritis is thought to be a response to over-extension of one's resources, or if the sufferer has fixed, fanatical ideas.

Aromatherapy Try rubbing camomile onto painful joints. Ten drops each of rosemary, marigold and lavender oil in 3 tablespoons of almond oil make another massage oil. Pine, lavender or juniper oil can be added to a hot bath.

Osteopathy, Chiropractic, Massage, Alexander Technique and other manipulative therapies These can be effective, especially if begun in the early stages. However, they need to be practised with great care or harm may result. Always ask your doctor's advice before adopting any of these therapies and do not use them if there is inflammation – for example, in the acute phase of rheumatoid arthritis.

Reflexology Massage to the reflex areas relating to the joints affected may help relieve pain and inflammation. So, too, may direct massage to zone-related areas (shoulder for hip, elbow for knee, wrist for ankle, hand for foot and vice versa). Massage to the reflex areas for the pituitary, adrenals and parathyroid glands, the kidneys and the solar plexus may also be helpful. A good general treatment to all the reflex areas is also recommended. See chart, p. 295.

Yoga, Tai-chi Ch'uan and Dance Movement Therapy Gentle exercises such as these can help to prevent stiffness and keep the joints supple. They may also relieve STRESS and help you to relax. (Exercises are not recommended for severe cases of rheumatoid arthritis, for which rest is advised.) The improvement of breathing is also important and may assist severe cases of both rheumatoid arthritis and osteoarthritis.

Psychotherapy, Autogenics and Hypnotherapy These may help to overcome anxiety and depression, and encourage a more positive attitude to life. Some practitioners believe that unexpressed negative emotions such as fear, anger and grief may be a cause of rheumatoid arthritis and must be dealt with before a cure can take place.

An orthodox view

Doctors have made comparison tests of acupuncture and orthodox treatments for arthritic pain in joints such as the knee, back and shoulder, and have found it to be as effective as claimed. In general, however, little is known about the causes of arthritis, and doctors can only treat the symptoms. Drugs are prescribed to relieve pain and swelling, and physiotherapy is often recommended to keep the joints flexible and strengthen weak muscles.

In severe cases, arthritic joints can often be replaced with artificial ones; hip replacements are particularly successful. Where this is impossible, a range of aids and appliances is available to help sufferers remain independent.

Self-help yoga exercises

<u>Foot rotation (right)</u>: *Sit down and put one ankle across the other thigh. Rotate the foot using your hand. Rotate it in the opposite direction. Then exercise the other foot.*

<u>Shoulder rotation (below)</u>: *Sit down with your arm on the chair arm. Rotate the shoulder on that side using the other hand. Rotate the other way. Repeat for the other shoulder.*

ART THERAPY
Healing through self-expression

People with emotional problems can be helped to express their deepest thoughts and feelings visually through art therapy. Instead of being given drugs to suppress their symptoms, patients are encouraged to communicate their feelings to others by way of drawing and painting.

Often fears and needs are expressed that are so deeply buried that the person is not normally even aware of them. Giving these a visual form in paint, clay or some other art medium may be the first stage in the healing process of helping the patient to recognise and eventually overcome his problems.

This relatively new form of therapy was first practised in England during the 1940s, mainly as a result of the work of the artist Adrian Hill and psychotherapist Irene Champernowne (see box, p. 42), and has grown steadily since then. Today art therapy is practised in many parts of the world.

Who it can help Anyone with emotional or psychological problems, or who wants to find out more about themselves, may benefit, especially if they find it hard to express

Symbolic portraits

One way in which group members are encouraged to express their feelings about one another is by drawing 'symbolic portraits'. Each member draws the others not as they really appear, but in terms of the shapes, colours and images he associates with them.

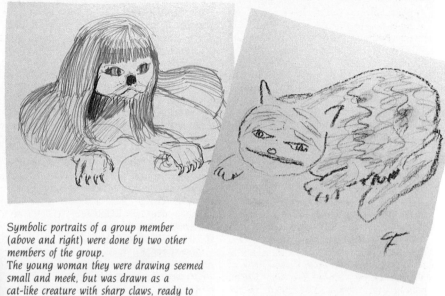

Symbolic portraits of a group member (above and right) were done by two other members of the group.
The young woman they were drawing seemed small and meek, but was drawn as a cat-like creature with sharp claws, ready to pounce. She was taken aback by this, but as she thought about it she came to realise that she was using her meek appearance to suppress her natural aggressiveness, and that this made her feel tense and knotted up inside. The realisation should help her to release her aggressiveness and channel it in a creative and positive way.

This clay mask (above) was made collectively by a small group of patients who had been drug addicts. At first, one member of the group, Aldo, dominated the others and insisted that they should use the clay to make a model prison. At first they agreed but soon became dissatisfied and lost interest, and began to bicker among themselves. The therapist urged them to find a way to resolve the problem and would not let them leave the room — even for a cigarette. Eventually, the group smashed up the prison and began discussing what they should make instead. They hit enthusiastically on the idea of masks and each made one. They then joined in creating a group mask, which was made with great care, loving attention, and lavishly applied colouring.
They ended satisfied with their achievement, pleased at finding a creative solution to their problem by working together. Even Aldo felt relieved that he had been able to cooperate with the others, instead of having to dominate them.

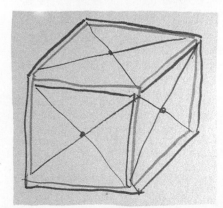

Another man drew the woman therapist as a conductor in charge of the group (above). She looks quite fierce, and the patient explained that he had been afraid when he found out that the therapist would be a woman, since he feared women in authority.

One patient in the group was drawn as a closed box, tied up with string (left). He agreed that he felt cut off from others and unable to be open with them, and decided that he wanted to change.

themselves in words. Group art therapy is particularly recommended for people who have difficulty relating to others, or who suffer from such ailments as ALCOHOLISM, drug ADDICTION, ANOREXIA, BULIMIA, or physical or mental handicaps which interfere with communication.

Long-term hospital patients can be helped to return to the community by learning to communicate better with others, and people with a low opinion of themselves can gain self-confidence and a sense of achievement.

Finding a therapist   Art therapy is still a fairly small profession in Britain and there are only about 600 practitioners registered with the British Association of Art Therapists. They practise in hospitals, clinics and special schools, seeing patients individually and in groups. Art therapy is available in the National Health Service and patients are usually referred to a practitioner by their doctors or psychotherapists.

All registered practitioners have either a postgraduate diploma or university master's degree in art therapy, as well as qualifications or long experience in some area of art, craft or design.

Consulting a therapist   Most patients are referred to an art therapist only when their emotional difficulties become so severe that they are admitted to hospital, either as outpatients or in-patients. Often they find it hard to talk about their personal problems because deep or frightening feelings are involved, or they do not understand why they are troubled or unhappy.

Therapists are trained to be sensitive – and, when the time comes, good listeners – who recognise a patient's need to share his problems, but also understand how difficult it can be to express innermost feelings, especially when distressed and confused.

Patients who are worried about not being able to draw or paint very well are reassured from the beginning. They are told that they do not need to be 'good at art', because making images, marks and symbols is a natural human activity which all children do spontaneously at play, but tend to give up as they grow older. Patients are helped to rediscover the ability to play creatively, and by doing so express and understand themselves and their problems better.

The patient is offered various art materials such as easy-to-use paints, crayons, charcoal, coloured and plain paper, clay, Plasticine, and old magazines and newspapers with which to make collages. 'Junk' material such as scrap wood, boxes and plastic containers which can be used to make three-dimensional constructions may also be provided. The patient is free to use the materials in any way he wishes, with the therapist offering help only if he seems stuck.

At first some people may find it hard to work spontaneously with unfamiliar materials and in front of a stranger. But most patients, once they begin to use paint, clay or whatever, become so involved in their creation that they forget fears and inhibitions, and express themselves freely.

Often the images created are unexpected, frightening or disturbing, and even the patient may be surprised or shocked at his work. Sometimes first attempts are just nervous doodles or splodges of colour, but the therapist will always be responsive, encouraging the patient to talk about himself through his work, though never offering an over-simplistic judgment or interpretation.

Art therapy is often used with groups of about eight to ten patients, each member working on individual pieces but also being encouraged to help others and cooperate on group projects. As members get to know one another, they become a sort of 'family' – and start to behave as they would with their own families. Then, as old conflicts, fears and needs emerge in their work and relationships with each other, the therapist helps the patients to work through their feelings and resolve their problems.

Self help   After receiving art therapy from a qualified practitioner, patients are encouraged to continue to paint and draw on their own, as a way of understanding and developing themselves.

An orthodox view

Art therapy is considered to be 'alternative' because it combines visual arts such as painting and collage with psychotherapy in a way that is still new and unusual in medicine. However, art therapy is accepted by doctors as an effective form of treatment, and many patients have been helped by it, even when more conventional psychiatry or psychotherapy has failed. The profession is recognised by the National Health Service in Britain, and practitioners hold official posts in many hospitals, schools and social service departments.

ASTHMA

Attacks of asthma occur when inflammation or muscular spasm causes the bronchial passages of the lungs to contract, making breathing difficult and causing a WHEEZING sound as the breath is exhaled. Other symptoms may include coughing, a fast pulse – up to 90 beats a minute – and, in serious attacks, going blue in the face. Often the victim feels restless and panicky, and may turn pale, rather than blue. While most attacks last just a few minutes, serious bouts may go on for hours and must always be treated by a doctor or there is a risk of collapse or death from lack of oxygen, strain or exhaustion.

Asthma is usually due to several interacting inherited or environmental factors such as ALLERGY (especially to pollen, house dust, animal hair, feathers, or mould and fungi spores), climate and temperature, or to infection, STRESS, ANXIETY, or any kind of physical exertion.

Asthma that runs in families tends to start in childhood or adolescence, and is sometimes associated with ECZEMA or HAY FEVER. Often it disappears after a year or two. Among adults, asthma sometimes develops after recurrent chest infections or as a result of HEART DISORDERS.

What the therapists recommend
NATUROPATHY

Self help Keep to a wholefood diet (see EATING FOR HEALTH) and avoid eating anything containing FOOD ADDITIVES such as the colouring agent tartrazine – which can trigger allergic reactions – refined products such as white flour and sugar, and reduce your intake of dairy products.

Include plenty of fresh fruit and vegetables – especially garlic and onions, said to counteract the production of mucus – and raw juices such as carrot, celery, spinach and grapefruit. One or two teaspoons of cider vinegar with a little honey in a glass of water three times a day may also help.

OSTEOPATHY may be recommended to keep the rib cage moving freely to help with normal breathing.

Consultation You will be advised about a suitable diet, and also about RELAXATION AND BREATHING techniques and reducing stress. The therapist will usually test for allergies – possibly by using KINESIOLOGY – and tell you to cut out any otherwise harmless foods to which you may be allergic – dairy products and wheat, for example.

If you also have THRUSH or are taking antibiotics, you will be advised to eat plenty of live yoghurt or take acidophilus tablets, which are believed to restore friendly bacteria to your digestive tract. Vitamins A, C and E, propolis tablets and honey may all be prescribed against coughing and inflamed bronchial passages.

BIOCHEMIC TISSUE SALTS

Self help _Kali phos._ is recommended for nervous asthma or a tight chest and difficulty in breathing; and _Kali mur._ alternated with _Kali phos._ for thick, white phlegm that is hard to cough up. If asthma is caused by muscular spasms in the bronchial tubes, alternate _Magnesia phos._ with _Kali phos. Calcarea phos._ is a general remedy believed to be suitable for all types of asthma.

HERBAL MEDICINE

Self help Generally, asthma is best treated by a practitioner, but infusions (see p. 184) of euphorbia and thyme are recommended to relax muscular spasms and loosen phlegm; and passion flower and pasque flower (always the dried herb, not the fresh plant) to relieve TENSION.

Elecampane is held to be good for the lungs and to loosen mucus when used in an infusion made from elecampane root that

has been soaked for eight to ten hours in water. Add 1oz of root to 1 pint (30g to 600ml) of water, bring to boiling point and allow to cool before drinking. Camomile is said to have an anti-inflammatory action, and may be helpful if stress is a problem.

HOMOEOPATHY

Self help _Arsenicum album_ is used to treat difficult breathing; also when the sufferer needs to bend forward to breathe, or feels restless or exhausted and finds the symptoms worse between midnight and 2am. If attacks peak between 3 and 5am, _Kali carbonicum_ is recommended, and _Aconite_ if they occur after exposure to cold or a dry wind. _Ipecacuanha_ can help acute breathlessness and may assist if there is a rattling cough or loose mucus in the chest.

Other alternative treatments

Massage To allow mucus to drain out during massage, the patient should lie face down with head lower than chest. Massage the back with long, gliding strokes, and knead the shoulders. Then use cupping movements on the middle and upper back, paying special attention to the lung points between the shoulders. See MASSAGE.

Ionisation This has eased difficult breathing for some asthma sufferers. Keep an ioniser switched on whenever possible – at home or at work.

Osteopathy, Alexander Technique and Chiropractic These manipulative therapies can help by teaching asthma sufferers how to breathe properly. By correcting the posture and breathing of asthmatic children, therapists aim to reduce the risk of spinal and chest deformities resulting later from years of difficult breathing.

Reflexology Massage to the reflex areas relating to the lungs and bronchi, plus areas relating to the solar plexus, diaphragm, adrenal glands, heart, digestive system, spine (cervical and thoracic regions) and pituitary gland is recommended. See chart on p. 295.

Biofeedback and Yoga These are thought to help, especially attacks brought on by tensions or stress. Yoga postures to open the chest include corpse posture, shoulder stand, mountain, fish, pelvic lift, back roll and cobra. Attention is usually given to deeper breathing and prolonging breathing out.

Hydrotherapy Hot and cold compresses (see p. 193) applied to the back and chest are believed to help the lungs work better, by stimulating circulation and muscular activity.

Aromatherapy A few drops of oils such as eucalyptus, juniper and wintergreen can be added to a teaspoon of carrier lotion and applied to the chest nightly. The same oils, plus peppermint or rosemary, can be inhaled from a tissue when breathing is difficult.

Acupuncture Some sufferers have found that treatment reduces the number of attacks they experience. The acupuncture is often applied to the ear.

Bach Remedies Mimulus is recommended if the sufferer is generally fearful and oversensitive; Rescue Remedy for a sudden attack, plus Olive for exhaustion afterwards. If attacks are brought on by anger, try Holly. Try Aspen for apprehension, or Rock water for self-restricting attitudes.

An orthodox view

Doctors recognise that allergies can play a part in causing asthma, and a doctor may offer allergy tests. Asthma itself is controlled mainly by cortisone and other drugs – often in the form of aerosol inhalers – that reduce inflammation in the bronchial tubes and open up the air passages. Antibiotics are used if the cause is a chest infection.

ASTIGMATISM

This is a common eyesight defect causing distortion and blurred vision, and sometimes headaches and aching eyes, and is due to irregularities in the shape of the eye's lens. It may be hereditary, or caused by problems in the lens or in the transparent cornea of the eye, through which light passes. See EYESIGHT PROBLEMS; BATES METHOD.

ATHLETE'S FOOT

Keen runners and swimmers are among the typical victims of this common foot infection. It is a type of RINGWORM caused by the fungus _Tinea pedis_, which is often picked up in public places such as changing-rooms and swimming pools, and once contracted it can be hard to get rid of. It is commonly found among adolescents and young men.

The skin on and between the toes becomes inflamed and itchy, and may crack or flake off, exposing red, tender skin underneath. Sometimes small blisters and rashes appear. In time, the nails may also be affected and may start to crumble or separate from the nail beds.

What the therapists recommend
NATUROPATHY

Self help Apply propolis ointment or vitamin C powder to affected areas, or bind cotton wool containing honey or cider vinegar into place over the area and leave it on overnight. Go barefoot whenever possible – except in public places where reinfestation could occur – and wear socks made from natural fibres such as wool or cotton, which allow the skin to breathe. Make sure when you remove your socks that you put them back on the same feet to avoid spreading the infection to the other foot. A skin tonic can also be made from the juice of fresh strawberries mixed with pulped fresh dates – drink about two cups a day.

HERBAL MEDICINE

Self help Daily herbal footbaths may be recommended for fungal infections – either a strong infusion (see p. 184) of golden seal root or a mixture of 1oz (30g) each of red clover, sage, calendula and agrimony, with 2 teaspoons of cider vinegar added to the water. Bathe the feet for half an hour, then dry well and powder with arrowroot or powdered golden-seal root. Calendula cream is said also to soothe irritated skin and combat infection. In addition, essential oil of tea tree applied neat to the affected area may be of help.

Other alternative treatments

Aromatherapy Add two drops each of lavender, tea tree and tagetes oil to a bowl of warm water. Soak the feet for ten minutes each night. Alternatively, make a small compress with the same oils. Place it on the affected area and keep in place with a cotton bandage or a sock.

Each morning, add a tablespoon of calendula oil to the same essential oils and apply to the affected area.

Reflexology Although reflexology treatment cannot be given to the areas of the foot affected by athlete's foot, sometimes the general effect of the treatment in stimulating the body's healing forces may encourage the condition to clear. This is particularly so if other alternative treatment is being given.

An orthodox view

The antifungal properties of certain herbs have been demonstrated by herbal practitioners in experiments. However, doctors prefer to rely on more powerful chemical preparations, whose effectiveness has been proven. Chemists keep a selection of these proprietary foot powders and creams, which can be bought over the counter without a prescription.

In cases of minor infection, doctors usually prescribe a cream such as Exelderm (sulconazole nitrate) or Ecostatin (econazole nitrate) and, if this does not work or if the infection recurs, tablets such as Fulcin or Grisovin (griseofulvin).

The aura around the hand of an aura therapist is shown on this Kirlian photograph. The photograph is thought to show the extra level of electromagnetic energy that is emitted during the act of healing.

AURA THERAPY
Using visible magnetism to fight disease

Practitioners who use this therapy describe the aura as a magnetic field around the body that interacts continually with other auras in the environment. These individual auras are said to be in contact with a universal field of spiritual energy, from which they draw their power. Many practitioners – particularly spiritual healers – say that they can see auras as areas of light around their patients, and use them to aid treatment. See also KIRLIAN PHOTOGRAPHY.

Artists and mystics have claimed from ancient times to have seen and portrayed this effect – for example, works of art as diverse as ancient Indian sculptures, aboriginal rock paintings in Australia, and American Indian totem poles all show figures surrounded by areas of light or lines emanating from their bodies. The halo in Western religious art is also believed to derive from a golden aura seen glowing around the subject's head.

Aura therapists say that although we are not usually aware of it, the aura determines our first responses to people and situations, and is a quicker and more sensitive gauge than many more rational faculties. They believe that the unease you sometimes feel in certain people's company may result from an aura that vibrates out of harmony with your own, and that a sense of peace in a particular place probably means you are surrounded by harmonious auras there.

The auras of plants, animals and minerals are said to communicate and interact continually with one another as part of a single living system. Each person's aura is thought to be made up of all the radiations from the cells and chemicals in his body, and their interactions.

The visible aura is said to be an oval extending from a few inches to several feet around the body, and sometimes more at the head. The light is composed of seven different coloured rays, each associated with particular organs of the body as well as higher functions; and the shapes, colours and strengths of the rays are said to vary from person to person, reflecting each individual's unique make-up.

Who it can help Aura therapists say that anyone may be helped, particularly those interested in developing themselves spiritually and those whom conventional medicine cannot help. Like other spiritual healers, aura therapists do not accept that anyone's condition is incurable.

Finding a therapist There are no formal qualifications in aura therapy, but people who practise it are usually healers or qualified alternative therapists who have a particular interest in spiritual awareness. Generally their ability to see and use auras therapeutically has been developed over many years of practical experience with

Learning to see auras

While some people believe that only specially gifted psychics can see auras, others think that we can all develop the ability to some degree. We could therefore start by training ourselves to be perceptive to subtle effects we do not normally notice.

Begin by setting aside all doubts about auras and try to believe sincerely that they are there and that you can see them. Try to react to people and situations with as much empathy as possible. People who see auras speak of the ability as a subtle process of 'tuning in' to life forces.

Learn to look at people carefully. Watch their movements: are they tense and jerky or smooth and flowing? Do their clothes look comfortable on them, and do the colours suit the person and his personality?

Try to understand the sort of messages people are sending out about themselves, and what they may be holding back. Try to imagine yourself in another person's position – how would you feel in similar circumstances and what would your reactions be?

patients, as well as with much work on their own spiritual development.

Finding an aura therapist can be difficult, as there is no national association in Britain. If you are consulting an alternative practitioner such as a naturopath, homoeopath or healer, he may be able to refer you to someone who practises aura therapy. If not, you may get advice from the National Federation of Spiritual Healers, Old Manor Farm Studio, Church Street, Sunbury on Thames, Middlesex TW16 6RG, or from the Institute for Complementary Medicine, 21 Portland Place, London W1N 3AF.

Consulting a therapist A therapist starts by observing – or, more rarely, actually touching – a patient's aura to interpret his state of health. A dull aura, for example, could show poor health or a need for change, which is exhausting the patient, while dark patches over certain organs are said to indicate the presence of disease.

Therapists believe that personality and emotions can also be interpreted from auras. For example, an aura with soft, fringed edges may be seen as a sign that the person is too susceptible to the influence of others; firm but fluid boundaries mean openness but not vulnerability, and a hard, distinct outline may indicate a defensive attitude and a tendency to view the world as hostile, owing to a

deeper insecurity. Colours, too, are held to be important: lots of red in an aura is believed to indicate anger, and blue, idealism.

Once the therapist has achieved a clear view of the patient's aura, and feels he understands the problem, he can offer treatment in a number of ways. Sometimes this could involve 'feeding' extra colour into a dull or depleted aura, or introducing a complementary colour to help balance one that is too strong. Therapists say that they do this not by using the energy of their own auras, but by making themselves into channels through which universal spiritual energy can flow into the auras of others. This can be done by touching the patient's aura or using visualisation to transmit the energy.

Self help Practitioners who use auras therapeutically tend to emphasise the need for patients to take an active part in the healing process. Part of the therapy usually involves helping the patient to become more self-aware and more in touch with his own spiritual nature. This can involve learning to see and strengthen your own aura by means of visualisation, COLOUR THERAPY, SOUND THERAPY or even by drawing, writing or keeping a journal. However, they emphasise that support and guidance from an experienced therapist are usually also needed.

Colours of the aura   Colours emanating from an individual are believed to reveal his or her nature and physical and emotional state. Here are some basic guidelines, though a proper interpretation of someone's aura can be complex since the colours have to be interpreted in relation to one another:

Red The colour of life and physical vigour, red represents strength, energy and passions, and is associated with the coordination of the individual as a whole. Tension or nervousness may show as light red; anger or sensuality as dark red. An excessive amount of red in an aura is said to indicate selfishness, wilfulness or an overvaluing of material things. Therapeutically, red is associated with the nerve endings, excretory functions and the sex glands.

Orange This is associated with energy and health and indicates a strong personality which is also considerate of others. But too much orange shows an overemphasis on selfish goals or ambitions. Orange is also the colour of the adrenal glands, sexual functioning and the spleen; it can also indicate fear, illusion or disillusionment.

Yellow Intellect and optimism are indicated or, in some cases, frustration or worry. If the yellow is very pale there may be weakness or indecisiveness, but golden-yellow is a sign of spiritual development and insight. Yellow is also associated with the pancreas, digestive system and reproduction and childbirth.

Green The colour of nature, regeneration

and healing, green shows a lively, adaptable personality and a versatile mind. It is associated with the thymus gland, the heart and circulatory system.

Blue Idealism, integrity and inspiration are associated with blue. Pale blue indicates a potential for learning and scholarship. Physically, blue is the colour of the thyroid gland, and is associated with the ears, nose and throat, and with breathing and speech.

Indigo This indicates a tendency to act on intuition and a search for spiritual truth. It indicates moral values and transcendence of the physical world. A predominance of indigo in an aura signifies calmness and benevolence or, if it is not well balanced, irritability. It is also associated with the pituitary gland and the lymphatic system.

Violet The colour of spiritual enlightenment, insight and love. It represents the pineal body, the nervous system and the integration of the whole body.

Black and grey These colours show that the aura has been damaged by negative thoughts or emotions, STRESS or illness, or by undergoing anaesthesia.

White Perfection, the ideal and truth are represented by white. It has a balancing effect on black or grey in the aura.

An orthodox view

Although there is no scientific evidence for the existence of auras, some doctors believe that they exist – in the form of emissions of energy, from both living and dead tissue. The degree of emissions varies, but may indicate the presence of disease. However, orthodox practitioners do not feel that auras can always be detected, or that they can be 'interpreted' accurately.

AURICULAR THERAPY
Curing it by ear

By treating only one part of a patient's body – the ear – auricular therapists claim that they can cure sickness in other parts of his system. For instance, a painful right shoulder is usually treated by means of the right ear; but treatment given to the left ear is often just as effective.

The therapists' method is similar to ACUPUNCTURE, and they claim that the ear has more than 200 acupuncture points which are physically related to specific areas of the body. By stimulating nerve endings at appropriate points, a 'healing wave' is sent along the nerve to the part that is ailing. Therapists also contend that any problem or diseased part of the body has an effect on its corresponding point in the ear. This may show itself in the form of nodules, white marks, scars or ECZEMA.

While admitting that they do not fully understand how their art works, practitioners point out that it is being practised in many parts of the world as a significant therapy.

Who it can help The therapy is said to be very useful in controlling and alleviating various types of ADDICTION – including alcohol, drugs, food and tobacco. It can also help people suffering from ARTHRITIS, ASTHMA, INDIGESTION, MIGRAINE, and those with NERVOUS DISORDERS and URINARY PROBLEMS.

It is said also to be highly effective in controlling pain and is widely used as an anaesthetic in countries such as China and Sri Lanka – especially in childbirth, dentistry, and major surgical operations, during which the patients remain awake, relaxed and apparently free from pain.

Finding a therapist Auricular therapy clinics are on the increase in Britain and may be listed in your local *Yellow Pages* directory. A list of practitioners can be obtained from the Secretary of the Association of Auricular Therapy, 489 Lichfield Road, Four Oaks, Sutton Coldfield B74 4DL.

Therapists take a two-year training course which includes anatomy, pathology and physiology. Trainees come from the ranks of doctors, nurses, qualified acupuncturists, health care workers and so on. The qualifications are: Associate MAA (Member of the Auricular Therapy Association); Licentiate MAA; and FMAA (Founder Member of the Association).

For further information contact the Richardson Clinic, Westgate, Heckmondwike, West Yorkshire WF16 OHE.

Consulting a therapist The therapist will compile a complete case history. As well as general health details – and those of parents and, possibly, grandparents – the patient will be asked about his family life, work relationships, SMOKING, drinking, what he eats and how much, and also his hobbies and spare-time interests.

The patient's ear is then examined thoroughly for any unusual marks or deformities. The therapist will also inspect skin texture, by which he claims to learn a lot about a patient's state of health. For example, dry and flaky skin over the lung acupuncture point can indicate asthma or a lung infection.

Therapists will usually want to see patients once a week. However, in the early stages of an acute illness, this may well be increased to a daily visit for the first two or three days.

Diagnosing acupuncture points The therapist usually does this with a small, blunt-ended probe. He passes the probe over the skin of the ear until the patient feels discomfort. This indicates the point, or points, to be treated.

Another method employs an electrical point detector. The patient holds a metal bar electrode which is wired to a meter. The therapist holds another electrode which looks like a ballpoint pen with a blunt end. He passes this over the patient's ear points, and any abnormality is duly recorded on the meter.

Types of treatment Many therapists use acupuncture needles placed in the chosen acupuncture points and manipulated.

The therapist may pass a tiny electric pulse down the needles. No pain is felt and patients usually find the treatment relaxing. Electrical stimulation may also be given without needles. The patient holds a metal rod which is attached by wire to an electrical stimulator. Another wire leads from the stimulator to a pen-shaped electrode held by the therapist. He places the tip of the 'pen' on the chosen area and a mild, stimulating current is passed into the relevant point.

A third method – for very young children and people who are afraid of needles – is the use of a laser. Stimulation is carried out by the electrical frequency of the light source, and patients experience no sensations at all.

Self help Patients who cannot get to their practitioner regularly can treat themselves by using press needles, or semipermanent needles as they are also called. These are mainly used to treat conditions such as ANOREXIA and heavy smoking. Press needles are very fine pins with heads like drawing pins. Or else they may resemble small, pointed studs.

The needles are fitted by the practitioner and left in place for several days at a time, covered by a small piece of plaster to keep them clean. To stimulate the pressure points, the patient simply presses the heads of the needles gently. In cases of addiction the needles should be pressed every hour and whenever the craving comes on. Otherwise, they should be pressed once every hour, especially in cases of painful joints and certain forms of arthritis.

An orthodox view

Although auricular therapy has long been used in China with reportedly good results, it still has to prove itself in Britain. It should therefore be approached with caution.

Rediscovering an ancient art

In the 1950s Dr Paul Nogier of Lyons, France, noticed that many of his patients had strange cauterisation marks on their ears. They had been made by a local lay practitioner and were a 'certain cure' for sciatica.

Dr Nogier began seeking clinical proof of this, and he gradually discovered that each one of the acupuncture points on the ear could act as a reflex, or health mirror, of a particular part of the body.

His researches also showed him that joining the various points formed the outline of an unborn baby lying upside-down in its mother's womb. From this he concluded that the ear is a reflection in miniature of the entire human body. He has published books and developed a sophisticated system of treatment at his clinic in Lyons.

The art of 'needling' a patient's ear was a standard medical treatment in Mediterranean countries four centuries before the birth of Christ. There is also evidence of it being practised in ancient India, China, Greece and Egypt, though it had largely been abandoned until Dr Nogier revived it.

AUTISM

An autistic child lives in a world of its own, unable to communicate and relate to other people – including its parents, to whom this can cause great distress. Autism is a rare mental illness that appears without known cause during the first three years of a child's life. It affects more boys than girls and may be related to SCHIZOPHRENIA in adult life.

Cut off from normal, everyday life, autistic children often give the impression of being deaf or mute. However, they are not physically handicapped – though they are usually mentally retarded and therefore notoriously slow developers.

Temper tantrums are often their only sign of emotion, and they may react violently to any change in their daily routine or environment – for example, if a meal is late or if furniture in the home is rearranged.

Normal play is also impossible for the autistic child, who prefers simple, repetitive games, toys and mechanical objects to playing with other children. A few autistic children display exceptional ability at tasks such as computing numbers, working out dates, recognising addresses, or memorising pieces of music at first hearing.

What the therapists recommend

Dance Therapy Some autistic children are able to express themselves through dance, and by analysing their 'movement content' the therapist can then help them adjust to the condition.

Faith Healing A process called 'psychic-visualisation' is used. The healer 'visualises' both the child's illness and the energies that he believes can help to cure it. For example, the healer may choose to imagine the child's mind as a vast, dark city, that is gradually lighting up.

Hair Diagnosis As autism is difficult to diagnose, hair diagnosis is claimed to be useful as part of nutritional diagnosis.

Bach Remedies Water violet is recommended if the patient is withdrawn, aloof and does not seem to want contact; Mimulus if there is actual fear of contact; Aspen if there is apprehension; Crab apple if the patient performs obsessive rituals. Beech is advised if the individual seems impervious to others' love, and Pine if there is periodic violent behaviour, which tyrannises others.

Music Therapy The appeal of music has been found to arouse an emotional response in autistic children. The therapist uses the music to hold a 'conversation' with the child by playing an instrument and singing, usually improvising, while the child is encouraged to respond with its voice, a percussion instrument, or both. As the child's mood changes during the session, the therapist meets each change with a suitable style of music. The child's responses give it a means of expressing feelings and relating to something outside its closed world. Music therapy can also be used in conjunction with drama, ART THERAPY and DANCE MOVEMENT THERAPY and has helped some autistic children to improve.

Naturopathy Consultation is necessary, and usually a wholefood diet is recommended (see EATING FOR HEALTH), perhaps with vitamin and mineral supplements.

An orthodox view

Doctors did not recognise autism until the early 1940s; before that autistic children were often thought of as 'backward' or 'difficult'. Even today diagnosis remains lengthy and difficult, calling for close co-operation between parents, family doctor and a paediatrician.

Autistic children need specialist care and special schooling. There is no known cure, although children may be treated with PSYCHOTHERAPY, occasionally in the form of child psychoanalysis, or calming drugs such as Melleril (thioridazine hydrochloride). Doctors also consider alternative therapies – particularly those using music and art – to be helpful in many cases.

AUTOGENIC TRAINING
Exercising your mind towards health

The basis of this relaxation therapy is a series of six simple mental exercises (see box, p. 48) which are aimed at relieving STRESS and helping the body to cure itself. Autogenic comes from the Greek word for 'self-producing', or 'coming from within', and the training has links with AUTOSUGGESTION, MEDITATION and YOGA.

Three main autogenic positions

Using these positions, training exercises can be carried out in various places and situations – such as at work, on a train, or while taking it easy in the park. Each position is taken up with your eyes shut, thinking about something peaceful and pleasant.

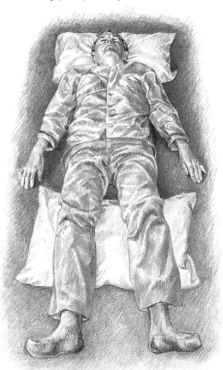

The reclining position This enables the patient to achieve a more beneficial level of sleep.

The armchair position This is particularly useful for practising the therapy in cars, trains and buses – and while relaxing at home and possibly at work.

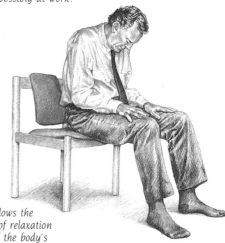

The simple sitting position This allows the patient to experience deeper levels of relaxation in the neck and shoulders – one of the body's main tension areas.

Training requires no special clothing, or the adoption of difficult and awkward postures, and has been compared by some of its practitioners to learning to drive a car: first make yourself comfortable behind the wheel; then start off properly (calmly and without jolts); next change gear (alter your physical and mental states); and finally come to a smooth, safe halt.

Before starting the therapy you will be given a brief checkup to make sure the training is suitable for you. You will also be asked to fill in a form giving your full medical and mental history. Some patients will only be treated under appropriate medical supervision – for example, those suffering from glaucoma or serious heart conditions. Modified treatment is given to asthmatics, diabetics, epileptics, expectant mothers, and people with emotional problems.

Who it can help Therapists claim that autogenic training has proved itself in treating a variety of ailments – including AIDS, ANXIETY, BRONCHITIS, COLITIS, DEPRESSION, ECZEMA, INSOMNIA, IRRITABLE BOWEL SYNDROME, high BLOOD PRESSURE, INDIGESTION, MIGRAINE and ULCERS. Its calming effect helps the body to cure itself, they say. It is also said to be particularly helpful to people who want to avoid or cut down on drugs such as sleeping pills and tranquillisers.

Athletes and sportsmen who want to relax mentally and emotionally are said to benefit; their bodies make more efficient use of oxygen, so improving their performances – and they also recover faster from injuries and exertions. Businessmen also use the therapy to help them relax; airline crews and passengers have had tuition to counter JET LAG.

Apart from children under six, the training is held to be suitable for people of any age. Children over six – an age when they are held to be capable of understanding the training – are said to behave better and do better at school after a course, with improved concentration and behaviour.

Finding a therapist As well as private clinics specialising in the training, certain

Six ways of willing good health

Therapists claim that by silently repeating a set of six phrases – such as 'My right arm is heavy' – patients can induce various physical sensations. In turn, these are said to lead to states of deep relaxation, promoting good health and preventing and curing illness. The exercises can be practised in all or any of the three main positions (see illustrations, p. 47).

<u>Heaviness exercise</u> *focuses thoughts on heaviness in arms, legs, neck, shoulders.*

<u>Warmth exercise</u> *concentrates on awareness of warmth in the limbs.*

<u>Heartbeat exercise</u> *involves concentrating on the heartbeat.*

<u>Breathing exercise</u> *cultivates an awareness of breathing.*

<u>Stomach exercise</u> *focuses on a feeling of warmth in the abdomen.*

<u>Forehead exercise</u> *concerns itself with coolness of the forehead.*

Increased energy

More than 3000 scientific papers have been published recounting the success of autogenic training as a medical aid, but nobody knows exactly how it works.

Medical research suggests that any stress on the body's immune system can contribute to making people ill. In addition, muscular tension caused by stress can lead to CRAMP, strained muscles and BACK PAIN. This can affect coordination, making people accident prone.

Practitioners claim that there is a link between repressed emotions such as grief and anger and the onset of several ailments, including FROZEN SHOULDER and PILES, and that autogenic training can be effective for such conditions.

A characteristic feature of the training is experience of so-called 'autogenic discharges' – fleeting impressions of touch, taste, smell and so on, related to past memories. These discharges are often intense and dramatic, and may be followed by feelings of increased energy.

general hospitals have their own therapists, and offer treatment on the National Health Service. A list of practitioners can be obtained from the Positive Health Centre, 101 Harley Street, London WIN 1DF. The practitioners are usually professionally qualified health workers such as doctors, psychologists, psychotherapists and nurses.

Consulting a therapist A therapist's technique varies according to the patient's individual needs, but it usually follows a general pattern. Once satisfied that the patient can be helped by the training, the therapist shows him the three main autogenic positions (see box) in which the basic exercises are done.

Autogenic training is usually taught in

The road to relaxation

Autogenic training was developed in Berlin in the late 1920s by a German neurologist, Dr Johannes Schultz, who treated his patients by means of hypnotism. He noted how they benefited from states of hypnotic relaxation, and wondered if he could get equally good results without hypnotism.

He devised a set of relaxation exercises based on his clinical observations. By the silent repetition of certain phrases, patients brought on feelings of heaviness, warmth, slowed heartbeat, regular breathing and a warm abdomen. To these he added a sixth sensation – that of a cool forehead – after observing how psychologically disturbed patients benefited even more from therapeutic warm baths when ice packs were put on their foreheads.

The system was so successful that it was taken up throughout Europe, North America and Japan. It was introduced to Britain in the 1970s by Dr Malcolm Carruthers, chairman of the British Association for Autogenic Training.

groups of six to eight patients. The sessions last for about 1½ hours and are usually held once a week for eight to ten weeks.

During the first two to four sessions the therapist focuses on _The heaviness exercise_, the first of six basic exercises (see box) in which the patients silently repeat phrases aimed to gradually produce feelings of deep relaxation and tranquillity. To begin with, they are performed in quiet, comfortable rooms with subdued lighting. Later on, the exercises can be done anywhere – at home in the patients' spare time, while stuck in a traffic jam, or waiting for a business meeting.

Each weekly session begins with patients comparing notes on how they spent their previous six days, and how they got on with their exercises at home. They are encouraged to keep a detailed diary as an aid to memory and a guide to the therapist. At this stage any special problems are solved by adjusting the therapy to meet individual needs.

As the sessions progress, the patients in the group may also perform a series of 'intentional exercises'. These are intended to throw off hitherto repressed feelings of sadness, bitterness, anger and fear, which otherwise may lead to physical discomfort.

Self help Although autogenic training is taught at a clinic or hospital, the therapist will ask you to practise the basic exercises at home or anywhere that is convenient. To begin with, the exercises need last for only a minute or two, three times a day. Towards the end of the course they will be extended to about 15-20 minutes three times a day. Once you have mastered the exercises, you can fit them conveniently into your daily routine.

An orthodox view

Autogenic training is a well-accepted approach to relaxation and has been extensively researched. It is particularly helpful in conditions where the sympathetic nervous system (which unconsciously stimulates certain bodily functions) is overactive, and in PSYCHOSOMATIC ILLNESS.

AUTO-SUGGESTION
Healing yourself by hypnosis

People can use this form of simple HYPNOTHERAPY on themselves. It is believed to work by releasing the unconscious healing powers of body and mind. Autosuggestion is also known as Couéism after Emile Coué (1857-1926), a French apothecary who developed the technique towards the end of the 19th century.

Coué's method is based on a form of meditation which aims to empty the mind of conscious thoughts by the repetition of words or phrases such as the maxim for which he later became famous: 'Every day, in every way, I am getting better and better.'

He believed that if this phrase was repeated regularly while in a relaxed state of mind, it would become implanted in the imagination, and would then direct the unconscious processes of the body and mind in a positive way.

Who it can help People who practise autosuggestion generally do so to enhance their overall well-being, health and happiness. It can also speed recovery and help to alleviate PAIN and suffering caused by physical and mental illnesses. TENSION, ANXIETY, PHOBIAS and ADDICTIONS (for example to food, alcohol or SMOKING) are said to respond well to autosuggestion. ASTHMA, ALLERGY and PSYCHOSOMATIC ILLNESSES may be helped, but take longer.

Autosuggestion can also be effective in controlling pain and FEAR – for example during childbirth (see NATURAL CHILDBIRTH) or among the terminally ill.

Finding a therapist This is a self-help technique, but if necessary a medically qualified hypnotherapist may be able to give you advice and instruction. A list of practitioners can be obtained from the Secretary, The British Society of Medical and Dental Hypnosis, 151 Otley Old Road, Leeds LS16 6HN.

Self help Learning autosuggestion is simply a matter of practising regularly on your own while relaxing. Find a suitable time and place to do so every morning and evening – Coué suggested in bed just before falling asleep and just after waking up.

Meditate if you know how to (see MEDITATION) or empty your mind of all distractions, and concentrate on Coué's formula, repeating it continuously at any speed, either aloud or silently. Do not, however, think about its meaning or imagine that it is a

How autosuggestion developed

From what Coué saw in his practice as an apothecary, he became interested in the role of the mind in healing illness. He observed the work of doctors who used hypnosis to help their patients and performed some experiments himself. From the results he drew two conclusions:

1 That the healing effects of hypnotism were not due to the hypnotist's skill, but rather to powers within the subject's unconscious mind – so that all hypnosis was, in a sense, autosuggestion.

2 That doctors paid too much attention to the will and ignored the patient's imagination, which Coué thought was more powerful.

Coué believed that having the will to live or get better was of no use if a patient had an imaginary fear that he could not recover. As an example of the effect of imagination on the body, Coué pointed to the process of salivating, which cannot be willed to happen but which is easily brought on by imagining tempting food.

Coué believed also that if the will did not interfere, the imagination could be influenced by autosuggestion, to help in healing physical and emotional problems of all types. He devoted the rest of his life to developing and teaching techniques of autosuggestion that people could practise on their own.

During the 1920s, Coué's methods became world famous and autosuggestion is now an integral part of many other therapies – particularly AUTOGENIC TRAINING and VISUALISATION THERAPY.

Emile Coué thought that 'education of the imagination' by autosuggestion led to cures.

command to yourself – just repeat it as an incantation. About 20 repetitions are all that is necessary on each occasion, but it is important to practise regularly *every* morning and evening, otherwise the suggestive effects will be weakened.

Coué believed that his formula was suitable for any circumstances, but followers have since developed other suggestions – for example, it is claimed that pain or tension may be relieved by repeating 'It is passing off', while passing your hand rapidly over the affected part. For relaxation and tranquillity, a phrase such as 'I am completely at peace' is recommended.

You can also experiment with your own suggestions, keeping in mind that some therapists believe suggestions should always be phrased positively.

For example, a suggestion such as 'I am not depressed' may not work as well as the more positive statement 'I am happy'. To stop smoking, eating or drinking too much you could try saying, 'Smoking is not good for my body', 'Overeating is not good for my stomach', or 'Drinking is harming my liver'.

Warning Some therapists warn that hypnotic states are not suitable for everyone, and you should always talk over any proposed treatment with your practitioner. Where the con-scious mind is opposed to the idea of hypnotism or suggestion, it is better not to try – in this state of mind you are not likely to be suggestible in any case.

There may also be a danger that some people with psychotic mental disorders or deeply repressed emotions could lose touch with reality – as a result of which their conditions could worsen. If in doubt, consult a qualified psychotherapist or hypnotherapist (see PSYCHOTHERAPY).

An orthodox view

The medical profession of the time was extremely hostile to Coué's theory. Though some doctors were prepared to admit that a patient's will might influence his health, they were more sceptical about the role played by the imagination.

Nowadays many doctors and psychologists are more sympathetic to this and other aspects of the therapy, and autosuggestion has been shown to influence both the mind and the body (see COGNITIVE THERAPY).

Autosuggestion is considered to be safe and can be used in conjunction with any other therapies. However, it should never take the place of orthodox treatment for serious disorders – particularly those which are life-threatening.

AVERSION THERAPY

This is a technique used in BEHAVIOURAL THERAPY. It is a type of learning by punishment in which the patient is taught to associate an undesirable habit or behaviour with an unpleasant experience. For example, alcoholics are sometimes given the drug Antabuse (disulfiram) which makes them violently sick when they drink – and heavy smokers are occasionally given similar treatment so that the very smell of tobacco makes them feel quite sick.

According to the therapists, the behaviour and the unpleasant experience that follows become so connected in the subject's mind that the habit of addiction is broken and his behaviour changes for the better.

However, much depends upon the patient's WILLPOWER and the determination he has to break his addiction, whatever it is. If he develops the right attitude of mind then aversion therapy stands a far better chance of working. With positive effort on the patient's part the technique is said to be successful in about one out of five cases.

AWARENESS THROUGH MOVEMENT

Group lessons in the FELDENKRAIS METHOD are known as 'awareness through movement'. During the lessons a teacher instructs the participants in a series of slow, simple movements which are performed while sitting or kneeling on the floor. The purpose is to improve the students' postures and bodily awareness. As a result, their self-image and emotional well-being are also frequently enhanced.

AYURVEDIC MEDICINE
The all-healing 'science of life'

Every aspect of people's physical, mental and spiritual health is dealt with in this all-embracing traditional Indian system of medicine. The name 'Ayurveda' comes from two Sanskrit words: *ayur* meaning 'life', and *veda* meaning 'knowledge'. It is the main form of medicine in India, where orthodox doctors and Ayurvedic physicians work alongside each other. Ayurveda is also growing in popularity in the West, where more and more patients are seeking advice from its practitioners.

Its doctrine of prevention means that people are often treated *before* showing signs of illness. This involves them keeping in constant, close touch with a therapist, who will monitor his patient's entire way of life – diet, hobbies, sex life, choice of spouse, conditions at home and work, religious beliefs, personal habits, and so on – and advise changes as necessary.

If illness does occur a wide variety of remedies and techniques is used – from conventional surgery to plant-based drugs and mineral supplements specially prepared for the needs of each individual. Altogether there are some 8000 different medicines designed to heal patients – and to keep them healthy and well adjusted.

Who it can help Practitioners claim that all can benefit from Ayurvedic treatments, which they believe are particularly successful in relieving STRESS and TENSION.

A host of illnesses including ARTHRITIS, ASTHMA, DIABETES, ECZEMA, INDIGESTION, tuberculosis and ULCERS, have reportedly been treated with particular success.

Finding a practitioner As well as Indian-trained practitioners, some 60-70 orthodox doctors are practising Ayurvedic medicine in Britain. For further information contact the Association of Ayurvedic Practitioners, 7 Ravenscourt Avenue, London NW11 0SA.

In India, there are three methods of training: by learning directly from a fully qualified teacher; by qualifying in orthodox medicine and then taking a course in Ayurvedic medicine; or by attending one of a hundred or so officially accredited colleges. A 5½ year college course leads to the degree of Bachelor of Ayurvedic Surgery and Medicine.

Consulting a practitioner The practitioner will start by finding out all he can about your personal and professional life, and details of your medical history and eating habits. He then helps you to relax by means of breathing exercises and takes your pulse, by which he aims to learn a great deal about your physical and mental condition.

Further diagnosis may involve examining your urine, stools, sputum, eyes, skin, nails, and tongue. The practitioner will also listen carefully to your voice. By all these means he can assess your condition and choose an appropriate treatment.

As Ayurveda is a holistic system, no disease is ever treated in isolation. However, all conditions are divided up into four principal categories:

Accidental These arise from any kind of blow, cut, sting, bite or physical accident. Treatment for such cases is usually by first aid or surgery.

Physical Internal ailments such as tissue degeneration, tumours, inflammations and blockages come into this category. These are treated by a carefully balanced combination of medicines, diets and practices (see *Treatments* below).

Mental These largely take the form of anger, fear, hatred, laziness, misery and pride. They are treated by a variety of means such as MEDITATION and COUNSELLING.

Ayurvedic medicine does not regard SCHIZOPHRENIA and manic-depression as purely mental diseases – but rather as a mixture of physical and mental states.

Natural The problems of birth, GROWING OLD and dying are included in this category and are treated by taking part in various religious ceremonies and rites. The natural consequences of hunger, thirst and tiredness have their own natural remedies of eating, drinking and sleeping.

Treatments These fall into three main sections: medicinal, dietary and practical.

Medicinal remedies The drugs used are made from natural substances such as herbs, vegetables and minerals. Getting the right balance of ingredients for each individual patient can take several weeks or even months of painstaking preparation.

In general, herbal and vegetable drugs are believed to start to lose potency if kept, and should be taken when fresh; on the other hand, mineral drugs are held to gain strength the longer they are kept. In addition, various homoeopathic and orthodox medicines and treatments are sometimes prescribed by Ayurvedic practitioners.

Dietary regimes Food is prepared in accordance with the season, weather, time of day, and – most importantly – the needs of the individual patient. For instance, to increase your energy you may be advised to introduce spices and meat into your diet; in order to lower your energy dairy products may be prescribed.

Food should be eaten slowly, well chewed, swallowed in a happy state of mind; patients are told to concentrate on savouring and enjoying their meals. In some cases, FASTING is recommended.

Practical aids These involve various practices including MASSAGE, emetics, enemas, oil treatments, steam baths, breathing exercises, meditation and YOGA.

An orthodox view

Many doctors agree that Ayurvedic medicine, with its emphasis on health as much as illness, is probably the most complete health system so far developed. Its underlying principles – such as the prevention of disease – are more important than its actual remedies and healing techniques.

However, any serious and potentially life-threatening illnesses – such as acute APPENDICITIS and heart attacks – should always be conventionally treated.

Ayurveda's three basic forces

According to Ayurvedic teaching, everyone and everything in the universe consists of three basic forces or elements. In Sanskrit they are called *Vata, Pitta* and *Kapha* (often pronounced Vat, Pit and Kaph). They are thought to control all physical and mental processes and are compared to the workings of the wind, the sun and the moon.

Vata is likened to the wind, which is constantly on the move, and controls the central nervous system.

Pitta is like the sun, a source of energy. It controls the digestive system and all biochemical processes.

Kapha governs the balance of tissue fluid, controlling cell growth and the firmness of the body – rather as the moon governs the tides.

Good health is believed to result from the three forces being in harmony – not unduly stronger or weaker than each other. Bad health is said to occur when they are out of balance. Their relative strength in a person is determined at the time of his conception, and continues throughout his life.

The practitioner's task is to discover the patient's inborn disposition and to pinpoint any imbalance that is causing him physical or mental distress.

Vata imbalance, for example, can be caused by irregular meals, too little sleep, leading a promiscuous sex life, outbursts of anger and jealousy, and any form of overexertion – physical, mental or vocal.

Pitta imbalance is often triggered by INDIGESTION, acidity, alcohol abuse, and feelings of grief or fear.

Kapha imbalance can result from lack of physical exercise, sleeping during the day, and the effects of the seasons.

Using the concepts of *Vata, Pitta* and *Kapha,* Ayurvedic physicians try to understand their patients' basic dispositions, taking into account their age and stage of development – childhood, maturity and middle age, and old age.

BACH REMEDIES
Flower treatments
for all disorders

This series of 38 preparations made from wild flowers and plants is called after its originator, an English physician named Dr Edward Bach (1880-1936). He began his career as a medical doctor and bacteriologist in London in 1915. In addition to orthodox medicine he also practised homoeopathy, and he believed that natural cures exist for every ailment.

After a severe illness of his own in 1917, Bach found he could intuitively judge the healing properties of different plants, and the illnesses they can cure. In 1930, he gave up his busy Harley Street practice and settled in Wales, where he continued to search for healing plants.

Bach believed that the dew on flowers was somehow 'impregnated' with their medicinal properties, and he collected it to give to his patients. Soon he found he could not collect enough for all who asked for treatment, so he experimented and decided that floating freshly picked flowers on clear spring water in sunlight could produce the same result as dew. This enabled him to bottle and sell his remedies, and the same production method is used today.

The remedies are designed to treat the whole person, not just symptoms of illness. The principle behind their use is that every disorder – physical or psychological – arises because of an inner imbalance for which nature has provided a cure in the form of healing plants, sunlight, spring water and fresh air.

Who it can help Users of the remedies say that anyone may benefit. Although they are chosen according to psychological and emotional symptoms, they may also help physical ailments, and are safe provided that orthodox treatment is given if necessary.

Self help Dr Bach intended his remedies to be simple enough for anyone to use without consulting a professional therapist. When choosing a Bach remedy, try to examine as honestly as possible your mental and emotional state, and your habits, attitudes and typical ways of behaving, and then select the remedy or remedies most suited to you (see box). Use no more than five at one time; generally, the fewer the better. Dr Bach believed that there is a 'type remedy' corresponding to each individual's nature and personality, and that this may need to be taken for a lengthy period, while other remedies can be used for temporary problems. Finding

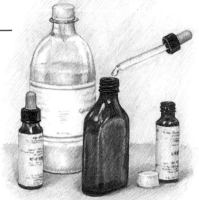

Bach stock remedies need to be diluted. Almost fill a 20ml dropper bottle with pure, uncarbonated spring water; then add two drops of each chosen stock remedy.

the right remedies can be difficult, but therapists advise users simply to select those that appeal to them and experiment.

Bach remedies can be bought from most health food and natural medicine shops, or from the suppliers: Bach Centre, Mount Vernon, Sotwell, Wallingford, Oxon OX10 OPZ. They come in a concentrated form known as a *stock remedy* – an infusion of flowers in water, preserved with alcohol. This must be diluted with spring water before use.

Take four drops of the dilute remedy four times a day, including first thing in the morning and last thing at night. The drops can either be taken in a little water or dropped straight onto the tongue, provided that your tongue does not touch the dropper, as this may transfer bacteria to the solution and cause it to spoil. Dr Bach advised that as you take each dose you should imagine it as a healing light penetrating your whole being.

Bach remedies are said to be safe for babies and children, and even for animals. A 20ml solution of the remedies will be enough for about ten days, after which you may want to try a different combination. Stop taking the remedies whenever you feel that you no longer need them, and resume doses if the problem comes back. If symptoms persist, see a doctor or psychotherapist, and never delay seeking such advice because you are taking a Bach preparation.

Although stock remedies last indefinitely if kept in a cool, dark place, dilute remedies last for only about three weeks: to prolong their life, add about one-third as much alcohol – brandy is traditionally used. In hot weather, keep dilute remedies in a fridge and add a little brandy or cider vinegar to prevent spoiling. Discard any solutions that develop a sediment or musty smell. When empty, sterilise all dropper tops and bottles by boiling them for a few minutes in water with a tablespoon of cider vinegar before re-use.

Finding a therapist Bach remedies are used in conjunction with other forms of treatment by many therapists who practise HERBAL MEDICINE, HOMOEOPATHY or NATURO-

PATHY. However, there is no register of these practitioners, and no Bach courses or qualifications are offered.

Consulting a therapist The therapist will encourage you to talk about yourself and your work, relationships, health and feelings, before choosing the most suitable remedies. He will explain what each one is for, how it should be taken and what effects it should have. You may be asked to keep a record of any changes in your general condition.

An orthodox view

Many case studies and personal accounts have testified to the effectiveness of the remedies. Scientists cannot explain these claims, for chemical analysis of the remedies shows only spring water and alcohol.

Some practitioners defend the remedies by saying that scientific research may not yet be sophisticated enough to measure their healing properties, and point out that some RADIONICS techniques show a distinctive energy field around the remedies. Many psychotherapists also believe the remedies to be beneficial since, when chosen with care, they encourage people to think about their behaviour, attitudes and lifestyles, and this self-awareness can help the healing process.

BACK PAIN

At some time in their lives, four out of five people in Britain have back pain. It is usually caused by damaged discs in the spine, or inflamed or strained muscles resulting from bad habits of lifting and carrying. See DEALING WITH BACK PAIN, p. 54.

BAD BREATH

This common but embarrassing symptom can have a number of causes. Simply eating spicy food, onions or garlic can leave an unpleasant smell on your breath for hours after a meal. Persistent bad breath, however, is usually caused by TOOTH AND GUM DISORDERS, or an infection such as THRUSH.

What the therapists recommend
Herbal Medicine Try chewing parsley, drinking infusions (see p. 184) of peppermint or fenugreek, or taking chlorophyll tablets.
Homoeopathy *Kali phos.* is recommended to remove any bitter taste in the mouth on waking. For a metallic taste, try *Merc. sol.*, in the 6X potency, twice a day for ten days.

The 38 Bach remedies

The Bach Centre gives the following rough guidelines for using the remedies:

Agrimony Those who hide worries behind a cheerful face.

Aspen Apprehensive for no known reason.

Beech Critical and intolerant of others.

Centaury Weak willed; easily exploited or imposed upon.

Cerato Those who doubt their own judgment, seek confirmation from others.

Cherry plum Tension, fear, uncontrolled or irrational thoughts.

Chestnut bud Refuses to learn by experience – continually repeats same mistakes.

Chicory Possessive (self-centred), clinging, overprotective, especially to loved ones.

Clematis Inattentive, dreamy, absentminded, escapist.

Crab apple The 'cleanser'; for self disgust, prudishness, or shame at ailments.

Elm Feelings of inadequacy, overwhelming responsibility.

Gentian Despondency.

Gorse Feelings of hopelessness, pessimism, defeatism.

Heather Talkative (obsessed with own troubles and experiences).

Holly Hatred, envy, jealousy, suspicion.

Honeysuckle Living in the past, nostalgia, homesickness.

Hornbeam 'Monday morning' feeling, mental fatigue, procrastination.

Impatiens Impatience, irritability.

Larch Lack of self-confidence, feelings of inferiority, fear of failure.

Mimulus Fear of known things. Shyness, timidity.

Mustard 'Dark cloud' that descends, feeling sad and low for no known reason.

Oak Naturally strong/courageous, but no longer able to struggle bravely against illness or adversity.

Olive Exhaustion, feeling drained of energy by long-standing problems.

Pine Guilt, blaming oneself even for the mistakes of others. Always apologising.

Red chestnut Obsessed by care and concern for others.

Rock rose Suddenly alarmed, scared, panicky.

Rock water Rigid-minded, self-denying.

Scleranthus For those with uncertainty/indecision/vacillation; fluctuating moods.

Star of Bethlehem For all the effects of serious news, or fright following an accident, shock and grief.

Sweet chestnut Utter dejection, bleak outlook, despair.

Vervain For those with over-enthusiasm, fanatical beliefs.

Vine Dominating, inflexible, tyrannical, autocratic, arrogant. Usually good leaders.

Walnut Assists in adjustment to transition or change – eg, puberty, menopause, divorce, new surroundings.

Water violet Proud, reserved, aloof; enjoys being alone.

White chestnut Persistent unwanted thoughts. Preoccupation with some worry or episode. Mental conflict.

Wild oat Unsure of direction in life.

Wild rose Resignation, apathy.

Willow For those who are resentful, embittered, always thinking 'poor old me!'

Dr Bach also combined five of the remedies – Cherry plum, Clematis, Impatiens, Rock rose and Star of Bethlehem – into an all-purpose treatment he called Rescue Remedy. It can be used for any kind of SHOCK, illness, injury or trauma, and is said to help restore calmness after accidents or bad experiences. Rescue Remedy is available as a stock remedy or a cream – for use on cuts, grazes, burns and bites, as well as skin conditions such as ECZEMA. It is not intended for long-term use and does not replace medical treatment.

An orthodox view

As with alternative therapies, bad breath is treated conventionally according to its underlying cause. Occasional symptoms can be alleviated by using proprietary breath fresheners and mouthwashes containing perborate. These are available from chemists and some other stores.

If bad breath persists for more than a week or two, you should see a dentist or doctor for investigation and treatment. As well as treating your teeth and gums, a dentist will be able to teach you the best way to care for your teeth – one very effective way of preventing bad breath.

BALDNESS

The problem begins when new hair does not grow fast enough to replace the normal daily loss caused by the body's fluctuating rhythms and hormone levels. As the thinning process continues, new growth stops altogether in certain parts of the scalp.

Most permanent baldness is due to a common hereditary condition – sometimes combined with other factors such as STRESS,

poor diet or poor circulation – that affects men more than women. Thinning usually begins at the temples and crown, and can start as early as the teens, although it is generally most noticeable in middle age. Hair loss is often slow and all the hair is seldom lost. Women are rarely as severely affected, and usually not until after the MENOPAUSE.

Temporary baldness or loss of hair (see HAIR PROBLEMS) can be caused by ANAEMIA, a deficiency of the thyroid hormone, scalp infection, illness, pregnancy, or drugs such as the contraceptive pill, steroids or antibiotics. People aged between about 12 and 40 occasionally develop bald patches for no apparent reason, but usually their hair grows back after six to 12 months.

What the therapists recommend

NATUROPATHY

Self help To improve your general health, try a wholefood diet (see EATING FOR HEALTH) rich in protein foods such as pulses, fish, lean meat, eggs, cheese and nuts – and a cup of fresh lettuce juice every day may also help.

Consultation The naturopath will give advice about diet, coping with stress and learning to relax. He will tell you about HAIR CARE and recommend the best products for you. Supplements may be prescribed – brewer's yeast, vitamin B-complex, multiminerals or kelp, for example. To improve your circulation, you will be advised to take regular outdoor exercise and not smoke.

Other alternative treatments

Traditional Medicine To improve the condition of the hair and scalp, try massaging it with warm almond oil. Leave it for an hour and then wash it out with a mild shampoo.

Aromatherapy Mix five drops each of sage and cedarwood essential oils in 1fl oz (30ml) of surgical spirit and massage a sprinkling firmly into the scalp every day. Keep the fingers in the same place and rub so that you feel the skin moving over the bone beneath.

Homoeopathy _Lycopodium_ is said to help premature baldness and greying – take the 6X potency twice a day for a month. Hair loss caused by hormones after childbirth or at the menopause, and accompanied by feelings of indifference to loved ones, may be helped by _Sepia 6X_ twice a day for a week.

An orthodox view

Doctors support the use of vitamin supplements and tonics for patients who seem run down, but appear to have no other reason for their hair loss. Where these do not help, the baldness is probably hereditary. If you are worried about your appearance a hair transplant or a wig may be suggested. If an illness or some other factor is the cause, the doctor will treat it and your hair should grow again.

Dealing with back pain

At some time in their lives, 80 out of every 100 people in Britain will be stricken with back pain. In all, some 33 million working days are lost each year because of it – more than in all the strikes, go-slows and works-to-rule put together. Back pain makes more people, including many doctors, seek alternative treatment than any other ailment. However, back pain seldom lasts for more than a few days or weeks. If the pain persists, see a doctor in case there is a serious underlying cause. But in most cases back pain is caused by sprains, strains and bad posture. Alternative practitioners believe that back trouble can be reduced by at least 70 per cent by adopting some simple exercises or therapies.

Most back pain has a simple physical cause – such as inflamed or strained muscles, restricted joints, or pressure on nerves. It can keep recurring, and may not be helped by the routine conventional treatment of painkillers such as aspirin and paracetamol, muscle relaxants and anti-inflammatory drugs such as steroids.

Conversely, simple expedients such as applying heat and cold can help. A hot-water bottle placed on the painful area can bring temporary relief – as can a pack of crushed ice cubes. Hold the ice against the area immediately after injury to prevent tissue swelling. After a few days, alternating hot and cold applications can be most effective.

ACUPUNCTURE and MASSAGE, postural training as taught in the ALEXANDER TECHNIQUE, and the manipulative work of osteopaths and chiropractors often prove effective. They also give the victim an opportunity to take an active part in treating the problem himself.

Nevertheless, always see a doctor before undertaking any

You and your spine

Think of your spine as the central pole that holds up a tent (your body) and the ligaments and muscles supporting it as the guy ropes. If they are tense or distorted they tilt the 'tent', making your back ache.
The spine consists of 24 small bones called vertebrae. There are seven in the neck (cervical); 12 in the upper back (thoracic); and five in the lower back (lumbar). In addition, five fused bones form the continuation of the spine called the sacrum; and four more small bones form the 'tail bone', or coccyx.

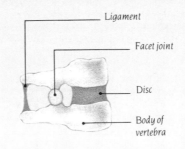

Ligament

Facet joint

Disc

Body of vertebra

The spinal cord runs through a hole in each of the vertebrae. The body's nerve roots are attached to the cord, linking them to the brain. Pressure on the cord can cause anything from pins and needles to acute pain and even paralysis.
Spinal joints are held together by a network of ligaments, or tough bands of fibre, and a series of facet joints. Together they restrict the movement of the spine in any given direction. The vertebrae are protected by fibre disc 'shock absorbers'.

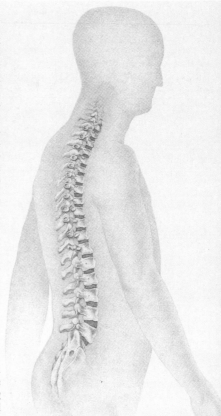

Spinal muscles Each joint is surrounded by tough, fibrous muscles that receive messages from the brain, making the muscles contract. In turn, this causes the various joints to move as required, usually in pairs, with one contracting while the other one relaxes.

alternative treatment – if the back pain does not have a simple physical cause, but is a symptom of something more serious, inappropriate treatment could be dangerous.

If conventional treatment fails – or if it is not called for – many doctors are now willing to help you find a reliable alternative practitioner.

Finally, although back pain is such a physical ailment, psychological elements should not be overlooked. STRESS and ANXIETY can contribute significantly to back problems, and you are more likely to damage or weaken your back if you, and your back muscles, are tense (see TENSION).

It strikes in many forms . . .

The pain is usually in the lower back, but it can lead to SCIATICA in the leg. Sudden (acute) back pain is usually associated with an injury or with a SLIPPED DISC, pulled muscle or torn ligament. It can strike when you are playing games, lifting heavy objects, or simply moving awkwardly. Continuous or recurring (chronic) back pain is mostly caused by poor posture when sitting, standing and walking. Sleeping in the wrong position or on the wrong sort of bed often adds to the problem (see BEDS AND BEDDING).

Self-help exercises – designed to bring relief

The following exercises have been specially designed to relieve acute back pain. Start them as soon as you can move without too much discomfort – probably within a day or two of the start of the attack.
Repeat the exercises every few hours daily, until the pain goes. Once you have recovered, Exercise 4 will help to stop further pain.

If you cannot straighten up fully, or if the pain is appreciably worse when you are standing or walking, do not attempt the exercises. Go to bed, rest, and get medical advice as soon as possible.
If the exercises make the pain worse or it spreads to other parts of the body, stop immediately and see a doctor.

Exercise 1
Lie face down with your arms beside your body and head to one side. Take a few deep breaths and relax for four or five minutes.

Exercise 2
Remain lying face down. Place your elbows under your shoulders and lean on your forearms. Take a few deep breaths, then allow your lower back to relax completely, and remain in this position for five minutes.

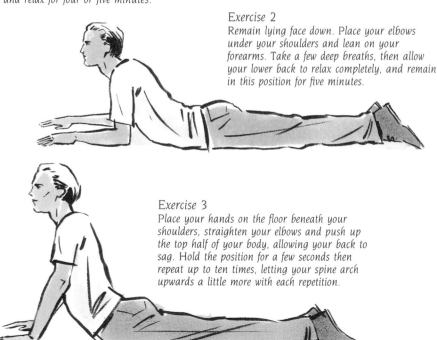

Exercise 3
Place your hands on the floor beneath your shoulders, straighten your elbows and push up the top half of your body, allowing your back to sag. Hold the position for a few seconds then repeat up to ten times, letting your spine arch upwards a little more with each repetition.

Exercise 4
Stand upright, feet slightly apart, and hands in the small of your back. Bend your trunk backwards as far as you can, keeping the knees straight. Hold for a second or two, then straighten up. Repeat up to ten times, each time trying to bend back as far as you can without losing your balance. Use this exercise also to prevent further back pain, doing it once in a while when working in a forward bent position.

Back Pain

Taking avoiding action

Since his beginnings several million years ago, man has been coping with the discomfort and inconvenience of back pain. Evolution has not completely adapted his spine, which was originally intended for four-legged movement and stance, to functioning on two legs. The spine is involved in every muscular effort, no matter how small, which is why many people cannot attribute their back pain to a specific cause. In some cases it disappears as mysteriously as it appeared. But some everyday activities – such as rising from a chair, getting out of bed and getting dressed – must be done correctly in order to avoid pain.

Getting in and out of an armchair

1 Bring your feet as close as you can to the front of the chair, if possible under the edge. Keep your knees at least a shoulder width apart to provide a good balance.

2 Keep your spine straight, and place your hands on the arms of the chair.

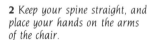

3 Slowly straighten your legs and at the same time bring your buttocks vertically above your feet. Then push yourself out of the chair with your arms.

4 To sit down in a chair, stand with your back to the chair and your feet a shoulder width apart, close to the front of the chair. Keep your back straight, and lower yourself slowly. Place your hands on the arms of the chair as soon as you can.

Getting dressed

Whatever the cause of your back pain, these tips will help you to start the day without straining your back. Avoid sitting down and bending over to put your clothes on – it will strain your back needlessly.

1 Roll your clothes up so that you can put your arms or legs through quickly and easily.

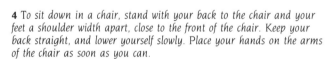

2 If you have difficulty pulling on tights or trousers, try dressing while lying on your back on the bed. Pull your knees up to your chest to get the clothes over your feet, then straighten your legs as you pull the clothes up. Do not arch your back to pull the clothes over your hips.

Alternative treatments

Many victims of back pain despair of ever finding a cure. Alternative treatment can help in many such cases, often providing immediate relief and avoiding prolonged bed rest and time off work. Among the treatments offered are:

Osteopathy A registered osteopath should be able to diagnose the problem and advise on suitable treatment. This may mean manipulating the spine and surrounding tissue by gently twisting, pressing and pulling. Only one session may be needed to correct a ricked back, but a course of treatment to eradicate a deeper seated problem such as a SLIPPED DISC may call for six or more sessions.

But if the osteopath cannot help you, or suspects that an underlying illness may be causing the back pain, he will send you to a doctor.

Chiropractic A qualified chiropractor should also be able to diagnose back pain as well as treat it. First of all, he will determine if the cause is mechanical – or if another medical condition is to blame. If mechanical, he will apply precise and gentle manipulation to restore normal movement to the joints of the back, allowing them to function properly.

Massage Techniques These are gentler than those of osteopathy and chiropractic – and may provide lasting help in dealing with occupational stress and strain, postural tension and muscle fatigue. The aim is to relax the muscles and so relieve and prevent recurrence of pain. Although massage does not solve certain structural back problems, it works well against LUMBAGO and chronic muscle tension. The basic techniques are easily learned and can be practised at home (see p. 225).

Acupuncture As well as providing relief, this has been found useful when the back pain is too severe for other treatments to take place. For example, muscle spasms and tension can be eased enough to allow massage to be used.

Alexander Technique You can be taught during a course of lessons to use your body in a more natural way – and so prevent or alleviate back pain.

See also ACUPRESSURE; HYDROTHERAPY; REFLEXOLOGY; ROLFING; T'AI-CHI CH'UAN.

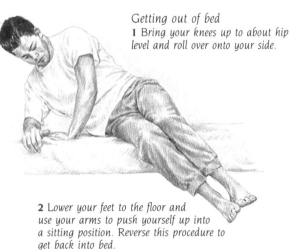

Getting out of bed

1 Bring your knees up to about hip level and roll over onto your side.

2 Lower your feet to the floor and use your arms to push yourself up into a sitting position. Reverse this procedure to get back into bed.

What the therapists can do

Most forms of back pain can be treated by any one of several alternative therapies – including acupuncture, the Alexander Technique, chiropractic and osteopathy. Most back pain occurs in the lower back, where strained ligaments are often the cause, and this can be relieved – if not cured – by therapists. However, if there is another and more fundamental reason for the pain – such as a kidney complaint (lower back pain) or pleurisy (upper back pain) – then it should be treated by conventional means.

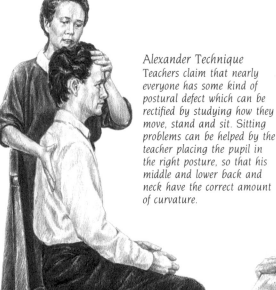

Alexander Technique

Teachers claim that nearly everyone has some kind of postural defect which can be rectified by studying how they move, stand and sit. Sitting problems can be helped by the teacher placing the pupil in the right posture, so that his middle and lower back and neck have the correct amount of curvature.

Chiropractic

A physical examination will be carried out in order to reach a diagnosis. In the treatment of back pain, the patient may be manipulated while sitting upright or lying on one side so that it is easier for the therapist to work on the affected joint. A rapid thrust, without much force, is used to open up the joint and allow it to move.

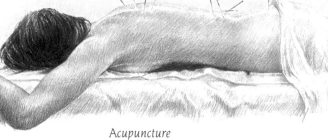

Acupuncture

At the first consultation, the acupuncturist will ask the patient for a full history of his back pain symptoms, as well as details about his personal life. He will lie the patient on a couch and insert sterilised needles into the appropriate points in the back and legs. The depth of penetration of each needle is said to help to restore body balance and treat the pain.

Osteopathy

An initial physical examination will be made. If a protruding disc is the problem, the therapist will first relax the contracted spinal muscles and then gently stretch the spine to relieve pressure on the injured disc. The patient must avoid bending or lifting until the affected tissues have healed. More than one treatment session will often be needed.

Caring for your back

Many people who suffer from back pain for short or long periods do so because they do not know how to take care of their backs. Any kind of physical activity – from running to catch a bus, to sneezing – can affect the back. In addition, heavy work such as digging in the garden and carrying loaded shopping bags can result in severe and sometimes long-lasting pain. In most cases this is cleared up by rest and basic treatment such as the application of heat to the affected area. However, it is better to try to avoid pain altogether by taking the following precautions.

Carrying heavy loads

Wrong If you have a heavy load when out shopping do not put all your purchases into one large shopping bag to be carried in one hand (below right). If you do this, it makes you lopsided and puts undue strain on the spine.
Right Carry two evenly loaded shopping bags, one in each hand, so that you are well balanced (below). Do not overtire yourself and rest if necessary, putting the shopping bags down on the ground.

People who are prone to back pain

There are several 'high risk' occupations associated with a painful back. If you fall into any of them, take extra care.
Manual workers About 22 per cent of miners, furniture removers, construction workers, dockers and other manual workers are regular sufferers.
Nurses About 17 per cent of nurses – who regularly have to lift bedridden patients, and carry and bend in their work – are stricken each year.
Office workers Typists and computer operators are prone, because they often use badly designed chairs that do not give enough support to the small of the back, and so encourage the operatives to slouch.
Drivers Long-distance truck drivers, tractor drivers and those who spend a lot of time behind the wheel are liable to get lower back pain due to poor posture and the vibration they experience in their vehicles.
Housewives and mothers Bending to make beds, cleaning, lifting and carrying babies and small children frequently cause back problems. Many women start getting back pain during pregnancy (see Relieving back pain in pregnancy).
Athletes Any sport that involves vigorous activity (for example, football, tennis, or squash), or one that makes great use of a particular set of muscles (for example, weightlifting or golf), can put undue strain on the back.
The elderly The older you are, the less supple your joints and muscles are likely to be. Back pain and stiffness may result – and there is a risk of OSTEOPOROSIS developing.
Previous sufferers If your back has already pained you, it is liable to 'go' again. Exercise and good posture (see illustrations) help to strengthen the spine and prevent recurring trouble.

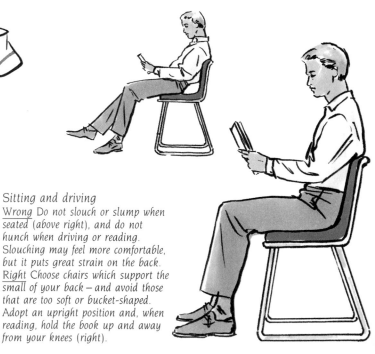

Sitting and driving

Wrong Do not slouch or slump when seated (above right), and do not hunch when driving or reading. Slouching may feel more comfortable, but it puts great strain on the back.
Right Choose chairs which support the small of your back – and avoid those that are too soft or bucket-shaped. Adopt an upright position and, when reading, hold the book up and away from your knees (right).

Working in the garden

Wrong Do not bend from the hips with straight legs to pick out weeds (above left). This action, and not the digging itself, is the commonest cause of backache in the garden.

Right Go down on one – or both – knees as close to the weeds as possible to save stretching (above right). This applies to picking up any object, not just pulling weeds in the garden.

Lifting an awkward object

Wrong Never stoop when lifting an object such as a tea chest or packing case (below left). Lifting and handling in the wrong way are common causes of back pain.

Right Squat by the object to be lifted (below right). Keep your feet about 12in (30cm) apart. Keep close to the load and pull it into your body while carrying. Wear loose clothes.

Relieving back pain in pregnancy

Many women suffer from low back pain during pregnancy – particularly in the last three months. This is caused mainly by poor posture as the baby gains weight. The mother leans backwards to counterbalance the change in weight distribution – and this often makes the ligaments supporting the spinal joints overstretched and slack. In addition, the ligaments naturally become more elastic so that the pelvis can expand at the moment of birth.
The following exercises should help to relieve back pain. If they prove too uncomfortable or difficult, try sitting crosslegged for short periods; or sit on the floor with your legs slightly apart and straight out in front of you; or get on your hands and knees and arch your lower back a few times.

Standing extension (right)

1 Stand up straight with your feet pointing directly forwards, about a shoulder width apart. Place your hands on the small of your back and breathe in deeply.
2 Breathe out slowly. As you do so, bend backwards, supporting your back with your hands, so that your lower back is arched. Repeat ten times.

Pelvic tilt (below)

1 Lie on the floor with your arms at your sides, your feet flat on the floor and your legs bent.
2 Gently press the back of your waist against the floor and tilt your pelvis forwards by tightening your abdominal and buttock muscles. Hold for six seconds, relax slowly, and repeat up to ten times.

Postnatal leg rolls

Practise this toning-up exercise daily from about a week after the birth until your check-up at six weeks. Lie on the bed with arms outstretched, knees bent and feet together. Roll your legs from side to side, and each time you reach the midway position, press your back against the bed.
Make sure you feel no discomfort and slowly repeat several times.

BATES METHOD
Can you improve your eyesight without glasses?

Most people who have failing eyesight regard it as part of GROWING OLD, and become resigned to wearing stronger spectacles. Followers of the Bates Method, however, assert that some simple eyesight exercises can help to keep your eyes strong and healthy and prevent them from being misused. The exercises were created by Dr William H. Bates, a New York eye specialist.

To achieve and maintain healthy eyesight, most Bates practitioners also recommend a well-balanced diet – not necessarily vegetarian – along with nutritional supplements (see EATING FOR HEALTH) and the use of HOMOEOPATHY. This should be done under the appropriate professional guidance.

The exercises have an educational and not a medical basis. Therefore they are not intended to cure eye diseases such as CATARACTS and glaucoma. In such cases expert medical help should always be sought.

Who it can help Anyone, no matter how good or poor their sight may be, may benefit.

Finding a teacher Most Bates teachers are located in the south-east of England, and a list of practitioners can be obtained from

Seven Bates eye exercises

The seven basic exercises were devised and developed by Dr Bates between 1900 and 1931. Below, the first three are not illustrated, and 'Remembering' is done while you are doing the fourth – 'Palming' (right).

Remembering (not illustrated)
While palming your eyes, try without straining to recall an object or experience in great detail and bright colours. According to Dr Bates, at least one patient found his eyesight was improved by visualising a beautiful yellow buttercup. Remembering things in the mind's eye helps people to see them more clearly in reality, said Dr Bates.

Shifting (not illustrated)
Do not stare fixedly at an object (as spectacle wearers tend to). Instead, move your gaze constantly from one point of interest to another. As your eyes become more relaxed, so the movement becomes smaller, helping your sight to become clearer.

Blinking (not illustrated)
Get into the habit of blinking regularly, once or twice every ten seconds, to clean and lubricate the eyes – especially if you wear glasses or contact lenses.

Palming
Sit comfortably and relaxed at a desk or table. Close your eyes, rest your elbows on a cushion on the table, keeping your back and neck straight and your head level. Then cover your eyes – without touching them – with your cupped palms. Think of something pleasant, such as a favourite holiday spot, or listen to a radio talk, show or play. Do this exercise for about ten minutes, at the very least twice each day – or whenever your eyes feel tired or ache.

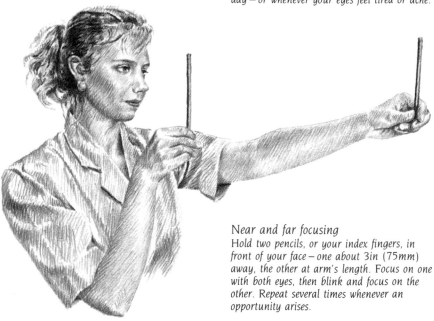

The doctor who healed himself

At the end of a particularly tiring day in 1900, Dr William H. Bates (1860-1931), a New York ophthalmologist and specialist in children's eye complaints, noted how much his own eyes ached. It reminded him of how often his patients complained of eyestrain and headaches – even after they had responded well to medical treatment.

In the quiet of his darkened office, he rested his elbows on his desk and cupped his palms over his eyes. After ten minutes his eyes stopped aching and he felt mentally refreshed.

Uncupping his hands, he found that objects in his room seemed much clearer and brighter. His observations led him to evolve his 'method of eyesight training', described in his best-selling book of 1919, *Better Eyesight Without Glasses*. By the time he died his method had gained disciples and practitioners on both sides of the Atlantic.

Near and far focusing
Hold two pencils, or your index fingers, in front of your face – one about 3in (75mm) away, the other at arm's length. Focus on one with both eyes, then blink and focus on the other. Repeat several times whenever an opportunity arises.

Splashing
First thing every morning, splash your closed eyes 20 times with warm water and then 20 times with cold water to stimulate circulation. Reverse the process last thing at night.

Swinging
Stand with feet apart and sway gently from side to side, letting your eyes swing along with your body's movement. Be aware of the visual movement as this relaxes your eyes and helps them to become more flexible. Repeat whenever an opportunity arises. It often helps to play music while doing this exercise.

The case of Aldous Huxley

In 1939, when the writer Aldous Huxley was 45 years old, he was rapidly losing his eyesight, and needed thick magnifying spectacles to read. Then he heard of the Bates Method, and within two months of starting lessons, reported that he was able to read without spectacles, and was doing so without strain or fatigue.

Later he wrote a book, *The Art of Seeing*, in which he reported that the opacity in the corneas of his eyes, which had remained unchanged for 25 years, was beginning to clear up. 'My own case is in no way unique,' Huxley continued. 'Thousands of other sufferers from defects of vision have benefited by following the simple rules of that Art of Seeing which we owe to Bates and his followers.'

Anthony Attenborough, 128 Merton Road, London sw18 5sp, sending a stamped addressed envelope. Although the teachers have no medical qualifications, they have been trained by other practitioners.
Consulting a teacher Practitioners base their treatment on Dr Bates' principles.
Self help Once the basic exercises have been learned, they can easily be practised at home or at work. The simplest ones – such as blinking every few seconds to lubricate the eyes – can be done at any time.

An orthodox view

Eye exercises have proved their value in treating several eye conditions. The Bates Method is, however, a very systematic approach and may be difficult to follow, but anecdotal evidence does suggest that it can be a helpful therapy.

Do's and don'ts about your eyes

Bates teachers recommend the following do's and don'ts for those who want to take up the exercises:
Do practise regularly – success is said to depend on persistence.
Do your best to relax when doing the exercises: a stiff neck or tensed shoulder muscles will not help your eyes to relax.
Do read in a good light, blink often and look up briefly at the end of every page.
Do rest your eyes – preferably by palming – when using visual display units (VDUs), for one minute in every twelve.
Don't do the exercises while wearing spectacles or contact lenses.
Don't overwork or strain your eyes while doing the Bates exercises – the aim is to ease tension and relax them, not to force them.
Don't do anything – such as watching a lot of television with the lights off – that hurts the eyes or blurs vision.

BATHING
Invigorating cures for body and mind

Bathing of many different types has long been practised for its reputed relaxing and health-giving effects. The best known form is probably HYDROTHERAPY, which uses steam or water baths of various types to treat illness, improve circulation and aid the elimination of many impurities from the body. Sunbathing is also very popular and can help some skin conditions such as ACNE. However, great care is needed to avoid SUNBURN.

Herbal baths – particularly hand and foot baths – are an important part of HERBAL MEDICINE and combine the curative powers of herbs with those of water. Many SPAS are famous for their mineral-rich waters, and sea water is used therapeutically – see THALASSOTHERAPY. Mud baths and MUD THERAPY with specially rich soils are also used to treat a variety of complaints including SKIN DISORDERS, ULCERS, ARTHRITIS and RHEUMATISM.

BEDS AND BEDDING
Getting a good night's rest

Most people spend about a third of their lives asleep but pay relatively little attention to their choice of a bed. In fact, everyone has different needs and finding just the right bed for each member of the family is most important. Your bed affects how deeply you sleep and how rested you feel when you wake up. If chosen carefully it will protect your health and speed recovery from illness. A badly chosen bed, however, or one that provides little support, can cause chronic BACK PAIN or muscular TENSION, and may leave you feeling tired after a restless night.

Hard or soft?

It is not always true that the harder a bed the better it must be for your back – choosing the right firmness is often a matter of compromise. Too soft a bed will not provide enough support and you will sink into the mattress, twisting your spine and suffering discomfort. However, if a bed is too hard, your muscles will not be able to relax fully and your sleep will be disturbed and restless as you try to get comfortable. You may also suffer from pins and needles or numbness on pressure points such as the hips, shoulders, base of the spine or heels, where the blood flow can become restricted.

Thin people generally need softer mattresses than weightier ones, but people with back problems often prefer hard beds.

Choosing a bed

Base Whatever type of mattress you use, it is advisable to put it on some kind of a base and not just on the floor. Every night your body loses over a pint of moisture in breathing and sweating, and much of this is absorbed by your mattress. Placing a mattress on the floor prevents air from circulating through it and traps moisture, encouraging the growth of bacteria which may eventually cause rot or mould.

Three main types of base are available:
Solid-topped bases These are hollow, wooden bases which are usually perforated to allow air to circulate. They are covered with a single layer of padding to provide very firm support.
Slatted bases The wooden slats allow air to circulate through the mattress. Some slatted bases are more flexible than others, but generally they provide good support.
Sprung bases These are less firm than the other types, but will support you well if combined with the right mattress. They also help the mattress to last longer, as they absorb some of the nightly wear and tear. Avoid sprung bases with firm edges, for although they are cheaper they reduce the sleeping area of the bed and when the springs in the middle start to wear, the edges will remain firm, creating a central hollow.
Mattress In the past, mattresses were just fabric covers filled with whatever was available – straw, horsehair or feathers. Today, a variety of different types is made to cater for our different needs. The mattress is the most important part of any bed and it is essential to take time and care over your choice.
Pocket spring mattresses About a thousand small springs in individual calico pockets support each part of your body independently. These mattresses come in a range of different firmnesses which combine comfort with support, but they need to be used on a spring base and are expensive.
Open-coil spring mattresses These come in a variety of different firmnesses and designs, and are by far the most popular mattresses. They are cheaper than the pocket spring sort, and contain from about 300 larger springs. They do not mould quite as well to the body, but many are still excellent. Special advantages are lightness and good ventilation.
Foam mattresses Many different varieties of these mattresses are available and you need to choose carefully. The best are made from layers of rubber latex or polyurethane which mould to the shape of your body while also providing good support. They are available in different firmnesses and are good insulators, although latex allows more air to circulate and is cooler.

These mattresses will help if you suffer from ALLERGY or ASTHMA as they do not

Night-time comfort

The perfect mattress combines an underlying firm support with sufficient softness to give where your body presses hardest. In this way you can relax without sagging (right), and can turn over easily. Elderly and heavy people, children and bedridden invalids should have a firm mattress; thin people need more softness. Put the mattress on the correct type of base, which absorbs a proportion of the stress and also enables the mattress to breathe, and it should last the 10-15 years you can expect from a good-quality product.

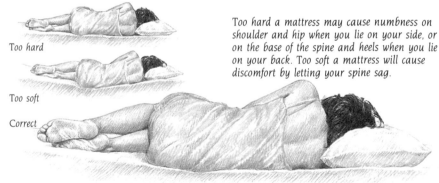

Too hard

Too soft

Correct

Too hard a mattress may cause numbness on shoulder and hip when you lie on your side, or on the base of the spine and heels when you lie on your back. Too soft a mattress will cause discomfort by letting your spine sag.

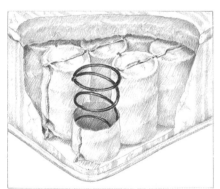

Pocket spring mattress *There is maximum independent movement for the springs in this construction, which makes for greatest comfort, particularly for couples of differing weights.*

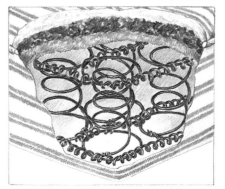

Open-coil spring mattress *Fewer and larger springs are linked to hold them in place – which reduces individual adjustment to your body contours and weight.*

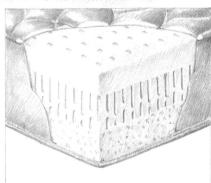

Foam mattress *A sandwich construction of soft and firm foams is best for combining comfort with support. Foam is dust free but the base must allow thorough airing.*

collect dust, but if you are extremely sensitive it may be better to consider one of the special sterile non-allergenic foam mattresses that are available. Whatever your needs, avoid the very cheapest type, which distort permanently after only a short time.

Natural-fibre mattresses Wool, horsehair, cotton flocking and coir fibre from coconuts are still used in some mattresses. Many people find natural fibres more comfortable and better ventilated than other types, but these mattresses do tend to be expensive.

Orthopaedic mattresses Very firm mattresses of all designs are sold as 'orthopaedic'. In fact, they cannot cure an orthopaedic condition, but do provide excellent support and can sometimes relieve or prevent back pain.

Futons These Japanese mattresses are becoming increasingly popular in the West. Futons are not sprung, but simply consist of layers of cotton or wool felt, sometimes mixed with synthetic fibres. They need a slatted base to allow air movement, and come in different thicknesses. Three layers is the best thickness for a futon, but to get firm, comfortable support you will need to stack two of them, one on top of the other.

Futons need to be aired and rolled up every day, and a regular shaking out helps to keep the layers even and separate. On the right sort of base they can also be used to sit on and are very useful if you are short of space. They are claimed to help backache and improve health generally, although fragile and elderly people may find them too heavy to handle easily.

Do's and don'ts for buying a bed

Do make sure the bed is at least 6in (15cm) longer than you are – or than the taller partner if you are buying a double bed.

Don't buy a bed or a mattress without lying down on it to see that it supports you well and is comfortable. Couples should try out beds together.

Do buy the best and largest bed you can afford and that will fit into your bedroom. Space is essential, as we move about constantly during sleep and a comfortable bed is necessary for good health.

Do remember that someone who sleeps on their side actually takes up more space – not less – than someone who sleeps on their front or back.

Don't economise on your bed or you may pay the price in terms of health and discomfort. Buy the best you can afford.

Waterbeds These can be effective in providing firm support evenly to all parts of the body, and are used in some hospitals for patients with burns or bedsores.

Double beds Choosing a double bed can be difficult as the needs of both partners must be taken into account. If the springs on a double bed are weak or there is a weight difference of more than about 7olb (30kg) then the heavier partner is likely to end up sleeping in the middle of the bed and the lighter to be pushed to one side. Even with a smaller weight difference the heavier partner may create a dip in the mattress into which the lighter one rolls. In such cases you may need to buy a good pocket spring mattress or – if there is a big weight difference – separate single units which can be zipped together to form a double bed suited to each partner.

In constant use, a good bed should last about ten years, a cheap one less, and a really expensive one a bit more. After that, it is unlikely to be giving you the comfort and support you need.

RESISTANT

Bed safety Since September 1990, *all new beds and mattresses sold in Britain have had to meet strict fire safety standards. To make certain, look out for this label.*

Pillows

The choice of pillow is very important. The purpose of a pillow is to support the neck more than the head, and you should never sleep with only your head on the pillow, or you may strain your neck and upper back muscles. Choose a feather pillow for air circulation, foam if you suffer from allergies, or a contoured one for extra neck support. Herb pillows may help defeat INSOMNIA.

Bed coverings

Duvets are lighter and warmer than blankets, and allow more air to circulate while you are sleeping. If properly looked after they should last for many years. When buying a duvet, choose the filling that suits you best. Down is warmest and lightest but most expensive, a feather and down combination is adequate for most needs and allows good ventilation, but if you are allergic to house dust or feathers look for a synthetic filling.

Care for your duvet by shaking it out regularly to keep the filling evenly spaced, or it will collect in the edges and corners and you may feel cold.

BEDWETTING

There are two sorts of bedwetters – children who are never dry, and those who are sometimes dry but then start wetting the bed again. The medical terms for their conditions are primary and secondary enuresis. Both alternative and conventional practitioners stress the importance of not making the child feel shame, and of avoiding all forms of punishment or forceful methods of trying to make the child overcome the problem. Indeed, bedwetting should not even be considered a problem before the child is three or four years old, as children develop bladder control at differing times.

By the age of two and a half, two out of every three children are usually dry in the daytime, and half of them are dry through the night. Six months later, 85 per cent are dry by day and night, barring an occasional accident. At the age of five, only 9 per cent of children are bedwetters; by the time they are 15, only 2 per cent are.

However, though relatively few children have the problem, it can cause much misery and disrupt family relationships. It has been around for as long as clothes have been worn, and some bizarre and painful remedies have been suggested in the past – placing burning leaves between the child's legs; making the child eat the crop from a cock; sprinkling dried sow's bladder over its head.

Only in recent times has a more enlightened and understanding approach been followed. Most primary enuresis is caused by a slow development of bladder control – much as some children are slower than others in learning to read. The usual cause of secondary enuresis is some ANXIETY or psychological upset, such as parental rows or a new baby arriving. Parents can also foster anxiety by starting pot training too soon, or being too fussy or insistent about it.

Other causes of bedwetting are urinary infections (see BLADDER PROBLEMS) or a congenital bladder abnormality. Occasionally there may be complex causes – certainly if the child has been punished or abused the problem may not only get worse, but his distress and psychological disorder may deepen. Finally, bedwetting can also be used by the child as an attention-seeking ploy. Until the problem is overcome, fit the bed with a waterproof sheet or mattress.

What the therapists recommend

BEHAVIOURAL THERAPY

Self help Gentle conditioning, in which the child is encouraged to become involved, has proved very successful. A special pad is placed under the sheet in the bed. Any water (urine) penetrating to the pad activates a buzzer, which wakes the child who can then switch it off. Three out of every four bed-wetters given a buzzer become dry. See also *An orthodox view*, below.

COUNSELLING
Consultation Both parents and the child are involved, and the child is given a positive role – for example, keeping a calendar or diary in which stars are awarded for 'dry nights', with perhaps a small prize or reward for stars accumulated, and praise and encouragement offered for each dry night.

HERBAL MEDICINE
Consultation If there are psychological factors, such as anxiety, a herbalist would probably concentrate on trying to relieve them. St John's wort may be prescribed as a gentle relaxant and antidepressant. Horsetail tea may be suggested to help empty the bladder and gently tone the muscles.

An orthodox view

A doctor may well recommend the counsel-ling or 'buzzer' conditioning treatments out-lined above, and can advise on where to obtain a pad. But he will first encourage both parents and child to keep in mind that the problem is most likely to disappear of its own accord, and to accept bedwetting as part of the child's natural development. This may give the child enough confidence to talk about his worries or fears (of darkness, perhaps), and he should be urged to do so.

On a practical level, the child may be told not to drink just before going to bed, and to visit the lavatory last thing. Those who fail to respond to the buzzer (some sleep so soundly they never even hear it) may be given an antidepressant drug to reduce wet-ting – though whether this works by relieving some subconscious depression or by a direct effect upon the bladder is not known. In difficult cases, perhaps involving a physical abnormality, the doctor may call for a specialist opinion.

BEE STINGS

When a bee stings it leaves both its sting and a poison bag in the skin. The poison is not dangerous unless it causes an allergic reac-tion (see ALLERGY), but pain is immediate and lasts from three to six hours. Swelling, inflammation and itching follow – usually clearing up after a few days.

If the sting becomes infected, the victim may become feverish and have painful joints for two or three days. An allergic reaction will cause severe swelling, which can spread over the body. In rare cases, where the victim is extremely sensitive, there may be anaphy-lactic SHOCK, with difficulty in breathing, unconsciousness and sometimes even death. See a doctor as soon as possible if symptoms indicate an allergic reaction.

Self help Remove the sting by easing it out with a fingernail in the opposite direction to the line of entry, taking care not to burst the poison bag.

What the therapists recommend
Traditional Medicine Apply crumbled leaves of plantain – the common, broad-leaved weed – to the wound. Alternatively, heat crumbled or broken plantain leaves gently over a match flame until they wilt (do not burn), then squeeze them and apply the juice. Apply ice to the area to reduce the inflammation and a few drops of lavender oil to relieve the pain.

Homoeopathy *Ledum* is believed to be most effective, helping to relieve redness, swelling, stinging and pricking pains. Take a dose every one to three hours until the discomfort stops. *Apis mellifica* is recommended if *Ledum* has not reduced the pain and swelling after four hours, or if the site of the sting is painful, swollen, red and feels hot. Take one pill every four hours. For very severe reactions, use the remedies in the 200X potency, taken every half hour for two or three doses. Otherwise, use the 30X potency.

Naturopathy Plunge the affected area into a bowl of water, with a teaspoon of baking soda and ice cubes – cold slows the circu-lation and helps to stop the poison spread-ing. Swift relief may also be obtained by holding or taping a freshly cut slice of raw onion over the area, or smearing the site with wheat-germ oil, placing an ice bag on top, then applying soothing calendula cream.

An orthodox view

Except in serious cases, the only treatment needed after removing the sting is to clean the area with an antiseptic or smooth on an antihistamine cream, available from chem-ists, to prevent infection. Itching can be relieved with calamine lotion.

If there is a severe reaction to the sting, a doctor will prescribe steroids, antibiotics, antihistamine tablets or painkilling drugs to combat inflammation or infection. An anti-histamine injection will be given for acute allergy and the victim taken into hospital and treated for anaphylactic shock using steroid injections.

Insect repellents available from chemists may help to prevent bee stings. See also MOSQUITO BITES, WASP STINGS.

BEHAVIOURAL THERAPY
Learning to overcome problems

When you laugh at a friend's joke, raise your voice in anger, punish a naughty child or reward a good one, you are practising a subtle sort of behavioural therapy. In dozens of everyday situations like these we all encourage other people to behave in the way we would like them to. We want our friends to be amusing, our enemies to feel intimi-dated and our children to get on with others and to do well.

In the same way, behavioural therapists use rewards – and sometimes punishments – to help people to overcome harmful or antisocial behaviour such as SMOKING, drinking too much, personal violence or giving in to unreasonable FEAR.

The therapy is based on the idea that bad behaviour is often something that has been learned – from whatever source or example – and can be 'unlearned' by training, to be replaced by something better. Accordingly, children may actually be taught to behave badly by parents or teachers, who reward disruptive behaviour with extra attention; or young people may learn to drink heavily to conform and win acceptance among their drinking friends.

Many disaster victims have found that their experiences leave long-lasting behav-iour problems, such as a fear of enclosed spaces (see CLAUSTROPHOBIA). Therapists aim to overcome these difficulties by teach-ing victims to respond to them in different and more constructive ways.

Finding a therapist Behavioural therapy is practised by specially trained clinical psycho-logists, psychiatrists and nurses, most of whom work within the National Health Ser-vice. Patients are usually sent for treatment by their doctors, but may also consult thera-pists privately. Names and addresses of prac-titioners are available from the British Psychological Society, St Andrew's House, 48 Princess Road East, Leicester LE1 7DR.

Consulting a therapist The therapist will talk over your problem in detail, asking when it began, exactly what happens on each occasion, and how you and others cope with it. He will then choose an appropriate treat-ment and begin a course of behavioural retraining, usually involving one visit a week. A typical course might last for three months.

PHOBIAS and fears can often be overcome using a technique known as *systematic*

The theory behind the therapy

In the late 19th century, a Russian scientist named Ivan Pavlov (1849-1936) became famous for experiments in which he trained dogs to salivate at the sound of a bell, which they associated with the arrival of food. He called this process *conditioning* and used it to study how some human behaviour was learned. In America J. B. Watson developed similar ideas in the early decades of the 20th century, and they became known as Behaviourism. Many of the principles that the two psychologists established still form the basis of modern behavioural therapy.

After the Second World War, another American psychologist, Burrhus Skinner, got animals and people to play an active part in the learning process – unlike Pavlov, whose dogs were passive participants. Skinner developed the theory of *reinforcement* – a kind of reward or pleasant experience that makes it more likely that the behaviour required will be repeated. For example, AGORAPHOBIA, a fear of open spaces, may become more entrenched by the relief a person experiences when staying indoors. This relief encourages him to keep indoors more and more, until he cannot go out at all.

Skinner's solution to this sort of problem was to get the person to associate his unwillingness to go outside with bad experiences, while associating ventures outdoors with some sort of reward. Today, these methods are still used to help people overcome their difficulties.

However, Skinner took Behaviourism to extremes by suggesting that it could be used to control *all* human behaviour and so create a perfect society run by psychologists. Fortunately, most behavioural psychologists never took these extreme ideas seriously, but behavioural techniques are still used on a purely personal level, with the patient's full knowledge and consent.

desensitisation. The patient practises relaxation exercises while imagining increasingly disturbing or frightening situations. When he is able to stay completely calm, the therapist gradually allows him to experience the real situations, while still helping him to relax. Eventually the relaxed response becomes so well learned that it comes naturally, and the fear or phobia is overcome.

A quicker 'shock' method of dealing with some fears is called *flooding* or *forced exposure*. The patient is confronted with the situation he most fears. At first he is terrified, but as time passes and he comes to no harm, the fear begins to exhaust itself and rational control takes over again. Many patients have learned to tolerate insects, heights, confined spaces and snakes in this way.

ALCOHOLISM is sometimes treated by AVERSION THERAPY, a method which involves taking a drug such as disulfiram (Antabuse) that causes nausea when you drink. Eventually the mind associates drinking and nausea so closely that all desire for alcohol is lost. A less drastic form known as *imaginal aversion* uses imaginary unpleasant associations to break bad habits – for example, it may be easier to stop smoking if you imagine each cigarette smeared with something repulsive before putting it to your lips.

Who it can help Therapists claim most success in treating specific problems such as smoking, excessive drinking, OBSESSIVE-COMPULSIVE BEHAVIOUR, phobias and fears, and children's problems such as BED-WETTING, school phobias and social adjustment difficulties such as stealing or indecent exposure. Some techniques such as desensitisation work best for children and adults who do not think too much about their motives and why they behave as they do; other techniques, such as *imaginal aversion*, are used for highly motivated and imaginative patients.

Like most forms of PSYCHOTHERAPY, the training is most effective when you *like* the therapist and feel that he is genuinely helpful, kind and interested in your problem. It is also more successful when the undesirable behaviour is not pleasurable – it is easier to overcome a fear of snakes than to give up smoking or heavy drinking.

An orthodox view

Behavioural therapy is based on scientific research into how people learn, and doctors accept that it can often help patients to overcome problems which conventional medicine cannot treat.

BILIOUS ATTACK

Bile, also called gall, looks like motor oil and is a bitter, yellow-brown or yellow-green fluid produced by the liver, and stored in the gall bladder. About a pint or more is produced daily, and its job is to break down food passing through the duodenum (the first part of the intestine), allowing it to be digested and absorbed. Bile also helps the liver to detoxify poisonous substances. During a true bilious attack, bile is brought up from the duodenum into the mouth, but this is rare. The term is often used loosely by lay people for any episode of NAUSEA AND VOMITING, particularly one from an ACID STOMACH.

BIOCHEMIC TISSUE SALTS
Mineral remedies for everyday ailments

A correct balance of the natural mineral salts found in the body is essential for health, and biochemic tissue salts can help to maintain or restore that balance, say practitioners who prescribe them.

They believe that an imbalance or lack of these salts can cause a range of illnesses, while replacing them in small, easily absorbed doses restores balance and allows the body to heal itself.

Biochemics was developed in the 1870s by a German homoeopathic physician, Dr Wilhelm Schuessler, who coined both the terms 'biochemics' and 'tissue salts'. He named 12 tissue salts as being vital for health, and described exactly what each of them did in the body. He also listed the ailments he claimed could be cured by using tissue salts as medicines in tablet form.

The 12 tissue salts (see box) are also listed in the homoeopathic range of medicines, and are prepared in the same way – but the two therapies are quite different. While biochemics makes good the mineral deficiency believed to be causing the disease, the homoeopathic philosophy of 'like cures like'

Dr W.H. *Schuessler* (1821-98), *who developed the tissue salts, was a physician in Oldenburg, near Hamburg in Germany.*

The tissue salts and their uses

Here is a list of Schuessler's 12 tissue salts with their numbers, names, chemical names, what they are claimed to do and the conditions for which they are believed to be useful.

1 *Calc. fluor.* Calcium fluoride
Helps promote elasticity of tissues. Used for PILES, ruptures, strained tendons, VARICOSE VEINS, muscle weakness, stretch marks, CIRCULATION PROBLEMS, COLD SORES at the corners of the mouth, cracked tongue and lips.

2 *Calc. phos.* Calcium phosphate
Helps build new blood cells, strengthens bones and teeth, aids digestion. Used for poor circulation, CHILBLAINS, indigestion, lowered vitality, iron-deficiency ANAEMIA, and during convalescence. Also for decaying teeth and teething problems.

3 *Calc. sulph.* Calcium sulphate
Blood constituent and purifier. Used for spots during adolescence, sore lips, slow-healing skin and wounds.

4 *Ferr. phos.* Iron phosphate
Constituent of red blood corpuscles which helps to distribute oxygen in the body. Used for inflammation of the skin, feverishness, chestiness, sore throat, coughs, colds, chills and muscular RHEUMATISM.

5 *Kali mur.* Potassium chloride
Used for respiratory disorders such as ASTHMA and BRONCHITIS; also for CATARRH, colds, WHEEZING, sore throat, TONSILLITIS, sluggish digestion.

6 *Kali phos.* Potassium phosphate
A nerve soother and nutrient. Used for tension, HEADACHES, indigestion, DEPRESSION, loss of sleep and irritability due to worry or excitement.

7 *Kali sulph.* Potassium sulphate
Promotes and maintains healthy skin. Used for minor skin eruptions with scaling, sticky or yellowish discharge, discharge of the nose or throat, catarrh, and poor condition of nails, hair and scalp.

8 *Mag. phos.* Magnesium phosphate
Nerve and muscle fibre nutrient. Used to relieve darting pains, CRAMP and menstrual pains, acute spasms, HICCUPS, COLIC and WIND.

9 *Nat. mur.* Sodium chloride
Controls distribution of water in the body. Used for watery colds with flow of tears and runny nose; loss of smell or taste.

10 *Nat. phos.* Sodium phosphate
Acid-alkaline regulator of the cells. Used for acidity, HEARTBURN, gastric indigestion and rheumatic pains.

11 *Nat. sulph.* Sodium sulphate
Balances body water. Used for queasiness, MORNING SICKNESS, DIGESTIVE PROBLEMS, BILIOUS ATTACK, colic, INFLUENZA symptoms and headaches.

12 *Silica* Silicon dioxide
Conditioner and cleanser, eliminates waste. Used for toxic accumulations, PIMPLES AND SPOTS, BOILS, STYES.

The combination biochemic tissue salts
The following are combination remedies – in which several salts have been chosen for their effects on different aspects of a problem – and their uses.

Combination A, for NEURALGIA, neuritis, SCIATICA.
Combination B, for nervous exhaustion, edginess, general debility and during convalescence.
Combination C, for acidity, heartburn.
Combination D, for minor skin ailments.
Combination E, for flatulence, indigestion and colic.
Combination F, for nervous and MIGRAINE headaches.
Combination G, for backache, LUMBAGO and piles.
Combination H, for hay fever.
Combination I, for fibrositis, muscular pain.
Combination J, for COUGHS, colds and chestiness.
Combination K, for brittle nails, hair loss.
Combination L, for VARICOSE VEINS.
Combination M, for rheumatic conditions.
Combination N, for menstrual pain.
Combination P, for aching feet and legs, and also chilblains.
Combination Q, for catarrh, sinus disorders.
Combination R, for infants' teething pains.
Combination S, for biliousness and stomach upsets.

tissue salts when they believe that the body is not producing enough mineral salts for good health, but biochemics is principally a self-help treatment. However, if you are already being treated by a doctor or an alternative practitioner, you should consult him or her before using any of the biochemic remedies.

Self-help Tissue salts are available from health stores and some chemists. They are prepared in highly diluted doses – their usual potency being 6X, which means one part of the active ingredient is mixed with nine parts lactose (milk sugar) and the process repeated a further six times, as in HOMOEOPATHY. The patient notes his symptoms and takes the salt or combination of salts recommended for them – though time and patience may be needed to find exactly which salts work best for individual cases.

Each salt is known by a number and an abbreviated name, and combination remedies are known by a letter. Homoeopathic chemists can supply them as required. The small, moulded, lactose-based tablets are dissolved in the mouth. The frequency and regularity of doses is considered to be most important – every half hour if the symptoms are sudden and short-lived; every two hours if they are long-lasting. The tablets are absorbed quickly into the bloodstream, and are said to give prompt relief in sudden, short-term conditions such as colds and flu. Response to long-standing ailments can be slow, taking six months or more.

It is claimed that the tissue salts will not mask any symptoms they cannot treat; instead the symptoms will persist – an indication that the patient should seek orthodox medical advice.

Warning Because the tablets are lactose-based, anyone with a milk-sugar intolerance (see ALLERGY) should buy them in another form in case of side effects. Diarrhoea, a bloated stomach and FLATULENCE occurring after drinking milk can be indications of lactose intolerance.

An orthodox view

Research has now shown that there are at least 12 tissue salts in the body. Doctors do not agree that all diseases treated by biochemics are due to tissue salt imbalance, however, and there is currently no scientific evidence that biochemic remedies have any therapeutic effect. But it is generally agreed that the salts are gentle, non-toxic and non-habit-forming and that Schuessler's dozen are basic to good health.

There are no side effects unless a person is allergic to lactose (see above). If there is a danger, it is that someone with a serious condition may continue self-treatment when they are in need of medical attention.

prescribes remedies to induce the symptoms of the disease in a healthy person, and is also concerned with the patient's mental and emotional levels.

Who it can help Biochemics claims to help alleviate many everyday aches and pains, and the tissue salts should be used to treat only simple, easily recognised symptoms that are usually self-healing, such as those associated with INDIGESTION, COLDS, HAY FEVER, TENSION, muscular PAIN, minor SKIN DISORDERS, cuts and burns. It may be possible to use tissue salts alongside medications prescribed by a doctor.

Consulting a therapist Naturopaths, herbalists and homoeopaths often prescribe

BIOENERGETICS
A healthy integration of body and mind

Those who practise bioenergetics believe that a form of energy creates an interaction between our body and mind, governing both our physical and our mental states. Although nobody has yet been able to find or measure this energy force – known variously as *Qi (chi), prana*, life force, vitalism, and so on – it is said to affect everyone. Therapists cite as one example of its effect the common experience of 'up' days, when we feel bright and full of energy, and 'down' days, when we feel dull and lethargic.

The concept of a body-mind energy forms the basis of Eastern therapies such as YOGA, T'AI-CHI CH'UAN and ACUPUNCTURE. Sigmund Freud, the founder of psychoanalysis, made use of a similar idea – which he called 'libido' or psychic energy. This concept was taken further by one of his followers, Wilhelm Reich, who renamed it 'orgone' and identified it with sexual energy (see REICHIAN THERAPY and ORGONE THERAPY).

Although Reich's theories eventually fell into disrepute, one of his American pupils, Dr Alexander Lowen, used aspects of Reich's work as a basis for the theory of bioenergetics. He first developed these ideas during the 1960s, and bioenergetics is now recognised as a legitimate form of therapy by many psychotherapists.

Our everyday language is full of expressions that acknowledge how our emotions affect our bodies. We speak of being 'flushed with pride' and 'overburdened with grief', and sometimes even talk of having 'butterflies in the stomach'.

Bioenergetic therapists believe that personal psychological problems, STRESS, negative attitudes and emotions such as anger and FEAR all affect the way we sit, stand, move and breathe. For example, therapists observe that an obstinate, defensive type of person tends to adopt a characteristic body posture which involves almost literally 'digging his heels in'.

The purpose of bioenergetic therapy is primarily to help people to become aware of their habitual postures and body movements – known as 'character armouring' – and the emotions that are associated with them. By doing certain exercises they are then taught ways of 'unlocking' this armouring, so that the body regains its ability to function freely and naturally.

In effect the original emotional problem is 'released' and COUNSELLING can then help.

Bioenergetic exercises

Some typical exercises performed in bioenergetic classes include:

Grounding The way you stand and 'ground' your feet is seen as a sign of your emotional security. Bioenergetics regards the legs and feet as the primary way we maintain contact with the reality of our lives. Exercises in grounding include getting group members to explore different ways of using their feet – such as tiptoeing or stamping – and then discussing how each person responded to them.

Animal game Each member of the group chooses an animal with which he identifies, and then imitates its stance and behaviour. For example, a person may find that he readily identifies with a leopard, which is 'always on the hunt', and this may help him to understand more about his personal relationships.

Breathing This plays an important part in bioenergetics, and the ability to breathe freely and fully is held to reflect emotional well-being. Nervousness fear, anger and depression can all cause unnatural breathing patterns such as hyperventilation. The subject will be encouraged to correct these through regular diaphragmatic breathing.

Who it can help As with many newer therapies, bioenergetics offers a range of different benefits to different people. Because of its focus on personal growth rather than the treatment of illness, many people use bioenergetics simply to learn more about themselves. Others, however, have reported that it has helped them with complaints such as MIGRAINE, ASTHMA, IRRITABLE BOWEL SYNDROME and peptic ULCERS.

Some people also practise bioenergetics as a Western form of yoga, using it to keep fit and increase their general bodily awareness. It claims to help those who suffer from a poor self-image – those who may feel too fat or too thin, or are otherwise unhappy with their looks – to develop a more positive attitude to their bodies.

Nearly all participants – whatever their reasons for joining a group in the first place – report having 'more energy' or feeling 'more alive' after a bioenergetics class.

Finding a therapist Although bioenergetics is popular on the Continent, there are few therapists as yet in Britain and classes can be difficult to find. One teacher is Geoffrey Whitfield, Westmount House, 146A Eastern Road, Brighton, East Sussex BN2 2AE, who will also offer advice to people living in other parts of the country.

The Gerda Boyesen Centre, Acacia House, Centre Avenue, Acton Park, London W3 7JX, offers a related type of therapy called Biodynamics. This includes bioenergetics classes as well as PSYCHOTHERAPY and MASSAGE sessions.

Seeing a therapist The first consultation is usually an individual one, but for later sessions the subject normally joins a group of about eight or ten people for either a two-day workshop or a series of weekly meetings. There is no set procedure for the way that groups are conducted, but classes usually combine a series of exercises (see box) with a period of discussion.

An orthodox view

Since no way has yet been found to measure bioenergy objectively, scientists and doctors have not been able to confirm or repudiate the claims made for bioenergetic therapy. The only evidence that exists is the accounts of participants, and these are considered too subjective to constitute scientific proof.

BIOFEEDBACK
Machines to measure body and mind

The lie detector used by police and courts in the United States is just one of many biofeedback machines and instruments developed to monitor changes in people's physical and mental states. Therapists use the machines to let patients actually observe these changes – for example, in their body temperature and brain wave patterns. The patient is then taught to control these bodily functions by techniques such as VISUALISATION THERAPY, RELAXATION AND BREATHING, and MEDITATION. This is called biofeedback training.

The instruments themselves do not affect the body in any way, but simply provide information. As the patient becomes increasingly expert at recognising and altering his responses, he is able to avoid conditions such as ANXIETY or raised BLOOD PRESSURE.

How biofeedback training techniques work is not fully understood, but it is clear that they can affect the part of the nervous system that determines how active or relaxed our bodies are. This is known as the autonomic nervous system, and governs responses such as blood pressure, skin temperature, digestion and muscular TENSION, which until quite recently were thought to be entirely involuntary. Biofeedback has shown that this is not so, and that most people can learn a certain amount of control.

Who it can help Biofeedback training can be used to learn relaxation and meditation techniques or to help a number of illnesses. For example, MIGRAINE attacks and tension HEADACHES – which are associated with cold hands – have been prevented by teaching patients to raise the temperature of their hands. Many people have used it to reduce their blood pressure without taking drugs.

HYPERVENTILATION – a symptom of panic or anxiety – may be controlled by learning breathing techniques with the aid of biofeedback. Therapists also claim that many illnesses and stress-related conditions can be avoided by using biofeedback techniques to learn how to relax at times during the day.

Finding a therapist The Institute for Complementary Medicine, 21 Portland Place, London W1N 3AF, can usually name a therapist near to you. Therapists do not have official qualifications; some are attached to hospital psychological departments.

Consulting a therapist Patients are usually seeking help in learning to relax, or to overcome specific physical or psychological problems. The therapist selects the most suitable equipment – an electrical skin resistance gauge for anxiety, or hand-held thermometer for headaches, for example – and explains how it works. The patient is then attached to the equipment so that he can see or hear a continuous signal measuring his responses.

However, before training starts, the therapist may demonstrate that the act of willing alone is not enough to bring about changes in the physical states being measured.

Depending on which responses are being tested, the patient will be asked to try to cause a change – for example, to raise the temperature of his hand or lower the tension in his facial muscles. Most people find that the harder they try, the more they tense up.

To overcome this problem, the therapist can use a number of special techniques that work at a deeper, less conscious level. These include diaphragmatic breathing (see p. 299), progressive muscular relaxation (see p. 301), autohypnotic suggestion, visualisation and meditation. Most of these involve suspending the conscious will and trying to change the physical state indirectly or by using imagination – a process called 'passive volition'.

When the patient does this successfully, the signal from the biofeedback equipment changes, indicating that his physical state has been influenced. This makes it easier to learn the passive volition techniques, for the patient knows when he is making progress and can adjust his behaviour accordingly.

For treatment to be effective, the patient must also practise the new techniques at home without the aid of biofeedback equipment. Training sessions – usually six, one a week – continue until physical responses can be controlled at will. After that, continued good health depends on regular practice.

Self help Biofeedback equipment for use in the home is available and it is possible to teach yourself to relax.

An orthodox view

Biofeedback training is one of the few alternative therapies that is based on scientific principles. Most of the instruments were originally designed for use in scientific and medical research, and the effects they

measure are accepted by doctors as accurate indications of bodily processes. Even though doctors do not know how activities such as meditation and breathing can influence these processes, they accept that measurable changes do often occur.

One scientific study in the mid-1970s found that after biofeedback training, about a third of patients taking drugs for high blood pressure were able to bring their pressure ratings down to normal without drugs. Another experiment in a Birmingham clinic found that biofeedback helped four out of five migraine patients to relieve their symptoms.

BIORHYTHMS
Explaining life's ups and downs

We all have our 'up' days, when everything runs smoothly, and 'down' days, when however hard we try, nothing goes right, we lack concentration and feel accident prone. These physical, emotional and intellectual ups and downs are thought to be controlled by three internal body clocks or 'cycles', called 'biorhythms'. The physical and emotional cycles were charted quite independently by two doctors, Wilhelm Fliess and Herman Swoboda, around 1900, and the third was discovered by an engineer, Professor Alfred Teltscher, 20 years later.

The physical cycle lasts 23 days, and is said to govern vitality, strength, endurance, confidence, sex drive, and immunity to and recovery from illness. The 28 day emotional (sensitivity) cycle is held to govern moods, nervous reactions and creative ability, and the 33 day intellectual cycle decision-making, memory and learning ability.

An individual's cycles can be shown on a graph as waves moving above and below a horizontal line called a 'caution' line. The graph gives an at-a-glance picture of the kind of ups, downs and caution (or 'critical') days the person may expect in the weeks ahead.

Who they can help It is believed that everyone can benefit from understanding the relationship between their pattern of biorhythms and their pattern of behaviour. A chart cannot predict whether someone is going to have an accident or catch a cold, but it may help them to avoid one. It is held that the date of a surgical operation, if chosen with care using a chart, can enhance the patient's chances of making a good recovery, although this has not received any orthodox approval, or been proved scientifically.

Finding out about biorhythms Individual

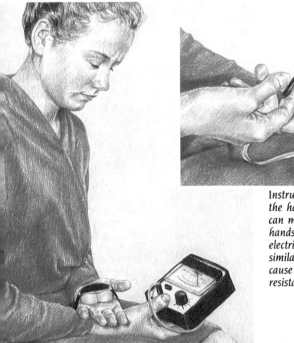

Instruments used in biofeedback include the hand-held thermometer (above), which can measure anxiety levels because the hands grow colder as anxiety rises. The electric skin resistance (ESR) gauge (left) is similar to a lie detector. Anxiety and fear cause the hands to sweat, reducing the skin's resistance to a small electric current.

Sample biorhythm chart

The purple, green and red waves show respectively the subject's fluctuating intellectual, emotional and physical cycles for a particular 33 day period. When a wave is above the caution line, it is in an active, high-energy phase; when below the caution line, in a passive phase storing energy for the next peak; and when crossing the line a 'caution' day occurs and accidents or mistakes may happen. The most difficult days are when two curves cross the caution line – June 2 on the chart, for example – and the most favourable days those such as June 7 when two cycles are high and one is low.

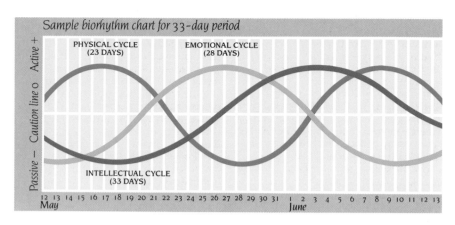

Sample biorhythm chart for 33-day period

PHYSICAL CYCLE (23 DAYS)   EMOTIONAL CYCLE (28 DAYS)

INTELLECTUAL CYCLE (33 DAYS)

Active + / Caution line 0 / Passive − Caution line

12 13 14 15 16 17 18 19 20 21 22 23 24 25 26 27 28 29 30 31 1 2 3 4 5 6 7 8 9 10 11 12 13
May   June

biorhythmic forecasts calculated by computer for six to 12 months ahead are available from various agencies which advertise in alternative and health magazines, and in the personal columns of some newspapers. Alternatively, you can work out your own chart with the aid of books which contain charts to make this process easier, or calculators, such as the Kosmos, that work out your cycles when you key in your birthdate.

An orthodox view

Biorhythms offer a scientifically acceptable theory for human mood swings. However, while many scientists accept the concept of biorhythms, most do not consider it a sufficiently accurate basis on which to predict or treat patients.

It is well known that life is influenced by a number of rhythms – the body has internal 'clocks' that regulate temperature, hormone levels, the female menstrual cycle and other functions. The Earth's rotation induces a daily rhythm for sleeping and waking, and the seasons bring changes of pace and mood. Scientific research has shown that there are certain times of day when people are able to function at their peak in different ways. For example, the best time to study is said to be just before going to sleep, and the best time to make important decisions is said to be at midday.

Further research is required, however, before a precise role for biorhythms in health and disease can be established. Although there are many well-documented cases to support the theory that critical days affect our health – such as the unexpected death of Christina Onassis on a critical physical day immediately after all three cycles were low – there is still no positive proof.

A study by the British Transport and Road Research Laboratory into the biorhythms of drivers involved in road traffic accidents showed no significant correlation. However, American airline authorities funded research at Missouri Southern State College in the 1970s, when laboratory-controlled biorhythm tests on pilots yielded different results.

Each pilot was asked to press a button ten times at five different times in their personal biorhythm cycles. Their reaction times averaged 5.13 seconds, but when their cycle was below the critical line, the times rose to 5.32 seconds – and, on critical physical days, to 5.41 seconds. Given that pilots are often called on to perform many tasks at once, it was deduced that they were more accident-prone on their low and critical days.

BLACKOUT

This momentary loss of consciousness happens when the brain does not get enough oxygen. There are a number of causes, a common one being a drop in BLOOD PRESSURE – for example, when you stand up suddenly or have to stand for long periods. If you suffer from blackouts, see a doctor for diagnosis and treatment. See also DIZZINESS and FAINTING.

BLADDER PROBLEMS

Embarrassing symptoms such as INCONTINENCE make sufferers reluctant to talk about bladder problems, so they are much more common than is generally realised. Over the age of 65, one woman in every 12 and one man in every 70 is bladder incontinent – making it by far the most common problem. It takes several forms:

Stress incontinence Women are the main sufferers – the condition is usually the result of childbirth or a surgical operation weakening pelvic muscles. The first symptom may be a few drops of urine leaking whenever you cough or strain; eventually any physical effort such as bending can cause a leakage.

Urge incontinence Both sexes are vulnerable. Sufferers cannot reach the lavatory in time when need arises. This can happen several times an hour and be exhausting.

Dribbling incontinence This is more common among men – a leakage of urine can occur at any time without the man even being aware of it. PROSTATE PROBLEMS are the usual cause: the bladder is never properly emptied, so urine continues to dribble out.

Incontinence can also result from a bladder infection (see CYSTITIS), or a stroke or spinal injury, so it is important to see your doctor if you develop the condition. Many of the measures that help to combat incontinence can also help to prevent it.

Problems other than those of incontinence include bladder CANCER and bladder stones – both relatively rare. Bladder cancer can result from working near certain dyeing chemicals, and SMOKING can also increase the risk of contracting it. Symptoms may not appear until the cancer has grown quite large, and include blood or mucus in the urine.

What the therapists recommend

Naturopathy A practitioner will recommend a diet high in FIBRE, and the avoidance of CONSTIPATION, which aggravates bladder problems. The diet will also be low in calories (see EATING FOR HEALTH), as being overweight puts extra pressure on the bladder. Regular EXERCISE, especially any designed to strengthen the abdominal and pelvic muscles, will also be recommended.

Herbal Medicine A herbalist will also advise a naturopathic diet and exercise, and may also prescribe arbutus (ground laurel). This is an astringent and has the effect of contracting tissues. Soak 1oz (30g) of the leaves in a pint (600ml) of boiling water for 15 minutes, cool, strain and drink freely during the day for as long as necessary. A practitioner may also prescribe other herbs, for example bilberries to reduce the accumulation of gravel in the bladder: pour 1 pint (600ml) of boiling water over 1oz (30g) of dried berries, cool, strain and drink daily.

An orthodox view

Many doctors feel that with most common bladder problems, prevention is much more effective than cure, and will recommend the same sort of general good health guidelines on diet and exercise as a naturopath.

If a doctor suspects a bladder infection, the urine will be tested and if necessary an antibiotic prescribed. If prostate problems are diagnosed, an operation may be required. In the case of bladder stones, large ones can be removed surgically; sometimes they can be disintegrated by powerful sound waves.

Useful address Incontinence Advisory Service, Disabled Living Foundation, 380-384 Harrow Road, London W9 2HU.

See also BEDWETTING.

BLISTERS

These small swellings are formed by pockets of watery fluid collecting under the skin. They can be caused by friction (for example, by wearing badly fitting shoes), burns, SUNBURN, insect STINGS AND BITES, or contact with irritating substances. Some infections, such as COLDSORES, CHICKENPOX, SHINGLES and IMPETIGO, may also cause blisters.

Usually only the top layers of skin are affected, and heal within a week. Consult a doctor if blisters become painful, red or inflamed, or if they have no apparent cause.

Do's and don'ts for blisters

Do keep a blister clean and protect it from pressure and irritation of all kinds.
Don't burst a blister unless it is causing severe pain, in which case . . .
Do wash and dry the area, then puncture the blister carefully with a sterilised needle. Simply put the needle tip in a flame for a few seconds, then allow to cool before using it.
Do keep the area clean to prevent infection.
Do expose it to the air as much as possible, but . . .
Do cover it when there is a danger of dirt getting in.

What the therapists recommend

Traditional Medicine To help blisters to heal, simmer cabbage leaves in milk for five minutes, leave them to cool down and then apply them to the skin in a poultice (see p. 184). Leave it in place for five to ten minutes. Alternatively, apply a strong decoction (see p. 184) of walnut leaves as a lotion or compress (see p. 184).

Biochemic Tissue Salts For immediate relief adults should try four tablets of *Nat. mur.* half-hourly until the pain has gone. For children two tablets half-hourly is advised.

Aromatherapy Dab the blister carefully with lavender essential oil.

An orthodox view

If there is an infection antibiotics may be prescribed. Tests may also be made to determine the cause of infection.

BLOOD PRESSURE
Treating the highs and lows

By taking your blood pressure it is possible to tell how hard your heart has to work to pump blood through your body. Depending on what you are doing, blood pressure changes slightly through the day, although the brain has to receive a constant supply of about 1½ pints (900ml) of blood every minute. Abnormally high blood pressure is known as hypertension; low blood pressure is called hypotension. Regular medical checks on blood pressure levels (see box) are advisable, as both conditions may require treatment – though hypertension is usually regarded as the more dangerous.

A blood pressure reading of 140/90 or more is generally considered high. However, most doctors now regard a systolic (upper) reading of 100 plus the age of the patient as acceptable and will not treat a 70-year-old whose systolic blood pressure is 170. The condition is more common among middle-aged people – about one in every ten is affected – and among men. Often they do not know that they have a problem, as there are usually no symptoms – although some report headaches, dizziness and ringing in the ears.

Most cases of hypertension are the result of interacting factors: drinking too much, eating too much salt, being overweight and taking too little exercise. Narrowing or hardening of the arteries (see ARTERIES [HARDEN-

Measuring blood pressure

This is done by placing an inflatable cuff around the upper arm. The cuff is pumped up until it exerts enough pressure to stop the flow of blood in the arm's main artery. As the cuff is slowly deflated and the blood begins to flow again readings are taken on a gauge at two points in the heart's pumping cycle. One reading, called the systolic pressure, is taken at the moment when the heart actually beats and it measures the peak pressure; the other, called the diastolic pressure, is measured between heart beats and shows your lowest level of blood pressure.

The two readings are combined as a fraction – systolic pressure over diastolic pressure – to give your blood pressure measurement. Normal for an adult is a systolic pressure of about 120 and a diastolic pressure of about 80 – or a blood pressure reading of 120/80 ('120 over 80'). Systolic pressures of 100-140 and diastolic ones of 60-90, slightly less in children, are usually considered within normal bounds.

ING]), taking the contraceptive pill, SMOKING, or an inherited tendency to hypertension are other factors. Rarely, the cause may be a kidney disorder, and some pregnant women develop dangerously high blood pressure.

If tests show that you have high blood pressure it is important to take steps to bring it down, or it may contribute to serious conditions such as ANGINA, heart attack, stroke, haemorrhage or KIDNEY COMPLAINTS.

What the therapists recommend

NATUROPATHY

Self help Adopt a wholefood diet based on fruit, vegetables, wholegrain cereals – brown rice is particularly recommended – beans, fish and chicken (see EATING FOR HEALTH). Onions, GARLIC and strawberries are believed to lower blood pressure, and HONEY may also help by calming the nerves.

Include plenty of fibre in your diet and reduce salt, sugar, animal fat and red meat to a minimum. Replace tea, coffee and cola drinks with herb tea, fruit juice, coffee substitutes or mineral water. See also LOW-FAT DIETS; SALT-FREE DIETS.

Consultation You will be given individual advice about diet, and supplements such as vitamin E, lecithin, garlic, pollen and magnesium or green buckwheat (rutin) may be recommended. Sometimes rutin tea or raw juices are recommended – about two to four cups a day of celery, grapefruit, orange, cucumber, pear or pineapple juice, separately or in combination.

The therapist will also advise you on reducing STRESS – by changing your daily routine, for example, to allow more time to relax or exercise; by adopting a cooperative rather than competitive attitude to others; or by practising RELAXATION AND BREATHING techniques. The practitioner will monitor your blood pressure, but may at times insist that you take medication from your doctor to aid in the safe control of the problem.

AROMATHERAPY

Self help Add a few drops of lavender, lemon and/or ylang-ylang essential oil to your bath water, or to a base oil (see p. 37) for MASSAGE. Clary sage, melissa and marjoram can also be used. Or you can try three or four drops of essential oil taken in tea (see p. 52) two or three times a day.

HOMOEOPATHY

Self help _Arg. nit._ may help if you suffer from nervous tension, worry or overwork, but consulting a homoeopath who could get to the root of the problem is advised.
Consultation Homoeopathic remedies are designed to treat the whole person, not just an illness, so your overall physical and emotional state will be assessed, and medicines prescribed for your circumstances.

ACUPUNCTURE

Consultation Acupuncture has been used successfuly to help lower blood pressure, although it is not known whether it does so by adjusting the overall functioning of the body, or simply by promoting relaxation – usually it does both. Treatment is combined

Do's and don'ts for high blood pressure

Don't smoke.
Don't take the contraceptive pill; try other methods of contraception instead.
Do increase the amount of FIBRE in your diet.
Do lose weight if you need to (see SLIMMING THE NATURAL WAY).
Do restrict alcohol consumption to two to four glasses of wine a week.
Do take regular aerobic EXERCISE of a non-competitive kind such as walking, swimming or cycling. Begin gently if you are not fit and never push yourself beyond what feels comfortable. Ask your doctor if you are uncertain.

Low blood pressure (hypotension)

This is not generally as serious as high blood pressure, and is usually temporary, caused by getting up suddenly after sitting or lying down. It affects mostly elderly people, and the symptoms are momentary giddiness or FAINTING on standing up, due to slower than normal response to changes in position. Persistent low blood pressure may be due to an underactive adrenal gland.

The symptoms can sometimes be alleviated by standing up more slowly, but a number of alternative therapies may help to treat the underlying causes.

What the therapists recommend

Acupuncture For a systolic pressure lower than 100, accompanied by symptoms such as tiredness, lack of energy, headaches, dizziness, palpitations or cold hands and feet, points in the abdomen, back, neck, upper arm and lower leg would probably be treated. Further specific treatment would depend on individual symptoms.
Naturopathy Adopting a wholefood diet (see EATING FOR HEALTH) and eating regular meals may help. It is also important to see that you get plenty of rest and take regular gentle exercise. Avoid artificial stimulants such as tea, coffee, alcohol and

with advice about diet and lifestyle, and varies according to how serious the condition is. Generally points in the abdomen, lower trunk, back, foot and head are stimulated, sometimes giving immediate relief.

BACH REMEDIES

Self help Oak and Elm for those feeling overwhelmed by responsibilities; Impatiens for irritability and impatience; Agrimony for the 'life and soul of the party', who hides his anxieties; Vervain for over-enthusiasm and strain; Vine for those who are ruthless and driven by ambition; Rock water for those with impossibly high standards; Beech if advice from others is refused. The last three are also for those who find relaxation difficult. If the condition is rooted in repressed emotion: Holly for anger, hatred and desire for revenge; Mimulus for fear of poverty; Star of Bethlehem for shock and grief.

Other alternative treatments

Hydrotherapy Try hot and cold foot baths twice a day.
Reflexology As high blood pressure is often caused by stress, the general relaxing effect of a full treatment is often beneficial.

tobacco. A naturopath would give advice on a healthier diet and lifestyle. Supplements such as vitamin E and MINERALS may be suggested.
Herbal Medicine A herbalist may recommend infusions (see p. 184) prepared from herbs such as broom, which is said to increase blood pressure. Other herbs may be used to tone and stimulate the whole system – kola, oats, gentian and wormwood are a few.
Aromatherapy You are advised to add hyssop, rosemary, sage or thyme essence to a massage oil or to your bath, or take them in a tea (see p. 37).
Bach Remedies Olive is prescribed for general exhaustion and depletion; Wild rose for resignation and apathy; Star of Bethlehem for uncompleted mourning, chronic sadness; Willow for resentment and self-pity; Clematis for loss of interest in life and mental confusion; Honeysuckle for nostalgia or regrets about the past.

An orthodox view

Hypotension for reasons other than those given above is not a diagnosis recognised by orthodox medicine. Recommendations by alternative therapists – although not harmful – would not be seen as affecting this condition.

The most important areas requiring massage will be those relating to the heart, kidneys, adrenal glands, solar plexus, head, eyes, lungs, neck and spine. See chart on p. 295.
Yoga The corpse pose and YOGA meditation are likely to help. Practising yoga regularly can also relieve stress (avoid inverted postures). See also BIOFEEDBACK, MASSAGE, ACUPRESSURE.

An orthodox view

Doctors agree that diet is important and that cutting down on salt intake and reducing excess weight should help. They make tests to find the cause of the hypertension and determine if it has had any effects on the body that need treating. You will be advised to cut your alcohol intake and stop smoking.

If these measures do not help, drugs such as beta blockers (which lower the heart rate), diuretics (which increase production and excretion of urine) or vasodilators (which enlarge blood vessels) may be prescribed. However, these treat only the symptoms and not the underlying cause, so they have to be taken until the condition is cured by some other means. All can cause serious side effects, such as IMPOTENCE and TIREDNESS.

BOILS

These inflamed, pus-filled areas of infection on the skin often start in a hair follicle – the minute hollow in the skin where a hair grows. The follicle and surrounding cells in the skin are killed by bacteria – usually staphylococci – and form thick yellow pus. As the pocket of pus gets bigger, the boil gradually comes to a head and, usually within a week or two of starting, the pus bursts out and disperses.

In some cases several follicles become infected, giving rise to a cluster of boils, called a *carbuncle*. Both boils and carbuncles are a form of *abscess*, and generally erupt in hairy areas such as the neck, nostrils, armpits and wrists. They may also erupt where there is friction, such as between the legs and buttocks. The most common place for abscesses to form is in the gums, where they are commonly called gumboils (see TOOTH AND GUM DISORDERS).

Boils are most likely to appear when you feel run down, are extremely tired, weakened by poor nutrition, or suffering from DIABETES.

Although boils are a common minor disorder, they should not be ignored. If untreated, the infection can spread, eventually causing fever and general debility, particularly if pus enters the bloodstream. And it is for this reason that boils should never be squeezed. Medical treatment should be sought for carbuncles or a series of boils; if the boils are particularly painful; if the inflammation spreads without coming to a head; or if no pus is discharged even though a head has formed on the boil.

Warning Bacteria from boils can also find their way into warm food, where they rapidly multiply and can cause food poisoning. Sufferers should wash their hands thoroughly before dealing with food – and should not use anyone else's towel, as discharging boils are highly infectious.

What the therapists recommend

Traditional Medicine Apply a kaolin or magnesium sulphate poultice – available from chemists – to bring the boil to a head. Draw out the pus with a magnesium poultice. Or apply a bread poultice every three to four hours. Crumble a slice of bread into boiled milk or water, wrap it in gauze, drain and apply hot.

Naturopathy Practitioners regard a wholefood diet as the key to treating boils – or avoiding them altogether (see EATING FOR HEALTH). A cleansing diet of raw vegetables and fruit is recommended for the first two to seven days. Naturopaths also recommend

that close attention should be paid to personal hygiene and skin care (see NATURAL AIDS TO BEAUTY).

A poultice can be made from crushed fenugreek seeds, obtainable at health shops. Wrap a teaspoonful in foil and simmer for about ten minutes in a cup of water. Strain and then apply the seeds on a piece of lint, lightly held in place. Alternatively, apply a hot, softly baked onion to bring boils to a head – or lightly bandage a thin slice of juicy lemon on the area.

Homoeopathy *Hepar sulph.* is used to help a boil to come to a head, and *Silica* to speed the discharge of pus once it has burst.

Biochemic Tissue Salts Among those recommended by practitioners are *Ferr. phos.* and *Kali mur.* Given alternatively in the early stage they are said to prevent swelling and pus formation. In cases where the boil bursts but the discharge continues and the wound is slow to heal, practitioners recommend taking *Calc. sulph.*

Herbal Medicine Herbalists traditionally believe that boils are the manifestation of internal impurities – and that the blood can be purified by drinking strong teas made from herbs such as barberry, burdock, cayenne, echinacea, golden seal and yellow dock. Use a teaspoonful of the chosen herb to a cup of boiling water and, when the tea is cool enough, drink a tablespoonful every two to three hours.

Poultices made by mixing a paste of slippery elm and hot water and applied warm over several days are said to help clear up boils and heal the wounds.

An orthodox view

If a boil refuses to burst, a doctor may lance it so that the pus drains away. He may also prescribe an antibiotic such as penicillin to kill the bacteria and prevent the infection spreading. If he thinks that diabetes is the underlying cause, he may make a urine test.

BONESETTING

The art of bonesetting – the treating of broken bones and dislocated limbs by manipulation – dates back to the Stone Age. The bonesetters' skills reached a peak in the 18th and 19th centuries, when their relatively gentle use of hands for correcting bone and muscle problems was preferred to the more vigorous methods of conventional physicians and surgeons.

Today traditional bonesetters have mostly been replaced by practitioners of OSTEOPATHY and CHIROPRACTIC – whose methods are partly based on those of their predecessors.

BOWEL DISORDERS

There are a number of bowel disorders, all of which have pronounced symptoms. The two most common of these are CONSTIPATION and DIARRHOEA. In some cases there may be bleeding, with blood in the faeces or discharged from the anus. Both can indicate the presence of PILES or, more seriously, CANCER. Any such symptoms – or any marked changes in otherwise well-established bowel habits – should be reported to your doctor as soon as possible.

See also COLIC, COLITIS, DYSENTERY, INCONTINENCE, IRRITABLE BOWEL SYNDROME, WIND and WORMS.

BREAST PROBLEMS

Most women will have a breast problem at some time in their lives. Fluctuations in hormone levels – associated with the menstrual cycle or with the rise and decline of fertility over the years – generally cause the problems. These frequently right themselves as the hormone levels stabilise.

The breasts consist of glandular tissue and fat, which fibrous bands called ligaments support on the chest wall. Hormones in the female bloodstream make the breast tissue develop during puberty, produce milk after childbirth, and dwindle after the menopause.

Men have little breast tissue and rarely suffer breast problems. A man who has any pain or swelling in the breast area should get professional advice.

The most common disorders are mastalgia (painful breasts) and fibrocystic disease (lumpy breasts). The most serious is breast CANCER. Some women who are breastfeeding experience discomfort or difficulties that will respond to simple treatment (see below and box, p. 74).

Many women have painful breasts before a period. Some pregnant women have pain early in pregnancy. The raised level of oestrogen and of sodium in their blood causes water to be held in the fatty tissue of the body. Since there is a large amount of fat in the breasts, so much water is retained that the breasts feel overfull, tight and sore.

In about half the women aged 30-55 increases of fibrous (*fibro-*) and glandular (*-cystic*) tissue occur in the breasts, which

Examining your breasts

Set aside 10-15 minutes each month to check your breasts. Immediately after a period is the right time to do it. In the week before and during a period, your breasts may feel swollen and sore but this is not abnormal. After the menopause, carry out the examination at a fixed time each month — perhaps on the first day of the month. Once you have done a few monthly checks, you will know what is the normal appearance and structure of your breasts and notice immediately anything unusual. Some women are made too anxious by carrying out their own examination and prefer to have a six-monthly checkup by a health worker.

1 Strip to the waist and face a mirror in a good light. Look for any changes in the shape of either breast, for any puckering or dimpling of the skin, and for changes in the condition of either nipple.

3 Raise and lower your arms and see if both nipples move by the same amount.

4 Squeeze each nipple gently to make sure there is no discharge. Look for any rash or flaky skin on the nipples.

5 Lie flat with a small cushion or a folded towel under your left shoulder blade and with your left hand behind your head. Keeping your right fingers flat, use them to work round and round your left breast in tiny circles, pressing firmly as you go and gradually spiralling from the outermost part towards the nipple. Make sure you cover every part.

2 Put your hands behind your head and look again. Turn sideways for another look and then lean forward and check again.

6 Again working the flat of your fingers in tiny circles, test from your armpit down towards your breast. Then use your left fingers to check your right breast.

If you find anything unusual, see your doctor within a few days. Do not keep feeling any lump while you wait to see the doctor and remember that the great majority of breast lumps are harmless.

73

may then feel tender and lumpy, especially before a period. A soft, sore lump (an adenoma) may develop in a breast. Because the lump moves easily and seems to slip away when you try to grasp it, it is often called a 'breast mouse'. Sometimes an olive-sized cyst develops, most often in the upper and outer part of the breast towards the armpit. An excess of oestrogen, deficiency of vitamin E, and xanthines in the diet (from coffee, tea, chocolate and cola drinks) are thought to cause the condition.

Avoiding and relieving problems

Women can reduce the risk of some breast problems by examining their breasts regularly (see illustrations, p. 73) for early warning of troubles, and by following a healthy lifestyle with a few extra measures added specifically to aid breast care.

Diet Cut down on salt and salty foods. This will help to curb the retention of water in the fatty tissue, which is one cause of mastalgia. Eat plenty of fresh fruit and vegetables to make sure you get enough VITAMINS. Vitamin B6 eases WATER RETENTION by acting as a diuretic (making you pass more urine) and it may restore your oestrogen balance. Cut down on coffee, tea, chocolate and cola.

Give up smoking and regular drinking of alcohol, which seem to increase the risk of contracting cancer. Cut down on animal fats – many researchers believe that as the body breaks down these fats, by-products are formed that can encourage breast cancer. Eat soya bean products, which are thought to counteract the harmful by-products of fat.

Exercise Fat will be burned off instead of stored in the body if you take regular exercise. The tension that can increase premenstrual discomforts, and seems to be a characteristic of people at risk from cancer, is often dispelled by exercise.

Swimming, especially breaststroke, and skipping are good general muscle toners and particularly good for firming the chest muscles behind the breasts. Strong muscles and a well-fitting bra help to prevent sagging, which can make sore breasts more uncomfortable – and which in time causes stretch marks on the skin.

An effective exercise for the muscles round the breasts is to put your hands together as hard as you can while you count to five. Relax, then repeat four or five times.

Make sure you do not let your chest muscles sag. Maintain a good posture with a straight back whether you are standing or sitting. Breathe properly to help to open up your chest: as you fill your lungs deeply, your diaphragm should move down and your abdomen, not your shoulders, rise.

YOGA can help to relieve tension and exercise chest muscles. The most useful

Remedies to ease breastfeeding

	LACK OF MILK	CRACKED NIPPLES	BLOCKED MILK DUCT (pain in one segment)	ENGORGEMENT (over-full breast; poor flow)
Self help	Take extra drinks and rest. Eat pears and strawberries. Have your back massaged.	Make sure the whole areola is in the baby's mouth and the nipple well back in the mouth. Use a softening cream.	Soak breasts in a warm bath. Stroke breasts towards nipples to express milk. Empty breasts after feed.	Apply hot compresses before and during feeds, cold compresses after feeds. Encourage baby to feed from affected breast.
Acupressure	Use a matchstick to stimulate the outer side of both little fingers just below the nail.	As for lack of milk.	Stimulate inside the wrist in the central hollow, on the breastbone, halfway along the shoulder slightly towards the back, on the chest wall beneath each breast.	As for blocked duct.
Aromatherapy	Massage with oil of aniseed, caraway, fennel, verbena.	Massage with oil of camomile.	Massage with oil of geranium or mint.	Massage with oil of garlic.
Herbal medicine	Take infusions of milkwort, fenugreek, holy thistle, fennel or borage.	Rub in calendula cream.	As for cracked nipples.	Massage with calendula cream, honey, almond oil.
Homoeopathy	Take *Causticum*, *Urtica urens* or *Pulsatilla*.	Take *Caster equii*.	Take *Silica*.	Take *Phytolacca*.

postures for this are the bow, the cobra and the head of a cow.

Breastfeeding You need plenty of rest and a nourishing diet while breastfeeding, with ample vitamins, calcium and iron (see EATING FOR HEALTH). As well as your usual fluids, drink a glass of water after each feed.

While feeding, sit up straight in a high-backed chair and support the baby on a pillow on your lap to lift it well up to the breast without straining your back and arms. Make sure you are relaxed with plenty of time and no distractions so that the milk will flow. A warm bath and your favourite peaceful music may help you if tension is making feeding difficult.

You can ease many discomforts yourself, as shown in the chart, but if you are feverish with hard, painful breasts and greenish milk, you may have MASTITIS and should get professional help. If you have the same symptoms and a localised swelling, you may have an abscess and should again seek help.

What the therapists recommend

NATUROPATHY

Self help Maintain a healthy weight and eat plenty of cress, turnips, cabbage and all other plants of the cabbage family. Make up a vegetable juice from half turnip and half cress and then add an equal quantity of carrot juice. Have some of the juice each day.

Splash or spray your breasts with cold water every day.

Consultation A diet will be worked out to rid your body of waste that has accumulated. A course of BIOCHEMIC TISSUE SALTS may be suggested and vitamin supplements prescribed as required for your individual diet – perhaps A, B1, B6, C and E. Capsules of calcium, arginine, kelp, oil of evening primrose or flaxseed oil are claimed to relieve the discomforts of fibrocystic disease.

Other alternative treatments

Aromatherapy Make up a cream of one part essence of geranium, five parts white wax, 12 parts water, 20 parts sweet almond oil. Massage the cream into your breasts at bedtime to ease soreness. Alternatively, bathe them with a bowl of water, boiled then cooled to a pleasant warmth and three to four drops of essence of geranium added.

Homoeopathy *Calc. ostrearum* and *Calc. phos.* are generally recommended to ease painful breasts and *Conium flaculatum* for pregnant women whose breasts hurt.

Reflexology Massage is applied from the second to the fifth zone on top of the feet to treat fibrocystic disease.

An orthodox view

For mastalgia, a doctor is likely to prescribe a diuretic drug to relieve the water retention; or a synthetic hormone may be prescribed to balance out the excess oestrogen level.

For cysts that cause pain in fibrocystic disease, your doctor may send you to a hospital to have fluid drawn off from the cyst by a syringe, or to have the cyst removed. Occasionally a biopsy may be recommended to confirm that any breast lumps are not malignant. A small sample of the suspect tissue is removed under a local or a general anaesthetic so that cells can be examined under a microscope. Even if the lump is not malignant, and is fibrous tissue, you may still be advised to have it removed.

Women with fibrocystic disease have a rather higher risk of developing breast cancer – as have women whose near relatives develop breast cancer, or who have recently lost someone close to them, or who habitually suppress angry feelings. Three-yearly screening for early detection of breast problems is recommended for all women of 50 to 64 years, and for women at greater risk.

The screening is usually by mammogram, an X-ray taken with the breasts held firmly between two photographic plates, or by an ultrasound scan, in which a small high-frequency sound instrument is passed over each breast. If a cancerous lump is found, you will be referred to a specialist unit for surgery, radiotherapy, chemotherapy or a combination of these treatments.

BRONCHITIS

When the large air passages (bronchi) which carry air from the windpipe to the lungs become inflamed the result is bronchitis. It can be brought on by a variety of viruses and bacteria.

Symptoms include persistent COUGHS, WHEEZING, breathlessness, chest pains, FEVER, HEADACHES and loss of appetite. The condition may come on suddenly (acute bronchitis), or develop in a more serious form, as a prolonged disorder (chronic bronchitis) that gets progressively worse. In its serious form, the lining of the bronchi narrows and the lungs' air sacs are gradually destroyed, cutting down the supply of oxygen to the blood. This form occurs in occupations where air pollution is common, such as coal mining and in the building trade.

Warning Anyone developing symptoms of bronchitis should see a doctor before seeking alternative treatments. Both conventional and alternative practitioners will recommend smokers to stop SMOKING – the most common cause of the disease.

What the therapists recommend
NATUROPATHY

Self help Avoiding dairy products and eating only wholefoods (see EATING FOR HEALTH) is believed to help in reducing mucus. Also avoid dry, overheated rooms.

Consultation Naturopaths believe that bronchitis is generally caused by poor living habits, which poison the system and can lead to the build-up of poisonous waste in the bronchi. Lowered resistance caused by overwork, EXHAUSTION, a sudden CHILL, or exposure to coldness, is thought to trigger the symptoms.

Many practitioners do not agree with the prescription of conventional drugs or medicines for bronchitis except in severe cases, but may suggest such supplements as GARLIC capsules and vitamins B and C.

For prolonged cases, an all-fruit diet for three to five days is recommended (under constant supervision), followed by ten to 14 days on a diet of raw salads, vegetables and sweet fruit – all to be eaten according to appetite. After this, a more varied, normal diet of fish or poultry and fresh vegetables may be resumed, but still with no dairy products and with two or three days each month on the all-fruit diet.

For a sudden onset of bronchitis, an initial fast until the fever and other symptoms have eased is recommended. This can be followed by two or three days on an all-fruit diet.

Naturopaths also recommend measures such as dry friction 'baths' – self-massage with a brush or sponge – Epsom salt baths (see HYDROTHERAPY), RELAXATION AND BREATHING exercises, and outdoor exercise.

HERBAL MEDICINE

Consultation Practitioners may prescribe one or more plant-based remedies including gum plant, coltsfoot, squill, liquorice, comfrey, boneset, white horehound, heartsease, wild thyme, ginger and elder flower. The exact prescription will depend much on the individual patient. Echinacea may be added, to build up the immune system and improve the patient's circulation.

These herbal prescriptions may be supplemented with vitamin C, plus iron to help form haemoglobin, the blood's oxygen carrier.

Once the patient is well enough, the practitioner will recommend a combination of rest and gentle exercise, such as walking, gradually going on to more vigorous activities such as swimming.

Prescriptions are reviewed regularly during consultations, with emphasis on healing the damaged bronchial tissues, restoring the body's resistance and building up the nervous system.

Other alternative treatments

Aromatherapy Essential oils of eucalyptus, hyssop and sandalwood are recommended as inhalants. Eucalyptus is considered good for clearing the head, hyssop as a decongestant and sandalwood as a relaxant. Use them as drops on a paper towel or in a bowl of hot water in the following proportions: six eucalyptus, two hyssop, two sandalwood.

The same oils can be applied during massage, in a ratio of 15:10:5. Many less expensive oils may also help, including pine, cajuput and niaouli.

Biochemic Tissue Salts In the first stages of bronchitis, *Ferr. phos.* 6X potency is recommended. If the condition worsens, *Kali mur.* 6X potency should also be taken, along with *Nat. mur.* 6X potency.

Homoeopathy For sudden attacks, when the patient finds movement difficult and wants long, cool drinks, try *Bryonia*. Chronic sufferers should consult a homoeopath personally. Other aids recommended are *Aconite*, at the onset of feverishness; *Kali bich.* if the mucus is stringy, tough and thick, and difficult to cough up; and *Pulsatilla* if the cough is dry, or the mucus is loose and green and the patient does not feel thirsty.

Acupuncture Points on the lung, bladder, stomach and spleen meridians are treated.

Reflexology Massage to the reflex areas relating to the bronchi, lungs and throat, together with the solar plexus, adrenal and pituitary glands, lymphatic system and spine is recommended. See chart on p. 295.

An orthodox view

While many alternative therapists disagree with using drugs to treat bronchitis, a doctor may prescribe medicine to ease the cough, a balsam inhalant to aid breathing, and antibiotics to fight the infection. However, some doctors reject cough-suppressing drugs, because coughing and spitting prevent infected matter being inhaled.

The patient will be advised to get plenty of rest in a warm room, to avoid moving from a hot to a cold atmosphere, and to avoid dusty places. Smokers with progressive bronchitis will be advised to give up, otherwise their health will continue to deteriorate, leading to complications such as EMPHYSEMA, PNEUMONIA and HEART DISORDERS.

A conventional doctor would be concerned if someone with a cough were treated by an alternative practitioner without an orthodox diagnosis being made. All patients should consult a doctor if a cough persists.

BRUISING

Most bruises are the result of a fall or blow which causes bleeding in the tissues under the skin. This can be slowed down – reducing discomfort and the extent of the bruising – if you apply an ice pack or a cold, damp cloth over the bruise with moderate pressure for about ten minutes. Aspirin or paracetamol will relieve the pain. Do the same for a 'black eye' – despite popular belief, putting raw steak on it is a waste of time.

A badly bruised limb should be rested for 24-48 hours. In the case of a leg, lie down and raise it on pillows to reduce blood flow.

Unless bruising appears for no apparent reason, or does not clear up within about a fortnight, there is no need to see a doctor.

What the therapists recommend

Naturopathy Many naturopaths believe that people who bruise easily may lack vitamin K, a vital blood-clotting protein. Eating 5oz (150g) of yoghurt daily is thought to stimulate the microorganisms that produce the vitamin. Fresh green vegetables are recommended, with fresh pineapple or its juice, which contain enzymes that are said to speed the disappearance of bruising.

As an immediate measure, spray the area with cold water to stimulate local circulation.
Herbal Medicine A cold compress soaked in comfrey infusion (p. 184) or oil of lavender, or comfrey ointment is recommended.
Homoeopathy Rub *Arnica* oil or ointment gently into the bruised area.

BULIMIA
The consequences of compulsive eating

Strict dieting or an overpowering desire to be thin can bring on bulimia – which, like the closely related ANOREXIA, is an eating disorder with a psychological basis. The victim has sudden uncontrollable cravings for food, which lead to periodic bouts of overeating, called 'bingeing', which are followed by the taking of laxatives or self-induced vomiting to get rid of the food.

Strangely, victims are usually of normal weight for their age and height, and seldom appear to be ill. But beneath the surface they conceal a constant fear of food and of their inability to stop eating.

Bulimia has become a more common eating disorder than the much better known anorexia, and can affect both men and women of any age – although most of its victims are women in their twenties. It has been estimated that about 45 per cent of those suffering from anorexia will later develop bulimia.

It is a dangerous condition that can cause a variety of physical and mental symptoms such as low BLOOD PRESSURE, PERIOD PROBLEMS, TENSION, ANXIETY and DEPRESSION. Regular use of laxatives and vomiting can cause KIDNEY COMPLAINTS, URINARY PROBLEMS, dehydration and poor circulation. In extreme cases, overeating itself may eventually lead to death.

Warning Anyone who thinks they may be suffering from bulimia – or is trying to help a family member with the disorder – should consult their doctor before any of the alternative treatments are embarked upon.

What the therapists recommend
NATUROPATHY
Self help See SLIMMING THE NATURAL WAY for advice about how to stay slim while also taking in all the nourishment your body needs. Include plenty of raw foods (see RAW FOOD DIET) and freshly squeezed raw fruit and vegetable juices in your diet. In addition, avoid the use of laxatives, which can cause dehydration and deplete the body of its necessary minerals.
Consultation The naturopath will help you to work out an individual diet plan. It will be supplemented with extra vitamins and minerals where necessary. The practitioner will also give advice about coping with STRESS and taking EXERCISE, especially outdoor exercise. The naturopath may well work alongside a psychotherapist.

Other alternative treatments

Bach Remedies Complex emotions may underlie this condition. Crab apple is recommended for self disgust and anxiety about weight and appearance; Heather for being self-obsessed and craving love; Scleranthus for instability and mood swings; Beech for difficulty in receiving food and love in appropriate measure; Pine for guilt about the condition; Aspen for fear of being found out; and Holly for negative feelings such as jealousy, hatred and the desire for revenge.
Psychotherapy Patients are often started on BEHAVIOURAL THERAPY, followed by COGNITIVE THERAPY to deal with underlying causes such as a poor self image, fear of failure, and social or personal problems.

Among other therapies, DANCE THERAPY, YOGA, T'AI-CHI CH'UAN and BIOENERGETICS may also help by making bulimia victims feel more positive about their bodies.

An orthodox view

Doctors agree that bingeing, taking laxatives and vomiting can do serious damage. Your general practitioner can help you to work out a safe diet if you want to lose weight or avoid putting it on. If deep psychological problems are an underlying cause, you will be referred to a psychologist or psychotherapist.

BUNIONS

Like CORNS, bunions are nearly always caused by ill-fitting shoes which put pressure on the big toe. The joint swells, the skin over it becomes hard, red and sore – and the toe is forced inwards. Middle-aged women who have always worn narrow shoes, children, teenagers and young adults are particularly prone to bunions. Unless treated, an operation may eventually be needed to cure them.

What the therapists recommend

Naturopathy   Bathe the feet for 20 minutes daily in a bowl of hot water in which a tablespoon of Epsom salts is dissolved. Alternating footbaths of hot and cold water may also help, and gentle, circular massage helps to keep movement at the joints.

Herbal Medicine   Bio-Strath Willow formula – a modern preparation made from extract of willow and primula – is said to relieve inflammation. It can be taken long-term in liquid form – available from health shops – and is said to have no side effects. Celery seeds are also thought to help. Make an infusion (p. 184) with 1 teaspoon of seeds. Take 1 tablespoon three times daily, cold (but _not_ during pregnancy). Celery helps you to lose more uric acid, so it is also appropriate for GOUT and related conditions.

Aromatherapy   Massage the feet every night with oils of patchouli (if the skin is dry) and lavender. Camomile and geranium are also helpful.

Acupuncture   Therapists say that pain can be relieved – but only if the source of pressure on the big toes, such as tight shoes – is avoided.

An orthodox view

A doctor may recommend the wearing of felt pads to ease the inflammation – as long as they are not so bulky that they put unwanted pressure on the affected area. The patient would then probably be sent to a chiropodist.

If the foot is seriously deformed, the doctor may prescribe painkillers, or an operation may be advised.

BURSITIS

Housemaid's knee and TENNIS ELBOW are two common forms of bursitis. This is the name given to any inflammation of the small liquid-filled sacs – or bursas – which lubricate the joints, helping skin, muscles and tendons to move smoothly over the bones.

In bursitis, excess liquid collects in the sac, and this prevents the free movement of the joint, causing heat, swelling and pain. The condition is usually caused by repeated bumping or overuse of the joint, ARTHRITIS, GOUT or infection.

What the therapists recommend

NATUROPATHY

Self help   Rest the joint as much as you possibly can, and stop any activities that may be causing pressure or bumps at the joint. If the elbow is affected, it may help if you put the arm in a sling. Use a crepe bandage or tubular bandage as a support for the joint, and apply cold (not ice) compresses (see p. 193) for five to ten minutes three times daily.

When the pain and swelling begin to decrease – usually after about seven to ten days – start using the joint again. Go carefully at first, gradually increasing the range of movements until you are using the joint normally again.

A nourishing wholefood diet supplemented with vitamins A and C is also recommended (see EATING FOR HEALTH and VITAMINS). If symptoms persist for ten days or more, see your doctor.

HYDROTHERAPY

Self help   Apply cold compresses (see p. 193) to the joint during the first few days, when swelling and pain are worst. Leave them on overnight and for several periods of about 20 minutes during the day, renewing them whenever they no longer feel cold. Alternate or replace with hot compresses once improvement begins.

For acute inflammation, a bag of frozen peas can be applied as an ice pack (it will conform to the contours of the affected part). First smear the skin with olive or cooking oil to prevent frostbite. Apply three times daily, on for five minutes, off for five minutes, then on for ten minutes.

HERBAL MEDICINE

Self help   After the first few days, hot herbal poultices (see p. 184) may help. Comfrey, linseed, marsh-mallow and slippery elm are recommended, either individually or in combination. If you find that heat is helpful, gently boil a tablespoon of cayenne pepper in 1 pint (600ml) of cider vinegar for ten minutes. When it is cool, soak a clean hand towel in the mixture, wring it out slightly and wrap it around the joint. If the skin begins to burn, protect it by applying a thin layer of oil or diluting the mixture with water.

Drinking herbal infusions (see p. 184) may also help. Camomile is particularly recommended – add some hops or passionflower if taken at bedtime as a relaxant, to help you sleep if disturbed by discomfort. Seek medical help if the problem persists.

Other alternative treatments

Aromatherapy   Mix five drops each of lavender, juniper, eucalyptus and rosemary essential oils in almond or peanut oil and massage into the affected area every day.

Homoeopathy   For swelling, redness and pain, _Apis_ 6X potency every two hours is recommended. If attacks recur, try _Rhus tox._ 6X potency twice a day for two weeks.

An orthodox view

Doctors support the naturopathic advice to rest the joint at first and avoid banging or applying pressure to it to prevent further attacks. Orthodox treatment involves anaesthetising the area and draining excess fluid from the bursa with a fine needle. Sometimes cortisone is injected to reduce the risk of another attack, and antibiotics are given if there is an infection. If the bursitis does not clear, the bursa may be removed under local anaesthetic.

Avoiding bunions

Make sure socks are not tight, and that shoes are wide enough for comfort, with plenty of room for the toes.

Remove shoes whenever possible and do toe-flexing exercises.

Wiggle and massage your toes when you are in the bath.

Loop a strong rubber band around both big toes and move the feet outwards to try to make a 'V'. Do it as often as is practicable.

Let children go barefoot as much as you possibly can.

Recovering from bursitis

Once the swelling begins to go down, the affected joint must be used and exercised every day, or the bursitis may develop into a permanent condition. Begin by swinging the arm or leg freely in every direction possible, supporting it if necessary. Exercise frequently during the day, but for only a minute or two at a time. As the pain subsides, do the exercises for longer and enlarge the scope of the movements.

Prevent further attacks by avoiding pressure or knocks to the joints. If you have to kneel for long periods, use a foam-rubber mat.

When the body's cells go out of control

Cancers can develop when the body's own policing system fails to destroy cells with the wrong genetic code and allows them to multiply unchecked. Orthodox medicine recognises that environmental factors seem to stimulate faulty cell division and that prolonged grief or depression makes the policing system less efficient. But it is still far from unravelling the complexities of this multi-form illness. It can see also that factors outside hospital clinics and operating theatres play a vital part in the outcome of orthodox treatment. Alternative therapies concentrate on this aspect – fostering positive control by patients over their bodies and boosting a determined and assertive mental approach.

Helpful, balanced discussion of cancer is often difficult because, for many people, the very word conjures up an image of pain and death. They shun the topic and shy away from learning more about it. But the term 'cancer' is used for many different sets of symptoms, some of them almost invariably curable.

The causes, treatments and chances of a cure differ widely for the different forms of cancers. SMOKING, for example, is a cause of lung cancer; too much ultraviolet light a cause of skin cancer; and diet a cause of bowel cancer. The rigorous diet that may be appropriate in treating bowel cancer is quite unlike treatments recommended for skin cancer. While 98 per cent of people with skin cancer survive, only 7 per cent of lung cancer victims survive longer than five years.

Statistics about survival can be misleading. Death rates generally take no account of how late the condition was diagnosed and the treatment was started. In many forms of cancer, early diagnosis greatly improves the success rate of treatment, as measured by survival time.

What is cancer? The factor that all forms of cancer have in common is the development of abnormal cells in some part of the body.

Body cells are constantly reproducing – more than 90 per cent of the body's cells are replaced every six months. Cells reproduce by dividing in two, each half taking its share of the nucleus (see illustrations below). Within the nucleus is the genetic code which controls what kind of cell develops and how it behaves.

A dividing cell sometimes produces mutant (abnormal) cells which are not properly coded and multiply uncontrollably, developing into a cancer. It is one of the tasks of the

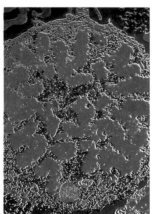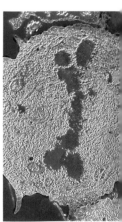

The orderly process that makes a matching pair of body cells

The stages in normal division of a human cell are shown in the series of photographs above. Magnification and staining with strong colour have made the process easier to see.
1 In a cell about to divide, the chromosomes (stained pink) of the nucleus, which carry the genetic code, are contained in an encircling envelope (orange). Cytoplasm (green) makes

up the rest of the cell. The chromosomes – each consisting of two matched chromatids – have begun to grow shorter and thicker.
2 The envelope around the nucleus has disintegrated and the chromosomes begin to move towards the midline – the 'equator'.
3 All the chromosomes have lined up along the equator, where the cell will divide.

body's white blood cells to kill abnormal cells. A white blood cell has to make contact with a mutant to kill it, but the mutant will try to prevent contact by putting out a barrier of blisters on its surface.

Some research scientists believe that the production of mutant cells is not unusual, but that a regulating system in the body usually kills them off. When this regulating system breaks down or is swamped with more mutant cells than it can cope with, cancer is able to develop.

Certain mutant cells multiply much faster than others: cancer of the womb grows slowly, while cancer of the cervix (neck of the womb) is fast-growing. Mutant cells may also travel in the body and start other cancers – so-called 'secondaries' – away from the original site.

There are more than 200 forms of cancer, and doctors give them special names according to the part of the body or the body system mainly affected. The largest group are carcinomas – cancers of the external and internal linings of the body, its cavities and most of its organs, such as the lung and the breast. The second group, sarcomas, affect connective tissues such as muscles and bones. Individual cancers include LEUKAEMIA (cancer of the blood), lymphoma (cancer of the lymph glands), osteosarcoma (cancer of the bones), encephaloma (cancer of the brain) and melanoma (a form of skin cancer).

In Britain there are about 250,000 new cases of cancer each year. Approximately a quarter of these will be lung cancer in men; about one-fifth, breast cancer in women; and about one-tenth will be skin cancer in both sexes. Some 150,000 cancer victims die each year – almost half of them from lung, breast or bowel cancer.

About two-thirds of cancer victims who die are 65 or more years old. As the population avoids or survives infections such as diphtheria, scarlet fever and tuberculosis, which were the big killers of previous generations, more of them eventually die from cancer.

Causes of cancer Heredity may be a factor with certain cancers. For example, a woman is four times more likely than average to develop breast cancer if her mother, aunt or sister has had it. People who are only light smokers themselves are 15 times more likely than other light smokers to develop lung cancer if their parents have had lung cancer. People with fair or ruddy skin, red or light hair and blue eyes – all influenced by heredity – are more likely to develop skin cancer than dark-skinned people. Some leukaemias also run in families.

People who suffer from certain diseases, including ulcerative COLITIS, pernicious ANAEMIA and viral hepatitis B, also run an extra risk of developing cancer.

However, much more important than heredity or disease are environmental factors. We may take up the same occupation or adopt the same unhealthy diet or lifestyle as our parents and so develop the same illnesses – but not through heredity. The world we live in and the way we treat our bodies play a large part in the development of cancers.

Smoking, inhaling asbestos particles, excessive fat in the diet, heavy alcohol consumption, overexposure to sunlight or radiation from nuclear waste or leakage (as at Chernobyl) and contact with benzopyrenes (chemicals used in dry cleaning) are all known to increase the likelihood of developing cancer. See HEALTH HAZARDS.

We can avoid or limit our exposure to some of these so that they are not such a danger. Basking in the sun for an hour or two is unlikely to cause skin cancer, but frequent sunbathing without using a protective cream might – especially if you have a fair or ruddy complexion.

The occasional alcoholic drink will not give you liver cancer, but frequent and excessive drinking, especially with heavy smoking, could well do so.

Psychological factors also seem to play a part. People who bottle up their feelings are at greater risk than those who release them. DEPRESSION, GRIEF at bereavement or some other loss, and other forms of mental STRESS make people more likely to develop cancer.

What the therapists recommend

Most alternative therapies aim to stimulate a patient's life force, or will to live, and so bring to bear the body's natural defences. It is these defences that prevent cancers from developing in most people most of the time. The mutant cells are regarded not only as the cause of cancer but as a symptom that the body's balance has been

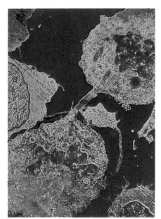
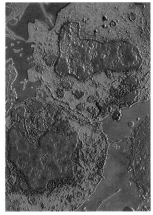

4 Division has begun with a deepening furrow forming around the cell. The matched pairs of chromatids have separated, with one from each pair moving to opposite ends of the cell. Two separate but identical groups now exist, each carrying the same genetic code.
5 Only a narrow neck of cytoplasm is left connecting the two parts of the cell. The chromosomes within each part of the cell start to lengthen again and there is the beginning

of an envelope forming around each cluster.
6 The cells, now completely formed, have their chromosome clusters contained in envelopes. Before division starts again, the chromosomes will duplicate their genetic material so that matched chromatids exist ready for the next division. Cancer may begin when a fault occurs somewhere in the replication process, so that a cell receives a faulty genetic message.

disturbed. Some practitioners concentrate particularly on diet to restore a proper balance; others give more emphasis to the patient's mind and emotions.

NATUROPATHY

The emphasis is on a healthy diet and lifestyle, not with the claim of curing diagnosed cancers, but of preventing cancer from developing and for use alongside or as a follow-up to orthodox methods of treatment.

The various regimes developed by alternative therapists have several recommended courses in common: a largely vegetarian or vegan diet (see VEGETARIANISM); a high proportion of raw, and preferably organic, foods; a low intake of sugar and salt; and the clearing of poisonous waste from the body – by FASTING or by enemas, for example.

Much medical research has shown that bowel, breast and stomach cancers in particular occur less in societies where the diet is low in fat and meat, and high in FIBRE. The benefit of fibre may be that it speeds up the movement of waste products through the digestive tract so that cancer-causing substances do not linger in the body.

Both the Gerson diet and the Bristol diet, the best known of the regimes used to help cancer patients, are based on these principles.

Gerson Therapy The diet that is the basis of this treatment was devised in the 1920s by a German physician, Dr Max Gerson, to bring his own migraines under control. He recommended it to his patients and many benefited, including some with tuberculosis or cancer.

His treatment was designed to clear the body of accumulated poisons, stimulate enzyme production to improve the digestion, correct the body's balance of VITAMINS and MINERALS, and promote a positive attitude to the body – and to life in general.

Carrying out the strict regime is time-consuming. Every hour, 13 freshly made juices are taken, one made from oranges, four from leafy greenstuff, four from carrots and apples and four from calves' liver. All items must be organically grown or reared. Caffeine enemas and castor oil are taken regularly to cleanse the system. Meals are mainly based on salads, oats and baked potatoes.

For full details of the dietary treatment, contact The Gerson Institute, PO Box 430, Bonita, California 92002, USA. Patients may suffer vomiting, diarrhoea and skin sores while the cleansing process goes on. Therapists support them with COUNSELLING.

Bristol Diet A strict diet devised by Dr Alec Forbes was a major part of the treatment originally offered by the Bristol Cancer Help Centre. Patients started by eating a low-fat

Signs to watch for

You should report any of the following signs and symptoms to your doctor at once. They are among the first indications of cancer, which is more likely to be treated successfully if it is discovered in the early stages.

These symptoms can also indicate a number of other, non-cancerous conditions, so do not be fearful and mistakenly assume that you have a serious illness if you notice one of the signs. Instead, find out its cause and have it treated promptly.

Persistent coughing; coughing up blood.
Skin sores (ulcers) that do not heal.
Blood in the urine or faeces.
Persisting changes in bowel habits.
Lump or puckered area in a breast.
Blood-stained vaginal discharge.
Vaginal bleeding between periods, after intercourse or after the MENOPAUSE.
Lump in the neck.
Unexplained weight loss.
Indigestion with no known cause.
Persistent tiredness for no reason.

vegan diet with a high proportion of raw food and, as they improved, were slowly allowed to add small quantities of vegetable oil, eggs, poultry and fish.

In recent years, however, the centre has modified this regime and patients now adopt a basically vegetarian diet of fresh fruit and vegetables, whole grains and pulses, with a little fish, free-range poultry or eggs, or even organically farmed red meat for those who wish. More of the food is cooked, and organically produced goat's-milk yoghurt is included for the friendly bacteria it supplies.

For cooking, cold-pressed or virgin olive oil is preferred, and herbs, spices and fruit juice replace salt and sugar. Patients are advised to cut down on tea and coffee, and to switch to herb teas, fresh juices, mineral water, or grain substitutes.

More information about the diet is available from the Cancer Help Centre, Grove House, Cornwallis Grove, Clifton, Bristol BS8 4PG, where cancer patients can also receive aid in the form of MEDITATION, VISUALISATION THERAPY, counselling and PSYCHOTHERAPY.

Megavitamin Therapy This is an extension of the corrective diet therapies. Even with a healthy diet, cancer patients may not get enough of the vitamins and minerals they need because their bodies cannot absorb them properly. So much larger amounts than the usual recommendations are given, to ensure that enough get through. More than 1000 times the usual daily 30mg of vitamin C is prescribed, for example. Large doses of vitamins A, B and E, and of the minerals selenium, zinc, calcium, magnesium and molybdenum may also be given.

PSYCHOTHERAPY

Substantial evidence from studies of cancer patients shows that psychological factors play a part not only in causing their illness but also in their chances of survival. People who are positive, self-assertive, cheerful and able to express their feelings are less likely to develop cancer. Among people who do develop it, those who deny that they have a life-threatening illness and adopt a fighting attitude have a significantly higher chance of surviving longer than those who accept their cancer stoically or feel helpless and hopeless.

Psychological therapies that are used to help cancer patients generally focus on shifting their mood and emotional state. They also give social support that can reduce patients' anxiety and depression. The assumption is that thoughts, feelings and mental images affect bodily states, particularly the IMMUNE SYSTEM.

Immunologists now believe that some cells in the immune system possess what is called natural killer activity. Stress and loneliness can lower natural killer activity while positive attitudes and a belief in one's well-being enhance it, so that the body's own defence mechanism will destroy cancer cells. Therapies to generate such attitudes include RELAXATION AND BREATHING, meditation, mental imagery or visualisation therapy, and HYPNOTHERAPY.

The best known is Dr Carl Simonton's visualisation technique. The patient is asked to see in the mind's eye a battle in which powerful immune cells hunt down and kill weak, confused cancer cells. Many patients say they have felt better after this treatment and have learned to cope with their illness well enough to improve the quality of their life to a significant extent.

Other alternative therapies

Immunoaugmentative Therapy In an attempt to boost the immune system, extracts from human blood known as 'immune protein factors' are injected into the muscle. Some of the blood is from healthy volunteers and some from people with cancer. Dramatic improvements have been claimed.

Acupuncture This has been used to combat the effects of radiotherapy for cancer of the cervix and has produced good results. It has also improved the number of white blood cells – responsible for destroying cancer cells – in patients after radiotherapy. It is mainly used, however, to relieve symptoms or minimise the discomforts that may be caused by orthodox treatment.

An orthodox view

Surgery to remove tumours, radiotherapy to kill cancer cells by radiation, and chemotherapy to stop the multiplication of mutant cells with drugs are the treatments that orthodox medicine considers most effective. But these treatments do not constitute a complete answer to all forms of cancer.

It is becoming increasingly clear that by the time a tumour has grown large enough to be detected, the cancer cells will have been growing for several years and may have spread to other parts of the body, so that surgery may not remove all the cancerous tissue. Nevertheless, removal of the cancer may be necessary to relieve symptoms caused by obstruction as well as to control local spread. Cancers of the breast, lung, bowel, womb and testicles are among those where surgery is most likely to be recommended.

Radiotherapy is often the first choice of treatment in skin cancer and early cancer of the cervix. Not all cancers are sensitive to radiation and the farther away from the skin, the more difficult is the treatment. The techniques in radiotherapy, as in surgery, have improved considerably but there may be unwelcome side effects. Their severity depends partly on the patient's level of well-being before treatment

Monthly check for men

Cancer of the testicles is almost always cured if it is discovered and treated in its early stages. A simple check which you can carry out at home once a month will detect it.

Make the test just after a warm bath when the skin is relaxed. If you find anything unusual, go to see your doctor as soon as possible.

Use the thumb and fingers of both hands to press gently all round the testicles one at a time.

After you have made a few regular checks you will be familiar with what is normal for you and notice any variation from normal. It is normal for one testicle to be a little larger than the other.

The soft lump you will feel at the top and towards the back of each testicle is the epididymis, the sperm-carrying tube to which it is attached.

Check that the testicles are smooth and without swellings. They should be of about matching weight, and no harder or softer than usual.

begins. Tiredness and nausea are by far the most common. Both can be alleviated by drugs. Depression is another frequent side effect. Many radiotherapy centres now employ counsellors to support patients during treatment.

In some cancers, chemotherapy is the preferred treatment, and the response can be excellent. Twenty years ago leukaemia was almost invariably fatal. Now many children are cured simply with chemotherapy. Chemotherapy is also used in treating Hodgkin's disease and for tumours of the testicles and of the bone marrow. More than 50 drugs have been used for treating cancer, and the greatest success has come from giving drugs in combination as a 'cocktail'. Recently, drugs have been developed which attack the cancer cells only. This reduces the side effects, but chemotherapy can still be an unpleasant form of treatment.

Although orthodox treatments do not guarantee a cure, they can halt the spread and should not be discarded. Alternative therapies are controversial and cannot replace normal treatment.

Many patients say that anticancer diets have helped by giving them some positive action they can take. However, there is no scientific evidence that they work. One recent study has even found that some patients who followed the Bristol Centre's programme in addition to receiving orthodox treatment had a poorer survival rate than those with similar cancers who had only conventional therapy. The reason is not known, but some doctors have suggested that a strictly vegan or vegetarian diet may be too extreme.

Opinion varies as to the worth of large vitamin supplements. Clinical trials have failed to show increases in survival time. However, doctors do recommend them for patients who have an increased risk of developing stomach cancer.

Herbal extracts are not regarded as effective, and one containing Laetrile (bitter almond) is dangerous because it contains cyanide. There are dangers also in injecting supposed immune factor extracts from blood: some extracts have contained the hepatitis B virus.

Orthodox doctors do not accept that visualisation, hypnotherapy or meditation have been proven to affect tumour growth or the survival time of patients. But they recognise that individual and group psychotherapy can show an individual and group effect on survival time. It is generally accepted in orthodox medicine that psychological support is a vital component in treating cancer.

As with diet therapies, any benefit may be in taking positive steps that increase belief in one's power to recover. Such belief, with its presumed effect on the immune system, may account for instances of 'spontaneous regression' (reduction of a tumour) by SPIRITUAL HEALING.

CANDIDA

This is a fungal disorder more commonly called THRUSH. It is caused by an excess amount of the yeast-like fungus *Candida albicans*, which lives on the skin and vulva, and in the mouth, bowel and vagina.

Normally the fungus is harmless. However, it sometimes sets up an infection characterised by sore white patches which usually affect the mouth or vagina.

CARPAL TUNNEL SYNDROME

Tissues inside a space in the wrist called the carpal tunnel can sometimes swell, pinching a nerve and causing the painful condition known as carpal tunnel syndrome. There is a feeling of numbness, tingling and pain in the index finger and first finger of the affected hand, and also weakness in the thumb.

Middle-aged and pregnant women are the principal sufferers, especially those who use their fingers a lot, such as typists, housewives and pianists. The condition is often worse at night, when the pain and tingling may spread up the forearm and interrupt sleep. Hanging the affected arm – or arms – over the side of the bed sometimes brings relief; a splint on the wrist may also help.

Without treatment, the symptoms will gradually worsen over the months or years. Anyone developing the symptoms should see an orthodox doctor before using any alternative treatment.

What the therapists recommend
NATUROPATHY
Self help The cause can be either fluid pressure on the median nerve within the carpal tunnel, or inflammation of the tissues making up the tunnel itself. When there is fluid build-up, vitamin B6 is believed to be effective in reducing the local swelling.

Using cold packs for ten minutes twice a day can also help. However, in persistent cases surgery may be recommended, as in orthodox medicine.

An orthodox view
A doctor will usually prescribe painkillers – or, if the condition is particularly troublesome, inject the wrist with cortisone to reduce the tissue swelling. In severe cases, he may recommend a minor operation to relieve the compression.

CATARACTS

One or both eyes can be affected by a cataract – a cloudy area in the lens which causes blurred or impaired vision. Cataracts usually appear in old age, as advancing years bring a deterioration in the blood supply to the lens. In many cases, one eye is affected more than the other, and most elderly people who have cataracts have little trouble with their vision. But if seeing becomes difficult they should consult a doctor.

What the therapists recommend
Naturopathy Some naturopaths believe that cataracts are partly the result of a deficiency of riboflavin (vitamin B2), which must be rectified. Vitamin C is also thought to be useful in protecting the eye lenses against harmful effects of sunlight.

An orthodox view
In severe cases – especially if the sight in the 'best' eye is impaired – a doctor may refer his patient to an eye specialist. An operation may then be performed to remove the cataract or cataracts. The operation is simple and vision is restored with a contact lens or a plastic lens implanted within the eye.

CATARRH

Any inflammation or irritation of the membranes that line the passages of the throat, nose and lungs can cause catarrh – a thick mucus. A little watery mucus is necessary to protect and lubricate the membranes, but too much and/or too thick mucus can cause a blocked or runny nose, COUGHS or earache. If the symptoms last more than a few days they may point to an infection (if the mucus is yellow or green) or COLDS, SINUS PROBLEMS, a poor diet or ALLERGY.

What the therapists recommend
NATUROPATHY
Self help Eat a nutritious wholefood diet including plenty of fresh fruit, salads, vegetables, fish, nuts, honey and wholegrain cereals. Drink plenty of spring water or fresh juices. GARLIC is said to help.

Take regular outdoor exercise and make sure you are getting enough sleep (see SLEEP DISORDERS). Try to avoid foods that are thought to encourage mucus production, such as milk and milk products, meat, eggs, animal fats, pulses, and those containing white flour, white sugar or FOOD ADDITIVES.

A treatment which can provide effective relief is to add the juice of half a lemon to a cup of warm water in a bowl, and inhale the mixture gently through the nostrils, right up to the back of the nose. It may make you sneeze and splutter, but is a good way of clearing catarrh from the nose. Repeat several times a day.

Consultation Advice will be given about diet, eliminating impurities from the body and treating CONSTIPATION – which naturopaths say is often associated with catarrh. Tests for allergies – especially milk and dairy products – may be done and, if necessary, a special diet will be drawn up. Supplements such as the vitamin B-complex, vitamin C, bioflavinoids and zinc are sometimes prescribed. Initial FASTING or a RAW FOOD DIET may be suggested, but must be supervised.

HERBAL MEDICINE
Self help Infusions (see p. 184) of hyssop, slippery elm, marsh-mallow, elderflower, ribwort or catmint seeds are believed to help. Add honey or lemon juice if you prefer – they are also good for the mucous membranes. Some herbalists recommend a combination of equal quantities of hyssop, eyebright and yarrow taken as an infusion. Other helpful herbs include rosemary, *Echinacea*, white horehound, Irish moss and elecampane.

HOMOEOPATHY
Self help Homoeopaths recommend *Nat. mur.* for catarrh that has the consistency of egg white and causes sneezing; *Kali bic.* for stringy yellow or white catarrh; *Hydrastis* for continual dripping at the back of the nose and blocked ears; *Arsenicum iodum* if you feel run down and have a runny nose; *Graphites* for catarrh with constipation, skin irritation around the nose and a chill; *Pulsatilla* for a head cold and thick yellowish-white mucus, and *Euphrasia* for a cold with watering eyes and runny nose. In each case take one tablet (6C potency) every two hours six times, then three times daily until better.

Other alternative treatments
Aromatherapy Use basil, eucalyptus, black pepper, hyssop, lavender, lemon, marjoram, peppermint, thyme or cedarwood oil in a bath or steam inhalation. A gargle said to be effective can be made from one drop each of eucalyptus, lemon and tea tree or cedarwood essential oils in half a cup of water; stir before each mouthful.

Biochemic Tissue Salts *Kali sulph.* and combination remedy Q are advised for all types of catarrh. In addition, *Ferr. phos.* and combination remedy H may help to get rid of nasal catarrh, and *Kali mur.* is recommended if the secretion is white.

Acupressure Pressure is applied to points at the back of the skull, on either side of the nose, and on the web of the hand.

Acupuncture Treatment usually involves acupuncture at points on the large intestine, stomach and lung meridians.

Massage Facial massage can help to drain the sinuses. If mucus is lodged in the bronchial tubes, superficial stroking massage of the upper back, vibratory petrissage (picking up) over the shoulder muscles and vibratory friction over the lower tip of the breastbone may help to bring it up.

Hydrotherapy Treatments such as mustard footbaths, hot and cold compresses, friction rubs and cold hip-baths may help. Nasal douches and gargling with a teaspoon of salt or baking powder dissolved in a glass of warm water may also give relief.

Reflexology Therapists recommend massage to the reflex areas relating to the nose and sinuses, plus areas relating to the head, eyes, upper lymph nodes and digestive system. See chart, p. 295.

An orthodox view

Doctors do not usually treat catarrh by changing your diet or dealing with allergies. Instead, you may be given antibiotics if there is an infection, or advised to use decongestant nose drops to alleviate the symptoms.

CELLULITE

The term 'cellulite' was coined by certain French doctors for what they believe is a form of fat that accumulates in women, causing the thighs, bottom, upper arms and stomach to look lumpy and dimpled. It afflicts women – even slim ones – mostly at the MENOPAUSE, and is difficult to get rid of.

The cause is believed by many European doctors and many health and beauty experts to be a build-up of waste materials in the body tissues, creating pockets of water, fat and impurities, and encouraging the formation of a 'sludge' in the blood, leading to CIRCULATION PROBLEMS. However, the theory is controversial, and most doctors in Britain and the USA do not believe that cellulite is a special form of fat, and do not acknowledge it as a medical condition (see below).

What the therapists recommend

NATUROPATHY

Self help A 75 per cent raw food diet is claimed to prevent cellulite forming, to eliminate existing cellulite and to prevent a further build-up (see EATING FOR HEALTH and RAW FOOD DIET). Eating two or three pieces

of citrus fruit a day – including the pith – is also said to help.

These foods are also recommended:

<u>Beetroot juice</u> to help the liver to break down stored fats. Make fresh beetroot juice with an extractor, or buy it from health food stores, and drink a 4fl oz glass (120ml) daily.

<u>Celery</u> to help remove excess fluid from the body. Eat it raw, or make a fresh juice cocktail with celery, beetroot and carrots.

<u>Cucumber</u> to make the kidneys eliminate more wastes. Extract and drink the juice or eat a large cucumber salad every day.

<u>Seaweed</u> contains minerals, proteins, vitamins and iodine. It is said to promote a smooth skin and to get fats moving in the body. Kelp (seaweed) tablets are available from health food stores and some chemists; other edible sea plants can be found in some health food stores and oriental food shops.

<u>Spirulina</u> is a blue-green algae plant, available as tablets or capsules from health food stores. It is held to be highly nutritious, while also suppressing appetite. It can be taken safely in doses of up to ¼oz (8g) a day.

<u>Watermelons</u> are said to help remove excess fluid from the body.

Skin-brushing

This is a technique claimed to remove toxic wastes directly through the skin, and to stimulate the lymphatic system. Use a long-handled, natural-bristle brush or a friction glove – available from chemists – and follow a daily routine, brushing after getting up in the morning and before going to bed. Brush your whole body – except your face – starting gently, then using a firmer action as you get used to the feel of it.

Consultation Naturopaths believe that the underlying cause may be the typical Western diet, containing too much starch, fat, protein and sugar. A practitioner will prescribe a diet that includes lots of fresh raw vegetables.

He may also advise you to combine the diet with 30 minutes' general EXERCISE three times a week to improve circulation and general fitness. But check with your doctor first, to see if you are fit enough.

Finally, a skin-brushing regime (see illustrations below) and, if you are in good health, an occasional SAUNA BATH could be recommended, or alternating hot and cold sprays on the thighs and pelvis.

An orthodox view

Most British and American doctors believe that cellulite is simply ordinary fat pulled downwards by gravity, and that when this is lost, so are the dimples. Because of its link with the menopause, doctors also believe that hormonal changes may be a contributing factor.

However, research in France, Italy and Germany has revealed that CONSTIPATION, a poor lymphatic system, poor circulation and

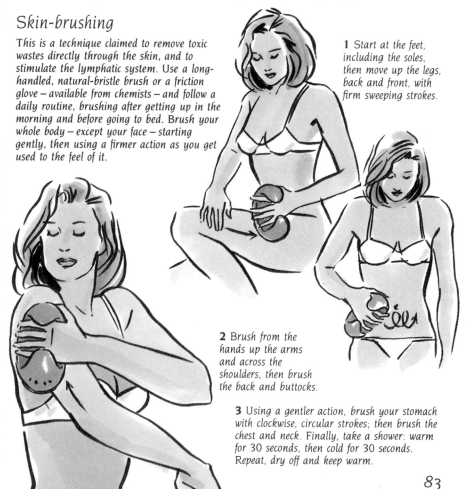

1 *Start at the feet, including the soles, then move up the legs, back and front, with firm sweeping strokes.*

2 *Brush from the hands up the arms and across the shoulders, then brush the back and buttocks.*

3 *Using a gentler action, brush your stomach with clockwise, circular strokes; then brush the chest and neck. Finally, take a shower: warm for 30 seconds, then cold for 30 seconds. Repeat, dry off and keep warm.*

weak functioning of the kidneys and liver are all common in women prone to cellulite.

The orthodox cure in Britain is simply to lose weight. European commercial cellulite creams, which are massaged into affected areas, are available from most chemists, but the general opinion of the majority of health and beauty experts is that these cannot work on their own, and that any good results obtained are probably due mostly to the massage involved.

CHAPPING

In cold weather, people are often troubled by chapped skin – especially if they have to wash their hands frequently because of their work. In some cases the skin becomes inflamed and cannot tolerate soap and water.

Wind and cold may also affect the lips, which become cracked and inflamed.

What the therapists recommend

Traditional Medicine Mudpacks – especially those made from clay-rich earth – have been used to treat dry and chapped skin since the Middle Ages. They are said to soften the skin and, as the mud becomes harder and shrinks, to draw impurities in the skin to the surface, and to pull off the top layer of dead cells. They are available at chemists and health food stores. Do not use them if your skin is inflamed.

Glycerine mixed with rosewater is said to prevent rough and chapped hands even in the coldest weather. Rub the mixture well into the fingers and backs of the hands and then dry them with a paper towel. For very fine and sensitive skin, mix a little cocoa-butter with half its quantity of pure olive oil and rub gently into the skin.

Aromatherapy Benzoin and patchouli are strongly recommended, lavender and geranium are also useful. Add 15-20 drops of the chosen oil to 2fl oz (60ml) of base white carrier lotion and apply to the skin.

An orthodox view

Most doctors feel that there is no need to use anything more than the proprietary creams, lotions and lip salves from a chemist.

For housewives or kitchen workers, whose hands are often in water, a barrier cream applied in the morning, before starting work, can help. Otherwise, ordinary vanishing or cold creams should help (see also NATURAL AIDS TO BEAUTY).

Lanolin cream has also proved effective, but as it comes from wool fat some people may be allergic to it (see ALLERGY).

CHARISMATIC HEALING
The curative power of prayer

The treatment of disease by charismatic healing is based on Christian faith and prayer. Meetings at which people pray for their own good health, as well as that of relatives and friends, are held in churches of many denominations. In Catholic churches they often form part of a normal Sunday service. At any time during the week such meetings are sometimes held in the assembly places of Quakers and other religious groups.

The therapy – which comes from the Greek word *charis*, meaning 'grace' – dates back to Biblical times and Christ's miracles. Charismatic healing seeks to carry on this work through the Holy Spirit. Healers may be laymen or priests, who appeal to the Holy Spirit to release healing forces and direct them at the sick – whether they are aware of it or not (see ABSENT HEALING). Prayer sessions can last from five minutes to several hours. See also HEALERS AND HEALING.

As well as praying for divine healing, many believers use personal prayer to help prevent sickness. They feel this brings about a more positive and optimistic approach to life – one in which physical and mental illness does not so easily occur.

Who it can help Most believers in charismatic healing are practising Christians who go regularly to church. However, anyone who believes in God can pray at home for the blessing of good health.

How healing helped Sir Francis

Perhaps the best-known case of charismatic healing is that of British round-the-world yachtsman Sir Francis Chichester (1901-72). He developed lung CANCER at the age of 56 and spurned conventional surgery. Instead, he relied on the prayers of his second wife, Sheila, and of his friends to cure him. He also received treatment at a NATUROPATHY clinic.

Miraculously, he said afterwards, he made a complete recovery and in 1960 won the first solo transatlantic yacht race. His record-setting solo voyage around the world took 226 days' sailing time in 1966-70.

An orthodox view

Although doctors recognise that so-called 'miracle cures' have sometimes occurred, they think of them as 'spontaneous remissions', in which the body heals itself. However, many people do receive comfort by attending prayer meetings, and their suffering becomes easier to bear.

CHICKENPOX

This highly infectious disease – with its irritating, itching rash and blisters – usually affects children. It is milder in childhood, so it is best not to keep children away from school during an outbreak, for catching chickenpox also brings immunity from it later in life, when its effects can be more serious.

Known medically as *varicella*, it is caused by the virus which also causes SHINGLES. Symptoms show between 12 and 14 days after infection, starting with a raised temperature and an itchy rash – usually on the body – which spreads to the limbs, face and head. The pink spots soon turn into watery blisters, then burst or shrivel and, after about five days, form scabs. Adult sufferers feel quite ill for the first few days.

The virus can be passed to people in close contact with the sufferer from about four days before the rash appears until the spots have gone. Although the sufferer becomes immune to the disease, the virus may remain in the system and cause shingles later.

What the therapists recommend
NATUROPATHY
Self help Raw fruit and vegetable juices are recommended: fresh orange and lemon juice, sweetened with honey if necessary, and a daily intake of about 1 pint (600ml) of carrot juice, mixed with ¼ pint (150ml) of watercress juice to prevent dehydration. During convalescence, a modest wholefood diet (see EATING FOR HEALTH) is held to be beneficial.
Consultation Practitioners see the symptoms as the natural reaction to infection. A supervised fast may be advised, with the aim of raising the blood's white cell count – and in doing so, the temperature – to kill the virus and stimulate the IMMUNE SYSTEM. Sponging the spots with tepid water during the first few days may also be suggested.

HERBAL MEDICINE
Self help To soothe irritation, an infusion (p. 184) of elder flowers sponged on the spots is said to help. Alternatively, try tincture of comfrey, or essential oil of lavender on the

spots, being careful to avoid the eyes. Aloe vera gel can reduce the itching.

To ease the fever for children between six and ten, try a dessertspoon of herbal tea four times daily: yarrow, lime blossom, camomile flowers or meadowsweet, with honey. For younger children give 2 teaspoonfuls.

Consultation A practitioner may advise taking GARLIC – either raw or in capsule form – and eucalyptus, as an infusion. Boil 1oz (30g) of eucalyptus leaves in 1¾ pints (1 litre) of water. Cover for ten minutes, strain, cool and give 1 teaspoonful three times daily.

Other alternative treatments

Homoeopathy At the onset of symptoms, *Rhus tox.* is said to soothe restlessness and ease the irritation. Other recommendations include *Antimonium tart.* if the child is irritable and has large blisters, a cough and cold symptoms; *Pulsatilla nigricans* if the child is weepy and not thirsty, and *Aconitum napellus* if there is fever, or the pulse rate increases.

Aromatherapy Try lemon tea, made with three drops of essential oil of lemon, one teabag and 1½ pints (900ml) of water. Drink a cupful three times daily.

Biochemic Tissue Salts *Ferr. phos.* is recommended to combat feverishness and restlessness; and *Kali mur.* once the fever has cleared and the spots blister.

An orthodox view

Many doctors feel that some alternative treatments may help and that they will not do any harm. However, they say that most cases can be treated at home by keeping the rash clean and dry, and easing itching with calamine lotion. Avoid picking spots – this can result in permanent pockmarks. There is no immunisation against the virus.

Liquids are important, rather than solid food, and the patient should get plenty of rest. Consult your doctor only if the eyes are affected; if there is a high fever or excessive coughing and vomiting; or if the spots become overinflamed. If the lungs, skin or ears are infected, a doctor may then prescribe antibiotics.

Once the infection is overcome, recovery is complete – and the spots will leave scars only if they are scratched or become infected.

CHILBLAINS

Exposure to the cold can give people with sensitive skin or poor circulation chilblains – reddish-blue swellings that itch and burn. They occur when blood vessels shrink so severely that the skin's supply of blood and oxygen is severely reduced. Chilblains mostly break out on the toes and fingers, but they may affect the ears and other parts of the body. Never scratch chilblains – it only makes them worse.

What the therapists recommend

Traditional Medicine According to folklore even severe chilblains can be eased – if not cured – by a paste made of glycerine and honey. Mix a tablespoon of each with the white of an egg and a tablespoon of flour. Beat the ingredients into a fine paste and spread it over the swellings – first making sure they are clean and dry. Cover the sticky paste with a cloth or bandage and leave in place for 24 hours.

Naturopathy Many therapists believe the best cure to be a form of HYDROTHERAPY. First bathe your feet in warm water for about three minutes – then dip them in cold for one minute. Repeat for about 20 minutes morning or evening, always finishing with cold.

It may also help to massage your feet afterwards in a footbath containing 1 tablespoon of calendula or mustard oil to 4 pints (2.3 litres) of warm water. Vitamins E and C may also be prescribed for people particularly susceptible to chilblains.

Homoeopathy Recommended remedies involve rubbing the chilblains with *Tamus* ointment when the chilblains are cracked; *Rhus tox.* applied twice a day when chilblains are inflamed and itch; and *Agaricus muscaria*, applied every three hours when there is much burning, itching and redness. Use *Petroleum* when the skin is cracked and broken, with a tendency to ulcerate or chap, or where there are split fingertips. *Carbo veg.* is also for itching, burning, and when the chilblains feel worse in a warm bed. Apply the chosen remedy, in the 6th potency, three times a day for two weeks.

Nutritional Therapy Chilblains are said to respond well to a calcium-rich diet, particularly fresh green vegetables and oranges, almonds, yoghurt and sesame seeds. Vitamin supplements held to be beneficial include vitamin B-complex (500mg a day).

An orthodox view

Doctors point out that, provided you do not expose susceptible areas to the cold, chilblains usually clear up without treatment in two to three weeks. However, they feel that alternative treatments may help. The best way to prevent chilblains is to wear warm clothing – especially gloves, trousers and shoes. Do not smoke, as nicotine reduces the blood circulation in the skin (see SMOKING). People with poor circulation should take regular EXERCISE to stimulate the blood flow.

To soothe the burning and itching, doctors may prescribe E45 cream.

CHILL

A chill is often the first sign of a number of ailments but usually heralds COLDS or a FEVER – especially if accompanied by raised body temperature and alternating bouts of shivering and sweating.

Some people believe wrongly that a nip of brandy or whisky will 'take the chill off'. Alcohol dilates blood vessels just beneath the skin, bringing extra blood to the surface, causing you to lose body heat. An immediate feeling of warmth is soon replaced by an even greater chill – particularly if the 'nip' is taken outside. Better simply to stay indoors and keep warm.

CHIROPRACTIC
Relieving pain by joint manipulation

By the skilful use of their hands, chiropractors set out to correct disorders of the joints, muscles and – particularly – the spine. Spinal problems can cause pain not only in the spine itself, but in other parts of the body – including the shoulder, arm, hip and leg. In addition, the disorders can also sometimes bring on SCIATICA as well as back problems such as LUMBAGO and SLIPPED DISC. In some cases they are even said to cause ASTHMA, ARTHRITIS, CATARRH, CONSTIPATION, MIGRAINE, PERIOD PROBLEMS and STRESS.

In some ways chiropractic is similar to OSTEOPATHY – for example, neither therapy uses drugs or surgery. But the major difference between them is that chiropractors make far greater use of X-rays and conventional diagnostic methods than osteopaths.

Who it can help More than 90 per cent of a chiropractor's patients suffer from some kind of musculo-skeletal pain – especially low BACK PAIN and NECK PAIN. People with whiplash injuries from car accidents – in which the head has been abruptly jerked backwards or forwards – are also high on the list of those seeking treatment.

HEADACHES are another common ailment treated by chiropractic. In most cases treated the headache is caused by TENSION contracting the neck muscles – for example, those which help to balance the head on the neck joints at the top of the spine.

Sportsmen suffering from a range of injuries – including strained muscles, sprained joints, damaged ligaments, injured tendons, wrenched knees and TENNIS ELBOW –

may also benefit from chiropractic. In some cases heat or ice applications are used, as well as specific joint manipulation.

There are no age barriers as far as chiropractic is concerned and anyone from babies to senior citizens can be treated.

Difficult births involving the use of forceps can injure a baby's neck or strain its spine, although this may not be apparent at the time of birth. Chiropractors say that it can, however, lead to neck problems or headaches later on in life.

Sometimes, in infancy or early childhood, a baby may fall from a cot, be accidentally dropped, or stumble against furniture when learning to walk. This can jar its spine, causing back pain to develop long afterwards. In some cases a baby's spine can adapt after a short period of pain only to prove troublesome later on. Many childhood or adolescent discomforts are wrongly attributed to 'growing pains', when the root cause may be musculo-skeletal injury.

If a child has had any such accidents, or suffers from puzzling aches or pains, it could be that he or she needs to see a qualified chiropractor – ask your doctor's advice. In any case, chiropractors advise periodic checkups in childhood, to help to avoid spinal or pelvic problems later.

Many older people suffering from back or joint pain rely on painkillers to give them relief. However, this only deals with the symptoms – and the real cause of the pain is often not treated. Chiropractic, it is said, can often help these people considerably.

David Daniel Palmer (1845–1913)

Chiropractic's birth

In 1895 a 'magnetic healer' named Daniel David Palmer treated his office janitor for deafness. The man told Palmer that he had lost his hearing when bending down – he had felt a click in his back, and shortly became deaf. Palmer found that some small bones in the cleaner's spine were misaligned. He manipulated them and the janitor's hearing was restored.

The healer founded the Palmer School of Chiropractic – from the Greek *kheir*, meaning 'hand', and *praktikos*, meaning 'practical'. 'Displacement of any part of the skeletal frame,' he stated, 'may press against nerves, which are the channels of communication, intensifying or decreasing their carrying capacity, creating either too much or not enough functioning, an aberration known as disease.'

During pregnancy, women often suffer from backache due to the increased weight on the spine and difficulty in maintaining their balance. And in childbirth itself changes occur in the pelvis and the sacroiliac joints (the joints at the base of the spine which carry the weight of the body to the legs). Again, this can cause back pain; and the spine can be further damaged after childbirth, when the baby is lifted and carried.

In all these cases chiropractors say that they can help to ease, if not banish, the pain.

Finding a practitioner Increasingly, British doctors are sending patients with back pain to chiropractors for assessment and possible private treatment. Most people are recommended to practitioners by others who have benefited from the therapy themselves.

Always make sure that a practitioner is fully qualified. Most chiropractors today will have the letters DC (Diploma in Chiropractic) after their name, but from 1991 those who have undergone a four-year Bachelor of Science course at the Anglo-European College of Chiropractic in Bournemouth will be able to use the suffix BSc Chiropractic. Alternatively, contact the British Chiropractic Association, Premier House, 10 Greycoat Place, London SW1P 1SB, who will provide a list of registered practitioners in Britain.

Consulting a practitioner At the first consultation the chiropractor will want to know about your medical history, as well as the current problem. He will then examine you, feeling for areas of muscle spasm, pain and tenderness – and discovering which joints are moving properly and which are not.

An X-ray will probably be taken to determine the condition of the spine. This may also reveal signs of arthritis, bone disease or fractures. Finally, the practitioner will decide whether chiropractic treatment will help, or if a fracture or disease means that you should rely on a doctor.

Treatment usually begins at the second visit, after the full diagnosis has been revealed to you. You will be asked to strip to your underwear and women patients may put on a robe. You will stand, sit, or lie on a chiropractic couch – specially designed for manipulative therapy, and various manual treatment techniques may then be used.

A chiropractor at work

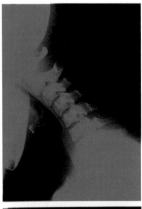

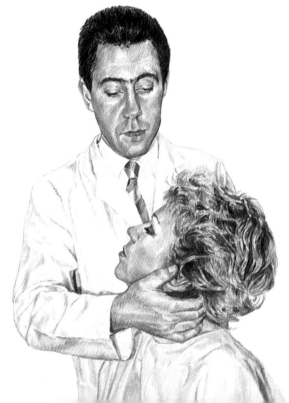

This 16-year-old suffered a whiplash injury, which seriously impaired movement in the vertebrae of her neck (top X-ray). Constant pain and the side effects of the drugs she took made her too ill to go to school.

The chiropractor is shown manipulating the bones in the patient's neck. He was able to restore normal movement (bottom X-ray), and she made a complete recovery.

For example, to adjust (or manipulate) a painful lower lumbar or low back joint, the patient lies on one side. The chiropractor then manually rotates the upper spine one way, and the lower spine the other way. The rotation partially locks the joint to be adjusted. Usually, the patient's uppermost leg is flexed to help in the locking.

The chiropractor then feels the vertebra either just above or below the joint. The patient's position, plus slight pressure by the chiropractor's hand, now takes the joint to the end of its normal range of movement.

Next, the chiropractor makes a very rapid thrust to the vertebra, taking the joint slightly beyond its present range. This restores normal movement to the joint, and by suddenly stretching the muscles which are in spasm around it, helps to relax the deep spinal muscles that control the joint.

The adjustment should not be painful, and afterwards the patient is re-examined. The locked joint should now be moving more freely and, because the muscles have been relaxed, the area should be more flexible.

Some patients will feel relief from pain immediately; others may experience aching, soreness and stiffness later that day, or the day after. In certain cases four or more treatments may be necessary before the pain starts to go. Generally speaking, chronic (long-lasting) cases need more treatment than acute (severe and sudden) cases.

An orthodox view

There is an increasing amount of co-operation between doctors and chiropractors. It is limited, however, due to the comparatively small – though growing – number of practitioners in Britain.

Like osteopathy, chiropractic is now a well-accepted method of dealing with musculo-skeletal problems. If the practitioner is well trained, most doctors would have no difficulty in accepting the validity of the assessment and treatment carried out. However, orthodox practitioners do not approve of chiropractors treating general disease states, such as asthma or DIABETES.

CIRCULATION PROBLEMS

Poor circulation – when the body's flow of blood is restricted – can lead to a range of ailments, including ANGINA, CHILBLAINS, CRAMP, DIZZINESS, FROSTBITE and VARICOSE VEINS. A severe circulation problem such as blood clotting can lead to HEART DISORDERS.

What the therapists recommend

Naturopathy A diet which includes plenty of FIBRE and fresh green vegetables is recommended to avoid circulation problems (see EATING FOR HEALTH). A diet rich in fish and fish oils may be prescribed in certain cases. In addition, you should take plenty of EXERCISE – such as walking and swimming – and not let yourself become overweight (see SLIMMING THE NATURAL WAY). It is also advisable to stop SMOKING, as nicotine damages the arteries.

Many practitioners believe that vitamin supplements – especially vitamins C and E – can play a vital part in preventing the build-up of cholesterol in the body – see ARTERIES (HARDENING).

Herbal Medicine Practitioners recommend several remedies to improve circulation, depending on the cause, including cayenne, hawthorn and prickly ash. They are normally prescribed in tincture form, amounts depending on individual circumstances. Advice on diet and exercise may also be given.

An orthodox view

In general, orthodox doctors think that diet, exercise, weightwatching and the giving up of smoking are key factors in preventing circulation problems.

CLAUSTRO-PHOBIA

One of the most common forms of ANXIETY is claustrophobia – a phobia (exaggerated fear) of crowded places and being shut up in small spaces, such as lifts. When the sufferer feels confined, symptoms of TENSION, HYPERVENTILATION, rapid pulse and SWEATING are experienced. Everyday life is disrupted because the sufferer avoids the situations that make him tense.

The condition is often an expression of an underlying mental problem of which the sufferer is not aware, such as STRESS, FEAR or an emotionally traumatic experience during childhood. It may also be hereditary.

What the therapists recommend

HYPNOTHERAPY
Consultation After discussing your problem, the hypnotherapist will place you in a trance, during which he will suggest changes that will affect your behaviour and the way you react to the world. These will be remembered by the unconscious mind. The hypnotist would also gradually take you out of

your home in your imagination, and repeated sessions would eventually desensitise you to the problem. Hypnotherapy is said to be able to cure phobias, and to work faster than conventional psychotherapy.

NATUROPATHY
Consultation A naturopath will suggest a mainly raw wholefood diet (see EATING FOR HEALTH) and may use KINESIOLOGY muscle-testing techniques to find any food allergy that may be causing the problem.

Self help For stress, high potency vitamin B complex tablets, available from health food stores, are suggested – up to 50mg two or three times daily, reducing gradually to one daily. Vitamin C is also said to help guard against stress – take 200mg with each meal. Zinc and magnesium mineral supplements may also be helpful in a 100mg zinc and magnesium combination. A naturopath will often work alongside a psychotherapist and help in teaching specific relaxation exercises.

Other alternative treatments

Acupressure You can help yourself to relax by gently massaging an acupressure point in the web of either hand – between the thumb and the index finger.

Autogenics This simple system of mental exercise can help the body and mind to relax, releasing you from stress and the abnormal pattern of behaviour it has been causing. Training is with a qualified practitioner and, once learned, autogenics is a technique you can use at home.

Homoeopathy A general remedy is _Argentum nitricum_, and _Aconite_ is said to help people who are fearful and apprehensive before an ordeal and fear closed spaces and crowds. Take the 30th potency every ten minutes until relief is found.

Reflexology The generally relaxing effect of this treatment may well be helpful, but professional treatment should be sought.

Bach Remedies Mimulus if the fear is well-defined; Aspen for vague apprehensiveness; Rock rose if it escalates into panic; Rescue Remedy for an acute attack.

An orthodox view

A careful case history is prepared and tests may be made to check whether the problem is caused by anxiety or is inherited. Treatment for severe anxiety may include COUNSELLING, with tranquillisers to relieve symptoms and help the sufferer to relax and cope better in small, crowded spaces.

BEHAVIOURAL THERAPY may also be prescribed by doctors, and during it you are faced with claustrophobic situations for gradually longer periods. This may be combined with PSYCHOTHERAPY involving both the sufferer and his family. See also PHOBIAS.

CLINICAL ECOLOGY
Overcoming sensitivities to food and other substances

The idea that people are made ill by their environment – the basis of clinical ecology – is far from new. The father of medical science, Hippocrates, a Greek physician of the 5th century BC, knew of reactions to certain foods. Foods are the most common of the environmental factors that cause illness, but pesticides, fungicides, weedkillers, dust, pollen, petrol and diesel fumes, cleaning agents and many other chemical pollutants take their toll (see HEALTH HAZARDS).

Medical interest in patients' abnormally sensitive reactions to foods and chemicals swelled in the United States from the 1920s. In Britain, clinical ecology began to attract the attention of doctors in the 1970s. Many now accept that physical sensitivity short of ALLERGY does cause illness, but others find a major obstacle in the fact that no conventionally acceptable test for true allergy helps in diagnosing ecological illnesses.

Research into food and chemical sensitivity is slow. It is an unpromising area for the pharmaceutical companies that fund much medical research, since the treatments are unlikely to involve drugs that they could market. But investigations made so far suggest that patients have abnormalities in their IMMUNE SYSTEM.

People with true allergy have abnormally high amounts of a blood protein called immunoglobulin E (IgE). People with food and chemical sensitivities have increased amounts of the more common immunoglobulin G (IgG). The IgG molecules seem to lodge in certain parts of the body and produce inflammation. Depending on where they lodge, different symptoms are produced. If they lodge in the lining of the nose, they may cause a constantly streaming nose and frequent SNEEZING; in the intestine they may cause chronic DIARRHOEA; in the brain they can produce MIGRAINE.

The mechanisms that set off the abnormal reactions are of several kinds. The lining of the stomach or intestine may be irritated, especially by wheat, bran or spicy foods and especially when the lining is unsound. An enzyme deficiency may make a patient unable to cope with a food: insufficient lactase, for example, leaves the system unable to cope with milk, which then acts as a poison. In some people a psychological reaction to food sets off the abnormal immune response. Other patients can react almost like drug addicts in their craving for certain substances, for example the tyramine in chocolate or the caffeine in coffee.

Abnormal bowel bacteria cause sensitivity in a large number of people. The bacteria may be there as a result of taking antibiotics, which can kill friendly as well as harmful organisms. In the bowel, friendly bacteria are often not replaced, or the balance of bacteria is disturbed and too much of a yeast known as *Candida albicans* is produced.

In appropriate cases, a clinical ecologist identifies the foods or chemicals to which a patient is sensitive, to ascertain if possible what mechanism sets off the abnormal reaction, and to advise on treatment to avoid or reduce the reaction. Medical specialists, including doctors, involved in clinical ecology believe that ecological illness is affecting more and more people: at present 10-30 per cent of the population.

As a rule, the foods patients eat most are those to which they are sensitive. Milk and dairy products head the list, followed by sugar, then wheat, coffee, tea, chocolate, eggs, and lastly yeast. But outside these commonly occurring items are many others that trigger trouble in some individuals. Similarly with chemical triggers, the substances people are exposed to most are the likeliest sources of their intolerance. The trigger items, whether foods or chemicals, will occur not only singly, but often combined with others. Patients need to know the contents of prepared foods, household cleaning preparations and other products that could contain the source of their intolerance.

Who it can help Numerous symptoms may indicate ecological disease. Completely different symptoms are often triggered in different people by the same cause. Wheat, for example, will cause migraine in one person who is intolerant to it but COLITIS in another. In children, HYPERACTIVITY, disturbed sleep, stomach upsets, COELIAC DISEASE (a sensitivity in the bowel to gluten), ECZEMA, ASTHMA and migraine are among the symptoms. In adults, the symptoms include HEADACHES, DIGESTIVE PROBLEMS, night sweating, PALPITATIONS, RHEUMATISM, INSOMNIA, fatigue and BLADDER PROBLEMS.

People who suffer repeatedly from any of these symptoms, especially without apparent cause, may find a clinical ecologist able to pinpoint the source of the trouble. Sensitivity is increased after a prolonged viral infection such as GLANDULAR FEVER or INFLUENZA, and such cases can also be helped.

Finding a therapist Ask your doctor for the names of any medically qualified colleagues who practise clinical ecology – or of alternative practitioners who have effectively treated cases similar to yours. If your doctor is not helpful, you are recommended to contact Action Against Allergy, 43 The Downs, London SW20 8HG, asking for the names and addresses of any experienced clinical ecologists working in your area.

The methods used by clinical ecologists vary widely. Choose a therapist who is a skilled tester, not one who relies solely on the elimination diet. A therapist experienced in KINESIOLOGY, electrical testing (see below) or the ACR technique (see below) would be cheaper than one using more time-consuming methods – and may give you a quicker solution to your problem.

Do not go to practitioners who are not medically qualified unless they are recommended by a most reliable contact; they are unlikely to be skilled and safe in diagnosis. While some alternative practitioners are safe and effective, they tend to be in the minority.
Consulting a therapist Identifying the food or chemical to which you may be sensitive will be the first task. Give all the information you can about your diet and habits to help the therapist compile a list of suspect items. The list may be long and it could take time to establish an order of priority for testing. Often there are several items that cause illness, not just one. Eight techniques are in the repertoire of testers:
Radio-allergic solvents test This is the test most likely to be used in conventional medicine – a blood test that can show that IgE has been produced as an allergic reaction to a particular food. However, the RAST, as it is usually called, does not show whether IgG has been produced in people who are sensitive or intolerant to a substance rather than allergic to it.
Elimination diet In everyday life the patient has no distinct, obvious reaction to the substances that cause illness. The reaction becomes obvious after the patient has taken only fluids (usually as a hospital in-patient) for at least five days, and has then had suspect items reintroduced one by one. The fast puts the patient in a clinically hypersensitive state, in which there is usually a strong reaction within a few minutes to the offending food or chemical.

A similar but less drastic method of identifying food sensitivity is to spend five days on a diet unlikely to cause adverse reactions. This will most commonly be lamb and pears. The suspect foods are then reintroduced one by one. First, the less commonly eaten foods are reintroduced, with the initial meal consisting of one food alone.

If no adverse reaction (such as migraine or sweating, or whatever symptom is usual) occurs within ten minutes, then the next meal can consist of two foods. If the second food is cleared then a third can be introduced, and so on. The most commonly eaten foods such as wheat products, milk and dairy products, yeast and sugar are the last to be reintroduced.

Cytotoxic testing A blood sample is taken and tested by introducing concentrates of substances to which the patient may be sensitive. Changes occur in the white blood cells of patients who are sensitive. One drawback of this technique is that the findings are difficult to interpret, as so many foods and chemicals appear to be implicated in each patient. Another drawback is that it can be expensive, costing anything from about £50 to £100.

Sublingual drop testing The patient exists on fluids for five days, then one drop of a solution containing the suspect food is placed under the tongue. If there is a sensitivity to it, symptoms develop within minutes. This method also works for chemical sensitivity. It takes time to carry out all the necessary tests, so again the technique can prove expensive.

Intradermal testing Small, diluted amounts of the suspect foods or chemicals are injected just under the skin. The troublesome symptoms will occur two or three hours after injection of a substance to which the patient is sensitive. The technique is very time-consuming and therefore expensive. An average testing session may take five or six hours and cost anything from £100 to £200.

Auricular cardiac reflex The ACR test, as it is called, relies on the movement of any pulse, most commonly the wrist pulse, when a food or chemical to which the patient is sensitive is placed within the body's electrical field. In skilled hands the test is believed to be about 80 per cent accurate, equalling the accuracy of other tests. Its advantage is that it is quick and cheap. Some 50 substances can be tested in a 15 minute consultation.

Electrical testing A small electrode is used to apply a low-voltage electrical current to the patient at an ACUPUNCTURE point, generally on the tip of the toe. The electrical reading is taken over the acupuncture point. A glass bottle containing a suspect food or chemical is then incorporated in the circuit. If the patient is sensitive to it, the reading over the acupuncture point changes. In skilled hands, this method is said to be about 80 per cent accurate and, like ACR, it is quick and cheap.

Kinesiology This is a muscle-testing technique. When a food or chemical to which the patient is sensitive is placed in the patient's hand or under the tongue, muscle power is affected – as a result of changing the body's electrical field, much as in ACR and electrical testing. In skilled hands, kinesiology is said to be about 80 per cent effective.

Treatment The simple treatment for ecological illness is to avoid foods and chemicals that cause the trouble. Many people, however, are sensitive to several – even many – substances and where they are foods, avoidance can lead to serious nutritional problems. Either the patient has to be desensitised to the offending items or the underlying causes must be treated.

Desensitisation involves giving a patient different dilutions of the food or chemical as a drop under the tongue to find out what the body will tolerate without harm. This process probably works in a way similar to homoeopathy. Once a tolerance level has been established, the patient will usually be able to take limited exposure to the harmful substance without ill effect.

Treatment of an abnormal balance of bowel bacteria aims principally at replacing normal bacteria and treating an overproduction of _Candida albicans._ This may simply involve the avoidance of sugar and yeast or, in more severe cases, the use of conventional antifungal drugs.

An orthodox view

Many conventional doctors do not accept that sensitivity to foods or chemical pollution causes illness. Some would accept that there are true allergies to food, but many sufferers do not have allergic reactions when given a test acceptable to orthodox medicine. For example, there is no instant red weal on the skin as when pollen or a mould is injected under the skin of an allergy sufferer. NEUROSIS or emotional STRESS are seen as the likeliest causes of the symptoms presented by sensitive patients.

Some tests which produce results for clinical ecologists are, moreover, shunned by conventional doctors. But there is a growing acceptance among impartial doctors that a sensitivity that falls short of allergy can make people ill.

CO-COUNSELLING

A form of COUNSELLING introduced to Britain from the United States during the 1970s, co-counselling is regarded as a tool for personal development. It pairs together people who want to significantly enhance their sense of identity and personal effectiveness. They take turns to be counsellor and client to each other, with the client choosing the subject and the depth of feelings he or she wishes to explore. The participants are given a short training course – Fundamentals of Co-counselling – after which they usually meet about once a week for a few hours.

COELIAC DISEASE
A dietary disorder of the bowel

Children are the most likely victims of this rather rare disorder of the small intestine, which usually strikes before they are three years old. Symptoms are diarrhoea, with soft but bulky, foul-smelling stools and sometimes a stomach swollen with wind. The child gradually becomes weaker and weaker through malnutrition.

The cause is an inability to absorb gluten, a form of protein found in wheat, rye, barley and perhaps oats, and their products. Just why some children are unable to absorb gluten is not known, but the disease runs in families and sometimes occurs after a bowel infection. Some adults develop it after the age of 30, but are often found to have had it in mild form during childhood.

The remedy, a gluten-free diet, was discovered soon after the Second World War, when it was noticed that Dutch children with the disease became much better when they could not get bread to eat.

Medical researchers eventually pinned down gluten as the culprit. Once gluten has

Do's and don'ts for coeliacs

Don't eat bread, cakes, biscuits, and any food cooked or thickened with flour, such as meat or fish in batter or breadcrumbs, or oatmeal dishes such as porridge. Gluten is usually present in frozen and tinned foods, and also processed foods, because flour is used as a thickener. Milk can also upset some coeliac disease sufferers.

Do eat fresh vegetables (including potatoes and other root vegetables for bulk), dried beans, fruit (either fresh or tinned), cream, nuts, eggs, bacon, fresh meat, plain fish (or fish in brine or oil), plain cheese, butter, honey, jam, plain marmalade, tea or coffee. Rice is also free of gluten, and gluten-free sausages are available.

Special diet counters usually carry a range of gluten-free foods. Information and advice on food and diets is available from The Coeliac Society, PO Box 220, High Wycombe, Bucks HP11 2HY.

been removed from the diet (see box, p. 89) coeliacs usually return to normal health within weeks or a few months.

What the therapists recommend

HERBAL MEDICINE

Consultation Many herbalists think there is a link between coeliac disease and bottle-feeding babies. But the treatment prescribed, which attempts to restore the imbalance of beneficial microorganisms in the gut and of the IMMUNE SYSTEM that has led to the disorder, varies according to the person.

A detailed history of the patient's way of life, medical problems and diet will be compiled before arriving at a course of treatment. Herbs that are likely to be recommended to coeliacs include soothing agents such as marsh-mallow or slippery elm, or such anti-inflammatory remedies as meadowsweet or camomile.

An orthodox view

Long-term sufferers are given vitamin and mineral supplements to help restore health. Sometimes child coeliacs develop a tolerance for gluten by the time they are grown up, and can return to a normal diet. In some cases, a GP will send the patient for tests.

COGNITIVE THERAPY
Learning to believe in yourself

The aim of cognitive therapy is to boost people's self-confidence. It is a form of PSYCHOTHERAPY, and seeks to alter the perceptions, memories and thoughts of people who have a poor opinion of themselves, so that they feel and act in an outgoing and confident way. Therapists believe that negative thoughts produce negative results – for example, if you believe yourself to be unattractive and boring, so will other people; their attitude strengthens your belief and you are trapped in a vicious circle.

The therapy reverses this process by teaching you to like yourself and to think and act positively. When people respond by taking an interest in you, your feelings about yourself are strengthened and you realise that you are likeable after all.

Cognitive therapy was introduced in the late 1960s by an American psychologist named Aaron Beck. It can be practised singly or in groups run in many cases by teachers of BEHAVIOURAL THERAPY.

COLDNESS

Apart from the obvious cause – exposure to cold, damp weather in inadequate clothing – coldness can be a sign of poor health, particularly CIRCULATION PROBLEMS, and EXHAUSTION. Old people and those immobilised by illness are particularly susceptible, and need warm clothes and properly heated accommodation if they are not to become victims of HYPOTHERMIA, which can be fatal.

It is important not to stay cold for long periods, or you may develop a CHILL, CRAMP, CHILBLAINS or FROSTBITE.

What the therapists recommend

HERBAL MEDICINE

Self help Infusions (see p. 184) of ginger and prickly ash are thought to stimulate blood circulation, and increase the body's ability to withstand cold. An infusion of cayenne has a warming effect and may also stimulate circulation – to make it, pour a cup of boiling water onto ½ to 1 teaspoon of cayenne powder, and leave for ten minutes. Drink 1 tablespoon of the infusion mixed into a cup of hot water as often as necessary.

NATUROPATHY

Self help The heart, circulation and nervous systems are believed to be strengthened by eating a diet high in magnesium-rich foods such as almonds, cashew nuts, Brazil nuts, whole grains, sweetcorn, spinach and bananas. Potassium may help by improving nerve functioning – it is found in fresh fruits such as bananas, grapes, melons and peaches, dried fruit, seeds and raw or baked (not boiled) vegetables.

EXERCISE can also help – regular running is said to be particularly good for cold feet. Cold showers can help to draw more blood into the capillaries under the surface of the skin, which warms the area.

Warning Always consult a registered naturopath to ensure that such treatment is suitable for the individual.

HOMOEOPATHY

Self help *Arsenicum album* is recommended for those who suffer from anxiety, and have to sit next to a heater to stay warm; *Calcarea carbonica* for cold, clammy hands in those who tend to be overweight. *Hepar sulphuris* may help those who are very sensitive to pain and feel the cold severely.

An orthodox view

Doctors agree that warm clothing, exercise to improve circulation, and good heating are the most efficient ways of staying warm. In

Do's and don'ts to guard against cold

Do wear a warm hat – it will keep your whole body warm, since a great deal of body heat can be lost from the head. A nightcap may help if you feel cold in bed.

Do wear warm woollen socks in winter, bedsocks at night and insulated inner soles in shoes if you have particularly cold feet. Electrically heated socks are available from some motorcycle accessory shops.

Do keep your hands warm with a good pair of gloves and wear a scarf to protect your neck, particularly in cold wind.

Do check ski and outdoor activity shops for jackets, hats, gloves, socks and thermal underwear which give maximum protection against cold and rain.

Don't try to get warm too quickly. If you get very cold, warm up slowly – take a bath that feels just slightly warm to the hand, because hot water may cause serious harm. Then take a warming drink such as hot milk, and wrap yourself up well.

Don't smoke – it constricts the blood vessels and causes poor circulation (see SMOKING).

addition, have at least one good hot meal a day, and take hot drinks at regular intervals – especially at night. Patients with serious circulation problems may be given drugs called vasodilators to open up blood vessels that have become constricted by cold.

COLDS

That coughs and sneezes spread diseases is an old maxim, but a true one – especially in the case of the common cold. Colds are caused by VIRUS INFECTIONS and are highly contagious, particularly in enclosed places. Because the mucus in the nose and throat of cold sufferers is full of viruses, coughing, sneezing – even breathing in a confined space – can easily spread the infection.

Cold viruses are in a constant state of change, so immunity acquired from one infection does not necessarily protect you from further attacks. Any run-down condition or general debility can leave you more liable to catch a cold. Babies and young children, the elderly, or those already ill are particularly at risk.

Symptoms include a runny nose, sore throat, headache, stuffed-up feeling, dry cough, sneezing, loss of appetite and a general lack of energy. These may last for up to three days, then die down over the following seven days, although the stuffed or runny nose may last for up to three weeks.

Being physically cold or getting wet does not cause a cold, but the chances of infection are heightened by STRESS, EXHAUSTION, DEPRESSION or chronic sickness, all of which lower resistance.

What the therapists recommend

NATUROPATHY

Self help The advice of naturopaths is to avoid all foods said to be mucus-forming, such as dairy products, eggs, starch and sugar. In the early stages of a cold, an Epsom salts bath (see box) is recommended. If the cold becomes feverish, either FASTING or a raw fruit and vegetable diet – including GARLIC and onions or leeks – for two to three days may help to reduce CATARRH. See also RAW FOOD DIET; EATING FOR HEALTH.

HERBAL MEDICINE

Self help Hot drinks and a good sweat seem to ease cold symptoms, and one recipe is: 1/8 teaspoon of cayenne pepper, the juice of a lemon, a minced clove of garlic and a gram of vitamin C, all mixed in half a cup of hot water. Sip it slowly. Both the garlic and cayenne should make you sweat; the lemon juice is rich in vitamin C and bioflavonoids, which are claimed to help your system to absorb the vitamin.

A variety of herbal teas are also said to be

Do's and don'ts when you have a cold

_Do_ drink plenty of fluids – especially cool drinks – for a slight fever. This replaces fluids lost through sweating.
_Do_ take painkillers such as paracetamol in recommended doses for a headache, or other aches and pains.
_Do_ inhale steam to relieve a stuffed-up nose: half fill a bowl with hot water, put a towel over your head to trap the steam and inhale for a few minutes at a time. Take care not to upset the bowl.
_Do_ get some fresh air – take a gentle walk – as soon as you feel able.
Don't wrap up in extra clothes or blankets, do not overheat the room or sit in front of the fire – let the body lose heat naturally.

Epsom salts bath

Fill the bath with water as hot as you can comfortably bear and enough to lie in immersed to the neck. Dissolve two handfuls of unpurified Epsom salts in the water. Soak in the tub for as long as you can comfortably stay, with a compress wrung out in cold water on your forehead. On getting out, dab yourself gently dry, wrap yourself in a sheet and get into a warm bed.
Warning This treatment should not be used by the elderly, the very young, or those with high blood pressure.

beneficial – including camomile, lemon balm, boneset (especially for fever), coltsfoot (for coughs and congestion), elder, pennyroyal and vervain. Also recommended are infusions (see p. 184) of yarrow, peppermint, ginger and catnip.

HOMOEOPATHY

Self help Colds treated homoeopathically are held to occur less frequently, but prolonged ones should be treated by a doctor. However, for an occasional infection, the following preparations are recommended:

Early stages: _Aconitum napellus_ will often stop a cold if taken on the first sneeze when feeling suddenly chilly. _Ferrum phosphoricum_ is also useful at the outset, and _Arsenicum album_ if there is much painful sneezing with watery discharge, which makes the skin sore, or if the patient is very chilly and thirsty. _Kali iodatum_ is recommended for a cold due to exposure, especially damp, when the eyes smart and water, there is much sneezing and the nose is red and sore.

Persistent cold: _Sambucus nigra_; or _Teucrium marum verum_ and _Wyethia_ to relieve chronic catarrh and LARYNGITIS, and _Kali bichromium_ or _Silica_ for SINUS PROBLEMS. When the cold is severe, the chosen remedy can be taken hourly for up to 12 doses. Stop as soon as the condition improves.

Other alternative treatments

Acupressure To relieve nasal congestion and clear the sinuses, apply the thumb or index finger to two points, below the cheekbones, directly beneath the eye pupils when looking straight ahead, and about a finger's width from the end of the nose. Use a gentle, circular massaging motion.
Aromatherapy You are recommended to add six to eight drops of cinnamon oil to a warm bath, and rub the oil undiluted into the temples, the sinus area and chest four times a day. For a steam inhalation, put two drops of the cinnamon oil into a bowl of hot water

and breathe in the steam for a few minutes, four times daily.
Traditional Medicine Chopped or crushed garlic taken in small amounts several times a day is said to help repel colds – especially head colds. If a cold has developed, you are advised to go to bed and drink the juice of a lemon in a glass of hot water with a teaspoon of honey. If desired, two aspirins can also be added.

An orthodox view

Despite years of research, there is no effective cure for the common cold or any sure way of shortening its duration. Some people have great faith in the curative power of vitamin C (see MEGAVITAMIN THERAPY), but so far this has not been medically proved.

The general view among doctors is that colds should be allowed to clear up naturally at home – which they normally do after a week to ten days. But if the symptoms last for longer than that you should see your GP. There are, however, certain measures you can take to relieve the worst symptoms of a cold (see _Do's and don'ts_ box).

COLD SORES

These small blisters usually appear on the lips and are caused by the _Herpes simplex_ virus. The virus is common and infectious, and can also attack other parts of the face, the genitals (see GENITAL HERPES) and other skin areas.

It is usually picked up from someone during childhood, sometimes causing feverishness and sickness as well as blisters. The virus remains dormant in the body, sometimes without causing symptoms for years, but it can be reactivated at any time by FEVER, STRESS, exposure to cold, SUNBURN, lowered resistance – or even menstruation.
Warning Always see a doctor immediately for cold sores near the eyes – they can cause great pain if not treated quickly.

What the therapists recommend

NATUROPATHY

Self help Some supplements believed to help your body fight the virus include vitamins A, B3, B5, B-complex (which includes the previous two, plus five others) and C. Bioflavonoids, zinc, the amino acid lysine, and acidophilus tablets are also recommended. In addition to these general supplements, vitamins B6, B12 and E, folic acid, pantothenic acid, calcium, magnesium and selenium are favoured by some practitioners.

A mix of equal quantities of lemon juice

and water may promote healing if applied directly to lip sores. To prevent further attacks, a wholefood diet which cuts out refined foods and sugar and includes plenty of FIBRE and alkali-forming foods such as fruit, vegetables, honey, milk and yoghurt is recommended (see EATING FOR HEALTH).

HOMOEOPATHY

Rhus tox. and *Natrum muriticum*, one or the other, morning and evening, are thought to help. Take the 30th or 6th potency every four hours for two days, then morning and night for two or three days.

An orthodox view

Chemists stock creams and lotions that can relieve the pain of the blisters and help them to heal. Doctors sometimes prescribe anti-viral drugs to reduce the symptoms and shorten an attack. But once infected, there is no way of ridding yourself of the virus, and further attacks are always possible.

When the eye is affected, the doctor will put a drop of yellow dye in the eye to show up any ulcers (dendritic ulcers) that have formed. Antiviral drops and ointment will clear the attack, but corneal ulcers may recur. If you wear contact lenses, always moisten them with sterilising solution, never with saliva, which can cause reinfection.

Do's and don'ts about cold sores

Do avoid all forms of skin contact – such as kissing – when others come close to the affected area while sores are still moist.

Don't share towels, face cloths or pillowcases.

Don't touch the blisters unnecessarily or more may develop. If you do touch them accidentally, or when applying a salve, wash your hands afterwards.

COLIC

Parents with very young babies often have their nights ruined by loud, persistent crying. Often this is caused by colic – spasmodic stomach pains – and colic is in turn usually caused by the milk used in feeding.

Breastfed babies do not often suffer from colic – provided that their mothers do not themselves drink much milk. But whether bottle or breastfed, babies generally grow out of colic attacks by the time they are three months old. If they do not, medical advice should be sought – especially if a baby suffers also from DIARRHOEA or vomiting, or if there is blood in the bowel motions.

In growing children colic may sometimes be brought on by fear of a coming event or 'ordeal'. In some cases going to school in itself can cause an attack; sometimes 'nervous colic' can strike when an examination is due, or – in older children – a career opportunity has to be discussed, or a job interview arranged.

Adults are affected less often by colic, but when they are, the intermittent pain comes and goes like a fist being clenched and unclenched in the abdomen, and can make them double up in agony. The pain occurs when an organ such as the bile duct or intestine contracts and becomes inflamed when trying to expel poisoned food (see FOOD POISONING), or to pass an obstruction such as GALLSTONES.

What the therapists recommend

HERBAL MEDICINE

Self help Babies' colic is said to be relieved by a teaspoon of warm herbal tea every hour. The infusions can be made from catmint, camomile or fennel seed. The mother can also take the infusion if she is breastfeeding.

Adult colic sufferers should drink infusions by the glass, three times daily. Seed tea is also recommended: mix a teaspoon each of aniseed, caraway and fennel in enough boiling water to fill a cup. Cover the cup and infuse for about ten minutes. Then strain and drink the tea while it is hot.

AROMATHERAPY

Self help For babies, use gripe water which already contains the essential oil of fennel – check on label. One drop of fennel oil mixed with ½ teaspoon of honey can ease severe attacks, or gently massage the baby's stomach clockwise with two drops of fennel in ½ teaspoon carrier oil.

Several other oils which are said to help ease the pain for adults, and to aid digestion generally, include camphor, cinnamon, juniper, lavender and patchouli.

An orthodox view

For a child, a doctor will probably prescribe an antispasmodic medicine to relax the affected organs, which will work quickly and safely. However, if the colic is severe or long-lasting the child may have to be examined in hospital.

For adults, a painkilling drug may be prescribed, and the patient told to avoid rich foods and alcohol. Usually it is better not to eat at all during an attack and take only sips of water until the colic finally clears up.

COLITIS
Inflammation of the bowel

This disorder – the cause of which is unknown – is marked by chronic inflammation of the large bowel, which becomes ulcerated (see ULCERS). Symptoms include pain in the abdomen and intermittent bouts of blood-streaked DIARRHOEA which, in severe cases, can occur up to 20 times a day.

If the bouts increase in number and severity – or if the condition persists – you should seek medical advice.

What the therapists recommend

Acupressure Apply downward pressure to a point on the outside of the leg, immediately below the knee. This is thought to control the muscular movement of the abdomen and so relieve colitis. In severe cases, pressure should be applied on a point midway between the breastbone and navel.

Acupuncture The practitioner will concentrate on the gall bladder, liver and stomach meridians. He may also pack warmed salt into the navel, and use MOXIBUSTION which is believed to relax the abdomen in general.

Naturopathy Diet is held to be the key to preventing or combating colitis. This involves cutting out milk and dairy products such as butter and cheese, and eating mainly moderately cooked vegetable broths and vegetable stews, and a mixture of slippery elm and mashed bananas. The disorder should clear up within a few weeks.

Colitis is often accompanied by STRESS – and a consultant may teach a patient relaxation exercises.

Herbal Medicine A favoured way of soothing inflamed or irritated intestinal walls is a twice-daily cup of slippery elm drink. Mix one part of powdered bark – available from health shops – in eight parts of water. Heat the water, pour on powder and drink warm.

An orthodox view

In general, doctors tend to view ulcerative colitis more seriously than do alternative practitioners. In severe cases, the patient may be sent to hospital for a barium enema, X-rays and a bowel examination. Occasionally, an operation to remove part of the colon may be advised.

Usually, however, a doctor will prescribe steroids to reduce the number and intensity of attacks. He will also probably recommend a suitable diet – avoiding vegetable roughage and raw fruits – and stress the importance of rest and relaxation.

COLOUR THERAPY
Casting light on your body's ills

The sun gives out a variety of electromagnetic rays with different wavelengths, some of them visible to the human eye as natural light. Light can be separated into its component wavelengths by a prism or filters, and the human eye then sees each component as a different colour.

The sun also emits wavelengths not visible to the human eye – infrared rays, ultraviolet rays, X-rays, for example. Although the eye is not sensitive to these invisible rays, the body is – and may be helped or harmed by them. Ultraviolet rays, for instance, enable the body to manufacture essential VITAMINS, but too much of it can cause severe burning and skin CANCER.

People are affected also by the visible rays – psychologically and physically. Red light has been found to speed up the circulation and raise BLOOD PRESSURE, while blue light is calming. The effect is the same even if the patient is blindfolded or blind. Colour can affect people's mood, perception of temperature and time, and their ability to concentrate. It is being used increasingly to produce desired responses in mental health clinics, hospital recovery rooms, prison cells and in work places.

Colour therapists attach even more significance to colours, and believe that specific ailments can be cured by adjusting the colour input to the body. They believe that the body receives the various electromagnetic components of light, absorbs them to some degree, and gives out its own aura of electromagnetism (which KIRLIAN PHOTOGRAPHY is believed to record) in a pattern of vibrations that the skilled therapist can pick up.

An unhealthy body is said to give out an unbalanced pattern of vibrations, and the colour therapist works to restore the balance. Colour, through light, food and surroundings, will work through the nervous system to stimulate the production of hormones that control the chemical and energy balance of the body.

Who it can help Colour therapists will treat any disorder be it mental, emotional, metabolic or physical, but they emphasise that their therapy is complementary to qualified medical treatment, not an alternative to it. Patients should always seek the advice of their orthodox doctor. Therapists offer an extra means of promoting well-being which

requires sustained effort from the patient. Sufferers from MIGRAINE, ECZEMA, ASTHMA, inflammation, rheumatic pain, ARTHRITIS, INSOMNIA, STRESS, high blood pressure, DEPRESSION and lack of energy have, according to therapists, benefited from treatment.

Finding a therapist Colour therapy is in its infancy in Britain, where there are only a few dozen therapists. A national register of them is being compiled by the Institute for Complementary Medicine, 21 Portland Place, London W1N 3AF. Get in touch with the institute for a list of therapists, or contact Hygeia Studios, Brook House, Avening, Tetbury, Glos GL8 8NS; or the International Association of Colour Therapy, c/o The Institute for Complementary Medicine (see address above); or Living Colour, 33 Lancaster Grove, London NW3 4EX.

Consulting a therapist Diagnosis of your condition will occupy the first consultation and take well over an hour. The therapist will record details of your medical history, lifestyle, diet and colour preferences, and study your skin. A skilled therapist will concentrate on these details and use extrasensory perception to tune in to your electromagnetic field and assess any imbalances there.

As an aid in deciding on treatment, the therapist dowses with a pendulum (see DOWSING) or strokes the length of the spine (or a chart of a spine) while concentrating on your condition, and so picks up vibrations from individual vertebrae which reveal where the colour balance is wrong. Each vertebra is related to an organ or part of the body and also to one of the eight colours of the spectrum, which are repeated in sequence down the vertebrae, increasing in density of colour from the neck to the base of the spine.

The therapist compiles a detailed spine chart and uses it to explain to the patient which colours will be used for the therapy and why. Seven or more weekly treatment sessions are required. A colour therapy instrument beams coloured lights on the patient through shaped apertures. A main colour and a complementary colour are used: the complementary pairings are red and turquoise, orange and blue, yellow and violet, green and magenta.

During the session the instrument gives increasing time to the main colour and decreasing time to the complementary colour in a carefully worked out irregular rhythm; a regular rhythm soon becomes ineffective. The total time before the instrument is 19¾ minutes per session.

Some therapists prefer to direct the colours at specific parts of the body instead of bathing the whole body in colour. As treatment progresses, the colours or their intensity may be adjusted to suit the patient's

changing condition. Music or a particular range of notes may be used to reinforce the colour therapy.

The therapist also advises on what colours to wear and use for furnishings, and what colours of foods to eat to help in rebalancing the patient's energies. Patients are also taught to visualise the treatment colours.

An orthodox view

Few doctors doubt that colour does affect mood and can affect behaviour. Many accept that an individual's choice in colour points to personality traits. Psychologists attach more significance to colour and are engaged by some employers to make detailed assessments of job applicants by testing their colour preferences.

Although doctors have long known that the body is affected by radiation outside the visible spectrum (infrared, ultraviolet and X-rays), they see no scientific proof that visible colour rays affect particular parts and disorders of the body. However, the work of colour therapists is not regarded as harmful.

CONJUNCTIVITIS
Pink eye

A sensation of grittiness and irritation in the eye is usually the first symptom of this common condition. The conjunctiva – a delicate membrane that covers the white of the eye and inside of the lids – becomes inflamed, causing redness and pain. Sometimes the eye is also sticky and crusted, especially after a night's sleep.

Most cases are caused by bacterial or VIRUS INFECTIONS, but ALLERGY, foreign bodies in the eye and irritants such as tobacco smoke, aerosol sprays and some eye products can all be causes. In babies, blocked tear ducts are sometimes responsible, and in a few rare cases conjunctivitis may be a symptom of some more serious eye disorder.

Consult a doctor as soon as possible if you suspect another disorder, if the eye is very painful, particularly if the swelling and pain have not started to get better after two or three days, or if you have recently visited a tropical country where you may have picked up an eye virus.

What the therapists recommend
HERBAL MEDICINE
Practitioners recommend bathing the eyes with decoctions (see p. 184) of cornflower, marigold, elderflower, camomile, chickweed,

eyebright or plantain, or using infusions to make compresses (see p. 184) for the eyes. Use separate eye baths and compresses for each eye. Do not bathe more than three times, to avoid irritation.

HOMOEOPATHY

Self help Bathing the eye three times a day in a solution of one part *Euphrasia* mother tincture (see p. 184) in ten parts boiled or distilled water is thought to help. *Ferrum phosphoricum* is also recommended – take five tablets of the 6X potency dissolved in hot water four times a day.

Aconitum napellus is recommended in the initial stages when the eyes are red, hot, gritty and swollen, and water after exposure to cold, wind and light; *Apis mellifica* when there is stinging pain, itching, blistering on the white of the eye and pus; *Euphrasia officinalis* when the eyes burn and water, causing blinking and dislike of bright light; *Mercurius corrosivus* when the lids stick together and there is pus in the eye; *Pulsatilla nigricans* when there is a thick, yellow discharge with itching, burning and a tendency to Styes; *Arsenicum album* when the eye is hot and waters.

NATUROPATHY

Self help Vitamin A is recommended for many eye disorders, but needs to be taken under supervision if large quantities are used or if it is taken for a long time, because in large quantities it can be poisonous. For safety, always take in combination with vita-

mins D and E – a total of 5000-10,000iu a day. Some therapists also suggest vitamins B2, B3, B6 and C.

An orthodox view

Most conjunctivitis heals by itself within a week or two, but doctors usually give prescriptions for antihistamine or antibiotic eye-drops to speed up the process.

CONSTIPATION

A typical Western diet does not usually contain enough of the FIBRE that the body needs to help rid itself of waste products. Constipation is the all-too-frequent consequence. The strain of passing hard motions from the bowel can lead to BOWEL DISORDERS, PILES – and even APPENDICITIS.

Bowel action varies from person to person – from three times a day to once every three days – but irregular and infrequent small, hard motions are the usual signals that you are constipated. If constipation lasts more than two weeks, see your doctor.

Apart from lack of fibre in your food, other causes include eating too much meat or dairy produce, not drinking enough fluids (fibre needs water to form soft motions), food ALLERGY, lack of EXERCISE, ignoring the 'call of nature', dependence on laxatives, the side effects of some medicines, PREGNANCY (when intestinal muscles often weaken), ANXIETY, STRESS and TENSION.

What the therapists recommend
HERBAL MEDICINE

Self help A herbal laxative should only be used as a short-term solution. Make one by crushing up to six senna pods (but start with only one or two per dose) into a cup of boiling water and adding a small piece of liquorice root. Leave to soak for ten minutes, strain and drink at night. Senna takes about eight hours to work and can cause a griping pain in the stomach – add a teaspoon of fennel seeds to relieve this.

Another strong laxative is cascara, which is believed to tone the bowel. You can make an infusion by soaking ½ to 1 teaspoon of cascara bark in a cup of hot water for one hour. Strain and drink before bedtime. This also takes about eight hours to work and may have a griping effect.

Linseeds make a gentler laxative, acting to provide soothing bulk in the gut. Soak a tablespoon of seeds overnight in ¼ pint (150ml) of cold water and add to your breakfast cereal. Or soak a tablespoon of seeds in ¼ pint of hot water for two hours,

strain and drink sweetened with honey; eat the seeds. An infusion of dandelion leaves or chopped dandelion root (see p. 184) has a gentle laxative effect. Take three or four tablespoonsful daily.

NATUROPATHY

Self help A high fibre diet or RAW FOOD DIET is recommended; chew the food well and never rush meals. Get plenty of fibre from peas, beans, brown rice, wholemeal bread, jacket potatoes, raw vegetables, fresh and dried fruits; and drink plenty of fluids. Naturopaths believe it is far better to eat more food in its natural state than to sprinkle bran on top of food.

If possible, take regular exercise to condition your stomach and back muscles. This, in turn, aids bowel movement. If you are constipated through resisting the 'call', visit the lavatory regularly after a cereal breakfast and try to relax – read a book or magazine if necessary. Stay for ten minutes, whether or not a motion is passed, and your body should resume its regular habit.

TRADITIONAL MEDICINE

Bran absorbs up to nine times its own weight in water and so helps to form good motions. Added to food it helps to regulate the bowels, but you need to drink at least three glasses of water a day to make it work. Take 1 to 3 teaspoons of bran – always with some liquid – a day and slowly build up to a maximum of ½oz (15g) a day.

Do not rely on bran as a long-term cure, however, as it has been found to contain ingredients which prevent useful minerals being absorbed into the body. Bran may also cause WIND and a bloated feeling, but these effects normally pass within a week or two.

Prunes and prune juice work as a natural laxative, but should not be taken regularly in place of a fibre diet. Soak prunes in water overnight, and eat night and morning. A regular daily teaspoon of mineral-rich molasses is also said to help combat constipation.

Other alternative treatments

Homoeopathy *Alumina* is recommended for dry motions, when there is no 'call of nature' or movement of the bowels for days; *Nux vomica* if you feel the call but no motions are passed, or if poor bowel habits are due to laxatives (good for those who overeat and drink too much); *Plumbum metallicum* for long-term constipation with stomach pain; *Collinsonia canadensis* when hard motions are passed and when piles are present.

Reflexology Massage to the reflex areas relating to the small and large intestines, plus areas relating to the adrenal glands, solar plexus, liver and lower spine is recommended. See chart, p. 295.

Do's and don'ts about conjunctivitis

Do stay away from cut grass, smoky rooms, dusty atmospheres or anything that irritates your eyes.

Do wear goggles if you work where metal is being cut or where there are wood shavings or other splinters that may enter the eye.

Do use your own towels and face cloths and don't lend them to others.

Do remove blockages from babies' tear ducts by gently massaging the bottom lid near the nose.

Don't cover a sore eye with an eye patch – this can spread infection.

Don't use eyedrops or eyewashes unless necessary – they can sometimes cause irritation.

If you get conjunctivitis Touch your eyes only when necessary, and wash your hands before and afterwards to prevent the infection from spreading.

An orthodox view

Bran is now approved by doctors for constipation. In general they will recommend a diet containing plenty of fluids and fibre. Laxatives or suppositories may be prescribed to help retrain the bowels, and an enema may occasionally be needed.

For babies, a doctor may prescribe small glycerine suppositories and recommend adding an extra teaspoon of sugar to every 6fl oz (180ml) of milk feed.

CONTRACEPTION

Throughout history, couples have tried to control their fertility – to have children or not as and when they wish. Modern medicine has developed highly effective means of preventing conception, but many couples prefer traditional methods either for religious reasons or because they wish to avoid the side effects of drugs or other artificial contraceptives. See NATURAL FAMILY PLANNING, p. 96.

CONVULSIONS

Although not always dangerous in itself, a convulsive fit or seizure is frightening and disturbing for victims and their families, and if it happens while crossing a road or operating machinery the sufferer may be in danger of injury. The cause is thought to be a temporary loss of control in the brain, leading to uncoordinated and uncontrollable muscular jerking and twitching, often while the victim has lapsed into UNCONSCIOUSNESS.

There are a number of disorders that can induce convulsions, including EPILEPSY, a high FEVER, injuries and reactions to some FOOD ADDITIVES.

Warning Convulsions are a serious symptom, and a doctor should always be seen so that the cause can be diagnosed and treatment given before using any alternative therapies. However, it is quite common for young children to suffer from 'febrile' convulsions as a result of a high temperature. A single attack is not a cause for alarm, but if it recurs or persists, seek medical help.

What the therapists recommend

NATUROPATHY

Self help Treatment depends on the cause of the convulsions. Some epileptics have found that supplements of vitamin B6, vitamin D or calcium and magnesium prevent or

---

Do's and don'ts for convulsions

Do turn the victim so that he is lying on his side, without a pillow.

Do loosen any clothing or jewellery around the neck.

Do move furniture and other objects away from the patient, so that he cannot injure himself on them.

Don't try to force his mouth open or give any food or drink.

Don't hold the person down or restrict his movements.

Do make sure, once the convulsions have stopped – when the patient will probably sleep – that he is able to breathe properly by grasping him under the jaw and extending his neck. And allow him to rest as long as necessary.

Do make sure the family, teachers and colleagues of an epileptic know what to do when a seizure happens.

Don't drive a vehicle, operate any machinery or take part in sports such as skiing or swimming if you suffer from convulsions, without first getting your doctor's advice.

---

lessen their convulsive attacks. Vitamin B6 should be taken in large quantities only under the supervision of a doctor, or a naturopath who is also a doctor, since it may interfere with the effectiveness of other antiepileptic medicines.

In other cases, convulsions may be an allergic reaction to artificial additives in processed foods, such as the flavouring agent monosodium glutamate used in some preserves and Chinese food, and the nitrates used to preserve many meat products.

It is often difficult to identify the exact ingredient that is responsible, but switching to a wholefood diet based on fresh fruit, vegetables and wholegrain cereals (see EATING FOR HEALTH) and excluding all processed foods may cure the problem. Alternatively, keep a written record of everything you eat and the time you ate it, as well as the times of the convulsive attacks. If the cause is something in your diet, a pattern should soon emerge.

Consultation A naturopath will always examine the patient to exclude the risk of a serious neurological problem. If one is found, the patient will be referred to a neurologist.

An orthodox view

Many doctors accept that vitamin B6, vitamin D, or calcium and magnesium supplements can help some epileptics. One trial in Den-

---

mark showed that vitamin D treatment reduced patients' fits by about one-third, and research is continuing into this.

Orthodox treatment for convulsions depends on the cause. Epilepsy can be controlled with a range of drugs, and other types of convulsions usually disappear once the cause has been removed.

COPPER THERAPY

Traditionally, wearing a copper bracelet is thought to be an effective way of relieving the pain of ARTHRITIS and RHEUMATISM. Although doctors tend to dismiss the idea as an old wives' tale, research in Australia in the late 1970s showed that three out of every four volunteers who wore a copper bracelet for at least a month found their arthritic aches and pains considerably eased. It is said that traces of copper from the bracelet penetrate the skin and make up for any lack of essential copper in the body. See also MINERALS; BIOCHEMIC TISSUE SALTS.

CORNS

Badly fitting shoes are the most common cause of corns, which are formed by a thickening of the skin on toes or soles. Comfortable shoes which do not squeeze or rub the feet will prevent corns. Any already formed should go once the cause is removed.

What the therapists recommend

Naturopathy Wash your feet regularly and remove any rough skin with a pumice stone. Alternatively, bathe your feet for five to ten minutes night and morning in a small tub of hot water in which 4oz (120g) of Epsom salts is dissolved. Some practitioners recommend soaking the feet in sea water (or water to which sea salt has been added), for ten to 15 minutes, twice daily.

Herbal Medicine Paint the corns with fresh lemon juice, or crush a garlic clove onto the gauze patch of a sticking plaster and put it on the corn. Alternatively, soak the feet for five to ten minutes in a mixture of one-third vinegar and two-thirds warm water.

An orthodox view

A chiropodist will probably pare the corn with a sharp, sterile blade – and perhaps advise corn plasters and salicylic acid ointment or tincture. A doctor will almost certainly recommend a change of footwear.

Natural family planning

There are many different ways of preventing pregnancy, but those favoured by most doctors and clinics involve taking drugs or using chemical preparations and artificial devices which can cause a range of side effects. Many couples have become dissatisfied with these methods or do not use them for religious reasons, and there is a growing interest in more natural forms of contraception.

Recommended methods of natural family planning depend on charting the woman's menstrual cycle and avoiding intercourse on the days when she is likely to be fertile. There are three main ways of keeping track of your cycle. The principles on which the methods work are given here, but details of how to apply them to your case should be sought from a doctor or family planning clinic.

Recommended methods

Calendar (or rhythm) method   Record the dates of your periods on a calendar for six to 12 months – the longer you do so, the more reliable the method will be. Then calculate the length of each menstrual cycle by counting the number of days from the first day of each period to the day before the first day of the next (inclusive).

Find the first 'unsafe' day of your cycle by subtracting 19 from the length of your shortest cycle, and the last unsafe day by subtracting 11 from the length of your longest cycle. Avoid intercourse between these dates. For example, if your shortest cycle is 26 days and your longest 33, your first unsafe day will be 26 − 19 = day 7, and your last unsafe day will be 33 − 11 = day 22.

Warning The method may fail if something such as acute stress substantially alters the length of your cycle.

Temperature method   This involves taking your temperature to find the time when you ovulate – usually 12-16 days before your next period. Again, the more cycles over which you do this, the more reliable the method will be.

Take your temperature every morning at the same time for at least three minutes before getting out of bed, and record it on a chart. An ordinary thermometer can be used, but special fertility thermometers available free from doctors and family planning clinics make the task easier. Free charts are also available from these sources.

From the first day of your period until around the day you ovulate, your resting temperature is 0.3-0.6°C (0.5-1°F) lower than from ovulation until your next period, so a 'step' will show on your chart (see sample chart below). You will be fertile for three to four days before and after the temperature change, so avoid intercourse during this time.

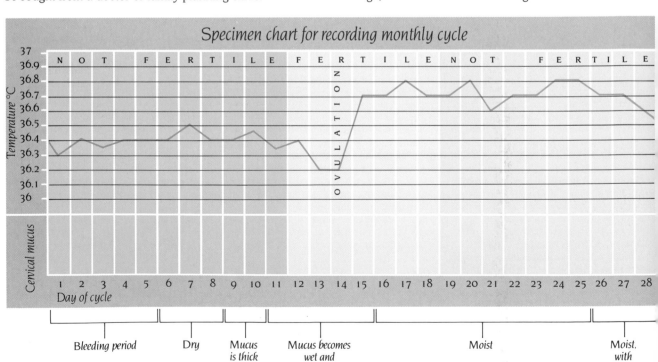

Specimen chart for recording monthly cycle

Warning This method is unreliable if illness affects your temperature, or if your cycle is disrupted for any reason.

Cervical mucus method This depends on noting subtle changes that accompany ovulation, including changes in the mucus produced by the cervix. After a period, the vagina is usually dry for a few days, and then thick, cloudy mucus is produced. Before and during ovulation, the mucus increases in quantity and becomes thin and clear.

If you know how to locate it, the condition of your cervix can also be a guide. On unsafe days the cervix feels higher up in the vagina, softer and more open than on safe days. Some women also notice other signs of ovulation such as abdominal pains, tender breasts or slight vaginal bleeding.

Used in combination, the calendar, temperature and cervical mucus methods provide the best guide to ovulation and the safest form of natural birth control. The combination is known as the 'sympto-thermal method'.

Other methods

There are also two traditional methods of natural contraception which have long been practised. However, one is possible only for women who have recently had a baby, and the other is not always suitable. Further, neither method is very reliable:

Breastfeeding Nursing mothers who breastfeed their babies frequently and regularly – every two to four hours day and night, with no supplement feeds – are less likely to become pregnant than others. Even so, some may conceive.

Withdrawal ('coitus interruptus') This requires the man to withdraw his penis before ejaculating. Many couples find this unsatisfactory, but it works well for others. However, care must be taken afterwards to prevent semen from coming anywhere near the woman's vagina. What is more, some sperm may escape from the penis before ejaculation.

Principal methods of contraception

METHOD	ADVANTAGES	DISADVANTAGES	EFFECTIVENESS
Natural methods			
Calendar	No cost; no side effects.	Needs long period of attention; long periods of abstinence.	Good when combined with other natural methods.
Temperature	No cost; no side effects.	Needs long period of daily attention; doesn't work when ill.	Good when combined with cervical mucus method.
Cervical mucus	No cost; no side effects.	Not reliable on its own; examining cervix not always easy.	Good when combined with calendar or temperature method.
Breastfeeding	No cost; good for baby; no side effects.	Not suitable for everyone; not a long-term solution.	Not completely reliable.
Withdrawal	No cost; no preparation needed; can be used at any time of cycle.	Can interfere with sexual fulfilment.	Unreliable.
Artificial methods			
Condom	Easy to use; no side effects; protection from sexually transmitted diseases.	Can interfere with spontaneous sex; diminished sensation for some men.	Very good, especially when used with spermicide.
Diaphragm and cap	Easy to use; no side effects.	Must be fitted by doctor or nurse, and user taught to insert and remove it.	Very good when used with spermicide.
Spermicidal vaginal sponge	Easy to use.	Expensive.	Good.
Intrauterine device (IUD)	Needs no attention once fitted, except for occasional checks that it is still in place. Can be fitted up to five days after unprotected intercourse (eg, rape).	Must be fitted by doctor or nurse; may cause infections and heavy periods; not suitable for some women.	Excellent.
Contraceptive pill (various types)	Lighter, shorter periods; reduced premenstrual tension; protection from some disorders.	Requires daily attention; can cause weight gain; may increase risk of breast cancer and blood clots; prolonged use by smokers or other risk groups may be inadvisable.	Almost completely effective if taken as instructed.
Morning-after pill	Effective up to 72 hours after unprotected intercourse.	Not suitable for routine use; may cause nausea or other side effects.	Very good.

COUÉISM

In the late 19th century, a French apothecary named Emile Coué (1857-1926) developed a form of self-hypnosis based on repeating certain phrases, the most famous of which was: 'Every day, in every way, I am getting better and better.' His principles formed the basis of AUTOSUGGESTION.

COUGHS

The best way to treat a cough is to get rid of what is causing it, not to suppress it. Coughing helps to expel congested phlegm or inhaled dust from the lungs, bronchial tubes or windpipe. A cough may be caused by infection or an irritant such as cigarette smoke or dust. A hoarse cough may be a symptom of LARYNGITIS or, in a child, CROUP. If a child is wheezing after a coughing spasm, the cause may be WHOOPING COUGH.

If the cough is persistent – lasting more than two or three weeks – or is accompanied by a high temperature, chest pains or blood in the sputum, see a doctor.

What the therapists recommend

ACUPUNCTURE

Consultation A cough is believed by practitioners to be caused by an imbalance in the flow of energy to the lungs. An acupuncturist will treat it by inserting needles into points on the lung meridian in the arms. Needles may also be inserted in the meridian for another organ with a related rhythm in the body's 24 hour cycle – for example, the bladder meridian (see p. 14).

AROMATHERAPY

Self help In the early stages an inhalant is generally recommended to soothe the cough and help expel phlegm. Essential oils to use include eucalyptus, thyme, cypress and sandalwood. Generally, two or three drops are added to a bowl of hot water and the steam inhaled for periods of about ten minutes, two or three times a day until the cough clears.

For a sore throat caused by a dry, hard cough, gargle with three drops of the same essential oils in half a glass of water.

BIOCHEMIC TISSUE SALTS

Self help Different salts are recommended for different types of cough: for a hard dry cough with FEVER, *Ferr. phos.*; cough with thick white phlegm, *Kali mur.*; cough with yellow phlegm and worse at night, *Kali*

sulph.; spasmodic, painful cough, *Mag. phos.*; loose, rattling cough with watery phlegm, *Calc. sulph.* alternating with *Ferr. phos.*

Some of the salts are available in combined packs: Combination J, containing *Ferr. phos.*, *Kali mur.* and *Nat. mur.*, is a general remedy for coughs and colds. The salts are taken as small tablets, and the recommended dose is given on the container. Tablets are generally taken three or four times a day, or every half hour in chronic cases.

HERBAL MEDICINE

Self help White horehound is one of the most highly recommended herbal cough remedies. Make an infusion (p. 184) of the dried leaves in a cup of boiling water, and take a teaspoonful three times daily. LIQUORICE can be added to offset their bitterness.

Other herbal infusions that can be used are: for hard coughs, mullein; irritating coughs, wild lettuce or, for children, wild cherry bark, which is a mild sedative; coughs with fever, yarrow or angelica; catarrhal coughs, elecampane or elder flower.

NATUROPATHY

Self help Recommended remedies include two garlic tablets three times a day, and vitamin A, B, and C supplements daily. Hot lemon juice with a spoonful of honey and glycerine added should soothe the throat. A towel soaked in three parts hot water to one of cider vinegar and applied as a compress to the throat and chest is said to help get rid of phlegm.

An orthodox view

If the cough is not a symptom of something more serious, a doctor will simply advise you to stay quiet in a warm room and take cough medicine, usually a linctus. These medicines may contain compounds such as codeine to suppress the cough, and expectorants such as triprolidine, pseudoephedrine and guaiphenesin, which help to get rid of phlegm. Linctuses also contain something soothing, such as syrup or glycerol.

COUNSELLING
When just talking to someone can help

There are times when we all need to talk over a problem that life has thrown at us. It may be a crisis of the moment requiring a decision – accepting a move at work, what to do after an exam failure, how to pay a debt. Or the trouble may have been deep or long-

standing, darkening the whole of life – the threat of incurable illness, bereavement or splitting up with a partner, for example.

Because body and mind are inseparable, a physical cause can give rise to psychological symptoms and vice versa. Muscle pains or CONSTIPATION, for example, can result from STRESS and DEPRESSION, while loss of confidence and concentration may stem from helplessness after an operation. Counselling is one way of coming to understand such problems and learning to manage them.

Although counselling is a treatment for the mind – a form of PSYCHOTHERAPY – it is not aimed principally at sick people, but at healthy people who want to deal with a crisis or improve their lives and relationships with others. Counselling does, however, form an important part of helping the terminally ill and their relatives to come to terms with impending death (see TERMINAL ILLNESS).

For people with mental illnesses, or who want extensive analysis and exploration of their own personality, different forms of psychotherapy are more suitable – for example, treatment by a psychologist, psychiatrist or psychoanalyst, all of whom have academic and often medical training in treating the mind. However, counselling may well form part of the treatment they offer.

Supportive counselling for clients who are basically healthy but are in crisis or at the end of their tether may be given by lay people who have had a course of training over a period of some months. The temperament of the counsellor is more important than academic or medical qualifications.

Many difficulties can be eased by a talk with a sympathetic friend or relation. Even a moan to a hairdresser or a letter to a magazine's advice column can lift the load. For more persistent problems, and when friends or relations are the problem, you may need professional help from an independent trained counsellor. But first be sure that you have made the most of your own resources.

Who it can help Anybody who feels that they have no one to turn to, or that they cannot cope with life, can benefit from counselling. Specific legal, educational or social problems can be taken to specialist counsellors. Even people with family and friends about them can receive more help from a totally objective, neutral 'ear' – and may find it easier or less embarrassing to talk to someone who is in no way involved.

Recently counselling has been offered to people who have been involved in a large-scale disaster such as a train collision, shipwreck or air crash. Uninjured survivors and members of the emergency services as well as the victims and their relations suffer long-term distress after such events. Counselling and support groups have been of great help.

Finding a counsellor Spend some time thinking about what your problem really is. Do you want someone just to listen and sympathise, or do you want advice for a particular problem? If you need specific advice, a specialist counsellor is best – someone from a local law centre, careers office, student counselling centre, company personnel office or rape victims' centre, for example. Your local telephone directory will list such centres, or your local Citizens Advice Bureau will help you to find them.

The bureau or your local reference library should have the _Someone to talk to directory_, published by the Mental Health Foundation. It lists counselling services of many kinds – covering bereavement, depression, divorce, marriage guidance, SEXUAL PROBLEMS, stress problems – as well as contacts for people needing help with ADDICTION, educational difficulties, disabilities, family problems, housing and a range of medical disorders. The Mental Health Foundation can provide updated information on counsellors.

For more general counselling you may find a sympathetic ear at your church, synagogue or temple. Or your doctor may refer you to someone suitable. Some health practices have a counsellor on the team. If your doctor cannot help, your Citizens Advice Bureau or the _Someone to talk to directory_ will.

The Westminster Pastoral Foundation, 23 Kensington Square, London w8 5HN, can supply a list of counselling centres all over the country. An introductory interview will sort out which type of counselling would be best for you. A fee is charged but no one is denied help because they cannot pay.

The British Association for Counselling, 37a Sheep Street, Rugby, Warwickshire CV21 3BX, can also supply information on counselling services countrywide and on counsellors in private practice. Where a fee is charged it may vary from about £3 to £15 an hour.

During the 1970s, CO-COUNSELLING was introduced to Britain to give help without the long-term expense that trained counselling can incur. People needing a counsellor are themselves trained as counsellors and then paired with a fellow client-cum-counsellor. The two make their own arrangements for sessions in which they take turns to be talker and listener. For details, send a stamped addressed envelope to Co-counselling International, c/o Westerly, Prestwick Lane, Chiddingfold, Surrey GU8 4XW.

Seeing a counsellor Listening is the chief role of a counsellor. A skilful one will quickly

Relatives and rescuers as well as the victims of disasters – such as the 1988 south London rail crash (right), in which 35 people died – can suffer psychological after-effects that counselling can greatly help.

make you feel sufficiently at ease to talk freely. Your readiness to talk is vital. When you feel trust in the counsellor, you can reveal your thoughts and emotions fully, knowing that what you say will be in confidence. No judgment or criticism will be made, nor will you be cross-examined on matters you are not ready to deal with.

The counsellor may sum up and feed back to you what you have revealed, and point out recurring patterns in your behaviour. If a decision has to be made, the counsellor may outline the case for and against the various options, but any decisions are left to you.

The opportunity to talk without interruption or contradiction is a beneficial release in itself. It boosts self-confidence, clarifies your situation and allows you to assess past actions and work out priorities for the future. The counsellor aims to help you gain insight into your motives and needs, but this will not of itself make your situation different or your future actions easier.

If you have gone to a counsellor for help with a specific problem, the counsellor may do more than just listen. Letter-writing skills, role-playing, practising new behaviour, discussing your problems and progress in a group or other useful techniques may be incorporated in the sessions.

Be prepared to give the counselling a fair trial, but do not persist if the counsellor is not right for you – go to a different one. It is vital to feel that the counsellor is genuinely interested in you and your situation.

Self help To get the most benefit from counselling, you must be prepared to back it up with your own everyday efforts. Eat a healthy, nourishing diet (see EATING FOR HEALTH) and cut down on coffee and tea, which can make you jumpy and irritable. Take some brisk EXERCISE and learn to calm yourself through RELAXATION AND BREATHING exercises. Set aside time for hobbies or other activities you enjoy so that you can forget your problems for a time.

Do not bottle up your feelings between counselling sessions. Pour them out with a good cry, stamp your feet, punch a cushion – or express them in a diary. If writing about your anger and misery is not enough, talk to a discreet friend, an older relative or a priest.

An orthodox view

Doctors do not dispute the benefits of counselling, indeed many would like to have time enough to act as counsellors themselves. If there is no counsellor in their particular practice, they will readily suggest contacts for patients in need. Some, however, prefer not to be involved in what they regard as non-medical aspects of a patient's life. Or they may believe that patients come to them simply to be told what to do.

CRAMP

These agonising muscular spasms usually affect the legs, feet and (in writer's cramp) the hand. The muscles contract suddenly, causing severe pain that can last for several minutes. Such people as athletes and gardeners, who use certain muscles all the time, often suffer from it. Cramp is a recognised industrial disease that may entitle sufferers to a state benefit in some cases.

Other causes of cramp may include swimming in cold water, poor circulation to the muscles (see CIRCULATION PROBLEMS), and salt or other mineral deficiencies. Period pains, which are often called cramps, are not caused by muscular contractions (see PERIOD PROBLEMS).

What the therapists recommend

NATUROPATHY

Self help A diet rich in VITAMINS and MINERALS is recommended, including leafy greens, soya beans, nuts, buttermilk and yoghurt, wholegrain cereals, and seeds such as pumpkin, sesame and sunflower. Some therapists advise avoiding high cholesterol foods such as animal and dairy fats, because

First aid for cramp

Cramp can often be relieved by stretching the cramped muscles from their contracted state. For cases of thigh cramp, sit down, straighten the knee and get a helper to lift the heel of the foot with one hand while pushing firmly down on the knee with the other. For cases of hand cramp, gently force the fingers to straighten, then spread them wide and push the fingertips firmly down on a flat, solid surface.

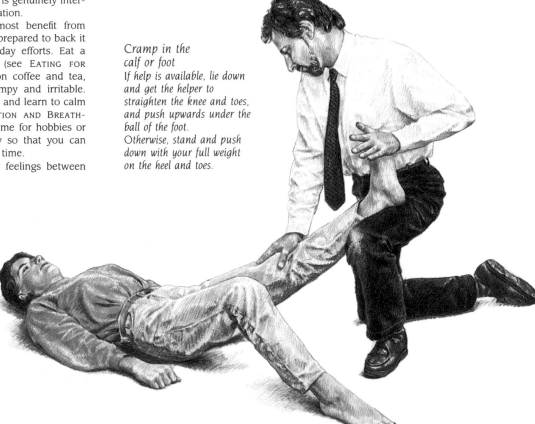

Cramp in the calf or foot
If help is available, lie down and get the helper to straighten the knee and toes, and push upwards under the ball of the foot.
Otherwise, stand and push down with your full weight on the heel and toes.

the cramp may be a sign of poor circulation caused by 'furred' blood vessels.

Supplements of calcium, magnesium, potassium, iron, vitamins B, C and D, and kelp tablets may help if a deficiency is the cause. In addition, vitamin E is recommended for cramps after EXERCISE or during the night. If you sweat a lot at work or exercise, you may need salt tablets to replace salt lost with the sweat.

A practitioner may advise you to make time for relaxation as well as exercise, since TENSION can make cramp more painful. Some victims have also claimed relief from bandaging a magnet loosely to the affected area, and from a tonic which is believed to stimulate the flow of blood to the calves. Make it from a teaspoon each of lemon juice, honey and cloves, mixed with a tablespoon of ginger wine and half a cup of boiling water. Allow it to stand for 24 hours. Take 3 tablespoonsful nightly before bed.

Other alternative treatments

Massage Treat the whole region, not just the affected muscles. Concentrate on stretching the muscles by using gliding and kneading movements (see p. 225) and finish off with chopping strokes, deep massage or effleurage to stimulate circulation to the affected area.

Homoeopathy *Cuprum metallicum* is used for severe cramp, especially in the fingers, legs and toes. *Colchicum* may help cramp in the soles of the feet, and *Nux vomica* is recommended when cramp occurs at night for no known cause. People who also have cold feet or are overweight may find *Calcarea carbonica* useful, and those who suffer from a general feeling of tiredness as well as cramp can be helped by *Arnica*.

Herbal Medicine Decoctions (see p. 184) of crampbark are said to have a relaxing effect on the muscles. Take one cup three times a day. For long-term treatment, decoctions of prickly ash and ginger are believed to improve circulation. Infusions (see p. 184) of ginger can also be used.

Biochemic Tissue Salts *Mag. phos.* is thought to nourish the nerves and muscles and to relieve cramp.

Hydrotherapy Mustard foot baths may help to relieve cramp in the legs, and applying hot and cold compresses is recommended for improving the blood supply to affected muscles.

Aromatherapy Three drops each of basil and marjoram and one drop of lemongrass essential oils are recommended for use in a bath. Alternatively, mix them into 20ml of carrier oil or lotion and rub it into the area immediately, twice daily if the problem is recurring. Regular aromatherapy treatment is said to be helpful for cramp.

An orthodox view

A doctor will advise rest as the best cure for overused muscles, and salt replacement for persistent cramp accompanied by sweating, diarrhoea or vomiting. Sometimes doctors are unable to find the cause, and prescribe small amounts of quinine to relieve the symptoms. In general, they are not opposed to naturopathic therapy.

CRANIAL OSTEOPATHY
Coaxing the skull bones into the right position

The dome of bone that protects the brain is not in one continuous piece. The eight separate bones that make up the skull – the cranium – have the finest of gaps between them. It was once thought that the bones are immovable after young childhood, but now it is known that they can move very slightly in relation to one another.

They move most during birth, and if they do not return to their proper position afterwards, they can distort the flow of 'shock absorber' fluid around the brain, cause pressure on parts of the brain or affect quite different parts of the body through nerves that originate in the brain. Later in life, blows to the head or dental work that displaces the jaw bones can cause the same problems.

Some practitioners of OSTEOPATHY aim to detect and correct pressures and displacements in the skull and facial bones, using the delicate form of manipulation called cranial osteopathy. The techniques were largely developed in the United States in the 1920s by William Garner Sutherland. During experiments to test whether the skull bones could move, he devised various contraptions to squeeze his own skull bones out of position. His wife saw marked changes in his behaviour while the pressure was on.

Who it can help People suffering facial NEURALGIA, MIGRAINE and other HEADACHES have been helped. Discomforts following blows to the head, whiplash injuries and dental work have also been relieved. Disturbances of balance and tinnitus resulting from slight displacement of the temporal bones at the sides of the skull often respond.

Slight pressure on the nerves in the brain can cause circulation and breathing problems, high BLOOD PRESSURE and stomach ULCERS – all of which, it is claimed, can be improved by cranial osteopathy.

Finding a practitioner Follow the recommendations under OSTEOPATHY or ask for a list of practitioners and their qualifications from The Cranial Osteopathic Association, 478 Baker Street, Enfield, Middlesex EN1 3QS.

Consulting a practitioner A careful assessment of your medical history and present symptoms will precede treatment. Manipulation is very gentle, some of it barely perceptible, consisting of tapping, moulding and holding the bones to coax them into the proper alignment. To correct wrongly positioned jaw bones, the osteopath may manipulate them from inside the mouth.

An orthodox view

Cranial osteopathy, like osteopathy in general, is far more widely practised and accepted in the United States than it is in Britain. Here many doctors who accept that osteopathy works do not agree with the fundamental concepts of cranial osteopathy. However, few of them would regard the treatment as harmful.

The only danger is that illnesses which could urgently need quite different treatment may not get it. This risk is avoided by consulting only a reputable osteopath, preferably one who is also a qualified doctor and who will not be too ready to give physical manipulation before checking whether symptoms are caused by a fracture, a tumour or an infection.

CROUP

A harsh, barking cough and strained, noisy breathing are symptoms of croup, which affects babies and children under five (see also COUGHS). It usually strikes in the winter and is often accompanied by FEVER, irritability and restlessness. Croup normally lasts for only about 12 hours, but if it persists – or if the child turns a pale grey-blue colour, or has difficulty in breathing – call a doctor.

What the therapists recommend
NATUROPATHY

Self help A hot, dry atmosphere is to be avoided, say practitioners, so lower or cut off any central heating in the child's bedroom, and see that the room is well ventilated. If you have room humidifiers, use them.

Consultation A naturopath will probably advise cutting down the child's intake of dairy foods such as butter, milk, cheese and yoghurt, which are believed to increase mucus (see CATARRH). He may also advise supplements of vitamin C to build up body defences, and recommend garlic or onions in the diet. Soya milk or proprietary milk formula can replace cow's milk for babies.

HYDROTHERAPY

Steam inhalation can help to relieve croup symptoms. Shut all bathroom doors and windows, and fill the bath or basin with hot water. Since steam rises, sit with the child on your lap so that his head is held as high as possible. Do not leave the child alone, and take care to avoid scalding.

Other alternative treatments

Herbal Medicine A soothing infusion said to ease croup can be made by adding a teaspoon each of coltsfoot and vervain to a cup of boiling water. Cover and leave for about ten minutes and then strain through muslin. Make sure it is not too hot, then give a teaspoonful to children under three, or a tablespoonful if the child is older.
Aromatherapy Two drops each of eucalyptus and sandalwood essential oils added to a teaspoon of carrier oil and rubbed into a child's chest is recommended as beneficial for croup.

An orthodox view

As croup is usually caused by a VIRUS INFECTION in the larynx, or voice box (see LARYNGITIS), a doctor will not prescribe antibiotics unless there are complications – such as a risk of PNEUMONIA. However, he may give an aspirin to reduce fever, and recommend cool drinks of milk, fruit juice or water.

A baby or child in great pain or discomfort may be sent to hospital for observation.

CUPPING
Suction cups for removing 'poisons'

This technique was used by practitioners of Western medicine for many centuries to treat a range of maladies. It is still part of traditional Chinese medicine, and is most commonly used to relieve BOILS or abscesses, some cases of ARTHRITIS and RHEUMATISM, ASTHMA, BRUISING, COLDS and a CHILL.

Cupping involves applying suction 'cups' made of bamboo or glass in various sizes to the body. Alcohol-soaked cotton held in forceps and set alight – or simply a lighted taper – is held at the mouth of the inverted cup. The heat causes the air inside to expand, and some of it escapes. The cup is then placed mouth down on the patient's skin, and as it cools, the partial vacuum inside makes it stick on and draw the flesh

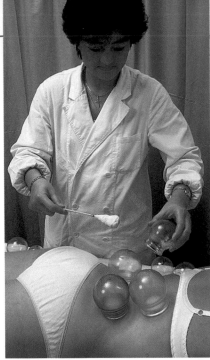

A therapist places glass suction cups mouth-down on the patient's back along the energy meridian lines. This aims to draw any 'bad energy' to the surface and bring relief.

into the cup. The skin becomes red with the increased blood flow that results.

To release the cup, pressure is exerted on the skin around it. The time the cups are left in place varies according to the age and constitution of the patient and the complaint.

Western doctors believed that the increased blood flow under the cup drew impurities away from nearby organs and tissues. Sometimes the skin under the cup was cut so that the 'poisons' flowed out of the body with the blood. Even in the early part of this century some doctors still used cupping to 'draw' boils.

The Chinese theory underlying cupping is that it gets rid of unwanted or 'perverse' *Qi* – energy, or life force – in the body. Practitioners believe cupping draws the perverse energy to the body's surface and disperses it.

CYMATICS
The healing effects of sound waves

Practitioners of this therapy compare the human body to a musical instrument which sometimes makes discordant sounds and needs to be 'tuned'. They claim to do this by directing high-frequency sound waves onto the affected area, restoring the body to a harmonious whole. The term cymatics

comes from the Greek word *kyma*, meaning 'a billow' or 'great wave'.
Who it can help It is claimed that cymatics is particularly beneficial for people suffering from ARTHRITIS, BACK PAIN, bone FRACTURES, LUMBAGO, RHEUMATISM, SLIPPED DISC, and forms of paralysis. The therapy is also given to people who are to have an operation such as a hip replacement (see HIP COMPLAINTS), to aid and accelerate the healing process.
Finding a therapist Cymatics was founded in England in the 1960s by Dr Peter Manners. Information is available from his clinic at Bretforton Hall, Bretforton, Vale of Evesham, Worcestershire WR11 5JH.
Consulting a therapist Patients are treated mostly by means of a hand-held instrument called a sound-wave applicator, which is used in much the same way as a massage vibrator. There may also be a warm-water treatment pool into which sound waves are transmitted. This, it is said, greatly enhances the healing effect of the water. Special therapeutic music which incorporates sound waves aimed to relax and increase feelings of well-being may also be played.

An orthodox view

Doctors have confirmed that fractures heal quicker if sound waves are applied to the broken limb, and this therapy is now used in several orthopaedic centres. Research is currently directed at finding further uses.

CYSTITIS

Burning pain on passing urine; repeated trips to the lavatory, often to pass only a few drops; pain in the abdomen and back – the distressing symptoms of cystitis are well known to many women. The cause is an inflamed membrane lining the bladder – usually the result of bacteria from the anus passing through the urinary passage.

Food ALLERGY, chemical sensitivity, bruising during intercourse and vaginal THRUSH can also cause the inflammation. Symptoms vary from mild to severe, sometimes disappearing within hours, sometimes dragging on for weeks. Many victims have only a single bout; others suffer repeated attacks. In all cases – especially if there is blood in the urine – it is advisable to see a doctor before seeking alternative treatments.

Men are rarely affected because anal bacteria have much farther to travel to reach a man's urinary passage and bladder (see also URETHRITIS). In children, cystitis is often associated with CONSTIPATION, which may cause pressure on the bladder.

First aid for cystitis

Start home treatment as soon as symptoms begin. Attacks can often be cut short by taking the following steps immediately:

Drink 1 pint (600ml) of water or mild camomile tea straight away, to flush germs out of the bladder.

Use hot-water bottles wrapped in towels to alleviate pain in the lower back or pelvic region.

Take a teaspoon of bicarbonate of soda in a glass of water every three hours. This makes the urine less acidic, which stops bacteria from breeding and relieves burning.

Warning Patients with high BLOOD PRESSURE or HEART DISORDERS should ask a doctor's advice before taking bicarbonate of soda.

If pain persists, take one or two mild painkillers (aspirin or paracetamol).

Apply live yoghurt to the affected area. The friendly bacteria it contains can help to fight invading germs.

Drink as much water or mild herbal tea as you can – at least ½ pint (300ml) every 20 minutes – and go to the lavatory as often as necessary.

Lie down or sit in a comfortable chair, keep warm and relax. After three hours most attacks should begin to wear off. See your doctor if the symptoms persist.

Do not eat citrus or sour fruit, and avoid foods containing vinegar, and animal proteins such as eggs, fish, meat and cheese: they make the urine more acid and painful to pass.

What the therapists recommend

NATUROPATHY

Self help After urinating, rinse away any germs by pouring cool, boiled water over the urethral and vaginal openings while leaning back slightly on the lavatory seat. Wipe from front to back with toilet paper, taking care not to touch the anal area. After passing a motion, wipe as before, from front to back. Afterwards, wash the anus with warm, soapy water and then carefully pat dry with clean cotton wool.

A diet of mild, non-irritating foods may also help. Cut out hot, spicy dishes, and replace tea, coffee and cola drinks with herb teas, fresh juices or coffee substitutes such as chicory and barley extracts. Two or three glasses a day of mixed raw apple and carrot juice are recommended, and some sufferers have found relief by taking dolomite or propolis tablets.

Consultation The naturopath will make tests and ask questions to try to find out what is irritating your bladder. Allergy tests are often made, and a diet is drawn up to cut out harmful foods. If you also suffer from thrush, the diet may exclude all yeast-containing foods such as bread, cheese, wine and beer. Sometimes a two-day fast is recommended, followed by a RAW FOOD DIET.

HERBAL MEDICINE

Self help Single attacks of cystitis are said often to be cleared up by drinking large amounts of yarrow infusion (see p. 184). The following herbal mixtures may be used to treat more persistent cases: A decoction (see p. 184) of equal amounts of marsh-mallow leaves, bearberry, sage and horsetail well mixed together: take one cup three times a day. An infusion made from corn silk, cherry stalks, bilberries and poppies in equal quantities: take two or three cups a day. An infusion made from equal amounts of corn silk, couch grass, bearberry and yarrow: take three times a day.

Barley water is also believed to have a soothing and mildly diuretic effect that can help. Put 4oz (120g) barley in enough water to cover it and bring to the boil. Strain it, then pour 1 pint (600ml) of cold water over the barley, add the rind of half a lemon and simmer until the barley is soft. Leave until lukewarm. Now remove the barley, add 1-2 tablespoons of honey, and drink as required.

HOMOEOPATHY

Self help _Cantharis_ is used to treat burning pains when passing urine, _Staphysagria_ for cystitis due to bruising or injury, _Aconite_ for the sudden onset of symptoms after exposure to dry cold, and _Sarsaparilla_ when pain is felt only after urinating.

When the cause is a chill caught by getting cold and wet. _Dulcamara_ is recommended. If you have a high temperature, try _Belladonna._

BIOCHEMIC TISSUE SALTS

Self help _Ferr. phos._ is recommended for early stages when there is frequent and burning urination; _Kali phos._ for a cutting or scalding pain, and _Mag. phos._ when there is a constant but unproductive urge to urinate.

Other alternative treatments

Aromatherapy Make a tea using juniper and eucalyptus oils and drink three or four cups daily. Also helpful are eight drops of essential oils in a warm bath lasting ten minutes once or twice daily. Other helpful oils include benzoin, bergamot, black pepper, cajuput, fennel, frankincense, lavender, naiouli, pine and sandalwood.

Hydrotherapy Spray the pelvic area for three minutes with warm water, followed by one minute of cold spraying, to relieve pain. Do the same over the upper part of the sacrum (between the two dimples in the lower back). Repeat three or four times in each treatment. Hot and cold sitz baths may also help (see HYDROTHERAPY).

Reflexology Massage to the reflex area relating to the bladder is recommended, plus areas relating to the kidneys, ureter, lymph nodes of the pelvis, adrenal and pituitary glands and, in men, the prostate gland.

An orthodox view

Doctors agree that rest and drinking large quantities of mild liquids will benefit many sufferers. However, they usually treat cystitis by prescribing sulphonamide drugs such as sulphafurazole. If attacks keep occurring, the bladder or urethra may be stretched while the patient is under anaesthetic.

Do's and don'ts for cystitis sufferers

_Do_ maintain a high standard of personal hygiene.

_Do_ take an allergy test and avoid foods that yield a positive response.

_Do_ avoid excessive vibration such as riding a motorbike for long journeys.

_Do_ try alternative methods of CONTRACEPTION if taking the Pill or using a condom, cap or diaphragm seems to bring on attacks.

_Do_ use sanitary towels instead of tampons.

Don't use perfumed soaps, powders or other toiletries on the skin or in your bath, and avoid vaginal deodorants.

_Do_ wash underwear with hand soap or soap flakes, as some washing powders can cause irritation. Always rinse out soap thoroughly.

_Do_ use a lubricating cream such as KY Jelly – available from chemists – or experiment with different positions if attacks occur after sexual intercourse. Passing urine immediately after intercourse can also help by flushing out any germs.

_Do_ wear pure cotton underwear and loose-fitting clothes, and wear stockings rather than tights, to allow air to circulate freely.

_Do_ go to the lavatory as soon as you feel the need. Holding back gives bacteria a chance to breed.

Don't expose the bladder to heat and cold: don't sit on icy ground or on radiators, and don't stand around in wet clothes or in a wind.

DANCE MOVEMENT THERAPY
Listening to the body's message

As small children we can readily express our feelings long before we learn to talk. One of the ways we communicate is through body movements. Once we can speak, we may forget that our bodies are still in touch with feelings that are worrying, embarrassing, or simply hard to talk about. Dance movement therapy uses the connection between body movement and emotion in order to help us express and manage feelings too deep to recognise or too difficult to explain in words.

Most tribal communities have recognised from earliest times the healing power of dance, but complex modern societies did not become aware of its relevance to modern ailments until the 1940s when dancers in the United States began to develop ways of using it to help people suffering from mental health problems. Dance movement therapy developed even later in Britain and by the late 1970s there were still few therapists.

Who it can help Adults are usually referred to a therapist because of emotional problems, including ANXIETY and DEPRESSION, and difficulties with relationships. Therapy can also help in more serious illnesses such as SCHIZOPHRENIA, MANIC DEPRESSIVE DISORDER, ANOREXIA and BULIMIA, and in drug or alcohol ADDICTION. Adults with learning disabilities can benefit from it, as can people with certain stress-related physical illnesses – HEART DISORDERS, for example.

Dance movement therapy is particularly effective for children, especially those with learning or emotional difficulties, those with limited ability to concentrate and those who find it hard to get on with other children. Children with behaviour problems resulting from family stresses, including physical or sexual abuse, and even severely mentally handicapped children and those with AUTISM are successfully treated. Physically disabled children, such as the blind and deaf, may also benefit from the therapy.

Finding a therapist Most dance movement therapists work in hospitals, day care centres, family welfare centres, homes for the elderly or in schools. Clients are referred to them at their own request or at the suggestion of a member of staff such as a doctor, psychologist, social worker or teacher. Treatment is free if it is available at one of these places.

Private sessions, for which you have to pay yourself, are not easy to find. If you do try to find a private therapist, make sure that the person you choose is reliable. The best guarantee of this at present is a recommendation from other clients, postgraduate training in dance movement therapy or recognition by a body such as The Association for Dance Movement Therapy, which was formed in 1982 and has a strict code of professional practice. You can get in touch with the association c/o The Arts Therapies Department, Springfield Hospital, Glenburnie Road, London sw17 7dj.

Classes or courses which you may see advertised in health magazines or fitness centres are sometimes helpful in promoting personal growth. However, many of them are not run by a qualified dance movement

Two members of the group, a man and a woman, became involved in moving together. When other group members join in, the man is shocked to discover how he suddenly feels inhibited. He realises that his problems in relating to women are connected to difficulties in coping with jealous and intrusive family members.

This young woman is going through a time when she feels overloaded by the claims life is making on her. She has asked for support from a group member while she struggles with a large bean bag. She is surprised to find support especially valuable as she rests between spells of more demanding activity.

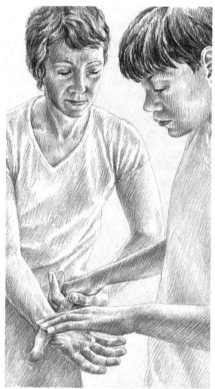

The therapist is working with a non-speaking 14-year-old boy to build a relationship through their movements. It has taken a long time for the boy to develop enough trust to let his hands be touched. In earlier sessions the therapist moved at a distance, echoing the shape and rhythm of the boy's movements.

therapist, and they are not generally suitable for people with the emotional and psychological problems or physical handicaps that are outlined above.

Consulting a therapist Treatment sessions may be individual or for groups. Before you join a group the therapist will usually wish to see you on your own. Some groups meet in the evening to suit people who work in the daytime. Others are run for hospital patients, day care clients or children at times more suitable for them.

Treatment varies according to the client's problems and the therapist's personal style, but some features are common. Clients need have no previous experience of movement or dance, nor is there any stress on competence in learning or carrying out sequences of movements. Instead, the emphasis is on exploring movements and expanding your vocabulary of movements as you discover resources within yourself.

You need not be young and active. Therapists are used to working with people who are anxious, elderly, frail or overweight.

Sessions always begin with movements that everyone can manage, sometimes even while sitting down.

If you begin dance movement therapy, always tell the therapist at the start about any difficulties you may have, such as BACK PAIN or high BLOOD PRESSURE. The therapist may advise you to see your doctor before deciding on suitable treatment. However, while a therapist will always be alert to physical problems, the main focus of the work is understanding your feelings and working out how to deal with them. Although some people are helped by treatment that lasts only a few weeks, it is usually necessary to continue for longer.

Sessions start with a warm-up period to loosen muscles. Music may be used during the session, but not always – it can distract clients from what they want to express. The therapist may suggest movements but clients are not expected to follow the suggestions rigidly. They are encouraged to contribute ideas of their own.

A theme will usually emerge from the movements and this may be explored by clients working separately, in pairs or in a group. A theme that emerges might be, for example, the way in which one person always makes movements that are very fast and forceful at first but then fizzle out; or the way that, in a group, the members always move at arm's length, never coming closer to one another or getting farther apart.

To begin with, the therapist may need to step in, picking up the themes that clients have introduced and helping them to explore and resolve the problems they encounter. Eventually, clients may begin to identify important issues and learn how to work through a problem by themselves. Clients may discuss the feelings aroused by the movement and try to integrate their insights into further movements so that there is continuing interplay between feelings, talk and movement.

Therapists working with seriously disturbed or handicapped clients use their highly developed sensitivity to movement to establish a relationship that does not rely on words. The relationship enables the therapist to support the client through the experiences of excitement, sadness, frustration and fear that are part of normal development.

An orthodox view

There are no risks involved in dance movement therapy with a qualified therapist. Evidence is growing that it has psychological and emotional benefits. It serves as an effective non-verbal form of psychotherapy. The therapy helps, in particular, patients who are mentally ill or mentally handicapped, or who have severe behavioural problems.

DANDRUFF

The exact cause of dandruff has long been uncertain. Some doctors believe it is the result of either too much or too little oil being produced by sebaceous glands in the scalp.

However, some dermatologists suggest that it is caused by an infection, and a yeast fungus has been isolated that is believed to breed in a combination of sebaceous oil and dead skin cells. Anti-fungal shampoos, developed in the 1980s, are now available in chemists and health stores.

What the therapists recommend

NATUROPATHY

Self help Natural 'live' yoghurt is recommended as a hair conditioner. First wash and rinse the hair, then rub yoghurt well into the scalp, and leave for 10-15 minutes. Rinse it out, then wash again, using as little shampoo as necessary. A strong infusion (p. 184) of thyme, nettle or sage with 2 tablespoons of vinegar can be used as a final rinse.

Consultation A practitioner will tell you that dandruff may indicate poisons in the system or nutritional deficiencies and imbalances in levels of minerals and/or trace elements. He will recommend a diet of plenty of fresh fruit and vegetables, wholegrains and wheatgerm, vegetable oils and high-protein food, such as lean meat and nuts. To be avoided are: sugar and starch products, alcohol, and fatty or highly spiced foods.

Other alternative treatments

Herbal Medicine For a scalp massage after shampooing, use infusions (p. 184) of rosemary or lavender, or a few drops of essential oil of these herbs, rubbed into the scalp. Alternatively, boil ½oz (15g) of sage leaves in 1¾ pints (1 litre) of water for five minutes. Leave to infuse for another five minutes – and then use it as a scalp massage.

Aromatherapy Mix essential oils of cedarwood (seven drops), cypress and juniper (each ten drops) in 50ml of carrier oil. Rub well into the scalp and leave for one hour. To remove, rub neat, mild shampoo into the hair then wash out with warm water.

To keep dandruff at bay, use the same quantities of the oils in a pint (600ml) of warm water. Stir well and use as a final rinse.

An orthodox view

A doctor will probably recommend washing the hair only once or twice a week in a mild detergent shampoo available from chemists. You will also be advised to avoid harsh hair dyes and scented hair creams; also brilliantines and other oily dressings.

DEAFNESS

Some people are born totally or partially deaf; others become deaf gradually, after the age of about 50. Both conditions fall into one of two main categories: *conductive deafness*, which is mostly curable, and *nerve deafness*, which is not.

Conductive deafness is due to something hindering the transmission of sound waves to the cochlea, the sound-sensitive organ of the inner ear. It can have a number of causes including infections, earwax, sudden loud noises, foreign objects such as a bead in a child's ear, and otosclerosis – a fusion of the small bones in the middle ear, which mainly affects women aged between 20 and 40.

Nerve deafness occurs when the auditory nerve which carries stimuli from the ear to the brain is damaged. This is usually caused by viral infections such as MEASLES, MUMPS and German measles (rubella). German measles can damage the hearing of babies whose mothers contracted the infection during the first three months of pregnancy.

Never attempt to relieve deafness yourself. Poking about in the ear to remove wax or foreign objects can lead to perforated eardrums and possibly permanent deafness.

What the therapists recommend
NATUROPATHY
Consultation Practitioners believe that diet can affect the functioning of the ears, and may recommend a diet rich in VITAMINS A and B1 (thiamine). Vitamin A comes in dairy foods such as cheese and eggs, as well as liver and carrots. Vitamin B1 is found in brewer's yeast, wholemeal bread, potatoes and peanuts, and is said to help repair damaged cell tissue in the ear and to strengthen the auditory nerve.
Self help In straightforward cases of earwax, soften it with a few drops of almond or olive oil and lemon juice, heated in a cupful of warm water to body temperature. Apply with a small dropper two or three times a day, taking care not to poke your ear with the dropper. Do not probe the ear with a cotton bud, as this can make wax harder to remove and may cause damage.

ACUPUNCTURE
Consultation Some cases of deafness – those caused by, or associated with, CATARRH, DIZZINESS, MOTION SICKNESS, RINGING IN THE EARS and Ménière's syndrome – are said to respond to stimulating the nerves regulating the workings of the ear. Acupuncturists relate these workings to the kidneys and bladder, so the practitioner may treat points on the meridians for these organs. MOXIBUSTION may also be applied.

The bladder meridian extends from the eye, round the back of the head and down the spine and back of the left leg. The kidney meridian is down the left front of the body and the front of the left leg (see chart, p. 14).

Other alternative treatments
Chiropractic By manipulating the patient's neck, chiropractors can sometimes ease tinnitus (see RINGING IN THE EARS).
Biochemic Tissue Salts Practitioners recommend *Kali sulph.* for deafness caused by catarrh and *Kali phos.* for deafness accompanied by nervous exhaustion (see also NERVOUS DISORDERS). Normal recommended dosage is four tablets dissolved on the tongue three times a day for adults, two tablets for children and one for babies. In acute cases, adults can take one tablet every half hour. Do not eat or drink anything for 15 minutes before and after each dose.

An orthodox view
Where deafness is conductive, and therefore curable, most doctors do not object to the use of alternative remedies as a supplement to conventional treatments. They agree with naturopaths in using warm oil to treat earwax and are not opposed to tissue salts as an added aid. If these methods are not sufficient, they may syringe the ears.

However, a conventional doctor would send any patient suffering from any form of nerve deafness or other severe hearing loss to an ear specialist. In most cases – such as old-age deafness – a hearing aid may be fitted; in others, such as otosclerosis, the fused bones may be separated by surgery.

Advice about deafness and its treatment can be obtained from the Royal National Institute for the Deaf, 105 Gower Street, London WC1E 6AH.

DEPRESSION

Each year about one person in every thousand in Britain is treated in hospital for depression. In addition, 15 in every thousand consult their doctors about feeling depressed, while far more do not seek medical advice and try to cope with the illness alone.

According to pscyhiatrists, there are two kinds of depression: *exogenous*, becoming depressed as a result of outside factors such as divorce, job loss, money troubles, or the death of a loved one; and *endogenous*, resulting from internal biochemical sources – a medical form of depression. Sometimes, spells of euphoria and hyperactivity alternate with periods of deep depression (see MANIC DEPRESSIVE DISORDER).

With such a complex and serious illness it is hard to separate normal and therapeutic feelings of sadness and GRIEF from clinical depression. In some cases, symptoms of straightforward ANXIETY may mask a state of depression. Depression is more common among women than men, and affects people of all ages – from young children to pensioners. It is also the cause of 50-75 per cent of all suicides in Britain each year.

Symptoms include feelings of worthlessness, inadequacy, isolation and despair – and the belief that no one understands or sympathises with you. This may be accompanied by loss of interest in work or home life, inability to concentrate on anything, and, in severe cases, sluggish thought processes and delusions (see also NERVOUS DISORDERS).

Physically, symptoms may include loss of energy, a sense of 'heaviness', difficulty or slowness in movement, a dryness in the mouth, INDIGESTION, sluggish bowel movements and CONSTIPATION. In some cases sufferers may lose weight and women may have PERIOD PROBLEMS.

Occasionally people may be prone to depression from birth due to irregularities in the biochemical make-up of the brain. With some patients depression is associated with ANAEMIA, hormonal changes, low thyroid activity (see THYROID DISORDERS), VITAMIN deficiencies or ADDICTION to drugs. Some women suffer from the so-called 'six-day blues' following childbirth, a depressive phase related to sudden hormonal changes.
Warning If symptoms – mental or physical – are severe or last for more than a few weeks, professional help should be sought.

What the therapists recommend
HOMOEOPATHY
Consultation A therapist should be consulted if bouts of depression are frequent or intense. For short-lived bouts, in which the sufferer is anxious, restless, or exhausted – especially in the small hours – *Arsenicum album* is recommended. To help overcome emotional upset or bereavement, try *Ignatia* immediately after the event. If the distress persists then take *Natrum mur.* All these remedies should be taken in the 6th potency, three times a day for two weeks.

If the sufferer feels suicidal, professional help must be sought without delay.

BACH REMEDIES
Self help If depression follows an illness or long-standing exhaustion, Olive is said to be helpful. For cases of sudden depression, accompanied by repressed anger, Mustard; when depression is caused by resentment or

bitterness, Willow. Gorse is said to be effective for feelings of hopelessness. Larch may help overcome lack of confidence, and Centaury aids those who put other people's interests before their own.

People in extreme despair, especially spiritually, are advised to take Sweet chestnut. Walnut is held to help cope with major changes in life, and for anyone who has lost interest in life, or is apathetic.

Beating the blues

Everyone feels depressed from time to time, especially if things start to get 'on top' of them and they feel they cannot cope. If this happens, the following self-help measures may help solve the problem. If they do not, consult a therapist or doctor.

Taking exercise Try to increase your energy level by taking up an activity such as cycling, jogging, or swimming. Alternatively, you could join a BIOENERGETICS group.

Expressing your feelings Sometimes depression may be caused by pent-up anger or the inability to cry. If this seems to be so, release your anger and let yourself weep.

Making physical contact Feelings of loneliness and isolation may sometimes bring on depression. If this happens, make arrangements to have a MASSAGE or SHIATSU treatment.

Keeping a diary Writing down your thoughts each day is a good way of obtaining relief, especially if you are feeling overburdened and overwhelmed by life.

Talking things over Depression can often be lifted by simply talking over your problems with a friend, perhaps while taking a walk together.

Thinking positively Depressing situations may be relieved by making positive statements about yourself and your circumstances. For example, tell yourself, 'I am *not* a victim', 'I *will* overcome', 'Tomorrow *is* another day'.

Breathing deeply Taking full YOGA breaths, or bellows breaths, can be an effective means of overcoming feelings of gloom and despair.

Visualising peaceful images Imagining you are in a tranquil, comfortable place can assist in banishing depressing thoughts.

Creating artistically Painting, drawing, dancing, singing and playing musical instruments are all effective ways of combating depression.

Other alternative treatments

Naturopathy Practitioners prescribe large doses of vitamin B to counteract depression. In particular, vitamin B6 is recommended for mood swings associated with period problems. If the MENOPAUSE is thought to have caused depression, some therapists will advise the patient to have hormone replacement therapy (HRT), the treatment that conventional doctors prescribe.

Hydrotherapy Therapists say that SAUNA BATHS and vigorous rubs have proved effective for some sufferers.

Acupuncture Depression is regarded as a LIVER DISORDER, and practitioners concentrate on points on meridians associated with the liver, gall bladder, pericardium (the fibrous sheath around the heart), ren, du, spleen and stomach.

Aromatherapy Aromatherapy body massage is said to be most effective in relieving depression. Several oils are also held to be beneficial. They include basil, clary sage, neroli, otto, Roman camomile, rose and thyme. The oils should be inhaled deeply from a tissue at regular intervals, or six to eight drops of any one of them can be put into your bath.

Herbal Medicine One or two cups of borage or vervain tea are believed to raise your spirits. Alternatively, try a hot cup of rosemary tea each day with a pinch of valerian. A recommended nerve tonic is an infusion of four to five flowering lavender tops, with relaxing honey added to taste.

Autosuggestion and Hypnotherapy Therapists who practice both of these techniques have claimed success in the treatment of depressive cases.

Massage The pleasant and relaxing effects of massage are said to help relieve those suffering from depression.

An orthodox view

Although most doctors are not opposed to alternative remedies, they feel they should go hand-in-hand with conventional medical or psychological treatment. For example, in cases of mild depression, tranquillisers or sleeping pills will probably be prescribed. With more serious cases a course of antidepressant drugs – lasting for several weeks or even months – may be advised. Anyone who feels suicidally depressed should seek immediate medical help.

Sometimes a course of PSYCHOTHERAPY will be advised. This involves the patient seeing a psychotherapist at regular intervals, either individually or as part of a group. Alternatively, a GP may send a depressive patient to see a counsellor, who will try to help him to come to terms with his problems and so overcome them (see COUNSELLING).

DIABETES

Unquenchable thirst and passing abnormal amounts of urine are among the first signs of diabetes. The disorder occurs when the pancreas, a gland situated behind the stomach, fails to produce enough insulin – the hormone that regulates the blood sugar level.

In some cases complications – such as ANGINA, blocked arteries (see ARTERIES [HARDENING]), CATARACTS and KIDNEY COMPLAINTS – may eventually occur. But most diabetics learn to live fairly comfortably with their incurable – but controllable – condition. No one knows what exactly causes the insulin failure. Some doctors believe the disorder may be hereditary; others think that VIRUS INFECTIONS could be to blame.

Warning Since diabetes is a serious illness, medical advice is imperative, especially if the sufferer is a child.

What the therapists recommend

Naturopathy Most naturopaths consider that a high-fibre diet – including wholemeal bread, jacket potatoes, spinach, bran cereals, almonds and baked beans – reduces the body's need for insulin. It is also said to lower fat levels in the blood and lessen the risk of accompanying heart disease.

Some practitioners believe that the complications associated with diabetes may be avoided by taking extra minerals and vitamins, including daily doses of vitamin C (1g), vitamin E (250iu), chromium (200 micrograms), manganese (4mg) and zinc (15mg).

Herbal Medicine As well as a strict, high-fibre diet, herbalists may recommend taking raw garlic. This is believed to help curb the increase of sugar in the blood, which otherwise causes the kidneys to produce large amounts of urine.

In addition, practitioners may offer various herbs to ease the condition. These may include: burdock (to help the kidneys to work properly); gentian (to stimulate the working of the pancreas); and goat's rue (to cut down sugar levels).

Aromatherapy A body and bath oil containing a mixture of six to eight drops each of camphor, eucalyptus, geranium, juniper, lemon and rosemary is said to help to balance secretions from the pancreas. Back massage with four drops of the mixture in a teaspoon of vegetable carrier oil is also held to be beneficial for some people.

Yoga Some exercises in Hatha yoga are believed to balance the body's natural processes and so help relieve diabetes.

Homoeopathy Remedies are chosen according to individual symptoms – for example, *Phosphoric ac.* when exhaustion makes them worse, *Silicea* when the feet are cold and sweaty, *Uranium nit.* when there are digestive problems and weakness, and *Arg. nit.* when the victim feels depressed. In each case, 6C potency is recommended.

An orthodox view

Provided that patients take daily doses of insulin, most doctors see no harm in the use of alternative remedies. In fact, they may well recommend special diets – especially those that are low in sugar.

Daily insulin injections are necessary for children and most adults. These replace the loss when the pancreas fails to produce insulin. Some older people – whose bodies usually produce some insulin – need take only insulin tablets each day, and mild cases can sometimes be controlled by diet alone.

Diabetics using insulin will sometimes feel the effects of low blood sugar due to an accidental overdose. Symptoms include fainting, unsteadiness, sweating and disturbed behaviour such as incoherence and loss of memory. Most diabetics recognise these warning signs and can cut short the attacks by eating sugar. If they do not, they may appear intoxicated and are at risk of going into a coma. If this happens, call a doctor or ambulance straight away.

People prone to such attacks should carry a card or wear a bracelet stating their condition and asking for immediate medical aid.

DIAGNOSIS

In any consultation, one of the first and most important tasks of a practitioner is to decide what the patient's problem is. This process is called *diagnosis*, and the ways in which it is done differ according to the kind of medicine practised. Having the problem diagnosed is obviously very important to the sick person, for it helps a patient to understand the situation and feel more in control.

However, not all practitioners make a formal diagnosis before beginning treatment. Some alternative therapists simply accept whatever reason the patient gives for the visit, since they view all illness as coming from the same source – the individual's separation from divine or natural healing forces (see HEALERS AND HEALING).

Conventional doctors view each illness as a separate problem with its own causes, symptoms and treatment. Their diagnosis is basically a scientific process of making observations of the patient and using logical reasoning to identify the illness.

In practice, however, many doctors tend to offer some sort of treatment *before* they make a formal diagnosis, and admit that they do not always use purely scientific methods. Like many alternative practitioners, they use their accumulated experience and subjective impression of the patient's condition to form an opinion. They recognise a pattern in his symptoms or behaviour, and feel able to see the whole picture from just a small part.

All practitioners begin by asking about the problem and the patient – a process known as 'taking a history'. A physical examination and, sometimes, tests follow. Here are some of the diagnostic methods that are used by alternative therapists:

Taking a history Questions are asked about the problem, how long it has been present, and how it began. The patient may also be asked for background information about family, work and past illnesses; also about personal habits and way of life – for example, patterns of sleep (see SLEEP DISORDERS) and any ADDICTION, such as SMOKING. The practitioner will listen carefully to the answers, and also hear the patient's own views regarding the problem.

Other specific questions are also asked by particular types of therapists.

Homoeopaths need to know about personality traits which they call 'mentals' – for example, whether you are anxious or easily upset – and also about unusual symptoms such as if pain is worse on one side of the body than the other, or if there is numbness or discomfort in an apparently unconnected area. Cravings for certain foods and responses to changes in the weather are also deemed important, as is your vaccination and immunisation record.

Naturopaths are more interested in diet and way of life. They will ask about sleep patterns, and the appearance of the urine and motions, as well as your sexual and, for women, menstrual history.

Oriental medicine considers weather factors and emotional states to be of particular importance. The practitioner – in ACUPUNCTURE, ACUPRESSURE or SHIATSU – will probably want to know how the changing seasons affect you, and how you respond to heat, cold, wind, dampness and dryness.

Osteopaths will ask about injuries and accidents, and will be interested in your posture and how you sit, walk, stand and sleep.

Physical examination Some of the alternative therapists also make different kinds of physical examinations.

Oriental medicine views taking pulses and examining the tongue as most important. The practitioner will also listen to your breathing, observe the brightness of your eyes, and consider the colour and texture of the skin. Acupuncturists measure 12 different

pulses – six in each hand – each of which is held to reflect the health of a different organ or bodily system.

Osteopaths carefully examine the spine, ask you to perform some simple movements, measure your legs to see if one is shorter than the other, and examine the working of your joints.

Tests As well as blood tests, X-rays and other conventional means, many alternative therapists use HAIR DIAGNOSIS to reveal any shortage of VITAMINS, MINERALS or other nutrients; KINESIOLOGY to test for ALLERGY; electronic instruments called biometers to show if there are ENERGY blocks; and KIRLIAN PHOTOGRAPHY to check the state of the aura. Cranial osteopaths, spiritual healers and some acupuncturists diagnose mainly by passing their hands over the patient's body to sense his aura and feel for blockages in the flow of vital energy (see AURA THERAPY).

The diagnosis To a practitioner who adopts a holistic approach, the diagnosis is seen as a way of understanding the patient as a whole person, rather than just labelling his illness. Nevertheless, most patients want to know what is wrong with them, and the practitioner may tell them that they have a particular condition, such as ASTHMA or ARTHRITIS, or say that the symptoms show that their systems are 'out of balance' and need to be restored.

Instead of treating the illness as something specific that happens to the patient and has to be treated in its own right, the illness is considered to be a sign that something is wrong with the person's *overall* health, and treatment should help them become wholly well again. The patient, and not the illness, is diagnosed and treated.

DIARRHOEA

Most cases of diarrhoea occur after eating infected food. The cause is inflammation of the large intestine which normally clears up within a day or two. More prolonged attacks can be serious, and babies and elderly, frail victims are particularly at risk, as the resultant fluid loss can cause dehydration.

If the diarrhoea lasts for more than 48 hours, call a doctor. See also DYSENTERY.

What the therapists recommend

NATUROPATHY

Consultation Practitioners tend to feel that diarrhoea is the body's natural reaction to unwanted substances – and should not be dealt with by suppressants such as kaolin for at least 36 hours. But they emphasise the importance of avoiding bodily liquid loss by keeping up the fluid intake.

Self help Victims are advised to avoid food for 24 hours, taking only mineral water or 2 tablespoons of apple juice at regular, 15-30 minute intervals. When symptoms subside, the advice is to eat boiled rice and water, vegetable juices or soups.

It is claimed that live yoghurt helps the large intestine to restore its protective bacteria in cases where they have been destroyed by the infection.

Return gradually to other solid foods such as steamed carrots, bananas, hard-boiled eggs and toast, then slowly resume a normal diet. This dietary procedure is claimed also to be effective for children, but the advice is to purée the food in a blender.

HOMOEOPATHY
If diarrhoea is caused by food poisoning, especially meat, take *Arsen. alb.*, or *Carbo veg.* if bad fish is the culprit, or if the attack occurs before a big event. Take the 6th, 12th or 30th potency every half hour for six doses, then hourly. Stop taking the treatment as soon as a definite improvement is felt.

For symptoms caused by sudden fright, or aggravated by cold, dry weather, try *Aconitum napellus*. For particularly severe attacks, with cold sweats, *Veratrum alb.* is advised, and *Arg. nit.* if worry or stress is the cause.

AROMATHERAPY
One drop each of peppermint and cypress oil on a sugar lump every two hours has been known to bring relief in attacks of diarrhoea. Or make a tea as in the advice for WIND, using one drop each of peppermint, cypress and sandalwood or camomile; drink a cup two or three hourly until symptoms subside.

Nervous diarrhoea should be treated with oils that are beneficial for stress. They include camomile, geranium, juniper, lavender and sandalwood. Use three to four drops in a tea. Alternatively, the same amount in a teaspoon of carrier oil or lotion should be massaged into the abdomen twice a day. Six to eight drops in the bath are also beneficial.

HERBAL MEDICINE
Herbalists advise taking a garlic oil capsule once or twice a day if the cause is a mild infection, and 3-4 tablespoonsful three times daily of an infusion (see p. 184) of agrimony, plantain or geranium, with a pinch of powdered cinnamon, ginger or crushed caraway seeds. Use 1 pint (600ml) of water to 1oz (30g) of chopped herbs. Cover, allow to stand for 15 minutes, then strain.

An orthodox view
Like alternative therapists, a doctor will probably recommend rest and plenty of

fluids, allowing the attack to subside naturally. However, in severe cases antibiotics, codeine or a suppressant may be prescribed. If the attack lasts longer than three days, the doctor will seek other causes, such as APPENDICITIS or COLITIS.

DIETS AND DIETING
What's on the menu . . .

Alternative practitioners consider diet to be one of the most important factors in health and disease, and in addition to the specific therapies they practise, most also offer dietary advice. Usually, they recommend a basic wholefood diet (see EATING FOR HEALTH), which consists mainly of fresh fruit and vegetables, unrefined grains, pulses such as beans and peas, and small quantities of dairy products, fish, lean meat and poultry. Depending on the patient's needs, special adaptations may be made.

Cleansing diets Some therapists, particularly those who practise NATUROPATHY, recommend highly restricted diets when they think the system needs to be cleansed and purified. These include FASTING and the RAW FOOD DIET.

Diets based on particular beliefs Certain diets are based on special beliefs or nutritional theories. Vegetarians avoid meat, while vegans will eat no animal products at all (see VEGETARIANISM). MACROBIOTICS depends on balancing so-called YIN AND YANG foods, and the HAY DIET is a way of eating designed to improve digestion by separating proteins and starches.

Slimming diets Anyone who follows a sensible, wholefood diet should avoid putting on weight (unless they are underweight). If you are overweight, you will find that you gradually become slimmer, but if the process seems too slow, see SLIMMING THE NATURAL WAY, for safe, healthy ways to lose weight.

Therapeutic diets Although the wholefood diet is believed to help in curing or preventing many illnesses, more specialised diets are also used to treat particular problems. LOW-FAT DIETS are often recommended for patients with ANGINA, hardening of the arteries (see ARTERIES [HARDENING]) or HEART DISORDERS; and high BLOOD PRESSURE may be helped by SALT-FREE DIETS. A diet containing plenty of FIBRE is important for people with BOWEL DISORDERS. Several rigorous, specialised diets have also been used in the treatment of CANCER.

DIGESTIVE PROBLEMS

Stomach aches, feeling too full, WIND, nausea and acid regurgitation are just some of the uncomfortable symptoms associated with digestive problems. The most common complaints are ACID STOMACH, HEARTBURN and INDIGESTION, usually caused by overloading the stomach, too much rich, fatty food or too much alcohol.

Treatment depends on individual cases, but simply sticking to a more sensible diet (see EATING FOR HEALTH) generally solves the problem. ALLERGY to certain cereals (see COELIAC DISEASE) and to dairy products (see LACTOSE INTOLERANCE) can also interfere with digestion.

In rare cases, symptoms such as stomach pains, vomiting (see NAUSEA AND VOMITING), DIARRHOEA or CONSTIPATION may indicate more serious conditions such as APPENDICITIS, ULCERS, FOOD POISONING or GALLSTONES, which need medical attention.

See a doctor immediately if pain is severe. Otherwise, seek medical advice if any digestive problem or abdominal pain persists for more than 48 hours, or if it is accompanied by loss of appetite or weight.

See also IRRITABLE BOWEL SYNDROME and COLITIS.

DIZZINESS

In most cases the spinning sensation and feeling of faintness brought on by a dizzy spell are caused by a slight change in BLOOD PRESSURE or posture – such as rising quickly from a chair, or jumping out of bed in the morning. The attacks are usually over in less than 30 seconds.

However, if they last for longer than that – and are accompanied by recurring HEADACHES with NAUSEA AND VOMITING – see a doctor as soon as possible: the symptoms could indicate a brain tumour (see CANCER).

What the therapists recommend

Acupressure In straightforward cases of dizziness, two main pressure points can be used – in the foot and neck. The foot point is located between the metatarsal bones about 2in (50mm) from the angle between the big and second toes. The neck pressure point is immediately below and behind the bottom of the ear lobe.

To use the foot points, press down hard with your thumb and massage in small circles for one to three minutes about six times a day. For the neck, use your index finger to massage in the same way.

Naturopathy Many practitioners attribute dizziness to low blood-sugar levels, and advise patients to change their eating habits. White sugar, white flour and all fatty foods are to be avoided, but lean meat, fresh fruit and vegetables, and whole grains are recommended (see EATING FOR HEALTH).

Using acupressure to treat dizziness

Firmly massage the foot point – about 2in (50mm) from the angle between big and second toe – moving the thumb in small circles for up to three minutes. Repeat six times daily.

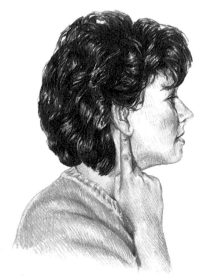

In the same way, massage the neck point – immediately below and behind the bottom of the ear lobe – with an index finger.

Chiropractic Chiropractors can sometimes help attacks of dizziness, which may be due to misalignment of the upper neck joints. These joints contain nerves which balance the head, so that the eyes are level for vision. If the upper neck joints are not correctly aligned, faulty nerve signals may give rise to dizziness. Manipulation of the upper neck, and often further down the spine, can be used to correct this.

An orthodox view

As dizzy spells can accompany more than 50 complaints and illnesses, a doctor will want to know what – if any – other symptoms you have had. For example, if someone staggers or is unable to stand up, the doctor may suspect VERTIGO or poor circulation (see CIRCULATION PROBLEMS).

Unless there *is* a more serious underlying cause, he will probably tell you to take it easy, get a good night's sleep and if another attack comes on, to stop whatever you are doing and sit or lie down until it passes.

DOCTRINE OF SIGNATURES

Medieval herbalists believed that the physical appearance of a plant – especially if some aspect of it resembled a part of the body – was a sign of its healing properties. For example, the creamy, toothlike scales on the roots of the toothwort plant led to it being used as a 'cure' for toothache, and yellow-flowered plants such as agrimony and broom for 'yellow' illnesses such as jaundice. This theory was called the doctrine of signatures, and is generally thought to have been popularised by the Swiss physician Philippus Theophrastus Bombastus von Hohenheim (1493-1541), better known as Paracelsus.

DO-IN
Massaging your way to health

This ancient form of Chinese self-massage – pronounced 'dough-in' – aims to prevent disease, rather than cure it. A series of exercises is said to strengthen 'energy channels' called MERIDIANS, linked to the heart, lungs, liver, gall bladder and other organs, keeping them in a healthy condition.

As a stimulant Do-In is best done first

Six basic Do-In exercises

The exercises are designed to make the organs involved stronger and healthier – and so help to ward off ailments such as stress, tension, rheumatism and arthritis. Before commencing the exercises you should limber-up for about five minutes.

Prelude to exercises
Start by sitting on the ground with your back rounded and holding your knees with your hands. Rock backwards and forwards. Finally, loosen your body by crossing your legs and briefly holding your toes.

Heart – small intestine
Sit with your legs open and the soles of your feet touching. Put your hands around your toes and breathe in. Then bend slowly forward, keeping your back straight and bringing your forehead down towards your toes. Breathe out, pause and repeat.

Liver – gall bladder

Sit up straight with your legs extended and as far apart as possible. Breathe in, stretching your arms along your left leg until you can grasp the sole of your foot. Be sure to keep your right buttock on the floor. Stay in position and take two deep breaths. Then repeat on the right side.

Circulation – pericardium

Sit with your legs and arms crossed. Hold your knees and bend forward, slowly trying to press your knees to the floor with your hands. Cross your arms and legs the other way and repeat the exercise.

Stomach – spleen

Face the wall and stand as close to it as you can. Raise your left arm as high as you can and place the palm of your hand against the wall. With your right hand, hold up your right foot and press the front of your thigh against the wall. Bend your head and neck backwards, stretching the whole of the front of your body. Stay in position and take two deep breaths. Then repeat on the other side of your body.

Lung – large intestine

Stand straight with your feet hips' distance apart. Put your arms behind your back and lock your thumbs together. Breathe in. Breathe out, stretching your arms out and up. Bend forward and straighten up.

Kidney – bladder

Sit up straight with your legs extended and your toes flexed upwards. Stretch your arms up and breathe in. Breathe out, bending your upper body forward and down, and grasp your toes. Stay in position and take three deep breaths. Then repeat.

Completing exercises

End by lying flat upon your back and relaxing. Open your legs to hips' distance and let your feet flop sideways. Stretch your arms by your side, palms up. Raise your head and look at your feet. Then gently and slowly lower your head. Gently shake your body and head to loosen your neck, arms and legs. Finally, close your eyes and rest for about five minutes.

thing in the morning when you wake up. And it can help to relax you when you get home from work and last thing at night before you go to bed. However, it can be practised at any time of the day, except after eating. You can spend as much or as little time on it as you like – and, as with SHIATSU, with which it is closely related, age and infirmity are not necessarily a barrier. Providing you are fit and mobile, all you need is a tracksuit, or loose, comfortable clothing, and a reasonable amount of free space.

Although Do-In is essentially a self-help technique, it is a good idea to attend some classes before attempting the exercises on your own, to make sure that you are on the right lines. For information about classes in Britain contact the Community Health Foundation, 188 Old Street, London EC1V 9BP.

DOUCHING

This is a form of HYDROTHERAPY in which a jet or jets of water are hosed onto parts of the body. Douching is believed to have many therapeutic benefits, including stimulation of the circulation, sedative effects and easing of muscular and other PAIN. The temperature and pressure of the water varies, as does the length of treatment, and there are several kinds of douche – an ordinary shower being one basic example.

In a Scottish douche, hot water is directed at the body for up to five minutes, followed

by cold water for up to 30 seconds. It is said to be a circulation stimulant, good for the body as a whole, and to help in cases of SCIATICA, LUMBAGO and related skeletal pains. An underwater douche, in which the patient stands in a pool or bath, is held to have a similar effect to deep finger kneading MASSAGE – another circulation stimulant and muscle and ligament relaxant. For muscular and joint pains, the Vichy and Aix douches – in which massage is applied under warm water sprays – are considered beneficial.

DOWSING
Diagnosis by rod and pendulum

In the 1920s a French priest, the Abbé Mermet, claimed to have extended the ancient art of dowsing, or water divining, into a means of locating and diagnosing illness. He believed that if dowsers could find water under the ground and assess its freshness, then healers could 'dowse' the body to locate and treat diseased and faulty organs.

He was particularly impressed by the claims of medieval dowsers that they could find underground 'black streams' containing

Traditional divining-rods came in a variety of shapes and sizes and could be used in many different ways, as these French dowsers of the 17th century demonstrate.

currents of 'evil energy', which brought illness to anyone living along them. Further, the dowsers claimed that they could destroy this evil power by driving their divining-rods into the ground.

Most dowsers use divining-rods and forked hazel twigs, but some use a pendulum suspended by a silk thread, and this was the diagnostic tool used by Mermet. He demonstrated his new technique in several French hospitals, and called his form of medical dowsing *radiesthesia*, or 'sensitivity to radiations' (see RADIONICS AND RADIESTHESIA).

His theory was that all substances, including those making up the human body, emit 'good' and 'bad' radiation waves which can be picked up – much as a radio picks up sound wave frequencies – and identified. Once a diagnosis was made, the patient could be treated with appropriate herbal, homoeopathic or other remedies.

Finding a therapist The British Society of Dowsers can put you in touch with your nearest practitioner: contact The Secretary, Sycamore Cottage, Tamley Lane, Hastingleigh, Ashford, Kent TN26 5HW, enclosing a stamped, addressed envelope.

Consulting a therapist In order to diagnose and treat disease, practitioners may dowse a lock of the patient's hair, or a sample of blood or urine.

Holding a pendulum over the specimen – or, in some cases, the patient himself – the practitioner may, for example, ask aloud if there is any organic or glandular imbalance. The way the pendulum swings is interpreted as either a 'yes' or a 'no' answer, and treatment is then given accordingly. Alternatively, the patient may be referred to a specialist in some other therapy.

An orthodox view

Doctors point out there is no evidence that dowsing can correctly diagnose disease. Attempts to show that bodies emit 'radiation waves' have proved inconclusive, and the claims made by practitioners are unacceptable to orthodox medicine.

DRUGS AND THEIR DANGERS

Since earliest times man has sought drugs – external substances that affect the composition or function of living organs – to relieve distress, discomfort and pain. Herbs – fresh, dried, cooked or pounded – infusions, liniments, ointments, balms, poultices and linctuses were all known to the ancients.

The Egyptians thought they had the 'ultimate cure', the golden pill: medicines were wrapped in gold (or silver) leaf – thus ensuring, in fact, that they were not absorbed at all by the alimentary tract and so had little or no effect!

The great expansion of knowledge in the European Renaissance augmented the contemporary physician's array of drugs with those of the ancients and the Arab and Asian worlds. By the 17th century, the apothecary – one who specialised in the preparation of drugs – was firmly established alongside the physician, traditional folk healer, quack and white witch.

The modern drug industry began with the invention of gelatine capsules by French apothecaries in 1834. At last, unpleasant medicines could be delivered in palatable form. Their effects lasted longer too, for the drugs were released slowly into the intestine as the gelatine dissolved. Traditional remedies began to lose their appeal, and by the end of the century the travelling quack peddling his elixir 'Beneficial for Rheumatiz, Ladies' indispositions, Colic, Stones and Baldness – and preserving saddles' gave way to the pharmaceutical or drug representative. He visited doctors and tried to convince them

that his firm's drug for a particular ailment was superior to all others on the market.

Medicines for all Today, nearly 12 per cent of the National Health Service (NHS) budget goes on drugs. Some £2 billion is spent each year – more than the cost of the Family Practitioner and Community Health services together. And, even allowing for inflation, the yearly cost of drugs prescribed by general practitioners is five times more than in 1948-9, when the NHS came into being.

How far the drug industry's efforts led to the change in doctors' prescribing or how far the change led to the industry's expansion is debatable. But expand it certainly did. Pharmaceutical firms now employ more than 70,000 people.

General practitioners prescribe more than 75 per cent of all drugs used in the United Kingdom, so the industry aims most of its promotion at them. They are bombarded with advertising literature, free samples, sponsorship schemes and visits from reps. Overall, about £7000 is invested in each practitioner each year, and as the doctor prescribes some £70,000 worth of drugs annually, the investment is well worth while.

The general public has played its part in the industry's expansion too. At any one time, 60 per cent of the population is taking at least one drug, and only half will have had it prescribed by their doctor. Most households stock at least one proprietary (over-the-counter) medicine, and even the advent of virtually free prescriptions with the NHS did not affect their sale.

The hidden dangers Doctors and patients increasingly have come to believe that treatment requires prescription of one or more drugs. But this does have dangers. Some result from bad medical practice, others from misunderstandings between doctors and drug companies, some from patient error, and a few from lack of adequate trials before drugs are released for general use.

Some practitioners over-prescribe. When 50,000 prescriptions in an American teaching hospital were analysed, one in eight revealed over-prescription – too much or too frequent use or both. Doctors' handwriting is not always legible, and incorrect copying of repeat prescriptions by receptionist staff sometimes occurs. The introduction of computers in general practice has been seen as a way of minimising errors, but the wrong medicine for the wrong person continues to be prescribed. Occasionally, pharmacists fail to tell patients all they should know.

Once patients are prescribed drugs, they may fail to have them dispensed; some 10-15 per cent of prescriptions are not fulfilled. Other patients obtain their medicines and then fail to take them. It is estimated that this is the fate of at least one in four NHS

prescriptions. More commonly, patients do not complete the course of treatment, usually because they note some improvement and think they are 'cured'.

The volume of hoarded drugs suggests that the true figures may be higher. Some 200,000 tablets were surrendered during a 'drug amnesty' in Dudley, Hereford and Worcester in 1976. The figure for a similar operation in 1979 was 300,000, and in 1982, 740,000. Other patients, particularly elderly ones, misunderstand prescription instructions, some continuing with one medication after beginning a new one.

Drugs are extensively tested before being put on the market. However, very occasionally the tests fail to reveal harmful side effects, sometimes with tragic results. The sedative thalidomide, which resulted in foetal abnormalities when taken in pregnancy, is an example. Other medicines produce harmful effects when taken together. There is now a 'Yellow Card' system of reporting by which doctors inform the Committee on the Safety of Medicines of their experience with drugs.

Occasionally, a practitioner may have a difficult choice and resorts to the risk/benefit ratio: the risk of taking the drug against the benefit derived from it. For example, in cases of serious infection such as typhoid fever, the doctor may give the antibiotic chloramphenicol despite the fact that it may cause bone marrow damage, less toxic drugs being useless in such cases.

Every year more than 200,000 adults and children are admitted to United Kingdom hospitals because of an overdose – accidental or otherwise – and 4000 of them die. In addition, it is estimated that at any given time one in every six people in hospital are there because of some side effect of their prescribed medication.

What makes the British use medications in such vast quantities despite the dangers? Perhaps the answer lies in the 'hidden functions' of the prescription – the unconscious reasons why doctors give and patients expect to receive prescriptions (see box).

DYSENTERY

There are two forms of this bowel infection, which causes severe DIARRHOEA. The most common type is bacterial dysentery; the other form, amoebic dysentery, is rare in Britain. In both cases, however, the disease is spread by poor hygiene, infected food and contaminated water.

Symptoms include FEVER, frequent bowel movements (up to 20 a day in children), griping stomach pains, WIND and vomiting. Both conventional and alternative practitioners stress the importance of personal hygiene and scrupulous cleanliness in handling, preparing and cooking food. Always wash the hands after using the lavatory.

Bacterial dysentery sometimes occurs in epidemics in schools, but usually passes within about a week. If it persists, or becomes worse, medical advice must be sought. Amoebic dysentery, contracted in tropical countries and often accompanied by blood, mucus or pus in the stools, should always be treated by a doctor.

What the therapists recommend

Moxibustion For bacterial dysentery, the practitioner (usually an acupuncturist) will probably treat points on the abdomen.

Naturopathy A practitioner would advise the patient to take plenty of liquids – particularly those such as milk and vegetable juices that are rich in minerals and salts – to replace lost body fluids. He would also advise him to avoid solid foods and eat bland dishes such as semolina, tapioca, porridge and pasta, or plain boiled rice with a little butter. These are believed to absorb much of the poisonous matter in the bowels.

Traditional Medicine Simmer 6 pints (3.5 litres) of fresh milk containing 1oz (30g) of cinnamon, 1oz of oak bark, two nutmegs, 20 cloves and 20 white peppercorns. Strain the mixture, allow it to cool and pour into four equal measures. Drink one measure every six hours for 24 hours.

An orthodox view

For bacterial dysentery a doctor will simply recommend a liquid diet and rest. Amoebic dysentery will call for antibiotics, and your stools will be examined for infecting organisms once a week for six months.

DYSLEXIA
Coping with learning difficulties

Children who have difficulty recognising words and letters when they are being taught to read and write are victims of dyslexia, a learning disorder once misleadingly called word blindness. It affects about one person in ten to some degree, and one in 25 are significantly troubled by it. One of the major causes is thought to be a disorganisation of the nerve cells in the areas of the brain dealing with language.

Dyslexic children can be diagnosed at the age of five or six, after starting school, when teachers discover that they are finding it hard to read. Often they have difficulty in learning sequences, such as the order of the days of the week, or the months of the year. In addition, they have trouble in distinguishing different sounds in words and in identifying the different letters.

Sometimes the victim also suffers from dyscalculia, or difficulty in learning numbers – for example, when writing his address, the child may give the house number as 27 instead of 72. Both problems last through life, but much can now be done to help dyslexics live with their disability – and sometimes to overcome it, at least in part (see box, *Do's and don'ts for parents of a dyslexic*).

In suspected cases of dyslexia it is important initially for the children's vision and hearing to be carefully tested, in case the learning fault lies there.

Finding a teacher First of all, see if your child's head teacher at school can put you in touch with an appropriate expert. If he can't, then contact your local education authority asking for the name and address of an educational psychologist in your area. Your GP may also be able to help by sending your child to a clinical psychologist at an NHS hospital. Alternatively, you can contact one of the 2000 or so specialist teachers in Britain – many of whom work in the private sector at a cost of around £10 an hour.

A number of organisations also offer

How hope came to the dyslexic

Dyslexia has existed for hundreds of years, but was not officially recognised until the late 19th century. The American psychologist William James wrote of 'word-blind' patients in his *Principles of Psychology* (1890). But the preferred modern term – from the Latin *dys* ('abnormal') and Greek *lexis* ('speech') – was first used in German in 1883.

Sufferers have mostly been male, and are thought to have included the artist and scientist Leonardo da Vinci, the sculptor Auguste Rodin, the inventor Thomas Edison, and Albert Einstein, father of modern physics.

However, in Britain it was not until the 1970 Chronically Sick and Disabled Persons Act that local authorities were obliged to provide educational facilities for dyslexic children. These include specially trained teachers and separate classes in which youngsters with learning problems can receive skilled help and encouragement.

Do's and don'ts for parents of a dyslexic

Do read to a dyslexic – even a teenager. He needs all the help and encouragement he can get – at home and school.
Do show an interest in the child's school notes and homework – and go through them with him.
Do try to get tape or video versions of books needed for English Literature lessons, and encourage the child to watch any required plays that come on television, or listen to them on radio.
Do develop a good relationship with the child's teachers, making sure they are aware of his special needs.
Do praise any achievements or improvements in performance. This can include something as seemingly simple as correctly dialling telephone numbers.
Do help a child who struggles to tell left from right – for example, put his bicycle bell on the left handlebar, reminding him to ride on the 'bell' side of the road.
Don't scold the child if he has trouble tying shoelaces or a tie – encouragement is the key.
Don't lose patience if the child has difficulty with the calendar – help him to work out the weeks and days.
Don't show favouritism towards 'normal' brothers or sisters.
Don't take the child from one expert to another for constant 'second opinions', which can be unsettling. Have faith in one and stick with him.

expert help and advice. For free nationwide advice, contact the British Dyslexia Association, 98 London Road, Reading, Berkshire RG1 5AU. For information about private lessons throughout the country, contact the Dyslexia Institute, 133 Gresham Road, Staines, Middlesex TW18 2AJ.

Consulting a teacher Teaching depends largely on the degree of each child's disability. Dyslexic children need a carefully designed, progressive programme based upon learning the structure of words.

What the therapists recommend

Osteopathy Practitioners claim to have helped sufferers in cases involving displaced vertebrae, or joints of the spine.

An orthodox view

Your family doctor will gladly discuss with you any learning problems that a dyslexic child may have, and will give all the help and support he possibly can.

EATING FOR HEALTH

Getting the balance right is the first essential of healthy eating. No matter how much you spend or to what lengths you go in shopping for or growing your own food, it will be to little purpose if the proportion of the various nutrients is not correct. The body needs carbohydrates, fats and proteins in varying quantities, plus smaller amounts of vitamins, minerals and fibre to function well and to maintain itself. All are essential, but too little of one and too much of another can lead to poor health. See CHOOSING THE RIGHT FOODS FOR VITALITY AND WELL-BEING, p. 116.

EATING PROBLEMS

These generally fall into three categories: ANOREXIA and BULIMIA, which are psychological illnesses, and OBESITY.

Anorexia usually affects teenage girls or young women who refuse food due to a morbid fear of gaining weight, or, in some cases, of growing up. In bulimia, bouts of compulsive eating are followed by self-induced and ultimately involuntary vomiting.

Obesity is the condition in which excess fat accumulates in the body. It is caused by overeating and is cured by adopting a diet of healthy, wholesome food (see EATING FOR HEALTH). Anyone seeking general advice on eating problems can contact the Maisner Centre for Eating Disorders, PO Box 464, Hove, East Sussex BN3 2BN.

See also SLIMMING THE NATURAL WAY.

ECZEMA

An eczema victim's skin not only becomes inflamed, but usually develops a persistent itchiness – often with blisters that weep and then form dry scabs and crusts. Mostly it strikes during childhood and clears up after PUBERTY AND ADOLESCENCE (p. 292). However, many people are affected in later life – especially housewives with an ALLERGY to bleaches, detergents, wax polishes and so on, who get eczema on their hands.

The two most common forms are *contact eczema*, which develops within minutes and is caused by reactions to anything from rubber shoes to metal watch straps, and *atopic eczema*, which usually affects people with a family history of ASTHMA or HAY

FEVER, and can take months, or even years to develop, appearing at any time.

Self help To relieve skin irritation, try putting two tablespoons of sodium bicarbonate in your hot bath.

What the therapists recommend

ACUPUNCTURE

Consultation Traditionally, acupuncturists believe that eczema is associated with exposure to heat, damp and wind. Treatment is based on counteracting the effect of the elements – and by trying to correct any blood and ENERGY deficiencies that may result.

Meridians treated would be those corresponding to the large intestine, lungs, spleen and stomach. If the practitioner believes that the liver is not functioning properly, and is failing to expel the eczema, a special diet is advised. This involves avoiding all alcoholic drinks, coffee, fats and dairy products.

HOMOEOPATHY

Consultation Practitioners view eczema as an outward sign of an underlying disorder. Treatment would depend on the individual case and requires expert help – especially if steroid creams have been prescribed by an orthodox practitioner (see below).

If the eruptions exude a sticky, honey-like fluid, *Graphites* is said to be effective. *Petroleum* is recommended if the eruptions itch at night and ooze a watery discharge in people with a tendency to chapped skin and cracked fingertips. If the itching gets worse with heat and the desire to scratch becomes irresistible: *Sulphur*. Only a few doses of the 6th potency are advisable – and the effect should be closely watched.

AROMATHERAPY

Self help Essential oils recommended include fennel, German camomile, geranium, sandalwood, hyssop, juniper and lavender. If the eczema is dry, use calendula oil as the carrier for the essential oils. If moist, use carrier lotion. The ratio should be 12 drops to 50ml of carrier. Apply to the affected area every morning and night.

Consultation Therapists will advise on diet and use the creams and lotions which do not contain lanolin – an oil derived from wool, which is a frequent cause of allergy, as are milk and milk products.

NATUROPATHY

Consultation Naturopaths, like conventional doctors, believe allergy to be a prime cause of eczema. They will recommend a diet of raw fruit and raw vegetables, washed down by mineral water, herbal teas or fresh fruit drinks. You will be advised to keep to it for a week, then fast for two or three days.

Warning Do not adopt the diet or fast

without first getting a doctor's advice. The diet is unsuitable for anyone who is weak or run down.

Other alternative treatments

Herbal Medicine Since eczema is a complex condition, a practitioner should be consulted and careful treatment of individual cases is required.

Marigold tea has long been recommended to relieve symptoms of itching, blisters and flaking skin. It is also said to help ward off eczema. Add 1oz (30g) of marigold flowers or petals to 1 pint (600ml) of boiling water, let it soak for five to ten minutes, then strain and drink as required. In addition, marigold ointment can be obtained from some chemists or health food shops.

Traditional Medicine Fresh green cabbage leaves – well washed and well pounded – are said to relieve even bad cases of eczema. Warm the leaves and use a bandage to hold several layers of them in place on the affected areas every morning and night. Savoy cabbages are believed to be particularly effective in relieving eczema.

Bach Remedies Therapists believe that Crab apple decreases feelings of embarrassment about eczema – and Clematis and Mimulus help to combat oversensitivity. If eczema sufferers experience irritability about their condition, Impatiens is said to help. Rescue Remedy cream is said to bring relief when rubbed on the affected areas.

Reflexology Massage to the reflex areas relating to the areas of skin affected, plus the areas relating to the solar plexus, adrenal and pituitary glands, liver, digestive areas, kidneys and reproductive glands is recommended. See chart, p. 295.

An orthodox view

For all types of eczema, a doctor will probably prescribe a corticosteroid cream or a course of antibiotics to help heal the skin. If unsure of the cause, he may send you to a dermatologist, who will make patch tests by applying suspected irritants to the skin. If contact eczema is identified – caused by a woollen jumper, perhaps, or a certain aftershave – you will be advised to avoid it.

Some doctors believe that eczema also has psychological causes – that it can be triggered by, for example, an unhappy marriage or unpleasant atmosphere at work. If so you may be sent to a psychiatrist to discuss your problem and find a way to resolve it.

Leaflets on eczema are obtainable from the National Eczema Society, Tavistock House East, Tavistock Square, London WC1H 9SR. They are especially useful for parents, teachers and anyone associated with child sufferers. The society also sponsors local self-help groups.

Choosing the right foods for vitality and well-being

There is no need to make sacrifices or go without anything to eat a healthy diet. Hearty and wholesome meals, simply cooked – or not cooked at all – can be varied to include all your favourites. It is only the balance you need to check. With plenty of bread and cereals, as much fresh fruit and vegetables as you can eat, and a moderate amount of protein, you will give your body all the nutrients it needs. Fuss, fads and extravagance are out, simple enjoyment is in.

Healthy eating means choosing food that gives all the nutrients your body needs to grow, repair itself and carry out vital chemical processes. A good diet must also provide you with enough energy to stay fit and active. People's needs differ, depending on their age, way of life and metabolic rate (how fast their bodies perform these functions), but there are certain nutrients that everybody needs.

Carbohydrates, proteins and fats are needed in relatively large quantities to provide energy and build body tissue. VITAMINS and MINERALS are needed in much smaller amounts to help the body to function properly. Lastly, a good diet must contain FIBRE to keep the digestion healthy.

Alternative practitioners and nutritionists both recommend a diet based on unrefined and unprocessed foods such as fresh fruit and vegetables, wholemeal bread, lean meat and salads. This is called a wholefood diet, meaning that as little nutritional value as possible is removed from food during preparation. For example, wholemeal (not wheatmeal) flour is used because it is made from the whole wheat grain, including the outer shell which contains valuable vitamins and fibre. Wholefoods should not contain FOOD ADDITIVES such as preservatives, colourings or flavourings. Wherever possible, they should be organic foods – crops grown without the use of chemical fertilisers and pesticides, and meat from free-range poultry and animals reared without antibiotics or artificial hormone supplements.

Immediate source of energy

Carbohydrates, especially in their natural, unrefined forms are highly nutritious, and are our most immediate source of energy. They should be eaten in substantial quantities, especially by sports people and by those whose work is physically hard.

The body eventually breaks carbohydrates down into the simple sugar glucose. This is then either used immediately to provide energy or stored for a short time in muscles and liver as glycogen or animal starch, whose molecules comprise branched chains of glucose molecules. A longer-term excess of glucose is converted and stored as fat, and can lead to OBESITY.

Carbohydrate molecules contain carbon, hydrogen and oxygen atoms only, and include starches and sugars. Thirty years ago, more of our carbohydrates came from starches than now. Refined cane and beet sugar is now our major source of carbohydrates and an important source of energy. It consists mostly of the sugar sucrose, and is the sweetest of the natural carbohydrates in our diet.

However, refined sugar does not make you feel full as easily as other carbohydrate foods, so it is easy to eat far too much, with the possible danger of obesity. It can also cause tooth decay. You should eat sugar and honey (mostly sugar) only in very small quantities, and only as a small proportion of any meal so that it is absorbed more slowly.

Starch molecules comprise chains of glucose molecules which the body must break down with digestive juices before it can absorb them. Although the process begins in the mouth, most of it occurs farther down the gut, so starchy foods are less likely than sugary ones to cause tooth decay.

They also tend to contain more fibre, vitamins and minerals than sugary ones, so they are more bulky and eventually provide the body with less glucose per ounce.

The hormone insulin is necessary for the oxidation of glucose – the process that produces energy for the body. When not enough insulin is produced, DIABETES results. Starchy foods are therefore an even more important component of the diet for diabetics than for other people.

Honey and many fruits such as figs (and some vegetables including carrots and beetroot) contain the sugar fructose, which is also known as fruit sugar. Metabolism of fructose does not require insulin, so the sugar is especially useful for diabetics. These foods contain other valuable nutrients too.

Starches should make up most of your daily carbohydrate intake. The best sources are breads, oats, rice and other grains, beans, peas and potatoes. Because the message has been stressed that wholemeal bread is good, it has been assumed that white bread is bad. In fact white is good, but wholemeal is even better. To make our diet better balanced, we should be eating more of the old staples bread and potatoes, and less red meat, fat and refined sugar. Whether bread is white or brown matters less than eating more of it. Most of the white flour used for bread in the UK is 'fortified' – calcium and several vitamins have been added to it. So white bread has about the same carbohydrate, protein, vitamin and mineral content as wholemeal – but it has only about half the fibre.

Occasional helpings of cakes, biscuits and puddings made with white sugar and flour do no harm, but should not form a regular part of the diet. Such foods are also usually rich in fat, so it is easy to consume too many calories if you eat them. Replace them with vegetables such as carrots, or a low-fat sandwich, when you feel the need of a snack. Many conventional recipes work successfully with wholemeal flour instead of white and, with fresh or dried fruit, require less (or no) sugar.

Vital roles

Body-building proteins form the basic structure of muscles, tendons, bones and other tissues. Without them the body cannot repair damaged tissues and generate new cells for growth and to make good the bodily wear and tear of daily life. Equally vital is their role as hormones and enzymes, which regulate the body's chemistry and functions.

A protein molecule contains carbon, hydrogen, oxygen and nitrogen atoms, and sometimes phosphorus and sulphur atoms too. It comprises a chain (or chains) of amino acids, which are built up by the body from the amino acids obtained by the digestion of the protein in food. Any excess of protein that the body does not need is converted into glucose to provide energy or be stored as fat. Proteins can give the same energy, ounce for ounce, as carbohydrates, but their prime value is as 'building materials'.

Proteins are needed in smaller quantities than carbohydrates – some 1½-2¼oz (40-60g) a day is enough for most adults. Since meat is about one-fifth protein (the rest is water and fat) this would mean eating about 8oz (225g) a day, if meat were the only source of protein. Bread, which is less than one-tenth protein, would have to be eaten at the rate of about 1lb (450g) a day.

Many people think – wrongly – that red meat is the best protein and that other forms are second class. In practice, most people in the West eat a variety of protein-containing foods which more than make up the daily need: meat, fish, eggs, cheese, yoghurt, milk, bread, peas, beans, oat-based or wheat-based breakfast cereals, nuts – even potatoes give a little protein to the diet. However, a great deal of protein is not recommended, mainly because any surplus is eventually converted and stored as fat.

Right combinations

The amino acids in proteins have to be present in certain combinations before the body can use them. Many animal foods, such as meat, eggs, cheese, milk and fish, have the right mixture, but many of them also contain much fat, so plant protein is better.

Pulses (beans, peas, lentils), oats, wheat and many other vegetables contain protein and starch with little fat, but need to be combined to provide the right mixture of amino acids. Particularly good combinations are vegetable proteins with small amounts of animal proteins – bread and cheese, or fish and rice, for example – and pulses with grains in dishes such as beans on toast or a lentil curry served with rice.

Vegans should take special care to include pulse-and-grain combinations in their diet as sources of protein, since they exclude all animal products (see VEGETARIANISM). However, in practice those who eat a wide variety of vegetable foods will get plenty of protein without worrying about combinations.

A healthy diet must contain some fats for they form vital parts of the structure of body cells. They are the main

---

Reducing sugar intake

White sugar contains no vitamins or minerals, and brown sugars and honey contain a very small amount of no nutritional importance. In large quantities sugar and honey are fattening, cause tooth decay and even become addictive, yet most of us still eat too much. Here are some ways to cut down:

Reduce sugar in hot drinks gradually until you no longer need it. As they get used to it, many people find that the taste of the drink is improved.

Cut out proprietary soft drinks. Have water or diluted freshly squeezed fruit juice instead.

Read the labels on packaged foods and drinks such as fruit juice, tomato sauce, breakfast cereals and peanut butter, and buy only those brands without added sugar.

As a rule finish meals with fruit or cheese, and break the habit of having sugary desserts.

Do not use sweets as presents or rewards for children, or they will come to associate harmful foods with happy occasions – fruit and small toys are good alternatives.

Do not keep sweets, chocolates or biscuits in the house.

If you want something to nibble between meals, try olives, raw vegetables, fruit – even cheese or nuts, in small quantities because of their fat content. All these are more nutritious and may help to cure your sweet tooth.

insulating material beneath the skin and around organs such as the kidneys. Fats are also necessary for the absorption into the body of the fat-soluble vitamins – A, D, E and K – from the gut. They make foods tastier and easier to swallow. However, fats must be eaten in only small amounts for they are the most concentrated form of food, giving more than twice as much energy for their weight as either carbohydrates or proteins. Excess fat leads to obesity.

Fats are made up of fatty acids – substances containing hydrogen and oxygen atoms attached to chains of carbon atoms, edible fats having an even number of carbons in the chains. Fatty acids in which all the possible chemical bonds are used up are known as saturated (or hydrogenated) fatty acids. Monounsaturated fatty acids have one unused bonding site for a hydrogen atom in the molecule, and polyunsaturated, several. Animal fats are mainly saturated and are generally solid at room temperature. Vegetable fats are mostly unsaturated; they are generally liquid at room temperature, and like all such fats are usually known as oils.

Saturated fatty acids seem to make the body form too much cholesterol. Some cholesterol is needed for a healthy brain and nervous system and for the producion of hormones. However, any excess can cause GALLSTONES and coat the inside of the arteries, eventually impeding blood circulation, causing heart attacks and strokes (see ARTERIES [HARDENING]). To avoid this danger, we should eat far less fat and try to make sure that the little we do eat is mainly unsaturated. In a diet where fat consumption is low, however, the occasional cake, fried food or slice of buttered toast presents no danger.

Cut down on meat, dairy products (especially cream and hard cheeses), eggs, hard margarines, some soft margarines, peanuts and peanut butter, and products containing palm or coconut oil; these are all rich in saturates. Olive oil and some fish oils are monounsaturates. Sources of polyunsaturates are oily fish such as herring, mackerel, trout and salmon, and oils from sunflower seed, maize (corn), walnuts, safflower seed, sesame seed and grapeseed. Eating oily fish and peas and beans is now thought to help in clearing cholesterol deposits already formed in arteries.

Whenever possible, buy oils that are labelled 'cold-pressed', 'virgin', or 'extra virgin' – other oils will have been treated with heat or chemicals, which

can convert unsaturates to saturates. Never eat oils that have a rancid smell or taste.

Virgin olive oil is excellent for salad dressings. The traditional Mediterranean cuisines that use it so much are among the world's healthiest. Corn oil has less flavour but is also suitable. Walnut and sesame oils are more expensive but give a distinctive flavour.

Olive oil is also suitable for gentle shallow frying – as are other cold-pressed or virgin vegetable oils except coconut or palm oil. For the occasional deep-fried food, for which a high temperature is needed, use sunflower or corn oil.

Many people now use soft margarines for spreading and in sauces and cakes. Although such margarines are made largely from unsaturated oils, they have been through heat or chemical processes which alter the unsaturated structure of the fat molecules or leave chemical residues in the margarine. There is no way of knowing whether good-quality oils have been used in the manufacturing process. Both margarine and low-fat spreads usually contain preservatives and other chemicals. It is better to use sparingly a natural food like butter. In baking, butter gives the best flavour and in a well-balanced diet where cakes and biscuits are not eaten often it will do no harm even though it is rich in saturates. Its advantage is that it is a natural food, not processed or high in additives. Choose a slightly salted or unsalted variety. Those who must avoid butter altogether, because of a heart condition for example, could use a soft margarine high in polyunsaturates, but would do better to cut out all cakes and biscuits.

Giving protection

The body requires many different vitamins and minerals to function efficiently. They are needed in small amounts only – the total daily requirements amount to about $\frac{1}{4}$oz (7g) of minerals and only about one-tenth of a gram of vitamins. However, they play essential roles in all bodily processes and provide protection against infection and disease.

The best sources of vitamins and minerals are fresh or frozen unprocessed fruit and vegetables, dairy products, cereal foods, meat, eggs and fish. Many of these nutrients dissolve in water or are destroyed by too much heat, so it is important to use good cooking methods and eat raw fruit and

---

How to cut down on saturated fats

Read the labels on oils and tinned, packaged or processed foods, and avoid those which list saturated or hydrogenated fats or oils.

Buy lean cuts of meat and trim off any visible fat. Poultry has little fat with the flesh, but the skin is fatty; remove it before sautéing, grilling or casseroling it. Game is lean meat: rabbit, venison and pheasant can be inexpensive.

Avoid fried food. Grilling, roasting, stewing and baking use a minimum of fat. If you do fry chips or other foods, cut them into large pieces to reduce the total area of fried surface. Use corn or sunflower oil at a high temperature – but not so high that the oil begins to smoke – so the food develops a crisp crust quickly and absorbs less oil. Pat off the excess oil with kitchen paper.

Eat more fish. White fish is low in fat and oily fish such as herring, mackerel, trout and salmon are rich in an unsaturated oil not widely available in other foods, and which helps to combat cholesterol. Try to have two servings of an oily fish every week.

Cut down on meat. Even the leanest beef is about 15 per cent fat and a juicy steak about 30 per cent. Replace meat with vegetable or fish dishes for a few meals a week.

Use yoghurt instead of cream, which is rich in saturated fat. If you want cream occasionally, use single rather than double or clotted cream.

Before serving meat casseroles, curries, soups and stews, remove surface fat with absorbent kitchen paper.

Look out for low-fat sausages, cheeses, milk and yoghurt. Cut down on crisps – although they are generally cooked in unsaturated oil, they contain as much as 38 per cent of it.

salads as much as possible. Many vegetables can also be eaten raw; try finely chopped broccoli, spinach, peas, carrots, cabbage and mushrooms sprinkled on salads.

Steaming, stir-frying, baking or adding vegetables to casseroles does not waste their nutrients so much as boiling can. If you do boil them, add the vegetables to a little rapidly boiling water and cook them for the shortest time, keeping them crisp. Add the cooking water – which contains some of their nutrients – to a soup or stew.

Cut down on the salt you use in cooking, or omit it altogether. Most people eat more than they need and those suffering from high BLOOD PRESSURE have to avoid it (see SALT-FREE DIETS). It makes the body retain water and waste products. Season food with GARLIC, herbs, spices, freshly ground black pepper or lemon juice instead. Your taste for salt will soon dwindle, but if you want an alternative to salt, there is a vegetable salt made from vegetable extracts.

Vitamins and minerals are needed in complex combinations by the body, but anyone who eats a balanced and varied diet of wholefoods, including plenty of fresh fruit and vegetables, will receive enough. It is rarely necessary to take vitamin or mineral supplements, nor are people who take them ensuring that their diet is healthy. They can still be eating too little fibre, for example. See pp. 361 and 242 for the food sources of vitamins and minerals.

Fibre adds bulk

Plant foods – bread, rice and other cereals, leafy and root vegetables, fruits, salads, beans, peas and other pulses – provide dietary fibre, especially if they are unrefined. Fibre has no nutritional value. The body cannot digest or absorb it, but it adds bulk to our diet which pushes waste products through the system faster, and absorbs dangerous substances. It keeps the digestive tract healthy and carries the waste away. Eating sufficient fibre prevents CONSTIPATION and helps to reduce the risk of CANCER of the bowel. Fibre also makes us chew food longer and fills the stomach, making meals more satisfying and thus preventing us from overeating.

Until the last few years, people were relying less on bread as a staple food and eating fewer vegetables. Of the vegetables we do now eat, far more are frozen or processed and fewer are fresh and leafy. There is now a marketing drive to promote foods to which fibre has been added. However, to get enough fibre it is not necessary to add bran to foods or to eat special breads, crackers or muesli. Simply eat a variety of wholefoods that are naturally rich in fibre. Bread, white or brown, and oats are good sources of fibre. The skin of potatoes is another, but it contains the natural pesticide solanine, which you may wish to avoid. Daily helpings of bread, porridge, fresh vegetables, raw and dried fruits and pulses will carry you to the daily fibre target of 1oz (30g).

Balancing your diet

Making up a balanced wholefood diet is not difficult and gives you plenty of choice. Whatever your age, you should have three servings a day of meat, fish, poultry, nuts, beans, peas or lentils; one serving of milk, cheese or yoghurt; four servings of bread, brown rice,

Healthy drinking . . . <u>Top shelf</u>: grapefruit juice, white wine, tomato juice, rose-hip tea. <u>Second shelf</u>: pineapple juice, decaffeinated coffee, pear juice, apple juice. <u>Third shelf</u>: mint tea, peach juice, fennel tea, papaya juice, beer. <u>Bottom shelf</u>: grape juice, orange juice, water and carrot juice.

Eating for Health

muesli, potatoes or wholewheat pasta; four servings of fresh fruit, vegetables or salads; and as little fat, oil and dressing as possible. The small amount of fat needed comes from the rest of the diet. Breastfeeding mothers and growing children need an extra daily serving of milk, cheese or yoghurt to provide the calcium they need.

Three meals and a mid-morning or evening snack will provide all you need. Adjust the size of servings to match body weight. Generally about 15 calories (kcal) a day per pound (0.45kg) of body weight is needed to maintain that weight. Thus someone who weighs 10 stone – 140lb or 63.5kg – and leads a moderately active life needs about 2100 calories (140 × 15) a day. Those who use more physical energy need more calories, those whose lives are sedentary need less. Protein and carbohydrates provide 4 calories per gram (113 per oz) and fat 9 calories per gram (255 per oz).

Many shops and supermarkets now sell organically produced foods. They are usually more expensive than similar non-organic products, and are generally identified by the symbol of the Soil Association (see p. 179), Organic Farmers' and Growers' Association, or similar bodies.

Besides the wholefood diet, many special diets are used for medical reasons. People with HEART DISORDERS, ANGINA or hardening of the arteries are usually advised to adopt LOW-FAT DIETS, and salt-free diets can help to lower high blood pressure. NATUROPATHY and nutritional medicine use diets to treat a range of illnesses – for example, therapists sometimes recommend highly restrictive regimes such as the RAW FOOD DIET or FASTING to cleanse the system.

Other diets are based on special nutritional theories. Vegetarianism maintains that meat is not necessary in man's diet, and veganism that all animal products should be avoided. Balancing so-called yin and yang foods is the basis of the way of eating known as MACROBIOTICS, and the HAY DIET shuns proteins and starches in the same meal.

You should be wary of extreme and restrictive diets. Concentrate instead on eating moderate amounts of wholesome unprocessed foods free as far as possible from chemicals. Variety, with more emphasis on fruits, vegetables and grains, less on meat and dairy produce, and avoidance of animal fats, will make the greatest contribution to your health. Enjoy your varied diet, eat your food slowly in relaxed surroundings, and savour to the full its colour, taste and texture.

Choose a wholegrain breakfast cereal free of refined sugar or honey. Add sweetness with the natural sugars of fruit. It can double as a snack instead of biscuits.

Pastas in strands, butterflies, hoops or nests are a base for quick and healthy meals. The darker wholewheat or buckwheat pastas have more flavour.

Brown breads contain protein, vitamins and fibre as well as starch. White is good too, just lower in fibre.

Starches for ready energy

Bread and potatoes were once the staples of the British diet and should be restored to pride of place. Their value is as starches – complex carbohydrates which satisfy the appetite, produce glucose to fuel the body's activities, and come in a package with other valuable nutrients. They can be varied now with many other starchy foods, including cereals, crispbreads, pastas and rice. Four substantial helpings a day of these foods are needed in a healthy diet.

Choose breads with distinctive tastes – black rye or rolls with poppy or sesame seeds – and they will not need spreading with fat or jam.

Rice, brown or polished, is a base for curries and vegetable casseroles as well as a good substitute for the hard-working potato.

Eating for Health

Melons, grapes, citrus fruits, pineapples and bananas that were once exotic imports are now familiar fare. Today's exotics are plum-shaped orange kumquats and soft-fleshed spicy mangoes.

Vitamins, fibre – and protein too

In a balanced diet we should enjoy four ample helpings a day of fruit and/or vegetables. Their value for most people is in the vitamins, minerals and fibre they contain, but vegetarians and vegans may also obtain sufficient protein from them. There is always a wide variety in season so that you can buy fresh foods rather than processed ones. Eat them raw for maximum food value, or cook for the shortest possible time.

Sweet golden papaya, knobby little lychees and tangy juice from dark green limes can be added to salads of homegrown top fruits and soft fruits.

Beans – a valuable protein source for vegetarians.

Sweet peppers, red or green, are becoming as common in salads as the traditional radishes, lettuces and tomatoes. Courgettes have largely ousted their older relatives, marrows, from vegetable stalls.

Fresh garden peas – a source of vitamins and protein – have become harder to find in young and perfect condition, but their flat-podded cousins, mangetouts, are more common. Eat pod and all, raw or lightly cooked.

Look for okra in larger supermarkets or in street markets with a cosmopolitan spread of customers.

Fresh asparagus is still an early summer luxury.

The familiar mainstays such as cabbage, carrots, leeks, cauliflower, white cabbage, onions, swedes, parsnips and turnips, have been joined for much of the year by varieties of broccoli and glossy purple aubergines.

Spring onions, celery and young broad beans add bite when used raw in salads, but globe artichokes need careful cooking and preparation.

123

Eating for Health

Hazel nuts, walnuts and other nuts are rich in protein – and also in high-calorie fat, but it is unsaturated. Peanuts and coconut are also rich in protein and fat, but their fat is largely saturated.

Trim the fat from meat such as pork chops and do not eat the fatty skin of chicken.

Game such as pheasant, and offal such as kidneys are low in fat.

Red meat is a valuable source of iron. Reduce its fat by casseroling it and skimming off the fat that rises to the surface.

The protein in pulses such as peas, beans, and dried haricots, red kidney beans and orange, brown and green lentils is absorbed more easily when combined with a cereal food such as bread or rice.

124

Limit your intake of dairy foods and choose those with reduced fat, such as skimmed milk, low-fat yoghurt, cottage cheese or such soft cheeses as camembert.

High-cholesterol eggs, butter and hard cheeses will do no harm if eaten occasionally.

In need of care and control

Our protein requirement is much more limited than generally thought. Just three helpings a day of meat or fish and one of dairy produce is quite enough – and the helpings should be small. Although these foods provide the protein we need for body-building and repairs, and contain several vitamins and minerals, many of them are high in the saturated fats that clog arteries with cholesterol. Nuts and pulses are rich vegetable sources of protein.

Eat more fish, a low-fat form of protein. Mackerel and sardines and other oily fish contain unsaturated fat that helps to clear the body of cholesterol.

ELECTRO-THERAPY
Stimulating the body against pain

The idea of using electrotherapy to alleviate pain originated when a Roman doctor treated GOUT by placing a patient's swollen foot on a live electric eel. In the 19th century, when it was possible to store static electricity, it became fashionable for doctors to discharge electric currents through their patients' bodies to relieve various aches and pains. Later, dentists used the same method to reduce the pain when extracting teeth.

Today, electrotherapy's most widely accepted form is transcutaneous nerve stimulation (TNS), which activates the nerves that block out pain. To do this, a small, battery-powered machine sends weak electrical pulses – machine output varies but is only in milliamps – through the skin by means of a pair of rubber pads. The pads are coated with jelly and taped around the area to be treated.
Who it can help The therapy is mainly used in physiotherapy to treat LUMBAGO, SCIATICA and SPORTS INJURIES. Many hospital maternity wards use TNS machines specifically designed to relieve pain in childbirth. As an alternative to drugs, TNS is also offered for non-painful conditions such as CIRCULATION PROBLEMS.

However, TNS merely reduces the level of pain, and does not cure the underlying cause of it. It is important, therefore, that a problem is medically diagnosed before any treatment is given.
Warning People with a heart pacemaker should *not* use the machines, as they can affect the pacemaker's action.

Self help TNS machines can be borrowed from most hospital physiotherapy departments and used by patients on a daily basis. Alternatively, they can be bought or hired from the manufacturer provided you have the approval of a doctor or physiotherapist – who will give you the manufacturers' names and addresses. The treatment is safe and effective, as long as proper instruction is given as to where the pads should be placed and how the machines are operated.

Small, hand-held electrical stimulators can also be bought. With these, the current is applied by a probe to a specific point on the body. However, they are less effective than proper TNS machines.
Finding a therapist Many fitness and beauty clinics use a variant of TNS for slimming. In this, electrical pulses are directed onto the skin over the 'motor' area of the muscles. This makes them twitch rhythmically, with the aim of burning up calories and eliminating excess fat.

Some clinics offer a similar form of therapy to TNS called electro-ACUPUNCTURE. This is also used mainly to treat pain and sports injuries. The machines employed pass electrical pulses into the body from up to eight needles, and they must be operated by a fully qualified acupuncturist. Before undergoing electro-acupuncture you should always consult your GP, as a more orthodox treatment may be advisable.

An orthodox view

As far as slimming is concerned, most doctors believe that EXERCISE is a more effective way of losing weight. However, the use of TNS is now a standard feature in many pain clinics, and electro-acupuncture is used in some special units. Surgeons also use a form of electrotherapy to destroy nerve tissue in cases of severe pain.

EMPHYSEMA
The gradual breakdown of the lungs

Heavy smokers and people living or working in polluted atmospheres are at risk from this progressive and incurable disease. It occurs when tiny air sacs in the lungs become distended and rupture. This damages the lungs' elasticity, making them less efficient and slowing down their flow of blood. As a result, the heart has to work harder to pump blood through the system, and the added strain can lead to heart failure.

The main symptoms are breathlessness and blueness of the lips. People with ASTHMA and chronic BRONCHITIS are also at risk. The disease is far more common among men than women.

What the therapists recommend

Acupuncture Although the disease cannot be halted, acupuncturists claim to have brought relief in certain cases, allowing the patient to breathe more easily and improving blood circulation in the lungs. But this can only be done in less advanced cases where the lungs are not too distended and the chest has not taken on a beer-barrel appearance.

Acupuncture points treated are similar to those for asthma and bronchitis.
Chiropractic Some breathing difficulties are believed to be the result of slight spinal problems which affect nerve impulses to the lungs. Chiropractors can treat these problems and sometimes ease difficult breathing.
Naturopathy Practitioners claim that vitamin and mineral supplements have helped long-term patients. For example, 7500iu of vitamin A taken daily is said to strengthen lung tissue; and 200iu of vitamin E taken three times a day to make breathing less arduous. Many emphysema victims also suffer badly from mucus; practitioners will advise them to avoid dairy products (milk, butter, cheese and so on).
Herbal Medicine Always discuss your health problem with a herbal practitioner before taking any teas or using liniment rubs. He will probably offer the same treatment as for bronchitis. However, a drink he may recommend specifically for emphysema is made from ½oz (15g) each of LIQUORICE root and comfrey, added to 1pint (600ml) of water. Simmer for about 15 minutes, allow to cool and take 4 tablespoonsful four times daily. Both herbs are relaxing, soothing expectorants to loosen and remove phlegm. Other remedies are also used, but these depend on individual consultation.
Aromatherapy A number of essential oils are said to make breathing less laborious for emphysema victims, including basil, cajeput, eucalyptus, hyssop and thyme. The best way to use the oils is in a diffuser, or an essential oil burner – six drops in water – in the bedroom at night. Or they can be inhaled from a kitchen tissue.

An orthodox view

Patients with severe breathing problems may be given oxygen, and antibiotics may be prescribed to control secondary infection in asthma and bronchitis – which aggravate the condition. A doctor will certainly advise a sufferer to stop SMOKING, take regular but moderate exercise in fresh air, and avoid polluted atmospheres.

ENCOUNTER GROUPS
Learning to know yourself and others

The principal aims of encounter group therapy are to raise self-awareness and improve an individual's ability to get on with others and form fruitful relationships. This is done by making people aware of their own feelings – of ANXIETY or aggression, for example – and of the true feelings of other people.

Layers of behaviour can build up over

years to hide feelings which people think make them unacceptable to others, and also to protect themselves from being hurt by other people's expression of feelings. Encounter group members are helped to discard these layers to reveal their true feelings freely within the group, and to become aware of and accept the feelings of others.

The American psychologist Carl Rogers was among the principal developers of the therapy, in the 1940s. He moved away from earlier methods, in which a medical expert had face-to-face meetings with a patient, and towards a freer group in which people used here-and-now, face-to-face interactions to help each other to uncover their problems and learn how to deal with them.

This type of therapy has now been taken out of the world of psychiatric clinics and developed by non-medical bodies into courses that ordinary people can use to develop their own self-awareness and self-esteem, and to move closer to fulfilling their own potential as human beings.

Who it can help Besides helping people receiving mental health care – sometimes in hospital or as outpatients – encounter group therapy can encourage confidence in people who find personal and business relationships difficult. Working out their feelings in the group has also been found to benefit some who have suffered distressing upheavals in relationships.

Finding a group Among organisations that hold encounter groups are: The Open Centre, 188 Old Street, London EC1V 9BP; Resonance, 18 Station Terrace, Great Linford, Milton Keynes MK14 5AP; and Spectrum, 7 Endymion Road, London N4 1EE.

Attending a group The numbers and activities in encounter groups are very variable. Some groups hold several short sessions on successive days, some have weekly sessions, while some have one continuous session lasting 24 or 48 hours.

Group members will have an initial period of getting to know each other, and may use simple exercises to help the process of 'letting go'. These may include physical contact, eye contact, communication exercises, group games and 'trust' exercises. As the group unfolds, members will be encouraged to be as honest as possible with each other about their feelings, thoughts and reactions.

The emotional climate may at times become intense. Anger and frustrations can well up and are voiced openly, and members will be encouraged to resolve conflicts as they arise. When they discover something about their own behaviour that is destructive or limiting, they will be asked to try more effective alternatives. For example, a quiet, withdrawn person may be encouraged to speak out and express himself openly.

There should always be a balance of challenge and support within a group. Usually there are regular pauses to review what has happened so far, and the therapist or group leader makes sure that the group concentrates on what the members are feeling there and then about each other. Problems involving people not in the group are dealt with by group members playing the role of the absent person.

An orthodox view

Many qualified psychiatrists and trained counsellors lead encounter groups, but there is no scientific proof that the therapy gives lasting help. Group courses to promote more skilled handling of colleagues at work rarely do harm, but allowing too much challenge and release of aggression can result in some members feeling humiliated and gaining no benefit. Some people can even be pushed towards mental illness by untrained probing of their mental scars.

Advice should always be sought from a doctor before joining any such group.

ENERGY

Alternative practitioners believe that energy – also known as _Qi_ or _chi, prana_, vitalism or life force in different healing traditions – circulates through the body in channels called meridians (see also ACUPUNCTURE). At certain points – called _chakras_ in YOGA – the energy becomes concentrated, affecting you both physically and mentally. Disease is thought to be the result of a 'blockage' or 'imbalance' (too much or too little) in the energy flow, which alters the molecules and cells of particular organs; also that this happens before any effects detectable by orthodox means occur.

Healers (see HEALERS AND HEALING) and Chinese practitioners say that they can often tell that something is wrong long before conventional doctors can. Some therapists believe that technical methods such as KIRLIAN PHOTOGRAPHY can also show the flow of energy in the body.

It is not fully understood how – or even whether – this view of energy is related to scientific definitions of physical kinds of energy. When spiritual healers talk about energy flowing between them and their clients, or Yoga teachers describe it circulating through the chakras of the body, no scientifically measurable changes have been shown to occur. Nevertheless, attempts continue to be made to find some objective evidence for these forms of energy.

Self help Alternative therapists say that good health does not mean being continually in a high-energy state – this would exhaust both body and mind and deprive us of time for relaxation, reflection and rest. It is also necessary to allow ourselves to feel sad and depressed at times; to live fully and healthily means accepting both positive and negative, high-energy and low-energy states of both body and mind. In a healthy person, energy should flow naturally and freely among all four of these states.

Different therapies offer a variety of ways to encourage the free flow of energy. Here are some simple self-help methods:

Exercise and self-expression These are said to increase low-energy states and reduce high-energy ones. Regular rhythmic EXERCISE of the 'aerobic' type – JOGGING, swimming and skipping, for example – releases physical and mental TENSION and encourages the production of chemicals in the brain which have a painkilling and uplifting effect. If practised regularly, this can help even long-standing DEPRESSION.

Expressing feelings by shouting, laughing, pummelling a punchbag or cushion, or crying also helps many people to relieve tensions. Crying, for example, has been shown to alter the breathing pattern and reduce high levels of STRESS hormones.

Diet Stimulants such as tea and coffee have the effect of increasing energy levels, as do sugary snacks such as sweets and chocolates. Many people who suffer from ANXIETY find that simply avoiding these foods reduces the problem considerably. Fasting decreases adrenal hormones in the blood, which may help to calm people who are in a state of agitation or tension. And in India, Ayurvedic practitioners use certain foods, such as milk, fats and FIBRE, to achieve this effect; other foods – meat, spices and sweets, for example – are prescribed to increase the energy levels of depressed patients.

Breathing One of the most immediate ways of altering the energy state is through special breathing exercises (see RELAXATION AND BREATHING). To aid relaxation, therapists recommend diaphragmatic breathing (see p. 299), which slows down the pulse rate and decreases BLOOD PRESSURE. The Full Yogic Breath practised early in the morning helps to get your system going and keep you wide awake. Even in the lowest energy state, the 'shining skull' exercise – rapid in-and-out diaphragmatic breathing – should rouse and invigorate body and mind.

An orthodox view

The concept of energy, in the scientific sense of the word, forms part of certain orthodox treatments such as radiotherapy and isotope medicine, used against CANCER. The body receives energy beamed at it, altering the structure of targeted cells.

Conventional doctors tend to reject alternative theories of energy because of a lack of scientific explanation and evidence for them. Recently, however, experiments with traditional healers seem to have demonstrated energy transfer between living things and between people and inanimate objects. The techniques for measuring this energy are still quite primitive and most orthodox scientists do not accept the evidence of methods such as Kirlian photography and intuitive DIAGNOSIS. However, although proof remains uncertain, the possibility of this kind of energy is now more widely acknowledged by doctors.

EPILEPSY

People with epilepsy suffer periodic CONVULSIONS, or fits, during which they lose consciousness for anything from a few seconds to several minutes, depending on the type of epilepsy involved. The two most common forms are called *grand mal* and *petit mal*.

Grand mal normally affects adults, who sometimes froth at the mouth and are in danger of swallowing their tongue. An attack, with its accompanying BLACKOUT can last for ten minutes. Petit mal affects youngsters aged between about four and their late teens. These attacks are usually so brief and undramatic that the victim is often not even aware of them. He loses consciousness for only a few seconds, during which time his eyes may flicker or blink rapidly.

The main cause of epilepsy is excessive electrical discharges among some of the brain's nerve cells. Head injuries or, in some adults, brain tumours (see CANCER) can also be causes. But in many cases the cause remains unknown. Rarely, a baby under six months may have an epileptic fit which is sometimes mistaken for COLIC.

Epilepsy sometimes runs in families and affects about four people in 1000. Sufferers should always carry a card or tag stating their problem, in case they collapse in public. In Britain, it is illegal for epileptics to hold a driving licence unless they have not had an attack for the previous two years.

What the therapists recommend

Naturopathy A well-balanced wholefood diet is favoured by practitioners, who say that it reduces the frequency and intensity of epileptic attacks. Mixed salads and raw fruit are said to be particularly effective (see EATING FOR HEALTH).

Bach Remedies Rescue Remedy may be used during a sudden attack of epilepsy, with Olive to help afterwards. Clematis may assist the victim regain normal consciousness. In addition, certain remedies may help to control various mental and emotional states which may herald an attack. For example: Holly if hatred or anger brings on an attack; Rock water if the victim tends to be hard on himself; Mimulus for fear of the condition itself; Hornbeam if the victim easily becomes mentally exhausted; Clematis for feelings of vagueness, dreaminess and lack of interest.

Aromatherapy Practitioners believe that relaxation is one of the keys to combating epilepsy. A cup of camomile tea at bedtime promotes a good night's sleep. And one drop of Roman camomile essence on a cube of sugar, taken three times a day between meals, is said to aid general relaxation. Basil, cajeput, rosemary and thyme are helpful oils, but hyssop, sage and possibly fennel should be avoided by anyone prone to fits.

Cranial Osteopathy Practitioners claim to have relieved symptoms by cranial massage.

An orthodox view

There is no evidence that any alternative therapy can reduce the frequency or severity of fits. However, some doctors favour the use of alternative medicines such as BIOCHEMIC TISSUE SALTS. The importance of healthy eating and relaxation is also stressed, and a course of YOGA may well be advised.

Anticonvulsant drugs may be prescribed as a conventional method of controlling fits. Once conventional treatment has begun, it usually has to be followed for life.

EURHYTHMY

This system of rhythmical body movements is performed in harmony with the rhythm of the spoken word. The vowel and consonant sounds each have their own type of movement. Eurhythmy was devised by Rudolf Steiner as part of the system of ANTHROPOSOPHICAL MEDICINE, which he pioneered.

The body movements are said to be especially helpful for children as aids to developing suppleness and rhythmic sense.

EXERCISE

Taking sensible, regular exercise can aid slimming, improve fitness and help the body resist many diseases and disorders. See IT'S YOUR BODY – USE IT OR LOSE IT, p. 130.

EXHAUSTION

Extreme and seemingly unshakable feelings of weariness and general depletion are the telltale symptoms of exhaustion. The condition has many causes and may take many different forms. ANXIETY which develops into STRESS is often responsible.

However, exhaustion may also be brought on by heat stroke (in which there is profuse sweating leading to the loss of body salt and causing muscle cramps and general weakness); extreme coldness leading to HYPOTHERMIA; various NERVOUS DISORDERS, including the depressive phase of MANIC DEPRESSIVE DISORDER; or intense TIREDNESS.

EYE DISORDERS

Easily the most frequent disorder affecting the eyes is a foreign object – anything from a speck of dirt to a gnat – in the eye. If such an object enters the eye, do not rub it as this will only increase the pain and cause swelling (see illustrations opposite).

Homoeopaths may recommend washing the affected eye in an eyewash made by mixing ¼ pint (150ml) of lukewarm water with four or five drops of *Hypericum* mother tincture, obtainable from most health shops. Blink repeatedly while washing to dislodge the object. If this fails, wet a small, clean piece of cloth or gauze with the eyewash and gently try to clear the eye. It may help if you pull the eyelid up or down.

If the object remains lodged, see a doctor or go to a hospital casualty ward. Never try to remove a loose or embedded foreign object by force – this could cause serious damage. And never even touch a foreign object that is embedded in the eye.

Other fairly common eye disorders apart from EYESIGHT PROBLEMS and EYESTRAIN include: CATARACTS (a misting of the eye's lens, affecting elderly people); CONJUNCTIVITIS (inflammation of the conjunctiva, the thin transparent membrane across the front of the eye); glaucoma (a gradual loss of vision which, if left untreated, can lead to blindness); and STYES (small boils near the base of the eyelashes).

A minor disorder is the appearance of floaters, black threads or dots that seem to float in the field of vision. They are caused by tiny amounts of blood leaking into the eyeball. They are not serious and usually disappear in a few weeks without treatment. If they persist, see a doctor.

Eye injuries

An injury to the eye, including a foreign object under the eyelid, is potentially dangerous and needs expert medical attention – as well as on-the-spot first aid. Never rub or touch an injured eye or eyelid.

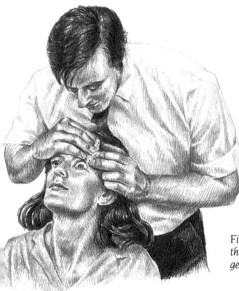

A homoeopathic treatment for a foreign object in the eye is to wash the affected eye in an eyewash of ¼ pint (150ml) lukewarm water containing about five drops of Hypericum mother tincture. Blinking helps to dislodge the object.

First aid: stand behind the victim and examine the injured eye (left). Prepare to carefully and gently remove any loose foreign object from it.

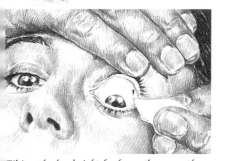

Tilting the head right back, gently grasp the lashes of the upper or lower lid and pull the lid back. Now carefully remove the object with the point of a clean handkerchief or piece of gauze.

Another method is to press down on the eyelid with a matchstick to pick up the object on the inner surface of the lid. The lid is then pulled up against the match and the object removed from inside the lid using a clean cloth.

EYESIGHT PROBLEMS

Among the most common eye problems are short-sightedness (_myopia_), in which only nearby objects are clearly focused, and long-sightedness (_hypermetropia_), in which the eye can focus only on distant objects. Short-sightedness often runs in families, affecting about one person in five. Long-sighted people often have blurred vision and EYE-STRAIN through overusing the eye muscles.

Long-sightedness is also a natural consequence of the ageing process, when it is known as _presbyopia_. Most people experience it by the age of about 45. Apart from wearing spectacles or contact lenses, both conditions are said to be helped by the BATES METHOD of eye exercises.

Another common eyesight problem is ASTIGMATISM, or distortion of vision. This occurs when the eye lens has different curvatures in different directions, so that the image on the retina is irregular. It can be corrected by the aid of specially made spectacle lenses, but the Bates method is believed also to help alleviate this problem.

EYESTRAIN

The growing use of visual display units (VDUs) at work and at home is one of the major causes of eyestrain. The eyes ache and feel tired, and the condition is often worsened by a HEADACHE. Eyestrain can also be caused – or aggravated – by working in artificial light, reading in poor light, and watching hours of television in the dark.

Self help People using VDUs should spend no more than two hours at a time in front of the screen, followed by at least one hour away from it. When reading, make sure that sufficient light falls onto the pages, and when watching television at night, always have a side light on in the room. In either case, relax your eyes by looking away from the page or screen for a few seconds every half hour.

What the therapists recommend

Homoeopathy Bathe the eyes with four drops of _Euphrasia_ mother tincture in ¼ pint (150ml) of lukewarm water. If the trouble persists, seek medical help.

Bates Method Practitioners recommend a series of basic eye exercises; they claim that these dispense with the need for spectacles.

Naturopathy Try a daily intake of vitamin A (7500iu) and vitamin B2 (10mg).

Acupressure Relief may be obtained by massaging a few key points on the face. Use the thumb and index finger of one hand to massage the bridge of the nose with an up-and-down motion. Use both thumbs to massage the top of the nose on both sides, keeping the other fingers flat on the forehead. Use the index fingers to massage beneath the eyes, just below the cheekbones.

Herbal Medicine Herbalists recommend various compresses – including chickweed, cucumber, eyebright and marigold petals – to combat eyestrain. Immerse a clean piece of cloth in an infusion (see p. 184) of the herb. Let the cloth cool and then hold it to your eyes. It is best to do this when sitting or lying down. Alternatively, cut thin slices of fresh cucumber and place them on the eyes. Leave the compress in place for about ten minutes.

An orthodox view

In cases of straightforward eyestrain a doctor will probably agree with bathing them in water. However, he is more likely to advise the use of a proprietary brand of eyedrops.

If reading presents problems – such as having to hold the reading material close to the eyes – he may send you to an optometrist for an eye test. If long or short-sightedness is diagnosed (see EYESIGHT PROBLEMS) you will be advised to wear glasses or contact lenses.

It's your body – use it or lose it

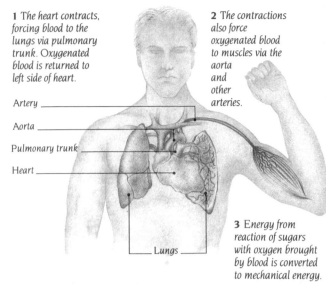

1 *The heart contracts, forcing blood to the lungs via pulmonary trunk. Oxygenated blood is returned to left side of heart.*

2 *The contractions also force oxygenated blood to muscles via the aorta and other arteries.*

Artery

Aorta

Pulmonary trunk

Heart

Lungs

3 *Energy from reaction of sugars with oxygen brought by blood is converted to mechanical energy.*

Sitting behind desks or minding machines, we in the West become less fit as we get older. But does it matter? It does, because with your body it's a case of use it or lose it. Good health – life itself – is put at risk by inactivity.

Power from heart to muscle

When you exercise, your muscles need extra oxygen and nourishment. The heart beats faster and more strongly to meet the demand, and in this way is itself exercised. The diagram shows how oxygen reaches a muscle, in this case the biceps muscle of the arm.

Physical activity is a natural part of human life – like sleeping or eating. Nobody who sees how children rush around can doubt it. But as adults, our inclination and capacity for exercise become gradually eroded by sedentary jobs, readily available transport and home-based leisure activities such as watching television.

So it becomes necessary to take planned exercise. For not only does the body simply deteriorate if it is not used, the health hazards of a sedentary life – such as high BLOOD PRESSURE and cholesterol build-up – need to be offset. Perhaps just as important, exercise simply makes us feel better. Getting fit relieves TENSION and STRESS, which boosts mental as well as physical health.

What getting fit means

Many people think mistakenly that fitness training is designed to develop a bigger heart or lungs. However, the amount of air an adult's lungs can hold is largely an inherited capacity, which cannot be changed much. Nor does a healthy person's heart get bigger through exercise – indeed, any such increase is a warning signal of possible heart failure (see HEART DISORDERS). What fitness training does, is make our lungs, heart, blood and muscles work more efficiently.

All human activity depends on moving muscles. The energy for this comes from the breakdown of sugars (and indirectly fats) in muscle tissue; the amount of energy produced there depends on how much oxygen reaches the muscle cells through the bloodstream.

If we exercise a group of muscles over and over again – say, by raising an arm overhead once every second – it soon

becomes painful. This is because we have used up the available oxygen and the muscle is now working without any. It can still produce energy, even without oxygen, but the process leads to a build-up of lactic acid in the muscles, which causes painful muscle CRAMP.

Physically fit people can transfer large amounts of oxygen from their blood to their muscles, allowing the muscles to work for longer than those of unfit people before cramp sets in. The large amount of oxygen results partly from increased carrying capacity in the blood. This capacity has been improved through improved oxygen exchange in the lungs and more efficient expulsion of carbon dioxide. The muscles also extract oxygen more efficiently from the blood, because physical training increases a muscle's number of mitochondria – microscopic parts of cells that exchange oxygen and sugar for energy.

The effect is that a fit muscle is capable of more work – and does not have to work as hard to do a particular task as it did before getting fit. It can work for longer and produce more energy before lactic acid builds up and causes cramp.

The heart is, of course, a major muscle. One effect of an exercise programme is to train the heart muscle along with others. The heart's job is to pump blood all over the body – first to the lungs where it picks up oxygen, and then back to the heart to be pumped out to organs and tissues. Each squeeze of the pump is felt as a heartbeat or the throb of a pulse with each fresh surge of blood.

The amount of blood reaching, say, the legs during one minute depends on how frequently the heart beats and also on how much blood it pumps out at each beat. Exercise makes the heart muscle more elastic, so at each beat it contracts more efficiently, forcing out more blood. This means that fewer beats are needed to supply the same amount per minute of oxygen-bearing blood to the legs. The heart can therefore afford to slow down.

You should be able to measure how much it does so. After a few weeks of training, your heartbeat – and consequently your pulse rate – should slow. A pulse rate of perhaps 65 beats a minute would come down to only 60 or less (see box, *Test your fitness*). In highly trained athletes it often comes down into the 40s. This more efficient heart pumping also means that when your muscles are working hard – to run for a bus or climb stairs, for example – your pulse rate does not go as high as before.

Choosing your exercise

Many people are now taking up weight training to get in better shape. The repetitive exercising they do with light weights works the heart and increases oxygen consumption – and so is a form of aerobic exercise (see p. 134). But not all forms of exercise are like this. People interested in getting strong lift heavy weights to build large muscles. They exercise in short bursts, exerting very high effort – which does little to train the heart.

However, people often combine the two – weights for strength, and aerobic exercise to make the heart more efficient through regular and repetitive routines. It is important to know the difference between the two, especially for unfit middle-aged people. Lifting heavy weights causes muscles to contract fiercely and puts pressure on the blood vessels – which can raise blood pressure quite dramatically. *This is a danger that would-be weight trainers should consider.*

When people who have not exercised for years decide to take up an exercise programme they are often confused about which kind it should be and whether they need their doctor's advice (see box, *Do's and don'ts about exercise*). Although you will often read and hear the advice that you should ask for your doctor's approval before beginning, you should remember that your doctor can only examine you for any obvious problems – no collection of tests can prove that you are immune to every problem that exercise could cause.

The best advice is to find a form of exercise that you like and can do easily. If you are unfit, you might decide first to introduce more physical exertion into your everyday life. When you move about, do it briskly. In shops and offices, walk upstairs instead of using lifts or escalators. Walk to the local shops or station instead of driving. Get off your bus one stop before your destination and complete the journey on foot. Unwind at the weekends by walking or gardening instead of sitting all the time.

When you are ready for exercise routines, start slowly and never push yourself to the point where you are uncomfortable – you should, for example, just be able to carry on a conversation with someone exercising next to you. Only if you are a professional sportsman and your living depends on winning is there any need to force yourself through the pain barrier. You can achieve a training effect well before that moment arrives.

The idea of a training zone – a heart rate that develops increased elasticity in the heart and greater oxygen uptake

in the muscles – is the basis of all exercise programmes. Such programmes try to make the body work close to its maximum rate of absorbing oxygen. This absorption rate is linked to heart rate, and consequently to pulse rate, which is easily measured and tells whether you are working hard enough to train the heart and other muscles (see chart).

Measure the rate by taking your pulse immediately you stop exercising, before the rate begins to drop. The simplest way is to take your pulse for just 6 or 10 seconds while the rate is at its highest – and multiply the number (by 10 or 6 respectively) to get the rate per minute. If you take your pulse for a full minute, the figure will be misleadingly low since the rate will drop rapidly during that minute. As you get fitter, your heart and pulse rate should drop from exercise to normal level more quickly, and this *recovery time* should eventually level out at about 1½ minutes.

Remember that any activity uses *some* energy, but much of it does not use enough to produce a training effect. The exercises that use large muscle groups such as the arms and legs – running, cycling, skiing or rowing, for example – are those that give a training effect and so increase fitness. Generally, exercise has to require 6-10 METs (metabolic units) to give a training effect. The MET is a unit for measuring the body's metabolic rate – that is the rate at which energy is used to maintain structure and activity. One MET is taken to be the body's metabolic rate when it is at rest. Carrying out everyday tasks multiplies this rate according to the amount of effort needed. It is only quite energetic activities that raise the rate enough to give a training effect – that is above 6 METs.

Brisk walking, cycling at 11mph (17.5km/h), competitive badminton, social tennis singles and water-skiing are among the activities that require 6-7 METs. Jogging at 5mph (8km/h), cycling at 12mph (19km/h), galloping on horseback, swimming, downhill skiing, ice hockey, mountain climbing, canoeing, football and disco dancing require 7-8

Do's and don'ts about exercise

Do ask your doctor's advice if you suffer from high blood pressure, DIZZINESS, BLACKOUTS, any HEART DISORDERS, DIABETES, BACK PAIN or ARTHRITIS.

Don't exercise for more than 20 minutes at a time at first. If you cannot manage 20 minutes, then build up your sessions slowly.

Do stop and rest if you become breathless or feel pain or discomfort. You should always be able to hold a conversation while exercising.

Don't exercise when you are tired, ill or feverish.

Do wait at least two hours after a meal before exercising.

Don't choose a competitive sport if you suffer from stress or tension.

Do warm up properly before strenuous exercise, to reduce the risk of strained muscles or ligaments.

Do wear loose, comfortable clothes for your exercise session, cotton if possible because it absorbs sweat better than synthetic fabrics and allows air to circulate more freely.

Do buy well-made, comfortable training shoes for exercising, to protect yourself from injury.

METs. Activities requiring 8-10 METs include running at 5½mph (9km/h), cycling at 13mph (21km/h), social squash, basketball, rowing and competitive tennis.

Running and JOGGING are undoubtedly the most popular forms of exercise in the Western world. You can do them more or less anywhere and with little equipment other than well-cushioned running shoes. But they still have drawbacks – apart from traffic and pollution hazards, they can be plain boring. Also, running on hard roads can cause muscle problems, SPRAINS and sometimes knee damage.

The second most popular exercise is aerobics (a term coined in the 1960s in the United States by Dr Kenneth Cooper). Essentially, this consists of movement to music, either alone, using exercise tapes now available, or with a teacher in a group.

Recently the value of walking has been rediscovered. Many doctors have recommended patients to walk more instead of going by car or bus, but sports specialists have doubted whether walking would put the heart rate up into the training zone. In the mid-1980s, a group of doctors in Massachusetts asked several hundred people, both young and old, to walk a mile (1.6km) briskly. Most of their heart rates rose enough for a training effect.

Walking also avoids many of the problems posed by more energetic exercise. However, it does not do much for the flexibility of the joints and muscles, so it should be combined with some form of stretch exercise, such as a hamstring stretch or a calf stretch. For a hamstring stretch, bend at the waist and clasp the backs of the calves with your hands, holding the position for 10 seconds and repeating it five times. For a calf stretch, stand 18in (46cm) away from a wall and press your hands against it while you push your pelvis forward (repeat three to five times).

How much exercise should we take?

Somebody unaccustomed to exercising – especially if in poor physical condition – should start cautiously, feeling out how the body reacts to exertion. You should not exercise for longer than you feel comfortable, even if this is only five minutes at first. Aim at building up steadily to three sessions a week, each of about 45-60 minutes. By the time you have become used to that amount, about half of each session should take you into the training zone, so that oxygen intake is increased and your heart rate is slowed.

A ten-week programme is usually required to reach this stage, and the effects of training will not show for the first few weeks. However, once you are fit, two exercise sessions a week are sufficient to maintain fitness. With less than that, you will quickly begin to lose fitness again.

Some people take exercise only occasionally, then do it as violently as they can in the hope of getting increased benefit. In fact, the opposite happens. For example, one game of squash every few weeks does little to improve fitness but increases the danger of injury. Getting into an exercise programme slowly and taking short, regular sessions is far more effective and far less risky than trying to achieve instant fitness in violent bursts.

Most exercise injuries involve muscles and the ankle,

knee and hip joints. Muscle injuries can be avoided by not driving yourself too hard, and by following a planned programme that makes sure you warm up properly and build up gradually to a peak effort. Joint injuries arise from constantly pounding the feet down on a hard surface, and they are a particular problem in running and aerobics.

A well-cushioned pair of training shoes is one answer to the problem – always buy the best you can afford. Many aerobics teachers provide another answer by specialising in

Test your fitness

A simple way to gauge your fitness is to take your pulse for a minute before you get out of bed in the morning. It is normal for individuals to have different pulse rates. In general, women have a slightly higher resting pulse than men. The fitter you are, the slower, stronger and more regular your pulse will be. A resting pulse rate higher than the 'unfit' level indicates that you should see a doctor as soon as possible.

FITNESS LEVELS FOR RESTING PULSE RATES

Age	20-29	30-39	40-49	over 50
Men				
Very fit	59	63	65	67
Fit	60-69	64-71	66-73	68-75
Fairly fit	70-85	72-85	74-89	76-89
Unfit	86	86	90	90
Women				
Very fit	71	71	73	73
Fit	72-77	72-79	75-79	77-83
Fairly fit	78-95	80-97	80-98	84-102
Unfit	96	98	99	103

If your resting pulse rate is slower than the 'unfit' level, you can test your stamina – but first read the *Do's and don'ts* box.

Step up with one foot after the other onto the bottom step of an ordinary staircase (with the step about 8in [20cm] high), then step down again with one foot after the other. Keep on doing this at the rate of twice every five seconds for three minutes. If you begin to feel dizzy, sick or uncomfortably out of breath, stop at once. After you have rested for 30 seconds, take your pulse again to assess your fitness for exercise.

FITNESS LEVELS AFTER EXERCISE

Age	20-29	30-39	40-49	over 50
Men				
Very fit	74	78	80	83
Fit	76-84	80-86	82-88	84-90
Fairly fit	86-100	88-100	90-104	92-104
Unfit	102	102	106	106
Women				
Very fit	86	86	88	90
Fit	88-92	88-94	80-94	92-98
Fairly fit	99-100	95-112	96-114	100-116
Unfit	112	114	114	118

Do the step test again after a few weeks of your regular exercise routine – you should see quite a difference.

'low impact' aerobics, where students learn how to move their feet up and down without jarring the rest of the body. A third development is to work against taut rubber belts that take the impact of feet and hands. These increase the effort you have to make against the resistance of the rubber, so you work harder but with reduced risk of injury.

There are more serious health problems to look out for. Occasionally newspapers carry stories about middle-aged businessmen who take part in violent exercise and then drop dead. Some years ago doctors in Scotland investigated the deaths of 29 men who expired after playing squash. All but six showed evidence of previous heart disease which they had chosen to ignore. This spotlights the need for a medical check for obvious signs of disease before taking up vigorous exercise. But, since no medical tests can spot an individual's risk of potential heart or other disease, it emphasises even more the need to listen to your body and *never exercise beyond a comfortable limit.*

The same Scottish doctors found that at least a third of squash players who died had been very aggressive, driving themselves to win at all costs. The investigation did not prove that squash is a dangerous game – only that some people find dangerous ways to play it.

The right training zone for you

An exercise session should raise your heart rate to between 70 and 90 per cent of maximum. Below that, there is little training effect, nor is there any point in pushing yourself above it into exhaustion. The fastest your heart will go is about 220 beats a minute, minus your age; the maximum rate declines as you get older. At 35 your maximum is about 185; by 50 it has fallen to about 170. If you are 40, your maximum is about 180 and the 70-90 per cent training rate you should be aiming for is 126-162 beats a minute.

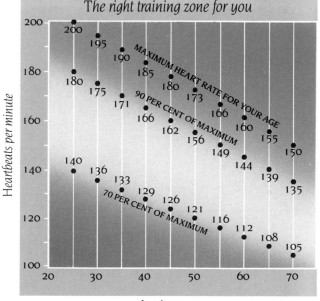

Age in years

Benefits of exercise

Combined with a sensible diet, fitness training can reduce your weight – one of the main reasons for overweight people to take exercise. There are no instant results – running a mile burns off no more calories than you get from a small piece of cake. In the long term, however, exercise increases the rate at which the body breaks down foods, so less of your intake is stored as fat reserves.

Exercise also affects cholesterol, the fatty substance in the blood that can build up inside arteries, blocking circulation and leading to the possibility of heart disorders or a stroke. Cholesterol exists in two forms. LDL (low density lipoprotein) cholesterol increases the risk of a heart attack, while the HDL (high density lipoprotein) form actually reduces it. Exercise is believed to increase the proportion of HDL in the bloodstream, and so should have a protective effect. At first it was thought that HDL increased only in people who took vigorous exercise – for example, running at least 6 miles (10km) a week. Now it seems that lower exercise levels may also increase HDL.

Exercise may reduce the risk of heart attacks in other ways as well. It may contribute to lowering blood pressure, if only by helping to reduce body weight. Some smokers find that exercise helps them to give up the habit (see SMOKING). It may also help by encouraging people to 'think healthy'. They start to see being fit as just one part of a healthy lifestyle that incorporates watching their diet and their weight, giving up smoking and trying to reduce stress.

Links between fitness and mental health are also emerging. The effect goes beyond lifting the mood of people in normal health. It certainly does that, but medical research in the USA in 1978 showed that exercise can be as effective as PSYCHOTHERAPY in treating patients with mild DEPRESSION. Patients with quite severe depression have also been helped by exercise that achieved a training effect.

Just why exercising makes people feel better about themselves remains a mystery, however. One theory is that it releases chemicals in the brain that give a sensation of pleasure. For example, many distance runners say that after a number of miles, their pain and fatigue suddenly change into a feeling of great well-being.

Scientists are now learning something about these brain changes, which may be due to the body's own tranquillising, painkilling group of hormones called endorphins. However, endorphins disappear from the body in a few hours, whereas the exerciser's feelings remain boosted long after the session has ended.

Another theory is that exercise simply distracts the mind from problems, that having got away from them briefly, the mind is refreshed and ready to face them again. Exercising in a group is particularly beneficial – a social activity where people get to know one another.

At the very least, exercise gives a feeling of accomplishment – a sense of mastery over at least one aspect of your life. You see your weight going down and your body shape starting to improve; you move more easily, can do more, and keep going longer: all satisfying proof of what you can do if you put your mind to it.

Exercise

Aerobics used wisely to achieve fitness

Working in a group is generally more enjoyable than exercising on your own – although there are many books and tapes that offer programmes planned to suit the age and fitness of anyone who cannot get to an aerobics class. One slight problem in a group is to avoid competing with others and pushing yourself too far. A good teacher will prevent this and keep students aware of their pulse rates. A well-planned class has three essential parts. First, the warm-up uses movements such as those shown on these two pages to accustom your muscles to exercise and reduce the chance of injury. Next, the most active part of the class progressively raises your heart rate into the training zone. Finally, a warm-down and stretch period allows your heart and pulse rate to return to normal.

Confident teachers will let you watch a class in action before committing yourself to one. Once you join, the teacher will advise you how to start slowly and build up if you are a beginner. Your age – whether it be 30 or 70 – will also be considered when a programme is worked out. People who take up exercise in their 40s or later can greatly improve their fitness, but usually they are not able to work as hard at it as younger people – nor should they try.

Shoulder warming
Standing erect with feet apart and hands hanging loosely at your sides, raise your left shoulder towards your ear while the right shoulder drops. Then raise the right one and drop the left. Repeat another three times.

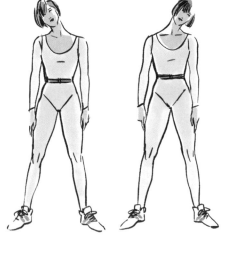

Neck loosener
Start your gentle warm-up of cold muscles by stretching the neck muscles. Drop your head first towards your left shoulder, then towards the right. Repeat three or four times.

Star jumps
Swing your arms out sideways and over your head while you jump and land with feet apart. Jump again to land with feet together and swing your arms out as you lower them to your sides. Do the jumps ten times.

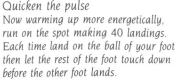

Quicken the pulse
Now warming up more energetically, run on the spot making 40 landings. Each time land on the ball of your foot then let the rest of the foot touch down before the other foot lands.

134

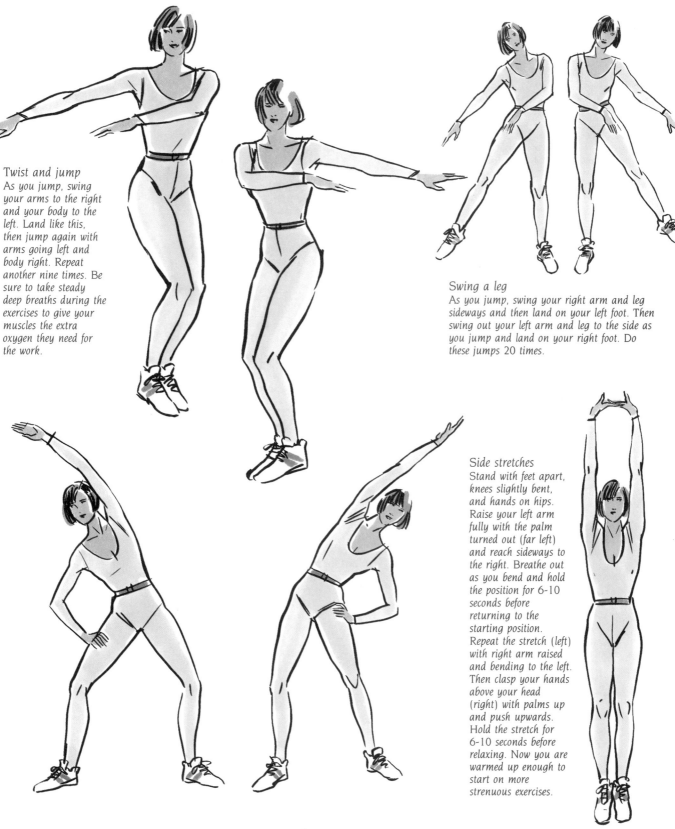

Twist and jump
As you jump, swing your arms to the right and your body to the left. Land like this, then jump again with arms going left and body right. Repeat another nine times. Be sure to take steady deep breaths during the exercises to give your muscles the extra oxygen they need for the work.

Swing a leg
As you jump, swing your right arm and leg sideways and then land on your left foot. Then swing out your left arm and leg to the side as you jump and land on your right foot. Do these jumps 20 times.

Side stretches
Stand with feet apart, knees slightly bent, and hands on hips. Raise your left arm fully with the palm turned out (far left) and reach sideways to the right. Breathe out as you bend and hold the position for 6-10 seconds before returning to the starting position. Repeat the stretch (left) with right arm raised and bending to the left. Then clasp your hands above your head (right) with palms up and push upwards. Hold the stretch for 6-10 seconds before relaxing. Now you are warmed up enough to start on more strenuous exercises.

FAINTING

Although books and films give the impression that it is ladies who swoon, in fact anyone can suffer the brief loss of consciousness which is generally called a faint. In medical circles the term syncope may be used. Lack of oxygen in the brain is the immediate cause of fainting, but there may be various reasons for that lack of oxygen.

Standing up too quickly is the commonest cause, especially in older people. In the short delay before the blood vessels adjust to the new position, blood (which carries the oxygen supply) is not circulated to the brain. When someone stands in one position for too long, blood tends to collect in the legs and circulation to the brain is slowed.

Fatigue, pain, emotional distress or SHOCK can all slow down the heart rate, and again the result can be a failure of circulation to the brain. A slow heartbeat – and consequent reduced oxygen supply to the brain – is common in people with heart disease or DIABETES, and in those who have been given certain drugs or anaesthetics.

A very rapid heartbeat, when the heart circulates blood that is inadequately supplied with oxygen, is characteristic of several conditions, including ANAEMIA, heart failure and some THYROID DISORDERS. It can also be the result of drinking too much coffee or alcohol, or of HYPERVENTILATION.

Self help Many faints can be prevented if you take the following precautions: If you have to stand in one place for a long time, tighten and relax your calf and thigh muscles from time to time and flex your toes to pep up the circulation. Do not stand up too quickly after lying down or slumping in a chair; first sit erect and then perch on the edge for a time before standing. Take care not to jerk your head to the side or tilt it back quickly to reach a shelf or peg; such movements can compress the arteries in the neck.

If you get the warning sensations that often precede a faint – weak legs, light-headedness and pale, cold skin – lie down for a time and get up slowly when the feelings have passed.

Anyone who faints frequently should seek medical advice to find out about the cause. If the fainting follows an injury or happens without any apparent cause, medical advice is certainly needed.

Where the victim recovers in a minute or two and the cause is clear – heat, cold, fatigue, distress or shock, standing still for too long, or standing up too quickly – medical help is not necessary. Prompt first aid is sufficient for recovery.

In both orthodox and alternative medicine the procedure is the same. Lay the victim down flat and prop up the legs slightly. This will quickly restore the blood supply to the brain. Make sure there is no tight clothing round the neck or chest and nothing in the mouth to block the airway. Turn the victim on one side and send for medical help if breathing seems difficult.

What the therapists recommend

Homoeopathy *Aconite* is given after a faint from fright, *Arsenicum album* after a faint from exhaustion or cold, and *Carbo vegetalis* after one from lack of air.

Bach Remedies A few drops of Rescue Remedy taken on the tongue, in water or in tea are given as the victim comes round. Do not give anything by mouth to a person who is unconscious; it can cause choking.

Acupressure A fingernail is used to stimulate strongly the point that is on the midline two-thirds of the way up, between the victim's top lip and nose.

An orthodox view

Prompt first aid (see above), without any other remedy, is the conventional treatment. The victim may like to take a sip of water and some fresh air after he has come round.

FAITH HEALING

The basis of faith healing is a belief in positive or 'right' thinking, which, it is held, can cure or relieve illness. This is particularly so when practised within a religious system such as Christian Science, which preaches healing through spiritual means.

In one form or another, healing – using a reliance on the subject's faith, either in a deity or the healer's own powers – has been practised for centuries in many parts of the world (see HEALERS AND HEALING).

In the early 1890s a French neurophysiologist, Jean Martin Charcot, asserted that his form of faith healing could cure most organic diseases, including CANCER. 'This,' he stated, 'is commonly known in medical circles as miracle healing. However, in the majority of cases, it is shown to be a natural phenomenon which occurs throughout history at all times at most levels of civilisation, and among most religions, however they may otherwise differ.'

In medical theory, faith healing activates and enhances the body's natural defences through reducing the body's response to STRESS. It may produce health-giving hormones – substances carried by the bloodstream which modify the structure and function of organs and tissues, promoting growth and so on. It may also strengthen antibodies – proteins in the blood which fight infection and disease. In addition, it can reinforce the mental attitudes of patients, so that they feel much better – even if their actual condition is not improved.

FASTING

A deliberate and controlled abstinence from solid foods for a certain period – fasting – should never be undertaken without your doctor's consent. Naturopaths are probably its keenest advocate in alternative medicine. A leading practitioner, the British naturopath Leon Chaitow, has described fasting as 'the oldest therapeutic method known to man', adding that 'primitive people stop eating instinctively when not feeling well . . . drinking as much as is needed and eating nothing, until health returns'.

The theory is that fasting makes the body concentrate its resources on ridding itself of disease and poisons rather than using them to digest food. However, naturopaths stress that it must be done under the supervision of a qualified therapist or dietitian.

The length and strictness of a fast is worked out in accordance with the person's age and the condition being treated. From middle age onwards, the system does not react to fasting in the same way as that of younger people – instead of using up body fat to keep going, it is thought to use up protein matter, the basic materials of skin, muscle and other tissues.

A practitioner may recommend short or extended fasts – from perhaps one or two days a week up to periods of 40 or even 50 days. Longer fasts are usually supervised in a residential clinic, health farm or spa. Patients are warned that their early reactions to an extended fast can be unpleasant: DIARRHOEA, HEADACHES, vomiting and BAD BREATH during the first days. However, these symptoms should then disappear, along with pangs of hunger.

An orthodox view

Doctors have tended to dismiss fasting as a healing process, but it has recently begun to earn some acceptance. Claims have been made that it has been effective in treating ARTHRITIS, high BLOOD PRESSURE, certain types of food ALLERGY, and RHEUMATISM. Fasting has also been used to treat SCHIZOPHRENIA, with encouraging results, at hospitals in Moscow and New York.

FEAR
It affects us all at times . . .

Walking through a deserted car park at night or facing a large, unfriendly dog – many common situations can arouse feelings of fear in even the most confident and capable people. The response is natural, normal and useful, because fear sharpens the senses, gives extra strength and quickens reactions, helping you to respond to danger.

Sometimes, however, fear seems to have no obvious cause, or to be excessive for the circumstances. Occasionally it continues long after the danger has passed, or becomes almost a way of life. In these cases, fear itself and not the frightening situation becomes a problem. People who suffer from this sort of unreasonable fear have difficulty coping with the demands of everyday life and work, and find it hard to relax or enjoy themselves. If the fear continues for any length of time, they experience physical and emotional STRESS.

Irrational fear takes many forms. When it is provoked by particular objects or situations such as spiders, heights or flying, it is known as a PHOBIA. In some cases the victim experiences sudden, severe panic attacks in crowded or closed-in public places, CLAUSTROPHOBIA, or finds it hard to leave the house, AGORAPHOBIA.

Often, however, there is just a vague, persistent feeling of ANXIETY, or dread, which either has no apparent cause, or has its roots in some forthcoming event – an interview or examination, for example.

Sometimes the causes of these irrational or exaggerated fears stem from events far in the past – even from such childhood terrors as fear of the dark and 'bogeymen' – which have been forgotten, or which may not even have made much of a conscious impression at the time. Repressed feelings or NERVOUS DISORDERS also play a part.

Mild attacks of fearfulness can be dealt with at home, but more severe or long-lasting feelings need to be treated by a doctor or qualified psychotherapist.

What the therapists recommend

Bach Remedies Rock rose is said to relieve extreme fear or intense panic which has reached crisis level. Mimulus is suitable for known fears, such as getting CANCER, being rejected, finding yourself alone in the dark, and dread of spiders, snakes, or heights. For feelings of foreboding, or of being punished for no good reason, try Aspen. Cherry plum may help with fear of insanity, of losing self-control, or feeling paralysed with fright.

Fear of being alone may be helped by Chicory or Heather.

Relaxation and Breathing; Meditation Both these therapies offer help in overcoming fears. Practitioners consider meditation an effective way of strengthening people's resistance to fear and anxiety. In addition, relaxing and breathing in an even and natural manner will help to prevent panic and the heightening of fear.

An orthodox view

Doctors see fear as a normal human emotion which can help to protect us from irrational behaviour and dangerous situations. When fear gets out of hand and becomes a phobia, doctors usually refer patients to a behavioural psychologist for 'desensitising' treatment (see BEHAVIOURAL THERAPY). The success rate is good for fears of specific things such as snakes or confined spaces, but less effective when the person has a generally fearful or timid personality.

FELDENKRAIS METHOD
Learning new patterns of movement

'A body that is organised to move with minimum effort and maximum efficiency' – this was the purpose for which Moshe Feldenkrais devised his lessons for helping people to learn how they are moving and methods of improving the way they move. Trained in engineering and applied physics, he took a practical scientist's approach to making the 'machinery' of his own body – and then others – work properly.

He came to believe that, in infancy or later, the brain develops an image or pattern of how movements should be made and that the body 'obeys' this image when it moves. He further theorised that this brain image could turn out to be less than ideal for some of the movements, instructing the body to move in ways that eventually cause it pain and damage.

His lessons aim to develop new patterns in the brain, so that movements are made more efficiently. Two techniques were developed: AWARENESS THROUGH MOVEMENT, taught in classes, is intended to make people aware of their habitual patterns and of new possibilities. FUNCTIONAL INTEGRATION uses gentle manipulation to do the same on a one-to-one basis.

Who it can help The gentle lessons given

Learning to free a shoulder

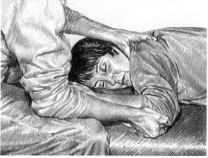

The student lies face-down as shown, with head turned towards the stiff left shoulder. The teacher holds the left elbow and shoulder, and moves them in relation to one another.

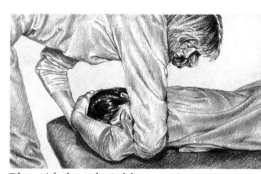

Then, with the student's left arm resting on the head, the Feldenkrais teacher raises and rotates the entire upper torso.

By rotating the left leg the teacher shows the student how the hip joint and entire spine are related to the left shoulder.

Feldenkrais Method

in awareness through movement classes have been found to help many people who suffer recurring pain in their muscles and joints. The lessons are designed to improve posture and hence breathing, circulation and general well-being. Athletes, dancers and other people whose lives involve them in a great deal of movement can, it is believed, lessen the risk of injury by learning efficient muscle use.

A functional integration lesson with a trained teacher aims to restore or control movement in stroke victims and people with cerebral palsy and spinal disorders, as well as easing ARTHRITIS, chronic BACK PAIN and muscle injuries.

Finding a teacher The Feldenkrais Guild UK can put you in touch with the nearest teacher of the method and can also advise on how to obtain lessons on tape. Senior teachers who were trained by Moshe Feldenkrais himself are now leading professional training programmes in England and elsewhere in the world. The training is concentrated in periods of three to five weeks, and is undertaken twice a year for four years. You can contact the Guild and Feldenkrais Professional Training Programmes Ltd at 188 Old Street, London EC1V 9BP.

Consulting a teacher At classes in awareness through movement the teacher leads students through sequences of movements. None of these movements is strenuous. The students usually lie down at first, in order to free them of the usual efforts involved in sitting and standing.

Pelvic clock

The purpose of the sequences of rotations known as the pelvic clock is to explore the possible range of movement of the pelvis. By becoming more aware of the possibilities students are able to improve the relationship of the pelvis to the spine, head and legs, create new patterns of action and develop a wider range of movement.

Copying the moves
The head naturally rotates in the same way as the imaginary dial — the pelvis (see below) — mimicking its movements.

6 o'clock

12 o'clock

3 o'clock

9 o'clock

Imaginary dial
Students imagine that fixed on the back of the pelvic girdle there is a clock dial (which from the front would appear to be reversed). On the dial, 6 o'clock is at the lowest point (the coccyx), 12 o'clock at the highest point (where the spine meets the pelvic girdle), 3 o'clock at the right hip joint and 9 o'clock at the left hip joint.

1 Lying as shown, the student lifts the lower back from the floor, arching as much as possible and putting the pressure on the 6 o'clock point. The weight is shifted to the 12 o'clock point, the arch disappears and the coccyx lifts from the floor. The student then rocks the pelvis from one position to the other several times, making the movements smooth and easy and breathing normally throughout.

2 The movement is repeated, paying attention to how the head copies the pelvic movement.

3 The pelvis is tilted to 3 o'clock, with the pressure on the right side while the left lifts. Then the weight is moved to 9 o'clock and the left side lifts. The sideways rocking is repeated several times.

4 Starting with pressure at 12 o'clock, the pelvis is moved to 1 o'clock and back, then to 1, to 2, and back, and so on until the pelvis is rolling smoothly to 6 o'clock and back. The head will again copy the movement.

5 The movement is repeated but this time on the left side.

6 With 3 o'clock as the starting point, the student rolls the pelvis back and forth, first to 2 o'clock, then to 4, and adds an hour at a time until rolling to 12 in one direction and 6 in the other.

7 The movement is repeated with 9 o'clock as the starting point.

8 The pelvis can then move all round the clock, first clockwise, then anticlockwise, with smooth movements every time. The student notices each time how the head moves in unison with the pelvis.

Between sequences, the student rests on his or her back with legs stretched out and feels the different sensations in the area of the pelvis just moved.

The lessons can be varied, sometimes with one leg drawn up and the other straight; with both legs straight; with one leg crossed over the other; in a sitting position with knees bent, leaning back on the hands.

After the lesson the pelvis feels flatter and the lower back closer to the floor while lying down. On standing, a change of position of the pelvis in relation to the spine and legs is felt.

They repeat the gentle movements over and over until they become easy and smooth, then students can concentrate solely on developing awareness of what they are doing. They quickly become sensitive to tiny adjustments made to the way they organise themselves for movement. More comfortable habits are easily learned – and can affect the way students think and feel.

At a functional integration lesson the teacher sees only one student and uses touch and manipulation to suggest new ways of organising movement. The movements are again very gentle, with no strain or effort.

An orthodox view

Posture, breathing and circulation have been improved by the method, as have muscle and joint disorders. The ALEXANDER TECHNIQUE and ordinary MASSAGE may be equally effective for these problems, as well as for STRESS and serious loss of muscle function, which Feldenkrais teachers also treat.

A teacher from the football field

A persistent knee injury lingering from enthusiastic amateur footballing days drove Moshe Feldenkrais (1904-84) to work out his own method of recovery. The Russian-born immigrant to Israel worked there as a labourer and surveyor before going to study in Paris. He proved to be a first-class student of engineering and physics and continued to be a keen sportsman.

He was one of the first Europeans to become a black belt in judo (in 1936). He was involved in the French atomic programme until the Second World War started, when he moved to Britain and worked on antisubmarine research.

Feldenkrais' success in curing his own knee pain was repeated in curing pains in his family and friends. He returned to Israel after the war, as an electronics consultant to the government. He also lectured on his work on movement at Tel Aviv University.

At the Feldenkrais Institute which he established in Tel Aviv, he practised his method with classes of 100 or more students, and with individuals as well known as David Ben-Gurion, who became Israel's first prime minister in 1948, and the violinist Yehudi Menuhin. Feldenkrais' book _Awareness through Movement_, published in 1972, and his lectures and classes spread his ideas through Europe and the USA.

FEVER

The onset of a fever is a symptom, rather than a particular illness. It is a sign that the body is fighting infection. Most people's body temperature is normally 98.6°F (37°C), although a few individuals may be 1°F (0.6°C) above or below this. At the outset of many childhood infections, temperature can rise up to 104°F (40°C), while among adults, it generally rises to a lesser extent.

However, elderly people may suffer infections and yet their temperature stays normal. This is a sign that the body's ability to fight infection has lessened.

If the patient has severe shivers, shakes and chattering teeth – a condition known as a rigor – call a doctor immediately. These can be symptoms of PNEUMONIA, pyelonephritis (kidney infection) or malaria.

What the therapists recommend

HERBAL MEDICINE

Self help A variety of herbal teas is recommended for fevers – here are three:

Cayenne The hot, red, powdery pepper may be added in small quantities to warm milk, water or tea. Alternatively, swallow a gelatine capsule of cayenne, washed down with a glass of water.

Willow bark This is also said to be helpful in lessening fever. The ancient Greeks used it, as did American Indians. The inner bark is boiled and the 'tea' is drunk in strong doses. Willow bark contains an ingredient which the human system converts into salicylic acid – a basic ingredient of aspirin.

Boneset Another American Indian herbal remedy: 1 or 2 teaspoons of the dried herb are infused in a cupful of boiling water for 10-15 minutes, and drunk every half hour until the fever subsides.

Consultation Like most alternative practitioners, a herbalist tends to regard fever as the process of the body 'burning up' poison wastes in the system. Intense sweating is taken as a good sign that the unwanted matter is being ejected, so treatment does not necessarily aim to suppress the fever.

A practitioner may recommend various preparations, depending on the intensity and stage of development of the fever. In addition to those already outlined, the herbalist may also advise – as an infusion, decoction or tincture – borage, German camomile, eucalyptus or marigold.

NATUROPATHY

Consultation Practitioners regard fever as a kind of 'healing crisis' – a process by which the natural protective functions of the body

Other herbal remedies for fever

To induce heavy sweating, drink an infusion of yarrow hourly. The dried herb – 1-2 teaspoonsful – is infused for 10-15 minutes in boiling water.

To relieve a feverish cold, make a herbal tea of elderflower and lime-blossom in equal proportions.

To ease fever during influenza or a cold on the chest, drink a tea made from lavender flowers.

To clear mucus from the lungs, hyssop tea is recommended. Most herbal teas can be drunk every one to two hours, as hot as possible, in 3-4 tablespoon doses until perspiration subsides. However, take only 1 tablespoon of hyssop.

are attempting to help it recover from some infection. They advise avoiding solid foods and suggest taking four to six glasses of natural unsweetened vegetable juices a day.

If the patient is feeling weak, but still has an appetite, a broth of mixed vegetables may be allowed. Once the feverishness dies down and normal appetite resumes, solid foods can be taken, beginning with natural yoghurts and fresh fruit.

If the patient is a child under five, sponging the neck, face and limbs with tepid water is advised, with the body covered to prevent chill. For older children and adults, a trunk or abdominal pack – that is, a blanket soaked in tepid water placed over the body, then covered with a second, dry blanket – may be applied for three hours or even overnight. Alternatively, regular cold compresses are placed on the forehead.

Other alternative treatments

Homoeopathy _Aconite_ is prescribed for the first signs of fever, accompanied by restlessness and intense thirst which is worse after midnight; _Belladonna_ for a 'burning up' feeling, with a hot, flushed face and dilated pupils; and _Bryonia_ for a dry mouth, intense thirst for large amounts of water at long intervals and irritability. If a child is restless, cries a lot and constantly seeks attention, _Pulsatilla_ may be prescribed. _Nux vomica_ if the patient is extremely irritable, oversensitive and feels chilly. If the condition is accompanied by oversalivating and there is bad breath, particularly worse at night: _Mercurius solubilis. Gelsemium_ when there is lack of thirst, chills up and down the spine, headache and the patient is worse at the least movement, has a feeling of heaviness in the eyelids and limbs, and wants to lie in the dark and be quiet.

Biochemic Tissue Salts *Ferr. phos.* is recommended when there is a rapid pulse, flushed face, with chilliness and vomiting of undigested food. Take every half-hour until the fever subsides. For fevers associated with nervous conditions and general weakness, *Kali phos.* is recommended.

An orthodox view

Like alternative therapists, general practitioners consider fever as a symptom of the body fighting infection. A doctor would first advise rest in a warm – but not hot – room, with plenty of liquids. Aspirin-type painkillers or an anti-infective medicine may also be prescribed – and an attempt would be made to find out the cause of the fever.

FIBRE
An essential part of healthy eating

For thousands of years, mankind was largely vegetarian, so roughage or dietary fibre formed an integral part of our diet. Cellulose, the main component of fibre, is found in all plant cell walls, while lignin supports the plant's cellulose structures. Pectins, the third component, are found in most ripe fruits.

However, with the increasing affluence brought by the Industrial Revolution, and especially after the lifting of food restrictions following the Second World War, preferences for white bread (from which much of the fibrous bran has been removed) grew, and meat gained a much larger place in the diet than vegetables. Fatty, sugary foods such as biscuits and cakes were preferred to fresh, raw fruits – especially as snacks.

Many nutritionists blame all this for the increase in BOWEL DISORDERS and HEART DISORDERS in the last two centuries. During that time, cases of CONSTIPATION, PILES and CANCER of both the upper and lower bowel multiplied apace. People became overweight and developed high BLOOD PRESSURE, placing undue – even fatal – strain on the heart.

Both conventional and alternative practitioners believe that a high-fibre diet helps to combat these disorders (see also EATING FOR HEALTH). Fibre is the part of the food intake that is not digested and absorbed by the body to produce energy. It comes in two forms: insoluble and soluble.

Insoluble fibre is mostly found in wholegrain cereals and bran. The indigestible cellulose and other components in the fibre

Ideal fibre intake

The average adult should aim at a total daily intake of about 1oz (30g) of fibre. This could be made up in the following way on an average day: bowl of muesli or wholegrain cereal (3.5g); slice of wholewheat toast (2.5g); wholewheat sandwich (5g); piece of fruit or handful of nuts and raisins (2g); helping of wholewheat pasta or of lentils, beans or peas, or medium jacket potato (7g); two helpings of vegetables (4g); fresh fruit salad (4g) – total 28g.

give bulk to the body's waste products and speed their passage through the bowel. It is held that the less time that cancer-causing waste stays in the bowel, the less chance there is of tumours forming.

Soluble fibre is contained in most ripe fruits and in vegetables, particularly beans, lentils and peas. It slows up the absorption of nutrients in food and delays the intake of sugar into the blood.

It is believed to help people with that form of DIABETES which is caused by too much blood sugar. In some cases diabetics on high-fibre diets have been able to reduce – and even forgo – their daily intake of insulin.

Soluble fibre also binds with cholesterol in food and helps in its elimination from the system. It is therefore thought to reduce the risk of heart attack and to cut down the likelihood of GALLSTONES. Excluding meat, almost any food which has not been pro-

cessed or refined should provide enough fibre for most people's needs. However, if desired, fibre in the form of bran or special high-fibre or high-bran biscuits, breakfast cereals, breads and other products can be obtained from health stores and some food stores, and taken as a supplement.

FLATULENCE

Gas building up in the stomach and intestine causes WIND, or flatulence. It can result in considerable discomfort – and can find embarrassingly audible means of announcing its presence and making its escape.

FLOATATION THERAPY
A 'weightless' way to relax

Total relaxation of mind and body and relief of STRESS are the basic aims of floatation therapy, but it can be combined with other therapies to treat a variety of problems.

During floatation therapy, the patient floats quite effortlessly because the high concentration of salts dissolved in the water in the tank greatly increases its buoyancy.

The client lies in an enclosed tank of water, which is 10in (25cm) deep, in total or semi-darkness and silence. The water is kept at skin temperature, around 34.2°C (93.5°F), and a blend of Epsom and other mineral salts is dissolved in it to ensure that floating is effortless.

The therapy evolved from experimental work in the 1950s by John C. Lilly, an American doctor, psychoanalyst and neuro-physiologist. Dr Lilly set out to discover how the brain reacted when it did not have to deal with normal outside sensations – not even with gravity. Lilly and another doctor named Jay Shurley made careful observations of each other, as they took turns to float in a tank, and by the early 1970s they had pioneered a floatation tank similar to those now in therapeutic use.

They evolved a theory that once the brain did not have to cope with outside sensations it tended to turn inwards. Then by becoming more aware of inner mental and biological processes, a person could possibly be able to control them consciously. For example, by focusing inwardly, a person might be able voluntarily to control BLOOD PRESSURE and heartbeat, ease PAIN – even strengthen the IMMUNE SYSTEM.

Who it can help Therapists claim that floatation can help to relieve STRESS or stress-related problems such as INSOMNIA or ANXIETY. The total relaxation said to be induced is also held to ease pain, help people stop SMOKING and to help heavy drinkers to cut down (see ALCOHOLISM).

Finding a floatation centre Floating is a relatively new therapy in Britain, so there are few float tanks available for public use. They include those at The Floatarium, 21 Bond Street, Brighton BN1 1RD, and the South London Natural Health Centre, 7A Clapham Common Southside, London SW4 7HA. Information can be obtained from: The International Floatation and Stress Research Association (address as The Floatarium, above), or The Floatation Tank Association, 3A Elms Crescent, London SW4 8QE.

Practitioners are usually qualified in other therapies, which they may use in conjunction with floatation sessions. For example, some tanks have underwater speakers and, while floating, the patient may also have live or recorded sessions in HYPNOTHERAPY, PSYCHO-THERAPY or MEDITATION.

Going to a floatation centre Sessions are usually booked in advance, and may last between 1-2½ hours. The tanks are in various shapes and sizes: a popular type is housed in a fibreglass pyramid, so that condensation runs down the inside walls, rather than dripping from a flat ceiling.

You take a shower before entering the tank, and then insert ear-plugs as a protec-tion against salts and minerals in the water. Once the door is closed, you float in complete or semi-darkness. Some centres have tanks fitted with video screens and offer films for self-improvement or hypnosis, or tapes, played through speakers in the tank, aimed at aiding meditation or as part of VISUALI-SATION THERAPY.

Patients have described the sensation of being in the tank as like lying in cotton wool or marsh-mallow. Therapists claim that the experience 'does not make you feel closed-in' (see CLAUSTROPHOBIA); but anyone who finds it uncomfortable in any way can get out – the tank door is not fastened.

An orthodox view

This technique is used more as a research method than a treatment, and most doctors would not recommend it unless it is super-vised by a well-qualified practitioner. It is potentially dangerous in certain psychiatric conditions (psychosis, severe DEPRESSION and PHOBIAS) – and people undertaking this form of 'treatment' should consult their doctor if they have any doubts.

FLOWER ESSENCES
Health-giving vibrations from petals

The aim of this therapy is to harmonise the mind, body and spirit – and so encourage people to express feelings of love and peace. The bottled flower essences, imported from California, are said to contain vibrations of the sun's energy, absorbed by the flowers' petals when immersed in sun-warmed water.

More than 70 essences are on sale in many British health food stores. They range from Aloe vera (said to increase sensitivity to others), to Zinnia (believed to promote laughter as a potent form of self-healing).

The flower essences are not in any way meant to replace any form of medical treat-ment. However, therapists claim that by working on a mental and emotional level, their vibrations are calculated to relieve conditions such as ANXIETY, DEPRESSION, NERVOUS DISORDERS and TIREDNESS.

A few drops of the essences, placed on the tongue, or in a glass of water, should be taken regularly until the condition eases.

Finding a therapist Courses are periodically held. For information contact The Flower Essence Association, Anubis House, Creswell Drive, Ravenstone, Leics LE6 2AG.

An orthodox view

Smell and emotions are well known to be closely linked and in so far as this approach is used with caution, most conventional doctors would not object to it. The dramatic claims made for the essences, however, should be viewed cautiously.

FLUORIDATION

Controversy rages among both conventional and alternative practitioners over the question of adding soluble fluorides to water supplies in order to reduce tooth decay (see TOOTH AND GUM DISORDERS).

Fluorides are chemical compounds containing the element fluorine. Those who support their use as water additives claim that fluoride ions prevent tooth decay (dental caries) in children.

Those opposed to using fluoride in this way point out that there has not been a single laboratory study proving that fluoridation alone prevents or reduces tooth decay, and is safe for human consumption. Civil liberties campaigners strongly object to fluoridation as an unacceptable form of compulsory mass medication.

Fluoride occurs in the human body, in animals, most foods, particularly fish, and in some plants – especially tea grown in fluoride-rich soil. However, its precise function in living matter is unclear.

Fluorides are contained in volcanic gases and are released by man in various industrial processes, including the steel and aluminium industries, oil refining, the manufacture of phosphate fertilisers and in nuclear power generation. Those who object to fluoridation argue also that industrialists see it as a convenient and lucrative way of getting rid of their waste fluoride.

However, the amount of fluoride put into drinking-water supplies is comparatively very small: usually one part fluoride to one million parts of water. Excess fluoride can permanently stain children's teeth.

Around half the population of the United States is supplied with fluoridated water, while in Britain only one-eighth of the 53.5 million population is supplied with it.

Warning A high intake of fluoride can be dangerous – and even fatal. Some children may eat toothpaste that contains fluoride, because of its sweet additives and pleasant taste and flavour. However, toothpaste itself is a powerful emetic, and long before anyone could eat enough to do any real harm, they would be violently sick.

Will chemicals make us safe or sorry?

Tiny amounts of chemicals are added to what we eat, for safety or to improve the appearance or extend the shelf life of convenience foods. But now they are causing anxiety. In the Western world 75-80 per cent of the food people eat has been processed, and in Britain we eat ten times more food additives than we did 30 years ago. Buyers should be aware of what they are, what they do, and whether they are safe or to be avoided.

An additive is any ingredient that you would not eat as food on its own. It must be approved by the government before food manufacturers can use it. Under the Food Act 1984, government ministers must not allow the use of substances that have no nutritional value unless they are considered necessary. The government's Food Advisory Committee (FAC) investigates the additives which manufacturers ask for permission to use. The committee applies certain criteria: the additive must be necessary; it must be pure and proved safe; the nutritional value of the food must not be lessened by the additive; and only the minimum necessary quantity of additive must be used. An additive is considered necessary if it will keep food wholesome until it is eaten, or make it look and taste good, or make it easier to prepare, store and pack.

The aim is to make it possible for people to have a nutritious diet all the year round. Without additives our food

would be less varied in winter and would cost more. Food poisoning would be more common. Whether we do ultimately benefit from the system is a tricky question. Few people dispute that preservatives are necessary to keep meat products safe to eat and antioxidants to prevent fats from going rancid. Many, however, believe that colours and flavour enhancers are not necessary even though grey margarine, khaki tinned peas and brownish strawberry yoghurt would result from leaving them out.

There is no evidence that the great majority of UK residents have been harmed by food additives, but some certainly have. These are people who have been made abnormally sensitive by some defect in body chemistry. More than 80,000 have suffered one of a range of ailments – skin rashes, dermatitis, ECZEMA, breathing problems (including ASTHMA), MIGRAINE, BOWEL DISORDERS and PALPITATIONS. Lumps and blotches on the skin are the commonest bad reactions. HYPERACTIVITY in children and some forms of CANCER have also been blamed on food additives, but the factors causing these conditions are so complex that there are no clear answers yet. At least six times as many people – perhaps 1 per cent of the population – are made ill by sensitivity to foods free of additives. Milk, eggs, wheat, shellfish, nuts, oranges and strawberries are among the many known to cause reactions. Without food preservatives even more people could be affected by food poisoning.

For most people, convenience outweighs the slight hazard of additives. A public that works more, travels more and eats a greater variety of foods at home and in restaurants demands attractive-looking food that is cheap, quick to prepare and has a long storage life. Manufacturers and retailers are anxious to provide this. Now that there is some public pressure for fewer additives, manufacturers and retailers have responded, cutting colourings from some crisps and some preservatives from bread, for example. The shorter shelf life for wrapped bread (reduced from five days to two) has brought complaints from some customers. The swift distribution of foods, fast turnover in supermarkets and strict control of hygiene and temperature throughout production and retailing should allow manufacturers to reduce the amounts of preservatives used, and under pressure from customers no doubt many of them would. There would then be a greater onus on the customer to store food safely and cook it properly.

Long-term worries

A large number of buyers would gladly accept that onus. They worry that, despite the efforts of the FAC, no tests are made on the cumulative effects of absorbing a range of additives over many years, or on possible interactions between the 3500 additives now approved for use in Britain. Some people assume that all additives are bad but nevertheless use the long-familiar bicarbonate of soda or baking powder in home baking. Some substances approved as additives are a natural, desirable part of foods. There is some carotene and monosodium glutamate in tomatoes, for example, but the colouring carotene and the flavour enhancer monosodium glutamate are viewed in a much less favourable way when they are added to processed foods.

The use of natural extracts rather than synthetic additives – which allows a manufacturer to claim a product is free from artificial additives – does not lessen the worry. If you suffer ill effects from a particular chemical substance, the effect will be the same when you eat it whether it has occurred naturally or been man-made.

People who are concerned to eat a healthy diet without being cranks balance the uncertain risks of additives against

The deep orange colour of many kippers is not the result of traditional curing and smoking over a peat or wood-chip fire but of a dye called brown FK. This is permitted for use as additive E154, but in sensitive people it may cause skin rashes, breathing difficulties, water retention, blurred vision or hyperactivity. Undyed kippers such as the Manx one on the left are distinguished by their silvery skin and pale golden flesh, and may be safer for people with sensitivities.

those of food being contaminated by bacteria. They reduce the risks by making up their diet from foods that have been interfered with as little as possible and by avoiding the additives that are suspected of causing bad reactions in sensitive individuals. Above all, consumers need accurate information on all the contents of foodstuffs so that they can make the choices that suit them.

Identifying foods containing additives

Ingredients of processed foods are listed on the wrapping or package in order of the amount used. Additives, which must be listed, are present in tiny amounts and so appear at the end of the list. They are grouped under category headings – and then itemised under the heading by their code number, their full chemical name, or both. The permitted flavourings are not itemised but are simply included as flavourings. Many of the code numbers are preceded by an E, which shows that the additive has been approved for use in all European Community (EC) countries. Additives whose code has no E have been approved only in the UK. At present about 20 additives approved in the UK are not allowed elsewhere in the EC. Others approved in the UK have no E because the EC committee controlling food additives has doubts about them, or lacks enough information to make a decision.

Foods often contain traces of substances that are not listed. These are substances that are not ingredients of the product but have previously been added to one or more of the ingredients to keep them in good condition – for instance, enzymes used to tenderise meat for pies and other meat products. Foods with only one ingredient – milk or honey, for example – are exempt from the regulations.

There are strange quirks in the labelling regulations. Butter, cheeses and cream list only the ingredients not essential to making them. Thus the colour in some cheeses is listed but not rennet, the enzyme that makes the milk coagulate. Cocoa products, coffee, tea and drinks with more than 1.2 per cent alcohol do not have to list their ingredients – even though several controversial additives are used. Some items such as vinegar and lemon juice are listed but not among the additives, because they are considered to be foods with nutritional value even though they act as preservatives in the product (vinegar has now replaced 'artificial' preservatives in some wrapped breads). Vitamins and minerals are not generally classed as additives but sometimes vitamin C or E is used as an antioxidant and is listed.

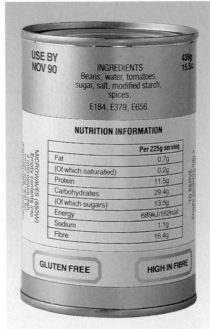

Additives appear at the end of the ingredients list on most processed foods. The full chemical name of the additive or its code number or both may be given. An E in the number denotes that it has been approved for use throughout the EC, and not just in the UK.

What additives are for

There are 17 categories of additive, grouped according to function. An additive may be in a product to do more than one job but will be listed only under the main one – which is not necessarily the one for which it was originally tested and approved. The categories are: acids, acidity regulators, anticaking agents, antifoaming agents, antioxidants, artificial sweeteners, colours, emulsifiers, flavour enhancers, flavourings, flour improvers, gelling agents, glazing agents, preservatives, raising agents, stabilisers and thickeners. The table on pp. 146-7 lists the main additives and their uses.

Preservatives are the most necessary of the additives. Food sellers have a legal duty to make sure that food stays uncontaminated up to its 'sell by' or 'best before' date. Most, but not all, preservatives are man-made. They slow the development of bacteria and other microorganisms that would make food go off and cause food poisoning.

The nitrates and nitrites (E249-252) are preservatives used in meat products, and in Edam, Gouda and some other cheeses – but not in Cheddar, Cheshire or Parmesan. They protect against botulism, a dangerous (often deadly) form of food poisoning. There is concern that we may be getting too much of them because of the multiplicity of sources. Tap water and fresh vegetables may contain more of these substances than processed foods because of residues from agricultural dressings. They are thought to have caused nausea, headaches and dizziness in some sensitive people. In laboratory animals they have produced reactions that could lead to cancer – but only rarely and only after massive doses beyond the possible intake in real life. Vitamin C (from citrus fruits, for example) eaten at the same time as the preservatives gives some protection from their harmful effects.

Benzoates (E210-219) are preservatives that can cause skin problems, hay fever and asthma. Sulphites (E220-227) can cause problems for asthmatics too. They are added to some frozen seafoods, fish products, fruit and vegetable products, dried fruits and vegetables, and white sugar. Go for foods with E270 lactic acid as the preservative instead. This is made by fermentation of the sugar occurring in milk. It is the natural preservative in yoghurt and is widely used in cakes and prepared meat dishes.

Some additives aid manufacturing. Antifoaming agents prevent liquids from boiling over or from frothing when they are bottled. Anticaking agents keep fine powders, such as salt, flowing freely. Flour improvers help to make bread rise.

also a cocoa substitute used in confectionery and drinks and, unlike cocoa, it contains no caffeine.

How to avoid additives

If you are worried about additives because of controversies about particular dangers or possible long-term cumulative effects, adapt your eating habits to avoid them. Eat more fresh foods and cut out processed ones to reduce your additive intake. Remember that foods without preservatives are more liable to bacterial contamination. Extra care is needed to store and cook them so as to avoid food poisoning. Learn how to store fresh foods safely and read your refrigerator handbook again. You may have to spend more time or money, but not necessarily. Extra money spent on organically grown vegetables can be saved by cutting out cakes, biscuits and prepared dishes. Time spent on shopping more often for fresh ingredients with a shorter storage life can be recouped by turning to foods that can be eaten raw, so reducing the time spent cooking. Using fresh fish and cheap cuts of meat trimmed of fat costs less than buying made-up dishes, and you can enhance their flavour with spices and fresh herbs.

Apart from fresh meat, fish, fruit and vegetables, you can buy additive-free tinned fruits and vegetables, cereals and biscuits for the store cupboard. Rice, pulses and pasta are usually additive free, and so are many cheeses and yoghurts. There are also additive-free beefburgers, canned fish and frozen meals on sale.

The growing interest in organic foods and healthy living has made more manufacturers seek alternatives to disputed additives, so a wider range of acceptable goods is available. Retailers, especially the large supermarket chains, are also keen to provide what an increasing number of customers want and to carry lines free of particular categories of additive – sausages free of preservatives, for example.

The lists of ingredients on processed foods give you another means of avoiding additives. Note down both code numbers and names of substances you want to avoid and take your notes when you go shopping. It will take some time to work out your own list of acceptable goods. In any one visit to a supermarket or store you will probably be able to deal with only one or two types of food. If you shop mostly in one supermarket, find out the company's policy on additives and ask for any booklets they produce, some of which are very useful. But remember, the company's policy may apply only to its own brand-name products.

The mineral hydrocarbons (E905-907) are used as glazing agents to seal and give a gloss to fresh citrus fruits, dried fruits and cheese rind. They can impede vitamin A, D, E and K absorption and can also cause itchiness of the anus. Cellulose, gums and gels (E450s and 460s) are not harmful but are used to add bulk to foods and allow them to retain more air or water. In this way, they act like dietary fibre.

Antioxidants prevent oils and fats from going rancid and some fruits from going brown when air gets to them. E320 butylated hydroxyanisole (BHA) and E321 butylated hydroxytoluene (BHT) are synthetic antioxidants used in many breakfast cereals, cheese spreads, margarines, ice creams, chewing gum and soft drinks. They may trigger hyperactivity in children. To avoid them, look for products with E306 as the antioxidant. This natural extract from soya beans, maize and other grains is rich in vitamin E.

Some of the 2000 permitted colours can cause problems – for example, hyperactivity – and a host of other disorders: rashes, blurred vision, respiratory problems, asthma and the allergic reaction of people sensitive to aspirin. The azo dyes, derivatives of coal tar, are responsible for many bad reactions. Chief among the suspects is E102 tartrazine, a yellow colouring used in desserts, drinks, sauces and crumb coatings. About half the permitted colours are extracts from natural sources: chlorophyll for green, beetroot for red, and carotene, xanthophylls and turmeric for yellow.

Emulsifiers and stabilisers are added to prevent oil and water from separating. Without them, salad creams, ice creams, margarine and many made-up dishes would disintegrate into separate liquids and be quite unrecognisable. Emulsifiers and stabilisers are usually extracts from natural foods and include E322 lecithin from egg yolks or soya beans. E410 carob (or locust) bean gum is another natural extract used as an emulsifier and gelling agent. It is

Identifying the additives – a checklist of those to watch out for

Only a few people have unpleasant reactions to food additives. Most of us never suffer the slightest ill effect. But for the unfortunate few, tracking down and learning how to avoid the offending ingredients can bring welcome relief from alarming asthma attacks or the maddening itch of a skin rash. These are among the worst effects of additives. Although the people affected are few, the symptoms they suffer are numerous and the additives that might trigger them make a long list. Other ill effects include fever, blurred vision, hay fever, stomach upsets, breathlessness, nausea, dizziness, headaches and palpitations.

Those who suffer them have defects in their metabolism – the chemical and physical processes within the body, whereby food constituents are broken down to produce energy, and complex substances are built up to form tissues and organs. The defects make them allergic or intolerant to minute amounts of food additives which are no problem to the vast majority with normal metabolism.

Three main groups of people can be picked out among the additive-sensitive: asthmatics, in whom additives may trigger attacks; people sensitive to aspirin, who may develop rashes, breathing problems or other symptoms; and hyperactive children. It is far from clear as yet how much hyperactivity (uncontrollably excited, energetic and unruly behaviour) results from food additives. Some doctors believe that it is the extra care and attention given to a child during the monitoring of its diet that brings about improved behaviour, not cutting out additives.

Listed below are the additives that are suspected of causing ill effects in sensitive people, and typical foods they are used in. The ingredients labels on foods may name the additives or simply list their numbers (see p. 144).

The symbols in the table below show which groups of people may have adverse reactions to particular additives:
■ *– hyperactives*
□ *– asthmatics*
☆ *– people sensitive to aspirin*
○ *– people with other allergies or intolerances*
★ *– babies*

ADDITIVE	FUNCTION AND USES
E102 Tartrazine ■□☆	Yellow/orange colour very widely used in drinks, cakes, biscuits, puddings, meat products, smoked cod and haddock, sauces, confectionery, snacks.
E104 Quinoline yellow ■	Greenish-yellow colour used especially in smoked fish and Scotch eggs.
107 Yellow 2G ■□☆	Yellow colour used in much the same way as E102.
E110 Sunset yellow ■☆	Yellow colour used in chocolate drinks, packet soups and desserts, biscuits, breadcrumbs and preserves.
E120 Cochineal ■	Natural red colour from dried insects and egg yolk. There is a synthetic form. They are used in confectionery and cakes.
E122 Carmoisine ■□☆	Reddish-purple colour used in raspberry drinks, jam, desserts and sauces, and in brown sauces and packet soups.
E123 Amaranth ■☆	Red colour used in drinks, fruit-pie fillings, jellies, cakes, puddings, packet soups, gravy mixes and beefburgers.
E124 Poncea ■□☆	Red colour used in meat pastes, tomato soup, strawberry products such as pie fillings, jellies and puddings, and in cake mixes.
E127 Erythrosine ■	Red colour used in glacé cherries, tinned fruits, packet desserts, biscuits, ham and pork products and some potato snacks. It is also used in tablets to reveal plaque on teeth.

ADDITIVE	FUNCTION AND USES
128 Red 2G ■	Red colour used in pork pies, sausages and other meat products.
E131 Patent blue V ■□☆○	Violet-blue colour used especially in Scotch eggs.
E132 Indigo carmine ■□☆○	Blue colour used in meat products and gravy mixes.
133 Brilliant blue ■	Blue colour used in bacon-flavoured snacks and tinned peas.
E142 Green S ■	Green colour used in tinned peas, asparagus soup, mint sauce, and lime drinks and jellies.
E150 Caramel ■	Brown colour produced from sugar and used in drinks, gravy mixes, soups, sauces, breads, cakes, biscuits, vinegar, marmalade and beef products.
E151 Black PN ■	Black colour used in fruit sauces and hence in cheesecake mixes.
E153 Carbon black or vegetable carbon ■○	Black colour from burnt vegetable matter used in fruit juices, jams and jellies.
E154 Brown FK ■○	Brown colour used in kippers and other smoked fish.
155 Chocolate brown HT ■□☆○	Brown colour used in a wide range of processed foods.
E200 Sorbic acid ○	Preservative to slow the growth of moulds and yeasts. Used in yoghurts, cheese products, wrapped cakes, cake fillings and toppings, sweet sauces, soft drinks and frozen pizzas.

ADDITIVE	FUNCTION AND USES
E210 Benzoic acid ■□○	Preservative that occurs naturally in tea and raspberries but is made synthetically for use in fruit products, pickles, marinated fish, salad dressings, beer and coffee essence. Also used as an antioxidant.
E211 Sodium benzoate ■□○	Preservative used in bottled sauces, soft drinks, sweets and prawns.
E212 Potassium benzoate E213 Calcium benzoate E214-219 Hydroxy-benzoate salts ■☆○	Uses as for E210.
E222 Sodium hydrogen sulphite (or bisulphite) ■	Preservative used in wine and beer. Also used as a bleaching agent.
E223 Sodium meta-bisulphite ■	Preservative used in sausages and bottled sauces, pickled onions, packet mashed potato and orange squash.
E224 Potassium meta-bisulphite ■	Preservative used in home-bottled fruit and homemade wine, and also in brewery beer.
E226 Calcium sulphite ■	Preservative used in cider.
E227 Calcium hydrogen sulphite ■	Preservative used in beer.
E249 Potassium nitrite E250 Sodium nitrite ■○★	Preservative used in cooked and cured meats and sausages.
E251 Sodium nitrate ■○★	Used in the same way as E249 and also in some cheeses.
E252 Potassium nitrate ■○★	Used for curing and preserving meat.
E270 Lactic acid ★	Preservative used in margarines, baby milks, salad dressings, confectionery and soft drinks.
E300 L-ascorbic acid (vitamin C)	Used as an antioxidant in fruit products, soft drinks, dried potatoes and beer.
E310 Propyl gallate E311 Octyl gallate E312 Dodecyl gallate ■□☆★	Antioxidants added to fats and oils, and hence found in fried foods and snacks.
E320 Butylated hydroxyanisole (BHA) ■□○★	Antioxidant used in raisins, potato snacks, biscuits, pastry, sweets, breakfast cereals, bottled sauces, ice creams, margarines, soft drinks and prepared fried foods.
E321 Butylated hydroxytoluene (BHT) ■□☆○★	Antioxidant similar in use to E320.

ADDITIVE	FUNCTION AND USES
E406 Agar ○	Thickener and stabiliser extracted from seaweeds and used in ice creams, frozen trifles and meat glazes.
E407 Carrageenan (Irish moss) ○	Emulsifier, thickener and gelling agent extracted from seaweed and used in ice creams, jellies, frozen trifles, spray creams, cake decorations and cheeses.
E413 Tragacanth ○	Emulsifier, thickener and stabiliser extracted from the gum in the trunks of certain *Astralagus* trees. Used in processed cheeses, cake decorations, sherbet and salad dressings.
E414 Gum arabic ○	Thickener, emulsifier and stabiliser from the gum exuded by the branches of some acacia trees. Used in some packet cream cheeses and gateau mixes.
E421 Mannitol (manna sugar) ○	Texture improver and sweetener extracted from seaweed and certain ash trees. Used in sweets and ice creams.
E430 Polyoxyethylene (8) stearate E431 Polyoxyethylene stearate ○	Emulsifiers and stabilisers used in baked goods.
508 Potassium chloride ○	Salt substitute and gelling agent.
510 Ammonium chloride ○	Used for flavour in yeast goods.
514 Sodium sulphate ○★	Used to dissolve other additives.
541 Sodium aluminium phosphate ○★	Raising agent used in cake mixes.
621 Monosodium glutamate (MSG) 622 Monopotassium glutamate ■□☆○★	Usually extracted from sugar beet but also occurs in seaweed. Used as flavour enhancer in meats, soups, savoury snacks and many prepacked meals.
623 Calcium glutamate ■□☆★	Used in the same way as 621.
627 Sodium guanylate 631 Sodium inosinate 635 Sodium-5-ribonucleotide ■☆○★	Flavour enhancer used in savoury snacks, packet soups, gravy granules and precooked rice dishes.
924 Potassium bromate ○	Used to bleach flour and so found in bread, cakes and biscuits.
925 Chlorine ○	Used as a bleach in white flour and so found in bread, cakes and biscuits.
926 Chlorine dioxide ○	Used in the same way as 925 and also to purify water.

FOOD POISONING

Symptoms of food poisoning are vomiting (see NAUSEA AND VOMITING), DIARRHOEA and cramp-like abdominal pains, which are often worse just before diarrhoea (see COLIC). Victims may also be feverish and sweaty.

The usual cause is germs that inflame the lining of the stomach and intestines. Reheating or only half cooking food encourages the growth of bacteria such as *Salmonella* and *Staphylococcus*, which are among the commonest causes of food poisoning. *Lysteria*, another bacterium, can be caught from soft cheeses and paté, but has little effect on most healthy adults – though unborn children are at risk. *Campylobacter* can be caught from contaminated poultry, fish or unpasteurised milk – and may cause bloody diarrhoea.

Other causes include rotaviruses, which are spread by direct contact with either vomit

Do's and don'ts against food poisoning

Do always wash your hands carefully before handling food, before meals and after using the toilet.

Do keep kitchen work surfaces clean, cook meat thoroughly and don't eat anything which you suspect to be 'off'.

Do keep all waste materials well away from food in firmly lidded bins.

Do cover any cuts or sores on your hands with waterproof sticking plaster when working in the kitchen.

Do wash all your dishes and kitchen utensils thoroughly, being careful to rinse off any detergents.

Do make sure you defrost frozen food – especially meat and meat products – thoroughly before preparing.

Do cook food thoroughly at a high temperature if you are reheating it.

Do make sure your kitchen is well ventilated; extractor fans or carbon filter extractors take out fumes.

Don't handle cooked meat after handling raw meat unless you have washed your hands in between.

Don't keep cooked meat near raw meat – it is a frequent cause of food contamination and poisoning.

Don't leave hot, cooked food in a warm place, such as a cooling cooker – it promotes bacterial growth.

or diarrhoea – not necessarily via food. They cause outbreaks of food poisoning in families, schools and at work.

Vomit and diarrhoea contain a lot of water, so the main danger of food poisoning is fluid loss – particularly in babies and the elderly. In any case, consult a doctor if abdominal pain is severe, if the patient is not passing much urine – a sign of dehydration – or if symptoms are severe or prolonged.

What the therapists recommend

Homoeopathy If there is severe diarrhoea resulting from tainted food, particularly meat, *Arsen. alb.* is recommended when there is also vomiting, acute prostration, chilliness and ANXIETY, which is worse between midnight and 2am. If, after eating bad fish, the flatulence and bloatedness are marked, the patient feels cold and clammy, collapses or needs air, take *Carbo veg.* For upsets from too much, or unripe, fruit, when there is weakness and colic, vomiting and painless diarrhoea, use *China off. Phosphorus* is advisable when there is diarrhoea, vomiting and a craving for iced cold water, which is vomited as soon as it warms in the stomach. In each case, try one tablet of 6th or 30th potency every hour for up to 12 doses.

Herbal Medicine In mild cases, taking three or four GARLIC capsules a day may help to fight infection, while camomile tea three times a day is said to reduce inflammation. Hot spices such as cayenne may help to give protection in tropical countries.

An orthodox view

A sufferer can rest the stomach and intestines by avoiding all solid food, and replace lost fluid by drinking small amounts of water or diluted fruit juice regularly. Recovery is usually complete within a few days.

Drinks of sugar and electrolyte solution such as Dioralyte, available from chemists, help to replace chemicals lost through vomiting and diarrhoea and are particularly effective for children and the elderly or infirm. Anti-diarrhoea medicines, such as kaolin, soothe the stomach and reduce diarrhoea.

FOOT PROBLEMS

Ill-fitting shoes are the cause of the most common foot problems, such as CORNS and BUNIONS. But there are other complaints with various different causes:

Ingrowing toenails These usually affect the big toe and cut into surrounding skin,

becoming painful and sometimes infected. Apart from being caused by tight shoes, they can also occur due to cutting down the side of the nail instead of across, so that when the nail grows, skin and nail are competing for the same space.

Flat feet This is a condition that tends to occur in small children and in older people whose ligaments are generally slack. Almost anyone who can bend back their fingers more than average or who is 'double-jointed' will flatten out the arches of the feet when standing. If the feet ache, arch supports worn in shoes might help; otherwise no treatment is necessary.

Veruccas Also known as plantar warts, these are contagious and often picked up in school changing rooms, showers or swimming baths. They are painful warts that grow into the skin of the sole of the foot. They sometimes disappear within 18 months without treatment.

What the therapists recommend

Aromatherapy Try dabbing undiluted lemon essential oil on a verucca three or four times a day, avoiding the healthy skin.

Hydrotherapy Cold and swollen feet and sprained ankles may benefit from cold baths and ice packs at first, followed by hot ones. Practitioners will advise on treatment and exercises for other disorders such as weak or flat feet, or getting over a FRACTURE.

Osteopathy A useful exercise to loosen the joints and flex the big toes of bunion sufferers involves looping a large, thick rubber band across both big toes. Sitting with heels together and legs outstretched, move the feet outwards so that they form a 'V'. Gentle manipulation by a qualified practitioner may also help to relieve other painful conditions.

Massage Try these simple techniques for problems such as tired, aching feet, flat feet and poor circulation or coldness. Hold the foot firmly and with flat fingers or the palm of your hand apply firm effleurage strokes (see p. 225) along the sole of the foot from toes to heel; then use the same techniques across the instep to strengthen the arch. Next, by kneading and friction with the thumbs and fingers, massage the foot muscles with deep upwards pressure to the sole, particularly the instep and inner edge of the foot. Finish off with finger kneading and effleurage to the top of the foot, thorough kneading of the calf muscle, and stretching petrissage to the front lower leg and ankle.

An orthodox view

For ingrowing toenails practitioners suggest properly fitting shoes and advise that nails should be cut straight across only. Antibiotics would be prescribed in the case of infection and, if severe, part of the base of the nail would be removed, or chemically destroyed, so that the nail would be narrower and therefore less likely to grow into the skin.

Standard treatment is to pare the dead skin from the surface of a verruca, then destroy it either with salicylic acid in collodion, in ointment or in paint form, or by heat (cauterisation) or cold (cryotherapy).

See also ATHLETE'S FOOT and CHILBLAINS.

FORGETFULNESS

After the age of about 50, many people have difficulty in remembering dates, names, telephone numbers and so on. In some cases, sufferers are unable to recall them at all; in others their MEMORY of them returns after some thought. Forgetfulness should not be confused with AMNESIA, which has physical or emotional causes. See also GROWING OLD.

What the therapists recommend

Autogenic Training This form of therapy, it is claimed, frequently results in a spontaneous improvement in memory. There have been cases of sudden flashes of recall during a session, resulting in articles that were mislaid weeks previously being found.

Hypnotherapy Treatment consists of producing relaxation, then taking the patient back in time and getting him or her to relive the period.

FRACTURES

Cracked or broken bones are usually caused by injury, and are more likely to occur if the bones are thin or porous. For example, elderly women with OSTEOPOROSIS are particularly prone. A bone broken into several pieces is called a comminuted fracture. In a compound fracture there is an open skin wound over the broken bone through which infection may enter.

What the therapists recommend

Cymatics The practitioner holds an instrument called a sound-wave applicator over the site of the fracture. Patients may also use a warm water treatment pool through which sound waves are passed.

Herbal Medicine Comfrey, also known as Knitbone, has long been used to treat fractures. The ointment helps to heal broken bones and tissues. The roots can be pounded into a sticky paste and bound around a fracture. When dry, this paste binds the bone.

An orthodox view

First aid immobilises the broken limb to prevent further damage and relieve pain. If possible, the joints above and below the fracture are supported. The patient can support a fractured arm with the other hand, and a sling provides support for a broken collarbone. The patient should then be taken to hospital immediately. There X-rays will reveal the extent of the fracture so that appropriate treatment can be given.

Practitioners have confirmed that broken bones heal faster if sound waves are applied to the broken limb, and CYMATICS is now used in several orthopaedic units.

FRIGIDITY

Men often say of a woman who is sexually unresponsive, 'She's frigid'. It is a derogatory and hurtful term, and is used less and less as understanding of sexual difficulties and their causes increases. The problem is properly called *general sexual dysfunction*. See also SEXUAL PROBLEMS.

Like IMPOTENCE in men, frigidity in women is when sexual excitement fails to occur or does not develop into arousal and responsiveness. The woman feels unresponsive to her sexual partner.

Sexual arousal in women results in an increased blood flow around the vagina, a swelling of the tissues surrounding it, and the production of vaginal lubrication. In frigidity, this lubrication hardly appears or is absent altogether. Production of lubrication is also dependent on an adequate supply of oestrogen, the most common cause of deficiency being the MENOPAUSE.

Psychological factors may also be involved, and they are usually related to conflict or fear about intercourse, or about the particular partner. The conflict may stem from early sexual abuse, or it may be caused by an insensitive or sexually aggressive man. If a woman feels uncertain about engaging in sex, then her body sends out signals based on the conflict or fear. Even though she feels loving towards her partner, she is unable to let it be expressed in her physical reactions, and frigidity is the distressing result.

What the therapists recommend

BEHAVIOURAL THERAPY

The aim would be to produce an atmosphere in which lovemaking is relaxed and enjoyable. Sexual contact is withdrawn, then progressively reintroduced, perhaps over a couple of weeks. This may start with an embrace, then kissing, caressing, oral stimulation and, finally, intercourse. Contact may become more intimate, moving from the face to the neck, shoulders, back, thighs, breasts and finally the vagina. When each stage has been mutually enjoyed, then the partners move onto the the next one.

AROMATHERAPY

Self help Several oils have been found helpful. One of the best ways of employing them is for the partners to give each other a relaxing back massage as an introduction to lovemaking, using jasmine, ylang-ylang, and clary sage.

Another way is to sprinkle a few drops of the oils on kitchen tissue and place it in the bed, just on and below (but not under) the pillow about an hour before retiring. It is also an excellent idea to use the oils in a room burner, in both the bedroom and rooms used before retiring.

Other alternative treatments

Acupuncture The aim of treatment is to remedy any hormonal imbalance and mental and emotional conflicts. The best results occur when acupuncture is combined with dietary changes and homoeopathic or herbal remedies. MOXIBUSTION is applied to points governing the kidney, bladder, stomach and conception meridians.

Bach Remedies The following are recommended: Crab apple for feelings of disgust with the body; Impatiens for impatience with oneself; Rock water for those who have repressive Victorian attitudes to sex and find it hard to relax; Pine for feelings of guilt and shame; Mimulus for fear of being rejected because of frigidity, and fear of physicality in general; Honeysuckle for those who idealise the past and cannot appreciate the present; Star of Bethlehem for shock; Rock rose for intense fear; and Holly for anger.

An orthodox view

A doctor will investigate and treat any physical conditions that are inhibiting or are likely to inhibit sexual arousal and response, such as vaginal dryness or pain during intercourse. He may, for instance, prescribe hormone replacement therapy (HRT; see p. 238) for vaginal dryness at the menopause.

A doctor will help a woman experiencing mental conflict about intercourse or her partner to work out for herself the nature of the conflict(s), and what she is going to do about the situation.

He may also refer her to a therapist, who may give behaviourally based treatments. In non-threatening circumstances, the senses are encouraged to respond sexually, so that arousal takes place and becomes not only a pleasure, but also acts as an inhibitor of fear.

FROSTBITE

An icy wind during a winter hill walk, a morning on the ski slopes, or even a long wait for a bus in a snowstorm can all cause frostbite. Ice crystals form in the body tissues when their temperature falls to about −5°C (23°F). They damage the tissues, restrict blood circulation, and eventually cause blood clotting. Without immediate treatment the frozen tissue will die, causing gangrene, and amputation may become necessary.

Good circulation and warm clothing usually keep body temperature above such a level, but areas of bare skin are at risk, and if circulation is impeded, body temperature may fall dangerously low (see HYPOTHERMIA).

Susceptibility to frostbite can be increased by an injury with bleeding and SHOCK, over-exertion that causes fatigue or dehydration,

clogged arteries or beta-blocker drugs (see ARTERIES [HARDENING]; HEART DISORDERS). Take special care if prone to CHILBLAINS.

Fingers, toes and the face – especially the nose and ears – are most likely to be affected. Frostbitten parts first feel cold and stiff, and prickle slightly. Then the skin goes hard and white, later turning blue. Soon it becomes numb and the victim feels neither cold nor pain – a dangerous stage.

To prevent frostbite, wear several layers of light, warm, loose clothing with a waterproof and windproof layer on top. Make sure socks, boots and gloves are not tight. Protect ears with muffs, keep your head warmly covered and wear a face mask. Do not go out in unusually severe weather unless it is essential, and do not risk getting stranded.

What the therapists recommend

Traditional Medicine For the early phase of minor frostbite apply slices of peeled cucumber dipped in warm water, slices of raw onion, or cold salted mashed potato.

Naturopathy Therapists aim to improve the circulation by regular EXERCISE, friction rubs, and making sure hands and feet are warmly wrapped in cold weather. It can help to bathe the feet in warm water for two to three minutes, then in cold water for 30 seconds, dry them thoroughly and put on warm, dry socks. People susceptible to chilblains may be prescribed vitamins E and C.

Autogenic Training Those experienced in AT can use it to protect themselves from fairly severe cold, for during the Heaviness and Warmth exercises blood flow to the skin is increased, raising surface temperature.

An orthodox view

Once frostbite has set in, swift treatment is essential. Both alternative and conventional first aid aims to restore circulation quickly but gently with indirect warmth. When this is achieved, the frostbitten area often blisters. Reddish blisters reaching to the tip of the area are a good sign of returning circulation – but the area may be left scarred and numb because of damaged nerves.

FROZEN SHOULDER

Reaching up to brush your hair, fastening a zip at the back of a skirt, or taking a wallet from a hip pocket can be agony – even impossible – if you have a frozen shoulder. The condition usually starts with inflammation of the tendons that move the

shoulder joint, or inflammation of the fibrous capsule of the joint, or swelling of the soft sac that cushions the joint (see BURSITIS).

The shoulder joint has an unusually wide range of movements because of its complicated mesh of muscles and bone. This and its almost constant use make the shoulder vulnerable to damage and slow to mend.

If you avoid using the shoulder because of discomfort, it may become stiff and even more painful to use. If it is not treated, the pain and stiffness may spread to the neck and upper arm, making lying down so uncomfortable that sleepless nights result. The pain will begin to ease after some months, but by then scarring of the joint capsule and prolonged immobility may mean that the full range of shoulder movements never returns.

What the therapists recommend

ACUPRESSURE

Self help The shoulder must be treated before stiffness develops. Apply pressure as in the illustrations. It may be uncomfortable at first but it should soon induce numbness.

In addition, press downwards midway down the front of the fibula (outer bone of the lower leg), then downwards midway down the back of the tibia (shinbone). Use a fingernail or a matchstick to stimulate the outer rim of the ear just above the point where the rim rises out of the lobe.

If you find the treatment difficult or the shoulder does not improve, see an expert.

Other alternative treatments

Chiropractic Treatment is given after an examination and probably an X-ray. In the acute, very painful stage, gentle manipulation will be applied. In many cases, there is a spinal neck lesion contributing to the problem and treatment of this may help considerably. In the later stages, when stiffness and restricted movement are the main symptoms, chiropractic manipulation may shorten recovery time significantly.

Herbal Medicine Gently exercise the joint to stimulate the circulation. Avoid possible build-up of deposits in the joint by cutting out acid fruits, white sugar, alcohol, tea and coffee. Eat plenty of celery.

Aromatherapy Take hot baths with ten drops of essential oil of rosemary or pine added, or rub the shoulder gently with warmed oil of thyme or rosemary.

Homoeopathy Try *Rhus tox.* if the pain lessens with continued movement of the shoulder, and *Bryonia* if it increases.

An orthodox view

Keeping the joint moving is the main aim in conventional medicine, so physiotherapy will be recommended. If the shoulder is very painful, manipulation under anaesthetic or a

---

steroid injection into the inflamed tendon or joint capsule may be preferred. Infrared heat treatment, painkillers and anti-inflammatory drugs will ease discomfort and allow more use of the shoulder. Your doctor may diagnose calcium deposits in one of the tendons and advise surgical removal.

See also HYDROTHERAPY.

FUNCTIONAL INTEGRATION

This is one of the two methods used in the FELDENKRAIS METHOD for retraining muscles to work properly. It involves gentle manipulation of muscles that are injured or do not work because of brain or spinal damage. A trained therapist uses the technique, which is aimed at introducing new brain patterns in the recipient and with them, new habits of moving his or her muscles.

Acupressure for a frozen shoulder

Allow 20 minutes daily for these treatments plus those given in the text. Use thumb or fingers to apply strong, deep pressure in the direction shown for two to three minutes at each point.

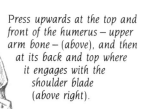

Press upwards at the top and front of the humerus – upper arm bone – (above), and then at its back and top where it engages with the shoulder blade (above right).

Press upwards at the innermost point of the elbow joint (left).

Press downwards midway between neck and shoulder, on the ridge above the collarbone.

FUNGAL INFECTIONS

The warm, moist areas of the body, such as the armpits, groin, beneath the breasts and between the toes, are ideal places for fungi to grow, and there they cause RINGWORM. If between the toes, it is called ATHLETE'S FOOT, and if in the groin, dhobie itch. Ringworm of the scalp _(Tinea capitis)_ is most common in children, and there is also a variety that affects the fingernails and toenails. THRUSH is a fungal infection of the mouth or genital area. Some diabetics are particularly prone to ringworm when there is more sugar in the system to feed the fungi.

Ringworm infections are highly contagious, and can be caught from cattle or pets. They occur as raised, inflamed patches with a definite ring around the edge – hence the name – and glow under ultraviolet light.

What the therapists recommend

Naturopathy Excluding white bread, cakes, biscuits, sweets and other refined sugars and starches, as well as alcohol, from your diet may help, since yeasts and fungi thrive on these foods. Seek qualified help to increase resistance to recurring infections.

Homoeopathy Recurrent infections are treated by boosting the IMMUNE SYSTEM. For ringworm, particularly on the scalp, _Sulphur_ may help, or _Tellurium_ if it is on the trunk only. Treat brittle, painful and inflamed nails with _Graphites_ four times a day for three weeks. If the skin at the base of the nail is red and inflamed, try _Thuja_, and if there is brittleness with horny thickening, _Antim. tart._ Try _Ranunculus scleratus_ three times a day for three weeks for athlete's foot. In all cases, 6C potency is recommended.

Herbal Medicine Thrush in the mouth may be helped by gargling several times a day with tincture of myrrh. For all fungal skin infections, try three or four GARLIC capsules a day or one clove of fresh garlic. Apply tea tree essential oil to the area several times a day. For recurring infections, seek treatment by a qualified practitioner to strengthen the immune system.

Aromatherapy For ringworm, mix 1 dessertspoon (10ml) of calendula oil in a dropper bottle with one drop of tea tree oil and two drops of marigold tagetes oil or myrrh. Apply three times a day.

An orthodox view

Fungal infections can be slow to go and may recur. Antifungal ointments usually help, and antifungal powders are of particular benefit in moist areas. Hydrocortisone creams relieve itching, but can cause the fungus to spread. All are available from chemists without prescription. Sometimes antifungal tablets such as griseofulvin are prescribed.

Do's and don'ts for fungal infections

_Do_ shower or bath at least once a day, and dry thoroughly. Wash feet twice a day, and pat dry, never rub.
_Do_ keep your towels and face cloths separate from those of the rest of the household.
_Do_ wear cotton socks and underwear, and change them frequently.
_Do_ wear leather shoes, not trainers as they encourage sweating.
Don't machine-wash linen and clothes at low temperatures; the fungus could survive and infect the whole load.

GALLSTONES

Small, hard, coloured pebbles known as gallstones form from liquid bile in the gall bladder, or in the bile ducts, which drain bile from the liver. These join the duct from the gall bladder to form the common bile duct, which carries the liquid to the small intestine, where it is essential for fat digestion.

Sometimes a stone gets stuck in a duct and causes biliary colic – severe pain in the upper abdomen which may radiate into the back. Blockage of the common bile duct causes jaundice. If the gall bladder becomes inflamed, fever with pain in the upper abdomen and tenderness under the ribs on the right side may result. Occasionally gallstones block the flow of fluids from the pancreas, again causing inflammation and pain.

Warning Gallstones are only one of many possible causes of severe abdominal pain. If such pain persists for more than four hours, see your doctor immediately. Do not follow alternative remedies without his approval.

What the therapists recommend

Acupuncture After determining the cause of the symptoms by questioning and examination, the practitioner stimulates points on the liver, stomach, bladder, gall bladder, spleen and conception meridians.

Herbal Medicine Bitter herbs are used, aimed at encouraging the flow of bile and reducing any inflammation of the gall bladder; a daily cup or two of centaury tea might be prescribed, and should also aid digestion. However, herbalists have a number of other remedies to choose from, depending on the exact nature of the problem: gentian, barberry, boldo, golden seal and dandelion are typical examples, usually taken as tinctures.

Since some liver and gall-bladder stimulants may also stimulate the muscles of the uterus, pregnant women should always seek medical advice before using any of them.

Naturopathy A very low fat diet, with no dairy products and no animal fats is advised, along with plenty of fresh vegetables and whole grains. Increased intake of polyunsaturated oils such as sunflower and safflower is also recommended, with extra vitamin C aimed at reducing cholesterol levels in the bile. Fresh lemon juice is held to be particularly beneficial, also bitter salads such as chicory, endive and globe artichoke.

An orthodox view

Small gallstones sometimes disappear without treatment; they simply enter the intestine and pass out of the body with the faeces.

Others remain in the gall bladder for years, causing neither harm nor pain.

Stones that do cause pain or inflammation are removed surgically, together with the gall bladder. Occasionally small stones – particularly those that are difficult to see on X-rays – can be dissolved by drugs. In some hospitals the stones are broken up by sound waves.

GALVANISM

In this early form of ELECTROTHERAPY, direct electric current (rather than alternating current) is passed through the body by way of electrodes attached to the skin. It was once widely used to treat SPORTS INJURIES such as sprains, strains and contusions, the aim being to improve circulation in affected parts and reduce inflammation. It was named after the 18th-century Italian anatomist, Luigi Galvani, who discovered that a severed frog's leg twitches when an electric current is passed through it.

GARLIC
The oldest herbal cure-all?

Without doubt, garlic is the herbalists' and naturopaths' favourite remedy – and has been used medically for something like 5000 years. It is regarded – with some scientific and medical approval – as one of the most versatile and effective plants in the entire herbal cornucopia.

Variously known as *Allium sativum* (its botanical name), 'poor man's treacle' and – to the ancient Greeks – the 'stinking rose', garlic is a member of the same group of plants as the onion, chive and leek.

The list of ailments for which garlic has been prescribed – as an oil, in soups or inhalants, eaten raw, crushed and applied to affected parts or, more recently, taken in tablet or capsule form – is extensive. Complaints treated range from ACNE, ASTHMA and ARTHRITIS to high BLOOD PRESSURE, various BOWEL DISORDERS, BRONCHITIS, DIGESTIVE PROBLEMS, KIDNEY COMPLAINTS, RHEUMATISM, insect stings, TENSION, toothache, tuberculosis, warts (see WARTS AND WART CHARMING), WHOOPING COUGH and WORMS.

Garlic is known to contain the VITAMINS A, B1, B2 and C, along with various natural antibiotics, antiblood-clotting agents and cholesterol-controlling ingredients.

Among the many beneficial effects claimed for garlic are: its ability to destroy harmful bacteria (pathogens) in the intestines, without any effect on the natural, beneficial organisms and fungal infections which help digestion; its power to break down cholesterol, the fatty substance which causes furring of the arteries and can lead to HEART DISORDERS; its effectiveness against bacteria which may be unaffected by other antibiotics; its capability for improving resistance to viral infections; and its use as a general preventive against many illnesses, especially those that people suffer in winter, such as COLDS, chills and INFLUENZA, SINUS PROBLEMS and bronchial complaints.

Garlic also apparently has the ability to lower blood pressure. A specialist working at the University of Geneva has claimed that it causes blood vessels to widen, so reducing the pressure inside them.

Home help with garlic

Garlic can be used in numerous ways to protect against, or to treat, many ailments. Here are a few preparations you can make at home:

To ward off colds Take one garlic capsule three times a day on a regular basis to keep you generally fit and healthy.

For coughs and bronchitis An old folk remedy is to make a garlic syrup. Pour a pint (600ml) of boiling water over 2oz (60g) of finely chopped garlic. Allow to stand in a sealed container for ten hours. Then add honey until a syrupy consistency is formed. Take a teaspoonful up to three times a day.

For sickness or diarrhoea Two garlic capsules a day are recommended – especially for those going abroad – to protect against stomach upsets caused by change of diet and climate.

For a sore throat or voice loss Try eating a single clove of garlic three times a day.

To reduce blood pressure Take between one and three capsules of garlic three times a day with water. However, make sure that you also seek qualified medical treatment for the condition.

Many people are embarrassed by having the odour of garlic on their breath. Capsules, which dissolve in the stomach and intestines, are less pungent than raw garlic. Another way to reduce the aroma is to chew fresh parsley after eating garlic.

Caution: If you are already consulting a general practitioner, always seek his advice, or that of a medical herbalist, before using herbal alternatives.

A herbal of 1385 shows the cultivation of garlic, which had been used for centuries. Clay models of garlic bulbs were found in an Egyptian tomb of 3750 BC, and when their garlic ration was cut, slaves building the Great Pyramid are believed to have gone on strike in the world's first industrial dispute.

GEM ESSENCE THERAPY
Stone vibrations that care for the emotions

Emotional health and spiritual well-being are said to be helped by this therapy. Practitioners claim that vibrations from gemstones can relieve or remove mental and emotional problems – for example, emerald is said to improve MEMORY.

The 'vibrations' of more than 200 different stones are sold as bottled essences, imported from the USA. They are made by immersing the stones in pure water and leaving them in the Californian sunshine. The sun's energy is said to percolate through the stones and into the water, taking the gems' vibrations with it.

The essences are said to be most effective if taken in a calm and relaxed state at least 30 minutes before or after eating. Take some deep breaths, relax the muscles of your face, jaw and throat, and hold the bottle for several minutes. Then place four drops directly from the bottle under your tongue.

Crystal Therapy This is a similar therapy using naturally occurring crystals. Its prac-titioners think it strengthens and speeds up other treatments. The crystals – which include precious and semiprecious stones – are said to contain 'positive energy', which can be channelled through healer to sufferer.

Most healers use quartz (for physical healing), rose quartz (for emotional healing) and amethyst (for spiritual healing). The various techniques include contact healing (in which the crystals are placed on body parts in need of treatment), and pressure-point healing (in which the crystals are placed on relevant ACUPUNCTURE points).

An orthodox view

There is no scientific basis to these therapies and most doctors would regard them as beyond the fringe.

GENITAL HERPES

The virus that causes genital herpes is very closely related to the one that causes COLD SORES. Both are types of _Herpes simplex_. A different herpes virus, _Herpes zoster_, causes CHICKENPOX and SHINGLES.

It is usually _Herpes simplex_ Type II that causes genital sores. The virus is caught only by direct contact with active sores. These may be visible on the genital area or buttocks but may be hidden in the vagina or anus. The virus can also be passed from around the mouth to the genital area and vice versa.

After an incubation period of 2-12 days, the infected area feels itchy and prickles. Painful blisters develop which burst and leave ulcers. These usually heal within three weeks, but sufferers may feel feverish or generally unwell during the attack.

After the first ('primary') infection, the virus lies dormant in a nerve root. At times of stress or other illness it may become active again and produce new crops of painful blisters at the original site of infection.

In rare cases, _Herpes simplex_ can cause inflammation of the brain. The patient develops severe headaches and confusion and may be very ill.

Self help To avoid infection, do not have sexual intercourse with a partner who has active sores. Use condoms if in any doubt.

If you develop sores, ease the discomfort by sitting in a shallow bath of gently warm water with half a cup of salt added. Try dabbing on witch hazel to dry up the sores – but only if it does not sting too much. Wear loose cotton pants instead of synthetic ones. Do not wear wool against your skin.

To help avoid a flare-up of a dormant virus, ensure that your diet is adequate in VITAMINS A, B and C. Get enough rest, and start YOGA or RELAXATION AND BREATHING exercises to reduce stress.

What the therapists recommend

Naturopathy Naturopaths consider that outbreaks of dormant genital herpes are triggered by a lowering of vitality. Naturo-pathic advice is aimed at correcting this imbalance. The amino acid L-lysine seems to help reduce an attack, and may be supplemented with vitamin B to support the IMMUNE SYSTEM. Lysine is found in lamb, chicken, fish, cheese, milk, brewer's yeast, beans and beansprouts, as well as in most fruits and vegetables. Salt washes or baths can reduce the irritation.

Aromatherapy Try a mixture of eucalyptus, thyme and geranium in the bath, and apply a lotion made from three drops of each of these oils in a tablespoon of carrier lotion.

An orthodox view

Doctors endorse the self-help preventive measures outlined above. They may pres-cribe anti-viral drugs such as acyclovir to clear up an attack. While these drugs can be effective during the primary infection, they are not able to prevent further attacks and are less effective during them.

GEOPATHIC STRESS
How the earth's energy may affect your health

Electromagnetic fields and other forms of radiation from the earth are believed by some practitioners – both orthodox and alternative – to have potentially stressful and unhealthy effects on people. This is called 'geopathic stress' and may contribute to illnesses ranging from INSOMNIA and MIGRAINE to RHEUMATISM and CANCER.

The idea that physical and geological features can affect people's health and well-being is not new. The Chinese have long practised _Feng-Shui_ – a way of positioning objects and structures such as houses, fur-nishings, roads and wells so that they are in harmony with what is seen as the natural flow of energy in the earth. Some people in the West believe that prehistoric standing stones such as those at Stonehenge and elsewhere in Britain were placed to protect dwellings from lines of geopathic stress.

Many different factors are thought to cause geopathic stress. Among those considered important are so-called 'ley lines' – lines of energy that are said to correspond to underground streams of water or small electrical currents produced by pressure on quartz crystals in the ground. Man-made structures such as railways, overhead power cables, large buildings and quarries may all interrupt the natural pattern of ley lines and cause further geopathic stress.

Another factor is the effect of magnetic storms on the surface of the sun – 'sunspots'. When sunspots are particularly active, they disturb the earth's magnetic field and these periods also appear to coincide with human disasters such as wars and famines. Heart attacks, too, are said to become more common during sunspot activity.

Certain minerals and rocks such as granite contain radioactive substances or release radioactive radon gas which can cause illnesses such as lung cancer. In Britain, the areas most affected are parts of Cornwall, Devon, Somerset, Grampian, Derbyshire and Northamptonshire, where special methods are sometimes used to make houses safer. See HEALTH HAZARDS.

Generally, geopathic stress is thought to affect city dwellers less than people in country areas, where there are fewer people to 'soak up' earth radiation. It is also said to be stronger inside buildings than outside, since electrical wiring systems can enhance the effect of other electromagnetic fields. This may be the reason why people sometimes feel better outside their homes than inside.

The most serious danger of geopathic stress is believed to be its weakening effect on the IMMUNE SYSTEM, which increases vulnerability to disorders such as cancer, MYALGIC ENCEPHALOMYELITIS (ME), ARTHRITIS, insomnia, migraine, MULTIPLE SCLEROSIS, LEUKAEMIA and AIDS. Many alternative practitioners also believe that geopathic stress can contribute to problems such as DEPRESSION, high BLOOD PRESSURE and ALCOHOLISM. In addition, certain types of geopathic stress have been associated with particular effects: underground water may disturb sleep, while strong electromagnetic fields have been related to higher rates of suicide and leukaemia. Sharply increasing or decreasing fields – such as are found close to overhead power lines – have been associated with migraine and depression.

What the therapists recommend

If a practitioner – of any sort – suspects that a patient's problems are caused by geopathic stress, he will probably call in a trained dowser (see DOWSING). Alternatively, the practitioner may use electronic equipment to examine the sick person's home.

Dowsers are thought to be particularly sensitive people who can detect small changes in the earth's magnetic field – whether caused by ley lines, underground water, sunspots or other factors – by holding a willow or hazel twig, dowser's rod or a pendulum over a suspected stress zone. Depending on how the instrument responds, the dowser is able to say where the energy lines are strongest.

This is thought to work because the twig, rod or pendulum exaggerates small muscle reactions caused by the field in the dowser's body, and makes them observable. Dowsers say that they can tell the difference between healthy and harmful energy lines, and some even claim to alter them by using objects such as crystals and electrical coils.

The first spot that is checked for geopathic stress is over a patient's bed, since vulnerability is thought to be greatest during sleep. A picture is drawn up of the field around the bed and, if necessary, the patient is advised to change its position or even move to another bedroom.

Sometimes simply switching to a foam rubber mattress or one without metal springs is enough – mattress springs are thought to reinforce the strength of electromagnetic fields in the bed.

Other parts of the house are also checked if necessary, and dowsers will offer advice on how to reduce geopathic stress in areas where electromagnetic fields are found to be strong. An IONISATION machine in the room is also believed to help.

An orthodox view

Although most conventional doctors still reject the idea that geopathic stress can cause illness, it has gained support in Germany, where research is being done into its connection with cancer and accident 'black spots'. Cancer specialists have known for years of certain 'cancer houses' where the disease occurs much more frequently than usual, and some think that geopathic stress may offer an explanation.

GESTALT THERAPY
Doing your own thing

A way of promoting personal growth through self-awareness, similar to but gentler than ENCOUNTER GROUPS, was developed by Friedrich (Fritz) Perls (1893-1970). The former Berlin psychoanalyst was practising in America after the Second World War when

he worked out his Gestalt therapy. It is based on the view that a person's ideas, feelings and actions are related aspects of his whole personality. (Gestalt comes from a German word meaning an organised whole.) Gestalt therapists argue that if someone's response to any event is not experienced by all aspects of their personality, that experience is incomplete and inner conflict results, which in turn causes distorted behaviour patterns.

Blocking out one aspect of your responses may have been learned in childhood – perhaps to please an adult – but may eventually leave your inner needs unsatisfied.

Gestalt therapy tries to remedy a distorted way of responding by teaching you not to analyse your past, as other psychotherapies may do, but to be aware immediately of thoughts, feelings, actions and gestures aroused by what is happening around you. The aim is to become fully aware of yourself, so that you see your life clearly, realise what you want from it, appreciate your own worth and feel free to be yourself.

Perls summed up his theory as: 'I do my thing, and you do your thing. I am not in this world to live up to your expectations and you are not in this world to live up to mine. You are you and I am I.'

Who it can help People who suffer from ANXIETY and TENSION, or who spend too much time explaining and judging what they have done, can benefit. Gestalt can also help those who repeatedly have difficulties in getting on with other people or in forming close relationships.

Finding a therapist For a list of therapists, contact the Gestalt Centre London, c/o 64 Warwick Road, St Albans, Herts AL1 4DL. This is one of the places where therapists can train, a process that involves a four-year part-time course. Qualifications are not hard and fast, but some formal training in psychology, COUNSELLING, social work or other related discipline is usually desired. Make sure that any therapist you consult has had similar training, which is approved by the UK Standing Conference on Psychotherapy.

The period of therapy is discussed before weekly sessions start. It is usually a few months, but some people choose to continue for longer periods. Treatment varies in price: £10-£25 or more a session may be charged.

Consulting a therapist Therapists use whatever means they think best for helping people to self-knowledge. Movement, ART THERAPY and BIOENERGETICS may play a part. Sessions may be on a one-to-one basis with the therapist in private; in a group using special self-awareness exercises; or in groups working in pairs. Early exercises may include focusing on your opposite number's hands and feet and then describing exactly what you notice.

One of Perls' techniques was to have one person facing an empty seat, supposedly occupied by someone close to him, and carrying on a discussion with that person, acting out both roles and moving from one seat to the other to do so.

Perls pointed out how not only what was said, but also vocal expression and body language, signified patterns of behaviour and facets of personality. The aim of all the methods of therapy is to work from what you do and say to a realisation of why you do it and what your real self is.

An orthodox view

With a skilled therapist, individuals who seek personal growth will come to no harm. However, relationships with others do not invariably improve since the emphasis is on being more aware and demanding of life – and this may work against forming safe and stable relationships.

See also HUMANISTIC PSYCHOLOGY.

GINGIVITIS

The gums are medically known as the _gingivae_, and gingivitis is inflammation of the gums caused by dental plaque – a layer of bacteria and other organic matter that forms on a tooth, usually at the neck, where it narrows into the root. Regular brushing – particularly after meals – and use of dental floss help to prevent plaque. But if untreated, it leads to dental caries (decay) and periodontitis, which loosens the teeth, and is probably a greater cause of tooth loss than decay itself. See TOOTH AND GUM DISORDERS.

GINSENG

For some 5000 years, the Chinese and Koreans have used the root of the ginseng plant – and credited it with many beneficial effects. The botanical name of this Asian variety – _Panax ginseng_ – derives from the Greek word _panacea_, meaning 'all-healing', but it is largely regarded as a supplement and all-round tonic as well as a curative.

The plant belongs to the Araliaceae family, which includes ivy and American spikenard. It is cultivated in China, Korea and the eastern USSR in damp, cool, wooded soil, rich in humus. Once the root has been carefully dug up, its outer tendrils are removed and it is washed. Some specimens are steam cured in a secret way, which

makes them turn red and almost translucent. The non-steamed variety ('white ginseng') remains a yellowish colour and opaque. It is dried slowly over a period of months in rooms of different temperatures, which preserves and hardens it.

Ginseng is claimed to relieve HEADACHES, TIREDNESS, EXHAUSTION and AMNESIA, to slow down the ageing process (see GROWING OLD), and to be a complementary aid in the treatment of HEART DISORDERS, DIABETES, tuberculosis, KIDNEY COMPLAINTS, NERVOUS DISORDERS and CIRCULATION PROBLEMS.

The root has also been held to have aphrodisiac properties (see APHRODISIACS), but most practitioners now feel that any such effects are a natural result of its tonic value. In any case it is relatively harmless, but is believed to help the body regain normality if stress or damage strike.

Active constituents Ginseng contains so many different ingredients that researchers have found difficulty in determining which ones, or what combinations of them, are responsible for the effects attributed to it.

Some of the main constituents and what they are thought to do include: various oils, such as sapogenin and panacen, that are believed to stimulate the central nervous system; a group called the saponin glycosides – plant substances that break down to produce sugars, and known as ginsenosides

to the Japanese and panaxosides to the Russians – that are believed to influence the IMMUNE SYSTEM, increasing resistance to infection, to reduce blood clotting, and help to balance the body's internal systems; panaxans – chemically called steroidal glucosides – that reduce blood sugar levels; and various plant phenols, in particular maltol, believed to help to protect the tissues, possibly reducing damage caused by ageing.

In addition, ginseng contains a range of hormones, VITAMINS (B1, B2 and D) and other substances, all of which are believed to combine with the above ingredients to result in the complicated overall effect.

Using ginseng Opinions vary among herbalists and those who take ginseng as to which type is most beneficial. Apart from the Asian variety, there is also an American type (_Panax quinquefolium_), and a root called pfaffia, which is known as Brazilian ginseng.

In addition, a root called _Eleutherococcus senticosus_ or _Eleuthero_, a Russian relative of the ginseng plant, is known as Siberian ginseng. Its saponins are slightly different, and make it a vasodilator – a substance that

Ginseng is usually available in Western health food shops and in some chemists in various forms: as a root to be chewed, in powdered form in tablets or capsules, or as loose powder or extracts to be made into decoctions or herbal teas.

Ginseng tablets

Ginseng tea

Ginseng extract

Ginseng tea powder

Ginseng powder

Dried ginseng root

Ginseng extract powder

Ginseng capsules

Sliced ginseng

causes widening of the blood vessels and increased circulation. Advocates make the same claims for its tonic, restorative and rejuvenating qualities as those made for Asian and American ginseng.

Herbalists suggest different doses, depending on the patient's general condition. However, the usual recommendation for those taking a month's course, simply as a tonic to improve their general well-being, is 60mg of the powdered root each day, taken as tablets, capsules or decoctions.

Although quite safe, ginseng may have side effects. These include headache, irritability and related symptoms.

An orthodox view

Many conventional doctors now accept some of the claims made for ginseng both as an overall tonic and a stimulant.

GLANDULAR FEVER

Children and young adults are most prone to glandular fever, which is caused by a virus infection and is passed on by close contact, such as kissing.

After an incubation period of up to seven weeks, the patient develops a sore throat with white seepage on the tonsils, FEVER and swollen lymph glands in the neck, armpits and groin (see IMMUNE SYSTEM). Sometimes the spleen is enlarged so that a doctor can feel it in the upper left abdomen when the patient takes a deep breath. There may also be a rash similar to that in German measles, and sometimes the liver is affected and the patient develops JAUNDICE. Diagnosis can be confirmed by a blood test.

Once the disease has manifested itself, the patient may be unwell for two to eight weeks or even more.

What the therapists recommend

Naturopathy During the feverish state, herbal infusions of yarrow and elderflower are aimed at inducing sweating and regulating temperature. A light but nourishing diet is prescribed – home-made soups, for example – until appetite and strength begin to return. High levels of vitamins B and C may also be given, aimed at boosting the immune system and maintaining a healthy nervous system. A long-term plan for greater health will be worked out according to individual needs.
Herbal Medicine Infusions of yarrow and elderflower taken three or four times daily are aimed at controlling the fever, inducing

sweating and maintaining an even temperature. Afterwards, the common problem of tiredness is tackled with tonics – two or three cups daily of yarrow or rosemary tea are recommended; also plenty of porridge.
Homoeopathy For a high fever with painful glands, *Belladonna* is prescribed; for a late-developer child with very swollen glands, *Baryta carb.*; and for dark red tonsils, with pain extending to the ears, *Phytolacca*.

Constitutional treatment is advised if the condition drags on. Other members of the family are said to be protected by taking Glandular Fever Nosode (available from homoeopathic pharmacies) daily for a week to ten days.
Biochemic Tissue Salts Practitioners prescribe *Ferr. phos.* hourly in the early stages of fever. If glands are affected, *Kali mur.* is advised – again hourly. If at a low ebb after infection, try *Calc. phos.* three times daily.

An orthodox view

As with most infectious diseases, doctors advise rest, plenty of liquids and a painkiller such as aspirin to relieve discomfort and reduce fever. The liver may be inflamed, so avoid alcohol. Children under 12 should not be given aspirin without advice, as it may affect the lining of the stomach, causing nausea, sickness and pain.

GLUTEN INTOLERANCE

For most people, gluten – a protein found in grains such as wheat, barley and rye – is a nourishing food. But people with a digestive disorder called gluten intolerance cannot absorb such food. See COELIAC DISEASE.

GOITRE

Swelling of the thyroid gland in the front of the neck is known as goitre It may be caused by insufficient iodine, which the gland needs for the production of hormones. If there is insufficient iodine, less hormones are produced, and the gland swells in an effort to produce more (see THYROID DISORDERS).

This form of goitre (endemic goitre) is rare now that iodised table salt (with added iodine) is widely available. In most parts of the world, iodine is also provided in vegetables, drinking water and seafood. However, in some areas, the soil and rocks lack iodine and goitre was common – in England, a 'goitre belt' ran through Derbyshire and the disease was known as 'Derbyshire neck'.

GOUT

Contrary to popular belief, gout is not usually caused by overindulgence, although excess alcohol and some medicines, such as diuretics (which encourage urine excretion), increase the risk. It is a disorder of the body chemistry in which too much uric acid and its compounds (urates) accumulate in the blood.

Acid and urate crystals collect in one or more joints, causing attacks of severe PAIN, swelling and redness (see ARTHRITIS). The joint at the base of the big toe is often affected. Repeated attacks can damage the bones of the joints. The crystals can also collect in the kidneys, causing kidney stones, kidney failure and high BLOOD PRESSURE, and in the skin where they form hard lumps, most commonly on the ears, fingers and toes. Diagnosis of gout is made by a blood test.

What the therapists recommend

Naturopathy A largely vegetarian diet with plenty of salads is advised to counter excess uric acid production. Red meat, coffee, alcohol and refined carbohydrates such as sugar are particularly to be avoided. During a severe attack cold compresses may help.
Homoeopathy When the pain feels like a bad bruise and the patient is frightened of the affected area being touched, *Arnica* is prescribed; and *Belladonna* when the joint is hot, red, swollen and unbearably tender. *Colchicum* is recommended when pain shifts from joint to joint and the patient is angry and irritable. *Urtica urens* is for intense itching, burning and swelling during a severe attack.
Acupuncture Points on the liver and spleen/pancreas meridians are stimulated.
Biochemic Tissue Salts The usual remedy prescribed is *Nat. phos.* taken four times

Traditionally, as this 19th-century illustration shows, a gout sufferer was seen as a rather ridiculous, pathetic, overindulgent person. The view was entirely unfounded, for overindulgence is rarely a cause of the condition.

daily, aimed at neutralising acid present. It can be alternated with *Nat. sulph.*, which is believed to help eliminate toxins.

An orthodox view

The usual treatment of gout is to relieve pain and inflammation by prescribing anti-inflammatory drugs. Further attacks can be prevented by avoiding excess alcohol and medicines that raise the blood urate level. Drugs that increase urate excretion may be prescribed. Allopurinol, also available only on prescription, reduces urate production and the risk of further attacks. It normally has to be taken daily over a period of years.

GRIEF
Coping with the shock of losing loved ones

Our greatest suffering frequently comes with the death of people we love – an experience for which modern society gives us little training. Death is not talked about and is rarely witnessed, as the severely ill and the elderly are taken into professional care. Only a minority die in their own homes. Advances in medicine and technology have made hospital wards the focal point of treatment with drugs, drips, monitor screens and nurses staving off the end as long as possible.

Previous generations saw more of death. Children and adults gathered in the family home at the bedside of aged grandparents, fevered infants, tubercular adolescents and others, as they neared death. The dead person lay at home until the funeral. Rituals of mourning were observed, with the bereaved wearing black and avoiding company. Some fear and hypocrisy doubtless hid beneath the outward show, but at least death had to be thought about and confronted.

Now our first sight of death may be when someone very close dies in a laboratory-like ward. Within days, the normal routines of life are apparently restored, with acquaintances shunning mention of the person who has died and the bereaved often forced to carry on almost as if nothing has happened. Even so, the emotional progress of those who are bereaved follows a general pattern which they have to work through before they can face the future. Obstructing this emotional progress leads to psychological and physical problems. Without a sufficient period of grieving, the survivor of a close partnership can become ill: widows seem to show an increased tendency to develop breast cancer and widowers to have heart attacks.

Those who grieve should be helped, comforted and supported by relatives and friends around them: even if someone very elderly – say, a person of 95 years or older – dies and it was more or less expected, their 75-year-old son or daughter might still find it difficult to accept the loss.

Self help Do not try to numb yourself to the pain of bereavement by blotting it out with tranquillisers or sleeping pills. Let the process of grieving follow its course, remembering that it may take many months.

Do not be afraid to talk to family and friends about your feelings. Often they avoid mentioning the dead person for fear of upsetting you, but will gladly listen and reminisce when they know this is what you want. You may feel a need to talk again and again about what has happened; perhaps feel guilt for what you did or did not do, and anger at your loss.

Do not let everything from your relationship with the dead person be lost. Remember happy times and shared achievements. Look at photographs and other mementos that remind you of the value of the life that has ended.

Mourning other losses Death is not the only loss that we need to mourn, although it is likely to be the greatest. Women who have had a miscarriage, stillbirth, hysterectomy or mastectomy suffer a deep feeling of loss. Equally a person who loses a limb may be stricken by the loss. Being made redundant or uprooted – even evicted – from one's home can cause similar feelings.

Getting help Coming to terms with the permanence of loss is at the heart of grieving. COUNSELLING can play a significant role here, offering a sympathetic ear and time to listen. You have an opportunity to recount what has happened and how you feel, over and over if necessary, without worrying whether you are imposing on a friend, and without the counsellor showing impatience or losing interest.

Gentle questioning may lead you to explore feelings you find hard to acknowledge. The general pattern of emotions that develops when people are grieving is familiar to counsellors. Denial of the death is a typical first reaction – 'I can't believe it; it's not true!' Usually this stage passes quickly, but sometimes it is prolonged and becomes an obsession – for example, the dead one's clothes are kept or their room is left undisturbed for year after year.

Often the next stage is anger – perhaps directed against a doctor for not working miracles, against relatives for still being alive, or against the dead person for taking risks or deserting you. Bereaved people can also feel guilty about *being* angry, and about their own real or imagined failures to care

properly for the dead one. A few can become trapped in the anger and bear a bitter grudge for the rest of their lives.

Some people are spurred to raise funds or agitate for laws or safety devices that would prevent similar deaths. Such hectic activity helps to pass the time but also staves off the essential painful stage of sadness and depression, where the extent of loss is acknowledged and accepted. This stage has to be worked through before normal zest for life begins to return.

The many organisations that can help you to find a bereavement counsellor include: Cruse – Bereavement Care, Cruse House, 126 Sheen Road, Richmond, Surrey TW9 1UR; National Association of Widows, 54-57 Allison Street, Digbeth, Birmingham B5 5TH; Stillbirth and Neonatal Death Society, 28 Portland Place, London W1N 4DE; and Age Concern, Bernard Sunley House, 60 Pitcairn Road, Mitcham, Surrey CR4 3LL, and 54A Fountain Bridge, Edinburgh EH3 9PT.

What the therapists recommend

Homoeopathy Practitioners believe homoeopathic remedies to be especially useful for the immediate effects of grief, as well as long-term problems arising. *Arnica 30* is prescribed for sudden shock when the person insists that he is all right, and wants to be left alone and not touched; *Ignatia 30* for someone who is hysterical with grief.

When the person is cold, shaky and frightened, try *Aconite 30*; and a few doses of *Pulsatilla* if weepy and emotional. For shock, the medicines can be taken hourly for up to 12 doses, then morning and night for two to three days if necessary.

A homoeopathic doctor should be consulted for problems in the later stages of grief, but three self-help remedies are offered: *Natrum mur. 6* when tears result if sympathy is offered, or the sufferer prefers to hide his feelings; *Ac. phos. 6* for depression and apathy; *Nux vomica* for those who become angry and critical. Take three times daily for up to three weeks.

Massage Applied in a comforting, caressing way, rather than 'mechanically', massage can help in cases where a need for physical contact and companionship is felt. Light stroking of an arm, the shoulders or back of the neck can be tried, avoiding any friction or drumming movements.

An orthodox view

It must never be forgotten that grief is normal after the loss of someone we love, so it is important to accept the painful symptoms. Any therapy which attempts to deny or avoid the process of mourning is likely to result in long-term, health-threatening problems for the bereaved.

Making the most of our autumn years

Scientists now believe the potential human lifespan to be between 110 and 120 years – yet very few people live to this age. True, the proportion of elderly people in the developed world is at a record high, but this is mainly due to low birth rates and improved medicine and living conditions.

While people in their forties no longer consider themselves 'middle aged', and expect to still look and feel good in their fifties and early sixties, the current retirement age in Britain of 60 for women and 65 for men is still associated with the spectre of boredom and inactivity, loss of independence, and loneliness through bereavement. But are these really inevitable? Our way of life and circumstances clearly affect how quickly we age, but many psychologists maintain that state of mind plays a significant role – that if we expect to go into a decline in our seventies, it is likely to happen.

Gerontologists (experts in ageing) have found that the process is a combination of many changes – for example, internal 'body clocks' switch off functions, slowing the production of a number of important hormones; and the IMMUNE SYSTEM weakens and we become less resistant to illness. There is also general wear and tear on the body from the sun's ultraviolet light, pollution, drugs, pesticides – and the physical exertions of a lifetime. All these factors cause the formation of highly active atoms or atom groups which react with others to damage body cells and collagen (protein fibre). This in turn leads to 'cross-linking', which causes the protein fibres to become tangled and the skin to lose its suppleness. Wrinkles develop, veins and arteries harden, muscles soften and limbs stiffen.

However, research has shown that some primitive peoples living on sparse diets of natural foods such as fish and grain live to advanced ages and feel healthy and energetic, little troubled by the Western diseases of degeneration such as ARTHRITIS and HEART DISORDERS. Nutrition may therefore play an important role in longevity. Several alternative therapies are particularly concerned with countering the ageing process.

What the therapists recommend

HERBAL MEDICINE
Russian scientists believe that GINSENG strengthens the body's resistance to illness, TIREDNESS, STRESS and ageing. Siberian ginseng roots are a mild stimulant and are believed to improve memory and protect against cell and collagen damage and cross-linking. Korean ginseng is thought to help rid the body of poisons, and to ease tiredness and DEPRESSION. (However, some Western doctors feel that people with high BLOOD PRESSURE should not take ginseng.)

Mexican herbalists claim that sarsaparilla and damiana (available from specialist herb shops) have the same restorative effect as conventional hormone replacement therapy (HRT; see MENOPAUSE), but with none of the potential side effects. These herbs also help to restore the function of the reproductive system, especially in men. They are less potent than pure hormone treatment and therefore less disturbing to the system.

A tea can be made by soaking a teaspoon of dried damiana leaves in a cup of boiling water for five minutes. Strain before drinking. Make a sarsaparilla infusion by putting 1oz (25g) of sarsaparilla root in a pint (600ml) of water and boiling for 25 minutes. Then strain and drink. Herbalists believe that these two herbs are best taken by 40 to 50-year-olds for a period of two to six weeks: two tablespoons (40ml) twice a day. But it is advisable to consult a herbal practitioner, since dosage depends on the individual.

NATUROPATHY
Too much protein, lack of exercise and being overweight are all thought to speed up the ageing process. People in the West eat an average of about 3500 calories a day. Naturopaths believe that about 1800 calories is sufficient, with little salt, fat or refined sugar and mainly consisting of raw food, with wholegrain cereals and bread, pulses and seeds, and moderate amounts of protein (see EATING FOR HEALTH). This type of diet is believed to strengthen the immune system, slow the ageing process and keep you mentally alert. Avoiding highly processed foods, FASTING for a maximum of 24 hours about once every three months, and taking EXERCISE are also advised.

Various special vitamin and mineral-rich foods that are recommended include liver, egg yolks, sunflower seeds, blackstrap molasses, seaweed (available as kelp tablets from health stores), GARLIC, cabbage, raw green vegetables and wheatgerm (sprinkled on salads and wholegrain cereals). It is important to eat a variety of the foods. Unless there is gastric irritation, garlic can be eaten quite freely, and unless otherwise prescribed one kelp tablet should be taken each day. Fresh pineapple and pawpaw fruits eaten raw once a week, on an empty stomach, are said to improve the skin and promote fresh skin protein fibre.

A naturopath may also advise you to take nutrients known as 'antioxidants', which are said to prevent, among other things, the destruction of vitamin C and to slow down the destruction of body cells. Antioxidants are also said to strengthen the immune system. The naturopath will advise you on personal daily dosages, or you can buy combination formulas as tablets from health stores.

The following nutrients are said to complement each other and can be taken in a good quality multivitamin and mineral tablet with breakfast each day: vitamin A, aimed at stimulating the immune system; vitamin C, said to boost the immune system and stimulate production of interferon (a natural antivirus chemical); zinc, believed to rebuild skin proteins; bioflavinoids, said to promote strong, smooth, unlined skin; vitamin E, aimed at slowing the ageing of body cells, and warding off infection and damage from air pollution; and a mixture of B vitamins to prevent a range of deficiencies from loss of appetite to tiredness.

Naturopaths also recommend aerobic exercise to stimulate the endocrine glands (which produce vital hormones, such as those for growth), to improve circulation, and to help prevent cross-linking, high blood pressure and depression. Or go walking, dancing or swimming for at least 30 minutes, three to five times a week.

Warning Elderly or middle-aged people should always consult a doctor before embarking on a new exercise routine, particularly if it will include strenuous activities.

VISUALISATION THERAPY
Therapists believe that the more you expect the future to hold for you, the more likely you are to resist illness and grow old gracefully. They recommend that you take ten minutes a day for regular relaxation and MEDITATION, visualising an image of yourself feeling healthy, happy, playful, active, creative and full of love and hope. You can also use COUÉISM and each day repeat to yourself positive thoughts such as: 'I am well and will continue to be so as the years pass.'

Other alternative treatments

Acupuncture Regular acupuncture sessions, four or more times a year including at the change of the seasons, are said to help keep you young. The therapist will give your entire system a tune-up, aimed at promoting health and energy. Acupuncture is also said to relieve diseases of ageing such as arthritis and RHEUMATISM.

Alexander Technique Bad posture adds years to people's appearance. This technique improves posture and is said to give agility, energy, a feeling of well-being and relief from BACK PAIN.

Aromatherapy Therapists believe that ageing involves a slowing down of the body's natural 'rhythm', and that essential oils can stimulate and restore rhythm, delay the

ageing process of the skin and help promote regeneration of cell tissues which are out of balance and cause arthritis and SINUS PROBLEMS. Certain aromas are believed to sharpen the mind, improve perception and aid MEMORY.

Biorhythms A personal biorhythm chart claims to tell the ups and downs – the good days and bad days – that you are likely to face in the near future. Older people can use it to work out which days are best for conserving energy, and which are best for activity – so preserving mind and body for a longer and more rewarding life.

T'ai-chi Ch'uan This Chinese daily meditation routine, which involves slow and continuous movements, is suitable for every age, and is said to make the elderly feel young again. It aims to promote good posture, flexibility, balance, energy and general well-being.

Yoga Yoga postures are said to relax the mind, ease TENSION and help people grow old stylishly.

An orthodox view

Scientists have been able to double the lifespan of some laboratory animals using fasting and low-calorie diets, and believe that these nutritional approaches can also rejuvenate and protect the human immune system. They believe, too, that if they could fully understand the nature of our internal 'body clocks', which begin switching off our vital functions as we grow older, it might be possible to reprogramme them in such a way as to slow down the process of ageing.

An orthodox science called psycho-neuroimmunology (PNI), which studies the connections between mind and body, has shown that your state of mind affects your immune system. The immune system of someone who constantly feels helpless and depressed does not work as well as that of a person who generally feels happy and hopeful. So it is possible that techniques such as meditation and visualisation, which can alter mental and emotional states, could be used to encourage a healthy immune system and longevity.

It has been noted also that artistically creative people tend to lead longer and healthier lives – perhaps because they remain mentally active and open-minded, and retain their curiosity and wonder about the world they live in.

More than 18 per cent of people in Britain are of pensionable age and are spending the last quarter of their lives in retirement. Increasingly, these people are in good health and enjoying the opportunity to make new friends and to take up fresh interests. Instead of being the twilight of a busy and purposeful life, retirement is a time of freedom in which there is at last the leisure to follow pursuits that earlier responsibilities ruled out.

Do's and don'ts for staying young

Do exercise for 30 minutes, three to five times a week.

Do eat a fresh, mainly raw diet with ample vegetables and wholegrain foods for vitamins and minerals.

Do go easy on alcoholic drinks.

Do practise relaxation techniques such as meditation to combat everyday stress and promote well-being.

Do take up a hobby or other interest that keeps your mind active as well as your body after retirement.

Don't overeat.

Don't smoke.

Don't take drugs unnecessarily.

Don't drink too much non-decaffeinated coffee or tea.

Don't expose yourself to the sun for too long, or use a sunbed.

HAIR CARE
Keep your head
– the healthy way

The basic character of your hair depends on four features that are due to heredity: density, texture, pattern and colour. But its condition depends largely on variable factors, including your general health, hair hygiene, care in choosing shampoos, conditioners and any other treatments, and the use of grooming equipment – combs, brushes, curling tools and so on.

Along with skin, hair is one of the fastest-developing cellular constituents of the human body. On average, hair grows about ½in (13mm) a month – more at night than in daytime, and faster in summer than winter. When healthy it should be supple, and shiny from a thin coating of sebum – a natural oily substance secreted by the scalp's sebaceous glands, near the root of each hair. Sebum keeps the outer layer of scalp supple, helps to prevent skin moisture evaporating, lubricates the hair itself and is thought to prevent harmful bacteria breeding on the scalp.

To maintain a healthy head of hair – provided there are no obvious HAIR PROBLEMS – simply keep the scalp clean by washing and adopt a balanced and adequate diet (see EATING FOR HEALTH). There are no hard-and-fast rules about washing your hair: whenever you feel it necessary – which differs from person to person – is a good general rule. Those with particularly greasy hair, because of overactive sebaceous glands, obviously need to wash the hair more often – even daily. However, people with a dry scalp may need pre-shampoo treatment with natural oils (see box).

Hair can be damaged by the wear and tear of over-grooming. If you wash your hair frequently, use a mild shampoo – preferably non-detergent – and avoid using heated, spiky rollers, plastic brushes and sharp metal combs, which can all cause damage. Do not use elastic bands to tie up your hair – they can tear it and damage the roots. Also to be avoided are electric tongs, strong sunshine and chlorinated or sea water, all of which can dry the hair and scalp.

Hair can also be damaged by dyeing, bleaching, perming and massage. Perming at home should be done strictly according to the instructions on the package. Temporary dyes and rinses are not harmful, but permanent dyes can damage the scalp and penetrate the hair shaft, creating harmful chemical compounds there. The scalp may become swollen and inflamed as a reaction.

Warning Always test a hair dye by dabbing a small amount on the scalp behind your ear. If there is any sign of inflammation within 48 hours, do not use the dye.

Repeated bleaching with hydrogen peroxide-based preparations can make the hair rough, dry and brittle, with split ends. It can also become thin or shortened. The ends split because they are short of sebum and divide into a Y-shape; and the farther the ends are from the scalp, the drier they become – although greasy hair can also split. Mid-length fractures are also common, causing the hair to break off.

To avoid split ends, snip off the ends cleanly every couple of weeks. Otherwise the split may travel back along the hair towards the scalp. Ragged ends that prove difficult to remove may be treated temporarily with conditioner applied only to the ends.

Going grey Your hair colour is determined by the ratio of two pigments in the hair – brown-black and red-yellow. As you grow older, less pigment is deposited in hair shafts as they grow, and grey hairs appear. These usually start appearing at the temples, then gradually spread over the rest of the scalp. However, the speed and extent of greying depends much upon hereditary factors.

Loss of hair Some loss of hair is quite normal; a hair drops out because a new one has grown under it. However, there are some ailments (see BALDNESS; HAIR PROBLEMS) which can cause abnormal hair loss. Women sometimes lose hair due to hormonal changes after childbirth, or after giving up using the contraceptive pill. Some drugs given to CANCER patients can also cause loss of hair. Though such cases can be distressing, gradually with time the hair tends to grow back in all of them.

Olive oil for dry hair

Put 2 tablespoons of olive oil into a cup, warm it in a pan of hot water, then massage the oil thoroughly, but gently, into the scalp, using your fingertips.

Steep a towel in hot water, wring and wrap it around the head. On cooling, immerse the towel once more in hot water and repeat the process two or three times, until the scalp is completely saturated. Finally, shampoo in the normal way.

If this does not clear up the dry condition, see your doctor for a check-up. Alternatively, see a trichologist (an expert in hair and scalp disorders). A list of such experts can be had by sending a stamped addressed envelope to the Institute of Trichologists, 228 Stockwell Road, Brixton, London sw9 9su.

Women's hair tends to thin – and remain so – during the menopause. Other causes of hair loss include tight hair styles, such as a pony tail, tight and too frequently applied hair rollers, repeated, vigorous massage and over-zealous brushing.

Never use sharp combs or brushes, which may tear the hair, do not brush or comb vigorously when the hair is wet and always towel it dry gently. Never hold a hair dryer too close to the head – at least 6in (15cm) away is best – and set the heat control on low or medium, rather than high.

As a measure against mild cases of DANDRUFF, halve a lemon and rub the two halves into the scalp. Leave for ten minutes, then wash the hair. Alternatively, carry out a similar procedure with sour milk. Try each treatment – and decide which one is most suited to you.

HAIR DIAGNOSIS

Laboratory tests on a lock of your hair – preferably taken from the nape of the neck, where hair grows quickest – are used in hair diagnosis to detect whether your body contains any harmful mineral imbalances.

Hair is made of a type of protein called keratin, which contains large amounts of sulphur. Practitioners believe that the sulphur attaches itself to minerals – both harmful and beneficial – and holds them in the hair. Poisonous minerals such as aluminium, arsenic, lead and mercury can, in excess, give rise to disturbed behaviour – such as acts of violence. In addition, mineral imbalances can cause a variety of ailments, including ALLERGY, DEPRESSION, DIGESTIVE PROBLEMS, HYPERACTIVITY and TIREDNESS.

Hair analysts say they can determine mineral deficiencies or excesses by putting hair samples in a chemical solution for 36 hours and then examining them by a sophisticated electronic procedure called atomic absorption spectroscopy. This will reveal what, if any, harmful minerals have been absorbed into the body from such things as hair dyes, perm lotions, shampoos and sprays. Air pollution – which can affect city joggers and cyclists – is another potential cause of mineral imbalance. In addition, the minerals absorbed from aluminium cooking utensils may also prove harmful.

But before any analysis is undertaken, patients must get their doctor's approval and cooperation. The results of the tests – which are printed out on charts – are interpreted by the laboratory, which also usually supplies the treatment.

An orthodox view

There is much scepticism among doctors and some trichologists (hair experts) as to the reliability of hair analysis, and many will not accept the readings as valid. However, some doctors will use the tests as a guide, and advise patients about diet, work and leisure environments, which can have a bearing on the balance of essential minerals that we need to help us to stay healthy.

HAIR PROBLEMS

Only the skin on the palms of the hands, soles of the feet, ends of the fingers and toes, umbilicus and parts of the genitals is without hair. Hair conserves heat by trapping air to form an insulating layer. It has no nerve endings, so although the skin hurts when hair is pulled, there is no pain when it is cut.

Hairs eventually fall out; eyelashes and armpit hairs have the shortest life (about four months) and scalp hairs the longest (four years). This is why there is a limit to the length hair will grow, and why dead hairs frequently appear on hairbrushes and combs. Healthy adults normally shed between 50 and 100 hairs each day. However, the number of hairs on the average head varies between 90,000 and 100,000.

The condition of the hair and scalp reflects the general well-being of the body and mind (see HAIR CARE). Almost any illness or emotional stress can cause lifeless, dull hair; ANAEMIA, lack of VITAMINS and thyroid hormone deficiency (see THYROID DISORDERS) can result in hair loss.

BALDNESS of the scalp, beginning with a receding hairline and thinning of the crown, is normal in many men, and so is thinning of the hair in older women. Most women experience a thinning of the hair two or three months after giving birth, but there is usually improvement over the following months.

Alopecia – a sudden and generally temporary, patchy loss of hair – can occur in men and women, boys and girls, sometimes at times of STRESS. The hair usually regrows, but the colour may be different. This form of alopecia may occur as a side effect of cytotoxic (anti-cancer) drugs and radiotherapy. Generalised alopecia, in which all the hair drops out and does not regrow, is rare.

DANDRUFF – scales of dead skin from the scalp – commonly occurs in teenagers and young adults. Severe cases are sometimes caused by a type of ECZEMA called seborrhoeic dermatitis.

Highly infectious lice can infest the hair, leaving nits – tiny, white eggs – stuck to individual hairs. Lice thrive in clean hair and they often spread among family members and in schools.

What the therapists recommend

NATUROPATHY
Self help Gently massaging the scalp will stimulate circulation. Try using plain YOGHURT as a conditioner, rinsing off with an infusion of rosemary, nettle or thyme to combat dandruff.

However, practitioners regard hair condition as an early warning indicator of lowered vitality and ill health, and see any disorders as signs of a possible underlying imbalance. Taking more EXERCISE and adopting a wholefood diet (see EATING FOR HEALTH) are held to be useful measures to take, but individual consultation is advised.

HERBAL MEDICINE
Self help To encourage the hair follicles and promote growth, try massaging a few drops of oil of rosemary into the scalp, then rinse; or use a strong infusion of nettles to rinse off shampoo. For an itching, flaky scalp and dandruff, try massaging it with infusions of rosemary, thyme, lavender or juniper, as cleansing and antiseptic treatments.

Herbalists regard hair and scalp problems as often reflecting inner disorder, and may prescribe camomile as a relaxant or skullcap to counter STRESS.

AROMATHERAPY
Self help For lank, lifeless hair, try regular rinsing with 1 pint (600ml) of water containing five drops each of lemon, rosemary and lavender oils. Therapists warn, however, that poor health may be the underlying cause and that this, too, should be treated.

For thinning hair, the prescription is three drops each of rosemary and ylang-ylang oils in a teaspoon of vodka or other strong alcohol, made up to a tablespoonful with orange-flower water. Apply a few drops to the scalp daily and massage firmly for two to three minutes.

Dandruff may be treated with a mixture of three drops of cedarwood and two drops each of rosemary and lemon oils in a tablespoon of carrier oil or lotion. Apply sparingly to the scalp and leave for two hours or overnight before shampooing and rinsing.

TRADITIONAL MEDICINE
Self help For hair loss, use a bay rum and jaborandi lotion, following the manufacturer's instructions. Alternatively, massage the scalp with castor oil at night, shampoo in the morning, and repeat the process once or twice a week. Safflower oil or wheat-germ oil may be used in the same way.

To reduce dandruff, cut a lemon in half and rub the juicy sides liberally over the scalp. Leave for ten minutes, then rinse off with plenty of cold water. Repeat weekly.

An orthodox view

Doctors sometimes prescribe minoxidil solution, which when rubbed into the scalp daily for at least four months produces a temporary improvement in male baldness. The baldness returns when the treatment is stopped, and minoxidil is not suitable for treatment of hair loss in women.

Small areas of alopecia sometimes respond to steroid injections or creams. A steroid scalp lotion often benefits sufferers from seborrhoeic dermatitis.

Hair lice can be killed by rubbing in malathion or carbaryl lotion – but *not* garden insecticides containing these – and leaving it for 12 hours before washing it out. The whole family and, ideally, school classmates should be treated at the same time.

HAKIMS

This is the name given to Indian and Muslim herbal therapists, who in Britain generally work only in their own communities. The word comes from the Arabic for 'learned' or 'wise'. Treatment is similar to that used in AYURVEDIC MEDICINE. However, instead of preparing herbal mixtures for each patient's needs, Hakims use ready-prepared patent mixtures. See also HERBAL MEDICINE.

HAND CARE
Simple measures to keep hands in trim

For housewives and manual workers especially, the hands are the most overworked part of the body, and yet they are often the least cared for. The back is covered with soft skin, with fine hairs and sebaceous (oil) and sweat gland openings. The palm has tougher skin, no hairs or sebaceous glands, but plenty of sweat glands, which are often set into action by heat or stress to produce sweaty palms.

The exposed parts of the fingernails – the nail plates – are made of inert keratin. They grow throughout life, not always at the same rate, the average time for a nail to grow from quick (base) to tip being 16–20 weeks.
Self help Constant pressure or friction may cause calluses – small patches of thickened

skin. Use a dry-skin remover according to the maker's instructions, and rub in hand/body lotion or night cream.

Sometimes the top layers of nails separate and flake off, or the nails split easily due to contact with detergents, solvents and other preparations; using an emery board that is too coarse or a metal file; too little protein in the diet; or extreme old age. Keep the nails short and follow the *Do's and don'ts of hand care* and remedies below for very dry hands.

Alternatively, rub nail cream or oil into the nail bases each night and increase your protein and vitamin intake. Eating two cubes of concentrated jelly or a dessertspoon of gelatine a day helps the problem in some people. Nail varnish will act as a 'splint' for broken nails, but do use a moisturiser base coat. Avoid using nail-varnish remover as much as possible; add more coats of moisturiser and/or varnish instead.

If nails become dry or brittle, immerse them in warm olive oil for 30 minutes daily.

For minor ridges and furrows on the nails, use a ridge-filling base coat. The problem will eventually 'grow out'. More serious ridges and furrows may result from an injury or cyst near the cuticle. The furrows may split and become infected. If there is any inflammation or swelling, see your doctor.

Constant immersion of hands in water may cause hangnails – splits where the outer skin has come away from the cuticle, often allowing infection to enter. Carefully snip off the hangnails with scissors and apply a proprietary antiseptic cream. To prevent hangnails, apply hand cream nightly.

A heavy blow or pressure will cause bleeding underneath a nail and turn it black. With minor injuries, the problem will grow out. If the nail falls off, is very painful or the bleeding continues, see your doctor.

Some nail varnishes, especially if used without a base coat, turn nails yellow. Again, the condition will grow out, and so will white spots or flecks.

What the therapists recommend

Traditional Medicine For dry hands, soak 3 tablespoons of linseed in 1 pint (600ml) of warm water overnight. Boil, strain and retain the gel. Add a pint of white vinegar and 2–3oz (60–90g) of glycerine. Heat to boiling, remove from the heat, beat for one minute, and then bottle the mixture while still warm. Store in a cool place and rub a little into the hands as required. Alternatively, apply an unperfumed hand cream (a perfumed one may cause further irritation).

For very dry hands, soak them in warm olive oil for 30 minutes. Alternatively, apply vitamin E, either as wheat-germ oil, or by cutting open a vitamin E capsule and rubbing the contents well in. Cod liver, safflower or

sunflower oil will also help. Either rub it into the hands at night, or drink a teaspoon of oil before retiring. See also CHAPPING.

To remove discoloured areas such as the stains acquired by smokers, rub the hands with the juicy side of half a lemon. Leave for one minute, rinse off thoroughly, dry carefully and massage with hand cream.

An orthodox view

Extreme cases of chapping may lead to ECZEMA. If this happens, or if there is an

---

Do's and don'ts of hand care

Do avoid all detergents and highly alkaline soaps (over pH 7.5).

Do wet your hands as little as possible.

Do wear rubber gloves when doing wet jobs, preferably cotton-lined ones. If you are allergic to rubber, use plastic gloves instead. If the job cannot be done in gloves, apply a barrier cream first.

Do wear cotton gloves for dry tasks.

Do brush your nails once a day with a soft brush and warm, soapy water.

Do have a manicure at least weekly.

Do buff your nails as often as possible, working in one direction only.

Do use a nail moisturiser as a lacquer base and top coat.

Do use an emollient at night, if necessary wearing cotton gloves in bed.

Do dry your hands thoroughly and apply hand cream after each wash.

Do eat a healthy, well balanced diet, with plenty of calcium, vitamin B1, iron and fresh fruit and vegetables (see EATING FOR HEALTH).

Don't expose the hands to harsh sunlight, extremes of hot and cold or very dry atmospheres.

Don't use creams and lotions containing lanolin if you think you may be allergic to it.

Don't bite your nails.

Don't pick at the cuticles, or push them back too hard.

Don't cut your cuticles; if it is necessary, have a professional do it.

Don't cut your nails except when they are soft and pliable after a warm bath.

Don't use nail varnish/lacquer remover containing acetone unless it also contains oil to prevent overdrying.

Don't use base and top coats containing formaldehyde; they are too drying.

Don't apply nail-varnish hardeners containing formaldehyde too near the cuticle, as this will cause drying.

Do-it-yourself manicure

You will need: cotton wool; emery boards; a hoof stick with a blunt point at one end for cleaning, and a rubber 'hoof' at the other for easing back cuticles; nail or cuticle cream; chamois-covered nail buffer, and some oily nail-varnish remover.

1 *Remove any nail varnish: put some oily nail-varnish remover on a swab of cotton wool, hold it on a nail for a second or two, then gently rub until all the varnish is removed.*

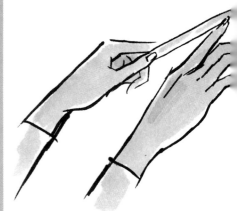

2 *Shape the nails with an emery board, using the fine side only. Movements should be from side to centre only. Do not file down the sides so far that strength is impaired.*

5 Gently ease the cuticles back from the nails using the rubber end of the hoof stick.

3 Massage nail or cuticle cream all over the nails, and wait two minutes.

4 Soak the fingers in warm soapy water for two minutes, and dry thoroughly.

6 Wrap a little cotton wool around the pointed end of the hoof stick, dip it in the soapy water, and run it around under the tips of the nails to clean them. (If you are not going to apply a highly coloured nail varnish, run a white nail pencil under the nail tips.)

7 Buff the nails, using strokes in one direction only.

8 Massage cream into the hands (and wrists, forearms and elbows, if desired). Run nails along a piece of fabric to find any snags, and smooth with the emery board.

9 If you are going to apply nail varnish, dip a piece of cotton wool in soapy water, squeeze almost dry, and gently rub each nail to remove traces of cream.

10 Apply one coat of base coat or moisturiser, two coats of varnish and one top coat. Use long straight strokes from base to tip, one in the centre and one on either side. If necessary, remove any smudges of nail varnish on the skin by wrapping a little cotton wool around the pointed end of the hoof stick, dipping it in oily remover, and running it around the nails and under the tips. Allow at least 20 minutes to dry.

allergic reaction (see ALLERGY), consult your doctor immediately.

Sometimes a whitlow – a small, painful abscess – forms at the side of a nail if the hands are in water a great deal. The skin becomes abnormally soft and infection enters. This too needs the attention of a doctor, who will lance it to drain out the pus. Antibiotics may be prescribed, and patients should keep their hands as dry as possible, and not handle food or dress wounds.

Sometimes the skin around the nails becomes cracked, usually because of an allergen. If a doctor cannot find the cause, he may prescribe supplements of vitamin C and cod liver oil (vitamins A and D).

Children and young people are especially prone to WARTS on the hands. They are caused by a virus and are therefore contagious. If they persist, see a doctor.

Liver spots – large brown spots on the backs of the hands – are the result of the ageing effects of climate. Mild bleaching creams are available from most cosmetics counters. If the spots appear before old age, have them checked by a doctor immediately, for in rare cases they·can be malignant.

Excessive sweating of the palms may cause embarrassment at times. Try to remain calm, and avoid stimulant drinks such as coffee and cola. If the problem becomes very severe, a doctor may prescribe a cream or lotion to reduce sweating, or even sedatives or tranquillisers for important occasions.

HANGOVER
Remedies for the morning after

Drinking too much alcohol usually results in a hangover. If the overindulgence takes place in the evening, the hangover may not be apparent until the next morning. A person with a hangover is suffering from dehydration – or loss of fluid – and the symptoms include NAUSEA AND VOMITING, thirst, TIREDNESS and HEADACHES.

Often the hangover is heightened by a group of substances called congeners. These are formed during fermentation, especially in drinks such as red wine, brandy and lager, and irritate the lining of the stomach. In addition, smoking usually adds to the severity of a hangover.

Self help One of the best ways of helping to prevent a hangover is to make sure that you do not drink on an empty stomach, and to drink plenty of water – up to a pint (600ml) of it – beforehand. Some people find a glass of

milk to be an effective substitute, while others swear by a dessertspoon of oil.

Having got a hangover, water – pints of it – is probably the best drink to replace lost fluids; and eating something light, such as a slice or two of dry wholemeal toast will help to replace the blood sugar which the alcohol has destroyed, and so help reduce weakness, dizziness and trembling. A walk in the fresh air should also help to clear the head.

Activated charcoal is known to absorb congeners, and is available in tablet form from most chemists and health shops. Take several tablets as directed before you go to bed after an evening's drinking.

To 'cure' a hangover some people drink black coffee. This is a mistake, for like alcohol, coffee itself is a diuretic (a substance that increases the flow of urine) and only prolongs the discomfort.

What the therapists recommend

Herbal Medicine   After drinking, take plenty of water before going to bed to prevent dehydration. Herbalists suggest that throughout the next day you drink peppermint, nettle, camomile or yarrow tea to help settle the stomach and liver.

Naturopathy   If you are going to drink, then you are advised to make sure to eat something at the same time. This will slow down the absorption of alcohol. Then drink at least a pint of water just before going to bed. If you still get a hangover afterwards, have a glass of water or a peppermint tea to help settle the stomach.

Traditional Medicine   One of the oldest and most popular folk remedies is 'the hair of the dog that bit you' – that is, more alcohol. Although this will not cure a hangover, it may make the victim feel slightly stronger. But if more than just a 'nip' is taken it could lead to another and even worse hangover.

A 'prairie oyster', made of a raw egg immersed in liquid – usually Worcestershire sauce or vinegar – and swallowed whole is another supposed cure. Honey is also a remedy of long standing: try 12 teaspoonsful, either neat or in a little warm water. The honey will help to replace the blood sugar lost, and its potassium content is also said to be beneficial.

An orthodox view

Although doctors are not opposed to alternative hangover cures, they mostly agree that time is the best cure. If you are able to, stay in bed, keep warm, and take painkillers such as soluble aspirin or paracetamol. (Ordinary aspirin tablets may cause nausea or sometimes, with a severe hangover, bleeding in the stomach.) If you must drink, it is safer to take white wine, vodka or gin, as they contain comparatively few congeners.

HAY DIET
Avoiding the foods that fight

An American doctor, William Howard Hay (1866-1940), devised a diet aimed at combating DIGESTIVE PROBLEMS. He recommended that carbohydrates (starches and sugars) should not be eaten with proteins and acid fruits at the same meal. He pointed out that protein stimulates the production of acid in the stomach, and that the acid interferes with carbohydrate digestion, which needs an alkaline medium.

While many foodstuffs contain both protein and carbohydrate, virtually all of them are 20 per cent or more one or the other, and can be classified as such. The exceptions are peas, beans, lentils and peanuts, and these Hay excluded from his diet. However, modern vegetarian proponents now include them as proteins.

Hay's foods for a protein meal include meat, poultry, game, fish (including shellfish), eggs, cheese, yoghurt, milk, and acid fruits such as apples, apricots (both fresh and dried), gooseberries, oranges, pears and prunes. His carbohydrate group includes bread (whole grain), flour, rice, sweet fruits such as ripe bananas, dates, figs, currants, raisins and sultanas, and potatoes and Jerusalem artichokes.

Hay's third group of 'neutral foods' combines well with either of the other two. Nuts (excluding peanuts), butter, cream, egg yolks, olive oil, safflower oil, sunflower and sesame seeds and oils, salads, herbs, and all green and root vegetables except potatoes and Jerusalem artichokes belong to this third neutral group.

Hay did not ban alcohol. He recommended dry red or white table wine or dry cider with protein meals, and ale or beer for carbo-

Do's and don'ts of the Hay diet

Don't eat carbohydrates with proteins and acid fruits in a single meal.
Do make vegetables, salads and fruits the major part of your diet, and cut down on proteins, starches and fats.
Don't eat refined or processed foods, including white flour, white sugar, margarine, or things containing them.
Don't eat a meal of one type within four hours of a meal of the other type.

A new lease of life

In 1942, the actor Sir John Mills left the Army with a painful, debilitating duodenal ulcer. Complete bed-rest in hospital and the traditional bland diet of potatoes and milk puddings gave no relief. In fact, things got worse. His digestion almost came to a halt and, as he himself has said, be became a walking zombie.

Then his sister suggested the Hay diet, and Sir John 'remembers with gratitude' his first Hay meal: a small minute steak, large salad and a glass of claret. He has followed the diet ever since, and has never looked back. His distinguished career of stage, film and television, and active, rewarding lifestyle have continued into his eighties.

Sir John finds other diets 'a crashing bore', but while following the Hay diet, he can eat most of any meal put before him. Often it means simply foregoing the potatoes and pudding.

hydrate meals. Whisky or gin may be drunk with either type of meal. Of course, all must be taken in moderation.

An orthodox view

Tests by the Russian physiologist Ivan Petrovich Pavlov (1849-1936) proved that meat mixed with starch takes twice as long – or more – to pass through a dog's stomach than either of them does alone, and that sluggish digestive action continues through the rest of the alimentary canal. Hay's diet therefore gives some relief to people sufferering from indigestion, stomach and duodenal ulcers and constipation.

Any well-balanced diet, taken in moderation as Hay recommended, promotes good health, avoiding obesity and related heart disease, diabetes and arthritis. See also DIETS AND DIETING; EATING FOR HEALTH.

HAY FEVER

In spite of the name, hay fever is neither caused by hay nor associated with fever. It is usually an ALLERGY to pollen released by grasses, flowers and trees in spring and summer. The pollen causes cells to release histamine and other chemicals, resulting in a running, itchy nose; blocked sinuses; SNEEZING; redness, prickling and watering of the eyes, and/or a sore, itchy throat; and sometimes ASTHMA.

But allergic rhinitis, as it is medically named, may also be caused by allergy to things such as house dust, mites, the fur or feathers of animals or birds, or by moulds, plants or chemicals.

What the therapists recommend

NATUROPATHY

Consultation A practitioner may prescribe vitamin B as a preventive in late spring and early summer. He will also recommend that you cut down on dairy products (cheese, milk and so on) and refined carbohydrates such as sugars. These are all held to encourage excess mucus, and a sensitivity to dairy foods is believed to exacerbate the pollen reaction itself. Large doses of vitamin C – 1 or 2g daily – are prescribed for an antihistamine effect.

HOMOEOPATHY

Self help *Allium cepa* is prescribed for an acute attack, with running eyes and nose, sneezing and sore lips and nose, which is worse indoors and towards evening. For violent, painful sneezing, with a ticklish spot in a running nose, try *Arsen. alb.*; *Sabadilla* may be a better choice for an itching, stuffy or running nose, red eyes and frequent sneezing spasms. A practitioner may offer individual treatment in winter to reduce the tendency to hay fever later.

Other alternative treatments

Acupuncture The therapist stimulates points on the large intestine governing lung and spleen meridians.

Hypnotherapy The patient is put in a relaxed state, then instructed in appropriate breathing techniques. Suggestions are made under hypnosis which take effect at times when the patient needs them. Hypnosis has been used to prevent attacks in people susceptible to certain allergies, even though skin tests remain positive (see ALLERGY).

Traditional Medicine Use small lumps of honeycomb as a chewing gum all through the winter and spring. Brewer's yeast tablets taken according to the manufacturer's instructions are said to be beneficial.

An orthodox view

Doctors often prescribe or advise their patients to take antihistamine tablets during the hay fever season. Drowsiness may be a side effect of these and, if so, patients should not drive a car or operate machinery. The regular use of cromoglycate eyedrops, nasal sprays and/or inhalers, available on prescription, can also prevent or reduce the allergic response of the body.

Cortisone inhalers and nose sprays can help to reduce inflammation and swelling of the sensitive membranes of the lungs and nasal passages. In severe cases, or when hay fever might interfere with a critical event such as an important examination, a course of cortisone tablets or a long-acting cortisone injection can relieve hay fever symptoms dramatically.

However, steroids such as cortisone should not be used as a routine treatment because of long-term side effects, such as bruising and bone thinning. The side effects depend on how long the particular substance has been taken.

Courses of desensitising injections are no longer given because patients can die from anaphylactic shock, a severe allergic reaction to protein in the injection.

HEADACHES

Almost everyone experiences headaches at times. Most are caused by TENSION in the muscles of the scalp and neck after periods of concentration or STRESS. Some result from EATING PROBLEMS or alcohol abuse (see HANGOVER). Others are the forerunners of COLDS or INFLUENZA. MENSTRUATION can be another cause.

EYESTRAIN only rarely produces headache, despite popular belief, and if it does, it usually arises from ASTIGMATISM. MIGRAINE can cause severe headaches, often on one side of the head only, and sometimes associated with numbness or weakness down one side of the face or body. Headache is common after head injury (concussion), and it can also be caused by SINUS PROBLEMS or problems involving the lower jaw muscles that may result from TEETH-GRINDING.

A sudden, severe headache, like a blow to the back of the head, often followed by unconsciousness, may indicate internal bleeding underneath the brain known as a subarachnoid haemorrhage. Meningitis produces a headache aggravated by bright light, and accompanied by fever and neck stiffness. The headache caused by a brain tumour is worst in the mornings or when lying down, and may be associated with nausea and mental disturbances. However, all of these are very rare complaints.

Warning If a headache persists or recurs frequently, see your doctor at once; do not attempt to treat yourself.

What the therapists recommend

NATUROPATHY

Consultation The cause of the headache should always be sought. A consultant will therefore inquire about the patient's way of life to try to discover any factors which may aggravate the problem. Diet can also be a

Demons with corkscrews, red-hot pokers, trumpets and mallets torture a headache victim at his fireside in this cartoon by George Cruikshank published in 1835.

trigger, especially in cases of migraine. Cheese, chocolate, alcohol or coffee can all be causes, but each case will be assessed on its merits.

Hot and cold compresses to the forehead and neck, depending on the type of headache, may also be applied.

BEHAVIOURAL THERAPY
Consultation For a stress-induced headache, the aim is to relieve tension in the muscles of the body. This can be done through progressive muscular relaxation, in which all the muscles are tensed, and then relaxed in turn starting with the toes and working up the body.

The patient becomes aware of the tension and relaxation of the muscles and can then aim at maintaining relaxation as much as possible. Particular emphasis is placed on the muscles around the shoulders, neck, jaw and face.

Other alternative treatments

Acupuncture Headaches are held to be due to an energy blockage in the yang channel of the head. Those that do not respond well to conventional medicine are thought to respond best to acupuncture. Depending on the type of headache, points on the meridians relating to the gall bladder, large intestine, stomach, small intestine governor and bladder are treated.

Massage Certain kinds of headaches – particularly those which tend to start at the back of the head – may be helped by firm effleurage strokes down the back of the neck, and gentle petrissage and kneading of the muscles over the upper part of the shoulders. Follow by deep friction with the thumbs over the tight muscle band on either side of the spine of the neck, and friction with the fingers behind the ears.

Then apply firm stroking across the forehead, from one temple to the other, using the ends of the fingers. Finish with more firm stroking down the neck towards the shoulders, avoiding completely any contact with the front of the neck and the throat.

Osteopathy Many headaches are believed to be caused by muscle tension, which can result from poor posture, eyestrain and the pressures of everyday living. Osteopaths may therefore try to free the contracted muscles at the base of the skull, and improve the mobility of the neck joints.

An orthodox view

The main role of the doctor is to reach a diagnosis and treat serious causes of headache. Orthodox painkillers such as paracetamol and aspirin are of only limited value in the treatment of tension headaches.

HEALERS AND HEALING
Summoning inner powers to fight disease

For at least 3000 years healers throughout the world have been seeking to cure people of illness – physical and mental – by various non-physical means. By concentrating their attention solely upon their patients, healers claim that they can sometimes relieve pain, soreness and tiredness within minutes – and so help the body to heal itself. For example, swellings may quickly diminish, wounds rapidly get better, and infections speedily clear up; patients are also said to spend less time recuperating.

Very occasionally healers are said to achieve so-called 'miracle cures', in which

the blind are able to see again and the crippled able to walk. But although these 'miracles' are often widely reported in the popular Press, they are generally viewed with scepticism by many doctors and scientists (see FAITH HEALING).

Some healers believe that their powers of healing are channelled through them by an outside 'spiritual' source. This often results in a spirituality developing in the patients, which is thought to speed up the cures and make them more effective. Even so, belief in the healer and his particular therapy does not always seem to be necessary as in some reported cases infants, unconscious patients, animals and plants are said to have responded positively to healing. By observing their growth patterns, it has even been demonstrated that healing has had a beneficial effect on bacteria and yeasts.

In the late 1980s controlled experiments in healing were conducted at London University by two lecturers in physiology, Dr David Hodges and Dr Tony Scofield. They scientifically tested the curative powers of a psychic healer and medium who claimed he could take 'sick' organisms such as cress seeds – whose ability to grow had been hampered by soaking them overnight in salty water – and make them 'well' again.

The healer held half of the seeds in his hands and directed 'healing energy' at them for a couple of minutes. The treated and untreated seeds were laid on wet filter paper and placed in a laboratory for almost a week. A series of tests then showed that the 'treated' seeds grew at a significantly faster rate than those which the healer had not touched. From this, Dr Hodges and Dr Scofield concluded that the healer was somehow able to transmit a healing power which enabled the sick seeds to throw off any ill effects and grow almost normally.

Some medical experts dismiss the work of healers and say that unexplained cures are due to 'spontaneous remission', in which the body heals itself (if only temporarily), or AUTOSUGGESTION, whereby patients heal themselves by self-hypnosis. The experts also suggest that healing is similar to parapsychology, in which clairvoyance (the supposed power to see things not present to the senses) and telepathy (the awareness, even at a distance, of someone else's feelings and thoughts) play a significant part (see PARANORMAL THERAPIES).

In some cases, it has been suggested that the healers go into medium-like trances in which they are possessed by the spirits of the dead, who do the healing for them. In addition, the sick have reportedly been cured by ABSENT HEALING, in which healers apparently project their powers from another room or even another continent – and some patients are not even aware that they are being treated. Other healers use the LAYING ON OF HANDS and THERAPEUTIC TOUCH, whereby powers appear to be activated through their hands. In some cases this is done simply by making a series of 'passes' around the patients' bodies without physically touching the affected areas.

Finding a healer Most people contact a healer through the personal recommendation of friends or relatives. There are more than 20,000 healers practising in Britain – some of them in National Health Service hospitals. About a third of the healers are registered with the Confederation of Healing Organisations (CHO), and are governed by a code of conduct approved of by the General Medical Council. The CHO also requires the healers to undergo training, the duration of which varies according to the natural gifts involved, and to practise for at least two years under skilled supervision.

For information about healers who are practising in your area write to the CHO at Suite J, The Red and White House, 113 High Street, Berkhamsted, Herts HP4 2DJ.

Consulting a healer Healing is generally regarded as a two-way process, and the first thing a healer will do is talk soothingly to a patient to induce relaxation and open his mind to the possibility of getting well again. Once a mutual bond has been established the healer will focus his mind on his powers, allowing them to flow freely from – or through – him and onto his patient. He may also instruct the patient to visualise projections of white or coloured light, which are said to aid the healing process (see COLOUR THERAPY and VISUALISATION THERAPY).

During healing sessions – usually held once a week until improvement is shown – the patient should gradually become less tense and nervous. He may have sensations of heat, cold and tingling (like small electric shocks) – especially on the skin over the site of an illness, such as the liver or kidneys. This is taken as a sign that a beneficial form of energy is being transferred from the healer to the patient – although no known form of energy or healing power has so far been scientifically identified. However, if such sensations do not occur healing may still be taking place.

Some patients begin to feel better as soon as healing begins, or shortly after. Others do not feel any benefit until hours or days later. Occasionally healing may take weeks or months before it has any effect. Frequently symptoms which the patient has omitted to mention are cleared up – while the original illness remains unchanged. In such cases, further healing may be carried out.

Many registered healers – especially those who work part-time – do not charge a fee for treatment, although a small 'donation' may be requested. But full-time professionals, who sometimes have a waiting list of several months, may ask a fee from £10 TO £15 a session – about that of a professional chiropractor or osteopath. As a general rule, avoid any healer who demands exhorbitant fees, or who is not registered with the CHO.

An orthodox view

Spiritual healing, significantly older than Western medicine, is still widely practised throughout the world. No scientific basis to the claims made for healing have been identified, but many doctors believe that faith and hope are important ingredients in recovery. Insofar as spiritual healing encourages these factors, it can do no harm. However, doctors are justifiably concerned if false hopes are raised and if patients do not seek orthodox treatment for complaints because they are seeing a spiritual healer.

HEALTH FARMS

People visit health farms for a rest and a general tone-up, or for naturopathic cures for ailments such as ARTHRITIS and BACK PAIN. See GETTING FIT – AWAY FROM IT ALL, p. 170.

HEALTH FOODS
Balancing fads and true food values

It is tempting to expect extra benefits from eating what we call health foods and from increasing our intake of the VITAMINS and MINERALS vital in our diet. They are today's equivalent of the elixirs and magic potions of bygone days. But is there as much nutrition – equal magic – in ordinary fresh foods if they are chosen and combined wisely?

Some foods have a powerful health image. Wholegrain cereals and pulses, nuts and seeds, dried fruit and honey, natural yoghurt and cottage cheese are among the goods people seek out in health food stores. They are there in abundance – and with them is a bewildering array of pills and potions promising convenient bottled health: vitamins, minerals and oils to supplement your diet, GINSENG, ROYAL JELLY and amino acids to act as tonics or lift your mood. Some shops also have a pharmacy selling herbal, homoeopathic and other remedies.

What are you to do faced with such a wide choice and with that persuasive 'health' tag backed by potent advertising? Are these special foods, supplements and tonics necessary for your health?

How healthy are they?

Cereals and pulses Wholegrain cereals and pulses are undoubtedly valuable foods that play an essential part in a healthy diet (see EATING FOR HEALTH). Indeed, they sustain much of the world's population. They have a similar nutritional content – protein, starch, dietary FIBRE, vitamins and minerals – in differing permutations and amounts. You should eat a wide variety of them to ensure that you get a supply of all essential nutrients. It is best to eat a cereal and pulse at the same meal since the usable proteins in them are enhanced in combination.

Pulses (seeds from pods) such as beans and lentils have, when dry, more protein than meat, but you cannot eat them dry. Once they have been soaked, washed and thoroughly cooked (which removes the poisons most beans contain), they have far less protein than meat but still make a useful protein contribution to the diet: they contain about the same amount as bread. Fresh and frozen peas also have a similar protein content; nutritionally, peas are simply wet beans without the poisons and with the bonus of vitamin C.

Nuts and seeds Nuts, like cereals and pulses, contain useful amounts of protein, dietary fibre, vitamins (especially B, E and folic acid) and minerals (including potassium, calcium, magnesium, iron and zinc). Seeds such as sesame, poppy and melon are similar but are eaten as garnishes rather than a main constituent of a meal.

The energy stored in nuts and seeds is in the form of fat instead of starch (as in cereals and pulses), so they should be eaten in moderation. As nuts are eaten dry, they appear – weight for weight – to contain more nutrients than pulses and cereals, but in practice we eat nuts in smaller helpings so the end result is similar.

Dried fruits and honey It seems curious that dried fruit, rather than fresh fruit, should find such favour as a health food. Dried fruit is only fresh fruit with much of the water and some of the nutrients lost in the drying process. Dried fruit makes a concentrated food package but is eaten in smaller helpings (by weight) than fresh fruit, so its nutritional contribution is about the same. Dried fruit is often used as a sweetener, and is to be preferred to sugar or HONEY. Despite all the virtues attributed to honey, it is little more than sugar in another guise. Both provide calories, but with only tiny amounts of other nutrients for maintaining the body.

Yoghurt and cottage cheese These both

Pulses, cereals, dried fruits and nuts are all part of a well-stocked 'health kitchen'. To get the most benefit from the food, they need careful weighing for a balanced diet.

contain protein, vitamins (especially B) and minerals (including calcium and potassium) without an unhealthy excess of fat – provided you choose the right yoghurt. Yoghurt made with full-cream milk and sweetened fruit certainly cannot qualify as a health food.

Tonic supplements

What of pills? The massive increase in the sale of nutritional supplements indicates an upsurge of interest in personal health – an encouraging trend but one that is being satisfied by 'pill popping' rather than by sound dietary practices.

Should vitamin supplements be taken at all, or singly, or in combined 'multivit' forms? What is a health-promoting vitamin when supplied in tiny quantities by nature can, in overdose, become a dangerous poison. Vitamins A and D taken in excess can kill. Too much vitamin C can cause kidney stones. Minerals too carry dangers. Iron can inflame the bowel and selenium is poisonous at quite modest overdose levels.

Even bran, source of the dietary fibre that Western-style eating lacks, has its dangers. It is widely available in health food shops as a concentrated, refined product that makes it easy to take in too much at one time – far more than you would eat in natural foods. Too much interferes with the absorption of iron, calcium, zinc and other essential minerals and nutrients.

Equally risky is taking every new fad substance that man's ingenuity brings onto the market. Individual amino acids have been offered as nutritional supplements in

recent years. They are the basic building blocks of food and body proteins, but also serve as transmitter substances in the brain, passing information from one nerve cell to another. The body has sophisticated mechanisms to regulate the flow of the 22 different amino acids it needs and ensure that only those required are allowed to penetrate the brain, and even then only in suitable amounts. The amounts and balance of amino acids that you would take in from the proteins in foods are safe, but to load the body with individual amino acids can overwhelm its protective mechanisms and disrupt normal brain function.

A significant number of new fad substances are later withdrawn as useless, dangerous or both. The most recent is the mineral germanium, at first promoted as a wonder drug to stimulate the immune system and boost vitality. Now it has been withdrawn because it may cause kidney damage. In any case, there is serious doubt that it ever did anything beneficial. An earlier example was Laetrile, the so-called vitamin B17, that was supposed to cure cancer and produced cyanide in the body.

If you feel certain that you need supplements because your diet and lifestyle are so poorly managed, or because of illness, stick to safe and beneficial low-dose mixtures of minerals and vitamins from a reputable chemist or health shop. High-dose, high-potency single nutrients are quite likely to create more problems than they solve, by disturbing your metabolic balance. Mega-dosing, especially of individual nutrients, is nothing to do with nutrition. It is far better to use nature's supplements: milk, cheese or yoghurt for calcium, red meat for iron, carrots for vitamin A, greens for so many things.

Natural tonic supplements, such as ginseng, honey and GARLIC, have been used for thousands of years in the hope of improving strength and performance. Ginseng contains pharmacologically active substances that do something – but precisely what is not clear. There is no evidence that it does harm so long as the dosage is modest, and many people believe it has done them good. Honey is just a mixture of sugars with minute amounts of nutrients. There is no evidence that it does anything more than act as a fuel and taste nice. There is growing evidence, however, that garlic can reduce blood fats, blood pressure and blood clotting – all of which are helpful in the fight against coronary heart disease.

Another popular supplement, evening-primrose oil, has done well in some trials and may help PREMENSTRUAL TENSION, breast tenderness, ALCOHOLISM and ECZEMA. It contains the fatty acid GLA (gamma linolenic acid) which the body converts into hormone-like substances. These appear to reduce inflammation, decrease cholesterol levels and regulate the female reproductive system. Side effects are rare, but epilepsy sufferers should not take the supplement.

In your search for a sound approach to health, observe three simple rules for nutritional sanity: Firstly, avoid extremes and overdoses. Just because a little is good, it does not mean that twice as much or a lot is better. Secondly, avoid single-nutrient supplements. In nature, micronutrients occur and work in complex groups, not individually. Thirdly, eat a well-balanced mixture of natural, fresh, nourishing foods – and put your trust in nature's delicate balance.

HEALTH HAZARDS

How to cope with some of the hazards – such as aerosols and lead pollution – which daily threaten our health? See IS THE ENVIRONMENT MAKING YOU ILL?, p. 172.

HEART DISORDERS

The heart is one of the most efficient pumps ever evolved, beating approximately 2.5 billion times in a lifetime of 70 years. But like any other pump, if it becomes clogged it becomes less efficient – or even stops working altogether, threatening life itself.

Plaques of the fatty substance cholesterol are deposited on the walls of blood vessels from early adulthood onwards. Eventually this deposit may block the coronary ARTERIES that supply blood to the heart muscle itself and cause heart disease.

Partial blockage may result in ANGINA. More seriously, if a blood clot lodges suddenly in a coronary artery and blocks it completely, part of the heart is starved of oxygen, causing a 'heart attack' or even stopping it beating altogether.

Other complaints are associated with old age. Hearts become 'tired' and susceptible to both heart failure (weakening) and heart block, a condition which causes the heart to beat very slowly, sometimes only 30-40 times a minute. The rate does not increase on exertion, so the patient tires very easily. Heart valves may also become ineffective later in life, often as a result of rheumatic fever. Typical symptoms are breathlessness and WATER RETENTION, when the ankles swell towards evening.

Some babies are born with congenital heart disease in which the chambers or valves of the heart are not properly formed. Cardiomyopathy is general weakness and enlargement of the heart. There are many causes, and the condition can develop at any age.

Warning Anyone suspecting that they have a heart disorder should see their doctor before undertaking any alternative regimes or remedies.

What the therapists recommend

Autogenic Training This has been found helpful in reducing high BLOOD PRESSURE and cholesterol levels, and in steadying the heart rate and increasing blood flow to the body's extremities. All these things can help to increase the efficiency of the circulatory system and so help the heart to recover.

Naturopathy Practitioners will advise seeking orthodox treatment for heart disorders, but can advise on preventive measures. Reducing fats – especially animal fats – sugars and salt will be part of a dietary regime which includes increased intake of fresh fruit and vegetables, also whole grains. Regular EXERCISE is advised to maintain heart and lung fitness, and time should be set aside for relaxation and gentler exercises such as YOGA to combat STRESS.

An orthodox view

Doctors are concerned to try to prevent heart disorders by encouraging their patients to exercise regularly, eat sensibly and avoid SMOKING. Early detection and treatment of high blood pressure and raised blood cholesterol also helps some people who otherwise would be at risk.

Doctors can prescribe a variety of medicines to relieve angina. If they are ineffective, bypass surgery to reroute the blood around the clogged coronary artery to the heart may help. Modern medical treatment of a heart attack includes 'clot-busting' drugs such as streptokinase which reduce damage to the heart muscle.

Increasingly ambulances, paramedics and doctors are equipped with defibrillators, which electrically shock the heart out of potentially fatal conditions. Heart block is usually treated successfully by inserting a battery-powered pacemaker under the skin of the chest wall. It produces tiny electric stimuli to keep the heart beating regularly and at the right rate – an average of 70-72 beats a minute for an adult male, awake but at rest, and 78-82 for a woman.

The risk of having a baby born with congenital heart disease is reduced if the mother has been immunised against German measles, and if she avoids smoking, drugs and medicines, particularly around the time of conception and during early pregnancy. Many of the congenital abnormalities and those of later life can be corrected by delicate surgery. Surgeons can save the lives of people suffering from cardiomyopathy by heart-transplant operations.

Diuretic medicines, which make patients produce more urine, relieve the symptoms of heart failure, as do vasodilators, which take pressure off the heart by allowing blood to flow more easily through its vessels.

HEAT RASH

This harmless, but irritating, pimply skin rash most commonly affects babies and overweight people in hot weather. Also known as 'prickly heat', it appears around skin creases and where clothing is tight. The skin rapidly recovers on a return to cooler weather.

What the therapists recommend

Herbal Medicine You are advised to bathe the area with a cold infusion of marigold or lavender to reduce the inflammation. The leaves of many fleshy plants, such as the houseleek (_Sempervivum_, hen-and-chickens), may cool and soothe when applied to the affected area.

An orthodox view

There is no quick, conventional remedy. Doctors usually advise sufferers to wear loose clothing, avoid direct sunlight and take frequent baths or showers. Calamine lotion gives some relief. See also SUNBURN.

HELLERWORK
Realigning the balance of your body

The basis of this therapy is a series of 90-minute sessions of manipulation, movement and discussion designed to restore the body's balance, returning it to a more relaxed and youthful state and so releasing built-up TENSION and STRESS.

Hellerwork was founded in 1978 by a former American aerospace engineer, Joseph Heller. It does not set out to cure illness but to prevent it by freeing people from their set patterns of moving and thinking, thereby allowing them to adapt more easily to life's changes. The aim of the therapy is to release tension and rigidity, and – by improving the body structure – to prevent it from occurring in the first place.

It concentrates on a form of connective body tissue called fascia, which wraps the individual fibres and bundles of fibres that become muscle. Fascia comes together at the end of the muscle and forms the tendon, which attaches the muscle to the bone.

Finding a practitioner Although most Hellerwork practitioners are in the USA, British teachers can be contacted through Roger Golten, The Peak, Hyatt Carlton Tower, Cadogan Place, London SW1 9PY.

Consulting a practitioner Hellerwork is a combination of three main elements: Bodywork, Movement Education, and Dialogue. In Bodywork the practitioner uses his hands to manipulate and release any tension in the fascia and to stretch it back into its normal position. In Movement Education the patient is shown how to become aware of his body and to make it supple and tension-free. And in the Dialogue, the client and practitioner discuss how mental attitudes, beliefs, feelings and opinions may affect the body.

An orthodox view

Many physical therapies are similar in their approach, although they are known by different names. Hellerwork, ROLFING and the ALEXANDER TECHNIQUE, for example, all aim to improve mind-body integration.

HERBAL MEDICINE

The popularity of medicinal herbs is booming as more and more people are turning to nature for their health's sake. See USING THE HEALING POWER OF HERBS, p. 182.

Getting fit – away from it all

Modern health farms are run on naturopathic lines, with treatment centred on diet and fasting (see NATUROPATHY), and many people go there to lose weight and generally improve their health, fitness and appearance. However, most farms – or clinics, as they are more properly called – also offer a wide range of therapies such as ACUPUNCTURE, AROMATHERAPY, EXERCISE, HYDROTHERAPY, OSTEOPATHY, REFLEXOLOGY and YOGA.

Their facilities include gymnasiums, saunas, solariums, swimming pools and whirlpools – and often the means to play croquet, golf, snooker and tennis, and to go cycling, dancing, JOGGING and swimming. For women guests there may be hairdressing and beauty salons and, for men, even the occasional assault course or pigeon shoot.

Some clinics insist that guests must be at least 16 – in some cases 18 – years of age; some prefer guests who have been recommended by a doctor. An initial consultation and physical examination by a doctor or state registered nurse is normally held, and a report from the guest's GP may be used to help and confirm any clinical diagnosis.

If necessary, X-rays and an electrocardiogram (showing any possible HEART DISORDERS) will be taken, and outside specialists may be called in. Then, in certain cases, a personal course of treatment will be prescribed.

Guests may be treated by professionally qualified staff for conditions as diverse as ANXIETY, ARTHRITIS, BACK PAIN, LIVER DISORDERS and SCIATICA. But there are many more who spend anything from a night or a weekend to two or three weeks at a clinic simply to tone-up their bodies through EXERCISE and MASSAGE, or to escape from the STRESS of business and domestic life.

Most such clinics impose strict, calorie-controlled diets (see EATING FOR HEALTH), with mainly vegetarian cuisine. Others are more relaxed and allow guests to drink undecaffeinated coffee occasionally, to eat the odd slice of cake at teatime, to have a cigarette in the smoking room, and even to take a little wine at weekends. In addition, guests are generally allowed to wander about the premises in dressing gown and slippers, and to fall asleep whenever and almost wherever they choose.

However, all the concentrated treatment and personal attendance can be expensive. Guests at some clinics can pay up to £800 a week or up to about £260 a night. But others charge as little as £250 a week, with prices from about £50 a night and £115 for a weekend. Certain clinics insist on a minimum stay of three to five nights.

A list of recommended health clinics and hydros, with details of their prices and facilities, can be obtained from the British Tourist Authority, British Travel Centre, 12 Regent Street, London SW1 4PQ.

Hot packs, cold showers – and a puff in the 'Butt Hut'

An hour-by-hour account of a young businesswoman's intensive day's toning-up at the medium-priced Tyringham Clinic, near Newport Pagnell, Bucks:

9am On arriving the visitor is seen by the senior state registered nurse and asked if she has ever had any serious illnesses, if she is currently taking any form of medication, and what – if anything – she feels is wrong with her. In this, as in many cases, the nurse is told that the client simply wishes to relax, tone-up, and leave that evening feeling fitter and fresher than when she came.

The nurse takes her BLOOD PRESSURE to make sure it is not too high or too low, and gives her an on-the-spot physical and mental

Seen from the air, Tyringham Clinic looks like a stately home set in its own grounds. It is typical of most country health farms.

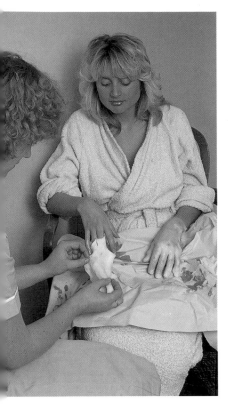

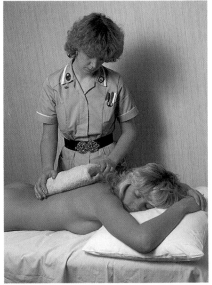

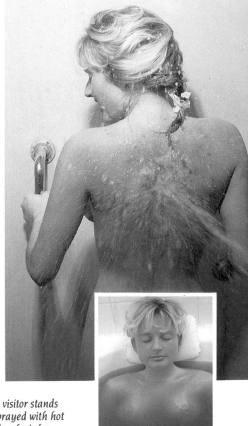

A day's treatment at a health farm involves several therapies for toning-up and generally stimulating the body. (Left) The visitor has her hands covered with hot paraffin wax to soothe and refresh them.
(Centre) The visitor lies down comfortably on a couch while hot packs containing crystal gel are applied to her back and shoulders to relieve tension and draw out pain.
(Top right) Holding onto steel bars for support, the visitor stands naked – her back covered with salt – while she is sprayed with hot and cold water alternately. The so-called Scottish douche is for stimulating the circulation. (Right) The visitor relaxes for half an hour in a warm bath of specially imported Irish seaweed which generally soothes the skin and the body.

assessment. It confirms that she is suffering from tiredness and TENSION, and needs to 'get away from it all', if only for a day. A busy schedule of therapies is drawn up and the visitor is issued with a bathrobe, soft shoes and a swimsuit.

9.30am The day starts with an invigorating session with a masseur. Stripped to her underwear, her back covered with vegetable oil, the visitor spends half an hour having the knots and pain nodes kneaded out of her shoulders and back.

10am She goes to her next appointment: hot-pack therapy. This consists of lying face down on a couch and having piping-hot packs filled with a gel of crystals placed on her shoulders. The aim is to draw out any remaining deep-seated pain and also iron out areas of tension.

10.30am Day visitors and longer-term guests gather in a spacious drawing room for a glass of fresh fruit juice.

11am The visitor moves on to her next therapy: a 30 minute workout in the Bethesda indoor swimming pool, named after the Biblical healing pool at Jerusalem.

Here swimmers and non-swimmers alike are put through their paces by a lifeguard cum swimming instructress. The exercises include running through the water forwards and backwards; arm and leg raising holding onto the side of the pool; underwater pedalling; and floating on the surface. This is followed by a short lie down in the warmth of the adjacent solarium.

12.30pm The visitor reports for a wax bath – hands, knees or feet only according to where, and if, she is experiencing any discomfort or pain. In the case of the hands, hot paraffin wax is poured over them and left for about five minutes until it hardens and feels like a pair of tight-fitting gloves. It is specifically designed to combat arthritis, and afterwards the hands feel soothed and refreshed.

1pm Lunch is served in the dining room, overlooking ornamental gardens and a large outdoor swimming pool. Tyringham specialises in nutritious vegetarian fare, and the meal consists of corn and lentil soup (delicious) and ratatouille and rice (filling).

Afterwards the visitor is free to stroll in the grounds, read in the library, or, if she so chooses, smoke in the so-called 'Butt Hut', in which the walls are lined with empty cigarette packets and notices declaring 'YOU CAN STOP SMOKING'.

2pm The visitor reports for balneotherapy – a warm bath in Irish seaweed – designed to soothe and relax the body.

2.30pm It is time for ten minutes of intensive foot massage, in which the feet are placed on a vigorously vibrating 'biocomfort pedio machine'.

2.45pm Next comes a bracing Scottish douche, for stimulating the circulation. Standing naked in a small cubicle, the visitor has salt spread across her back and shoulders and is then hosed down by a nurse, using hot and cold water alternately.

3.30pm There is a short tea break in the drawing room (rosehip tea with honey).

4pm The day ends with an hour-long Yoga class. This concentrates on the importance of breath control, posture and MEDITATION – all of which can help to combat feelings of tiredness and stress.

Is the environment making you ill?

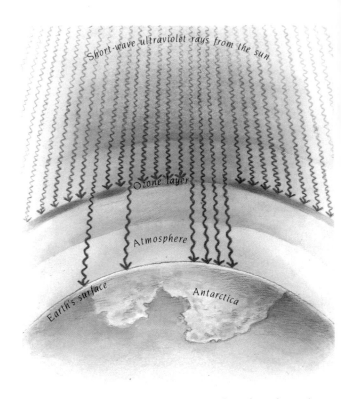

The ozone layer lies 6 to 20 miles (10 to 30km) above the earth, and protects us from cancer-causing short-wave ultraviolet radiation. Gases such as CFCs destroy ozone, and a large 'hole' in the layer – a thinning of the ozone – occurs each spring over Antarctica and a smaller one over the Arctic. However, by mid-1990, about 60 nations had agreed to phase out CFC production by the year 2000.

Daily life exposes us to all sorts of situations, substances, machines and gadgets that the human body was never designed to cope with. From aerosols to air conditioning and exhaust fumes to X-rays, hundreds of ordinary things can damage our health. Less direct but equally serious risks come from industries, agriculture, power stations, mines and waste disposal, in the form of water and air pollution, noise, stress, exposure to dangerous chemicals, and even increased levels of radiation. There also exist longer-term perils, such as the greenhouse effect, that may not pose an immediate threat but promise to affect the health, safety or comfort of future generations.

Although many of these hazards are beyond the power of individuals to control, there is still much that each person can do to make the environment healthier.

Air pollution

Poisons are continually being pumped into the air by industries, traffic, agricultural spraying, power stations, aircraft, aerosols, and wood, coal and garden rubbish fires.

Health risks include HEADACHES, EYE DISORDERS and irritation of the throat, lungs and respiratory tract, which can contribute to illnesses such as ALLERGY, ASTHMA, BRONCHITIS and EMPHYSEMA. Some chemicals may enter the blood from the lungs, eventually damaging the IMMUNE SYSTEM, causing CANCER, and contributing to defects in newborn babies.

Air pollution can have other serious consequences:

Lead from petrol Three-quarters of the lead that poisons our air comes from vehicle exhausts. Lead can damage the brain and nervous system. It has also been associated with HYPERACTIVITY and lower intelligence in children, and may also be particularly dangerous for pregnant women and their unborn babies.

<u>What to do</u> Cut down car use if possible. Cycling, walking, public transport and car-sharing all help. Wrap a fine silk scarf over your mouth and nose or use a surgical mask when walking, cycling or jogging on roads with heavy traffic, but avoid such routes as much as possible.

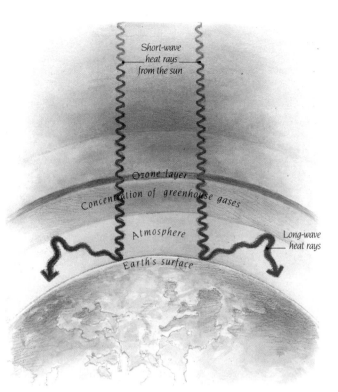

Short-wave
heat rays
from the sun

Ozone layer

Concentration of greenhouse gases

Atmosphere

Long-wave
heat rays

Earth's surface

The earth is turning into a gigantic hothouse, for carbon dioxide, CFCs and other gases in its atmosphere act like the glass of a greenhouse. Short-wave heat rays from the sun pass through, but when the heat is re-radiated by the earth as long-wave radiation, the gases trap it. Significant global warming has begun: four years in the 1980s were the warmest since reliable records began.

From 1990 all new cars in the UK must be able to use lead-free petrol. If your car is older, get it converted, and switch to lead-free fuel.

Acid rain A more correct name for this would be acid deposit or acid fallout, because the damage is done by pollutants in dry as well as wet form. Sulphur dioxide, nitrogen oxides and ozone are the main acid deposit gases. Sulphuric acid and nitric acid are chief among the wet deposits, which are formed when the pollutants are dissolved in rainwater. The burning of coal and oil in industry, and especially fumes from power stations and refineries, manufacturing (especially of chemicals), and vehicle exhausts are major sources of the pollution. Domestic users of fuels also play a part.

The pollutants may be carried hundreds of miles from their source by air currents before they are deposited. For example, Norway and Sweden receive some 60 per cent of their acid rain from abroad, mostly from Britain. Apart from the direct harm acid deposits do to health by causing respiratory diseases, they also alter the ecological balance of an area. They cause leaf loss and the eventual death of trees, increased acidity of soils, lakes and rivers, and the release of aluminium in soils where the underlying rock is granite. The aluminium runs into the rivers where it poisons

fish, with a consequent increase in life-forms the fish would have eaten and a decrease in creatures that feed on fish.

What to do Individuals can reduce pollution by cutting their own consumption of coal and oil, and especially of petrol in cars. There is not much they can do about industrial pollution except to ask a local environmental officer to check the level of air pollution coming from factories in the area, and to monitor the acidity of rain and water in lakes and rivers. Environmental groups such as Greenpeace, 30-31 Islington Green, London N1 8XE, and Friends of the Earth, 26-28 Underwood Street, London N1 7JQ, publish informative leaflets on the subject.

Carbon monoxide When carbon fuels are burnt in an inadequate supply of oxygen, carbon monoxide results. The colourless, odourless gas combines more readily with the haemoglobin in blood than oxygen does, and can cause suffocation. Most appliances produce some carbon monoxide, but motor vehicles are major producers.

What to do Cars that can use lead-free petrol are suitable for catalytic converters, which convert the carbon monoxide, nitrogen oxides and hydrocarbons in the exhaust to less harmful carbon dioxide, water and nitrogen.

CFCs Chlorofluorocarbons (CFCs) are nonflammable, virtually nontoxic gases widely released into the atmosphere. They are used mainly as propellants in aerosols, as coolants used in refrigerators and air-conditioning plant, in the manufacture of plastic foam packaging, and as solvents in the electronics industry. They are very stable, and some last for more than 100 years. However, when they break down in the strong sunlight of the upper atmosphere they release chlorine, which persistently destroys ozone.

Although ozone is one of the acid deposit gases in the lower atmosphere, it is essential in the upper atmosphere, where it forms a layer that shields us from too much ultraviolet light (see p. 174 under *Radiation*). The ozone layer has already been damaged by CFCs. If the damage continues, cases of skin cancer and of CATARACTS will increase in number and agriculture may be harmed.

About 60 countries have signed the Montreal Protocol, under which they have agreed to phase out use of CFCs by the end of the century. What is not certain, however, is whether the countries will be able to carry out their undertaking, or whether cutback by just these countries will be enough to prevent further damage to the ozone layer.

What to do Buy 'ozone-friendly' products instead of CFC aerosols and products in plastic foam packs. CFC-free refrigerators are becoming available.

Global warming As well as damaging the ozone layer, CFCs are among the gases that are causing the 'greenhouse effect' by trapping heat in the atmosphere.

Carbon dioxide is another 'greenhouse gas'. The burning of wood and fossil fuels such as coal, natural gas and petroleum products – including oil, paraffin and petrol – produces carbon dioxide, and its output is increasing worldwide. Vehicle exhausts are a major source in the West.

At the same time, large-scale destruction of tropical forests in land-clearance schemes in the Amazon and other areas is worsening the situation. Trees and other green plants use up carbon dioxide and release oxygen as they manufacture their food, but now the earth's natural capacity to process carbon dioxide cannot keep pace with the increased emission.

The average global temperature has been rising very gradually over the last century. It is not clear how far this is part of natural fluctuation or how far it is due to the greenhouse effect. Rising sea levels from the expansion of water as it warms and from the melting of land ice are threatening to flood low-lying areas and submerge some islands. Many large cities and much prime farming land could be affected.

The food supply may be severely affected. A warmer climate may produce droughts in some areas, more rain in others. The distribution of plants and crops would change, and fish and animal populations would be different.

What to do Individuals can use less of the energy sources and goods that produce carbon dioxide in their generation, manufacture or use. Switch off lights and electrical appliances when they are not necessary; draught-proof and insulate the home – you may be eligible for a local authority grant towards the cost of having the work done; make garden rubbish into compost instead of burning it; cut out unnecessary driving and use a car with low fuel consumption; and stop using CFC aerosols.

Water pollution

Rivers, lakes, reservoirs, domestic water Some of the main pollutants are: the run-off from nitrate fertilisers, pesticides, silage and slurry used in agriculture; phosphates from detergent washing powders; and industrial wastes such as dioxin, which is a by-product from manufacturing chemicals and from bleaching paper products. Nitrates convert to other substances in the body, where they reduce the amount of oxygen in the blood. Bottle-fed babies are at risk, even if the water used to make up their feeds is boiled before use. Some scientists believe they can also cause cancer of the oesophagus and stomach, but the evidence on this is not conclusive. Even small quantities of dioxin can result in SKIN DISORDERS such as chloracne, miscarriages, cancer and birth deformities; larger quantities can kill.

Chlorine is added to water to rid it of bacteria, but although the water may smell and sometimes taste of chlorine, the amount permitted is not usually a health hazard. However, some people may be allergic to it.

Aluminium is added in some areas to make the water clear, and fluoride in some areas to help prevent tooth decay (see FLUORIDATION). The amounts permitted are minute – but there is controversy about how much is harmful. Some studies have suggested that ALZHEIMER'S DISEASE could be linked to aluminium. Mottling of teeth can be caused by large doses of fluoride, and in laboratory animals huge doses have caused genetic defects and cancer, though there is no conclusive proof of such damage to humans. Fluoride occurs naturally in the water in some areas.

For the problem of lead in domestic water, see p. 175 under *Hazards in the home*.

What to do An efficient, properly maintained water filter can remove many chemicals from drinking water. Always take drinking water direct from a cold tap on the mains, not from a storage tank, and run the tap for a few moments first – hot water and water that has been standing in the pipes tend to contain more dissolved impurities.

To make sure you do not contribute to pollution you can avoid garden fertilisers and household goods that produce toxic wastes. Many supermarkets now sell unbleached paper towels, disposable nappies, toilet paper and other items, as well as phosphate-free, biodegradable washing powders and liquids. You can also make your own non-polluting cleaners – see box on p. 178.

Sea water The sea has a limited capacity to break down waste, and much of Britain's shoreline is badly polluted. Industrial and agricultural waste, oil spills and the radioactive by-products of nuclear power stations are all problems. But by far the greatest threat to health is the discharge of raw or only partially treated sewage into the sea, leading to dangerously high levels of bacteria, algae and viruses, and contaminating shellfish. Stomach upsets are the most common dangers, but swallowing or bathing in badly polluted water, or eating contaminated shellfish, can cause stomach upsets, ear and eye infections or hepatitis.

What to do Avoid swimming in the sea if you have doubts about the quality of the water. Look for sewage outlet pipes, and check with the tourist board before bathing.

Radiation

Nuclear radiation We are all exposed to nuclear radiation from many sources, some natural, some man-made. Particles from space, rocks (see *Radon* under *Hazards in the home*, p. 176), soil, plants and other natural sources are responsible for 87 per cent of the radiation, and man-made items for only 13 per cent. Of the man-made radiation, 11.5 per cent comes from medical sources such as X-rays, and the rest from miscellaneous sources, including nuclear weapons tests, mining and processing radioactive matter, power-station discharges, high-altitude air travel (where there is less protection given by the atmosphere), and some household items such as luminous clock and watch dials and smoke detectors.

The maximum permitted dose of nuclear radiation per person per year in the UK is 500 microsieverts, but it is planned to reduce this to 100 microsieverts. (The permitted maximum dose for workers in the nuclear industry is 5000 microsieverts a year.) It is estimated that the Chernobyl nuclear power-station disaster in the Ukraine in the USSR in 1986 will give UK residents 50 microsieverts during their lifetime – with most of it already received during the year following the accident. A chest X-ray gives a dose of approximately 20 microsieverts.

High doses of nuclear radiation can kill. Lower doses can cause NAUSEA AND VOMITING, DIARRHOEA, bleeding, hair loss and eventual death. Radiation can also cause damage to human cells which makes them reproduce abnormally. This can give rise to cancer and genetic defects that can affect future generations. The long-term effects of continual exposure to small amounts of nuclear radiation are not yet fully understood, but some researchers believe that it can cause allergies, asthma, high BLOOD PRESSURE and muscular or bone defects.

<u>What to do</u> If you are worried about nuclear processing or the storage or transport of nuclear waste in your area, contact an environmental health officer through the local council, or get in touch with an environmental group such as Friends of the Earth, who may be able to help.

Before having an X-ray, ask your doctor or dentist if it is essential, and make sure a protective bib or sheet shields the rest of your body. If you fit a smoke detector in your home, make sure it is well out of reach of children. Avoid luminous-dial clocks and watches.

An extra precaution is to make sure you are getting enough iodine (see MINERALS) – it helps to eliminate any radioactive matter in the body.

Ultraviolet light Too much ultraviolet light, whether from natural sunlight or from a sunlamp, can cause eye disorders such as cataracts. It can also cause skin cancer; the greatest danger is to people with a fair complexion whose skin does not produce a protective tan but burns and freckles.

<u>What to do</u> Instead of baring yourself to strong sun, protect yourself with a broad-brimmed hat, a loose shirt, and trousers or a skirt. Use an effective sun-blocking cream on parts that are exposed to the sun for any length of time (see SUNBURN). Report to your doctor immediately any changes in moles or dark patches of skin, or skin sores that do not heal. They are easily treated in their early stages.

Electromagnetic fields A multitude of high and low-frequency electromagnetic waves emanate from man-made equipment – high-voltage cables, radar systems, microwave communications systems, domestic cables and appliances, computer and word processor terminals (see *VDUs* under *Hazards at work*, p. 179). We are only beginning to recognise the effects that long-term exposure to these fields may have. The evidence is growing, but not conclusive, that they may cause headaches, nausea, impaired concentration, STRESS, cataracts, disturbances of the nervous system, and even cancer and genetic damage.

<u>What to do</u> It is difficult to avoid the effects of electromagnetic fields set up by power cables. However, you can reduce the fields in your home by remembering always to turn off unnecessary lights and appliances.

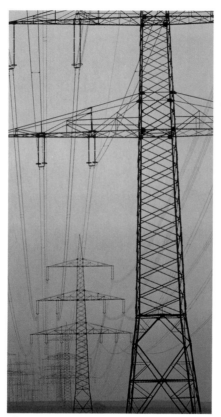

There is increasing evidence that the invisible electromagnetic fields around electrical appliances and power lines can be hazardous. The fields of 240V domestic power cables extend only a few inches. However, those around high-power lines such as those of the National Grid, which operate at 400,000V, can extend hundreds of yards. The extremely low-frequency electromagnetic radiation from such lines has been linked with depression, insomnia, headaches and cancers.
Our exposure to electromagnetic radiation from all sources – from the extremely low-frequency rays emitted by power lines and VDUs, through radio, microwaves, infrared (heat), light and ultraviolet rays to ultra high-frequency, ionising X-rays and gamma rays – has increased nearly 10,000 times in the last 50 years. Nowhere is unaffected.

When watching television, sit at least 6ft (2m) away from the screen, where the field is weaker. Some manufacturers are now producing computers with shielded parts, to reduce the electrical fields set up.

Hazards in the home

Lead in water Chlorine, aluminium and fluoride may be present in drinking water (see p. 174 under *Water pollution*), but the greatest hazard is lead. This occurs in old properties which have lead pipes, and in some newer properties where copper pipes have lead soldering. The lead may be in the pipe from the local water main to the house.

The mains water, especially soft water, picks up lead from the pipes, and it accumulates in the body through drinking and cooking food in it.

<u>What to do</u> Ask your water company to test your tapwater for lead content. You may be eligible for a grant towards the cost of replacing pipes, should that be necessary. If you cannot afford to replace them at once, let the tap run for a time whenever you draw water, so that you do not use water that has been standing in the pipes. A proprietary filter jug with the filter changed frequently will remove lead.

Carbon monoxide See p. 172 under *Air pollution* for the dangers of this gas. Paraffin heaters and gas appliances – including cookers, boilers, water heaters and fires – all produce it, along with small amounts of nitrogen dioxide, formaldehyde and sulphur dioxide, which can aggravate bronchitis, emphysema, asthma and ANGINA.

<u>What to do</u> Check that all appliances are properly adjusted – their flames should burn blue with no orange showing. If a gas appliance is not burning efficiently and you cannot adjust it, your local gas board will help. Use all appliances only in well-ventilated rooms; if doors and windows are sealed for insulation, make sure there is an efficient ventilator. Have the flue cleaned regularly. Do not use a paraffin heater constantly. Have all appliances serviced regularly by professionals.

Fumes from open fires Carbon monoxide is also among the gases given off by burning wood and coal, and wood smoke also contains cancer-causing fumes. Burning plastic and rubber, on a garden fire for example, may give off the deadly gas dioxin.

The plastic foam filling commonly used for furniture and mattresses will give off deadly cyanide fumes if it catches fire. Latex is less hazardous, and a fire-retardant plastic foam has been developed in the last few years, but furniture already in the home or on sale secondhand may contain the more dangerous type.

<u>What to do</u> If you use an open fire in your home, make sure the chimney is swept regularly and is not letting smoke drift back into the room. Closed stoves are safer. Ensure that the room is well ventilated.

If you buy new foam-filled furniture look for the fire-safety symbol on it (see BEDS AND BEDDING). Older furniture would be safer with a fire-retardant fabric put over it.

Install smoke detectors in your home. They will give occupants the crucial time to get away from dangerous fumes, which kill more people – and kill them sooner – than are killed by flames.

Radon This colourless, odourless, radioactive gas comes out of the ground, where it is produced by the decay of the element radium in rocks. Although radon is present in minute quantities everywhere, it comes mostly from granite rocks, which contain small amounts of radium. Radon can seep into homes through floors and walls, remaining trapped there until there is a dangerous build-up. It accumulates in people's lungs, and can cause RESPIRATORY DISORDERS and lung cancer.

About 75,000 homes in Britain are in the higher-risk granite areas, but even neighbouring houses can build up widely differing amounts. Cornwall, Devon, Somerset, parts of Derbyshire, Northamptonshire and Grampian are the areas most severely affected. The concentration of gas is measured in becquerels per cubic metre. A count of more than 200 calls for the home to be treated.

<u>What to do</u> Houses in high-radon areas should have floors, walls, pipe inlets and mains inlets well sealed. Ground-floor and under-floor ventilation should be efficient; sumps and fans are sometimes installed.

For advice on whether you are at risk, contact the Radon Survey, National Radiological Protection Board, Chilton, Didcot, Oxon OX11 0RQ, who can test your house if necessary; or write to the Department of the Environment, 2 Marsham Street, London SW1P 3EB, for their free booklet, *The householder's guide to radon*.

Alternatively, people living in high-risk areas can ask for advice from their local council's environmental health officer on how to stop the gas seeping into the home.

Formaldehyde Pressed timbers and plastic goods contain this chemical in the adhesives used to make them, and it is also used in some types of plastic foam, including some cavity-wall insulation. It gives off a vapour that can irritate the eyes, throat and skin, cause headaches and fatigue, and is a suspected cause of cancer.

<u>What to do</u> Use as many solid and natural materials as you can to avoid an accumulation that causes discomfort. Make sure there is adequate ventilation in rooms where you detect the sharp smell of the vapour.

Air imbalance The natural balance of positive and negative electrically charged particles (ions) in the air is disturbed by electrical fields from television sets and other

Efficient heating
A combination of low background central heating and extra heat from gas or electric fires in rooms when needed, keeps air circulating through the house – balancing warmth and ventilation.

Good air flow
Fresh air is necessary for good ventilation, even in a heated house. To conserve heat, open windows in parts of the house which are unheated or not in use at the time; the air will be drawn through the house on currents created by heat sources in other rooms without cooling them down too much.

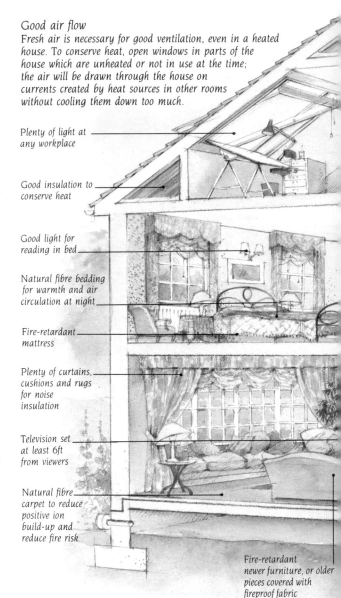

Plenty of light at any workplace

Good insulation to conserve heat

Good light for reading in bed

Natural fibre bedding for warmth and air circulation at night

Fire-retardant mattress

Plenty of curtains, cushions and rugs for noise insulation

Television set at least 6ft from viewers

Natural fibre carpet to reduce positive ion build-up and reduce fire risk

Fire-retardant newer furniture, or older pieces covered with fireproof fabric

Radon-proof flooring
Protection from naturally occurring radon gas is important in all high-risk areas. For a suspended floor – such as that shown beneath the living room, entrance hall and dining room – seal all cracks around floor edges and where pipes or vents emerge. Cover the floor with a layer of heavy-duty sealed polythene, or other radon-proof material, and place protective boards over it. It is a good idea to install an extractor fan and ventilator outlet beneath the floor to disperse any radon build-up underneath the house.

Cutting down risks in the home

You cannot get rid of every health risk in the environment but, with a little care, you can make your home a much safer place – and one that produces less waste, conserves energy and protects the environment. Even steps as small as keeping houseplants, making better use of natural light and recycling household waste can make an important contribution. Other, more extensive alterations such as improved heating and ventilation systems can be incorporated as gradual home improvements.

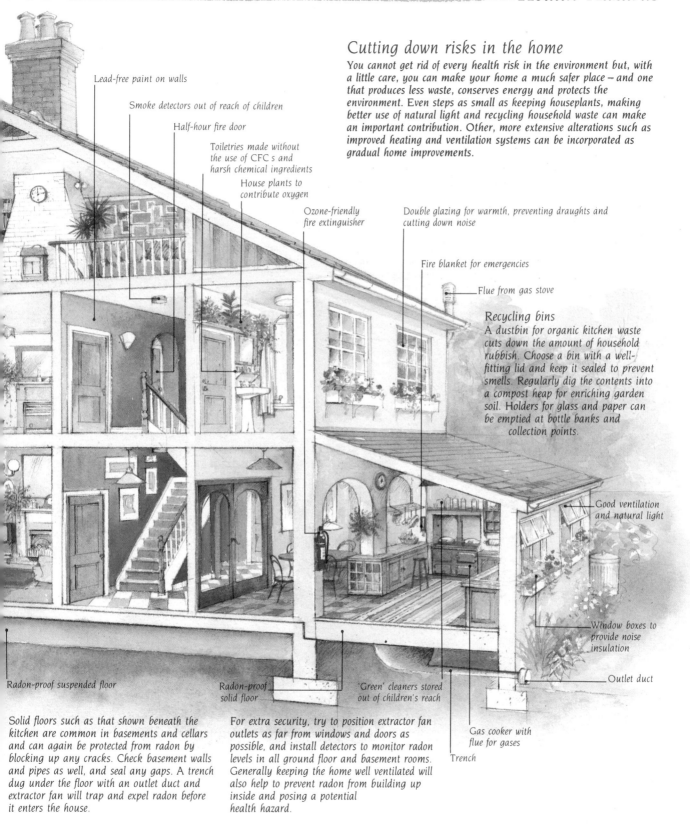

Lead-free paint on walls

Smoke detectors out of reach of children

Half-hour fire door

Toiletries made without the use of CFCs and harsh chemical ingredients

House plants to contribute oxygen

Ozone-friendly fire extinguisher

Double glazing for warmth, preventing draughts and cutting down noise

Fire blanket for emergencies

Flue from gas stove

Recycling bins

A dustbin for organic kitchen waste cuts down the amount of household rubbish. Choose a bin with a well-fitting lid and keep it sealed to prevent smells. Regularly dig the contents into a compost heap for enriching garden soil. Holders for glass and paper can be emptied at bottle banks and collection points.

Good ventilation and natural light

Window boxes to provide noise insulation

Outlet duct

Radon-proof suspended floor

Radon-proof solid floor

'Green' cleaners stored out of children's reach

Gas cooker with flue for gases

Trench

Solid floors such as that shown beneath the kitchen are common in basements and cellars and can again be protected from radon by blocking up any cracks. Check basement walls and pipes as well, and seal any gaps. A trench dug under the floor with an outlet duct and extractor fan will trap and expel radon before it enters the house.

For extra security, try to position extractor fan outlets as far from windows and doors as possible, and install detectors to monitor radon levels in all ground floor and basement rooms. Generally keeping the home well ventilated will also help to prevent radon from building up inside and posing a potential health hazard.

electronic appliances, by static from synthetic fabrics and by polluted or dry air. The negative ions are reduced from their normal fresh-air proportion of four parts for every five parts of positive ions. A similar reduction occurs before thunderstorms. A drop in negative ions may cause TENSION, irritability, MIGRAINE and HAY FEVER.

What to do Choose natural fibres such as wool and cotton rather than synthetics for clothes, home furnishings, carpets and curtains. Turn off television sets, computers and other electronic equipment when not in use. Good ventilation is another way of preventing positive ions from building up, as is a negative ionising machine (see IONISATION).

Cleaners Most commercial cleaners such as detergent washing powders, bleaches, scouring powders, window cleaners, polishes and air fresheners can cause health problems, including skin and eye irritations, and allergies. Many cleaners are poisonous if swallowed, and some give off fumes that can irritate the nose and throat – chlorine bleach and ammonia-based products are particularly dangerous.

What to do Use cleaners sparingly, following the instructions and ensuring the room is well ventilated. Wear gloves if you are going to touch them. Use hydrogen peroxide bleach rather than chlorine. Do not mix different products, especially chlorine and ammonia-based ones. For example, do not put bleach in the sink if you have been using scouring powder; the combination gives off chloramine vapour.

If sprays such as window cleaners irritate your eyes, nose or throat, look for alternative products that are used as solids or liquids. 'Green' cleaners are now available in most supermarkets, and cause fewer health problems, as well as less pollution. Alternatively, you can make your own simple cleaners by following the instructions in the box.

Note Store all household cleaners upright and out of reach of children.

Toiletries Cosmetics, perfumes, soaps and other toiletries can cause allergies, skin irritations and rashes in sensitive people; and if hairspray is used regularly it can collect in the lungs, causing breathing trouble. Frequent use of some hair dyes that contact the skin is suspected of causing cancer.

What to do Read the labels before you buy toiletries and choose those made from plant extracts rather than mineral oils. The plant extracts are less likely to have ill effects, especially if they are also free of added colours and scents. Many toiletries can be simply and cheaply made at home

Greener cleaners

Some simple ingredients can be used to make safe and inexpensive household cleaners. Soap and water is the most useful and can replace many special-purpose cleaners. Stubborn dirt will often yield to soaking in soapy water – or you can wipe it at intervals over dirty surfaces until the dirt softens.

Washing-up liquid Put small slivers of hand soap in a warmed jam-jar, cover with boiling water and let them dissolve. Add 1-2 tablespoons of washing soda in hard-water areas. Use the mixture for washing up. Add a tablespoon of washing soda or vinegar to the washing-up water for greasy dishes.

Washing powder Use equal quantities of soap flakes and washing soda. A few tablespoons of washing soda also makes commercial biodegradable washing powders work better.

Bleach Borax is a good bleach and disinfectant, although not as strong as a chlorine bleach. Keep borax out of children's reach.

Scouring powder Mix salt and sodium bicarbonate in equal quantities and rub on with a moist cloth.

Mirrors and tiles Use equal quantities of white vinegar and water. Mix and use for wiping off splash marks.

Fabric softener Combine one part bicarbonate of soda, one part white vinegar and two parts water. Use as you would a commercial softener.

Air freshener Good ventilation is best. For a pleasing scent use fresh flowers, herbs, potpourri or essential oils (see AROMATHERAPY).

(see NATURAL AIDS TO BEAUTY). Use hair dyes that give paint-on highlights or treat selected areas only.

Insecticides Household insecticides such as fly killers, mothballs and house plant sprays are poisonous if swallowed or inhaled. Many contain chlorine or hydrocarbons – naphthalene in mothballs is a hydrocarbon. Even when correctly used, they can cause rashes, allergies, breathing problems, and eye, nose and throat irritations.

What to do Do not attract insects. Cover food, empty rubbish bins often and do not let washing up accumulate. See box for natural insect repellents.

You can often rid house plants – and garden plants – of pests by washing them with soapy water, taking care to treat both sides of the leaves. Or treat them with derris powder or permethrin.

DIY products Many glues, paints, paint strippers, wood preservatives, varnishes, fillers and sealants, and other decorating and hobby products give off poisonous vapours until completely dry. If inhaled, these can cause sickness, dizziness, respiratory disorders and allergies. Flexible sealants which are not meant to harden completely continue to give off minute amounts of vapour. Glue or solvent sniffing can also become a dangerous ADDICTION.

Dust from timber, asbestos and cement sheets, bricks, and glass-fibre insulation material can irritate the lungs and cause chest disorders. Asbestos dust can also cause cancer.

What to do Follow the instructions carefully when using DIY products and wear gloves, safety goggles and a face mask whenever necessary. Do all possible jobs outside and make sure any indoor work area is well ventilated. Use glues that dry hard whenever possible. Do not work on any asbestos products or installations – it is a job for professionals only.

Food

Agricultural methods Unless they are labelled as organically grown, nearly all fruit and vegetables have been sprayed with chemicals, and grown with artificial fertilisers. Some of these substances are absorbed, and traces are found in most foods. Animals reared for meat are often given drugs such as antibiotics and artificial hormones to prevent disease and increase their weight. Some of these accumulate in the animal's body, along with chemicals that it absorbs by eating sprayed crops.

Intensive rearing methods often confine animals in

unhygienic spaces and feed them the ground-up remains of other animals – sometimes of their own species – not thoroughly sterilised and even containing animal droppings. In these conditions salmonella, listeria and bovine spongiform encephalopathy (BSE) have passed down the generations and from one species to another. Salmonella and listeria cause food poisoning; listeria also damages unborn babies. The effects of BSE are not yet known; there is no evidence so far that it is a hazard to humans, but some scientists fear that it might affect the human brain.

Many doctors and alternative therapists believe that allergies are often a reaction to small quantities of impurities and chemicals in food. Other long-term effects of consuming these substances are not known, nor is it known how they may interact in the body with other chemical FOOD ADDITIVES.

The Soil Association mark on fruit, vegetables, meat and dairy products in supermarkets and food stores is a guarantee of high standards of organic production, processing and distribution. To be able to use the symbol farmers have to adhere to rigorous standards, including farming without artificial fertilisers and sprays for at least two years, and keeping to strict guidelines for the rearing of animals. Regional guides to outlets of approved produce are available for £2.50 each from the Soil Association, 86 Colston Street, Bristol BS1 5BB.

What to do The best solution is to buy or grow as much organic produce as you can. It will also help to buy fruit and vegetables that are in season, since these need less spraying. Wash and peel non-organic produce, and trim fat from meat, since this is where most impurities accumulate.

Unless you have an organic butcher, avoid liver and kidneys, as high concentrations of drugs and other chemicals can build up in these organs. Fish, game and free-range poultry are said to be safer than other types of meat.

Packaging, cooking and storage Many soft plastics, especially some types of thin, transparent film, contain minute traces of cancer-causing substances which may contaminate food. Traces of dioxin have been found in some cartons of fruit juice and milk.

Alternative ways to deal with insects

Some safe and simple insecticides can be made at home.

Ants Although they do not spread diseases, ants make for any food or food debris. To deter them, block up visible holes, then sprinkle dried mint, chilli powder and borax where they are coming in. Keep out of children's reach.

Cockroaches Food can be contaminated by the droppings of cockroaches. To deter them, put down a mixture of cocoa powder, borax and flour; icing sugar and sodium bicarbonate; or plaster of Paris and flour. Keep out of children's reach.

Flies Bacteria are spread by flies. If you do not want to use a fly swatter or sticky fly paper, make bunches of bay, mint, pennyroyal or eucalyptus leaves, or crush them and sew into cheesecloth bags with some cloves and a few drops of citrus or eucalyptus oil. Hang them in windows or doorways to deter flies.

Moths The destruction that moths cause to fabrics is not a health hazard but mothballs are. Put sachets of lavender, camphor, rosemary, peppercorns, conkers or cedar chips in drawers and wardrobes with woollen clothes. Before packing clothes away, wash and air well, then tumble in a drier or iron with a steam iron to kill moth eggs.

Weevils Stores of starchy foodstuffs are where weevils live and breed. Place a bay leaf in each container of rice, lentils or other dry goods – including flour, if the slight flavour of bay is acceptable.

What to do At home, store or pack foods in lidded glass, china, glazed earthenware or stainless-steel containers. Wrap food for taking out as packed lunches or picnics in Cellophane or kitchen foil. Never use cling wrapping or plastic containers in a microwave oven. Avoid paper containers of milk and fruit juices. Buy your milk in bottles, and squeeze fresh fruit juice at home whenever possible.

Irradiation Treating food with radiation kills bacteria that would normally cause it to go bad after a certain time. Irradiated foods can be kept for longer 'on the shelf', so producers and manufacturers save on the costs of spoilage.

If, after much controversy, irradiated foods are allowed in the UK, they will be clearly labelled as irradiated. Those who prepare foods – restaurants, for example – must make it clear when irradiated produce has been used. People who do not want to eat irradiated food fear that the rules will be flouted. There is at present no way of telling for certain which foods have been treated, since the appearance and texture are not altered. There are also fears about imports of unmarked irradiated foods from countries where such treatment is allowed.

Other fears are that irradiation is used to disguise poor quality or soiled produce by keeping it looking good. Although all bacteria are destroyed, some of them leave dangerous substances behind which can still cause FOOD POISONING.

What to do To avoid irradiated food, shop in stores that have guaranteed not to sell it; or buy from small, local suppliers whose procedures you can question; or buy organic foods.

Hazards at work

Offices and factories Various aspects of the indoor environment can affect the comfort and health of workers in offices and factories, causing the so-called 'sick building syndrome' in serious cases. Possible causes include insulating materials, cigarette smoke, poor ventilation, artificial lighting, temperatures that are either too high or too low, excessive dryness of the atmosphere, pollen, viruses, bacteria, moulds and other fungi, and chemical fumes from correcting fluids, glues, paints, industrial processes and even some photocopiers.

The most common symptoms caused are dizziness, headaches, EYESTRAIN, skin irritations, allergies, breathing problems, COLDS, stress and TIREDNESS. In and near air-conditioned buildings a type of PNEUMONIA known as legionnaires' disease can be spread if there is inadequate cleaning of the cooling system and its water.

What to do Employers have a statutory responsibility to provide a safe place of work, to control air pollution and noise, and to keep machinery and work practices safe. There are also strict rules about the amount of air space each individual worker should have. The Health and Safety Executive publishes useful leaflets about the law on workplaces, which you can obtain from HMSO, 49 High Holborn, London WC1V 6HB.. They include *Advice to employers, Advice to the self-employed* and *Advice to employees*. See under *Noise*, p. 181, for details of permitted noise levels.

Tell your employer, personnel officer or head of department about anything you may feel is a health risk. If nothing is done about the problem, contact your local environmental health department or the nearest office of the Health and Safety Executive.

Something you may be able to control is your own lighting. To reduce eyestrain, work in natural or non-fluorescent light as much as possible, or if fluorescent lighting is unavoidable do not use the ordinary tubes, whose flickering can cause headache, eyestrain and disturbance of vision. Instead, use a full-spectrum tube, in which the flickering is too rapid to be perceptible.

The Department of Health's Froggatt Report recorded evidence that passive smoking carries risks similar to SMOKING itself. Some of the smoke – if not all of it – that smokers exhale has not been 'filtered' by their lungs, and still contains tar and other cancer-causing substances.

If cigarette smoke is a problem, ask your employer to designate nonsmoking zones in the office. If separate zones are not possible, try to sit next to a window or use a desk fan to clear your immediate area of smoke.

VDUs The electromagnetic radiation from the visual display units (VDUs) of computers and word processors is still being studied, but it is known that pregnant women who work mainly at VDUs are more likely than others to miscarry. The World Health Organisation considers VDUs a health hazard, and the European Community is drawing up regulations for their use. The length of time spent at them is likely to be limited, and safe distances from terminals at which others can work safely will be designated.

Eyestrain, BACK PAIN and tendon strain in the arms and hands can also be caused by constant work at VDUs.

What to do Make sure that terminals near you emit only low-level electromagnetic radiation and that you are not within a yard of other people's terminals. Make sure the position and height of your chair and of the terminal are

adjusted for you. Glare on a VDU screen can be reduced by using special shielded lights, attaching a clip-on protective filter, and placing the screen at right angles to a window – never facing it. Have a break of at least ten minutes in every hour you spend at the VDU.

Dangerous substances People who work with acids and other irritating chemicals can develop disorders ranging from ECZEMA to skin cancer. Asthma, allergies, lung cancer and other lung complaints can all be caused by breathing in chemical fumes or dust containing particles of asbestos, coal, sand or brick.

Leukaemia and other cancers can result from exposure to some products refined from petroleum (crude oil), dyes, X-rays, radioactive materials, and chemicals used in paints, glues and plastics. In other industries, heavy metals such as lead, cadmium and mercury are a danger. They accumulate in the body, causing damage to the brain and nervous system.

What to do The safest course is obviously to avoid or reduce contact with potentially harmful substances, if that

A good working environment: it is well lit by natural light; the plant absorbs carbon dioxide from the air; the worker's desk and chair are the right height for good posture, and he is outside the electromagnetic field of his VDU.

is possible. Follow the instructions for use issued with such substances, and make sure your employer observes the regulations and approved codes of practice for work systems and equipment. These are laid down in the Health and Safety at Work Act. Wear protective clothing, including masks and gloves, where necessary to reduce the risks.

People who work in or around substances likely to cause a risk to health should get regular medical checks, which should include blood tests. If you work with or near radioactive materials, make sure your personal dose recorder is checked frequently to ensure you are not receiving more than the permitted radiation. See p. 174 under *Radiation* for permitted levels.

Noise

The environment is fast becoming noisier. People in cities suffer the effects of traffic, trains, aircraft and sirens; while motorways and farm machinery make even the countryside far from peaceful. Noise level is measured in decibels and the noise perceived by listeners is adjusted and recorded as dB(A). The noise of ordinary conversation heard one stride away is 60dB(A). Street traffic produces about 70dB(A)

The Health and Safety Executive's official safety level in Britain is 90dB(A). Levels above that will cause damage, be it ringing in the ears, sound distortion or loss of hearing. The length of exposure to the noise plays a part in the severity and duration of damage. Permanent damage to hearing can result from four hours at 93dB(A), or from just a few seconds at 110dB(A).

The decibel scale does not rise evenly but multiplies: 90dB(A) is ten times louder than 80, and 100dB(A) is 100 times louder than 80. Caps in a toy pistol (up to 170), a screaming baby (up to 117), a pop concert (110), a food blender (up to 100) are among the many noises above the danger limit. Many young people have experienced temporary deafness after an evening at a disco, and workers in heavy industry or construction suffer some permanent loss. Power tools used at home carry the same dangers but they usually operate for short periods.

Apart from the dangers to hearing, loud noises cause instinctive reactions which tense the muscles and increase the heart and breathing rate. If they are persistent or occur often, the results can be tiredness, stress, high blood pressure, headaches, ULCERS, SLEEP DISORDERS and even HEART DISORDERS.

What to do Reduce noise at home by improving the insulation of floors, walls and lofts. Fit solid doors and double glazing; plant hedges and even trees, if possible, to block off noisy roads. Carpets, curtains, rugs and cushions also absorb sound. Wear earmuffs at home when you use noisy tools or machines, and at work if your job or workplace has dangerous noise levels.

Noise is measured in decibels (dB), but the dB(A) scale takes into account the impact on our ears. The UK official safety level is 90dB(A), but anything over 80db(A), especially if prolonged, can damage hearing. The decibel scale rises by multiples – 40dB(A) is 10 times louder than 30dB(A), and 50dB(A) is 100 times louder.

Jet engine at 100ft (30m): 135dB(A)

Pop group at 4ft (1.2m): 110dB(A)

Train on steel bridge: 110dB(A)

Thunder 100dB(A)

Inside average factory: 90dB(A)

Telephone bell at 3ft (1m): 80dB(A)

Moving traffic in the street: 68dB(A)

Talking at 3ft (1m): 60dB(A)

Quiet street: 50dB(A)

Whispering at 3ft (1m): 30dB(A)

Rustling leaves: 10dB(A)

Using the healing power of herbs

The medicinal use of herbs is said to be as old as mankind itself. Until the 18th century it was the usual form of medical treatment in the West. Today the World Health Organisation estimates that, worldwide, herbalism is three to four times more commonly practised than conventional medicine. And even conventional doctors rely heavily on plant-based medicines – in Britain about 15 per cent of all GPs' prescriptions are plant-based.

Primitive tribes still use their traditional knowledge of plants and their healing properties, which has been passed on from generation to generation for thousands of years. In the early civilisations, food and medicine were inextricably linked, and many plants were eaten for their health-giving properties. For example, the armies of slave workers who laboured to build the Egyptian pyramids took a daily ration of GARLIC in order to ward off the pestilential fevers and infections that were rife at the time. And by this time, written records of herbs and their beneficial properties – the first 'herbals' – were being produced.

Most of Britain's knowledge and use of herbs can be traced back to the ancient Egyptians, whose priests were also herbal practitioners. A papyrus from the city of Thebes, dating from 1500 BC, lists hundreds of medicinal herbs – including many that are still in use today, such as caraway seed and cinnamon.

As well as the Egyptians, the ancient Greeks and Romans were practitioners of herbal medicine. As their armies conquered the then known world, military doctors took the plants and their uses with them – and also gained new skills as they travelled. For example, the Roman conquerors of Britain brought with them many Mediterranean herbs, including lavender and rosemary.

Two more cultures which have always relied heavily on herbal medicine are the Chinese and the Indians. To this day in China herbs play a vital part in health care, and there are numerous schools of herbal medicine and herbal dispensaries in most hospitals. In India, the use of herbal drugs is part of the all-embracing system of AYURVEDIC MEDICINE.

In Britain from the Dark Ages well into medieval times, herbals were painstakingly hand-copied in the monasteries – each of which had its own physic garden for growing herbs to treat both monks and local people. In rural areas, particularly in the west and Wales, the Druids are believed to have had an oral tradition of herbalism, mixing medicine with mysticism and ritual.

Setting up shop

The advent in the 15th century of the printing press encouraged the compilation and publication of herbals. John Parkinson of London, a herbalist-physician, listed 3000 useful plants in a publication of about 1630. Such herbalists set up their own apothecary shops, and the most renowned of Britain's herbalists in the medieval tradition was Nicholas Culpeper (1616-54). He wrote several books, including his famous herbal, *The English Physician Enlarged* (1649), which have been in print ever since.

By the time Henry Potter established himself as a 'Supplier of Herbs and Dealer in Leeches' in London in 1812, a vast amount of traditional lore on the medicinal use of herbs was available from Britain, Europe and, in addition, the Middle East, Asia and the Americas. The opening up of the world following the advances in navigation had made this

Herbalism flourished in ancient Egypt. Queen Hatshepsut travelled to the Land of Punt around 1490 BC, and this wall painting in her temple at Deir el-Bahari shows her men returning with herbs.

possible. And by this time, too, preparations containing not just one herb, but a combination of several, were in use. Potter's firm continues today, and *Potter's Cyclopaedia of Botanical Drugs and Preparations* is still published.

However, soon after Potter founded his firm, the growth in popularity and power of scientifically inspired conventional medicine sent the profession of herbal medicine into a decline – although as the main element in folk medicine it continued to flourish in the countryside. Then, in 1864, a number of herbalists – including several trained in the USA – founded the National Association (later Institute) of Medical Herbalists, an organisation for training and maintaining standards of practice which remains in existence today.

In its early years – and until well into the present century – the Institute resisted attempts by orthodox medical pressure groups to have herbal medicine banned. Public opinion was with the herbalists, helping them to stay in business. Gradually interest in herbalism increased – especially over the last 20 years – as more and more people questioned the use of synthetic drugs and their prolonged and sometimes alarming side effects.

International research

Increasingly, the apparently safer approach of herbal medicine matched the growing support – in Britain and throughout the world – for ecological matters and natural remedies. Today, herbal medicine is once again widespread and popular. Countless people buy over-the-counter herbal remedies for minor complaints and ailments. Health shops abound and many high street chemists have special herbal and health food sections. In addition, an ever-increasing number of professional herbalists treat patients for most illnesses – often in herbal clinics.

However, while owing a large debt to traditional herbalism over the centuries, herbal medicine in Britain has not stood still. The incorporation of American herbs and practices in the 18th and 19th centuries has been followed by a continuing investigation of various other plants. International scientific research not only confirms the healing powers of herbs, but also enlarges herbalists' knowledge with new ones.

As medical herbalists have become more scientifically minded in their research, so a new word has been coined to describe their work: phytotherapy, from the Greek words *phyton*, meaning 'plant', and *therapeuein*, 'to take care of, to heal'. In Europe, most phytotherapists are conventional doctors who believe in the effectiveness and safety of herbs. Organisations such as The European Scientific Cooperative for Phytotherapy (ESCOP), in the Netherlands, promote the study of plants for healing purposes – and the use of plant-based medicines.

Because herbalists use only natural sources, they consider the pharmaceutical industry's search for 'active ingredients' in plants – which are then extracted or produced synthetically to make medicines – to be misguided. In many cases, they say, the whole plant offers a safer and more effective treatment than isolated ingredients which are artificially bound together.

Herbal therapy

Herbalism claims to treat the patient as an individual, with individual weaknesses and needs, and not as just another medical case history. So its treatment is tailored to specific and varying requirements – and there is no such thing as an 'automatic' repeat prescription.

Who it can help Herbalists state that their medicines may benefit most people suffering from most kinds of illnesses, including long-standing conditions such as ARTHRITIS, MIGRAINE and SKIN DISORDERS. In some cases, where plant medicines alone will not effect a cure, patients may be advised to undergo another therapy, such as CHIROPRACTIC or OSTEOPATHY.

Finding a herbalist A list of qualified herbalists can be obtained by sending a stamped addressed envelope to: The Honorary Secretary, National Institute of Medical Herbalists, 41 Hatherley Road, Winchester, Hants SO22 6RR.

Practitioners have undergone a four-year course at the School of Herbal Medicine, near Hailsham in East Sussex, either as full-time or outside, part-time students. Members of the Institute have the letters MNIMH after their name, and Fellows of the Institute have FNIMH.

Consulting a herbalist At the initial consultation, a herbalist will ask the patient about his medical history, eating habits, how much EXERCISE he takes, if he feels under STRESS – as well as questions about his present state of health. His BLOOD PRESSURE will be taken and he will be given a physical examination. Then he will receive advice about improving his general health. Finally, the herbalist will prescribe a suitable treatment – which may take the form of a herbal tincture, lotion, cream or ointment. Individual prescriptions may be modified or changed after further consultations. An initial consultation usually lasts about an hour, later appointments about half an hour.

As a general rule, herbal medicines work more slowly than some conventional drugs, because they are less concentrated. This is particularly so with long-standing ailments. However, as the herbs begin to enhance the body's natural healing powers, it is claimed that patients often soon feel better in themselves.

In addition to curing or relieving specific illnesses, herbalists aim to restore the patient's overall health and vitality. Herbal medicine has much in common with NATUROPATHY, sharing its concern for the importance of preventing – as well as treating – disease.

An orthodox view

Herbal medicine can be viewed as the precursor of modern pharmacology, and many powerful drugs are indeed derived from herbs. Like drugs, herbs are not always as safe as the practitioners suggest. In addition, the claim to be 'holistic' is somewhat spurious, as a glance through a herbal book will show – like orthodox medicine, herbalists will treat 'just the symptoms'. Nevertheless, there is much wisdom and know-how in the general approach of herbal medicine and there are undoubtedly fewer side effects.

For further information on the use of herbs, see pp. 184-7.

Making the most of herbs

The best way of using herbs as a means of keeping healthy – or of clearing up minor ailments – is in your daily diet. They provide extra minerals and vitamins, as well as giving additional flavour to the food.

Medicinally, one of the most valuable herbs is garlic. It contains a variety of nutrients and is a potent protection against bacterial, fungal and viral infections – particularly those affecting the digestive and respiratory systems.

However, it is not always practicable or pleasant to use herbs in food. For example, many people dislike the taste or smell of garlic. But some of the commoner herbs can be bought from a health shop in tea-bag form – and drunk as a refreshing beverage.

Alternatively, you can make your own drink, putting a heaped teaspoon of the herb in a cup of boiling water. Leave

To make a decoction: Put a dessertspoon of powdered dried herb into a stainless steel or enamel (not aluminium) saucepan. Add about half a pint (300ml) of boiling water. Bring to the boil and simmer for 10-15 minutes. Strain while hot, and drink.

To make a tincture: Put about 4oz (120g) of ground or chopped dried herb into a container. Pour on about a pint (600ml) of 40 per cent alcohol such as gin or vodka, and seal the container. Leave in a warm, dry place for two weeks, shaking well twice a day. Then decant the liquid into a dark wine bottle. Seal, and use when required.

it to steep for two to three minutes and then drink it without milk or sugar, using a little honey to sweeten it if desired.

Although decoctions and infusions (see below) are for home medical use, they should only be used for up to a week. After that a herbalist should be consulted.

Herbal drinks There are four main ways in which herbs can be taken as liquids:

Decoction Suitable for preparations made from roots or bark, so that their soluble contents enter the water. To make a decoction put a heaped tablespoon of powdered dried herb into a stainless steel or enamel – not aluminium – saucepan. Add about a pint (600ml) of boiling water. Bring to the boil and simmer for 10-15 minutes. Strain while the tea is hot, and drink.

Infusion Popular in the home for drinks or gargles. Fresh or dried herbs can be used in loose or tea-bag form. To make an infusion, warm a teapot and put in 1 dessertspoon of herb for each cup required. Pour in a cup of boiling water for each cup of tea; allow to steep for 10-15 minutes.

Tincture Herbalists prescribe more alcohol-based tinctures than any other form of medicine. They are long-lasting, highly concentrated and taken in small doses. They can be made at home with a 40 per cent spirit such as vodka or gin. Put about 4oz (120g) of ground or chopped dried herbs into a container. Pour 1 pint (600ml) of alcohol on the herbs and seal the container. Leave it in a warm, dry place for two weeks, shaking it well twice a day. Then decant the liquid, leaving the residue, into a dark wine bottle. Seal and leave until needed.

Tisane Essentially a milder version of an infusion. It is sold in tea bags and is made with boiling water. It can be drunk straight away, without long steeping.

Herbal dressings Herbs can be used in two ways to dress wounds, bruises, injuries and local infections:

Compress To make a compress, soak a clean cloth, or piece of cotton wool, in a hot herbal decoction or infusion made from various anti-inflammatory herbs, such as marigold and flax seed. Place the cloth on the affected area and maintain the heat by holding a hot-water bottle against it. Helps cuts and bruises to heal more quickly.

Poultice To make a poultice, soothing herbs such as comfrey root and slippery elm bark can be used. With fresh, untreated herbs, apply the leaves directly to the skin. Alternatively, put the leaves on a piece of gauze and place on the skin. With dried herbs, make a paste with hot water and apply accordingly. Maintain heat by holding a hot-water bottle against the poultice. Used to draw out pus, promote healing and reduce inflammation.

Other herbal preparations Herbal products are also sold by chemists and health food shops in a variety of other forms. Some of the best known include:

Creams, ointments Used externally for helping wounds to heal and for relieving skin inflammations. Comfrey and marigold ointments, for example, can be bought in most health shops.

Essential oils For external use only. They have many healing properties, from treating infected wounds (camomile, lavender) to clearing and concentrating the mind (basil, rosemary). See AROMATHERAPY.

Creating your own herb garden

Fresh, tasty herbs are a welcome part of a healthy diet – and planning and growing a herb garden can be a rewarding experience in itself. Most herbs are quite easy to grow, and some, such as garlic and parsley, are often already part of an average vegetable plot. All the common herbs shown here – and more – are available at garden centres.

Most of the commoner herbs need a fairly sunny aspect, and this should be borne in mind when choosing a plot. In general, the soil should be moderately fertile and well-drained. Herbs are best grown organically and should not be overfed. To obtain the maximum aroma and flavour, a light mulch of garden compost is all that is needed.

Herbs can be ornamental. A patch of golden marjoram lies behind a border of box (left), wild strawberry, germander and dropwort. Clockwise behind are purple-leaved sage, sorrel, wormwood, lady's mantle, fennel (top left), purple meadowsweet (top right), fennel.

Most herbs can flourish in pots, as the wild strawberry (left), and bay and parsley here.

A good spot for a herb bed is on the sunny side of a wall or hedge. The one shown here is roughly 7ft (2m) long and 3ft (1m) wide, with the groups of plants about 18in (45cm) apart. (Use several plants of smaller types.) Make sure that tall plants will not shade shorter ones.

Fennel

Comfrey

Lemon balm

Lavender Chives

Borage

Camomile

Marigold

Garlic

Basil

Herbal Medicine

Herbs for your health's sake

You do not have to be an expert gardener to grow health-giving herbs – which can be used for cooking, brewing herbal teas, or making poultices and compresses. The following list includes growing advice and recommended culinary and medicinal uses.

Basil Best treated as a half-hardy annual, often most successfully grown in pots, in greenhouses or on windowsills. Aids the digestion and eases stomach cramps.

Borage Will self-sow easily; simply pull out the excess seedlings. As a tisane it is used against rheumatism and respiratory infections. Its flowers can be eaten in salads.

Camomile Grow from seed. The flowers can be used fresh or dry to make a refreshing tea, which is good for digestive troubles. Apply as a poultice for inflammations.

Chives Buy a plant or grow from seed. Divide it each year or so to promote new growth. It stimulates appetite and helps digestion during convalescence. It is said to be effective against infections and anaemia.

Comfrey (or Knitbone) Unearth the roots each spring or autumn, split them down the middle and dry in a moderate temperature of about 50°C (122°F). Comfrey ointment is used to mend broken bones and tissue. The pounded sticky roots are wrapped around a fracture and, when dry, hold the bone in place.

Fennel Start with a plant, or obtain a seedling. Place at the back of a border or plot. Do not grow near dill, as cross-pollination will occur and seedlings will be hybrids. Both seeds and feathery leaves can be used against excessive wind, as well as indigestion, insomnia, nausea and vomiting.

Garlic Fairly heavy feeder needing plenty of organic matter. Divide a bulb into its cloves and plant in early October or March. Harvest the following summer. Try using your own bulbs to repeat growth. See GARLIC.

Lavender Buy a plant or take cuttings. The flowers contain a very relaxing essential oil. Can be drunk as a tisane, or used as an infusion in the bath. Good for coughs, headaches, wind and rheumatism – and as an antiseptic for cuts.

Lemon balm Very easy to grow from seeds or cuttings. Makes a refreshing tea, good for anxiety and nervous exhaustion, as well as indigestion, headache, nausea and vomiting.

Marigold The old English variety, *Calendula officinalis*, is easily grown from seeds. It should be thinned out to about 9in (23cm) apart. The flower heads are held to be ideal for treating local skin inflammations, as well as minor burns and scalds.

Marjoram Pot marjoram and wild marjoram (oregano) can be grown from seeds, cuttings or divisions of roots. Perennials, they prefer a dry, warm soil. They are good for relieving colds, indigestion and minor respiratory infections.

Mint Fast-spreading, it ideally needs its own border. Prefers moist, fairly rich soil. It greatly aids the digestion, and hot infusions can be helpful at the start of a cold. Black peppermint is used against headaches, stress, constipation, wind, insomnia, and nausea and vomiting.

Nasturtium Easy to raise from seed. Its peppery-tasting leaves are rich in vitamin C. Take for minor respiratory infections. Use in salads. The dried seeds can be ground in a pepper mill and used for seasoning.

Rosemary Needs a light, chalky, lime-rich soil. Some ground-up chalk or a few eggshells should provide enough lime. A useful, space-saving variety is Miss Jessup's Upright. Good as a tisane for headaches, neuralgia, colds, and as an antiseptic gargle.

Sage Purple or red sage makes a useful gargle, or a lotion for wounds. Sage tea is recommended for indigestion, anxiety and depression, and excessive sweating.

Thyme Essential to any herb plot. It takes up little space, growing in pots, tubs or window boxes. It is propagated by cuttings or layered side shoots. A highly antiseptic gargle or expectorant for coughs and catarrh. Lemon thyme makes a pleasant tisane, with similar medicinal effect.

Mint

Comfrey

Lavender

Chives

Marigold

Garlic

Oregano

Fennel

Rosemary

Basil

Lemon balm

Nasturtium

Camomile

Borage

Sage

Thyme

HICCUPS

The longest bout of hiccups on record affected an American, Charles Osborne of Iowa. He started while slaughtering a hog in 1922 and continued for 60 years, hiccupping an estimated 430 million times. Nonetheless, he led a comparatively normal life and died in 1982, aged 88. Fortunately, prolonged bouts are very rare.

Hiccups are repeated sharp inhalations of breath caused by involuntary spasms of the diaphragm – the powerful muscle that separates the chest from the abdomen and which increases the volume of the chest when air is breathed in – accompanied by involuntary closing of the larynx (upper windpipe). They are caused by irritation of the diaphragm, for example by an overfull stomach or inflammation of the membrane around the heart.

If hiccups recur frequently or an attack lasts longer than a day, see your doctor.

What the therapists recommend

Traditional Medicine Traditional and folk remedies are numerous. Here are some: Breathe in deeply and hold your breath while slowly counting to ten, or as long as possible. Gargle for a couple of minutes with hot or cold water. Sip several cups of cold water slowly. Drink a glass of water slowly, from the side of the glass farthest from you. Surprise the sufferer with, for example, a sudden slap on the back or by dropping something cold down the back of the neck – a door key or an ice cube often works.
Herbal Medicine Sipping peppermint or lemon balm tea may reduce the spasms.

An orthodox view

Doctors sometimes recommend inhalation of increased concentrations of carbon dioxide – an easy way is to cover nose and mouth with a paper bag (*never* a plastic one) and breathe in and out into it for a couple of minutes. Or a tranquilliser such as chlorpromazine may be prescribed to control the symptoms.

HIP COMPLAINTS

The head of the femur – the thigh bone – forms the ball of the ball-and-socket hip joint. It can be damaged by Perthe's disease (inflammation and softening of the top of the thigh bone) in children, or by a FRACTURE or

ARTHRITIS in older people. The bone and joint surfaces become deformed so that movement is limited and painful.

Pain in the hip is also commonly caused by a back or knee complaint because of a common nerve supply to these areas.

Physical examination of the hip, sometimes aided by X-rays, helps to diagnose the cause of the pain.

What the therapists recommend
MASSAGE
Self help Massage is considered to be a valuable treatment for post-traumatic and post-operative conditions of the hip joint, in the relief of stress and strain around the joint, and as an aid to improving mobility in the stiffening, ageing joint.

Firm upward effleurage strokes (p. 225) are made over the front, outside and back of the thigh to improve circulation and nourishment, followed by wringing and kneading of the same areas to improve muscle tone.

Lifting, squeezing and wringing over the buttocks should precede deep kneading and frictions over the hip joint. Once the muscles are softened and relaxed, intersperse the massage with passive mobilisation, moving the joint as far as possible both ways, providing the movement is pain-free.

Never force a movement and never massage an inflamed arthritic joint, but be content to persevere with treatment, daily if possible, and with just a little improvement at a time in cases where the joint has been stiff for some years.

OSTEOPATHY
Consultation Pain in the hip is often seen as an early sign of wear and tear or the beginnings of arthritis in the hip joint. An osteopath can give relief by helping to maintain mobility of the joint and improve general muscle tone. Advice would probably be given on weight control and taking regular non-weight-bearing exercises, such as swimming, cycling or rowing.

ACUPUNCTURE
Consultation Hip joint pain is said to respond well to acupuncture. Points along the gall bladder, stomach and large intestine meridians may be treated. MOXIBUSTION may also be used.

An orthodox view

Doctors may prescribe anti-inflammatory painkillers such as ibuprofen and naproxen to relieve symptoms, but these can have side effects – rashes or digestive upsets. If pain is persistent and severe, surgeons replace a damaged joint with a metal artificial one. Hip replacement operations have proved to be extremely successful.

HIVES

Itchy red weals on the skin are the major symptom of hives – also known as urticaria or nettlerash. They can appear anywhere on the body and vary in size from small, pimple-like spots to raised patches several inches across. Sometimes the weals disappear after only a few minutes, but in other cases they can last for days or even weeks, and may move to different parts of the body.

Hives is the result of histamines and other substances being released by the body into the skin. Often the cause is an ALLERGY to certain foods such as strawberries or fish, FOOD ADDITIVES, or drugs such as aspirin and codeine. Sensitivity to cold, house dust, pollen or even sunlight can also trigger an attack, but in many cases there is no identifiable cause.

Hives is not dangerous unless swellings around the mouth or tongue make breathing difficult. See a doctor if this happens, or if itching is intense.

What the therapists recommend

Herbal Medicine A cool infusion (see p. 184) of chickweed or camomile can help to alleviate itching. As well as treating the symptoms, a herbalist may use herbs such as yarrow, golden seal, gentian and camomile to improve the functioning of the liver and digestive system.
Naturopathy Relief may be gained by having cool baths or using a vitamin E cream. A naturopath may also recommend high levels of vitamin C, taken internally: 1g or 2g daily. In the longer term, exclusion diets (see DIETS AND DIETING) are advised to find and eliminate any food causes.
Homoeopathy If the sufferer is restless and full of anxiety, try *Arsen. alb.* If the rash is caused by stinging nettles, give *Urtica urens*. If there is burning and swelling, made worse by warmth, *Apis mel.* is recommended. When a rash burns and itches, there are blisters and the patient is restless, try *Rhus tox.*

An orthodox view

The symptoms are usually treated with anti-histamines such as terfenadine, many of which are available from chemists without prescription. Doctors also try to help patients to pinpoint the cause of their hives. Sometimes this may be obvious, but in other cases careful experiments with diet and exposure to substances to which a patient may be allergic might be necessary.

In rare emergencies, where a swollen mouth, tongue or throat prevents breathing, an adrenaline injection can be lifesaving.

HOMOEOPATHY
Boosting the body's healing powers

By using natural remedies to boost the body's own healing ability, homoeopathy aims to treat the whole person. Illness is seen as a sign of disharmony or inner imbalance, so homoeopaths try to resolve underlying problems rather than simply dealing with particular symptoms.

To do this they use special homoeopathic remedies which are highly diluted forms of natural substances that, in a full-strength dose, would actually produce the symptoms of the illness in a healthy person. This is thought to help, since symptoms are seen as the body's way of fighting illness.

Homoeopaths say that the more closely a remedy imitates a patient's symptoms, the better it promotes healing; and the more dilute the dose, the greater its effect, since the remedies are prepared in a special way that is said to strengthen them with each dilution (see box, p. 191).

Each remedy is carefully tested ('proven') on volunteers who take very dilute mixtures for up to a year, and record all their symptoms in detail. This includes subjective impressions of sleeping and eating habits, moods and relationships, since homoeopaths believe that the body functions as a whole. Once the remedy has been proven it can be prescribed to patients, who usually receive only one high-potency dose. Remedies rarely cause any effects other than the symptoms already present, although occasionally these may worsen at first – known as a 'healing crisis' – but usually this does not last long, and is taken to herald improvement.

Homoeopaths pay most attention to symptoms that have the greatest effect on the patient's overall ability to function – particularly mental or emotional symptoms. Disorders of the heart, for example, are regarded as more important than disorders of the skin.

The severity of symptoms within each bodily system is graded in order of importance, but unusual symptoms have greater significance. So a person's mental and emotional state, general problems such as INSOMNIA, and any additional 'peculiar' symptoms (such as a tingling sensation on the left side of the body only) may receive more attention than a symptom such as a rash, although this may have been the original reason for seeking help.

Who it can help Unlike conventional medicine, homoeopathy stresses the uniqueness of the individual, and holds that the indivi-

dual's make-up determines which diseases he or she is most susceptible to and which symptoms are likely to occur. Homoeopathic remedies must be matched both to the symptoms and to the individual. So the same symptom, a cold for example, may be treated differently if the victim is a jovial, outgoing, overweight person, than in the case of a thin, nervous patient with few friends. Conversely, the same remedy may be used for different symptoms in different people.

Finding a therapist Most British homoeopaths practise privately, but some who are qualified doctors work in the National Health Service. There are five NHS homoeopathic hospitals – in London, Bristol, Tunbridge Wells, Liverpool and Glasgow – and a private homoeopathic clinic in Manchester, each one staffed by medically qualified homoeopaths.

The qualifications held by homoeopaths vary widely. Those who are also doctors have usually taken a postgraduate training course followed by a written examination or thesis to become a Member or Fellow of the Faculty of Homoeopathy, although all doctors in Britain are free to offer any form of treatment they wish, including homoeopathy. To find a practitioner on the Faculty's register, contact them at Royal London Homoeopathic Hospital, Great Ormond Street, London WC1N 3HR.

There are also many homoeopaths who are not medically qualified. At present, anyone is allowed to set up as a homoeopath in Britain – although this may change with EC regulations after 1992 – with the restriction that only medically qualified people may treat certain conditions, such as sexually transmitted diseases (venereal diseases).

A growing number of colleges now offer diplomas and certificates in homoeopathy, but none has yet received legal recognition. Registers of homoeopaths are kept by the Hahnemann Society – contact them at Hahnemann House, 2 Powis Place, Great Ormond Street, London WC1N 3HT – and by the Society of Homoeopaths, 2 Artizan Road, Northampton NN1 4HU.

Consulting a therapist The homoeopath will carefully assess not only your symptoms, but also your manner and appearance; your mood and state of mind; how worried or anxious you are; and your personal circumstances, emotional responses, fears and beliefs. This usually takes an hour or more.

In most cases, homoeopaths give only a single dose of one remedy, and wait to see what effect it has before offering further treatment. Any change is thought to show that the remedy has boosted the body's healing process, and that no other treatment should be necessary. For simple, temporary problems such as a HEADACHE, the remedy should be effective almost at once. Patients

How homoeopathy began

The origins of homoeopathy go back to 1810 when a German physician, Samuel Hahnemann, first proposed a new system of medicine as an alternative to the orthodox practices of the day. These practices included bloodletting and purging, which Hahnemann thought were too harsh and often weakened patients more than did their illnesses. By contrast, the new system was to be based on gentle ways of helping the body to cure itself.

Hahnemann's ideas of how this could be done were inspired by the discovery that a herbal remedy for malaria, cinchona tree bark, actually *produced* symptoms of the disease, such as headache and FEVER, when taken by a healthy person. He concluded that symptoms were the body's way of fighting illness, and that medicines which produced the same symptoms as an illness could help recovery. (It was later discovered that cinchona bark contains quinine, the first drug used against malaria.)

Hahnemann's ideas were in effect a rediscovery of an ancient principle first expressed by the Greek physician Hippocrates in the 5th century BC – 'like cures like'. Hahnemann called the new system homoeopathy (meaning 'like disease'), in contrast to conventional medicine, which he termed allopathy (meaning 'against disease') since it uses medicines to suppress or prevent symptoms (see ALLOPATHIC MEDICINE).

Hahnemann thought that small doses of homoeopathic remedies would be safer than large ones, while still being effective. He spent many years experimenting on himself and his family and friends with a wide range of natural substances in dilute forms. His approach was 'holistic', for it concentrated on the whole person – mental, emotional, spiritual and physical – and his homoeopathic remedies aimed to restore the body's natural balance and to strengthen it to fight disease.

The first homoeopathic hospital in London opened in 1850. Although interest declined in the early 20th century, the popularity of homoeopathy has recently begun to increase, spurred on by concern about the side effects of conventional drugs and publicity about its use by the royal family.

with more long-term conditions such as RHEUMATISM, need to be monitored over many months, and extra doses or different remedies would be given if improvement stops or new symptoms develop.

Homoeopaths believe that in the course of a cure, symptoms change from more important to less important bodily systems, and from the inside of the body outwards – so, for example, heart symptoms may 'move' to the skin as healing occurs. Symptoms are thought to disappear in the opposite order to their appearance, the most recent being the first to go.

This is known as the 'law of direction of cure'. Sometimes symptoms get worse before they improve, or symptoms of old complaints may reappear briefly, this time to be healed permanently.

Homoeopathic remedies are sold in many health food and chemists' shops.

An orthodox view

Although homoeopathy is available on the NHS, it is not yet taught in British medical schools, where it is often mentioned only disparagingly. Many doctors find it particularly difficult to accept the homoeopathic notion that the greater the dilution of a remedy, the greater its effectiveness, because this is contrary to orthodox medicine and orthodox medical thinking. Many homoeopathic remedies are so dilute that they are likely to contain very few molecules, if any, of the original substance.

Homoeopaths say that the power comes from the dilution process itself, which leaves 'footprints' of the original extract in the solution even if none of the substance itself remains. But since there is no scientific explanation of how this is possible, many doctors reject the theory.

It is especially difficult to compare homoeopathy, which uses a variety of different remedies to treat the whole person, with orthodox medicine, which relies on specific remedies for particular diseases with established and accepted symptoms.

Many doctors attribute any benefits of homoeopathic treatment to the PLACEBO effect – the idea that some treatments are effective simply because the patient believes in them, rather than because they do any good themselves.

Nevertheless, a few scientific trials have shown that homoeopathy has benefits greater than can be accounted for simply by the placebo effect – although these findings have been hotly disputed.

Even if relatively few doctors believe in the effectiveness of homoeopathy, most say that the remedies are so dilute that they must be completely safe.

Common homoeopathic remedies and their uses

Aconite (wolfsbane, blue monkshood): for COLDS and COLDNESS, especially when there is dryness and thirst; CROUP; ANXIETY and anguish; also recommended for gastric complaints.

Allium (from red onions): symptoms of a cold, including sneezing, running nose and headache; also HAY FEVER.

Antimonium tart. (tartar emetic, potassium antimony tartrate): for STOMACH COMPLAINTS, especially if there is NAUSEA AND VOMITING from sour food or drink.

Arnica (leopard's bane): BACK PAIN, SPRAINS, NOSEBLEEDS, BRUISING (as ointment), sore muscles and toothache.

Arsenicum (arsenic trioxide): DIARRHOEA or vomiting from FOOD POISONING; cold symptoms such as fever, sore throat, thirst, disturbed sleep; also restlessness, anxiety, panic attacks and DEPRESSION.

Belladonna (deadly nightshade): throbbing headaches, especially when worsened by light; earache; fever; flushed or irritable teething baby.

Calcarea (calcium carbonate: a mineral extracted from oyster shells): said to be good for INDIGESTION, CONSTIPATION, OBESITY, ECZEMA, ARTHRITIS and heavy menstrual periods.

Chamomilla (German camomile): for teething babies, especially when they are irritable or will not sleep.

Drosera (common or round-leafed sundew): a remedy recommended for COUGHS which are accompanied by spasms and constrictions and are painful and frequently exhausting; usually a dry cough with tickling in the throat.

Dulcamara (bittersweet, woody night-shade): said to help to clear up CATARRH, when there is also ulceration of the mucous membranes.

Eupatorium (boneset or thoroughwort): recommended for winter colds, when there is severe aching in the bones.

Euphrasia (common eyebright): for catarrh, especially when accompanied by headache, and tired, light-sensitive eyes.

Gelsemium (yellow jasmine): FEAR and PHOBIAS may be treated with this preparation, especially if there is trembling and a need to urinate; also, if there are fears of falling, attending a dental surgery, or a sensation of the heart stopping suddenly. It is also recommended for dullness and drowsiness – as well as for the opposite: excitement, nervousness, inability to sleep and a feeling of inadequacy.

Physical complaints which may be treated include: headaches which lift after vomiting, sleeping or urinating, but which are aggravated by bright light; DIZZINESS, faintness, earache, double vision, summer colds, catarrh, sore throat, dry coughs and, in women, painful periods.

Glonoinum (trinitroglycerine): may be prescribed for dizziness and headaches triggered by extreme heat or cold, hot flushes during the MENOPAUSE and the cessation of menstrual periods.

Hepar sulph. (calcium sulphide): a preparation used to treat sinusitis, CONJUNCTIVITIS, COLD SORES and mouth ULCERS, TONSILLITIS and INFLUENZA. It may also be prescribed for irritability caused by anxiety, for hypersensitivity to touch, and for restlessness beneath a calm exterior.

Hypericum (St John's wort): used as an ointment or tablets for burns and SUNBURN, small cuts and grazes, and insect bites (see STINGS).

Ipecac. (ipecacuanha): prescribed for fainting, nosebleeds, nausea not eased by vomiting, ASTHMA, back pain, a weak pulse, and copious bleeding, of blood that is slow in clotting.

Lachesis (bushmaster, sutucucu snake): sore throat; BOILS and abscesses; sinusitis; headaches; sore muscles; painful periods.

Ledum (marsh tea, wild rosemary): prescribed for anxiety, timidity and aloofness; also recommended for black eyes, stiffness of the joints and cold, purplish complexion during cold weather.

Lycopodium (wolfsclaw club moss): prescribed for ACNE; recurrent colds, lymphatic disorders (see IMMUNE SYSTEM), moodiness, premature ejaculation (see SEXUAL PROBLEMS), and HEARTBURN.

Nux vomica (poison nut tree): DIGESTIVE PROBLEMS, especially when caused by a poor diet or by overeating; constipation; PILES; influenza and colds with blocked nose and sore throat; MOTION SICKNESS; CYSTITIS; CRAMP; period pain; MIGRAINE.

Pulsatilla (Pasque flower): prescribed for colds that keep coming back, wheezy coughs, hay fever, obesity, depression, PAIN, swellings, headache.

Rhus tox. (poison ivy): recommended for arthritis, backache after physical exertion, SCIATICA, sprains, RINGING IN THE EARS, children's fevers. It is also prescribed for restlessness, nervousness, irritability, depression (especially for those who burst into tears for no apparent reason, or have thoughts of suicide).

How homoeopathic remedies are made

Plant, mineral and animal substances are all used to make homoeopathic medicines. The substance is first soaked in alcohol to extract its active ingredients. This solution (called the 'mother tincture') is progressively diluted many times over in measures of tens or hundreds, with a vigorous shaking after each dilution.

The shaking is said to 'potentiate' the mixture and increase its therapeutic powers by transferring energy to it. This means that homoeopathic remedies are held to become _more_ powerful with each dilution, ending up with a very low concentration of the original substance, but with a very high energy level. Sugar is then added to the final diluted and energised solution to make small homoeopathic tablets.

Successive ten-fold (also called decimal or X potency) or hundred-fold (centesimal or C potency) dilutions are indicated on remedies as 1X, 2X, 6X or 3C, 12C, 30C and so on. Sometimes 1M is used instead of 1000C, and sometimes the X is omitted.

HOMOEOPATHIC POTENCIES
The decimal scale
$1X = 1/10^1 = 1/10$
$2X = 1/10^2 = 1/100$
$6X = 1/10^6 = 1/1,000,000$
and so on.

The centesimal scale
$1C = 1/100^1 = 1/100$
$2C = 1/100^2 = 1/10,000$
$3C = 1/100^3 = 1/1,000,000$
up to:
$6C = 1/100^6 = 1/1,000,000,000,000$
and beyond.

A 3C dilution is a 1:100 dilution of the original mixture, further diluted in the same proportion and shaken twice more. A typical homoeopathic remedy for a mild condition might have a potency of 6C, while higher potencies of up to 200C or more are used for severe symptoms. As well as selecting a remedy suitable for the individual and his symptoms, the practitioner also has to decide which potency to prescribe.

HONEY
'Food of the gods'

Man has prized honey as a sweetener and food since the days of the Stone Age hunter-gatherers. The viscid liquid is produced by bees from the nectar they collect from flowers – a single pound of honey requiring the nectar of some one and a half million flowers. The foraging bees carry the nectar, a mixture of sugars and water, together with pollen, back to the hive. There, worker bees add enzymes that reduce the water content to less than 20 per cent and break down the larger sugar molecules. The honey is then sealed in the honeycomb, and later fed to the larvae or saved for winter food.

The smaller sugar molecules, including glucose and fructose, are readily absorbed by the human digestive tract, so honey soon gained a reputation as an instant high-energy food. The ancient Egyptians, Persians and Chinese all knew its value. King Solomon recommended it, saying: 'My son, eat thou honey, because it is good; and the honeycomb, which is sweet . . .' (Proverbs 24, verse 13.) The Greeks and Romans called it 'ambrosia', and thought it was the food of the gods that ensured their immortality.

The honey sugars break down into substances that inhibit the growth of bacteria, and the ancients used it to treat wounds, burns and skin problems – a practice that continued into the Middle Ages. The Celts and Anglo-Saxons made mead, their reviving drink, from fermented honey and water.

Besides sugars (about 75 per cent) and water, honey contains small amounts of calcium, iron, magnesium, potassium, sodium, sulphur, phosphorus and protein.

Traditionally, honey has been used as a 'tonic' or 'pick-me-up', and in the treatment of ANAEMIA, KIDNEY COMPLAINTS and CIRCULATION PROBLEMS. Its soothing effects are well known. Try a glass of hot milk with a teaspoon of honey for a sore throat, and the same with an added measure of brandy to relieve the symptoms of INFLUENZA. A glass of hot water with 2 teaspoons of honey and the fresh juice of half a lemon is a soothing bedtime drink. Use honey as a skin softener and conditioner: spread it over the face and hands, leave for 15 minutes and then wipe off with a damp flannel.

Honey may also help HAY FEVER victims. But to be effective it must be gathered in the area where you live, so that you ingest the local mix of pollens. When taken regularly through the winter and early spring, the pollens may give a measure of desensitisation to the same pollens in the air during the 'season'. Chewing small pieces of honeycomb – also pollen-rich – may help too.

Pure honey makes an admirable substitute for refined (white) sugar in tea, coffee and in cooking. Use it for basting roast meats. Replace 10oz (300g) of white sugar with 8oz (240g) honey when making cakes, breads and biscuits, but remember to cut down on the amount of liquid added accordingly.

An orthodox view

Doctors recognise honey as a high-energy foodstuff. A few think its antibacterial properties sufficient to warrant its use in the treatment of bedsores, BURNS and the like. Claims that honey slows down the ageing process or has particular therapeutic effects are generally rejected. See also ROYAL JELLY.

HOSPICES

In recent years, specialist care for the dying has increasingly been provided by hospices. Few nursing homes and hospitals are equipped to care for terminally ill patients for any length of time, and families may find it difficult to cope with a dying relative's needs. Patients, too, may prefer to spend their final days or weeks in a hospice where they are cared for in a positive spirit, and are less of a burden to others.

In addition, the hospice staff are skilled in dealing with the emotional and spiritual pain – along with any physical pain – that the dying may suffer. Patients, whether visited and cared for at home by hospice staff or in an actual hospice, are treated with respect and compassion, and their personal needs are attended to. Hospice staff also try to help relatives to cope with their own emotions.

To obtain a directory of hospices in Britain, send a large self-addressed envelope (stamped for 200g) to The Hospice Information Service, St Christopher's Hospice, 51-59 Lawrie Park Road, London SE26 6DZ.

See also TERMINAL ILLNESS.

HOUSEMAID'S KNEE

As its name suggests, this complaint was once common among housemaids, who spent much of their time working on their hands and knees. It affects the front of the kneecap, where an inflamed sac of fluid forms (see BURSITIS). It is still found among roof slaters and carpet layers, whose work involves rubbing and pressure on the knees.
Self help The condition can be avoided by wearing protective kneepads, and swelling can be reduced by strapping the knee.

HUMANISTIC PSYCHOLOGY
Taking responsibility for your life

Every living person is different from everyone else and must therefore accept final responsibility for his or her own actions and behaviour, regardless of influences exerted by genetic make-up, family, society and circumstances. This is the basic philosophy behind humanistic psychology – a reaction against what are seen as the dehumanising effects of today's technological society. Theories that behaviour results mainly from unconscious fears and desires, childhood experiences, social pressures and environmental forces are rejected.

The main driving force behind an individual's behaviour is held to be the need for personal growth – or 'self-actualisation' as it is called. Humanistic PSYCHOTHERAPY aims to help people to achieve this. While everyone is influenced by their genetic make-up, family background, society and environment, it asserts that the individual alone is responsible for choosing how he reacts to these, and what he makes of his life.

Unlike many other psychologists who study only certain types of behaviour – and those mainly in artificial laboratory settings – humanistic psychologists prefer to concentrate on the overall well-being and feelings of those who come to them – often called 'clients' rather than 'patients'. When they do try to analyse society, they usually do so in terms of its effects on individuals and their personal responses to social pressures.

Humanistic psychotherapies The different therapies within the humanistic movement concentrate on current problems and on individuals' own feelings about themselves and events. They do not try to find objective explanations for people's behaviour, and avoid deep examination of childhood experiences or inner motives. Instead, they try to develop clients' self-knowledge and ability to communicate, and to help them to feel more positive about their lives.

Humanistic psychologists embrace different theories, but all are based on a belief in the individual's freedom to direct his own life. They reject psychoanalytic and behaviouristic approaches as dehumanising, since they portray people as helpless victims of internal instincts or external circumstances.

The two most important spokesmen of humanistic psychology have been the American psychologists Carl Rogers and Abraham Maslow. Rogers pioneered a method of so-called 'client-centred' therapy – more often called COUNSELLING in Britain – in which the therapist tries to help the patient to make his own decisions without directing him – to assist him to develop his own view of a situation and how to handle it.

Rogers thought that problems arise when patients get out of touch with their true selves by being surrounded (especially in childhood) by others whose affection and approval are conditional – for example, a parent who implies: 'I will love you only if you are good.' He believed that trying to live up to such demands can leave people with a sense of failure, make them unable to admit their true feelings, and cause long-lasting psychological problems.

His methods became known as ROGERIAN THERAPY, and aim to decrease dependence on the judgment of others, restore the value of self, and help people to take charge of their lives. This is not a selfish attitude, say therapists, since self-reliant, fulfilled individuals can be more caring towards others and have better relationships with them and with the community (see ENCOUNTER GROUPS).

Abraham Maslow became interested in finding which characteristics make some people more mature, fulfilled and successful. He drew up a list of human needs, from basic biological necessities such as food and warmth, through psychological needs such as love and security, and ending with the need for self-development and personal growth. Fulfilment, he decided, depends on meeting all these needs and keeping all aspects of the personality in harmony.

From a study of successful public figures, Maslow formed a general idea of the self-fulfilled personality, and defined the characteristics and ways of behaving associated with it. He took an optimistic view of human nature, viewing people as innately sociable and cooperative and reasoning that destructive or antisocial behaviour occurs only when people cannot meet their basic needs.

The different types of humanistic therapy all aim to help people who are unhappy with the way they are leading their lives by encouraging them to make changes to improve matters. Therapists generally try to get some idea of the individual's view of himself – whether he is confident or fearful about his own abilities, for example. They try to match this self-image with what he would *like* to be and how he actually behaves in the real world. Discrepancies between how a person feels and how he appears to others are discussed. For example, someone holding a good job may still lack confidence in himself; or a person may think himself helpful while others see him as interfering. The individual's ability to share his true thoughts and feelings, and to portray himself honestly to others is encouraged as characteristic of a healthy personality.

Who it can help Most clients helped by humanistic psychotherapists are people who have emotional problems that they want to talk about without delving into complex childhood experiences. People who feel that they tend to react inappropriately to circumstances, or who have problems in their day-to-day lives and relationships may also benefit, as may those who just want to make more of their lives or who feel that they have simply lost sight of their goals.

Finding a therapist As with all forms of psychotherapy, there is no single recognised qualification for a humanistic psychotherapist. Some psychiatrists or other medically qualified doctors offer this form of treatment, either privately or on the National Health Service. But usually the therapist does not have medical training. The amount and quality of training that therapists receive can vary greatly, so unless you have a personal recommendation from a doctor or friend, consult someone who is registered with an organisation such as one of the following:

The Norwich Centre for Personal and Professional Development, 7 Earlham Road, Norwich NR2 3RA; Association for Humanistic Psychology, 26 Huddlestone Road, London E7 0AN; The British Association for Counselling, 37A Sheep Street, Rugby, Warwickshire CV21 3BX. Lists of this last association's own accredited counsellors, as well as other counselling and psychotherapy organisations, are available if you write to it enclosing a stamped-addressed envelope.

Consulting a therapist Usually client and therapist sit in comfortable chairs facing each other, in an informal, relaxed atmosphere. Therapists tend to be flexible, seeing you as often as you wish. However, many require one or two meetings before letting you commit yourself – or them – to further therapy, and some will suggest a contract for a certain number of sessions.

At the first session, the therapist generally

Carl Rogers (1902-87) (above) and Abraham Maslow (1908–70) developed humanistic psychology.

asks about your reasons for seeing him, and what your main problems are. He will usually stress that responsibility for change during therapy will be yours, but that he will be there to help and to act as a sounding board.

In further sessions he will try to build a relationship in which you can come to terms with the anxiety and confusion that can result from challenges to your view of yourself. A sense of personal value, openness to new experiences and feelings, trust in yourself, and freedom to develop in accordance with your true self should then grow.

An orthodox view

Doctors and conventional psychiatrists believe that the humanistic view of each person as responsible for his or her own life encourages a healthy, helpful self-reliance. Many clients report feeling more complete, fully alive, and better able to take charge of their lives after therapy.

Recently, psychotherapy as a whole has moved away from deep analysis of the childhood roots of unhappiness towards a more humanistic approach. However, some humanistic therapists may give the impression that people who feel trapped by circumstances are avoiding making choices, and that saying they feel unable to change things is just a way of not facing up to the truth. For some people this can create anxiety about choice and responsibility, or make them feel a failure if changes are not achieved.

HYDROTHERAPY
Water to stimulate the body into curing itself

We have all eased ourselves into a comforting bath of warm water to soak stiffness and pain from overworked limbs; or we have splashed on invigorating cold water to make ourselves alert. Hydrotherapy – water treatment – is much more specific in its use of water's properties to cure ailments.

At the root of hydrotherapy is the belief that water is the essence of life. It forms the major part of our bodies and is a constituent of most foods. We can live only a few days without it. In its various forms – liquid, solid ice, steam or gas – it can be used to induce relaxation, to stimulate blood flow, to remove impurities, drugs or alcohol, to ease pain and stiffness and to treat diseases.

Your body may benefit from water in several ways – in a compress, as a spray or from a bath, for example – but the most significant point is its temperature. Hot water

or steam dilates blood vessels, encourages sweating, relaxes muscles and joints, and draws heat to the surface. Cold applications constrict blood vessels, reduce inflammation and congestion on the surface and stimulate the flow of blood to internal organs.

The beneficial powers of water have been valued since ancient times, and used by physicians for specific ailments as well as for general well-being. Many of the ancient Greek temples built to honour the god of medicine, Asklepios, were at the sites of hot springs renowned for their healing properties. Steam baths were popular among the Romans and Turks, and both the ancient Chinese and the American Indians knew about the healing effects of water.

In Europe, the use of springs, and mineral springs called Spas, to restore health led to the establishment of hydros and fashionable resorts. A hydro is a hotel that offers treatments with curative waters. Towns such as Spa in Belgium, Baden-Baden in West Germany, and Bath, Buxton and Tunbridge Wells in Britain attracted the smart set as well as cure seekers. At Lourdes, in France, seemingly miraculous cures have occurred at the spa's Christian shrine.

The first hydrotherapy centre established in Britain to give a range of water treatments was founded by Sebastian Kneipp (1821-97), a Dominican monk from Bavaria. It was Champneys, near Tring – now one of many Health Farms. Kneipp believed that the body could regulate and cure itself. Water was the principal means of stimulating or soothing the body's own healing powers.

Hot and cold baths, vapour baths, hot and cold compresses, showers and foot baths were complemented by a strict regime of diet and exercise which Kneipp recommended to cleanse the body of impurities. Many of the treatments he popularised are now incorporated in Naturopathy, but others have been added – aerated whirlpools and underwater massage among them.

Who it can help People with Back Pain, Joint Problems and Rheumatism may find their discomfort eased by water treatment as part of their physiotherapy. It is also beneficial to people with muscle injuries and paralysis after disease, injury or a stroke.

In naturopathy, hydrotherapy is used to treat a range of diseases from Gallstones to diphtheria. The cleansing effects of various types of steam baths may help Headaches, while hot and cold water sprays help those with Period Problems, Anaemia, Arthritis or Asthma. People with minor strains and Sprains find cold compresses effective.

Anyone who is feeling run down, anxious or exhausted should be relaxed and start improving after most forms of hydrotherapy. Women are increasingly asking for water

births when they have babies, because of the comfort and gentle support they get from being in water (see Natural Childbirth). Some hospitals have birth pools and small pools can be hired for home births.

Finding a therapist If you have painful joints or other conditions that your doctor feels might respond to hydrotherapy by a physiotherapist, he can refer you to a suitable hospital or a recommended private physiotherapist. National Health Service and private physiotherapists must have a recognised qualification and most are experienced in using hydrotherapy.

Naturopaths and others who offer hydrotherapy need no registered qualifications, and the length and quality of training varies. Many advertise in _Yellow Pages_ and popular health magazines, but a recommendation from a reliable acquaintance is best. Or you can get a list of accredited therapists, some of whom practise hydrotherapy, from The British Naturopathic and Osteopathic Association, Frazer House, 6 Netherhall Gardens, London NW3 5RR.

Consulting a therapist There are many different forms of treatment, depending on the nature of your problem:

Physiotherapy For patients whose muscles have become weak or wasted by lack of use after an operation or injury, or through disease or a stroke, the physiotherapist is likely to include water therapy as part of the treatment. A patient immersed in warm water is partly supported by the water, so that muscles and joints can relax. The warmth also dilates the blood vessels, increasing blood flow and making more oxygen available to aid healing.

Patients generally have daily sessions lasting up to half an hour. They can exercise muscles and joints more easily in water to build up strength and improve mobility. When massaging in water, the therapist can apply greater pressure without causing discomfort and so speed progress.

Compresses To increase the blood flow to a diseased area or organ and to flush out impurities by opening the pores and promoting sweating, the therapist may apply hot compresses. You can use hot compresses at home to ease stiff muscles. Wring out a cloth in water that is hot, but not uncomfortably so. Wrap the cloth round the painful spot and leave it there until it has cooled.

To constrict the blood vessels and so reduce inflammation – at a sprained ankle or arthritic knee, for example – the therapist may use a cold compress. You can use one at home, wringing out a cloth in water running very cold from the tap and applying it to the inflamed area for several hours. Pin or bandage round the affected spot.

Iced water compresses or ice cubes

wrapped in a cloth can be used – but only for severe inflammation and swelling.

Wrapping Cold wraps are used for SKIN DISORDERS, COLDS and feverishness, strained back muscles, chronic BACK PAIN and chronic BRONCHITIS. You can use one at home for minor ailments, but for chronic conditions a trained therapist should supervise the treatment. In such cases it may be necessary to apply wraps daily for several weeks.

A sheet wrung out in cold water is wrapped round the body. A dry sheet and a warm blanket are in turn wrapped over the wet sheet. The patient lies in the wrap until the wet sheet dries out. A hot-water bottle may be needed to keep the feet warm. When the wrap is removed, the body is sponged with tepid water, then rubbed with a dry towel.

A wrap applied from waist to hips only is said by therapists to help ease DIGESTIVE PROBLEMS and CONSTIPATION.

Baths A common treatment in hydrotherapy is 20 minutes in a hot bath with the water just above 38°C (100°F) and deep enough to cover the shoulders – it relaxes muscles, eases pain, and promotes sweating, which removes impurities from the body. Because BLOOD PRESSURE may fall, you should leave the bath slowly and lie down for about half an hour when you are dry. A bath at about

body temperature will give many of the same benefits, but sweating will be much less.

Adding Epsom salts to a bath is believed to help drive off chills and colds; adding salt to help flesh injuries to heal. Oats or bran (tied in muslin or thin cotton) put in the bath is thought to help in clearing up ECZEMA and other skin complaints. Seaweed may also be added for soothing relaxation.

Cold baths with the water at about 16-20°C (60-68°F) are given to reduce inflammation and improve circulation, so that oxygen and nutrients are carried around the body more efficiently. You will not be immersed in cold water, but sit in a shallow bath for only a minute or two while the water is splashed over the upper part of the body. Vigorous towelling afterwards makes you glow. Cold baths are not suitable for children, elderly people or those with HEART DISORDERS.

Sitz baths For conditions such as CYSTITIS, CONSTIPATION, PILES, anal fissures and problems with the reproductive organs, a therapist will often recommend sitz baths. Two baths – each about the size of a baby's bath and having a ledge to sit on – are used. One is filled with hot water, the other with cold.

You sit in hot water covering the hips and abdomen for three minutes, with your feet in the cold bath, then sit in the cold bath for one

minute with your feet in the hot one. The process may be repeated. You can improvise sitz baths at home.

Sprays A jet of water – hot, cold, or alternately hot and cold – sprayed on part or all of the body is used for a wide variety of conditions, from anaemia and arthritis to DIABETES, gallstones and headaches.

Water temperature is the most important ingredient of the treatment; its benefits are the same as those of baths, but the impact made by a spray increases the effects. Whirlpool and aerated baths also increase the effects, but not as much as sprays. Sea water and the mineral-rich waters at spas make particularly effective sprays.

Young children, old or frail people and anyone with blood-pressure problems should not have spray treatment – and nobody should have it until two hours after a meal.

Although a hand-held shower at home can give some of the benefits of spray treatment, an experienced therapist should supervise a course of treatment for curing particular ailments, so that the best combinations of temperature and duration are used.

Steam bath TURKISH BATHS and SAUNA BATHS are recommended when problems arise from impurities in the body, such as drugs or anaesthetics. The profuse sweating caused

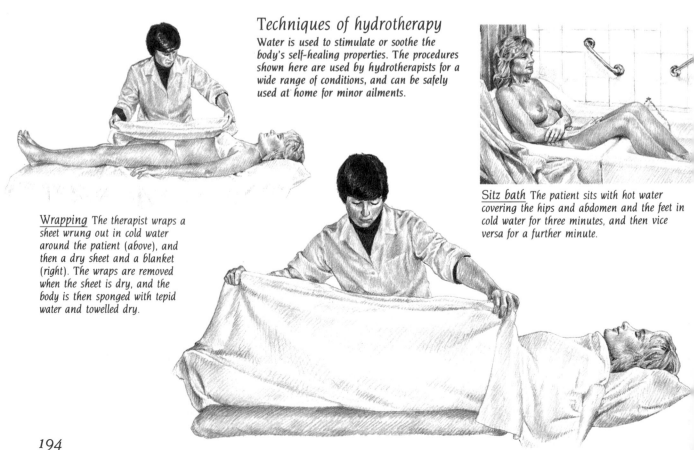

Techniques of hydrotherapy

Water is used to stimulate or soothe the body's self-healing properties. The procedures shown here are used by hydrotherapists for a wide range of conditions, and can be safely used at home for minor ailments.

Wrapping The therapist wraps a sheet wrung out in cold water around the patient (above), and then a dry sheet and a blanket (right). The wraps are removed when the sheet is dry, and the body is then sponged with tepid water and towelled dry.

Sitz bath The patient sits with hot water covering the hips and abdomen and the feet in cold water for three minutes, and then vice versa for a further minute.

helps to carry impurities out through the skin pores. The sweating can also be a short-term answer to water retention.

The atmosphere in a sauna is less humid than in a Turkish bath, so perspiration dries on the skin and the process may feel more comfortable. Sometimes an individual steam cabinet is used, so that the head is kept out of the steam and the steam is not breathed. The treatment finishes with a cool – not cold – dip or shower and a rub-down. Do not have any steam bath with a full stomach.

Inhalation Blocked nasal passages and catarrh on the chest may be treated by INHALATION THERAPY, especially with eucalyptus, menthol or another pungent oil added to the water. CROUP in children and bouts of coughing during WHOOPING COUGH are also eased by breathing steamy air. Skin conditions such as ACNE are improved because the facial pores open and sweat out impurities.

An orthodox view

Except in physiotherapy or for childbirth, hydrotherapy is rarely recommended by conventional doctors in Britain. They are often sceptical about the benefits claimed for minerals in spa water, and for hot or cold-water treatments – except for joint injuries. However, doctors do not doubt the general benefit for body and mind of a warm bath, and fully accept that exercising in water is easier for those who find movement painful.

There are some dangers to avoid in hydrotherapy. Anyone allergic to iodine should avoid any treatment with seaweed or its extracts. Patients with heart disease or high blood pressure should see a doctor before having hydrotherapy. Take care when choosing a hydrotherapist to find out about qualifications and experience. Hot and cold-water treatments always need to be administered with caution to avoid dramatic changes in blood pressure, or fainting. There are similar hazards in taking too cold a shower or dip after a steam bath.

HYPERACTIVITY

An abnormally active child can be anything from a 'bit of a handful' to one who is aggressive, violent and who may, if not helped, come into serious conflict with school authority and eventually the law. The hyperactive child is constantly on the go, does not know its own mind, will not settle to anything for any length of time, cries and shouts a good deal, will not sleep, and has no or little fear and so can be a danger to itself and others. The child also has problems of thirst and body temperature regulation.

Rearing such a child can be highly stressful, especially if those doing the rearing get little sleep and little sympathy from friends, teachers and doctors. Fortunately there is an organisation that can help: The Hyperactive Children's Support Group, 71 Whyke Lane, Chichester, West Sussex PO19 2LD.

Hyperactivity affects about 2-5 per cent of children, and ten times as many boys as girls. It is generally thought to be an allergic reaction (see ALLERGY) to certain foods and chemicals, and sufferers often have other problems, such as ASTHMA, HAY FEVER, ECZEMA and CATARRH.

Foods that have been implicated include dairy products; sugar; wheat products; citrus fruits, especially oranges, tangerines, clementines and satsumas; substances with a high content of salicylates – aspirin-like chemicals – such as most fruits (including apples and grapes), peas, dried fruits, almonds, vinegar and alcoholic drinks; and FOOD ADDITIVES, especially E102 (tartrazine).

Other substances suspected of causing hyperactivity include cadmium (from cigarette smoke), aluminium, copper, mercury (including amalgam tooth fillings), household chemicals, deodorants, perfumes, fluoride (see FLUORIDATION), vehicle exhaust fumes and chlorine (in treated water). Deficiencies of magnesium, manganese, zinc, vitamin B6 and fatty acids may also play a part.

What the therapists recommend

Many therapists give nutritional therapy, with mineral, vitamin and other supplements, such as evening primrose oil, and exclusion diets to find allergens. The procedure can be lengthy, and may induce tantrums, but persevere. See DIETS AND DIETING, EATING FOR HEALTH, FOOD ADDITIVES.

Naturopathy Practitioners consider consultation essential. They see food intolerance as a major source of hyperactivity, with certain food additives posing significant problems. Careful thought is given before changing a child's diet, and non-food factors are considered and eliminated before any diet restrictions are advised. Simply switching from high-additive foods to those with natural ingredients has been known to help.

Homoeopathy Individual treatment will include advice on avoiding food additives, and also toxic metals in the atmosphere.

Dance Therapy The child is given an opportunity to express himself energetically and without criticism. The therapist moves in harmony with him, and as their relationship develops the child is encouraged to explore new movement skills. He is led to organise and focus his energy more productively.

An orthodox view

This condition has been diagnosed more frequently in the last 20 years, and doctors feel that allergy to dyes in sweets may play a large part in it. Family medical problems may also be present. A doctor will advise a diet that cuts down on sugar, and may suggest seeing a child psychologist or health visitor.

HYPERTENSION

This is the medical term for high BLOOD PRESSURE, which increases the risk of HEART DISORDERS, KIDNEY COMPLAINTS and stroke. About one middle-aged person in every ten is thought to suffer from hypertension.

HYPER-VENTILATION

It is not unusual at moments of great nervousness or ANXIETY for people to find that their heart starts thudding and their breathing becomes hard and rapid, as though they had been running for a bus. Hyperventilation, or overbreathing, is particularly common at moments of social tension – before making a speech in public, for instance, particularly if the speaker is not practised in the art. It happens because too much carbon dioxide is expelled from the bloodstream through the lungs.

Although the condition is basically harmless, it can result in DIZZINESS, FAINTING bouts, and feelings of light-headedness. In addition, sufferers feel pain or tightness in the chest, and tingling or numbness in their fingers, toes and sometimes lips. Excessive sighing and yawning is common.

Strangely enough, another symptom of hyperventilation is shortness of breath. To compensate for this, sufferers tend to breathe even faster and so make the condition worse. In extreme cases, they hyperventilate until they collapse. On some occasions, victims of hyperventilation are taken to hospital, mistakenly thought to be suffering from HEART DISORDERS such as ANGINA, in which chest pains are a symptom.

If public speaking is an ordeal, you can combat hyperventilation by taking several deep breaths beforehand – each time expelling as much air as possible from the lungs, then breathing in as deeply as possible.

What the therapists recommend

Yoga Therapists encourage patients to relax as much as possible and to practise calm, rhythmical breathing, using the free movement of the lower ribs to activate the pumping action of the diaphragm. They should then aim to develop a slower breathing rhythm, relaxing in the pauses between inhaling and exhaling.

Biofeedback Practitioners believe that biofeedback instruments can literally show patients how to breathe properly, by providing the precise information needed to correct the mode of breathing, its rhythm and its gaseous composition. A tube around the belly, or one to breathe into, is connected to a computer which can display the extent of chest and diaphragmatic movement taking place, or show whether carbon dioxide levels in the breath are abnormal. The information provided can increase the patient's awareness of what is involved in his problem and – perhaps with some simple breathing exercises – help him to fight and overcome it.

An orthodox view

First of all, a doctor will examine the patient to make sure that there is nothing seriously wrong with him. He may then tell the patient to breathe into and out of a paper bag so that the exhaled carbon dioxide is returned to his bloodstream. (*Never* use a plastic bag, which could cause suffocation.) He may also send the patient to a physiotherapist to learn how to breathe correctly.

HYPNOTHERAPY
Seeking cures at a deeper level of consciousness

Somewhere between wakefulness and sleep is the state of consciousness that hypnotherapists use to try to improve a person's health. The trance-like state induced by therapists is similar to the one that occurs spontaneously in sleepwalking or daydreaming.

Someone in this condition can perform tasks efficiently, avoid hazards, obey instructions and speak lucidly. A sleepwalker, however, has not handed over control to another person, whereas someone in a hypnotic trance temporarily hands over a large measure of personal control to the therapist.

The therapist uses it to bring about physical or mental changes in the patient. Such changes can include healing physical illness, reducing pain, inducing relaxation, and gaining insight into present difficulties and past events that may have a bearing on them.

The word 'hypnosis' (based on the Greek *hypnos*, 'sleep') was coined for such induced trances in 1843 by James Braid (about 1795-1860), a Scottish surgeon working in Manchester, who revived the use of mesmerism (see box) for some of his operations. Other practitioners were, at about the same time, also making use of hypnotism as a painkiller. James Esdaile (1808-1859), a surgeon in Calcutta, performed many operations with hypnosis as the only anaesthetic. These surgeons were flouting established medical opinion, which had for some 60 years condemned Mesmer's theories and practices.

Although the effectiveness of hypnotism in deadening sensation was apparent from the surgeons' work, the technique once again fell into disfavour – ousted this time by the introduction of ether, chloroform and other such anaesthetics which were quick and reliable.

At the turn of the century, the British Medical Association looked into the subject of hypnotism and disapproved it. Only in the last 50 years has it been used again. Practitioners now see the trance as a healing state that allows the mind and body to achieve a calmness and tranquillity in which changes can be created that are inaccessible in the fully conscious state.

There is no question of the hypnotherapist simply waving a magic wand and taking control of the patient. Instead, the therapist and the client work on a problem together.

Who it can help Hypnotherapy has successfully treated SKIN DISORDERS, MIGRAINE, peptic ULCERS, IRRITABLE BOWEL SYNDROME and other conditions caused by ANXIETY and STRESS, including hysterical illnesses (see HYSTERIA). ASTHMA, INSOMNIA and PHOBIAS (of heights, air travel, exams, for example) are commonly treated. Pain can be relieved, and childbirth made easier.

Patients gain self-confidence from reliving and coming to terms with past events. The confidence gained often eases difficulties in relationships. Hypnosis can help to control habits such as SMOKING, and give some help with drug and alcohol ADDICTIONS.

Finding a therapist The first requirements in a therapist are competence and adequate training, but almost as important are personality and character. You must trust and feel comfortable with a therapist with whom you may well discuss sensitive areas of your life.

Mesmerised by magnets

Centuries ago, medicine men, shamans and the priests of ancient Greece seem to have used hypnotic powers to treat bodily and mental ills. Modern Western hypnosis, however, began its chequered history with an Austrian doctor, Franz Anton Mesmer (1734-1815).

His investigation of the natural phenomenon of magnetism led him to believe it existed as an invisible fluid flowing through and connecting everything in the universe, and that ill health occurred when the flow was distorted.

Mesmer believed that by using magnets he could restore a proper balance of fluid and cure illness. He became a celebrity in his fashionable Viennese practice by successful use of his 'animal magnetism', as he called it. But failures led to condemnation by Vienna University and in 1778 he moved to Paris.

Again he built up a circle of influential admirers who came just to be amused by his theatrical demonstrations. Patients clustered round a tub of water and iron filings, holding on to the tub while music and dim lighting relaxed them into a trance. Mesmer, holding an iron rod, would then practise his 'magnetism' on them. Modern investigators think that it was Mesmer's magnetic personality and powers of suggestion that brought about cures in patients who were in fact 'mesmerised'.

This time the French establishment was provoked by Mesmer's methods and notoriety. After scrutiny, they failed to find a scientific basis for his cures. Mesmer was eventually branded a charlatan and his treatments faded from the medical scene.

In Britain, anyone can set up as a hypno-therapist, and some virtually worthless diplo-mas are gained after the briefest training courses. For a list of well-trained therapists, contact one of the following: British Society for Medical and Dental Hypnosis, 151 Otley Old Road, Leeds LS16 6HN; or Dr Michael Heap, British Society of Experimental and Clinical Hypnosis, Psychology Department, Middlewood Hospital, Sheffield S6 1TP.

Hypnotherapy is not usually offered on the National Health Service, partly because of the time needed for each session. The cost of private consultations varies from about £20 to £50 per session. Generally, five to ten sessions are required, but some conditions can take a great deal longer.

Consulting a therapist The procedures followed in hypnotherapy sessions vary widely from one therapist to another. At the first session the therapist will take a detailed history of your case, of past and current treatments and of any more general matters that may be relevant.

You will be given a full explanation of what will happen at sessions and should be ready to take part in discussions of what you are both trying to achieve. The therapist is unlikely to use hypnosis at the first session, but may test your susceptibility to it.

At following sessions, you will sit com-fortably or lie down while the therapist puts you into a trance, usually by talking quietly and making repeated suggestions that you are tired and that your eyelids are gradually becoming heavy.

You may be asked to look at some parti-cular thing – a pool of light or a slowly turning wheel, perhaps – which will increase your wish to close your eyes.

The feeling is similar to dozing off to sleep. While in this state, a patient can be led to recognise positive abilities, be guided by the therapist to view problems from a better perspective, and gain insight into past and future behaviour. The entire session usually lasts 30-60 minutes.

Very occasionally a client may pass from a trance into a natural sleep; this is only a sign of tiredness and the need for sleep. Clients should have no fear that they will remain in a trance or that they will be controlled by the therapist. Therapists have no wish to control their clients – and in fact work to return control to clients whose illness or condition demonstrate loss of control

It is common for a hypnotherapist to teach a client to carry out self-hypnosis after an illness has been brought under control. This is particularly suitable for asthmatics, insomniacs and many others who may need frequent or on-the-spot help with their con-dition (see also AUTOSUGGESTION). With half an hour's practice a day between sessions, a

Overcoming a fear of flying

Mrs C was a fine musician whose career had taken a distinct turn for the better. However, many of the invitations to perform came from abroad, and she had a phobia of flying. She had to turn them down, and it seemed she would not have an international career. In desper-ation she went to a hypnotherapist.

At the first consultation she was put into a trance and the therapist told her to imagine she was going on a trip to the airport. At the next session she was again hypnotised and told to visualise herself at the airport and getting onto a plane. At the third hypnotic session she saw herself boarding a plane and taking a short flight around the airfield. And at the fourth and fifth sessions, while again in a trance, she visualised herself making a flight to and from a foreign capital. In addition, the therapist made a short tape-recording of the sessions, which Mrs C afterwards played at home.

Soon after she flew to Vienna to give her first concert outside Britain. On her return to London she was overjoyed and said, 'The only thing that bothered me was the long delays at the airport!' Her career is now well established and she travels abroad extensively – her fear of flying a thing of the past.

client can reinforce and re-explore points reached during sessions. Some therapists supply a tape-recording to give the familiar lead-in to the trance state.

An orthodox view

Many doctors still have doubts about the scientific basis of hypnosis, but others are themselves qualified hypnotherapists who use hypnosis as one of their standard tech-niques. It is best to find a hypnotherapist who is also a doctor. This avoids the danger of hypnosis being used for a wrongly diagnosed condition which needs different treatment.

Tests show that physiological signs during hypnosis match those that would be expected if events being recalled were actu-ally happening; pulse rate and brain activity in a person reliving a traumatic accident, for example, will be the same as during the accident itself. Patients who are taken back to earliest infancy will display one reaction that occurs only in small babies: if stroked under the foot, their toes curl upwards – a reaction that changes after the age of six months to curling the toes downwards.

Despite such evidence, some doctors dis-pute that anyone really goes into a hypnotic trance, although they do not suggest that there is deliberate faking. It may be that the part of the consciousness that is geared to reality stops functioning and a part in which intuition and imagination flourish takes over.

Normally a self-critical aspect of full con-sciousness would reject ideas allowed to surface and develop under hypnosis. There is concern that pseudo-memories are woven into actual memories to produce what the therapist or the client think desirable.

Doubts about the nature of a hypnotic trance do not, however, prevent recognition of its effectiveness in giving drug-free release from pain, cures of many forms of PSYCHO-SOMATIC ILLNESS and easing of a variety of conditions rooted in stress and anxiety.

HYPOGLYCAEMIA
Lack of sugar

The brain cannot store glucose, the energy source it uses for all its functions, so it must get it from the bloodstream. If it is starved of glucose because the bloodstream contains too little of this sugar – a condition known as hypoglycaemia – the patient rapidly becomes sweaty and confused, and has a rapid pulse. Without treatment, unconsciousness and brain damage may follow.

Hypoglycaemia is most commonly caused by uncontrolled DIABETES, when there is an imbalance in the dose of insulin taken and the patient's carbohydrate intake. It can also be caused by ALCOHOLISM, and its symptoms are mimicked by excessive adrenaline pro-duction in ANXIETY. Rarely, non-diabetic people can suffer from hypoglycaemia, experiencing hunger, confusion, irritability, and sometimes sweating, but these symp-toms are relieved by eating.

Self help If you are diabetic, always carry barley sugar or glucose tablets around with you in case of emergency. Eat a suitable snack or meal every two or three hours, especially if you are about to do something strenuous. Avoid becoming over-tired and try to get a full night's sleep.

What the therapists recommend

Naturopathy Avoid refined carbohydrates (sugary and starchy foods); instead eat whole grains that are digested slowly and thus maintain a more stable blood sugar level, Eat regularly to avoid wild swings in energy. Bitter salad vegetables, like chicory and endive, play a part in stimulating liver functions and digestive processes; the liver stores glucose in the form of glycogen, releasing it again as glucose when required.

An orthodox view

Doctors treat acute hypoglycaemia in diabetic patients by giving sugar, if necessary by intravenous injection, or by a glucagon injection. A glucose tolerance test, in which blood glucose levels are measured regularly for several hours after ingestion of 100g of glucose meal, confirms the condition in nondiabetics. Doctors may then do further biochemical tests to exclude serious hormone or enzyme disturbances.

Minor symptoms can be relieved by regular, light meals. Symptoms in non-diabetics are more commonly caused by anxiety than by a disturbance of glucose metabolism.

HYPOTENSION

People with naturally low BLOOD PRESSURE – known medically as hypotension – tend to live longer than those with high blood pressure, but sometimes suffer from DIZZINESS and FAINTING. A drop in blood pressure during an illness or after an accident can be a serious sign of SHOCK.

HYPOTHERMIA
Cold that can kill

Elderly people and babies are the most vulnerable to hypothermia or abnormally low body temperature. However, mountaineers, sailors and anyone exposed to extreme cold can be affected.

Normally, body temperature is regulated at about 37°C (98.6°F) – by shivering, if necessary, to produce heat. But if someone stays cold or wet for long, his temperature may fall and hypothermia occur. The situation becomes dangerous when the temperature drops to about 35°C (95°F) and body metabolism starts to slow down. At about 33°C (91.4°F) shivering stops and the victim becomes confused and unsteady. Unconsciousness occurs at about 30°C (86°F), and then death if help is not urgently received.

What the therapists recommend

Naturopathy Maintaining adequate circulation becomes more difficult with advancing age. Naturopathic advice is aimed at preventing any deterioration reaching a critical level.

How to prevent hypothermia

Always wear plenty of warm clothes when outdoors in severe weather and indoors when heating is inadequate – several thin layers are better than one thick one. Thermal underwear, long socks, scarves and gloves can help even indoors – or in bed, if necessary.

Wear a hat, for much heat is lost from the head. This is particularly so for children, whose heads have a proportionately larger surface area.

Keep the heat up to 21°C (70°F), even if this means using fewer rooms, or living and sleeping in one room.

Eat at least one good hot meal daily, and take hot drinks when needed.

Keep active – staying in one position for a long time makes you feel colder.

Check for draughts from doors and windows, and block up any gaps. You may be eligible for a local authority grant to improve your home insulation – ask at the local Department of Social Security (DSS) office.

Use a hot-water bottle or an electric blanket – never both – in bed. Electric blankets are cheap to run, and an overblanket can be left on. A woollen or fleecy underblanket also helps.

People who move around little during the day may find electric heating pads and footwarmers cheaper and more effective than extra heaters.

Visit elderly neighbours during cold weather. An offer to help with shopping or ordering fuel is often welcome. Further advice for those in need can be obtained from the local DSS office.

EXERCISE is important at all ages, even when it is too cold to go outdoors. Hot drinks or soup give a boost to body heat.

Autogenic Training This can help prevent hypothermia in the elderly; it is not a substitute for adequate food, clothing and heating.

An orthodox view

Anyone suffering from hypothermia needs urgent medical help – call an ambulance or a doctor immediately. While waiting, wrap the victim's head and body in blankets, and place him in the recovery position if unconscious. Warming up too suddenly can be dangerous, so avoid direct heaters and hot water bottles. If the victim is conscious, offer a sweet, warm – not scalding – drink and comfort.

Never give alcohol to a hypothermia victim, or massage the body – these draw blood away from the vital organs to the skin.

HYSTERIA

Anxiety built up by conflicts during the formative years is the usual cause of hysteria – a medical term for a far more serious, deep-rooted disorder than is implied by its everyday meaning. Susceptible people under STRESS can become hysterical to avoid facing a difficult situation, or to divert attention from what they see as their inadequacy.

The symptoms are genuinely felt and not in any way faked. The subconscious mind has converted the individual's anxiety into physical symptoms. These take many forms, from uncontrolled screaming and thrashing about to loss of sight or memory, or apparent paralysis of a limb. However, sufferers see themselves as gaining in some way, however crippling the symptoms may seem to others. The gain is the ability to opt out of a situation that is too difficult to deal with.

What the therapists recommend

Yoga Emphasis is on relaxation and natural breathing to calm the overactive, easily aroused nervous system. Restoring steady breathing is of primary importance, to reduce TENSION. Relaxation and MEDITATION can benefit longer-term conditions.

To those who study yoga, its philosophy can offer a new interest and motivation in life, which may help to free them from the conflicts at the root of their condition.

An orthodox view

No treatment will be effective unless the root of the anxiety is found and recognised by the patient. It is not enough to treat current symptoms. They may go, but the underlying cause will tend to produce new ones. And accurate diagnosis by a doctor is essential in case what are thought to be hysterical symptoms are those of a real physical ailment.

Tranquillisers will give relief for a time while PSYCHOTHERAPY tries to get to the root of the problem. HYPNOTHERAPY has proved a successful form of psychotherapy for many hysteria cases – but only when carried out by a qualified hypnotherapist who is also a doctor. Patients are taken back to the origin of the anxiety and allowed to vent feelings they suppressed at the time. Once the patient is freed from the unacknowledged anxiety, the symptoms go.

When faced with a fit of hysterics, be calm, firm and reassuring. Take practical steps to deal with whatever has triggered the attack. Get rid of any onlookers.

Warning Never slap a hysterical person – the shock can cause psychological damage. Get the victim to see a doctor.

IATROGENIC ILLNESS

When seeing the doctor brings its own problems

Illnesses that arise as a direct result of medical treatment itself are called 'iatrogenic' – from the Greek words _iatros_ meaning 'physician' and _genesis_ meaning 'origin'. Since orthodox forms of treatment such as drugs and surgery involve interfering with the body's normal functioning in ways that may lead to iatrogenic conditions, doctors and patients have to weigh the advantages and risks of treatment before starting it.

In some cases, iatrogenic illness may be unavoidable – as, for example, when anti-CANCER medication causes the patient's hair to fall out, or when lifesaving steroid drugs lead to swelling of the face and easy bruising. Occasionally, iatrogenic disorders can be the result of accidents and errors or of rare and unexpected reactions to treatments.

Concern about the side effects of orthodox medical treatment is often an important part of a decision to consult an alternative practitioner such as a herbalist, homoeopath or acupuncturist, rather than a doctor. Not all alternative treatments are completely free of side effects – some herbs, for example, can be dangerous or even fatal if incorrectly used – but in general if you consult a suitably trained and qualified practitioner the chances of developing iatrogenic problems are less.

An orthodox view

Doctors say that as conventional medicine becomes increasingly sophisticated, the incidence of iatrogenic disorders will inevitably increase. However, by improving training and holding regular reviews – called 'medical audits' – they hope to reduce the risks. In Britain, doctors can report bad reactions to particular drugs to the Committee on Safety of Medicines, which will then issue a warning if they suspect a new iatrogenic illness.

IMMUNE SYSTEM

The body has a system of organs, cells and antibodies to fight a constant attack of bacteria, viruses, fungi and parasites. It both resists first-time attackers and recognises previous ones. See THE SECRET SERVICE THAT DEFENDS OUR BODIES, p. 204.

IMPETIGO

This is a highly contagious bacterial skin infection, common among children, and minor epidemics sometimes occur in nurseries and schools. Red spots with yellow crusts usually affect the victim's face, hands or knees, but they may spread over other parts of the skin. Usually, the child does not feel ill; but without treatment the sores can linger for weeks.

If impetigo is suspected, consult a doctor immediately, because of the high risk of spreading the infection.

What the therapists recommend

Herbal Medicine Local applications of antiseptic herbs, such as infusions (see p. 184) or tinctures of marigold, myrrh and thyme, are said to be effective. Most essential oils – especially eucalyptus, lavender, lemon and thyme – are also said to work. Put ten drops of an oil in a dessertspoon of water and dab onto the spots with cotton wool.

Herbalists may also prescribe internal treatment with tinctures of burdock or echinacea to cleanse the system.

Naturopathy Attention to hygiene is vital to prevent the spread of this infection. Use separate face cloths and towels, and even boil clothes. Natural antibiotic effects may be gained from GARLIC – three or four cloves or capsules a day might be needed. Extra vitamins A, B and C may help to boost healing and resistance.

Aromatherapy A mixture of essential oils is said to kill the bacteria that cause impetigo and so prevent the infection from spreading. Dilute three drops of thyme, three drops of savory, and six drops of tea tree oils in three tablespoons of carrier lotion and apply to the affected area three times a day.

An orthodox view

A doctor will probably prescribe a course of antibiotics in tablet, medicinal, or ointment form, and advise that the child should be kept at home.

IMPOTENCE

A strong association exists between a man's ability to have and maintain an erection and his image of himself. Partly this is due to the common assumption – whether right or wrong, instinctive or conditioned – that the man should take the initiative in sexual intercourse. Partly it is because, unlike a woman, he is not able to complete the sexual act without being fully aroused, with an erect penis.

Add to this the thought that normal reproduction is impossible unless the man can perform effectively through to ejaculation and it is not surprising that men are both proud of and fearful for their erections. There is so much that can go wrong. . .

In both sexes, sexual arousal or excitement is marked by increased blood flow to the genital and pelvic areas. In a man, blood pumps into the spongy tissues of the penis, causing them to swell and become stiff, making the penis erect.

The process depends on a complex arrangement of blood vessels in the penis and pelvic region, on the nerves controlling them and the central nervous system itself, on the correct balance and sequence of hormones triggered by the brain, and on an erotically focused mental state.

If any one of these should go wrong – whether for physical, neurological, chemical or psychological reasons – an erection may be impossible to achieve or may subside at a crucial moment. This is commonly called impotence but is medically termed _erectile insufficiency_. No wonder, then, that many causes of STRESS and disease, as well as more subtle psychological factors, can lead to impotence (see also SEXUAL PROBLEMS).

Many drugs such as tranquillisers, antihistamines, spironolactone (prescribed for high BLOOD PRESSURE) and so on can also impair or prevent erections, yet doctors and pharmacists rarely warn about such effects. The result can be very troubling to the man concerned, and may even create the kind of secondary anxiety about performance that makes the impotence worse.

Self help Many of the recommendations given under SEXUAL PROBLEMS will be beneficial. In addition, it is particularly important, in order for your body to re-establish sexual responsiveness, that when erections begin to return after a period of impotence, you allow them to subside without insertion, so that you have the experience of an erection coming and going in response to the flow of sexual stimulation.

What the therapists recommend

Autogenic Training This can help many kinds of sexual disorders, including impotence. Standard exercises are often enough, but sometimes the use of a personalised formula added to the exercise may be needed. Even better results occur when the training is used with orthodox techniques.

Behavioural Therapy With impotence, the important aim is to try to reduce any anxieties about sexual intercourse, and take away the pressures involved. Therapy usually focuses on physical contact – kissing, caressing, massage and foreplay – rather than intercourse itself, placing emphasis on the pleasant sensations. When an erection can be successfully produced and maintained, then sexual contact is made increasingly intimate until intercourse can take place.

An orthodox view

Effective diagnosis depends upon distinguishing between physical and psychological causes of impotence; or, if both are present, how they are interacting. Consequently treatment may involve both physical and psychological methods. As with all treatments for sexual problems, relaxed circumstances free from anxiety are crucial.

In recent years, surgical methods of treating erection failure have been developed – such as implants of permanent flexible splints; inflatable devices, and vacuum systems applied to the outside of the penis, to promote blood flow and cause an erection.

There are also drugs which, when injected into the penis, relax muscles and encourage blood flow. This technique is seen by doctors as best used as a way of breaking the cycle of anxiety and fear which persistent loss of erection can produce.

INCONTINENCE

The inability to control the passing of urine and/or faeces can be embarrassing to adults, teenagers and older children. It can be hard to cure and a doctor should be consulted.

Incontinence in children may result from insecurities (see also BEDWETTING). In women, urine incontinence may be caused by a PROLAPSE, or organ displacement, sometimes as a result of childbirth. In men, PROSTATE PROBLEMS may be the cause. Either sex can be made incontinent by a stroke that damages the nervous control of the bladder (see BLADDER PROBLEMS).

The most common cause of faecal incontinence is, oddly enough, CONSTIPATION, in which the bowel can become so obstructed by solid faeces that only liquid faeces can be discharged.

Looking after an incontinent person – particularly one who is elderly or bedridden – can be a trying and difficult chore. The unpleasant odours of wet or soiled clothes or bed linen can cause embarrassment and distress to both the sufferer and the carer.

A health visitor or district nurse should be able to offer advice about home care. A wide range of aids is available on doctors' prescriptions, including incontinence pads. There are also special deodorants that can be used on affected items to get rid of the smell.

What the therapists recommend

Herbal Medicine To clear the bowels herbalists may prescribe a mild astringent such as marigold or meadowsweet, taken three times a day.

Naturopathy You are advised to see a doctor first. Naturopathic measures that may help are hot and cold sitz baths (see HYDROTHERAPY), or alternating hot and cold compresses over the lower abdomen and back to improve local circulation and muscle tone. Also, pelvic floor exercises (see PREGNANCY) may help the patient to regain control.

An orthodox view

Bladder and bowel incontinence need careful examination, especially with the elderly, and expert treatment should be sought.

INDIAN MEDICINE

Traditional Indian medicine, AYURVEDIC MEDICINE, has developed over 4000 years. It deals with all aspects of life – physical, mental and spiritual – and treats the whole person, not just diseases. Methods involve herbal remedies, diets, and practical aids such as MASSAGE, MEDITATION and YOGA.

INDIGESTION

Eating too quickly and too much is one of the main causes of indigestion, or discomfort in the upper abdomen or in the chest. It is often accompanied by belching WIND and the bringing up of acid through the gullet and into the mouth (see ACID STOMACH). Other causes include a diet of rich, fatty foods, smoking, and drinking too much alcohol and drinks containing caffeine.

Occasionally indigestion is the result of stomach CANCER, but this is unusual in anyone below the age of 40. Symptoms of indigestion can also be caused by a variety of other ailments, including GALLSTONES, hernia, OBESITY and ULCERS.

What the therapists recommend

Herbal Medicine For short-term indigestion, drink hot teas such as peppermint, camomile, fennel, lemon balm or cinnamon.

For recurrent, long-term indigestion, a herbalist should be consulted. He will treat each case individually, and may prescribe from a range of herbs, including dandelion, ginger, golden seal, marigold, marshmallow, meadowsweet and thyme.

Acupuncture An acupuncturist will usually treat the bladder, conception governor, spleen and stomach meridians.

Acupressure First treat a point on the lower leg, four fingers' width from the crown of the inner ankle bone, against the shin bone. Press inward beside the bone. Also, press inward on the knee, three thumbs' width from beneath the kneecap, in the hollow on the outer edge of the shin.

Naturopathy For simple causes such as overeating or an excess of rich foods, fasting for 24 hours, taking only liquids such as apple juice or herb teas, may help the digestive tract to recover. Longer spells of indigestion, however, require a consultation. In general, slippery elm powder in hot water may give some relief if the digestive tract is inflamed, while warm compresses over the abdomen ease COLIC or stomach cramps.

An orthodox view

People who develop indigestion for the first time after the age of 40, or whose bowel movements change (see BOWEL DISORDERS), or if there is weight loss or frequent pain, should see a doctor. To reach a diagnosis a practitioner may send you to hospital for a barium meal and X-ray, or to have an endoscopy (an examination of the stomach and first part of the intestine by means of a flexible, lighted tube). He may also, as with other cases, prescribe an antacid or a drug to reduce the amount of stomach acid.

Indigestion may be aggravated by aspirin and most anti-ARTHRITIS medicines.

INFERTILITY

Difficulty in conceiving a baby, commonly called infertility, may be more properly termed 'subfertility', since most couples with this problem do eventually manage to have children. The condition is quite common, affecting about one in every ten couples in the West. Some women naturally take longer to conceive than others, so infertility is not diagnosed until a couple have been having regular sexual intercourse without using contraceptives for at least a year.

A variety of causes can reduce a couple's fertility: SMOKING, drinking too much alcohol, illness, and strenuous exercise by women may all play a part, as well as more specific physical disorders. Worry, STRESS and ANXIETY – especially about trying to have a baby – can also make things worse. In about a quarter of all cases, doctors can find no sure reason for infertility; for another quarter the problem lies with the woman; for another quarter with the man; and in the remaining quarter with both partners.

The normal process of fertilisation

In most fertile women, one of the two ovaries produces an egg every month in about the middle of the menstrual cycle, although this varies greatly between individuals. The egg then travels down the uterine tube (Fallopian tube or oviduct) and into the womb.

For fertilisation to occur, the couple must have sexual intercourse shortly before or after ovulation, so that the man's sperm can pass from the vagina through the cervix – the muscle at the entrance to the womb – into the womb and the uterine tubes, where one of them must fertilise the egg. Since the egg survives for only about 36 hours after ovulation, and sperm for only about two or three days, fertilisation depends on timing.

The best chance of a woman becoming pregnant is to have intercourse 12 to 24 hours before ovulation, although this can be hard to estimate. Nevertheless, many women experience pain or discomfort when they ovulate; sometimes they notice a little blood in the vagina, and a woman can identify

---

How good health can be a help

Good general health will make conception easier. Both partners should eat a balanced diet (see EATING FOR HEALTH), take a reasonable amount of EXERCISE – though very active women may need to cut down – get ample sleep, and make plenty of time for rest and relaxation (see RELAXATION AND BREATHING).

Women can find out when their fertile days occur by taking their temperature every morning first thing before getting out of bed. When ovulation occurs, the temperature will rise by about 0.2 to 0.5°C (0.5 to 1°F). Conception is possible for about two or three days before and after the day of ovulation. Special kits are available from pharmacies which allow women to detect ovulation by testing urine samples. (See also CONTRACEPTION , for more information on telling when ovulation occurs.)

Men with a low sperm count are sometimes helped by splashing their testicles with cold water several times a day, since too high a temperature can interfere with sperm production.

---

fertile days by taking her temperature regularly, first thing every morning (see box). Once an egg has been fertilised it embeds itself in the womb lining as a foetus, and gradually develops into a baby.

Many physical problems – some of them quite small – can interfere with the process of fertilisation and pregnancy. Here are some of the most common ones:

Problems affecting women

Failure to ovulate About one-fifth of all infertility occurs because the woman ovulates very infrequently or not at all. The cause can be a hormonal imbalance, a problem affecting the ovaries, sudden weight loss, or even simply stress and anxiety. Usually the woman has irregular periods, or these may have stopped altogether.

Too little progesterone The hormone progesterone prepares the lining of the womb to receive the embryo. If too little is produced by the woman's body, the embryo cannot implant itself into the womb.

Blocked uterine tubes Usually an infection – either at the time or one which occurred in the past – is the cause. Conception is prevented as sperm are unable to reach the egg, and the egg to travel to the womb.

Endometriosis Pieces of the womb lining begin to grow around the ovaries or uterine tubes, reducing the woman's chances of becoming pregnant.

Problems with cervical mucus To prevent germs from reaching the reproductive organs, sticky mucus is secreted around the cervix at the entrance to the womb. Normally it becomes thinner during ovulation, to allow sperm to pass through, but if this does not happen infertility may be the result. In a few rare cases a woman's cervical mucus may contain antibodies which actually attack and destroy her partner's sperm.

Abnormalities of the womb Sometimes these can prevent the fertilised egg from implanting itself into the womb. The most common problems are fibroids (non-malignant tumours in the womb), adhesions (old scars in the womb lining, which are often the result of previous infections) or an abnormally shaped womb.

Problems affecting men

Sperm abnormalities Some men have a low sperm count or produce abnormal sperm which cannot fertilise an egg. Many factors can cause this, including illnesses such as MUMPS, VARICOSE VEINS near the testicles, OBESITY, tight clothing, and allowing the testicles to get hot – for example, by working in an overheated environment. In other cases, stress or hormone imbalances affect sperm production. About one in ten infertile men produce antibodies which make their

---

sperm clump together so that they cannot move freely; this can occur after a vasectomy operation has been reversed.

Difficulties with ejaculating sperm Infertility can result from blockages in the sperm ducts, premature ejaculation which occurs outside the vagina, and so-called 'retrograde ejaculation' when semen is passed into the bladder instead of out through the penis – a condition which affects some diabetics and men who have had prostate surgery.

What the therapists recommend

Acupuncture Treatment depends on the cause of the problem, and generally includes advice on diet and vitamin supplements as well as acupuncture or MOXIBUSTION treatment to the bladder, kidney, stomach and conception meridians.

Autogenic Training This may help when infertility is related to stress or TENSION.

Naturopathy The nutritional intake of the couple trying to conceive may need improving. A high-potency, multivitamin and mineral supplement is often very valuable. Hot and cold splashes of the genital area will stimulate local circulation (but hot baths should not be taken before intercourse). It should also help to avoid alcohol and tobacco; to take plenty of exercise; and to get adequate rest and sleep.

An orthodox view

Once a couple have been trying to have a baby for about a year without success, the doctor will begin tests to investigate the causes. Most of these can be treated by means of drugs, artificial hormones, surgery or special techniques such as *in vitro* ('test tube') fertilisation – where eggs are removed from the woman's body, fertilised with the man's sperm in the laboratory and then replaced in the womb.

If no cause can be found, couples are simply advised to improve their general health as much as possible, stop worrying, and keep trying – sooner or later many of them will manage to have a baby. If this does not happen, or the cause of infertility cannot be treated, the doctor may suggest that the couple consider adoption.

INFLUENZA

Winter epidemics of this virus infection are common. Many people incorrectly refer to COLDS as flu, but true influenza is more severe. It produces high FEVER with a sensation of feeling cold, sweating, HEADACHE, aching muscles, weakness, loss of appetite,

The chart shown above gives a selection of alternative methods of treating influenza – and the specific effects that each particular remedy has. For example, taking garlic eases sore throats, reduces fever, combats infection and acts as an expectorant.

If you stay at home and choose the right remedies, you can stave off the worst miseries of flu, from the shivers and soreness of the early days to the tiredness and cough that may linger. Wise treatment avoids spreading the virus and cuts the risk of complications.

COUGHS and pain behind the breastbone. It is caused by any of numerous influenza VIRUS INFECTIONS, which change with time to produce new strains so that long-term immunity is impossible.

Symptoms may last up to a week, and a period of depression is common afterwards.

What the therapists recommend

HOMOEOPATHY

Self help Medicines prescribed include: *Baptisia*, when there is severe prostration, gastric symptoms, stupor, and the patient has a red face and feels 'in pieces'; *Eupatorium perf.* when the bones feel broken, the eyeballs are sore, and the patient dare not move; and *Gelsemium* when there is a bursting headache, great heaviness of head and eyeballs, absence of thirst, and hot and cold waves alternate down the back.

HERBAL MEDICINE

Self help In the early, shivery stages, hot ginger, cinnamon – or even cayenne pepper – teas are recommended to increase the circulation and warmth. When there is a fever, try infusions (see p. 184) of elderflower, yarrow and peppermint, to regulate the temperature; take a tablespoon of hot infusion every hour. Two or three cups of yarrow and lemon balm tea a day are said to improve the appetite during convalescence.

NATUROPATHY

Prevention would be ideal, although during epidemics this is not easy. Taking only fluids during the early stages may help. When aching and chilled, try a hot bath, perhaps with 2 tablespoons of Epsom salts, just before retiring. At the feverish stage, take elderflower tea and/or fruit juices, and apply a cold pack on the trunk. As always with cold packs and compresses, immediately cover with a thick towel or blanket to encourage warmth and sweating. Vitamins, especially vitamin A (about 5000iu) and vitamin C (3-4g) may be prescribed.

BIOCHEMIC TISSUE SALTS

When there is feverishness, *Nat. sulph.* is recommended hourly, in alternation with *Ferr. phos.* during the early stages. *Kali sulph.* may be alternated with *Ferr. phos.* when there is stuffiness, yellow discharge and a desire for cool air. It should help to reduce the temperature. *Calc. phos.* may be taken during convalescence.

An orthodox view

With rest, extra drinks and paracetamol or aspirin as required – usually two tablets every four hours, up to a maximum of eight in 24 hours – most healthy young people recover from influenza without medical treatment. Antibiotics are ineffective against viruses, but doctors prescribe them for secondary bacterial infections such as BRONCHITIS or PNEUMONIA, or to prevent complications in the elderly or infirm.

Flu sufferers should not struggle to work. They only spread the disease – by coughs and sneezes – and increase their risk of complications.

Every autumn, vaccines against the viruses that are expected the following winter are produced. Immunisation may be offered to high risk groups such as people over 65 and those who have DIABETES, lung disease or heart disease. However, the vaccines give protection only against the particular viruses, not against other strains of flu – or against common colds.

INHALATION THERAPY

Many practitioners of HYDROTHERAPY as well as orthodox doctors recommend steam inhalations to clear CATARRH and to improve skin conditions such as ACNE.

Various aromatic oils or proprietary remedies, often with a eucalyptus or menthol base, are added to hot water to increase the effect of the vapour. You can use the treatment at home, breathing in the steam deeply over a bowl and holding a towel over your head and the bowl to keep the steam in. Take care not to have the water too hot, in case the steam scalds you, and be careful also not to upset the bowl.

INSOMNIA

Almost everyone experiences insomnia – or sleeplessness – at times. Noise, pain, coffee, irregular hours, unfamiliar surroundings and worry can all lead to restless nights. Because time drags when they are trying to sleep, most people overestimate their sleeplessness. There are no rules about how much sleep is necessary: everyone's needs are different. Babies – and some teenagers – may sleep for up to 18 hours each day, but elderly people may require only five or six hours.

There are two types of sleep: orthodox sleep and rapid-eye-movement (REM) sleep, during which dreaming occurs (see SLEEP DISORDERS). Both types of sleep are necessary if a person is to start the next morning feeling refreshed.

Lack of sleep causes irritability, inefficiency and inability to concentrate at school

Do's and don'ts of insomnia

Do note your sleep pattern in your diary; it will help you to find the causes of your insomnia.

Do persevere to find the alternative therapy that suits you.

Do take plenty of fresh air and EXERCISE.

Do try to relax as often as possible during the day, and try to follow a regular routine.

Do keep regular sleeping hours.

Do ensure that your bedroom is well ventilated but warm, quiet and dark.

Do make sure that your bed is comfortable and gives your body proper support (see BEDS AND BEDDING).

Do allow yourself time to relax and unwind before trying to sleep.

Do listen to soft, 'easy' music while preparing for bed.

Do take a warm, not hot, relaxing bath.

Do put the bedside clock out of sight.

Do relax in bed. For example, imagine doing something peaceful, such as sunbathing on a deserted beach.

Don't take alcohol or stimulants such as tea, coffee and cola drinks before going to bed.

Don't eat anything immediately before going to bed, or a heavy meal less than three hours before bedtime.

Don't over-stimulate your mind near bedtime – for example by smoking, taking a hot drink or watching a violent film on television.

Don't put off going to bed.

Don't lie awake for hours worrying; get up and do something relaxing for 20 minutes or until you feel tired again.

or work. However, the body can make up for sleep loss without catching up on every lost hour. People who have had several nights' broken sleep can recover after a single sleep of about 12 hours.

Some insomnia sufferers become so wound up that they cannot relax enough to sleep. A vicious circle of overtiredness and insomnia develops and the victim becomes exhausted.

Insomnia, particularly early waking, may be a symptom of DEPRESSION. Sufferers also lack energy, finding everything an effort.

What the therapists recommend

HOMOEOPATHY

Self help Treatment of general health with homoeopathic remedies is said often to bring about an improvement in sleeping habits. In

the meantime, one of the following may help: *Aconitum* when kept awake by a sense of fear and panic, possibly following a shock or fright; *Arnica* when overtired mentally and physically, and when the bed feels too hard and constant movement is necessary to get relief; *Coffea* when wide awake with an active mind.

HERBAL MEDICINE

Self help Infusions of camomile or lime blossom (see p. 184) are gently relaxing, so take 2 tablespoonfuls at night.

Consultation Individual treatment and counselling may be needed for chronic insomnia due to STRESS and TENSION. In short-term (acute) cases, herbalists may prescribe 1 teaspoon (5ml) of passion flower or cowslip tincture each night.

MASSAGE

Self help Provided the insomnia is not a result of indigestion or a medical condition, a soothing, relaxing, sedating massage can work wonders if applied at bedtime, or as near as possible before that.

The patient's head rests gently on the pillow during treatment, and the body is kept well covered and warm. The therapist uses mainly slow, rhythmic stroking movements, with fairly deep kneadings using the palms of the hands. Contact is maintained throughout, as removing the hands or even changing the stroke can be irritating or disturbing to the person.

A full massage of the legs and back is applied, taking extreme care to avoid hypersensitive areas and the abdomen. The person carrying out the massage concentrates on the two movements of stroking and kneading, applied with comforting firmness. The intention is to apply firm upward strokes in rhythm with the patient's breathing.

Once this is achieved, the movement is slowed down a little and then maintained at that same gentle rhythm until the patient falls asleep.

Other alternative treatment

Traditional medicine A glass of warm milk with a teaspoon of honey helps induce sleep.

An orthodox view

Doctors can treat some forms of depression by prescribing antidepressant drugs, and so relieve insomnia. Other diseases that interfere with sleep, particularly painful ones, can also be diagnosed and treated.

Sleeping pills may be effective in breaking a vicious cycle of sleeplessness and overtiredness. However, users can become addicted within as little as three weeks of regular use, and the pills must therefore be used only for short periods.

The secret service that defends our bodies

A host of 'germs' – microorganisms from the environment – constantly attack and invade our bodies, where our immune system is ever at war with them. The complex system acts as a secret army which begins preparing for war before we are born. When invaders strike they activate teams of chemical dispatch riders – messengers that carry the orders for deployment of the troops and their engagement with the enemy. And once an engagement has been fought, the troops remain in reserve against any future attacks by the same invader.

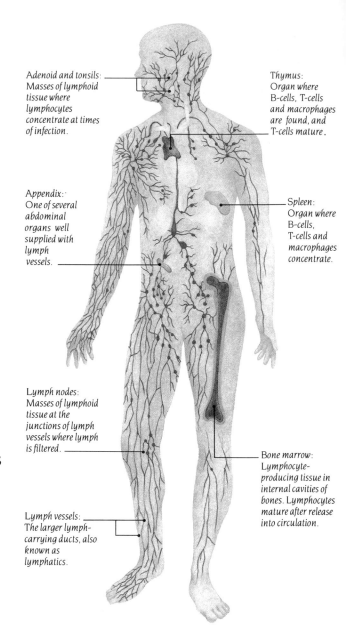

Adenoid and tonsils: Masses of lymphoid tissue where lymphocytes concentrate at times of infection.

Thymus: Organ where B-cells, T-cells and macrophages are found, and T-cells mature.

Appendix: One of several abdominal organs well supplied with lymph vessels.

Spleen: Organ where B-cells, T-cells and macrophages concentrate.

Lymph nodes: Masses of lymphoid tissue at the junctions of lymph vessels where lymph is filtered.

Bone marrow: Lymphocyte-producing tissue in internal cavities of bones. Lymphocytes mature after release into circulation.

Lymph vessels: The larger lymph-carrying ducts, also known as lymphatics.

The lymphatic network – the body's one-way drainage system

The lymphatic system consists of a network of vessels extending to all parts of the body. The fluid in them is colourless lymph, containing white but no red blood cells, and valves ensure that it flows only one way, away from the body's extremities. (Lymph also bathes the body's tissues and is very similar to blood plasma.) Disease-fighting white blood cells called lymphocytes originate in bone marrow, and develop and mature in other parts of the lymphatic system, such as the thymus and spleen. The tonsils, adenoid and other organs are made of lymphatic tissue, but their exact role remains unclear.

The 'germs' that invade the human body and live there as parasites include fungi such as *Candida albicans*, which causes THRUSH, and protozoa such as *Plasmodium*, the cause of malaria. However, by far the commonest are bacteria and viruses which are responsible for a whole host of infectious diseases, ranging from COLDS and INFLUENZA to SHINGLES, PNEUMONIA and POLIOMYELITIS.

Our first line of defence is the skin and mucous membranes, which keep out many would-be invaders. However, close behind is a complex defensive system which allows us to remain immune to most infections, even when they do get into the body. That is why it is called the *immune system*.

This system must be ready to neutralise or destroy microorganisms and the poisons they make wherever they attack the body, and the extensive lymphatic system fills the bill. The spleen, thymus gland, tonsils, bone marrow and other bodily organs are vital to it, and its network of capillaries and lymphatics, or lymph vessels, drain the clear body fluid known as lymph from the body's tissues and into the bloodstream (see diagram). And it is by special cells called *lymphocytes* – a type of white blood cell originating in bone marrow – and complex blood protein molecules called *antibodies* that the immune system mostly does its job.

Two types of immunity

We have two kinds of immunity. The first is a very general form of defence that we are born with or acquire through our mother's milk. This is called *passive* immunity, and it protects young babies while they are developing their own

How the antibodies, lymphocytes and macrophages act to destroy invaders

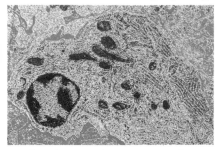

A B-lymphocyte is shown in section above. The parallel red bands (right) are the system of membranes where antibodies are made.

A computer graphic (right) shows an antibody-antigen complex. At the top is the antigen – the 'foreign' substance or bodily invader (red). The green is the part of the antigen that the antibody has recognised. The antibody itself is below (blue).

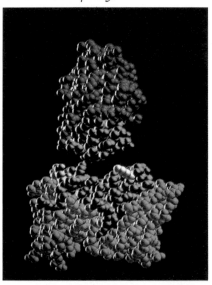

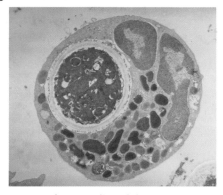

A macrophage engulfs and digests a yeast cell (large oval), a type of fungus. Macrophages – similar to white blood cells – occur in connective tissue, liver and the central nervous system as well as in the lymphatic system. The process by which they destroy invading cells is called phagocytosis.

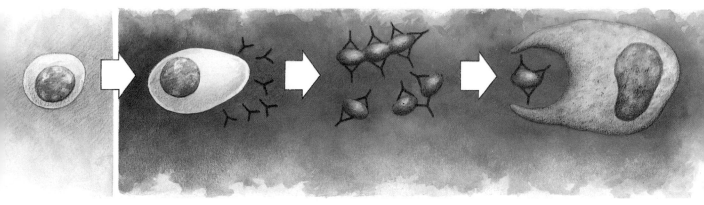

1 A B-cell detects invading bacteria, producing antibodies specially tailored to deal with the invaders.

2 Antibodies specific to the invading antigen (bacteria) are then released into the bloodstream.

3 Antibodies attach themselves to the invading bacteria, marking them for the macrophages.

4 Macrophages – scavenger white cells – engulf and digest the marked bacteria.

much more powerful system of *acquired* immunity. It is called 'acquired' because it develops in response to contact for the first time with some new virus or bacterium. Having been acquired, this immunity remains with us, so that the next time we encounter the same organism we can mount a defence against it very quickly.

This is one of the immune system's key features: its ability to 'remember' attackers (or *pathogens*) encountered in the past, recognising them so that it can instantly switch on a set of ready-made defences. A second feature is its diversity: its ability to develop a whole range of immune defences against different pathogens.

Immunising babies against, say, MEASLES or WHOOPING COUGH involves exposing them to a small amount of the dead or weakened pathogen. The body recognises this as a 'foreign' substance, or *antigen,* and creates a defence against it (see also ALLERGY). In later life, if the child encounters live measles viruses, the defence system is ready and needs only to be activated and directed against those particular invading organisms. But the defences against measles give no protection against, say, polio. Whether by vaccination or direct contact with disease, the immune system has to develop a host of programmes, each defending the body against a particular invader.

In the front line

The actual defences of the immune system consist of two closely connected main parts – the lymphocytes, white blood cells which are found in lymph as well as the bloodstream, and

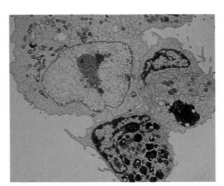

A cytotoxic T-lymphocyte attacks a virus-infected cell (the large cell at top). Such T-lymphocytes recognise antigenic components on the surface of invaders. They then bind directly to their outer cell membranes, and destroy the invader cells by a process called lysis. In this the invaders' outer membranes are broken, so allowing their cell contents to escape.

antibodies, which are produced by certain types of lymphocytes and circulate in the blood.

Antibodies have a branching structure with special sites shaped to lock on to invading microorganisms, or to the poisonous substances they are producing, and neutralise them. But the process goes further than that: scavenger cells called *macrophages* are constantly on the lookout for antibody-coated antigens. Any they encounter they engulf and destroy. In fact, antibodies act as 'markers' to ensure that invading material is destroyed by the macrophages.

Antibodies also act in other ways. When they stick to a foreign cell, the process mobilises groups of blood proteins known as *complement*, which have the ability to break up cells and so kill them. It may also be involved in the 'calling' of scavenging cells to the site of the ongoing conflict.

The body's production of antibodies depends on two types of lymphocytes. The *B-lymphocytes* (or *B-cells*), are the ones that first recognise the foreign antigens in the body and produce the first antibody reaction against them. During any subsequent attack by the same microorganism, particular B-cells specialised for that antigen mature rapidly and produce the appropriate antibodies in large quantities.

However, they cannot do so on their own. They are controlled by a second group of lymphocytes known as the *T-lymphocytes* (or *T-cells*), so called because they develop and mature in the thymus in the upper chest. There are several types of T-cells. Helper T-cells 'switch on' B-cells, and suppressor T-cells switch them off again (see diagram, p. 207). So the balance of

An enemy cell is recognised, and a 'killer cell' locks onto it

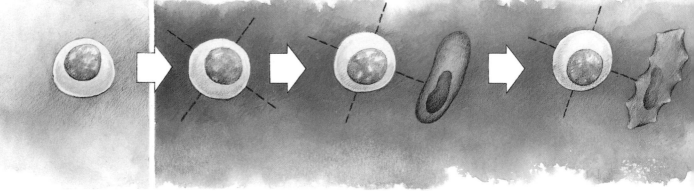

1 A T-cell in the thymus is activated in response to the invading antigen – virus, fungus, parasite or cancer cell.

2 The activated killer (or cytotoxic) T-cell is released into the bloodstream to home in on the invader.

3 Now the alerted T-cell attacks the target antigen cell, or virus-infected body cell, binding itself onto it.

4 The invader's cell wall is then broken down by the T-cell and the disease-producing antigen is destroyed.

helper to suppressor cells is vital for controlling immunity. The AIDS virus (HIV) attacks the immune system at this point, infecting and destroying the helper T-cells. The same mechanism is used to prevent the rejection of transplants.

Apart from the helper and suppressor cells, other types of T-cells play a direct part in destroying invading organisms or even the body's own cells once they have become infected – with a virus, for example. One type is the so-called *cytotoxic* ('cell-poisoning') T-cells, which learn to lock on to particular antigens on the surface of infected cells in much the same way as B-cells learn to make antibodies, which also lock on to antigens. The cytotoxic T-cells then break down the outer walls of the infected cells, thus causing their destruction. Other T-cells are known as *natural killers*. They do not need to be programmed, and can recognise and destroy any foreign materials even if they have not encountered them before.

Some CANCER cells are recognised as foreign by natural killer T-cells and are destroyed, but unfortunately not all. One of the great challenges of cancer research is to find out why, and to devise ways of boosting the immune system so that it can fight cancerous tumours.

Why your 'glands' swell

The B and T-cells and the macrophages, which together make up the body's system of cellular immunity, are found in high concentrations in the thymus and spleen. They constantly monitor the contents of body fluid as it flows through the lymphatic system, where lymph nodes (junctions in the network) filter it. If foreign material is detected, mature lymphocytes concentrate in large numbers in the nodes and migrate to the bloodstream to deal with it. (This concentration causes the swollen 'glands' – in fact, lymph nodes – in the neck, armpits or groin during some illnesses.)

The way the body coordinates cellular immunity through chemical messages has only recently been discovered. Helper T-cells stimulate B-cells to produce antibodies by secreting a particular chemical substance called an *interleukin*. Other interleukins stimulate cytotoxic T-cells and natural killer cells into activity, and suppressor T-cells similarly exert their influence chemically.

So do macrophages, which produce similar substances when they encounter foreign cells; the result is to boost the activity of T-cells nearby. And other chemical messengers act as 'help' signals. They make lymphocytes concentrate at the site of an infection.

Chemical signals may also maintain links between the immune system and the brain. This traffic is apparently two-way, implying that the brain somehow monitors or responds to the condition of the immune system, and that state of mind can influence resistance to disease.

There is plenty of circumstantial evidence that this is true, and doctors have long known that a 'positive' attitude can help patients to overcome diseases ranging from common infections to cancer. But they have never been able to measure the effect or explain how it happens. The discovery of the chemical messengers involved may help us to both understand and influence this aspect of the body's defences.

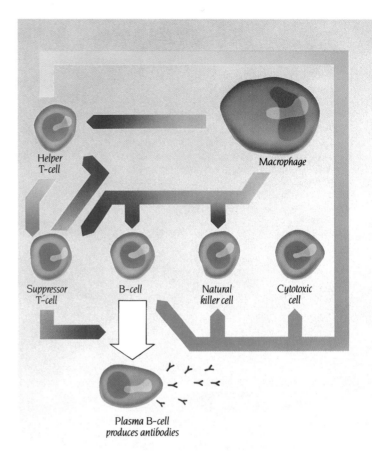

Plasma B-cell
produces antibodies

Chemical messengers

The various types of cells involved in the immune system – and, it now appears, the brain too – signal to and influence each other by a system of chemical messengers. Among the most important are the interleukins, by which helper T-lymphocytes (T-cells) stimulate other kinds of lymphocyte into action (green arrows), and the suppressor factors that suppressor T-cells use to keep helpers and B-lymphocytes (B-cells) under control (red arrows). Macrophages signal for help in a similar way (blue arrows).

Strengthening the defences

A number of alternative therapies suggest ways of boosting the immune system, to make the body better able to fight disease. Most conventional doctors would endorse the need for a good, balanced diet – though there is disagreement as to whether additional zinc (see MINERALS), VITAMINS A and C, and/or certain essential fatty acids are beneficial, as some claim. Similarly, the immunity-boosting effect of EXERCISE is difficult to prove or disprove.

The recent discoveries mentioned earlier – as well as commonplace experience – point to the importance of avoiding stress and adopting a positive mental attitude in overcoming disease, whether it is the common cold or AIDS, influenza or cancer.

IONISATION
Mountain air from a machine

The well-known feeling of tension that builds up before a storm, and the sense of relief afterwards; headachy irritability after a day at work; or vigorous good health on a mountain holiday – these are some of the most common effects that different kinds of air seem to have on our well-being. One explanation – accepted by many doctors and scientists as well as by alternative practitioners – is that electrically charged particles in the air, called ions, are responsible.

Most air particles are electrically neutral, or contain no charge, but others can acquire a positive or negative charge. When there are too few negative ions or too many positive ones – before a storm, for example – many people experience HEADACHES, lethargy, DEPRESSION, irritability and a general feeling of being unwell. By contrast, a good supply of negative ions – as occurs after a storm – is associated with feeling alert and uplifted.

Charged ions are mainly the result of radiation from the sun and from space, but negative ions are also created by lightning, ocean waves and running water. Fresh mountain and seaside air is rich in negative particles, but most city air contains few or none. Pollution, air conditioning, central heating, dust, synthetic fibres and electrical appliances are all said to destroy negative charges, and may account for the oppressive atmosphere in many houses and offices.

Self help People in environments likely to be low in negative ions and those who are particularly sensitive to weather conditions – some ASTHMA sufferers, for example – often find ionising machines helpful. These are small electrical devices which use very little current but produce a constant stream of negative ions when turned on.

Small ionisers cost about £35-£50 and are available from chemists, health food shops and electrical stores. They have a range of about 3-4 metres (10-13ft), so need to be plugged in at the bedside or placed on a desk or table where you work. Some manufacturers also make more powerful units for use in offices and larger areas.

Ionisers work best when doors and windows are closed, and should be no less than about 50cm (20in) from walls and floors to allow a free flow of ions into the air. Wherever possible, avoid placing ionisers near windows or on polished surfaces, as static electrical charges on these can make the machines work less efficiently.

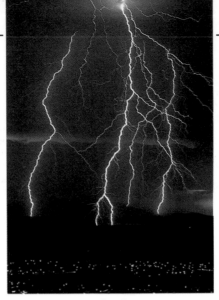

Pure air for the home

The most effective ionisers are supplied by nature. For example, an electric storm fills the air with negative ions, making us feel refreshed and reinvigorated once the storm is over. Fresh running water – such as a mountain stream – is another highly successful way of providing the atmospheric ions that do us good. The balance of positive and negative ions in the home can be restored by installing an air ioniser in the living-room or bedroom. Bedroom ionisers should be placed no more than about 2m (6½ft) from the head of the bed, and you can go to sleep knowing that you are breathing balanced-ion air. Home ionisers are believed particularly to help people suffering from chest and lung problems.

Keep ionisers and the surfaces around them clean, as they tend to attract dust particles – and sticky tar if you are a smoker – which may eventually interfere with their functioning. Ionisers are also more effective if air conditioning and central heating are used sparingly, and if electrical appliances are turned off when not in use.

Alternatively, taking a shower is a cheap and effective way of receiving negatively charged ions – which is one reason why most people feel refreshed and reinvigorated after a brisk shower.

Who it can help Regular night-time use of a bedside ioniser is said to benefit respiratory disorders such as asthma, BRONCHITIS, HAY FEVER and CATARRH. Depression, INSOMNIA, MIGRAINE and headaches have also been helped, and one study has even shown that burns may heal faster when there are more negative ions.

Ionisation is also thought to prevent illness by cleansing the air of bacteria and impurities such as cigarette smoke, pollen, dust and small fibres that can irritate the respiratory tract and cause ALLERGY. However, these impurities tend to collect on furniture and household surfaces, which then need to be cleaned more often.

An orthodox view

There are no known side effects or dangers associated with negative ionisation machines, and many conventional doctors and scientists accept the claims made for them. Studies by Dr Leslie Hawkins at the University of Surrey have shown that many people with respiratory conditions, skin allergies and headaches were helped by ionisers at their places of work.

Dr Hawkins's research suggests that air rich in negative ions has a stimulating effect, while too many positive ions have a depressing effect. The levels of the hormone serotonin in the blood, brain and other body tissues also seem to be reduced by negative ions, having a calming influence on the nervous system. This may explain why ionisers seem to help in cases of asthma, irritability and STRESS.

IRIDOLOGY
Diagnosing by eye

Studying the markings on the irises of the eyes and observing changes in them is the basis of iridology. It is a method of DIAGNOSIS and health monitoring used by iridologists and other alternative therapists. Iridology

relates precise positions on the irises to parts of the body, and from changes at those positions, practitioners claim to locate and diagnose problems in the body – and mind.

Although early medical men sought clues in the eye for their patients' ailments, modern iridology began with the Hungarian doctor Ignatz von Peczely (1826-1911). As a boy he had cared for an owl with a broken leg. He noted a black line form in the owl's iris and gradually change to white marks around a black dot as the leg healed.

Later, as a doctor, von Peczely became convinced that the same illness produced a telltale mark at the same point on the iris in patient after patient. After he published his findings in 1881, interest in them spread across Europe and, in the early 1900s, throughout the United States. It was there in the 1950s that Dr Bernard Jensen worked out a detailed chart of the irises, pinpointing the precise part of the body that each iris area is said to reflect.

The iris is divided into sections (like portions of a cake) linked to parts or functions of the body, and also into six rings or zones linked to bodily systems (see p. 210). The first and innermost zone relates to the stomach, the second to the intestines, the third to the blood and lymph systems, the fourth to glands and organs, the fifth to the muscles and skeleton, and the sixth and outermost to the skin and elimination.

The left iris corresponds to the left side of the body and the right iris to the right side. Many parts or functions are reflected in both irises. Generally, organs and functions in the upper body will reflect their condition in the top part of the iris and lower body organs and functions in the lower part.

White marks are thought to develop through inflammation, too much stimulation and STRESS; and dark ones when a part of the body does not work properly. A dark rim round the edge of the iris may indicate that poisons are accumulating in the skin because of inefficient elimination of waste.

Iridologists recognise ten different types of constitution with a different balance of strengths and weaknesses in their body systems, organs and glands. Each type of constitution has a basic fibre pattern in the irises. A fine-grained pattern like woven silk indicates a strong constitution, an open hessian-like pattern indicates a weak one.

When the abnormal marks have been studied, the iridologist or other therapist may devise a suitable treatment to restore the correct balance for that particular patient's constitution. An experienced iridologist also looks for early warning of problems.

Who it can help People who do not like the more invasive techniques of conventional medicine – blood tests, swabs, X-rays, biop-

sies and the like – feel more at ease with an examination of the eye. Those who want early warning of a condition before it shows unpleasant symptoms or who want a regular check on what progress they are making with a more healthy life style, may also benefit from iridology.

Finding a therapist Many alternative therapists use iridology as one of their diagnostic methods and will use it as a matter of course when you consult them, or refer you to the iridologist they normally use.

If you want to go independently to an iridologist, the British School of Iridology, PO Box 205, Cambridge CB3 7YF, will supply a list of members of the British Register of Iridologists. The school runs a training course lasting one to three years to prepare students to become members (MBRI). Many are already professionals in one or more type of natural treatment (some are conventional doctors), and the school also offers diploma courses in HERBAL MEDICINE and NATUROPATHY. The National Council and Register of Iridologists, 80 Portland Road, Bournemouth BH9 1NQ, can also give you a list of trained iridologists.

Before embarking on any consultations, ask how long consultants have practised, how long their training was, and whether they are trained in anatomy and physiology. Many iridologists give diagnoses only, not treatment. If you require treatment, make sure your preferred form of therapy is on offer, be it homoeopathy, acupuncture, or some other.

Consulting a therapist A practitioner who examines your irises as only one of several diagnostic techniques is likely to use a torch and a magnifying glass, and make a detailed record of your markings. A specialist iridologist may also use a camera with a close-up lens and side lighting to take slides of your irises for a permanent record.

When the slides are projected onto a screen, the iridologist will explain the significance of the various markings and advise you what treatment will correct any disorders, or recommend you consult a suitable therapist. At follow-up consultations further slides can be compared with the originals to show progress.

If signs of degeneration, malignancy, or chronic disease are found, patients are advised to see their GP.

An orthodox view

Although doctors often find the general appearance of the eye – yellowing, dullness or unnatural brilliance, for example – an indication of ill health, few of them accept the detailed links between parts of the body and areas of the iris that iridologists do. Most doctors consider iridology to be unscientific

Right Iris

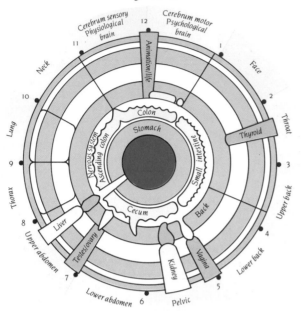

Left Iris

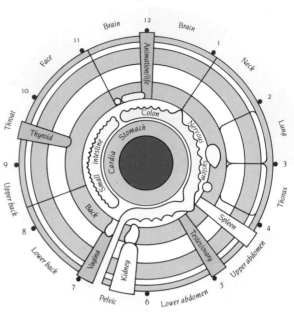

Seeing the body in the eyes

An American pioneer of iridology, Dr Bernard Jensen, drew up comprehensive iris charts showing, in sections, how the different parts of the body are related to the eyes. The left iris reflects the left side of the body and the right iris the right side.

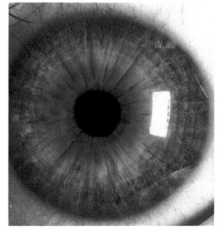

Studying the eyes of this patient, the iridologist decided that she was disposed to weakness in the nervous system (shown by the tightly stretched fibres radiating from the pupil) – prone to headaches, swollen glands and ulcers as her nervous system was subjected to stress. The patch of white light at three o'clock is a camera light reflection.

When consulting an iridologist, a special camera is used to photograph the irises. It can move in three different directions: left-to-right, up-and-down and forwards-and-

backwards. The contours of the eyes are lit from the sides so that the therapist can capture all their aspects on film – and then assess the patient's strengths and weaknesses.

and therefore of no use. The white fibres in the iris are only part of the layers of muscle that open and reduce the pupil. Neither they nor the flecks of colour have any more meaning than the texture or colouring of hair – except in a few instances. Minute pale lumps may develop on the iris of people with tuberculosis, for example.

Conventional doctors do not generally consider iridology harmful. They feel that the chief danger may lie in failure to diagnose a condition that needs urgent surgery or control by a drug.

IRRITABLE BOWEL SYNDROME

Young and middle-aged adults are those most prone to this bowel disorder, commonly called IBS. It is more common in women of 20 to 45 years than in men of the same age, but children can also suffer. The symptoms come and go, and there may be many years of respite between bouts. However, in some cases IBS persists for months or years, even with treatment.

The condition has also been known by such names as spastic colon and mucous colitis, and the causes are still not firmly established, though it is thought that STRESS may play a significant role in many cases.

IBS restricts the contraction and relaxation of the rings of muscle in the walls of the gut, which push down through the intestines, into the colon and rectum, and finally out through the anus. When the sequence of muscle action is weak or disturbed, spasmodic pain with explosive, watery DIARRHOEA or CONSTIPATION results. Bouts of the two often alternate. Usually the diarrhoea is worse in the morning, and it may also contain slimy mucus.

Cramp-like pain in the lower abdomen is commonplace, but this is sometimes relieved by passing WIND or evacuating the bowel. Other symptoms may include BACK PAIN, a feeling of bloatedness, and general weakness and TIREDNESS.

The muscles of the bowel are controlled by the autonomic nervous system; they are not consciously directed. This means that IBS can be brought on and aggravated by ANXIETY, stress and NERVOUS DISORDERS. Tests in which balloons and tubes were introduced into the colon have shown that sufferers have rapid, jerky contractions there, instead of a smooth sequence of muscle activity. IBS may also be the result of a

severe infection affecting the intestines. **_Warning_** If you have any bleeding from the bowel, see your doctor immediately. It may be the result of an unusually severe type of IBS, but it could also indicate something more serious. In any case, if you experience IBS symptoms together with a rapid loss of weight, especially if you are over 60, seek expert advice at once.

What the therapists recommend
NATUROPATHY
Consultation The problem is often associated with imbalanced diets and/or food intolerance, and not just a matter of nervousness affecting the bowel. A wholefood diet (see EATING FOR HEALTH) is usually recommended to maintain regular bowel action. You will be asked to avoid stimulating laxatives, and instead rely on dietary FIBRE and bulk laxatives, such as linseed or psyllium seed, for restoring regularity.

A practitioner will also be concerned to rule out any food sensitivities. In any case, potential irritants such as alcohol, coffee and strong spices should be avoided.
Self help Abdominal massage can be helpful, and attention to ways of relaxing generally is considered vital (see RELAXATION AND BREATHING).

HERBAL MEDICINE
Self help Initial measures include hot infusions of peppermint or camomile, possibly with a little ginger added, two or three times a day. Use linseed as a soothing bulk laxative: put a dessertspoonful on a serving of cereal, and eat it with at least ⅓ pint (200ml) water.

HOMOEOPATHY
Self help One of the following remedies may help. Take a dose three to four times a day for 10-14 days. For griping pains, which are better when the sufferer is doubled up or pressing on his abdomen, and to give warmth, _Colocynthis 6_ or _30_. This is also helpful if the condition is brought on by anger. When constipation alternates with diarrhoea, and there is flatulence, colicky pain and mucus in the faeces, _Argentum nit. 6_. If there are nausea, tearing pains and watery stools with jelly-like mucus, and an aversion to food, _Colchicum 6_.

An orthodox view
Doctors diagnose irritable bowel syndrome by testing samples of faeces, by X-raying the bowel after a barium enema (or meal), and/or by inserting an endoscope up into the rectum. These procedures eliminate any possibility of LACTOSE INTOLERANCE, diverticular disease – in which 'pockets' develop in the wall of the colon in which its contents

become trapped – or CANCER of the bowel being the cause of the problem.

Treatment is aimed at controlling the abnormal activity of the bowel-wall muscles and relieving stress, if that is a factor. Doctors may tell the patient to eat more dietary fibre, and may prescribe antispasmodic and antidiarrhoeal drugs.

ITCHING

Many skin disorders, including ECZEMA, HIVES and scabies, cause itching. Chronic itching and scratching of exposed areas can be symptoms of some psychological problems, and in jaundiced patients, some LIVER DISORDERS that cause excess bile in the blood can also give rise to itching. PILES, threadworms (see WORMS) and ANXIETY can cause itching around the anus – which is more common among men. This sometimes persists or recurs for months or years, despite treatment.

In addition, lice and nits cause severe itching of the scalp (see HAIR PROBLEMS).

What the therapists recommend
Herbal Medicine Full treatment depends on the cause of the itching, but local application of chickweed, as an infusion (see p. 184), oil or ointment, may reduce itching considerably. A dry skin aggravates the problem, so an oil such as sweet almond can help if gently massaged into the skin regularly.
Naturopathy The advice depends very much on the cause. In skin conditions such as eczema, the excessive dryness of the skin aggravates the itchiness and this may be relieved with oils such as sweet almond, avocado or wheat germ.

An orthodox view
If itching persists for more than two or three days, see a doctor, who may be able to diagnose and treat the cause. Hydrocortisone cream or ointment, available without prescription, may relieve symptoms, but should be used only for conditions such as eczema that have already been diagnosed. Antihistamine tablets such as terfenadine or chlorpheniramine, also available without prescription, may give some relief, but may also cause drowsiness.

If anal itching is caused by threadworms, or scalp itching is caused by lice and nits, all members of the household should be treated at the same time to prevent recurrence. A daily bath or shower and the use of soft wipes instead of toilet paper may relieve anal itching.

JAUNDICE

In cases of jaundice, the patient's skin – and the whites of the eyes – turn a sickly yellow. This is due to the presence in the bloodstream of a yellow pigment called bilirubin, which is produced in the spleen when old or damaged red blood cells are destroyed. Normally, the pigment is passed by the liver into the intestine, where it causes the stools to be coloured brown. There are various reasons why bilirubin may accumulate in the blood, causing jaundice.

The yellowing may be a symptom of a serious underlying disease – often of the liver – such as CANCER, cirrhosis or hepatitis. In addition, GALLSTONES in the bile duct can block the outflow of bile from the liver, preventing the excretion of bilirubin.

The most common type of jaundice in young, healthy people is a virus disease, infectious jaundice, or hepatitis A. Patients usually recover within three weeks without any specific treatment. Less common, but much more dangerous, is hepatitis B. See LIVER DISORDERS.

Otherwise healthy babies often suffer from jaundice during the first week of life, but in their case the condition is not serious and quickly passes. It is a normal result of the destruction of excess red blood cells that are not needed once the baby can breathe.

Warning Jaundice is often hard to recognise in its early stages, and may take anything from a few days to several weeks to develop. It can indicate serious (possibly fatal) disease so, as soon as it is suspected, medical advice should be sought.

What the therapists recommend

Herbal Medicine Medical herbalists have a range of remedies for helping the liver, including balmony, dandelion root, golden seal and milk thistle. They are usually prescribed as tinctures or decoctions.

Naturopathy Practitioners advise treating liver imbalance by avoiding fats and alcohol. Two or three glasses daily of fresh vegetable juices – celery or carrot, for example – may also be recommended.

Reflexology Massage is given to the reflex areas relating to the liver and gall bladder; and also to areas relating to the solar plexus, and the adrenal and pituitary glands.

An orthodox view

Once jaundice has been diagnosed, a doctor will try to determine the root cause of the disease. Tests may include taking blood samples, X-rays, or a scan of the gall bladder or the liver. See liver disorders.

JET LAG

Fatigue and feelings of sluggishness are normal after east-west or west-east air journeys that cross any of the world's 24 different time zones. The body's natural 24-hour cycle (known as the circadian rhythm) is disturbed. This causes sleepiness at the 'wrong' time of day. With north-south or south-north flights time changes do occur, according to how far east or west your destination is, but they are not as great as when travelling long distances from east to west or west to east.

One of the problems in dealing with jet lag is that the condition varies from one person to another. However, researchers at the University of Surrey have discovered that doses of melatonin, a hormone produced in the body during sleep, can help some people's systems to adjust to time changes on arrival in other countries.

Contributory causes that have been suggested include the body's overproduction of 'free radicals' – toxic chemicals. This is thought to be caused by factors such as low cabin pressurisation (generally equivalent to the air at about 10,000ft; 3000m) and exposure to radiation through flying at heights where earth's protective atmosphere is thin. (It has been estimated that a trip across the Atlantic, for example, exposes a passenger to the equivalent of two X-rays.)

One way of getting rid of excess free radicals after a flight, suggested following research at the University of Toronto, is EXERCISE, such as JOGGING or AEROBICS. This is thought to produce enzymes which help to counter unwanted chemicals in the body.

Other suggested ways to avoid the effects of jet lag include eating only light salads during a flight, sleeping as much as possible, and resting again on the first day after the flight. Supplementary VITAMINS are also believed to help: during a journey, try one 50-100mg strength extra-stress B complex in the morning and another in the evening, along with 1g of vitamin C with bioflavonoids, and 400iu vitamin E.

It is also worth noting that both airline crews and passengers have attended courses in AUTOGENIC TRAINING, intended to help relax the traveller and to counter jet lag.

An orthodox view

Doctors say that jet lag can be greatly reduced by drinking plenty of non-alcoholic fluids during long air flights, and so avoiding dehydration. Do not drink alcohol, which not only dehydrates but has a stronger effect in low-pressure conditions. If possible, try to arrive at your new destination in the evening

(local time). Then take a mild sedative or sleeping pill and go to bed early.

For a short visit – say a few days – try to eat and sleep according to your clock back home. For longer visits of a week or more, start to live according to local times as soon as possible. Set your watch to the new time as soon as you are seated in the aeroplane, and then go to bed at the same time as the residents at your destination.

JOGGING
Pacing yourself to fitness

Many people go jogging as their main form of EXERCISE, preferring its easy movement to that of running or more energetic sports and pastimes. Ideally, jogging should last for no more than 20-30 minutes at a gentle, comfortable pace. Run at a pace that allows you to have a conversation. If you cannot, then you are jogging too fast. As your fitness improves you will find that you will be able to jog faster for the same rate of breathing.

Although jogging on grass or tarmac is generally regarded as a 'safe' activity, injuries such as SPRAINS and strains can occur – especially if you do not wear the right kind of shoes, socks and clothing.

Jogging, or sports, shoes should be flexible enough to promote a springing step and firm enough to give good support around the heel. Buy them from a specialist sports shop, where you can get expert guidance. A well-cushioned inner sole reduces impact shock and supports the arches. Make sure the shoes fit comfortably. There should be about a thumb's width of space between the big toe and the front of the shoe to allow the toes to move freely. Break in the shoes by wearing them at home or when out shopping or going for a walk.

The shoes will cost £25-£50. They will be the most expensive and the most important investment. Remember, you get what you pay for; the higher the price, the better the quality and the more support they will give you. Good quality shoes should last for many months, or even a year or two.

Sports socks should be made of cotton to absorb sweat – nylon socks do not do this. Again, make sure they fit comfortably and do not wrinkle up. A cotton (or cotton-mix) T-shirt and shorts are best for jogging in warm weather, and a well-fitting tracksuit when it is cold.

Before you start jogging, it is important to warm up for about five minutes with bending and stretching exercises (see illustrations). This prepares the heart and lungs for the effort to come, helps the muscles to work well, and cuts down the chance of injury.

When jogging, never ignore any pain or signs of breathlessness, discomfort, weakness or fatigue. If these feelings are experienced, slow down or stop. Carrying on regardless may lead to further distress, pulled muscles, stiff muscles and joint damage (see SPORTS INJURIES).

Jogging is a safe activity in terms of serious health risks such as heart attack. But, if you are aged over 35, or suffer from bad health, do not take up jogging without first consulting a doctor. Remember, vigorous activity never harmed a healthy body; it is _inactivity_ that causes the damage. However, vigorous activity following years of inactivity may just bring unseen damage to the surface.

Warming up for jogging

Ease into the stretches, and go only as far as is comfortable. Stretch in straight lines and breathe normally. Hold each for 10 seconds, and if comfortable, continue to time given.

JOINT PROBLEMS

People with inflamed or worn joints find it increasingly difficult to move as the areas become stiffer and more swollen and painful. Most joint problems are caused by ARTHRITIS in one form or another. Sometimes a joint may be damaged by injury, and the tough, fibrous ligaments that hold it together become weak and painful. This may occur during games, for example (see SPORTS INJURIES; SPRAINS).

Usually, different diseases affect different joints. For example, OSTEOARTHRITIS affects mainly the hips, spine and knees of the

Calf Gently push through the hips, keeping heels on the floor. Hold for 30 seconds each leg.

Hamstring Pull knee towards the chest, hips on floor. Keep knee straight, as far as possible. Hold each leg for 20 seconds.

Shoulder Push arm gently back with hand. Don't arch the back; keep it rounded by bending the knees. Hold for 15 seconds each arm.

Groin Push knees down with elbows, feet together. Hold for 30 seconds.

elderly. RHEUMATOID ARTHRITIS affects mainly the hands, knees and feet of the middle-aged. And GOUT affects mainly people's finger, leg and big toe joints.

What the therapists recommend

Osteopathy The aim is to remove abnormal stress from an injured joint, and improve overall mobility and muscle tone. But manipulation is _not_ advised for acutely inflamed joints, as in rheumatoid arthritis.

Hydrotherapy For stiff and/or painful joints, therapists advise cold baths or packs for acute cases; and underwater douching, vortex baths, warm paraffin wax, Vichy massage and supervised exercises in the warm hydrotherapy pool for less serious cases.

Homoeopathy An experienced homoeopath will probably prescribe one or more medicines – for example, _Rhus tox._ for aching and stiffness which wears off as the patient gets moving, and which is worse after rest; _Colchicum_ for pain and stiffness which is worse during the night; _Dulcamara_ for pain which is worse in damp weather.

Acupuncture The practitioner will treat points on the abdomen, gall bladder, liver, spleen and stomach meridians. MOXIBUSTION may be applied to the abdomen, bladder, gall bladder and liver meridians.

Acupressure For knee pain, a therapist will treat the outer side of the knee, four fingers' width down from the kneecap in the hollow between the shin and smaller leg bone.

Massage A therapist will show the patient how to start the treatment with deep stroking of the limb and, if there is joint swelling, to concentrate on the part of the limb nearest to the trunk. Kneading and wringing follows to tone the muscles. Friction is then applied, gentle at first, then firmer, deeper movements around the affected joint.

Reflexology Massage is given to reflex areas related to the affected areas, and direct massage to the zone-related area – shoulder for hip, elbow for knee, wrist for ankle, hand for foot and so on. Areas relating to the solar plexus and the adrenal and pituitary glands are also treated. See chart, p. 295.

An orthodox view

If a joint is painful or swollen with fluid, a doctor will strap it with a crêpe bandage. He will then raise the limb – on cushions or a stool, for example – and apply an ice pack to reduce inflammation and swelling. In hospital a special hoist may be used.

If a FRACTURE is suspected, or if the symptoms are severe or last for more than a week, an X-ray or physiotherapy may be advised. If arthritis is suspected, blood samples may be taken to identify the cause.

See also BACK PAIN, CHIROPRACTIC and NECK PAIN.

KIDNEY COMPLAINTS

Most people have two kidneys, although very occasionally a baby may be born with only one, or a kidney may be lost due to illness or an accident. Their job is to filter waste products from the blood into the urine, which then passes to the bladder and out of the system. They also play a vital role in controlling fluid balance in the body (see WATER RETENTION) and BLOOD PRESSURE.

Several disorders can affect the kidneys. The most common is kidney stones, small lumps of calcium and uric acid that crystallise in the kidneys or the ureters (the tubes that carry urine to the bladder). They result from urine that is too concentrated, or from an infection.

Usually the stones do not cause pain while in the kidney, but can do so when they become dislodged and start to travel down the urinary tract, or block it. When this occurs, there can be short bursts of severe BACK PAIN in the kidney region (see illustration below), sometimes spreading to the abdomen and genitals. This is also known as renal or ureteric colic. Other symptoms include pain on passing urine, and sometimes blood in the urine.

The kidneys may also become infected by bacteria, causing a disorder called pyelonephritis. This is usually the result of another condition, such as CYSTITIS or PROSTATE PROBLEMS. The sufferer experiences pain over the kidneys and in the sides, waist and sometimes the abdomen. There is usually a FEVER, and blood, protein and white blood cells are found on analysis of the urine. There may be a frequent need to urinate.

Nephritis is a rare but more serious kidney complaint. The cause is generally a disorder of the IMMUNE SYSTEM, in which antibodies produced by the body attack kidney tissue. The symptoms are red or smoky-coloured urine passed in small quantities, water retention, HEADACHE and backache, along with high blood pressure. A few cases eventually lead to kidney failure, making a transplant or regular treatment on a dialysis machine – a type of filter system – necessary.

Other problems include CANCER of the kidney, in which there is blood in the urine, but no pain, and kidney failure brought on by DIABETES. Always consult a doctor about any kidney trouble, since it can become serious without attention.

Warning Untreated infections can cause permanent damage. It is vital to exclude them before seeking alternative treatments.

What the therapists recommend

Acupuncture Kidney problems are often thought to involve a deficiency of the yang element (see YIN AND YANG). If the symptoms include burning heat, severe pain or FEVER, the disorder is usually regarded as an excess of heat disturbance of the bladder. If there is an infection, the patient will also be advised to seek orthodox medical treatment.

Acupuncture for kidney problems is given at points on the governor, conception, bladder, large intestine, kidney and spleen meridians (see chart, p. 14). MOXIBUSTION may be applied at points on the gall bladder, bladder, kidney, liver and spleen meridians to strengthen the kidneys.

Herbal Medicine Responsible herbalists advise orthodox treatment for kidney complaints, although they may also recommend remedies such as gravel root, parsley piert and wild carrot when there is inflammation or tiny kidney stones. These plants are said to have a soothing, diuretic effect and to help flush out the urinary system.

Acupressure The therapist will apply firm pressure at appropriate points on the kidney,

Waste-disposal system

Many times a day the blood passes through the kidneys, which adjust its content of water, salts and acids.

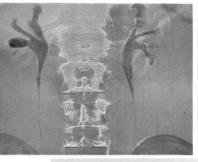

The X-rayed kidney on the left has a stone blocking the entry to the ureter. An inadequate flow through the ureter has allowed damaging deposits to form there.

Kidney
A mass of tubes in the kidneys processes the waste filtered from the blood and produces urine.

Ureter
A ureter from each kidney carries the urine to the bladder, where it can be stored before being expelled through the urethra.

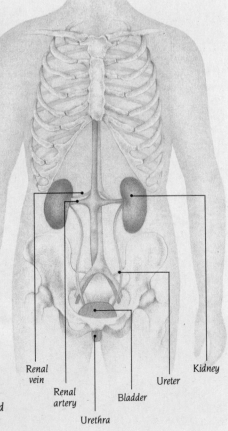

Renal vein

Renal artery

Bladder

Urethra

Ureter

Kidney

Caring for your kidneys

Drink up to 3 pints (1.75 litres) of liquid a day, especially when hot weather or activity increases perspiration. Dehydration makes the urine highly concentrated, increasing the risk of kidney stones and disorders such as cystitis.

Do not take diuretics – drugs that increase urination – unless they are essential. In that case, ask your doctor to prescribe those that do not increase uric acid levels in the blood.

Empty your bladder as soon as you feel the need. The longer urine remains in the body, the more likely minerals are to crystallise into stones, and the greater the chance for bacteria to breed.

If you suffer from kidney stones, avoid dairy foods, which are calcium rich, and drink low-calcium bottled mineral water rather than tap water.

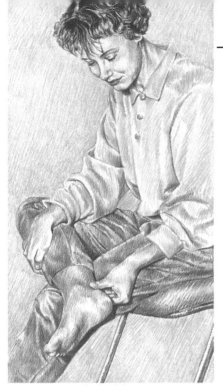

Acupressure can be helpful in countering incontinence – apply strong pressure upwards in the hollow between the inner ankle bone and the Achilles tendon.

spleen, conception and bladder meridians (see also illustration above).

T'ai-chi Ch'uan This is said to help by balancing the energy flows of the body and mind, and improving the circulation of body fluids and the expulsion of waste. The gentle, co-ordinated movements of T'ai-chi Ch'uan, coupled with full abdominal breathing and good posture, are said to release TENSION and to have the effect of internally massaging the kidneys. A teacher would also be likely to advise the patient on a more suitable diet and about possible causes of tension.

Naturopathy Small stones and gravelly deposits are usually calcium based, and patients will be advised to reduce their intake of calcium-rich foods such as dairy products – and also foods high in oxalic acid, such as spinach, rhubarb and chocolate. Naturopaths may advise patients to take a little cider vinegar each day, or possibly a magnesium supplement. They will also be encouraged to drink plenty of fluids – in a hard-water area this may necessitate the use of a water filter to remove calcium.

Reflexology Manipulation would be applied to reflex areas that correspond to the kidneys, the bladder, and the pituitary and adrenal glands (see chart, p. 295), and to areas that relate to the lymphatic system.

An orthodox view

Kidney complaints can be serious if left untreated, so alternative therapies, although they may help to get rid of infections, should be used only alongside orthodox treatment. When consulting a doctor about kidney trouble, take a sample of urine along to help with the diagnosis. The doctor will probably also examine the abdomen to see if the kidneys are enlarged or tender, and may use blood tests, a kidney scan or X-rays to discover more. The urine will be analysed for evidence of blood, protein or cells. Sometimes it is also necessary to take a sample of kidney tissue for testing.

Treatment depends on the individual problem. Stones can be broken down with ULTRASONICS, while infections can usually be cleared up quickly by antibiotics. More serious disorders are treated in a variety of ways and, if all else fails, a kidney transplant can restore good health in certain cases.

Despite doctors' caution about alternative medicine, much of the advice from alternative therapists on diet and care of the kidneys is useful and appropriate. Naturopathy, herbal medicine and acupuncture, which help both to diminish toxin build-up and to increase the expulsion of toxins, can be useful on a long-term basis.

KINESIOLOGY
Balancing health by testing muscles

Most people are familiar with the 'knee-jerk' test, when your knee is tapped to test your reflexes. If they are working properly, your leg will involuntarily jerk upwards. A system of diagnosis and treatment based on this and similar reactions was developed in 1964 by an American doctor of chiropractic named George Goodheart. It became known as kinesiology from the Greek word *kinesis*, meaning 'motion'.

Practitioners believe that each group of muscles is related to other parts of the body – the organs, digestive system, glands, bones and circulation – and that when the muscles are in good working order, so is the body. How a muscle responds in tests to gentle, manual pressure, reveals to the practitioner how the whole body is functioning.

Kinesiologists do not diagnose illness. They look for imbalances or deficiencies in nutrition and energy, or locate physical problems. Having pinpointed any trouble spots, practitioners try to revitalise them by giving a light, fingertip massage to 'pressure points' on the body and scalp. Most of these points are some distance from the muscles they relate to. The pressure points for the main leg muscles between the hip and knee, for example, are along the border of the rib cage.

The theory is that because muscles rely upon good supplies of blood and lymph (a body fluid which carries away poisons and drains the tissues), stimulating appropriate pressure points enhances the blood flow to the muscles concerned and balances the lymphatic system.

It is also believed that our bodies contain an invisible energy, like an electric current, running through 'computer circuits' that control bodily functions – a stomach circuit, a pancreas circuit and so on. The energy flow may be compared to the electrical impulses that make a washing machine run through a series of functions according to a programme. These circuits are said to 'blow a fuse' under stress or during illness, and you become weak if you use up more energy than they can generate.

Muscle testing is seen as a way of checking the circuits to give a practitioner a clear picture of the patient's state of health. The practitioner then tries to 'reset' the circuits found to be out of balance.

Kinesiology is also used as a preventive measure. Practitioners claim that they can identify imbalances which, if neglected, could lead to problems in years to come.

Who it can help Practitioners believe that this therapy can help anyone, but it is perhaps best known for aiding people who have an ALLERGY or sensitivity to certain foods. The body is thought to recognise and react instantly to nutrients and chemicals, and these reactions affect (among other things) the way muscles work. If certain foods cause instant muscle weakness, then the patient is said to be allergic to them (see box, p. 217). The allergy can result in many symptoms, such as CATARRH, COLDS, DEPRESSION, HEADACHES, TENSION, TIREDNESS and a weakened IMMUNE SYSTEM.

Muscle tests are said to monitor the effect of foods on the body, and patients can use the techniques at home with the aid of a partner (see box). Kinesiology also claims the ability to pinpoint deficiences in VITAMINS and MINERALS and digestive problems.

Conditions such as lack of ENERGY, frequent minor illnesses, and being generally run down are believed to be made worse by internal stagnation of body fluids. Practitioners claim to treat the conditions by balancing the lymphatic system and improving blood flow. They treat BACK PAIN and NECK PAIN using muscle balancing techniques without the danger of stretching ligaments or loosening joints. Patients can learn to use some of the techniques at home – for example, massage of the inner thigh, which is said to strengthen many weak muscles which cause or aggravate back pain.

Kinesiologists also claim that their

How did kinesiology develop?

The chiropractor George Goodheart discovered kinesiology while trying to help a patient who had severe leg pains. As he was massaging along a muscle called the *fascia lata* – which runs down the outside of the leg, from the hip to just below the knee – the patient felt the pain easing.

Goodheart found that the muscle had been strengthened, but massaging the fibres of other muscles did not produce similar results. He then recalled research that had been done by an osteopath named Dr Frank Chapman at the turn of the century. Chapman had shown that massaging specific 'pressure points' could improve the flow of the lymph fluid in various parts of the body.

Goodheart patiently matched Chapman's pressure points to the sets of muscles to which they were related, and found that the pressure point for the *fascia lata* was the only one which lay over the muscle that is affected – nearly all the other points were some distance away in other parts of the body.

An American osteopath named Terrence J. Bennett had claimed in the early 1930s that blood circulation to various organs could be improved by lightly touching certain pressure points on the skull. Bennett used a type of moving X-ray machine to monitor changes in the body after touching points on the head. Goodheart found that touching these points with his fingertips for a few seconds also strengthened specific muscles; eventually he mapped an association between 16 different pressure points on the skull, just above the breastbone and behind the knee, and all the major muscle groups.

Wondering how such a light touch could strengthen a muscle so quickly, Goodheart studied ACUPUNCTURE, which is also concerned with particular points on the body, located on invisible channels or 'meridians'. He concluded that these meridians are common energy channels for both organs and muscles. Kinesiology channels are identical to the meridians that are used in acupuncture.

methods can relieve or resolve PHOBIAS and FEAR. For example, gently tapping the bone under the eye in line with the pupil is said to help relieve fear.

Finding a practitioner Information and a register of those who belong to the Association for Systematic Kinesiology is available from The Academy of Systematic Kinesiology, 39 Browns Road, Surbiton, Surrey KT5 8ST. Classes in self help are also available there. Members of the association may have qualified in other fields – orthopaedic surgery, physiotherapy or MASSAGE, for example. Most have completed at least 200 hours of kinesiology. Some use kinesiology along with other professional skills.

A number of osteopaths, chiropractors, physiotherapists, naturopaths, homoeopaths and herbalists use kinesiology. If the problem relates to bones, muscles or ligaments, an osteopath or chiropractor who uses the therapy may be able to help. For digestive problems a dietician-kinesiologist or a herbalist who uses muscle testing can be consulted. For mental or emotional disturbances, a psychotherapist or counsellor who uses kinesiology is the logical choice.

Consulting a practitioner The therapist starts by asking about your case history. Then your major muscle groups are systematically tested – a painless procedure. You are shown how to put an arm or leg into a particular position and hold it steady. The kinesiologist presses gently for a few seconds to assess your ability to exert an equal and opposite pressure. If the muscle does not respond normally, the practitioner makes a series of touch tests to find out why it is not 'firing' properly.

More tests will determine which imbalance is most in need of correction, then the therapist works on the appropriate pressure points. Some points will be sore or tender when touched – due, it is believed, to poisons building up in the tissues and preventing proper nerve impulses from going to and fro between brain and muscle. This in turn affects the working of the muscle – tight shoulder muscles which cannot relax are a common example.

Soreness may persist for a day or two as poisons disperse, but an improvement of the main discomfort and in well-being should be felt almost immediately.

An orthodox view

An increasing number of doctors use kinesiology as an aid to diagnosis, but the therapy has not yet been the subject of much research that orthodox medicine would consider valid. Most conventional practitioners still take the view that the body's flow of electrical energies cannot be adjusted by mechanical means.

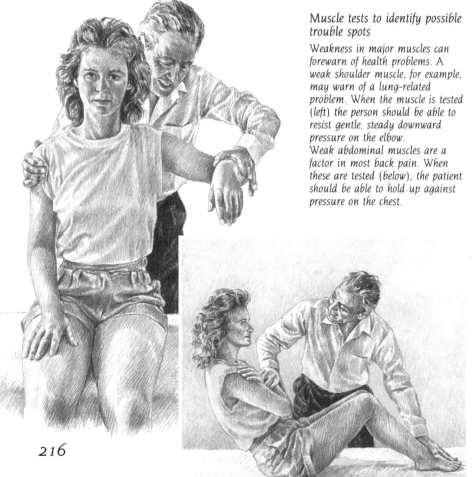

Muscle tests to identify possible trouble spots

Weakness in major muscles can forewarn of health problems. A weak shoulder muscle, for example, may warn of a lung-related problem. When the muscle is tested (left) the person should be able to resist gentle, steady downward pressure on the elbow.

Weak abdominal muscles are a factor in most back pain. When these are tested (below), the patient should be able to hold up against pressure on the chest.

Self-help test for food allergy

Kinesiology therapists often use a simple test made on a strong chest muscle (the pectoralis major, clavicular muscle) to check whether a patient has an allergy or sensitivity to a particular food.

You can carry out the test at home with the aid of a partner – but note that this is *not* a trial of strength, and actions must remain firm but gentle. First, however, you must test the muscle itself.

The muscle test

1 Hold your body upright and stretch your left arm out in front of you with the elbow turned outwards and fingers and thumb hanging down.
2 Your partner faces you, resting two fingers of the right hand on your outstretched left wrist and placing the left hand on your right shoulder.
3 Now ask your partner to push your wrist downwards while you resist by exerting pressure upwards. Breathe normally (do *not* hold your breath) while your partner applies firm but gentle pressure for as long as it takes to say 'One thousand, two thousand and off'.

If you matched your partner's pressure and the muscle felt firmly locked, not 'spongy', go on to the allergy test. If,

however, your arm moved downwards under pressure, the muscle is unsuitable for the allergy test. In this case, try the test on the other arm or test a different muscle. For example, hold your arm straight by your side with the palm turned outwards and resist your partner's pressure to pull the arm away from your side. If you cannot match the pressure again, you should contact a trained practitioner.

The allergy test

1 Take up the same position as before, with left arm extended, elbow outwards and fingers and thumb hanging down.
2 Place a sample of the suspect food – cheese, for example – under your tongue, or even just between your lips.
3 Your partner places the first two fingers of his or her left hand on a point in the soft tissue just under your right ear, while applying downward pressure on your left wrist. As before, you resist.

If you match the pressure and the muscle remains firm, it is believed that you are not allergic or sensitive to the suspect food; if your arm feels less strong, or moves, practitioners say you should avoid the food or eat it only occasionally – and never in excess.

If you are sensitive or allergic to a food, you may not be able to keep your arm raised against steady downward pressure when that food is held to your mouth.

KIRLIAN PHOTOGRAPHY
Capturing auras on film

The aim of Kirlian photography – named after a Russian engineer, Semyon Kirlian, and his wife Valentina – is to produce prints of the auras that reveal people's mental and physical disorders before they display any outward symptoms (see AURA THERAPY). Diagnosing from the photographs, practitioners may suggest appropriate treatments ranging from ACUPUNCTURE to YOGA.

For centuries, mystics, spiritual healers and psychics have been fascinated by the 'auras' – luminous, misty outlines – said to surround people, animals, plants and other animate or inanimate objects.

The auras are said to reflect the subjects' general well-being, and their colours and brightness to be open to medical interpretation. Kirlian high-voltage photography, or electrophotography, is a development of this; it claims to capture the interference pattern created when the high-frequency electrical sweep comes in contact with the subject's electromagnetic field, or aura.

Semyon Kirlian made his discovery in 1939 while repairing machinery in a laboratory. A spark flew off the machine, there was a vivid flash and he received a jolting electric shock. On recovering, he wondered what would happen if he put a sheet of light-sensitive paper between another electric spark and his bare hand – and had a photograph taken at the very instant of shock.

This was done and the developed film showed that his fingers were fringed with glowing streaks of light. The Kirlians then set up their own laboratory and spent the next 40 years taking their mysterious pictures.

To begin with, the Kirlians put two similar leaves, one from a diseased plant, the other from a healthy one, between photographic plates and high-voltage, high-frequency electrical charges. No light sources were used. When developed, the photographs showed a vivid aura around the leaf from the healthy plant. The other leaf had only a weak aura.

In another experiment, a leaf from which a section had been cut was photographed. This time the picture showed a faint outline of the missing section. The so-called 'phantom-leaf' phenomenon was compared to the experiences of many amputees who have had an arm or leg removed, and who later feel pain or tingling in the 'phantom limb'.

Semyon Kirlian also photographed his own hand at a meeting of scientists and doctors. His equipment consisted of an electric coil which sent a high-voltage charge to an aluminium plate, on top of which were a glass plate and a sheet of photosensitive film. The film was covered with a clear sheet of plastic to protect it from salt in the skin.

Kirlian placed his hand firmly on the plate for a few seconds – and the photograph was taken. To his alarm, however, his aura was shown to be vague and cloudy, with dull, blurred colours. His wife's hand was then photographed and her aura came out strong and clear. A few hours afterwards Semyon Kirlian went down with a bad case of INFLUENZA, while his wife remained well.

From this it was deduced that sickness in humans could be detected at an early stage, before symptoms became evident – and that preventive treatment could be taken.

The Kirlians continued their work in relative obscurity until, in the early 1960s, their findings were publicised. By then Russian and American disciples of Kirlian photography were making big claims for it – such as that it could detect the onset of CANCER.

By examining the colours and patterns of an aura, Kirlian photographers claimed to determine the subject's state of health. An even, regular aura indicated a well-balanced, healthy person but someone who was upset and ill had a jagged aura. In this case, the illness would be identified according to the aura's finer points and treated accordingly.

Critics, however, asserted that various unaccounted-for factors could affect the size, density and colour of the photographed auras. For example, the subject could vary the pressure of hand or foot on the photographic machine. This could distort the image – as could any intake of alcohol, food, and drugs such as painkillers or tranquillisers. Human sweat could also interfere with the flow of electromagnetic energy.

Sceptics have also pointed out that any fault or deviation in the photographic machine itself – as well as changes in room temperature – could alter the aura. However, modern machines are not affected by pressure or sweat, and alcohol or drug intake can be identified in the print and is therefore not confused in the general interpretation. The machines are consistent, and temperature and humidity are constantly monitored where the tests are taking place.

An orthodox view

Conventional doctors do not believe that Kirlian photography can accurately detect and record human auras. Nor can auras – providing they exist – be used as a reliable means of diagnosis. However, some doctors agree that dead and live objects give off 'energy emissions', which vary in intensity and degree. And that these emissions may indicate the presence or absence of disease.

Kirlian photographs of the menstrual cycle

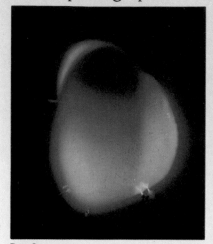

Day 3

Day 7

Day 12

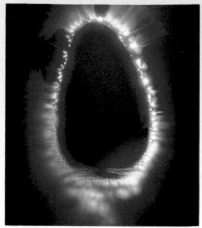

Day 21

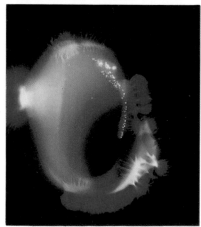

Day 3

These Kirlian images show finger-pad auras which are claimed to reflect the hormonal changes that occur during a woman's monthly cycle. The colours all have a meaning. Red-yellow within a dotted halo represents follicle-stimulating hormone (FSH), which stimulates the follicles in the ovary to ripen into ova (or eggs). Blue denotes luteinising hormone, which stimulates ovulation (release of an ovum from an ovary). White represents the level in the blood of oestrogen, one of the steroid hormones that promote the functioning of the female sex organs.
On day 3, menstruation is in progress. Day 7 shows increasing hormonal activity. By day 12, hormonal activity has reached its peak before ovulation (about day 14). The activity has subsided by day 21, and by day 3 a new cycle has begun.

LACTOSE INTOLERANCE

This condition – the inability to absorb lactose, or milk sugar – results in watery DIARRHOEA. The sugar is a baby's main source of energy. Normally, more than 99 per cent of the lactose in a baby's feeds is digested and absorbed into its bloodstream. As a result, there is virtually no sugar in the baby's normally solid faeces. However, if not enough is absorbed, lactose and water remain in the faeces, causing diarrhoea.

Lactose intolerance is usually temporary, and most commonly occurs in babies and children after an attack of gastroenteritis (diarrhoea and vomiting). Taking milk only makes it worse. In rare cases, the condition is present at birth and lasts for life.

What the therapists recommend

Naturopathy As with any food intolerance, the practitioner will make sure that this really is the problem before advising a restricted diet, particularly if the patient is a child. You will be asked for details of everything that is eaten, and changes will be suggested to improve digestion generally. If lactose is found to be the cause of the upset, foods containing it will be excluded from the diet.

An orthodox view

A doctor will determine if lactose intolerance is present by testing a baby's faeces for sugar. As the condition is intensified by taking milk and other dairy products such as cheese, he will advise avoiding them until the digestion of lactose is back to normal. In the meantime, the baby can be fed on soya milk substitute, which contains no lactose.

Short-term lactose intolerance following gastroenteritis usually lasts two to three weeks. Milk can then be safely reintroduced into the diet. Adults with lactose intolerance should avoid many pharmaceuticals, confectionery and bakery products, which also contain lactose, as well as dairy products.

LARYNGITIS

Loss of voice and hoarseness are the two main effects of laryngitis, or inflammation of the larynx (voice box). There are two main types of laryngitis: acute, which is infectious, short-lived and usually accompanied by pain or discomfort in the throat; and chronic, which is longer-lasting or keeps recurring, and affects only adults.

Acute laryngitis is usually caused by a VIRUS INFECTION. Chronic laryngitis is frequently the result of emotional STRESS and strain. It can also be brought on by irritating the vocal cords through singing or shouting – as well as by smoke, fumes or dust.

What the therapists recommend

Herbal Medicine For immediate relief, gargle with marigold, myrrh, raspberry leaf, sage or thyme. These are most effective in tincture form. To boost resistance to infection, take two to four garlic capsules a day for a few days. Herbalists may also prescribe herbs such as echinacea or wild indigo to fight infection, and may also advise you to take extra vitamin C.
Acupressure The points to be treated are the bottom corner of the nail on the outer side of the thumb, press upwards and inwards; and at the end of the crease in the web between the forefinger and thumb, press towards the finger bone.
Homoeopathy For a harsh cough and dry, ticklish throat try _Drosera_. For a dry, hard cough and loss of voice, try _Phosphorus_.

An orthodox view

In cases of acute laryngitis doctors advise patients to rest their voice, drink plenty of fluids, and, if needed, take painkillers such as aspirin or paracetamol. Antibiotics are not normally prescribed unless the infection has spread to the lungs (see BRONCHITIS).

With chronic laryngitis, patients are advised to avoid smoke, dust and irritants – and not to shout or sing until the voice returns to normal.

If hoarseness lasts for more than three weeks, you should consult a doctor in case there is a more serious underlying cause. He may send you to an ear, nose and throat specialist, who will examine your throat for a non-cancerous polyp or nodule on the vocal cords and remove it if necessary.

LAUGHTER
How it does us good . . .

We share our ability to laugh with our fellow primates – for example, chimpanzees 'laugh' when tickled – and this behaviour goes back to earliest times. Primitive man bared his teeth as a sign of aggression or warning. But by screwing up his face at the same time – and making strange, inarticulate, rhythmic noises – he turned aggression into friendliness, and warning into welcome. 'Do you want to fight?' became 'Do you want to play?'

Laughing together is a way of strengthening social bonds between people, for laughter brings us out of ourselves and provides the human contact we need in order to survive. But it has other benefits – both physical and psychological.

When we laugh we draw air in and out of our lungs more than during normal breathing. So laughing may push more oxygen into the bloodstream, stimulating the circulation. Our heart rate often goes up at the same time, helping the process. And studies of blood samples taken from people while they were laughing show higher levels of the 'arousal' hormones, adrenaline and noradrenaline. During a bout of laughter we become physically more aroused and, as a result, afterwards we may be mentally sharper.

Finally, when we laugh we experience a burst of activity followed by a period of relaxation, when our muscles are less tense than they were before. These alternating cycles of tension and calm stop us getting physically keyed-up about daily problems.

The mental benefits relate more to our underlying sense of humour than to the act of laughing. Seeing a problem as funny breaks the overwhelming sense of TENSION that often goes with it, and an intimidating difficulty suddenly becomes manageable.

Psychologists regard humour as a vital way of dealing with day-to-day problems. It helps promote and sustain mental good health, for people with a well-developed sense of fun usually have fewer emotional problems than those who find it difficult to laugh . . . particularly at themselves.

And mental good health can boost our physical health, as a 30 year study in the United States recently showed. Medical researchers observed a group of males from boyhood to middle age. They found that young men who enjoyed good mental health had comparatively few illnesses after 40. In contrast, those who had suffered emotional problems as college boys had far more physical problems in middle age. From this, the researchers concluded that sound mental health – shown by a good sense of humour – slows down the inevitable deterioration in physical health later on in life.

So laughter has a curious and contradictory history. Originally a sign of hostility, it became a sign of mutual attraction. People who laugh together – such as husbands and wives – have a better chance of staying together. And laughter on the surface is a sign of something deeper and more significant – it reflects a particular way of looking at the world which makes us feel better, and may even help us to live longer.

LAYING ON OF HANDS

Since earliest times, some people have believed that they have the ability to bring about cures for physical and mental illness by placing their hands on or near the affected person or part, so transferring some sort of power. The early Christians developed such a 'laying on of hands' using God's power through the Holy Ghost (or Spirit), and it is still practised by Christian healers, especially those of the charismatic churches (see CHARISMATIC HEALING). A similar 'hands on' technique, sometimes called 'hand healing', 'contact healing' or 'touch healing', is an integral part of SPIRITUAL HEALING.

LEUKAEMIA

This uncommon form of CANCER affects the blood cells. If not treated, most cases are fatal, but with appropriate treatment many patients are cured. There are two forms, depending on the type of blood cells affected: *lymphoblastic* and *myeloid*. Either of these can be acute (rapidly developing) or chronic (slow-developing and long-lasting).

The most common childhood leukaemia – which starts between the ages of three and six – is acute lymphoblastic leukaemia, in which major advances in treatment have been made. Symptoms develop rapidly and include FEVER, ANAEMIA, HEADACHES and excessive NOSEBLEED. In adults, symptoms include fever, loss of energy, loss of appetite, weight loss and weakness. Women may menstruate excessively (see PERIOD PROBLEMS). Chronic leukaemia, especially in the elderly, can be relatively harmless.

If leukaemia is suspected, you should consult a doctor without delay.

LIQUORICE
A magic medicine and confection

For more than 3000 years, Chinese physicians have been using liquorice to treat LIVER DISORDERS, and it is still their popular remedy for hepatitis, JAUNDICE, a distended abdomen and NAUSEA AND VOMITING. The liquorice plant, *Glycyrrhiza glabra*, and the similar wild liquorice, *Astragalus glycyphyllos*, are native

Herbalists collect liquorice in this Italian illustration of about 1385. It has been grown in England since the 16th century.

to southern Europe and western Asia, and have been used in Mediterranean lands for centuries. Chinese or Manchurian liquorice, *G. uralensis*, is closely related. *G. glabra* is most commonly used, and today, most of the world's imports of it come from Spain.

The liquorice root and stolon – creeping underground stem – are dark reddish-brown and wrinkled, with a yellow, fibrous interior. They are often sold cut into sticks some 6in (15cm) long and ½in (13mm) in diameter, and may be chewed raw. The hard, though pliable, black solid used in medicine and confectionery is prepared by crushing and boiling the roots, then reducing (evaporating down) the resulting juice. Medicinal extracts are then prepared from this solid, and sold in liquid, powder and lozenge form.

Modern research has confirmed many of the medicinal properties claimed for liquorice. A major active ingredient is glycyrrhizin, a sweet, white crystalline substance when pure. It is 50 times sweeter than sugar, and gives liquorice its agreeable sweet taste.

Liquorice is a demulcent (soothing agent) and spasmolytic (countering muscle spasms such as those that cause COLIC and some bronchial disorders). It is an expectorant (increasing the production of sputum so that it may be coughed up more easily), an antitussive (suppressing coughing), and an anti-inflammatory and antiallergic substance, making it particularly useful in the treatment of ASTHMA. It is generally 'hepato protective' (protecting the liver), and may be used in the short term to relieve stomach ULCERS. Recent research has shown that it counters bacterial

growth and plaque, and so helps to prevent dental decay.

The other ingredients of liquorice may give it antidepressive properties, inhibit histamine release and act as muscle relaxants. It is a mild laxative, and may have detoxifying effects on poisons such as strychnine.

Liquorice root, either from your garden or bought from a chemist's or herbalist shop, may be prepared as a decoction. Put ½-1 teaspoon of the root in a saucepan. Add a cup of water, boil, and allow to simmer for 10-15 minutes. Drink when cool, and repeat three times a day.

LIVER DISORDERS

The liver is the largest gland in the body. Situated in the upper right part of the abdomen, it weighs 2½-3½lb (1.1-1.6kg) in adults. It performs more than 500 different functions, ranging from storing VITAMINS and carbohydrates to excreting waste products from the bloodstream.

The liver produces bile, which aids food digestion and makes the faeces brown. It metabolises proteins and carbohydrates, and helps to regulate the amount of sugar in the bloodstream. It stores and metabolises fats, producing cholesterol.

It also produces blood-clotting chemicals and heparin, an anticoagulant. It synthesises vitamin A, and stores it together with vitamins B12, D and K. One of the liver's most important roles is the removal of drugs, poisons and worn-out red blood cells from the bloodstream.

Because the liver is such a complex organ, it has a vast number of possible disorders. Inflammation of the liver is called hepatitis. 'Infectious hepatitis' (hepatitis A) is caused by a virus and is transmitted by food and drink. It causes FEVER, sickness and the yellowing of the skin known as JAUNDICE, which may last up to three weeks. It is rarely serious, but is frequently followed by a period of post-viral DEPRESSION, and your doctor should be informed.

The much more serious 'serum hepatitis' (hepatitis B), also a virus infection, is spread by sexual intercourse and by infected blood and blood products, syringes or needles, and drug addicts who share syringes are particularly vulnerable. Its symptoms – HEADACHES, fever, chills, general debility and jaundice – appear suddenly after an incubation period of one to six months. Even with treatment, recovery may be slow or incomplete – and in about one case in ten the disease is fatal.

Cirrhosis, in which scar tissue replaces dead or injured liver cells, has several causes, including ALCOHOLISM, hepatitis, blockage of the common bile duct by GALL-STONES or other obstructions, disorders of the IMMUNE SYSTEM and chronic heart failure. Or it may occur for no known reason. Because of the organ's importance, CANCER of the liver is extremely serious.

Warning If you suspect any liver disorder, consult your doctor before embarking on a course of alternative treatment.

What the therapists recommend

Acupuncture Practitioners give treatment at a combination of points on the liver, gall bladder, stomach and spleen meridians.

Homoeopathy Treatment of chronic (persistent) hepatitis is constitutional and must be carried out by an experienced homoeopath. For acute (brief but severe) hepatitis, *Phosphorus 30* is indicated. *Chelidonium 30* is indicated for jaundice when the abdomen feels distended and there is right-sided pain extending to the shoulder.

Naturopathy You are advised to avoid fatty foods and alcohol, and take two or three glasses of fresh vegetable juice every day. Cold packs on the abdomen and exercises such as YOGA can help to stimulate the liver, and in some cases supplements such as multivitamin and mineral tablets or lecithin to counteract cholesterol may also help.

Reflexology Massage is applied to the reflex areas relating to the liver, gall bladder, small and large intestine, spleen and lymphatic system, and also to the areas related to the solar plexus and adrenal and pituitary glands. See chart, p. 295.

An orthodox view

Patients with hepatitis A are advised to rest, eat little or nothing – or a fat-free diet (see LOW-FAT DIETS) – and to take plenty of fluids. Since the condition can be spread by faeces, people should avoid water that could be contaminated by sewage. Pay careful attention to hygiene – especially when travelling to places where the disease is prevalent, such as poorly developed tropical and sub-tropical countries. An injection of gamma globulin before going to high-risk areas gives some protection against hepatitis A.

Corticosteroids may reduce the inflammation in cases of hepatitis B. The disease can be prevented by immunisation, by avoiding contaminated needles, and by the use of condoms.

There is no cure for cirrhosis, but it can be halted by removal of the cause – alcohol, hepatitis, blockage of the common bile duct (removed by surgery), or heart failure (see HEART DISORDERS).

LOW-FAT DIETS
Helping to keep arteries clear

Small quantities of fats and oils are essential for a balanced diet, but in large amounts they are thought to contribute to ailments such as heart disease (see HEART DISORDERS). About 45 per cent of the calories – or energy value – of the average British diet comes from fat. Doctors and alternative practitioners agree that this is far too high, and a figure more like 30 per cent is generally recommended.

Reducing fat intake to about this level is particularly important for patients with conditions such as hardening of the arteries (see ARTERIES [HARDENING]), heart disorders or ANGINA. This is because excess fat in the bloodstream can build up on the inner walls of the arteries, obstructing the flow of blood and straining the heart and circulation.

Low-fat diets may also be recommended for OBESITY, or for people who just wish to lose weight. Weight for weight, fat is the most concentrated form of food energy, containing nine calories per gram, while proteins, starches and sugars – the other main energy-giving food components – contain only about four. This means that fat helps to keep us warm and gives us energy for activities (though it is digested much more slowly than sugars). But it also makes it easy for us to put on weight if we eat a lot of it.

Nevertheless, a certain amount of fat is necessary. It contains essential substances known as fatty acids, some of which the body cannot make and must get from food. In addition, fat-containing foods are sources of vitamins A, D, E and K, and fats can make food tastier and more satisfying. Most people can easily cut down on fat in their diets and still meet their needs, but if in doubt, ask a doctor, nutritionist or naturopath for advice.

Different kinds of fat Whether or not you need a low-fat diet, you can benefit from careful choice of the type of fats you consume. Depending on their chemical structure, the fatty acids in food oils and fats can belong to three groups: saturated, mono-unsaturated or poly-unsaturated (see EATING FOR HEALTH). Most fats contain a mixture, usually with more of one than the others.

Nutritionists advise eating mainly mono-unsaturates such as olive oil and the oils in fish, and polyunsaturates such as sunflower, corn and rapeseed oil. In moderate quantities these unsaturated oils are safe even for people who are on low-fat diets, and mono-unsaturates are believed even to reduce the risk of artery disease.

Saturated fats can damage the circulatory system and are generally reduced to a minimum on a low-fat diet. They come mainly from animals, and include butter, lard, suet, cheese and the fat on meat, all of which are highly saturated. Coconut and palm oil, which are used in hard margarines, though vegetable oils, also fall into this category (see table on p. 222).

Warning Low-fat diets are not suitable for babies and children (who have high energy needs) unless they are obese. Pregnant and nursing women should ask their doctors' advice before starting any special diet.

Cutting down on fats

Some simple changes to an ordinary diet will reduce fat intake considerably:

Butter, margarine, low-fat spreads Reduce or stop using spreads altogether. Although most soft margarines and low-fat spreads are made from mainly unsaturated oils – check the labels – they also tend to contain additives and preservatives, and have been highly processed.

Meat, chicken Although the flesh of red meat contains fat, the overall amount can be reduced if you choose lean cuts, trim off any visible fat and remove the skin from chicken. Skim fat from soups, stews and curries before serving, and look out for low-fat products such as special sausages. Eat meat sparingly, substituting with fish or occasional vegetable dishes.

Milk, cream Skimmed milk and buttermilk are low-fat alternatives, as are some soya milks and plain yoghurts, but you will need to check the labels to make sure.

Hard, full-fat cheeses such as cheddar Cottage cheese or even medium-fat types such as Brie, Camembert and Edam are better.

Mayonnaise, salad dressings Homemade dressings containing low-fat yoghurt or cottage cheese are less oily than bought products. Flavour them with herbs, garlic, mustard, lemon juice or other seasonings.

Cooking oils and fats Reduce your intake by frying, sautéing and roasting food only occasionally. Baking, boiling, grilling, poaching, steaming and stir-frying all use less or no oil or fat.

Snacks Avoid nuts, crisps, chocolates, biscuits and cakes, all of which are high in fat. Go instead for fresh or dried fruit, carrot or celery sticks, or eat a wholewheat or wholemeal sandwich.

Fat content of foods

This table gives the amount of fatty acids – saturated and unsaturated (including both poly and mono-unsaturates) – and the total fat (including glycerol) per 100g (3½oz) of food. No one is likely to eat 100g of butter at a time, but for foods such as meat and chicken 100g is about the size of an ordinary portion. In some prepared foods, the saturated and unsaturated content depends on the fat or oil used.*

FOOD		SATURATED FATTY ACIDS (g)	UNSATURATED FATTY ACIDS (g)	TOTAL FAT(g)
Cheese	Camembert	13.9	8.0	23.2
	Cheddar	20.0	11.6	33.5
	cottage	2.4	1.4	4.0
	processed	14.9	8.7	25.0
Cream	single	12.7	7.3	21.2
	double	28.8	16.7	48.2
Milk	whole	2.3	1.3	3.8
	skimmed	0.04	0.03	0.1
Yoghurt	low-fat	0.6	0.3	1.0
Butter		49.0	28.3	82.0
Chocolate		17.7	10.8	30.3
Lard		41.8	50.6	99.0
Margarine	soft, vegetable oil	25.6	51.7	81.0
Oil	corn	16.4	78.6	99.9
	olive	14.0	80.9	99.9
	rapeseed	6.6	88.7	99.9
	sunflower	13.1	81.8	99.9
Bacon	grilled	13.6	17.6	33.8
Beef	lean grilled steak	2.5	3.1	6.0
	roast (lean only)	3.8	4.7	9.1
Chicken	roast with skin	4.6	8.4	14.0
	roast, no skin	1.8	3.3	5.4
Egg		3.4	5.4	10.9
Lamb	roast (lean only)	4.0	3.5	8.1
	grilled chops	14.1	12.3	29.0
	kidney	0.9	1.0	2.7
	liver	3.2	4.2	10.3
Pork	roast (lean only)	2.7	3.6	6.9
	grilled sausage	9.7	13.6	24.6
Rabbit		3.1	4.0	7.7
Cod	raw, no skin	0.1	0.3	0.7
Mackerel	smoked	4.0	10.4	16.3
Prawns		0.2	1.0	1.8
Sardines	tinned	2.7	10.1	13.6
Almonds		4.2	46.7	53.5
Hazelnuts		2.6	31.7	36.0
Peanut butter		10.6	40.7	53.7
Peanuts		9.2	37.4	49.0
Bread	wholemeal	0.5	1.6	2.7
Muesli		1.3	5.8	7.5
Oatmeal porridge		0.1	0.7	0.9
Biscuits	plain	7.9	7.7	16.6
Fruit cake		3.9	6.3	11.0
Most fruits, eg, apples, pears				Traces only
Avocado		2.6	18.6	22.2
Most vegetables, eg, carrots, beans, peas				Traces only
Potatoes	boiled, baked	0	0.1	0.1
	roast*	–	–	4.8
	chips*	–	–	10.9

LUMBAGO

The pain of lumbago in the lower back, or lumbar region, can be so severe that the back 'locks' – and the patient is stuck in a bent position. Symptoms may be caused by strained back muscles or ligaments, a SLIPPED DISC or displacement of a vertebra. The pain is often triggered by stooping, sitting or lifting, and may also accompany SCIATICA.

What the therapists recommend

Acupuncture In addition to points that are painful, other channels treated are gall bladder, bladder and large intestine. MOXIBUSTION may also be used.

Acupressure The pressure point in the centre of the back of the knee-crease should be used – but *not* if the patient has VARICOSE VEINS. Press inwards at this point.

Massage Before the pain becomes acute, deep effleurage and frictions should be given to the lumbar region, extending the movements upwards, to improve general circulation. This should be followed by petrissage, concentrating on kneading and rolling movements over the muscles at the sides of the waist and upper buttocks. Next, friction is applied along each side of the spine. Later, as the pain subsides, a general back massage should help re-tone the affected muscles.

Hydrotherapy Ice packs are recommended for severe pain. Other treatments offered include hot packs, needle sprays (for relaxation), underwater douches and specific exercises in the hydrotherapy pool.

Osteopathy Treatment is aimed at reducing spasm in the small muscles of the back and increasing flexibility in the joints of the spine. Exercises to ease the pain may also be suggested – for example, lying on your back and slowly pulling your knees towards your chest with hands clasped around your legs.

Reflexology Reflex areas corresponding to the lumbar region of the spine are massaged, as well as areas corresponding to the solar plexus and adrenal glands (see chart, p. 295).

An orthodox view

Doctors often advise rest in bed – with a board under the mattress for extra firmness. They may prescribe painkillers or occasionally, for short-term use, muscle relaxants such as diazepam. EXERCISE to maintain muscle strength and the natural curvature of the spine can help, as does traction, physiotherapy, and advice about lifting and sitting properly (see BACK PAIN).

Some conventional doctors may also use alternative treatments such as MANIPULATIVE THERAPIES or acupuncture.

MACROBIOTICS

The aim of a macrobiotic diet is to help you get the most out of life in terms of health and enjoyment. It is based on a regime of vegetables and whole grains. See EATING YOUR WAY TO INNER HARMONY AND HEALTH, p. 228.

MANIC DEPRESSIVE DISORDERS

Everyone has changes of mood – feeling 'high' sometimes and 'low' at others – but those who suffer from manic depressive illness experience excessive mood swings, ranging from extreme elation (mania) to profound DEPRESSION.

Symptoms of mania may include overconfidence, talkativeness, extravagance, HYPERACTIVITY, and the ability to remain extremely lively with little or no sleep. Such sufferers may make grandiose plans and be interfering and difficult. Although tolerable for short periods, relatives and friends eventually find manic behaviour exhausting.

When they are depressed, sufferers may be withdrawn and introverted, lacking in confidence and self-reproachful. They may even contemplate suicide. Swings from mania to depression may be sudden or gradual, and are usually unpredictable.

Some sufferers' mood may swing to only one extreme: at one end of the swing they behave normally, but at the other they are either manic or depressed. So some cases of depression are caused by manic depressive disorder, despite the fact that the sufferer is never manic.

Symptoms of manic depressive disorders may resemble those of SCHIZOPHRENIA.

What the therapists recommend

Aromatherapy A drop of thyme and two of clary sage in a teaspoon of carrier lotion, applied to the back of the hands every two hours and inhaled, is said to be helpful in balancing extreme emotions. A total of six to eight drops of basil and bergamot with sandalwood or patchouli in the bath or inhaled from a tissue may also be beneficial.
Bach Remedies For treatment of the manic state: Scleranthus for general instability, and for being introverted and out of touch with one's feelings. Vervain for overenthusiasm,

fanaticism (especially if religious mania is apparent) and overextension of oneself. If there is impatience with others' slowness, try Impatiens. Give Chestnut bud for haste and an inability to control the repeating cycle of moods. Walnut may also help to regulate the cycle. Try Gorse for a feeling of despair that things may never change. For treatment of the depressive state, see DEPRESSION.
Homoeopathy Practitioners regard the condition as too serious for self help, and advise consultation with a qualified homoeopath. Remedies are available for both the manic and depressive stages and treatment is prescribed according to individual needs.
Biochemic Tissue Salts *Kali phos.* is believed to help sufferers to cope with the nervous STRESS that may accompany the manic depressive condition.
Naturopathy Since depression and other psychological imbalances may have a physical basis in part, naturopaths will encourage changes to provide more energy for the central nervous system. Cutting out alcohol, strong tea, coffee and sugar, and increasing protein as part of a wholefood diet may help. FOOD ADDITIVES should be excluded as far as possible.

An orthodox view

Without treatment, a manic patient's behaviour may be so bizarre and antisocial that he finds himself in trouble with the law, or being detained involuntarily in a psychiatric hospital. Doctors treat attacks of mania with tranquillisers such as haloperidol or chlorpromazine, and depression with antidepressant drugs.

The mainstay of medical treatment is lithium carbonate which, taken daily, is a mood regulator and prevents dramatic swings from mania to depression and vice versa. Regular blood tests ensure that the dose of lithium is adequate, but not so great as to produce adverse effects such as drowsiness, tremor, blurred vision or DIARRHOEA.

COUNSELLING may help the families of sufferers to cope with the stress caused by the sometimes irrational demands and other burdens of living with a manic depressive.

MANIPULATIVE THERAPIES

This group of therapies includes any system of treatment in which the practitioner uses his hands to bring about beneficial changes either in the patient's muscles and skeleton or, through them, in other parts of the body. Diagnostic therapies using the same techniques are also included. The group includes

the ALEXANDER TECHNIQUE, KINESIOLOGY, CHIROPRACTIC, FELDENKRAIS METHOD, MASSAGE, OSTEOPATHY, REFLEXOLOGY and ROLFING. Sometimes other 'hands on' therapies such as LAYING ON OF HANDS and THERAPEUTIC TOUCH are also included.

MANTRAS

Among the early Hindus, mantras were sacred words (or groups of words) used in prayers and incantations to invoke the gods. Later, similar formulas were repeated, either aloud or silently, in order to clear the mind for MEDITATION. They are now also used in YOGA, and were an integral part of COUÉISM. It was Emile Coué who coined the famous mantra: 'Every day, in every way, I am getting better and better.'

Sitting crosslegged in the Lotus position is an ideal way in which to say your daily mantra, aloud or to yourself. This helps to induce a state of contemplation.

MASSAGE
Perhaps the oldest way of healing

As probably the oldest therapy known to man, massage has been practised in the Middle and Far East since at least 3000 BC. Physicians in ancient Greece were skilled in massaging stiff and painful joints – and Hippocrates, known as the 'Father of Medicine', wrote in the 5th century BC: 'The way to health is to have a scented bath and an oiled massage each day.'

Oil is still used for all forms of massage, which became increasingly popular in Europe from the 19th century onwards, when the Swedish gymnast Per Henrik Ling devised the aesthetic and scientific principles of what is now called Swedish massage. Based on various ancient massage practices, it combines therapeutic massage with exercises for muscles and joints.

The next major step forward came in the early 1970s, when the American massage therapist George Downing published his trend-setting work, *The Massage Book*. In it he formulated the idea of massage as a therapy taking into account a person's whole being – his physical, mental and emotional make-up. Downing also incorporated into his system the beliefs and techniques of two other well-known massage therapies, REFLEXOLOGY and SHIATSU.

Since then, therapeutic massage has grown into the art of creating and maintaining the best possible health for its devotees. It aims to do this by, in turn, relaxing, stimulating and invigorating mind and body.

Who it can help The most common – and most effective – use of massage is to relax the body and mind and so relieve the strains and TENSION of daily life. It is also used to treat people with some CIRCULATION PROBLEMS and HEART DISORDERS – as well as those suffering from high BLOOD PRESSURE, HEADACHES, HYPERACTIVITY, INSOMNIA and sinusitis (see SINUS PROBLEMS).

Physically, its therapies are aimed at improving the blood, muscular and nervous systems, and also helping the body to assimilate food and get rid of waste products.

On the simplest level, massage can ease the kind of BACK PAIN and NECK PAIN people frequently suffer from at the end of the working day – especially if they have been hunched over a desk, or sitting awkwardly behind the wheel of a car.

Athletes, sportsmen and dancers can also benefit greatly from massage – which eases the stiffness they often experience when their work is over. It does this by 'milking', or draining, the muscles of toxic chemical waste products which accumulate after strenuous activity.

Mentally, on a psychological and emotional level, its calm and soothing effects have helped people plagued by ANXIETY or DEPRESSION, allowing them to deal more constructively with everyday worries and problems – and to regain self-confidence.

Traditionally, hospital nurses and physiotherapists have used massage on patients to help relieve pain or physical discomfort – and to promote circulation to the muscles of the bedridden. This is now also practised on patients suffering from CANCER. It helps to relieve the discomfort they may experience from their treatments, and from the effects of the illness itself. In addition, it is proving beneficial to people recovering in hospital from heart attacks.

However, massage is not suitable for people who suffer from phlebitis (vein inflammation), thrombosis (blood clotting), VARICOSE VEINS (swollen and lengthened veins, usually in the leg), or any form of FEVER. In such cases you should consult your doctor before undergoing massage.

Finding a practitioner Contact is best made through personal recommendation, or at the suggestion of your GP. Alternatively, trained and qualified practitioners can often be contacted through your local health centre, or Citizens Advice Bureau.

Do not simply pick a name from *Yellow Pages*, or advertisements in a local shop window. Treatment by an unqualified masseur or masseuse could do more harm than good. There are a number of reputable massage centres throughout Britain, including The London College of Massage and Shiatsu, 21 Portland Place, London WIN 3AF, and the Northern Institute of Massage, 100 Waterloo Road, Blackpool, Lancs FY4 1AW.

Consulting a practitioner Increasingly, practitioners are incorporating methods from other therapies into their work. These include ACUPUNCTURE and ROLFING (tissue massage), as well as AROMATHERAPY, reflexology and shiatsu.

Basically, however, massage takes four main forms: effleurage (or stroking), friction (or pressure), percussion (or drumming), and petrissage (or kneading). See illustrations.

Used individually or in combination, these techniques – and variations of them – aim to help people through the use of 'caring touch'. Practitioners stress that massage is fundamentally a two-way process, in which the therapist – by using his or her hands with skill and sympathy – benefits in terms of well-being just as much as the patient.

In most cases, people visit a masseur at his work place, or else attend a massage clinic. However, some private practitioners will visit clients at their homes. Whichever it is, the same basic procedure is followed. The client strips to undershorts or briefs and lies – usually face down – on a massage table or the floor. A thorough massage is then given, lasting for some 20-60 minutes.

Usually, the treatment consists of a mixture of the four basic techniques, in which problem areas are attended to, and the entire body is worked over. At the end of the time any trouble should have been reduced or expelled, and your mind and body should feel relaxed and at peace.

An orthodox view

This form of therapy – one of the oldest and most humane in the world – has wide applications for many conditions. However, it should not be seen as a treatment for a specific disease – or as a substitute for conventional medical treatment. Its effect has more to do with its soothing, relaxing qualities and the close and sympathetic contact with another human being.

A danger arises if its practitioners believe it can actually cure. As a complementary therapy, however, it is finding favour with many doctors in various forms of treatment.

Do's and don'ts about massage

After attending classes given by an experienced and qualified practitioner, some people may like to give some simple massage – perhaps for a stiff neck or aching back – to their spouse or a close friend. There is probably no harm in this as long as you do know what you are doing – and follow some basic principles. For example:

Do make sure to work in a quiet, warm room, free from draughts or damp.

Do use a firm but comfortable surface, such as a well-carpeted floor. For added comfort use folded blankets or a special yoga mat.

Do ensure that both you and your partner are relaxed and receptive to the process. If desired, some restful background music will help set the scene.

Do maintain a firm and regular rhythm, with your hand movements flowing naturally into each other. For continuity, keep one hand on your partner's body from start to finish.

Do see that your partner wraps up warmly afterwards in a tracksuit or bathrobe. Fits of shivering will undo the good work.

Don't use anything but pure vegetable oil or baby oil – a teaspoonful rubbed into the hands to warm it will be enough. Mineral and unrefined oils will only clog the pores.

Don't pour oil directly onto your partner's body.

Don't continue massage if you start to feel tired or short of breath. Rest and wait until you have recovered. Still keep one hand on your partner.

Don't wear tight-fitting clothes or jewellery such as rings, bracelets and necklaces.

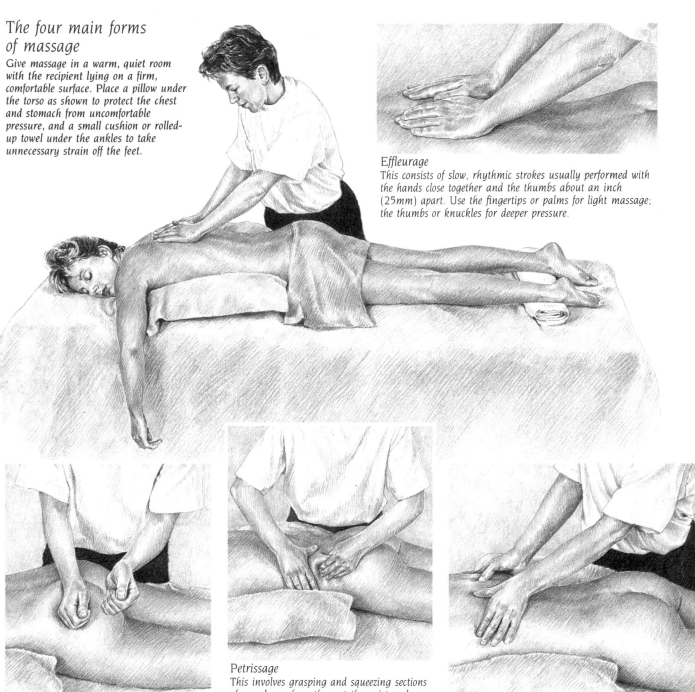

The four main forms of massage

Give massage in a warm, quiet room with the recipient lying on a firm, comfortable surface. Place a pillow under the torso as shown to protect the chest and stomach from uncomfortable pressure, and a small cushion or rolled-up towel under the ankles to take unnecessary strain off the feet.

Effleurage

This consists of slow, rhythmic strokes usually performed with the hands close together and the thumbs about an inch (25mm) apart. Use the fingertips or palms for light massage; the thumbs or knuckles for deeper pressure.

Percussion

These short, fast rhythmic movements are also known as tapotement, from the French word 'tapot', meaning 'to drum' (on a table). The percussive strokes are usually performed with the sides of the hands on the back or any broad, fleshy part of the body – such as the thighs, waist, buttocks and shoulders. Deliver them like little karate chops – briskly but lightly so as not to cause pain.

Petrissage

This involves grasping and squeezing sections of muscle, such as those at the waist and across the stomach. The flesh is kneaded like dough as it is picked up, 'rolled', and then released – with the masseur's hands moving steadily across the area. It stimulates circulation, and helps sportsmen to stretch and relax hard, contracted muscles. It also helps to 'milk', or drain the lactic acid that builds up in their muscles during periods of exertion. It is the build-up of lactic acid that is often the cause of cramp.

Friction

Here a series of small, circular movements are made by one or more fingers, the heel of the hand, or the pads of the thumbs. The pressure stimulates circulation and enables joints to move more freely. It is particularly helpful to sportsmen and dancers, who tend to strain or damage tendons and ligaments. Do not apply to bruises, injuries, or sore areas without a doctor's approval.

Massage

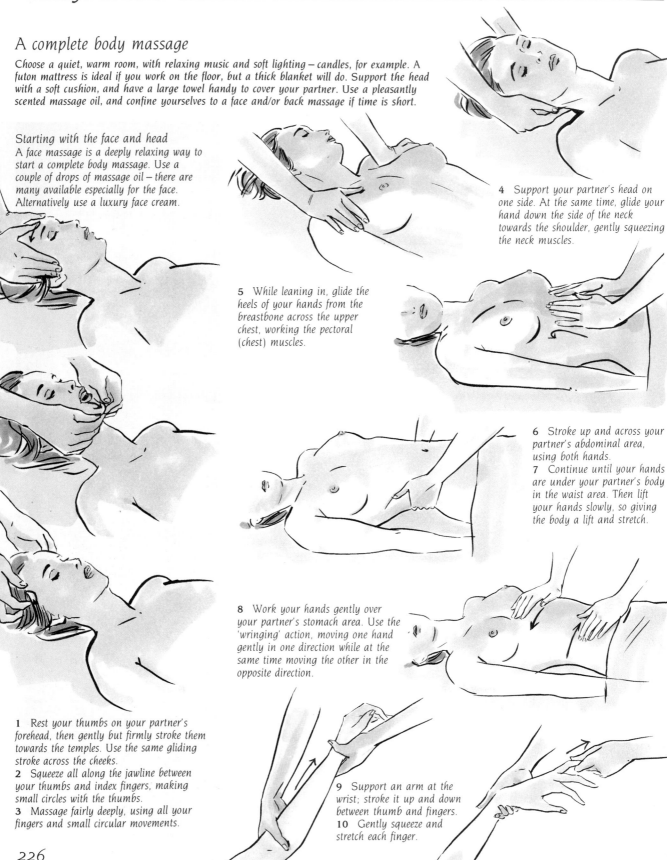

A complete body massage

Choose a quiet, warm room, with relaxing music and soft lighting – candles, for example. A futon mattress is ideal if you work on the floor, but a thick blanket will do. Support the head with a soft cushion, and have a large towel handy to cover your partner. Use a pleasantly scented massage oil, and confine yourselves to a face and/or back massage if time is short.

Starting with the face and head

A face massage is a deeply relaxing way to start a complete body massage. Use a couple of drops of massage oil – there are many available especially for the face. Alternatively use a luxury face cream.

4 Support your partner's head on one side. At the same time, glide your hand down the side of the neck towards the shoulder, gently squeezing the neck muscles.

5 While leaning in, glide the heels of your hands from the breastbone across the upper chest, working the pectoral (chest) muscles.

6 Stroke up and across your partner's abdominal area, using both hands.
7 Continue until your hands are under your partner's body in the waist area. Then lift your hands slowly, so giving the body a lift and stretch.

8 Work your hands gently over your partner's stomach area. Use the 'wringing' action, moving one hand gently in one direction while at the same time moving the other in the opposite direction.

1 Rest your thumbs on your partner's forehead, then gently but firmly stroke them towards the temples. Use the same gliding stroke across the cheeks.
2 Squeeze all along the jawline between your thumbs and index fingers, making small circles with the thumbs.
3 Massage fairly deeply, using all your fingers and small circular movements.

9 Support an arm at the wrist; stroke it up and down between thumb and fingers.
10 Gently squeeze and stretch each finger.

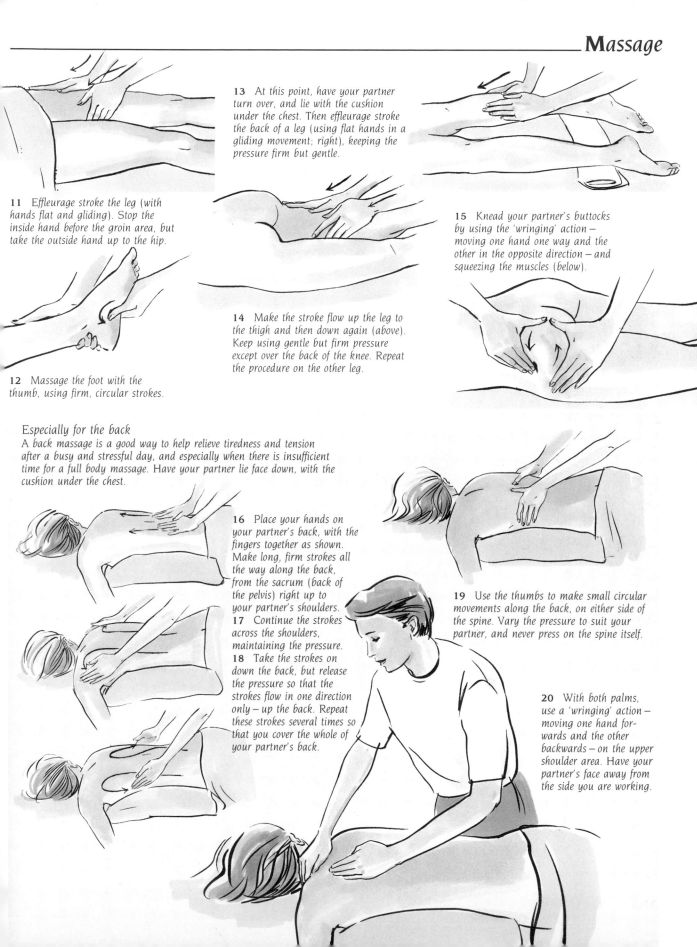

13   At this point, have your partner turn over, and lie with the cushion under the chest. Then effleurage stroke the back of a leg (using flat hands in a gliding movement; right), keeping the pressure firm but gentle.

11   Effleurage stroke the leg (with hands flat and gliding). Stop the inside hand before the groin area, but take the outside hand up to the hip.

15   Knead your partner's buttocks by using the 'wringing' action — moving one hand one way and the other in the opposite direction — and squeezing the muscles (below).

14   Make the stroke flow up the leg to the thigh and then down again (above). Keep using gentle but firm pressure except over the back of the knee. Repeat the procedure on the other leg.

12   Massage the foot with the thumb, using firm, circular strokes.

Especially for the back
A back massage is a good way to help relieve tiredness and tension after a busy and stressful day, and especially when there is insufficient time for a full body massage. Have your partner lie face down, with the cushion under the chest.

16   Place your hands on your partner's back, with the fingers together as shown. Make long, firm strokes all the way along the back, from the sacrum (back of the pelvis) right up to your partner's shoulders.
17   Continue the strokes across the shoulders, maintaining the pressure.
18   Take the strokes on down the back, but release the pressure so that the strokes flow in one direction only – up the back. Repeat these strokes several times so that you cover the whole of your partner's back.

19   Use the thumbs to make small circular movements along the back, on either side of the spine. Vary the pressure to suit your partner, and never press on the spine itself.

20   With both palms, use a 'wringing' action — moving one hand forwards and the other backwards — on the upper shoulder area. Have your partner's face away from the side you are working.

Eating your way to inner harmony and health

In the 1880s a Japanese doctor, Sagen Ishizuka, found that he could treat many common health problems with a diet based on wholegrain cereals and vegetables, and without white rice and refined sugar products. He kept case histories and published his ideas in two books. Early in this century the Japanese writer George Ohsawa put these ideas into practice and claimed that the diet had cured his tuberculosis. Ohsawa went on to develop a whole dietary system based on Ishizuka's methods, which he named macrobiotics – from Greek words meaning 'large' and 'life', as he believed that it could make everyone healthy enough to enjoy life to the full.

Macrobiotics is based on the Chinese philosophy of YIN AND YANG, two qualities which complement and balance each other, and which are held to be part of every natural object. Yin represents the flexible, fluid and cooler side of nature, and yang the strong, dynamic and hotter side. Everyone has both yin and yang elements in combination – as does each type of food – and macrobiotics is aimed at balancing the two in the right way for each individual.

People who are more yin than yang are thought to be calm, relaxed, peaceful, creative and social; those who are more yang are active, alert, energetic and precise. A balance between the two is said to be needed for good health, and an excess of either to result in illness. Too much yin is supposed to bring lethargy, DEPRESSION and difficulty in concentrating; too much yang to induce TENSION, irritability and inability to relax.

To overcome these problems – as well as more serious illnesses – the macrobiotic diet recommends foods with yin and yang qualities that complement the person's condition. For example, someone who needs to be alert at work but who lacks energy would be advised to eat more yang foods such as fish or bean stews, whole oat porridge and root vegetables. Someone who needs to relax and stay calm under STRESS should eat more yin foods such as salads, steamed vegetables and fresh fruit (see chart, p. 231).

Temperature and climate are also said to play a part – yang foods are warming and strengthening during a cold, wet winter; yin foods are cooling and refreshing in hot summers. Even so, extremely yin and yang foods are not recommended: these include sugar, spices and alcohol (very yin), and meat, eggs and cheese (yang). Such foods are believed to have too strong an effect on the system, and may eventually cause illness.

The macrobiotic way of life involves other factors such as EXERCISE and environment as well as diet. For example, YOGA and T'AI-CHI CH'UAN are considered yin in effect, and 'aerobic' exercise, such as JOGGING or skipping, yang.

Followed consistently, macrobiotics is said to help in preventing or treating nearly all illnesses, and there are many case histories which claim cures for CANCER, ARTHRITIS, DIGESTIVE PROBLEMS and other serious disorders. But macrobiotics is not only for those who are ill – everyone may benefit from the increased energy, healthy appearance and greater resistance to illness that it is said to bring.

Anyone wishing to try this way of eating is advised to attend a cooking course. Pregnant women, breastfeeding mothers, children, people who are ill, and anyone with special requirements should see a doctor before visiting a macrobiotic counsellor, who can draw up an individual diet and health plan. To find a counsellor contact the Community Health Foundation, 188 Old Street, London EC1V 9BP, which will also provide information by post if you send a stamped addressed envelope.

Warning During the 1960s and 70s an extreme form of macrobiotics was widely followed. It involved eating almost nothing but brown rice. This dangerous diet gave macrobiotics a bad name. However, the version of the diet given here is much more moderate, and meets the requirements of normal, good nutrition.

The macrobiotic larder

Most macrobiotic foods are everyday ingredients found in supermarkets and grocers' shops, but some special oriental products are also used – buy them from a health food shop or oriental grocers. Here are some of the most important ingredients to keep in stock:

Wholegrain cereals Brown rice, barley, oats, wheat, buckwheat, corn (maize), millet, rye, and products made from these such as wholewheat flour, bread and pasta; whole oat porridge; couscous.

Vegetables Fresh, seasonal vegetables are used, preferably those that grow in the local soil and climate. A mixture of root, ground and leafy green ones is recommended.

Fruit Like vegetables, these should be bought often, to ensure freshness. Choose seasonal and local varieties of both fresh and dried fruit.

Pulses Some of the best include lentils, chickpeas and adzuki beans.

Nuts and seeds Peanuts, almonds, hazelnuts, walnuts, dried chestnuts, and sesame, sunflower and pumpkin seeds are all used.

Oils Polyunsaturated or monounsaturated, cold-pressed vegetable oils such as sesame, sunflower, corn and olive oil are used (see EATING FOR HEALTH).

Seasonings Sea salt, ginger, mustard, tahina (sesame seed paste), cider vinegar, garlic, lemon juice and apple juice are recommended in moderation.

Spreads Natural, sugar-free jams, tahina, barley malt, peanut butter and other nut butters can be used.

Snacks Always useful to have around are rice cakes, roasted nuts and seeds, and raisins.

Sweeteners Use barley malt or corn and barley malt, rice syrup – buy it at a health food shop – or fruit juice.

Beverages Natural drinks such as apple or carrot juice, real ale, organic wine, spring water and herbal TISANES are all allowed.

Special oriental ingredients

Bancha twig tea This is made from the twigs of the bancha bush. It contains virtually no caffeine or tannin, and is slightly alkaline – useful in counteracting the effects of stress. It has a mild, soothing taste and does not need milk or sugar.

Brown rice vinegar A tasty seasoning for vegetable dishes.

Kuzu This vegetable powder can be used to thicken sauces and desserts, and is said to settle the digestive system.

Miso A rich, salty seasoning for soups and sauces, made from fermented soya beans. It is said to fortify the blood and improve digestion.

Seaweed Use this to enhance the flavour and nutritional value of just about any savoury dish. Try wakame or dulse in soups or salads, kombu with beans, and arame or hiziki with vegetables. All of them are rich in calcium and iron.

Shoyu This dark, naturally fermented soya sauce is a good seasoning for bean and vegetable dishes.

Tempeh Use this high-protein, rich soya bean pâté fried or in stews.

Tofu A soft, white soya-bean curd, which is high in calcium and protein. It is quick and easy to prepare, and can be fried, steamed, boiled or grilled.

Umeboshi plums Salty, sour pickled plums which can be added to grain or vegetable dishes, or stirred into bancha tea. Umeboshi plums are also recommended for HEADACHES, INDIGESTION, upset stomachs and HEARTBURN.

Utensils in the macrobiotic kitchen

Using the correct tools is just as important in macrobiotics as having the right mix of ingredients to start with. Pots, pans and other utensils are chosen with care and treated with respect. Most kitchens already contain many of the essential items, but you may find that you need to buy one or two. Basic equipment includes:

Pots and pans Cast-iron utensils are generally preferred because they distribute heat evenly, but they are also very heavy and can be hard to lift when full. Stainless-steel pots – particularly those with a heavy, reinforced base – are a good alternative, but need to be used on a lower heat or food may burn. Enamel pots can also be used – treat them gently to avoid chipping, and do not use harsh scouring pads which can scratch the surface.

Copper and aluminium kitchenware is not advised, as traces of the metals may contaminate food and affect its vitamin content.

Ovenware In addition to stainless steel, enamel and cast iron, ceramic and Pyrex are suitable for baking utensils and oven dishes. These materials are more fragile, however, so avoid

A doctor's road to recovery

In January 1987 a retired English doctor living in Italy, Hugh Faulkner, was told after tests in London that he had cancer of the pancreas. The tumour was already the size of a cricket ball and could not be operated on, but a bypass operation was performed to prevent it blocking the passage of food from the stomach. Dr Faulkner knew that drugs and radiation treatment would be unlikely to help, and that he would probably die within a few months.

However, while recovering from the bypass operation, Dr Faulkner began to receive SHIATSU massage treatment, which he found greatly relieved his pain and stiffness. The shiatsu therapist mentioned that she thought a macrobiotic diet could help his condition further. After discussing it with friends and family, the doctor decided to try it, since orthodox medicine had nothing more to offer. He contacted the Community Health Foundation, which provided advice, books, cookery lessons and food supplies.

When the doctor and his wife Marian got back to Italy, they began to follow the macrobiotic diet as carefully as they could. They grew many of their own vegetables and drank water from a well on their land. In addition, they practised self MASSAGE and took lessons in shiatsu and the ALEXANDER TECHNIQUE.

Three years after the operation, at the age of 77, the doctor was not only still alive, but fitter and more energetic than for many years. He was engaged part-time in local health work and was also doing research, writing, and learning woodcarving and the jazz harmonica.

He has admitted that there is no scientific proof that macrobiotics cured him. However, a scan showed that the tumour on his pancreas was shrinking and that its centre was being destroyed – and spontaneous regression is rare in pancreatic cancer.

exposing them to strong direct heat. Sudden changes of temperature such as transferring dishes straight from refrigerator to oven or pouring cold water on a hot dish can also cause breakage.

Knives A good knife – or several if you like to use different sizes – is an indispensable part of macrobiotic cookery. Carbon steel blades are best, followed by stainless steel, which cuts well but chips more easily. Sharpen knives regularly on a whetstone or butcher's steel.

Vegetable chopping board Choose a good-quality wooden board of the biggest size that you can handle comfortably. If possible, avoid scrubbing or washing with soap and hot water – instead, wipe down with a damp cloth before and after use, and between chopping different vegetables. Rubbing in a little sesame oil occasionally will help to keep the wood in good condition.

Steamer Few methods of cooking vegetables are better for retaining taste, texture and vitamins than light steaming. Special steamer pot sets are available, but a folding steamer rack that fits inside an ordinary pot works just as well. Whichever method you use, stainless steel is recommended.

Vegetable brush Brushes of natural bristle are available from many health food shops and stores that sell kitchen equipment. Use them gently to remove sand and grit from root vegetables.

Containers and jars Airtight containers made of natural materials such as glass, ceramic or even wood are recommended for storing dry goods such as nuts, seeds, pulses, rice, other grains and flour.

Pestle and mortar Use these for all mixing, crushing and grinding jobs, such as pulverising nuts and seeds, making sauces and salad dressings, and blending herbs.

Spoons, spatulas and ladles Wooden or bamboo ones are preferred as they do not scratch pans or taint food.

Cooking and preparation methods

Macrobiotic cooks believe that the way food is prepared affects both its nutritional value and its yin and yang qualities. In general, raw foods are considered more yin than cooked foods, and the more heat and the longer the cooking time the more yang food is thought to become. Different kinds of food respond best to different methods of preparation and cooking:

Vegetables The freshness of vegetables is of great importance in macrobiotic cookery. Buy small quantities regularly rather than occasionally stocking up with large supplies. Store vegetables carefully, removing plastic bags so that they can breathe, and keep them in a cool, dry place such as a refrigerator vegetable box.

To preserve their vitamin content do not remove soil or

Legumes
Lentils
Beans
Peas
Tofu

Fruit

Soups

Seafood

Wholegrains
Wholewheat bread
Oatmeal porridge
Wholewheat pastry
Brown rice
Couscous
Wholewheat pasta

Vegetables
Green vegetables
Salads
Seeds
Seaweed

Balancing your diet

This diagram indicates approximately the proportions of different types of foods that should be eaten in a balanced macrobiotic diet. However, they do not need to be followed rigidly.

wash vegetables in advance. Treat vegetables gently when preparing them and, if possible, scrub off soil with a vegetable brush rather than peel them. Avoid lengthy soaking which will leach nutrients into the water. When cutting, use a sharp knife that slices cleanly rather than a blade that has to be drawn back and forth.

Because the upper parts of plants are considered more yin than the lower parts, vegetables are usually cut from top to bottom or diagonally to get a cross-section of yin and yang in each piece. Make the pieces quite small and use different shapes such as triangles, matchsticks, rolled strips, semicircles and cubes to add variety to your meal.

Vegetables are often eaten raw in a macrobiotic meal, usually with a sauce or savoury dip to accompany them. When cooked, they are generally steamed, boiled or stir-fried. Leafy green vegetables need only a minute or two, while root vegetables will take a little longer, but no vegetable should be cooked so long that it loses its crunchiness and texture. Save the water from boiled or steamed vegetables to use in soups, stews and sauces, and when stir-frying use just enough oil to coat the pan, never heating it so much that the oil smokes.

Grains In their whole form grains can be kept for a year or even longer, but as soon as they are ground into flour or pressed into flakes they begin to lose some of their freshness and nutritional value, and will last only a few months. Many macrobiotic cooks dislike buying ready-milled flour for this reason and prefer to use a small hand mill to grind fresh flour.

Grains and grain products are best stored in airtight containers and kept in a cool, dark place. Whole grains should be cooked slowly and thoroughly, using just enough water so that the pot is left dry at the end of cooking – about four measures of water to every one of grain. Remember that the unpolished grains used in macrobiotic cooking take longer to cook than polished ones – about 40-60 minutes for brown rice, for example, compared with 15-20 for white (which also needs less water).

To add variety, sprinkle rice or other grains with roasted nuts or seeds before serving, or serve them with a sauce made from miso, fried onion and a little water or stock.

Pulses Beans, peas and lentils are a rich and inexpensive source of protein. Stored in airtight containers away from heat and moisture, they can last for several years, but careful preparation is necessary to avoid indigestibility.

Begin by spreading dry pulses on a clean tea towel and picking out any stones, husks or broken pieces. Then rinse thoroughly and leave to soak for 4-8 hours or overnight in plenty of water. Before cooking, throw out the soaking water, rinse the beans and bring them to the boil in a saucepan with four measures of fresh water to every measure of beans. Sometimes a strip of kombu or wakame seaweed is added to improve digestibility. Reduce the heat and simmer gently until soft, about 40-60 minutes or even longer in some cases. When soft add soya sauce or sea salt to taste and cook uncovered until the remaining water has evaporated. Adding salt any sooner will harden the skins and increase cooking time.

Beans and other pulses can also be baked. Soak as above and boil for 20 minutes. Place a strip of kombu seaweed in the bottom of a baking dish, pour in the beans and cooking water, cover and cook in a medium oven (180°C or 350°F; gas mark 4) for 3-4 hours. Top up the water halfway if necessary, and add diced vegetables such as onion and carrot if wished, or miso, salt or soya sauce to season.

Fish and shellfish Many people who follow a macrobiotic diet are strict vegetarians, but for those who are not, a little fish and shellfish can be included. They should make up no more than 5 per cent of a macrobiotic diet – only a couple of small portions every week – and their yang qualities should be balanced by helpings of vegetables, grains or pulses in the same meal. Buy only the freshest seafood, if possible on the day you are going to eat it.

Fish can be baked or roasted whole, or skinned, filleted and sautéed in a little hot – but not smoking – oil, with stock, vegetables, seasonings or even fruit added to make a sauce. It can also be chopped into smaller pieces and used in dishes such as paella, or stir-fried with vegetables – also good ways to use prawns or other shellfish. Another tasty way to prepare seafood is in a casserole, with seasonings such as herbs, spices or miso, vegetables, and a little liquid such as stock or wine. Cook covered at 150°C (300°F; gas mark 2) for about an hour, or until tender.

Corresponding yin and yang foods

MODERATELY YIN	MODERATELY YANG
Fruit	Wholegrain cereals such as brown rice, wholewheat bread and flour, whole oat porridge
Leafy green vegetables	Root vegetables such as carrots, potatoes, parsnips
Nuts and seeds	Fish and shellfish, cottage cheese
Tofu and tempeh	Beans, peas and lentils
Fruit and vegetable juices	Salt
Jams (made without sugar)	Miso
Barley malt	Shoyu soya sauce

Extremely yin and yang foods to avoid

YIN	YANG
Sugar, sweets, cakes	Meat, poultry
Strong spices	Hard, salty cheeses
Alcohol, tea, coffee	Eggs

A *macrobiotic meal to try*

The three recipes below have been chosen to give an idea of the different tastes and textures which everyday macrobiotic dishes can provide. Together with rice or other grains they make up a light, well-balanced meal, with a good mixture of yin and yang ingredients. The quantities given should be sufficient for four average servings.

Miso Soup
2 pints (1.1 litres) water
3-4in (7.5-10cm) strip wakame seaweed, plus a little water for soaking
8oz (225g) sliced vegetables (try combinations of carrot, onion, celery, leek, broccoli, cauliflower or others)
1½ tablespoons miso
Lemon juice or crushed ginger to season (optional)
Chopped spring onion or parsley to garnish

Soak the wakame in water for a few minutes, then remove and slice, retaining the soaking water. Bring the 2 pints of fresh water to the boil, add onion if used and simmer for 10 minutes. Then add the other vegetables, wakame and soaking water, and simmer for another 5 minutes. Turn the heat right down, mix the miso into a little of the soup liquid and add. Simmer gently for 3-4 minutes without boiling, add seasoning, pour into bowls, garnish and serve.

Chickpea and Vegetable Stew
6oz (175g) chickpeas (dry measure), soaked overnight
6in (15cm) piece of kombu seaweed
1½ pints (900ml) water
1 chopped onion and 2 chopped carrots
¼ teaspoon sea salt or 1-2 teaspoons shoyu soya sauce
Parsley sprigs and lemon slices to garnish

Boil or bake the chickpeas and seaweed in the water as described in *Cooking and preparation methods* for pulses. When nearly done, add the chopped vegetables and seasonings, and cook until the water has evaporated and everything is soft. Serve with rice, couscous, pasta or other wholegrains, and a dish of steamed, blanched or raw vegetables, or a salad.

Fruit Compote
Fresh or soaked dried fruit – use the equivalent of 2-3 whole fruits per person, or more if using small fruit such as berries, apricots or prunes
Water or apple juice to cover fruit
3-4 tablespoons raisins
Pinch sea salt
Pinch ground cinnamon or ginger
1 teaspoon arrowroot
Roasted almonds and lemon slices to garnish

Peel fresh fruit if not organically grown, core and chop. Place fruit, including raisins, into a pan with the water or apple juice and salt. Simmer gently until soft – 5-10 minutes for fresh fruit, longer for dried, depending on soaking. Stir in the arrowroot to thicken, remove from heat, add the cinnamon or ginger, and scoop into individual bowls. Serve cool, decorated with the nuts and lemon slices.

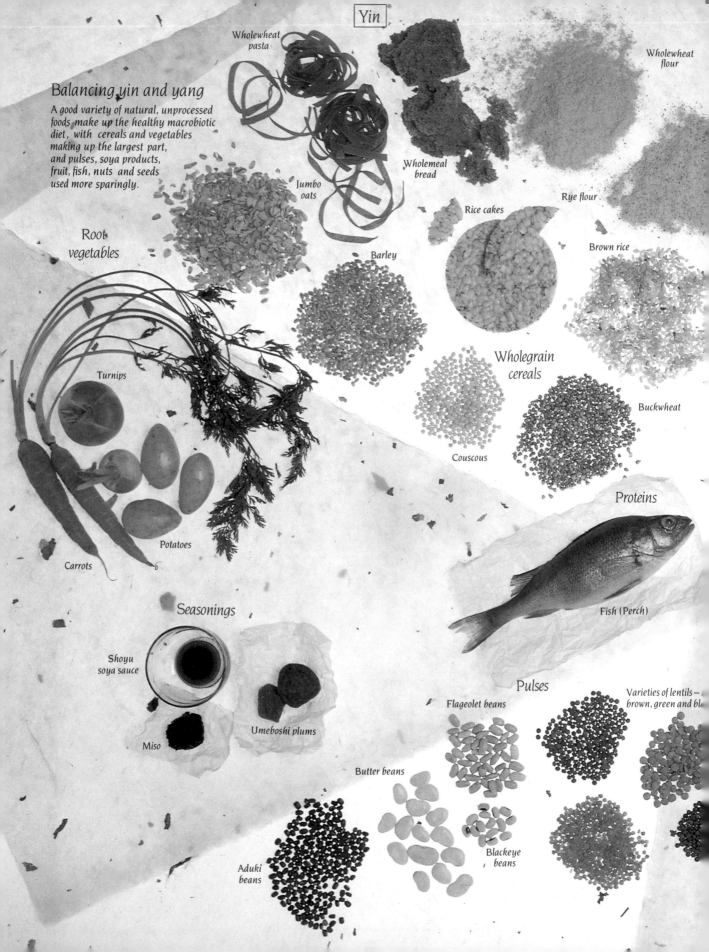

Wholewheat
pasta

Wholewheat
flour

Balancing yin and yang

A good variety of natural, unprocessed foods make up the healthy macrobiotic diet, with cereals and vegetables making up the largest part, and pulses, soya products, fruit, fish, nuts and seeds used more sparingly.

Wholemeal
bread

Rye flour

Rice cakes

Brown rice

Jumbo
oats

Root
vegetables

Barley

Wholegrain cereals

Buckwheat

Turnips

Couscous

Proteins

Potatoes

Carrots

Fish (Perch)

Seasonings

Shoyu
soya sauce

Pulses

Miso

Umeboshi plums

Flageolet beans

Varieties of lentils –
brown, green and bl

Butter beans

Aduki
beans

Blackeye
beans

Yang

Sweeteners

Barley malt

Brown rice vinegar

Fruit

Lime

Tomato

Kumquat

Apple

Lychees

Orange

Grapes

Nuts

Chestnuts

Walnuts

Peanuts

Hazelnuts

Vegetables

Soya products

Tempeh

Tofu

Watercress

Seeds

Sesame seeds

Hiziki seaweed

Spinach

Melon seeds

Mustard and cress

Cabbage

Lettuce

Sunflower seeds

MASTITIS

Many women suffer nodular mastitis, or fibroadenosis – tender, lumpy breasts, particularly in the week before a period (see PERIOD PROBLEMS). It is an uncomfortable and often worrying condition – but harmless. It is caused by the effect of female hormones on breast tissue. Another form of mastitis is a breast abscess, which sometimes occurs in a nursing mother. Any woman who discovers a lump in her breast should seek medical advice immediately – see BREAST PROBLEMS.

MEASLES

One of the most common infectious diseases in the world is rubeola, or measles – a major cause of death in less-developed countries. The virus is spread by direct or close contact and, after an incubation period of eight to 15 days, causes FEVER, a dry cough and sore eyes, followed by a characteristic brownish-pink rash over the entire body.

White spots, known as Koplik's spots, on the insides of the cheeks, may be visible a day or two before the skin rash appears.

Recovery is usually complete within about ten days, although adults who catch the disease may take up to four weeks. Complications arising from measles, which are more common in adults, include ear infections, PNEUMONIA and, rarely, brain inflammation (encephalitis).

Warning Measles is a notifiable disease, and you must report any suspected case to your doctor whether or not you also seek complementary remedies.

What the therapists recommend

HERBAL MEDICINE
Self help   To relieve the feverish symptoms, make infusions (see p. 184) of yarrow, elderflower or boneset; drink a cupful hot every three to four hours. For restlessness and aching, add camomile to the mixture.

To relieve itching, sponge the skin with a cool infusion of lavender, or a teaspoon of distilled witch hazel added to half a pint (300ml) of water.

NATUROPATHY
Consultation   You will be advised to avoid dairy produce and take plenty of fruit and vegetable juices both to replace fluids and provide nutrients. A practitioner may prescribe 1-2g of vitamin C per day to improve resistance to the viral infection.

HOMOEOPATHY
Self help   The aim is to aid recovery, relieve distress and reduce the risk of complications. *Apis mel.* is prescribed for a high temperature, when the patient is hot but wants to be uncovered, has sore eyes and/or ears, and is tearful and irritable. *Euphrasia* is for streaming, sore eyes and sensitivity to light. *Gelsemium* is given for high fever and extreme prostration – even delirium. If a child is restless and irritable, needs to be comforted, has a troublesome cough and wants cool air, try *Pulsatilla*.

An orthodox view

There is no cure for measles, although secondary ear infections or pneumonia respond to antibiotics. Measles vaccine, given in the UK, along with MUMPS and German measles (rubella) immunisation, to two-year-olds, is 95 per cent effective as a preventative. The side effects of the vaccine are the same as those of measles, but the risk is less after vaccination than after infection.

Conventional advice to measles patients is to rest, drink extra fluids, and to take paracetamol to reduce fever and ease discomfort. To ensure that there are no complications, consult your doctor.

MEDITATION
Finding your way to the still, calm centre

When life heaps upon us problems that must be solved, decisions that cannot wait and changes that disrupt settled ways, we sometimes feel unable to manage, lose confidence in ourselves and become plagued by TENSION and ANXIETY. These may persist beyond immediate crises, robbing us of energy, setting a pattern for INSOMNIA, raising BLOOD PRESSURE, and causing many other physical ailments. To gain relief, millions of people go to their doctors for help and are given tranquillisers, sleeping pills and anti-depressants; such drugs are by far the commonest prescribed for patients.

Meditation is seen as a way of shedding your cares and strains – reaching, without drugs, a tranquil state that refreshes the mind and relaxes the body. Such a respite, which you can take as frequently as you wish, is aimed at restoring both the will and the ability to manage your life. A little time spent simply staring into space and pleasantly daydreaming may give an inkling of the feeling and benefits.

In India and much of the rest of Asia, meditation has been practised for thousands of years as a way of achieving spiritual enlightenment. YOGA developed from it. There have long been small numbers of people in the West who practised it, mostly people who were interested in Buddhism. But meditation was thrust into the limelight in the 1960s, when Eastern music and culture attracted pop musicians, among them the Beatles, and masses of young people looking for new approaches to life's problems.

Maharishi Mahesh Yogi was the best known of their teachers, and his MANTRAS for transcendental meditation attracted devoted followers – an unusual occurrence because the association of meditation with Oriental or eccentric religions, and descriptions such as 'transcendental', which wrongly imply that unearthly powers are involved, tended to put off most Westerners.

However, forms of meditation have been, and are, practised by members of various Christian religious orders – the retreats of Jesuits, and the spiritual exercises of their founder, St Ignatius Loyola, for example, may be considered to involve elements of meditational techniques.

Meditation is regarded by its practitioners as a supreme self-help method. Using nothing more than your own powers of concentration, you control your thoughts and calm and slow your body. This is not to say it is easy. Switching off racing thoughts and keeping worry at bay may at first prove difficult, but practitioners offer simple procedures which they say help most people to reach the utterly relaxed but self-controlled meditative state.

Who it can help   Meditation requires concentration, persistence and time – anything from ten to 20 minutes a day. Most people can learn to meditate without too much difficulty. Although some benefits – such as lowering of the pulse and blood pressure – may occur immediately, long-term benefits require regular practice. For some people, this can be difficult.

A large group among those who benefit are people with high blood pressure: many are able to cut down or even cut out the drugs prescribed for them. The exaggerated reactions which their bodies have to everyday stresses diminish and their blood pressure remains lower as long as they continue with meditation, especially if they also practise RELAXATION AND BREATHING.

Machines that record the electrical impulses sent out by muscles show that muscular tension drops almost to nil during meditation. As a result, chronic pain and discomfort from injury are relieved – for tension causes, or at least worsens, many pains.

Circulation has been shown to improve during meditation, so conditions as comparatively minor as CHILBLAINS or as serious as RAYNAUD'S DISEASE may be helped by meditating. It can also relieve tension HEAD-ACHES, where the blood supply to the scalp is affected.

The slower, deeper breathing and the reduced rate of consuming oxygen that occur during meditation are beneficial to people with chest complaints. Combined with the relaxation of muscles, this is particularly good for asthma sufferers.

Pain, breathing difficulties, tension and a mind racing uncontrollably are all common causes of insomnia. Monitoring the brain's pattern of electrical activity with an EEG (electroencephalograph) machine shows that brain activity during meditation becomes similar to that during sleep.

Meditation makes people sufficiently relaxed to go off to sleep. It breaks the pattern of sleeplessness which is particularly difficult to alter. Insomniacs who meditate will not necessarily sleep longer, because their need to switch off is partially satisfied by the meditative state itself. They will, how-ever, be able to get to sleep and feel properly rested by the sleep they have.

Finding a teacher Traditional meditation techniques intended to empty the mind with the aim of allowing consciousness to expand and reach a higher reality require formal programmes of teaching. A special posture and a mantra (a phrase or sound chanted over and over) are used in transcendental meditation, with a teacher to lead and super-vise. People rooted in Western cultures often find this difficult to accept, and simpler methods may suit them far better.

Some people find it impossible to start meditating on their own and welcome join-ing a group where they can seek advice and practise suggested techniques. Your local library may include such groups in its list of local societies.

How to meditate Whether you choose to meditate on your own or in a group, the procedure will be similar. Details may vary, but the basic rules are common.

It is best not to eat or drink in the half hour before meditating. Choose a quiet room where you will not be interrupted. Some people lie down and close their eyes, but many teachers say that you should sit com-fortably but upright, with eyes open and hands resting in your lap. In this way you can relax but remain alert and controlled; lying with eyes closed, your mind may simply wander or you may fall asleep.

What you are aiming to do is stop trouble-some or stimulating thoughts from entering your mind. This is most easily done by filling up your mind with one neutral or calmly pleasing thought. Breathing is made the focus in some methods, by feeling the air

entering your nostrils, moving it down to fill your lungs completely and then slowly expelling it. Concentrate on making your diaphragm move down and your abdomen (not chest) swell out as you breathe in. Count as you breathe in and out, taking as long to expel the air as you did drawing it in – and making sure it is all expelled.

When this breathing pattern becomes automatic you may find unwanted thoughts creeping in. You can shift your concentration from breathing to relaxing every area of your body. With one breath, check that your forehead is not tight, with the next that you are not clenching your teeth, then that your shoulders, elbows, knees, calves and feet are loose.

If thoughts keep intruding, do not follow them up. Merely acknowledge that they have come and then resume concentration on your chosen focus. When you can easily follow the breathing and relaxation pattern, you may prefer to focus on an object – a favourite ornament perhaps, or a photograph of a tranquil place whose smell, sounds and air you can feel surrounding you.

You may find that playing a soothing tape-recording helps you into the meditative state. Special meditation tapes can be bought at health food shops or specialist book shops, or you could compile your own.

Maintain your meditation for ten minutes or more. As you become practised you will be able to fall into it almost anywhere – on a train going to work, between chores, or at your desk during your lunch break. At the end of your meditation, shuffle about a little and exercise your muscles gently for a minute or two before you stand up, other-wise you may feel giddy because of lowered blood pressure.

Obviously you must not practise medi-tation while driving or using tools of any kind. But otherwise it holds no dangers and is a useful way of improving well-being, whether or not you are receiving any other form of treatment.

An orthodox view

The key to meditation probably lies in man-aging to concentrate on just one thing at a time instead of on a welter of things as we normally tend to do. Reducing the flow of information and sensations we are trying to accept reduces the mental responses we have to make.

Research shows that breathing, brain activity, blood pressure, and heart and pulse rate are all affected by meditation. The calm and rested feeling it produces should not only ease disorders of the moment, but also improve your ability to cope physically and mentally with forthcoming activities or future problems.

MEGAVITAMIN THERAPY
Treatment based on large doses of vitamins

The American biochemist Linus Pauling (1901–) first attracted popular attention to the use of huge doses of VITAMINS to improve health. His book _Vitamin C and the Common Cold_ (1970) described for ordinary readers what he discovered.

It was research into the way MEMORY works that led Pauling to investigate the role of vitamins. His findings during studies of vitamin C led to his claim that large doses of the vitamin could ward off the common cold. The medical establishment rejected his claim – but many people tried the vitamin remedy and have found it effective.

Pauling's researches went much wider into other vitamins and MINERALS. He gave the name ORTHOMOLECULAR MEDICINE (_ortho_ means 'correct') to a new approach to health which came out of his work. It was based on preserving and restoring good health by finding the right level of vitamins and min-erals to suit each individual.

He claimed that orthomolecular medicine could add 20 years of good health to people's lives. He also claimed benefits for large doses of vitamin C that went far beyond fighting the common cold – chiefly in helping people with CANCER. He said that it could improve healing and strengthen the IMMUNE SYSTEM – especi-ally the resistance of tissue around a cancer, so that malignant cells cannot spread.

Although Pauling's fertile mind and com-munication skills drew attention to the potential of vitamin megadoses, he was not the first in the field. From the early 1950s his compatriots, Dr Abraham Hoffer and Dr Humphry Osmond, had been using high doses of vitamin B3 to treat SCHIZOPHRENIA, and claimed success rates of more than 75 per cent in some 2000 cases. A whole field of 'orthomolecular psychiatry' has grown since, to treat mental illnesses.

At the core of all these treatments for physical and mental ills – now generally referred to as megavitamin therapy – is the belief that the daily intakes at present recom-mended by orthodox practitioners for vita-mins and minerals are only a very rough guide. Individual needs can vary enormously – many people are said to need quantities ten times greater than the recommended amount, and some are thought to need doses 100 or more times greater.

Taking vitamins as remedies is now

common practice. Vitamin C supplements aimed at preventing VIRUS INFECTIONS are available from chemists and health shops without prescription; the amounts taken are much smaller than megavitamin doses. Vitamins and minerals are also prescribed as part of standard medical practice – for example, for ACNE, ANAEMIA, DIABETES, high blood cholesterol, ALCOHOLISM and PREMENSTRUAL TENSION (PMT) – but again the doses do not reach megavitamin proportions.

Who it can help Megavitamin therapists take the view that most people's illnesses will be relieved by their therapy because a principal cause of illness is metabolic abnormality resulting from an incorrect intake of vitamins.

The therapy also helps those people who are unable to absorb enough vitamins and minerals even from a diet that would normally be adequate. Megadoses are prescribed so that the tiny proportion absorbed by their faulty system will approach their required level.

Some illnesses and medical treatments are believed to alter the ability to absorb vitamins and minerals, and very large doses are prescribed in such cases; conventional chemotherapy and radiotherapy, for example, are said to triple the needs of cancer patients for vitamins B and C.

Megavitamin therapists have worked out complex combinations of vitamins to treat cancer patients, especially after they have had orthodox treatments.

Vitamin C and the B vitamins are also claimed to restore the biochemical balance in the brain of people with mental illnesses including schizophrenia and DEPRESSION. HYPERACTIVITY and drug dependency (see ADDICTION) have also been found to respond to megavitamin treatment.

Finding a therapist For information on where megavitamin therapy is available, contact The Institute for Optimum Nutrition, 5 Jerdan Place, London SW6 1BE. The institute can supply a list of graduate nutritionists. Graduates will have spent two years studying biochemistry and physiology in relation to nutrition and completed at least 50 case histories along with a three-month research project. Once these criteria have been met and a final examination passed, graduates may use the letters Dip ION.

Consulting a therapist Large doses of vitamins and minerals should never be taken without qualified advice and supervision. They interact in complex ways which it is the therapist's job to know. Indeed the most important part of a series of consultations will be devoted to drawing up an accurate profile of your particular needs. This will take time and may involve skin tests and hair analysis. Only then can a suitable course of

high-dose supplements be decided upon. The therapist will want to keep a close check on your progress because vitamins can cause uncomfortable, even dangerous, side effects from quantities that can easily be eaten.

An orthodox view

Despite the many individual cases where megavitamin treatment has been successful, orthodox practitioners view the therapy with suspicion. This is largely because it works in the dark. Very few controlled trials have been done on matched groups of people to pinpoint the effects of vitamins and minerals, alone or in combination, compared with other treatments.

Trials which have been carried out, mainly in the United States, have produced poor or confusing results. There are so many variables in the biochemistry of individuals, whether in normal or in ill health, that it may never be possible to get enough answers to predict the effects of treatment.

Meanwhile, the possible harm done by megadoses is causing concern. If vitamin D, for example, is taken in excessive amounts it can quickly cause muscle weakness, bone pain, hypertension, irregular heartbeat and kidney deterioration. If vitamin A is taken in excessive quantities for a long period it can cause painful joints, cracked skin, anaemia and amnesia in adults; in children it can cause severe visual disturbance and painful swellings over bones; and in unborn children it is suspected of causing deformities.

There are also doubts about the skill of those who prescribe, and fears that big business interests are misleading the public in order to make profits.

At present it would be better to educate the public on what the daily requirements of vitamins and minerals are, what common foods contain them, and how to avoid destroying them during cooking or storage.

MEMORY
Ways of giving it a jog . . .

The brain may be likened to a computer, for in both a 'good memory' involves the successful input, storage and retrieval of information. Barring some forms of mental problems, we learn throughout our lives, receiving and storing information and experiences. This is thought to involve changes in the way nerve impulses are routed through the brain.

There are two kinds of memory, based on two kinds of changes. Short-term memory is

thought to involve reverberatory activity in groups of nerve cells – a kind of 'echo' or 'bouncing back' effect. Long-term memory probably involves a more permanent 'trace' in the brain, in the way the nerve cells are connected to each other at the so-called synaptic junctions (relay stations between the nerve cells).

The two types of memory have different properties. For example, at any one time only about seven items can be retained in the short-term memory. Most people can read and remember a seven-digit telephone number, provided they keep rehearsing or repeating it. Larger numbers are not so easily remembered, for the items become jumbled or lost. And without repetition, short-term memory lasts for only about 30 seconds.

Another difference is that specific items or detailed content tend to be stored in the short-term memory while usually only the general idea or meaning is retained in the long-term memory. For instance, most people will remember for about a day the actual words of a sentence that someone said. After that, they will be able to recall only the gist or meaning of the sentence.

Generally, the more easily recalled items fit into an existing framework, the more successfully they are stored in the long-term memory. All adults have built up a framework of the human face, and when confronted with a new one, need only to remember its distinguishing features to recognise it again.

Generally, too, recognition – or storage – is easier than recall or retrieval. We have all had someone's name 'on the tip of the tongue'; we feel we know the name, yet cannot recall it. Then as soon as the name is said, we instantly recognise it.

On the whole, the more easily a new item can be associated with earlier items, the more easily it is learned or stored. And this association works for new material too, for items are more readily learned if associated in groups. However, association with earlier information may confuse what we store. We may have preconceived ideas about a situation and these may affect what we remember about it.

Normally, the more interesting we find an experience, the better it will be remembered. This is probably because we concentrate on it and rehearse it more, so that a more permanent 'trace' is made in the brain.

Several factors can impair the memory. Head injuries often result in a total or partial loss of memory – a condition known as AMNESIA. Alcohol, nicotine, and the side effects of certain drugs, such as the tranquillisers prescribed for INSOMNIA and medications for BLOOD PRESSURE problems, adversely affect the memory. So do STRESS,

DEPRESSION, ANXIETY, SHOCK and fatigue, which affect concentration. Amnesia may also be a symptom of HYSTERIA.

We all experience deterioration of our mental faculties – including memory – to a greater or lesser degree in old age (see GROWING OLD). In its more drastic form, this is called senile dementia and is associated with loss of brain cells and synaptic junctions. Elderly people more readily recall things experienced in the distant past than recent happenings. However, in some people, severe dementia develops in middle age, and this condition is known as ALZHEIMER'S DISEASE.

Self help There are several ways in which you can improve your memory. Some people find MEDITATION or the SILVA METHOD to be of help.

Dietary supplements of choline have been proved beneficial in tests carried out at the National Institute of Mental Health in Bethesda, Maryland, USA. Subjects given 10g of choline were able to memorise a list of unrelated words more quickly than before. Choline is a substance that the body produces and converts into acetylcholine, which is essential for the smooth flow of nerve impulses. Victims of Alzheimer's disease are deficient in the enzyme that produces acetylcholine, so the evidence for a link between choline and memory seems strong.

Lecithin, a fat sometimes included in the vitamin B-complex, is the main dietary source of choline. It is found in soya beans, maize, egg yolks and liver. It is best to try an unsaturated type, such as that made from soya beans, available in granule or capsule form. Take as directed by the manufacturer. Alternatively, take 1 or 2 tablespoons of the granules each day, sprinkled on food or mixed in drinks. (Lecithin also has the property of dissolving cholesterol deposits, so it may also be helpful for HEART DISORDERS and GALLSTONES.)

Do not smoke, and cut out alcohol and any drugs that are not absolutely essential to your well-being (see ADDICTION, ALCOHOLISM and SMOKING).

Use 'tricks' of association. For example, conjure up a pleasing image for each of the numbers 0 to 9. You should find it easier to remember the images than the numerals, and through them, recall the digits more easily. When introduced to someone, imagine something connected with them, their name or their occupation, for example – a gigantic pen for a writer, or a green light for someone named Green.

Try to associate things to be remembered in groups. For example, you may find it easier to remember the shopping list if you group the items according to their location in the supermarket – and you will save time, too.

Try to imagine things in a setting that you already have imprinted in your memory. Associate them with happy events or some pleasing scene.

These images need not necessarily be visual; they can be sounds, feelings, moods or postures. You will remember happy events better if you put yourself into a happy mood. Conversely, unhappy episodes will come to mind more readily if you are sad. Whatever you do, the more outrageous and unusual your images and associations are, the more effective they will be. The more you practise, the better your memory will become.

Mnemonics – devices such as formulas or rhymes – also aid memory by association. In music the notes of the treble clef can be remembered by the formula 'Every Good Boy Deserves Favour'. An example of a mnemonic rhyme lists the sovereigns of England from the Norman conquest: 'Willi, Willi, Harry, Ste; Harry, Richard, John, Henry' and so on.

Finally, arrange your 'memory training' according to the time of day. Short-term memory gets worse as the day wears on, possibly because of increasing tiredness. On the other hand, long-term memory improves as the day progresses.

MENOPAUSE

Technically the term menopause refers to the permanent ending of monthly periods, but in general use it often embraces the wide range of accompanying symptoms which make up the climacteric, or 'change of life'. This phase of a woman's life, when her ovaries stop producing eggs and her fertility declines and eventually ceases, may begin anywhere from the early forties to the mid-fifties and usually takes two or three years.

Bound up with this physical process are several psychological factors – fear about losing attractiveness, uncertainty about a purpose in life for middle-aged women, perhaps sadness that the fertile prime of life is over. These feelings are added to, and may outweigh, any physical discomforts or disturbances caused by complex changes in hormone balance.

In a few women, menstruation may stop suddenly with no previous change in the cycle, but in most women the menstrual cycle becomes irregular. Often, periods become less heavy and occur farther apart. But they may also occur more often, or follow the usual timing but with some missing altogether. Bleeding or spotting between 'normal' periods, or after sexual intercourse,

should always be discussed with your doctor promptly – as should any bleeding which occurs a year or more after the last period.

During the menopause, the ovaries reduce and finally cease production not only of eggs but also of oestrogen, the hormone that maintains the female reproductive function. Some oestrogen is still made elsewhere in the body, particularly in the layers of fat beneath the skin, so plumper women generally experience fewer effects.

Loss of oestrogen brings symptoms such as hot flushes, sweating at night, uncomfortable lack of lubricating fluid in the vagina, and a more frequent need to pass urine. About seven in every ten women suffer these effects in varying degrees.

One result of the menopause in all women initially goes unnoticed – a gradual but progressive loss of bone mass, or OSTEOPOROSIS. This leads to a greater risk of FRACTURES, particularly of the hip, in later life. After the menopause, women also lose the greater protection against heart attacks, compared with men, which their higher oestrogen level may have given them previously.

During the menopause, many women suffer with ANXIETY, irritability, lack of concentration, INSOMNIA, swings of mood, or even DEPRESSION. As it often coincides with children growing up and leaving home, women who have had families may feel an acute loss of identity. Women who go out to work tend to have fewer menopausal problems than those whose life revolves around the family home.

Symptoms may be made worse by the STRESS, lack of zest for life and curtailment of activity and exercise which can result from the psychological hurdles.

For many women, however, the problems are few and the compensations welcome. They feel fit, vigorous, and glad to be rid of the slight (or considerable) nuisance of monthly periods (see PERIOD PROBLEMS). They find their sex life enhanced by knowing they will not become pregnant and being free at last of the need for contraception.

Vaginal dryness and shrinkage are greatly lessened by a regular sex life. And as lifespans have increased, the process of GROWING OLD has been slowed. Where once both men and women were considered elderly at 55, a postmenopausal woman can now expect many years of active life. There are many natural and medical ways of enhancing well-being during this time.

What the therapists recommend
NATUROPATHY
Self help A healthy diet, regular exercise and sufficient sleep will ease many menopausal symptoms.
Consultation Naturopaths may suggest a

short period of supervised semi-fasting, taking only fresh vegetable juice or fruit juice, to cleanse the body of impurities. This is followed by a diet with a high proportion of raw foods, and a planned programme of EXERCISE and relaxation.

Some naturopaths also recommend vita-min and mineral supplements, particularly vitamins B, C and E and calcium.

ACUPUNCTURE

Consultation Although treatment varies according to the individual and her symp-toms, menopausal disorders are generally treated at points on the bladder, conception, stomach, kidney and liver meridians. MOXI-BUSTION to the governor, stomach and bladder meridians may also be suggested.

The practitioner may also be able to treat digestive disorders, peptic ulcers and gall-stones, to which older women are more

Replacing lost hormones through HRT – panacea or meddling with nature?

An increasingly popular, but somewhat controversial, conventional treatment for menopausal problems is hormone re-placement therapy (HRT).

Women using HRT are usually given oestrogen tablets which they take for three weeks out of every four-week cycle – or continuously for the whole four weeks if, for example, menopausal symptoms appear in the week in between. If the tablets cause nausea or DIARRHOEA, oes-trogen pellets can be implanted under the woman's skin. This is done under local anaesthetic, and once in place the pellets release small amounts of the hormone continuously for up to six months, when a replacement is implanted.

Since it can be absorbed through the skin, oestrogen is also available in the form of creams, pessaries and stick-on skin patches for women who prefer not to take tablets or have an implant.

Whatever type of oestrogen is used, most women are also given a second hormone, progesterone, to take in tablet form for one or two weeks every month. This protects against the major side effect of HRT: overstimulation of the womb lining leading to a possible increased risk of CANCER. This does not affect women who have had a hysterectomy, and they are given oestrogen only.

HRT can make a dramatic difference to women who find coping with the meno-pause a real struggle, but not all doctors approve of it. They agree that it does relieve hot flushes and vaginal dryness, and it may improve skin tone, lift depres-sion and increase energy. But against this are slightly increased risks of some can-cers and the possible inconvenience of continued monthly bleeding – similar to a normal menstrual period but without an egg being produced each month.

The greatest benefit of HRT is that it reduces OSTEOPOROSIS and the risk of hip, wrist and spine fractures of brittle bones that are common among postmenopausal women. Since hip fractures in particular are a major cause of disability and death in women over the age of 65, HRT can literally save lives.

There is also some evidence that HRT brings down the risk of heart disease and strokes to premenopausal levels, because of the protective effects of oestrogen. However, other studies show an increased risk – pos-sibly due to progesterone – so that HRT is not given to women who have had a heart attack, stroke or blood-clotting problems.

It is also unsuitable for anyone with a history of cancer of the breast or uterus, a family history of breast cancer, or undiag-nosed vaginal bleeding.

Before prescribing HRT, your doctor must take all these factors into account and con-duct a thorough medical examination. He will then be able to advise you on the different options available, and their advan-tages and disadvantages.

Women receiving HRT need regular medi-cal check-ups and should mention any symp-toms (such as an unusual vaginal discharge, headaches, dizziness or pains in the calf muscles) as soon as they notice them. Regu-lar breast self-examination is another impor-tant safety check (see BREAST PROBLEMS).

For and against Here are the contrasting views of two women who have had HRT: FOR . . .

Mrs Theresa Gorman, MP, began to suffer pains in her wrists, ankles and back during her late 40s. At first she thought they were signs of early ARTHRITIS, but then hot flushes and other menopausal symptoms developed. She became forgetful, felt tired and lost interest in life. MIGRAINE occurred for the first time. Eventually she turned to hormone treatment for help.

'As soon as I started taking HRT, all the symptoms disappeared, including joint pains,' Mrs Gorman says. 'That was ten years ago, and they have never returned. I felt absolutely marvellous, restored, almost resurrected, with a terrific feeling of well-being, confidence and energy. I may be old but I feel just as I did in my twenties. I'll never stop taking HRT.'

Mrs Gorman believes that ignorance about HRT still condemns many women to unnecessary suffering, and she campaigns to publicise its benefits. A biologist by training, she views HRT as restoring something which nature takes away too soon. 'It's not just vanity,' she says. 'The body begins to age very rapidly when oestrogens are lost. The hormones are completely natural, and enable women to stop worrying about their physical state and get on with life.'

An added benefit, she says, is that HRT is the only known antidote for osteo-porosis, and could prevent much of the pain and suffering older women currently endure through osteoporotic fractures. She believes also that the zest for life which HRT gives is important, especially for the increasing numbers of elderly women to whom it might offer new hope and vigour – and prevent them from being placed in a home. 'If we don't take care of women as they get older, we will face the social consequences', she warns.

AGAINST . . .

Dr Margaret White, a retired general prac-titioner with a special interest in women's health, had a natural, trouble-free meno-pause at 48, without any unpleasant symptoms such as hot flushes. Two years later she was persuaded by a drug com-pany representative to try HRT.

'I took the lowest possible dose for a year,' she says, 'but then an American medical professor advised me in the strongest terms that not enough research had been done on HRT and its long-term effects, which might include cancer.'

Following this advice, Dr White grad-ually reduced her doses until she even-tually stopped altogether. 'Immediately I had all the awful symptoms which I hadn't had during the natural menopause: hot flushes, sweating every two or three minutes, giddiness. I felt depressed and awful, and bitterly regretted ever taking it.'

The symptoms gradually subsided, but it was another year before Dr White felt normal again. Now she advises women to avoid HRT or use it only temporarily, to get over the worst symptoms of the meno-pause. 'There just isn't enough research to show what happens to women if they take HRT for 20 years or more,' she cautions. 'Until we're sure, we shouldn't be handing it out like Smarties to healthy women. We should only use it for a short time to help women who do have symptoms.'

prone, in addition to OBESITY, raised BLOOD PRESSURE, SMOKING and ALCOHOLISM which can sometimes affect them.

HERBAL MEDICINE

Self help Regular drinks of camomile tea and lime-blossom tea act as general relaxants. Passiflora tablets may also reduce tension and anxiety. Oats included in the diet should provide a gentle tonic. Hot flushes may be relieved by taking liquid sarsaparilla, ginseng tea, life root or St John's wort. Hormonal disturbances can be treated with herbs such as chaste tea, wild yam and false unicorn root. A bedtime drink of honey and hot water, with three drops of essential oil of sage added, is used to relieve night sweating.

Other alternative treatments

Homoeopathy Treatment is individually tailored for the woman's personality, circumstances and overall symptoms.

Pulsatilla may be recommended to stabilise the menstrual cycle of women with fair complexions, but *Sepia* for those women who are dark-skinned brunettes. *Glonoine* and *Lachesis* are believed to be most useful for reducing severe hot flushes.

Aromatherapy Essential oils of sage, cypress and geranium are said to ease physical symptoms – carry a mixture of the oils with you for inhaling if symptoms start while you are out. At home, put six or eight drops of the oils in your bath. For massage, add a total of 15 drops of the oils to 5 dessert-spoons of carrier oil.

An orthodox view

Regular exercise and a balanced diet help to minimise menopausal symptoms, and reduce to some extent the risk of osteoporosis. Drugs such as clonidine can alleviate hot flushes and oestrogen cream eases vaginal dryness. Orthodox medicine also offers hormone replacement (HRT; see box).

MERIDIANS

Followers of Chinese medicine believe that *Qi* – the body's life-activating internal energy – flows through 12 channels known as meridians. These link related organs and body parts, and when they become blocked, energy imbalances result; it is these that cause disease. In order to restore the flow, practitioners of ACUPUNCTURE insert needles at points along the meridians, while practitioners of ACUPRESSURE and SHIATSU apply finger pressure. REFLEXOLOGY has ten similar meridians, which link the massage points of the feet with their related body parts.

MESMERISM

The Austrian doctor Franz Anton Mesmer (1734-1815) was the pioneer of HYPNO-THERAPY, which was known as 'mesmerism'. Mesmer claimed to magnetise his patients.

METAMORPHIC TECHNIQUE
Manipulation as a means to health

A relationship between the foot and the body's development during the first nine months of life in the womb forms the basis of the metamorphic technique. Its practitioners believe that gentle manipulation of the feet, hands and head can help recipients to come to terms with many long-standing problems.

They do not claim an ability to heal or cure, but many of their clients say that they experience physical and emotional benefits, and are helped to develop a more positive and creative outlook.

In particular, people who feel trapped in a rut, or are aware of a need for change but cannot see what to do, may find that the technique opens up new ways of transforming their lives.

The metamorphic technique began in the 1960s as a result of the work of a British naturopath, Robert St John (1912-   ). He was disappointed that many people who had been helped by treatment later fell back into their old ways of behaving and their former illnesses recurred.

Seeking a way to help these people to gain permanent benefits, St John turned to REFLEXOLOGY – a method of massaging areas of the feet thought to correspond to particular bodily systems and organs.

In addition to the normal reflex areas,

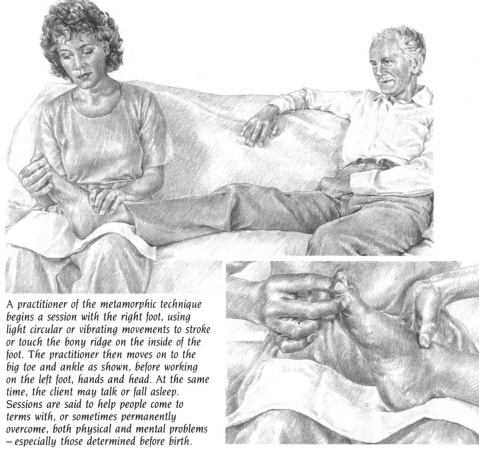

A practitioner of the metamorphic technique begins a session with the right foot, using light circular or vibrating movements to stroke or touch the bony ridge on the inside of the foot. The practitioner then moves on to the big toe and ankle as shown, before working on the left foot, hands and head. At the same time, the client may talk or fall asleep. Sessions are said to help people come to terms with, or sometimes permanently overcome, both physical and mental problems – especially those determined before birth.

however, St John came to feel that parts of the foot – particularly the reflex areas relating to the spine (see chart, p. 295) – also reflect the individual's development before birth. He attached great importance to this period, and thought that many of our physical and psychological characteristics develop during the nine month gestation period.

He decided that for people to receive lasting benefits, treatment should go right back to these early patterns, removing and correcting problems that began in the first stages of life.

Who it can help The technique is designed to help anyone who feels mentally blocked, stuck or unable to make a necessary change. People who cannot shake off long-standing health problems, children and the handicapped are said to derive particular benefits – even those with such severe conditions as Down's syndrome and AUTISM.

Finding a practitioner Practitioners have usually attended courses run by The Metamorphic Association, but need not have any medical or other qualifications. They practise privately and, although the technique is not available on the National Health Service, voluntary as well as private work is done in many hospitals.

For information about metamorphic classes, books and practitioners in your area, get in touch with The Metamorphic Association, 67 Ritherdon Road, London SW17 8QE.

Consulting a practitioner No attempt is made to diagnose or treat problems directly. Instead, practitioners of the metamorphic technique call themselves catalysts – agents of change and healing who remain personally detached from the processes which they spark off in the client.

Sessions begin with the client sitting comfortably, with legs raised and well supported. The practitioner sits at right angles and gently manipulates first the right and then the left foot. Using a light circular or vibrating finger movement, he strokes or touches the bony ridge on the inside of each foot, then moves on to the big toe and ankle areas. Later, the thumbs, wrists and top of the head are worked on.

The feet are considered to represent movement and energy; the hands and head, respectively, to express action and thought. As each is touched, old patterns of behaving, feeling and thinking are said to be loosened, allowing new and better ones to develop.

Throughout the process, the practitioner remains detached, allowing the client simply to express whatever he feels. Acceptance is offered, but not approval, disapproval or advice, since practitioners do not see themselves as therapists. Instead, their attitude encourages the client to take responsibility for his or her own health, and believe that their work simply helps to activate clients' own inner healing powers.

Sessions usually last for about an hour and take place weekly until the client feels ready to stop. However, daily sessions may be arranged in certain cases where the clients are, for example, children, mentally or physically handicapped people, or patients in hospital.

Family self help Practitioners encourage their clients to learn a simple form of the technique and to practise it on family members – a parent on a child, for example. Although you can use the technique on yourself, there is a slight drawback since this creates what practitioners call a 'closed circuit' of energy, and you lose the sense of 'sharing' with another person. Ideally, at least two members of each family should learn and take part.

An orthodox view

This is a variant of many of the mind-body therapies available, and differs from them in that the practitioners aim to help people to cure themselves.

MIASM THEORY
Treating the roots of disease

The belief that illness can signify an underlying disease that is not directly apparent was proposed by the founder of HOMOEOPATHY, Samuel Hahnemann (1755-1843), of Meissen, Germany. He noted that many patients would recover only to become ill again later, and reasoned that some deep-seated condition was creating within them a predisposition to develop certain diseases.

He used the word 'miasm' – from the Greek *miainein*, meaning 'to pollute' – to describe the condition. He felt that various diseases, including SKIN DISORDERS and tuberculosis, were 'miasmatic' in character. Accordingly, he sought to get to the roots of his patients' illnesses, and to treat them with appropriate homoeopathic remedies.

Hahnemann also tried to improve their ways of life. For example, he told them not to smoke or drink too much, not to eat rich food, or to waste their energies on such pursuits as gambling and horse-riding.

Some homoeopaths believe that miasms are the underlying causes of ANXIETY, DEPRESSION, CANCER, MIGRAINE and STOMACH COMPLAINTS. However, other homoeopaths reject the theory of miasms.

See also RADIESTHESIA AND RADIONICS.

MIGRAINE

One of the most common ailments of the nervous system, migraine causes recurrent HEADACHES and sometimes other neurological symptoms, such as numbness, tingling or weakness on one side of the body.

The first sign of a migraine may be an 'aura', or a premonition that an attack is imminent. There may be visual disturbance, such as bright spots or zigzag lines before both eyes. An aura is caused by temporary narrowing of the blood vessels supplying part of the brain. Minutes later, when the blood vessels, which had been tightly constricted, suddenly open up to allow a gush of blood to the brain, a severe, one-sided, throbbing headache follows, often with an aversion to light, and vomiting. Symptoms may last from a few hours to several days.

However, not all migraines follow the same pattern – and in some cases only the headache occurs.

Typically, migraine occurs after, rather than during, times of STRESS – for example, after an examination or important interview. It may also be related to sensitivity to certain foods (see ALLERGY and FOOD ADDITIVES). Women are prone to migraine during menstrual periods. The oral contraceptive pill can also cause migraine, particularly during the pill-free week.

One of the three acupressure points for treating migraine is the area at the top of the neck. To gain relief, the sufferer should press inwards and upwards below the skull and near to the sides of the spine.

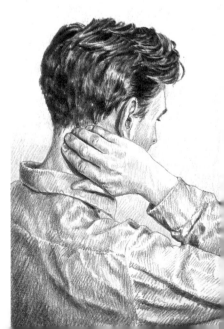

What the therapists recommend

ACUPUNCTURE
Consultation Practitioners ascribe migraine to a blockage of _Qi_ energy in the yang channels of the head. Individual treatment depends upon the location of the pain, but the stomach and the large and small intestine meridians would probably be treated. MOXIBUSTION is also said to be effective.

ACUPRESSURE
Self help There are three points to be treated for migraine: on the hand, press at the end of the crease between finger and thumb towards the first finger bone; press in and upwards at the top of the neck beneath the skull and close to the sides of the spine; on the feet, press the web between the big and second toe inwards and up towards the centre of the foot.

BIOFEEDBACK
Consultation By visualising comfortable surroundings (see VISUALISATION THERAPY), such as being on the beach, in the bath, or in front of the fire, patients can relax – and, in doing so, restore normal blood circulation. This technique, it is claimed, can be learned by using a biofeedback instrument that measures the temperature of the fingers – and informs the user when warmth is restored. With practice, sufferers are said to be able to ward off a migraine attack when they feel one coming on.

HOMOEOPATHY
Consultation Advice is given according to individual diagnosis, but one of the following remedies may be prescribed: _Iris vers._ for blurring of vision before the onset of headache, vomiting and/or when the scalp feels tight; _Nat. mur._ for throbbing, burning headache, or when tingling or numbness in the face signals an attack; _Sanguinaria_ for a right-side headache which starts at the back of the head and extends to the right shoulder; and _Spigelia_ for a left-side headache made worse by bending or movement, and when pain pulses in time with heartbeats.

IONISATION
Whether related to stress or sensitivity to some foods, a migraine attack is thought to release a substance called 5-hydroxytryptamine (serotonin) from blood platelets. Negative ions are believed to reduce the amount of serotonin carried by the platelets, so that when something triggers an attack, less of the substance is released and both the chances of an attack or the severity of it are reduced. A survey of sufferers using ionisers revealed that the frequency and severity of attacks had been reduced.

Other alternative treatments

Reflexology Massage is given to the reflex areas relating to the head, and to the spine, eyes, sinuses, pituitary, thyroid and reproductive glands, the digestive system, liver and solar plexus (see chart, p. 295).
Massage The treatment is the same as that recommended for HEADACHES.

An orthodox view
Anyone who suffers severe, recurrent headache should consult a doctor, who can make a diagnosis and check the patient's BLOOD PRESSURE. If migraine attacks are preceded by an aura, the doctor may prescribe ergotamine tablets. Ergotamine can be dangerous if taken in excess or during pregnancy, but if it is taken early, during the blood-vessel-narrowing stage of migraine, before headache develops, it can prevent the development of a full-blown attack. For frequent sufferers, a doctor may also prescribe a drug such as pizotifen, to be taken every day to reduce the frequency of attacks.

If it is not possible to prevent or avert an attack in the early stages, doctors advise rest in a darkened room, painkillers and, if necessary, medicines to control vomiting.

A woman who has ever experienced numbness, tingling or weakness of part of the body during a migraine attack should tell her doctor, because some oral contraceptive pills may be inadvisable.

MIND AND BODY
Ways of keeping them in harmony

Most of us know only too well that illness and DEPRESSION often go hand in hand. We also know that when we feel at our best physically, we tend to be brighter, more optimistic and to have more mental energy.

Everyday language is full of phrases that link feeling with physical states. We speak of having 'butterflies in the stomach', 'shouldering a burden' or 'having a lump in the throat'. Similarly, physical factors both inside and outside the body (muscle tension, TIREDNESS, light and WEATHER, for example) can influence our thoughts and feelings.

Despite this, orthodox Western medicine generally makes a sharp distinction between mind and body. Doctors tend to confine their care to bodily illnesses and psychiatrists confine theirs to the mind.

Alternative therapies, however, are nearly always directed at the interaction of the two.

From ACUPUNCTURE and BIOFEEDBACK to YOGA and ZEN, they tend to view the person as a whole, needing harmony between body, mind and feelings to be completely healthy.

Most alternative therapies use one – or more – of four basic approaches to influence body and mind: food and drink, breathing, EXERCISE, and mental activity.

Of these, the food and drink approach is probably the most familiar. In alternative medicine, herbal extracts, vitamin supplements or HEALTH FOODS are likely to be recommended. Fasting for 24 hours is known to lower the adrenaline level in the blood and so reduce STRESS. In AYURVEDIC MEDICINE, particular foods and drinks are used to produce mental and emotional changes, and many spiritual traditions believe that certain diets can enhance spiritual well-being.

Like food and drink, breathing is essential for life. Again, language reflects the link between breath and state of mind. We speak of being inspired (from the Latin _inspirare_, to breathe in), we sigh when depressed, or talk of someone being a 'breath of fresh air'. In alternative medicine, rhythmic diaphragmatic breathing (see RELAXATION AND BREATHING) forms the basis of most relaxation techniques, from NATURAL CHILDBIRTH exercises to HYPNOTHERAPY.

Exercise is a less-common form of mind-body therapy in the West, where it is generally used simply to tone the muscles or to improve stamina. However, exercise can be very effective in relieving unpleasant moods and altering our state of mind.

Try going for a long walk next time you feel low or depressed – and notice how much better you feel. Or try a brisk run or some other form of demanding exercise to forget anger and frustration. Alternative medicine makes use of these effects in therapies such as T'AI-CHI CH'UAN, yoga and BIOENERGETICS.

The process also works in reverse – changing the way we think can bring about changes in the body. MEDITATION is one of the most effective of these thought therapies, but it can be difficult to learn and keep up regularly. Easier, and more convenient to practise, is positive thinking – focusing on thoughts such as 'Every day, in every way, I am getting better and better'. Images may be used as well as words, for example, in VISUALISATION THERAPY where a CANCER patient creates a mental picture of the body's defences attacking invading cancer cells.

Since alternative medicine is based on the idea of promoting well-being as a way of warding off (though often also curing) diseases, each of the four approaches is seen not just as a therapeutic measure, but as a vital part of daily life. Good health and a harmony of body and mind require the right balance of all four.

MINERALS
Getting enough of the essential traces

Your body contains about 25 essential minerals – chemical elements found mostly in inorganic (non-living) matter, but which are present in small proportions in living things. They are needed in small amounts for your body's chemistry to work properly. A diet with too little of any vital mineral, or anything that prevents it being absorbed into the body, can lead to deficiency disease and eventually to death.

Certain minerals, such as phosphorus and calcium, are present in the body in larger quantities than others. Phosphorus makes up about 1.5 per cent – just over 2lb (1kg) – of an average 11st (154lb or 70kg) healthy adult, mostly in bones and teeth, and the total body content of the mineral is replaced every three years. Calcium accounts for about 2 per cent of body weight, and again it is present mostly in bones and teeth.

Iron forms only some 0.006 per cent of body weight, the average adult body containing only 0.15oz (4.2g). Yet it is critical for life. About half of it is contained in the haemoglobin of the red blood cells. The iron is part of the pigment haem, which gives the cells their colour. Combined with the protein globin this forms the haemoglobin molecule, which has the unique ability to combine reversibly with oxygen, and is the means by which the gas is carried from the lungs to the

Major minerals: what they do and how we obtain them

MINERAL AND NATURAL SOURCES	RECOMMENDED DAILY AMOUNT (RDA) AND BENEFICIAL EFFECTS	EFFECTS OF DEFICIENCY
Calcium Dairy products; hard tap water; fish, and especially sardines, pilchards and other fish whose bones are eaten; watercress; fortified cereals, white flour and its products.	RDA: 500mg; 1200mg for pregnant women and nursing mothers. Growth and maintenance of healthy bones and teeth. Several essential processes, including nerve function, muscle contraction and blood clotting.	Deficiency of calcium is very rare. Its uptake is facilitated by vitamin D, and deficiency of the vitamin may cause rickets in children and osteomalacia (equivalent of rickets in adults).
Iron Red meat, kidney, liver; pulses; dried apricots and figs; cocoa; fortified white flour and products; fortified breakfast cereals; nuts, especially almonds.	RDA: 10mg for men, 12mg women, 13mg pregnant women, 15mg nursing mothers. Healthy blood function: distribution of oxygen to and removal of carbon dioxide and other waste products from body tissues by haemoglobin.	ANAEMIA. Extreme cases: depression of IMMUNE SYSTEM.
Magnesium Most foods, but especially green vegetables; wholemeal flour, cereals and products; milk; eggs; meat; nuts, especially peanuts; pulses; shellfish.	RDA: 300mg; 450mg for pregnant women and nursing mothers. Healthy bones and teeth. Proper functioning of muscles, nerves, metabolic enzymes, and vitamins B1 and B12.	Loss of appetite; nausea; weakness; ANXIETY; muscle cramps and tremors; INSOMNIA; rapid or irregular beating of the heart; HYPOGLYCAEMIA. Also PREMENSTRUAL TENSION.
Phosphorus Nearly all foods, but especially high-protein foods such as meat, dairy products, pulses.	RDA: 800mg; 1200mg for pregnant women and nursing mothers. Healthy bones. Conversion and storage of energy in all cells. Muscle function. Function of some enzymes. The intestinal absorption of some foods.	Loss of appetite; weakness; bone pain; stiff joints; central NERVE DISORDERS; respiratory failure. **Excess** can prevent intestinal absorption of calcium, iron, magnesium and zinc.
Potassium Most foods, but especially fresh fruit; vegetables, including potatoes; meat; wholemeal flour, cereals and products; milk; coffee; tea. Salt substitutes.	RDA: 1875-5625mg. Maintenance of body's balance of fluids, especially water. Maintenance of body's acid-alkali balance. Functioning of nerves and muscles.	Vomiting; abdominal distension; muscular weakness, paralysis; 'pins and needles'; loss of appetite; low BLOOD PRESSURE; thirst. Extreme cases, drowsiness, coma. **Excess** may be dangerous for people with some heart conditions – consult doctor.
Sodium Common salt (sodium chloride); baking powder; most foods, but especially cured meats, smoked fish, milk; tinned meats and vegetables; bakery products.	RDA: 2000mg (5g common salt). As potassium.	May accompany dehydration, which causes low blood pressure. **Excess** causes oedema; hypertension (high blood pressure); HEART DISORDERS; some KIDNEY COMPLAINTS. In babies, DIARRHOEA and dehydration.

Trace elements: the minerals we need in minute amounts

TRACE ELEMENT AND NATURAL SOURCES	RECOMMENDED DAILY AMOUNT (RDA) AND BENEFICIAL EFFECTS	EFFECTS OF DEFICIENCY
Chromium Unrefined and unprocessed foods, but especially wholegrain flour, cereals and products; fresh fruits; nuts; liver; kidney; beef; brewer's yeast.	RDA: 0.05-0.2mg. Metabolism and storage of fats and sugars; functioning of skeletal muscles; partial control of body's IMMUNE SYSTEM.	Very rare, but may cause irritability, confusion, weakness, DEPRESSION.
Cobalt Meat, liver, kidney; eggs.	RDA: none laid down. Essential component of vitamin B12.	Lack of vitamin B12 leads to pernicious ANAEMIA, weak muscles, BOWEL DISORDERS, NERVE DISORDERS.
Copper Most foods, but especially shellfish (particularly oysters), nuts (brazils), cocoa, liver, kidney; brewer's yeast; tap water supplied through copper pipes.	RDA: 0.05-0.2mg. Functioning of many enzymes; red blood cell formation; bone growth.	Very rare, but may cause low white blood cell count, changes in hair colour and texture (not normal greying), DIARRHOEA.
Fluorine Fluoridated tap water, toothpastes and the like; tea, especially China tea; fish such as sardines and pilchards whose bones are eaten; cereals; meat.	RDA: 1mg. Probably for healthy bones and teeth.	Dental caries (decay); OSTEOPOROSIS. **Excess** causes fluorosis – mottling and discoloration of teeth; calcification of ligaments; increased density of bones in spine, pelvis and limbs.
Iodine Iodised table salt; seafood, including seaweed (kelp); meat, fruit and vegetables produced where soils contain iodine.	RDA: 0.14-0.15mg. Production in the thyroid gland of hormones that control metabolism, and therefore healthy growth and development.	GOITRE; drop in metabolic rate, leading to drowsiness, lethargy, fatigue, increased weight. In pregnancy and from birth can lead to cretinism.
Manganese Many foods, but especially wholegrain cereals, nuts, tea, pulses, avocados.	RDA: 2.5mg. Control of growth; the functioning of many enzymes, nerves and muscles; strong, healthy bones.	Decreased growth rate; bone deformities. **Excess** may cause brain damage.
Molybdenum Many foods, but especially buckwheat, barley, oats, liver, pulses.	RDA: 0.15-0.5mg. Prevention of dental caries; iron metabolism; male sexual function.	Increased dental caries; IMPOTENCE; in extreme cases, irregular heartbeat, coma.
Selenium Unrefined foods, especially wholegrain flour, cereals and products; seafood; egg yolk; liver; kidney; brewer's yeast; GARLIC.	RDA: 0.05-0.2mg. Healthy liver function; with vitamin E selenium is an antioxidant, and detoxifies elements such as cadmium, lead and mercury; the proper functioning of red and white blood cells.	Cardiovascular disease; possibly infant cot death and some types of ANAEMIA
Sulphur Animal and vegetable proteins (meat, dairy products, pulses).	RDA: none laid down. Normal protein synthesis; strong hair, nails and skin.	
Zinc Most foods, but especially liver and red meat; egg yolk; dairy produce; wholegrain flour, cereals and products; seafood, particularly oysters.	RDA: 15mg; 20mg for pregnant women; 25mg for nursing mothers. Functioning of many enzymes, and thus normal growth and development; the release of insulin (see DIABETES) and of vitamin A; healthy reproduction; the healing of cuts and wounds.	Slow physical, mental and sexual development; INFERTILITY; and the slow healing of wounds

body tissues. There it combines with glucose and other 'fuels' to produce energy for essential metabolic processes.

Some elements present are needed in even smaller quantities. These minerals are known as 'trace elements'. See the tables of the most important minerals and trace elements on pp. 242 and 243.

The amount of a mineral needed by the body varies with age and circumstances. Generally children require less than adults, but growing children – those under 17 years – need more calcium than adults. Women need more iron than men, and pregnant women and nursing mothers need more iron and calcium again.

Some minerals, notably sodium, can create problems because people tend to consume too much of them. Many doctors believe that too much sodium can be a cause of high BLOOD PRESSURE in some people. Excess sodium is usually taken as too much salt (sodium chloride). You can easily cut down the amount of salt that you add to your diet, but beware of manufactured foods. Salt is added to many of them, so read the labels and go for those items whose labels state that none has been added. Avoid also foods containing monosodium glutamate (MSG). This flavour enhancer has a meat-like taste, and is used in soups and similar products.

On the whole, a healthy, well-balanced diet will provide you with all the essential minerals that your body requires. The only possible exception is selenium. It is estimated that the average British adult gets only 20 per cent of the recommended daily amount (RDA) of selenium.

Several things affect the amount of food minerals that the body absorbs. One factor is the form that the minerals take. For instance, you will absorb far more of the iron present in meat than the iron which is contained in green vegetables.

Another factor is the combination of mineral sources at a single meal. For example, vitamin C from fresh fruit and vegetables will enhance the uptake of iron, but the tannin in tea will reduce it. Too much bran (see FIBRE) reduces the absorption of several minerals, including calcium and zinc. In addition, anyone lacking vitamin D cannot absorb calcium properly.

Generally, refined foods have lost many of their minerals, including potassium, chromium and selenium. Refined flours and cereals have a greatly reduced calcium and iron content, so if you do eat these and their products, go for the fortified varieties to which calcium and iron have been added.

See also BIOCHEMIC TISSUE SALTS, HERBAL MEDICINE, HOMOEOPATHY, MEGAVITAMIN THERAPY, NATUROPATHY, EATING FOR HEALTH and FOOD ADDITIVES.

MINERAL WATER
Better from bottles than your tap?

Drinking spring water for therapeutic reasons is mentioned in early Chinese writings, and in Britain, the Celts and Romans practised a form of what is now called HYDROTHERAPY, notably at Aquae Sulis (Bath). However, it was on the Continent that 'taking the waters' or 'cure' became really popular, and by the 18th century it was the fashionable thing for the rich to do. Numerous medicinal properties were claimed for rival waters, especially as cures for RHEUMATISM and similar ills.

The bottling and sale of spring – or natural mineral – water soon followed, and now the industry is 'big business' following expansion in the 1970s and 1980s, and all bottling and sales are strictly controlled. One of the world's largest firms is Source Perrier near Nîmes in southern France, which normally sells more than 2000 million bottles a year. However, sales were affected early in 1990, when the company withdrew its entire stock of 160 million bottles (including 10 million in Britain) from the market. This followed the discovery that the water was contaminated with the petroleum-derivative benzene,

Visitors to Karlsbad (now Karlovy Vary in Czechoslovakia) in about 1895 drink from the Vridlo (der Sprudel), the best known of the spa's 17 active springs. Its alkaline, sulphurous water issues at 72°C (160°F).

which is thought to induce CANCER. The company blamed the problem on inefficient filtration at its spring at Vergèze, but resumed normal production once the filters had been cleaned.

Natural mineral water is not healthier than good, clean tap water – you may simply prefer the taste of bottled water, and with ice and a slice of lemon or lime it makes a refreshing alternative to alcoholic drinks.

The most common MINERALS found in bottled waters are bicarbonates, sulphates, nitrates, chlorides, calcium, magnesium, potassium and sodium. Of these, calcium and bicarbonate are by far the most common. A few mineral waters contain iron and/or iodine.

The European Community (EC) has strict laws governing 'natural mineral water'. To qualify, the water must be taken from an underground source at an officially recognised site. It must not be chemically treated, but mechanical filtration is allowed. (This may not be necessary, for the water may be naturally filtered by percolating through sand or gravel, perhaps for several years.) If a bottled water is a natural mineral water, it must by law be bottled at source.

The water's composition must be determined by an officially recognised analysis, and the content may be displayed on the label; only slight variations of content are permitted. The water must be free from harmful microorganisms and chemical pollutants. No reference to 'medicinal' qualities may be made in advertising the water, or on its label – though some labels come close.

Natural mineral waters are either 'still' or 'sparkling' – that is, naturally bubbly with carbon dioxide, or made fizzy (or fizzier) with added carbon dioxide. The bubbly ones are usually more expensive than the still, but the differences in composition between them and still waters are slight. Again, strict regulations apply.

Naturally sparkling water must have the same amount of bubbles as when it left the ground. If the label says, 'fortified with gas from the spring', carbon dioxide from the water's own source has been added. Very fizzy waters may cause flatulence, but otherwise, whether you choose still or sparkling water is a matter of taste.

MORNING SICKNESS

Feelings of nausea and sickness which are common in early PREGNANCY are caused by increased hormone production, triggered by the woman's condition. This so-called morning sickness can actually strike at any time of the day or night. It usually comes during the first three months of pregnancy, but can happen even before the woman has missed a period – and it very occasionally persists right into late pregnancy.

In severe cases – known as *Hyperemesis gravidarum* – the mother vomits so much that she risks becoming dehydrated and must receive medical attention.

What the therapists recommend

Herbal Medicine   Make an infusion (see p. 184) of fresh ginger and sip frequently. Since morning sickness may be associated with lowered blood sugar levels, ginger biscuits may give relief. Also held to be beneficial are peppermint or camomile teas.

Homoeopathy   These remedies are believed to be particularly appropriate because their great dilutions mean they pose no risk to mother or child. *Ipecacuanha* is recommended for constant NAUSEA and VOMITING and lack of thirst; *Argentum nitricum* for nervousness and panic, and a craving for sweet foods. *Sepia* may help if the vomit is pale and full of mucus, but the appetite is good and the mother feels sad and indifferent. Try *Pulsatilla* when fatty foods aggravate the condition, symptoms are worse late in the day and the mother is tearful but better for fresh air.

Naturopathy   Eating small, frequent meals and avoiding fried, fatty foods may be helpful. Wholemeal toast or a dry biscuit in the morning can often relieve the problem, and the woman should take plenty of fluid – but not milk – to counteract dehydration if she is actually being sick.

An orthodox view

Conventional doctors are extremely reluctant to prescribe medicines in early pregnancy because of potential adverse effects on the developing baby. Practitioners can, however, examine the mother-to-be to ensure that the pregnancy is progressing normally, offer reassurance and give advice about the importance of small, regular meals. In severe cases it is sometimes necessary to admit the patient to hospital and give her fluids through an intravenous drip to prevent dehydration.

MOSQUITO BITES

Travellers to many regions, including the subarctic and southern Europe, run the hazard of mosquito bites. These are usually more of a nuisance than a danger, producing pain and skin irritation. However, in some parts of the world – particularly the tropics – they transmit parasites that cause serious diseases, such as malaria.

When a female mosquito bites, it injects its saliva into its victim's skin before it sucks blood. If the mosquito takes blood from a person infected with the parasites, it will carry the disease, which will be spread each time it bites and injects infected saliva into another victim.

Of the many diseases spread by mosquitoes worldwide, malaria is the most serious. It is endemic in large areas of Africa, Asia, and South and Central America.

Do's and don'ts of mineral water

Do read the label carefully.

Do use a brand of bottled water that you know if there is any question about the purity of local tap water.

Do boil bottled water and allow it to cool before making up babies' feeds with it.

Do remember that mineral waters, like all water, have a mild diuretic effect – they increase your flow of urine – and the greater the mineral content, the greater the effect.

Don't drink natural mineral water if you are on a SALT-FREE DIET, for sodium chloride is one of the most common minerals in bottled waters. If you are on such a diet, you should read the label carefully and seek professional advice on what you can and ought not to drink.

Don't drink waters with more than 20mg sodium/litre if you are on a low salt diet.

Don't regularly give water with more than 1.5mg fluoride/litre to babies or children, as it can cause mottling and weakening of the teeth.

Don't assume that bottled water will necessarily help those people who are allergic to tap water – mineral water may also contain chloride and other substances that are implicated in the allergy. Seek professional advice.

Don't drink bottled waters instead of milk as a substitute source of calcium – even the most calcium-rich mineral waters contain only about 12 per cent of milk's calcium. And the content of other minerals is also much less.

Attempts at global eradication have so far failed, and there are more than 1500 cases (and some deaths) each year in the United Kingdom among travellers who have caught the disease overseas.

Dengue fever (breakbone fever), yellow fever and some forms of encephalitis, including St Louis encephalitis, are all spread by mosquitoes. However, it seems the AIDS virus is not transmitted by them, probably because the virus is killed by mosquito saliva.

What the therapists recommend
HERBAL MEDICINE
Self help Dab the affected areas with distilled witch hazel, or with a drop of essential oil of lavender, to reduce the irritation and inflammation. If susceptible to insect bites, sponge exposed areas of skin with camomile infusion, which will help deter the insects. To prepare the infusion, put 2 teaspoons of dried leaves in a cup and fill it with boiling water. Allow it to infuse for five to ten minutes, strain and use when cold.

An orthodox view

Visitors to affected areas of Africa and South America should be immunised against yellow fever at least ten days before they travel. One dose gives protection for ten years.

Do's and don'ts if mosquitoes are troublesome

Do sleep in properly screened rooms and use a knockdown flyspray to kill any mosquitoes that may have entered the room during the day.

Do use mosquito nets around the bed at night, checking that there are no holes, and tucking the edges under the mattress before nightfall. Protection may be enhanced by impregnating the material with permethrin. Use 0.2g per square metre every six months.

Do burn mosquito coils or use an electric mat to vaporise synthetic pyrethroids in the bedroom overnight.

Do wear long-sleeved clothing and long trousers, and avoid wearing dark coloured clothes when out of doors after sunset, as such garments can attract mosquitoes.

Do use adequate insect repellants, such as diethyl toluamide, on exposed skin.

Don't rely only on electronic buzzers to ward off or kill mosquitoes because they are inadequate.

If you are visiting malaria-infested areas, your doctor will prescribe daily or weekly tablets and will select them carefully, for some strains of the disease parasite have become resistant to certain drugs. It is vital that the antimalaria treatment starts a week before travel and continues for four weeks after you leave the malaria zone.

If you are bitten, calamine lotion and antihistamine creams or tablets will relieve the symptoms. After returning from an area where malaria or other serious diseases are endemic, seek medical advice without delay if you develop a feverish, sweating illness, particularly if accompanied by headache. Some malaria parasites have an incubation period of ten months, so the symptoms may develop up to ten months after your return from foreign parts.

MOTION SICKNESS

Seasickness can be the most uncomfortable manifestation of this all-too-common problem, and many sailors remain affected by it throughout their careers – Nelson, Britain's greatest naval hero, was a lifelong sufferer. However, as many know to their cost, motion sickness can also affect travellers by road, rail or air.

The cause is an imbalance between what the eyes see and what the delicate inner ear balance mechanisms feel during movement. The eyes adjust to motion, but the inner ear does not, and the resulting signals to the brain from eye and inner ear do not tally. Symptoms are usually less severe if the eyes can see dry land or the horizon.

The symptoms cease quickly at the end of a journey, but may last up to 72 hours during long journeys. Children are more vulnerable than adults. However, some people adapt to regular travel, and the sickness diminishes on subsequent journeys.

What the therapists recommend
Acupressure A widely used remedy is to press a point three fingers' width above the wrist crease on the inner wrist, centrally, in line with the middle finger (Pericardium 6; see p. 13). Apply the pressure towards the centre of the wrist. Wristbands are available from chemists and at seaports, airports and railway stations, which perform the same function and have proved effective.

Homoeopathy If sickness is worse for the smell of food, try taking *Cocculus*. Use *Tabacum* for giddiness, weakness, nausea,

---

sweating, the feeling of a tight band round the head, and if the smell of cigarette smoke is particularly nauseating.

Petroleum is recommended for nausea, vomiting and increased salivation by a patient who feels better when eating or lying down and worse in bright light. *Borax* is advised for a fear of sudden downward motion – such as is experienced when travelling by air and there is turbulence.

Aromatherapy Two drops each of peppermint and ginger essential oils on a tissue, inhaled regularly on a journey, are said to ease the discomfort.

Naturopathy Ginger is said to be one of the best remedies: chew a few pieces of fresh or crystallised root during a journey. Some practitioners also recommend taking vitamin B6 – 25mg every two hours for adults, 10mg for children.

An orthodox view

Do not talk about being sick in the presence of someone who is susceptible to motion sickness. Anticipation makes sickness more probable, whereas regular breaks and fresh air make the condition less likely. Try to ensure that susceptible children can see out of a window and stay warm.

There are several anti-sickness medicines which help if taken before symptoms begin. Some contain atropine or related substances and may, as well as preventing sickness, cause a dry mouth and constipation. Others such as cinnarizine are antihistamines and may result in drowsiness, particularly if taken with alcohol.

If sickness does occur, lie down if at all possible and take small amounts of fluid regularly to prevent dehydration. Vomiting may in fact give some relief.

MOUTH ULCERS

Painful, small, shallow, round or oval ulcers, often with a grey base and yellowish edge, occur inside the lips or cheeks, on the tongue or elsewhere in the mouth. Sometimes known as 'aphthous ulcers', they can appear for no apparent reason, but may indicate that you are run down, or they may be STRESS-related. Other causes can be ill-fitting dentures, or over-vigorous brushing of the teeth, which causes abrasions that can then turn ulcerous.

A more serious cause is the herpes virus (see COLD SORES). The first attack can be severe, with sore throat and several unpleasant looking ulcers inside the mouth. Subsequent attacks are less severe, with fewer, smaller ulcers. So-called hand, foot and mouth disease (which is nothing to do with foot and mouth disease in cattle) is a common infectious disease of childhood in which there are small blisters on the hands and feet, as well as in the mouth.

Self help If the ulcers coincide with feeling run down, check that your diet is a well balanced one (see EATING FOR HEALTH), and take more rest, with a general vitamin and mineral supplement. The ulcers may possibly be due to GLUTEN INTOLERANCE, so try a gluten-free diet for a week or two.

Use a soothing mouthwash several times a day: add two to three drops of essential oil of lemon, tea tree, camomile, sage or fennel to a cup of warm water.

What the therapists recommend

Herbal Medicine As herbalists generally see mouth ulcers as a sign of being run down, treatment looks at the underlying health as well as the ulcers themselves. A mouthwash of tincture of myrrh, available from herbalist stores and chemists, should clear up the ulcers in 48 hours if used every two hours or so. Chewing a piece of LIQUO-RICE root is both soothing and healing.

Homoeopathy If there is bad breath and increased salivation, try *Merc. sol. 6*. When the ulcers feel like sharp splinters, try *Nitric acid 6*. When the ulcers are on the soft palate and bleed when touched or during eating, and the mouth feels tender and hot, *Borax 6* is recommended.

Naturopathy Practitioners consider that mouth ulcers are often caused by lowered vitality, stress and inadequate nourishment. Fresh vegetables and fruit are recommended to cleanse the system, although some foods may add to the acidity in the mouth. Occasionally, the problem may be related to vitamin B2 deficiency; in this case wheatgerm or brewer's yeast, together with extra vegetables, are recommended in the diet. Practitioners may also recommend vitamin C with zinc.

An orthodox view

Most mouth ulcers disappear in a few days. Mouthwashes or local anaesthetic lozenges such as benzocaine (available without prescription) help to keep the mouth clean and relieve pain. However, take care that you do not numb the mouth before a meal as this might lead to choking.

If the symptoms are persistent or severe, you should see a doctor to exclude any underlying cause. The doctor may prescribe local steroids such as Corlan lozenges or Adcortyl in Orabase paste.

If you find a hard lump in your mouth and it persists for more than two weeks, consult your doctor or dentist.

MOXIBUSTION

Practitioners use this technique as well as the insertion and manipulation (or electrical stimulation) of needles in ACUPUNCTURE. It is a way of applying heat locally to regulate, tone and supplement the body's flow of *Qi* (vital energy). The practice is particularly popular in China and Japan, and has been found especially useful for relieving post-operative pain and for chronic conditions such as ARTHRITIS.

There are two methods of moxibustion, both of which employ moxa wool. This is prepared either by drying and shredding leaves of the common mugwort (*Artemisia vulgaris*, Chinese wormwood), or by drying the down from its leaves.

In the heated needle method, the practitioner inserts acupuncture needles, then places small cones of moxa on the needle heads and ignites them. (The needles are sometimes inserted through discs of cardboard or similar material to prevent any ash falling onto the patient's skin.) The gentle heat so generated passes down the needles into the body.

In the other method, the therapist fills a roll of paper some 6in (15cm) long with moxa, lights it, holds the glowing tip safely above the acupuncture point until it becomes too hot and then withdraws it. The number of times this is repeated varies according to the condition of the individual patient and the nature of the complaint.

Roll of paper method
The practitioner fills a roll of paper with moxa wool and then lights it. She holds the lighted tip above the appropriate acupuncture point. The practitioner withdraws the tip when the heat becomes too hot for the patient's comfort.

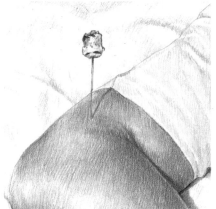

Heated needle method
First of all, the practitioner inserts an acupuncture needle – or needles – in the selected acupuncture point. She then puts a small cone of moxa wool on the head of the needle and sets it alight. As a gentle heat is generated, it travels down the needle and into the patient's body. Sometimes the needle is inserted through material such as a cardboard disc so that hot ash does not fall onto the patient's skin. Both methods attempt to cure or relieve specific ailments and allow the unimpeded flow of good health.

247

MUD THERAPY

The ancient Greeks discovered the therapeutic value of certain muds rich in dissolved minerals and plant substances, and mud baths are still available at certain British SPAS and HEALTH FARMS. On the Continent, Black Sea resort spas in particular have long specialised in this form of treatment. See HYDROTHERAPY.

The benefits derived from the many different sorts of mud used are said to come from health-giving substances in decayed plant matter and soil that accumulate in them at certain sites over hundreds of years. The composition of each differs, according to the minerals and plants found in the area.

Mud at one of the most famous mud spas, Neydharting in Austria, has been shown to contain natural antibiotics, VITAMINS in large quantities, as well as MINERALS, trace elements and other organic matter.

Apart from taking mud baths, mud packs can be applied to the skin. Packaged mud products – including shampoos and cosmetics – from well-known spas such as Neydharting can also be bought from health shops for use in the home.

No one knows exactly how mud therapy works, but most theories assume that the beneficial substances in it penetrate the skin,

Patients of both sexes wallow in a therapeutic mud bath in the south American republic of Colombia. Such baths are recommended treatment for arthritis and rheumatism.

possibly entering the bloodstream and circulating throughout the body. In addition, tiny nerve fibres in the outer layers of skin may be stimulated, so that the whole nervous system benefits.

The drying, abrasive action of mud on the skin is thought to augment the cleansing and invigorating effects of mud baths which have been compared to taking vigorous exercise – increasing the heart rate, speeding up circulation and encouraging sweating, helping to rid the body of impurities.

The mud treatment can be used not only for toning the system generally, or for easing particular complaints – RHEUMATISM, ARTHRITIS, SKIN DISORDERS, INFERTILITY and other disorders of the female reproductive system. Some mud extracts can even be drunk and are claimed to relieve stomach ULCERS and other DIGESTIVE PROBLEMS.

MUESLI
Making your own good-health food

The German-Swiss doctor Max Bircher-Benner (1867-1939) initiated muesli's present popularity. He discovered that a staple part of the diet of the exceptionally fit and long-lived inhabitants of certain country areas of Switzerland was muesli. This was made from various combinations of wheat, oats or barley with nuts, fresh fruit and berries,

honey and milk. The doctor's discovery confirmed his own faith in a RAW FOOD DIET, and he introduced at his small clinic in Zürich his own recipe – a simple mixture of oatmeal, grated apples or berries and milk.

Today there are many brand versions of Dr Bircher-Benner's original low-fat, protein and fibre-rich muesli on sale. 'Swiss-style' mueslis are soft and usually have added salt, milk powder and sugar – up to about 20 per cent. So-called 'natural' mueslis contain no added salt and sugar. 'De luxe' brands have higher proportions of fruit and nuts, while 'crunchy' mueslis include toasted or cooked ingredients, frequently coated with honey or sugar.

A bowl of your favourite muesli at breakfast makes a good start to the day, and making your own is both easy and much cheaper than relying on brand varieties. It allows you to use fresh fruits and berries in season, and to include different ingredients to ring the changes and suit your preferences. It also allows you to control the amount of sugar or salt – if any – that you add.

A useful basic recipe contains: 12oz (360g) mixed cereals – rolled oats or oatmeal; rye, barley or wheat flakes; millet; 8oz (240g) dried fruit – sultanas, raisins, chopped dates or figs, apple, banana, apricot, pineapple; 2oz (60g) seeds – sunflower, sesame, pumpkin; and 1oz (30g) chopped nuts – almonds, brazils, hazelnuts, walnuts, coconut. These quantities will be sufficient for about eight to ten average portions.

Mix the ingredients and store in an airtight container. Then serve as required, adding fresh fruit and/or berries and milk, preferably semiskimmed milk for adults. When buying the cereals, make sure that they contain no added sugar or salt. Additional oat bran flakes or wheatbran will provide extra dietary FIBRE if needed, while wheat germ will boost the muesli's content of vitamins B and E.

See also EATING FOR HEALTH.

MULTIPLE SCLEROSIS

Known for short as MS, multiple sclerosis results from damage to the sheaths surrounding the nerve fibres of the central nervous system. Like electric wire without insulation, affected nerves are unable to function properly. The cause is unknown and subject to much research. About one person in 2000 is affected, women more often than men. The average age of onset is about 30.

Symptoms usually develop over a period of hours or days. The disease may attack only once, but usually runs a course of relapses (attacks) and remissions (periods of recovery) over many years. Some 40 per cent of cases begin with blurred, dimmed or double vision. Sufferers may develop weakness, numbness or lack of coordination. They may also become clumsy, develop slurred speech or lose full control over their bladder and bowels (see INCONTINENCE).

Self help MS sufferers should make sure that their diet is low in fats and high in FIBRE. Avoid sugar and all sugar-containing items such as chocolate. Do not drink stimulants such as coffee, tea and cola drinks; use fructose (fruit sugar), weak lemon tea, decaffeinated coffee, herb teas and fresh fruit and vegetable juices. Avoid pulses (beans, peas, lentils), white bread and pasta, peanuts, salted nuts, hot spices and other such flavourings. Stop SMOKING and avoid other people's smoke. Cut out all alcohol, especially if your balance is impaired.

What the therapists recommend
YOGA
Self help Effective breathing, in which the diaphragm is the body's pump, is said to enhance the electrical charge running through the nervous system and stimulate activity. Where muscles are constricted, relaxation and relaxed breathing may help to ease the tension.

The stress factor in MS is severe, and yoga provides a force to counter this. The postures, linked with calm mental processes and improved breathing, are said to provide an important stimulus to the patient's use of the affected limbs.

MASSAGE
Consultation General massage of the entire body is applied, if possible using slow, rhythmic and fairly deep movements of effleurage and kneading. Massage of the legs is most beneficial in maintaining some degree of muscle tone and, equally important, abdominal massage helps avoid constipation, which is often suffered by those unable to take normal exercise.

In the early stages, regular treatment – on a daily basis if possible – helps the nourishment and tone of the muscles, and encourages patients to persevere with light trunk exercises. In later stages, when the sufferer is confined to bed, massage of the legs and abdomen continues as long as the patient derives benefit from it.

NATUROPATHY
Consultation This is not a complaint for which self help can be advised, but there may be scope for individual advice on nutrition, to support the nervous system. In recent years, some benefit has been claimed with evening primrose oil capsules – but see a qualified practitioner first.

An orthodox view
The first task of a conventional doctor is to diagnose the disease. As well as performing a thorough neurological examination, including testing skin sensation, muscle power, coordination and reflexes, the doctor may recommend a lumbar puncture. A local anaesthetic is given, and fluid is withdrawn for testing from around the spinal cord through a needle inserted into the small of the back.

Treatment includes courses of steroid injections such as prednisolone or ACTH (adrenocorticotrophic hormone), physiotherapy to maintain bodily function, and occupational therapy to help the patient cope with disabilities.

Although doctors, nurses, therapists and counsellors can help sufferers, there is no orthodox medical cure for MS. The Multiple Sclerosis Society of Great Britain and Northern Ireland, 25 Effie Road, London SW6 1EE, is a valuable source of support and advice for affected people and their families.

MUMPS

The most common recognisable sign of mumps is swelling in front of the ear and over the angle of the jaw as one of the saliva-producing (parotid) glands becomes enlarged. The corresponding gland on the other side may also swell a day or two later.

Mumps is an infectious disease which occurs in epidemics and mainly affects children over the age of two. Along with the swollen glands, there may be earache, particularly when eating. Other saliva-producing glands under the tongue and jaw may also become swollen.

Since the incubation period is 15 to 21 days before the visible symptoms appear, it is impossible to stop the infection from spreading. The virus, which is similar to that of INFLUENZA, is carried through the air, so the disease can be caught simply by being close to an infected person.

Adult men who catch mumps can suffer painful complications – swelling and inflammation of the testicles. In girls, inflammation of the ovaries or pancreas can cause abdominal pain. In some rare cases, encephalitis or meningitis – inflammation of the brain or its surrounding membranes, or meninges – can result.

What the therapists recommend
Herbal Medicine If there is an increase in temperature, infusions (see p. 184) of yarrow or elderflower are advised, to induce sweating; try a cupful, hot, every few hours. Marigold added to the infusion is said to relieve the swollen glands. Medical herbalists may use more potent remedies, such as poke root, which requires careful dosage.

Naturopathy Because of the difficulty in eating that can arise due to the swollen glands, it is sensible to increase liquids, such as soup, in the diet. However, it may not be advisable to drink too many fruit juices that are acidic. Supplements to boost the IMMUNE SYSTEM may be prescribed, and a cold compress will reduce swelling.

Homoeopathy For the early, acute stages, when there is pain, fever, restlessness and thirst, *Aconitum 30* is suggested; if the testicles are affected, *Pulsatilla 6*. Try *Belladonna 3* when fever is accompanied by throbbing pain, worse on the right side. When worse on the left side, and in cold, damp weather, *Rhus tox. 6* is indicated.

Biochemic Tissue Salts Try *Ferr. phos.* alternating with *Kali mur.* hourly while the fever lasts, *Kali mur.* alone for glandular swelling and pain when swallowing, and *Calc. phos.* during convalescence.

An orthodox view
Doctors recommend immunisation with MMR vaccine against MEASLES, rubella (German measles) and mumps, for all babies during their first year. As mumps becomes less common through immunisation, so too should serious complications, such as meningitis and inflamed testicles, which in adult males occasionally causes sterility.

There is no specific cure for the disease, but a few days of rest and, if necessary, paracetamol or children's aspirin to reduce fever and ease discomfort are all that are required. Consult a doctor if earache or HEADACHES are severe, if the neck becomes stiff, or if the testicles in adult males become painful or swollen.

MUSCULAR DYSTROPHY

Alternative therapists can offer both practical help and psychological support to victims of this progressive, muscle-wasting disease; but like conventional doctors, they cannot promise a cure. For the disease – commonly called simply MD – is hereditary and cannot be reversed. It usually appears in one of three distinct forms:

The Duchenne-type begins in childhood and affects only boys between four and ten years old. It starts with weakness in the legs. The child tends to waddle, cannot climb stairs properly, and can rise to his feet only by using his hands to 'climb up' his legs. In facio-scapular-humeral MD, the face, shoulders and arms are mostly affected. The disease tends to strike during the teens or young adult life of both sexes. Limb girdle MD affects the shoulders or hips during the twenties or thirties in both sexes. This type runs a slower, less-severe course than other forms of the disease.

In certain cases of MD, there is *pseudo-hypertrophy* of the muscles, meaning that they are enlarged, but weak. Generally, the best outlook is for those who develop the disease late in life.

What the therapists recommend

MASSAGE
Consultation A brisk, but very brief, full body massage is probably of most benefit. Otherwise, the massage should be confined to only a few minutes' treatment of the affected limbs: effleurage stroking and kneading movements should be given, with the aim of toning up the muscles and improving blood supply, and delaying atrophy and contraction for as long as possible.

Physical therapy is extremely important in the treatment of muscular dystrophy and massage can be a valuable element of it. However, on a long-term basis, its value is largely in making the condition seem less severe, rather than in bringing about actual improvement.

HYDROTHERAPY
Consultation Needle spray or vortex baths would be advised, to promote or improve circulation in the affected limbs. This would be followed by specific exercise programmes, suited to each patient's particular condition, in a HYDROTHERAPY pool.

An orthodox view

Despite intense medical research, there is still no cure for muscular dystrophy, or any sure means of determining whether affected potential parents will pass it on to their offspring. Doctors confirm their diagnoses by finding raised levels of muscle enzymes, or ferments, in blood samples, and by surgical removal and examination of a small sample of muscle. Sufferers may benefit from advice from specialist therapists, such as occupational therapists, and from support and advice from The Muscular Dystrophy Group of Great Britain, Nattrass House, 35 Macauley Road, London SW4 OQP.

MUSIC THERAPY
The rhythm of life as a healing force

The need for self-expression is satisfied not only by speaking but also by music. Its rhythms and harmonies, the pattern of its sounds and silences make a powerful impact on our senses, often touching feelings too deep or difficult to express in words. Continually bottling up such emotions can cause distressing mental – even physical – problems. See also PSYCHOTHERAPY and HUMANISTIC PSYCHOLOGY.

Since ancient times music has been closely connected with healing – an association that declined as a scientific basis for treatments became the test of acceptability. Only recently has the use of music in therapy been researched and found valuable. Individual responses may vary, but many of us are deeply affected by music. And actually making music – however crudely – allows us to express a range of emotions, from anger and frustration to tranquillity and joy.

It is these expressions and responses that music therapists, who are trained musicians, can observe and work with. The therapy depends much upon the therapist and his client reacting to each other as shared music-making frees the client to reveal deep – sometimes totally submerged – feelings and problems.

The improvised music that they play or sing together is ideally chosen or initiated by the client (who may, through disability, be unable to ask directly), no matter how simple the music or the means of making it may be. This improvised music, composed for that particular moment in the therapy, is considered an essential factor in the treatment.

It is not only in the psychotherapeutic approach that music is valuable. Physically handicapped people who may need to improve their movement or breath control, for example, are often more enthusiastic about playing even a simple instrument or singing than about doing pure exercises.

Who it can help The mentally handicapped, the mentally ill or the physically disabled can all benefit. Children referred by education authorities to child development and assessment centres, or who are being given special education, are treated. Elderly people – in care units and day centres – can also benefit, as can people attending community health centres, and those who need help in coping with STRESS. Even prison inmates have responded to treatment.

The client does not need to have any

How music can help an autistic child

Geoffrey is a seven-year-old child suffering from AUTISM. He can't talk, although he can make a wide range of vocal sounds. Like all autistic children, he finds it extremely difficult to establish relationships with other people; he prefers to relate to objects. He loves music and for the past three years has been receiving music therapy at home – with his mother taking an active part in the sessions.

Each week the therapist fosters a special bond between the two, by encouraging Geoffrey's mother to respond to him on his own level, singing to him and imitating and developing his vocal sounds. Through sharing a musical experience, Geoffrey feels that someone is showing an interest in him and that he can participate in a family activity.

'These sessions,' says Geoffrey's mother, 'have been an opportunity not to be missed. With the aid of the therapist, I have been able to help Geoffrey to open out and have developed a brand-new relationship with him. It is the one time in a busy week when he and I can share an experience which means a great deal to both of us.'

musical experience. Striking results have been obtained from people claiming not to be musical and having never learned to play an instrument.

Finding a therapist There are only about 200 trained music therapists in Britain, many working in therapeutic teams within the National Health Service, some in the education service, but only a few in private practice. Demand for therapy is much greater than the supply.

To find your nearest therapist, write to The Coordinator, The Association of Professional Music Therapists, The Meadow, 68 Pierce Lane, Fulbourn, Cambs CB1 5DL. You can also get information and help from The Administrator, The British Society for Music Therapy, 69 Avondale Avenue, East Barnet, Herts EN4 8NB; its members include therapists, teachers, medical practitioners, students, relatives of disabled people and anyone who has a particular interest in music therapy.

A music therapist must be a trained musician with a university degree or diploma from a recognised British music college, and have completed a postgraduate one-year course at one of three therapy centres: the

Guildhall School of Music and Drama, the Nordoff-Robbins Music Therapy Centre, or the Roehampton Institute of Higher Education, all in London. The therapy courses include the study of communication skills; psychology; physical, mental and emotional disorders; and practical clinical work under supervision. The courses are recognised by the NHS. Therapists working in the education service must also have completed a teacher-training course.

Consulting a therapist What happens at a session varies according to individual needs, but the broad approach is the same no matter what your age or problem. The therapist first observes the client's musical responses, asks questions aimed at discovering his needs, and assesses what music therapy programme would best serve those particular needs.

This is an important time for therapist and client to get to know one another and feel comfortable together. A variety of instruments, such as piano, xylophone, glockenspiel, keyboards, guitar and drums will be available, and the therapist will also have an instrument.

For those with physical problems, the music is used to motivate movement. With someone whose problems are emotional or physical rather than intellectual, the therapist may discuss music, to find out what the client enjoys and to agree on a starting point for the therapy.

For a client who has difficulty speaking and understanding speech, the relationship has to begin with the music-making. This may be as simple as sharing an instrument and playing together, or beating 'messages' to one another on drums.

The client's responses are carefully observed so that the therapist can follow them up, so it becomes important that the client is brought to realise that the therapist is communicating through the music. But always the therapist aims to let the client choose and control what happens in the music, and realise that he can express what cannot, perhaps, be put into words.

The music is seen not as an end in itself, but as a means of building confidence and self-esteem and facing inner conflicts.

An orthodox view

Music therapy with a qualified therapist is a completely safe and very effective form of treatment. Research has shown that it is beneficial for people with mental disorders that prevent communication through speech, and also for people with physical disabilities. It is increasingly becoming part of the treatment provided by the National Health Service in psychiatric, mental, community and educational centres.

MYALGIC ENCEPHALO-MYELITIS
ME – a mysterious, exhausting illness

Extreme exhaustion is the most characteristic symptom of myalgic encephalomyelitis – usually referred to simply as ME. But a number of other symptoms may afflict sufferers: muscle pains, especially after exercise; a persistent itchy skin rash; twitching of the muscles and limbs; chest pains; localised sweating; FEVER and shivering fits; HEADACHES; visual disturbances and RINGING IN THE EARS; nausea and STOMACH COMPLAINTS; INSOMNIA; swollen glands; frequent need to pass urine; and a strong body odour.

Patients feel generally unwell and often experience worrying mental symptoms such as loss of memory and inability to concentrate, or psychological effects such as mood swings and DEPRESSION.

The symptoms develop following a failure to recover fully from VIRUS INFECTIONS. The initial infection, such as INFLUENZA or gastroenteritis, may be fairly trivial, and sometimes passes unnoticed by the patient. After virus infections people are often tired and lethargic for some weeks. In ME, however, the symptoms are more severe: even the slightest exertion may make the sufferer's muscles so weak that they need several days' rest to recover.

Medical researchers have found a number of abnormalities in ME sufferers, particularly changes in the IMMUNE SYSTEM and in the composition of muscle cells; but they have not yet been able to pinpoint the cause. A genetic defect in the immune system or an unusual reaction to one particular virus may be what triggers off the condition. The virus that causes GLANDULAR FEVER has been found in some ME sufferers, and many ME symptoms resemble the prolonged debilitation which often occurs after glandular fever. Other viruses implicated include enteroviruses (which enter the body and multiply in the bowels) and the CHICKENPOX virus.

These viruses, however, may only be triggers for certain people. Another factor frequently shared by ME sufferers is recent physical or emotional STRESS. Whatever symptoms affect individual ME sufferers, they usually follow a fluctuating course, with some easing between severe bouts.

The condition often strikes active, successful people, and those in their late twenties and early thirties are the most frequent victims. When ME was first recognised it was often dismissed as over-dramatised debility or as psychological in origin, a result of high-pressure modern lifestyles. The media rather scathingly dubbed it 'yuppie flu', but as more cases were reported to doctors and scientists began to take it seriously, it was more often called postviral fatigue syndrome. In many cases this was more appropriate than its current cumbersome full name, which literally means inflammation of the brain and the spinal cord with associated muscular pain, and is quite erroneous.

The wide range of symptoms added to the difficulty of recognising the condition. The sufferers seemed to be affected by totally different ailments. In fact, most patients suffer many of the same symptoms but in numerous permutations of severity.

However, although some doctors remain sceptical, ME is now recognised as an illness by the Departments of Health and of Social Security, which means that sufferers are entitled to treatment and benefits in the same way as people who have other recognised if more straightforward illnesses.

The ME Association supports a network of self-help groups for sufferers. For information

Do's and don'ts for ME *patients*

Do get an accurate diagnosis before following any programme of treatment.
Do take plenty of rest and avoid stresses, both mental and physical.
Do avoid alcohol, and cut out any foods that make the symptoms worse.
Don't have an anaesthetic or a vaccination unless it is essential.
Do keep your own notes about your diet, activities and symptoms. You are the best person to pinpoint what improves or worsens your condition.
Don't take supplements of the trace element germanium, which some have claimed boosts the immune system. Tests suggest it can cause severe kidney damage. And no thorough clinical tests have yet been made of claims that vitamin B12 injections, capsules of evening primrose oil, or antifungal drugs are safe for treating ME sufferers, who should avoid them.
Do find an activity to occupy you in your weakest periods to stave off loneliness and depression – simple card games, jigsaw puzzles or keeping a scrapbook, for example.

about a group near you or for other advice, you can contact the association at PO Box 8, Stanford-le-Hope, Essex SS17 8EX. The ME Action Campaign, PO Box 1126, London W3 0RY, offers up-to-date information in a journal and leaflets.

What the therapists recommend

Naturopathy Poor functioning of the immune system is seen as an underlying cause, and a proliferation of yeasts – especially *Candida albicans* – in the intestines has often been found in ME patients. A radical, long-term change in eating habits and lifestyle may be recommended to deal with both these problems.

A wholefood diet based on unprocessed, additive-free, raw foods is usually suggested. You will be asked to keep a note of what you have eaten, to identify foods that provoke symptoms or worsen them, so that you know what to avoid. Fresh air is generally thought to be helpful, but exercise should be avoided. Some practitioners prescribe supplements of MINERALS and VITAMINS to boost the body's defence system.

Acupuncture A practitioner will advise treatment according to individual needs. Generally this is aimed at stimulating the immune system, ensuring that breathing and digestive problems do not develop, relieving pain and increasing strength and energy. Stimulation is given to the points diagnosed as appropriate on the spleen, governor, liver, conception, heart and kidney meridians.

Aromatherapy Try oil of lavender, which relaxes and soothes, to alleviate tiredness, weakness, pain and shiveriness. Oil of lemon is said to calm the mind and, combined with oil of lavender, to promote refreshing sleep. Oil of orange or oil of geranium can be uplifting and stimulating.

You can put drops of any of these oils on a tissue to inhale, or take a ten-minute warm bath with six or eight drops of oil added.

For a drink, put two drops of geranium, thyme, lemon or sage oil on a tea bag, put the bag in a jug or teapot, then pour onto it a pint (600ml) of boiling water. Drink this infusion without milk, keeping any that is left over in the refrigerator, to reheat as and when required.

Hydrotherapy Russian, Turkish or sauna baths, or ordinary hot baths at home, are used to stimulate circulation and promote relaxation. They are seen as particularly helpful for ME patients who feel shivery at night or have difficulty in getting to sleep. Hot and cold sitz baths may bring relief where muscular pains are troublesome.

Herbal Medicine Gentle relaxants and tonics such as wild oats, skullcap, vervain and St John's wort are recommended to aid rest and increase vitality.

Homoeopathy ME patients are said to have gained considerable relief of symptoms through the care of an experienced homoeopath, but no general remedies are prescribed, as the condition is so complicated. The practitioner starts by making a detailed assessment of the patient's constitution and the symptoms causing most trouble, and seeking information about the illness which triggered the onset of ME.

Bach Remedies Wild rose is recommended to combat exhaustion and Crab apple to purify the system. Feelings of confusion and low vitality may be helped by Clematis, while Heather may help to alleviate depressive symptoms. Walnut and Willow are suggested to overcome feelings of resentment and help acceptance of the newly restricted lifestyle while the illness lasts.

An orthodox view

Because neither physical examinations nor laboratory tests produce findings specifically related to ME, some doctors are still sceptical about the illness. Many have in the past dismissed it as malingering, or seen it as a psychiatric condition, but it is now generally recognised as a distinct clinical condition. There is increasing evidence that it is caused by an enterovirus. Diagnosis is not easy, for tests must be made for other causes of muscle weakness and possible stress disorders, in order to rule them out.

In April 1990, Dr Elizabeth Dowsett, a consultant microbiologist and expert on ME, told a conference on the condition held in Cambridge that there may be as many as 150,000 ME sufferers in Britain. General practitioners have reported that among them are schoolchildren, whose complaints of feeling unwell may have been disregarded as unwillingness to go to school, or put down to many other causes before their true condition is recognised. Delay in diagnosis and unsympathetic treatment can have particularly severe consequences for children. They may fall far behind their classmates and even have to take an extra year at school – by which time the disease has taken hold.

Although there is no proven remedy, many patients do benefit from a course of antidepressant drugs. Some people are reluctant to take antidepressants because they do not wish their problems to be seen as psychological. But where mood swings, disturbed sleep, poor concentration and memory loss are occurring, this treatment may help, whether ME has a physical or a psychological cause.

Symptoms commonly persist for months – and may go on for years. Doctors can explain the likely course the illness will take and reassure sufferers that they should recover without specific treatment – albeit slowly.

Trial and error treatment for a schoolgirl sufferer

It was in the autumn of 1987 that schoolgirl Flavia Boyd's mother began to suspect that her daughter had ME. By Friday each week, 13-year-old Flavia would be exhausted and ashen-faced, and sleep all weekend to recover. At first Mrs Boyd thought overwork could be the trouble. Flavia – able, conscientious, and very keen to do well at her schoolwork – would stick at her books until 10pm.

Then a bout of flu and severe gastroenteritis struck Flavia. Once she was back at school the gastroenteritis recurred and she became very depressed. Mrs Boyd had seen similar symptoms in her own sister, who was suffering from ME, and so was alert to the danger. Both the school and the family doctor were sympathetic to the problem, but the doctor knew little of how to treat ME – a new and little understood disease.

Low point By December, Flavia was too ill to go to school and it was six months before she returned. She was constantly fatigued and her muscles ached; she was bewildered by her condition and resentful about the time lost at school. Her tiredness and depression were made worse by poor nights, when frightening, technicolour nightmares disturbed her sleep.

In the absence of firm medical guidelines for treatment, the Boyds tried whatever they could – vitamin and mineral supplements in case there was some deficiency, and a diet made up of wholefoods, avoiding any items that might foster an abundance of yeasts in the bowel. Treatment for a suspected liver condition only made her worse. Flavia had made no improvement by March, when she had colonic irrigation to wash out the bowel.

On the mend This proved to be the turning point for her. During the early summer she made such progress that in June she went back to school part-time. The school, still cooperative, kept her workload down when Flavia pushed herself too hard to catch up on the work she had missed.

Flavia, who lived in Bradfield, Berkshire, has made a complete recovery. She is not afraid to be active at her wide range of interests – but has learned not to overtax herself at them.

NAIL PROBLEMS

Nails serve a protective purpose and, like the skin and hair, their condition reflects your overall state of health, as well as the treatment they receive.

To keep your nails strong and healthy, wear rubber gloves for household chores, avoid soaking your hands in water for long periods, eat a balanced diet (see EATING FOR HEALTH) and follow the instructions for HAND CARE on p. 162. Particular problems can be dealt with as follows:

Deformed nails Hollow, spoon-shaped nails may show iron deficiency (see ANAEMIA) while with RESPIRATORY DISORDERS or HEART DISORDERS nails can become clubbed or grow around the fingertips. Pitted nails can be a result of PSORIASIS. Treatment can prove difficult and, like the skin rash in psoriasis, the problem can recur.

Flaking, splitting or chipping Rough treatment or lengthy immersion in water is usually to blame, or sometimes a shortage of unsaturated fats in the diet.

These problems can generally be overcome by massaging a moisturising cream into the nails every day, and wearing work or rubber gloves for gardening and indoor tasks as necessary. Keep nails fairly short and file them in one direction only, never to a point. Always use an oil-based polish remover if you paint your nails.

Practitioners of HERBAL MEDICINE regard nail problems largely as a sign of nutrient deficiency – such as calcium or silica – in the diet. But a consultation and full treatment is advisable to investigate the underlying cause of the problem.

Naturopaths also regard such conditions as split or brittle nails often to be the result of inadequate nourishment. Calcium and vitamins A, B and D are recommended and a multivitamin and mineral supplement might be suggested.

Hangnails Frequent soakings in water can make the outer layer of skin pull away from the cuticle, causing painful splits called hangnails. Prevent them becoming infected by snipping dead skin off with sharp nail scissors, and keeping the hands scrupulously clean. Wear rubber gloves for washing up and other domestic chores, and moisturise the skin with hand cream and cuticle cream every night.

Loose nails Regular use of commercial nail hardeners containing formaldehyde can separate nails from the skin underneath, opening the way to germs. Psoriasis and ECZEMA may cause a similar condition. The problem takes time to heal, but is helped by trimming the nails as short as possible and by avoiding the use of any hardeners which contain formaldehyde.

Nail biting This is a common habit of both adults and children, and often stems from ANXIETY, TENSION or insecurity. It weakens the nails and may damage sensitive skin underneath. Painting the nails with one of the bitter-tasting products sold by chemists and keeping the hands occupied when idle – by knitting, for example – may help to break the habit.

PSYCHOTHERAPY and HYPNOTHERAPY have been used to help nail-biters come to terms with any insecurity or anxiety at the root of the problem. In some cases, however, the best remedy is to appeal to the individual's vanity or self-respect.

Nails turn black or purple Dark discoloration under a nail is a sign of bleeding due to prolonged pressure or to a blow. Usually such spots just grow out, but if bleeding is extensive the nail may loosen and fall off. Pain caused by pressure can be relieved by having a doctor lance the nail. A new one should grow in due course – the actual rate of growth varies between individuals.

Pale nails Anaemia may be responsible. Whitish nails may show a liver condition which should disappear when the underlying cause has been treated.

Red, inflamed cuticles A bacterial or yeast infection at the base of the nail is to blame (see FUNGAL INFECTIONS). The cuticles become swollen and sometimes small blisters develop. Eventually nails may become discoloured or deformed. Self-help measures include taking supplements of zinc, vitamin C and vitamin B-complex, but it is usually necessary to see a doctor, who will use antibiotics or other drugs and ointments to clear the infection.

Belladonna 30C is used by homoeopaths when skin at the nail base is red, painful and throbbing; the biochemic tissue salt _Hepar sulph. 6C_ is advised if the tenderness is acute and there is pus.

Ridges Crosswise ridges are the result of a calcium or zinc shortage, illness or injury to the nail – for example, from pushing cuticles back too hard. The ridges grow out with time, and may be prevented by protecting nails from further damage and taking a multimineral supplement. Women can use a commercial ridge-filler to smooth the surface before applying varnish.

Lengthwise ridges sometimes develop in old age or illness, possibly because of vitamin and mineral shortages, and supplements may be of help.

White flecks These are usually a sign of too little zinc or vitamin A in the diet. Eating more spinach, whole grains and sunflower seeds may help, or taking vitamin and mineral supplements.

White, soft and crumbly nails Fungal infections are the cause. Eventually nails may thicken or grow ridges. Orthodox treatment with antifungal drugs and ointments is usually necessary. Homoeopaths recommend treating brittle nails that are red and swollen at the base with _Thuja 6_, three times daily for ten days. For slow-growing, white-spotted nails take _Silica 6_ twice a day for a month.

Yellow nails Staining can result from SMOKING, dyes in nail polish, or chlorine in swimming pools. Rub gently with a nail buffer and soak nails in lemon juice (or paint it on) to lighten the stain. Women should use a base coat before applying nail polish.

Four common kinds of nail disorder

Deformed, spoon-shaped nails may indicate an iron deficiency in the diet. It may help to eat iron-rich foods such as broccoli, watercress, raisins and parsley.

Painful splits called hangnails may occur if the hands are frequently immersed in water. To prevent this, rubber gloves should be worn when doing washing up.

Loose nails are often caused by using nail hardeners containing formaldehyde. This can separate the nails from the underlying skin, allowing germs to enter.

White-flecked nails are mostly the result of a diet containing insufficient vitamin A or zinc. They may be remedied by eating spinach and sunflower seeds.

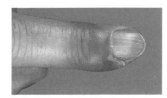
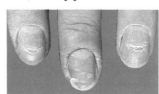

NATIONAL HEALTH SERVICE

Which alternative therapies you can get

In Britain, conventional medicine operates largely through the National Health Service (NHS), and at present HOMOEOPATHY is the only form of alternative medicine that is integrated within it. About 2000 doctors, most of them GPs, practise homoeopathy.

They can write prescriptions for homoeopathic remedies and can refer patients to any of the five hospitals in the UK that have homoeopathic units or departments (London, Glasgow, Liverpool, Bristol and Tunbridge Wells). These will accept referrals from other doctors, so virtually any patient who so wishes can get homoeopathic treatment.

OSTEOPATHY and CHIROPRACTIC have not yet received official recognition – due partly to disagreements among practitioners and partly to opposition from conventional medicine. However, some doctors take courses in these therapies and practise them.

Indeed, hospital trials using these treatments have shown good results, and several orthopaedic outpatient units now have osteopaths and chiropractors attached to them. A report in 1990 recommended considering making chiropractic generally available on the NHS. In addition, the British School of Osteopathy in London offers 'reduced fee' consultations at teaching clinics.

HERBAL MEDICINE is probably the longest established alternative therapy, going back to the apothecaries of old. Although herbalists operate outside the NHS, their organisation, the British Herbal Medicine Association (BHMA), works closely with the Department of Health and submits all herbal preparations to the Committee on Safety of Medicines for approval before members use them.

Since 1971, when the Medicines Act became law, herbal remedies have had to obtain licences like any other medicines, certifying that they are safe, effective and of good quality. Over 90 per cent of the BHMA's remedies have passed this test.

Despite these advances, doctors have in general tended to view unconventional healers as dangerous and unscrupulous quacks. However, increasing numbers of people do not share this view. Unorthodox forms of medicine continue to be practised and in recent times many have actually increased their following – even among GPs.

Of all alternative therapies, ACUPUNCTURE has gained most respectability, largely because a scientific explanation has been offered to account for its effect. It is thought that acupuncture stimulates the brain to release natural painkilling and tranquillising substances, called endorphins.

Many trials have been carried out on acupuncture, and it is now recommended by some orthodox practitioners for anaesthetic purposes, to relieve pain during PREGNANCY and in cases of recurring, long-term pain. The results are moderately successful, but treatment is not offered on the NHS and is not widely available.

Some alternative treatments such as MASSAGE, REFLEXOLOGY, AROMATHERAPY and relaxation techniques are given by specially trained nurses and physiotherapists in many NHS hospitals. Indeed, doctors often encourage these treatments – but this does not make them generally accepted forms of therapy. Hypnosis, by contrast, has become almost an orthodox therapy and is used by many doctors, dentists, psychologists and psychiatrists (see HYPNOTHERAPY).

One other alternative approach, SPIRITUAL HEALING, is also widely available, although not part of the NHS. Most healers do not charge a fee, and The Confederation of Healing Organisations provides hospitals and doctors with lists of registered healers.

A unique experimental clinic combining both conventional and alternative treatments was opened by Prince Charles in 1987. The Marylebone Health Centre in London houses an ordinary general practice, with 4000 patients, and operates several additional research units. Among those working there are a homoeopath, massage therapist, osteopath, traditional Chinese practitioner and a counsellor. All patients in the NHS general practice have access to these therapists, and several research studies identifying the outcome of this approach are underway.

NATURAL AIDS TO BEAUTY

Creams, lotions, face packs and shampoos to make at home

Nothing you put on your skin or do to your hair can take the place of good health when it comes to looking your best. But with a balanced diet (see EATING FOR HEALTH), regular EXERCISE, a good night's sleep and satisfying work and relationships, cosmetics and toiletries made from natural ingredients can help a woman make the most of her looks.

The recipes given here are easy and inexpensive to follow. Many of the ingredients may even be found in your kitchen; the rest can be bought from a chemist or health shop. They do not include any of the chemical dyes, perfumes and preservatives that can cause ALLERGY when used in certain commercial products. You will also have the satisfaction of knowing that none of the preparations has been tested on animals.

A double boiler is useful for some of the recipes, but a heatproof bowl placed over a pan of boiling water will work just as well. Otherwise you need only ordinary kitchen utensils, storage jars and bottles. Wash and dry all utensils and containers thoroughly before using.

When buying the recommended essential oils, make sure that they are pure, and not synthetic or adulterated (see AROMATHERAPY). Always count out the stipulated number of drops.

Note Allergies to these preparations are rare, and a simple test will soon show sensitivity. Dab a little of each cream or lotion on the inside of the forearm and leave for 24 hours. If there is no reaction, it is safe to use. All these preparations are intended for external use only, and should not be swallowed.

Caution Remember that, because no preservatives are used in the homemade preparations given here, the creams and lotions will not last as long as commercial products. Always store your preparations in a cool, dry place, and use a spatula to extract and apply them, since putting your fingers into jars can promote the development of bacteria.

Moisturiser Suitable for face and hands, a simple mixture using equal quantities of glycerine and rose water has been a favourite moisturiser for many years. Reduce the proportion of glycerine to make a less greasy cream for oily skins, or increase it if your skin is dry.

To make a moisturising gel, dissolve a teaspoon of gelatine in ¼ pint (150ml) of hot water, then mix in a teaspoon of rose essential oil and 3 tablespoons of glycerine. If you prefer, use lavender, orange or another flower water in place of rose.

Facial cleansing cream Finely pare about 8 tablespoons of beeswax – bought from a hardware or health shop – with a sharp kitchen knife or grater. Heat gently with ¾ pint (450ml) of liquid paraffin in the top of a double boiler until melted. Allow to cool to 50°C (120°F), while separately heating ½ pint (300ml) of water to the same temperature. When both are hot, slowly add the water to the wax and oil mixture, stirring continuously. Leave to cool until it begins to solidify, then pour it into storage jars.

Cold cream Pure aloe vera gel is available from most health shops and gives a pleasant texture to this cleansing and moisturising lotion – make it as shown in the illustration on the right.

Facial toning lotion This contains sage to tighten the skin, close the pores and soothe any spots of inflammation. Use the lotion after cleansing the skin and before applying any moisturiser.

To make the lotion, place 4 tablespoons of dried sage – or 8 of the fresh herb – into a clean jar, and pour on it ¼ pint (150ml) of vodka. Tightly screw on the lid and leave it to stand. After a week strain off and discard the sage, replacing it with a similar new measure of the herb and leaving it for another week.

The liquid should now have a strong herbal smell, but for an even stronger lotion, repeat the procedure once more. Finally, strain the liquid into a clean bottle, using a fine sieve or a coffee filter. Add four or five drops of tincture of benzoin – available from chemists – screw on the lid and shake well.

To make a milder lotion, dilute with distilled water or use a less astringent herb such as camomile instead of sage. Stronger herbs such as yarrow, or the addition of 2-4 tablespoons of witch hazel, will strengthen the mixture.

Skin refresher Papaya (papaw) fruit contains enzymes that help to remove dead skin, leaving the face fresh and clean. Apply pulped fruit all over the face, leave for a few minutes and then wipe off. Splash with cool water and apply moisturiser, as papaya tends to dry the skin.

Facial masks These will cleanse and tone the skin, drawing out impurities and soothing sore or inflamed spots. Make them as shown in the illustration on the right, mixing dry and liquid ingredients chosen to suit your skin.

Oatmeal and ground almonds are good all-purpose dry bases, suitable for any skin type; wheatgerm and brewer's yeast are said to nourish the skin; and kaolin clay to draw impurities to the surface, heal spots and improve circulation.

Other clays may also be used: bentonite to soothe and heal, and fuller's earth to absorb excess oil and stimulate the skin. Sulphur is sometimes used to treat ACNE and oily skins, but it can cause allergies so use with caution and test on a small area first.

Liquids to use for a greasy skin include witch hazel, beaten egg white, yoghurt, lemon juice or an infusion of yarrow, agrimony, raspberry leaf or lady's mantle. Dry skin can benefit from an application of egg yolk, honey, sour cream, pulped bananas or avocado, rose water, almond oil, or melon or carrot juice.

To invigorate the skin and improve circulation, try using rosemary, peppermint,

Making cold cream

Using a blender or whisk, thoroughly mix together a tablespoon of aloe vera gel and ¼ pint (150ml) corn, olive or other vegetable oil. Then, in the top of a double boiler, melt a tablespoon of white beeswax and 2 tablespoons of anhydrous (water-free) lanolin. Slowly stir in the oil and aloe mix, remove from heat and add 2 tablespoons of rose, lavender or other flower water, and two or three drops of any essential oil you like. Stir until the mixture cools and thickens, then pour into storage jars.

Homemade face packs

To make these, combine 2½ tablespoons of a suitable dry base with enough liquid to make a thick paste, choosing ingredients to suit your skin type – see text.

Before applying, wash your face and either steam it (see p. 194) or cover with a warm, wet facecloth for a few minutes to open the pores. Then spread the paste all over the face, not neglecting, as some women do, the neck and décolleté area; but avoid eyes and lips. Allow to dry completely – about 15-30 minutes – before washing off with warm water and a soft cloth.

nettle, elderflower or eucalyptus infusions in the mixture; to soften rough, dry skin, use aloe vera gel or 1-2 tablespoons of linseed or kelp gently heated in ¼ pint (150ml) of water until it thickens.

Herbal shampoo Choose the right herbs for your hair type when making this gentle shampoo: sage to condition and enhance dark hair, camomile to lighten and soften fair hair, mullein to intensify blonde highlights, parsley to thicken hair and enrich its colour, southernwood to stimulate hair growth, burdock root and nettle to control dandruff, and kelp or yarrow to encourage growth and check hair loss.

Into a heatproof jar place 1½ tablespoons of your chosen herbs, a teaspoon of pure-grade borax and 3 tablespoons of dried soapwort leaves or 2 tablespoons of dried root. Pour on ¾ pint (450ml) of boiling water and stir well, cover loosely and leave to cool. Allow the mixture to stand for a day or two, shaking regularly; then strain and use.

In this recipe, soapwort takes the place of the soap or detergent used in most shampoos. It has a good cleaning effect, but you will need to use a little more of the shampoo than of most proprietary types.

Soap shampoo A gentle, effective shampoo which rinses out better than commercial ones can be made with castile soap, which is made from olive oil.

For fair hair, place 8 tablespoons of dried camomile flowers into a saucepan with 1 tablespoon of dried peppermint, 2 tablespoons of dried rosemary and 1 pint (600ml) of distilled water.

For dark hair, substitute dried sage for the camomile flowers. Bring the mixture to a boil, reduce the heat and simmer for ten minutes. Turn off the heat, cover, and allow it to soak for half an hour.

Strain the liquid into a mixing bowl, squeezing out as much as possible from the herbs before discarding them. Put 2oz (60g) of flaked or grated castile soap into the saucepan and pour the herbal water back in. Heat gently until all the soap has dissolved, stirring with a wooden spoon. Leave and allow to cool.

Stir three drops of peppermint or eucalyptus essential oil into 2 tablespoons of vodka. Add this mixture to the soap solution. Pour into a jar and leave for three to four days in a warm place before using.

Herbal hair oil Place 12 tablespoons of suitable herbs (see herbal shampoo recipe above) in the top of a double boiler and add ½ pint (300ml) of safflower, soya, peanut, corn or sunflower oil. Olive oil may also be used if you do not mind the smell. Heat for half an hour, then pour the mixture into a wide-necked jar. Cover with a few layers of cheesecloth or muslin held by a rubber band.

Natural hair colours from herbs and flowers

Test these tints on a strand of hair to check the colour before using. The infusions need to be used as regular rinses to keep up the effect, but a single 15-30 minute application of the paste colourings is usually enough, with retouching every four to six weeks to colour new growth at the hair roots.

COLOURING AGENT	EFFECT ON HAIR COLOUR
Henna mixed to paste with hot water.	Comes in different colours, but red is most popular.
Henna mixed to paste with hot camomile infusion, red wine or lemon juice.	Enhanced red tints.
Henna mixed to paste with hot black coffee.	Deeper colour.
Strong camomile infusion.	Lightens fair hair.
Camomile mixed to paste with kaolin powder.	Highlights mid-brown hair.
Infusion of marigold flowers, or saffron roots or flowers.	Gives reddish-yellow tint to white hair.
Infusion of powdered walnut bark or shells.	Darkens hair slightly (good for grey hair).
Rhubarb root infusion.	Lightens any hair slightly.
Sage infusion.	Gives brown tint to grey hair.
Sage infusion mixed with tea.	Deeper brown colour.

Leave in a warm place for about a week, stirring every day. Then strain and store in a clean container.

To use, pour out 5 tablespoons of the oil – 8 if your hair is very long or thick – and warm it gently for a few minutes. Wet your hair with warm water, squeeze out, then spread the oil evenly through the hair using your fingers. Cover the hair with a shower cap, and wrap around your head a wrung-out towel that has been soaked in hot water. When the towel cools down, remove and wet it with hot water again, wring it out and replace around the head.

Leave the oil on your hair for about half an hour, then shampoo it out twice and rinse well.

Egg and oil conditioner Use this mix like the oil above, or just warm it slightly and apply 15 minutes before washing your hair.

Beat together an egg, 2 teaspoons of lemon juice and 1 teaspoon of honey. Pour into the top of a double boiler and heat until creamy, stirring continuously. Remove from heat, and when cool slowly whisk in 4 tablespoons of safflower or other vegetable oil – or the herbal hair oil above – into which you have stirred two or three drops of rosemary essential oil.

Green clay body treatment Mixed to a paste with water and two or three drops of an essential oil of your choice, green clay can

be applied to the whole body to cleanse and tone the skin, draw out impurities and invigorate your circulation. It removes dead cells, leaving the skin smooth and soft, and will not irritate even a sensitive skin.

A course of regular applications can be used to treat spots on the back and help dry out excessively oily patches. Leave the treatment on for at least five minutes, and up to a maximum of 15 minutes, depending on the sensitivity of your skin.

Pre-bath body rub To remove dead skin cells and improve circulation, rub your body all over – excluding your face and neck – with fine sea salt. Use it by the handful and apply it with a circular motion. Rinse off with cool water, then bathe.

Beauty baths Almost any herb can be used in the bath – choose according to the list on p. 186. To prepare, steep 2oz (60g) of herbs in a pint (600ml) of boiling water for 20-30 minutes, strain and add to your bath water. Alternatively, tie the herbs in a muslin bag and hang it from the hot tap so that water runs through it. One bag will do about three or four baths.

Half a pint of cider vinegar added to a bath, with one or two drops of peppermint essential oil added, may help to relieve dry, itchy skin, and both cider vinegar and sea salt in a 3 per cent dilution in your bath are said to be helpful against THRUSH or other yeast infections. Alternatively, try four or five drops of tea tree oil.

Oatmeal and bran baths are prepared in the same way as herbal baths and have a cleansing, soothing and whitening effect on the skin. For a rich, nourishing bath, try adding about 2oz (60g) of powdered milk to the water or, for a fragrant treat, a few drops of aromatherapy oil.

Natural deodorant If chemical sprays and roll-ons irritate your skin, try using an alunite crystal moistened with a little water and rubbed under the arms for a few seconds.

You may also find that you have less need for deodorant if you eat plenty of foods that contain chlorophyll, such as green, leafy vegetables and salads. You should also make sure that your diet is balanced by supplements of zinc, aluminium and manganese (see MINERALS).

NATURAL CHILDBIRTH

More and more women are choosing to have their children delivered without artificial aids. Many doctors endorse this, and most hospitals now provide suitable facilities. See A GENTLER WAY INTO THE WORLD, p. 260.

NATUROPATHY
Helping your body to heal itself

The first man to bathe his sprained ankle in a cool stream was practising naturopathy – as was the first woman to stop eating food to rest an upset stomach, and the first person to sit tight and sweat out a FEVER.

Since its earliest days, when it was known as 'nature cure', naturopathy has concentrated on helping the body to cure itself. It aims to do this by means of various therapies, which today include CHIROPRACTIC, DIETS AND DIETING, EXERCISE, HYDROTHERAPY, MASSAGE, OSTEOPATHY, RELAXATION AND BREATHING, and YOGA. It also encourages people to think positively in terms of good health, rather than of pain and illness – and to live as naturally as possible amid the pressures of our modern, everyday world.

When, for whatever apparent reason, our health breaks down, naturopathy sets out to identify the underlying cause of illness – and to treat this, rather than trying to suppress or merely alleviate the symptoms.

Basically, disease is thought by naturo-

paths to have one major cause – the breakdown of the body's normal balance. The particular type of illness a person suffers may be the result of various bacteria, viruses, ALLERGY, or other outside factors. But these are held to be of secondary importance to the patient's weakness and lack of resistance.

By treating each case as unique, and each person as an individual, naturopaths take into account the patient's entire physical, emotional, biochemical and social circumstances. They seek to complement and support conventional doctors – providing help and comfort whenever severe illness requires surgery or drastic orthodox treatment.

Who it can help Naturopaths believe that their holistic approach can help all kinds of people with all kinds of medical problems. Age is no barrier, and patients range from infants to the elderly.

Naturopathy is said to be particularly effective against degenerative diseases such as ARTHRITIS and EMPHYSEMA (damaged, inefficient lungs). It has reportedly been used to powerful effect on patients with ULCERS and various forms of inflammation. In addition, it aims to speed up recovery in cases of COLDS, INFLUENZA, DIARRHOEA, and rashes (see SKIN DISORDERS).

It is often used in dealing with cases for which no clear medical diagnosis can be made – such as ANXIETY and TIREDNESS. And naturopathy is believed to be highly successful in helping to prevent disease in bodily tissues and organs such as the lungs, kidneys and heart.

As naturopaths concentrate on the person, rather than the disease, they emphasise that their success depends upon their patients' ability to heal themselves, as well as the amount of physical damage already done. For example, a young person full of vitality should respond well to treatment for, say, BRONCHITIS. On the other hand, a frail, elderly person with the same complaint may not get better as completely or as soon. Even so, naturopaths believe, old people should be able to cope with the illness effectively without the need for drugs.

Finding a therapist A list of qualified naturopaths can be obtained for a small charge from the General Council and Register of Naturopaths (GCRN), Frazer House, 6 Netherhall Gardens, London NW3 5RR. Its members have the initials MRN after their names, showing they have passed a four-year, full-time training course at the British College of Naturopathy and Osteopathy. They hold a Naturopathic Diploma (ND); and some also hold a Diploma in Osteopathy (DO).

Most naturopaths work in private practice, and will see patients only by appointment. Some therapists attend HEALTH FARMS and

Naturopathy in the home

The advice given by a naturopath will be directed at you as a person, rather than at a specific disease you may have. And most of what the practitioner recommends can be carried out in your own home.

For example, you may be told to make changes to your diet – such as eating more salads and fresh fruit, and avoiding caffeine in coffee and tea. In some cases of allergy you may be told to avoid dairy products and wheat. And people with arthritis and skin disorders may be prescribed dietary supplements of anti-inflammatory fatty acids (see EATING FOR HEALTH).

You may even be put on a short, water or juice-only fast designed to cleanse your system and give your organs a chance to rest. You may also be advised, if necessary, to stop SMOKING and give up alcohol.

Simple advice on hydrotherapy may also be given – such as taking hot and cold foot baths to help control high blood pressure, or applying cold compresses to the throat and waist to try to relieve TONSILLITIS. Other measures may include the use of herbal medicine and HOMOEOPATHY.

During the first few weeks of home treatment you will need to see your naturopath regularly so that the effect of any dietary changes can be checked, and for special muscle reflex treatments, counselling, or instruction in relaxation and breathing. But after that fewer consultations should be needed.

clinics – especially those where hydrotherapy is available and where dietary and exercise programmes are conducted under strict professional supervision.

Consulting a therapist Since naturopathy deals with you as a whole, a therapist will first take your complete case history, possibly by means of a questionnaire. He will want to know how you – and your symptoms – are affected by such things as changes in the weather, different times of day, the areas in which you live and work, the various events that make up your daily routine, your eating habits and sleeping patterns, and physical factors such as menstrual cycles and bowel activity.

This will be followed by a routine medical examination of the pulse, heart, lungs and BLOOD PRESSURE. The practitioner may also

The natural birth of naturopathy

Fig.1. The Knee-jet.

Fig.2. The Head-affusion.

Fig.3. Walking barefoot in wet grass.

The origins of naturopathy go back more than 2000 years to the Greek physician Hippocrates, known as the 'Father of Medicine'. He laid down the principle of 'first do no harm' – implying that cures should work with the body and be as natural as possible – and maintained that good health is based upon eating and exercising with moderation.

Modern naturopathy was pioneered in Germany in the early 19th century by therapists such as Vincent Preissnitz (1799-1851), who believed in the 'miraculous' healing power of water and founded hydrotherapy as it is now called. Towards the end of the century a Bavarian monk, Father Sebastian Kneipp, successfully treated an ailing American named Benedict Lust. After studying with Kneipp at his clinic, Lust returned to the USA and founded his own particular form of therapy – naturopathy.

Lust believed that, as far as health is concerned, man is his own worst enemy – hampered by 'narrow thinking' and beset by 'criminal eating, foolish drinking, sagged standing [and] congested sitting'.

The Kneipp water cure was recommended to people of all ages suffering from muscular aches and pains. Hosing, sprinkling with water and walking barefoot in wet grass were all part of the therapy.

check the spinal joints and other parts of your musculoskeletal system to make sure that they are working freely.

Many naturopaths also use various special diagnostic techniques – such as IRIDOLOGY (examining the irises of your eyes for signs of illness) and HAIR DIAGNOSIS. Samples of your blood and urine may also be taken for laboratory analysis.

Naturopathic diagnosis is more concerned with establishing why your health has broken down than with putting a name to the illness. For the practitioner, the diagnostic findings are only part of the assessment he makes. He will also take into consideration your own particular physical, emotional and environmental circumstances.

Many people are frightened of illness, feeling it is something over which they have no control. Naturopaths try to dispel this fear by explaining what the body is telling us when it is unwell.

For example, sudden or severe symptoms are indications that it is dealing with a particular illness and therefore the symptoms

must not be suppressed – unless, of course, the patient's life is at risk. Sometimes during treatment of long-standing conditions such as bronchitis or skin disorders, there may be a short return of phlegm or irritation for a few days. These aggravations of old symptoms are known as the 'healing crisis', and are regarded as a good sign.

Measures may include changes in diet or herbal treatment (SEE HERBAL MEDICINE). In all cases, care is taken to ensure that the symptoms do not overcome the patient's reserves of energy or hinder his ability to make a satisfactory recovery. If necessary, therapists may arrange for patients to have emotional and spiritual COUNSELLING.

An orthodox view

Many of the treatments offered by naturopaths form the basis of good health care, both preventive and curative. Several are now advocated in health education programmes. Treatment of complex medical problems will respond well to a combination of orthodox approaches as well as naturopathy.

NAUSEA AND VOMITING

If you feel sick, it is called nausea. Vomiting is simply the physical outcome. Nausea may be a symptom of many conditions, including overeating, MORNING SICKNESS, MOTION SICKNESS, MIGRAINE, VERTIGO and uncontrolled DIABETES. One of the most common causes is FOOD POISONING, or gastroenteritis, in which bacteria from contaminated food inflame the lining of the stomach and intestine – often resulting in DIARRHOEA, too. By ridding the body of the harmful agents, vomiting can make you feel much better.

But prolonged or excessive vomiting (with or without diarrhoea) can result in dehydration – the loss of too much body fluid.

What the therapists recommend

Acupressure Press towards the centre of the wrist, three fingers' width above the inner wrist crease, centrally, in line with the middle finger (Pericardium 6). Alternatively, press firmly inwards, centrally, on the midpoint on the stomach, between the breastbone and navel (Ren 12).

Herbal Medicine If the symptoms are persistent or inexplicable, seek advice and treatment. Sipping an infusion of ginger and/or peppermint can bring ease. A herbalist may also prescribe black horehound to give relief, while simultaneously treating the cause.

Naturopathy Once the cause is discovered and the vomiting controlled, some foods can be reintroduced, starting with clear vegetable soups, followed by wholemeal toast or boiled rice and vegetables, before gradually resuming a normal diet.

Homoeopathy For constant nausea and vomiting after meals, with a clean tongue, griping pains, headache and perspiration, homoeopaths recommend *Ipecac. 6*. If it follows rich fatty food and afflicts a weepy person who tends to feel better outdoors, try *Pulsatilla 6*. If the vomit is very acidic and occurs soon after a meal, with burning pains, chilliness and exhaustion, *Arsen. alb. 6* is recommended. Dosage in each case is every half hour until improvement is felt.

An orthodox view

Nausea and vomiting are symptoms – not diseases. The most important role of a conventional doctor is to diagnose and treat the cause of these symptoms. For example, it would be dangerous – and could even be fatal – to treat the vomiting of uncontrolled diabetes without giving insulin.

Pending professional advice, take little or

no solid foods and plenty of fluids, such as water, weak tea or barley water.

Medicines such as metoclopramide or pro-chlorperazine in tablet form, suppository or injection, may control vomiting, once the cause is known. But medicines should be avoided during pregnancy.

NECK PAIN

Most people have neck pain and stiffness at some time in their lives. The cause can be trivial or serious – and it can be difficult to tell which.

The neck is the most mobile part of the spine, with seven bones separated by discs of cartilage and joined by ligaments. Wear-and-tear changes in the bones and joints, known as cervical spondylosis, begin at the age of about 25 and may result in pain and stiffness from bony fringes, called osteophytes, growing around the joints. ARTHRITIS can also develop in the joints between the vertebrae (spinal bones).

Ligament SPRAINS may occur after 'whiplash' injuries to the neck caused, for example, when a car is shunted from behind.

Neck pain is frequently accompanied by pain in the shoulder or arm caused by trapped nerves (see NERVE DISORDERS). It is also often aggravated by reflex muscle spasm in the neck, with increased stiffness and restricted movement.

Tension HEADACHES may also cause neck pain. If it occurs suddenly and the patient shows signs of general illness, it can also be a symptom of meningitis – infection of the membranes surrounding the brain – or a brain haemorrhage.

What the therapists recommend

Acupuncture Treatment can be given for most types of neck pain and stiffness. Points treated are on the small intestine, gall bladder, lung, bladder and large intestine meridians (see chart, p. 14). MOXIBUSTION may also be beneficial.

Massage If the pain stems from the neck muscles or joints – but is not glandular or disease-related – apply firm, stroking effleurage movements down the back of the neck and over the shoulder area. Also give deep frictions with the pads of the fingers along the band of muscle at each side of the vertebrae of the neck. But avoid the front of the neck and throat regions.

Reflexology Massage is given to the reflex areas relating to the neck, with rotation of the toe joints, plus massage to areas relating to the upper spine, the side of the head, the

shoulders, the arms and the adrenal glands (see chart, p. 295).

Osteopathy Poor posture can often lead to pain and stiffness in the neck. Gentle manual traction and mobilisation may bring rapid relief. Some simple exercises are recommended to help to maintain mobility of the neck. First, when sitting, drop the chin to the chest and then slowly stretch the head up and backwards. Second, with the head upright, turn round as far as possible to the left and then to the right. Third, again with the head upright, bring the left ear slowly down as far as possible to the left shoulder, then the right ear to the right shoulder. Repeat all three exercises five times.

An orthodox view

X-rays are not particularly helpful in diagnosing the cause of neck pain, because they frequently reveal cervical spondylosis in patients over the age of 25 even when there are no symptoms of stiffness and pain. On

the other hand, severe symptoms sometimes occur in people whose X-rays appear to be fairly normal.

After taking a patient's history and physically examining the neck, a doctor may recommend a course of physiotherapy (often including massage), heat treatment, traction or a cervical collar. Painkilling medicines such as aspirin, paracetamol or ibuprofen sometimes help, but they do not relieve muscle spasm.

Many neck problems can be avoided by maintaining an upright posture, lifting and carrying loads properly (see ALEXANDER TECHNIQUE and POSTURAL INTEGRATION), and being careful not to overextend the neck – for example, when painting ceilings or washing high windows.

Poor work conditions in which the neck is bent for long periods – such as working at a desk at the wrong height – should also be avoided. Car headrests reduce the risk of 'whiplash' injuries to the neck.

Exercises to avoid neck pain

Maintaining flexibility is the key to keeping your neck free of tension and pain. To achieve this, try the following daily exercises. Make sure to move only your neck and head.

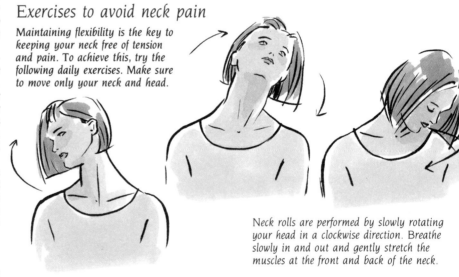

Neck rolls are performed by slowly rotating your head in a clockwise direction. Breathe slowly in and out and gently stretch the muscles at the front and back of the neck.

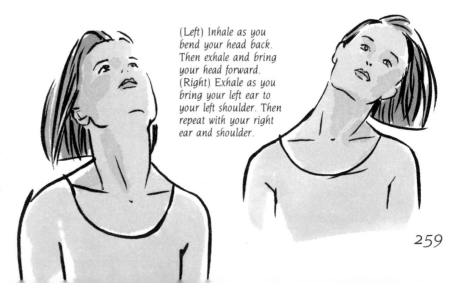

(Left) Inhale as you bend your head back. Then exhale and bring your head forward. (Right) Exhale as you bring your left ear to your left shoulder. Then repeat with your right ear and shoulder.

A gentler way into the world

Nothing is more natural than having a baby, yet few natural events have been more interfered with. In 1982, 6000 women met on London's Hampstead Heath to protest at being made to give birth lying down. They were supporters of the natural childbirth movement, which upholds the right of women to follow their instincts in the matter of childbirth. Since then women have increasingly opted for natural deliveries. Many doctors are sympathetic to the idea, and most hospitals now make provision for women who want a minimum of medical interference while still ensuring the safety of their babies.

All births were natural until the 17th century, when King Louis XIV of France made his mistresses lie on their back during labour so that he could witness the birth of his children. Although childbirth is difficult and painful in this position, it soon became so fashionable that French doctors had to develop forceps to overcome some of the problems it caused. Soon so many special instruments were introduced that doctors came to regard childbirth as an emergency requiring medical intervention for the best results.

Women may give birth squatting, sitting or even standing up; there is no general rule. But even in the most primitive societies, first-time mothers usually get the advice of other women who have been through the experience of childbirth.

In Britain, natural childbirth was pioneered by Dr Grantly Dick-Read (1890-1959), after he assisted at a delivery in a Whitechapel slum. The woman refused to have chloroform. Later, when asked why, she replied: 'It didn't hurt. It wasn't meant to, was it doctor?' From this and other deliveries, Dr Dick-Read came to believe that women who stayed calm and had faith in the natural process of birth tended to have a relatively painless experience.

He developed relaxation techniques to help women overcome their fears and these, with advice on posture, EXERCISE and diet, became basic principles of the National

Water births are increasingly popular. Some hospitals have pools big enough for both partners to enter, as shown here. The baby does not breathe until its head is out of the water, so there is no danger of drowning.

Childbirth Trust (NCT). The organisation still provides counsellors and classes to help women prepare for childbirth.

A French obstetrician, Dr Michel Odent (1930-), went a step further. Instead of teaching women what to do, he encouraged them to believe that if they trusted their instincts they could all be natural experts at giving birth. He gave his patients the freedom and privacy to act as they wished during labour, including the chance to sit in a tub of warm water to ease painful contractions – and so the idea of water births was introduced to the West (see below).

Another recent development is the 'Leboyer method', named after Dr Frederick Leboyer (1918-), who considered birth from the point of view of the baby. He believed that instead of emerging into a world of bright lights and raised voices – and even being held upside down and slapped – a baby should enter the world as gently as possible.

Today, many women opt for natural childbirth because they feel it will be less traumatic for the baby, and give them more control over the birth.

Preparing for natural birth

Start immediately – even before you are pregnant – to take regular exercise and eat a well-balanced diet rich in proteins, VITAMINS and MINERALS (see EATING FOR HEALTH). During PREGNANCY, choose gentler types of exercise such as swimming and walking, which tone the muscles and improve fitness without strain. Some simple YOGA exercises can help to increase suppleness and flexibility.

Choosing where to have the baby is the next step – the most 'natural' place is wherever you feel most comfortable. For some mothers – particularly if it is their first baby or there are any problems – this is in hospital, where modern technology is available. Some women prefer the familiar surroundings of home, with the midwife present as a guest. Others opt for a 'domino' (domiciliary-in-out) delivery, where the midwife stays at home with the mother through the first stages of labour, then drives her to hospital for the actual delivery and brings her home again soon afterwards.

Natural childbirth advisers recommend that every mother-to-be should draw up a 'birth plan' well in advance, setting out what she would prefer. Some hospitals provide ready-made forms to fill in, or you can easily make your own (see box, p. 263).

Natural labour and birth

Birth positions If squatting appeals to you it may be a good idea to practise during pregnancy (see illustrations, p. 262). Your partner can help by holding you up. You may also find that a birth cushion or kidney-shaped birth stool or birth chair helps you to stay in position, but ask your midwife's advice, as some modern birthing chairs can restrict movement and may increase bleeding and tearing.

Alternatively, you could adopt a South American Indian method and stand up just as the baby's head is about to emerge – half the women who do this have no tears at all.
Water births The first recorded underwater birth was mentioned in a medical report of 1805, but it was not until

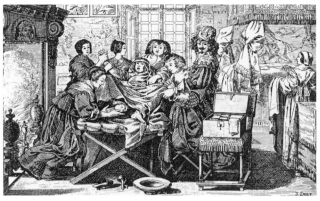
Louis XIV of France began a long-lasting fashion by insisting that his mistresses give birth lying down in spite of the problems it caused.

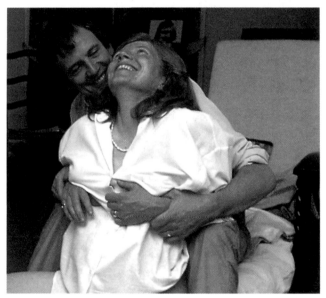
Childbirth can now be a happy, relaxed experience in which partners increasingly play an active, supporting role. In natural childbirth, the mother-to-be usually chooses where and how she will be delivered. The days when women had to give birth on their back are over.

the 1960s that the idea started becoming popular. Now some modern hospitals can provide receptacles for women who want to try this method. Hospitals that do not have tubs or pools will sometimes allow you to bring in one that you have hired. They can be obtained from: Birthworks, Hill House, Folleigh Lane, Long Ashton, Bristol BS18 9JB; The Active Birth Centre, Dartmouth Park Road, London NW5 1SL; and Splashdown Birth Pools, 68 West Street, Harrow on the Hill, Middlesex HA1 3ER.

The tub or pool is filled with about 15in (38cm) of body-temperature water – enough to reach the armpits when sitting. When contractions become painful, the mother-to-be eases herself into the water. Some receptacles are even big enough for her partner to get in with her and

Natural Childbirth

Preparing for the birth

Two positions which can help women prepare for childbirth are the squatting pose (right) and the so-called 'frog position' (below). The first increases flexibility and gives a good stretch to thigh, groin and back muscles, while the second is said to enhance suppleness and aid relaxation, especially when combined with labour breathing exercises.

Gently lower yourself from a standing position into the squat, keeping your back straight and your feet flat on the ground if possible. Rest elbows on thighs and clasp hands together. Remain in the position as long as is comfortable.

Kneel on a soft carpet, rug or mat with your toes touching and knees a little apart. Keep your back straight and arms, neck and shoulders relaxed.

Place hands on the floor, palms down, and lower your bottom as far as possible. Slowly 'walk' hands forward, stretching out the spine and lowering the body towards the ground.

When you are stretched out as far as you can go, rest your forehead on a cushion. Hold for a minute or two, taking slow, rhythmic breaths with the emphasis on the out-breath.

Two simple ways of helping to make labour more comfortable for you

A gentle massage from a nurse, therapist or partner can soothe away pain and help women in labour to relax. It is said to work best for women who have had massage before, and who find the touch of human hands reassuring.

A birth cushion or beanbag moulded into shape can help women to find the best positions for giving birth. These simple aids are available in many hospitals and provide a useful combination of comfort and support.

(Right) A mother-to-be tries out the V-shaped birth cushion developed by Dr Jason Gardosi in 1987 at the Milton Keynes General Hospital.

(Left) The mother lies on her side or sits if she prefers, while the therapist or nurse massages her back and buttocks, relieving muscle tension and labour pains.

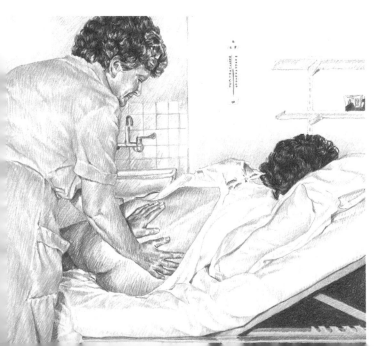

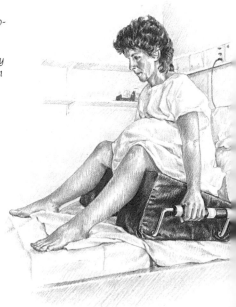

A birth plan for you and your baby

Prepare your plan well in advance with your partner, and try to include every aspect of the birth. Discuss the details of it with a midwife or your general practitioner, and prepare to be flexible, accepting that unforeseen circumstances can upset even the best laid of plans.

Try to include the following information:

Other people   Many women enjoy having a partner, relative or friend with them during labour. Your midwife can tell you if this is possible. If you would rather be alone, note this instead.

Induction   This is not used in natural childbirth, as once contractions are artificially induced they become faster and more painful, increasing the need for painkillers. If induction is unavoidable – for example, if the baby is two or three weeks late, or if mother or baby shows signs of distress – you can still say that you want to try alternative methods first. Acupressure, acupuncture or homoeopathy may be able to balance your system so that your labour begins naturally.

Lovemaking, nipple stimulation, a long walk or a drink of castor oil and orange juice may all increase production of the hormone prostaglandin, sometimes causing labour to start. However, labour should never be induced except on the advice of a doctor or midwife.

If artificial induction is necessary, you can ask for it to be done by the gentler method of prostaglandin vaginal pessaries, rather than by having the waters broken or being given the hormone oxytocin by injection or through a drip.

Shaving and enemas   These days, women's pubic hair is usually shaven only for a Caesarean section, and an enema is given only for CONSTIPATION. Even so, if you do not want either of them, say so in your plan.

Moving around   Freedom to move around and change position at will can relieve pain and assist labour, so put that in your plan. Electronic monitoring of the baby can restrict movement, and you can choose to have it done only intermittently, or with an instrument called a Pinard stethoscope, which allows you to move most of the time.

Pain control   Painkillers are often administered without asking the mother, so say in writing if you want them only on request. However, in case natural methods such as relaxation and breathing prove inadequate, you should say which of the alternatives you would prefer.

The usual options are gas and air (a mixture of laughing gas – nitrous oxide – and air); injections of the drug pethidine; or an epidural injection of an anaesthetic which goes into the outer lining of the spinal cord. This numbs the lower half of the body while leaving you fully conscious.

Cut or tear   Neither may happen, but your plan should allow for all possibilities. In natural childbirth, natural tearing of the vagina is usually preferred to an episiotomy – a deliberate cut at the entrance of the vagina to help the baby out. Natural tears are said to heal faster, but episiotomies are common in some hospitals, so say if you don't want to have one. They are avoidable unless forceps are used.

Giving birth   Say what equipment you want available – birth chair, cushions or a water receptacle, for example. Indicate also what sort of conditions you would like for the birth – with lights dimmed and the room quiet, or perhaps with a favourite piece of music on a tape recorder. Talk it over with the midwife and, if necessary, phone around to find a hospital that offers everything you want.

Delivering the placenta   In a natural birth the placenta – often known as the afterbirth – is left to be delivered naturally after the baby's birth. However, most hospitals inject a drug called syntocinon to speed the process. Should you not want this, say so in your birth plan. If syntocinon is not given, then there is no immediate necessity to cut the umbilical cord, and you can wait until it stops pulsing or even until the placenta appears, if you wish.

After delivery   You can choose to hold and breastfeed your baby immediately, and to have some time in private with your partner and the baby. You may also want to bath the baby yourself soon after birth. If both mother and baby are well, you can leave hospital after just a few hours, or you can choose to stay in for a couple of days.

give support. The water's warmth tends to soothe away pain, and its buoyancy supports her weight. The water also provides a gentle transition from the womb for the baby.

Coping with pain   The first choice during a natural birth is to rely on RELAXATION AND BREATHING exercises to control pain. Simply concentrating on your breathing can have a soothing effect and is a well known MEDITATION technique. During contractions, breathe rhythmically in to a count of four and out to a count of four.

Once labour begins in earnest, your breathing pattern will change naturally, as you breathe more deeply in through the nose and out through the mouth. Practising during pregnancy will help to make this pattern familiar and natural.

Gentle MASSAGE can also be tried to ease labour pain, especially in the lower back. Downward strokes are particularly calming and soothing, but not everyone enjoys being touched during labour. For anyone anxious or worried about being unable to relax, HYPNOTHERAPY can be used to teach simple calming techniques.

Many alternative therapists are happy to attend births and, if labour is tiring, painful or slow, ACUPUNCTURE, HOMOEOPATHY or ACUPRESSURE can often help. Some hospitals can also provide transcutaneous electrical nerve stimulation (TENS) instruments for ELECTROTHERAPY. These use electrical impulses to block the body's pain signals and stimulate the production of natural painkillers called endorphins in the brain. Your doctor can advise on whether TENS is suitable for you.

Welcoming baby

A great advantage of natural childbirth is that it leaves mother and baby free from the aftereffects of drugs, and feeling well – which makes bonding more successful.

Fathers are encouraged to participate – for example, by washing and cuddling the baby soon after birth, or even by cutting the umbilical cord. The baby is generally put to its mother's breast as soon as possible. The sucking stimulates contractions of the womb so that the placenta is then expelled naturally. It also stimulates the production of milk containing colostrum, a substance rich in antibodies that give the newcomer protection from disease.

NERVE DISORDERS

Messages to and from the brain and around the body are conducted by nerves. The messages consist of electrical impulses that travel from one end of a nerve to the other and are then chemically transmitted to other nerves or to muscles. Sensory nerves carry messages to the brain or spinal cord about sensations such as PAIN, ITCHING and COLDNESS. Motor nerves deliver orders from the brain to the muscles.

Any interference with the operation of nerves can cause such symptoms as pain, numbness or paralysis. NEURALGIA is pain arising from an irritated or damaged nerve and is felt in the part of the body served by the nerve – not necessarily at the site of the problem. Neuralgia felt in an arm or leg that has been amputated is caused by the severed nerves and is known as 'phantom pain'.

Trapped nerves can also produce pain, numbness and tingling sensations in the part of the body supplied by the particular nerve. Compression of the median nerve at the wrist causes symptoms in the fingers, sometimes spreading up the arm, particularly at night (see CARPAL TUNNEL SYNDROME). Spinal problems may irritate nerve roots, causing pain in the shoulder, arm or down the back of the leg (see NECK PAIN; SCIATICA; SLIPPED DISC; LUMBAGO).

SHINGLES, caused by the CHICKENPOX virus infecting a nerve to part of the skin, produces a painful, blistering rash, especially on the chest.

Neuritis is inflammation of a nerve. Optic neuritis, for example – inflammation of the optic nerve which carries visual signals from the eye to the brain – results in temporary deterioration of sight. It can be a sign of MULTIPLE SCLEROSIS. Other types of neuritis may produce neuralgia.

Myasthenia gravis is a rare condition in which antibodies – part of the body's defensive IMMUNE SYSTEM against infection – interfere with the chemical connections between nerves and muscles. The muscles feel weak and tire easily. The eyelids droop towards the end of the day, and chewing and swallowing may be difficult.

What the therapists recommend

Herbal Medicine Infusions of rosemary or peppermint make gentle tonics. However, in individual cases herbalists may use stronger restoratives such as vervain, wild oats or St John's wort.

Naturopathy A naturopath will probably advise relaxation methods, such as YOGA and MEDITATION, as long-term self help to maintain a calm and balanced attitude. MASSAGE may also be recommended to reduce TENSION and fatigue.

Many herbal teas – for example, lemon balm or rosemary – are held to be of great value in calming and restoring nerve function, and patients may be referred to a herbal practitioner. Vitamin B taken as a supplement is said to be particularly effective for nervous exhaustion.

Biochemic Tissue Salts For nervous debility, *Kali phos.* is suggested as a nerve nutrient. *Mag. phos.* is prescribed when motor nerves are involved and there are cramps, nerve pains and twitching.

An orthodox view

To diagnose nerve disorders, a doctor may carry out nerve conduction studies by placing electrodes at different points along a nerve and measuring the passage of impulses along it. Treatment depends upon the cause.

Trapped nerves can sometimes be released by steroid injections, by surgery or, in the spine, by traction.

Prescribed early enough, antiviral drugs may reduce the pain of shingles. So-called anticholinergic medicines – which enhance the effect of chemical transmitters between nerves and muscles – help myasthenia gravis sufferers. Sometimes an operation to remove the thymus gland at the base of the neck (which influences metabolism in muscles) also provides relief.

NERVOUS DISORDERS
Anguish of the disturbed mind

The distressing complaints known as nervous or psychiatric disorders are mental problems that are serious enough to be called illnesses – as opposed to the minor psychological problems that still permit the sufferer to lead a more or less normal life. They fall into two main groups.

The first group, known as neuroses, are generally less severe, and sufferers to a large extent recognise their problem. Their responses to situations – sometimes including physical symptoms – may seem exaggerated or inappropriate to outsiders, but they remain in touch with reality.

In the second and more severe group, the psychoses, patients are cut off to a greater or lesser extent from the reality of the world around them. Not only is their behaviour irrational, but they themselves cannot see that it makes no sense.

Neuroses When normal thoughts and feelings of vulnerable individuals are exaggerated to such a degree that they interfere with daily life, the result is known as a neurosis. The most common form is an ANXIETY state. Everyone feels anxious at times, and the increased circulation of the hormone adrenaline around the body and the heightened awareness and responsiveness that it causes are a useful reaction to STRESS. A neurosis occurs when the anxiety is aroused without adequate cause, or when it is excessively severe or persistent.

Anxiety neurosis may lead to panic attacks with PALPITATIONS, shortness of breath and a sensation of imminent disaster. Other sufferers develop PHOBIAS – unreasonable fears of going outdoors (see AGORAPHOBIA), of confined spaces (CLAUSTROPHOBIA), of heights and so on.

Neurotic DEPRESSION is another excessive response to stress. Unlike psychotic depression (see below), which can occur with no apparent cause, there is usually a reason for neurotic depression – although it may not be obvious. Sufferers find everything an effort, cannot get to sleep, feel worse as the day goes on, and may have either an increased or decreased appetite.

OBSESSIVE-COMPULSIVE BEHAVIOUR is also a neurosis. As a response to stress, a sufferer's mind is preoccupied, or is unable to shake off certain thoughts or impulses. Sufferers may feel extremely anxious if, for example, ornaments are out of their usual places. Or they may feel compelled to perform rituals, such as washing their hands many times a day.

HYSTERIA is another neurotic condition, in which a person subconsciously develops symptoms of physical disease – such as paralysis of an arm or leg – or displays unusual behaviour in order to attract attention or to avoid an unpleasant situation. Unlike a malingerer, the hysteric is unaware of the true psychological cause of his or her physical symptoms.

Psychoses Unlike neuroses, psychotic illnesses often occur for no apparent reason, although they do tend to run in families. The two most common psychoses are SCHIZOPHRENIA and MANIC DEPRESSIVE DISORDER.

Psychotic people experience life in a distorted way. Schizophrenics may suffer delusions or hallucinations and can be unreasonably suspicious. Manic depressive illness produces uncontrollable mood swings, varying from profound depression to mania – a state of excessive cheerfulness and overconfidence accompanied by overactive (and often extravagant) behaviour.

Most people regarded as 'mad' are actually suffering from some form of psychotic illness. Unfortunately, some psychotics do not realise that they are ill and strongly decline all treatment.

What the therapists recommend

A number of alternative therapies offer help for sufferers of nervous disorders, particularly the less severe neuroses. For specific recommendations, see main entries on individual neuroses and psychoses.

MASSAGE

Depending on how the neurosis shows itself, such therapy – whether rhythmic and relaxing, or rapid and tonic – may have some sedative, soothing, stimulating or other psychological effect. If the neurosis is accompanied by physical symptoms, such as PAIN, the massage will aim at improving circulation, mobility, relieving spasms, or whatever the complaint may be in the affected area.

MUSIC THERAPY

The sharing of music-making between the therapist and client can encourage the expression of deep and sometimes previously unrecognised emotions. Music therapy may reduce anxiety and build up self-esteem. The cathartic (the 'cleansing' or 'purgative') effect of the music may make it much easier for patients to express their pent-up feelings.

ART THERAPY

The process of creating an image can be a valuable first step in sharing the distress of a neurotic condition. Art therapy often provides a means of uprooting buried feelings, in a process which may be described as 'dreaming on paper'. The art work can be kept and discussed either at the time of making it or later. It gives a tangible record of progress which can be useful for both the patient and therapist.

Other alternative treatments

Hypnotherapy Psychoanalysis originally made great use of hypnosis in analysing the deep causes of neurotic disorders, and, properly used, it is still held to be of great value. The therapist can use posthypnotic suggestion to instruct the patient in self-help measures that are undetectable after coming out of the trance.

Dance Movement Therapy The aim of therapists in this field is to help clients to regain contact with their deep feelings, to discover the personal resources that are needed to cope with their emotional problems and (when done in a group) to develop the ability to make positive, satisfying and lasting relationships.

Herbal Medicine Therapies vary according to the exact condition, but an infusion of camomile, lemon balm and/or lavender is held to aid relaxation. In some cases, herbalists may suggest stronger relaxants such as valerian, passion flower, skullcap or cowslip.

An orthodox view

As with physical illnesses, the treatment of nervous disorders depends on DIAGNOSIS, and this usually needs the skills of a psychiatrist (a doctor specialising in mental problems) and possibly a psychologist (a person who studies people's minds and behaviour).

Psychiatric treatment may include PSYCHOTHERAPY, drug treatment, or both. The behavioural approach (see BEHAVIOURAL THERAPY), which aims to teach patients to understand and cope with their problems, involves skilled psychologists, psychiatric nurses and counsellors in individual or group therapy sessions.

At one time, tranquillisers and sleeping pills were widely prescribed for neuroses and lesser psychological problems, but they are losing favour because of the risk of ADDICTION. However, there are non-addictive antidepressant drugs, such as amitriptyline and imipramine, which may help in the treatment of depression.

A sufferer from schizophrenia or manic depressive disorder requires skilled psychiatric help – sometimes as a hospital inpatient. If the illness is a potential danger to the sufferer's life, or to that of someone else, it may be necessary to detain the individual in hospital against his will. Treatment with antipsychotic drugs, such as chlorpromazine, haloperidol or lithium, may allow the sufferer to lead a reasonably normal life, although medical supervision and treatment may always be needed.

NEURALGIA

When pain signals reach your brain along a nerve, you sense the pain as coming from whatever part of your body is served by that nerve. If the real cause is irritation or damage to the nerve itself, anywhere along its route, the pain still seems to come from that part of your body.

For example, inflammation of the trigeminal nerve, which is a carrier of sensations and which enters the skull near the ear, produces spasmodic pain in one side of the face. This kind of pain is called neuralgia.

See also NERVE DISORDERS.

What the therapists recommend

Acupressure For trigeminal neuralgia, press inwards at the inner end of the eyebrow, or press downwards towards the jaw at the points near the corners of the mouth.

Acupuncture When the pain is acute, neuralgia is best treated every day. The points

Acupressure can relieve the pain of neuralgia. Try pressing inwards with an index finger at the inner end of the eyebrow on the affected side of the face for trigeminal neuralgia.

Alternatively, press downwards with the index fingers at the points close to the corners of the mouth. For both treatments press lightly for 5-10 minutes, and repeat half-hourly.

manipulated are on the governor, gall bladder, bladder, large intestine, stomach and liver meridians. In addition, the corresponding points on the other side of the body to that of the pain are used.

Aromatherapy Facial pain may be helped by applying, when required, a mixture of two drops of clove oil, one of basil and one of eucalyptus in a tablespoon of carrier lotion.

Biochemic Tissue Salts The principal remedy recommended is *Mag. phos.* taken every half hour until the pain subsides. *Kali phos.* is prescribed when it is accompanied by irritability or sleeplessness, and alternate *Mag. phos.* with *Ferr. phos.* when neuralgic pains are due to a fever or chill.

An orthodox view

Having diagnosed the cause, a doctor may then prescribe painkillers. Alternatively he may apply transcutaneous nerve stimulation – electrical impulses passed through the skin from a portable instrument which anaesthetise the nerve (see ELECTROTHERAPY). Another method of providing relief is a 'nerve block' – an injection of phenol into the nerve to destroy the hypersensitive fibres. Drugs normally used to treat epilepsy may reduce the pain of trigeminal neuralgia.

Many hospitals now have 'pain clinics' to provide specialist advice and treatment for sufferers from neuralgia and other chronic types of pain.

NOISE POLLUTION

Increasing noise levels are a fact of modern life, so much so that even our homes are often far from peaceful. Yet noise is not just a nuisance – doctors now know that at high levels or over long periods of time noise can be a major cause of STRESS and related problems, as well as a danger to hearing.

See HEALTH HAZARDS.

NOSE AND THROAT AILMENTS

The symptoms of a sore throat and a blocked nose have many different causes. Viral and bacterial infections are responsible for COLDS, LARYNGITIS, TONSILLITIS, ADENOIDS and QUINSY. HAY FEVER, on the other hand, is a seasonal allergy to grass and other pollens.

Laryngitis often results in temporary hoarseness, but if prolonged it may be caused by polyps or 'singer's nodes' on the vocal cords, particularly if the voice is abused.

A NOSEBLEED can be caused by injury or infection, but most commonly it just happens for no clear reason.

Cleft palate – a readily seen gap in the roof of the mouth – may be associated with a hare lip, and is present from birth. The baby has difficulty sucking from the breast or bottle, and will go on to develop a characteristic speech impediment.

What the therapists recommend
AROMATHERAPY

Self help For CATARRH and a blocked-up nose, mix four drops of eucalyptus oil with the same amount of cajeput and half the amount of peppermint, and inhale either from a kitchen tissue or a basin of warm water (see p. 37) – provided you are not asthmatic. Diluted in a carrier oil or lotion, this mixture can be applied to the outside of the nose for immediate relief.

For a runny nose, mix three drops of eucalyptus with equal quantities of cypress and lemon oil, and inhale from a kitchen tissue. However, do not do this if you suffer from ASTHMA.

To relieve a sore throat, try three drops of eucalyptus, one of tea tree and two of sandalwood oil, either gargled in a glass of water or mixed in a tablespoon of carrier oil or lotion and rubbed around the throat and behind the ears. Do it three times during the day and before retiring at night.

The same techniques can be used with various oils from eucalyptus, aniseed, camphor, hyssop, cedarwood and cinnamon to ease a cough. Two drops each of thyme, sage and geranium oil can soothe swollen glands.

Other alternative treatments

Naturopathy For many problems such as nasal congestion and catarrh, or recurrent throat infections, you are advised to avoid dairy produce and sugars and eat more fresh fruit and vegetables. Vitamin C can be helpful – a gram a day for a short period, then half that amount in the long term – for chronic catarrh or infection.

Herbal Medicine Gargles of tincture of sage, thyme or myrrh can ease sore throats. Catarrh is relieved by steam inhalations (see p. 37), using one or two drops of the essential oils of eucalyptus, pine, cypress and lavender. Infusions (see p. 184) of catmint can help to clear a blocked-up nose.

An orthodox view

Most nose and throat ailments eventually clear up by themselves, so although antibiotics are sometimes given to speed recovery

from a bacterial infection, most doctors recommend just rest and simple home remedies, such as inhalants, camphor oil and nasal sprays.

Serious or continual problems, however, require other medical treatment. For recurrent tonsillitis or swollen adenoids, and also nasal polyps, surgery may be the answer. And through plastic surgery most babies with a cleft palate can now develop normally.

NOSEBLEED

Many people, especially the young and middle-aged, occasionally suffer from bleeding from one or both nostrils. The bleeding usually comes from the superficial blood vessels just inside the nostril, on the septum, which divides the nose in two.

Nosebleeds can be caused by COLDS, HYPERTENSION, SINUS PROBLEMS, blood disorders, injury, nose-picking, or SNEEZING, but sometimes occur without obvious cause. In most cases, they stop within an hour.

What the therapists recommend
TRADITIONAL MEDICINE

Self help Most nosebleeds can be stopped by the sufferer sitting upright in a chair with the head tilted slightly forward and firmly pinching the soft part of the nose for at least 15 minutes. Any blood that goes down the back of the nose should be swallowed or spat out. Breathe through the mouth. If the bleeding restarts, squeeze the nose for a further 15 minutes. An ice-pack applied to the bridge of the nose may help to reduce bleeding.

NATUROPATHY

For persistent nosebleeds, a general investigation of health, including BLOOD PRESSURE, may be required. If there is swelling over the nose, an ice-cold compress may help. Causes such as severe CATARRH or sinus congestion will call for treatment through diet, supplements and, perhaps, inhalations, although excessive heat is not desirable in recurrent nosebleeds, so seek advice.

An orthodox view

If a nosebleed does not stop, the sufferer – especially if he is elderly or feeling faint – should consult his GP. The doctor may numb the nose with a local anaesthetic and pack it with gauze or an inflatable balloon. He may then take the patient's blood pressure to check for hypertension, and test the blood to see if there is any underlying cause for the bleeding. He may also cauterise any blood vessels that are prone to bleed.

OBESITY

In Britain, about one adult in three is obese. Seriously overweight people have an above-average chance of developing any of several diseases, including high BLOOD PRESSURE, CIRCULATION PROBLEMS, DIABETES, gall bladder problems, GOUT, HEART DISORDERS and heart attack. They also may not live as long as slim people, and their excess weight may damage joints, causing OSTEOARTHRITIS, particularly of the knees and hips.

Obesity is caused by eating more food and drink than the body can use up in energy. The surplus energy is then stored as fat. See SLIMMING THE NATURAL WAY.

What the therapists recommend

NATUROPATHY
Consultation Individual treatment is considered vital, because a number of factors can combine to create the problem. Differences in metabolic rates are believed to be largely responsible, but emotional, psychological and social pressures will need to be assessed.

Generally, a simple crash diet is held _not_ to be the answer to obesity, as it can lead eventually to weight gain as the metabolic rate slows even further.

A naturopath's advice will be that increasing EXERCISE at the same time as changing diet is important for speeding up metabolism. Multivitamin tablets may be prescribed to help replace any lost nutrients.

HOMOEOPATHY
Consultation Practitioners stress that there is no such thing as a 'wonder cure', but that constitutional help can be of value. A change of eating habits and extra exercise will be recommended.
Self help For the type of person who is flabby and inclined to perspire a lot, _Calc. carb._ may prove helpful, especially if he is depressed and has cravings for foods, particularly eggs. If there is WATER RETENTION, try _Natrum mur._ in the 6th potency twice daily for three weeks.

DANCE MOVEMENT THERAPY
Consultation Therapy will not be aimed directly at reducing weight (though it may help) but at aiding understanding of how your body is expressing itself, and allowing you to discover and work through underlying feelings relevant to your weight problem. Alternatively, you may be taught how to come to terms with your weight and shape, and achieve a more harmonious relationship with your body.

Other alternative treatments
Acupuncture Treatment is aimed at reducing the heightened appetite that springs from a weakened stomach-spleen system, by restoring the 'energy' flow along the spleen meridian. Points on the stomach, spleen, heart and lung meridians may be treated. Treating ear points is said to help overcome cravings for food. MOXIBUSTION, or the healing use of burning herbs, may also be used.
T'ai-chi Ch'uan Over a period of time, the exercises should tend to streamline the body. The everyday use of T'ai-chi's principles of balance, creativity and harmony should also reduce the urge to overeat and produce feelings of well-being.

An orthodox view
Most doctors will advise obese patients to lose weight by eating a balanced diet in moderate proportions (see EATING FOR HEALTH). Weight-losing drugs are not usually prescribed as they can become addictive and have dangerous side effects. Exercise is another effective way of losing and keeping down weight.

OBSESSIVE-COMPULSIVE BEHAVIOUR
Therapy for obstinate ideas and irrational acts

Obsessions are thoughts that are persistent, intrusive and difficult to control. Compulsions are actions and habits that a person feels driven to perform, and these, too, are usually persistent, difficult to stop and often unwanted. The two are often associated, and are then known medically as obsessive-compulsive behaviour.

Most people develop particular habits or routines at an early age. Sometimes these are based on superstitions such as touching a lucky horseshoe or always stepping over cracks in the pavement. Often they become parts of daily routine – dressing in a particular order, for example. Other actions are based on safety or security, and these include repeatedly making sure that the car doors are locked before leaving it, or checking that the cooker is switched off before going out. Sometimes a particular thought or idea, such as a certain tune or a reminder to do something, keeps running through the mind.

Most of these thoughts and behaviour

patterns are acceptable because they are not unduly worrying or disruptive in daily life; they are, in fact, fairly rational and sensible – or at least harmless. However, in some people thoughts and actions get exaggerated and out of control, and become a problem.

In most cases, obsessive-compulsive behaviour is associated with strong feelings of ANXIETY. The anxiety may be based on a fear that something bad or untoward will happen if the thoughts and actions are not carried through. The sufferer may think that if he fails to keep himself and his house scrupulously clean, he will catch some infection or disease. He may feel compelled to wash his hands, body, clothes and all surfaces in the house repeatedly and thoroughly.

If he does not do this, he becomes increasingly anxious and uncomfortable, until eventually the need to engage in these activities overwhelms him, and he gives in. Other sufferers repeatedly check that doors and windows are locked, or arrange objects and ornaments in particular order. Others avoid certain objects, places or situations, or repeatedly check that they have not dropped or mislaid something.

The fear or anxiety may be logical. For example, it is reasonable to fear that if a gas fire is left on, it may start a blaze. However, the fear may lead to an irrational action – one that is not necessary or helpful – such as constantly checking that the gas fire is off.

Obsessional thoughts are also usually based on anxiety or FEAR. The obsessional person may repeatedly recite lists or numbers. If particularly anxious about his physical well-being, he may mentally run through a lengthy and involved checklist, making sure that every part of his body is all right. Some obsessional thoughts arise from the fear that something repulsive or abhorrent may be done, such as typing swear words into a letter, or standing up in church to blaspheme, or hitting someone, or performing some indecent act in public.

If unchecked, obsessive-compulsive behaviour can lead to a very disrupted life, and even to serious illness – mental disorders such as DEPRESSION and physical maladies such as malnutrition, for example.

Treatment in severe cases is difficult and should be left to professionals. However, one or two alternative therapies have proved helpful, and PSYCHOTHERAPY – particularly BEHAVIOURAL THERAPY – has been shown to be of some benefit in alleviating and controlling the condition.

What the therapists recommend
ART THERAPY
Self help This can be helpful in enabling a patient to 'let go' of some of the underlying fear, TENSION and anger, which lead to

ritualistic behaviour. The resulting art work, however simple, provides a channel for communication and an outlet for deeply repressed anger. Using modelling clay, or other malleable materials, can be particularly helpful in the safe release of emotion.

BEHAVIOURAL THERAPY

Consultation Repeated thoughts and actions are seen as short-term ways of dealing with fear and anxiety. The therapist aims to teach the sufferer to manage his anxiety in more productive ways – for instance, by relaxation training. Response prevention is also part of the treatment: the client is encouraged not to repeat the thought or action, so discovering that nothing bad or untoward will happen – that, in fact, his irrational fears do not come true.

AUTOGENIC TRAINING

Consultation Obsessional conditions are usually difficult to overcome, but autogenic training has a lot to offer for those with this kind of problem. In the hands of an experienced practitioner, great progress is said to be made in many cases.

Other alternative treatment

Colour Therapy The practitioner may find that old, unresolved difficulties are at the root of the problem, and very careful COUNSELLING is required to go over and try to break through the patterns formed in the mind of the client. This may be difficult, since the obsessive-compulsive behaviour is often rooted in the subconscious.

It may manifest itself in small, stupid, harmless actions at which most people might laugh – or, at the other end of the scale, as serious crime. Counselling with colour has, it is claimed, shown that a soft magenta, along with relaxation, given by an experienced, professional practitioner, can turn what may be a vicious circle into a spiral of growth. Tactful recognition of the self – through the counsellor – is vital. Relaxation, colour, music and counselling are said to prove very successful.

An orthodox view

An obsessional personality is unlikely to change and does not require treatment. But if it leads to depression, doctors can help by diagnosing and explaining the problem and, if necessary, prescribing antidepressant medicines. Severe obsessive-compulsive behaviour is difficult to treat, although it naturally improves in time. The results of medicines and psychotherapy tend to be disappointing, so successful management of the condition depends upon the sufferer adjusting his way of life to reduce or eliminate the stresses that caused the problem.

ORGONE THERAPY

The idea that there is a universal energy present in all living creatures, in the atmosphere, in all matter and even in space was the theory behind orgone therapy. The treatment was developed in the first half of this century by Wilhelm Reich (1897-1958), an Austrian psychiatrist and follower of Freud, and it formed a part of REICHIAN THERAPY.

According to Reich, this force – which he called 'orgone energy' – is stored in units termed 'bions'. These, he said, can be trapped in machines known as 'orgone accumulators' and then used to help to heal diseases.

Reich achieved some remarkable results, but his controversial ideas brought him into conflict with the medical and legal authorities in the USA, where he had gone to practise – and where he died in prison. People objected to his linking of orgone energy with orgasm and sexual fulfilment, and in particular to his claims that patients placed in boxes containing orgone accumulators could be cured of CANCER and other serious diseases.

Although much of Reich's equipment and many of his papers were destroyed after his death, some European therapists have recently started to use orgone therapy again. Sometimes they include so-called 'vegetotherapy' which, like BIOENERGETICS, is a more widely accepted technique based on Reich's idea that muscular tensions – particularly of the abdomen – and unnatural breathing patterns can be signs of emotional problems. By manipulating the body, therapists aim to relieve both physical and psychological tensions.

See also HUMANISTIC PSYCHOLOGY.

ORIENTAL DIAGNOSIS
Clues in the pulse and on the tongue

Like Western doctors, traditional oriental practitioners begin every consultation by trying to identify the patient's problem. However, since they have a very different view of how the healthy body functions and of what causes disease, they rely on completely different methods of DIAGNOSIS.

Most of the oriental techniques come from traditional Chinese medicine, which views good health as a state of harmony between YIN AND YANG – stages in the processes of change that constantly occur in the body – and balance in the body's energy, or Qi (chi).

Qi is said to flow along an invisible network of pathways called MERIDIANS that link all bodily organs and systems. Any blockage or imbalance in the network is believed to cause physical or mental illness. The purpose of diagnosis in oriental therapies such as ACUPUNCTURE, ACUPRESSURE and SHIATSU is to identify any trouble spots or blockages on the meridians, so that appropriate treatment can be given.

A variety of sophisticated techniques are used to make the diagnosis, many going back thousands of years. As well as asking questions about the patient's symptoms, history, habits and way of life, the practitioner makes careful notes about the sound of the voice, texture and colour of the skin, breathing patterns, posture and even smell.

All are used together to build up a detailed picture of the person's health, but most weight is given to two particular procedures: pulse diagnosis and tongue diagnosis.

Pulse diagnosis At least 12 different pulses are usually measured in Chinese medicine, corresponding to the major organs and systems of the body.

The practitioner finds them by pressing lightly with three fingers – each of which can detect a different pulse – along the artery on the inside of the wrist. Different pulses are measured by pressing a little deeper, and the procedure is then repeated on the other wrist, giving a total of 12 pulses. Medium pressure is sometimes used to read six more pulses that are believed to reflect the energy level of the blood.

Each pulse is interpreted in terms of 28 different qualities or descriptions – such as 'rapid', 'slippery', 'choppy', 'full', 'scattered' and 'empty'. On the basis of these interpretations and the strength or weakness of each pulse, the practitioner decides where energy imbalances lie and how to correct them. Using deduction, based on their observation of signs and symptoms, skilled practitioners claim to find evidence of past diseases and can suggest the likelihood of any future health problems.

The pulses are said also to be affected by factors other than illness, such as time of day, season, nervousness and physical exertion. An experienced practitioner will be aware of all these influences and able to link them to information about the patient's state of health.

Tongue diagnosis Practitioners consider the colour, shape and coating of the tongue as well as how moist or dry it is, whether it has surface markings, such as cracks or 'thorns', and whether there are any scars or ulcers on it.

Different parts of the tongue are examined

to provide information about different organs. For example, a bluish-purple tip is said to show a particular energy state in the heart, and teeth marks around the edge may indicate a digestion problem.

A light white coating is considered to be normal, but a thicker grey, yellow or white 'fur' to show some disturbance. A healthy tongue should be slightly moist, indicating that body fluids are flowing freely; if it is too dry or too moist, an imbalance is diagnosed.

The exact type of imbalance is decided by considering other signs such as whether the tongue is cracked, swollen, stiff or quivering, together with all the other information obtained from the patient.

ORTHOMOLECULAR MEDICINE

The term was first used by the American biochemist and double Nobel prizewinner Linus Pauling (1901–), to describe treatment centred on giving individuals the best possible concentrations of vitamins and minerals for their physical and mental health. Individual needs for these nutrients vary widely, he said, and doses recommended could be dozens or even hundreds of times greater than the amounts generally thought suitable. Such treatment is now called MEGAVITAMIN THERAPY.

OSTEOARTHRITIS

Wear and tear on the joints, which eventually damages shock-absorbing cartilage between the bones, is the usual cause of this condition. Symptoms include pain, stiffness and deformed joints, and affect mainly the hips, knees, spine and fingers. See ARTHRITIS.

OSTEOPATHY
Your skeleton key to fitness . . .

The body's largest system is its framework of bones, joints, muscles and ligaments. It is this framework that allows us to walk, run, drive, speak, write, build, play sports – in fact, carry out any physical activity. Osteopathy, one of the most widely used of all the

Andrew Taylor Still

Making the body's machine run smoothly

An American doctor, Andrew Taylor Still (1828-1917), founded osteopathy in the mid-1870s after he became dissatisfied with orthodox medicine. He felt that stimulating the body's natural powers of self healing would be preferable to using the often dangerous drugs of his day.

His detailed knowledge of human anatomy, combined with his earlier study of engineering, made him interested in the body as a machine. He became certain that many illnesses arise when part of the body's structure gets out of alignment. Manipulation could, he decided, restore the balance and cure the illness.

Strong initial opposition to Still's ideas gradually dwindled in the United States, and now osteopathy is an accepted part of established medicine. Most modern research into osteopathy has been carried out in the United States, which now has 15 osteopathic medical schools and some 20,000 osteopathic physicians.

Osteopathy came to Britain at the turn of the century, and the British School of Osteopathy was established in London in 1917 by Dr Martin Littlejohn, one of Still's pupils. Today the school is one of the three accredited British training schools, but there are still only about 1400 registered osteopaths in Britain.

complementary forms of medicine, aims to diagnose and treat mechanical problems in the framework.

These problems may be caused by injury or STRESS, for example, and they prevent the framework from functioning comfortably and efficiently. Osteopaths believe that when the structure of the body is sound, it will work just like a well-tuned engine, with the minimum of wear and tear.

Standing upright imposes a great and constant strain on the mechanism. The force of gravity is particularly severe on the vertebrae of the spine and the cushioning discs between them. The spinal joints and their

discs have become weight-bearing in the upright position, a burden which poor posture increases, so making mechanical problems more likely to occur. Osteopaths use their hands for massaging and manipulating the framework to restore normal, more comfortable function.

Who it can help People with spinal problems, such as low BACK PAIN and NECK PAIN, account for more than half of an osteopath's workload. But practitioners also bring relief to mechanical problems in many other parts of the body – often resulting from stresses at work. TENSION headaches caused by contraction of the small muscles at the base of the skull are another problem frequently treated by osteopaths.

Many patients have sustained SPORTS INJURIES to muscles or to the joints of the hips, knees, ankles, feet, wrists, shoulders or elbows. Older people suffering the onset of OSTEOARTHRITIS can also find treatment beneficial. During PREGNANCY many women develop back pain because of a change in posture, and they, too, can often be helped by osteopathic treatment.

Finding a practitioner The General Council and Register of Osteopaths (GCRO) was established in 1936 on the recommendation of the health minister to produce a register of qualified osteopaths. The GCRO monitors the training and ethics in practice of its members, who can put the letters MRO (Member of the Register of Osteopaths) after their names and use the title registered osteopath. They have successfully completed a four-year full-time degree or diploma course at one of the three osteopathic colleges accredited and monitored by the GCRO.

Osteopathic treatment is not readily available on the National Health Service, but general practitioners are increasingly referring their patients to registered osteopaths. The patient will be asked to pay a fee, which can vary from one practitioner to another. However, most private medical insurance schemes cover fees for treatment carried out by a registered osteopath.

You can ask at your local doctor's surgery whether patients are referred to a particular osteopath in the area. If you cannot get advice there, look in _Yellow Pages_ for the names of registered osteopaths; or ask for a list from the General Council and Register of Osteopaths, 56 London Street, Reading, Berkshire RG1 4SQ.

Consulting a practitioner The osteopath will first want to know how your symptoms began and what makes them better or worse. Your medical history and any current treatments you may be receiving will be noted.

Then the practitioner will carry out a detailed physical examination. He will observe you standing, sitting, lying down and

Self help on wheels

Car drivers often have a poor and restricted posture behind the wheel, which can lead to back pain, stiffness in the neck and shoulders, and tension headaches. To help people avoid these discomforts – and so take the 'pain' out of driving – osteopaths suggest a set of procedures which are easy to follow and put into practice.

Make sure that the car seat is adjusted so that the steering wheel and pedals are all within easy reach. You should be sitting up straight with your knees slightly bent but not so bent that they interfere with the steering wheel. To remind you to sit up straight, every time you get in the car make sure that your bottom is as far back in the seat as possible. Then straighten up and, if necessary, adjust the rear-view mirror to your needs.

As your hands hold the steering wheel (preferably at between nine and ten o'clock and at between two and three o'clock, if you imagine the wheel as a clock face), your arms should be slightly bent. Adjust the seat to lean very slightly back, as this will make it easier for you to maintain a well-balanced and comfortable position for your neck and back.

If you do have a back problem, you can buy or make a simple lumbar roll to tuck behind you and support the curve of your lower back. This will help to prevent strain being placed on your spine and shoulders.

When you are driving, check from time to time that your shoulders are relaxed. Keep your head upright with your chin tucked in; if it juts forward, the muscles at the back of your neck are under strain.

There are several relaxation exercises that you can do in a traffic jam or at traffic lights:
1 Shrug your shoulders towards your ears and then roll them backwards with your head bent slightly forward. Repeat two or three times.
2 Tighten and relax your stomach muscles two or three times – you can do this while you are driving as well as at stops. It improves your posture and helps circulation in the legs.
3 Tuck your chin close to your chest and then relax it back to normal. Repeat this several times and you will feel the muscles at the back of your neck stretching gently.

performing certain movements such as bending forwards, backwards and to the side. The range and quality of movement in particular joints will be assessed, and the osteopath will examine by touch the soft tissues, muscles and ligaments to see if they are abnormally tense or stressed.

During this 'structural survey' the osteopath diagnoses any abnormalities in the body's framework, which may be confirmed by other tests, such as the conventional testing of reflexes with a small hammer. In some cases an osteopath will ask for an X-ray, particularly if there has been a recent accident or major health crisis.

Treating an injured knee

Sports injuries account for many joint problems, and here a patient is examined by an osteopath after twisting a knee while playing tennis. By making a 'structural survey' of the problem area, the practitioner diagnoses the extent of the injury. He also asks the patient for her full medical history – in particular, if she has previously suffered any pain or discomfort in the knee.

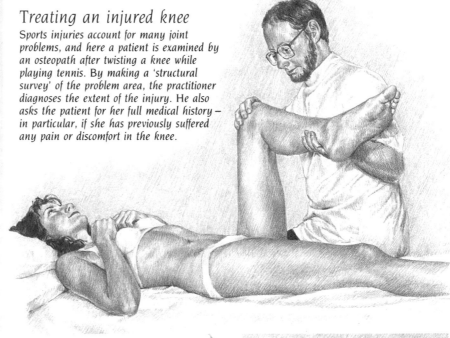

If the examination shows that your condition is suitable for treatment, a course will be planned. If not, the osteopath may recommend that you see your doctor again. Length of treatment by an osteopath varies enormously. It may last over several sessions for a long-standing condition, but a recent, acute problem may be relieved immediately.

A treatment session usually lasts 20-30 minutes, and most people find it relaxing and enjoyable. Several techniques may be used. MASSAGE of soft tissue relaxes taut muscles and improves circulation. Gentle, repetitive movement of joints increases their mobility and reduces tension in surrounding muscles.

After assessing the damage – and deciding that the patient is a suitable case for treatment – the osteopath sets to work on the injured knee. He manipulates the malfunctioning joint back into working order and guides it through its normal range of pain-free movement. In addition, the gentle manipulation of the joint eases tension that has built up in the nearby muscles.

Fixed or malfunctioning joints may be released by guiding the joint rapidly through its normal range of movement. This produces the clicking that many people associate with osteopathic treatment. EXERCISE, advice on posture, and relaxation techniques are often recommended; patients implement these at home between treatment sessions.

For some conditions, including head and facial pain, CRANIAL OSTEOPATHY may be used. This involves applying gentle pressures to the head and upper neck. Areas where there is strain or where movement is restricted are held painlessly at the point of tension until the condition is relieved.

An orthodox view

Many doctors recognise the benefits of osteopathy for people suffering from mechanical problems and strains. More and more general practitioners refer patients to registered osteopaths, and some doctors have themselves taken postgraduate osteopathy courses accredited by the GCRO. There are now more than 40 doctors in Britain who are also qualified as registered osteopaths.

Conventional doctors would dispute the value of osteopathy for patients with non-mechanical symptoms. They see correct diagnosis by a qualified medical practitioner as essential before it can be decided whether osteopathy is the right treatment.

OSTEOPOROSIS
Thinning and weakening of the bones

Women who are past the MENOPAUSE are the principal sufferers of this disorder, in which the bones become progressively thinner, weaker and more brittle – due in part to loss of calcium in the bones. Osteoporosis can, however, begin to affect people who are in their mid-twenties.

The spine gradually becomes shorter and more curved, resulting in loss of height and the characteristic hunching of the shoulders often known as 'dowager's hump'. The brittle bones are easily broken, especially at the hip or wrist, even by minor injuries or normal everyday activities (see FRACTURES).

Although persistent BACK PAIN is common, there are often no warning symptoms and the condition is sometimes discovered in its early stages only if an X-ray is taken for some other reason. Osteoporosis can be caused by prolonged treatment by steroid drugs and is aggravated by lack of EXERCISE or insufficient care over diet.

What the therapists recommend

Yoga Practitioners believe that osteoporosis – and other bone problems – can be combatted by more efficient breathing. Diaphragmatic breathing is said to help the body to deal with changes in bone structure. In addition, relaxation techniques are employed to help ease the condition.

T'ai-chi Ch'uan The graceful movements of T'ai-chi help patients to adapt to changes in their bodies and to maintain a positive and creative outlook. This is particularly important in middle age, when diseases such as osteoporosis may occur and the female body is undergoing disturbing hormonal changes. T'ai-chi is said to promote the use of mental, emotional and physical energies, helping the patient to function normally.

Naturopathy Regular exercise is thought to be essential in preventing osteoporosis, or stopping the condition worsening. Plenty of protein is recommended, and a wholefood diet with additional seeds such as sesame and sunflower, nuts, grains and pulses will probably be suggested. Calcium and vitamin D may also be prescribed.

Homoeopathy Consultation with a therapist is recommended, for individual treatment including advice on diet and exercise.

An orthodox view

Doctors recommend regular exercise to prevent the onset of osteoporosis – although once the disease has taken hold it increases slowly with age.

The most successful conventional treatment is hormone replacement therapy (HRT; see MENOPAUSE), which can alleviate osteoporosis if taken for several years. It is particularly effective for women who reach the menopause before the age of 45. However, in some cases it can have unwanted and occasionally serious side effects.

OVARIAN PROBLEMS

A woman has two ovaries in the lower abdomen, one on either side of the womb. They produce eggs (ova) almost every month from the commencement of monthly periods until periods stop at the MENOPAUSE. Sometimes the ovaries are painful at the mid-point of the menstrual cycle when they release eggs, and this is known as ovulation pain.

Growths on or in the ovaries are usually benign, but are occasionally malignant (see CANCER). Fluid-filled swellings called cysts are common. The vast majority are small and benign, and may persist for years without symptoms. Others cause intermittent pain in the lower abdomen, often during menstruation or ovulation. Some ovarian cysts become very large, and others twist, rupture or bleed, causing severe pain and sickness.

Consult your doctor immediately if there is any pain or swelling in the lower abdomen, or if pain is felt during sexual intercourse – as this could indicate the presence of cysts.

The ovaries also release female hormones into the bloodstream. Imbalance of these hormones can cause various symptoms, including INFERTILITY and PREMENSTRUAL TENSION (PMT). The organs naturally cease to produce hormones at the menopause, and this sometimes leads to OSTEOPOROSIS.

What the therapists recommend

Naturopathy Practitioners consider that poor functioning of the ovaries can be a result of poor general health, STRESS, long-term use of the contraceptive pill, and other factors. Serious disorders such as ovarian cysts require qualified help. But for general disorders which can cause PERIOD PROBLEMS, improvements to diet and EXERCISE levels are advised. These are aimed at benefiting the reproductive system and general well-being.

Herbal Medicine Many herbs have hormonal effects. A professional herbalist may use chaste tree, false unicorn root, blue cohosh or wild yam, among others, to restore ovarian activity to normal.

Aromatherapy If you suspect that the problem is hormonal, the essential oils recommended are: clary sage, true melissa, lemon, pine and orange. Mix a total of four to six drops in a tablespoon of carrier oil, and massage into the abdomen and small of the back each night and morning.

An orthodox view

The doctor can examine the ovaries and feel any growths or cysts by performing an internal pelvic examination through the vagina. He may recommend an ultrasound scan, in which very high frequency sound waves are passed through the body to build up a picture rather as an X-ray does, or a laparoscopic examination, in which internal structures are examined with a lighted instrument passed through a small cut in the abdominal wall. These will usually reveal whether a growth is benign or cancerous. If necessary, growths can then be removed by surgery.

A doctor may recommend a blood test for hormone levels at a certain point in the menstrual cycle in order to diagnose hormonal problems or the cause of infertility. Hormone treatment, usually taken by tablet or suppository, may restore fertility or relieve symptoms of PMT.

PAIN
Nature's early warning system

The first indication of an unseen malady within the body is usually pain – a natural early warning system. This unpleasant – at times agonising – sensation afflicts most people at some time as a result of injury, disease or emotional disorder. Yet pain can at times be of great benefit to the body.

It tells the brain to take avoiding action against whatever is causing the pain. This is usually an involuntary action, as when your hand jerks away when pricked by a pin, or when you touch something very hot. It thus prevents further injury.

Though the sufferer finds pain all too real, it is often difficult to describe. However, it is important to try, for a description will help a therapist or doctor to make a DIAGNOSIS.

Continuous throbbing pain indicates swelling or inflammation in a restricted space, as in a carbuncle or tooth abscess. Intermittent stabbing pain results from the stretching or swelling of a tube-like part of the body such as the intestine. In certain cases, such as ANGINA and gangrene, disruption of the blood supply produces continuous severe pain in the affected part. Burning pain is felt when heat, friction or chemicals destroy body tissues. A dull continuous ache can signal strained muscles and ligaments.

Exactly where you feel the pain is also important in diagnosis – it may not necessarily be felt at the site of the actual injury or disease. This 'referred pain', as it is known, can be felt down the left arm and fingers in some HEART DISORDERS, for example, while an abscess under the diaphragm gives pain in the shoulder.

The pain threshold Tests have shown that the 'pain threshold' – the point during the painful stimulus at which pain is first felt – is roughly the same among all ordinary, healthy people. On the other hand, the 'pain tolerance' point, when pain becomes unpleasant, varies greatly.

However, several factors, other than the immediate cause of pain, can influence the threshold. Illness, hunger, extremes of climatic temperature, swings in temperature and pain caused by another condition all work to lower the threshold, giving greater pain. For example, many arthritics find their pain worse in spring and autumn, when swings in temperature are at their greatest.

Psychological conditions, including worry, FEAR, ANXIETY, fatigue, STRESS, DEPRESSION and INSOMNIA all play a similar role. For

instance, a pain often gets worse as the day progresses, and your tiredness increases.

Other psychological factors work in the opposite way to raise the threshold and ease the pain. When you believe strongly that a pain will get better, it often does; and faith in your doctor, therapist or treatment to make it better may have the same effect. And so do concentration of the mind, and emotions such as happiness and excitement. You may be so absorbed in catching your train that you fail to notice that your shoes are giving you blisters. Then there are the physical pain relievers, such as analgesics, anaesthetics, and a host of conventional and alternative remedies and treatments.

However, all practitioners are only too aware that pain is often an early warning that something is wrong, whether it is a physical problem or an emotional condition, such as hypochondria or PSYCHOSOMATIC ILLNESS, and will aim to diagnose and treat the root cause. Sufferers should bear this in mind too – if a pain persists, see a doctor.

Killing pain the natural way The body produces its own powerful painkillers. Endorphins and encephalins are examples – proteins occurring naturally in the brain which have effects similar to those induced by opiates. The body synthesises them from amino acids in the proteins in your diet.

Dopamine and the so-called stress hormones adrenaline and noradrenaline, which are produced by the adrenal glands, are similar proteins. Their release is triggered by stress and EXERCISE, and can prove very effective. For example, a rugby player may not become aware that he has been injured until an exciting and strenuous game is over; and many wounded people have little or no pain at the time of their injury. The hormones can also relieve chronic (long-lasting) pain.

Dopamine and the hormones are produced by the body from the amino acid phenylalanine or DL-phenylalanine (DLPA). The body cannot synthesise this, and it is an 'essential amino acid' – one that must be provided by the diet. Cheese, nuts such as peanuts and almonds, avocados, bananas, lima beans, herrings, and sesame and pumpkin seeds are good dietary sources.

Like vitamins and minerals, DLPA is available as a dietary supplement from health shops. However, you should follow the manufacturer's instructions carefully, and ask your doctor about taking the supplement if you are pregnant or are being treated for high BLOOD PRESSURE. You should not take DLPA if you suffer from MIGRAINE, are taking tyrosine as a supplement, or are taking certain drugs used to treat depression.

Besides the therapies covered below, the following may also help to relieve your pain: VISUALISATION THERAPY, OSTEOPATHY, HYP-

NOTHERAPY, PSYCHOTHERAPY, AUTOGENIC TRAINING, BIOFEEDBACK, YOGA, RELAXATION AND BREATHING, HEALERS AND HEALING, and HOMOEOPATHY. Different ones will benefit different people and different types of pain.

What the therapists recommend
The therapists investigate and treat the condition causing the pain. For the pain itself they recommend the following:

ACUPRESSURE
Self help For general pain, apply pressure in the hollow behind the outer ankle bone, pressing inwards and a little towards the ankle bone. For pain in the upper body, apply pressure at the end of the crease in the web between the finger and thumb, pressing towards the finger bone. For pain in the lower body, apply pressure one hand's width above the crown of the inner ankle bone just behind the shin bone, pressing inwards beside the bone.

AROMATHERAPY
Self help For muscular pain, use six to eight drops of essential oil in a bath, and stay in it for ten minutes. Choose two or three oils from the following: camphor, cajuput, eucalyptus, ginger, juniper, lavender, marjoram, rosemary or sage, all of which warm and relax painful tissues. A most effective application lotion can be made by using a total of 15 drops in 5 dessertspoons (50ml) of a base carrier lotion or carrier oil. Apply night and morning or as required on the affected part.

For stomach pain, apply a teaspoon of carrier oil or lotion mixed with two drops of fennel and two drops of peppermint if due to indigestion. If it is due to constipation or wind, substitute two drops of rosemary for the peppermint. A nervous stomach will respond better to aniseed and basil.

For period pains, use oils of Roman camomile, true melissa and rose otto. These are expensive, but you can use less-expensive oils mixed with them. However, if you do use them, mix a few drops of each together in a dropper bottle for ease of application and enhanced results. Alternatively, use cajuput, sage, aniseed, cypress and marjoram. Apply the mixed lotion or oil to the abdomen and small of the back twice a day, from the tenth day before the period is due to start.

Other alternative treatments
Herbal Medicine Several herbs can reduce the level of pain. Some such as meadowsweet and willow bark are similar to aspirin. Others such as wild yam and black cohosh have a steroidal effect. If an infusion of meadowsweet and camomile does not give relief, seek qualified help for the problem.
Massage It is instinctive to rub a part of the

body when it hurts, so do this initially if it helps to lessen the pain. However, in some painful situations, massage would definitely be inadvisable, and the therapist will decide whether this is so when making a diagnosis.

Acupuncture A point on the large intestine meridian and other distal points are used for the rapid relief of pain.

An orthodox view

Doctors aim to find the root cause of the pain and treat it, or refer patients to a specialist consultant. They have a battery of drugs at their disposal. Mild pain usually responds well to non-narcotic drugs such as aspirin, which can also relieve inflammation. This can cause irritation of the stomach lining, but the use of soluble aspirin and taking it with or after food – never on an empty stomach – helps to some degree. Paracetamol does not have this side effect, but it does not relieve inflammation, and an overdose – even a small one – can cause severe liver damage.

Narcotic drugs that dull the senses and induce sleep are prescribed for more severe pain. Many of them, like codeine, are opium derivatives, and most can lead to ADDICTION.

Always follow very carefully the manufacturer's instructions on dosage for over-the-counter painkillers, and tell your doctor what you have taken if you consult him later.

Anti-inflammatory drugs ease arthritic and rheumatic pain. Apart from aspirin these fall into two groups: steroids and non-steroidal anti-inflammatory drugs (NSAIDs), such as ibuprofen. One or two of these, such as ibuprofen (Nurofen), are available without prescription. The side effects of steroids include increased appetite, weight gain, digestive disorders, NAUSEA AND VOMITING and change in sleep patterns. NSAIDs may cause DIARRHOEA, gastrointestinal irritation and bleeding, and HEADACHES. If you experience any such side effects, see your doctor at once; another drug may suit you better.

A further group of drugs reduce the formation of uric acid and are prescribed for GOUT pains. Side effects include digestive upsets with stomach pains, nausea, vomiting and loss of appetite, and itching or rashes.

See also ULCERS, INDIGESTION and TOOTH AND GUM DISORDERS.

PALPITATIONS

Healthy people are usually conscious of their heartbeat after strenuous exercise – such as running for a bus, or up a flight of stairs – or while experiencing ANXIETY or FEAR. Awareness of the heart beating at other times, known as palpitations, may sometimes be a sign of heart disease. There are three main types of palpitations: rapid heartbeat, irregular heartbeat, and extra heartbeat.

If you have prolonged or persistent palpitations, you should see a doctor before undertaking any alternative therapy.

Rapid heartbeat, or tachycardia, can be a sign of an overactive thyroid gland (see THYROID DISORDERS), and may occur in short bursts called paroxysmal tachycardia. It particularly affects anxious people whose bodies produce a lot of adrenaline. Caffeine in coffee sometimes causes rapid heartbeat.

Irregular heartbeat, accompanied by an irregular pulse, is common in elderly people. It can also be caused by ALCOHOLISM, thyroid disorders, or disease of the heart valves or blood supply (see HEART DISORDERS).

Extra heartbeat affects everyone at times. A premature heartbeat is followed by a pause before the next normal beat, causing the sensation of a 'dropped' or missed heartbeat. An excessive number of extra beats may be caused by anxiety, or may be a symptom of a heart disorder.

What the therapists recommend

Massage Before undergoing massage you should consult a doctor to make sure there is no underlying disease, especially of the heart. If there is no heart disorder, however, slow stroking of the limbs may help to ease the palpitations.

An orthodox view

Most cases of palpitation can be relieved by cutting down on the consumption of non-decaffeinated coffee and alcohol. However, if another cause is suspected, a doctor will take a patient's pulse and BLOOD PRESSURE. If necessary, he will arrange for an electrocardiogram (ECG) to be taken to determine if there is any heart disorder, and blood tests to detect any thyroid disorder.

Palpitations caused by heart disease usually respond to drugs such as beta-blockers, digoxin, or verapamil.

PARANORMAL THERAPIES

This group of therapies is known to the various practitioners simply as 'healing'. It includes FAITH HEALING – a term not used by the practitioners themselves – and also some therapies in which faith in the healing method or practitioner on the part of the patient is not necessary. Indeed, in some paranormal therapies the patient may not know that therapy is taking place. See HEALERS AND HEALING.

Healers all believe in the existence of a healing force or forces. These may be supernatural forces invoked by the participants and transcending the forces of nature or able to alter them, or psychic forces of the participants which, while natural, have yet to be explained.

There are several aspects of paranormal therapies. Some people are believed to have the power to 'tune in' to the healing force(s), and to channel or 'beam' them through themselves or directly to others. Such therapies include CHARISMATIC HEALING; SPIRITUAL HEALING; LAYING ON OF HANDS, which is also known as 'hand healing'; ABSENT HEALING, or 'prayers for the sick'; THERAPEUTIC TOUCH; and Christian Science.

Another aspect is the use for diagnosis of extrasensory perception (ESP) – that is, perception other than by the five normal senses of hearing, sight, taste, touch and smell. In radiesthesia (see RADIESTHESIA AND RADIONICS) and similar therapies, some form of equipment is used to tap ESP in order to diagnose and treat diseases.

PARKINSON'S DISEASE

Muscular stiffness, along with slowness and difficulty in moving about, are among the symptoms of Parkinson's disease, or parkinsonism, a disorder of the nervous system.

These symptoms become progressively worse. The muscles of the face stiffen, so that sufferers may develop a blank stare or a frowning expression. Walking becomes increasingly slow and difficult. Patients stoop and shuffle, taking short steps. Some find it easier to walk backwards than forwards.

Although many people associate the disease with a shake, or tremor, this is not always the case. If it does occur, the head may nod rhythmically and the fingers may tremble involuntarily, as if a pill were being rolled between thumb and fingers. Patients often suffer from DEPRESSION, sometimes severely, or they may have hallucinations.

Parkinson's disease is caused by degeneration of the ganglia – groups of nerve cell bodies – and shortage of dopamine, a substance which is thought to be a transmitter of nerve impulses.

What the therapists recommend

Yoga Many people suffering from Parkinson's disease allow the malfunctioning of the muscular system to seize them up and make them increasingly inactive. A well-balanced programme of yoga postures (*asanas*) is aimed at providing an effective counter to the stiffening process. Relaxation while lying down, and full attention to the most suitable posture, reduce twitching and calm the body. Visualisation of the brain repairing the dopamine deficiency is said to have been used effectively by some sufferers.

Counselling This can be important for anyone in a chronic, progressive, incurable condition, because the individual may need help to come to terms with the dysfunction and disability.

An orthodox view

If you suspect you have Parkinson's disease – which can develop gradually and may go unnoticed at first – consult your doctor. He may prescribe drugs containing levodopa (L-dopa) as a substitute for the brain's dopamine deficiency, or anticholinergic drugs to reduce tremor and muscle stiffness. Another useful drug is bromocriptine, which stimulates dopamine receptors in the brain.

However, between 10 and 20 per cent of patients do not respond to drug treatment, and even when treatment is effective, the disease causes progressive disability, so that sufferers become increasingly dependent on relatives and others. The Parkinson's Disease Society, 36 Portland Place, London W1N 3DG, offers useful advice and support.

PATTERN THERAPIES

The belief that patterns or shapes profoundly affect the mind and body arose in early times, and today many people believe that the shape and pattern of things – from subatomic particles to the universe itself – affect homes and other properties.

Some healers claim that pattern and shape help in curative processes, and many state that a fundamental part of healing is the transfer of a healing pattern (an energy or thought pattern) from healer to patient, where it stimulates the patient's intrinsic healing force.

For example, they believe that the pattern of dials as set by a healer on a radionic instrument is the healing pattern in radionics (see RADIESTHESIA AND RADIONICS). Others make homoeopathic and BACH REMEDIES by imprinting patterns on water or inert tablets by means of their mental efforts, channelled through instruments. Others say that patterning is the curative basis of ACUPUNCTURE, SHIATSU, PARANORMAL THERAPIES and orthodox medications – even of PLACEBO ones.

PERIOD PROBLEMS

Every woman's menstrual cycle is different, and although symptoms such as pain or irregularity can be unpleasant, they are usually the result of natural hormone changes and not illness. Some of the most common problems are:

Painful periods (dysmenorrhoea) Sufferers tend to be girls or young women. They experience cramp-like pains in the lower abdomen at the beginning of a period and sometimes also feel ill or faint. Symptoms usually pass after one or two days, and are only rarely a sign of illness. Most often, the cause is a 'tight' cervix (the muscle at the neck of the womb), which generally loosens after the first pregnancy, putting an end to the problem. An intrauterine contraceptive device (IUD) or a menstrual cycle in which no egg is produced is also sometimes to blame.

Lack of periods (amenorrhoea) This condition is natural during PREGNANCY and MENOPAUSE. In other cases, it may follow use of the contraceptive pill (see CONTRACEPTION) or be a symptom of ANOREXIA.

Heavy periods (menorrhagia) Some women have naturally heavier periods than others, but greater than usual blood loss may also be due to a hormone imbalance, use of an IUD, small non-cancerous growths in the womb known as fibroids, or to an infection of the womb or uterine tubes.

Other problems MIGRAINE headaches are more common during a period than at other times of the month. PREMENSTRUAL TENSION (PMT) and its associated symptoms are also a common complaint.

Self help Take adequate EXERCISE and eat a well-balanced diet with plenty of iron, calcium and vitamin B1. Rest and relaxation will help to alleviate pain at period time, and a hot bath or hot-water bottle on the lower abdomen may also provide relief.

What the therapists recommend

AROMATHERAPY

Self help Oils of Roman camomile, true melissa and rose otto are recommended for dealing with most menstrual problems – irregular or scanty periods, painful ones, PMT, and menopause. These particular oils are expensive, but it is possible to combine them with less costly ones.

If using Roman camomile, rose otto and/or true melissa – not the compound melissa oil – mix a few drops of each in a dropper bottle, for easy use and enhanced results. To prepare an application oil or lotion, blend a total of 15 drops of the chosen essential oils in 5 dessertspoons (50ml) of carrier oil or lotion.

For irregular and scanty periods try clary sage, fennel and thyme. Apply a mixed lotion or oil to the abdomen twice daily.

For painful periods, cajuput, sage, aniseed, cypress and marjoram are recommended. A mixed oil should be applied to the abdomen and small of the back twice daily, from the tenth day before the period is due to start.

For PMT use clary sage, geranium and lavender. A bath containing a total of six to eight drops of these essential oils should be taken daily for two weeks before the period is due. It is also said to be beneficial to inhale regularly and deeply during those two weeks, using either a few drops on a tissue (or one drop in the palm of the hand, if using Roman camomile, rose otto or melissa, cupping your hands over your nose). An application lotion or oil can be mixed and used as an after-bath lotion all the time as a preventive measure.

NATUROPATHY

Self help Painful periods may be relieved by taking more exercise and eating a wholefood diet (see EATING FOR HEALTH) rich in FIBRE-containing foods such as raw fruits and vegetables. This helps to prevent CONSTIPATION during periods. In addition, alternate hot-and-cold compresses to the lower abdomen and back may help. Leave the hot compress in place for two to three minutes and the cold for about 30 seconds, alternating them two or three times.

Consultation Treatment will depend on the individual's symptoms and the diagnosis of their cause. Supplements of calcium or oil of evening primrose, taken just before the period begins, are sometimes prescribed for painful periods.

HERBAL MEDICINE

Self help Herbalists recommend a hot infusion of camomile with perhaps a little ginger added to relieve period pain.

Consultation A range of remedies is used, depending on the problem. For instance, the herbalist may choose antispasmodics such as cramp bark, motherwort or wild yam, or uterine tonics such as false unicorn root, white deadnettle or lady's mantle.

Other alternative treatments

Homoeopathy A homoeopathic doctor may recommend the following. For scanty and late periods: *Viburnum op. 30* when accompanied by severe cramping pains, which extend down the thigh. For painful periods: when accompanied by cramping pains similar to birth pangs and much bright red blood, *Belladonna 6* every 15 minutes until relief is obtained; when the pain is relieved by bending double and applying pressure and warmth, _Mag. phos. 6._

Acupuncture A wide range of gynaecological disorders can be treated after any underlying problems have been ruled out. Points on the conception channel are most commonly used, and points on the stomach, spleen, bladder and kidney meridians are also treated. For the best results with painful periods, treatment should be given about a week prior to commencement of a period.

Reflexology For menstrual problems, massage would be applied to the reflex areas related to the ovaries, Fallopian tubes and uterus, along with those relating to the pituitary, thyroid and adrenal glands, and the solar plexus (see chart, p. 295).

An orthodox view

A general practitioner will analyse the pattern of periods, and examine the womb and ovaries by an internal examination through the vagina. A cervical smear – a sample of cells from the cervix – may be taken to detect early signs of CANCER there. If necessary, a blood sample is taken, and its hormone levels measured.

A dilatation and curettage ('D and C') operation, in which the neck of the womb is widened and samples are taken from the lining of the womb, may help to form a diagnosis and to relieve painful and heavy periods. This should always be performed when there is vaginal bleeding or pain after the menopause.

Medicines such as mefenamic acid (Ponstan) may help to relieve period pains. Progesterone tablets or suppositories, or the oral contraceptive pill, may relieve heavy periods and premenstrual tension. For women who have completed their families, a hysterectomy, or a minor surgical procedure known as TCRE (transcervical resection of the endometrium) to remove the womb lining, can provide relief from heavy periods, but leaves the patient infertile.

PERSONALITY AND DISEASE
The emerging links between mind and body

Many alternative therapists feel that there is a strong connection between the type of people we are and the sort of illnesses that we get. However, conventional doctors are generally not so sure. They find it hard to accept the idea that some people have an ARTHRITIS personality, or that others are especially prone to CANCER.

Only recently have these two views started to take account of each other. It is now known that personality does influence health, but the link is seldom obvious. The old idea of 'one type of personality – one pattern of disease' has now given way to a more holistic view.

What is personality? By 'personality' doctors and psychologists mean simply the consistent patterns of behaviour, thought and feeling that people follow throughout their lives. Some seek out company, while others would rather be alone, for example; some can handle a crisis well, while others go to pieces under pressure. The first is said to have a sociable, outgoing personality, and the second a more withdrawn or introverted one. The third is probably emotionally stable, and the last unstable or slightly neurotic.

Obviously, the way people behave depends on many factors, but you have only to observe your friends or family members to recognise that each has persistent tendencies to respond in their own particular ways.

Some psychologists believe that constant personality traits are genetically built in. For example, being emotionally stable or unstable might depend on the sort of sympathetic nervous system – the part of the nervous system that controls BLOOD PRESSURE, heartbeat, breathing and so on – that is inherited.

Others believe that we are not born with fixed personalities but develop them as we grow up, in response to the people and situations we encounter. Nowadays most psychologists believe that a mixture of the two views is probably correct, and that an individual's personality springs from both genetics and environment.

Personality and mental health The clearest effect of personality on disease is the link with mental health. For example, it is known that outgoing, gregarious people tend to be happier than quieter, more inward-looking ones. Individuals with an emotionally unstable personality tend to be easily upset, have a low sense of their own value, and are more likely to suffer from serious DEPRESSION than those who are more stable.

In a way, links between personality and mental health are hardly surprising. After all, instability and depression overlap to some extent, and things that upset us may equally be depressing. But even allowing for this overlap, psychologists have found that an unstable personality is still a strong predictor of who is likely to suffer from depression.

The link with physical illness Thirty years ago it was believed by some doctors that particular personality types tend to suffer from particular disorders such as arthritis, raised blood pressure or peptic ULCERS.

Today the picture is thought to be more complicated, although there is evidence that the theory still holds true for problems such as HEART DISORDERS and cancer.

In recent years heart specialists have come to believe that as well as physical risk factors such as high blood pressure or raised cholesterol levels, a particular way of responding to the world can also be a cause of heart disease. People with the 'Type A' personality – ambitious, aggressive and with an exaggerated sense of time passing – are twice as likely to have a heart attack as more placid, easy-going 'Type B' personalities.

In one study, Californian psychologists successfully used COUNSELLING to reduce Type A traits in men who had already had one heart attack. The results showed that the rate of second attacks was significantly lowered, as compared with heart-attack victims who had not had counselling.

Similar links have also been found between personality and cancer, another major killer in the West. Showing the link is difficult for two reasons, however. Firstly, cancer is not one disease but many, and it is unlikely that different personality patterns have the same effect on them all. Secondly, many biological factors such as diet and exposure to dangerous substances also affect susceptibility to cancer.

Sometimes these other external influences are so strong that they override the effect of personality, although there is now evidence that people with certain personality types tend to live longer than others even when they get cancer.

Nurses who work with cancer patients often describe them as 'very nice people', meaning that they put others first and do not express strong emotions, particularly not anger. This has given rise to the idea that cancer may be at least partly due to 'anger turned inwards'.

Whether this is true or not, specialists in London have found that breast cancer patients who had had surgery survived longer if they developed a 'fighting spirit' and decided not to let the illness dominate their lives. Those who felt helpless or hopeless, by contrast, tended to die sooner. Researchers in San Francisco have found a similar pattern among patients after surgery for skin cancer.

A disease-resistant personality? Although a direct link with personality is generally accepted among practitioners for heart disease and cancer, a new, more subtle version of the old 'psychosomatic' idea is now emerging for other diseases.

Rather than different personality types being associated with particular illnesses, personality traits are now seen as factors which can reduce – or enhance – the body's overall resistance to disease. The actual symptoms people go down with – HEADACHES, PALPITATIONS or HEARTBURN, for example – depend on which body systems are the weakest ones.

During the break up of a large American company, researchers studied the personality traits of middle managers, as well as their disease patterns. They discovered a personality type that they called 'hardiness'. These were people who believed that they could exert some control in the world, who were committed to what they were doing, and who welcomed change because of the opportunities it could bring.

The managers who showed this hardy personality were found to be less prone to illnesses of all sorts than those whose hardiness was lower. The researchers concluded that a hardy personality could be a general protection against physical illness.

How personality exerts an influence There are two different ways in which personality appears to affect physical health. The first is directly related to behaviour. The way we express emotions, for example, influences the secretion of hormones which may reduce immunity or increase susceptibility to disease. Severely depressed patients, for example, are thought to have a less effective IMMUNE SYSTEM.

The second link depends on how personality affects the way in which we see and react to the world. People who are hardy can accept difficult situations and try to change them for the better. They recognise health problems early on and usually get treatment in good time.

People with low levels of hardiness, however, tend to ignore unpleasant situations, including symptoms of illness. As a result they remain ill for longer and seek help only when they have to. Unfortunately, that may sometimes be too late.

PESTICIDES

The use of chemicals to kill pests, particularly insects and rodents, and the use of fungicides have escalated since the 1950s. People have become increasingly concerned that poisons find their way into our air, water, soil and food. Illnesses that have been associated with exposure to pesticides include ALLERGY and HYPERACTIVITY. Cases of miscarriages and male INFERTILITY have also been reported. Despite legal controls on what chemicals farmers use, how they use them and the amount of residues allowed in foods, many people prefer to buy 'organic' food grown without chemicals.

See HEALTH HAZARDS.

PHOBIAS

People with intense, irrational fears called phobias live in perpetual dread of things which would not bother the average person. Anything from spiders to railway trains can set the heart pounding and their breathing racing. They may turn dizzy and start sweating with fright. Often they want to flee in terror from the scene. Phobia comes from the Greek word *phobos*, meaning 'fear', or 'flight'.

It is estimated that about one person in every ten in Britain has his own personal phobia, causing attacks of panic which can strike at any time and any place. Among the most common phobias are AGORAPHOBIA, the fear of being in open places, and CLAUSTROPHOBIA, the fear of being in confined or crowded places. In many cases the two conditions overlap.

Most phobias affect men and women equally, though in varying degrees. For example, some people suffer so badly that they cannot leave their home or lead a normal life. They often make excuses to avoid going out or joining in activities that their family and friends enjoy. They have trouble holding down their job, and may be terrified of travelling. Some people are even frightened of work itself; while others can get to work and back provided they do not have to travel in the rush hour.

A morbid fear of illness prevents some sufferers from visiting a doctor. And the most recently recorded medical phobia – rivalling that of CANCER – is the dread of contracting AIDS. In extreme cases, such phobias can drive people to suicide. See ANXIETY and NERVOUS DISORDERS.

What the therapists recommend

HOMOEOPATHY

Self help For agoraphobia take one dose of *Aconite 30* or *200* three times a day for ten days. If improvement is felt before the period is up, stop the medicine. If the condition is due to severe SHOCK, and you feel weak and faint, take *Arnica* in the 6th potency three times a day for seven to ten days.

For claustrophobia, the fear of being trapped, possibly by a tall building falling on you, try *Argentum nitricum 30*. If the phobia involves closed, crowded, hot places such as lifts or the Underground, try *Pulsatilla 30*. Both remedies should be taken three times a day for ten days.

BEHAVIOURAL THERAPY

Consultation On seeing a therapist, you are encouraged to face up to and deal with

How to beat phobias on your own

Recent research in Britain suggests that phobia victims can, in many cases, cure themselves. Tests were conducted on three groups of patients suffering from phobias, and the results published in the *British Journal of Psychiatry*.

All three groups were assessed by a psychiatrist. The first group then received exposure therapy (confronting their fears) under the guidance of the psychiatrist; the second group practised self-administered exposure therapy; and the third group received instruction from a specially programmed computer. The recovery rate among the three groups was similar – and afterwards the patients had no trouble in maintaining their progress.

Here is a guide to help you to escape from your phobias. It is based on the book *Living with Fear* by Professor Isaac M. Marks, whose studies formed part of the three-group test. Along with other researchers, he maintains that by exposing yourself to your fears you can learn how to cope with them.

The techniques are not suitable for people who drink heavily, or who take large amounts of sedatives. Anyone suffering from anxiety, ASTHMA, COLITIS, HEART DISORDERS or peptic ULCERS should see their doctor before starting.

Stage one Write down exactly what form your phobia takes. For example: 'I'm frightened of cats and can't be in the same room as one!' If you suffer from more than one phobia, rate them on the following scale: 0, would not avoid the situation or object; 2, would tend to avoid it; 4, would definitely avoid it; 6, would markedly avoid it; 8, would always avoid it. Then prepare to treat the main one, or ones. If possible, get support from a relative or close friend.

Stage two Write down exactly what you want to achieve. For example: 'I'll overcome my fear and visit friends with cats. I might even get one for my children.' Set aside up to two hours a day for treatment. Remember, one two-hour session is more effective than four half-hour ones.

Stage three Expose yourself to the object or situation you fear most. Immediately after each session write down the amount of fear you experienced on the following scale: 0, no fear; 25, mild fear; 50, moderate fear; 75, severe fear; 100, total fear. Discuss your progress with someone close to you, and record what you hope to achieve next time.

Recording your fears

According to some psychiatrists, the best way to conquer your fears is to face up to them each day for weeks or even months on end. Keep a daily record of how you do this. Here is part of a record kept by a housewife with agoraphobia and claustrophobia.

The woman describes the tasks, the time spent on them, her 'anxiety score' out of a possible 100, and how she coped.

As she becomes more self-confident, the sufferer finds she can spend longer in situations which normally are full of dread for her.

The more the sufferer exposes herself to her phobia the less it begins to affect her. Her 'anxiety score' goes down.

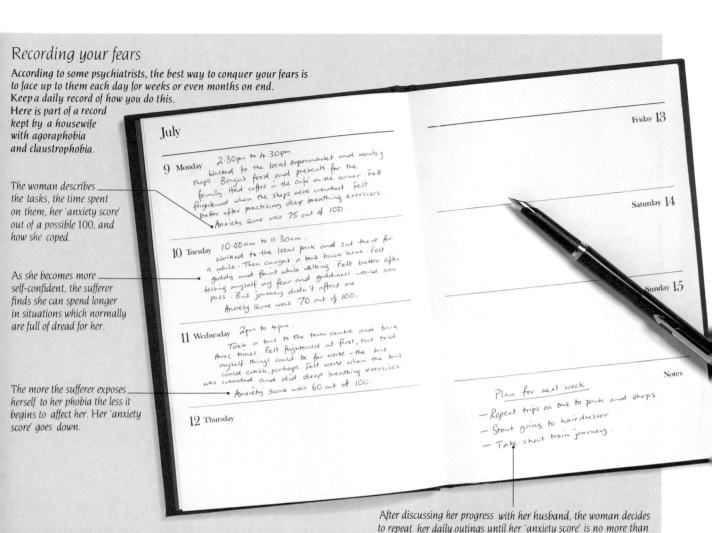

July

9 Monday 2.30pm to 4.30pm. Walked to the local supermarket and nearby shops. Bought food and presents for the family. Had coffee in the café on the corner. Felt frightened when the shops were crowded. Felt better after practising deep breathing exercises. Anxiety score was 75 out of 100.

10 Tuesday 10.00am to 11.30am. Walked to the local park and sat there for a while. Then caught a bus back home. Felt giddy and faint while walking. Felt better after telling myself my fear and giddiness would soon pass. Bus journey didn't affect me. Anxiety score was 70 out of 100.

11 Wednesday 2pm to 4pm. Took a bus to the town centre and back three times. Felt frightened at first, but told myself things could be far worse – the bus could crash, perhaps. Felt worst when the bus was crowded and did deep breathing exercises. Anxiety score was 60 out of 100.

12 Thursday

Friday 13

Saturday 14

Sunday 15

Notes

Plan for next week
- Repeat trips on bus to park and shops
- Start going to hairdresser
- Take short train journey.

After discussing her progress with her husband, the woman decides to repeat her daily outings until her 'anxiety score' is no more than 30 out of 100. Within a few more weeks, she hopes to have conquered her fears.

Stage four Write down on cards the sensations you have when frightened, such as:

(a) I want to scream or run away.
(b) I freeze in my tracks.
(c) I tremble and shake.
(d) My stomach tightens or turns over.
(e) I can't breathe properly.
(f) My heart pounds and beats fast.
(g) I feel dizzy and faint and about to fall.
(h) I break into a cold sweat.
(i) I feel I'm going insane.

Carry the cards always. Refer to them when you panic to help you take the sensations for granted, and so cope with them.

Stage five From the following tactics, choose three you feel will help you most:

(a) I must breathe slowly and steadily, gradually learning to deal with the situation.
(b) I'm very tense. I'll tense and relax my muscles until I gradually feel more relaxed.
(c) I'm thinking of the worst possible things that could happen to me. Perhaps they're not so bad after all.

(d) I must stay here and bear this panic, even if it takes an hour. Meanwhile, let me experience the fear openly and fully.
(e) I have to get away, but I know I must stay here.
(f) I feel awful. I could be better if I thought of something relaxing and pleasant, such as lying on a beach in the warm sun.
(g) These sensations are frightful, but I can change their meaning. My heart is pounding because I've been running in a race. I feel dizzy because I've just got out of bed.
(h) I'm terrified, but I'll get over it in time.
(i) I'll never get over this, but that is just a feeling, and in due course I'll feel better.
(j) I'm so embarrassed, but it is something I'll get used to.

Once you have chosen your three tactics, imagine that you are in the grip of your most terrifying fear and use the first tactic to deal

with it. Keep this up for three minutes. Then repeat with the other two tactics in turn. Write down what happens and how you feel afterwards. Slowly, with patience and perseverance, you should overcome the things that used to terrify you.

For information about local self-help groups in Britain, contact Phobic Action, Greater London House, 547-551 High Road, Leytonstone, London E11 4PR.

Five golden rules

1 Remember that anxiety is unpleasant but seldom harmful.
2 Don't flee from frightening situations.
3 Tell yourself to face up to your fears.
4 The longer you spend confronting your fears, the better you will feel.
5 The sooner you confront your fears, the sooner they will disappear.

your fears and anxieties, rather than trying to avoid them. Gradually, you are shown how to overcome your fear of a dreaded object or situation through a technique called desensitisation.

For example, if you are morbidly frightened of spiders you might start by looking at pictures of the creatures. You will then move on to looking at and handling dead spiders, and watching live ones. Finally, you will be asked to handle live spiders.
Self help As part of confronting your phobia, you may be taught some loosening-up techniques, such as deep breathing.

HYPNOTHERAPY
Consultation A hypnotist will try to take you back in time to when a particular phobia first showed itself. He will then attempt to 'will' you to conquer the fear. Alternatively, he will expose you to the phobia by visualising it stage by stage. That way you may be able to withstand and then dismiss your fear.

ART THERAPY
Consultation Therapists believe that phobias are often the result of childhood terrors – and that these can be dispelled by recalling them through drawing and painting. Once your worst fears and the panic that accompanies them have been re-created in pictorial form, an art therapist will try to help you to relax and to lead a normal life.

An orthodox view

Rather than prescribe tranquillisers – which give rapid, short-term relief, but which can prove addictive – some doctors recommend PSYCHOTHERAPY or BEHAVIOURAL THERAPY (see also box, pp. 276-7).

PHYTOTHERAPY

This recently coined word describes the work of medical herbalists. It refers to the healing powers of plants, which are now more widely used throughout the world than at any time in history. See HERBAL MEDICINE.

PILES

Haemorrhoids, the medical name for piles, are caused by swollen veins inside or on the outside of the anus. They can cause ITCHING and pain, and are the most common source of anal bleeding.

Internal piles may protrude from the anus

during straining when passing motions – and may even stay permanently outside in the form of small, soft, purplish lumps. These external piles – which usually clear up within a week or two – often leave irritating 'skin tags' which cause further itchiness. Sometimes a blood clot, or thrombus, turns a pile into a hard, extremely painful lump.

What the therapists recommend

Naturopathy Practitioners consider that most cases of piles are a result of the way of life prevalent in the West, where diets low in FIBRE and inadequate EXERCISE are the norm, and CONSTIPATION, straining and the use of laxatives are often a part of daily life.

The naturopathic approach to piles is to deal with these basic causes by adding high-fibre foods such as linseed to the diet in order to soften the motions. Maintaining a good posture and exercise are also considered to be important ways of reducing strain on the lower bowel. In addition, hot and cold packs may be used to improve the circulation and to reduce discomfort.
Aromatherapy Essential oils recommended for piles are cypress, camomile, juniper, frankincense or myrrh – any two of these plus one drop of peppermint should be used.

Make a sitz bath by adding four drops of the oils to half a washing-up bowl of water and sit in it for five to ten minutes. Apply a lotion or oil both after the evening sitz bath and every morning. For the application lotion or oil, use 2 dessertspoons (20ml) of white base lotion or vegetable oil mixed with ten drops of pure essential oil.
Herbal Medicine Herbalists aim to relieve the discomfort of piles with astringent ointments such as comfrey, horse chestnut and witch hazel.

An orthodox view

In cases of anal bleeding, a doctor should be seen so that he can test for any more serious, underlying cause. Medical advice should also be sought if there is a disturbing change in bowel habits, such as constipation or DIARRHOEA (see also BOWEL DISORDERS).

Piles can be avoided by eating adequate amounts of dietary fibre, or roughage, and by drinking sufficient liquid to avoid constipation. If they do occur, the itchiness and pain can be relieved by taking hot baths, using hydrocortisone ointments or suppositories, and using moist wipes instead of ordinary toilet paper. Sufferers should also avoid straining when relieving the bowels.

In severe cases, if piles persist or recur, an operation can be performed under local anaesthetic to remove them. A minor hospital operation can also be carried out to remove a painful blood clot and so give rapid relief from a thrombosed pile.

PIMPLES AND SPOTS

Everyone has pimples and spots at some time, particularly during adolescence. They are small, raised, inflamed areas on the skin containing pus. They usually occur singly at the roots of hairs when natural hair oil and skin keratin (a tough, fibrous protein) clog skin pores. The blocked glands continue producing oil which can become infected or leak into the skin, causing redness and inflammation. When there is a rash of pimples, the condition is called ACNE.

In some cases, pimples and spots are caused by certain foods, cosmetics, soaps and other toiletries to which people may have an ALLERGY, and which they should therefore avoid. Pimples can also be helped by spending time outdoors, taking regular EXERCISE, and adopting a sensible and nutritious diet (see EATING FOR HEALTH).

What the therapists recommend

Herbal Medicine Inflammation and further infection may be reduced by sponging the affected areas with infusions of lavender or marigold, or with diluted witch hazel.

Remedies that are given internally by herbalists – usually as tinctures – include burdock, echinacea and red clover. These preparations are thought to cleanse the body and so reduce the likelihood of pimples and spots occurring.
Naturopathy Practitioners often recommend a short, supervised fast (see FASTING) to cleanse the body of impurities. This is usually followed by a diet based mainly on fresh fruit and vegetables, and excluding sugar, fried and fatty foods, alcohol, and strong tea and coffee. Skin brushing (see p. 83) to invigorate circulation in affected areas may also be helpful.

Hygiene is another important factor, but gentle methods may be more effective than harsh skin scrubs. Moderate EXERCISE taken in fresh air and, according to individual needs, supplements such as vitamin A are often advised.

An orthodox view

Apart from possibly recommending various skin creams and lotions that are on sale at the chemist, conventional doctors have little to offer for commonplace pimples and spots. In cases of acne, however, they may advise the sufferer to avoid oily or fatty foods, and may also prescribe creams and antiacne preparations. In some severe cases, oral antibiotics are prescribed.

PLACEBO

Before the scientific testing of drugs, a placebo was simply an inactive medication or therapy given to humour the patient. (The word comes from the Latin *placere*, 'to please'.) The treatment itself had no effect on the illness or complaint – real or supposed – but the patient believed that it would cure. And it sometimes did, for the sufferer's faith in the prescription brought about a change of mental attitude to the illness, and the body's powerful self-healing potential then came into play. This is known as the placebo effect or placebo response.

Today, placebos are used in the clinical testing of new drugs. One group of patients is given the drug under test, while a similar group of 'controls' is given an inactive placebo. The drug's effect is then compared with the placebo effect to give a measure of the new drug's activity.

Sometimes a 'double-blind' trial is conducted. In this neither the patients nor their doctors know who is receiving the drug and who is taking the placebo. Only the researchers conducting the trial have that information during the test period. This ensures complete objectivity on the part of those actively involved in the trial.

PLEURISY

Sharp or stabbing pains in the chest or shoulder – felt with every breath – can be a sign of pleurisy. The condition is caused by inflammation of the pleura, two delicate membranes which separate the lungs from the chest wall. The pleura are lubricated by a thin film of fluid which allows them to move smoothly against each other as the lungs expand and contract during breathing. In pleurisy, the fluid becomes sticky, and a doctor may hear through his stethoscope a 'pleural rub' like two pieces of sandpaper rubbing together. The patient may have a raised temperature and feel generally unwell.

Pleurisy is usually caused by a virus infection of the pleura. But other causes can include PNEUMONIA, injury to the chest wall where there is bruising beneath the ribs, pericarditis (inflammation of the pericardial lining of the heart after a heart attack, or because of infection), a blood clot in the lung or, rarely, lung CANCER.

Warning If pleurisy is suspected, consult a doctor before undertaking any form of alternative treatment.

What the therapists recommend

Traditional Medicine A drink of home-made wheat bread is said to relieve the pain of pleurisy. Oven-dry the bread, break it up into powder, and then boil it in water with salt and butter. Drink the resulting 'toast water' while it is warm.

Naturopathy Self help alone must not be practised, and naturopaths may recommend a course of HYDROTHERAPY, with chest and back compresses to help reduce the internal inflammation. A daily dose of 2-3g of vitamin C may be prescribed to try to boost the body's IMMUNE SYSTEM, and possibly about 5000iu a day of vitamin A.

Homoeopathy If the pain is worse when you move, and you are irritable and thirsty, try *Byronia 30* each hour for up to 12 hours. If the attack comes on suddenly after exposure to cold wind – and is accompanied by anxiety, restlessness and fear of dying – try *Aconite 30* once an hour for up to 12 hours. If your face is flushed and you are very hot and thirsty with dilated pupils, a similar dosage of *Belladonna* is a better remedy.

An orthodox view

When examining a patient with suspected pleurisy a doctor may hear a pleural rub. He may then arrange for an X-ray to help to determine the cause.

If pneumonia is found, it usually clears with a course of antibiotics. If there is a blood clot in the lung (pulmonary embolism), the doctor will recommend blood-thinning drugs such as heparin and warfarin. The treatment will probably start in hospital.

In cases of virus infections there is no specific medical treatment. The GP will tell his patient to rest, and may prescribe pain-killers to give relief and speed recovery.

PNEUMONIA

A virus or bacterial infection is the usual cause of pneumonia, when one or both lungs become inflamed. It develops with a cough and shortness of breath.

Bacterial pneumonia is considered a serious health hazard, although viral pneumonia can also be dangerous – especially in the elderly and the young. Legionnaires' disease is a form of viral pneumonia.

Acute lobar pneumonia usually affects only one lobe of one lung. It develops quickly, often in children and young people, and causes high FEVER, rapid breathing and a persistent, dry cough. There is usually little phlegm, but the patient may cough up blood.

Bronchopneumonia often affects both lungs, and the victim produces large quantities of green or yellow phlegm. It can be a complication of SMOKING or infections such as INFLUENZA, and mainly affects elderly people or those who are weakened or bed-bound through other illness. It is often the final cause of death in people dying of CANCER or old age.

Pneumonia is sometimes a feature of AIDS. In its viral form, it is often the result of CHICKENPOX or MEASLES.

Warning If pneumonia is suspected, consult a doctor before undertaking any of the alternative treatments.

What the therapists recommend

Herbal Medicine Herbalists advise pneumonia sufferers to seek expert medical help. But they prescribe expectorants to loosen the phlegm, including lobelia or thyme combined with anti-infective herbs such as echinacea or GARLIC. Any fever is treated by herbs such as elderflower and yarrow.

Homoeopathy When the illness begins suddenly in cold, dry weather and the patient experiences fever, ANXIETY and FEAR, *Aconite 30* may help – give up to 12 half-hourly doses. If chest pains get worse with movement and improve when lying on the affected side, *Bryonia 30* may give relief. Therapists advise *Phosphorus 30* hourly or half-hourly as required for chest pains with a dry cough, blood in the sputum, and symptoms that worsen when lying on the left side.

Naturopathy Treatment should be attempted only under the supervision of a fully qualified therapist, especially in the case of elderly patients. A diet of nothing but fresh fruit and vegetable juices is usually recommended for a few days, and then fruit, vegetables, grains and a little protein are slowly added. Dairy products and sweet foods are avoided to decrease mucus production, and supplements such as vitamin C and vitamin A in fairly large doses may be prescribed to boost the IMMUNE SYSTEM.

An orthodox view

In cases of bacterial pneumonia, lifesaving antibiotics should be given as soon as possible. The patient's lungs will be sounded and a chest X-ray arranged. If the illness is present there will be a characteristic shadow across one or both lungs on the X-ray.

Many cases can be treated at home with antibiotics taken by mouth. Severely ill patients may need an intravenous drip in hospital, together with physiotherapy to help clear the lungs of phlegm.

Elderly people, particularly if they smoke, may be advised to have a follow-up chest X-ray after treatment to make sure that there is no underlying lung cancer.

POLARITY THERAPY
Balancing the body's vital energy

The basis of this wide-ranging therapy – which incorporates Eastern and Western healing techniques – is that most illness is caused by 'blockages' of the body's energy currents. By removing the blocks, and allowing the currents to flow naturally, it is said that people can overcome illness – and that once eliminated it should not recur.

The therapy was developed in the United States over a period of some 50 years by the Austrian-born Dr Randolph Stone (1890-1983), who trained in CHIROPRACTIC, NATUROPATHY and OSTEOPATHY. In addition, he studied various Eastern healing systems, including ACUPUNCTURE, AYURVEDIC MEDICINE and YOGA. Early in his career he noted that after curing patients by manipulation, there was often an underlying, residual condition that made them ill again later.

Seeking a solution, he adopted the oriental belief in a form of 'life energy' known in China as *Qi* (or *chi*), and in India as *prana*. In the West it is usually regarded as the spirit, or soul. The energy is thought to govern people's physical, emotional and mental processes. Pain and illness arise when it fails to function properly. These blockages or imbalances are also caused by bad eating habits, irrational behaviour patterns, psychological problems and STRESS.

He asserted that good health depends upon 'polarity relationships' – positive, negative and neutral – between different parts of the body and its five energy centres. According to ancient Indian thinking, these centres are: air (governing respiration and circulation); earth (bladder and rectum); ether (throat and ears); fire (bowels and stomach); and water (glands and pelvis).

The aim of Dr Stone's polarity therapy is to balance all these complex factors. To do so, it uses four basic techniques: manipulation and touch; stretching postures; diet; and thought and mental attitude (see box).

Who it can help According to its practitioners, anyone who is ill can benefit to some degree from the therapy. However, it concentrates on achieving balance, or polarity, in the patient – rather than dealing with specific symptoms. For polarity therapy to succeed, it calls for the patient's full cooperation, commitment and belief.

Finding a therapist Lists of qualified practitioners can be obtained through the three

Exercises to balance the body

As well as receiving instruction in polarity therapy from a qualified therapist, you can do the following basic self-help exercises at home. They are designed to let you work in depth to cure your particular forms of imbalance or energy blockage. The exercises should also help to boost your vitality and increase your general well-being.

Basic squat
Lower yourself slowly into the squatting posture. Then circle and rock gently to and fro to 'open up' and stretch your body. If necessary, support your heels with pillows or cushions.

Neutral sitting
Sit with your legs bent in front of you. Cross your hands and grasp your right ankle with your left hand; your left ankle with your right hand. Close your eyes and let your mind be at peace.

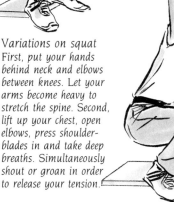

Variations on squat
First, put your hands behind neck and elbows between knees. Let your arms become heavy to stretch the spine. Second, lift up your chest, open elbows, press shoulder-blades in and take deep breaths. Simultaneously shout or groan in order to release your tension.

Woodchopper Ha!
Put your feet slightly apart, bend knees and put your hands above your head as if wielding an axe. Bring your hands down between your legs in the 'woodchopper' action, at the same time shouting 'Ha!' to release tension. Repeat the action as often as you like, providing that you are comfortable with it.

main training centres for the therapy: Polarity Energetics Practitioner Training, 15 Bath Street, Lancaster LA1 3PZ (practitioners have the initials PEPA after their name); The International School of Polarity Therapy, 12-14 Dowell Street, Honiton, Devon EX14 8LT (practitioners have the initials MISPT); and the Polarity Therapy Educational Trust, 11 The Lee, Allesley Park, Coventry CV5 9HY (practitioners have the initials RPT).

Consulting a therapist First you are asked for a full medical history. The therapist then

---

Four paths to health

Dr Randolph Stone, who developed polarity therapy, devised four techniques designed to help the body to balance and heal itself, which are practised by therapists today.

Manipulation and touch The therapist uses his hands to release and then 'polarise' blocked energy currents said to be a cause of ill health. Three types of pressure are applied: _positive_, involving manipulation of various parts of the patient's body, from the toes to the back of the neck; _negative_, involving deeper pressure and manipulation, particularly of the tissues; and _neutral_, involving a light, soothing touch with the fingertips.

Stretching postures Exercises such as squatting, sitting with legs crossed, and clasping hands behind the head aim to open up energy currents, tone muscles, sinews and ligaments, and strengthen the spine. To help release TENSION, the patient is asked to shout and groan while doing the exercises.

Diet To clear the system of poisons accumulated through bad eating habits and pollution, the patient will be put on a 'cleansing diet' for anything up to 14 days, depending on condition. Basically, the diet consists of fresh fruit and vegetables and plenty of natural fruit drinks (see VEGETARIANISM). In addition, there is a special 'liver flush' – a drink created by Dr Stone, made from olive oil, lemon juice, root ginger and garlic.

Once the system has been cleansed, the patient is put on an extended 'health-building' diet, followed by a 'maintenance diet', intended to maintain fitness and health.

Mental attitude Through counselling work, negative attitudes which may predispose the patient to ill health are explored and an openness to new possibilities is encouraged. This is of prime importance in balancing the body and stabilising the mind.

---

analyses your energy patterns and physical structure, searching for any blocks by testing the body's pressure points and reflexes. Touch and manipulation techniques are used which are aimed at balancing these energy patterns and their physical repercussions.

The importance of being aware of the body's healing processes is also stressed. For example, during treatment for low BACK PAIN, you will be asked to concentrate on the site of the pain and to note the emotions, thoughts and mental images you experience. This, it is said, will help you to build up a complete picture of your state of health – physical, mental and emotional. In turn, this self-knowledge is claimed to hasten your return to fitness.

In addition, you may be asked to keep a record of the food you eat. From this, the therapist can assess how diet is affecting your health. In some cases, a special 'cleansing diet' devised by Dr Stone will be prescribed (see box).

If necessary, you will be offered COUNSELLING to help change any personal habits, attitudes, or ways of life that are seen as harmful to health. Some therapists may also use HERBAL MEDICINE and BACH REMEDIES to help in the overall healing process.

An orthodox view

Polarity therapy, like many alternative therapies, draws on Eastern views of 'energy' and health. Such therapies have much in common, using a combination of diet, EXERCISE, touch and MEDITATION. Little harm and much benefit can result from their use, but it is vital to get a competent DIAGNOSIS first.

POLIOMYELITIS

Early symptoms of poliomyelitis – a virus infection – are very like those of INFLUENZA. There is generally FEVER, a sore throat or HEADACHES, lasting a few days. Fortunately, most people only suffer the early symptoms and do not develop the full-blown version of the disease. They do, however, become immune to further infection.

Only a minority of those infected go on to develop encephalitis – inflammation of the brain – with its accompanying fever, severe headache, drowsiness and neck stiffness. Cramping muscle pains and spasms may develop, possibly leading to paralysis and muscle wasting, particularly affecting the muscles that were most active during the early stages of the disease.

Polio, as it is commonly called, usually strikes in epidemics – and because of wide-

scale vaccination, is mostly restricted to developing countries and areas where sanitation is inadequate. The virus is excreted in the faeces of someone infected, and infects others who come into direct – or even indirect – contact with the faeces, through sewage, contaminated drinking water or poor personal hygiene.

Note Polio is a notifiable disease and suspected cases _must_ be seen by a doctor.

What the therapists recommend

T'AI-CHI CH'UAN

Consultation Holding the spine vertically and allowing the quiet flow of all energies is said to help the relaxation of the joints, and T'ai-chi breathing exercises (_Ch'i kung_) are said to be beneficial. They may be either in the form of meditation or the directing of mind-breath energy (_Qi_) through the spine and limbs, or subtle breathing-movement exercises, aimed at smooth muscle coordination and spinal mobility.

Correctly carried out with guidance, all of these have produced encouraging results. T'ai-chi's inspirational elements of beauty, philosophy, creativity and harmonious ease of movement are believed to give the patient vital psychological support. However, it is important that the instructor should have experience of therapy – not merely of teaching T'ai-chi movements.

Other alternative therapies

Yoga Although there is little evidence of yoga having a direct effect on polio, it can play a major part in keeping the body and mind in order – and in doing so, help in fighting infections and other conditions which may cause grave problems.

Hydrotherapy Needle spray or vortex baths are recommended, to promote or improve lower limb circulation, before specific exercise programmes and patterns in a hydrotherapy pool.

An orthodox view

Polio can be prevented by adequate sanitation and personal hygiene, and by immunisation of children and travellers. In the UK, all children are recommended four doses of oral vaccine, usually at the ages of three, five and nine months – at the same time as those for diphtheria, WHOOPING COUGH and tetanus – along with a booster dose before starting school.

When polio develops, there is no specific cure, but rest, skilled nursing – and, if breathing muscles are affected, artificial respiration on a life-support machine – will aid the patient until recovery. If there is paralysis, it is permanent, but physiotherapy and mobility aids, such as callipers, may help a victim to lead as normal a life as possible.

POSTURAL INTEGRATION

Practitioners of postural integration believe that the body quite literally 'embodies' experiences as well as emotions and thought patterns. Through injuries, trauma, or prolonged stressful patterns of use, muscles and the connective tissues surrounding them will lose their natural responsiveness. The result is loss of flexibility, TENSION, and often PAIN.

Practitioners aim to restore the natural flow of energy, healthier breathing, and less stressful patterns of alignment. Physical, mental and emotional patterns are therefore encouraged to change together, reducing tension and increasing well-being. A more functional posture with better balance may be the result.

Postural integration practitioners use techniques similar to ROLFING, REICHIAN THERAPY, ACUPRESSURE and other forms of movement in an integrated manner. For more information contact The Centre for Release and Integration, 62 Twickenham Road, Teddington, Middlesex TW11 8AW. The centre can put people in touch with recognised practitioners.

PREGNANCY
Preparing for a new member of the family

Some women become pregnant as soon as they want to start a family, but others take longer, and one couple in ten may have to wait a year or more (see INFERTILITY). Most babies are conceived around the middle of the woman's menstrual cycle, following sexual intercourse taking place just before or after her ovaries produce an egg – known as ovulation. Once the egg has been fertilised by a sperm from the man, it implants itself into the lining of the womb and becomes a growing embryo.

By the time the first period is missed, the embryo is usually about two weeks old and its heart is already beginning to beat. Twelve weeks after conception, it is recognisable as a human baby and all the organs are formed. Birth usually occurs about 40 weeks after the first day of the last ordinary period, but any time from 38 to 42 weeks is normal.

Most pregnancies follow a smooth course, but all women need regular check-ups by a doctor, midwife or antenatal clinic to monitor their health and that of the baby. Alternative practitioners can provide extra help

and advice, but cannot replace conventional medical care.

Preparing for pregnancy All women should have a blood test for German measles before trying to start a family – catching the disease in the first three months of pregnancy can damage the baby's hearing, eyesight, heart and mental development. Even if you believe you have had the disease or been inoculated against it, you may still be at risk. Only if a blood test shows that you are immune is a vaccination not necessary.

A healthy way of life is important for both partners right from the start: stop SMOKING, eat a balanced diet (see EATING FOR HEALTH), take moderate EXERCISE, and allow plenty of time for rest and relaxation. Women should preferably avoid alcohol altogether, never taking more than four units a week (see ALCOHOLISM), and should stop taking any medicines or drugs that are not essential. See your doctor as soon as you think you may be pregnant, to ensure proper care for you and your baby.

During pregnancy Most women agree that they feel 'different' when pregnant. Some feel wonderful, others miserable, and most find themselves easily tired and more emotional than usual. A healthy diet and way of life will help to reduce these problems, but it may also be necessary to reschedule daily tasks to make time for resting, without giving up regular exercise.

Minor health problems often include MORNING SICKNESS – common in the first three months, but usually better after that – CONSTIPATION, BACK PAIN, PILES, INDIGESTION and HEADACHES. Avoid taking medicines to deal with these – doctors and alternative practitioners can offer other treatments. A few pregnant women develop dangerously high BLOOD PRESSURE, for which medical attention is essential.

Pregnancy demands emotional adjustment from fathers too, and it is important that they are not left out. Involving both partners in visits to the doctor or clinic, antenatal classes, making decisions and preparing for the baby at home, will help to make men feel part of the event.

Sex is safe for most couples during pregnancy, although you may need to experiment to find a comfortable position. Some doctors advise against sex in the first three months if there has been a previous miscarriage or if there are other problems – ask advice from your doctor if in doubt. In late pregnancy, an orgasm may set off contractions, but it is unlikely to induce labour.

Where to have your baby Early on in pregnancy the doctor will discuss various options for having the baby. In Britain, most couples choose a hospital delivery by a doctor – or a community midwife in areas

which operate the Domino (domiciliary-in-out) system.

Under this system, the midwife looks after the mother during pregnancy and the early stages of labour, takes her to hospital and delivers the baby – with the help of a doctor, if necessary. If neither mother nor baby need special care, they are allowed to leave hospital after only a few hours, and the midwife continues to look after them at home.

Some couples prefer a home birth, believing that it will be more 'natural' and less stressful. Doctors will sometimes agree to this, except for first babies or if problems are possible. Hospitals generally try to make childbirth as pleasant as possible, and many allow women quite a lot of freedom in choosing how they give birth – ask your doctor or telephone around yourself to find out the policies of different hospitals before booking into one.

Childbirth and after See NATURAL CHILDBIRTH for information on making the experience as easy and rewarding as possible.

After giving birth, women will experience vaginal bleeding or discharge which may last for a few weeks. Afterpains, rather like period pains, can also occur as the womb shrinks back to its normal size. Piles are common, so include high-fibre foods in your diet (see FIBRE) and drink extra fluids to avoid constipation. Get plenty of rest and do postnatal exercises as soon as possible, to tone the abdominal muscles (see box, p. 284).

Tiredness and depression are normal in the weeks following birth, and mothers who feel unable to cope can get help from their doctor or health visitor. Readjustment can be difficult for other members of the family too, but patience, a sense of humour and tolerant attitude will overcome most problems. A special effort to give other children time and attention will help to prevent jealousy and build good family relationships.

Making time for each other, sharing feelings and listening sympathetically will also help a couple to strengthen their relationship at what can otherwise be a difficult time. Sharing baby care and household chores will help fathers to feel more involved, and mothers less exhausted. Sexual intercourse can be resumed as soon as the woman feels comfortable. Some women may be fertile again straight away, so consider using contraception. Breastfeeding reduces – but does not eliminate – the chances of becoming pregnant again.

When pregnancy fails Although many problems can be treated if detected early on, as many as one in six diagnosed pregnancies – and many more unrecognised ones – may end in a miscarriage, sometimes experienced as a late, heavy period. Consult a doctor at the first sign of bleeding or lower abdominal

Exercises for pregnancy and birth

These gentle exercises are safe for most pregnant women, but ask your doctor's advice before beginning any exercise programme, and never push yourself beyond what feels comfortable.

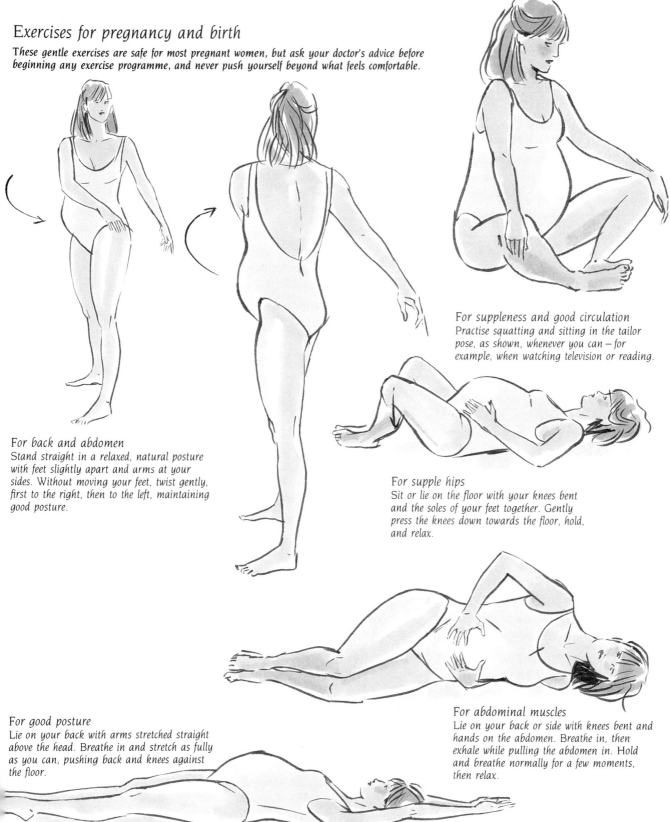

For suppleness and good circulation
Practise squatting and sitting in the tailor pose, as shown, whenever you can – for example, when watching television or reading.

For back and abdomen
Stand straight in a relaxed, natural posture with feet slightly apart and arms at your sides. Without moving your feet, twist gently, first to the right, then to the left, maintaining good posture.

For supple hips
Sit or lie on the floor with your knees bent and the soles of your feet together. Gently press the knees down towards the floor, hold, and relax.

For abdominal muscles
Lie on your back or side with knees bent and hands on the abdomen. Breathe in, then exhale while pulling the abdomen in. Hold and breathe normally for a few moments, then relax.

For good posture
Lie on your back with arms stretched straight above the head. Breathe in and stretch as fully as you can, pushing back and knees against the floor.

Pregnancy

Getting back into shape after childbirth

Begin gentle exercise as soon as you feel ready. Stop whenever you feel tired, sore or uncomfortable, and ask your doctor's advice if in doubt. Frequent short periods of exercise are better than occasional longer sessions.

First days after birth
Lie on your back with knees bent and hands resting lightly on the abdomen. Breathe in and out slowly and rhythmically; on each out-breath pull the abdomen in gently and tilt the pelvis upwards. Hold for a count of four, then relax.

Stand with feet a little apart, knees slightly bent. Place one hand on the abdomen, the other on the lower back, fingers pointing down, as shown. Breathe in, then out, and tilt the pelvis forwards and upwards, pulling the abdomen in and tucking in your bottom. Hold for a few moments while breathing normally, then relax.

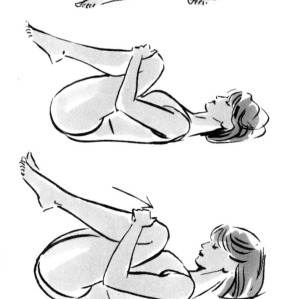

After a few days
Sit on the floor with knees drawn up and arms folded, but held away from the body. Breathe in, then exhale, tilting the pelvis forwards. Allow yourself to lean back until you feel the abdominal muscles tighten. Hold and breathe normally for a short time, then sit up and relax.

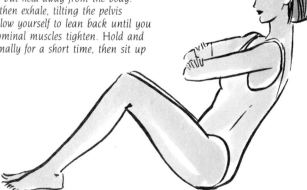

Lie on your back with knees drawn up and clasped to your chest as shown. Breathe in, then out while pulling in the abdomen and pressing the knees to the chest. Breathe in again, and relax.
Other exercises to tone abdominal muscles include leg rolls (see BACK PAIN) and breathing techniques (see RELAXATION AND BREATHING).

pain in the pregnancy, since these can signal miscarriage.

Occasionally it can happen that a fertilised egg is prevented from reaching the womb and begins to grow in the uterine tube instead. This is known as an ectopic pregnancy. It causes pain and bleeding about two weeks after the first missed period, and requires urgent surgery to prevent further internal bleeding and the possibility of fatal complications.

Women who lose their babies in these or other ways need time to come to terms with the loss, and a chance to express their feelings to sympathetic listeners. For more information and help, contact the Miscarriage Association, 18 Stoneybrook Close, West Bretton, Wakefield WF4 4TP.

What the therapists recommend

Apart from their advice on dealing with specific conditions, described in the relevant entries, a number of alternative therapists offer suggestions for general health care during pregnancy.

NATUROPATHY

Eat well-balanced, nourishing meals at least three times a day – or as many as six smaller meals if you prefer. Smaller portions more often will also help if you suffer from nausea (see NAUSEA AND VOMITING), HEARTBURN or indigestion. Base your diet mainly on fresh vegetables, salads, whole grains, pulses and protein foods such as lean meat, chicken, fish, eggs and dairy products. Drink plenty of spring water and avoid tea, coffee, alcohol, sweets, cakes and other products made with refined sugar and flour. If you want a snack, go for nuts or fresh or dried fruit instead.

Some women find multivitamin and multimineral supplements helpful for problems such as TIREDNESS or STRESS. Vitamin E is recommended for reducing stretch marks after the birth: take 100iu a day for up to three months. Brown skin discoloration on the face may be helped by PABA (para-aminobenzoic acid), which is found naturally in wheatgerm, whole grains, liver, mushrooms, fresh fruit and vegetables. It can also be taken as a supplement in doses of up to 500mg a day.

HERBAL MEDICINE

Infusions (see p. 184) of black haw root are said to help prevent miscarriage, or three drops of false unicorn root tincture taken four or five times a day from the time you start trying for a baby until the 14th week of pregnancy. Pain in the legs and feet may be helped by a decoction (see p. 184) of cramp bark, and headaches by infusions of poppy heads, or equal parts of balm (lemon balm), lavender and meadowsweet.

AROMATHERAPY

Sprinkle a few drops of lavender or peppermint essential oil onto a handkerchief or tissue and keep it near you to smell if headaches are a problem. Do the same with lavender, camomile or rose oil to relieve nausea. For sciatic pain in the leg, mix a massage oil (see p. 36) with a few drops of lavender or wintergreen essence and rub in as often as necessary.

HOMOEOPATHY

Treatment is said to help with many minor problems of pregnancy. For FAINTING caused by heat try _Belladonna 30C_, for fear and nervousness _Aconite 30C_, and for a euphoric mood that interferes with sleep _Coffea 30C_. False contractions in the last few months may be helped by _Pulsatilla 6C_, _Coffea 6C_ or _Nux vomica 6C_, and heartburn by _Capsicum 6C_ or _Sulphur 6C_.

Take _Sepia 6C_ for brown or dark yellow skin discoloration over the bridge of the nose, and _Sulphur 6C_ for dry, itchy, flaking skin. Take four doses a day for up to a week. A sweet, metallic taste in the mouth accompanied by excessive saliva production may be helped by _Mercurius 6C_, and large amounts of saliva together with feelings of nausea by _Pulsatilla 6C_.

Other alternative remedies

Moxibustion Babies in a difficult birth position may be helped to turn in the womb after the 35th week by burning moxa close to the outside edge of the nail of each little toe. Hold it close enough to feel the warmth but not burn. Repeat twice a day for ten minutes on each foot.

Traditional Medicine A drink made by pouring 1 pint (600ml) of boiling water over 1oz (30g) of raspberries was traditionally believed to ensure a plentiful supply of milk and a safe delivery. Begin the treatment after the third month and continue until birth.

PREMENSTRUAL TENSION

As many as three out of four women suffer from premenstrual tension (PMT) – a troublesome but largely harmless range of symptoms whose effects become evident in the run up to a period. For some the symptoms must be endured for up to half of every month. Problems include physical ailments such as WATER RETENTION and swollen joints (especially ankles), food and alcohol cravings, weight gain, skin problems, weakness

and HEADACHES. There are also psychological disturbances such as irritability, poor concentration, decreased sex drive, insomnia, tearfulness and even DEPRESSION.

The main cause of PMT is a change in the balance of female hormones during the menstrual cycle which results in an accumulation of salt and water in the system and a shortage of progesterone, the hormone that prepares the uterus to receive a fertilised egg. Lack of essential fatty acids such as linoleic acid (see EATING FOR HEALTH) can also upset this balance and lead to hormone deficiency. Vitamin B6 is known to regulate the menstrual cycle, so lack of it may be another cause of distress.

Not every sufferer experiences all the symptoms of PMT, and degrees of suffering can vary from mild discomfort to complete misery. A few women become so disturbed that they act like a completely different person – irrationally moody and even physically violent towards those they love. So family and friends may suffer accordingly from these irrational spells.

The condition also affects judgment, and women may be prone to accidents during this time. Many industrial concerns try to avoid such accidents by temporarily transferring women employees to safer jobs during the premenstrual period.

PMT is a well-known problem – most people are aware of its effects and are sympathetic to the sufferer, making allowances for her uncharacteristic behaviour. See also PERIOD PROBLEMS.

What the therapists recommend

Aromatherapy Take a daily bath containing the essential oils of clary sage, geranium and lavender during the two weeks before a period is due. The same oils may also help if inhaled from a tissue. As a preventive measure, try mixing them with a carrier lotion and using the mixture constantly as an after-bath lotion. Oils of Roman camomile, rose otto or melissa are said also to be beneficial – inhale the scent of a single drop of any of them from the palm of the hand, cupping it over your nose.

Massage Some sufferers have found that a massage can help to relieve PMT – perhaps a full body massage for its all-round relaxation and tonic effect. A neck and shoulder massage is recommended for headaches, and a light, abdominal massage to ease discomfort in that region.

Herbal Medicine Try infusions (see p. 184) of camomile two or three times a day in the week or so before a period. It is gently calming and a diuretic, removing some of the fluid that may have been retained.

A consultant herbalist may use stronger diuretics, such as couch grass, together with hormonal treatment, especially chaste tree, to encourage progesterone secretion.

Bach Remedies Crab apple is suggested for feelings of disgust towards menstrual blood; Cherry plum for tension and for a fear of being overtaken by emotion and moodiness. Water violet is prescribed when the tension is caused by an unfulfilled need for solitude and withdrawal; Aspen for fear of the heightened sensitivity which many women experience. Holly is advised for intense, negative emotions; Beech for feeling intolerant towards one's condition, and Rock water for those who try to deny their feelings.

Acupuncture The important meridians to treat are the kidney, liver, conception and sometimes stomach and governor (see chart, p. 14). MOXIBUSTION to points on these meridians may also help.

Homoeopathy Start taking the following remedies either morning and night or every four hours, according to severity, for the appropriate symptoms 24 hours before the symptoms are expected to appear. If the sufferer bursts into tears easily, has painful breasts and irregular periods and possibly nausea, *Pulsatilla 30* is advised. If chilly, depressed and weepy, with indifference to sex and a tendency to turn against loved ones, try *Sepia 30*. *Nat. mur. 30* is recommended if there is sadness, irritability, much fluid retention and swollen breasts.

Naturopathy EXERCISE usually helps general well-being and reduces fluid retention. It is also advisable to cut down the intake of salt, sugary foods and alcohol. Supplements

that might be prescribed include vitamin B, especially B6, magnesium and oil of evening primrose. MASSAGE is of great benefit in relieving TENSION and congestion.

An orthodox view

Hospital trials in London in the early 1980s and some doctors' experiences have shown that a course of evening primrose oil helps many women, and treatment is usually timed to begin a few days before symptoms are expected. Extra vitamin B6 is also prescribed in some cases, especially for women taking oral contraceptive pills, who are more likely to lack this vitamin. Doctors can help to restore hormone levels more directly by prescribing progesterone in various forms during the second half of the menstrual cycle.

Exercise and a healthy diet (see EATING FOR HEALTH) may help a sufferer to 'weather the storm' if symptoms are persistent and relief remains difficult to attain.

PRENATAL THERAPY

The belief that the pattern of our mental, emotional, spiritual and physical attributes is laid down during gestation underlies prenatal therapy, now usually known as the METAMORPHIC TECHNIQUE. Therapists of the technique focus on the spinal reflex areas of the head, feet and hands, claiming to unlock that pattern and so release life energy blocked in the prenatal period.

PRIMAL THERAPY
The 'scream' of release from childhood trauma

As children, many people suffer hurtful and frightening experiences which, although they may be soon forgotten or pushed into the unconscious mind, cause pain, insecurity and emotional problems such as NERVOUS DISORDERS in adulthood. This is the theory behind primal therapy, which tries to offer a way of coming to terms with such experiences. See also HUMANISTIC PSYCHOLOGY.

Primal therapy was developed by the American psychiatrist Dr Arthur Janov, who was interested in the intense cries produced by patients as they came face to face for the first time as adults with needs for parental love that had not been fulfilled in childhood.

Janov found that simply voicing this 'primal scream' was often enough to cure people. Janov's work was influenced by the ideas of the psychoanalyst Wilhelm Reich (see REICHIAN THERAPY) – who believed that mental pain was reflected also in bodily posture, breathing patterns and muscular tensions – as well as by those of the Swiss psychotherapist Alice Miller.

Miller thought that in many societies children were brought up and educated in ways that caused great pain – they were shown too little affection, had impossible demands made of them and were ridiculed, ignored or punished when they failed to meet those demands. Sometimes children who were physically ill-treated or sexually abused could not help themselves or express their pain for fear of losing their parents' love and sympathy. The childhood traumas and suppressed feelings that resulted were thought by Miller to be the root of later emotional difficulties and unhappiness.

Primal therapy aims to help the lonely suffering child within the adult to express his long-ignored needs, hurt and anger, to grieve if necessary, and finally to come to terms with his feelings so that he can begin to live freely and fully again.

Therapy is usually intensive – generally carried out at weekends, for two to three hours, over a period of several weeks – and can be extremely traumatic. However, many patients report that it has changed their lives permanently. For further information and the names of practitioners, contact The London Association of Primal Therapists, 18A Laurier Road, London NW5 1SH.

PROLAPSE

The most common type of prolapse – the forward or downward displacement of part of the body – occurs in a woman's vagina after childbirth. However, the displacement may not occur for many years.

Weakness of the ligaments supporting the bladder, womb or rectum causes the patient to feel a lump in her vagina – particularly when she coughs or strains. In severe cases the lump protrudes through the vaginal opening. Even when there is no actual prolapse, the ligament weakness may affect the neck of the bladder, causing INCONTINENCE.

In both women and men, SLIPPED DISC is a frequently encountered form of prolapse.

What the therapists recommend

Acupressure For prolapse of the womb, press diagonally inwards two fingers' width above the pubic bone and one hand's width out from the centre line. For a prolapsed rectum, press firmly inwards two fingers' width below the navel on the centre line.

Naturopathy Treatment would concentrate mainly on EXERCISE and posture. Pelvic floor muscle exercises in particular are considered invaluable, and a regular class in YOGA may be advised. At the same time, it is vital to avoid lifting weights and so bearing down on the lower abdomen. Correct posture can also be maintained with sessions of the ALEXANDER TECHNIQUE.

Prevention is much better than cure, and it is advisable to give attention to these factors before, as well as after, childbirth.

An orthodox view

After childbirth, the risk of a woman developing a prolapse is increased by OBESITY. Frequent or difficult childbirth and large babies can also cause the problem. In the postnatal period, therefore, it is important to do pelvic floor exercises to strengthen the muscles supporting the bladder, womb and rectum. See also PREGNANCY and NATURAL CHILDBIRTH.

If incontinence is only a problem during times of particular strain – such as when playing sports – a tampon worn during the activity may give a woman sufficient support. Doctors sometimes fit temporary plastic ring pessaries to women at risk, or advise an operation to provide physical support for the bladder, womb and rectum.

PROSTATE PROBLEMS

The chestnut-sized prostate gland lies at the neck of a man's bladder. Through the middle of it runs the urethra, which passes urine from the bladder to the penis. In men over 50, the prostate gland often grows to the size of an apple, upsetting the flow of urine.

In some cases, the sufferer passes smaller amounts of urine; in others, he passes urine more frequently, particularly during the night. There is an embarrassing tendency to dribble afterwards, and a feeling that the bladder is not completely empty. Sometimes he finds it difficult and painful to urinate – particularly during the day.

An enlarged prostate may also develop malignant growths (see CANCER). Even if the original symptoms are mild, a doctor should be seen so that routine urine and blood tests can be taken – and, if necessary, a more detailed examination made in hospital.

Inflammation of the prostate gland, or prostatitis, normally occurs in younger men, causing pain in the lower abdomen, back, testicles, or the area between the scrotum (the pouch containing the testicles) and the anus. The patient may feel unwell, with a raised temperature – and his urine, which may be cloudy, bloody or smelly, is passed more often and more urgently. Prostatitis is caused by infection, which is sometimes sexually transmitted.

What the therapists recommend

Acupuncture Practitioners claim success in relieving prostate problems by using pressure points on the bladder, large intestine, spleen, kidney, conception and governor meridians. In addition, treatment by MOXIBUSTION may be applied.

Herbal Medicine For non-cancerous enlargement of the prostate, and difficulty in passing water, herbalists may use diuretic herbs such as couch grass, horsetail or saw palmetto, to promote the discharge of urine.

Naturopathy Hot and cold compresses, or sitz baths, are a key part of naturopathic treatment of prostate disorders. Regular EXERCISE is a preventive measure for enlarged prostate symptoms, and supplements of zinc may reduce the swelling: about 15mg a day is the usual recommended dose, or perhaps eating 1oz (30g) of pumpkin seeds daily. Plenty of fluids may also help – but cut down on such drinks as alcohol, strong tea and coffee.

Biochemic Tissue Salts Try *Nat. sulph.* when it is difficult or impossible to retain urine; *Calc. phos.* for a frequent need to urinate; and *Mag. phos.* when the need is constant when walking, or even standing.

An orthodox view

Older men with an enlarged prostate often benefit from an operation allowing urine to pass more freely. If the growth is cancerous, hormone treatment may control the condition for many years. In cases of prostatitis doctors will prescribe a course of antibiotics, which could last for several weeks.

PSIONIC MEDICINE

Aimed at treating the basic cause of illness, rather than using drugs to suppress symptoms, psionic medicine was founded in the late 1960s by a retired British GP, Dr George Laurence. As well as drawing on the experience gained in some 40 years of practice, Dr Laurence based his technique on several established alternative therapies. These included DOWSING (diagnosing disease by

rod and pendulum), HOMOEOPATHY, and MIASM THEORY (which asserts that illness is often a symptom of a deep-rooted disease).

The therapy – which involves helping the body to heal itself – takes its name from the Greek letter *psi*, generally used to denote some psychic or paranormal phenomenon. However, Dr Laurence declared that psionic medicine should be practised only by qualified and experienced doctors, who had the knowledge to diagnose and treat the imbalances which cause disease – usually by homoeopathic means.

For further information, get in touch with The Institute of Psionic Medicine, Hindhead, Surrey GU26 6HU.

PSORIASIS

The raised, red scaly patches caused by psoriasis can appear anywhere on the skin, but most often affect the knees or elbows. It is a common disorder, affecting as many as one person in 50. The cause is unknown, but it sometimes runs in families. It is uncommon before the age of ten, usually erupting between the ages of 15 and 30.

The rash begins as small red spots, which may merge to form circular or oval patches 2-3in (50-75mm) across. It often affects both sides of the body symmetrically – for example, if one elbow is affected, so is the other. Fingernails and toenails are frequently involved, becoming pitted and thickened, and sometimes separating from the nail bed. About one in 20 psoriasis sufferers also develop a mild form of RHEUMATOID ARTHRITIS, often in the fingers, knees and ankles.

The complaint sometimes follows two or three weeks after a throat infection and can also be triggered by drugs such as chloroquine, which may be prescribed for rheumatoid arthritis, some SKIN DISORDERS, liver infections and malaria. Although it is not caused by STRESS, worry and ANXIETY may trigger or aggravate an attack.

What the therapists recommend

Herbal Medicine Traditionally, herbalists have prescribed blood-cleansing herbs for the condition: an infusion (see p. 184) of dandelion root, red clover flowers and burdock may help the purification process.

Bach Remedies Crab apple is suggested for feelings of disgust and shame; Willow for resentment over the condition. Rescue Remedy cream or Impatiens applied externally may help to relieve itching.

Homoeopathy Psoriasis should be treated by an experienced practitioner. However, the following remedies may be helpful, taken three or four times daily for 14 days in the 6th potency. Try *Sulphur* for dry, red, itchy patches, which are worse after taking a bath, in someone who feels the heat; and *Graphites* when the skin exudes a sticky, honey-like discharge, particularly behind the ear. *Petroleum* is prescribed when the skin is dry, rough and cracked and the condition grows worse with each winter.

Aromatherapy It is said that pure essential oils of bergamot and lavender can keep the condition at bay when used both in the bath and applied in a lotion or oil. A white lotion base is recommended if the psoriasis is not over-dry or flaky. However, if the skin is very dry and the patches very scaly, then a vegetable oil may be better (and sandalwood essential oil can also be used). If in doubt, first try a lotion.

An orthodox view

While there is no cure for psoriasis, doctors can confirm the diagnosis, give general advice and prescribe creams and ointments to give relief. Coal tar, dithranol and steroid preparations are often effective, particularly if applied under a plastic dressing. Sunlight or artificial ultraviolet light may also help. Many sufferers improve dramatically if they are able to move to a sunnier climate.

If arthritis develops, doctors can take blood samples to check if another disease such as rheumatoid arthritis is the cause. They can prescribe anti-inflammatory painkillers, which help to ease pain and stiffness.

In 1990, researchers at the Finnish National Public Health Institute in Helsinki linked alcohol consumption with psoriasis. They found that 144 men with the complaint drank an average of 42.9g of alcohol a day compared with 21g a day in men with other skin disorders. One unit of alcohol (see ALCOHOLISM) equals 8g.

PSYCHODRAMA

An actress, who became much more pleasant in private life when she was able to play unpleasant roles on stage, provided the inspiration for the idea of psychodrama. Jacob Moreno, a psychiatrist who lived in Vienna at the time of Freud (see PSYCHOTHERAPY), and who had noticed the actress's behaviour, reasoned that the change occurred because acting out her true hostile feelings on stage left her free to express the more positive side of her nature in real life.

Moreno developed a theory that if people could get together in groups to act out frightening and difficult situations, they would be able to express true feelings that might never be released in real life. He turned this into a form of psychotherapy.

In psychodrama, groups of patients – guided by a therapist – take it in turns to act out each other's real-life roles and situations. Because they are acting, participants feel free to express their emotions to each other much more freely and safely than they often can in real-life encounters.

Psychodrama can be a powerful experience, exposing strong emotions, so the guidance of a qualified and experienced therapist is essential. The therapist's role is to help the group to interpret the events they act out, and to clarify participants' feelings about the real people involved. Many patients claim that psychodrama enables them to come to terms with their feelings in a constructive and supportive setting.

See also HUMANISTIC PSYCHOLOGY.

PSYCHO-SOMATIC ILLNESS
It's not all in the mind . . .

There are two extreme and contradictory schools of thought among doctors regarding psychosomatic illness – the belief that physical illness can be caused by the workings of the mind. The first school believes that *all* illness is psychosomatic, in that it affects both mind and body. The second school, on the other hand, dismisses psychosomatic illness entirely, and it is not even mentioned in their medical textbooks.

The term psychosomatic – from the Greek words *psyche*, meaning 'soul', and *soma*, meaning 'body' – became current at the beginning of this century. It replaced phrases such as 'organic neurosis' and 'cardiac neurosis', which suggested that bodily illness was the result of neurotic feelings.

According to believers in psychosomatic illness, STRESS-related ailments such as ASTHMA and MIGRAINE have two main 'self-induced' causes. These are an excessive release of hormones into the bloodstream (causing changes in various parts of the body) and hyperactivity of the nervous system releasing too much adrenaline into the bloodstream.

Both these conditions occur when emotions such as anger, DEPRESSION, guilt and hate are bottled up or belatedly released. For example, if you cannot express your anger towards someone close to you – such as your husband, wife or boss – you may channel the unreleased tension to different parts of your body.

In turn, this can give rise to a variety of symptoms, including rapid blinking, tics, TEETH-GRINDING, HEADACHES, stomach rumblings and DIARRHOEA. If the symptoms persist they may lead to more serious complaints such as high BLOOD PRESSURE and peptic ULCERS.

Psychosomatic illness is often associated with feelings of not being 'in charge' of oneself. Many self-help therapies therefore aim to give a greater sense of control over MIND AND BODY. This is particularly useful to the small number of patients who suffer from more than one psychosomatic illness at a time. Until recently, treatment was based upon a combination of tranquillising drugs and PSYCHOTHERAPY. These have now been augmented by numerous alternative remedies, which are said to be highly effective.

Despite an increasing acceptance of genuine pain and worry caused by psychosomatic illness, many patients object to the term – which, they think, smacks of perfectly healthy people imagining that they are ill. However, as long as we remember how closely linked the mind and body are, it is relatively easy to understand how the one can affect the other. For example, suppressed GRIEF – the inability to mourn the loss of someone we loved – can lead to RESPIRATORY DISORDERS.

As the saying goes: 'If the eyes do not weep, then other organs will.'

What the therapists recommend

Autogenic Training Teachers say that physical problems caused by stress have responded extremely well to the training. However, some psychosomatic problems – for example, where there is pain without an obvious physical cause – need longer than normal periods of treatment.

Dance Movement Therapy By concentrating on the links between people's emotions and their bodies, the therapy tries to provide a helpful approach to psychosomatic problems. It claims to open up new ways of understanding the feelings that cause physical symptoms – and aims to explore more positive ways of expressing and communicating these feelings.

Hypnotherapy Numerous studies have shown the effectiveness of hypnotherapy, and the relaxation it produces is said to be particularly helpful for bronchial asthma. Therapists try to get to the source of the problem, and say that getting the patient to relive the event that triggered it is often a necessary part of the cure. Self hypnosis is also said to be particularly beneficial.

Bach Remedies Therapists say that it is important to deal with any obvious link between physical illness and your mental or emotional state. Examine your feelings as honestly as you can, and do not ignore any emotional condition which may persist and deepen, causing physical distress. Then you should be able to choose the best remedies.

PSYCHO-SYNTHESIS
Bringing out the best in yourself

An Italian psychiatrist, Dr Roberto Assagioli (1888-1974), began to develop the principles of psychosynthesis around the time of the First World War. Although originally a follower of Sigmund Freud, Assagioli took a more optimistic view of human psychology, believing that it was in each person's nature to develop a harmonious and balanced personality, and to realise his fullest potential.

While he accepted the vital importance of the lower unconscious – those aspects of ourselves related to early childhood that we have yet to become aware of, or that we ignore because they are uncomfortable or frightening – Assagioli believed that man also has a 'higher' unconscious often ignored by psychologists. In psychosynthesis he tried to correct this by giving more weight to spiritual needs and the development of a so-called 'transpersonal self'. This was what might almost be termed a 'new identity' for each person. He would no longer be concerned just with satisfying his own needs, but his actions would be guided by a sense of love, unity and cooperation with others and the whole of nature.

This process of self-development, the essence of psychosynthesis, requires imagination and will – not just in the sense of 'will-power' but also as 'goodwill' and a genuine desire to change. Assagioli believed that although man has an innate drive to develop his own potential, his behaviour is not determined but free, and each individual has to choose and take responsibility for his own development.

Who it can help Since it concentrates both on curing disorders and on developing a healthy personality, psychosynthesis tends to attract a broad range of clients, some of whom are interested in personal growth and, in particular, those suffering from a mid-life crisis of meaning. It is also said to be helpful for conditions such as STRESS, MIGRAINE,

PSYCHOSOMATIC ILLNESS and PHOBIAS. Anyone suffering from troubled relationships or who simply wants to understand others and communicate better with them may also benefit from psychosynthesis.

Finding a practitioner Practitioners should have completed a three or four-year course and have either a Psychosynthesis Counselling Diploma or a Psychosynthesis Psychotherapy Diploma. To find a qualified practitioner, contact the Institute of Psychosynthesis, The Barn, Nan Clark's Lane, London NW7 4HH, or Psychosynthesis and Education Trust, 48 Guildford Road, Stockwell, London SW8 2BU.

Consulting a practitioner Psychosynthesis is usually given in courses of six or more sessions, depending on individual need. A wide range of different methods can be used, depending on the needs of each individual. These can include analysis, imagining, considering yourself in different ways, movement, MEDITATION and keeping a diary.

Whatever methods are used, the goals of psychosynthesis remain the same: attaining knowledge and control of all aspects of your personality, discovering a new – and true – identity, and integrating every part of yourself into it.

An orthodox view

This approach is more educational than therapeutic, and is not usually regarded as a treatment for specific diseases.

PSYCHOTHERAPY
Someone to talk you out of trouble

Talking your way through problems, the basis of psychotherapy, is a natural way of coping with everyday difficulties. Everyone knows that a heart-to-heart chat with a trusted neighbour or an evening spent pouring it all out to a sympathetic friend can make you feel better. At a slightly more formal level is COUNSELLING from a trained but non-specialist counsellor. However, in their way these procedures are all simple forms of psychotherapy.

But psychotherapy itself does more than this and can help when problems are too difficult or too deep to be solved by normal means. Like ordinary conversation, talking to a psychotherapist can have many aspects – discussing your experiences, revealing personal feelings, trying to understand your own behaviour and that of others, receiving advice and encouragement, and even some-

times getting angry or having an argument.

Where psychotherapy is different, however, is in the therapist's professional training and experience, which enable him to organise and guide each session, so that the patient makes the most out of his time with the therapist. Unlike orthodox psychiatrists, psychotherapists are not usually medically trained and cannot prescribe treatments such as drugs and shock therapy.

Whether the problem is longstanding difficulties in a marriage, coping with PHOBIAS or other forms of neurosis, or simply a feeling of being unfulfilled or unhappy, psychotherapists see symptoms such as ANXIETY, TENSION, OBSESSIVE-COMPULSIVE BEHAVIOUR and DEPRESSION as a sign of some sort of inner disharmony.

The task of psychotherapy is to help the person to understand and correct this, so that he breaks out of his pattern of destructive behaviour and thoughts, has a stronger sense of his own identity, and is happier and more in control of his life and relationships. To do this, most forms of psychotherapy rely on the patient talking to a trained therapist, but some also use other means of expression such as ART THERAPY, BIOENERGETICS, DANCE MOVEMENT THERAPY and MUSIC THERAPY.

Who it can help Anyone with personal, emotional or behavioural problems may benefit. Depression, tension, INSOMNIA, STRESS, obsessive-compulsive behaviour and irrational fears may all be symptoms of psychological problems which could be helped by psychotherapy. In addition, many physical ailments such as ANGINA, stomach ULCERS, PSORIASIS and COLITIS may be related to emotional stresses and conflicts that psychotherapy can help.

Finally, psychotherapy is not just for the sick or troubled – many people want simply to find out more about themselves, to enrich their lives and improve their relationships.

Choosing a form of therapy Psychotherapy is a very wide field, including a great range of different approaches. Choosing the right therapist is difficult at the best of times, and more so when you are troubled. Nevertheless, the choice should be made with care, since mistakes can be costly and also time-consuming. New patients are advised to consider the following issues before opting for a particular course of therapy:

Long or short-term therapy? People with fairly simple problems – a phobia, perhaps, or a single difficult relationship – but whose lives are otherwise satisfying, may find short-term BEHAVIOURAL THERAPY, COGNITIVE THERAPY or PRIMAL THERAPY most suitable. Sessions are directed at achieving particular goals, with the therapist taking charge and the patient following instructions.

For suitable cases, this can yield quick

results. The drawbacks, however, are that once probed, seemingly simple problems can turn out to have roots that go much deeper – and which the patient is often unaware of – so short-term therapy may not be enough. There is also less time to build up a good relationship with the therapist – an important factor in determining whether treatment will be successful.

Note Short-term therapies overlap to some extent with counselling, but in general this is more suitable for problems of adjustment – to divorce or retirement, for example – while psychotherapy deals with issues that involve some aspect of the patient's personality.

Difficulties involving basic problems with attitudes and relationships – for example, conflicts over security and independence in a marriage, or long-term depression and a sense of meaninglessness – generally call for more lengthy treatment such as that offered by GESTALT THERAPY, Freudian psychoanalysis and practitioners of HUMANISTIC PSYCHOLOGY (although these often offer shorter treatment as well).

These approaches concentrate on helping you to understand why you feel and behave as you do, believing that change can only grow out of self-knowledge. The patient is expected to take responsibility for his own treatment and to play an active role. Sessions tend to be freer and less directed by the therapist than with shorter therapies, and there is plenty of time to talk about feelings and responses as they occur.

A deep and trusting relationship between therapist and patient is essential and is believed to enhance and enliven the patient's own inner healing powers. In psychoanalysis, the relationship is even thought to mirror the person's original relationship with his parents, giving him an opportunity to work through early problems that were never resolved during childhood.

Lengthier therapies also enable the therapist to help analyse in depth his patient's unconscious fears and longings, suppressed emotions, past traumas, dreams, and even his hopes for the future and sense of purpose. However, this can take a long time and may not offer any immediate solutions to problems. Patients must be prepared to put a great deal into their therapy themselves, and must not look to the therapist to provide all the answers.

Working with thoughts, feelings or behaviour? Most psychotherapists have a holistic approach, believing that thoughts, feelings and physical actions are all expressions of the same underlying personality, and that a change in one will bring about corresponding changes in the others. Different therapies adopt different approaches, so thought must be given to choosing which would be most comfortable to get along with, bearing in mind that feelings can change as treatment progresses.

Shorter therapies tend to approach problems from a single viewpoint. Behaviourists work with actions, cognitive therapists with ways of thinking, and primal therapists with feelings. Lengthier treatments generally use a greater variety of approaches: both thoughts and feelings are important factors in psychoanalysis, while TRANSACTIONAL ANALYSIS concentrates on thoughts and behaviour. Gestalt therapy is broad enough to tackle all three.

How much change do you want? The longer psychotherapy of any sort goes on, the more different aspects of the patient's life can be examined, and the more challenges are presented to his view of himself and others. While short-term therapy is aimed at making just a few changes, longer types can involve fundamental shifts in attitudes, behaviour and way of life.

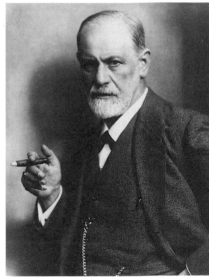

Psychotherapy arose from the work of the Austrian psychiatrist Sigmund Freud (1856-1939). In his psychoanalysis, patients relive the traumatic episodes they have repressed, and so help to overcome the cause of their nervous problems. Psychotherapy is a shorter version of Freud's method – one in which therapist and patient are much closer. Freud came to England in 1938 to escape Nazi persecution. His house in Hampstead, now the Freud Museum, preserves his consulting room with its famous couch (left).

Deciding on the right type of treatment and how long to carry on may require the insight of the evangelist who wrote:

Lord, Grant me
The courage to change
What can be changed,
The serenity to accept
What cannot,
And the wisdom
To know the difference.

Finding a therapist Psychotherapy is rarely available on the NHS except for patients with diagnosed mental disorders, but your GP may be able to recommend or refer you to a therapist privately. Alternatively, contact the British Psychological Society, St Andrew's House, 4 Princess Road East, Leicester LE1 7DR, or the British Association for Counselling, 37A Sheep Street, Rugby, Warwickshire CV21 3BX. If you send a stamped addressed envelope they can put you in touch with organisations for various types of psychotherapy. Lists of qualified practitioners are also available from the organisations given in entries on specific therapies.

Remember that in Britain anyone may practise as a psychotherapist, and there is no single registering body, so it is up to the client to check the credentials of a therapist.

Seeing a therapist What happens depends on the therapy involved. You may be asked to join a group or get personal attention; therapy may involve just talking, or talking and acting out your feelings, moving, drawing or making music; you may be treated as an equal partner in a process of discovery, or simply be expected to follow instructions.

Ensure at the first session that you know which approach to expect, or you may be disappointed. However, your needs may change once a process of change begins.

Generally, at this first session, you will be asked why you have come, what your view of the problem is and what you hope to gain from treatment. This is also your chance to ask questions about the therapist's training and qualifications, his methods and how he can help you. If he cannot do this in language you can understand, beware!

Never allow yourself to be rushed or pressured into a lengthy course of psychotherapy – of all treatments, this is the one where personal feelings and compatibility with the therapist matter most. If you feel uncertain, visit two or three therapists for one session each before deciding – no more, or you may end up even more confused.

An orthodox view

Short-term psychotherapy for particular problems is accepted by many doctors as a valid, often successful treatment for conditions such as phobias, anxiety and obsessive-compulsive behaviour. It is also generally accepted that there is a psychological or emotional factor in many illnesses (see PSYCHOSOMATIC ILLNESS; PERSONALITY AND DISEASE) and that psychotherapy may be a useful additional treatment for them.

See also NERVOUS DISORDERS.

PUBERTY AND ADOLESCENCE

The period of physical and psychological changes that herald adulthood – adolescence – is often difficult. It starts with puberty, when sexual maturity begins. See COPING WITH THE PROBLEMS OF GROWING UP, p. 292.

PULSE DIAGNOSIS

This method is an important diagnostic aid in traditional Chinese therapies. Practitioners interpret the strength and 'quality' of the pulses in a patient's wrists as a clue to past, present and future health – and as a guide in deciding treatment. See ORIENTAL DIAGNOSIS.

PYRAMID POWER

A cat in the Great Pyramid at Giza near Cairo was the unlikely starting point for discovering the seemingly 'magical' potential of pyramids built to similar proportions. In the 1930s a French holidaymaker, Antoine Bovis, saw the cat, and was struck by the fact that it had not decayed, but dehydrated. He later experimented with small models of the Great Pyramid – itself covering 13 acres (over 5 hectares). He reproduced its proportions correctly and positioned his model in the same way, with the sides facing due north, south, east and west. He placed a dead cat in his pyramid and found that it also dried out – and so did fruit and vegetables.

Scientists generally regarded his findings as worthless at the time, but some remained interested. They and many lay people pursued the investigations, particularly in the United States. There in the 1970s Bill Schul and Ed Pettit reported that the growth of sunflower seedlings in a pyramid was speeded up – but not equally throughout. The area just below the apex produced the fastest growth and that on the floor along the sides had least effect. They found that seeds kept in pyramids germinated more quickly too.

Schul and Pettit tested milk in pyramids a number of times. They reported that while control samples outside the pyramid went sour and mouldy within days, those inside turned into a creamy yoghurt-like substance with no mould after six weeks. Tomatoes, grapes, eggs, calf's liver, sirloin steak and fish were also tested. Again controls outside the pyramid went 'off', while items inside dehydrated and shrank, but did not go mouldy. Pyramids of glass, wood, cardboard and plastic have all produced similar effects.

This lack of decay suggested that bacterial growth was halted. This was also borne out by an unusually quick healing of cuts, burns and bruises on people who spent time in a pyramid model. Toothache, headaches, cramps, rheumatic pains and tension have also been relieved in a pyramid.

Their experiments confirmed similar findings by Boris Vern, director of a pyramid research centre in Washington, DC. Two more US researchers, Bill Kerrell and Kathy Goggin, did similar tests. In addition they found that patterns of brain activity on electroencephalographs changed markedly in people inside a pyramid, even though they wore blindfolds and did not know when or whether a pyramid was placed over them. Many reported a warm, tingling sensation when inside a pyramid. Sounder sleep, increased vitality and improved well-being have also been reported.

A peculiar energy flow, a change in IONISATION or an electromagnetic force is considered by some scientists to be involved in the mysterious powers of pyramids, but a confirmed source of those powers has yet to be pinpointed. Researchers are testing theories that the pyramid shape creates a heightened energy field that alters the rate of physical, chemical and biological processes.

One experimenter put Bovis's findings to practical use. Karel Drbal, a Czechoslovak radio and television engineer, extended the experiments to metal, and found that minute pockets of moisture that cause weaknesses in metal dried out in a pyramid.

In the late 1940s he patented a pyramid-shaped razor-blade preserver that has sold widely, and it is said to keep a blade sharp for many weeks. The blade lies in the pyramid between shaves with its edge pointing north-south. Drbal's explanation is that minute pockets of moisture remaining along the fine edge of the blade swiftly evaporate, halting the corrosion of the edge.

An orthodox view

Most scientists view proponents' claims for pyramid power with considerable scepticism.

Coping with problems of growing up

The teenage years are well known as a time of upheaval and stress for young people and their families alike. Girls and boys face rapid and uneven changes to every area of their lives; parents have to cope with their children's erratic behaviour and sometimes baffling choice of friends and clothes. Parental authority may be seriously questioned as happy, well behaved children change suddenly into moody adolescents, spending more time alone or with friends than with the family.

Disruptive as adolescence can be, it is a natural and necessary part of growing up. Understanding, love and acceptance by other members of the family can do much to smooth the rocky path to adulthood.

Although the words are often used interchangeably, adolescence and puberty are not the same. Puberty refers to the physical changes – such as breast development in girls, for example, or deepening of the voice in boys – which mark the start of adolescence, and which transform the child's body into that of a sexually mature adult. Adolescence, by contrast, refers to the whole process of growing up, including all the mental, emotional and social changes that must occur before the person is accepted as an adult member of society.

Puberty This process of development takes about two years, and is usually completed between the ages of 12 and 17. It is a period of rapid growth, boys gaining about 4in (10cm) and 13lb (6kg) a year and girls about 3in (8cm) and 11lb (5kg). It is also a time of rapid sexual development.

For boys, the first sign is an increase in the size of the testicles and penis, followed by growth of hair around the genitals and in the armpits, and the beginnings of a beard. The voice box increases in size, causing the voice to 'break' and eventually to deepen to a man's pitch. By the age of 13 most boys have experienced their first ejaculation and find themselves easily aroused.

In girls, puberty begins with breast development, growth of the reproductive organs, genital and armpit hair, and an increase of fat around hips and thighs, giving a more womanly appearance. The first period usually occurs about a year later – on average, at around 12 or 13, although it can be as early as 10 or as late as 17.

Adolescence This continues for some time after puberty, often into the twenties – and is not considered completed until the individual achieves physical maturity, emotional independence, a sense of identity (including sexual identity), education and training for a job, financial independence and a full sexual relationship.

These changes can take a long time and prove very demanding. Even so, most adolescents cope well and emerge as mature, well adjusted adults. However, some areas can cause particular problems . . .

If puberty arrives early or late Boys especially tend to worry if they seem to be developing more slowly than those around them. In fact, although on average puberty starts at 13 or 14, any time up to about 17 can be considered normal. Unless malnutrition or illness is interfering with normal development, reassurance and time are all that are needed. Hormonal treatment may be considered if puberty has not begun at 18, or in rare cases of hormone deficiency.

Unusual conditions such as premature hormone production may lead to puberty beginning as early as five or six. Affected children develop physically and sexually, while retaining the thoughts, emotions and social status of infants. Drugs or surgery may be needed to prevent too-rapid development from overwhelming them and causing behavioural problems.

Coping with periods Most girls view the approach of their first period with a degree of fear and apprehension, and even those who look forward to their entry into womanhood can be frightened or embarrassed when it actually happens. However, these doubts and fears are usually short-lived and girls soon learn to cope, needing only a little extra attention and understanding from parents, and advice about using sanitary pads or tampons.

Better to be active

In some girls considerable PAIN, NAUSEA, HEADACHES, DIZZINESS, WATER RETENTION, sore breasts and irritability may be associated with their periods. These symptoms tend to lessen or disappear as the hormonal cycle becomes more regular over the years, but until then periods can often be heavy, irregular or painful. Even after the cycle has settled down, it can easily be disrupted again by STRESS, travel, illness or excessive dieting.

Period pains can usually be relieved by hot-water bottles or mild drugs available from chemists – doctors advise that it is better to take these and remain active than to stay at home feeling ill and sore. Slight tension and irritability before a period is normal and needs no treatment.

Hormonal drugs are given only if periods are extremely heavy or irregular, or cause serious feelings of illness. For less severe cases, alternative remedies such as the herbal oil of evening primrose may be helpful. See also PERIOD PROBLEMS; PREMENSTRUAL TENSION.

Spots and pimples They can make life a misery for both boys and girls during puberty, causing them to feel self-conscious and unattractive. The problem usually disappears as puberty progresses and hormone levels settle down. For help and guidance, see ACNE; SPOTS AND PIMPLES.

Learning to relate
During adolescence boys and girls enjoy each other's company more than they did as children. At this stage they need frequent opportunities to get together in groups, make new friends and practise social skills without adults being present. Parents can help by providing safe places to meet and not intruding too much.

Breast worries   Girls often worry if one breast appears to grow faster than the other during puberty. This problem seldom lasts, usually correcting itself as hormone production stabilises. A slight difference in size is, in fact, quite normal and needs no treatment.

Tender and slightly enlarged breasts can also affect some boys as a result of hormonal changes during puberty. The condition usually disappears without treatment. Simple reassurance that it is not a sign of 'sex-change' or homosexuality is generally all that is needed from parents.

Weight problems   As hips and breasts grow and take on a rounded, feminine form, teenage girls often worry about putting on weight and getting fat. The changes happen in sudden spurts – some girls putting on as much as 20lb (9kg) around the time of the first period – which can be alarming and hard to accept.

This weight gain is normal, however – the hormone oestrogen is the cause, so although many girls start dieting, cutting down on food does little to help. Unfortunately, a few girls and boys want so desperately to stay thin that they resort to extreme dieting and end up suffering from the so-called 'slimmer's disease', ANOREXIA.

Most adolescents, however, find that they can stay slim enough to feel and look good simply by eating a well-balanced diet (see EATING FOR HEALTH), including plenty of FIBRE; cutting down on sweets and snacks; avoiding alcohol; and taking regular, moderate exercise. Weight worries often disappear too as teenagers grow taller and start to take on their full adult proportions.

Masturbation   Young people sometimes feel guilty about masturbation, or worry that it can harm them. In fact, masturbation is a natural form of safe sex. And not only does it relieve sexual tensions, it can help both boys and girls to understand their bodily responses and contribute to a happy sex life in adulthood.

Identity crisis   The many changes that adolescence brings can be quite bewildering to teenagers. Friends and society generally may treat them as responsible and grown up, while parents still expect obedience and fitting in with rules at home. Adolescents may also reject parents' beliefs and standards, while still needing support and guidance for they may not yet be sure of their own values.

The situation is made even more difficult by the powerful sexual feelings adolescence brings, while hormonal fluctuations mean that even sexual feelings change rapidly, adding to teenagers' uncertainty.

That sense of identity, however, becomes more and more influenced by friends and less by parents. And unlike parental love, acceptance by friends depends on ability and personality. Trying to win acceptance can be a source of stress and anxiety.

Most young people emerge from these difficulties with a strong sense of their own identity. Very few remain unsure of themselves, unable to relate to others – particularly to the opposite sex – or lacking in confidence. There is a danger that these teenagers may become withdrawn, rebellious or resort to drugs or alcohol. For them, sensitive help from a counsellor (see COUNSELLING) may be needed. Families and friends can help by giving understanding and support.

When help is needed

A stable, loving and accepting family, support from friends, and people to look up to as good examples will usually prevent teenage difficulties from becoming serious problems. Those who lack these protective factors may find themselves in trouble or needing help. Even then explanation, time and reassurance are usually enough.

Very few need medical help for conditions such as hormonal imbalances, and PSYCHOTHERAPY is recommended only for serious emotional or behavioural problems. Among other alternative therapies that may alleviate less serious problems are the BACH REMEDIES.

QUINSY

Occasionally during an attack of TONSIL-LITIS, an abscess forms behind one tonsil – an uncommon condition known as quinsy. Pain is worse on the affected side of the throat and may also be felt in the ear. There may be difficulty swallowing and speaking.

Diagnosis of quinsy is made by looking into the mouth and seeing that one side of the throat is red and swollen, so that the tonsil and the uvula – the fleshy lump that hangs down from the back of the palate – are pushed towards the other side.

What the therapists recommend

Naturopathy Plenty of fluids, especially cold fruit juices, should be taken. Herbal gargles, particularly red sage, are recommended. In addition, a cold compress around the neck may help to ease the inflammation and any swelling. Extra vitamin C is likely to be prescribed: 500mg to 1g a day, with zinc or vitamin A.

An orthodox view

Although an ordinary sore throat does not usually require medical attention, consult a doctor if you suspect quinsy. He can arrange for an ear, nose and throat surgeon to release the pus from the abscess under local anaesthetic, providing rapid relief. Antibiotics may be given to clear up the infection and reduce fever.

To prevent further attacks, some surgeons advise removing the tonsils after the inflammation has cleared up.

RADIESTHESIA AND RADIONICS

The Abbé Mermet, a Swiss priest, applied the ancient art of DOWSING to medicine in the 1920s. He coined the term *radiesthesia*, 'sensitivity to radiation', for his technique. See also PARANORMAL THERAPIES.

Radionics is a method of healing at a distance using specially designed instruments in conjunction with radiesthesia. Radionics is concerned with the 'energy patterns' thought to be emitted by all forms of matter. Any disharmonies or distortions in these patterns, it is claimed, can be identified and measured so that the practitioner using the instruments for analysis builds up a 'holistic blueprint' of the patient covering his

mental, emotional and physical aspects. It is said to be possible to determine some diseases before they are physically obvious.

When a patient applies to a practitioner, he is sent a case-history form, and a list of charges. The patient fills in the form and returns it. The practitioner then carries out an analysis, and sends treatment(s) to the patient. In giving treatment, the practitioner seeks to correct the fundamental causes of disharmony identified by the analysis by stimulating the natural healing forces inherent in all living things, and so to return the patient to good health.

Further information can be obtained from the Confederation of Radionic and Radiesthetic Organisations (CRRO), The Maperton Trust, Wincanton, Somerset BA9 8EH.

An orthodox view

Although there is increasing acceptance of the 'energetic' level of human function, very few if any of the claims made by the practitioners are verifiable, and caution and scepticism are appropriate.

RAW FOOD DIET

A naturopathic, or 'nature cure', diet that has been in use for about 100 years is one in which 80 per cent of the food (measured by weight) is eaten raw, mainly as fruit and vegetables. This sounds more extreme than it really is. Fruit and vegetables contain a relatively large amount of water and are usually eaten in heavier portions than more calorie-concentrated foods such as fish, dairy foods, eggs and meat. As a result, considerable variety can be included in even the 20 per cent of non-raw foods that are permitted in the diet.

Although fruit and vegetables provide the bulk of the diet, raw foods with a higher concentration of calories – nuts, seeds (sunflower, pumpkin, sesame and poppy), uncooked cereals such as MUESLI, and sprouted pulses and grains, for example – ensure that the diet provides an adequate supply of protein and energy. No more than 66 per cent of the total number of calories are obtained from fruit and vegetables, so the intake of proteins and fats can still be maintained in line with the national recommendations for healthy eating (see EATING FOR HEALTH).

There are two main ideas behind the raw food diet. The first is that the human digestive tract is not designed for a high-meat diet. It is long in proportion to body size, like those of plant-eating animals. Food

takes a relatively long time to pass through it, which is ideal for the good digestion of vegetable matter, but which gives meat or fish time to start decomposing. Such unsuitable food, the theory goes, upsets the body's ability to maintain its health.

The second aim of the raw food diet is to avoid the loss of VITAMINS, MINERALS, enzymes and FIBRE that occurs in most cooking and processing methods. In addition, supporters of the diet often divide food into two groups according to its effect on the body. Fruit and vegetables are classed as so-called 'alkali-forming' foods; and meat, egg yolk, fish and dairy products as undesirable 'acid-forming' foods. A diet with a high proportion of raw ingredients naturally promotes the eating of alkali-forming foods and reduces the amount of acid-forming ones that are eaten, since these are generally foods that require cooking.

A raw food diet can supply every nutrient except vitamin B12, which is virtually confined to animal foods – although, in practice, it is added to many breakfast cereals and yeast extracts. However, to ensure a wide range of nutrients takes careful meal-planning, especially where children are concerned. In practice, it is much easier and more sociable to ensure a suitable intake of calories, iron, calcium, zinc, protein and vitamins B12 and D by adding small amounts of oily fish, dairy foods, meat and cooked beans, peas and lentils. The fruit and vegetables included should be as varied and fresh as possible, and eaten only when in season.

RAYNAUD'S DISEASE
'Cold hands' complaint

People who are very sensitive to the cold can be affected by this condition, in which the fingers, hands and sometimes feet suddenly turn pale and numb. In severe cases they may turn blue and there may be burning pains. Very occasionally the sufferer may develop gangrene (death and decay of the fingers or toes when the blood supply to them is cut off), or ULCERS.

About 5 per cent of the people in Britain suffer from the disorder at some stage in their lives, the vast majority of them women. Attacks usually last for no more than 15 to 30 minutes, providing the cause is treated.

In most cases the disease is caused by the contraction, due to cold, of the small arteries supplying blood to the surface of the skin.

Occasionally it can result from the vibration caused by using power tools or drills; from drugs prescribed for other ailments; from the pressure of gripping or carrying something; or from cigarette SMOKING.

Raynaud's disease (or Raynaud's syndrome, as it is also known) was named after Maurice Raynaud (1834-1881), a distinguished French physician who discovered the condition in the early 1860s – when he described it as 'a case of local asphyxia of the hands and feet, leading to gangrene'.

Self help Wear long thermal socks, gloves, fleece-lined shoes and a hat in cold or wet weather. Use warm bedding and seal bedroom doors and windows against draughts. If necessary, wear a nightcap, bedsocks or gloves in bed and keep a vacuum flask of hot tea or coffee by you in case you wake up cold. Take some EXERCISE every day, and eat regular hot meals. Avoid smoking, which narrows the arteries and restricts blood flow, and cut out any activities that you find trigger attacks. For further advice on keeping warm see COLDNESS and HYPOTHERMIA.

More information can be obtained by sending a stamped addressed envelope to Anne Mawdsley, The Raynaud's Association, 112 Crewe Road, Alsager, Cheshire ST7 2JA.

What the therapists recommend

Biofeedback Practitioners believe that worry or nervous upset may reduce the amount of blood flowing to people's extremities – especially their fingers and toes. This is thought to apply particularly to anyone who is prone to Raynaud's disease.

Therapists recommend sufferers to train themselves to warm their extremities using a hand-held thermometer which indicates when warmth is restored to the affected areas. By relaxing and imagining being in a warm situation (such as on a sunny beach or in a warm bath), and observing the effect on the instrument, it is possible to learn quite quickly to control the condition.

An orthodox view

If the patient's symptoms are extreme, and do not respond to ordinary warming, a doctor may prescribe drugs to stimulate the circulation. To exclude any underlying disease, such as inflamed arteries, he may also arrange for X-rays and blood tests.

A new drug called iloprost has recently been introduced, which is given by infusion with a drip. By mimicking a natural hormone, prostacylin, in the blood vessels, it prevents blood cells from clotting and blocking the circulation. The treatment, given to hospital outpatients, lasts for a total of 72 hours, spread over several days. Meanwhile, trials are taking place in Britain on a tablet form of the drug, taken orally at home.

REBIRTHING

A technique of bringing patients to re-live the process of birth as a form of PSYCHOTHERAPY is known as rebirthing. It is based on the idea that traumatic experiences at birth have long-lasting effects which can lead to psychological problems in later life. Therapists say that re-living the pain and anxiety of the experience helps to release patients' tensions and heal disorders in a way similar to PRIMAL THERAPY.

See also HUMANISTIC PSYCHOLOGY.

REFLEXOLOGY
Treating illness with foot massage

By massaging what they call 'reflex areas' found in the feet, reflexologists treat diseases in parts of the body they claim to be related to those areas. Exactly what happens when the reflex areas are massaged is not fully understood, and cannot be explained scientifically. But it is thought that illness occurs when 'energy channels' in the body are blocked, causing damage to one area or another. Massage is aimed at destroying these blocks, allowing the energy to flow freely again and so heal the damage.

Reflexologists regard the feet as a 'mirror' of the body, with the left foot representing the left-hand side, and the right foot the right-hand side. Different parts of the sole connect in some way to such organs as the bladder, kidneys and lungs; the big toe to the head and brain; and the little toe to the sinuses. The massage alone is said to prompt the body to heal itself – no drugs or instruments are used.

Reflexology is said to have originated in China some 5000 years ago, when pressure therapies were used to correct energy fields in the body (see ACUPRESSURE; ACUPUNCTURE; SHIATSU). The ancient Egyptians also used a form of reflexology, as shown in a wall-painting in a tomb dating about 2330 BC at Saqqara, south of Cairo.

But it was not until around 1913 that the therapy was introduced to the West by an American ear, nose and throat consultant, Dr William Fitzgerald. He devised a method termed ZONE THERAPY, which involved applying healing pressure either with the hands or with special instruments to certain parts of the body.

He divided the body into ten zones, or

Major reflex areas on the soles of the feet

Reflexologists use charts like the one below to show how zones of the feet are thought to mirror various parts of the body. They believe that illnesses show up as tender spots on the reflex areas of affected organs, and that by *applying special foot massage techniques to the correct points they can treat almost any organ or area of the body. Most but not all parts of the body have corresponding (though not necessarily identical) points on each foot.*

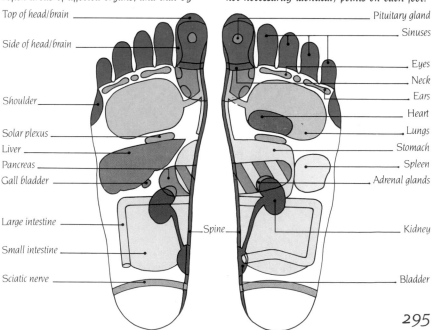

Top of head/brain — Side of head/brain — Shoulder — Solar plexus — Liver — Pancreas — Gall bladder — Large intestine — Small intestine — Sciatic nerve — Spine — Pituitary gland — Sinuses — Eyes — Neck — Ears — Heart — Lungs — Stomach — Spleen — Adrenal glands — Kidney — Bladder

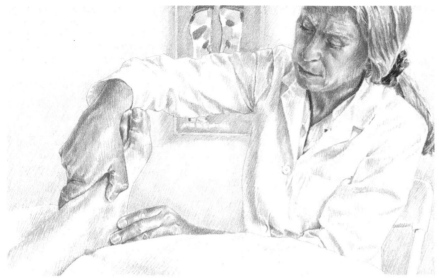

channels, through which, he said, flowed the person's vital energy. The zones extended from the toes, up through the body to the head, and back down again to the hands. Each of the zones was of equal width, covering each organ and part of the body.

By applying pressure to, say, an area in the same zone as the ear, he produced an anaesthetic effect which deadened any pain that might be there. It is similar to someone automatically gritting their teeth when in pain, or gripping the sides of the chair at the dentist's. Unwittingly, they are using a form of reflexology to deal with discomfort in an everyday situation.

In the early 1930s Dr Fitzgerald's work was taken up by another American therapist, Mrs Eunice Ingham, who published two popular books on reflexology called *Stories the Feet Can Tell* and *Stories the Feet Have Told*. Unlike Dr Fitzgerald, however, she did not work on different parts of the zones, but treated the body by concentrating on the feet.

In turn, the therapy was introduced to Britain by a student of Mrs Ingham's, Mrs Doreen Bayly, who set up her own practice and training courses in 1960.

Who it can help   While not claiming to be a 'cure-all', reflexology has been used to treat a host of common ailments, including BACK PAIN, DIGESTIVE PROBLEMS, MIGRAINE, PERIOD PROBLEMS, SINUS PROBLEMS and STRESS. It has also reportedly helped patients with more serious conditions, such as HEART DISORDERS, MULTIPLE SCLEROSIS and strokes.

In addition, reflexologists claim that they can sometimes detect an impending or potential illness, then give preventive treatment, if appropriate, or advise the patient to see a specialist. By having treatment every month or two, good health may be maintained – and early warning signs spotted.

The often powerful effects of the therapy may mean it is not always suitable during PREGNANCY or for anyone suffering from ARTHRITIS in the feet, DIABETES, certain heart disorders, OSTEOPOROSIS (thinning bones), phlebitis (vein inflammation), or THYROID DISORDERS. In such cases, treatment will be given with extra care – or not at all.

Finding a therapist   Whenever possible, treatment should be carried out by a fully trained practitioner – especially for patients with more complicated or serious disorders. A list of qualified private practitioners can be obtained by sending £1.50 to the Secretary, British Reflexology Association, Monks Orchard, Whitbourne, Worcester WR6 5RB. Members of the association have the letters MBRA after their name.

Consulting a therapist   At your first visit you are asked for a full medical history. You are then asked to lie comfortably in a reclining chair, with feet raised. Shoes and socks

Basic reflexology techniques

Stimulating a reflex point (above) The therapist applies pressure with the side and end of the thumb – in this case to a point on the side of the foot. Either the right or left thumb may be used, whichever is most comfortable, while the fingers gently hold the foot in place and the other hand provides support. The thumb joint is kept bent.

'Kneading' the foot (left) This involves pressing the arch area of the sole of the foot with the flat side of a clenched fist, while applying pressure from the top with the other hand. The hands are moved around the whole arch area in a kneading motion to give a generally stimulating and toning effect.

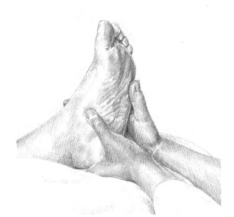

Locating treatment points Pressing with her thumbs, the therapist probes the reflex areas on each foot in turn, looking for spots of special sensitivity. The points are no bigger than a pinhead so movements have to be precise. To move from one point to another the thumb is eased back from the first point and then slid forwards to the next one, keeping in contact with the skin all the time but not exerting pressure while moving.

are removed and the feet quickly examined for CORNS or calluses, which can interfere with the blood supply, or infections which could indicate disease, such as ATHLETE'S FOOT (a fungal disease), or poor nutrition.

Before starting treatment, the therapist will gently massage talcum onto your feet to get you used to the 'feel' of the technique. Reassuringly, massage does not tickle.

Whatever the ailment, all the reflex areas on both feet are massaged. Using the thumb to apply pressure, the reflexologist examines the soles, sides and tops of the feet, feeling for areas of tenderness. If one is found, then the corresponding part of the body is believed to be out of balance, or sick. Where there is no discomfort, the corresponding part is in balance and working efficiently.

Any tender areas receive extra attention, and the therapist will deal with the causes of the condition – as well as its symptoms. By treating the whole body, it is possible to treat more than just one problem at a time.

The first treatment lasts for about an hour. As well as the good that this should do, you may well benefit from just sitting back and relaxing. Six to eight sessions are usually needed to deal with a specific ailment. To

begin with, the sessions will be given once a week; but later they may be spread out at intervals of every two or three weeks.

In some cases a patient may feel better after just one treatment. But at least another two treatments are recommended to prevent a relapse or recurrence of the complaint. In other cases, improvement may not occur until the second or third treatment. However, if the patient does not start to improve after three treatments, this may mean that reflexology is not going to help him, in which case he would probably be referred to another alternative therapist or to his doctor.

Usually there are no unpleasant side effects after treatment. However, some form of healing reaction may occur as the body starts to right itself. For example, treatment for a congested sinus may result in a cold; and CONSTIPATION treatment can cause increased bowel movements. However, providing the therapy has been used correctly, such reactions should not be severe.

An orthodox view

No clinical trials have been conducted to prove the claims made by reflexologists, but doctors believe that little harm can come from this therapy and many people find the massage particularly soothing.

Reflexology in the home

Although the best results are obtained through a complete treatment by a therapist, people can treat themselves at home by using a few simple techniques. Even so, a practitioner should advise on which techniques to use and how to perform them.

Only comparatively minor conditions are suitable for treatment, including: low back pain, catarrh, headaches, migraine, neck pain, sinus problems and tension. If you find _it awkward to work on your own feet, corresponding reflex areas in the hand can be used instead._

To massage the feet, sit comfortably on the floor or on a bed in a warm, quiet room, with your back supported by cushions.

Begin by massaging the whole foot, and do not overwork any reflex areas that might unbalance the body, causing possible unpleasant effects.

Reflexology for the aged – on the NHS

In January 1990 a group of nurses in a National Health Service hospital in Manchester carried out a study indicating that reflexology can significantly reduce ANXIETY and STRESS. Nine elderly patients were divided into three groups of three. The first group had foot massage for an hour a day, the second group had an hour of COUNSELLING a day, and the third group received no treatment at all. At the end of eight days the guinea-pig patients were asked to record their anxiety levels on a scale from zero to ten.

Those who had received reflexology showed a marked decrease in anxiety – in one case from eight to four, and in another from five to one. The patients who had received counselling had a lower drop in anxiety, of one or two points. And the patients who had received only conventional nursing – with no special treatment – had, if anything, higher anxiety levels than before.

Of the 14 nurses who took part in the study – none of whom had previously considered reflexology to be of value – 12 afterwards said that foot massage had proved to be a useful technique.

Sinus (left) Massage the reflex areas found in the back and sides of the smaller toes for complaints such as catarrh, colds, hay fever and sinusitis.

Tension (right) Massage the solar plexus reflex as shown. Then massage the adrenal reflexes in the middle of the feet, and pituitary reflexes in centre of pads of big toes.

Headaches (below) Massage head reflexes on the tips of the big toes and along their outer edges.

Neck pain (above) Apply pressure to the neck reflex area on the base and along the inner edge of each big toe.

Back pain (right) Treat the spine reflexes along the inside edge of each foot sole.

REICHIAN THERAPY

The psychiatrist Wilhelm Reich (1897-1957) began his career as a follower of Freud, practising psychoanalysis in Vienna. Later he broke away from the Freudian school, moved to the USA, and developed the ideas and methods known as Reichian therapy.

Reich extended and challenged Freud's views, believing that when frightening or hurtful experiences and feelings are repressed into the unconscious mind this can create physical tensions as well as psychological problems. He thought that certain physical movements can release these tensions while freeing repressed emotions.

In Reichian therapy, the therapist helps the patient to become aware of how his posture, muscular tension – called 'body armouring' – and breathing patterns reflect his emotions. Therapy often includes physical manipulation aimed at relaxing body armouring and releasing tension – methods which have been further developed in BIOENERGETICS.

Later, Reich incorporated sexuality into his theory, suggesting that psychological problems stem from blockages of 'orgone energy', a life force associated with the experience of orgasm (see ORGONE THERAPY). He devised an 'orgone accumulator', a box in which patients sat, supposedly to have this energy restored.

Most psychologists and scientists rejected this theory and after conflicts with US legal and medical authorities, Reich was jailed for selling prohibited medical equipment and defying a ban on publishing his theories. He died of a heart attack in prison. However, many of his ideas are still widely respected, and his methods have undergone a revival.

See also HUMANISTIC PSYCHOLOGY.

RELAXATION AND BREATHING
Simple ways to calm body and mind

Regular periods of relaxation are an essential part of physical and mental well-being, yet STRESS often prevents us from entering a naturally relaxed state. One of the simplest and most effective ways of counteracting this is by means of breathing exercises designed to ease TENSION and promote calmness. Many ancient traditions such as YOGA and MEDITATION make use of special breathing techniques to alter mental states, and Western medicine, too, is increasingly coming to recognise the way in which different breathing patterns are connected with general health. For example, anxious people are known to breathe more rapidly than others, using only the upper part of the chest, and talking with the lungs full of air (see HYPERVENTILATION), while depressed people sigh more and tend to talk after exhalation.

Breathing is a unique way of directly influencing the unconscious processes of the body, since of all the functions directed by the autonomic – or involuntary – nervous system it is the easiest to control by will. Some yogis and experienced meditators are said to be able voluntarily to lower their heart rate and BLOOD PRESSURE, but few of us realise we have such control over our own bodies. Everyone, however, can alter their breathing patterns and, through them, other parts of the nervous system, giving them control over their general level of bodily relaxation or tension.

The fundamental purpose of breathing is to provide the lungs with a constant supply of air from which essential oxygen can be

Relaxation and breathing techniques

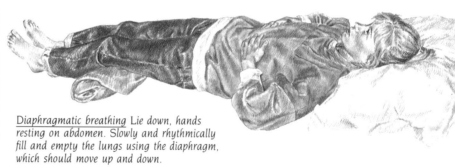

Chest breathing Lie on a firm, comfortable surface, hands lightly resting on upper chest. Breathe slowly in and out using chest muscles, so hands rise and fall with each breath.

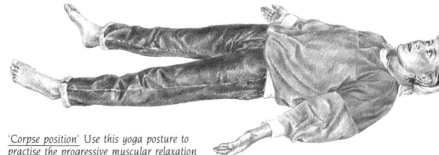

Diaphragmatic breathing Lie down, hands resting on abdomen. Slowly and rhythmically fill and empty the lungs using the diaphragm, which should move up and down.

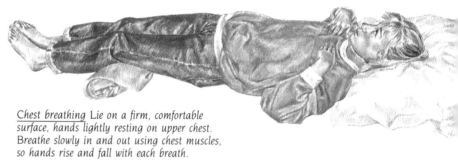

'Corpse position' Use this yoga posture to practise the progressive muscular relaxation exercise on p. 301. Lie with your head, neck and back aligned, feet about 18in (450mm) apart, and hands turned up and held about 6in (150mm) away from your body.

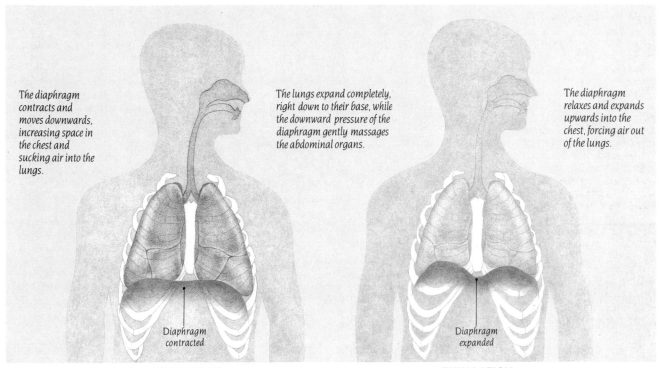

The diaphragm contracts and moves downwards, increasing space in the chest and sucking air into the lungs.

The lungs expand completely, right down to their base, while the downward pressure of the diaphragm gently massages the abdominal organs.

The diaphragm relaxes and expands upwards into the chest, forcing air out of the lungs.

Diaphragm contracted

Diaphragm expanded

INHALATION   EXHALATION

How to breathe naturally

The habit of breathing from the diaphragm, or midriff (as shown above), often has to be relearned in adult life. Too often children are taught to breathe in the 'chest out, stomach in' manner, which hampers natural breathing patterns and causes tension.

absorbed into the blood and circulated to all the body tissues. Breathing out empties the lungs for the next breath and additionally allows the body to expel waste gases such as carbon dioxide.

The respiratory rate changes naturally at different times of the day and in different situations, such as walking, sitting, or running for a bus, to accommodate changing needs for oxygen intake and carbon dioxide expulsion. These correspond to different levels of relaxation and tension, and are reflected in the two basic types of breathing that can occur: chest breathing and diaphragmatic (or abdominal) breathing.

Chest breathing This is the fastest way of getting a quick injection of oxygen into the blood. It usually occurs during vigorous EXERCISE, excitement, FEAR, ANXIETY or emergency situations which call for immediate action, but it can also be used to get the system going in the morning or give a boost when energy is low.

During chest breathing the rib muscles

contract, forcing the chest to expand upwards and outwards so that air is drawn quickly into the upper chest. Breathing is shallow and fast, with the emphasis on inhalation, and a general stress response, including increased muscular tension, occurs throughout the body.

This is appropriate in some situations – it may even save life by allowing split-second action in an emergency on the road, for example – but if it continues for too long or becomes a regular breathing pattern, the body may enter a permanently stressed state with serious consequences for health. It may also become hysterical overbreathing, with too much carbon dioxide expelled and metabolic changes in the body, leading to feelings of faintness and 'pins and needles'.

Diaphragmatic breathing This is the normal, natural way to breathe when you are relaxed – which should be most of the time. Instead of using the rib muscles, breathing occurs by the rhythmic contraction and relaxation of the diaphragm – a dome-shaped sheet of muscle separating the chest and abdominal cavities.

As you inhale, the diaphragm contracts and flattens, increasing space in the chest and sucking air into the lungs. The lungs expand completely, right down to their base, and the movement of the diaphragm gently massages the abdominal organs. On exhaling, the diaphragm relaxes and moves

up into the chest, forcing air out of the lungs. You can feel the movement of the diaphragm as you breathe by lying down and placing a hand on the abdomen, as shown on the previous page.

Diaphragmatic breathing is more efficient than chest breathing, promoting relaxation rather than tension. The lungs are more completely filled and emptied with each breath, so providing more oxygen for metabolism. At the same time, there is no build up of waste products such as carbon dioxide in the lungs and lactic acid in the blood, which can cause nervousness and TIREDNESS.

Unfortunately, diaphragmatic breathing may have to be consciously relearned by adults. This is because we all tend to be tense, and habitual chest breathing is often taught to children with instructions such as 'chest out, stomach in', which restrict natural breathing patterns.

Why relax?

The human body, like that of other animals, is adapted to cope with brief periods of arousal or stress that occur in the natural state – for example, when danger threatens or when prey has to be caught. At such times, irregular, shallow chest breathing occurs, muscles become tense, and panicky, anxious feelings may be experienced.

In nature, stressful situations usually last only a short time, and tension is quickly

Relaxation and Breathing

Quick relaxation at work

Office workers can relieve neck and shoulder tension and correct poor posture in just a few minutes with a good stretching session. Here is how to do it in under five minutes.

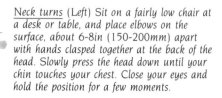

Chest and back stretch (Below) Stand up straight with neck and shoulders relaxed and feet slightly apart. Slowly raise arms, bend elbows and touch fingertips to the breastbone. Next lower the arms and straighten them out behind you as high up as you can, hands clasped together and head tilted as far back as comfortably possible.

Neck turns (Left) Sit on a fairly low chair at a desk or table, and place elbows on the surface, about 6-8in (150-200mm) apart with hands clasped together at the back of the head. Slowly press the head down until your chin touches your chest. Close your eyes and hold the position for a few moments.

Unclasp hands and turn head slowly until chin rests in palm of right hand. Push slowly down with the left hand and up with the right to turn head as far as possible. Hold for a few moments, return slowly to centre and relax. Then repeat in the opposite direction.

Shoulder rolls (Right) Sit comfortably in a chair, fingers pressing down onto shoulders. Keeping shoulders down, circle elbows up away from the body, back, down and forwards several times. Repeat in opposite direction.

(Above) Stretch the back by bending forward, raising your arms up over your back and allowing your neck to relax and hang down. Hold for a few moments, then slowly straighten up, unclasp hands and drop arms to your sides.

Lower back and leg stretch (Above) Sit on a low chair and draw one leg up so that the foot rests on the chair seat. Keep back straight and clasp knee as close to the body as you can. Hold for a few moments, relax, lower foot and repeat with the other leg.

Whole body stretch (Right) Stand up straight and take a deep breath to fill the lungs right to the bottom. Throw your arms out behind you and tilt your head back to look at the ceiling. Relax, breathe out slowly and bend forward from the waist with knees slightly bent, hands hanging loosely down and neck relaxed. Hold for a few seconds, slowly straighten up and return to first position, inhaling deeply.

dissipated in action of some sort, leaving body and mind free to return to their normal relaxed state. But in modern life, with its continual pressures and strains and few physical outlets, aroused states can be less easy to get rid of.

In continually stressful situations such as a high-pressure job or a troubled marriage, long periods of stress may be experienced, and these may eventually result in the development of ailments such as high blood pressure, heart and lung disorders, MIGRAINE headaches and anxiety.

The most effective way of combating stress and preventing these illnesses is to make time for regular relaxation. This can take the form of 'active' relaxation such as MEDITATION, taking exercise or practising rhythmic breathing techniques, or 'passive' relaxation such as listening to music.

In the relaxed state, there is regular diaphragmatic breathing, muscular relaxation and mental calmness. The body uses up less energy than usual and there is less work for major organs such as heart, lungs and brain to do. Regular relaxation exercises have been shown to lower blood pressure and improve performance at work. Participants in studies also report that they sleep better, learn new skills more easily and feel more energetic. Their stamina and fitness improve and they experience greater involvement and enjoyment in family life.

Relaxation through breathing

The first step in learning to relax is being able to recognise physical or mental tension. Breathing patterns provide one of the best indicators – shallow, uneven chest breathing is a sign of stress, and can occur in ordinary situations, such as waiting at traffic lights, making decisions or queueing for a bus.

Stress experts say that a good way to introduce relaxation into everyday life is to watch your breathing patterns so that you start to notice stressful points during the day. Whenever you find yourself breathing from the chest, take a deep breath in and then let it out slowly. You should feel tense muscles relax throughout the body as you exhale.

In addition, a daily relaxation routine of 10-15 minutes is said to improve physical and mental well-being and help to counteract many harmful effects of stress. Begin by finding a quiet, well-ventilated room where you will not be disturbed. Loosen any tight clothing and lie down on the floor with your feet about 18in (45cm) apart. The head and neck should be aligned with the back.

Close your eyes and practise diaphragmatic breathing with one hand gently resting on the abdomen to check that the diaphragm is moving rather than the chest muscles. Concentrate on the rhythm of your breathing,

letting it become smooth and regular so that there are no gaps. As you practise slow, rhythmic breathing, focus your attention on the coolness of the air breathed in and the warmth of the air breathed out. When thoughts come into your mind, let them go again without dwelling on them, so that you stay focused on your breathing rhythm.

After seven to ten minutes your mind should feel clear and your body relaxed. Gradually allow yourself to become aware of outside sounds and gently open your eyes. When you feel ready, slowly get up.

Progressive muscular relaxation

In times of stress the nervous system becomes overactive and stimulates the muscles more than usual, causing them to contract and become tense. The technique of progressive muscular relaxation is designed to undo the effects of stress, relax muscle groups one by one, and lead to a healthier, less stressed state if practised regularly. It works by first tensing and then relaxing each part of the body in turn.

Choose a quiet room where you will not be disturbed for about 10-15 minutes. Remove your shoes, loosen tight clothing and lie down on a bed or carpet, with head, neck and trunk in a straight line.

Begin by raising your eyebrows and tensing the forehead muscles for a count of five; then relax, feeling the difference in the muscles. Repeat, then go through the same procedure for different muscle groups, first with eyes squeezed tightly shut, then with mouth wide open, face muscles stretched and lips, eyebrows and chin puckered up. Repeat with jaw muscles tightened and teeth clenched; then with shoulders raised and neck and shoulders tense; then with left arm raised, arm muscles tensed and fist clenched; then with right arm tensed.

Now contract your rib muscles, noticing how your breathing changes. Relax, then pull in and tighten the stomach muscles, hold for a count of five, relax and breathe out. Lift the left leg a little and push the foot away from you so that the muscles tense. Hold for a count of five, relax, then let the leg drop. Repeat, then do the same with the right leg.

RESPIRATORY DISORDERS

Many different conditions can affect the respiratory tract and make breathing difficult. The most common are virus and bacterial infections such as COLDS of the nose and throat, INFLUENZA, LARYNGITIS (inflamed voice box), TONSILLITIS and BRONCHITIS.

Other viruses and bacteria are responsible for tuberculosis, PNEUMONIA and PLEURISY, which affect the lungs and surrounding tissues. Recurrent infections – and exposure to dust or cigarette smoke – can cause the lungs to become overinflated, resulting in EMPHYSEMA.

The respiratory system is particularly susceptible to ALLERGY because irritating substances such as grass pollen or house dust are easily breathed in, and may trigger HAY FEVER or ASTHMA attacks.

CANCER of the mouth or throat is rare, but lung cancer – caused by SMOKING in nine out of ten cases – kills 41,000 people a year in England and Wales alone. Heart failure (see HEART DISORDERS) is common in old age and may cause difficulty in breathing, especially when lying flat.

RESTLESS LEGS

Some people feel a constant need to move their legs, particularly when they are lying in bed. The condition is known as restless legs and is harmless, except that it disrupts sleep and leads to TIREDNESS. The cause of the condition is not known.

What the therapists recommend

Massage Provided there is no related problem, such as a skin rash or infection, or such conditions as phlebitis or VARICOSE VEINS, a general massage of the legs may help circulation and ease the restlessness.

A therapist would probably use light lifting and petrissage (kneading) of the calf muscles, ending with particular attention to the feet (see FOOT PROBLEMS).

Acupressure The point therapists recommend to be treated (known as 'gall bladder 34') is on the outer side of the knee, four fingers' width down from the kneecap, in the hollow between the skin and the smaller leg bone. You should press inwards and against the upper bone.

Naturopathy Therapists consider that the most common cause of restless legs is iron deficiency and chronic mild ANAEMIA through loss of blood – for example, in women who have heavy periods. A diet that is rich in iron, especially from green, leafy vegetables, would be advised. Naturopaths may prescribe iron and vitamin E supplements, and suggest hot and cold sitz baths (see HYDROTHERAPY) to improve the circulation.

An orthodox view

Apart from commonsense measures, such as keeping warm and avoiding coffee in the evenings, the only orthodox medical treatment that works is a dose of diazepam (Valium) at bedtime. However, like other benzodiazepine drugs, diazepam is addictive and most doctors today are reluctant to prescribe it, except in very short courses.

RHEUMATISM

Pain and stiffness of the joints and muscles are commonly referred to as rheumatism – a word more often used by laymen than doctors. It in fact covers a large number of distinct medical conditions, including fibrositis (inflammation of the connective tissues, especially those of the muscles in the back), rheumatic fever, and various forms of ARTHRITIS – in particular OSTEOARTHRITIS and RHEUMATOID ARTHRITIS.

Rheumatism is common in old age, and a significant cause in over 65s is a condition called polymyalgia rheumatica. This comes on suddenly, with severe neck and shoulder pain, morning stiffness and HEADACHES. A rare complication is temporal arteritis, an inflammation of arteries supplying blood to the eyes which, if not treated quickly, can lead to blindness.

What the therapists recommend

Acupuncture Practitioners claim to have cured rheumatism by treating points on the patient's gall bladder, large intestine, kidney, governor and stomach meridians. MOXIBUSTION is also said to help.

Traditional Medicine One of the most popular country remedies is garlic oil – 'devil's mustard' – which is made by crushing GARLIC with oil and lard. To relieve pain it should be rubbed firmly and deeply into the affected area.

Some people wear copper bracelets in the belief that this will relieve rheumatic pain. See COPPER THERAPY.

Massage To begin with, massage of the neck and shoulders should be applied gently. As the treatment progresses, deeper frictions and kneading, or petrissage, techniques can be employed. However, deep massage can be painful at times – and to ease this you should always finish with slow, soothing, rhythmic or effleurage strokes.

Hydrotherapy Practitioners claim success when rheumatism is treated with underwater douches, relaxing needle sprays, hot or cold packs, Vichy massage and hot paraffin wax for the hands or feet. The treatments are used in various permutations according to the patient's condition at the time.

Herbal Medicine Initially, patients can help

themselves by cleansing their systems (see EATING FOR HEALTH) and reducing their consumption of alcohol, red meat and sugar. Massage with diluted oil of lavender or rosemary – two or three drops to a teaspoon of vegetable oil – may help to reduce rheumatic inflammation.

Herbalists will give dietary advice and may prescribe remedies such as buckbean, celery seed, devil's claw, lignum vitae, wild yam and willow bark, as appropriate.

Homoeopathy Where the patient has a fear of being touched, the prescription is *Arnica*; and where the rheumatism is greatly aggravated by movement, *Bryonia*. If rheumatic pain is worse on beginning to move, but improves with continued gentle movement, try taking *Rhus. tox.*

Reflexology Massage is recommended to the reflex areas relating to the parts of the body affected, and also to areas relating to the solar plexus and the pituitary, parathyroid and adrenal glands (see chart, p. 295).

An orthodox view

Most cases of rheumatism respond to simple measures such as keeping warm or applying a hot-water bottle to the affected area. Anti-inflammatory painkillers such as aspirin or ibuprofen (Nurofen) may help.

If you suspect polymyalgia rheumatica, see your doctor, as a blood test is needed for diagnosis. If necessary, he will prescribe a course of steroid tablets which should provide dramatic relief. In some cases, it may be necessary to have regular blood tests and take further courses of steroids.

RHEUMATOID ARTHRITIS

One of the most common forms of arthritis, rheumatoid arthritis is estimated to afflict about one person in 20 in Britain at some time in their lives. Unlike OSTEOARTHRITIS, which is progressive and irreversible, rheumatoid arthritis may come and go spontaneously – though there is as yet no sure cure, and the underlying cause is not properly understood.

Most cases start between the ages of 25 and 55, often with swelling, stiffness and pain in the knuckle joints of the hands or in the feet. In some cases, the inflammation of rheumatoid arthritis may spread beyond the joints, to the lungs or eyes. Blood tests and X-rays may be needed to distinguish it from osteoarthritis or GOUT.

See ARTHRITIS.

RINGING IN THE EARS

In the condition known medically as tinnitus, the sufferer is conscious of a constant ringing or buzzing noise in one or both ears, which only he can hear. In some cases it is caused simply by a blockage of wax in the outer ears. But other more serious causes include DEAFNESS, HYPERTENSION, Ménière's disease (progressive deafness and dizziness caused by inner-ear disease) and otosclerosis (a type of deafness that runs in families).

In yet other cases, it is brought on by old age or by certain drugs such as aspirin or quinine. Often there seems to be no obvious cause, although the condition may be aggravated by ANXIETY or DEPRESSION.

Rarely, ringing in the ears is the result of a benign tumour of the nerve from the ear to the brain, called an acoustic neuroma. If a serious underlying cause is suspected – or if the patient is emotionally disturbed – a doctor should be seen as soon as possible.

What the therapists recommend
ACUPRESSURE

Self help Ringing in the ears may be relieved by pressing inwards with the fingers one finger's width in front of the ear at the top of the cheekbone.

ACUPUNCTURE

Consultation Traditionally, acupuncturists believe that ringing in the ears is caused by liver disorders or gall-bladder problems. They therefore treat pressure points on the liver, gall bladder and governor meridians. In addition, MOXIBUSTION – the therapeutic use of burning herbs – is applied to the bladder and kidney meridians.

Acupuncture is said to be particularly effective for treating tinnitus if previous attempts have not worked.

NATUROPATHY

Consultation Some practitioners consider CATARRH and sinus congestion (see SINUS PROBLEMS) to be common causes of tinnitus. Patients would be advised to cut down on dairy produce and refined starchy foods, and to avoid tobacco and smoky atmospheres. Steam inhalations may also prove helpful in relieving the condition.

HOMOEOPATHY

Consultation Many remedies are claimed to be effective. When there is pain in the cartilages of the ears with roaring, giddiness and deafness, *Salicylic acid 6* may be recommended as one of the most useful. For ringing, hissing or tinkling in the ears that is worse for movement, try *China off. 6*.

An orthodox view

A doctor investigating a case of tinnitus will first examine the patient's ears and perform simple hearing tests using a tuning fork. If necessary, he will arrange for a hearing specialist to conduct a test called an audiogram. If acoustic neuroma is suspected, he will send the patient to hospital for an X-ray examination of the bone between the ear and the brain.

Regular drug treatment may give relief, especially in some cases of Ménière's disease. Severely affected patients may benefit by wearing a 'masker', an instrument that looks like a hearing aid but produces a low background noise to block out the ringing.

For advice and information about the disease, and news of support groups in all parts of the country, patients should contact The British Tinnitus Association, 105 Gower Street, London WC1E 6AH.

RINGWORM

The highly contagious infection of the skin known popularly as ringworm is also medically called tinea. The term ringworm is somewhat misleading, since no worm is involved – it is caused by a FUNGAL INFECTION. However, as the infection spreads, inflammation extends in a ring shape, while the centre reverts to the appearance of normal skin.

Ringworm can occur anywhere on the body, but warm, moist areas – such as the armpits, groin, beneath the breasts and the feet – are the commonest places.

ROGERIAN THERAPY

The work of Carl Rogers (1902-87) has been a major influence on modern PSYCHOTHERAPY since the 1950s, when he began to publish his ideas. Rogers was one of the first to begin using techniques completely different from the Freudian psychoanalysis favoured by most therapists at the time.

The new approach became known as Rogerian therapy. Rogers himself called it 'client-centred' or 'person-centred' therapy, since he wished to emphasise the active, responsible role of those people who sought

therapy, refusing to view them as patients.

In Rogerian therapy, the client's own point of view and experiences are given primary importance, rather than the therapist's views. This is known as 'non-directive' treatment, since instead of offering advice, the therapist tries to help the client to develop his own view of the situation and work out what options are open to him.

The aim is to strengthen the individual's sense of his own identity, to help him find a compatible way of life and to develop himself as fully as possible in all respects.

See HUMANISTIC PSYCHOLOGY.

ROLFING
Tissue treatment to improve body posture

According to the founder of Rolfing, the American biological chemist Dr Ida Rolf (1896-1979), many health problems are caused by poor body posture – for example, hunched shoulders and stooped backs. Sufferers are constantly striving to rectify this, and as a result they are drained of vitality and the normal working of their bodies is impaired – leaving them open to illness.

To combat this, Dr Rolf devised a complex manipulative system which she called 'structural reintegration', and which is now known as Rolfing. By massaging the body's connective tissue and muscles, she aimed to realign the body so that its physical structures were

The American biochemist Ida Rolf spent 40 years formulating her technique of manipulation, aimed at aligning the body.

in a straight vertical line. She believed that only then could the earth's field of gravity properly support the body's own energy field, and physical and psychological well-being be re-established.

After treating patients for some 35 years in comparative obscurity, Dr Rolf began training therapists in her techniques in California in the mid-1960s. See also HELLERWORK.

Who it can help Rolfing is said to be suitable for anyone who feels his body structure is in any way out of line, and finds this a cause of physical or psychological distress.

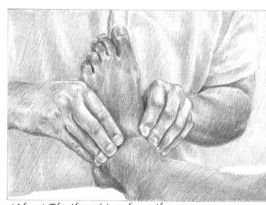

(Above) The therapist works on the connective tissue around the ankle joints. This aims to improve flexibility.

To relieve the strain of carrying the head too far forward, the practitioner eases the shoulder muscles towards their normal position.

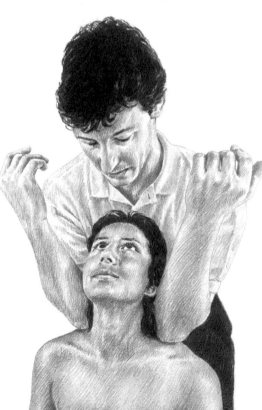

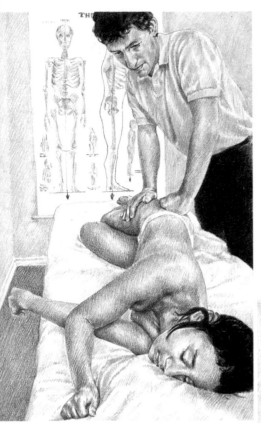

Finding a therapist Information about Rolfing teachers in Britain can be obtained by contacting The Institute of Structural Bodywork, The Peak Health Club, Hyatt Carlton Tower, 2 Cadogan Place, London SW1X 9PY.

Consulting a therapist A standard Rolfing course comprises ten hour-long sessions spread over a number of weeks.

An orthodox view

Rolfing combines a CHIROPRACTIC/osteopathic approach with BIOENERGETICS. It is a variant of many similar mind-body therapies and should be seen more as a way of learning about the body than as a specific treatment for any particular disorder.

During Rolfing, clients lie, sit or stand in various positions. (Left) The client lies on her side while the practitioner works on the limbs with the aim of improving the hip joint to change the relationship of the leg and pelvis.

After the first three sessions, the practitioner moves on from the outer muscles to the deeper layers closer to the backbone. This work on the front of the body affects the back. (Above) The diaphragm is worked upon, together with the muscles that flex the hip joint. These muscles can all contribute to back and neck pain.

During the sixth session, the entire back is worked upon. In this technique (left), the practitioner is moving the client's leg to articulate the hip joint, while holding on to various other muscles, including those that are sometimes involved in causing the pain of sciatica. Advanced sessions can continue the process of improving posture.

ROYAL JELLY
Good for us, or just good for queen bees?

Worker bees excrete this nutritious, milky substance from their salivary glands as food for the select bee larvae that are to develop into queen bees. The queens grow to be twice the size of the workers and live for up to six years, laying as many as 2000 eggs each day of their lives. By contrast, the worker bees, which do not receive the 'wonder food', live for only about six weeks and are sterile.

Analysis of royal jelly has revealed some 20 amino acids, some of which are 'essential amino acids' – ones the human body cannot synthesise but needs for growth and tissue replacement. VITAMINS, including most of the vitamin B-complex and vitamin C, are also present, along with the MINERALS iron, potassium and sodium, and minute traces of chromium, manganese and nickel.

The attributes of the queen bee and the presence in the jelly of several essential human nutrients is probably the basis of the claims currently made for it. Among other things, royal jelly taken daily over three to five months has been claimed to provide unprecedented energy, rejuvenate the body and combat malnutrition in infants and ANAEMIA following childbirth.

It is said to help reduce high BLOOD PRESSURE and to relieve hardening of the arteries (see ARTERIES [HARDENING]) in the elderly. It is also believed to treat DEPRESSION, dermatitis, ANOREXIA, MYALGIC ENCEPHALOMYELITIS (ME) and the pain associated with RHEUMATOID ARTHRITIS. And it supposedly revitalises the hair and complexion, curing spots, ACNE and stretch marks.

Royal jelly is available as a pure yellowish-white liquid, which must be kept refrigerated. Some people dislike its taste and mix it with honey. Capsules of the jelly are a more palatable form. Dosage recommendations are supplied with the product, and vary from one capsule (containing 100-500mg) to a measure of the liquid form (650mg) per day. Skin creams and lotions containing royal jelly are also on sale.

An orthodox view

The amount of vitamins and other nutrients that royal jelly provides is extremely small, but medical research suggests that it is their proportions which may account for its supposedly beneficial effects. Taking it can do no harm, and it may even act as a PLACEBO – albeit an expensive one.

SALT-FREE DIETS

Common salt, or sodium chloride, is the body's main source of sodium. Although sodium is an essential MINERAL, the average Westerner eats 12g – almost ½oz – of salt a day, compared to the recommended daily amount of 5g. About 70 per cent of this intake is sodium not naturally present in food, but added in manufacture and processing. For example, common prepared foods such as bread, cheese, yeast extract, delicatessen meats, breakfast cereals, biscuits, soups, stock cubes, sauce mixes, convenience meals and tinned vegetables are all heavily salted or contain other sodium compounds. Flavour enhancers such as monosodium glutamate, bicarbonate of soda, baking powder and certain other FOOD ADDITIVES all add large amounts of sodium.

A high salt intake has been shown to encourage high BLOOD PRESSURE in those prone to it. As a result, salt-free diets are often suggested for those with a tendency to HEART DISORDERS, high blood pressure, CIRCULATION PROBLEMS or KIDNEY COMPLAINTS.

What are commonly referred to as 'salt-free diets' are really 'low-salt diets', however. A totally salt-free diet is difficult to achieve because most foods naturally contain salt. In any case, such a diet should be followed only under the supervision of a doctor or medically qualified therapist. But food without added salt provides all the sodium the body needs (see EATING FOR HEALTH).

Instead of salt, you can flavour food with citrus juice, vinegar, herbs, spices, GARLIC, onions, wine or vegetable purées. Salt substitutes are also available, but some contain potassium chloride and should not be used by people with certain heart conditions, so check with your doctor first.

SALT-WATER TREATMENTS

Bathing in salt water is recommended for people suffering from stiffness and a variety of aches and pains. The treatments are aimed at soothing the body and encouraging it to use its own healing powers.

See HYDROTHERAPY; THALASSOTHERAPY.

SAUNA BATH
Turning on the heat to get fit

When taking a steam sauna bath, bathers sit in an insulated pine cabin and are subjected to hot, moist air produced by throwing water over heated stones on a stove. The treatment is based on increased humidity rather than increased heat, and is calculated to expel moisture from the body, eliminate waste

products and poisons, stimulate the circulation, and help people to relax.

It is best to take a sauna unclothed, as wearing trunks or swimsuits – or draping yourself with a towel – will impede the flow of perspiration and make you feel uncomfortably damp and sweaty.

Most saunas operate at temperatures of 27-38°C (80-100°F). For safety's sake, the heat is thermostatically controlled at a limit of about 43°C (110°F). The cabins contain wooden benches of differing heights, the lower benches being exposed to less heat than the higher ones. Knot-free benches are preferred as the resin in them does not escape and burn your skin.

Saunas originated in Scandinavia in the Middle Ages, and in Finland bathers still gently beat themselves with birch leaves to help cleanse the skin and get the blood flowing. In Britain saunas are now available at many HEALTH FARMS, health clubs, and sports and leisure centres. Some enthusiasts even have a small sauna cabin, holding two or three people, installed in their home. Firms supplying home saunas are generally listed in _Yellow Pages_.

Once you are used to taking saunas, and know that they have no bad effects on your system, you can spend an hour or longer in the cabin. Some experts claim that 30 minutes will eliminate as much waste as your kidneys normally dispose of in 24 hours. Depending on your fitness, it is possible to take gentle EXERCISE while in the sauna.

Before entering a sauna you should give

This 19th-century etching shows bathers enjoying the benefits of the Russian sauna, or 'bagne russe'. Some are striking their bodies with birch twigs while others douse themselves with pails of cold water. Water thrown on the fire at left produces billows of steam.

Do's and don'ts for sauna bathing

_Do_ wait for about three hours after a large meal before taking a sauna.

_Do_ see your doctor before taking a sauna if you suspect you are not in perfect health.

_Do_ wash or shower thoroughly during sessions in the sauna. This gets rid of perspiration and any impurities it may contain. If you wish, you can use a sponge, body-brush or loofah to cleanse your skin and stimulate the circulation even further.

Don't take saunas if you suffer from ANGINA, hardening of the arteries, high or low BLOOD PRESSURE, EPILEPSY, DIABETES or SKIN DISORDERS (except ACNE). Ask your doctor if in doubt.

Don't take saunas if you are pregnant – or in the first few days of a period.

Don't take a sauna more than twice a week, unless medically approved.

your skin a preparatory cleansing with a tepid shower. After a sauna you can take an invigorating cold shower or swim, provided that you are 100 per cent fit – ask your doctor's advice if uncertain. In Scandinavia some healthy and experienced bathers roll naked in the snow after a sauna.

Beginners, however, should spend about five minutes inside the cabin to start with – preferably on the less hot, lower benches – and build up gradually from that. Anyone who feels sick, faint, dizzy, or whose heart beats uncomfortably fast while taking a sauna, should leave the cabin and rest for a while. See also HYDROTHERAPY.

Warning Be sure to follow the *Do's and don'ts for sauna bathing.*

SCARLET FEVER

This highly contagious disease is a severe form of streptococcal TONSILLITIS. The sore throat is accompanied by fever, sickness and a rash of tiny, bright-red spots which starts on the neck and chest, and gradually spreads over the entire body. Patients should be kept in isolation for seven days from the start of the rash – by which time it has usually disappeared. Antibiotics speed recovery and prevent complications such as kidney infections. Scarlet fever is a notifiable disease, so call your doctor if you suspect it.

SCHIZOPHRENIA

In Britain, about one person in a thousand is affected by this serious mental illness. It is a form of psychosis that strikes – often suddenly and without any warning – usually between the ages of 18 and 30, causing behaviour that seems bizarre to other people but often perfectly normal (or at worst confusing) to the sufferer.

His symptoms may include delusions (for example, that a television set is sending messages to him, or controlling his mind); hallucinations (hearing imaginary voices, or seeing things that are not there); displays of irrational bad temper and violence; oversensitivity and paranoia (a feeling of being persecuted); or catatonia (complete inability to communicate and cooperate with others). In addition, a schizophrenic's conversation may be unreal and disturbing to the listener – and his ideas seem confusing, vague, extravagant and even comical.

A lack of initiative and drive is also commonplace, and this sometimes results in the sufferer losing his job and becoming virtually unemployable. His emotions may become unpredictable and perverse – for example, he may laugh at bad news and weep for no apparent reason. (This, rather than the existence of two differing personalities, is the basis of the common term 'split personality'.) The schizophrenic may also suffer simultaneously from DEPRESSION.

Severe bouts of schizophrenia can last for a few weeks or longer. Some people have a single attack and no more. But usually the condition tends to recur after a sometimes prolonged period of normality. But even with treatment, schizophrenia may grow progressively worse over the years and even become permanent.

As well as being extremely distressing for the sufferer, schizophrenia can have a devastating effect on other family members – who may become depressed and ill themselves owing to the victim's abnormal behaviour.

What the therapists recommend

Music Therapy By encouraging schizophrenics to listen to music, and possibly to play music themselves, therapists aim to develop a sense of self-identity in their patients. In other words, to allow them to see themselves as they really are – or should be – and to help them regain their true normality.

Art Therapy With some patients, painting or pottery is their only way of finding a personal language and of communicating with other people. Their work therefore helps to counteract the sense of isolation and confusion that schizophrenics feel. In addition, their creations may have a symbolic significance and so provide an insight into their chaotic world.

Colour Therapy Even mild cases of schizophrenia require long and painstaking professional help. The use of the colour violet – along with RELAXATION AND BREATHING and MUSIC THERAPY – is said to help patients recover their mental balance.

Counselling Trained counsellors are able to help families and victims by providing support, advising on day-to-day problems, and putting them in touch with social services and self-help groups.

Psychotherapy Treatment may help in some cases but should be given as a supplement to orthodox psychiatric help. Support rather than in-depth probing is needed at first and during serious bouts of the illness, but psychological exploration may be undertaken later if appropriate. Sometimes the therapist may wish to see the whole family, not just the victim.

Homoeopathy According to homoeopathic practitioners, the following remedies may help: *Belladonna 200* when there is violent, manic excitement with great restlessness and hallucinations; *Stramonium 200* when the patient is talkative, uses swear words, spends time praying, hears voices, and is afraid of the dark; *Hyoscymas 200* when there is obscene talk or behaviour, paranoid behaviour and hysterical laughter, suspicion of other people, and the desire to be naked.

An orthodox view

Before the advent of modern drugs, many schizophrenics spent long periods – in some cases most of their lives – in psychiatric hospitals. Drugs such as chlorpromazine (Largactil) and haloperidol (Haldol) now help to relieve symptoms and prevent the illness from recurring. They allow many patients – with the support of doctors, nurses, social workers, family members and friends – to lead a reasonably normal life in the community. But others, without family or continuing medical support, become outcasts sleeping rough in big cities.

Some patients forget or simply refuse to take their medication – often because they do not believe they are ill. If necessary, a patient may be committed to hospital, so that nurses or doctors can administer the drugs through regular, long-acting injections.

SCIATICA

This pain running down the back and outside of the thigh, leg and foot is caused by irritation of the sciatic nerve at its root in the spine of the lower back. The onset may be sudden – following a twisting of the body, for instance – and is worse on bending forwards, coughing or sneezing. Common causes include a SLIPPED DISC, when the displaced disc presses on the nerve, and displacement of joints between the vertebrae of the spine. See also BACK PAIN, LUMBAGO, and NERVE DISORDERS.

What the therapists recommend

Acupuncture Points on the meridians relating to bladder, gall bladder, kidney, spleen and large and small intestine governors may be treated. MOXIBUSTION applied to the bladder and kidney meridians may also be advised.

Acupressure Apply pressure inwards on the outside leg, one hand's width plus a thumb above the crown of the ankle bone, between the shin and smaller leg bone.

Osteopathy Sciatica may often be relieved by stretching the spine in the lumbar region – the part of the back between the lowest ribs and the top of the pelvis – and by reducing spasm in the local muscles. Gentle mobilisation to improve the mobility of the joints in the lower back can also be helpful. But osteopathic treatment may not be appropriate in very severe cases where sciatica affects both of the legs.

Hydrotherapy If the symptoms are severe, try an ice pack at the base of the back. For less severe, long-standing pain, try a hot pack. The therapist may suggest an underwater douche and teach specific postural and remedial exercises in the hydrotherapy pool.

An orthodox view

Doctors often advise sufferers to rest in bed on a firm mattress or with a board under the mattress. Back X-rays are not usually much help, but may show narrowing of the space between two vertebrae where the disc has been squashed. In severe cases, special X-rays such as a three-dimensional CAT scan or a myelogram (in which dye is injected around the spinal cord) may be used to reveal displacement of the disc.

Usually the offending portion of the disc shrivels so that the pain disappears in time. If it does not, a surgeon may operate to remove it, possibly using a fibre-optic instrument to avoid major surgery.

Many conventional doctors are now trained to use alternative treatments such as manipulation and acupuncture to treat joint displacement between vertebrae.

SCIENCE AND ALTERNATIVE MEDICINE

The scientific validity of alternative treatments is still a hotly contested issue, with some studies showing good results, some inconclusive, and some therapies never subjected to scientific tests. See TRYING TO MEASURE A THERAPY'S SUCCESS, p. 312.

SENSITIVITY TRAINING

A type of group PSYCHOTHERAPY aimed at helping people to relate to each other more truthfully is called sensitivity training. Under the guidance of a trained therapist, participants explore their attitudes and motives as they interact with one another, in ways designed to make them more aware of their own feelings, release tensions and build better relationships. See also HUMANISTIC PSYCHOLOGY; ENCOUNTER GROUPS; T-GROUPS.

SEXUAL PROBLEMS

The most common group of sexual problems stems from disturbances of the normal sexual response cycle that occurs in sexual intercourse. The cycle has three phases: desire; excitement/arousal; and resolution/ orgasm (climax). The stages tend to happen in sequence, for each is designed to trigger the next. However, they need not necessarily do so, and a disorder may arise in any phase.

It is possible to function sexually without feeling desire; or to feel desire and not be able to function; or to experience an orgasm without the changes – erection or secretion of lubrication – that occur in the excitement/ arousal phase.

The main difficulties arising from the normal sexual response cycle, each phase of which is served by different physical, chemical, nervous and psychological systems of the body, are as follows:

Both men and women may suffer from *inhibited sexual desire*. In this state desire is completely absent or is so weak that no sexual behaviour is initiated and/or sexual overtures from others are rejected. Problems connected with the excitement/arousal phase are *erectile insufficiency* or IMPOTENCE in men, and *general sexual dysfunction* or FRIGIDITY in women.

In the next phase of the cycle, resolution/ orgasm, men may experience *premature ejaculation* or *delayed/inhibited ejaculation*. In the first, the orgasm happens too soon. However, this is a rather subjective definition, for the 'best' time for ejaculation depends as much on the partner's satisfaction as on that of the man.

In the second problem, ejaculation is difficult to achieve and the difficulty destroys the pleasure of intercourse. In some cases the cause may be a specific malfunction of the man's sexual organs. For example, there may be the sensation of an orgasm, but the semen is ejaculated internally into the bladder instead of out through the shaft of the penis.

The equivalent problem in women is known as *general orgasmic dysfunction*. Orgasm does not occur, so sexual arousal results in a dissatisfied feeling. Sometimes there is also dull or intense pain. This is because the pelvic blood vessels become engorged by arousal, but the blood is not released at orgasm. However, it usually disappears as arousal subsides.

There are two more problems that men may experience. One, *specific loss of erection*

upon attempting intercourse, may have psychological causes – for instance, a fear of creating a pregnancy or fear of penetration itself. However, it is more likely to stem from a physical cause. For example, the man may become more active as he prepares for penetration; blood then flows away from the penile tissue to other muscles, so depriving the man of his erection.

The other problem is *pain upon intercourse*, a condition known medically as *dyspareunia*. The cause is nearly always physical in origin. The pain may only occur at ejaculation, and in a few rare cases of this kind the cause is a psychological one.

Women may experience *vaginismus*, a condition equivalent to the male specific loss of erection. The lower (outer) third of the vagina contracts very sharply when the vulva (vaginal lips) or vagina are touched – as in any attempt at intercourse – making penetration impossible. It is often caused by adverse sexual experiences or clumsy internal medical examination through the vagina. However, women who experience vaginismus may achieve an orgasm by other means, such as stroking of the clitoris (the rudimentary female penis).

Many physical conditions such as ulceration or inflammation result in vaginal pain, and the sudden contractions of the vagina may be an avoidance response to such pain.

Women can also experience dyspareunia. There are even more possible causes than in men, and they are mostly physical. Common conditions that may cause painful intercourse include ulceration of the sex organs, pelvic or vaginal inflammation or infection (see CYSTITIS), vaginal injury, and dryness or shrinking of the membrane lining the vagina. In a few cases the condition may have a psychological cause.

Self help There is a great deal that individuals can do to counter inhibited sexual desire, impotence, frigidity and other sexual problems. First of all realise that these problems can affect even the best of relationships, and can do so at any time. So try not to worry, for ANXIETY is one of the main causes of the difficulties; often fear of failure results in failure. DEPRESSION, STRESS and fatigue also play a part.

Try to talk freely and listen sympathetically to your partner. Express your needs and preferences and try to understand your partner's. For example, men often underestimate the importance of foreplay in female arousal, and hiding sexual dissatisfaction often aggravates the problem.

Try not to expect too much from sex. At certain times, for example, after illness, an orgasm may not be 'necessary'; kissing, cuddling, hugging, comforting, gentle massage, concern and attention for your partner –

even simply holding hands – may be equally satisfying. They are also an aid to discovery of a partner's needs and preferences.

One of the main problems in sexual relationships is the differing libidos (sexual drives) of the partners. And in both sexes, the sex drive may be different at different times. Again, couples need to work out their own understanding and compromise. For instance, women often experience less interest in sex at certain times in their menstrual cycle, after childbirth and at the menopause. Partners should try to realise that this is not a rejection of them, but of sex generally.

The ability to relax is all important (see RELAXATION AND BREATHING). Allow yourself time to 'unwind' from the cares of daily life – office work, travel, looking after children, housework, for example. Get 'in the mood'. You may find dimmed lights, soft music or dancing helpful, but again, each couple must find their own preferences.

Cut out alcohol, smoking and any drugs such as tranquillisers, antihistamines and the like, that are not essential for your wellbeing. All impair desire and performance, often causing impotence. Eating a heavy meal just before lovemaking often has the same effect.

Take EXERCISE – you will soon find how much you need – and eat a healthy diet (see EATING FOR HEALTH). Loss of desire and ability to perform sexually are some of the earliest effects of malnutrition. Zinc is a particularly important MINERAL, as both the female and male body need it to produce testosterone, a hormone necessary for sexual desire. Try a daily supplement of 20-30mg for a month or two. Men also need it for the healthy functioning of the prostate gland, which produces the liquid in which sperm are carried out of the body.

Iodine and thiamine are essential for a healthy thyroid gland, which produces a hormone that controls metabolism; deficiency leads to lethargy, tiredness, lack of desire and lowered interest in sex. And all glands need the amino-acid constituents of proteins. Choline is another essential, and its precursor is found in egg yolks, meat, maize and soya beans.

Brewer's yeast tablets may also be a helpful supplement. The yeast contains the glucose tolerance factor, without which the body develops glucose intolerance, which is believed to be another cause of impotence. However, if you are diabetic, you should consult your doctor before taking this supplement (see DIABETES).

Finally, discount the numerous myths about sex that have arisen. Perhaps the commonest is that 'good sex' is the right of all, and that it is entirely a question of performance and technique. And with

changes in moral attitudes over the last 30 years, increased availability of birth control, and despite the spread of AIDS, a myth persists that people who do not indulge freely in sex are freaks. Both these attitudes can place intolerable stress on individuals.

Another common misconception is that interest in sex is absent in older people, and that sex is actually bad for them. This is not true. You may not be able to do at 65 what you did at 25, but a happy, rewarding sex life can be enjoyed by the over 60s.

Another myth is that sexual intercourse puts undue strain on the heart. Tests in Britain and the USA have shown that the amount of physical energy spent during the sex act is below the energy required for most jobs. Even after a heart attack, by the time most patients return home they are ready for sex – but consult your doctor to make sure that this is true in your particular case. Usually a heart attack that occurs during or immediately after sex is due to some other factor, such as excessive indulgence in alcohol or food, or the stress associated with an extramarital affair.

Getting advice Should you feel that you need outside help for your problem(s) and do not want to consult your doctor, your local branch of Relate (The Marriage Guidance Council) can be found in the telephone book. Or you may find a therapist or counsellor through one of the following: The British Association for Counselling, 37A Sheep Street, Rugby, Warwickshire CU21 3BX; The London Centre for Psychotherapy, 19 Fitzjohns Avenue, London NW3 5JY; or The Institute of Psychosexual Medicine, 11 Chandos Street, London W1M 9DE.

What the therapists recommend

BEHAVIOURAL THERAPY

Consultation The course of therapy depends on the exact nature of the problem(s) involved. Basically, treatment consists of education (providing information about sex); communication (encouraging partners to discuss and agree on their sexual contact); sensate focusing (concentrating on the physical sensations of various aspects of foreplay and intercourse); and desensitisation (ensuring a relaxed and pleasurable sexual union by progressing through various stages of intimacy).

BACH REMEDIES

Self help Therapists suggest: Clematis if the problem is obsessive sexual fantasy with no action; Honeysuckle for being oversentimental and romantic; Mimulus for fear of experiencing intense sexual desire; Centaury for feeling one does not have a right to have sexual needs, or for feeling used, unable to say 'no'; Heather for being over-

demanding in a self-obsessed way; Water violet for shyness and reluctance to make intimate contact; Crab apple for feeling the body is unclean or shameful; Pine for guilt; Chicory for jealousy and possessiveness.

HYPNOTHERAPY

Consultation Once organic disease is ruled out, investigation is carried out by hypnoanalysis. If the problem is based on anxiety, then relaxation techniques are used. Patients may be taught ego-strengthening techniques to be used at home.

An orthodox view

The causes of problems related to the normal sexual response cycle may be physical, drug-induced or caused by nervous or psychological disorders. The doctor may ask to see both partners at the same time, or separately, for a full discussion of the problem.

A physical examination will be made. A diagnosis may be difficult, as in the case of pain that occurs only on arousal or ejaculation. If this is so, try to describe exactly what happens at these times. The doctor may then refer the patient(s) to a sexual function specialist. Physical conditions such as a dry vagina or cystitis will be treated, or the patient(s) may be referred to a consultant.

Certain drugs impair sexual performance, so the doctor will review any that have been prescribed. Drugs that may have such a side effect include phenelzine, used to treat depression and anxiety, and spironolactone, prescribed for high BLOOD PRESSURE

If the difficulty persists, the patient(s) may well be referred to a neurologist (nerve specialist) or psychotherapist.

See also CONTRACEPTION.

SHIATSU
Pressing the vital points for health

Although the Japanese name *shiatsu* means literally 'finger pressure', this stimulating form of massage is given by much more than fingers. The palms and heels of the hands, forearms, elbows, knees and feet are used, but thumbs most of all. Like ACUPRESSURE, shiatsu uses pressure on hundreds of surface points (*tsubo*) along the body's meridians (energy paths) to stimulate the flow of the Qi (life force) through the paths.

Shiatsu style therapies have been practised in Japan for centuries and developed (as did the Chinese acupressure) from *amna*, an ancient oriental massage system of rubbing and manipulating the hands and feet. Unlike the later development ACUPUNCTURE, shiatsu and acupressure were used as home treatments handed down the generations and practised by one family member on another.

Despite its long history, shiatsu was not formulated as a comprehensive therapy until early this century. Tokujiro Namikoshi was among the first to popularise the system. Now it has become rather more widely used than acupressure in the West.

It is a safe and effective technique, largely preventive but also used as a form of physiotherapy for specific ailments. It is said to act on the subtle electromagnetic forces of the body, which are particularly high or low in the areas used as pressure points. By stimulating or calming these points, shiatsu aims at rebalancing the quantity and quality of electromagnetic energy being distributed along the meridians – benefiting not only the body but also the mind, feelings and spirit.

Who it can help Practitioners claim that a wide variety of everyday ailments can be relieved by shiatsu – including HEADACHES and MIGRAINE, BACK PAIN and toothache. Treatment is said to be effective also for DIGESTIVE PROBLEMS, CONSTIPATION and DIARRHOEA. Convalescents and others have found their vitality and stamina restored. People suffering from STRESS and TENSION, DEPRESSION or INSOMNIA are believed to benefit. The general mobility and comfort of joints and muscles has been found to increase in people with chronic stiffness, and injuries resulting from sport or other physical exertion have responded well to treatment.

Shiatsu is also a whole-body programme designed to prevent these conditions, to tone up the circulation, nervous system and IMMUNE SYSTEM, to promote the elimination of poisons, and to help to strengthen bones.

Finding a therapist There are shiatsu therapists in most parts of the British Isles. Consult only an experienced, qualified person, registered with The Shiatsu Society, who has the initials MRSS (Member of the Register of The Shiatsu Society) after his name. For information about therapists in your area, write to The Shiatsu Society of Great Britain, 19 Langside Park, Kilbarchan, Strathclyde PA10 2EP; or The British School of Shiatsu-Do, East-West Centre, 188 Old Street, London EC1V 9BP.

The Shiatsu Society can also provide a list of approved teaching centres which offer training in the use of shiatsu. About 50 hours of instruction are needed for treating family and friends with minor problems, and about three years of part-time study for an average professional qualification.

Consulting a therapist Diagnosis comes before any treatment – and determines its exact form. The therapist will watch you, listen to your medical history, ask questions and perhaps touch affected areas to test their condition. Symptoms that affect you in everyday life will be of particular interest and allow the therapist to tailor the treatment specifically to your needs.

Treatment sessions last about an hour. No instruments or equipment are used. The only requirements are a firm surface and a warm room. You need to wear loose, comfortable clothing during the session. Do not have a large meal or drink any alcohol beforehand.

The session sometimes begins with stretching, turning and stimulating exercises, to set the energy flowing. You may be advised to practise them between sessions; they are routines used in DO-IN. One example is to curl your hand into a loose fist and, with the wrist relaxed, tap along the inside of your other arm from armpit to hand. Then tap along the outside of the arm from hand to shoulder. Repeat this three or four times and compare the sensation in the treated arm with that in the untreated side.

Continue the tapping all over the body including the head, and the back as far as possible. As a general rule, the tapping should move upwards on the front of the body and inside the legs and arms, and downwards on the back and the outside of the legs and arms.

When the therapist treats pressure points, the pressure will be deep but pleasant, though there may sometimes be pain. This signals energy blockage, and subsides with treatment. The strength will differ for different points, and the duration of pressure is determined by the energy flow response. It is applied as you breathe out, because the body is most relaxed then.

Pressure is applied mostly by the thumbs – not the tips but the pads of the top joints. This is the most sensitive part used to give therapy, so is the easiest to control. Control

Manipulating back and leg to stimulate the flow of 'life force'

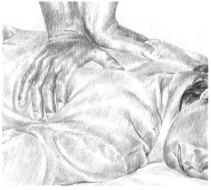

A shiatsu therapist sometimes begins a treatment with a preparation technique, such as this one to loosen and relax the back. A broad pressure is applied by using the palms with focus on the heels of the hands. No set order is laid down for shiatsu sessions.

The 'Hara' (or abdomen) is thought to be the centre of the body energy or life force, and important in both diagnosis and treatment. Below, the therapist seeks to activate the flow of life force along the inside leg meridians to stimulate its flow to the Hara.

Later in the session, the therapist applies more direct pressure to the back using the thumb pads (above). This is done in order to penetrate deeper and provide more focus to the treatment. It is said to stimulate the flow of Qi – or life force – along the bladder meridian close to the spinal column.

Shiatsu

Exercises that you can do

Treatment of certain 'tsubo' (points) is said to relieve the symptoms of specific disorders, and here a shiatsu therapist shows you how to treat some of them. The exercises are part of the system known as Do-In, and are claimed to improve general well-being as well.

Apply pressure on the palm where the tip of a completely flexed middle finger touches it. Press for 10-15 seconds, then repeat three times. This is claimed to relieve exhaustion, low vitality, stomach disease, high blood pressure.

Lightly, then gradually more firmly, tap the top of the shoulder, side of the neck, and down the back as far as you can. Do this for 15-20 seconds, then repeat on the other side. The method is said to relieve stiffness and aches anywhere when used on the affected area.

When nauseous or to prevent travel sickness, try pressing hard and inwards with one thumb two thumbs' width above the wrist, in the fold between the two tendons in the middle of the wrist. Press for 7-10 seconds three times.

Press hard and inwards with the thumb for 7-10 seconds, three times on the point on the inside of the lower leg, four fingers' width up from the tip of the ankle bone, just behind the shin bone. Therapists claim that this relieves period pains, insomnia and digestive problems. Don't do this if pregnant.

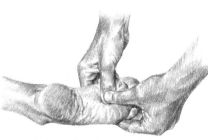

For revival, shock, epilepsy, period pains and dizziness, try the point on the sole of the foot about one-third the distance from the middle toe tip to the heel, midway across the ball of the foot. Press hard and inwards with two thumbs for 10-15 seconds, three times.

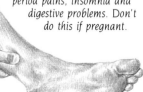

Press in and upwards on the points directly below the pupils when looking straight ahead, in the spaces under the cheekbones. This is said to relieve sinus and nasal congestion, facial tension and paralysis and toothache.

is increased by bracing the rest of the hand lightly on the client's body. You may be asked to sit, or lie face down, face up or on your side as various points are treated.

As the energy flow changes you may feel elated or depressed for a time, either during or after the session. Seemingly adverse reactions such as 'cold' symptoms are common, but are part of the healing process and usually disappear within a day or two as energy blockages dissolve. Treatment may be once a week to start with, then at fortnightly or longer intervals to maintain the correct energy balance.

An orthodox view

This is a useful home technique, particularly for relieving pain. It may be that the strongly applied pressure stimulates the body to produce endorphins, its own painkillers. The

---

Shiatsu at home

Among the many pressure points easily treated at home are those used to relieve INDIGESTION and sore throats.

For indigestion The tsubo is on the web between the thumb and index finger. Spread your left hand and put your right thumb on the back of the web and the index finger on the corresponding area of the palm. Massage gently for 10-20 seconds. Repeat on the other hand. (Do not use if you are pregnant.)

For a sore throat The pressure point is 2in (50mm) below the centre of the collarbone, between the first and second ribs. Press your thumbs on both sides together for 7-10 seconds.

To improve your suppleness and stimulate the energy flow, try these two exercises. The first is believed to reduce all stiffness, but especially that in the neck; the second to relieve tense shoulders and 'open up' the chest.

1 Sit with back straight and bend your neck sideways, bringing the right ear towards the right shoulder. Bring your right arm up over your head so that the hand covers your left ear. Rotate your left shoulder ten times clockwise then ten anticlockwise, gradually increasing the amount of stretch. Repeat the exercise on the other side.

2 Stand upright with your feet a little apart and hands clasped behind your back. Bend forward from the hips without curving your upper body. Raise your clasped hands as high as you can. Then lower your hands, stand upright, bend your head back and again raise your hands as high as possible.

therapy is unlikely to cause harm in most people – especially if only the thumbs, fingers and palms are used – but should not be used on inflamed, infected or damaged areas or on a person who has a FRACTURE or SLIPPED DISC, or who is taking steroids such as cortisone.

SHINGLES

This painful, blistered rash can develop only in people who have had CHICKENPOX at some time in their lives. The chickenpox virus lies dormant in a nerve root for years, only to be reactivated later in life. As a result, shingles develops on the area of skin supplied by the particular nerve. The reactivation can sometimes be the result of contact with someone – usually a child – who has chickenpox; or it can arise from STRESS following, say, the death of a husband or wife.

Shingles is known medically as *herpes zoster*, from the Greek words *herpes*, meaning 'to creep', and *zoster*, meaning 'girdle' or 'belt'. There is a mistaken belief that if the rash stretches all the way around the body and meets in the middle, the patient will die.

The first symptom of shingles is severe pain, without any apparent reason, on one side of the body – usually the chest or back. A few days later this is followed by a skin eruption, or rash, in the painful area. The rash normally goes after two or three weeks – often leaving scars where crusts have formed. However, the pain – which is known as post-herpetic NEURALGIA – can persist for months if not years afterwards.

Always see a doctor if you think you have shingles – and as soon as possible if it affects the forehead near the eyes, as sight can be damaged if treatment comes too late.

What the therapists recommend

Homoeopathy If shingles is caught in its early stages, homoeopaths claim the attack can usually be cut short. If the skin is blistered, red and itchy *Rhus tox. 6* should be used. If the skin burns and stings, apply a cold application such as *Apis mel*. For severe pain and itching, use *Mezereum*. If the patient finds it uncomfortable to move, and his appetite declines, *Ranunculus* may help.

Aromatherapy To be at all effective, treatment should start as soon the symptoms occur. Three drops each of geranium, sage and thyme in 20ml of carrier oil or lotion may be rubbed onto the affected area. If the skin is sensitive to the touch, the oil should be dabbed on gently. Alternatively, the same number of drops in a small glass of water

may be helpful when poured onto the shingles, or applied as a compress.

Acupuncture After the initial rash has subsided, the neuralgic pain can be treated by strong manual stimulation at points on the following meridians: stomach, large and small intestine, and governor. Pain points next to the rash may also be used to relieve the neuralgia.

Naturopathy As sufferers are often in a run-down condition, and the illness itself can be extremely weakening, treatment aims to restore vigour. Therapists may advise a high-dosage of the vitamin B-complex. In addition, up to 1g a day of the essential amino acid L-lysine may be prescribed. Post-shingles pain can linger for a long time, often causing depression, and natural therapies are claimed to be very effective against this.

An orthodox view

If shingles is diagnosed early and treatment begins within 24 hours or so of the rash appearing, antiviral drugs will shorten the course of the illness and reduce the risk of post-herpetic neuralgia. If necessary, strong painkillers will be prescribed – although these can result in side effects, including CONSTIPATION.

The patient should wear loose clothing such as a large shirt or pyjama jacket, so that the blisters are not rubbed and irritated. Two or three cool baths a day may help relieve the pain. Do not shake talcum powder onto the affected area, as it will irritate any places where the blisters have broken.

If shingles affects the forehead, a doctor will examine the patient's eyes to make sure that the cornea (the transparent membrane covering the eye) has not been harmed. Special eyedrops will be prescribed to protect the eyesight.

SHOCK

It is important to distinguish between emotional fright, which can be caused by sudden bad news, panic or minor injuries, and clinical shock, a dangerous condition which can even kill.

Clinical shock usually has a physical rather than a psychological cause, and results when insufficient blood is circulating to vital organs, particularly the brain and kidneys. It can be caused by bad burns or by an accident where there is serious external or internal bleeding.

Extreme PAIN or distress, severe vomiting (see NAUSEA AND VOMITING) or DIARRHOEA, near drowning, a blood infection and severe

ALLERGY (such as to a vaccine) can also cause clinical shock. The patient is pale or grey, and has a weak pulse which is rapid and may be irregular.

Warning The use of alternative remedies applies only to cases of emotional fright not involving clinical shock.

What the therapists recommend

Homoeopathy For emotional shock, after bad news, *Ignatia 30* or *200* is recommended every five minutes until calm is restored.

Massage Effleurage technique (when the hands are passed continuously and rhythmically over the skin in one direction only) and petrissage (kneading of the skin) should be used, and not percussive movements.

Bach Remedies Star of Bethlehem may ease shock and trauma. The Rescue Remedy (a combination of five separate remedies) can be applied if there are intense feelings or fainting fits.

An orthodox view

People may quickly recover from emotional fright. Comfort and attention are the best remedies. However, it is important to remember that extreme distress can lead to clinical shock.

In the event of clinical shock, seek medical assistance immediately. Lie the patient down so that the head is below the level of the heart, to ensure that sufficient blood goes to the patient's brain to prevent unconsciousness. Make sure that his airway is clear and that he is breathing. Give artificial respiration if necessary. Unless it interferes with breathing, raise the patient's legs to drain blood to vital organs.

If he is unconscious, place him on his stomach with his face on one side in the recovery position. This prevents his tongue from falling into the back of his throat and choking him, and allows fluid – such as blood or vomit – to drain from his mouth. If the patient is bleeding badly, press firmly on the wound to slow or stop the loss of blood.

A doctor or paramedic can help the patient by giving oxygen, fluids through an intravenous drip and, in cases of allergic shock, possibly an injection of a stimulant drug such as adrenaline.

SHOWERS

Water jets and sprays can be used to treat a whole range of ailments, from HEADACHES and GALLSTONES to ARTHRITIS and DIABETES. Even an ordinary bathroom shower or hand-held shower attachment can be therapeutic if used correctly. See HYDROTHERAPY.

Trying to measure a therapy's success

Many patients are worried that technology seems to be taking over more and more in conventional medicine. As it does so, the general practitioner's role is often reduced merely to deciding which clinic or consultant to pass patients on to. Further, patients are worried that busy doctors have so little time to talk to them that the traditional relationship of trust between doctor and patient does not develop.

Faced with this situation, many people have turned to alternative practitioners and have been helped – which has created in orthodox medicine a greater readiness to consider alternatives to its science-based approach. The readiness has been reinforced by orthodox doctors' recognition of shortcomings in their system. There are qualms about its 'infallibility'. If the removal of tonsils and radical mastectomies – once standard treatment – are no longer thought necessary, the scientific method that advocated them is not infallible. So questions arise: are there flaws in other orthodox treatments? Should alternatives be considered?

The medical establishment is now beginning to show more interest in them. In 1983, a survey of general practice trainees in Britain found that 80 per cent of them wanted to train also in at least one alternative therapy, and 21 per cent had already used one. If alternative therapies were to be wholeheartedly embraced and monitored by the establishment, one difficulty for patients would end – judging whether a therapist is properly trained. Many therapies have associations that accredit practitioners, but it is still possible for untrained people to practise.

Also in 1983, the British Medical Association (BMA) set up a committee to look into alternative medicine. One of the committee's aims was to see whether there are acceptable ways to measure the effects of alternative therapies. This has always been the greatest barrier to cooperation between orthodox and alternative medicine.

Science-based orthodoxy demands of its system of medicine measurable proof that a patient's condition has been changed for the better, and an understanding of why the change has happened. Advanced technology is used to aid DIAGNOSIS, and lengthy trials are held to test the effects of orthodox treatments. Diagnosis and treatment have altered as more has been discovered of the natural laws governing the body's biology and chemistry.

Much of alternative medicine, however, is built on completely different beliefs about what disease is and what causes it. Stimulating the life force or restoring the body's proper balance is at the core of many alternative therapies. Science finds such approaches unacceptable, since they are not always based on its knowledge of how the body works.

During its inquiry, the BMA committee saw more than 600 submissions from doctors and lay alternative therapists, plus replies to questionnaires sent to organisations. Some alternative disciplines chose not to participate, feeling that the committee's purpose was not appropriate to their methods. The ALEXANDER TECHNIQUE, IRIDOLOGY, ACUPRESSURE, SHIATSU and T'AI-CHI CH'UAN were among these. Perhaps not surprisingly, the doctors stuck strictly to the criteria demanded in their own discipline, and gave no credence to alternatives based on assumptions contrary to conventional knowledge of the body – classical ACUPUNCTURE and REFLEXOLOGY, for example.

The committee did not itself try to measure the effectiveness of alternatives, but noted what evidence there was and regretted that the alternative disciplines themselves had not reviewed their practices in the light of current scientific knowledge. The doctors also pointed to dangers that were being overlooked – in HERBAL MEDICINE, for example (see below) – because scientific tests were not being held.

Clinical trials

To be convinced of the value of alternative medicine, doctors demand the kind of clinical trials their own treatments are judged by – including a clear definition and diagnosis of the condition being treated. There must be enough cases, widely distributed, to provide valid statistics relating to the general population.

In one type of trial, those being given treatment are split into two randomly chosen groups, one to be given a genuine treatment, the other a PLACEBO (a substance containing no active drug). The results of both treatments are carefully noted, and allowances made for errors in procedure and coincidence. If enough of those getting genuine treatment show measurable improvement, the treatment is counted effective.

Just feeling better is not considered proof enough – you may feel better after taking a painkiller, for example, but the cause of pain remains. Some of those given a placebo also show improvement – the placebo effect is powerful. So clinical trials do not *guarantee* effectiveness. Even when the overall findings are favourable, some individuals tested – and patients treated later – do not respond to the treatment.

Alternative medicine has an ambivalent attitude to clinical trials. It questions their usefulness, finds them impracticable and points out that only mainstream medicine or drug manufacturers have laboratories equipped to carry out large-scale trials. Yet alternative practitioners are often eager to cite findings favouring their own therapies.

Therapists usually deal with patients who have chosen their own treatment, and so are not a random group. Symptoms are often unspecific and the therapist's diagnostic method may not follow orthodox procedures. The results of treatment also are often generalised – an improved sense of well-being rather than a measurable change in a blood count, for example.

The doctors' findings

The BMA committee findings, published in 1986, showed odd anomalies: some therapies gave measurable benefits, and had even been adopted by doctors, but sprang from unacceptable theories about the body and disease. OSTEOPATHY and acupuncture, for example, were found effective for some purposes. On the other hand, practitioners of HOMOEOPATHY and medical herbalists, whose training in diagnosis, anatomy and physiology is along lines of orthodox training, were said by the BMA to be giving many useless – and even some dangerous – treatments.

Many homoeopaths have also had conventional medical training. They treat the same range of conditions as orthodox medicine, and 80 per cent of those treated are satisfied (according to a *Which?* report). The scientific view is that homoeopathic remedies are given in such tiny doses and are so diluted that little or no trace of the original substance remains. 'Cures' are considered to be due entirely to the placebo effect; conditions treated successfully would usually have followed the same course with no treatment at all, say doctors. Practitioners argue that homoeopathy does not lend itself to clinical research, because diagnosis and treatment have no norms, being tailored to the individual.

Herbs have been the source of many drugs used in orthodox medicine, which has isolated their active constituents. However, the report said that medical herbalists, while traditionally paying attention to the time of day a plant is picked and to its exact place of origin, have not been so meticulous in analysing its constituents, and that some herbal remedies can be both beneficial and dangerous.

For example, herbal teas such as Maté, senecio and heliotrope can cause liver damage, and so can extracts or oils of comfrey, sassafras, mistletoe and pennyroyal. Amygdalin, from apricot and peach kernels, can cause cyanide poisoning, and some herbal mixtures contain lead or arsenic. Further, some herbal remedies interact dangerously with drugs prescribed by orthodox doctors. Lily of the valley, for example, increases the effect of digitalis, which is prescribed for heart conditions but is dangerous in excess.

Acupuncture has been adopted by many doctors as an extra tool – but only to support modern Western concepts of medicine, not to affect energy flow along meridians as held by traditional oriental medicine. Doctors use it simply for pain relief whereas most acupuncturists regard their therapy as a comprehensive treatment for all disorders. Scientific research has shown that it works by stimulating nerve fibres to send pain-blocking messages. It also stimulates production of endorphins and encephalins, the body's natural painkillers. Acupressure may well work in the same way.

MASSAGE, HELLERWORK and AROMATHERAPY may also stimulate in ways similar to acupuncture, but there is little scientific proof of what they do. Some electrocardiogram and electroencephalogram readings suggest that the rhythmic massage strokes have a sedating effect.

Of all the 'touch' therapies, osteopathy and CHIROPRACTIC are the most acceptable to doctors – but only for properly diagnosed muscle and joint disorders, not as comprehensive therapeutic systems, as some practitioners claim. Even so, they have given swift relief of long-term pain for many patients when orthodox medicine has failed. A Medical Research Council trial, reported in 1990, showed chiropractic to be significantly better than conventional physiotherapy for patients with low back pain.

Osteopaths claim that their sensitive hands feel sources of pain that science cannot measure. A possible explanation has been discovered by Professor I.M. Korr, of Kirksville College of Osteopathy and Surgery, in Missouri, USA. He found a higher measure of electrical resistance than is normally present on the skin over painful areas. The measure also became higher or lower according to the load put on the painful area, and was detectable before orthodox medicine could detect the injury.

One therapy that seemed unlikely to produce scientific proof has nevertheless allowed tests to be made. SPIRITUAL HEALING has been the subject of several small trials in the USA. Among them was one conducted among heart disease patients and another which used persistent headache sufferers. Patients were treated either by healers or by people only seeming to give healing, while actually concentrating on something else. In these, as in other tests, the genuine treatments gave significantly greater improvements. In Britain a controlled trial with RHEUMATOID ARTHRITIS sufferers is in progress at Leeds General Infirmary.

Healing in the mind

Sympathetic talk and touch may not be scientific treatment, but are undoubtedly beneficial to patients – and often what patients seek when they turn to alternative medicine. The fact that a patient who feels better still shows the same degree of disease in tests may be unsatisfactory from a scientific standpoint; but for the patient, feeling better is of prime importance. Relief from PAIN, ANXIETY or other symptoms boosts confidence and builds a positive attitude in the mind. The placebo effect itself testifies to the power of a believing mind to bring about improvement in the body.

Scientific medicine has been reminded recently of what a potent health factor the mind can be. Follow-up studies of patients treated by orthodox methods for breast CANCER found that despite having the same treatment, those least likely to survive were the resigned and hopeless ones. Those who survived longest – at least 15 years – were the fighters who refused to accept that their life was threatened, and showed a fierce will to live. Is this the unmeasurable life force that alternative therapies are all about?

SILVA METHOD
The power of mind over matter

By consciously taking control of the mind, followers of the Silva Method – a form of dynamic MEDITATION – claim to cure conditions such as STRESS and TENSION.

The method compares the brain to a vast computer, which is controlled by the mind. The brain emits electrical impulses called brainwaves, which operate at different frequencies and are linked to different states of consciousness. The method works on the assumption that most people are aware only of the surface, everyday level of the mind. The Silva technique is said to put them in touch with deeper, more creative levels.

The therapy was launched in 1966 by José Silva, a self-educated Mexican American.

Who it can help According to its teachers, the method can assist people of almost any age or profession. However, it may not be suitable for anyone with severe emotional or mental problems. In such cases, always check with a doctor or psychiatrist first.

Finding a teacher Courses in the Silva Method are held regularly in London, Manchester, Glasgow and other major British cities. For details, get in touch with The Silva Method, BCM Self Management, London WC1 3XX. The teachers are registered with the headquarters and have all been students of the method themselves.

Consulting a teacher Each course consists of a 42 hour seminar, or series of lectures, held over two consecutive weekends.

An orthodox view

The method is an approach to integrating the body and the mind, using techniques taken from other therapies.

SINUS PROBLEMS

The sinuses are air-filled spaces lined with mucous membrane in the bones of the face. Normally, mucus is channelled through tiny air ducts from the spaces to the nose, but during COLDS the ducts can become congested and the circulation of air and mucus impeded. If mucus builds up in the sinuses and they become inflamed, sinusitis results.

HAY FEVER can also cause sinusitis, and

ALLERGY or exposure to dust and irritants such as tobacco smoke can cause persistent symptoms, or chronic sinusitis.

Symptoms include pain in the forehead and cheeks, which worsens on stooping, lying down or coughing. There may be a green, yellow or bloody discharge from the nose, and the nostril on the affected side is blocked. The patient may suffer HEADACHES and the sense of smell is diminished. If the sinus is infected by bacteria the bone over it is tender, the skin may be red or swollen and the patient may have a raised temperature.

What the therapists recommend

Acupuncture Points on the governor and the large and small intestine meridians are treated, and on the spleen meridian when allergy is the cause.

Aromatherapy You are advised to inhale a drop or two of eucalyptus oil and/or peppermint oil, together with either lavender, bergamot or lemon, from a kitchen tissue for immediate effect.

To improve the sinus condition in the long term, apply a lotion every night made up of 60ml (2fl oz) white base lotion and 15 drops of any one or more of the same oils. If congestion is severe, press with the fingertips along the cheekbone from the nose to the temple, after applying the lotion. Repeat a little lower down on the same bone. Also try six to eight drops of oil in the bath.

Herbal Medicine Steam inhalations with essential oils of eucalyptus, pine, lavender, camomile, cinnamon, thyme, peppermint or cypress may be beneficial. You may also take infusions (see p. 184) of elderflower, ginger, peppermint or eyebright.

GARLIC is recommended as a general preventive against sinus problems, as well as being effective against colds, CHILL, INFLUENZA and bronchial complaints.

Homoeopathy For chronic sinusitis a therapist should always be consulted. He may recommend the following remedies taken every two hours for two days – less if relief is quickly obtained.

When there is yellow, stringy catarrh and heavy congestion try *Kali bich. 6*. If the face is very sensitive and tender, the patient is chilly and irritable, with yellow discharge, try *Hepar sulph. 6*. If the area of pain keeps changing, the symptoms are worse when indoors, there is a tendency to weep, the nose is sometimes stuffed up and there is yellow catarrh, try *Pulsatilla 6*.

Ionisation Dust makes mucus more viscous, and so ionisers are said to help mucus to drain more easily.

Reflexology You are advised to massage areas relating to the sinuses, head, nose, eyes, upper lymph nodes, neck, upper spine and adrenal glands (see chart, p. 295).

An orthodox view

Decongestant medicines from the chemist open up the air passages and help drain mucus. For infected sinuses, doctors may prescribe a course of antibiotics, and for chronic sinusitis, regular use of nasal sprays.

SKIN DISORDERS

The skin is a vital body organ which protects everything inside it from the elements, allows us to sense touch, pain, heat and cold, and, through variations in blood supply and sweating, helps to control our body temperature and fluid loss.

Skin disorders may reflect various diseases of the skin itself (see, for example, ACNE; ECZEMA; PIMPLES AND SPOTS; SHINGLES; COLD SORES; IMPETIGO) or they may result from disorders affecting other parts of the body (for example, PSORIASIS, ALLERGY, BEE STINGS, excessive BRUISING or CHICKENPOX). Areas of skin can also become malignant (see CANCER), may develop CIRCULATION PROBLEMS, or form ULCERS.

See also NATURAL AIDS TO BEAUTY.

SLEEP DISORDERS
Overcoming problems

In an anxious world, full of pressures, challenges and stresses, sleep should be a restoring antidote to daytime cares – a chance to rest the mind, repair the body and prepare for each new day. Yet as many as ten million Britons suffer regular night-time disturbances such as sleeplessness, restlessness, or troubled dreams.

Scientists still do not fully understand what makes us sleep, but certain 'sleep centres' have been found in the brain – a sort of 'body clock' which is thought to control the timing of rest and wakefulness. A number of natural sleep-promoting chemicals in the body also appear to play a role. See also INSOMNIA; JET LAG.

Individuals need different amounts of sleep and, throughout our lives, as well as from day to day, each person's needs are constantly changing. Many people – especially as they grow older – worry about not getting enough sleep. But as we age it becomes normal to sleep less, to take longer to get to sleep, and to tend to wake more often during the night.

It is thought that with age the body's processes slow down naturally, reducing the need for long rests at night. In the same way, people who practise deep relaxation exercises – which can slow down bodily processes even more than deep sleep itself – may also get by with less. On the other hand, if you are ill or under STRESS, your need for sleep is likely to increase.

The natural pattern of sleep can be disturbed for many reasons, but the most common problems are as follows:

Insomnia Difficulty in falling asleep, frequent waking and restlessness during the night, and early waking that leaves you feeling tired are common problems that can have many causes.

Hypersomnia Sleeping too much and continually feeling tired can be as troublesome as not being able to sleep. These symptoms may be a sign of DEPRESSION, and often go hand in hand with lack of ENERGY during the day. See also TIREDNESS.

Nightmares and troubled dreams Usually a sign of ANXIETY, strange or frightening dreams occur to nearly everyone at some time and are only a problem if they continue for prolonged periods. Restoring peaceful sleep depends on coming to terms with the underlying worries.

Nightmares sometimes make children afraid to go to sleep, while other children wake suddenly during the night in a state of fear and may cry, scream, speak incoherently or simply stare into space. The best response is to stay calm and give comfort at the time. Later you can discuss the child's fears with him and offer reassurance and help – often anxieties about separation from parents or problems at school are responsible for the troubled nights.

Restlessness Many sleepless nights are due to tossing and turning, and feeling unable to find a comfortable position in bed. The cause can be anything from illness to an uncomfortable bed or being too hot or too cold. See BEDS AND BEDDING.

Sleepwalking This is a rare problem that affects mainly children. Anxiety is sometimes to blame, but often there is no identifiable cause. Guide the victim gently back to bed without waking him if possible, but there is no danger if he does wake up.

Snoring People who snore habitually sometimes stop breathing altogether for short intervals – a symptom of some HEART DISORDERS. See SNORING.

What the therapists recommend

Massage This should be given last thing at night in a warm room with dimmed lights. First, lie on your back while your partner applies soothing effleurage strokes to the legs, then gentle, rhythmic petrissage to the abdominal area.

Next lie face downwards, while your partner gives gentle effleurage to your whole back, followed by rhythmic wringing, rolling and squeezing petrissage over the shoulders – if possible in time with your breathing – slowing gently to a finish, allowing you to roll over again and drift into sleep.

Herbal Medicine For mild sleeplessness due to minor worry or stress, a bedtime infusion (see p. 184) of lavender, lime blossom, lemon balm or camomile is often all that is needed.

A hot bath with a few drops of essential oil of lavender added may help you to unwind after a tense day. Individual advice from a practitioner will depend on the causes and symptoms of the problem. Herbs such as valerian, skullcap, cowslip or hops may be used to reduce high anxiety levels.

Homoeopathy If sleep is disturbed by fear, panic or the aftermath of a shock, *Aconitum* is recommended; or *Arnica* if overtired physically or mentally and the bed seems too hard. When your mind will not rest – after sudden good news, for example – and you feel wide awake, *Coffea* may help. For 3am sleeplessness due to strain or overindulgence of any kind, when you drop off only to wake up irritable and unrefreshed, try *Nux vomica*.

Take a dose of the indicated remedy half an hour before going to bed, and repeat half hourly as necessary. In each case, try taking potency 6 or 30.

Hypnotherapy Practitioners can teach methods of relaxation which are said to be very effective for inducing sleep. Analysis while under hypnosis may also be used to help poor sleepers who have underlying emotional problems.

Behavioural Therapy A good sleep pattern should be based on good sleeping habits and routines. Where a disturbed sleep pattern is a symptom of some greater problem, such as depression or severe anxiety, the therapist will aim to deal with this as well as re-establishing good sleep routines.

An orthodox view

Doctors are able to treat some causes of sleep disturbances such as sickness, pain and depression. In other cases, you are likely simply to be offered sleeping pills or tranquillisers. Taking these occasionally does no harm and many people find them a great help, particularly at times of stress. But they are not a long-term solution and some can disrupt the natural sleep cycle, adding to your problems.

Anyone who regularly relies on drugs for sleep should seek further advice from a doctor (see also ADDICTION).

Getting a good night's rest

First find the cause of your sleeplessness. It can be any kind of physical or emotional strain – illness, PAIN, heat, noise, a new or uncomfortable bed, depression, overeating or drinking.

Many sleep problems can be avoided simply by taking steps to cope with these problems – for example, doctors can provide medication to relieve pain, depression and unpleasant symptoms such as a blocked nose if they keep you awake. Installing double glazing will cut down street noise. However, this is an expensive business, and wearing wax ear-plugs is economical and fairly effective. If you get hot or cold at night, it may help to change your bedding.

A calming bedtime routine should also help anyone with sleep problems. Listen to music, take a walk, or read a book before bed, to help you to unwind and forget daytime tensions. Avoid late meals and arguments or serious discussions late at night. If something is on your mind, try writing it down, or making a list of your worries, so that you recognise them as problems to be set aside and dealt with at another time.

You could also practise RELAXATION AND BREATHING exercises, take a hot bath or ask a partner to give you a MASSAGE. In addition, you could try herbal TISANES such as camomile, rose hip or cinnamon, perhaps with a little honey added; or a milky drink. Avoid tea, coffee and cocoa, however – they contain caffeine which may keep you awake. Do not take any drinks at bedtime if you tend to wake during the night to go to the lavatory.

If you do find yourself lying awake in bed, again practising breathing exercises, or concentrating on a pleasant, detailed image or memory, may help. Or try listening to soothing music or a relaxation tape through earphones.

If sleep difficulties continue for any length of time, think about whether you are getting enough EXERCISE and eating a good diet (see EATING FOR HEALTH). If you have serious marital problems, money worries, depression or other emotional strains, try talking to a close friend, who may at least be able to offer comfort, and possibly advice. Or consider seeking professional guidance through COUNSELLING or consulting a doctor or psychologist.

Painless ways to lose weight

The slim body beautiful is the goal of many today, and undoubtedly thinner people suffer less illness and live longer than those who are overweight. Fads and fancy diets often fail; slimming the natural way is a good alternative.

From high-protein to low-fat diets, from fibre diets and single-food regimes to strange combinations and milkshake meals, people who want to lose weight come in for a great deal of bewildering – and sometimes bizarre – advice.

Mostly the advice is harmless enough – much of it so impractical or unsociable that no one can stick to it for long – but in a few cases it could be dangerous or even make you put on more weight in the end. And for seasoned slimmers who have already tried other regimes there is the guilt and despair of yet another failure, as unrealistic eating gradually drives them back to their old, bad ways yet again.

Fortunately, slimming need not involve fad diets or peculiar eating patterns. On a sensible, balanced diet of natural foods low in fat and sugar it is possible for most people to lose weight safely and simply – and establish healthy eating patterns to last a lifetime.

Note This is not true for people taking certain drugs – steroids and some antidepressants, for example. In any case, anyone receiving any form of treatment should consult their doctor before embarking on a diet.

For some people the change to a low-fat, low-sugar diet needs only small adjustments to their eating habits; for others it means changing their whole way of life if the results are to be permanent. The changes can take time to get used to, but the effects in terms of better health, increased vitality as well as weight loss are strong incen-

Are you overweight?

It all depends on the build of your body. To measure your natural frame size, try the wrist test below or the shoulder-arm comparison on the right, then plot the ideal weight range for your build and height on the graph opposite.

Wrist test
Measure your wrist at its narrowest point, just below the joint bone. For women, less than 5½in (14cm) indicates a small build, 5½-6½in (14-16.5cm) a medium build, and above 6½in a large build. For men, any measurement under 6½in indicates a small build, 6½-7in (16.5-18cm) a medium build, and above 7in (18cm) a large build.

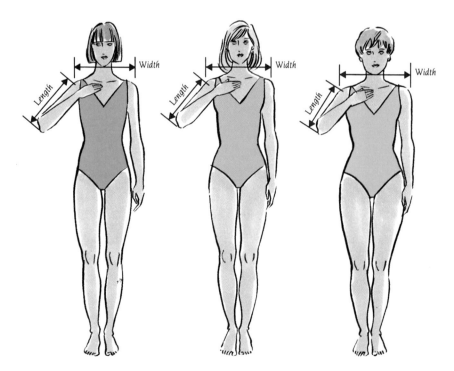

Shoulder-arm comparison
<u>Small frame</u> *The width of the shoulders is less than the length of the upper arm.*

<u>Medium frame</u> *The width of the shoulders is about the length of the upper arm.*

<u>Large frame</u> *The width of the shoulders is greater than the length of the upper arm.*

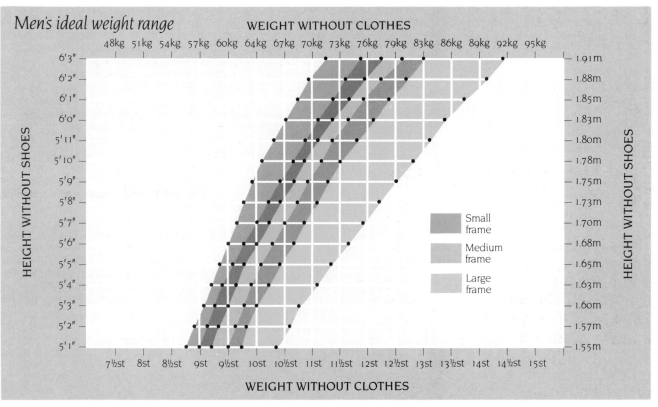

Men's ideal weight range

WEIGHT WITHOUT CLOTHES

48kg 51kg 54kg 57kg 60kg 64kg 67kg 70kg 73kg 76kg 79kg 83kg 86kg 89kg 92kg 95kg

HEIGHT WITHOUT SHOES

6'3" — 1.91m
6'2" — 1.88m
6'1" — 1.85m
6'0" — 1.83m
5'11" — 1.80m
5'10" — 1.78m
5'9" — 1.75m
5'8" — 1.73m
5'7" — 1.70m
5'6" — 1.68m
5'5" — 1.65m
5'4" — 1.63m
5'3" — 1.60m
5'2" — 1.57m
5'1" — 1.55m

7½st 8st 8½st 9st 9½st 10st 10½st 11st 11½st 12st 12½st 13st 13½st 14st 14½st 15st

WEIGHT WITHOUT CLOTHES

Small frame
Medium frame
Large frame

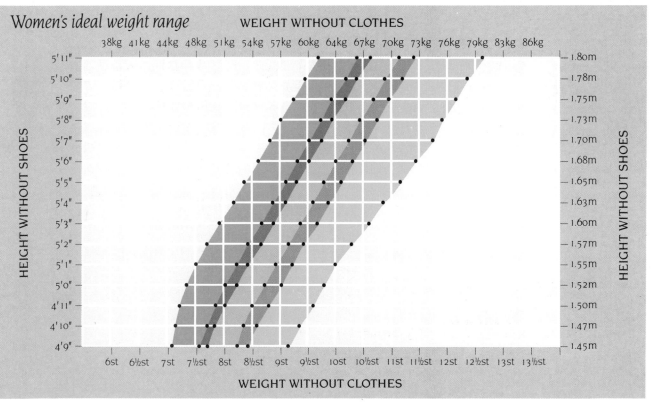

Women's ideal weight range

WEIGHT WITHOUT CLOTHES

38kg 41kg 44kg 48kg 51kg 54kg 57kg 60kg 64kg 67kg 70kg 73kg 76kg 79kg 83kg 86kg

HEIGHT WITHOUT SHOES

5'11" — 1.80m
5'10" — 1.78m
5'9" — 1.75m
5'8" — 1.73m
5'7" — 1.70m
5'6" — 1.68m
5'5" — 1.65m
5'4" — 1.63m
5'3" — 1.60m
5'2" — 1.57m
5'1" — 1.55m
5'0" — 1.52m
4'11" — 1.50m
4'10" — 1.47m
4'9" — 1.45m

6st 6½st 7st 7½st 8st 8½st 9st 9½st 10st 10½st 11st 11½st 12st 12½st 13st 13½st

WEIGHT WITHOUT CLOTHES

tives for persevering, even if occasional lapses do occur.

Like all slimming diets, losing weight naturally depends on keeping track of calories. A calorie is a unit of energy, and to lose weight you must take in fewer calories every day than are burnt up in activities, building and repairing tissue, and carrying out essential bodily processes. (Strictly speaking, food energy is measured in 'big' Calories – with a capital C – 1000 'small' calories equalling 1 Calorie or kilocalorie, sometimes abbreviated *kcal*. But the normal convention – followed here – is to refer simply to calories while always meaning the 'big' kind.)

Energy is stored in the body as fat, each pound (450g) representing 3000 to 3500 calories. So to lose one pound of body weight you have to eat about 3000 calories less than you burn up. The amount of energy you use each day depends on your metabolism, way of life and type of work. A slightly built woman who travels to work by car or bus and spends the day sitting at a desk may use up as little as about 1800 calories a day, while a 12 stone (76kg) miner or manual labourer may burn up twice as much. (However, it is not necessarily entirely dependent on size and weight, since people with a very fast metabolic rate may burn up more calories.)

This means that different people will lose weight on different dietary regimes – the miner, for example, would lose weight if he reduced his intake to 2000 calories a day, while the office worker would actually gain weight if she ate this much. While bearing this in mind, nutritionists generally tend to recommend diets of 1000 to 1200 calories a day for anyone wishing to slim.

A thousand calories is thought to be about the lowest safe daily intake for any length of time, as less is unlikely to provide the body with adequate nourishment. Crash diets of 600 calories or even fewer are unhealthy and often do not work any faster since the body reacts by conserving energy, slowing you down and making you feel tired rather than active and fit.

Making your daily intake as satisfying and nutritious as possible is the secret of natural slimming. A thousand calories a day is not a lot if you eat mainly junk food and snacks – one chocolate bar alone may be 300 calories, a quarter of your whole allowance. On the other hand, if you choose wisely, 1000 calories will go much further – an apple is only about 50 calories and a slice of bread about 70.

Eating normal, healthy foods like these means that slimmers can have the same meals as the rest of the family, but take smaller portions. No one need even know you are dieting. By avoiding processed and refined foods, you will get more vitamins and minerals too, boosting your health even though you eat a smaller amount. And when you feel well it is easier to carry on eating less. In addition, your new way of eating teaches good habits that will help you stay slim in the future, even when you are no longer on a diet.

What you can eat

The natural slimming diet is based on the same foods that make up any healthy diet: fruit, salads, vegetables, wholegrains, pulses and small quantities of fish, lean meat and dairy products (see EATING FOR HEALTH). You eat more high-fibre foods such as wholewheat bread, oats and potatoes (see FIBRE) and more fresh foods, while cutting down on sugary and fatty ones.

The average daily British diet contains about 3½oz (100g) each of sugar and fat – far more than is necessary for good health (see LOW-FAT DIETS). Cutting each by half will not take away any essential nutrients – provided the rest of your diet is balanced – but it will save about 640 calories a day, or one pound of body weight every five days. You could cut out all added sugar without losing *any* nutrients. But no one should ever try to cut out all fat, since it 'carries' essential fatty acids and vitamins A and D. But eating only half as much fat leaves you with enough of these, provided you get vitamin D from sunlight.

Do not be afraid of so-called 'stodge' foods such as bread, pasta, rice and potatoes – they are low in fat and because they are filling you are less likely to top up with unhealthy snacks. Choose wholegrain varieties for their extra fibre, vitamins and minerals.

Eat plenty of fresh fruit and vegetables. They are low in calories and rich in nutrients, and the variety of colours, flavours and textures means that your diet need never be boring. Including something fresh in every meal leaves less space for sweets and fatty foods, and adds vitamins and minerals which prevent the 'run-down' feeling that makes so many slimmers give up before the diet has time to succeed.

Dressings and mayonnaise are traps for slimmers eating salads. Just two tablespoonsful can add up to 250 calories – probably more than the salad contains – so experiment with low-fat dressings instead. Low-fat plain yoghurt makes a good substitute – flavour it with fresh herbs, pepper, mustard, tomato purée and lemon or orange juice.

Eat meat only sparingly – even the leanest is about one-tenth fat – and choose fish, chicken, turkey, rabbit or game in preference to red meat. Try not to fry food, but bake,

---

Dieting do's and don'ts

Do try to work out why you overeat. If it is for emotional reasons – to make up for DEPRESSION, unhappiness or boredom, for example – you could consider joining a slimming club or self-help group (see your local *Yellow Pages*), or even having PSYCHOTHERAPY.

Do leave the table as soon as you have finished to avoid the temptation of second helpings or nibbling away without noticing.

Do use a smaller plate to suit your smaller helpings.

Do make sure you are getting enough EXERCISE. It boosts your metabolic rate and burns up calories, makes you look better and feel better about your body, and provides an alternative emotional outlet to eating.

Do eat slowly and chew your food well.

Don't eat while watching television or concentrating on something else – it is all too easy to eat more than you mean to without noticing.

Don't be tempted by very low-calorie meal-in-a-glass diets. They don't provide the same balance of nutrients as ordinary healthy food, and most of the weight you lose is thought to be lean tissue and fluid, not fat. If you put on weight again later it will be as fat, making weight loss more difficult.

---

steam, poach, grill or roast it instead, and add no more than a light brush of oil. Avoid pastry products, even wholemeal ones – they can be up to one-third fat.

Drinks can be another pitfall for slimmers – alcohol and sweetened cold drinks in particular add extra calories that are often overlooked. A pint of beer contains around 200 calories and a can of soft drink about 120. Slimmers are usually advised to avoid alcohol altogether and choose mineral water or fresh vegetable juices such as carrot or tomato instead. However, if you want something alcoholic try an occasional glass of dry wine (90-100 calories) or a small tot of spirits (55-75 calories), avoiding sweet mixers.

Starting the diet

To diet effectively you will need a calorie-counter booklet listing the energy values of different foods by weight, kitchen scales to weigh your helpings, and a notebook for keeping track of what you eat.

For the first few days, use the notebook simply as a food diary. Eat normally, but write down everything that passes your lips, as well as the time of day, and what you were doing when you ate it. After two or three days, go through your records, marking any foods that are high in fat or sugar, and writing down healthier alternatives.

For example, most people consume about 3 pints (1.75 litres) of milk a week in drinks, cooking and on cereal. Changing to skimmed milk will save about 200 calories per pint (600ml) – or semiskimmed about 100 – and if you choose carefully you can find varieties with the same vitamin and mineral content as full-cream milk. However, all low-fat milk has the same B vitamin and calcium content as full-fat, and although it has less A and D vitamin content, milk is not an important source of these.

Sugar comes in many disguised forms – for example, in such so-called 'health foods' as fruit yoghurts, crunchy breakfast cereals, and dried fruit and nut snack bars. It is cheaper and healthier to buy plain yoghurt and chop in a little fresh fruit, mix your own cereals (see MUESLI) and eat fresh fruit or crisp raw vegetables when you want a snack. Read ingredients labels and avoid products with added sugar. Items such as glucose, any sort of syrup, dextrose, sucrose and fructose are all types of sugar.

The food diary will also show up any occasions when you tend to eat more high-calorie foods than usual. For some people, watching television is a signal to nibble nuts or crisps, while others look to chocolates to cheer themselves up or as a reward after a hard day's work. Once recognised, such danger times can be avoided or other activities planned to take your mind off food – for example, relaxing with a book, going for a walk or telephoning a friend instead of watching television.

When you are ready to begin the diet, you will need to plan healthy, low-calorie meals in advance. Weigh and record all your portions. Write down the weight and number of calories, ensuring that your daily intake is less than 1200. After a while you will be able to judge weight by sight, but start off by measuring accurately. The sample diet (right) gives an idea of how meals could be planned.

Sample diet chart

There are plenty of simple, nutritious ways to plan a daily diet of about 1200 calories and still allow room for variety:

APPROX CALORIES

Breakfast	
1oz (30g) wholegrain cereal (eg, porridge, unsweetened muesli)	100
Skimmed milk (from allowance below)	
7oz (200g) fresh fruit (or 4oz [115g] banana)	85
Or	
2 small slices wholewheat bread or toast	120
¼oz (7g) butter or soft margarine	50
1oz (30g) honey, or 2oz (60g) low-sugar marmalade or jam, or 2oz (60g) cottage cheese, or 1 boiled or poached egg	80
Or	
8oz (225g) plain, low-fat yoghurt	120
6oz (175g) fresh fruit (or 1 small banana)	75
½oz (15g) wheat germ and 2 teaspoons bran (optional)	45
	Total 185-250

Salad/Vegetable Meal	
Up to 1lb (450g) vegetables or salads, including no more than 1oz (30g) of either avocado, peas or sweetcorn	120
2 teaspoons of oil for frying or dressing	90
Lemon juice, herbs, vinegar, soya sauce, mustard for flavouring	negligible
2 large slices of wholemeal bread, or 7oz (200g) baked potato	180
2oz (60g) cottage cheese or ¼oz (7g) butter or soft margarine	55
	Total 445

Hot Meal	
Main dish based on unlimited green vegetables with 2oz (60g; raw weight) pasta, beans or brown rice, or 2 large eggs, or 8oz (225g) potatoes, or 6oz (175g) chicken or turkey, or 4oz (115g) grilled lean meat, or 8oz (225g) steamed fish	250
Fruit dessert (eg, baked stuffed apple, baked banana, dried fruit salad, fruit yoghurt, fresh fruit)	120
	Total 370

Snacks	
Unlimited fresh vegetables such as celery, carrot, cauliflower, cucumber	negligible
1 piece of fresh fruit (not banana) or 4 dried apricot halves	40
Any food left over from meal allowances	

Drinks	
½ pint (300ml) skimmed or ⅓ pint (200ml) semi-skimmed milk	100
Herbal TISANES such as peppermint or rosehip, tea or coffee (with milk from allowance, no sugar), mineral water, bouillon	negligible

DAILY TOTAL 1140-1205

SLIPPED DISC

The discs are the shock absorbers of the spine, pieces of cartilage which separate the top 24 vertebrae and help to cushion them from impact. Normal discs have a fibrous outer casing surrounding a soft pulpy centre, but occasionally the tough outer section is damaged, allowing part of the soft centre to bulge or burst out. This condition is known as a prolapsed or slipped disc.

The protrusion may irritate adjacent ligaments or the outer membrane of the spinal cord. It may also constrict the root of a spinal nerve. Symptoms include severe, dull, aching pain, and muscle spasm, nerve irritation and sometimes numbness in the leg or foot. Some sufferers are unable to stand erect.

Pain may be felt at the site of the problem or 'referred' to some other area served by the affected nerve. A slipped disc in the lower back, for example, often irritates or traps the sciatic nerve, causing pain down the back of

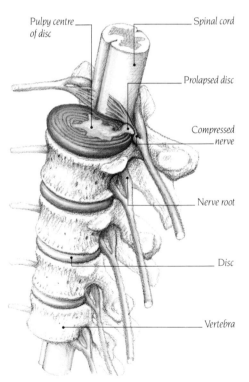

Pulpy centre of disc

Spinal cord

Prolapsed disc

Compressed nerve

Nerve root

Disc

Vertebra

The severe pain from a slipped disc can be caused when the disc 'pinches' the root of a nerve as it leaves the spinal column. Pain may also occur in the area served by the nerve – down an arm, for example.

Do's and don'ts for a slipped disc

Do use a hot-water bottle or heat lamp on the affected spot if you find that it relieves pain.
Don't sleep on a mattress that sags. Make sure that your bed is firm and flat (see BEDS AND BEDDING). In an emergency, use a thin mattress or a 2-4in (50-100mm) layer of plastic foam placed on the floor.
Don't take more than the manufacturer's recommended dose of pain-killers. Ask your doctor's advice if it seems insufficient for your pain.
Don't resume bad habits once you are well again. If the problem arose when you lifted something incorrectly, it could happen again. Take care of your back instead. When lifting objects keep your back straight and bend your knees, and avoid twisting as you lift.

the leg which worsens when the patient stretches the nerve by bending, coughing or sneezing (see SCIATICA; NERVE DISORDERS).

A prolapsed disc most often occurs in the lower back. It sometimes results from strenuous activity, especially if this is sudden, as when you lift something heavy or twist around violently. However, it more often comes about gradually, and generally occurs between the ages of about 20 and 50. Before 20 the discs are so strong that – except for some severe neck injuries – pressure will fracture the bony vertebrae before damaging the discs. In late middle age the soft disc centres begin to harden and again become resistant to damage.
Note The term 'slipped disc' is often incorrectly used to refer to BACK PAIN caused by joint displacement or muscle or ligament strain, properly known as LUMBAGO.

What the therapists recommend

Osteopathy Only some cases of disc damage can be treated by osteopathy. If pain is severe, practitioners advise bed rest and possibly traction.

In other cases, gentle MASSAGE and techniques designed to relax the contracted back muscles may be used, as well as treatment to improve mobility and reduce pressure on the affected disc.
Acupuncture The bladder, kidney, spleen, gall bladder and large and small intestine meridians are treated to ease pain.
Acupressure Press inwards on the 'bladder 11' point, on the back at the top of the rib cage, two finger widths out from the spine.

An orthodox view

A true slipped disc can heal only when the piece of soft disc centre that has escaped either shrivels up or is surgically removed. A doctor usually advises bed rest to take pressure off the disc and promote healing, which usually takes about six weeks.

If there is no improvement within that time, the doctor may arrange for you to have an X-ray or a test known as a myelogram, which involves injecting dye into the space around the spinal cord before X-raying it, to show how much of the disc is protruding. If necessary, a delicate operation to remove the protruding part can then be performed through an incision or an instrument inserted into the spinal column.

SMOKING

In spite of overwhelming evidence of its detrimental health effects, smoking continues to be one of our most popular addictions. For those who want to stop, however, help is available from natural medicine. See HOW TO GIVE UP SMOKING – FOR GOOD, p. 326.

SNEEZING

The world's longest recorded fit of sneezing happened to a young British girl, Donna Griffiths, of Pershore, Hereford and Worcester, who sneezed literally millions of times between January 13, 1981, and September 15, 1983 – a total of 976 days.

Sneezing – an involuntary expulsion of air from the nose and mouth – is the result of irritation or inflammation in the nasal passages. The most common causes of inflammation are COLDS, INFLUENZA and HAY FEVER. Irritation can come from accidentally breathing in such things as pepper or dust.

What the therapists recommend

Herbal Medicine In some cases, herbalists believe that sneezing may be, like hay fever, the result of an ALLERGY. If this proves to be so, try infusions of camomile, eyebright or plantain. Other remedies that may be useful include ephedra, ground ivy and hyssop.
Aromatherapy The following remedy may be of use when inhaled or put in bath water: one drop of peppermint oil in six to eight drops of cedarwood, cypress or hyssop.
Naturopathy Therapists concentrate on the cause of sneezing, such as colds or

allergic rhinitis (inflammation of the lining of the nose). Eating less dairy produce, such as butter and milk, is believed to reduce the amount of mucus produced, which could reduce sneezing. Allergic irritants such as pollen can be washed out of the nose by sniffing water. A short but high-level course of vitamin C – 3-4g a day – is also sometimes prescribed. It is thought to act in the same way as an antihistamine.

An orthodox view

Sneezing can be a sign of colds, allergy or emotional TENSION. It requires no specific treatment unless the sufferer is unable to stop. In most such cases, sedation with a mild tranquilliser should be enough.

SNORING

About one in every five adults snores – breathing in such a way that the soft palate of the roof of the mouth vibrates, making a harsh noise. Until recently, snoring was regarded as a social nuisance rather than a medical problem.

Sometimes, however, it can be a symptom of 'sleep apnoea', in which someone stops breathing – sometimes for as long as 90 seconds – when asleep. As a result, the body is deprived of oxygen and it produces too much adrenaline (a hormone which stimulates the system). In turn, this can lead to high BLOOD PRESSURE and increase the risk of ANGINA and other HEART DISORDERS.

Other major causes of snoring are OBESITY, alcohol abuse (see ALCOHOLISM), SMOKING and lack of EXERCISE.

What the therapists recommend

YOGA

Self help As there are several different causes of snoring, no single approach will necessarily be effective. However, you should always try to go to bed in a reasonably calm and tranquil state – especially if you have been to a party, had a hectic night out, or have been eating or drinking late.

Ideally, before going to bed you should relax on the bedroom floor, on a carpet or rug, with your arms and legs comfortably apart. Alternatively, lie on a firm bed. Become aware of your breathing and make sure it is fairly slow and rhythmical – and that you exhale for longer than you inhale.

Exhaling correctly is a vital part of relaxation. Concentrate on breathing out in a relaxed way to the exclusion of all other thoughts. Keep this up for no more than five minutes. Then, when you get into bed, think

about the peaceful way in which you have been breathing – and the tranquillity it has brought. The breathing exercise will not banish snoring immediately, but practised nightly, it should soon bring improvement.

HYPNOTHERAPY

Once obvious causes of snoring have been dealt with – such as alcohol intake, which may also benefit from this therapy – hypnosis can then be used to help reduce excess weight, and to enable the patient to go to sleep gently in a relaxed frame of mind.

TRADITIONAL MEDICINE

If snoring is caused by sleeping on your back, it may help to attach an object such as a small rubber ball to the back of your pyjamas, where it will cause discomfort when you turn onto your back.

An orthodox view

Although there is no specific remedy for sleep apnoea, doctors will give general advice covering the causes of snoring. If obesity or smoking is making you snore, it will help if you lose weight and cut down on or stop smoking altogether. In addition, do not drink large amounts of alcohol in the evenings. You should also ask your doctor to check your blood pressure.

If snoring becomes an embarrassment, special 'snore alarms' can awaken sufferers when they begin to snore.

SOMATOGRAPHY

Practitioners of this therapy believe that the body constantly sends out signals about itself. The signals come from every part – from the muscles, skeleton and other physical structures, and also from the 'aura' composed of the internal energy field, known to oriental practitioners as *Qi*, and the external energy field, which practitioners of KIRLIAN PHOTOGRAPHY claim to picture.

Therapists teach patients to recognise these body signals, especially those from the muscles, with their attendant stresses and tensions. Eventually, patients learn to do this without help, and the self-awareness that is generated should enable them to better understand thoughts and feelings about themselves, their way of life and their personal relationships. Once self-awareness is achieved, therapists aim to retrain body and mind to signal impending stresses and conflicts before they become deeply embedded.

Somatography is often used alongside other therapies, such as YOGA, NATUROPATHY, MASSAGE and GESTALT THERAPY.

SOUND THERAPY
Gaining health from good vibrations

In many ancient cultures the power of sound was considered an intimate part of the healing process, and had a central role in religious practices aimed at developing spiritual and physical well-being. In more recent times, growing interest in alternative therapies has revived some traditions such as healing chants and prayers; and modern 'sound therapists' say that they can relieve certain conditions by directing sound waves at affected parts of the body.

In everyday life the effects of different sounds are plain to see: singing before a soccer match heightens emotions and reinforces a sense of group unity; low-flying jets and rush-hour traffic cause ANXIETY, irritation and TENSION; and piped music in supermarkets is designed to make shopping more enjoyable so that people stay longer and spend more.

Sound is also a way of expressing yourself and communicating with others. Its quality often reflects the state of relationships between people. For example, it is natural to shout when angry, sing when happy, or murmur softly to express affection. Mothers all recognise the cries of their own babies, and most people are sensitive even to subtle variations in the timbre of familiar voices.

Sound waves from the outside reach the ear as vibrations that are converted into nerve impulses and transmitted to the brain, which interprets them as the sounds we hear. The waves also reach other parts of the body which, although they cannot 'hear' like the ear, are still affected by being rhythmically compressed and expanded at a microscopic level by the vibrations.

Sound therapy is based on the theory that organs and cells of the body respond in particular ways to particular patterns of compression and expansion. Each part of the body is thought to have a natural resonance and to respond well to sounds that vibrate in harmony with it. Dissonant vibrations, by contrast, may have harmful results.

Poor health and disease are believed to affect the frequency at which organs and cells vibrate, and in the most common form of sound therapy, practitioners try to restore and strengthen 'healthy' frequencies by directing harmonious waves at trouble spots.

Sound can be used therapeutically in a variety of other ways as well. It plays an important part in MUSIC THERAPY and DANCE THERAPY, and some practitioners teach singing and chanting as a way of altering breathing patterns, promoting relaxation and stimulating the body's own healing powers – similar to the effects of YOGA or MEDITATION. Done in groups or couples, it is said to strengthen bonds between people and help them to 'tune in' to each other.

One therapist, Fabien Maman, a musician, believes that by listening to the sound of the voice and the resonance of energy centres in the body he can find a particular sound to suit each individual and enhance his well-being. Maman also claims that carefully chosen sound waves may be able to attack diseased cells and strengthen healthy ones, helping to heal some illnesses.

The spiritual significance of sound

The power of sound has long been recognised by spiritual and mystical traditions the world over. In the East, meditative, spiritual exercises based on sound go back thousands of years, and many have been taken up by religions such as Buddhism and Islam. Today, chanting and rhythmic breathing and movements are still widely used in the East as a path to self-development and spiritual enlightenment.

Sound also plays a central, traditional part in Western religions. Experts say that intoning the liturgy, chanting prayers and singing hymns in church may all help to put people in touch with the spiritual side of life.

The way in which sound affects people's states of mind is not fully understood, but it is thought that certain vibrations and rhythmic breathing techniques may alter electrical brain-wave patterns, inducing relaxation or heightening awareness.

Another clue may be provided by the work of the Swiss doctor and scientist Hans Jenny, who developed an instrument called a 'tonoscope' which can depict any sound as a three-dimensional image. On the tonoscope the sound 'O' made by the human voice produces a perfect sphere.

It may be that this is the basis of the *om* or *aum*, one of the best-known MANTRAS that is chanted in many Eastern traditions as the expression of everything that is, as well as of the Christian and Jewish 'amen' and the Muslim 'amin'.

Who it can help Sound therapy using electronically generated waves is now being researched in some hospital orthopaedic departments as an aid to healing FRACTURES. It is also generally thought to be useful for other muscle and bone conditions such as fibrositis, RHEUMATISM, ARTHRITIS, BACK PAIN, strains and SPRAINS. NEURALGIA, MIGRAINE and sinusitis may also be helped.

Pre-surgical treatment is said to make hip replacement operations more effective, and the pain of a slipped disc may be reduced enough to allow manipulative treatment to take place.

Teachers of rhythmic singing and chanting say that anyone may benefit, particularly if suffering from STRESS or related disorders.

Finding a therapist The Royal London Homoeopathic Hospital, Great Ormond Street, London WC1N 3HR, or the other NHS homoeopathic hospitals – Bristol, Glasgow, Liverpool and Tunbridge Wells – may provide help or advice. Information about a similar therapy – CYMATICS – is available from Dr Peter Manners, Bretforton Hall, Bretforton, Vale of Evesham, Worcestershire WR1 5JH.

For information about courses in chanting and using sound as a form of meditation, contact Gillian McGregor, Garden Flat, 9 Yonge Park, London N4 3NU. Fabien Maman can be contacted c/o 31 Lisburne Road, London NW3 2NS.

Consulting a therapist The best-known form of sound therapy is the use of electronically generated wave signals directed at particular parts of the body in order to heal them. Before treatment can be given, a proper diagnosis of the problem is essential. It would probably be advisable to consult an orthodox practitioner first.

The therapist uses a machine to generate waves believed to be of the correct frequency to heal the patient's condition. Many different wave patterns can be generated, and choosing the right one requires skill.

The waves are transmitted to the body by means of a small hand-held 'applicator' placed over the affected region. A gel is smeared on the skin first to improve transmission of waves to the body. The applicator focuses the waves so that they supposedly home in on the problem area and leave healthy tissue unaffected. While treatment is in progress you may hear a sound or feel vibrations, but this does not always happen – sometimes the frequencies are too high or too low to be detected.

Other forms of sound therapy involve group or individual sessions where participants are taught to produce healing sounds by using their own voices. No singing ability or musical knowledge is needed, as sounds are generally chanted, hummed or 'vibrated' in a way that anyone can master.

An orthodox view

The basic principles of sound therapy are compatible with modern physics, according to which all matter is in a constant state of vibration, even at the smallest subatomic level. Conventional doctors accept that disturbances in electrical wave patterns produced by the heart can show if it has been damaged, but it is not generally agreed that other organs react in the same way, or that sound can be used to treat, as well as to diagnose, disorders.

While accepting also that chanting can have a soothing and relaxing effect, modern medicine has not developed the understanding which would allow it to evaluate the detailed claims made by those practitioners versed in this ancient therapy. So anyone seeking this form of therapy would be wise to approach it with caution.

See also ULTRASONICS.

SPAS
Taking the waters . . .

Although spas have declined in number and popularity in Britain, the mineral waters in which they specialised are available at many HEALTH FARMS, health clubs, hospitals, pump rooms and public wells. The word 'spa' comes from the Belgian resort of Spa, noted for its medicinal springs. See HYDROTHERAPY.

In Britain, spa treatments – mainly for ARTHRITIS and RHEUMATISM – are available at the following places:

Buxton, Derbyshire A National Health Service hospital, the Royal Devonshire, offers physiotherapy in warm spa water to people suffering from arthritis and rheumatism.

Droitwich, Hereford & Worcester In 1985 a new brine bath was opened at Droitwich Spa, with water pumped from an underground lake 200ft (60m) below the town. The natural brine is some 20 per cent more buoyant than fresh water and is heated to 33°C (92°F) – a little below normal body temperature. Visitors can float effortlessly in the water, allowing them to relax and gain relief from STRESS. There are also SAUNA BATH and MASSAGE facilities.

Royal Leamington Spa, Warks The Royal Pump Room has a heated therapeutic pool which usually contains a percentage of natural saline water. However, NHS treatment – mainly for joint and muscle problems – is given only to patients who have been referred by a GP within the South Warwickshire Area Health Authority, or by any hospi-

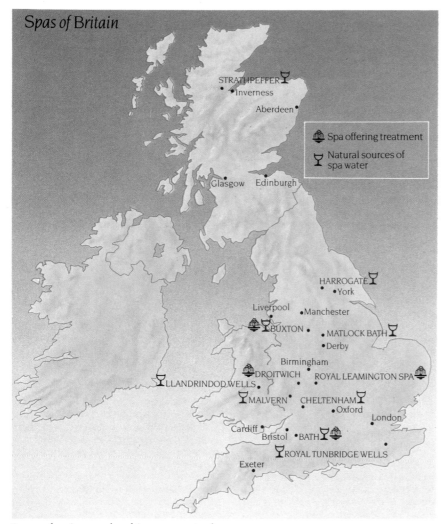

Spas of Britain

STRATHPEFFER
• Inverness
Aberdeen •

Spa offering treatment
Natural sources of spa water

Glasgow   Edinburgh

HARROGATE
• York
Liverpool   • Manchester
BUXTON
• MATLOCK BATH
• Derby
Birmingham
DROITWICH   ROYAL LEAMINGTON SPA
LLANDRINDOD WELLS
MALVERN   CHELTENHAM
• Oxford
London
Cardiff
Bristol   • BATH
ROYAL TUNBRIDGE WELLS
Exeter

Spas and springs are found in many parts of Britain, some offering full treatment facilities and others simply selling bottled water.

tal consultant. Private treatment is restricted to those who have a prescription from their GP. Physiotherapy is also available to people recovering from injuries.

Other spas Three baths featuring natural, hot-spring water are planned to reopen at Bath, Avon, in the early 1990s. The facilities will include an exercise and relaxation pool, a gymnasium, AEROBICS classes, beauty and therapy rooms, wet and hot treatments, as well as spa water for drinking.

In addition to the above, spa water can be obtained from natural sources in the following places:

Buxton, Derbyshire (St Ann's Well; bottled mineral water is also available); Cheltenham, Gloucestershire (alkaline spring water from the Pittville Pump Room and the Town Hall); Harrogate, North Yorkshire (sulphurous

water from the Royal Pump Room Museum); Llandrindod Wells, Powys (various spring waters from the Rock Park Pump Room); Great Malvern, Hereford & Worcester (water from springs in the surrounding hills; also bottled water); Matlock Bath, Derbyshire (spa water from The Pavilion); Royal Tunbridge Wells, Kent (iron-impregnated water from the Bath House portico on the Pantiles); and Strathpeffer, Highland (sulphur water from The Pavilion).

SPASTIC COLON

This distressing, but not serious, condition is caused by the abnormal action of the colon muscles, and is generally known as IRRITABLE BOWEL SYNDROME. Symptoms include pain, DIARRHOEA and CONSTIPATION.

SPIRITUAL HEALING

This form of healing – not to be confused with Spiritualism – uses a holistic approach, helping a person to return to the 'wholeness of being' – harmony of body, mind and spirit. By prayer and meditation healers channel divine healing energies, which are said to change the patient's personal life force for the better. The therapy can be a form of ABSENT HEALING or LAYING ON OF HANDS.

For more information – including self-help advice – contact the National Federation of Spiritual Healers, Old Manor Farm Studio, Church Street, Sunbury-on-Thames, Middlesex TW16 6RG, which is unconnected with any religious group. Alternatively, a doctor may refer you to a healer, and in this instance he will remain in charge of your case.

See also HEALERS AND HEALING.

SPORTS INJURIES
Coping with and avoiding damage to your body

Sport strengthens muscles, increases stamina, improves sleep patterns and helps to control OBESITY. However, sport and EXERCISE are only a part of good health, and contribute to fitness only when taken regularly in conjunction with a healthy lifestyle. Practised unwisely or to excess, sport and other physical activity can result in injury.

Fractured bones These common injuries usually follow accidents in which the bone is put under sudden strain. Skiers often break legs in this way, and cricket and hockey players their fingers.

Other fractures, known as stress fractures, occur without sudden impact. They usually take the form of a hairline crack that eventually causes so much pain that it interferes with movement. For example, as a result of repeated use, a long-distance runner may fracture a foot bone, or a high jumper his fibula (outer bone of the lower leg).

Sprains and dislocations Ligaments that hold joints together may tear, causing SPRAINS. An affected joint becomes painful and weak, and if the ligament is completely severed or torn, the joint becomes unstable.

A severe sprain may cause the joint to dislocate so that its surfaces are no longer aligned, the shoulder being the most prone to this type of injury. Repeated injury may cause the ligaments to become so lax that the joint becomes unstable and dislocates easily. See also JOINT PROBLEMS.

Muscle strains and bruises These account for ten to 30 per cent of all sports injuries. They occur when a muscle is damaged by impact – for example, a kick to a footballer's leg – or as a result of overloading when a player does not warm up properly. Reduced coordination and overextension due to fatigue, or deliberate efforts to overextend muscles may also increase the risk of strain. There is bleeding into the muscle and the muscle fibres may be torn. The muscle feels tender and painful on movement.

Tendon problems Muscles are attached to bones by tendons, which may also be damaged in sport. Most commonly they become inflamed as a result of friction caused by repeated strenuous movements. In severe cases, the tendon may rupture fully or partially so that the muscle becomes disconnected from the bone and is ineffective. The damage eventually repairs itself, but tendons with a relatively poor blood supply such as the Achilles' tendon at the back of the ankle may be slow to heal.

'Overuse syndrome' This is the name given to inflammation of tendons and other soft tissues as a result of being subjected to repeated strain, aggravated by training errors such as warm-up periods that are too short, together with faulty technique, incorrect equipment and prolonged training sessions.

One example of an overuse injury is TENNIS ELBOW, an inflammation of the outer elbow, where forearm tendons join the bone. Athletes, particularly when changing from one playing surface to another, may experience shin pain caused by another overuse syndrome called *periostitis* – inflammation of the covering membrane of a bone.

Bursitis Bursae are small sacs of fluid that are normally found around joints and where ligaments and tendons pass over bones. Their purpose is to reduce friction between the moving parts, especially around the hip, knee, foot, shoulder and elbow joints. When a bursa becomes inflamed, the condition is known as BURSITIS.

A bursa may also become infected to produce a fluctuant swelling – one in which wave motion of the liquid inside occurs when the swelling is pressed. Redness, pain and tenderness accompany the infection.

Cartilage injury This usually affects the knee joint, which is designed to move only in one plane, back and forth. However, in sports such as soccer, hockey, rugby and tennis, it is often forced to move from left to right as well. The rotation of the thigh bone acts like a wrench on the tough but relatively soft cartilage (packing tissue) in the knee, causing it to tear and giving rise to pain and

swelling. Because cartilage is poorly supplied with blood, it is often unable to repair itself, and surgery may be the only solution.

Back injuries Damage to the back is usually the result of poor lifting technique in sports such as weightlifting and during weight training, but it may also result from sports accidents. Most injuries involve damage only to soft tissues such as muscles and ligaments, and will heal themselves in time. Occasionally, however, the vertebrae may be damaged, causing spinal injuries which require immediate, specialist medical attention because of the risk of paralysis.

Other problems Blisters, CRAMP and stitches – pains in the upper abdomen, possibly caused by too little oxygen reaching the diaphragm – are common among sportsmen.

Preventing sports injuries

Never start playing a sport suddenly; rather go for regular, progressive training which gradually increases the strength and flexibility of your joints and muscles. This includes always allowing time for an adequate warm-up period before each session of sport. Learn and practise good technique so that you avoid unnecessary strain.

A well-balanced diet (see EATING FOR HEALTH), plus adequate fluid replacement during and after exercise will help; so will suitable clothing – especially footwear. Stop SMOKING, and avoid alcohol for at least 48 hours before playing any sport. Use appropriate protective clothing; for example, a helmet for cycling and horse riding.

Ask your doctor's advice before taking up a new sport or greatly increasing the amount of exercise you take. Regular health checks will also help to identify problems before they become serious.

What the therapists recommend

Massage This has long been recognised as valuable in both the prevention and treatment of sports injuries. Many Olympic and international sports and athletics teams use trained remedial masseurs for toning muscles and joints before events and for treating them afterwards.

Homoeopathy For aching muscles after overexertion at sport, as well as bruises and shock, try *Arnica 30*. Pulled tendons and sprains should first be treated with *Arnica* and then with *Rhus tox.* or *Ruta*, according to symptoms. For cases of tennis elbow try *Ruta 30* four times a day for a week.

Acupuncture Points local to the injury are treated. Points on the large intestine meridian are used for the rapid relief of pain. Treatment is also given at points on the governor meridian, which has a controlling effect on all the channels and points, in addition to its calming and sedative action.

Hydrotherapy All injuries – apart from severe lacerations, which need stitching – are treated by ice or at least cold packs initially, followed by special hydrotherapy massage, water jets, whirlpool baths, hot or cold packs, appropriate remedial exercises or combinations of these.

Acupressure Gentle pressure is applied at local points about 6in (15cm) away from the site of an injury, and not directly on the problem area itself.

An orthodox view

See your doctor or go to a hospital accident and emergency department if you think you may have sustained a head injury, fractured a bone, dislocated a joint, completely ruptured a tendon or have any other acute injury. A fracture will be revealed on an X-ray. It is treated by reduction of the fracture into the correct position ('setting') and immobilisation of the affected limb or part.

First aid for sprains and strains is to apply ice, and then compress and elevate the injured limb.

Anti-inflammatory painkillers such as aspirin can relieve pain, or if necessary a doctor may advise a stronger painkiller such as ibuprofen (Nurofen). Take care, however, that lack of pain does not encourage you to continue with harmful exercise and so do further damage – in particular, avoid repeating the movement that induced the injury. And remember that painkillers and many other drugs are banned in some competitions and may result in disqualification or suspension if detected.

Recovery from overuse syndromes can be slow. In the early phase, ice reduces swelling and inflammation. Once the acute phase – the period of severe pain – has passed, use local heat in the form of a heat lamp or hot-water bottle to speed recovery. Support the affected part with strapping or taping, and avoid activities that aggravate the pain.

Your doctor may help with a local anaesthetic and steroid injection, or refer you to a physiotherapist for massage, local shortwave or ultrasound treatment (see SOUND THERAPY; ULTRASONICS), and an exercise programme to aid recovery.

SPRAINS

Injury to a ligament which occurs when a joint is suddenly stretched beyond its normal range of movement is known as a sprain. Fibres within the ligament – which helps to hold the joint together – tear, causing pain and weakness of the joint. In a severe case, the ligament may tear completely, causing the joint to become unstable. See Joint Problems; Sports Injuries.

As well as causing bruising of the ligament itself, a sprain may also cause bleeding into the joint, and may be accompanied by other injuries such as cartilage damage. Symptoms of a sprain include swelling, tenderness and bruising around the joint, and pain on stretching the ligament – for example, by gently repeating the movement that caused the injury.

The ankle joint is commonly sprained during sports activities. Ligaments between the vertebrae in the neck may be sprained by a 'whiplash' injury, such as that caused to a car occupant when the car is suddenly shunted from behind.

What the therapists recommend
MASSAGE
Consultation Although firm strapping and padding may be necessary at first, massage should be commenced at the earliest opportunity to disperse swellings and prevent the formation of adhesions – the joining of internal surfaces that are normally separate – and also to encourage the normal free range of movement of the injured joint.

In the early stages of treatment, massage should be restricted to a firm effleurage stroking movement above and below the injured joint. At subsequent treatments, when the pain and swelling have subsided, the depth of treatment should be gradually increased and a gentle petrissage around the joint with the thumb and fingers introduced. Eventually, it will be possible to apply massage to the injured joint itself.

HOMOEOPATHY
Self help As soon as possible after the accident try *Arnica 30*, taken hourly for six hours. This should be followed by *Rhus tox. 6*, taken three times a day for about ten days. If the injury is close to the bone, *Ruta 6* may be more effective. If there is much swelling, distension and pain on the slightest movement, try *Bryonia 30* three times a day until the condition improves. Then use *Rhus tox.* to complete the treatment.

For a moist compress apply *Arnica* mother tincture – ten drops in about ½ pint (300ml) of water – and support with a firm bandage.

AROMATHERAPY
Self help As soon as possible after the injury has occurred, apply hyssop and marjoram oils to the area and massage gently: use two drops of each oil in a teaspoon of vegetable carrier oil. Then apply a compress held in position with cling film and leave for a few hours. Make the compress with five drops of each oil and just enough water to

soak all through the compress. (Old cotton vests, handkerchiefs and tea towels make good compress material.)

Other alternative treatment
Acupuncture Treatment is applied at local points. Points on the gall bladder, lung, bladder, and large and small intestine meridians are also used.

An orthodox view
First aid for sprains starts with applying ice, if available, or a cold compress to the affected area as soon as possible to reduce internal bleeding and inflammation. Compress the affected part with an elastic or crêpe bandage or elastic tubular bandage, and raise it to reduce swelling.

A damaged ligament must be protected from repeated overstretching. So avoid weight-bearing or unnecessary use of the affected part – for example by supporting an injured arm in a sling. Consult a doctor or physiotherapist as soon as possible.

In severe sprains, particularly of the ankle joint, the doctor may advise immobilising the joint in a plaster cast. However, when possible, prompt, active use of damaged joints and ligaments speeds recovery and reduces the risks of stiffness and muscle wasting.

Sprains generally heal more slowly than fractures, and recovery often takes six to eight weeks.

STAMMERING

The most commonly found speech problem is stammering, which in Britain affects about four people out of 100 – mainly men.

There are several possible causes for stammering, including an emotional shock or a distressing experience in childhood; a delay in the brain's mechanism for checking what it has heard; slow development of the co-ordination of tongue, palate and lips needed for speech; and, mostly among people over 50, partial paralysis of the mouth and face following a stroke.

In a child aged between two and five, stammering can be the result of overanxious parents making him feel that something is wrong if he has difficulty in speaking, or is stuck for words.

What the therapists recommend
YOGA
Self help Stammering can be treated by the regular practice of slow, relaxed breathing. For instance, a minute spent controlling your breath before making a speech may be

helpful. Many people may find that breathing practice combined with coordinated movement is also useful. Sit upright in a chair and raise your arms while breathing in. Hold your breath while stretching upwards, and breathe slowly out while bringing your arms down. Now try speaking.

BACH REMEDIES
Self help People who stammer and are frightened of speaking could try Cherry plum. For frustration and anger about stammering try Holly. Chestnut bud is advised if you speak too fast and fail to complete words. Take Vervain if you work too hard to overcome stammering and find it difficult to relax. If you are too self-critical over stammering try Rock water. Beech may help if you are too intolerant of the condition.

Parents of a child who stammers should take Vine if they are overauthoritative, and Beech if they are intolerant and harsh. Pine is said to help relieve feelings of self-blame.

HYPNOTHERAPY
Consultation Where appropriate, a patient can be taken back in time – regressed – to try to discover, and sometimes relive, the onset of the problem. In all cases, ego-strengthening techniques are used while the patient is in a hypnotic, relaxed state. Autohypnosis can, with the aid of prerecorded tapes, be applicable for speech and voice problems. Visualising difficult social situations under hypnosis, while at the same time receiving positive suggestions, may also help to desensitise some stammerers.

ACUPRESSURE
Self help Voice problems may be relieved by pressing down on the bottom, outside corner of the thumbnail.

An orthodox view
Although stammering cannot be cured by any single treatment, there are various techniques and aids which can improve fluency. A GP may send someone who stammers to see a speech therapist, who will select a method suited to the patient's personality and the cause of his condition. Techniques include speech exercises, ways of relaxing, and the use of headphones to stop the stammerer hearing his own voice.

Some National Health Service hospitals and clinics run residential courses in speech therapy in which patients are taught new speaking skills. A doctor or speech therapist will put sufferers in touch with these and other units dealing with their condition. Sometimes stammering can be helped by singing or acting in a play, when being part of a team can help to bolster self-confidence.

See also Voice Therapy.

How to give up smoking – for good

Deaths related to smoking are estimated at about 100,000 a year in Britain alone, and some two million worldwide. The dangers come mainly from chemicals inhaled in cigarette smoke – an astonishing 4000 of them, including tar, nicotine, carbon monoxide, hydrogen cyanide and ammonia.

Nicotine is the addictive agent in cigarette smoke, and makes it hard to quit the habit (see ADDICTION). It is a stimulating drug which elevates your mood, making you a little more confident with each puff – and a little more addicted to it. Nicotine and other chemicals in the smoke are responsible for three of the most deadly smoking-related diseases: lung CANCER, HEART DISORDERS and EMPHYSEMA.

Lung cancer is nearly always fatal and affects about 40,000 people in Britain every year, 90 per cent of them smokers. In fact, smokers stand a 1-in-12 chance of dying from this disease. Chemicals in cigarette smoke attack the lung cells, causing them to multiply out of control. The resulting growths eventually prevent the lungs from absorbing enough oxygen for the body's needs.

Smoking has a more complex effect on the heart and circulation. Although this is still not fully understood, doctors estimate that about 45,000 fatal heart attacks annually in Britain can be attributed to smoking.

It is believed that nicotine and carbon monoxide make the heart beat faster while at the same time thickening the blood and increasing the chances of clotting. This puts a great strain on the heart and, together with the narrowed arteries caused by cholesterol deposits on artery walls also caused by smoking, is responsible for heart disorders that eventually kill one in eight smokers. Add another risk factor such as OBESITY, too little EXERCISE, raised blood cholesterol levels or taking the contraceptive pill, and a smoker's chances of developing heart disease rise dramatically.

Emphysema and recurring bouts of BRONCHITIS account for nearly 30,000 deaths in Britain every year, about nine out of ten of them due to smoking.

Other risks include cancer of the mouth, throat and larynx – up to five times more common even among those who do not inhale, such as pipe and cigar smokers. Smokers also suffer more from strokes, blood clots, ULCERS, high BLOOD PRESSURE and, if they are women, cervical cancer.

The longer you smoke and the more heavily, the greater are your chances of getting one or more of these diseases. On average, smoking takes 12 years off a life, sometimes far more. The good news is that from the day you stop the risks begin to go down, and the longer you don't smoke the further they drop. If you stop smoking before developing a serious lung or heart condition, your chance of developing one in the future immediately drops by half. After five years without smoking, your risk of heart disease is about the same as if you had never started.

Dangers from other people's smoke

Estimates vary about exactly how much damage breathing in other people's cigarette smoke – passive smoking – can do to a non-smoker, but it is thought that the chances of lung cancer increase by about one-third. Compared with the risks to smokers, this is small, but it still amounts to several hundred lives lost every year in Britain. A recent study has shown that even if they do not develop a serious illness, non-smokers exposed to smoke at work show significantly reduced lung function.

One of the most worrying aspects of passive smoking is its effect on babies and children. Smoking during pregnancy increases the chances of a miscarriage, stillbirth, premature birth or death of the baby in the first week after birth – by about one-fifth if the mother smokes fewer than 20 cigarettes a day, and by one-third if she has more. Effects continue after birth too, since nicotine is concentrated in breast milk to two or three times its level in the blood. Women who do not stop smoking in early pregnancy should not give up hope, however. Stopping at any point, particularly before the sixteenth week, lessens the dangers.

Older children are also at risk. Studies have shown that the smoke they breathe is equivalent to smoking an average of 80 to 150 cigarettes a year. As a result, they suffer more attacks of ASTHMA, PNEUMONIA and bronchitis.

Strategies for stopping

The story goes that the American author Mark Twain found it easy to stop smoking: 'I've done it hundreds of times,' he is reputed to have said. Luckily not everyone finds it so hard to break the habit for good. Some simply make the decision and never look back; for others there may be setbacks. Even so, giving up is so worthwhile in terms of health and quality of life that no smoker should complacently accept his lot. Here are some helpful tips:

Make the decision If you are not yet sure that you really want to stop, remind yourself of the health risks. Imagine what life would be like with heart disease or lung cancer, dependent on others for the rest of your – probably shortened – life, and how that would affect your family. Add up what you spend on smoking and think what you could do with the money if you stopped. The advantages of stopping must outweigh the transient pleasure of a cigarette.

If you are still unsure, the inevitable bad attack of bronchitis will make you unable to smoke. Turn this to advantage by making it the time you give up altogether.

Choose a good time to stop Do not put yourself under extra strain by trying to stop smoking at times of stress – for example, when changing jobs, or facing a divorce or money problems. On the other hand, do not put it off too long; if everyday life is stressful, a holiday may be the best time.

Name the day Set a fixed day to stop smoking altogether rather than trying to cut down gradually. Make it a stress-free day, mark it on the calendar, and tell family, friends and colleagues the date. If you cannot face going 'cold turkey', plan a strict programme of 'tapering off': cut out at least one cigarette a day, and more if you smoke heavily.

Be prepared Start keeping a diary showing every cigarette you smoke, when you smoked it, what you were doing, whether you also ate or drank anything, and how badly you wanted each cigarette. As your pattern of smoking becomes evident, you will recognise danger times and be able to plan other activities or reschedule your day to avoid them.

If, for example, you smoke most when relaxing after a meal, start going for a walk instead, doing RELAXATION AND BREATHING or YOGA, or using the time for a hobby such as knitting or DIY. These both keep your hands busy and take your mind off cigarettes.

Eat a healthy diet Base meals on fresh fruit, vegetables and salads to help cleanse your system of impurities. Don't skip meals, and allow yourself healthy snacks if you want them. Be sure to get plenty of liquids such as fruit juice, herbal TISANES and water. Avoid tea, coffee, alcohol, cola, red meat and chocolate, which can all increase your craving. Supplements of vitamins A, B-complex, C and E, and zinc, are also said to help the body to cleanse itself, and reduce the desire to smoke.

Don't worry if you put on a little weight at first – this is best dealt with later, and should not be a serious problem (see EATING FOR HEALTH and SLIMMING THE NATURAL WAY).

Get others to help Tell friends, family and colleagues that you don't smoke any more. Ask them to help by not offering you cigarettes and by sitting with you in non-smoking areas of pubs, buses and other public places.

Think positively Tell yourself constantly that you no longer want to smoke, and that you feel better every day. Remember that it will get easier all the time, and after four to six weeks, *not* smoking starts to become a habit.

Reward yourself Use the money you save on cigarettes to treat yourself occasionally. Spending it on a hobby or activity is a good idea – it will take your mind off smoking.

Say no Avoid odd puffs or having a cigarette now and again; this is the fastest way to undo all your efforts. Do not give up if you do slip occasionally, but learn from your mistakes and say no next time. Think what a waste all the effort to stop would have been.

How alternative therapies can help

Acupuncture Provided you really want to stop, this can work well. Needles are usually inserted into the ear, on the addiction and lung points. Practitioners can also insert small needles which are left in the ear so that you can stimulate the points yourself every time you crave a cigarette.

Behavioural Therapy This can be very successful. Various methods are used, including rewards, better planning of your time, relaxation, habit-breaking techniques and AVERSION THERAPY.

Naturopathy A practitioner can help you by drawing up a diet, exercise and relaxation programme suited to you. This often includes dietary supplements, such as a daily 500mg dose of vitamin C, which is destroyed when you smoke.

Hypnotherapy The patient is put into a relaxed state, and given suggestions to strengthen his resolve to stop, remind him of the harm smoking does, and help him to change his behaviour. Post-hypnotic suggestions are also used to take effect afterwards.

Youth tempted

The temptation to smoke can be very strong for children and young people. Advertising associates cigarettes with grown-up sophistication, independence and sex appeal. Prohibitions at school and home can encourage the habit by making it seem daring and desirable, and many parents set a bad example by smoking themselves.

Even so, parents can do a lot to discourage children from smoking. Stopping smoking themselves may do more than any number of lectures – children from non-smoking families are less likely to start than others.

Another effective method is to offer a reward such as a new bike, a holiday or driving lessons if a child has not started to smoke by his or her 17th or 18th birthday. Be prepared to trust your child's word and, in any case, overlook the odd trial cigarette – curiosity and experimentation are natural during the teenage years.

Ten things to do when you want a cigarette

1 Consult your smoking diary – is this a danger time? Are you doing something or in a situation that always calls for a cigarette? If possible, do something else. If not, put your craving down to circumstances and try to change these or avoid them in future.

2 Go outside, stand up straight and practise deep breathing (see RELAXATION AND BREATHING). This gets more air into the lungs, and after a few minutes the craving should weaken.

3 Remind yourself of your reasons for stopping, one by one. Do you really need a puff enough to forgo all these?

4 Move to a non-smoking work area.

5 Tell yourself that you are saying no to just this cigarette. Don't look ahead – think only of the immediate situation.

6 Write a letter or make a telephone call you have been putting off.

7 Drink a large glass of fruit juice or water. If you like, have a high-protein snack such as a cheese sandwich.

8 Chew a piece of sugar-free gum. Some people find tranquillisers or anti-smoking tablets help too, but not everyone. Ask your doctor's advice.

9 Remember that just one cigarette will narrow your arteries, raise your blood pressure and put an extra strain on your heart for an hour and a half.

10 Remind yourself that there are ten million ex-smokers in Britain. *If they can do it, you can!*

STINGS AND BITES

As a natural form of defence, insects such as bees and wasps, other creatures such as jellyfish, and plants such as stinging nettles produce poisonous proteins which cause pain in human skin. The site of the sting or bite becomes red, painful and itchy. See BEE STINGS; WASP STINGS; MOSQUITO BITES.

TRADITIONAL MEDICINE abounds with cures for stings of all kinds. For example, one well-known folk remedy for nettle stings is to rub the affected area with crushed dock leaves, which tend to grow near beds of nettles. However, dock leaves should not be applied over long periods, as prolonged contact may cause skin ALLERGY.

In rare cases, stings cause a dangerous allergic reaction called anaphylactic SHOCK: the victim's BLOOD PRESSURE falls, and he becomes light headed and short of breath, with a rapid, weak pulse, and a widespread, itchy rash. Get immediate medical attention if any of these symptoms appear after a sting.

An orthodox view

Doctors and paramedics treat anaphylactic shock by an adrenaline injection, followed by an injection of antihistamine, together with basic life support if the patient is unconscious. If you are allergic to stings and at risk – for example if you are allergic to bee stings and live near a beekeeper – your doctor may provide you with your own pre-filled syringe of adrenaline to inject in an emergency.

STOMACH COMPLAINTS

The stomach is a bag-shaped organ in the upper abdomen where food is churned and the main processes of chemical digestion begin. The most common complaint of the stomach and the rest of the digestive system is INDIGESTION, which can have various causes ranging from over-eating and CONSTIPATION to feelings of STRESS and ANXIETY (see also DIGESTIVE PROBLEMS). Other common digestive complaints include COLITIS (inflammation of the large bowel), COLIC (spasmodic pain in the abdomen), NAUSEA AND VOMITING, and WIND.

Occasionally patients may suffer from ULCERS, often caused by an excess of acid in the stomach. (Ulcers in the stomach are called gastric ulcers; those of the first part of the small intestine are duodenal ulcers.)

More rarely there may be an attack of COELIAC DISEASE, in which the patient – usually a child – is unable to absorb essential foods from the intestines.

Persistent and painful stomach complaints should always be seen to by a doctor.

STRESS

Anything that is a threat to bodily health or which affects the body's functioning adversely is known as stress. Disease, injury and worry are the main causes. See LIVING WITH STRESS AND STAYING WELL, p. 330.

STYE

Bacterial infection of eyelash roots is the cause of styes – small boils on the glands that lubricate eyelashes. Symptoms are redness and a swelling on the eyelid, which comes to a head after a few days and discharges pus. Styes are common, irritating and unsightly, but do not affect the eye itself, so eyesight is not at risk.

What the therapists recommend

Naturopathy   As far as possible, avoid rubbing the eye. Hot compresses, with cotton wool or perhaps grated carrot wrapped in muslin or clean cloth, should help bring the stye to a head. Recurring styes are believed to indicate lowered vitality, so multivitamin and mineral supplements may be prescribed.
Herbal Medicine   A decoction (see p. 184) of eyebright or camomile used as an eyebath may help to reduce inflammation. A herbalist may also use remedies such as marigold or poke root taken orally, aiming to stimulate the lymphatic system and the body's defences (see IMMUNE SYSTEM).

An orthodox view

A stye usually heals on its own, but you can speed the process and help it to discharge by 'drawing' it with a hot compress every two or three hours. Take care not to scald it! Antibiotics may be prescribed if the stye is particularly severe or slow to heal.

A persistent lump on an eyelid may be a meibomian cyst which, though never cancerous, may prove troublesome and can be removed by minor surgery. It can, however, become infected and look like a stye: treatment is the same as for a stye, but the cyst discharges through the inner surface of the eyelid, rather than the rim.

SUNBURN

Prolonged or unaccustomed exposure to the ultraviolet (UV) radiation in sunlight produces this burning sensation of the skin. There are three types of UV radiation: UVA is the gentlest; while it may cause a suntan, it rarely burns. However, it does penetrate deeply, and may contribute to premature ageing of the skin and increased risk of skin CANCER. UVB radiation is more dangerous; it tans and can cause severe burning. UVC can cause ageing and skin cancer.

Minor sunburn causes red skin, with tenderness and itching. This is followed a few days later by a suntan, when more of the dark-brown to black pigment called melanin is produced by the skin as protection against further radiation. More severe sunburn can cause pain and fluid-filled blisters, followed by peeling of the outer layer of the skin.

Excessive exposure to any form of UV radiation increases your risk of developing skin cancer. Australian sun-worshippers are suffering a massive increase in the annual incidence of skin cancer, and in the USA there are 300,000-400,000 new cases each year. In Britain too the figures are increasing.
Self help   Follow the advice in the *Do's and don'ts for avoiding sunburn* box.

Choose sun lotions and creams carefully, and read the information given on the pack before buying; different products filter out different amounts of radiation. The strongest protection comes from the opaque 'sunshade' creams containing zinc oxide or titanium dioxide, which block out most UVB and UVC, and much UVA radiation. They can be messy to apply, so are best for small, sensitive areas such as the nose and lips.

Next come 'sunblock' and 'sunscreen' preparations which are graded in factors up to 20 or more according to how much protection they supply. The amount of sunlight you can take without burning is multiplied by the factor of the cream, lotion or oil – for example, a factor three means that you can take three times more than you could without protection, while with one of factor 20 you can take 20 times as much, provided you reapply the preparation regularly.

Your skin can never have too much protection, and even those who want to tan should use a sunblock. Low factors are suitable only for easy tanners; higher factors should be used for fair complexions which do not produce as much melanin. If you simply want to protect your skin, avoid lengthy exposure to strong sunlight as much as possible, wear protective clothing and use a high-factor sunblock whenever you are in the sun. The best preparations are the rub-in lotions and creams, which are said to remain on the skin longer than oils and mousses.

Products designed to promote tanning and creams which do not state a factor often offer very little protection and should be avoided unless you are going to be in the sun for only a short while or your skin is already tanned.

Take extra care in the mountains, for UV radiation is greater at high altitudes where the thinner air filters out less sunlight. Be even more careful if you ski. Snow reflects about 90 per cent of the light that falls on it, so you will be getting nearly twice as much radiation. And the reflected light from snow will affect unaccustomed areas of skin, such as that under your chin, so take extra care over these areas. Tropical and Mediterranean locations also call for extra protection since sunlight is stronger nearer the Equator.

The skin of your lips is very thin, with little melanin and few moisturising glands, so it is very vulnerable to UV radiation. Use a special lip screen to prevent painful burning.

Remember that cold air, especially winds, on your face and other exposed parts can counteract any burning sensation and disguise the fact that you are getting sunburnt.

What the therapists recommend

Herbal Medicine Treat as a burn, applying cold water initially; addition of one or two drops of oil of lavender can be helpful. Or

Do's and don'ts for avoiding sunburn

Do avoid excessive exposure to sunlight – more than 20-30 minutes a day – at the beginning of your holiday before your skin has produced extra melanin.
Do increase your exposure to the sun only gradually.
Do use a protective sunscreen lotion or cream, and reapply it regularly, particularly if you swim or perspire a lot.
Do remember that the fairer your skin (the less pigment it has) and the sunnier the location, the greater the protection you will need from sun lotion or cream.
Do remember that autumn and spring sun can also damage your skin.
Don't sunbathe for more than 1-2 hours a day during the period from mid-morning to mid-afternoon, particularly if you have a fair skin and particularly in tropical or subtropical regions. This applies even if you use a sunblock.
Don't use tanning preparations if your skin is fair – go for medium to high factor sunblocks instead.

apply a cold compress of marigold infusion. Herbs with fleshy leaves, such as houseleeks or plantain, are cooling if applied when fresh. A little comfrey or marigold cream will soothe large areas of mild sunburn.
Naturopathy Treat small areas as minor burns: immerse them in cold water for two to three minutes, then carefully dab dry. For large areas, a cold bath may help, followed by application of rich moisturising creams, such as vitamin E creams. The vitamin taken internally will help to heal damaged skin.
Traditional Medicine Folk remedies include a soothing mixture of water and vinegar, and a lotion made from dock roots.

An orthodox view

Treat sunburn as you would any other burn. Soothe the skin with a cool shower, take painkillers such as paracetamol, and have extra drinks to replace fluid loss. Do not burst blisters, and avoid clothes that chafe, and further damaging exposure to the sun.

SWEATING

Losing moisture through the skin is a vital part of the body's self-regulating mechanism and, although it can be troublesome at times, seldom indicates a medical problem. It is not known why some people sweat more than others, but the tendency may be inherited.

There are two kinds of sweat glands: the apocrine glands, found mainly in the armpits and genital areas, and stimulated by emotional and nervous changes; and the eccrine glands, which cover the whole body and are stimulated by heat to keep you cool.

Excessive sweating is usually harmless and affects mainly the armpits, hands and feet. It often begins at puberty and may last for life. Clothing becomes wet, but the main problem is the unpleasant body odour that accompanies this, mostly in areas where clothing prevents fresh air from circulating. Occasionally, heavy sweating is a symptom of THYROID DISORDERS. It can be made worse by ANXIETY, EXERCISE, OBESITY and heat.

What the therapists recommend
Naturopathy Therapists shun commercial antiperspirants, as one function of sweating is to eliminate body wastes. They believe that deodorants permit, but antiperspirants prevent sweating, forcing wastes to find another way out of the body – often causing PIMPLES AND SPOTS. They also hold that the aluminium salts used in some antiperspirants can prove poisonous, causing dermatitis or blocking pores and perpetuating odours.

Naturopaths also believe that strong body odour can be due to a zinc deficiency, which can cause KIDNEY COMPLAINTS, with excess urea being excreted by the skin. This may be indicated by white marks on the nails and a cracked tongue. They may suggest a supplement of 20-30mg a day for a few months.
Aromatherapy Certain essential oils such as rose oil, clary sage, ginger, lemon and nutmeg may be applied – diluted in a carrier lotion (see AROMATHERAPY) – as a natural perfume to disguise body odour. Cypress and nutmeg are recommended for bad cases. For sweaty feet, try rubbing a few drops of neat cypress oil into the soles and between the toes once a day until the condition improves.
Homoeopathy General remedies that may help are: *Hepar sulph.* for profuse, sour, sticky sweat during the day or night, where the skin feels very sensitive to touch – take in 6X potency, morning and night for two weeks, but stop before two weeks if there is an improvement; *Sepia* for profuse sweating of the chest, back and thighs at night, particularly during the MENOPAUSE.

Take *Sulphur* for body odour that is accompanied by unhealthy looking skin, and where sweaty feet are a particular problem. Take in 6X potency morning and night for two weeks, but stop before two weeks if there is an improvement.
Acupressure Press inwards on the thumb side of either hand, at a point three fingers' width up from the wrist crease, and in line with the thumbnail.
Autogenic Training Excessive sweating is often a symptom of anxiety, and the mentally calming effects of the training can be helpful. Night sweats are also often said to be relieved by this method.
Behavioural Therapy Anxiety is known to cause heavy sweating, and the therapy teaches people how to try and relax and avoid this. Apart from special relaxation techniques, sufferers are advised to slow down both physically and mentally.

An orthodox view
Anyone who sweats excessively will be advised by their doctor to lose weight if necessary, and try and improve their general level of health. The GP may prescribe antiperspirants to be applied at night and then washed off the following morning. He will also probably give advice on frequent washing and changes of clothing to keep the condition in check.

In severe cases, a surgeon can remove some of the skin in the armpit, so reducing the number of sweat glands.

Doctors do not approve of commercial vaginal deodorant sprays as these can cause allergic reactions, including itching, burning and blisters (see also VAGINAL DISORDERS).

Living with stress and staying well

The jet-setting executive with dangerously high blood pressure or the competitive businessman nursing his ulcer through endless working lunches are popular images of stress victims. Seldom do we think of a young couple excitedly planning their wedding, a new mother at home with her baby, or someone just retired and looking forward to freedom and leisure after a lifetime of hard work.

Yet all these people – in fact, anyone faced with important changes or new demands – may be at risk from stress and related disorders.

Stress itself is not bad or dangerous. It is part of the wear and tear of everyday life and cannot – indeed, should not – be avoided. Challenges and changes add spice to life, fire the imagination and spur us on to new achievements – if handled in the right way. Many of the happiest and most successful people are those who have learned to respond to high levels of stress in a balanced way.

A stress victim, by contrast, fails to adapt to pressures and problems as well as he might. For example, he may habitually bundle unpaid bills into a drawer and try to forget about them, or lose his temper and call his wife extravagant – or even obsessively write out a cheque the minute each new bill arrives.

Each response may sometimes be appropriate, but when one of them becomes a general way of coping, the result can be a serious stress problem. Luckily, help lies mainly in the victim's own hands.

Self help for stress victims

Coping with stress is a continual task of trying to respond in the best possible way to each new situation. There is no single, simple method, but stress experts recommend the following four-step approach:

Recognise the signs Stress affects the whole person – body, mind, feelings and behaviour – and symptoms can take many forms. Most result from increased tension in the muscles – NECK PAIN, lower BACK PAIN, HEADACHES, TEETH-GRINDING, feeling a 'lump in the throat', high-pitched or nervous laughter, trembling, shaking, a nervous TIC and blinking. If untreated, muscular tension can also lead to more serious symptoms and disorders such as high BLOOD PRESSURE, MIGRAINE, and DIGESTIVE PROBLEMS such as IRRITABLE BOWEL SYNDROME.

Other symptoms include a fast pulse, thumping heart, HYPERVENTILATION, PALPITATIONS, SWEATING, dryness of the throat and mouth, and difficulty in swallowing. INSOMNIA and other SLEEP DISORDERS are common, and there may also be FAINTING, DIZZINESS, a feeling of weakness and lack of ENERGY.

Mind, feelings and behaviour can also be affected – poor concentration, vague ANXIETY or FEAR for no apparent reason, and periods of irritability and perfectionism followed by DEPRESSION and lethargy are all signs of stress. Other warning signs include self-destructive behaviour such as eating and drinking too much, SMOKING excessively, relying on tranquillisers and even being unusually accident-prone.

Identify the causes If you recognise symptoms of stress, the next step is to become aware of the causes – called 'stressors' by doctors. These can be anything that throws you off balance, makes demands or initiates change – even for a short while.

Some stressors are internal – for example, worrying about how you are going to pay the mortgage or get to work on time, eating something that disagrees with you, or even being physically ill. Others come from outside – a noisy environment or a badly polluted one, a constantly ringing telephone, pressure at work or a baby that will not stop crying can all cause strain.

Modern life itself is often severely stressful – we move house, change jobs and end marriages more, we travel farther, are bombarded with more information, buy more and throw away more. At the same time, we worry about the effect on the environment of using up the earth's natural resources faster than ever and producing increasing amounts of waste and pollution.

Draw up a list of all the major stressors you currently experience, not forgetting that happy events can be just as stressful as unpleasant ones. As well as bringing joy into a home, a new baby, for example, can also bring broken nights, changed family relationships, new expenses and worries, and altered domestic routines. Even a get-away-from-it-all holiday can be quite demanding, as you cope with foreign money, worry about travel delays and deal with unfamiliar faces and languages.

Watch your reactions The same stressor can provoke different responses in different individuals; even one person may react differently at different times. There are three basic ways of reacting to stress – the so-called 'fight', 'flight' and 'flow' responses. Each works in some situations – none should be considered good or bad in itself – but trouble can start when you habitually rely on just one type of response, even when another might get better results.

Use the descriptions below to identify the ways in which you tend to respond to each of the stressors on your list. If you find that you nearly always respond in the same way, try writing down other ways; consider what the likely effects might be in each case – if they seem favourable, try out your ideas in practice.

<u>Fight response</u> This has two forms, external and internal. The external one involves assertively meeting problems head-on – sometimes even before they arise.

Those who rely on this type of reaction tend to be energetic, ambitious and competitive. Often they are high achievers, constantly pushing themselves to do better, and easily irritated or made impatient by others with a different approach. Typically, they may find it hard to relax and can be at risk from HEART DISORDERS.

Problems can be dealt with equally directly by the internal fight response, but people who use it appear unemotional, organised and in control, rather than outwardly aggressive. They tend to have particular, fixed ways of doing things and may object if anyone suggests a change. Imbalance in this direction can result in digestive disorders such as irritable bowel syndrome or a stomach ULCER.

<u>Flight response</u> Problems are avoided whenever possible, by pretending that they do not exist or by giving up and letting someone else deal with them. At best, this can make us careful and cautious; at worst, not in control of our lives and dependent on others.

Those who use the flight response too often may never realise their full potential or learn to express their feelings to others. Dangers include isolation, withdrawal and, in extreme cases, feelings of despair which some practitioners link with increased risks of CANCER.

<u>Flow response</u> This involves accepting the stressor without either fighting or running away from it. The idea is to 'flow with the tide', letting the feelings of the moment guide you.

Will changes make you ill?

In the early 1970s two stress experts at Washington University, Thomas Holmes and Richard Rahe, found that stress due to important 'life changes' was an accurate predictor of future illness. They drew up an index of 43 possible changes and rated each one for stressfulness on a scale from 1 to 100. (Financial factors have been generalised here to allow for inflation.)

To rate yourself on the scale, add up the scores for all the events listed that you have experienced during the past year. A total of over 150 gives a 50 per cent chance of a health change occurring in the near future, and over 300 a 90 per cent chance – unless effective antistress measures are taken.

Death of spouse	100
Divorce	73
Marital separation	65
Jail term	63
Death of close family member	63
Personal injury or illness	53
Marriage	50
Loss of job	47
Marital reconciliation	45
Retirement	45
Change in health of family member	44
Pregnancy	40
Sexual problems	39
Gain of new family member	39
Business readjustment	39
Change in financial state	38
Death of close friend	37
Change to different type of work	36
Change in number of arguments with spouse	35
High mortgage	31
Foreclosure of mortgage or loan	30
Change in responsibilities at work	29
Son or daughter leaving home	29
Trouble with in-laws	29
Outstanding personal achievement	28
Spouse begins or stops work	26
Beginning or ending education	26
Change in living conditions	25
Changed personal habits	24
Trouble with boss	23
Change in working hours or conditions	20
Moving house	20
Changing schools	20
Change in leisure pursuits	19
Change in church activities	19
Change in social activities	18
Low to medium mortgage or loan	17
Altered sleeping habits	16
Change in number of family get-togethers	15
Change in eating habits	15
Going on holiday	13
Approaching Christmas season	12
Minor violations of the law	11

You can also use the index to predict and plan changes in the future such as moving house or starting a new job so that stressful events do not all happen at once or build up to a crisis.

The danger here is one of appearing to be vague, without fixed values and beliefs. You may find it hard to make firm decisions and take action; you may even come to feel that nothing really matters. People who tend to just 'flow' can be susceptible to accidents and mild illnesses, and easily fall for passing health fads and fringe cults.

Develop a holistic approach Once your stress responses are under control, consider a wider, more long-term approach to the problem. Overall harmony and well-being is something to work for throughout life and is never complete, but stress experts suggest these first steps:

Be constantly aware of stressors and stress responses in everyday life. Look after yourself by eating a balanced diet (see EATING FOR HEALTH), taking regular exercise and getting a good night's sleep. Opt for compromises rather than extreme or one-sided solutions to problems. Get help from other people and suitable groups when you need it. Practise a form of RELAXATION AND BREATHING, YOGA or MEDITATION every day. Express your feelings to others – and if this is difficult, PSYCHOTHERAPY, ART THERAPY or BIO-ENERGETICS may help.

You can also draw up a personal 'life plan' – an overall view of your life as a whole, including your birth, achievements, major landmarks such as marriage and children, serious illnesses, where you are now, goals and aspirations for the future and, finally, your death. This can give a broader perspective on present problems and help you to plan ahead for future stressful times.

What the therapists recommend

NATUROPATHY
You are advised to eat a healthy diet, possibly supplemented by multivitamin and mineral tablets to replenish nutrients which are used up more quickly when under stress. Try not to look to cigarettes, alcohol, coffee or tranquillisers to make you feel better – take exercise or practise relaxation techniques or meditation instead, and give yourself regular 'time out' completely free of work pressures.

HERBAL MEDICINE
To help you unwind, try infusions (see p. 184) of lemon balm, camomile, catmint or lime blossom. Include oats in your diet – unless you suffer from GLUTEN INTOLERANCE. Practitioners may prescribe stronger relaxants such as skullcap, valerian or cowslip, or the restoring herbs vervain and St John's wort, as well as recommending changes in your way of life.

BEHAVIOURAL THERAPY
Practitioners say you should learn to relax – either through a specific technique such as yoga, or generally finding time to unwind and enjoy yourself by good use of your leisure time. Set limits on the amount and type of work you do. Learn to say 'no'. Take a break – a tea break or five minutes' rest every hour. Face up to and deal with your problems. There is a difference between worrying about a problem and thinking it through. Don't set your standards too high. They should be realistic and, most important, achievable.

HOMOEOPATHY
Ignatia 30 is prescribed for stress due to shock, bereavement, or an unhappy experience. If overwork, entertaining or eating and drinking too much lead to digestive troubles and irritability, try *Nux vomica 40*. For students under pressure, or anyone who feels weak and depressed as a result of stress, *Ac. phos.* may help.

ART THERAPY
Patients are given the opportunity to release tension and express their frustration in a creative way. Self-expression in art also helps to put people in touch with thoughts and feelings they may be unaware of, in an environment where there is no pressure on them to 'perform' or 'get it right'.

T'AI-CHI CH'UAN
The slow, flowing movements are aimed at balancing body, mind and emotions, releasing tensions and adjusting the energy flow. Correct breathing is taught, particularly a way of breathing out fully which promotes relaxation and calmness. Practitioners say that T'ai-chi improves posture as well as creating inner harmony in an uncompetitive, stress-free atmosphere.

Other alternative therapies

Dance Movement Therapy Individually or in a group, this can relieve tension and aid relaxation, while at the same time helping you to express pent-up emotions.

Colour Therapy Practitioners suggest that replacing fluorescent light at work with flicker-free, natural daylight bulbs may help to reduce stress.

Massage In cases where stress is due to physical discomfort and, on occasions, emotional disturbances, a gentle, caressing, 'caring' general massage may well help to bring about a more balanced state, enabling the sufferer to resist and, hopefully, eventually conquer the cause of the problem.

Reflexology The overall approach of the treatment is to induce relaxation, but reflexology can also treat physical symptoms by working on the relevant reflex areas.

Music Therapy Simply listening to music at home is often a good way to unwind after a stressful day. Attending therapy sessions can help stress victims to relax and share their feelings with others by using sound.

Autogenic Training Patients can be taught to relieve existing tensions and stresses, and to cope better with stressful situations in the future.

Hypnotherapy Suggestions are made under hypnosis which continue to be effective later, and techniques of self-hypnosis to aid relaxation are taught.

Yoga Postures and breathing patterns are taught to promote relaxation and balance of body and mind.

An orthodox view

Doctors can offer patients general advice on reducing stress – by cutting down their workload, playing sport or learning relaxation methods, for example – and may also prescribe tranquillisers for short-term relief.

Adding up your chances of becoming a victim

The physical and mental effects of stress are due not only to the amount of stress you experience, but also to how good your defences are and how well they enable you to cope with stressful situations. The tests below are designed to measure both factors, and are based on questionnaires developed by the American stress psychologists Lyle H. Miller and Alma Dell Smith of the University of Boston's Medical Centre. Test 1 measures the overall level of stress you are subjected to at the moment, and test 2 your ability to cope with it.

Test 1: Rate yourself for stress

The list on the right gives ten responses often made by people under pressure. Each response can be rated for stress from 1 (not stressful) to 5 (very stressful). If you can remember responding in any of these ways in the last six months, circle the number under the 'past' column that represents the amount of stress you experienced at the time. Under the 'future' column, circle numbers to represent the amount of stress you expect to experience from responses that may occur during the next six months. Add up both past and future scores, then add them together. A score over 30 indicates a potential stress problem, while more than 53 calls for a worked-out programme to fight stress.

Response	Past					Future				
1 Depression	1	2	3	4	5	1	2	3	4	5
2 Frustration	1	2	3	4	5	1	2	3	4	5
3 Guilt	1	2	3	4	5	1	2	3	4	5
4 Anxiety or panic	1	2	3	4	5	1	2	3	4	5
5 Desperation or hopelessness	1	2	3	4	5	1	2	3	4	5
6 Feeling out of control	1	2	3	4	5	1	2	3	4	5
7 Selfconsciousness	1	2	3	4	5	1	2	3	4	5
8 Irritation and anger	1	2	3	4	5	1	2	3	4	5
9 Restlessness	1	2	3	4	5	1	2	3	4	5
10 Feeling trapped or helpless	1	2	3	4	5	1	2	3	4	5

Test 2: Measure your resistance

This test measures how much your way of life supports you and bolsters resistance to stress. Rate yourself for each of the 20 items on the scale from 1 (almost always) to 5 (never) according to how often they apply.
Add up your total score. A score of 45 or less shows high resistance to stress and a healthy way of life; 45 to 55 indicates that you may be susceptible to the effects of stress and could benefit from adjusting certain aspects of your daily life; over 55 and stress could be a serious risk, calling for a reappraisal of your general way of life.

How much of the time are these statements true for you?	Almost always	Most times	Some-times	Rarely	Never
1 My health is good (including eyesight, teeth, etc.)	1	2	3	4	5
2 My income meets my basic expenses	1	2	3	4	5
3 I am about the right weight for my build and height	1	2	3	4	5
4 I give and receive affection regularly	1	2	3	4	5
5 I express my feelings when angry or worried	1	2	3	4	5
6 I have fewer than three caffeine-containing drinks (coffee, cocoa or cola) a day	1	2	3	4	5
7 I take part in regular social activities	1	2	3	4	5
8 I eat at least one full, well-balanced meal a day	1	2	3	4	5
9 I do something just for pleasure at least once a week	1	2	3	4	5
10 There is at least one relative within 50 miles (80km) of home on whom I can rely	1	2	3	4	5
11 I have some time alone during the day	1	2	3	4	5
12 I get seven or eight hours of sleep at least four nights a week	1	2	3	4	5
13 My religious beliefs give me strength	1	2	3	4	5
14 I exercise hard enough to work up a sweat at least twice a week	1	2	3	4	5
15 I have a network of friends and acquaintances	1	2	3	4	5
16 I discuss problems such as housework and money with other members of the household	1	2	3	4	5
17 I have at least one friend I can talk to about personal affairs	1	2	3	4	5
18 I smoke no more than 10 cigarettes a day	1	2	3	4	5
19 I organise my time well	1	2	3	4	5
20 I have fewer than five alcoholic drinks a week	1	2	3	4	5

T'AI-CHI CH'UAN
Meditation in motion . . .

The art of T'ai-chi Ch'uan – usually shortened to simply T'ai-chi, meaning 'wholeness' – is based on a series of slow-moving, circular, dance-like movements which are best performed in the open air. It aims to get people to focus on their mental and emotional state as well as their body.

Its practitioners say that, provided it is taught with insight, and studied responsibly, it is probably the most complete, natural and effective of all holistic therapies. It is a highly complex art form involving patience, perseverance and the ability to simplify, adapt and change – and should not be looked upon merely as a means of 'working out'.

T'ai-chi is based on the belief that, following emotional and/or mental disturbance, illness stems from imbalances such as energy (known as *Qi*) moving too quickly or too slowly through the body – or too much energy gathering in one particular area (for example, the head and chest) and too little elsewhere (such as the legs), so that the sufferer is 'top heavy'. Such imbalances may be corrected by mental focusing through the various movements of the therapy.

Deeply rooted in Chinese culture (see box, p. 336), T'ai-chi has been practised in Britain and the USA for much of this century. However, it came to wider public attention in the West following the visit by US President Richard Nixon to China in 1972. Outdoor practice of T'ai-chi was shown in television programmes, and within a few years the therapy was being practised daily in parks and gardens on both sides of the Atlantic.

However, practitioners say that the therapy cannot be self-taught, and you should receive instruction from a qualified teacher.

Who it can help As a natural process of healing, T'ai-chi has for centuries been considered both curative and preventive. Its graceful, flowing movements are particularly effective against ANXIETY and STRESS, because they encourage people to relax and 'let go'. They can also help improve breathing and posture, generally tone-up the body, and stimulate circulation. In many cases – particularly for people leading hectic,

In China even young children often join in T'ai-chi sessions – for many of them the beginning of a lifelong habit.

Parks such as this one in Beijing (right) are favoured among many thousands of ordinary Chinese as open-air venues for morning and evening T'ai-chi practice.

How the movements of T'ai-chi are performed

The movements illustrated below and on p. 336 make up just one small sequence in the 'long form' of T'ai-chi. They begin with the posture known as 'the bird's beak' (below left), which evolves subtly into 'strumming the lute' (below far right).

1   The bird's beak

2

3

4

5

6

*Strumming
the lute*

7

high-pressure lives – T'ai-chi is prescribed as an alternative to tranquillisers.

T'ai-chi can be practised at almost any age, and in China it is popular among young and old, who are said to find it physically, mentally and spiritually rewarding.

Finding a teacher Information about T'ai-chi teachers and classes in Britain can be obtained from The School of T'ai-chi Ch'uan, 5 Tavistock Place, London WC1H 9SS. Otherwise, try your local library, education authority, notice boards in specialist bookshops, health-food restaurants or shops, or health magazine advertisements.

Wherever possible, enrol with a teacher who has had sound training and at least four years experience with the therapy's 'long form' (see below).

Consulting a teacher Once you have contacted a teacher, you should ask to watch him – or her – conducting a class before enrolling. Classes should be peaceful, well-organised, and not crowded. Students dress in light, loose-fitting shirts and trousers, and wear socks or thin slippers which allow full use of the foot muscles. The teacher should be calm and perceptive. There should be plenty of opportunities for discussion of what

Riding the tiger and resisting the monkey

According to Chinese legend, the beginnings of T'ai-chi Ch'uan can be traced back to about the 11th century and a Taoist thinker named Chang San-feng. The aggressive nature of martial arts concerned him, and he sought a softer form which would help spiritual development.

One day while watching a magpie pecking at a snake, he was impressed by the way the snake moved slowly and continuously as it tried to evade its attacker. Its neat, circular movements and 'yielding' quality later formed the basis of a new form of *ch'uan*, or 'fist' – an exercise for developing self-mastery.

With this were incorporated the characteristic qualities of different animals, as developed by Taoist physicians such as Hua T'o in the 3rd century AD. These included the tiger (symbol of the ego), which had to be 'ridden' or 'mastered'; the monkey (symbol of mischievousness), which had to be 'resisted'; as well as the bear, the stag, the crane and others.

In about the 14th century, the more advanced form of this *ch'uan* acquired the name of *T'ai-chi Ch'uan* ('supreme ultimate fist') and was aimed at mastery of the whole self. It was adopted by Taoist monks in their monasteries and temple schools as a way of integrating body, mind and spirit by combining movement with breathing. The monks found that performing the movements focused their bodies and minds, and T'ai-chi was gradually transformed into a meditative healing process in which anyone could take part.

It is based largely on achieving a balance between YIN AND YANG, the two complementary life forces in Chinese philosophy: yin, the gentle, yielding and peaceful feminine force; yang, the firm, active and creative masculine force.

T'ai-chi was first performed by the public in the mid-19th century – and today millions of Chinese practise it in the early mornings and early evenings in parks and open spaces.

One movement flows into another as the T'ai-chi sequence begun on p. 334 progresses to 'holding the circle' (centre left, below) and 'the stork cools its wings' (far right, below).

Holding the circle

The stork cools its wings

8   9   10   11

is being experienced, studied and achieved.

From the start, you are taught that T'ai-chi is a 'growing' therapy which unfolds its benefits gradually. As such, it requires regular attendance – preferably in a class with group teaching – for at least 1½ hours a week. You should beware of teachers who progress too quickly. Insist on repeating and refining what you have been taught. Personal guidance is essential for correct body alignment (such as keeping your spine vertical, your hips level and your head upright), relaxation, and maintaining an active but peaceful mind – a prerequisite for a balanced personality and healthy body.

There are two forms of T'ai-chi movement, the long form and the short form, both of which should be performed slowly and with a tranquil mind – in the open air wherever possible.

The short form This has about 40 movements without repetitions, and takes from five to ten minutes. Although it is beneficial, practitioners believe that this more recent adaptation does not provide the full therapeutic value of the long form.

The long form There are more than 100 movements involved, and this complete exercise takes from 20 to 40 minutes, depending on its structure. This includes repetitions, which – in reflecting the rhythms of life – are considered essential to physical and psychological balance.

An orthodox view

T'ai-chi is a beautiful and elegant form of physical 'routine' which encourages body awareness and helps with balance and confidence. As a therapy, it can reduce much anxiety and stress.

TEETH-GRINDING

Misaligned or missing teeth, an uneven bite, or some other source of abnormal pressure on the jaw joints is usually responsible for this night-time symptom.

The two jaw joints are located in front of the mid-points of the ears, and connect the jawbone (or mandible) to the temporal bones of the skull. The principal movements of the joints are up and down, allowing the mouth to open and close, but the jaw can also move from side to side to some extent – as happens when chewing food. When the joints are under strain the jaw muscles contract and tense up, grinding the teeth together during sleep.

Teeth-grinding, like other problems such as ARTHRITIS and injuries to the jaw, may eventually lead to disorders of the jaw joint – known as temporomandibular joint dysfunction. Symptoms may include clicking and pain in the jaw, and sometimes referred pain, felt as HEADACHES, earache, painful sinuses, soreness of the throat or neck glands, or even shoulder pain.

If strain due to teeth-grinding persists without treatment, arthritis in the temporomandibular joints may eventually develop. Occasionally the jaw may even become dislocated, but this is most often the result of sudden violence, such as a blow to the jaw when the mouth is open, 'whiplash' produced in a car accident, or even a sudden muscular spasm when yawning. The jaw becomes locked in an abnormal position, the mouth will not fully open or close, and the head of the jaw can be felt in front of its usual position.

A dislocated jaw needs to be treated by a doctor or dentist, but alternative therapies may help to overcome the cause and subsequent pain.

What the therapists recommend

Acupuncture Treatment is given on the large intestine and stomach meridians to relieve pain; heart and bladder meridians as sedative points; points on the governor, stomach, heart, large intestine and bladder meridians as general treatment.

Autogenic Training This is said to be helpful in relieving excessive muscular tension in the region of the face and jaw. Grinding the teeth during sleep and facial pain resulting from tension in the jaw muscles is frequently eased or eliminated.

Osteopathy Often all that is required is for the osteopath to exert gentle but sustained pressure downwards on each side of the jaw. This has the effect of releasing contracted muscles and the osteopath can then gently guide the jaw into a better position.

Acupressure Apply pressure at a point two fingers' width in front of the ear in the hollow under the cheekbone, pressing inwards.

Massage The role of massage in this condition is largely to provide supportive extra treatment to the 'adjustment' performed by an osteopath.

An orthodox view

If you dislocate your jaw, your doctor or dentist can manipulate it back by pressing downwards on your molar teeth with his thumbs while lifting your chin with his other fingers. This overcomes muscle spasms and tension, and allows the joint to return to a normal position. Dislocation weakens the ligaments which hold the joints in place, so that recurrence is a possibility.

If you develop pain in one or both jaw joints, or a headache when chewing, see your dentist to check that your teeth and bite are even. If they are not, he can build up your teeth to protect you from arthritis in the joints and to relieve headaches and other associated pains. If the pain is severe, an anti-inflammatory painkiller such as ibuprofen (Nurofen) should help.

TENNIS ELBOW

Inflammation of the tendon which joins the muscles of the forearm to the lower end of the upper arm bone (or humerus) is known as tennis elbow. The muscles at the back of the forearm straighten and bend back the fingers and wrist, and they are all connected to the same point on the outer side of the humerus. It is not surprising therefore that repeated or vigorous use of those muscles produces inflammation, tenderness and pain, which may radiate down the forearm and upwards towards the shoulder.

Tennis is only one of many activities that can provoke the condition. Other repetitive actions such as typing, bricklaying and repeated lifting can also cause tennis elbow.

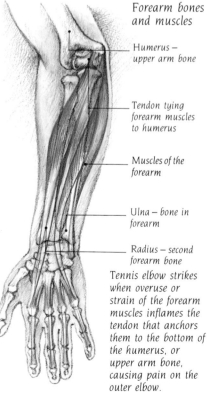

Forearm bones and muscles

Humerus – upper arm bone

Tendon tying forearm muscles to humerus

Muscles of the forearm

Ulna – bone in forearm

Radius – second forearm bone

Tennis elbow strikes when overuse or strain of the forearm muscles inflames the tendon that anchors them to the bottom of the humerus, or upper arm bone, causing pain on the outer elbow.

Poor technique is responsible for many tennis injuries. The player on the left risks straining his forearm muscles by locking the elbow joint in this backhand stroke. A two-handed stroke with the elbow slightly flexed would be safer. The young woman below has a common beginner's fault: getting so close to the ball that she is forced to play a cramped and awkward forehand. Not only her game suffers – the manoeuvre strains both arm and elbow muscles.

What the therapists recommend

Osteopathy In the early, very acute, inflammatory stage, ice packs and rest are recommended. However, osteopathic treatment is claimed to be very effective for this condition, which often lasts for months. Deep friction massage is given to the painful points in the muscles surrounding the joint. Restricted mobility of the joint may be corrected by gentle mobilisation.

Massage In the early stage, following an initial period of rest – particularly from the activity responsible for the condition – gentle effleurage and petrissage kneadings may serve to relieve the pain. They can also help to prevent adhesions (the growing together of normally separate surfaces) and the softening of tissue. After the acute stage has passed, deeper finger friction and kneading is usually applied.

An orthodox view

Despite treatment, tennis elbow can be a persistent and troublesome complaint, particularly if the sufferer continues the activity that caused it in the first place. Sometimes this is inevitable if the patient's livelihood depends on it.

Massage, painkilling tablets, steroid (cortisone) injections, injections of local anaesthetic, and strapping or elastic support around the elbow may all help. Exercises, manipulation and local short-wave or ultrasound treatment given by a physiotherapist may also be recommended (see ULTRASONICS).

TENSION

Designed to prime muscles for action, bodily tension was intended by nature to have a quick release. However, in the modern world, stresses and strains seldom find an immediate physical outlet, and tension easily builds up to a dangerous level. Never ignore warning signals such as HEADACHES, NECK PAIN, BACK PAIN, DIGESTIVE DISORDERS and raised BLOOD PRESSURE, or more serious disorders may develop.

Treatment and self-help measures for tension are the same as for STRESS.

TERMINAL ILLNESS
Breaking the final taboo

A terminal illness is, by definition, incurable – but this does not mean that it is untreatable. Most patients' fears are less to do with death itself than with the process of dying. They may be afraid of being in pain, of becoming dependent, of losing control over their bodily functions, or of being a burden to their relatives.

The best modern terminal care – whether at home, in hospital, or in a hospice – provides a supportive atmosphere for patients to come to terms with their illness. They have the reassurance that they will not suffer, that pain will be well controlled with drugs, and that they will die with dignity.

Nowadays fewer and fewer people die at home. Many die in hospitals, sometimes surrounded by high-technology equipment and often feeling frightened, alone and cut off from their families. They may even feel ignored, as if everyone has given them up and is concentrating on people who will get better – and sometimes this feeling is justified. If everyone is avoiding talking about death, the patient may feel that they are hiding some awful truth, and these fears may be replayed in the imagination until they assume horrific proportions.

Relatives too may lose the reassurance of being able to keep their loved one comfortable, and of knowing they will be on hand to help and to hold when the end comes. It can also be difficult for relatives to come to terms with a death when they have been unable to see the person and say their final goodbyes. Indeed, because dying and death seldom occur at home, comparatively few of us have ever seen anyone die, and may imagine what happens to be far worse than it really is.

Children especially are usually 'shielded' from the processes of birth and death, so most of us grow up with little sense of the continuity of the life cycle, and its beginning and end become shadowy, mysterious events, somehow removed from real life. This can help to produce an atmosphere of denial surrounding terminally ill patients, where medical staff and relatives feel that it may be cruel or traumatic to talk to them about facing death.

However, patients are often very aware that they have an incurable condition without being told so directly, and they too may shy away from mentioning it because they in turn do not want to upset their relatives.

When the subject is broached, almost everyone is greatly relieved to be able to talk openly about it, rather than constantly steering conversations away from the situation.

Talking about dying It is often said that dying has become the final taboo. Not only do people find it difficult and even embarrassing to talk about death and dying with those who are terminally ill, even doctors and nurses often feel uncomfortable about discussing it in a direct manner.

Because conventional medicine is mostly concerned with making people better and battling against disease, some doctors feel a sense of failure when they are no longer able to offer any hope of a cure. Some terminally ill patients do not want to know the truth; others welcome time to come to terms with their own feelings without having to discuss the prospect of death. But for many the 'conspiracy of silence' about death which is maintained by their families and those who care for them can be deeply distressing.

Many patients feel the need to talk about what is happening to them, to ask questions to relieve their fears and uncertainties, and to discuss both practical and emotional matters with their nearest and dearest.

Coming to terms Dr Elizabeth Kubler-Ross, a physician working at the University of Chicago, has done work aimed at dispelling the myths surrounding death and dying for patients and doctors alike. She describes five stages in the emotional response of patients with a terminal illness:

Denial On suspecting or being told the diagnosis, the patient's reaction is often 'This can't be happening to me', and a refusal to accept the verdict. Often doctors and relatives will collude in or even encourage this denial, leaving the patient unable to acknowledge what is really happening.

Anger The patient may now become angry at what is happening. This anger may be directed against himself ('Why didn't I stop smoking?'), or his doctors ('Why can't they cure me?'), or his relatives ('If I hadn't been so busy looking after them I would have seen the doctor more quickly'), or even against fate ('Why me?').

Bargaining At this stage patients try to extend the time left to them. They stick to treatments and diets, and may press for drastic surgery or extreme drug treatments. Some start seeking a miracle cure, visiting numerous doctors or alternative practitioners, or trying religious healers or shrines. Some try to strike a bargain with fate – 'If I am good and atone for my sins, I might get better'.

Sadness As patients start to accept the inevitability of their own death they begin to grieve for what they will lose – family, friends, possessions, years of life they might have had. Sometimes severe DEPRESSION will set in for a time.

Acceptance Many patients are lucky enough to come to terms with their illness before they die. They experience peace and tranquillity combined with a certain joy in what life still has to offer. Often, if they have been able to share their feelings, they experience an emotional attachment to their family which many describe as being closer than at any time in their lives.

Final stages The choice of where to spend the final stages of a terminal illness – at home, in hospital or in a hospice – will be determined by the nature of the illness, the degree of support relatives and friends are able to give, and the local facilities available. Many hospitals have specialists in terminal care, or there may be a hospice nearby. Alternatively, the hospital or hospice may be able to provide a home-care service, supplying doctors and nurses who can make regular visits to patients.

Some patients stay in hospital for a while, then go home when their symptoms are well under control, while others stay at home for as long as possible then go into a hospice. Whatever the decision, there is today no reason for a dying patient to suffer physically. Most patients fear pain, but with proper care,

The hospice movement

Many recent changes in attitudes towards the dying have come about as a result of the modern hospice movement. In the Middle Ages a hospice was a place where travellers could literally find hospitality – food, refuge and spiritual encouragement, administered by monks. In the 19th century, several religious orders set up special hospices for the dying, but these were few and far between. Today's hospice movement grew from a conversation between a social worker and a dying patient at a London hospital in 1948.

Realising the great and very special needs of dying patients, the social worker decided to train as a doctor so that she could prescribe proper pain relief for them. She is now Dame Cicely Saunders, who in 1967 set up St Christopher's Hospice in London. It caters for people with advanced or terminal cancer, providing treatment based on a philosophy of life and care radically different from that which operates in most hospitals.

Her aim is to relieve the distress of dying patients, whether physical, mental or spiritual. Full pain relief and treatment for symptoms are combined with a sympathetic, caring and communicating approach, in a supportive and cheerful setting.

In 1969 St Christopher's launched the first home-care team of visiting doctors and nurses, who help relatives to provide similar care for patients staying at home. Now there are hundreds of hospices, day-care units and home-care teams all over Britain, and many hospitals also have their own terminal care teams and support groups.

See also HOSPICES.

Support from alternative medicine

Those seeking comfort from alternative treatments have been known to benefit from MASSAGE. The Bristol Cancer Help Centre, at least one major London hospital and a number of hospices and care centres now use massage therapists or employ nursing staff trained in this therapy. The compassionate touching involved is seen as bringing both physical and psychological benefits.

Apart from toning muscles, massage is said to ease problems with breathing, circulation and digestion. However, these are held to be secondary factors compared with the value of the patient knowing that 'somebody cares'. Light back stroking seems to be a favoured technique in these cases.

Some homoeopaths recommend the BACH REMEDIES to help dying patients come to terms with difficult emotions and changed circumstances. They advocate Star of Bethlehem for shock on first learning of the situation, Walnut to help face death, Gorse for feeling helpless, and Sweet chestnut for despair. Honeysuckle is for regrets about the past, Willow for resentment of those who are well, and Rock water for those who try to be too brave and adopt a 'stiff upper lip' attitude.

People who struggle on without complaining may benefit from Oak, while Red chestnut can help to ease worry about others. If there are vague feelings of guilt or shame Pine may provide relief, and people who suffer in silence may find that Water violet makes it easier to reach out to others for comfort. Clematis is for unconsciousness and numbness, and Rescue remedy for pain or any crisis.

doctors can now control pain before it arises. Patients no longer have to ask for pain relief when needed as carefully timed regimes are worked out so that each dose of painkiller is given before the effects of the last wear off.

Terminal care doctors also have special expertise in dealing with other symptoms which may be troublesome, such as breathlessness, nausea or constipation. They can no longer offer the patient a cure but they will still treat his symptoms and care for him.

T-GROUPS

The growth of group PSYCHOTHERAPY has led to similar techniques being exploited to extend its use from solving personal problems to improving people's relationships with others, both socially and at work.

T-groups – or training groups – are often formed to improve relationships within large organisations. ENCOUNTER GROUPS and SENSITIVITY TRAINING use similar methods, but have different objectives depending on members' needs and the context in which therapy occurs. See also HUMANISTIC PSYCHOLOGY.

T-groups are usually made up of about 12 to 20 members who meet either for regular sessions over a period of weeks or for a single intensive weekend session. The group leader, who is sometimes called a 'facilitator', encourages participants to express attitudes, feelings and motives which they are usually unaware of or which they feel they have to conceal from others. Often T-groups adapt to their own use the principles of ROGERIAN THERAPY, in which more importance is attached to the experiences and points of view of the clients than to those of the therapist.

Although some people find T-group sessions extremely useful, many report deriving little benefit, and others find the experience unpleasant and disturbing. For this reason, responsible therapists recommend that individuals should be carefully assessed by a group leader or other psychotherapist before participating in a group.

THALASSOTHERAPY

This branch of HYDROTHERAPY relies on the healing powers of sea water or seaweed. Sea water has a buoyancy which partially supports the body, reduces the effort needed to move damaged limbs, and allows people to exercise stiff or diseased joints more fully.

Seaweed or seaweed extracts added to baths or used as compresses or poultices introduce a range of natural minerals, vitamins and trace elements which are believed to increase sweating and so help to cleanse the system of impurities. People allergic to iodine should avoid this therapy.

THERAPEUTIC TOUCH
Healing with the hands

Before attempting to locate and cure illness by therapeutic touch, those who consider themselves gifted with the power of healing, usually 'centre', or concentrate, their mind on a calm and beautiful visual image, such as a tranquil country scene. This, they say, lets them clear their mind of inessentials and harness psychic energy for their work.

They then run their hands over or near the patient's head or body seeking out any area of sickness. If anything is found to be wrong, the healer places his hands on the area so that the healing energy can flow through him to the patient, or so that any imbalances in the patient can be corrected (see LAYING ON OF HANDS). The treatment – which, ideally, should be done in a quiet atmosphere – takes about 10-15 minutes, after which the patient should start to feel better.

Therapeutic touch is particularly popular in the USA, and is practised mostly by trained nurses. See HEALERS AND HEALING.

THROAT PROBLEMS

The average sore throat lasts about three to four days, and is the commonest of throat problems. A virus or bacterium is generally the cause, and the throat is often the first area of the body to respond to the infection. See LARYNGITIS; NOSE AND THROAT AILMENTS; QUINSY; TONSILLITIS.

Some people are particularly prone to sore throats, but the likelihood of getting one does decrease with age. Several factors can lessen resistance to such infection, including TIREDNESS, an unhealthy diet, SMOKING, overindulgence in alcohol, or any form of STRESS – which often results from emotional problems, such as the loss of a partner or job.

Warning If a sore throat lasts more than four days, consult a doctor. It may be an early symptom of an illness such as GLANDULAR FEVER, MUMPS or SCARLET FEVER.

Self help Make sure that you get enough sleep, and follow a healthy diet (see EATING FOR HEALTH). Do not smoke or take alcohol.

A soothing drink can be made by adding the juice of half a fresh lemon, 1 teaspoon of honey and 1 tablespoon of glycerine to a glass of hot water. Alternatively, drink agrimony tea (available at health-food shops). Hot, damp air is also helpful, so put 1 teaspoon of friar's balsam in 1 pint (600ml) of hot water in a bowl, and inhale the steam under a towel for about ten minutes, up to three times a day.

What the therapists recommend
NATUROPATHY

Self help Plenty of fresh fruit juices are usually helpful. Avoid dairy products, sweets, cakes and similar foods. Sucking zinc lozenges is believed to be a good way to fight any throat infection directly, and this can be backed up by a vitamin C supplement. Steam inhalations ease congestion, and gargles with lemon juice or cider vinegar may be recommended.

HERBAL MEDICINE

Self help Sore throats and minor infections can be helped at home with regular gargles of sage or thyme, especially if fresh lemon juice is added. If you are prone to sore throats, it may be advisable to take one or two garlic capsules a day, particularly during the winter months.

Consultation For severe or recurrent throat infections, herbalists use gargles, notably tinctures of myrrh, sage, wild indigo or thyme. Remedies such as echinacea or wild indigo, to be taken internally, may be prescribed to boost the immune system. If your case is considered to be particularly serious, you will be advised also to see a doctor.

HOMOEOPATHY

Self help For a sore throat which is swollen, shiny and soggy looking, and which is worse with increasing heat, but when there is no thirst, therapists recommend *Apis mel. 30*. Burning pain in a raw throat, when the sufferer must keep swallowing and hoarseness is relieved by coughing, is treated with *Causticum 30*.

Hepar sulph. 30 is used for a sore throat with an established cold, when the patient has a sensation of something stuck in the throat, and pain shoots to the ears on swallowing, and when the sufferer is very irritable and sensitive to the least draught. For a congested, sore, dark red throat, when the patient cannot swallow even water and his neck muscles feel stiff, homoeopaths recommend a dose of _Phytolacca 30_ every two hours for a day, followed by four doses daily for two days.

An orthodox view

Most sore throats go away of their own accord. If necessary, a doctor may prescribe antibiotics to clear up bacterial infections, and in severe cases, painkillers such as paracetamol or aspirin.

THRUSH

This condition, also called candida, is caused by _Candida albicans_ or _Monilia_, a yeast-like fungus which thrives in warm, moist areas and may form white flaky patches. It may be present for long periods without causing symptoms, especially in men, but may then become troublesome due to hormonal changes, STRESS, emotional factors, an unbalanced diet and similar causes.

Thrush is particularly prevalent in babies, elderly people, fat people (see OBESITY), DIABETES sufferers, pregnant women and those taking antibiotics. It is also common where the IMMUNE SYSTEM is not functioning properly – for example, in people with AIDS or LEUKAEMIA, or those taking steroid drugs.

The thrush organism normally lives on the skin, so an infection can flare up without contact with another person. Such skin infection is common, particularly in the warm, moist skin folds of fat people. The groins, armpits and the skin under the breasts are most commonly affected, becoming inflamed and itchy. People whose work involves frequent wetting of the hands are susceptible to infection of the fingers. There is tender swelling and sometimes pus in the skin around the fingernails and, in chronic cases, deformed nails.

Babies frequently have white patches of thrush in the mouth or a red 'nappy rash' on their bottom, often with separate red spots around the rash and on their thighs. Adults sometimes get thrush in the mouth, especially if they wear dentures. If the immune system is not functioning properly, the thrush infection may spread down the oesophagus or gullet, causing pain and burning when the person eats or drinks.

Thrush infection of the vulva and vagina is common, recurrent and troublesome. It causes itching and soreness, with a white vaginal discharge, which may be thick, like curds. Although it is not necessarily sexually transmitted, a sexual partner may develop the infection, with redness and soreness of the end of the penis and under the foreskin.

Any clothing that limits the circulation of air around the body will make infection more likely, and will aggravate the condition once it is established. This is particularly true of tights, tight jeans, and underwear made from synthetic fibres.

What the therapists recommend

NATUROPATHY

Consultation Mouth and vaginal thrush has been known to respond well to natural treatments, and a practitioner may also aim to prevent a more widespread fungal invasion – of the digestive tract, for example.

You may be recommended to cut out all sugars and refined starches, alcohol, tea, coffee and chocolate drinks, but to eat plenty of vegetables, pulses and whole grains. Suggested supplements are likely to include garlic and acidophilus, in order to suppress excess fungal growth and restore the normal microorganisms in the digestive tract. Live, natural yoghurt or frequent salt washes are recommended for vaginal thrush.

HERBAL MEDICINE

Self help Tinctures of myrrh or marigold are recommended mouthwashes. A soothing vaginal wash can be made by dissolving up to 1 tablespoon of salt in 1 pint (600ml) of water. Alternatively, apply live, natural yoghurt on a sanitary pad.

Do's and don'ts for vaginal thrush

Don't wear tights, nylon pants or tight jeans or trousers.
_Do_ wear skirts, stockings or socks, and cotton pants – or none at all.
_Do_ use sanitary pads, not tampons.
Don't use perfumed toilet preparations such as soaps and bubble baths; and don't use vaginal deodorants, deodorant tampons or sanitary pads.
Don't use disinfectants in the bath.
Don't use strong detergents, particularly biologicals, when laundering linen and clothes, especially underwear.
Don't use soap if there is irritation; wipe the vulva with baby oil instead.
_Do_ wipe from front to back after using the toilet.
Don't take antibiotics unless absolutely necessary.
_Do_ tell your doctor that you are prone to thrush if he prescribes antibiotics or the contraceptive pill.
Don't bath, wash or shower more often; it will give only temporary relief.

Antibiotics are thought to upset the balance of microorganisms in the gut, allowing the _Candida_ fungus to thrive. So, after a course of antibiotics, take three to four garlic capsules a day for a week. If the thrush recurs, seek professional advice, for it may seriously damage your health.

AROMATHERAPY

Self help For oral thrush, try a mouthwash of three drops of tea tree essential oil and one drop of essential oil of myrrh in half a glass of water. Stir vigorously before use, swishing around the gums three times a day.

For vaginal thrush, dampen the tip of a tampon, add three to four drops of tea tree essential oil and insert it for one to two hours. Alternatively, use the oil in an application oil or lotion, and apply each night and morning. Regular sitz baths (see HYDROTHERAPY) with three to four drops of the above essential oils, or conventional baths with six to eight drops are also recommended.

Other alternative treatment

Biochemic Tissue Salts If cold sores on the lips accompany oral thrush, _Nat. mur. 6_ is often recommended.

An orthodox view

A doctor may check that there is no underlying cause for thrush. For example, he may test for high sugar in the urine which could indicate diabetes.

Oral thrush responds to nystatin (Nystan) drops, and skin thrush to nystatin, clotrimazole (Canesten) or imidazole (Daktarin) cream or ointment. If, as frequently happens, the thrush infection causes an ECZEMA-like reaction on the skin, the doctor may prescribe a cream or ointment containing both an antifungal agent to combat the infection and a steroid such as hydrocortisone to reduce the inflammation and itching.

Nail infections may require incisions to release the pus and prolonged treatment with antifungal agents. However, the most important measure is to avoid repeated soaking of the fingers, by wearing rubber gloves, for example.

Conventional treatments for vaginal thrush include pessaries or cream inserted high into the vagina, even during a period. Nystatin must be used for fourteen days, but newer drugs such as clotrimazole or imidazole may be effective in shorter courses – even in a single high dose. A single oral dose of fluconazole (Diflucan) is often effective when vaginal pessaries or creams fail, but it must not be used during pregnancy.

Recurrent vaginal infection is common, particularly if a sexual partner is harbouring the infection on his penis, and he too must be treated.

THYROID DISORDERS

The thyroid gland is situated in the lower part of the neck, immediately in front of the windpipe and just below the Adam's apple. It produces the thyroid hormones, iodine-containing substances that control the rate of metabolism (the body's chemical reactions and processes) and therefore our mental and physical growth and development. The thyroid is in turn controlled by the pituitary gland at the base of the skull, which secretes thyroid-stimulating hormone.

The main thyroid hormones are called T3 and T4 (also known as thyroxine). The main disorders of the gland are swelling, and under and overactivity, which can affect the body in disturbing ways.

Swelling of the gland is known as goitre. It may be caused by a lack of iodine in the diet, but this condition, known as endemic goitre, is now rare (see GOITRE). Swelling may also be due simply to overgrowth, or to a tumour, which in very rare cases may be cancerous. Unlike LEUKAEMIA, CANCER of the thyroid gland seems to be less common around nuclear installations.

Underactivity of the thyroid gland (called hypothyroidism) can begin at any age. Some babies are born with it. They have difficulty in feeding and sleeping, and suffer from CONSTIPATION and delayed mental and physical development. If it is not detected, sufferers develop coarse features. They grow short and fat, with a protruding tongue and sparse hair, and are known as cretins. Today, however, every baby born in the United Kingdom is given a blood test when only three days old, in order to detect the disease and ensure prompt treatment.

If the gland becomes underactive later in life, the symptoms develop gradually and may not be obvious at first. The patient becomes lethargic, sleeps more and unaccountably puts on weight. The hair and skin become dry, and the hair may fall out (see HAIR PROBLEMS). The eyes become puffy and the voice deepens.

In some cases, thyroid underactivity may be caused by inflammation of the gland (thyroiditis). The symptoms are similar to those of a sore throat (see THROAT PROBLEMS), but the gland is tender and swollen. The underactivity begins after an interval of weeks or months following the inflammation. Usually, however, the cause of an underactive thyroid is unknown.

Overactivity of the thyroid gland (called hyperthyroidism) results in too much of the thyroid hormones in the blood (thyrotoxicosis), the effects of which are the opposite to those of underactivity. The body's metabolism speeds up and, despite a good appetite, the sufferer loses weight, becomes restless and fidgety, and cannot sleep. There may also be a tremor – most obvious when the sufferer's hands are outstretched – along with PALPITATIONS and SWEATING. In addition, goitre may develop, and the eyes may protrude and appear to be staring.

What the therapists recommend

Acupuncture Treatment for thyroid disorders is given on the large intestine (neck area), gall bladder and governing meridians.

Herbal Medicine Iodine-rich foods such as kelp and other seaweeds may help mild thyroid disorders. As a tonic, herbalists may prescribe bladderwrack.

Severe thyroid disorders should always be diagnosed by means of blood tests and professionally treated.

Homoeopathy Overweight people with an enlarged thyroid should try *Fucus vesiculosus 3*, four times a day. Patients with an overactive thyroid are advised to try *Iodum 30* twice a day for two weeks. If the thyroid is swollen, feels hard, and the patient is constantly clearing his throat, try *Spongia 30* twice a day for two weeks.

Reflexology Thyroid disorders are said to be helped by massaging the reflex areas relating to the gland, and also those relating to the adrenal, pituitary and reproductive glands (see chart, p. 295).

An orthodox view

When it does occur, endemic goitre is treated with iodine supplements to the diet, but the use of iodised table salt has made this unnecessary in the United Kingdom.

A blood test in which low levels of thyroid hormones are found in the sample confirms diagnosis of underactivity of the thyroid gland. Doctors treat the condition in all ages with T4 (thyroxine) tablets. Patients usually have to take the tablets daily for the rest of their lives. The symptoms gradually disappear and there are no after-effects as long as the treatment is kept up.

A blood test that reveals antibodies confirms diagnosis of thyroid inflammation.

For overactivity of the thyroid gland, doctors usually prescribe a course of antithyroid tablets called carbimazole (Neo-Mercazole). Alternatively, a dose of radioactive iodine may be given to destroy part of the gland, or part of it may be removed by surgery.

As long as the patient's blood is tested regularly and any necessary treatment is given, the outlook for sufferers of both hypothyroidism and hyperthyroidism is now generally excellent.

TIC

People with a tic may repeatedly blink their eyes, clear their throat, twitch their mouth, or nod their head for no obvious reason. This nervous muscle twitch – also known as habit spasm – is a common complaint which can develop at any age.

It particularly affects children, who often are not aware there is anything 'wrong' with them. In their case it may be caused by strong feelings of insecurity, which should be understood and sympathised with. Calling attention to the child, or scolding him, will only make the condition worse. The best policy is to ignore the tic, which will disappear of its own accord, usually within a month or two. Sometimes, however, it may last into adulthood.

What the therapists recommend

Behavioural Therapy Family and friends are asked to avoid paying undue attention to the tic. The sufferer will be asked to try to achieve control over the tic by relaxation training at the times and in the situations when it is most pronounced. Another recommended technique might be to develop other physical responses that compete with the tic – for example, if the head twitches to the left, an alternative response could be to move the head to the right.

An orthodox view

There is no conventional drug treatment for tics, and no need to consult a doctor unless the condition causes undue distress or embarrassment. In some rare, extreme cases psychiatric treatment may be called for.

TIREDNESS
Combatting that tired-all-the-time feeling

All of us go through periods in our lives when we are always tired. We lose our zest for life, have no energy and are easily fatigued. We are tired when we wake up in the morning. It is hard to concentrate on daily tasks and to maintain interest in loved ones, friends and leisure activities. And we often become exceptionally irritable.

For some people, this unhappy state of affairs becomes a chronic, permanent condition. It may become overwhelming, leading to debilitating despair – and even to suicide.

Doctors sometimes call it the TATT (tired-all-the-time) syndrome.

Chronic tiredness is one of the most common reasons for a visit to a general practitioner or alternative therapist. It is also one of the most difficult to treat, because many factors can be involved in the condition, and both doctors and therapists find that the best results come from a truly holistic system of treatment – one in which the physical, psychological, spiritual and emotional facets of the sufferer and his lifestyle are considered.

Diagnosing the cause of tiredness A full case history will include details of the patient's past, particularly information about any recent traumas, such as a death in the family, the loss of a job, or a divorce. The practitioner will want to know if the tiredness occurs in bouts, and whether these can be related to any traumas or periods of 'feeling low'.

Physical aspects are also important. The practitioner will investigate the patient's diet, for one high in sugar can lead to Hypo-GLYCAEMIA, which could be the cause of the tiredness. Similarly, a lack of iron can lead to ANAEMIA, one of whose symptoms is tiredness, and which in women can also be caused by heavy periods.

Chronic tiredness can also be a symptom of PREMENSTRUAL TENSION or the MENOPAUSE, both of which are associated with hormonal imbalances. Some women experience a 'new lease of life' when put on hormone replacement therapy (see p. 238).

Other hormonal imbalances may be involved – for instance, hypothyroidism, in which the thyroid gland produces too little thyroid hormone (see THYROID DISORDERS), or Addison's disease, in which the body has too little adrenal hormone. These are rare conditions, but are easily treated.

On the other hand, MYALGIC ENCEPHALO-MYELITIS (ME) is difficult both to diagnose and to treat. Besides prolonged tiredness, patients also suffer from extreme exhaustion and muscle aches and pains, particularly after physical exertion. However, recent research has shown that a virus may be implicated in ME, and that information should at least aid diagnosis.

It has been estimated that in the UK some 10-15 per cent of the population suffer from HYPERVENTILATION, in which there is shallow, rapid chest-breathing. This leads to chemical changes in the blood – and chronic tiredness. This condition is also difficult to diagnose, but the remedy is simple: patients are retrained to breathe more slowly and deeply (see RELAXATION AND BREATHING). Hyperventilation is often a symptom of STRESS, and sufferers also need help with overcoming their personal problems.

In fact, doctors and therapists all recognise that one of the main causes of chronic tiredness is not a physical condition at all, but personal problems – often problems that the patient cannot face and has 'hidden'. Once physical causes have been eliminated, practitioners help patients to explore their personal lives, in order to uncover the cause.

For example, some people have unrealistic expectations of themselves – either too high or too low. Such people are often described as 'neurotic' or 'negative affective', and COGNITIVE THERAPY has been found to be helpful in such cases, for it teaches patients positive thinking.

Unexpressed GRIEF can also result in chronic tiredness. In such cases, people fail to mourn properly after a loss. This can be the loss of a loved one, or even a part of themselves – in the case of a woman, a breast or an unborn child; or in a man, IMPOTENCE. Grief over the loss of a job or a home can also be a cause.

Unexpressed anger often has the same effects as unexpressed grief. Many people are trapped in an intolerable life situation, and bottle up their rage. This repression uses up much of their energy, and they have little left for other things. Women are particularly prone to this condition. Many are trapped in a marriage or job where they are unable to make full use of their abilities, or their skills are not recognised. A partner may completely dominate them or fail to recognise their need to express their feelings.

In such situations, women lose their self-confidence and become prone to DEPRESSION, of which tiredness can be a symptom. Eventually they may become dependent on tranquillisers and sleeping pills. Assertiveness training will probably be able to help such patients. Women's groups are often of benefit too, for they help sufferers to talk through their problems and feelings, and to think more positively about themselves and their situation.

Today, many people face unemployment, money problems and poor, overcrowded living conditions. For example, a young family may have to share a home with their in-laws. These situations all put a strain on individuals, and they can all lead to depression. This may manifest itself as chronic tiredness, and in such cases the practitioner needs a great deal of skill to get to the heart of the matter.

The same is true of another condition in which sufferers have lost their faith or sense of purpose in life. They may be perfectly healthy, yet they feel that something is missing. Their life becomes empty of meaning, and chronic tiredness results. This frequently leads them to consult some type of therapist.

Chronic tiredness can, in itself, be both debilitating and a cause of worry – which in turn aggravates the condition. Great patience and effort on the part of both practitioner and sufferer are needed to find an effective cure.

Self help Ensure that you have adequate sleep (see SLEEP DISORDERS; INSOMNIA) and, if possible, practise relaxation and breathing exercises. Learn to express your feelings – to let go – and not keep them bottled up. Take sufficient EXERCISE.

Make sure that you eat a well-balanced diet (see EATING FOR HEALTH), with regular meals. Light, high-protein snacks between meals will probably help you to combat the tiredness. Cut down on sugar and avoid stimulants such as caffeine (in coffee, tea and cola drinks).

Make sure that your intake of MINERALS and VITAMINS is adequate – zinc, magnesium, potassium, vitamin C and folic acid are particularly important. To make sure, eat extra low-fat dairy products, yeast extracts, wheat germ, fresh and dried fruit, dark green leafy vegetables and soya products. Alternatively, take a proprietary general vitamin and mineral supplement for a month, preferably one including iron. Avoid heavy or stodgy meals at midday, and less than three hours before bedtime.

Some people experience chronic tiredness as a result of boredom. This is very often the case among those who retire from an active, totally absorbing and/or rewarding job. So, take up a new interest or hobby, or rekindle your interest in one that you know you have enjoyed in the past.

What the therapists recommend
HOMOEOPATHY
Self help If, following too much physical effort, you are unable to sleep and the bed feels too hard, try two or three doses of _Arnica 30_. After a long period of strain or study, _Phosphoric ac. 6_ three times a day for 21 days may help to restore lost energy. Two or three doses of _Kali phos._ may help when there is lack of nerve power, or mental and physical depression.

ACUPUNCTURE
Consultation Tiredness is believed often to be caused by some dysfunction of the internal organs, and treatment to those organs is given. General basic treatment consists of MOXIBUSTION combined with acupuncture to points on the bladder, gall bladder, conception, governing, large and small intestine, lung, kidney, spleen and/or stomach meridians.

MASSAGE
Self help When the tiredness is only temporary, and not a symptom of a medical condition or the companion of muscular

fatigue or exhaustion, then a brisk, light tonic, general massage is often the answer, and the means of sparking some new life into the various body systems.

A really vitalising massage could consist of rapid effleurage strokes in the direction of the venous return (towards the heart), working up the legs and arms, and over the entire back, from the lumbar to shoulder area. This is followed by stimulating petrissage wringing and squeezing techniques, and the clapping and finger hacking procedures for tapotement – all made at a brisk pace.

ACUPRESSURE
Self help Apply pressure at a point three thumbs' width from under the kneecap, in the hollow on the outer edge of the skin, pressing inwards. As an alternative, apply pressure to the centre of the palm at the point where the middle finger rests when the hand is folded inwards.

AROMATHERAPY
Self help If the tiredness is due to a physical cause, then try stimulating essential oils, such as black pepper, lemon, lemon grass and rosemary. Either inhale from a tissue, or put six to ten drops into a bath, and stay in the water for ten minutes. For mental exhaustion, use clary sage, savory or rosemary in the same ways.

For tiredness due to ME or postviral symptoms, regular use of essential oils of geranium, thyme, lemon or sage is recommended. Inhale them from a tissue or put them in a bath as above. Alternatively, make a tea by putting two or three drops of oil on a tea bag, and infusing in 1 pint (600ml) of boiling water; stir, remove the tea bag, and drink without milk as needed. Keep the surplus in the fridge, and reheat as required.

An orthodox view
The doctor will first seek any physical cause of the tiredness, and treat it accordingly. If this fails, he will help the patient to review his lifestyle, and help him to talk through any stress-causing situations. The doctor may then refer the patient to a psychotherapist or another specialist.

TISANES

This French word comes from the Latin *ptisana*, meaning 'barley', 'barley gruel' or 'barley water'. Originally it was used solely for barley water, but it gradually came to mean any weak herbal tea drunk for its mildly medicinal properties, or simply as a refreshing beverage. A herbal of 1544 recom-

mended: 'Drynke a ptisane made of barley, lyquyryce, prunes and the rotes of fenel.' Today, tisanes (or ptisans or tisans) are used extensively by herbalists; for instructions on how to make them, see HERBAL MEDICINE.

TOFU

Bean curd or tofu is used extensively in oriental cuisine. The word comes from the Mandarin Chinese *dòu*, meaning 'bean', and *fu*, 'curdled' or 'rotten'.

The curd is made by washing and rinsing soya beans, soaking them in water, then grinding them and boiling them for 15 minutes, after which the fibre is extracted by straining. The result is soya milk, which is further cooked and allowed to coagulate, calcium sulphate being added to curdle the milk. The curd is then pressed, separating the curdled milk into whey and tofu.

Tofu is now widely available, and is an important component of MACROBIOTIC diets. It is usually seasoned and steamed, sautéed, boiled or deep fried with vegetables.

TONGUE DIAGNOSIS

Traditional Chinese practitioners examine a patient's tongue to gauge the health of other parts of the body. In ORIENTAL DIAGNOSIS, each area of the tongue corresponds to a certain organ or body system, enabling a detailed diagnosis to be made.

TONSILLITIS

Children are the most common victims of tonsillitis, a highly infectious inflammation of the tonsils – two masses of tissue at the back of the throat. The complaint causes a sore throat and FEVER, sometimes accompanied by a HEADACHE and stomach ache. In addition, the neck glands are frequently swollen and there may be a dry cough.

Tonsillitis is usually caused by a virus against which children have not had time to develop a resistance. However, it may also be the result of bacteria called streptococci, of which some people are 'carriers' – even though they themselves may be perfectly healthy. Streptococcal tonsillitis with a rash which first appears on the neck and chest is called SCARLET FEVER.

Whatever the cause, tonsillitis tends to strike suddenly, and the worst of the illness is normally over within 48 hours. If the symptoms last for more than three days – or if the sufferer starts coughing up green or yellow phlegm – seek medical attention.

What the therapists recommend
Herbal Medicine Herbalists consider recurring infection and inflammation of the tonsils to be a key factor in illness in later life. They therefore treat the entire IMMUNE SYSTEM, aiming to eliminate this risk. For example, they may advise gargles made with myrrh, sage, thyme or wild indigo. Taking extra vitamin C may also help to boost the body's defence system, especially in the winter.

Homoeopathy If the tonsils are inflamed and bright red, and there is difficulty in swallowing, try *Belladonna 30*. If the throat is dark red and swollen, with unpleasant breath and thirst – and if the symptoms are worse when talking and at night – try *Merc. sol. 30*. Take one dose each hour for up to 12 hours; then three times a day for two days.

Naturopathy In cases of nasal congestion, and if the ADENOIDS are also affected, avoid dairy products. Naturopaths may prescribe sage or thyme gargles, with fresh lemon juice. One or two GARLIC capsules taken each day, especially in the winter, may also help.

An orthodox view
If tonsillitis has been caused by bacteria, and the symptoms are prolonged or the patient is ill with a raised temperature, a GP may prescribe an antibiotic such as penicillin. However, if there is no fever, and the patient is not ill – as is often the case – penicillin is unlikely to help and may provoke ALLERGY or THRUSH. If the disease is the result of a virus, antibiotics will not be effective.

For treatment at home, doctors will advise patients to drink plenty of fluids, not to worry if they don't feel like eating, take painkillers such as aspirin or paracetamol, and go to bed when the symptoms are at their height.

TOOTH AND GUM DISORDERS

We all suffer from toothache at some time or other – usually because we have not been taking proper care of our teeth and gums. The two most common diseases of the mouth are dental caries (decay) and GINGIVITIS (inflammation of the gums in which

Brushing and flossing your way to dental health

One of the most effective ways of taking care of people's teeth was devised in the 1950s by an American pathologist, Dr Charles C. Bass. The Bass method of brushing and flossing is concentrated against plaque, a thin film containing bacteria that forms between the teeth and where the teeth meet the gums – and which is a major cause of gum diseases. To remove plaque, teeth should be brushed for five minutes morning or night with fluoride toothpaste, and for two to three minutes at other times during the day. Put a dab of toothpaste on a nylon-tufted toothbrush with a small, flat head. Do not put water on the brush; the saliva in your mouth provides all the moisture you need, and too much paste and froth only hampers the cleaning process.

Even regular brushing, however, will not get rid of all the plaque that builds up between teeth and gums. As a supplement, run dental floss – a strong, unspun, nylon thread – between your teeth once a day for a few minutes. Some people may find flossing difficult to do and they should use wooden sticks instead – especially if they have gaps between their teeth. Although plaque is almost invisible, it can be seen by chewing a disclosing tablet. These tablets contain a dye that stains areas of plaque.

Everything you need for regular dental care can be bought at a good chemist's.

Brushing

1 Start with the upper, left-hand side of your mouth. Put the toothbrush at an angle of 45° against the top of your teeth and the bottom of your gum. Brush the outside surface of the teeth by moving the toothbrush head from side to side with short, vibratory strokes. The aim is to keep the bristles in the same area and so demolish the plaque. Then work the brush along the other side of your mouth. Take care not to brush too hard and bruise the gums.

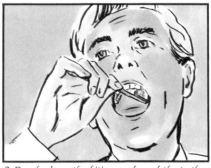

2 Brush the inside surface of the teeth in the same side-to-side way, tilting the brush to make access easier.

3 Brush along the biting surface of the teeth, holding the brush steady and using firm, horizontal strokes.
Finish the procedure – which should be carried out twice a day – by brushing your lower teeth in a similar manner.

Flossing

1 Take an unused length of floss about 1½ times the span of your hand.

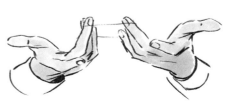

2 Make a loop of the floss and secure with a double-knot. Put the loop over the last three fingers of each hand in a cat's cradle. Leave your forefingers and thumbs free for controlling the floss.

3 Fit the floss in a straight line between the centre of your two upper front teeth. Draw the floss firmly between the sides of the teeth with a sawing action. When the floss moves easily take it to where the teeth join the gum. Hold the floss tightly against the sides of the teeth and wipe downwards. Take care not to damage the gum between the teeth. Floss all the way around your upper teeth.

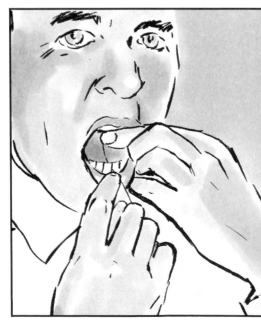

4 Repeat the process on lower teeth, wiping upwards. Afterwards, rinse your mouth, drawing the water through your teeth.

they turn bright pink and bleed easily). Dental decay can start in infancy and last throughout life, and gingivitis can occur as early as the age of five or less. Another troublesome (and very painful) condition is a tooth abscess, or gumboil (see BOILS) – a pus-filled sac which forms in the tissue at the tip of the tooth's root.

All these conditions can be avoided, or relieved, by having a dental check-up twice a year – and by taking thorough care of your teeth in between.

Self help A cheap and effective tooth-powder that you can make up easily at home is a mixture of two parts of sodium bicarbonate to one part of table salt. Alternatively, simply clean your teeth with pure lemon juice. First dip the toothbrush in warm water, then squeeze a few drops of the juice onto it. Be sure to rinse your mouth thoroughly after brushing with lemon juice.

What the therapists recommend

HOMOEOPATHY

Self help For an acute tooth abscess which is red, swollen and throbbing, try *Belladonna 200* hourly. Once the pus begins to drain away, take *Silicea*. For a less serious, or a chronic abscess, *Hepar sulph. 30* or *200* may help. *Silicea* is recommended when the abscess starts to drain.

Before and after a tooth is extracted *Arnica 30* is suggested to try and reduce shock, bleeding and the risk of blood-poisoning. Take the remedy hourly for three hours before the extraction and for three or four hours after it.

If splinters of tooth or bone are left in the gum after an extraction, *Silicea 6* taken four times daily may help to bring them to the surface. If there is still pain, *Hypericum 30* is said to be effective. In addition, a mouthwash of *Hypericum* mother tincture – ten drops in half a wine glass of boiled warm water – is said to help ease discomfort and speed up healing. The mouthwash can also be used for inflamed and sore gums.

For teeth which are painful and sensitive to cold after extensive dental work, try *Chamomilla 6* four times a day for two or three days. In the case of dental haemorrhage, when there is a lot of bright red blood, try *Phosphorus 30*. Take three doses, one every ten minutes, and then hourly as needed.

HERBAL MEDICINE

Consultation You will be told that decayed teeth should be treated by a dentist by means of fillings, or other dental work. However, herbalists believe that mouth disorders can be a sign of general ill health, and may recommend changes of diet – such as eating less sugar and fewer sweet things such as puddings, cakes and biscuits. Mouthwashes

or tinctures of marigold, myrrh and wild indigo may be prescribed to strengthen the gums and disinfect the mouth generally.

An orthodox view

Teeth should be cleaned regularly as shown in *Brushing and flossing your way to dental health*, p. 345.

Always see your dentist if your teeth or gums hurt, or if your gums begin to bleed.

TOUCH FOR HEALTH

This modified form of basic KINESIOLOGY seeks to channel energies in the body to enhance health and help to prevent sickness. It was founded in the early 1970s by an American chiropractor, Dr John Thie, who claimed that it could help to relieve aches and pains, release emotional TENSION, improve posture, increase energy, and promote a sense of well-being and relaxation.

It is a programme for lay people, who learn to use a series of muscle tests to detect physical imbalances and the effects of their emotions. They then try to correct the faults with deep MASSAGE or light touch, and so, it is said, restore the body's natural energy flow. Special classes are held in the method. For further information contact the British Touch for Health Association, 8 Railey Mews, London NW5 2PA.

TRADITIONAL MEDICINE
Folk remedies and country cures

From the earliest recorded times, people of all cultures have used plants for medicine as well as food. Before it became handed-down knowledge, our forebears must have learnt by a mixture of instinct and trial and error what was good to eat and what could heal them in times of sickness. Although some of this folk wisdom has been lost, much survives – particularly in Britain's rural areas – and many ancient plant remedies can be found among those still used in both alternative and conventional medicine.

Many animals have self-healing instincts; for example, dogs will search out couch grass to make themselves vomit when they have a stomach upset, while sheep will eat ivy leaves and horses chew the bark of

particular trees. Today, with so much known about the value of different plants, it is difficult to say if people still have similar instincts, but it may be that food cravings during pregnancy and the desire for fresh salads after winter are examples.

Some traditional cures have disappeared because in the past such knowledge was taken for granted and not considered worth writing down. The herbalist John Pechey wrote in the introduction to his *Compleat Herbal*, published in 1694: 'I have only described such plants as grow in England and are not commonly known; for I thought it needless to trouble the reader with the description of those that every Woman knows, or keeps in her garden.'

Even so, many traditional remedies remain in use. Until the NATIONAL HEALTH SERVICE began in 1948, professional medical treatment was a luxury not everyone could afford, and poor transport in many areas also meant that doctors were called only in a crisis. As a result, cheap and simple treatments that people could apply themselves often played a major part in healing even serious conditions.

In Scotland, for example, a letter from an 18th-century mother records how she successfully nursed her 11 children through smallpox – the letter does not specify the remedy, but saffron was frequently used – while pregnant with the 12th. And the story is still told of a Norfolk village woman who, in the 1930s, refused hospital treatment when she fell from a haystack and broke both wrists. Instead, she is said to have splinted them herself and healed them successfully by using comfrey.

Mostly, however, folk cures were used for treating common, minor ailments at home when it was thought unnecessary to call a doctor. Although many make use of plants we tend now to regard as weeds, much of the advice has turned out to have some sort of scientific basis, as in the case of feverfew and bark of willow (see below). Here are some common complaints and their traditional remedies:

Anaemia A tonic made from stinging nettles was a popular cure for ANAEMIA or loss of blood due to heavy periods. In spring the tops of young nettles were gathered and boiled in water, a small quantity of which was then drunk every day. Alternatively, young nettles could be steamed and eaten as a vegetable, or mixed with lemon juice and egg white in a spring pudding.

Arthritis In many places, drinking cod liver oil was recommended to relieve the pain.

Backache Muscular TENSION and BACK PAIN were treated by placing a thick piece of red flannel over the spot and ironing it with a slightly warm iron. Backaches resulting from kidney trouble were treated with an infusion (see p. 184) of juniper berries.

Boils Poultices were generally used to bring BOILS to a head. They were made from bread, cabbage leaves, or boiled up hedge mallow or groundsel, applied hot to the area.

Chilblains Some home remedies for CHILBLAINS were rather extreme, such as one which involved beating the feet with holly leaves until they bled. For those who could afford it, wine was a recommended soothing lotion, but the less well-off were advised to dip their feet into the contents of the chamber pot every morning. Another popular 'cure' was to rub the chilblains with a raw potato sprinkled with salt.

Colds For centuries onions have been regarded as a cure for COLDS and FEVER, and modern science has shown them to contain a large number of medicinal substances, some previously unknown. They were often taken as gruel made by stewing them in milk.

Other cures included horehound and peppermint infusions, and children were frequently given a tallow or goosegrease plaster at the beginning of winter to ward off colds. A piece of brown paper, often heart-shaped, was well coated, then wrapped around the child's chest or, in some instances, stitched in the vest. Some children would wear them throughout the winter.

Constipation Many people still remember the weekly dose of brimstone (sulphur) and treacle which was traditionally given to children to prevent CONSTIPATION. Rhubarb and the nut-like fruits of hedge mallow were also used as mild laxatives.

Coughs A simple, popular remedy was to cut a turnip into slices and coat them with brown sugar. Overnight this formed a thick syrup which was said to soothe COUGHS.

Cramp Keeping a cork in bed could relieve night CRAMP, according to popular belief.

Cuts The spores of the puffball mushroom were often relied upon to stop bleeding in animals as well as people. Many country families kept a dried puffball in the house as a first aid remedy, and barbers also used them when careless with the razor.

Even serious cuts were often treated with cobwebs, and in Suffolk a lotion made from madonna lily petals steeped in brandy was a popular treatment for both cuts and bruises.

Cystitis One soothing cure was an infusion made from 1oz (30g) of couch grass roots in 1 pint (600ml) of water.

Diarrhoea Apples, or acorns boiled in milk, were recommended to stop DIARRHOEA.

Earache In country districts a small onion was often roasted and placed in the ear, or a parcel of muslin containing boiled onions applied hot to it. The juice of leeks was sometimes also dripped into the ear.

Fever The juice of willow leaves has long been used to bring down a high temperature. When scientists analysed its contents they found that the active principle was a substance which they called 'salicylic acid' (*salix* is Latin for 'willow'). Today salicylic acid can be produced in the laboratory and is the raw material from which aspirin is made.

Headache One favoured cure is recorded in the well-known nursery rhyme:

Jack and Jill went up the hill
To fetch a pail of water.
Jack fell down and broke his crown
And Jill came tumbling after.
Up Jack got and home did trot
As fast as he could caper.
He went to bed to mend his head
With vinegar and brown paper.

Rhubarb leaves were sometimes used instead of vinegar and brown paper, and preparations made from the herb feverfew were also popular. Feverfew is now believed by scientists to contain substances which are effective HEADACHE and MIGRAINE relievers.

Influenza Elderberry wine and onion broth have a reputation for easing 'flu' symptoms.

An infusion or wine made from elder flowers is also said to induce sweating and bring about relief.

Insect stings The old wash-day 'blue-bag' was often applied to BEE STINGS, while WASP STINGS were generally treated with vinegar. Moistened or chewed tobacco was believed to relieve both pain and swelling, and crushed plantain or marigold leaves to soothe any sort of sting.

Nettle stings Dock leaves are the traditional cure. The victim rubbed them onto the sting while repeating the rhyme:

Nettle out, dock in.
Dock remove the nettle sting.

Nosebleeds Most folk cures involved giving the victim a mild shock of some sort, for example by dropping a large key or a cold coin down the back, or slapping a cold flannel onto the forehead. The success of such methods is probably due to shock causing the blood vessels to constrict and slow the bleeding. Remedies were also made from herbs such as yarrow and witch hazel.

Rheumatism Many country people liked to

The unhappy inmates of Dotheboy's Hall are dosed with brimstone and treacle in Dickens' 'Nicholas Nickleby'.

The royal touch

For many centuries there was a tradition in England that the monarch's touch could cure the King's Evil (scrofula) – agonising, often fatal tuberculosis of the lymph nodes, usually those in the neck.

The ability to cure the disease was believed to have begun with Edward the Confessor, who was said to have received it as a divine gift and to have passed it on to subsequent rulers. Confidence in the royal cure lasted until the time of Queen Anne, who reigned from 1702 to 1714 and was the last monarch to bestow her touch on sufferers.

Charles II confers his touch on a scrofula victim. A special coin in which the king's power was said to reside is being hung around his neighbour's neck.

carry a potato or an onion in their pocket to ward off RHEUMATISM. In East Anglia, white horse oils – their recipes were usually secret, although the common constituents included turpentine, vinegar and egg-white – were rubbed onto sore joints, and a liniment made from turpentine, vinegar and fresh beaten eggs was said to relieve pain. Small doses – usually a daily small sherry glassful – of an infusion of young nettle tops gathered in the spring were also claimed to help.

Sleeplessness Many people still find that a spoon of honey at night helps them to sleep. Other traditional sleep promoters include water in which lettuce has been boiled, and an infusion of lemon balm.

Sore throat One of the more unpleasant 'cures' was to tie a used sock around the victim's throat. Luckier patients received a teaspoon of blackcurrant jam diluted with a little hot water, a mixture of honey and fresh lemon juice in hot water, or a sage infusion to gargle with.

Sore eyes Cold tea and milk – particularly mother's milk – were reputed to soothe sore eyes, as were infusions of speedwell or eyebright flowers.

Spots and pimples Teenage skin problems have long been treated with oatmeal boiled in milk, strained, and the resulting liquid used to bathe the skin. Drinking an infusion of young stinging nettles is also said to clear the complexion, and rose water and cucumber juice are both valued traditional skin lotions.

Sprains Raw, bruised cabbage leaves were used to make a comforting dressing for minor SPRAINS. More serious injuries involving ligament or bone damage were treated with a comfrey poultice (see p. 184) – a centuries-old method of promoting healing and easing pain.

Sunburn Folk remedies include a soothing mixture of water and vinegar, and a lotion made from dock roots.

Teething troubles In the past, wild poppy seeds were given to babies to ease the pain of teething. They were also used as a HANG-OVER cure.

Toothache Traditionally, brown paper was moistened with vinegar, covered with pepper or mustard and tied around the face to relieve toothache.

Grated horseradish applied to the cheek was used for NEURALGIA as well as tooth-ache, and lavender water was also some-times dripped onto a painful tooth. Other trusted home remedies included chewing cloves or blackberry leaves.

Warts In many villages it was thought that WARTS could be charmed away, often by a particular person. Sometimes they had to be 'bought' for a penny, but on other occasions simply counting them was enough.

Another procedure involved getting an ash tree to 'buy' the warts. The warts were pricked with a pin, which was then stuck into the tree while the victim said:

Ashen tree, ashen tree,
Pray buy these warts from me.

Less superstitious cures were also used, for example applications of juice of spurge, dandelion and greater celandine were all thought to help get rid of warts.

Whooping cough In many places, eating fried mouse – said to taste much like rabbit – was the favoured treatment. Other unlikely remedies included hanging a fish around the victim's neck, or getting him to inhale fumes from the gas works or walk through a field of beans in bloom.

More promising was a traditional mixture of honey, ipecacuanha wine and friar's balsam. This was said to remove a lot of phlegm, but it often made the child vomit.

An orthodox view

Folk cures and traditional medicines will always form a large part of any approach to health care, no matter what culture is involved. Many modern medical drugs are derived from some of these traditional cures. Although certain ingredients in them have been known to prove harmful, the majority view is that these treatments are safe.

Several surveys have indicated very low levels of side effects, and many people continue to rely on these approaches to relieve disorders that are not serious and which usually clear up of their own accord.

TRANSACTIONAL ANALYSIS
How to build better relationships

An American psychiatrist, Dr Eric Berne (1910-1970), combined the here-and-now approach of HUMANISTIC PSYCHOLOGY and BEHAVIOURAL THERAPY – aimed at solving particular problems, rather than analysing a patient's whole personality – with the depth and insight of psychoanalysis. He developed his technique, transactional analysis, in the 1950s and 60s, and popularised it in his book, _Games People Play_, which was first published in 1961. The technique was intended to be a quicker, more practical way of treating patients than the traditional Freudian technique of psychoanalysis.

The result was a psychological theory and a type of PSYCHOTHERAPY which could explain people's development, their mental functioning and their relationships in simple, easily understood terms. Berne incorporated ideas from many different branches of psychology and put them together in an original, accessible way to form the new therapy.

According to transactional analysis, each person has three sides to his personality – or three 'ego states' – a 'parent', an 'adult' and a 'child', each with its own ways of thinking, feeling and behaving.

The parent is the responsible, caring side of the personality which tries to nurture and control both the person himself and other people around him. It is made up of all the attitudes, values and judgments learnt from authority figures such as parents and teachers, who have influenced us and whom we have imitated, even if unconsciously or in early childhood.

The adult, in contrast, is concerned with 'objective' functioning in the world and within ourselves. It allows us to reason, assess information and make realistic decisions. This side of the personality works rather like a computer, building up a picture of reality and of ourselves.

The child is a complex part of the personality, and consists of memories and early experiences that still exert an influence. It has two aspects, the 'natural child' and the 'adapted child'. The first is the source of all joy, creativity, intimacy with other people and capacity for play, as well as our needs for love, comfort and security.

The second aspect is composed of techniques we developed as children to cope with powerful grown-ups, and which we still use in dealing with others. The adapted child enables us to cooperate and participate in groups, but can also be more negatively expressed as rebelliousness or withdrawal.

A healthy personality means being able to use all three states as constructively as possible in daily interchanges with other people – called 'transactions' by Berne. In particular, a strong, well-functioning adult state is considered essential for psychological health and stability.

Berne believed that many emotional problems arise because people become locked in repetitive and destructive transactions with each other, where they regularly – but unconsciously – express negative aspects of their parent and child personalities, and provoke negative responses in return.

These destructive 'games', as he called them, were also thought to play a part in each person's 'life script' – a sort of half-conscious plan of how life should go that is built up in childhood and that influences later choices and decisions.

Who it can help Transactional analysis is said to be particularly suitable for those who have difficulty asserting themselves, or who constantly seem to undermine themselves, damage their relationships or are 'their own worst enemy'.

Its clear and easily understandable theory and methods appeal to many people who want fast, practical help with particular problems, but may frustrate those in search of a deeper understanding or self-knowledge.

Finding a therapist Treatment is not offered on the National Health Service, but the Institute of Transactional Analysis, BM Box 4104, London WC1N 3XX, can put you in touch with private practitioners in your area. All qualified therapists are Clinical Members of the Institute who have completed at least a four-year supervised training programme.

Consulting a therapist Before therapy begins you are usually expected to state definite goals that you want to achieve, and to commit yourself to them in a contract with the therapist. Goals are usually aimed at specific short-term results, but contracts can also be tailored to suit individual needs for deeper or lengthier treatment.

During therapy, patients are helped to understand the way their inner parent, adult and child personalities interact, and how they function in relationships with others, so that more constructive transactions can occur. They are also encouraged to build a more positive life script, and are shown how to stop playing destructive games in their everyday life.

Sessions are usually given in groups and tend to be well organised and directly aimed at achieving the laid-down goals. The therapist plays a more active role than in psychoanalysis and concentrates on patients' behaviour and ways of relating to others rather than on delving into deep or hidden aspects of the personality.

An orthodox view

This is a very helpful and easily accessible mental therapy. It avoids the complicated language of psychoanalysis and can bring psychological help to a far wider group.

TURKISH BATH

Unlike a SAUNA BATH, the heat from a Turkish bath is so moist that the perspiration it causes does not evaporate. The body, therefore, cannot cool down and perspires even more heavily. This is said to help flush impurities from the system and to aid people suffering from fluid retention. However, anyone with high BLOOD PRESSURE, a HEART DISORDER or a CIRCULATION PROBLEM should first consult their doctor. See HYDROTHERAPY.

ULCERS

There are many different kinds of ulcer – the medical term for a break in the skin or the mucous lining of the gut or mouth that does not heal. They range from peptic ulcers – painful and potentially serious ones in the digestive tract – to small mouth ulcers. Elderly people in particular can suffer extensive skin ulcers, caused by CIRCULATION PROBLEMS or VARICOSE VEINS.

Gastric (stomach) ulcers, duodenal ulcers (in the small intestine) and oesophageal (gullet) ulcers are caused by excess acid and/or the digestive enzyme pepsin. Small ones often develop, but cause no symptoms and heal without treatment. More serious stomach ulcers occur most often in men of 60 to 80, and result in recurrent upper abdominal pain and vomiting. A severe attack may last up to eight weeks.

On the other hand, duodenal ulcers occur mostly in young men subject to STRESS, and produce dull recurrent pain in the upper and central abdomen.

The pain of peptic ulcers is relieved by milk and alkalis, but aggravated by stress, excess stomach acid (see ACID STOMACH) and SMOKING, which increases acid production. The pain occurs after meals and there is tenderness below the breastbone.

Rarely, peptic ulcers bleed, causing bloody vomiting and black faeces. They may also perforate – rupture – and let the gut contents, including bacteria, into the abdomen, causing peritonitis, with severe pain and perhaps shock and a rigid abdominal wall.

Warning Any severe abdominal pain should be investigated by a doctor, and a perforated ulcer in particular demands immediate medical treatment. Leg ulcers, which are notoriously slow and difficult to heal, should also receive medical attention.

What the therapists recommend
HOMOEOPATHY
Peptic ulcers *Argent. nit.* is recommended when there is FLATULENCE and gnawing pain in the pit of the stomach, which is worse when pressure is applied and after food, and the sufferer craves sweet things that aggravate the pain. Try *Arsen. alb.* if the sufferer is anxious and meticulous, experiences DIARRHOEA and burning pain immediately after food, and has no appetite. *Lycopodium* is recommended for flatulence, and the sufferer feels full after the smallest amount of food, desires sweet foods and cannot bear tight clothing. When the sufferer has pain half an hour after eating, headache and constipation, feels better after vomiting,

and is irritable, especially in the morning, *Nux vomica* may help. These preparations should each be taken in the 6th potency.
Leg (varicose) ulcers The following remedies are said to promote healing; use the 6th potency and take three or four times daily for 21 days – or less if improvement occurs sooner: *Kali bich.* if the ulcer looks as if cut out with a punch and there is a white discharge; *Hamamelis* if varicose veins are prevalent; *Nitric acid* if the ulcers bleed easily and there are pains similar to those caused by splinters; *Merc. sol.* if the discharge is smelly; *Carbo veg.* if the sufferer is elderly with poor circulation and respiratory problems; *Lachesis* if the ulcer is deep and bleeds easily, there is a putrid discharge and the surrounding skin is purplish-blue.

NATUROPATHY
Peptic ulcers The advice is to eat little and often, gradually building on an initial bland diet by including more vegetables, especially cooked ones, pulses and grains. Avoid tobacco, alcohol and sugar. It is also important to find ways of relaxing and releasing tension (see RELAXATION AND BREATHING).
Leg ulcers Practitioners often suggest a vitamin E supplement to promote healing, for example 400iu a day.

ACUPUNCTURE
Gastric and duodenal ulcers Points on the liver, stomach, spleen, conception, bladder and governing meridians are treated.
Leg ulcers Local points are treated, and also the corresponding points on the other side of the body. Points on the meridians passing through the affected area – usually the lung and spleen meridians – and the large intestine and governing meridians are also treated.

Other alternative treatment
Herbal Medicine Liquorice or comfrey may be recommended for peptic and varicose ulcers. See also MOUTH ULCERS.

An orthodox view
Doctors can usually diagnose peptic ulcers from their symptoms. However, tests in an outpatients' clinic may be necessary. The patient fasts for 12 hours before his appointment, and is given a light sedative. A gastroscope is introduced into the gut. This is a type of endoscope – a fine rubber tube with an optical device for viewing inside the body – and allows identification of any abnormalities, such as ulcers, in the gut walls.

Modern drugs such as cimetidine (Tagamet) and ranitidine (Zantac) reduce the output of stomach acid and permit healing. Surgery for peptic ulcers has become unusual since the introduction of such drugs.

Do's and don'ts for peptic ulcers
Do eat a wholefood diet (see EATING FOR HEALTH).
Do try to relax and control your stress.
Do make sure that you have enough sleep (see SLEEP DISORDERS).
Do take regular EXERCISE.
Don't smoke.
Don't drink coffee, tea, alcohol or cola.
Don't eat refined sugar, refined flour or their products, or junk food.
Don't eat hot, spicy foods, or highly acid items such as apples.
Don't take aspirin or anti-inflammatory drugs if possible, especially on an empty stomach; they irritate the gut.

Skin ulcers can be prevented by regular exercise, wearing support socks, stockings or tights if you have varicose veins, and by avoiding injury to a fragile skin (see SKIN DISORDERS). Skin ulcers, particularly varicose ulcers, need skilled nursing. Regular dressings and compression bandages, which improve blood circulation, help, but healing can take a long time, perhaps years. In severe cases, skin grafts may be advised.

ULTRASONICS

The therapeutic use of ultrasound – sound waves too high-pitched to be detected by the human ear – is known as ultrasonics. The waves are produced by placing a quartz crystal in an electric field, which causes it to vibrate at a high frequency.

Ultrasonics is a form of SOUND THERAPY, and is said to be particularly effective for treating SPORTS INJURIES, SPRAINS and strained muscles. It is thought to work by producing heat when used in higher doses, and by bringing about direct changes in body cells at lower doses. Therapists who use the technique say that the effect is to speed up healing in soft tissues and bones, and to relieve pain by changing the way in which nerve impulses are conducted.

In orthodox medicine, ultrasonic waves are used to build up pictures of organs and tissues inside the body, for example, to diagnose the state of a patient's heart or check on the progress of a baby in the womb. High-frequency sound waves are directed at the appropriate part of the body and an image of its internal appearance is then created from the echo that comes back.

VAGINAL DISORDERS

Some discharge from the vagina is normal, but when it itches and the discharge is excessive and there is an unpleasant odour, there may be an infection. This is most frequently due to _Candida albicans_, the fungus that causes THRUSH. Alternatively, _Trichomonas_, a small oval microorganism, or a bacterium such as that causing gonorrhoea may be the cause. A tampon left in after a period has finished can also cause an unpleasant vaginal discharge, as can thread-worm infection (see WORMS). The vulva – the vaginal lips – may also itch as a result of a vaginal infection.

After the MENOPAUSE, lack of hormones may cause a dry, irritated, sore vagina, and there is often pain during sexual intercourse.

A tender swelling of the small mucus-excreting glands – known as Bartholin's glands – near the vaginal opening is known as Bartholinitis. The glands may become infected but will not become cancerous.

CANCER of the vagina is rare, but cancer can spread to the vagina from the cervix, the mouth of the womb. Regular cervical smear tests should detect any irregularity long before this stage, however.

What the therapists recommend
HOMOEOPATHY
Self help   Several remedies are offered:
Itching vulva   When the area is itchy with an unpleasant odour, and these are worse when the sufferer is hot and after washing, try _Sulphur 6_. For an itchy, red eruption which is relieved by heat, use _Rhus tox. 6_. Take the remedies three times daily for 14 days.
Menopausal dryness   Apply _Calendula_ cream to soothe and lubricate. _Bryonia 30_ is said to help the dryness in women who also tend to be constipated and have chest problems. _Nat. mur._ may be better for women who have tearful depression. In both cases, take the remedy morning and night for 14 days. If the condition continues, seek homoeopathic medical help.
Bartholinitis   Use _Belladonna 30_ during the early stages of the infection when the area is hot, red and swollen. If there is a discharge of yellow pus and the area is very tender, use _Hepar sulph. 30_. Take either remedy four times daily for three to four days.

Other alternative treatments
Naturopathy   A consultation is recommended, but local salt washes or applications of live yoghurt are often helpful.

Herbal Medicine   A consultation is recommended. Herbalists give local douches and washes, and use eliminative and/or hormonal remedies internally to restore the natural vaginal defences.

An orthodox view
If the discharge is caused by an infection, the cause will be revealed by laboratory examination of a swab taken from the vagina. Antibiotic or antifungal tablets or pessaries are then prescribed. Unfortunately, vaginal infections such as thrush tend to recur. Alternative remedies are often just as helpful as conventional medicine in the prevention of recurrent vaginal discharges, but if you do have one, consult your doctor to check that you are not suffering from DIABETES.

For menopausal vaginitis, doctors prescribe oestrogen cream to be applied regularly to the vagina, or oral hormone replacement therapy (HRT; see p. 238).

Swollen or infected Bartholin's glands are treated by a minor operation to drain away the fluid or pus.

VARICOSE VEINS

In this often painful condition, veins become distended, lengthened and 'knotted'. The surface veins of the legs are most commonly affected, but veins inside the rectum may also become varicose (see PILES), and varicose veins also sometimes occur around the vulva – female external sex organs – in PREGNANCY.

Obstruction of the blood flow is the prime cause of varicose veins, and this usually occurs when an organ presses on nearby blood vessels. In the case of leg veins, the problem usually arises in the rectum. The obstructed blood flow causes the veins' one-way valves to lose their efficiency, allowing blood to flow backwards, away from the heart. The result is increased pressure and distension of the veins.

Varicose leg veins are common from the teenage years onwards, and are particularly frequent in pregnancy. If only small they may cause no noticeable symptoms, but if extensive they result in aching legs – particularly after standing – and sometimes swollen ankles. People who spend long periods standing, such as housewives and police officers, are particularly susceptible. OBESITY can also be a contributory factor.

A varicose vein may become inflamed, causing pain and redness – a condition

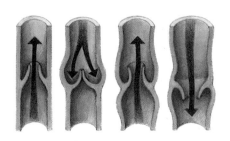

Valve in a healthy vein (left) halts the backward flow of blood. Faulty valve in a varicose vein (right) lets blood run back.

known as phlebitis. Sometimes blood clots form, and are felt as hard lumps in the veins. If the circulation is severely impaired, the blood supply to the skin may be inadequate and varicose (skin) ULCERS develop.

What the therapists recommend
NATUROPATHY
Self help   Hot and cold baths or splashes are useful. Sufferers are advised to take plenty of EXERCISE. They should avoid standing for long periods, and try to relax for short spells with legs raised on a cushion, especially in the evening.
Consultation   Dietary changes may be recommended, particularly if the sufferer is overweight. Supplements such as vitamins C and E, rutin and lecithin may be suggested.

An orthodox view
It is not possible to repair damaged blood-vessel valves, but doctors advise sufferers to help their circulation by taking regular exercise and wearing support socks, stockings or tights. They should avoid standing for long periods, and also sitting with legs crossed. A diet high in FIBRE will help to avoid constipation, and so relieve any obstruction of the blood flow in the pelvic region, where the rectum presses on the blood vessels.

A doctor may suggest injection of trouble-some veins with a chemical such as etha-nolamine to shrink or close them. In more severe cases, surgery may be necessary to strip out the veins through incisions in the leg. Once veins have been blocked by injection or stripped out, blood will reroute through other veins, which, under pressure, may in time also become varicose.

VEGANISM

The diet that vegans follow contains no animal produce. All their food is entirely of vegetable origin. See SENSIBLE WAYS TO 'GO VEGETARIAN', p. 352.

Sensible ways to 'go vegetarian'

People become vegetarians for a variety of reasons, from simple concern for animals or for their own health, to complex religious beliefs. A meatless diet is neither a cure-all nor an obstacle to health – which may be improved or damaged according to how the diet is managed.

True vegetarians do not eat meat or fish, but many will eat animal produce other than flesh, such as eggs, milk and cheese. Vegans do not eat any animal produce at all, so their diet consists entirely of foods of plant origin. A third group might be called partial vegetarians – people who have eliminated all or most meat from their diet, but who eat fish. All types of diet from regular meat-eating to wholly vegan can provide a basis for a healthy life – if properly managed. There are nutritional benefits but also risks associated with each style of eating. See EATING FOR HEALTH.

Eating lots of red meats, eggs and dairy foods may overload the diet with fat, though this need not be so if lean meats and reduced-fat cheeses are selected. The diet will ensure ample intake of iron and calcium but its content of starch and fibre may be low.

Vegans will not have fat, starch or fibre problems, but need to take care over vitamin B12, iron, calcium and zinc. Vegetarians who rely too much on eggs and cheese will, like big meat eaters, run the risk of too many calories and saturated fats. They will not, however, share the vegans' potential shortage of calcium, iron or vitamin B12. See the tables of foods rich in various nutrients on p. 357.

Vegetarian sources of vital nutrients

Protein   Meeting protein needs is rarely a problem for vegetarians in Britain. Many foods contain only small amounts of protein in themselves but together they make a useful contribution to overall protein intake. Beans, lentils, peas, bread, potatoes, porridge, rice and vegetables all contribute protein to the diet.

Vegetarians who also eat cheese, milk and eggs get ample protein, but vegans need to take a little care. Dried beans and other pulses are likely to figure prominently in their diet. Beans contain as much protein per pound as meat when dry, but when rehydrated and cooked they contain much less – about a third as much per serving as meat. This is about the same protein content as bread.

There are differences between the proteins in various foods. They all contain a mixture of more than 20 amino acids, but in varying proportions. The amino-acid profiles of some proteins make them easier for the body to use. Sometimes, combining different foods makes the protein easier to use. Pulse-and-cereal combinations such as beans and bread have a protein value that matches meat.

Vitamin B12   Only animal foods and microorganisms such as moulds contain vitamin B12. Vegans, therefore, have to take particular care to ensure their supply. Many decide to take vitamin pills. Breast-fed infants of vegan mothers will suffer a deficiency unless they are given a supplement; consult a doctor about what is suitable.

Many foods contain harmless traces of mould that yield some B12. Indeed, for the millions of vegans throughout the world these, together with fermented foods and drinks, are the source of their B12. Because vegetarian food in this country is much cleaner now than it once was, it provides less of the vital B12 via moulds. Vegans can increase their intake by spreading their bread with yeast extract.

Vegetarians will get ample B12 from milk and eggs.

Iron   Meat, especially red meat and offal, is the food that contains most iron. The iron in meat – reduced ferrous iron – is also easy for the body to absorb.

Fibre-rich foods such as vegetables, cereals and, to a lesser extent, fruits contain some iron, but as oxidised ferric iron which is not readily absorbed. To convert it to an easy-to-absorb form, you should eat vitamin C (in oranges or tomatoes, for example) at the same meal.

It is not only vegetarians and vegans who need to take care about this. Now that health promotion is urging people to eat less red meat to help reduce fat consumption, there is the accompanying risk of iron deficiency. Many people are already on a marginal iron intake that is barely sufficient to meet the body's needs. Women who experience heavy blood loss (hence iron loss) at menstruation should pay particular attention to boosting their iron intake.

Calcium   Milk and its derivatives butter, cream, cheese and YOGHURT are the main sources of calcium in a non-vegan diet; they provide more than half of most people's calcium. White bread, to which calcium is added to help ensure sufficient intake, accounts for a further one-fifth of most people's calcium. The remainder comes from greens and beans, fish bones – in tinned sardines and salmon, for example – and hard tap water.

It is vegans who may have difficulty maintaining an adequate calcium level. They do not eat milk products and their difficulty is even worse because fibre-rich foods – a mainstay of the vegan diet – tend to make calcium more difficult for the body to absorb. Hence, vegans need to eat even more of the source foods they find acceptable to get enough calcium. Eating plenty of greens, beans and white bread will help.

Zinc Zinc is found more in animal than in vegetable foods, and is usually associated with protein. Vegetarians get their zinc from wholegrain cereals which will normally be consumed in generous amounts. As with calcium and iron, dietary fibre makes zinc more difficult for the body to absorb, so a vegetarian's diet must include a plentiful supply of zinc before enough of it will be absorbed.

Making the change

Turning vegetarian does not necessarily solve all nutritional problems; it may solve some, but it raises others. What happens all too often is that would-be vegetarians simply switch from meat and fish to eggs and cheese; nuts too become a favourite food. The likely increase in calories, fat and body weight is quite the opposite of what they hope.

When you change to a new style of eating, your body will have to adapt. It does not like to change. Its metabolism and control systems are designed to maintain the status quo no matter what may be going on in the outside world. If you suddenly eat much more fibre, you will probably suffer from gas, abdominal bloating and discomfort. If you suddenly eat less saturated fat and more polyunsaturates, your liver has to make major changes in its working to cope with the new situation. Take up a new eating pattern gradually, just as you would a major exercise programme.

Adaptation takes time. Change your diet bit by bit, and your body will be able to retune without difficulty. Start with a few vegetarian dishes a week. Then have two or three entirely vegetarian days a week before you convert full-time. In this way you will make your mistakes while you can still rely on your meat and fish to provide essential nutrients.

Learn about true vegetarian recipes as well as egg and cheese dishes. Indian cookery includes a wide range of nourishing vegetarian recipes – as do Thai, Malay and Chinese cookery (see pp. 354-6).

If you prefer simple Anglo-Saxon dishes, start with beans on toast, a meal or snack which is nutritionally excellent. Do not worry about reports of the sugar content in tinned beans; the amount is small and unlikely to harm your teeth. You could then move on to bean and vegetable casseroles, preferably eaten with a cereal food such as bread, rice or corn. As you extend your range, try to mix as many ingredients as possible to ensure a good nutritional balance.

Any diet should include a wide variety of different foods to ensure a sufficient supply of all the nutrients, and to reduce the risk of excesses. This is even more important for vegetarians than for meat eaters.

Food combining has been made into a dietary cult by some food pundits, often with no logical basis. The best known combining system – the HAY DIET – is, however, nutritionally sound. Some others are unwise fads that abandon common sense and can be downright dangerous.

Vegetarians are as much a prey to fads and fashions in eating as anyone else – but must resist them. Bran with everything, especially concentrated bran or bran-fortified foods, can create nutritional imbalance. Too much is every bit as bad as too little, and could cause mineral deficiencies as well as intestinal discomfort.

Polyunsaturates too are being overvalued. The vegetable origin of most such oils makes them acceptable to vegetarians, but as yet we cannot predict the long-term effects of overloading the body with them. CANCER and GALLSTONES have been suggested as possible consequences.

In its report *Diet and Cardiovascular Disease* (1984), the Department of Health's Committee on Medical Aspects of Food Policy (COMA) urged a decrease in total fat consumption with an increase in the proportion of polyunsaturates. This was widely reported. What received little mention was that COMA also set an upper limit for the polyunsaturates. Uncontrolled consumption of safflower, sunflower, soya and corn oils or margarines made from them can provide an excess of polyunsaturates. Olive oil is thought to be safer.

Not peeling potatoes is another current fashion. It is believed this will improve nutrition by retaining more vitamin C and dietary fibre. In fact, the nutritional benefit is minimal or non-existent. More important, though, is that not peeling increases the consumption of solanine, the natural pesticide in potatoes, which is poisonous to humans in large amounts. So, on the whole, peeling is preferable.

When other factors count

Taking up a vegetarian or vegan diet should not be seen as a guarantee of health. Some people have been misled by scientific surveys that suggest good health is more frequent in vegetarian communities than in the population as a whole. Trappist monks and Seventh Day Adventists are often quoted as examples. They have long life, low incidence of cancer and HEART DISORDERS, and good BLOOD PRESSURE. However, they also have well-ordered lives that differ in other ways: strong religious beliefs, secure family or other supportive social groups, little or no SMOKING or drinking of alcohol contribute as much as – or more than – diet to their health. At the other extreme, the majority of the world's population is, of necessity, vegetarian and many of them are malnourished and sick. However, their health is poor not because they are vegetarian but because they cannot get enough food and their drinking water is unclean.

Eating the vegetarian way clearly demands skill. It has to be done properly if dietary balance is to be achieved. There are new shopping and cooking habits to be learned, new arts in menu planning to be acquired. But once the skills are mastered, the diet will be as nourishing and easy to manage as any other.

A varied diet containing ample vegetables, fruits and cereals is a good basis for health whether or not meat, fish or dairy foods are eaten as well. Vegetarians and vegans need the same nutrients as others and will easily obtain them if they have four helpings a day of staple foods (potato, bread, pasta, rice, for example); four of vegetables or fruits; and four of protein foods such as beans, peas, lentils, nuts, fresh milk, cheese or eggs. The ingredients should be as varied as possible and eaten in just sufficient quantities to maintain a healthy body weight.

Five vegetable feasts from around the world

Black-eyed beans and mushrooms from India (1)

6oz (180g) dried, black-eyed beans, soaked overnight
6oz (180g) fresh mushrooms
4½ tablespoons vegetable oil
1 teaspoon cumin seeds
1 stick cinnamon
4oz (120g) peeled and chopped onions
3 peeled and chopped garlic cloves
10oz (300g) peeled and chopped tomatoes
1½ teaspoons ground coriander
1 teaspoon ground cumin seeds
¼ teaspoon cayenne pepper
½ teaspoon powdered turmeric
2 tablespoons fresh parsley
Salt and black pepper

Bring the beans to the boil in a large pan of water. Cover and simmer gently on a low heat for 2 minutes. Then turn off the heat and leave the pan covered for 1 hour.

Chop the mushrooms lengthwise into thin slices. Heat the vegetable oil in a large frying pan over medium heat. When hot add the cumin seeds and cinnamon, and fry for 5-6 seconds. Add the chopped onions and garlic and stir-fry until the onions begin to brown. Next, add the mushrooms and fry until soft, stirring all the time. Add the tomatoes, coriander, ground cumin, cayenne and turmeric, and stir-fry for about 1 minute. Cover and leave on a low heat for 10 minutes, then turn off the heat.

Boil the beans again, turn down the heat and simmer until soft. Add the mushrooms and other ingredients, and season. Simmer for 30 minutes, stirring occasionally. Remove the cinnamon and serve with boiled or fried rice and Indian bread such as chapatti or nan. Serves four.

Spicy Thai salad (2)

2 large or 3 small limes
1 level teaspoon caster sugar
1 teaspoon anchovy essence
2 ripe mangoes
2 ripe papayas (papaws)
1 bunch spring onions, trimmed and sliced
1 red or green chilli, deseeded and chopped
1 large beef tomato, cut into 1in (25mm) cubes
½ cucumber, diced into 1in (25mm) cubes
4 sprigs of coriander leaves
8 fresh basil leaves, roughly chopped
2 Little Gem lettuces for garnish
Salt to taste

Squeeze the lime juice into a large bowl and mix in the sugar and anchovy essence. Peel the mangoes and papayas and cut into 2in (50mm) strips, discarding the mango stones and the papaya pips. Put the strips into the bowl with the lime juice. Then add the sliced spring onions, finely chopped chilli, diced tomato and cucumber. Reserving a few coriander leaves for garnishing, wash and chop the rest, and the basil, and add to the bowl.

Wash and arrange the larger lettuce leaves on individual plates. Chop the lettuce hearts, add to the salad, toss well and spoon onto the plates. Garnish with the remaining coriander leaves and serve immediately. Serves four.

Italian tagliatelle with mushroom and walnut sauce (3)

12oz (360g) fresh tagliatelle	½oz (15g) butter
4oz (120g) shelled walnuts	1 clove garlic, crushed
2 tablespoons virgin olive oil or walnut oil	8oz (240g) carton Greek strained yoghurt
½ medium onion, finely chopped	2 tablespoons fresh parsley, chopped (Italian flat-leaved parsley, if possible)
8oz (240g) field mushrooms, sliced	Salt and freshly ground black pepper to taste

Bring a saucepan of salted water to the boil. While you are waiting, wrap the walnuts in a clean tea towel and partially crush them with a rolling pin, leaving some large pieces. Melt the butter gently in a large, nonstick pan. Add the walnuts and cook them over a gentle heat for 2-3 minutes, stirring frequently and taking care not to burn them. Add the pasta to the boiling water and cook as instructed.

Remove the walnuts and wipe the pan clean. Add the oil and chopped onion to the pan and cook over moderate heat for 7-8 minutes until soft and golden, stirring occasionally. Add the sliced mushrooms and crushed garlic, turn to a high heat and cook for 5 minutes, stirring continually, until the juices run and the mushrooms are tender.

Remove the pan from the heat and add the walnuts and the yoghurt, 1 tablespoonful at a time, beating well to mix after each addition. Return the pan to a very low heat and stir until the yoghurt is heated through. Do not allow the yoghurt to boil or it will separate. Add half the parsley and season with salt and pepper.

Drain the pasta and mix with the sauce immediately. Taste and adjust the seasoning, then transfer onto heated individual plates. Sprinkle with the remaining parsley and serve with a light red wine and a mixed salad. Serves four.
Note This recipe is unsuitable for vegans, who may like to experiment with soya yoghurt instead of Greek yoghurt.

Ratatouille from France (4)

3 large courgettes	1 large onion
3 large aubergines	4 cloves garlic
6 large tomatoes	6 tablespoons olive oil
1 large green pepper	Salt and black pepper to taste
1 small red pepper	

Cut the stalks off the courgettes and aubergines, wash them and chop into ½-1in (13-25mm) slices. Place the slices in a colander with a weighted plate on top and leave for 1 hour to press out excess moisture. Skin the tomatoes and chop them into chunks. Wash the peppers, remove the seeds and white ribs inside, and dice the flesh. Peel and slice the onion, and coarsely chop the garlic.

Heat the olive oil in a large saucepan and fry the chopped onion and garlic for 5 minutes on a low heat until transparent. Add the peppers, cook for 10 minutes more, then add the remaining ingredients and season to taste. Cover the pan and cook over a low heat for 35 minutes, stirring from time to time. Season further if required.

Serve hot with rice, pasta or a jacket potato for a filling meal, or cold with salads for a lighter one. Serves four.

Stir-fried Chinese vegetables (5)

4 carrots	2 tablespoons yellow bean sauce
8oz (240g) cauliflower florets	2 tablespoons sherry
Two 8oz (240g) tins bamboo shoots	2 tablespoons brown sugar
10oz (300g) tofu	4 tablespoons soya sauce
¼ pint (150ml) vegetable oil	8oz (240g) mangetout
1 thinly sliced onion	8oz (240g) bean sprouts
2in (50mm) fresh ginger, finely chopped	1 red pepper, cut into thin strips
2 cloves garlic, crushed	Salt and black pepper
	2 tablespoons sesame oil

Cut the carrots into thin matchstick strips, and divide the cauliflower florets into small pieces. Blanch both vegetables in boiling water for 1-2 minutes. Drain the bamboo shoots and reserve 4fl oz (120ml) of the liquid. Cut the shoots into small strips and set aside together with the blanched carrots and cauliflower.

Drain the tofu, dry it with a piece of kitchen paper and cut it into squares. Heat the vegetable oil in a deep frying pan over moderate heat and fry the tofu pieces until crisp and slightly brown. Remove them from the pan and dry off excess oil with kitchen paper.

Pour off all except 1 tablespoon of oil from the frying pan. Add the onion, ginger and garlic to the pan and fry gently for 5 minutes. In the meantime, mix together in a jug the bamboo shoot liquid, the yellow bean sauce, sherry, sugar and soya sauce.

Slice the tips off the mangetout, and add mangetout, bean sprouts, carrots, cauliflower, red pepper and bamboo shoots to the pan. Turn up the heat and stir-fry the vegetables for 5 minutes. Add the mixed liquid ingredients and bring to the boil, stirring all the time.

Reduce the heat and add the fried tofu pieces, with salt and pepper to season. Simmer for 1-2 minutes, stirring continuously, then place in a heated serving dish and sprinkle with sesame oil. Serve immediately, with rice or noodles. Serves four to six.

(*Facing page*) *Food tables such as these contain valuable information that can help vegans and vegetarians to plan a healthy diet and make sure that they do not go short of protein or important vitamins and minerals. When using the tables, bear in mind that the nutrient quantities are given per 100g (3½oz) of food, so the amount you get depends on the weight of your portion.*
While 100g of pasta or eggs is not a big serving, it would be a lot of brewer's yeast or Marmite to consume, even over a period of several days. So although brewer's yeast and Marmite come higher up on the protein table, eggs and pasta will probably make a much greater contribution to your overall daily intake.
The more concentrated sources of nutrients are best used as supplements to enrich other foods – as when you sprinkle wheatgerm or brewer's yeast on cereal – or as alternatives to less healthy foods also eaten in small quantities – by spreading Marmite instead of jam on bread, for example.

Vegetarian sources of essential nutrients

PROTEIN
grams per 100g (3½oz)

Brewer's yeast	46.1
Marmite	39.7
Peanuts	26.9
Wheatgerm	25.2
Split peas	24.5
Cheddar cheese	23.9
Lima beans	20.7
Cottage cheese	19.2
Almonds	18.6
Walnuts	15.0
Oatmeal	14.2
Pasta	14.0
Eggs	12.8
Wholemeal bread	9.5
White bread	8.5
Cornflakes	7.9
White rice	7.5
Cream cheese	7.1
Peas	6.7
Baked beans	5.7
Dried apricots	5.2
Brussels sprouts	4.4
Sweetcorn	3.7
Milk	3.5
Broccoli	3.3
Raisins	2.3
Potatoes	2.0
Avocados	1.7
Cabbage	1.4
Bananas	1.2
Fresh apricots	1.0

By comparison, tinned tuna contains 23.9g, tinned sardines 21.1, chicken 20.2, calf's or lamb's liver 20.1, beef and lamb 18.5, and cod 16.5.

CALCIUM
milligrams per 100g (3½oz)

Cheese, Cheddar	873
processed	716
Almonds	254
Kale	225
Dandelion greens	187
Egg yolks	147
Broccoli	130
Milk	118
Brewer's yeast	106
Marmite	95
Dried apricots	86
Wheatgerm	84
Walnuts	83
Cottage cheese	82
Raisins	78

Peanuts	74
Split peas	73
Lima beans	68
Lettuce	62
Bread, wholemeal	60
white	56
Oatmeal	54
Eggs	54
Baked beans	49
Cabbage	46
Radishes	44
Brown rice	39
Brussels sprouts	34
Oranges	33
Onions	32
Strawberries	28
Dried apples	24
Pasta	22
Peas	22
Asparagus	21
Grapes	17
Fresh apricots	16
Tomatoes	11
Potatoes	11
Green peppers	11
Cornflakes	10
White rice	9
Bananas	8

By comparison, tinned salmon contains 67mg, tinned tuna 30, tinned sardines 29, cod 18, liver and chicken 16, and beef and lamb 11.

IRON
milligrams per 100g (3½oz)

Brewer's yeast	18.2
Wheatgerm	8.1
Lima beans	7.5
Egg yolks	7.2
Split peas	6.0
Brown rice	5.5
Oatmeal	5.2
Dried apricots	4.9
Almonds	4.4
Dried apples	4.1
Marmite	3.7
Baked beans	3.4
Raisins	3.3
Dandelion greens	3.1
Spinach	3.0
Eggs	2.7
Wholemeal bread	2.6
Cornflakes	2.5
Walnuts	2.1
White bread	2.0

Peanuts	1.9
Peas	1.9
Pasta	1.5
Broccoli	1.3
Lettuce	1.1
Processed cheese	0.8
Potatoes	0.7
Milk	0.7
White rice	0.7
Tomatoes	0.6
Cheddar cheese	0.6
Cabbage	0.5
Fresh apricots	0.5
Oranges	0.4
Green peppers	0.4
Fresh apples	0.3
Cream	0.2

By comparison, liver contains 12.1mg, beef and lamb 2.8, chicken 1.9, tinned sardines and tinned tuna 1.5.

ZINC
milligrams per 100g (3½oz)

All-Bran	8.4
Cheddar cheese	4.0
Split peas	4.0
Processed cheese	3.2
Almonds	3.1
Oatmeal	3.0
Walnuts	3.0
Peanuts	3.0
Brewer's yeast	2.6
Marmite	2.1
Wholemeal bread	2.0
Eggs	1.5
White rice	1.3
Sweetcorn	1.0
Pasta	1.0
White bread	0.8
Baked beans	0.7
Peas	0.5
Cottage cheese	0.5
Milk	0.4
Cabbage	0.4
Broccoli	0.4
Cornflakes	0.3
Bananas	0.2
Oranges	0.2
Potatoes	0.2
Tomatoes	0.2
Lettuce	0.2

By comparison, beef and lamb contain 5.0mg, chicken 1.0, tinned salmon 0.9 and tinned tuna 0.8.

VITAMIN B12
micrograms per 100g (3½oz)

Grapenuts	5.0
Egg yolks	4.9
Fortified cornflakes	1.7
Whole eggs	1.7
Cheddar cheese	1.5
Camembert cheese	1.2
Marmite	0.5
Cottage cheese	0.5
Processed cheese	0.3
Milk, whole	0.3
skimmed	0.3
Beer	0.2

By comparison, calf's liver contains 87.0 micrograms, tinned sardines 28.0, tinned tuna 5.0, pork 3.0, cod 2.0, and beef and lamb 2.0.

VITAMIN C
milligrams per 100g (3½oz)

Green peppers	120
Broccoli	118
Kale	115
Strawberries	60
Spinach	59
Cabbage	52
Oranges	49
Lemons	45
Grapefruit	40
Dandelion greens	36
Asparagus	33
Peas	26
Tomatoes	23
Lettuce	18
Potatoes	17
Apricots, fresh	16
dried	12
Sweetcorn	12
Dried apples	11
Bananas	10
Rhubarb	9
Carrots	6
Fresh apples	5
Baked beans	4
Grapes	4
Walnuts	3
Milk	3
Fruit cocktail	2
Lima beans	2
Split peas	2
Peanuts	2

By comparison, calf's and lamb's liver contains 10mg, cod 2mg and meat none.

VERTIGO

A sensation that the head is moving or spinning, when in fact it is still, is known as vertigo. The condition is often associated with NAUSEA AND VOMITING, and can be triggered by fear of falling from a height.

Vertigo can be caused by inflammation of the balance organ in the inner ear or by MOTION SICKNESS. It can also result from Ménière's disease, in which attacks of vertigo are associated with RINGING IN THE EARS and increasing deafness; the cause is unknown.

Rarely, vertigo and deafness result from a benign (non-cancerous) growth on the acoustic (or auditory) nerve, or – if it develops suddenly in an elderly person – from a stroke. High BLOOD PRESSURE, hardening of the arteries (see ARTERIES [HARDENING]) and ear disorders can also cause vertigo. See also DIZZINESS.

What the therapists recommend

Acupuncture The equilibrium of the body is affected, and the condition is treated by stimulating points on the governor, gall bladder and kidney meridians, and also by giving MOXIBUSTION to points on the governor, gall bladder and bladder meridians.

Acupressure Apply pressure at a point one finger's width under the outer ankle bone and press inwards.

An orthodox view

If you develop persistent vertigo, consult your doctor. He will measure your blood pressure, examine your ears and look for signs of an underlying cause. If your hearing is deteriorating the cause may be a growth on the acoustic nerve, and your doctor may arrange a CAT scan, in which a series of X-ray cross-sections are combined to give a three-dimensional view inside the body.

Conventional drugs such as betahistine (Serc) and cinnarizine (Stugeron) may relieve vertigo. However, they do not improve the hearing of Ménière's disease patients.

VIRUS INFECTIONS

A virus is a submicroscopic organism consisting essentially of a core of a single nucleic acid surrounded by a coating of protein. Viruses are on the borderline between living and non-living things. They can multiply only inside living cells, and in the process cause a wide variety of infections, from mild COLDS to life-threatening AIDS or POLIOMYELITIS. Virus infections also give rise to INFLUENZA, CHICKENPOX, SHINGLES and COLD SORES.

When vast numbers of a virus invade, the human body reacts, producing symptoms and signs of disease until its IMMUNE SYSTEM can produce enough antibodies – special kinds of proteins in the blood – to destroy the viruses. The antibodies then remain in the bloodstream as protection against another invasion by the same virus.

However, some viruses, such as those that cause the common cold, have the ability to mutate (change) so that the antibodies produced during one illness fail to give protection against future infections. Other viruses, including those causing MEASLES and MUMPS, very rarely mutate so that immunity usually lasts for a person's lifetime.

The human papilloma viruses (HPV) cause GENITAL HERPES, and may cause CANCER of the cervix (the neck of the womb). Another virus is thought to cause GLANDULAR FEVER.

What the therapists recommend

Homoeopathy The therapist gives remedies that, when correctly matched to the patient's symptoms, are said to enhance his body's ability to fight the particular infection.

Naturopathy Practitioners believe that natural therapies encourage the immune system, and that attention to overall health is of great value in combatting virus infections. A vitamin C supplement and two or three garlic capsules a day are generally recommended. However, consultation is advised.

Herbal Medicine If you are prone to frequent colds or influenza, try taking one to three garlic capsules daily as a preventive; double the dose if the infections occur very frequently. However, a consultation is recommended for all virus infections.

An orthodox view

Antibiotics are ineffective against virus infections, but they can alleviate accompanying bacterial infections. For example, if you develop a secondary bacterial infection such as BRONCHITIS or sinusitis (see SINUS PROBLEMS), penicillin will help you to recover.

Doctors now prescribe antiviral drugs for certain viral infections. For example, acyclovir (Zovirax) is effective against genital herpes, cold sores and chickenpox if given early enough in the course of the illness. Retrovir (Zidovudine or AZT) slows the progress of HIV infection and the resultant AIDS, but it does not cure the disease.

Conventional medicine cannot offer a cure for the majority of virus infections, though many – such as smallpox and measles – can be prevented by vaccination.

VISUALISATION THERAPY
Picturing your way to health

Mental pictures can be a powerful force for good or ill, depending on how they are used. In visualisation therapy, patients are taught imaginative techniques to benefit their health, to help along natural healing processes, and to reinforce positive feelings, behaviour and images of themselves.

In everyday life, people often tend to concentrate on fears and problems rather

How Ben, aged 8 solved his problem

The almost nightly BEDWETTING of eight-year-old Ben had not responded to several treatments – including an alarm system – when the family GP suggested that visualisation might help.

The doctor asked Ben where he thought the water was coming from. Ben replied that it came from a big river. So, guided by the doctor, he was asked to imagine going for a walk along the river and coming to a large dam which stopped the water from flowing any farther. The doctor asked Ben what happened at night, and Ben told him that there was a door in the dam which was a bit leaky.

The doctor then helped Ben to imagine ways in which the leak could be stopped. Together they visualised using Superglue to waterproof the door and then padlocking it. But Ben could open the lock with a key and remove the glue with a penknife.

Every night at bedtime Ben and his mother imagined going for a walk down the river, coming to the dam and making the door watertight. Then he gave the imaginary key to his mother to put under his pillow for the night.

In the first three weeks of treatment Ben wet his bed only three times, on nights when he said the water was particularly stormy. With the doctor's help he was able to overcome even this problem, by imagining in a visualisation session that there was a hole in the river bank which occasionally let water through. Once he had visualised filling it in, his nights became completely dry.

than on how they might improve things. For example, a young man going to a party may fear that no one will want to talk to him. He visualises himself entering a room full of guests and being totally ignored. And when he gets to the real party this image is so strong that he inevitably seeks out those people most likely to turn the imagined situation into reality.

Contrast this man's actions with those of someone who goes to the party believing that at least one guest will want to talk to him, and then seeks out that person.

Such imagined situations and the underlying beliefs that precipitate them tend to become self-fulfilling prophecies that influence mind, body and feelings. In the same way, people who practise creative visualisation believe that positive, health-promoting images will help them to create the sort of life they want.

Making images is a natural mental process that occurs every night during dreams. Visualisation is similar to dreaming, but involves making a deliberate attempt with the conscious mind to imagine particularly beneficial events. It is based on the belief that mind and body are not separate but affect each other directly, so that thoughts can have physical effects as well as mental ones.

A number of theories have been suggested to explain how visualisation works, mostly based on the idea that there is a close link between emotions, images and sensations. Just as emotions are accompanied by physical sensations such as deep sighs and a long face when you are unhappy, so images call up emotions and emotions are experienced in terms of images. For example, angry people are often said to 'see red'. By altering images, visualisation is believed to affect feelings and physical sensations.

It has also been suggested that visualisation may help to balance and integrate the

To help people create mental pictures, visualisation therapists use paintings such as this scene by Pieter Brueghel the Elder (c1515-69). A person would be asked to look at it for two or three minutes, and then, with eyes shut, to recall it in his mind's eye. With practice, he would be able to re-create the picture in detail. He would 'see' a man sharpening a scythe, a mounted lady carrying a basket, two horses feeding, three girls carrying rakes and five porters with baskets on their heads. He would then progress to imagining a real-life scene.

Rediscovery of an ancient art

The use of mental images to cure disease has played an important part in healing traditions from earliest times. It was used by witchdoctors or 'shamans' in Africa and South America, and viewed as an integral part of most early oriental therapies. In Western medicine its origins reach back to ancient Greece, and it exerted a powerful influence until the mid-1600s, sometimes being considered the single most important factor in healing illness.

With the birth of modern science in the 17th century, holistic therapies such as visualisation began to be replaced by more specialised medical approaches, which viewed mind and body as separate. For hundreds of years this view prevailed and most orthodox doctors considered there to be no rational basis for visualisation.

Recently, however, evidence of a link between body and mind has accumulated from observations and experiments in many different areas. Together with concern about the limitations and side effects of conventional treatments, this has led to a reawakening of interest in holistic approaches such as visualisation.

One of the earliest pieces of research was done in the 1920s by Edmund Jacobson, an American who discovered that when a subject visualised himself running, his leg muscles would twitch involuntarily.

Other work on visualisation was done by Carl Simonton, a doctor at Fort Worth in Texas, and his wife Stephanie. They got cancer patients to create mental images of healthy cells attacking and destroying cancer cells. They claimed that participants in the programme lived on average twice as long as others, and in some cases the illness stopped spreading, enabling them to resume normal lives. However, these findings have since been disputed.

Another American doctor, Bernard Siegel, a surgeon at Yale-New Haven Hospital and an assistant professor at Yale University Medical School, works with visual images produced by patients in dreams and paintings, which he believes often show that the patient unconsciously knows what is wrong with him.

Dr Siegel's work has led him to the conclusion that many people have the ability to heal themselves, but that often they lack the will to live or expect something outside themselves – a doctor, drugs or some other treatment – to cure them. For these patients he believes that visualisation therapy may be of little use, but for those who are prepared to take on responsibility it may help to activate inner healing processes.

hemispheres of the brain. The left side is believed to be concerned with logical thinking and tends to predominate in many people, while the more creative and intuitive right side is relatively little used. Thinking in images is believed to involve the right hemisphere and so help to correct the imbalance.

Who it can help Therapists say that visualisation is suitable for just about any sort of physical or emotional problem. In particular, it has been used to help patients with ASTHMA, HEART DISORDERS, CANCER and PHOBIAS, and is said to be an effective form of PAIN relief. It may also help in achieving personal goals such as an improved relationship or a more positive self-image.

Children make particularly good subjects (see box, p. 359) since they have vivid imaginations and find it easy to create mental pictures. Many live in rich fantasy worlds of dragons, knights, heroes and other mythical beings that can be used to help them overcome problems and express themselves, as well as to strengthen bonds with their parents.

Self help Therapists advise that it is usually best to learn the technique of visualisation from an expert and then practise it at home.

Most people learn quickly, but for a few it can take longer, sometimes because they tend to process information in terms of sounds or sensations rather than pictures.

If you find it difficult to build visual images at first, this simple exercise may help: Look at a picture or photograph for two or three minutes, then shut your eyes and try to re-create it in your mind in as much detail as possible. Once you can do this easily, repeat the exercise using a room instead of a picture, and then finally with a moving scene from real life.

Visualisation can also be an aid to RELAXATION AND BREATHING exercises. When you practise diaphragmatic breathing (see p. 299) try to visualise a circle right in front of you. Without moving, imagine that you are drawing one half of the circle with your breath as you inhale, and the other half as you exhale. Repeat several times until the circle seems as round and smooth as you can make it. Then spend a few minutes visualising each in-breath as travelling from the tips of your toes along the spine to the top of the head, and each out-breath as travelling down from the head to the toes.

To enhance the effect of the progressive muscular relaxation exercise on p. 301, try to imagine some special, peaceful place once you are fully relaxed. Notice as many details about the scene as you can and examine each part of it with care. Try to imagine sounds, smells and sensations as well as sights if you can. After five to ten minutes, let the image slowly dissolve.

For the relief of severe pain, visualisation is said to require practice and be best learned from a therapist, but this technique may be effective in less serious cases: Close your eyes and concentrate on slow diaphragmatic breathing. Visualise your breathing as coming in and out of the painful region, bringing a warm glow as you inhale and expelling pain with each exhalation.

Finding a therapist Visualisation is used by therapists of all types, almost always in combination with other treatments. Many practitioners are found in fields such as BIOFEEDBACK, AUTOGENIC TRAINING, PSYCHO-SYNTHESIS, REBIRTHING, HYPNOTHERAPY and PSYCHOTHERAPY. Conventional doctors are also beginning to recognise its value, spurred on by the work of Carl and Stephanie Simonton and Bernard Siegel (see box, this page).

Each therapy has its own registering body which can put you in touch with qualified therapists, but there is no national register of practitioners who teach visualisation techniques. As a result, personal recommendation may be the best – or the only – way to find a therapist.

Consulting a therapist The practitioner begins by listening carefully to your description of the problem, and then encouraging you to relax in a comfortable position with head, neck and trunk aligned. Most people like to sit in a firm chair, but you can lie down or sit crosslegged. The therapist may also teach breathing exercises to aid relaxation.

When you are fully relaxed you will be asked to imagine a scene that in some way relates to your problem. This may be a still from a film, a photograph or a painting, and the therapist will ask you to describe details of what you see, perhaps making changes to the original suggestion.

While you are exploring the scene, the therapist will help you to become aware of any feelings or bodily sensations that you experience. Subtle changes to what you visualise can then be used gradually to alter your responses in ways that will help you to solve your particular problem.

An orthodox view

Visualisation is a perfectly acceptable way to aid relaxation and reduce STRESS. Its use in specific conditions, especially cancer, is still controversial, although some studies have now established the benefits in a wide range of other conditions.

VITAMINS
Providing the body with the essentials for life

These vital substances, present in most foods in minute amounts, are needed for proper growth and development, body maintenance and general health. They control how your body makes use of other nutrients, and a serious deficiency of them can lead to a host of complaints ranging from HEADACHES and loss of appetite to rickets and sterility. Fortunately a well-balanced diet (see EATING FOR HEALTH) provides all the vitamins that the body normally needs.

There are 13 major vitamins, all essential to health. Only one – possibly two – of them can be made in the necessary amounts by the body itself. Vitamin D is produced by the action of sunlight on the skin, and vitamin K may be synthesised by bacteria in the large intestine. The other 11, and these two if not enough of them is produced by the body, must be obtained from an outside source: the food we eat.

Some vitamins are soluble in water and others are soluble in fat, and this makes an important difference to how they are used. The water-soluble vitamins (vitamin C and those belonging to the vitamin B-complex) can easily be lost in cooking, especially if the water in which the food source has been boiled is thrown away. It may pay to steam vegetables, or to follow the example of the Chinese and stir-fry them rapidly.

Our bodies cannot store water-soluble vitamins. Any excess not taken up and used by the body is passed out in the urine. This means that the C and B vitamins must be eaten daily. The fat-soluble vitamins A, D, E and K, on the other hand, can be stored in the liver, sometimes for weeks. There is no need to eat them daily, but the intake must be regular, to ensure that the supply in the body remains topped up.

The fresher the produce, and the nearer it is to its natural state, the higher its vitamin content. Vitamins can be lost by any form of cooking (because of the heat), by exposure to light or cold, by storage, and by many of the processes of food manufacture. Water-soluble vitamins are particularly 'fragile', deteriorating at high or low temperatures and in strong sunlight. Potatoes, for example, are a valuable source of vitamin C when fresh, but can lose about half of it when kept for five months. So store fresh foods carefully, and keep vitamin tablets or capsules in a cool, dry place, preferably in the dark.

If you are in good health and your diet is right, vitamin supplements are not normally needed. Indeed, an excess of some vitamins can be just as dangerous as a deficiency. Those that are fat soluble, and particularly vitamins A and D, can build up in the body to toxic levels. If you do take supplements, be sure to keep to the recommended dosage.

The times when supplements may be necessary are when there are extra demands or stresses on the body – during PREGNANCY, for example. Women taking contraceptive

Vitamins: what they do and how we obtain them

VITAMIN AND NATURAL SOURCES	RECOMMENDED DAILY AMOUNT (RDA) AND BENEFICIAL EFFECTS	EFFECTS OF DEFICIENCY
Vitamin A (retinol) Fat soluble.	RDA: 0.75mg; 1.2mg for nursing mothers.	
Found in: yellow/orange vegetables, especially carrots; green vegetables; tomatoes; full-fat dairy produce; liver; kidney; eggs; fish-liver oils; apricots and peaches (fresh or dried).	Vision, especially in dim light; healthy skin and mucous membranes; resistance to infection. Sometimes used to treat ACNE. _Warning_: Large doses can be toxic.	Night blindness (inability to see in dim light); damage to cornea and eventual blindness; ear, eye and respiratory infections; dry skin; dull hair and hair loss (see HAIR PROBLEMS); weight loss, and stunted growth.
Vitamin B1 (thiamin, aneurin) Water soluble.	RDA: 1-1.3mg	
Found in: wheat germ and wholegrain cereals, including brown rice; fortified white flour and products; brewer's yeast/yeast extract; seafood; liver, meat, poultry; pulses; nuts; potatoes; milk.	Metabolises (breaks down) carbohydrates to provide energy; healthy muscles and nervous system; countering pain; possibly, learning ability.	Loss of appetite, nausea (see NAUSEA AND VOMITING), CONSTIPATION; fatigue, weakness; DEPRESSION, irritability, lack of concentration; shortness of breath, slow heart. Severe: beriberi and eventual death.
Vitamin B2 (riboflavin, lactoflavin, vitamin G) Water soluble.	RDA: 1.3-1.6mg	
Found in: liver, kidney, meat, poultry; eggs, cheese, yoghurt; wholegrain cereals; fortified cereals; brewer's yeast/yeast extract; fish; green vegetables; pulses.	Metabolism of carbohydrates, fats and proteins; healthy skin and mucous membranes.	Inflammation of tongue and lips, lip sores; scaly scalp and hair loss (see HAIR PROBLEMS); sensitivity to light; trembling, DIZZINESS, insomnia.
Niacin (vitamin B3, nicotinic acid) Water soluble.	RDA: 18mg	
Found in: some cereals including rice, but not maize; fortified white flour and products; meat, liver, poultry, kidney; yeast extract/brewer's yeast; eggs; fish; nuts, especially peanuts; cheese; peas and beans; globe artichokes; dried fruit.	Efficient blood circulation; control of blood cholesterol; healthy adrenal glands; healthy skin and nervous system; healthy appetite.	Loss of appetite, nausea (see NAUSEA AND VOMITING), gastrointestinal ULCERS, DIARRHOEA; dermatitis; fatigue, HEADACHES; INSOMNIA, irritability, DEPRESSION. Severe: pellagra (dementia with dermatitis and DIARRHOEA).

Continued on p. 362

Vitamins: what they do and how we obtain them *continued*

VITAMIN AND NATURAL SOURCES	RECOMMENDED DAILY AMOUNT (RDA) AND BENEFICIAL EFFECTS	EFFECTS OF DEFICIENCY
Pantothenic acid (vitamin B5) Water soluble.	RDA: 4-7mg	
Found in all living matter and most foods, but especially beans, egg yolk, legumes, liver, oranges, peanuts, wheat germ, wholegrain cereals; also made in gut.	Use of fats and carbohydrates; healthy skin and hair; healthy nervous system; production of antibodies against infection.	Deficiency is unlikely in humans. Rare symptoms may include increased susceptibility to ALLERGY and infections; ASTHMA; CRAMP; fatigue; INSOMNIA.
Vitamin B6 (pyridoxine) Water soluble.	RDA: 1.5-2mg	
Found in: most foods, but especially green vegetables, brewer's yeast, yeast extracts, fish, pulses, prunes, raisins, soya beans and flour, nuts, wholegrain cereals, milk.	Production of antibodies against infection; red blood cell formation; metabolism of protein.	Deficiency not reported in humans.
Folic acid (vitamin B9, folate, vitamin B$_c$, pteroylglutamic acid) Water soluble.	RDA: 0.3mg	
Found in: liver, kidney, meat; green vegetables; fresh fruit; brewer's yeast/ yeast extract; wheat germ; pulses.	Proper functioning of vitamin B12; formation of red blood cells; use of proteins, fats and carbohydrates.	Lack of vitamin B12; ANAEMIA; fatigue, WEAKNESS, shortness of breath, irritability, INSOMNIA, FORGETFULNESS, confusion.
Vitamin B12 (cyanocobalamin) Water soluble.	RDA: 2 micrograms; 4 micrograms for pregnant women and nursing mothers	
Found in: foods of animal origin, especially liver, meat, kidney; fish; egg yolk; dairy products, especially cheese; fortified cereals; brewer's yeast/yeast extracts (traces only).	Proper functioning of folic acid; red blood cell formation; healthy nervous system; synthesis of nucleic acids and proteins; metabolism of fats, proteins and carbo-hydrates; prevention of cell degeneration.	Deficiency of folic acid; loss of appetite; fatigue, irritability; ANAEMIA. Severe: degeneration of nervous system, leading to moving and speaking difficulties.
Biotin (also one of vitamin B-complex) Water soluble.	RDA: 0.1-0.2mg	
Found in: egg yolk; liver, kidney; wheat germ; nuts; oats; yeast/yeast extract.	Metabolism of fats; synthesis of glucose when diet is low in carbohydrates.	Very rare.
Vitamin C (ascorbic acid) Water soluble.	RDA: 30mg; 60mg for pregnant women	
Found in (best raw): fruits and fruit juices, especially citrus fruits and blackcurrants; rose hips and syrup; vegetables, including potatoes; chillies and peppers.	Healthy skin, bone, tendons, cartilage, ligaments, blood vessels, gums, teeth; energy production and growth; resistance to infection; wound healing; iron absorption; control of blood cholesterol.	Bleeding and/or soft gums, loose teeth; low resistance to infections; tender joints, muscle degeneration; fatigue, weakness, irritability; ANAEMIA. Severe: scurvy, which can be fatal.
Vitamin D (cholecalciferol) Fat soluble.	RDA: 10 micrograms	
Produced by action of sunlight on human skin. Found in: liver; fish-liver oils and oily fish such as kippers, mackerel, sardines, tuna, tinned salmon; margarine; egg yolk; evaporated milk, full-fat dairy products; malted milk drinks; sprouted seeds.	Absorption of calcium and phosphorus for healthy bones and teeth. *Warning*: Large doses can be toxic.	Bone deformities, dental caries; CRAMP; muscle weakness. Severe: rickets and osteomalacia (equivalent of rickets in adults).
Vitamin E (tocopherol) Fat soluble.	RDA: 10 micrograms or 12-15IU	
Found in most foods, but especially vegetable oils, egg yolks, wholegrain cereals, wheat germ, green vegetables, nuts and seeds, pulses, margarine.	Healthy cell membranes, so may retard effects of ageing; healthy blood cells; blood clotting; resistance to infection; possibly fertility.	Rare: dull hair; muscle weakness; possibly: enlarged prostate gland (see PROSTATE PROBLEMS); miscarriage.
Vitamin K (menadione) Fat soluble.	RDA: 70-140 micrograms	
Synthesised by bacteria in large intestine. Found in: green vegetables, especially brassicas; seaweed (kelp); liver; potatoes; eggs; wheat germ.	Blood clotting.	Very rare, but may be caused by long-term use of antibiotics: bleeding beneath the skin, NOSEBLEED, DIARRHOEA.

pills may need extra vitamins, as may post-menopausal women, elderly people, and anybody who drinks much alcohol. Followers of VEGETARIANISM, and especially veganism, run the risk of becoming deficient in vitamin B12, which helps to maintain the nervous system in good working order. Vitamin supplements or brewer's yeast should make up the shortfall.

A theory was put forward in the 1980s that vitamin supplements could improve a child's IQ. This led to heated controversy in British medical circles, but in the early 1990s the claim was still unproven. Scientific tests were carried out in Wales and Scotland, but the results were conflicting.

See also MEGAVITAMIN THERAPY and FOOD ADDITIVES .

VOICE THERAPY
Retraining the vocal cords

The human voice reveals a great deal about our character or personality, not only through the way we speak, but also through the tone, pitch and rhythm of our voice. In addition to words, we express ourselves by how loud or soft, how high or low our voice is when we laugh, cry, become angry or apologetic. Our voice also reveals much about the way in which we deal with extreme situations involving ANXIETY, GRIEF, STRESS and frustration.

Some people are let down by their voice when seeking to express anger, or assert their authority. These 'betrayals' sometimes arise because they cannot change their tone of voice to suit the occasion.

For example, a young woman who has been brought up to be sweet, generous and accommodating, may develop a voice which is stuck in a high pitch with a soft and comforting tone. She therefore may find it extremely difficult – if not impossible – to have herself taken seriously when expressing more 'dominating' emotions.

Equally, a man who has been educated to believe he should be domineering and 'protective' may develop a low, booming voice which is incapable of expressing gentler and more sympathetic feelings.

A voice therapist aims to overcome these and other related problems through special vocal and breathing exercises, MASSAGE and psychological methods.

Who it can help People suffering from DEPRESSION may have difficulty in expressing themselves as their voice has become low, quiet and sad. Also, anyone beset with anxiety may find himself more or less gasping for breath, and his voice will be strained and unnatural. Even though the sufferers may be undergoing PSYCHOTHERAPY, their voice often needs separate attention.

Other problems with the voice may arise as a result of physical impairment or restriction, and the physically disabled can also sometimes benefit from the therapy. For example, someone confined to a wheelchair may have difficulty in being heard without getting a sore throat or experiencing TENSION. This is due to the often uncomfortable way in which he is forced to sit.

Difficulties of self-expression such as these do not necessarily mean there is a problem with talking itself. However, voice therapists may treat someone suffering from, say, STAMMERING, whom other therapists have been unable to help.

Finding a therapist There is no nationally recognised training course or institution for alternative voice therapists, and therefore no recognised qualification. Therapists – some of whom started off as psychotherapists, singers, or singing teachers – can be judged only by the degree of help which they can provide. Unlike speech therapy, voice therapy is not available on the NHS.

To find the nearest therapist to you, write to Paul Newham, Voicedance Laboratorium, 27 George Street, Leamington Spa, Warwickshire CV31 1HA.

Consulting a therapist The aim of the therapist is to release feelings and emotions in the patient which may have become blocked or submerged. In addition, he will try to 'liberate' the voice from the effects of extreme moods – such as depression – or ease the tension caused by any physical impediment. He does this by trying to improve the actual _sounds_ made by the patient, rather than by working on his pronunciation and manner of speaking as a speech therapist does.

The patient is asked to make a sound, or possibly sing a note which is played on the piano. The therapist listens carefully to the sound and then attempts to remove any physical factor which he thinks is restricting the voice.

The way this is done depends both on the individual therapist's approach and the patient's specific problem. Usually, however, the therapist tries to help the patient to breathe freely and easily. This may involve massaging the patient's back to realign the posture and the shape of the spine, and to relax muscles which are used in making sounds, in a manner similar to that used in the ALEXANDER TECHNIQUE.

In addition, the therapist listens to the moods and feelings which he says lie beneath any given sound. These are usually not apparent to the patient, who is not used to listening to the subtle intonations of his own voice.

The therapist encourages the patient's underlying emotions or 'deeper images' to emerge, often by making the patient imagine that he is experiencing different emotions, or pretending that he is a totally different person. In turn, this is said to change the sounds he makes.

The process has been compared to taking the patient's voice on a journey through his or her imagination. The mind contains a mixture of images, emotions, ideas, thoughts and feelings. These are often expressed in dreams and fantasies, or in the pictures we paint and the stories we tell.

Voice therapy aims at giving vocal expression to these notions, so that we can better understand the deeper workings of our minds – and therefore use our voice in a true and beneficial way.

An orthodox view
Voice therapy is regarded as a perfectly acceptable approach to the treatment of stress-related disorders. It is especially useful for those conditions in which breathing problems and emotional distress play a large part.

Sounds of war and peace

The first person to use alternative voice therapy was Alfred Wolfsohn (1896-1962), a German medical orderly who served in the trenches in the First World War. He was horrified by the agonised screams of wounded soldiers, and the heart-rending moans of the dying – and these sounds came back to haunt him in peacetime.

He suffered a nervous breakdown and sought ways to express vocally the deep psychological injuries he had suffered. Gradually, he healed himself by exploring the sound of his own voice.

Wolfsohn was a Jew, and in the 1930s he fled to England to escape persecution by the Nazis. Once there he taught emotionally disturbed people how to use their voice to overcome psychological problems and inhibitions. He founded the Alfred Wolfsohn Voice Research Centre (no longer in existence) at Golders Green, London.

His success encouraged other healers to take up his work, and today he is acknowledged by many voice therapists to be the master of their unorthodox art.

WARTS

Viruses cause the small, non-cancerous, solid growths on the skin which are known as warts. They are composed mostly of enlarged skin cells, and occur typically on the hands and feet. There are several types and most disappear of their own accord.

Common warts are rough, horny and skin-coloured or brownish. They occur mostly in children, usually on the hands. Scratching them spreads the virus and causes more warts to appear.

Plantar warts are also known as verrucas. They occur on the sole of the foot, and are similar to common warts. However, they grow into the skin instead of outwards and are therefore more painful. They spread rapidly from person to person in communal changing rooms for swimming and other sports, where people go barefoot.

Filiform warts appear as short, hard threads, and are often seen on the face, neck, chin and eyelids. They are harmless and tend to disappear with time, but can be unsightly. Plane warts are flat and light brown, and are also common on the face.

Warning Have a brown wart checked by your doctor if it feels soft, suddenly changes its shape, itches and/or bleeds, or produces a discharge. It may not be a wart at all, but a melanoma – a skin CANCER.

What the therapists recommend

Acupuncture In traditional Chinese medicine, the skin is related to the lung and large intestine, so treatment is given to points surrounding the wart(s), and also to points on the lung and large intestine meridians. Points on the governor and spleen meridians are also used as they are believed to produce anti-inflammatory and immune effects.

Hypnotherapy Under hypnosis the sufferer is given suggestions that the warts will gradually lose their food supply, fade away and eventually drop off.

Aromatherapy Onion and garlic oils are held to be effective, but because of their powerful aroma they are taken in capsule form. Raw, chopped onion or garlic applied regularly as an overnight compress is said also to remove warts.

An orthodox view

Most warts can be destroyed by carefully applying an acid, such as salicylic acid, or podophyllin (Posalfilin) – a resin obtained from the dried root of the May apple – and then covering the area with a plaster. If necessary, a thin layer of petroleum jelly is first applied to the surrounding healthy skin

Charming warts away

Traditional and folklore remedies for warts are legion, and some are ancient. Here are just a few:

Tie a hair from the tail of a piebald pony or from the mane of a grown horse around each one.

Rub each wart with seven white stones in turn.

Rub on bacon or raw meat and then bury the meat – but do not let anyone know where it is buried.

If you live in the country, try washing the affected skin in a blacksmith's trough – the bath in which he dunks horseshoes – every day for a week.

Saliva is a popular remedy. So, lick the wart with your tongue the moment you wake up. If you cannot reach the wart with your tongue, use your forefinger to transfer saliva to the wart.

See also TRADITIONAL MEDICINE.

in order to protect it. Before each treatment, dead skin resulting from the previous application is removed by rubbing the wart with a pumice stone.

These treatments may cause scarring, so they should not be used on the face. Both acid treatment and podophyllin should be avoided during pregnancy.

Warts are also sometimes removed by treatment with a heated instrument (cautery) or a very cold instrument (cryosurgery). The procedures require great skill.

WASP STINGS

Unlike bees, which leave their stings embedded in the skin, wasps simply inject poisonous protein into their victims and can go on to sting again. The poison causes redness, pain and itching, but wasp stings are seldom dangerous.

They can, however, cause a rare and serious allergic reaction called anaphylactic SHOCK. The victim's blood pressure falls, he becomes light headed, short of breath, with a rapid 'thready' pulse and a widespread, itching rash. Call a doctor as quickly as possible if you suspect anaphylactic shock.

What the therapists recommend

Traditional Medicine Vinegar dabbed on the sting was a traditional remedy; moistened or chewed tobacco was believed to relieve pain and any swelling. Crushed plan-

tain or marigold leaves were used to soothe all sorts of stings.

Herbal Medicine Ice-cold water (or even an ice cube) can be applied to the sting – a few drops of lemon juice in the water is said to help neutralise the alkaline nature of the sting. Marigold ointment is then applied, reducing the inflammation.

An orthodox view

A doctor may suggest calamine lotion or antihistamine cream, or tablets such as terfenadine (Triludan) or chlorpheniramine (Piriton) to relieve the symptoms. If anaphylactic shock develops, a doctor or paramedic will give basic life support if the patient is unconscious, with injections of adrenaline and antihistamine.

If you are allergic to wasp stings, your doctor may provide you with a syringe of adrenaline to inject in an emergency.

WATER RETENTION

Swelling of parts of the body can occur when water leaks from the blood and accumulates in the tissues. Puffiness of the feet and ankles is the most common sign of it. The medical term for the condition is oedema; it used to be called dropsy.

Mild water retention, with swollen ankles and a bloated feeling, occurs when the circulation is slow – for example, after a long period of sitting or standing in the same position. The circulation may also be slow because of VARICOSE VEINS – or even due to the tight elastic top of socks.

Women who suffer from PREMENSTRUAL TENSION may notice weight gain, puffy ankles and swollen breasts during the week or so before a period. Water retention is common during PREGNANCY; it is sometimes severe and may be associated with high BLOOD PRESSURE and toxaemia.

Severe water retention may be caused by some KIDNEY COMPLAINTS, HEART DISORDERS or LIVER DISORDERS. In such cases the sufferer is clearly ill and needs medical attention. Symptoms may include severe breathlessness and swelling of the ankles, legs, buttocks and abdomen. The blood pressure may be extremely high and JAUNDICE may develop.

What the therapists recommend

Naturopathy You are advised to cut out salt from your diet; it encourages water retention. Stimulate the circulation with

EXERCISE and lose weight if necessary (see SLIMMING THE NATURAL WAY).

Herbal Medicine Dandelion is a natural diuretic. You can add fresh young leaves to salads, or drink an infusion of the leaves, or take dandelion extract.

Acupuncture Stimulation of the kidney and bladder meridians may help.

Traditional Medicine Try taking a pinch of ground broom seeds in a spoonful of honey.

An orthodox view

Diuretic extracts or herbs will get rid of water by making you pass more urine, but they give only temporary relief and can lead to DIABETES, GOUT and potassium deficiency. Diuretic drugs (water pills) carry the same risks but are taken under supervision, for they are available only on prescription.

Regular exercise and a healthy diet can reduce premenstrual water retention.

See your doctor if water retention is severe, taking a urine sample to be tested for signs of kidney disease. You may also be examined for signs of heart or liver disease and your blood pressure will be measured.

WEATHER AND HEALTH
Climate affects more than your moods . . .

We seldom think of the expression 'being under the weather' as literally true, but in fact doctors and alternative practitioners believe that climate and weather conditions do exert an important influence on our health and sense of well-being. Although some people appear to be more sensitive to the effects than others, nearly everyone has experienced the invigorating quality of mountain air, or knows the effects of a sunny day on their mood.

Other health effects can be less obvious and may appear only at certain times of the year. Many involve a whole range of weather factors which all influence one another, making it difficult to establish precise cause-and-effect relationships. Even so, a variety of factors are known to have definite effects. Some of the most important include:

Temperature This affects respiratory rate and the body's overall metabolic rate – the speed of the vital bodily processes. In cooler climates such as that of Britain, body heat is dissipated relatively fast, increasing metabolic rate and stimulating feelings of vitality. The high temperatures of tropical climates,

by contrast, slow down the body's functions and decrease energy levels because heat is lost relatively slowly.

Although moderate heat and cold pose no direct health risks, people in hot countries appear to be more susceptible to intestinal disorders, and those in cold countries to respiratory problems. Exposure to extreme temperatures of either sort can have serious consequences: disorders such as prickly heat, heat exhaustion and heat stroke in the case of hot weather, and CHILBLAINS, FROSTBITE and HYPOTHERMIA in cold.

Temperature also affects health in a variety of other ways. For example, cold weather keeps many people indoors during the British winter and reduces the amount of EXERCISE they take. Crowded public places such as trains and shops are often overheated and poorly ventilated – perfect breeding grounds for germs of all sorts. And the temptation to warm up with extra food and drink – often in the form of sweet snacks, rich meals, coffee and alcohol – easily gives rise to bad habits.

Rainfall Amounts of rain vary greatly in different areas of Britain, from parts of the north and west which have more than 250 wet days a year, to the south and east coasts with fewer than 175. Despite the popular view that dampness gives rise to COLDS, there is no medical evidence that this is so. Most doctors do, however, accept that there is a connection with rheumatic complaints.

Humidity Although Britain gets most of its rain during winter, the humidity or level of water vapour present in the air is actually lowest at this time, and reaches a maximum in July. Some doctors believe that low winter humidity may lead to drying out of the mucous membranes of the upper respiratory tract, leaving them vulnerable to infections.

'Bracing' and 'relaxing' climates Certain areas have long had reputations for being bracing or invigorating, while others are considered soothing and tranquil. A number of factors are thought to be involved, including wind, humidity, temperature and possibly the frequency of changes in the weather, but there is no accepted scientific definition.

Invigorating areas are thought to be the east coasts of England and Scotland; most hill districts, particularly the Derbyshire Peak District and Scottish mountain areas; parts of the Sussex coast between Bognor Regis and Eastbourne; and the north coast of Cornwall. Places reputed to have relaxing climates include the south coasts of Devon, Cornwall and Wales; low-lying areas in the west of England; some western areas of the south coast; and the Western Isles and west coast of Scotland, including areas in Galloway and around Glasgow.

Sunshine Surveys show that both people who are ill and those in good health report

feeling better on sunny days, and the tonic effects of a holiday in the sun are well known. Doctors and psychologists now recognise a condition termed Seasonal Affective Disorder (SAD) which affects some people during periods of little natural daylight such as northern winters. Sufferers become depressed, moody and lethargic at such times, but return to normal once the days begin to lengthen.

In addition, sunshine enables the body to manufacture vitamin D – important for the prevention of rickets in children – but since this can also be obtained from the diet, deficiencies seldom occur. More serious are the risks of SUNBURN and skin CANCER if overexposure to the sun occurs, particularly in those with fair hair and skin.

Wind The direction and speed of winds influences the way in which sounds are carried or dispersed, and if persistent the sound of the wind itself can cause irritation.

Using the weather in alternative medicine

Many alternative practitioners believe that the way an individual responds to different weather conditions can give valuable information about the correct diagnosis and treatment of problems.

In HOMOEOPATHY, remedies are often prescribed according to the conditions under which symptoms improve or grow worse. For example, asthma which is worse in damp weather may be treated with *Nat. sulph.*, while if the same symptoms improve in these conditions, *Hepar sulph.* may be used.

Weather is also considered important in several oriental approaches such as ACUPRESSURE, ACUPUNCTURE and MACROBIOTICS, which are based on achieving a balance of the body's YIN AND YANG forces. Yin is associated with coolness and damp, and yang with dryness and heat. Depending on the patient's individual disposition, his way of life and the symptoms he is suffering from, the practitioner will offer treatment to restore the two forces to a state of harmony.

A condition that is exacerbated by cold weather, for example, or a patient who lives in a cold climate, may be treated in ways designed to strengthen the heating, yang principle. Someone whose main symptoms are inflammation and a high temperature, or who in some other way shows excessively yang symptoms may need yin-strengthening measures.

How weather affects common ailments

SHORT-TERM EFFECTS	LONGER-TERM OR SEASONAL EFFECTS
Asthma Bronchial asthma is generally worse when the temperature drops suddenly, particularly if air pressure falls and wind speeds rise at the same time. It often improves when there is a high air pressure and fog.	Attacks are infrequent in winter, but increase from June onwards, becoming worse in late autumn.
Bronchitis Usually worsens in fog, especially if air pollution is heavy and the temperature falls at the same time.	Many attacks occur in winter, few in summer.
Hay fever Tends to be worse when the temperature drops.	Attacks increase in the flowering seasons of certain plants, especially grass. Usually worse in May and June.
Rheumatism and arthritis Most forms worsen when exposed to falling temperatures or strong winds. Humidity alone has little effect.	Arthritis tends to be most common in autumn and early winter.
Heart disorders Many problems occur shortly after a sharp drop in temperature.	In Britain death rates from these disorders are highest in January and February and lowest in July and August. In hot countries, rates are lowest in winter and highest in summer.
Colds Weather changes that affect the body's heat-regulating mechanism, the conditions of the mucous membranes, and the strength of the cold virus can all increase infections. Cold periods followed by sudden warming, for example, may increase susceptibility.	Susceptibility increases from September onwards, reaching a peak in February and March.
Influenza Conditions of low humidity and low wind speeds are associated with outbreaks.	Most cases occur between December and February, but vulnerability is high from September right through to March.

Air pollution may also be carried by wind, causing problems such as smog and acid rain (see HEALTH HAZARDS) many miles away.

Wind also adds greatly to the amount of body heat lost at low temperatures – known as 'wind chill'. Wind chill accounts for about 80 per cent of heat loss and is a more accurate indicator of how cold you feel than temperature alone. For example, a gale-force wind of 45mph (72km/h) at a temperature of –7°C (19°F) will lower your body temperature to the same extent as a light breeze of 5mph (8km/h) at –24°C (–12°F).

Fog In the past the dampness of fogs was blamed for a variety of rheumatic complaints, but these days the main danger is thought to come from atmospheric pollution which is inhaled in foggy conditions. It is well known that periods of fog in Britain tend to be closely followed by increases in breathing problems and deaths from respiratory illnesses. People who suffer from these conditions are usually advised not to live in foggy places such as damp river valleys, and to avoid heavily polluted or industrialised areas.

Cold fronts These occur where warm currents of air are pushed out by cold currents, causing a change in the weather. In Britain cold fronts are a frequent occurrence, and some sensitive people find that they bring feelings of nervousness and mental tension.

NERVOUS DISORDERS such as EPILEPSY are also thought to be worse at such times, and studies have shown that the number of suicides increases. Changes in barometric pressure as a result of a cold front may be responsible for INSOMNIA, and for increasing the number of cases of blocked arteries resulting from blood clots.

Ionisation The relative proportions of electrically positive and negative particles – or ions – in the air vary from place to place and are thought to have a number of health effects. People tend to feel at their best in places with more negative ions, such as at the seaside, in the mountains or near natural running water such as rivers or waterfalls.

High concentrations of positive ions occur before storms, when pollution is heavy, and in indoor environments where electrical appliances, central heating and synthetic fabrics contribute to the problem. They can cause symptoms such as HEADACHES, TENSION and DEPRESSION, and may make breathing problems such as ASTHMA worse. People who suffer from these effects may find that a small home negative ionising machine makes a difference (see IONISATION).

WHEAT GERM

Weight for weight, this food supplement is one of the richest known sources of vitamin E. It is also rich in folic acid and biotin (VITAMINS of the B-complex). Wheat germ is the embryo of the wheat grain, and is separated during milling. The grain is ground and sieved several times to separate the wheat germ from the flour. See EATING FOR HEALTH.

WHEEZING

The noisy low-pitched breathing sounds known as wheezing are louder on breathing out, unlike CROUP, which is louder on breathing in. The symptom is caused by obstruction of the bronchial tubes (airways) in the lungs, and if severe it can be very unpleasant and frightening.

A foreign body such as an inhaled peanut can sometimes result in wheezing, which is also a symptom of BRONCHITIS. However, the commonest cause is ASTHMA. The walls of the airways swell and become inflamed, and the muscles around them contract. At the same time the bronchial mucous glands may produce excessive mucus. All these result in coughing, shortness of breath and wheezing.

Warning Wheezing can be a symptom of a serious condition such as a foreign body in the lung or a potentially serious lung disease. Sufferers, especially elderly people and children, should therefore see a doctor.

What the therapists recommend

Homoeopathy For remedies, see ASTHMA, BRONCHITIS and WHOOPING COUGH.

Acupuncture The commonly used points are on the lung, conception and large intestine meridians. If body acupuncture results in little response, ear acupuncture, head needle therapy and MOXIBUSTION are used in turn.

Herbal Medicine A professional herbalist will aim to find the underlying cause(s) of the symptom. For self help, try mixing two drops of oil of lavender in one teaspoon of vegetable oil and rub it into the chest. Inhalations of menthol and eucalyptus should also help.

Ionisation Many people suffering from heavy colds and persistent bronchitis find that using a negative ioniser reduces their wheezing and makes breathing easier. A humidifier in the room may also help.

An orthodox view

If there is a foreign body in an airway it must be removed before it causes partial collapse of a lung or PNEUMONIA.

When wheezing is caused by asthma, a doctor may prescribe a muscle relaxant such as salbutamol (Ventolin) to open the airways, an inhaled steroid such as beclomethasone (Becotide) to reduce swelling and inflammation, and a medicine such as cromoglycate to alleviate the allergy. Both patient and doctor can find out how well the sufferer is breathing – that is, measure the patient's 'peak flow' – when the patient blows into an inexpensive, simple peak flow meter.

WHOOPING COUGH

This infectious disease of childhood is also known as pertussis, and occurs in epidemics. It is caused by a bacterium, which is spread in the water droplets breathed out by an infected child, and attacks the mucous membranes lining the airways.

After an incubation of seven to 14 days, a mild fever, cough, runny nose and loss of appetite develop. The cough becomes worse, particularly at night, with 'whooping' – a noisy indrawing of breath – at the end of a cough. The child often vomits after a paroxysm of coughing, and may be very ill. The sufferer is infectious for 21 days after the onset of the 'whooping'. The illness may last up to four months, and the symptoms often recur when the child has a cough or cold.

Warning If a child develops a whoop, call the doctor immediately – whooping cough is a notifiable disease and the condition can in some cases prove fatal. Complications can include dehydration (which results from the vomiting), PNEUMONIA and encephalitis – inflammation of the brain.

What the therapists recommend

Homoeopathy If a violent tickle in the throat brings on a fit of coughing, which is worse at night, and the child must hold his chest when coughing, give _Drosera 30_. When the sufferer vomits frequently, try _Ipecacuanha 6_ every six hours. If the child is red, hot, has a bursting cough and is worse at night and when lying down, give _Belladonna 6_ every hour until there is improvement.

Herbal Medicine A consultation is recommended. The herbalist will use a choice of expectorants – preparations that aid the production of saliva and mucus so that they may be coughed up more easily. These include white horehound, mullein flowers, thyme and elecampane. He may also give relaxants such as hyssop or lavender if needed.

Naturopathy With other treatment, the naturopath will advise plenty of liquids, especially if the child is vomiting, and the avoidance of dairy products and large meals. He may also prescribe vitamin C, the dose depending on the child's age.

An orthodox view

Vaccination against whooping cough is recommended, despite possible side effects, as these are generally far less dangerous than the disease itself and its complications. Children should have a course of three injections during their first year. The whooping cough vaccine is now usually combined with those for diphtheria, tetanus and polio.

If ECZEMA results, the course should not be stopped. However, the doctor may advise against immunisation of a child who suffers from epilepsy or who has been brain-damaged since birth, or one whose parents suffer from epilepsy. The injections should not be given when a child is feverish or unwell, but may be given safely during a minor illness without fever. An attack of whooping cough usually gives the child immunity for life.

If a child develops whooping cough, a doctor may prescribe a course of antibiotics which, if taken early enough during the illness, may make it less severe. The child should be given extra liquids, regular doses of children's aspirin to reduce the fever and ease discomfort, and a proprietary cough medicine if it helps. Exposure to tobacco smoke will make the cough much worse. Hospital treatment may be necessary if the child is very ill.

WILLPOWER

By using our willpower in a positive way we may help ourselves to recover from – if not prevent – illness and disease. Doctors and nurses are familiar with patients who, instead of willing themselves to get well, give up. On the other hand, there are many recorded instances of sick people who, instead of worsening or dying, have 'miraculously' recovered of their own accord.

Self-help techniques such as AUTOSUGGESTION, COUÉISM and VISUALISATION THERAPY can aid people to achieve the will to live. To this Emile Coué, developer of Couéism, added another important factor – the imagination. This, he claimed, was even more powerful than the will. Even though people may have the will to recover, he said, they often _imagined_ that they would not. 'When the will and the imagination are at war,' he stated, 'the imagination invariably wins.'

He concluded that it was vital to train the imagination – by means of a YOGA-like concentration – to work in harness with the will. Between them, he contended, they could make the nervous system throw off any physical or psychological disease.

WIND

Excessive gas – or wind – in the digestive tract is known as flatulence. It can result in considerable discomfort – and can find an embarrassingly audible means of announcing its presence and making its escape.

The gas is sometimes air swallowed with hastily gulped food, so eating more slowly can reduce it. Or it can result from taking fizzy drinks, which can be cut out. A more complex cause is a failure of the digestive system to break down certain foods, leaving a residue that ferments in the bowel.

Beans are among the best known of these foods. Others which commonly give rise to the problem include Brussels sprouts, broccoli, cabbage, cauliflower, cucumbers, green peppers, lettuce, nuts, onions, peas, radishes, raw apples, melons and prunes. Sufferers should find out which foods are causing the trouble by cutting them out, then avoiding altogether those that induce wind.

A bloated feeling in the abdomen, frequent belching or breaking wind and CONSTIPATION are the usual symptoms. If wind persists or you also have pain, seek medical advice. An ULCER, hiatus hernia and other conditions can also cause similar symptoms.

What the therapists recommend

NATUROPATHY

Self help Practitioners recommend 24 hours' FASTING to clear the system, then simple meals, keeping carbohydrates (such as starches and sugars) and proteins (meat, fish, cheese) for separate meals (see HAY DIET). Use plenty of GARLIC, or take garlic capsules. Alternate hot and cold compresses on the abdomen may ease discomfort.

Consultation A diet to suit your needs will be worked out. Papain might be recommended. This enzyme, obtained from papaya (or papaw) fruit and taken as tablets, is held to aid digestion. You may also be given advice on gentle massage of the abdomen.

Other alternative treatments

Herbal Medicine Use thyme, sage, marjoram and rosemary in cooking, and after a meal chew caraway seeds or a clove, or sip peppermint tea. Between meals sip a small cup of camomile, meadowsweet or balm tea. Add 5g of dried camomile flowers (or 4g of meadowsweet or 3g of balm) to a cup of boiling water. Leave to infuse for ten minutes, strain and sip while still hot. If the flatulence persists, seek medical advice.

Homoeopathy For people who get wind after sweet food or when they are warm or worried, *Argentum nit.* is said to help. For those who suffer in damp weather, late in the day or after fatty food, *Carbo. veg.* can be an alternative. One tablet every half-hour should be taken up to six doses, whenever there is discomfort. *Lycopodium* is for those with ravenous hunger that is satisfied by only a few mouthfuls, who find cabbage indigestible, or have a strong desire for sweets.

Aromatherapy A therapist will blend essential oils to massage on your abdomen. Blend basil, sage, peppermint and myrrh in a teaspoon of carrier oil or lotion (see p. 36) to make a mixture you can apply yourself: rub on to the abdomen in a clockwise direction.

An orthodox view

Doctors agree that a simple diet, cutting down on sugar, fat and coffee, and eating slowly, should prevent wind. Better posture also helps. Massage and compresses will ease discomfort but charcoal tablets, available from chemists, are the preferred conventional remedy for quick relief – they are thought to absorb gas from the gut.

WORMS

Threadworms and tapeworms are the usual causes of worm infections in Britain. Threadworms are widespread, and children are particularly affected; tapeworms are less common. Contaminated food is a source of both types of infection.

Threadworms, also known as pinworms, can occur in even the cleanest homes and are one of the oldest human infections known – threadworm eggs have been found in fossils 100,000 years old. They commonly infect the human large intestine and cause inflammation and itching around the anus. They may be visible around it or in the faeces. At night female threadworms, each about ³⁄₈in (10mm) long, emerge from the anus, lay up to 10,000 eggs around it, and later die. The eggs live for up to three weeks and are highly infectious.

If the child victim scratches his bottom, eggs adhere to his hands and under his fingernails. They may then be transferred to his mouth, either directly or via food, and swallowed. If they reach the intestine, the eggs develop into adult worms and the cycle continues. Besides reinfecting himself, the victim may also infect other children and family members.

Threadworm infections sometimes cause abdominal pain and, rarely, APPENDICITIS. The infection may enter the vulva and cause a bloody vaginal discharge in girls.

Tapeworms live in the intestines of human beings and many other animals. They can grow up to 33ft (10m) long, and consist of a head, a neck and a ribbon-like body of separate segments. The worms attach themselves to the inner lining of the gut by suckers and hooks on their heads, and absorb food (intestinal contents) through their whole surface.

Segments full of eggs detach themselves from the worm and pass out of the body with the faeces. If the eggs are eaten by an intermediate host – for example, a cow or pig – they develop into cysts in its body tissues.

Humans become infected by eating tapeworm cysts in raw or inadequately cooked beef or pork. However, unlike threadworms, tapeworms cannot be passed directly from person to person.

Infection results in weight loss, nausea, upper abdominal discomfort, DIARRHOEA and irritability. Occasionally portions of the worm emerge from the anus, and appear in underclothes or bed linen.

A human being can act as the intermediate host for pork tapeworms. Cysts develop in his muscles, eyes and brain, causing muscle pains, weakness, fever, blindness, or symptoms that resemble those of EPILEPSY or a brain tumour.

What the therapists recommend

Naturopathy A consultation is necessary for threadworm infections. GARLIC, carrots and pumpkin seeds are all said to help clear the infection, and herbal medicines will be suggested. You will be advised to keep the fingernails short and well scrubbed, and to change your towels frequently.

Practitioners believe that garlic and raw carrots can weaken tapeworms, but that strong treatment is necessary to paralyse and expel them, so a consultation will be necessary in this case too.

Herbal Medicine A consultation is deemed necessary for threadworm infections. Regular intake of garlic and raw carrots is recommended to weaken the worms, making it easier for stronger remedies given by the medical herbalist to work.

A consultation is also advised for tapeworm infections as the remedies necessary to paralyse and expel the worms are potentially toxic. These remedies include wormwood, tansy and male fern, which are usually given with powerful purgatives.

An orthodox view

Threadworms are not dangerous and can be eradicated by treating the whole family with piperazine (Antepar or Pripsen) or mebendazole (Vermox). Careful hygiene, including the washing of hands and scrubbing of nails with a nail brush before meals and after each visit to the lavatory, together with a morning bath to remove any eggs laid overnight, will help control the spread of the infection. However, reinfection is common.

To avoid infection with tapeworm, do not eat raw or undercooked beef or pork. This is particularly important in the countries of Eastern Europe, Africa and South and Central America, where tapeworm infection is common. If you do become infected, a single oral dose of niclosamide (Yomesan) will eradicate the worm.

Do's and don'ts for wind

Do avoid any foods that you know give you wind, such as beans and sprouts.

Do eat more slowly, chewing well.

Do sit erect for meals and improve your general posture – with the ALEXANDER TECHNIQUE, for example.

Don't drink with your meals and avoid coffee and strong tea at any time.

Don't have protein and starch at the same meal – and go easy on sugars and raw vegetables.

Don't eat fat or too many pulses, especially soya.

Don't overeat.

YIN AND YANG

Ancient Chinese philosophy was based on the belief in two opposing but complementary forces, yin and yang, which together make up a balanced whole. Yin was the more passive, conserving force, yang the more positive, thrusting force. All understanding and explanation of the world, including medical science, was in terms of yin and yang.

The first treatise setting out a comprehensive system of medical symptoms and treatments according to the yin-yang principle was compiled by Chang Chung-ching about AD 200. The system was centuries old even then and is still followed.

When an individual's yin and yang are not in perfect balance, disease is said to result. Treatment is aimed not at symptoms, but at building up whichever of the two forces is deficient. Careful assessment (see ORIENTAL DIAGNOSIS) is needed to decide which is deficient before treatment is given. Treatment may be by stimulation of energy-flow channels as in ACUPRESSURE, ACUPUNCTURE, MOXIBUSTION, SHIATSU, REFLEXOLOGY and T'AI-CHI CH'UAN, by self-massage (see DO-IN), or by diet (see MACROBIOTICS).

YOGA
Teaching control of mind and body

In the last few years, yoga has begun to be used more and more as a therapy to help in the management of particular ailments, especially of STRESS and stress-related problems. Because it works on body and mind together, yoga is recommended for the relief of such conditions. HEART DISORDERS and ASTHMA are among other ailments said to respond to yoga therapy.

Taken in its entirety, yoga – the word is Sanskrit for 'yoke' or 'union' – is a system of spiritual, mental and physical training. It grew up originally in India. In Western countries it is the physical aspect – the postures and exercises called Hatha yoga – that is best known, but to the devotee other systems, such as Raja (which focuses on mind control), Jnana (which concentrates on intellect and understanding), Karma (moral action) and Bakti (a devotional aspect), are equally important.

Yoga exercises can, of course, be practised by people with all kinds of spiritual

The great violinist Sir Yehudi Menuhin suffered a frozen shoulder that threatened to end his career. Yoga exercises freed it and allowed him to continue playing.

belief, or by people with none. Nevertheless, yoga's underlying philosophy stresses the influence of mind over body, and holds that mental and spiritual development are necessary to reinforce the benefits that the physical exercises can bring.

It is only during this century that yoga has spread to Britain. Until the 1960s virtually the only people to practise it here were Britons who had lived or travelled in the East and those who were interested in oriental philosophies. A number of classical musicians were among them. Yoga helped to save the career of one of them – the violinist Sir Yehudi Menuhin, whose playing was threatened by a FROZEN SHOULDER.

With the guidance of his teacher, B.K.S. Iyengar, Sir Yehudi worked at yoga exercises that were reputed to be good for the shoulder. As a result of the publicity given to the recovery, yoga gained enormously in popularity. Through demonstrations on television and the founding of many local clubs and similar organisations, yoga has continued to spread. About half a million people in Britain now practise yoga regularly, and there are some 5000 teachers.

The ancient teachers of yoga worked out some of their postures through watching the movements of animals, which seem to move and relax so much more effectively than humans. The postures are designed to develop flexibility and controlled relaxation. The movements are done slowly and the postures held for a minute or more to build up awareness of the body and its tensions and patterns of behaviour. There should be no sense of extreme exertion or display during yoga exercises; the essence is inner, concentrated awareness.

Breathing plays an important part in yoga. According to yoga philosophy breath embodies the individual's *prana*, or life force. Although breathing is an unconscious function, it can be consciously modified – with a consequent effect on well-being. Breathing also reflects closely our various emotional states, so awareness and control of breathing patterns can play a part in creating mental and emotional harmony (see HYPERVENTILATION; RELAXATION AND BREATHING). Various yoga exercises càn be practised to develop different levels of breathing – diaphragm, rib cage and shoulder.

Who it can help Yoga teachers believe that anyone with patience and perseverance can benefit from taking up yoga. Provided that a realistic view is taken of physical capabilities, it can be practised from childhood into very old age. Nor is it designed just for unworldly people; indeed, teachers hold that the more disturbed someone's daily life becomes, the greater is the need for something that brings a compensating calm.

Until quite recently, yoga's role in the West was primarily to promote fitness of body and mind, to be a form of preventive medicine rather than a therapy for specific conditions. It has long been used to help people who suffer from TENSION. Both physical and psychological tensions are often expressed in tense muscles, which may remain contracted in a state of spasm throughout the day. Consciously stretching and releasing the muscles enables the mind to let go of the worries and stresses which

Salute to the sun

The 'sun salute' – a series of 12 yoga postures – is designed to relax and tone up the mind and body. Traditionally, it is practised facing the sun at sunrise and sunset. However, if this is not feasible, you can picture the sun rising or setting over a beautiful, tranquil scene, engulfing you with its rays.

The postures can be done with perfect safety on your own. But they should <u>not</u> be attempted by women who are pregnant or menstruating, except under expert guidance. And they are not suitable for anyone suffering from low back pain, high blood pressure, hernia (rupture), or blood clots in the veins. The postures are performed as illustrated, reading anticlockwise:

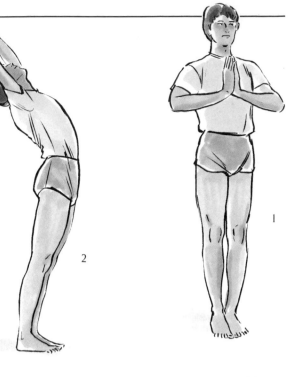

1 Stand upright with your knees and feet together. Place your palms together and hold them against your chest, with the fingers pointing upwards.

2 As you breathe in, raise your hands above your head and bend gently backwards. Your palms should be facing up and your head reaching back.

3 Breathe out and lean forwards without bending your knees. With practice, you will be able to touch the floor with your fingertips, or even rest your palms on the floor.

4 Breathe in, bending your knees and putting your palms flat on the floor. Push your left leg back, and rest the knee on the floor. Look up and push your hips forward.

5 Holding your breath, put your right leg back, next to the left. Use your arms to keep your body raised, with the palms still kept flat on the floor.

6 Breathe out and move your body backwards, keeping your hands in the same place, until your buttocks rest on your heels and your forehead on the floor.

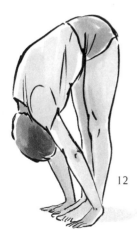

12

11

10

9

8

7

7 Breathing in and then out, come forward taking your weight on your hands. Rest your knees, chest and forehead on the floor. Keep your abdomen and pelvis off the floor.

8 Breathe in fully and straighten your arms. Stretch your head up as far as you comfortably can, arching your back.

9 Breathe out and push up your buttocks, keeping your hands and feet flat on the floor. Straighten your legs and your back so that your body forms a triangle with the floor.

10 Breathing in and then out, bend your knees, resting your buttocks on your heels and your forehead on the floor.

11 Breathe in, bringing your left knee up between your hands and stretching forwards and upwards. Keep your palms flat on floor.

12 Breathe out, bringing your right foot up to your left. Straighten your legs and bend from the waist. Then breathe in and stand erect. Now you can stop or repeat the salute once or several times if you like. In successive salutes, alternate the leg you take back in stage 4, and forward in stage 11.

originally brought about the muscle spasm.

People with problems in movement and posture benefit from the twisting and bending of yoga exercises which develop flexibility in the spine and the muscles of the back. Because the spine carries nerves from the brain to the trunk and limbs, its well-being is intimately involved in many reflex movements and in the control of PAIN. Yoga is especially useful for people whose problems result from a sedentary lifestyle. It also helps to keep the joints of the arms and legs healthy. It has helped people disabled by POLIOMYELITIS.

In its recent therapeutic role, yoga has been used particularly to treat ailments such as BACK PAIN, HEADACHES, high BLOOD PRESSURE and heart conditions, asthma and BRONCHITIS, HYSTERIA, ACID STOMACH, and PREMENSTRUAL TENSION.

It is also being tried for some cases of chronic illness, including RHEUMATOID ARTHRITIS, MULTIPLE SCLEROSIS and DIABETES, for cerebral palsy, for learning difficulties, for OSTEOPOROSIS, for postnatal depression, and to prepare pregnant women for childbirth (see NATURAL CHILDBIRTH).

Finding a therapist or teacher For difficult health problems you should make sure to consult a skilled yoga therapist. There is still a shortage of experienced therapists since therapeutic yoga is still in its infancy. Your regular doctor may be able to recommend a

Do's and don'ts about yoga

Do take lessons with a qualified yoga teacher, choosing one who concentrates on your particular interest.

Do practise regularly, preferably daily.

Don't compete with classmates; yoga should not be a strain.

Do consult a doctor before you take up yoga if you are taking medication, have a disability, or are experiencing abnormal physical symptoms.

Do wear loose or stretchy clothing for yoga and put a thick mat or folded blanket on the floor.

Don't practise yoga with a full bladder or bowels.

Do take a shower before and after yoga to complete the relaxation and refreshment.

Do fit in your practice before a meal — or wait for three hours after a heavy meal, one hour after a snack.

Don't do yoga immediately after exposure to strong sun or you may feel dizzy and sick.

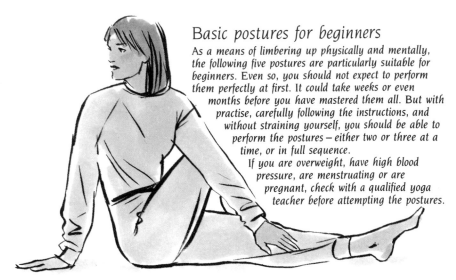

Basic postures for beginners

As a means of limbering up physically and mentally, the following five postures are particularly suitable for beginners. Even so, you should not expect to perform them perfectly at first. It could take weeks or even months before you have mastered them all. But with practise, carefully following the instructions, and without straining yourself, you should be able to perform the postures – either two or three at a time, or in full sequence.

If you are overweight, have high blood pressure, are menstruating or are pregnant, check with a qualified yoga teacher before attempting the postures.

1 <u>Spinal twist</u> Sit with your legs stretched out. Raise your right leg and put your foot on the far side of your left knee. Breathing out, turn your trunk to the right. Reach towards your left ankle with your left hand. Rest your right hand on the floor behind you and keep your back straight. Each time you breathe out twist a little further to the right. Hold for at least 1 minute, then repeat, twisting to the left.

2 <u>Bow</u> Lie face down with your feet together. Bend your knees and bring your feet towards your head. Grasp your ankles. Then, as you breathe in, pull on your ankles to raise your thighs, chest and head off the floor. Keep your arms straight and rest on your abdomen. At first, your legs will be apart, but bring them together as you gain skill. Hold the bow for 3-10 breaths. Then breathe out and release your legs.

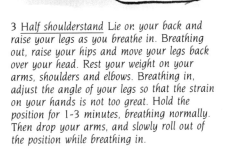

3 <u>Half shoulderstand</u> Lie on your back and raise your legs as you breathe in. Breathing out, raise your hips and move your legs back over your head. Rest your weight on your arms, shoulders and elbows. Breathing in, adjust the angle of your legs so that the strain on your hands is not too great. Hold the position for 1-3 minutes, breathing normally. Then drop your arms, and slowly roll out of the position while breathing in.

4 <u>Bridge</u> Lie on your back, arms by your sides, with knees bent and legs slightly apart. Breathe in and raise the mid section of your body. Interlock your fingers and stretch your arms out straight along the floor. Tuck your

shoulders under you as you lean towards one side and then the other. Push with your feet and arms to increase the bridge. Breathe in with your abdomen and hold for at least 1 minute. Lower your body and straighten legs.

5 <u>Triangle</u> (Above) Breathing in, raise your arms horizontally and place your legs comfortably apart. (Right) Point your left foot out and, breathing out, bend to the left without leaning forward and slide your left hand down your leg towards your ankle. At the same time, raise your right arm, palm facing forwards. Look up at your right hand. Hold the position for at least 1 minute, stretching a little further each time you breathe out. Then breathe in and return to your original position. Repeat the exercise, this time bending to the right.

therapist. If not, contact the Yoga Biomedical Trust, PO Box 140, Cambridge CB4 3SY. For a small fee (about £6) the Trust will find a suitable therapist for your condition. Send a stamped, addressed envelope if you write to the Trust.

Various training programmes are now under way to make up the shortage of therapists. Qualified yoga teachers attend courses on medical topics and on tailoring yogic practices to particular conditions; they also acquire extensive practical experience, usually over several years.

For minor problems, you will receive adequate help from an ordinary yoga teacher rather than a specially trained therapist. A teacher is also essential if you wish to take up yoga for general physical and mental health. In the more difficult early stages, a regular class with an experienced teacher will prove invaluable not only for physical guidance, but for helping you to strengthen your mental control and concentration.

It should not be too difficult to find a class since most towns in Britain now have several yoga teachers. Many classes are organised by adult education centres. Information about classes can also be found in sports centres, public libraries and health shops.

There are several schools of yoga, each placing its own emphasis on yoga's different aspects – postures, breathing, deep relaxation and MEDITATION. Be sure to choose a class to suit your interest; those who want to explore the spiritual side of yoga would not be content with what is principally an exercise class. Contact the Yoga Biomedical Trust for advice.

Seeing a therapist or teacher A yoga therapist will tailor routines to suit each individual case. No set pattern exists. The growing awareness and control of the patient and the insight of the therapist, as well as the condition itself, will determine the exact form of the therapy.

When you attend a yoga class, you will be expected to perform the exercises along with all the other class members, led by the teacher. Classes generally last about 1-1½ hours. Some classes are designed specifically for beginners, others for more advanced students. There is a spirit of friendly working together, rather than competition.

Self help Progress in yoga is said to come gradually through persistent development of flexibility, strength and mental poise. To aid this development, regular practice at home is recommended, as well as attending classes. Using the class work as the basis, you can plan a routine to follow at home. The following exercises, just three of the hundreds of yoga exercises, could form part of this home routine. Wear loose or stretchy clothing and do the exercises on a thick mat or folded

Yoga: a system for all that was once only for the few

The practice of yoga is extremely ancient. Seals made some 4000 years ago that have been excavated in the prehistoric city of Mohenjo-Daro (in present-day Pakistan) show men sitting crosslegged in positions resembling those adopted in yoga. From early times yoga had a wide-ranging influence on Indian culture; simple exercises, for example, are used as a form of therapy in the subcontinent's traditional system of AYURVEDIC MEDICINE.

One of the most influential yoga teachers, or yogis, was Patanjali, who drew up the formal classification of the discipline that is still in use today. Writing in about 300 BC, he divided the practice of yoga into eight parts. The first two parts are concerned with conduct – with living a peaceful and harmonious life devoted to study, simplicity and cleanliness, and shunning greed, excess and anything that caused harm to other creatures.

The next two of Patanjali's divisions set out the physical aspects of yoga and describe various exercises that calm and energise the body and the mind.

The last four divisions concern the development of various mental and spiritual qualities: detachment from worldly concerns; the ability to rise above the distractions of everyday life; concentration; calm expansion of the mind; and finally, realisation or *samadhi*, a spiritual transformation which brings about a deep insight into the nature of reality.

For century upon century the full practice of yoga was restricted to a small elite, to philosophers and meditators who lived apart from the world in forests or caves, sometimes entirely alone, sometimes in small groups. Each of these yogis would pass on his knowledge and methods to just a few devoted followers.

It is only during the 20th century that the situation has changed markedly. Indian teachers and doctors began to make yoga accessible to all at public centres, and now the change has been so radical that it is the policy of the Indian government that physical yoga exercises should be taught to all children in school. And the spread has not stopped at India's boundaries; yoga is now practised by millions of people in countries in every part of the world.

A picture to focus the mind
Devotional images were often used as an aid to yoga meditation. This painting dates from the 17th or 18th century and shows the sacred lotus flower surrounding a figure seated in the 'lotus position' with legs crossed and feet drawn up onto the thighs. The painting comes from Rajasthan in north-west India and belongs to the Jain religious tradition which acquired yogic teachings from Hinduism. Adherents of Jainism practise reverence for all forms of life, and believe that the soul is reincarnated many times before achieving perfection and being liberated from earthly existence.

blanket on the floor of a warm, well-ventilated room.

The cobra This exercise aims to develop flexibility and muscle tone in the back.

Lie face down with toes pointed, elbows bent and close to the body, and palms down on the floor beside your shoulders. As you

Conditions where yoga has been of help

In 1983 the Yoga Biomedical Trust conducted a poll of 2700 people who practised yoga and were suffering from one or more of 20 different ailments. For each condition, over 70 per cent of those polled said that yoga had helped them to improve.

The first column of figures shows the number of people who answered 'Yes' to the question 'Have you suffered from this condition?' and the second the percentage of those who answered 'Yes' to the question 'Has yoga helped this condition?'

DISORDER	NUMBER OF CASES	PERCENTAGE HELPED
Back pain	1142	98
Arthritis or rheumatism	589	90
Anxiety	838	94
Migraine	464	80
Insomnia	542	82
Nerve or muscle disease	112	96
Premenstrual tension	848	77
Menopausal disorders	247	83
Other menstrual problems	317	68
Hypertension	150	84
Heart disease	50	94
Asthma or bronchitis	226	88
Duodenal ulcers	40	90
Haemorrhoids	391	88
Obesity	240	74
Diabetes	10	80
Cancer	29	90
Smoking	219	74
Alcoholism	26	100

breathe in, raise your head slowly, looking upwards. Hold the position while you breathe out. Then, breathing in again, slowly raise your chest as far as you can, using your back and abdominal muscles to do so, not your arms. Breathe out.

Then, breathing in once more, slowly arch further upwards, using your arms to help. Arch up as far as you can without lifting your navel from the floor and hold the position for two or three normal breaths. Then lower yourself, uncoiling vertebra by vertebra until your face is back on the floor. Rest for a time with your head turned to the side.

Half shoulderstand This inverted posture benefits the abdominal organs and refreshes you when you are tired. But avoid it if you have high blood pressure, are overweight, or are pregnant or menstruating.

Lie on your back with legs together and arms by your sides. As you breathe in, raise your legs until they are vertical; bend your knees if necessary and keep your lower back close to the floor. Pause for a short time in this position.

Then, as you breathe out, continue the leg movement, taking your legs right back over your head and raising your lower back off the floor. Put your hands on your lower back, keeping your elbows on the floor, to give you support. Adjust the angle of your legs to give an easy, relaxed balance. Rest there for one to three minutes, breathing normally. Then lower your arms, breathe in, and gently roll out of the posture.

Tense and relax This exercise makes you aware of your muscles and helps you to relax them at will. The whole sequence should take about two minutes.

Lie on your back with legs together and arms by your sides. Tighten all your muscles, working from toes to head. As you breathe in deeply, tighten first your toes, then your feet, then ankles, calves, kneecaps, thigh muscles. As you breathe out, tighten your abdomen, clench your fists, then tighten your lower arms, upper arms and shoulders. Breathe in deeply and tighten your chest, throat and face. Make yourself tighter all over. Hold this as long as your breath lasts, then release all the muscles. Move your legs apart and your arms out with palms upwards. Relax your whole body completely so that you feel as if you are sinking into the floor.

An orthodox view

Yoga, like other forms of meditation and relaxation, helps to relieve many conditions. Provided the exercises are carried out properly, they will improve mobility and circulation; being non-competitive, they should pose no danger of injury.

If yoga is to be used to treat a specific condition, it is essential that the condition

should first be properly diagnosed by a qualified doctor. A few doctors do refer patients to yoga therapists and some doctors are taking part in controlled trials to measure the results produced by yoga. Most doctors, however, still see yoga only as a beneficial form of gentle exercise.

YOGHURT

The benefits of yoghurt come from 'acidophilus' bacteria in it. These convert milk into yoghurt by forming lactic acid, which partially curdles the milk and suppresses the growth of harmful bacteria. Eating live yoghurt strengthens the natural bacteria population of the gut, helping to fight off infections.

Most yoghurts are sold with these bacteria still alive but kept dormant by refrigeration, and develop a sharp, acid taste if the bacteria in them are allowed to be active. In heat-treated yoghurt – marked pasteurised, sterilised, long-life or UHT – the bacteria have all been killed off, but the lactic acid has by then already been produced and the growth of harmful bacteria inhibited. However, once the carton has been opened, the yoghurt is then still subject to bacterial contamination.

Yoghurt is a source of protein, natural sugars, fat, calcium and other minerals, as well as of B vitamins. The amount of fat it contains depends on the milk used. Yoghurts sold as low-fat are less than 2 per cent fat, compared with about 3.5 per cent fat in whole-milk yoghurt and up to about 10 per cent in thick Greek yoghurts.

Making your own yoghurt

Bring 1 pint (600ml) of milk slowly to the boil in a thick-bottomed saucepan. Let it cool to blood heat – test by sprinkling a few drops on the inside of your wrist; it should feel neither hot nor cold.

Stir in a tablespoon of live yoghurt (from your last bought carton), then pour the mixture into a clean vacuum flask, screw on the top and leave for six to eight hours. Alternatively, pour the mixture into a clean shallow dish, wrap it in a linen cloth and then in a thick towel, and put it in a warm airing cupboard for six to eight hours.

The yoghurt will keep for up to six days in the refrigerator. Use the last tablespoonful for the next batch.

ZEN
A Buddhist path to self-discovery

The Japanese form of Buddhism known as Zen is a system of MEDITATION and sustained self-discipline aimed at transforming completely the everyday experience of its adherents through teachings of insight and self-awareness.

Buddhism began in India in the 6th century BC, from where it was taken to China in AD 520 by a monk named Bodhidharma. The type of meditation he taught became known in China as *ch'an*. In the 12th century it was introduced into Japan, where it has flourished ever since as Zen.

Zen meditation is aimed at achieving direct insight into yourself at a level too deep to be expressed in words. When attained, this is known as enlightenment. Like other forms of Buddhism, Zen also teaches that unhappiness comes from longing for things to be other than they really are, and that learning to accept the real world is an important step on the road to enlightenment.

In Buddhism, the sense of a fixed personal identity is seen as the strongest illusion standing in the way of enlightenment. Everyone wants to believe that the 'self' or personality with which they identify is a permanent one, but Buddhism holds that everything has to change – including this. Teaching centres on helping you to see yourself as part of a never-ending process of change, and of loosening your attachment to a particular self-image.

Who it can help Zen meditation and training aims to help anyone who feels the need for a deeper level of insight and self-awareness in their daily life, or is dissatisfied with the materialistic 'I-centred' way of life that dominates Western society. The new perspective taught by Zen and the effects of practising techniques such as meditation may also help with problems such as STRESS, ANXIETY and DEPRESSION that are aspects of daily life for many Westerners.

Finding a teacher Zen is taught as a form of apprenticeship – each student gets personal tuition from a particular teacher. The teacher's role is to guide, encourage and, if necessary, challenge the pupil's progress. To find a teacher, or for further information, contact The Buddhist Society, 58 Eccleston Square, London SW1V 1PH.

Seeing a teacher Zen aims at developing a kind of direct understanding based on intuition and going beyond normal thought and reason. Three main techniques are used:

daily life practice, meditation, and special anecdotes, riddles and puzzles which are designed to carry thought beyond the limits of the intellect.

Daily life practice The aim is to apply the Buddhist principle of 'mindfulness' in every waking moment. This means being continually aware of your own responses, and devoting yourself fully to each activity as you perform it, rather than wishing you were doing something else or saying, 'I want . . .' or, 'If only . . .'

The difficulty here lies in overcoming the common desire to hang onto your illusions and desires – even though they can cause anger, frustration and disappointment.

Zen teaches that by seeing these negative feelings for what they really are, by accepting and 'suffering through' them, the wilful, demanding side of the personality can be tamed. In this state happiness and good fortune are gratefully accepted when they come, but the student does not become attached to them, since he knows that, like everything else, they will pass.

Meditation Known as *za-zen* (literally, 'sitting meditation'), this is really a special kind of daily life practice. Meditators sit crosslegged on cushions, with weight balanced equally on buttocks and knees, the spine erect and the head balanced upright.

At first, they learn to meditate by silently counting their breaths from one to ten. When other thoughts arise, the meditator must set them aside without dwelling on them, and start the count again.

Za-zen is often both physically and mentally uncomfortable. Maintaining the same posture for long periods can be painful, and meditation forces students to confront the turmoil of their own restless thoughts.

With practice, however, meditators learn to let thoughts come and go without making judgments about them. Eventually, a state is reached where the sitter is aware without there being a personal 'I' who is aware.

Za-zen is practised daily, either privately or in a group. Occasionally, there are longer periods of meditation known as *sesshin*, which can go on for hours or even days.

Anecdotes, riddles and puzzles Zen abounds with stories, conundrums, parables and paradoxes intended to 'trap' or jolt the rational mind, freeing the student for new ways of thinking. For example, one story tells of two monks looking at a flag flapping in the breeze and arguing. One says: 'The flag is moving.' The other insists: 'No, the wind is moving.' A passing master rebukes them, saying: 'It is your minds that are moving.' Even this, teachers say, is not the last word.

More advanced Zen students are sometimes given a *koan* to meditate on by their teacher. These are puzzles that cannot be

understood or solved by reason. Two examples are: 'What is the sound of one hand clapping?' and 'Show me your original face before you were born.'

The effect is to confront the intellect with a barrier which no amount of logical thinking can penetrate. Instead, insight may burst in with a response born of the immediate moment – a smile, a shout, the sight of raindrops trickling down a windowpane, for example. The answer is to 'un-ask' the question; the problem lies in calling it a problem.

Zen teaches that with each moment of insight, the stranglehold of the personal 'I' on the student's way of thinking is loosened and a new, deeper understanding grows. With this understanding comes an ability to live comfortably in the present – whatever the circumstances – and a feeling of 'travelling light', without strong attachments, in the everyday world.

An orthodox view

There is a danger that the very unfamiliarity of Zen could make it attractive to some people damaged by or out of touch with everyday life. However, Zen is not a form of psychotherapy and it cannot provide easy relief from mental or emotional troubles. The amount of self-confrontation involved may even make it dangerous for some people with weak psychological defences.

Zen encompasses an approach to life and living founded on an oriental view of the universe. Many of the methods practised by Zen monks have been introduced into Western stress-reduction programmes, but learning them through Zen itself involves embracing the underlying Buddhist philosophy as well.

ZEN GARDEN
Meditating amid beauty and peace

The main purpose of a Zen garden is to provide an ideal outdoor setting for MEDITATION – which Zen Buddhists regard as the basis of their religion and their chief way of reaching spiritual enlightenment. To this end the garden's traditional focal point is a rock, or small group of rocks, which are meant to take those who view them out of the immediate, everyday world and into a state of mind in which thought can flourish freely.

The rocks are framed in a setting – such as a small backyard, or a corner of a back garden – which separates and distinguishes them from their wider surroundings. The size

flanking flowerbeds; to the right amount of open space needed in the foreground (again not too much or too little); and to the height and bulk of the plants used to give the garden its privacy.

The exact balance between these various elements is up to you. If you wish, the arrangement can be a mixture of interwoven shapes, colours and textures – simple overall, but rich in complex and stimulating detail. On the other hand, it can be basic and uncontrived.

However, two important aspects must be borne in mind. Firstly, the rocks should be set off-centre so that they do not merely blend in with the symmetry of the walls behind and on either side of them. Secondly, to achieve the maximum, concentrated effect, the rocks should be arranged as simply and naturally as possible – their different shapes and sizes creating a pleasing but uneven pattern. (Rocks which are too 'perfectly' arranged leave little to the onlooker's imagination.)

The power of such simplicity is graphically shown in the gardens of the Zen Buddhist temples of Daitoku-ji and Ryoan-ji, on the outskirts of the former imperial capital of Japan, Kyoto. Laid out in the late 15th century, the Ryoan-ji garden consists of 15 large stones set in an expanse of grey-white gravel, which is raked daily. Apart from a few mosses, there are no plants. Even so, the bare beauty of the rocks and their surroundings inspire people throughout the world.

But whichever form of garden is chosen – the complex or the simple – it should provide the perfect setting to encourage and nurture deep and contemplative thought.

and nature of the setting, however, is immaterial. The important thing is that the spectator's eye is led up towards the 'shrine' by the layout of the area.

At its simplest, a Zen garden can consist of three or four strategically placed stones, with a foreground of smoothly raked gravel or closely cropped grass. If you already have a garden which is well-planted and secluded, all you need to do is put your 'shrine' in place and possibly put down some gravel or a short stretch of grass.

If you have the space, however, you can create a more elaborate garden, with converging lines of flowerbeds rising to form a mound behind the rocks. A backdrop of plants can be chosen to match and enhance the shape and size of the rocks. The picture can be 'framed' by an overhanging tree. Finally, the setting should be enclosed by a wall, fence, or dense, evergreen bushes which will cut it off from the outside world. This sense of privacy is essential for the setting to be free of everyday associations.

But no two Zen gardens are exactly alike, and a well-designed garden should reflect its creator's artistic and aesthetic tastes. To achieve this, careful thought should be given to the proportions of the various elements which make up the garden.

The size of the 'shrine' must fit in with the total size of the garden. It must not be so large that it dominates the scene, or so small that it may be overlooked at first sight. Consideration must also be given to the amount of earth used for the mound and

ZONE THERAPY

Dr William H. Fitzgerald, who introduced REFLEXOLOGY to the West around 1913, originally called it zone therapy. Fitzgerald, an American ear, nose and throat specialist, divided the body into ten zones, or energy channels, and applied healing pressure to points on them, using his hands or special instruments. The zones ran from the toes up through the body to the head, then down to the fingers. Later practitioners of reflexology concentrated on the feet, but some still call themselves zone therapists.

Alternative and orthodox action in emergencies

Knowing how to give first aid in emergencies can, and does, save many lives. Common emergencies and the techniques used to deal with them are listed alphabetically in this section of the book.

Whenever possible, alternative treatments accompany conventional ones; but where there are no appropriate alternatives, orthodox methods are used.

Remember, however, that it is essential to call a doctor — or an ambulance — for any serious injury or illness. If you are taking herbal or homoeopathic preparations, always tell your GP, as some orthodox treatments may not combine well with these medicines.

Using the list as a guide, conventional home or travel first-aid kits of plasters, bandages, antiseptics and so on can be supplemented by various alternative medicines — including calendula ointment, lavender oil, marjoram and Bach Rescue Remedy.

Artificial respiration

Mouth-to-nose: *most successful and easiest*
● Put casualty face up.
● Clear mouth with finger.

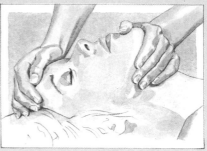

● Use one hand to hold casualty's chin forwards and mouth closed. Place other hand on forehead.

● Seal your lips around casualty's nose and breathe into it.

● Remove your mouth and turn your head to watch chest fall.
● Breathe into casualty's nose again. Give approximately 12-16 breaths a minute.
● If casualty vomits during resuscitation turn head to one side and clear mouth with finger.
● Tilt casualty's head again and resume resuscitation.

Mouth-to-mouth: *Kiss of Life*

● Clear casualty's mouth of blood or vomit.

● Tilt head up so that back is resting on ground with chin well up.

● Pinch casualty's nose shut with your fingers (above).
● Seal your lips around casualty's open mouth.
● Breathe into casualty's mouth until chest rises.
● Remove your mouth (below).
● Keep nose pinched shut with one hand.
● Turn your head to watch casualty's chest fall.

● Replace your mouth and breathe into casualty's again. Continue at normal breathing rate of 12-16 a minute (15-30 breaths a minute for children).
● If casualty vomits during resuscitation turn head to one side and clear mouth with your finger.
● Tilt casualty's head again and resume resuscitation.

Babies and small children

Perform resuscitation just enough to make chest rise. Give faster breaths – 15-30 a minute – depending on size of child. (The smaller the child the faster the breaths.)

Asphyxiation

Orthodox treatment
● Check casualty is breathing.
● Drag casualty from any danger.
● Untie or cut any cord or other material around neck.
● Clear casualty's airway by lying him on his back, supporting chin, and removing any debris from mouth with finger.
● If airway is blocked by food, treat for CHOKING.
● Check breathing and pulse, see PULSE AND RESPIRATION.

● If you can't see, hear, or feel any breathing, give mouth-to-mouth resuscitation, see ARTIFICIAL RESPIRATION.
● Once breathing is normal, turn casualty on side in recovery position, see UNCONSCIOUSNESS.
● Again make sure casualty's airway is clear.
● Keep careful watch on breathing and give artificial respiration again if it falters.
● Get immediate medical aid, if you can do so without leaving casualty unattended.

Bandages

Improvising with triangular bandage

● Lay out bandage on clean, flat surface ready for use.

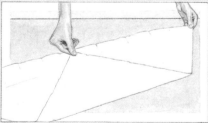

● Make broader bandage for emergencies by folding top point of triangle to middle of base.
● Fold bandage once more in same direction.
● To turn broad bandage into narrow one, fold it a third time in same direction.
● Use to bind hands, arms and legs.

Bandages: making raised pad
● Put clean cloth over wound.

● Make at least two curved pads by rolling cotton wool or other material in clean cloth.
● If possible, make pads higher than foreign body in wound.

● Place pads around foreign body and bandage on with diagonal strips of material.
● If foreign body is higher than pads, don't cross bandage over it.
● You then have raised pad to prevent pressure on wound that has foreign object in it, such as a piece of glass.

Bites and stings

Alternative treatment (bites)
Homoeopathy Clean all animal bites with pure tincture of Hypericum, or dilution in cold, boiled water.
● For pain and swelling, try Apis 6X.

Orthodox treatment (bites)
● Wash affected area with warm water and soap, or mild antiseptic.

● Dry gently, wiping down and away from wound.
● Cover with clean dressing. Fix dressing with sterile bandage or plaster.
● If wound is extensive or dirty, take casualty to hospital. Injections against tetanus may be needed, or course of antibiotics.

Alternative treatment (stings)
Traditional Medicine For insect stings in general, rub affected area with crushed dock leaves, found near nettle-beds.
● For bee stings – in which both sting and poison bag are left in casualty – apply crumbled leaves of plantain to area.
● Alternatively, heat crumbled leaves over flame until they wilt without becoming burnt, squeeze them and rub on juice.
● For wasp stings – in which only poison is left in casualty – dab sting with vinegar.
● Chewed or moist tobacco placed on sting may help to ease pain.
Homoeopathy For bee stings Ledum may help to relieve redness, swelling and pain. Take one dose every hour or two until discomfort stops.
Naturopathy Immerse affected area in bowl of cold water containing ice cubes and teaspoon of baking soda. This slows circulation and helps prevent poison spreading.
● Alternatively, hold fresh slice of raw onion over area, or cover with wheat-germ oil. Put ice bag on top and apply calendula cream to soothe.
Herbal Medicine For bee stings apply ice-cold water containing a little bicarbonate of soda on sting.
● For wasp stings put some drops of lemon juice in water and apply.
● Alternatively, apply plain ice cube.
● Marigold ointment may help to reduce swelling.

Orthodox treatment (stings)
● Scrape out bee sting and poison bag with fingernail, or any blunt edge.
● Avoid squeezing bag as this spreads poison.
● Apply antihistamine cream or calamine lotion to relieve itching.

● If casualty reacts strongly to bee or wasp sting, or if sting seems infected, get medical help.
● In rare cases, casualty may be allergic to stings. This can be fatal – get specialist help as soon as possible.
● If you know you are allergic to stings, ask your doctor for pre-filled syringe of adrenaline to inject in an emergency.

Bleeding

Orthodox treatment
Treat deep cuts to chest with casualty sitting up and inclined towards injured side.
Treat deep cuts to stomach, leg or back with casualty lying down as comfortably as possible.

● Gently remove clothing from around wound (above).
● Press down firmly on wound with clean, absorbent material or bare hands.
● If possible, raise injured leg, arm or head to slow bleeding (below).
● Maintain pressure on wound for 5-15 minutes.
● When bleeding stops, put absorbent pad – such as sterile gauze or clean, folded handkerchief – over wound.

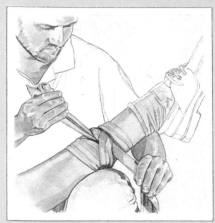

- Bandage firmly with scarf or clean piece of linen.
- If blood seeps through dressing, put another on top.
- Get medical attention, if you can do so without leaving casualty for more than a minute or two.
- Don't give anything to eat or drink.
- Regularly check casualty's pulse and breathing, see PULSE AND RESPIRATION.
- Be ready to give first aid for other injuries if necessary.

Warning Don't touch any foreign object firmly embedded in wound. Never pull out object that has made puncture – such as knife – as it may be plugging wound.
- Put raised pad of clean material around wound – preferably higher than object, to prevent pressure on it, see BANDAGES.
- Bandage pad with diagonally applied strips of material that don't go over foreign object.
- Get medical attention as soon as possible.
- If casualty bleeds from ear, mouth or nose, this can indicate serious injury to head or chest.
- In this case, put casualty in half-sitting position.
- If nose is bleeding, pinch bridge just below bone with your fingers and apply firm pressure for at least 5 minutes.
- Cover other bleeding points with clean cloth. Don't apply pressure.
- Get medical aid immediately.
- If casualty becomes unconscious, place in recovery position, see UNCONSCIOUSNESS.

Alternative treatment (cuts)
Herbal Medicine Apply calendula ointment after washing cut in running water, or warm, soapy water to remove any surrounding dirt.
- Alternatively, soak cut with calendula tincture.

Orthodox treatment (cuts)
- Take clean piece of cloth and press it on cut, or around edges if foreign body is in it.
- When bleeding stops, take pad away and remove any dirt or gravel that comes out easily.
- Gently wipe wound outwards with swab soaked in warm, soapy water. Use fresh swab for each wipe.
- Gently dry around wound with clean swab and apply plaster or bandage.
Warning Never apply tourniquet as this reduces supply of oxygen in blood and can permanently damage tissues, leading to gangrene and possible amputation.

Blisters

Alternative treatment
Biochemic Tissue Salts Take 4 tablets of Nat. mur. every 30 minutes until pain goes. For children, try 2 tablets every 30 minutes.
Aromatherapy Dab lavender oil on blister.

Orthodox treatment
- Gently wipe blister with cotton wool soaked in methylated spirit.
- Alternatively, wash it with soap and water, or antiseptic wipe.
- If blister is large and fluid-filled, sterilise sewing needle by passing once or twice through flame.
- Let needle cool for a second or two. Don't wipe or touch point.
- Hold needle flat on skin and press firmly into blister, bursting it.
- Remove needle and make second puncture in blister, opposite first.
- Remove needle and press gently on blister with clean swab.
- Wipe and apply dry dressing.

Burns and scalds

Alternative treatment (burns)
Homoeopathy For superficial burns apply *Hypericum* lotion to burnt area. Dosage is about 10 drops of lotion in glass of cold water.

Orthodox treatment (burns)

- Bathe burnt area in cold water for 10-15 minutes.

- Remove any jewellery or rings and cover area with clean bandages or clean handkerchief.
- Do *not* apply butter or fat.
Warning Don't try to treat deep burns or those that blister. Seek expert medical help without delay.

Alternative treatment (scalds)
Homoeopathy Apply *Hypericum* lotion to scalded area. Dosage is about 10 drops of lotion in cup of water.
- Take some drops of Bach Rescue Remedy in glass of cold water.

Orthodox treatment (scalds)
- Cool scalded area with cold water.
- Cover scald with clean, non-fluffy material such as linen handkerchief.
- If scald is serious, get medical aid.

Chest compression

Providing artificial pump for blood if heart has stopped beating

● Give 2 inflations of casualty's lungs and then feel for carotid pulse for at least 5 seconds, see PULSE AND RESPIRATION.

● If pulse can't be detected, and if casualty's complexion is blue-grey, place on firm surface and start chest compression.

● Feel for breastbone.

● Place heel of one hand on casualty's chest, two fingers up from bottom of breastbone.
● Keep thumb and fingers raised and off chest.

● Keep heel of your hand in place and put other hand over it, fingers interlocked, thumb and finger raised.
● Press down 40-50mm (1½-2in). Let chest rise.
● Give 15 presses, then inflate lungs twice by ARTIFICIAL RESPIRATION.

● Check carotid pulse after 1 minute.
● Continue chest compression until pulse returns, and give artificial respiration until casualty is breathing.
Adults Repeat pressure at normal pulse rate: 80 times a minute.

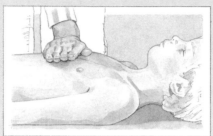

Children Lightly repeat pressure 80-100 times a minute, according to size of child. (The smaller the child the faster the rate.)
● Press lightly with heel of *one* hand on *lower* part of breastbone to depth of 25-40mm (1-1½in).
● After pressing breastbone down, let it rise.
● Give 5 presses followed by 1 lung inflation.
● Repeat until pulse beats unaided.
● Continue if necessary.

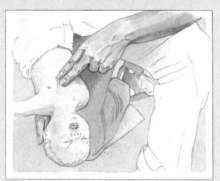

Babies Very lightly repeat pressure with two fingers 120 times a minute.
● Support baby along one arm, with your hand cradling its head, which should be tilted slightly down. (Artificial respiration can also be given in this position.)
● Press middle of breastbone down about 13mm (½in), using two fingers, and let it rise.
● Give 5 presses followed by 1 lung inflation.
● Repeat until pulse beats unaided.
Warning Chest compression should only be used if casualty's heart has

stopped beating and he seems likely to die. Ideally, it should be learned from a qualified instructor, and should be applied only by someone who's been trained. If applied wrongly or unnecessarily it could be fatal.

Choking

Orthodox treatment
Tell casualty to cough vigorously. If obstruction isn't cleared apply following:
Back slaps Give 3 or 4 sharp, flat slaps between casualty's shoulder blades with palm of hand.

● If casualty is young child, turn upside down while giving slaps.
● Rest older child face down across your thigh while giving slaps.

Abdominal thrust (conscious adult) Stand behind casualty and put arms around waist, making fist with one hand.

● Place thumb side slightly above casualty's navel and below rib cage.
● Hold fist with other hand and give 3 or 4 quick, strong pulls diagonally upwards and towards you.
● Use hands to exert pressure; don't just squeeze with arms.
● Once obstruction has been cleared, reassure casualty and give frequent sips of water. Adults should sip ½ cup of water over 10 minutes to help recovery.
Abdominal thrust (unconscious adult) Turn victim face up, kneel astride hips, put hand above navel.

● Push on it with your other hand, thrusting at an angle downwards and towards casualty's head.
● Clear mouth with finger. If necessary, give ARTIFICIAL RESPIRATION.
● Once casualty's breathing is normal, put in recovery position (see UNCONSCIOUSNESS) and get aid.

● Give casualty something to drink when fully conscious, but not before.
Abdominal thrust (self help) Below left: clench fist and place it, thumb side against abdomen, above navel.
● With other hand, jerk fist inwards and upwards several times.

Alternative method Above right: use back of chair or table edge.
● Lean over edge, supported by hands on either side.
● Thrust inwards and upwards 3 or 4 times.

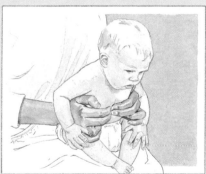

Abdominal thrust (conscious child) Sit child on your lap, facing away from you.
● Put tips of two fingers of each hand side by side, just above navel.
● Press gently but firmly upwards.
Abdominal thrust (unconscious child) Lie child face up.
● Put tips of two fingers of each hand side by side, just above navel.
● Press gently but firmly upwards.
● Clear mouth of any object with your finger.
● Give water to sip when consciousness returns.

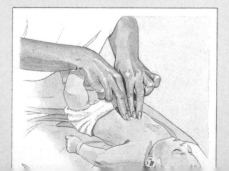

Concussion

A blow to the head can shake and disturb the brain, causing concussion. Symptoms may include confusion, slurred speech, vomiting, unsteadiness, inability to follow commands, or loss of consciousness.

Orthodox treatment
● Get expert medical help urgently.
● On recovery, casualty may suffer nausea and vomiting.
● Following head injury, any pressure on brain – from blood, fluid or fracture of skull – can cause compression, affecting casualty's alertness and level of consciousness.
● Compression may develop immediately after injury, or more slowly after casualty has apparently recovered from concussion.
● Again, get urgent medical help.

Drowning

Orthodox treatment
● Keep casualty's head and upper chest clear of water.
● Remove any debris from mouth with your finger.
● If casualty's breathing has stopped, start mouth-to-mouth ARTIFICIAL RESPIRATION.
● Move carefully towards dry land between breaths.
● Once in shallow water continue artificial respiration. Don't waste time bringing up water from lungs.
● Take casualty's pulse, see PULSE AND RESPIRATION.
● If there's no pulse, start CHEST COMPRESSION.
● Once breathing has re-started, turn casualty into recovery position, see UNCONSCIOUSNESS.
● Cover casualty with blankets or towels and treat any injuries.
● Get medical help as soon as possible.
Note Don't stop artificial respiration, even if situation looks hopeless. Recovery can be achieved even after apparent death for 25 minutes.

Electric shock

Orthodox treatment
● Turn off power.
● If casualty is holding frayed wire from electric lead, and power can't be switched off, rescuer may receive electric shock.

● With such accidents, lever casualty away from source of electricity with long, thick, dry piece of wood – such as broom handle.
● If possible, stand on dry, insulating material such as rubber mat or pile of newspapers.
● Once casualty is safely removed from contact with electric source, smother any burning clothes with blanket or towel.
● If impact of shock has thrown casualty to ground, check to see if breathing and heartbeat have stopped, see PULSE AND RESPIRATION.
● If necessary, apply ARTIFICIAL RESPIRATION.
● Once casualty is breathing naturally, place in recovery position, see UNCONSCIOUSNESS.
● Check for broken bones and give appropriate treatment, see FRACTURES.
● Treat minor burns by cooling with cold water, then cover with dressings or suitable material such as linen.
● Call ambulance as soon as possible.

Exposure

Orthodox treatment
● Wrap casualty in spare, dry clothes, blankets, or put sleeping-bags over clothes.
● Get casualty to tent or other spot sheltered from wind and rain.
● Lie casualty on blanket or groundsheet to prevent further heat loss.
● Remove wet clothes and put casualty into sleeping-bag, or cover with blankets or spare clothes.
● Wrap any windproof material – such as polythene or aluminium foil – on top of clothes for extra protection.
● Check casualty's breathing and pulse, see PULSE AND RESPIRATION.
● Be ready to give ARTIFICIAL RESPIRATION and CHEST COMPRESSION if necessary.
● Give warm, sweet, non-alcoholic drink and chocolate or biscuits if possible.
● Give warm (not hot) bath and get casualty into warm bed.

Eye injuries

Orthodox treatment
Chemical burns Tilt casualty's head with injured eye pointing down.
● Flood eye with gently running cold or lukewarm water.
● Alternatively, wash chemical away by splashing water from basin.
● Lightly put pad over eye and get casualty to hospital without delay.
Impaled objects Don't try to remove an impaled object from eye.
● Cut hole in piece of gauze and put over injured eye.
● Place soft pad, paper cup or similar object over gauze. This keeps gauze in place and should be secured by bandage.
● Cover uninjured eye as well to reduce eye movement.
● Get immediate medical aid.
Cut eyebrows Make casualty sit down with head erect. This will stop blood rushing to head.

● Firmly put gauze pad over cut.
● Once bleeding is controlled, leave pad in place and put retaining bandage over it. Be careful not to put pressure on eye itself.
● Get immediate medical aid.

Fainting

Alternative treatment
Bach Remedies As casualty comes round, place few drops of Rescue Remedy on tongue, or offer in water or tea.
Homoeopathy Give *Aconite* after faint from fright, *Arsenicum album* after faint from exhaustion or cold, and *Carbo vegetalis* after faint from lack of air.
Acupressure Use fingernail to stimulate firmly point on midline two-thirds of way up, between casualty's top lip and nose.

Orthodox treatment
● If casualty has passed out, but is breathing normally, lay on back with legs raised above level of head.
● Make sure casualty can still breathe, if necessary by supporting chin.
● Hold legs up, or prop them on chair or anything else suitable.
● Loosen clothing at neck, chest and waist and ensure casualty gets plenty of fresh air. If casualty is indoors, open windows.
● If casualty is out of doors, do the same and protect from sun.
● Casualty should stay lying down for a few minutes after recovering, before attempting to rise.
● If casualty has difficulty in breathing, ensure that airway is clear and, if necessary, apply ARTIFICIAL RESPIRATION.

Fractures

Alternative treatment
Homoeopathy To help relieve pain offer casualty *Asafoetida* 6 or 6X.
● Get expert medical help as soon as possible.

Orthodox treatment
● Gently remove clothing from any open wound over break, making sure to move affected area as little as possible.
● Cover wound with clean piece of lint. If bone protrudes, place gauze raised pad over area, see BANDAGES.
● Support injured part carefully, ensuring circulation is not restricted.
● If break is in leg, use uninjured leg as splint by tying it to other leg with bandages at knees and ankles and around feet. Pad between legs.
● Broken arm can be supported in sling, see SLINGS.
● Broken finger can be taped to adjacent finger.

Frostbite

Alternative treatment
Traditional Medicine For early stage of minor frostbite put slices of peeled cucumber dipped in warm water on affected area. Alternatively, use slices of raw onion or cold, salted, mashed potato.

Orthodox treatment
● Do *not* apply any form of direct heat – such as from fire – to frostbitten skin, and do *not* rub skin.
● Instead, warm area slowly between your hands until circulation returns.
● With frostbitten foot, remove casualty's shoe and sock and cover foot with linen pad.
● Cover foot with warm sock, blanket or sleeping-bag.
● Bandage frostbitten hands and cover in similar manner.
● Make sure casualty is wrapped warmly with coats or blankets and give plenty of hot, sweet drinks and painkillers as needed.

Head and facial injuries

Orthodox treatment
Scalp injuries Place clean pad or your hands on wound to stop bleeding.
● Cover wound with clean dressing. If foreign object is present, or if fracture is suspected, put dressing on lightly with pad on top of it to avoid causing further injury.
● Fix dressing or pad with bandage around head or chin, depending on position of wound.
● Keep casualty's head as steady as possible.
Broken jaw If jaw is broken or dislocated, make sure mouth is clear of blood or debris and that casualty can breathe.
● Put makeshift pad under point of chin.
● Put narrow bandage or scarf under chin.
● Tie ends of bandage on top of head in double knot.
● Make sure bandage is tight enough to support jaw, but not so tight casualty's teeth are clenched.
Bleeding face Press sterile pad or clean handkerchief against wound to stem bleeding.
● Seek medical aid.

Heart attack and stroke

Orthodox treatment (heart attack)
Symptoms are sudden crushing pain in chest, often spreading to arms, neck and jaw. Possibly breathlessness.

● Check victim's breathing and pulse, see PULSE AND RESPIRATION.
● If necessary, give ARTIFICIAL RESPIRATION and, if there's no pulse, CHEST COMPRESSION.
● If victim is conscious, put in half-sitting position, with head and shoulders supported with pillows or cushions, and cushion under knees.
● If there's loss of consciousness, lie victim flat.
● Loosen clothing at neck, chest and waist.
● Send for medical aid immediately.
● Comfort victim and stop any onlookers from crowding around.
● Give one soluble aspirin tablet to reduce blood clotting.

Orthodox treatment (stroke)
Symptoms may include paralysis down one side of body, difficulty in swallowing and speaking. Possibly confusion and loss of consciousness.
● If victim is conscious, lay down with head and shoulders slightly raised and supported with pillow.
● If victim is not conscious, place on side in recovery position, see UNCONSCIOUSNESS.
● Send for medical aid immediately.
● Comfort victim and stop any onlookers from crowding around.

Heat stroke

Orthodox treatment (heat stroke)
● Remove victim from source of heat, preferably to cool room.
● Undress victim and wrap in sheet or towels soaked in tepid water.
● Fan regularly.
● Take victim's temperature every 5 minutes.
● When temperature is down to 38°C (101°F), remove wet sheet, but continue fanning.
● If temperature rises again, restart cooling treatment.
● If victim is unconscious, place on side in recovery position, see UNCONSCIOUSNESS.
● If victim is conscious, give cup of weakly salted water every 10 minutes.
● Use quarter teaspoon of salt to each pint (600ml) of water. Add fruit juice to improve taste.

Motion sickness

Alternative treatment
Acupressure Press point three fingers' width above wrist crease on inner wrist, centrally, in line with middle finger. Apply pressure towards centre of wrist.
● Alternatively, wristbands applying similar pressure can be worn. Get them from chemists, airports or seaports and main travel stations.
Homoeopathy Try *Petroleum* for nausea and vomiting; *Tabacum* for nausea, sweating and giddiness; and *Borax* for turbulence during air travel.

Orthodox treatment
● Travel-sickness and seasickness tablets are available from chemists. Take one about ½-1 hour before setting out on a journey.
● If driving, do *not* take tablets containing antihistamine, which can cause drowsiness.
● Fresh air and regular breaks should help ward off sickness.

Overdose

Orthodox treatment
● If breathing stops start ARTIFICIAL RESPIRATION immediately, with CHEST COMPRESSION jf there's no pulse.
● If casualty is breathing but unconscious, place on side in recovery position and treat for UNCONSCIOUSNESS.
● If casualty is conscious, treat for POISONING.
● Get medical aid immediately, even if casualty seems to have recovered.
● Keep any vomit, tablets, bottles or containers which will help identify overdose drug.
Warning Try to keep casualty awake, but do not give coffee or help him to walk about. Wait until stomach has been pumped out.

Poisoning

Orthodox treatment
● If casualty isn't breathing give ARTIFICIAL RESPIRATION with CHEST COMPRESSION if necessary.
● If casualty is unconscious, but breathing, turn on side in recovery position, see UNCONSCIOUSNESS.
● Check that airway is clear.
● If necessary, hold chin forwards so that tongue doesn't fall back into casualty's throat.
● If casualty is conscious and has swallowed something caustic, give pint of milk to be sipped slowly to dilute poison in stomach.
● Don't deliberately make casualty vomit without medical advice.
● Get medical attention as soon as possible.

Pulse and respiration

Two places to take pulse

On inside of wrist (above) About 25mm (1in) below base of casualty's thumb and 13mm (½in) in from edge of arm.
● Place three fingers on pulse and press slightly.
● Time the beats.
On carotid area (below) On outer side of neck, by windpipe and just over halfway to jawline.
● Place three fingers on pulse and press slightly.
● Time the beats.

● Take casualty's pulse and respiration rates as you are treating him – except in cases of minor injuries.
● Bend casualty's arm at elbow so that it rests across chest near opposite shoulder, if that won't worsen injuries.
● Raise wrist slightly and feel for pulse with your fingertips – not your thumb.
● Count beats for 30 seconds and remember figure.
● Keep holding wrist and count number of times casualty's chest rises in next 30 seconds.
● Double pulse and respiration figures to express them per minute.
● Write them down, or have them noted by helper.

Normal pulse rate
Adults 60-80 beats a minute; average 72.
Children 90-100 beats a minute.
Babies Up to 140 beats a minute.

Normal respiration rate
Adults 12 times a minute when at rest.
Children and babies 20-40 times a minute.

Shock

Symptoms may include grey or pallid skin, cold and moist to touch; fast, shallow breathing and rapid, weak and thin pulse; dizziness or faintness; blurred vision; nausea or vomiting; thirst; anxiety and restlessness, sometimes leading to loss of consciousness.

Orthodox treatment
● Lay casualty down and treat any obvious injury or underlying condition which has caused shock.
● Reassure casualty.
● Loosen casualty's clothing at neck, chest and waist. Lightly cover with coat or single blanket.
● If possible, raise casualty's legs to return blood supply to brain.

● If casualty complains of thirst, moisten lips but don't give anything to drink.
● Give hot, sweet tea *only* in cases of emotional shock.
● Try to comfort and calmly reassure casualty.
● Don't move casualty unnecessarily.
● If casualty is unconscious, put on side in recovery position, see UNCONSCIOUSNESS.
● Try to get immediate medical aid, but don't leave casualty unattended.

Slings

Making triangular sling
● If casualty's hand or forearm is injured, raise arm so that hand rests on opposite shoulder. Get casualty to hold it in place if possible.

● Put one point of base of sling over casualty's shoulder on uninjured side, with point extended well beyond elbow. Sling should hang over injured arm (above).
● Gently push base of sling under hand, forearm and elbow of injured limb. Bring lower end of base up and around casualty's back on injured side (below).

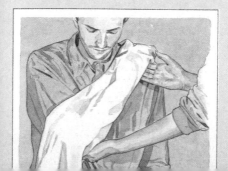

● Bring two ends of sling together round back of casualty on injured side. Tie at uninjured shoulder.

● Fold top of sling at elbow and fasten with pin or tape, or tuck it in.
● Check nail beds to make sure they haven't turned blue, indicating constricted blood supply. If they have, ease sling or bandage.

Improvising sling

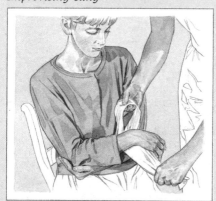

● Use belt, tie, narrow scarf, or roller bandage.
● For injured upper arm, wrap improvised sling round casualty's wrist on injured side.

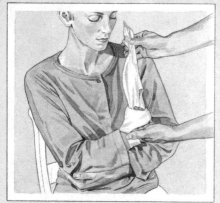

● Bring other end of sling across casualty's chest and around back of neck.

● Tie ends in hollow above collarbone on uninjured side.

Splinters

Orthodox treatment
● Sterilise pair of tweezers by passing them through flame. Don't wipe any soot from them.
● Alternatively, boil tweezers in water for 10 minutes.
● Wash skin around injury carefully with warm, soapy water. Wipe outwards from wound.
● Dry skin carefully.
● Using tweezers, pull splinter out.
● When splinter has been removed, wash wound with mild antiseptic and dry gently.

- Cover wound with plaster or sterile dressing.
- If splinter can't be removed, or becomes painful, get medical aid.

Warning Unskilled person should *not* put splint on broken limb. Fractures should only be splinted by skilled person if casualty has to undergo long or rough journey to receive medical aid.

- If casualty faces long or rough journey to receive medical aid, use five bandages.

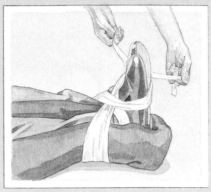

- Tie feet and ankles together with bandage.

Splints

Improvising bandage splint

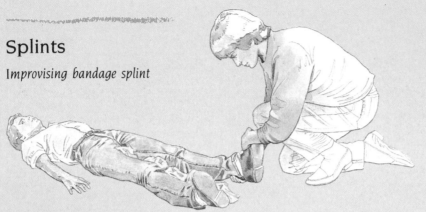

- If one leg is injured, prepare to bandage to other leg.
- Carefully and gently move uninjured leg to it.
- Place plenty of padding between legs – especially knees and ankles.
- Carefully and gently move uninjured leg to injured.

Improvising blanket splint
- Roll blanket lengthways as tightly as possible.

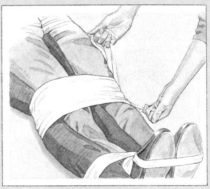

- Tie broad fold bandage around knees.
- Tie knot on uninjured leg.

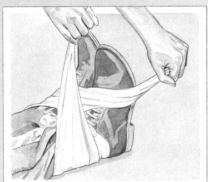

- Tie casualty's feet and ankles together (above).
- Tie knees together with bandage knotted on uninjured side (below).
- Tie extra bandages above and below fracture site.

- Place one end between casualty's legs, starting at crotch.
- Bring blanket around foot of injured leg and take other end alongside leg up to thighs.
- Tie legs together with two bandages.

- Tie third and fourth bandages above and below fracture site.
- Tie fifth bandage around casualty's thigh or calf, depending on where fracture is.

First Aid

Sprains and strains

Alternative treatment (sprains)
Homoeopathy Take *Arnica* 30 as soon as possible after accident, hourly for 6 doses.
Aromatherapy Apply hyssop and marjoram as soon as possible after accident and massage area gently.
● Use 2 drops of each oil in teaspoon of vegetable carrier oil.
● Apply compress made with 5 drops of each oil and enough water to soak through compress.
● Hold compress in place with clingfilm and leave for several hours.

Orthodox treatment (sprains)
● For indoor ankle sprains remove casualty's shoe.
● For outdoor ankle sprains leave shoe on.
● In either case, apply cold compress to injury and elevate foot.
● Place bandage over compress.
● Make one turn around ankle, then go over instep, under foot, back across instep, around ankle again and pin.
● Bandage over shoe.
● For wrist sprains, apply cold compress and bandage in place.
● Consult doctor to exclude fracture.

Orthodox treatment (strains)
● Steady and support casualty's injured part.
● Gently apply cold compress.
● Keep injured part steady and well supported.
● Bandage firmly but not too tightly as muscles may swell, causing further discomfort.
● Get medical aid.

Sunburn

Alternative treatment
Herbal Medicine Apply cold water then add 1 or 2 drops of lavender oil.
● Alternatively, apply cold compress of marigold infusion. Marigold or comfrey cream may ease large, mild burns.
● Apply fresh leaves of houseleeks or plaintain to small burns.
Naturopathy Immerse small burns in cold water for 2 or 3 minutes, then carefully dab dry. Immerse large burns in cold bath, then apply vitamin E moisturising cream.
Traditional Medicine Try lotion made from dock roots or mixture of water and vinegar.

Orthodox treatment
● Rest casualty in shade and give plenty of liquids to drink.
● Don't let casualty out in sun again without covering affected areas with light, loose clothing.
● Soothe mild cases of sunburn by bathing in cool water, or applying calamine lotion, witch hazel or proprietary after-sun lotion or cream to affected areas.
● If sunburn is severe, get medical help.
Warning Never deliberately burst blisters caused by sunburn.

Unconsciousness

Orthodox treatment
● Check to see if casualty is still breathing.
● Put your ear to casualty's nose or mouth and listen.
● Watch chest to see if it rises and falls, or rest your hand lightly on it to feel for movement.
● If there's no breathing, give ARTIFICIAL RESPIRATION.
● Check casualty's pulse, see PULSE AND RESPIRATION.
● If there's no pulse, start CHEST COMPRESSION.
● If and when casualty is breathing, loosen his clothing at neck, chest and waist.
● Turn casualty to recovery position (see illustration).
● Open doors and windows for fresh air.
● Check for injuries or bruises and stem any bleeding.
● Get medical assistance as soon as possible.

Recovery position
● Turn casualty on side by kneeling and tucking near arm under body, palm upwards.

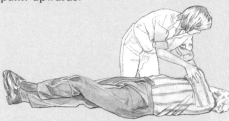

● Cross ankle farthest away from you over one nearest to you.
● Put other arm over chest.

● Turn casualty towards you, supporting head with your hand.
● Place your other hand on casualty's hip farthest away, and roll him gently towards you.
● Hold casualty's chin forwards. This extends neck and stops tongue falling back into throat.

● Bend casualty's knee to stop him rolling over too far.
● Pull the other arm out behind the body so that casualty is prevented from rolling back.

● Pull up casualty's arm nearest to you so that point of elbow is in line with shoulder.
● Don't leave casualty unattended.

389

Index

Herbal medicine – conditions treated

Homoeopathy – conditions treated

T'ai-chi Ch'uan 334-7
  for arthritis 40
  for kidney complaints 215
  for obesity 267
  for osteoporosis 271
  for poliomyelitis 281

Acknowledgments

The publishers wish to thank the following individuals, companies and organisations for their assistance in the preparation of this book.

Aleph One Ltd; ASH; Audio Ltd; Barbican Health Centre; Kenneth A. Beckett; The Biorhythm Co Ltd; British Association of Beauty Therapists and Cosmetology Ltd; British Nutrition Foundation; British Society of Dowsers; British Soft Drinks Association; Bronwen Burford; Cedar Falls Health Farm; Centre for Release and Integration; Crystal World; Cutler's Royal Jelly; Felicity Dawes; Peter Enkel; The Floatarium, Brighton; Victor N. Foster, British Acupuncture Association; Judith Fraser; Gestalt Centre; Roger Golten, The Peak Health Club; The Hale Clinic; Dr Brian Hammond; J.O. Harvey, Shen Tao Foundation; Dr J.L.M. Hawk, St Thomas's Hospital; Mike Hennessy; Highglade Naturopathic Clinic; Isabelle Hughes; Institute for Optimum Nutrition; Institute of Trichologists; International College of Oriental Medicine UK; Howard Kent, Yoga for Health Foundation; The Leaves Aromatherapy and Natural Therapy School and Clinic; The London Ioniser Centre; London Natural Health Clinic; Dr Michael McKee; Dr Peter Guy Manners, Bretforton Hall Clinic; The Maperton Trust; Mandy Metcalf; Milton Keynes General Hospital; National Anti-Fluoridation Campaign; National Back Pain Association; National Bed Federation; Garet Ann Newell, The Feldenkrais Guild UK; Northern Institute of Massage; Professor Richard W. Porter; Psionic Medical Society; The Radionic Association; Enid Segall, British Homoeopathic Association; Society of Homoeopaths; Margaret Taylor; Tyringham Clinic; Dr T.L.P. Watts, United Medical and Dental Schools of Guy's and St Thomas's Hospitals; John Whetton; Mike Wibberley; Ian Wilkie; L.A. Willcocks.

The photographs and drawings in *Family Guide to Alternative Medicine* were supplied by the following sources. Names printed in *italics* refer to illustrations that are Reader's Digest copyright. Where ambiguous, the position of an illustration on the page is indicated by letters in brackets, as follows: T = top; C = centre; B = bottom; L = left; R = right.

11 Biofotos; 13 *Biz Hull*; 14 *Rosalyn Kennedy*; 15 *Biz Hull*; 16 (T) Michael Holford, (B) ET Archive/National Palace Museum, Taiwan; 21 *Diana Miller*; 22 *Biz Hull*; 23 (L) *Rosalyn Kennedy*, (TR) *Glynn Macdonald*; 24 *Rosalyn Kennedy*; 31 *Biz Hull*; 32 (L) Mansell Collection, (R) P. Blundell-Jones/The Architectural Association; 35 The Ancient Art & Architecture Collection; 36 *Biz Hull*; 39 *Richard Bonson*; 40 *Rosalyn Kennedy*; 44 CNRI/Science Photo Library; 47-48 *Biz Hull*; 50 The Hulton Picture Company; 52 *Biz Hull*; 54 *Tim Pearce*; 55 *Rosalyn Kennedy*; 56-57 *Biz Hull*; 58-59 *Rosalyn Kennedy*; 60-62 *Biz Hull*; 65 Archiv fur Kunst und Geschichte, Berlin; 68 *Biz Hull*; 69 *Baird Harris Ltd*; 73 *Rosalyn Kennedy*; 78-79 CNRI/Science Photo Library; 83 *Rosalyn Kennedy*; 86 (T) The Scofield Chiropractic Clinic, (BL) Dr Brian Hammond, (BR) *Biz Hull*; 96 *Baird Harris Ltd*; 99 Peter Brooker/Rex Features.

100 *Biz Hull*; 102 John Walmsley/Impact Photos; 104-5 *Biz Hull* (from photos by Bronwen Burford); 110 (L) *Biz Hull*, (R) *Rosalyn Kennedy*; 111 *Rosalyn Kennedy*; 112 Mary Evans Picture Library; 119-25 *Diana Miller*; 129 *Biz Hull*; 130 *Tim Pearce*; 133 *Baird Harris Ltd*; 134-5 *Rosalyn Kennedy*; 137 *Biz Hull*; 138 *Rosalyn Kennedy*; 140 The Floatarium, Brighton; 142-3, 145 *Diana Miller*; 151 *Biz Hull*; 153 ET Archive; 155 *Diana Miller*; 156 Mary Evans Picture Library; 162-3 *Biz Hull*; 166 Mansell Collection; 168 *Diana Miller*; 170 Tyringham Hall; 171 *Andra Nelki*; 172-3 *Richard Bonson*; 175 Zefa; 176-7 *Richard Bonson*; 180 *Biz Hull*; 181 *Richard Bonson*; 182 Michael Holford; 184 *Rosalyn Kennedy*; 185 (T) Garden Picture Library, (BL) *Richard Bonson*, (BR) Elizabeth Whiting & Associates; 186-7 *Vernon Morgan*; 192 (L) Ted Lau/*Time* magazine; (R) The Bettmann Archive; 194 *Biz Hull*.

202 *Julie Busby*; 204 *Tim Pearce*; 205 (TL) CNRI/Science Photo Library, (TC) Oxford Molecular Biophysics Laboratory/Science Photo Library, (TR) Biology Media/Science Photo Library, (B) *Richard Bonson*; 206 (T) Dr Steve Patterson/Science Photo Library, (B) *Richard Bonson*; 207 *Baird Harris Ltd*; 208 (T) Gordon Garradd/Science Photo Library, (C) Julian Nieman/Susan Griggs Agency, (B) *Biz Hull*; 210 (T) *Baird Harris Ltd*, (BL) *Biz Hull*, (BR) Peter Enkel; 213 *Rosalyn Kennedy*; 214 (L) CNRI/Science Photo Library, (R) *Tim Pearce*; 215-17 *Biz Hull*; 218 Dr Leonard W. Konikiewicz; 220 ET Archive; 223 Françoise Sauze/Science Photo Library; 225 *Biz Hull*; 226-7 *Rosalyn Kennedy*; 230 *Joanna Walker*; 232-3 *Diana Miller*; 239-40 *Biz Hull*; 244 Mary Evans Picture Library; 247 *Biz Hull*; 248 Gamma/Frank Spooner; 253 National Medical Slide Library; 255 (T & BL) *Rosalyn Kennedy*, (R) *Andra Nelki*; 258 Mary Evans Picture Library; 259 *Rosalyn Kennedy*; 260 Petit Format; 261 (T) Mary Evans Picture Library, (B) Sally & Richard Greenhill; 262 (T) *Rosalyn Kennedy*, (B) *Biz Hull*; 265 *Biz Hull*; 269 Popperfoto; 270 *Biz Hull*; 277 *Shirley Harris*; Chapman/Collins & Partners; 280-4 *Rosalyn Kennedy*; 290 (R) Freud Museum, (L) Mary Evans Picture Library/Sigmund Freud Collection; 293 Zefa; 295 *Baird Harris*; 296-8 *Biz Hull*; 299 *Tim Pearce*.

300 *Rosalyn Kennedy*; 303 (TR & BR) *Biz Hull*, (BL) Karsh of Ottawa; 304 *Biz Hull*; 305 Ann Ronan Picture Library; 309-10 *Biz Hull*; 316 (L) *Biz Hull*, (R) *Rosalyn Kennedy*; 320 *Richard Bonson*; 323 *Malcolm Porter*; 333 *Joanna Walker*; 334-5 (T) Sally & Richard Greenhill, (B) *Biz Hull*; 336 *Biz Hull*; 337 *Richard Bonson*; 338 (T) Lorraine Rorke, (B) Dave Stock; 345 *Rosalyn Kennedy*; 347-8 Mansell Collection; 351 *Richard Bonson*; 356-7 *Diana Miller*; 359 Narodni Galerie, Prague/Bridgeman Art Library; 369 Rex Features; 370-3 *Rosalyn Kennedy*; 374 Werner Forman Library; 377 Marijke Heuff/The Garden Picture Library; 378-89 Andrew Aloof.

The publishers acknowledge their indebtedness to the following books and journals, which were consulted for reference.

The Alternative Dictionary of Symptoms and Cures by Dr Caroline M. Shreeve (Century); *The Alternative Health Guide* by Brian Inglis and Ruth West (Michael Joseph); *A-Z of the Human Body* (Reader's Digest); *Beating Back Pain* by Dr John Tanner (Dorling Kindersley); *Biochemic Tissue Salts* by Andrew Stanway (Thorsons); *Bloomsbury Good Health Guide* (Bloomsbury); *Chiropractice* by Arthur G. Scofield (Thorsons); *The Complete Manual of Fitness and Well-Being* (Reader's Digest); *The Complete Natural Health Consultant* by Michael van Straten (Ebury Press); *Concise Medical Dictionary* (Oxford University Press); *Coping with Old Age* by Pat Blair (Optima); *Cures that Work* by Janet Pleshette (Century Arrow); *The Dictionary of Medical Folklore* by Carol Ann Rinzler (Magnum); *The Encyclopedia of Herbs and Herbalism* edited by Malcolm Stuart (Orbis); *The Face and Body Book* edited by Miriam Stoppard (Windward); *The Family Guide to Homeopathy* by Dr Andrew Lockie (Elm Tree Books); *Family Medical Adviser* (Reader's Digest); *Grandmother's Secrets* by Jean Palaiseul (Penguin); *Gray's Anatomy* edited by Roger Warwick and Peter L. Williams (Longman); *Guide to Alternative Medicine* by Dr Vernon Coleman (Corgi); *A Guide to Chiropractic* by Susan Moore (Hamlyn); *The Handbook of Complementary Medicine* by Stephen Fulder (Coronet); *The Health and Fitness Handbook* edited by Miriam Polunin (Windward); *The Herb User's Guide* by David L. Hoffmann (Thorsons); *Here's Health* (Argus Health Publications; monthly); *Holistic First Aid* by Dr Michael Nightingale (Optima); *Holistic Living: A Guide to Self Care* by Patrick Pietroni (Dent); *Iridology* by Farida Sharan (Thorsons); *Journal of Alternative and Complementary Medicine* (Green Library Ltd; monthly); *Living with Fear* by Isaac M. Marks (McGraw-Hill); *McCance and Widdowson's The Composition of Foods* by A.A. Paul and D.A.T. Southgate (HMSO); *The Metamorphic Technique* by Gaston Saint-Pierre and Debbie Shapiro (Element Books); *Mitchell Beazley Atlas of the Body and Mind* (Mitchell Beazley); *Natural Choice* (Orbis; partwork); *The Natural Family Doctor* edited by Dr Andrew Stanway (Century); *The Natural House Book* by David Pearson (Conran Octopus); *The Polarity Process* by Franklyn Sills (Element Books); *Potter's New Cyclopedia of Botanical Drugs and Preparations* by R.C. Wren (C.W. Daniel Co); *Reflexology – A Way to Better Health* by Nicola M. Hall (Pan); *Stay Younger Longer* by Bronwen Meredith (Michael Joseph); *Thorsons Complete Guide to Alternative Living* by David Harvey (Thorsons); *Treat Your Own Back* by Robin McKenzie (Spinal Publications, New Zealand); *A Visual Encyclopaedia of Unconventional Medicine* edited by Ann Hall (New English Library); *Vogue Beauty and Health Encyclopedia* by Christina Probert (Octopus); *Vogue Complete Diet and Exercise* by Deborah Hutton (Octopus); *Which? Way to Health* (Consumers' Association; bimonthly); *Yoga for Common Ailments* by R. Nagarathna, H.R. Nagendra and Robin Monro (Gaia Books).

Page make-up: Apex Computersetting, London. **Separations**: Colourscan Overseas Co Pte Ltd, Singapore. **Paper**: Townsend Hook Ltd, Snodland. **Printing & binding**: Jarrold & Sons Ltd, Norwich. **Cloth**: Winter & Co London Ltd, Huntingdon.